InuYasha

Story & Art by
Rumiko Takahashi

INUYASHA

Volume 10
VIZBIG Edition

Story and Art by RUMIKO TAKAHASHI

Original Japanese edition "INUYASHA"
published by SHOGAKUKAN Inc.

English Adaptation/Gerard Jones
Translation/Mari Morimoto
Transcription/David Smith
Touch-up Art & Lettering/Steve Dutro, Leonard Clark, Primary Graphix
VIZ Media Series Design/Yuki Ameda
VIZBIG Edition Design/Sam Elzway
VIZ Media Series Editors (VIZ Media/Action Edition)/
Ian Robertson
VIZBIG Edition Editor/Annette Roman

Printed in China

Published by VIZ Media, LLC
P.O. Box 77010
San Francisco, CA 94107

10 9 8 7 6 5 4 3 2 1
First printing, February 2012

VIZBIG EDITION
viz media
www.viz.com

SHONEN SUNDAY
WWW.SHONENSUNDAY.COM

RATED T+ FOR OLDER TEEN

PARENTAL ADVISORY
INUYASHA is rated T+ for Older Teen and is recommended for ages 16 and up. This volume contains fantasy violence and partial nudity.
ratings.viz.com

INUYASHA

Volume 28
Resurrection

Volume 29
Inuyasha's True Feelings

Volume 30
Unique Among Women

Story & Art by
Rumiko Takahashi

Shonen Sunday Manga / VIZBIG Edition

CONTENTS

❧

Volume 30: Unique Among Women

CAST OF CHARACTERS

Kagome
A modern-day Japanese schoolgirl who is the reincarnation of Kikyo, the priestess who imprisoned Inuyasha for fifty years with her enchanted arrow. As Kikyo's reincarnation, Kagome has the power to see the Shikon Jewel shards.

Inuyasha
A half-human, half-demon hybrid, Inuyasha has doglike ears and demonic strength. He assists Kagome in her search for the shards of the Shikon Jewel, mostly because a charmed necklace allows Kagome to restrain him with a single word.

Naraku
This enigmatic demon is responsible for both Miroku's curse and for turning Kikyo and Inuyasha against each other.

Kagura
Kagura was produced as a doppelganger from part of Naraku's body. Kagura inherited her abilities from a demon that controlled the wind.

Bankotsu
The leader of the Band of Seven, a group of undead killers brought back to life by Naraku through the powers of the Shikon Jewel shards.

Kohaku
Naraku controlled Kohaku with a Shikon shard, then resurrected him after he was killed and used him as a puppet. Kohaku has regained his memories and is trying to redeem himself.

Miroku

An easygoing Buddhist priest of questionable morals. Miroku bears a curse passed down from his grandfather and is searching for the demon Naraku, who first inflicted the curse.

Kikyo

A village priestess who was the original protector of the Shikon Jewel. She died fifty years ago.

Sango

A proud Demon Slayer from the village where the first Shikon Jewel was born. Her clan and family lost, she fights on against the demonic Naraku along with Inuyasha.

Shippo

A young orphan fox demon. The mischievous Shippo enjoys goading Inuyasha and playing tricks with his shape-shifting abilities.

Koga

A wolf demon and leader of the wolf clan. Koga has Shikon shards in his legs, giving him super speed.

Sesshomaru

Inuyasha's half brother by the same demon father, Sesshomaru is a pureblood demon who covets the sword left to Inuyasha by their father.

InuYasha

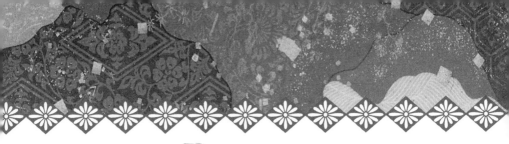

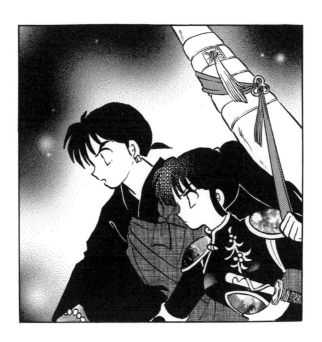

Volume 28
Resurrection

SCROLL ONE
INSIDE THE DARKNESS

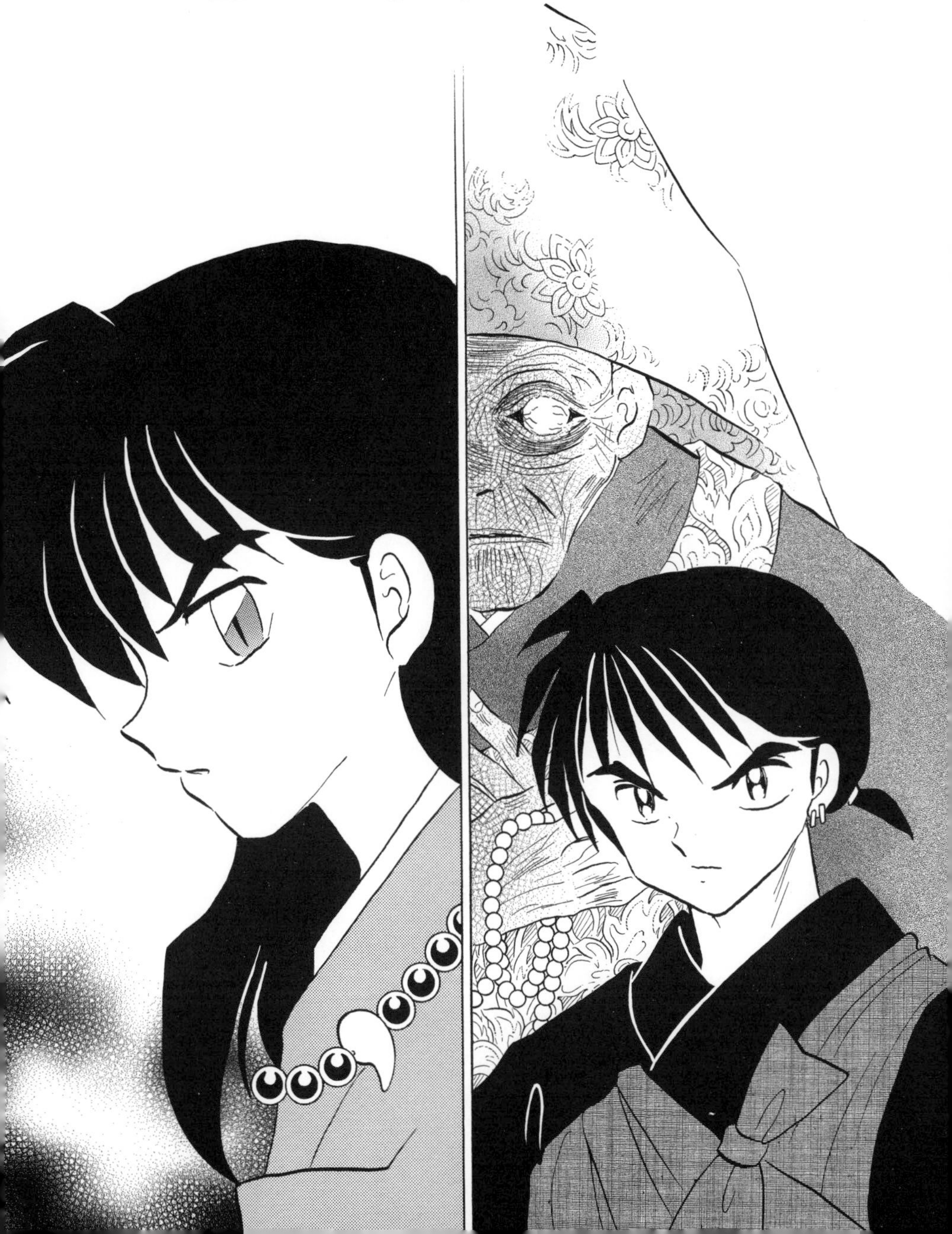

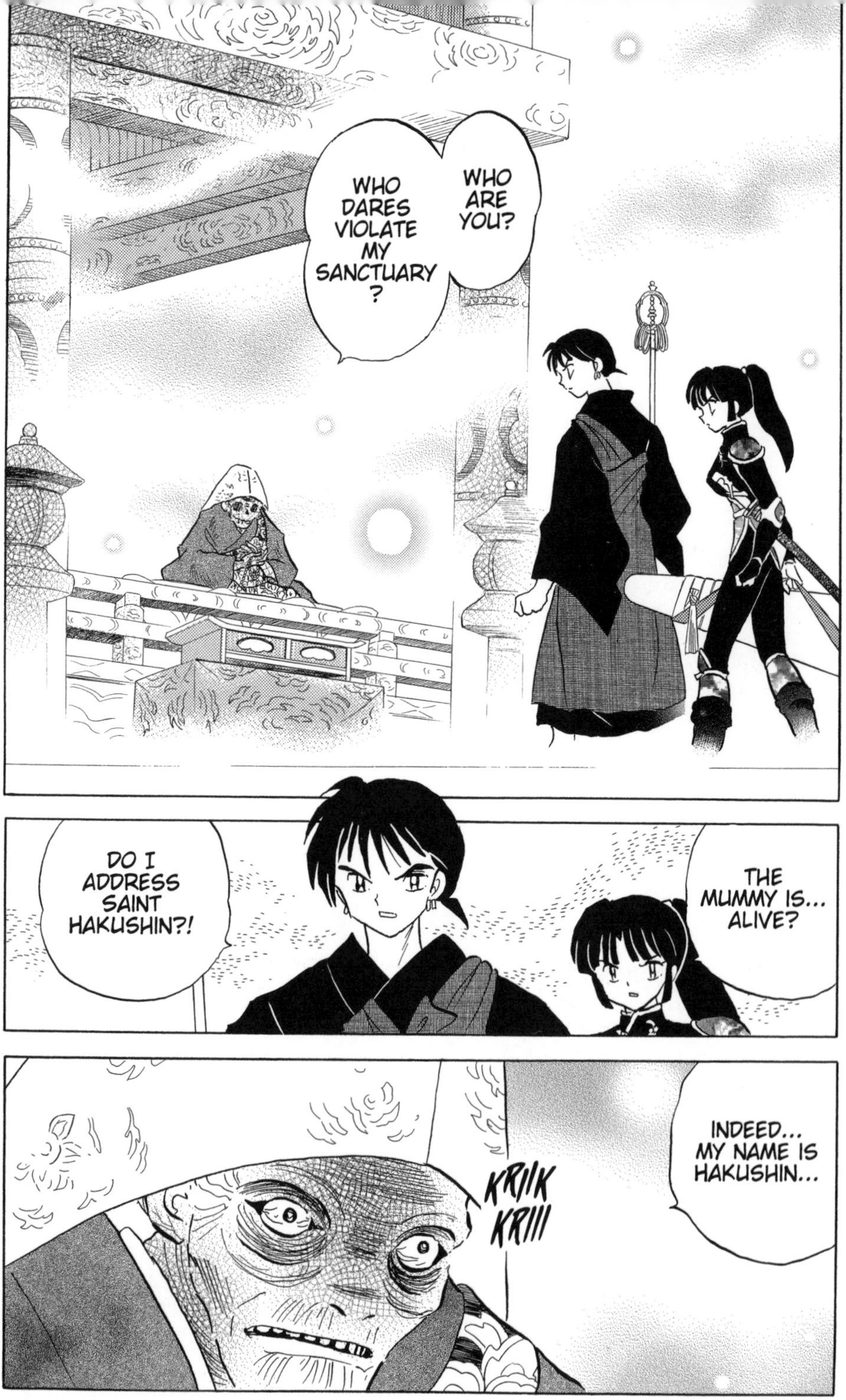
WHO ARE YOU?
WHO DARES VIOLATE MY SANCTUARY?
THE MUMMY IS... ALIVE?
DO I ADDRESS SAINT HAKUSHIN?!
INDEED... MY NAME IS HAKUSHIN...
KRIIK KRIII

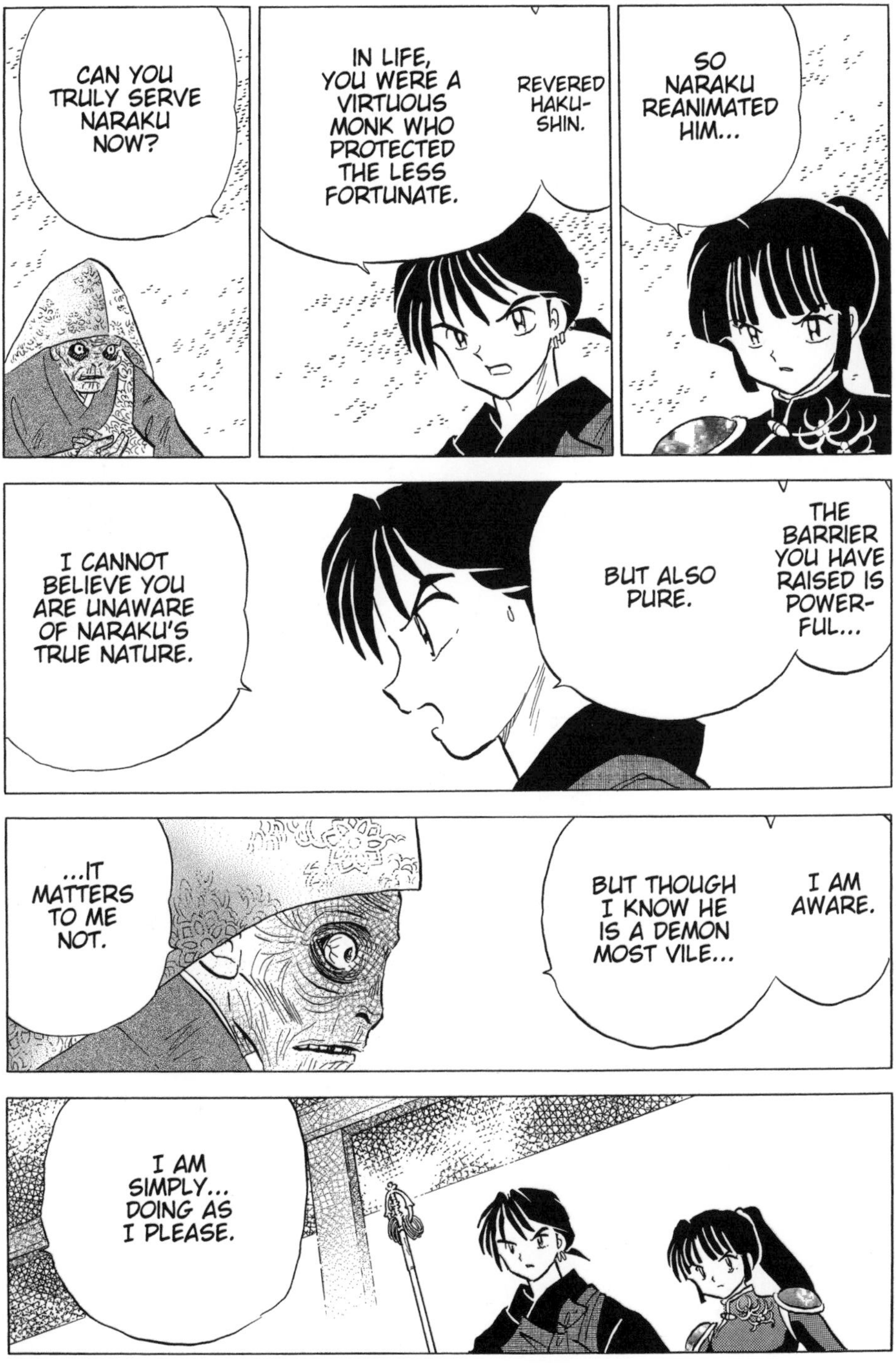
SO NARAKU REANIMATED HIM...
REVERED HAKU-SHIN.
IN LIFE, YOU WERE A VIRTUOUS MONK WHO PROTECTED THE LESS FORTUNATE.
CAN YOU TRULY SERVE NARAKU NOW?
THE BARRIER YOU HAVE RAISED IS POWER-FUL...
BUT ALSO PURE.
I CANNOT BELIEVE YOU ARE UNAWARE OF NARAKU'S TRUE NATURE.
I AM AWARE.
BUT THOUGH I KNOW HE IS A DEMON MOST VILE...
...IT MATTERS TO ME NOT.
I AM SIMPLY... DOING AS I PLEASE.

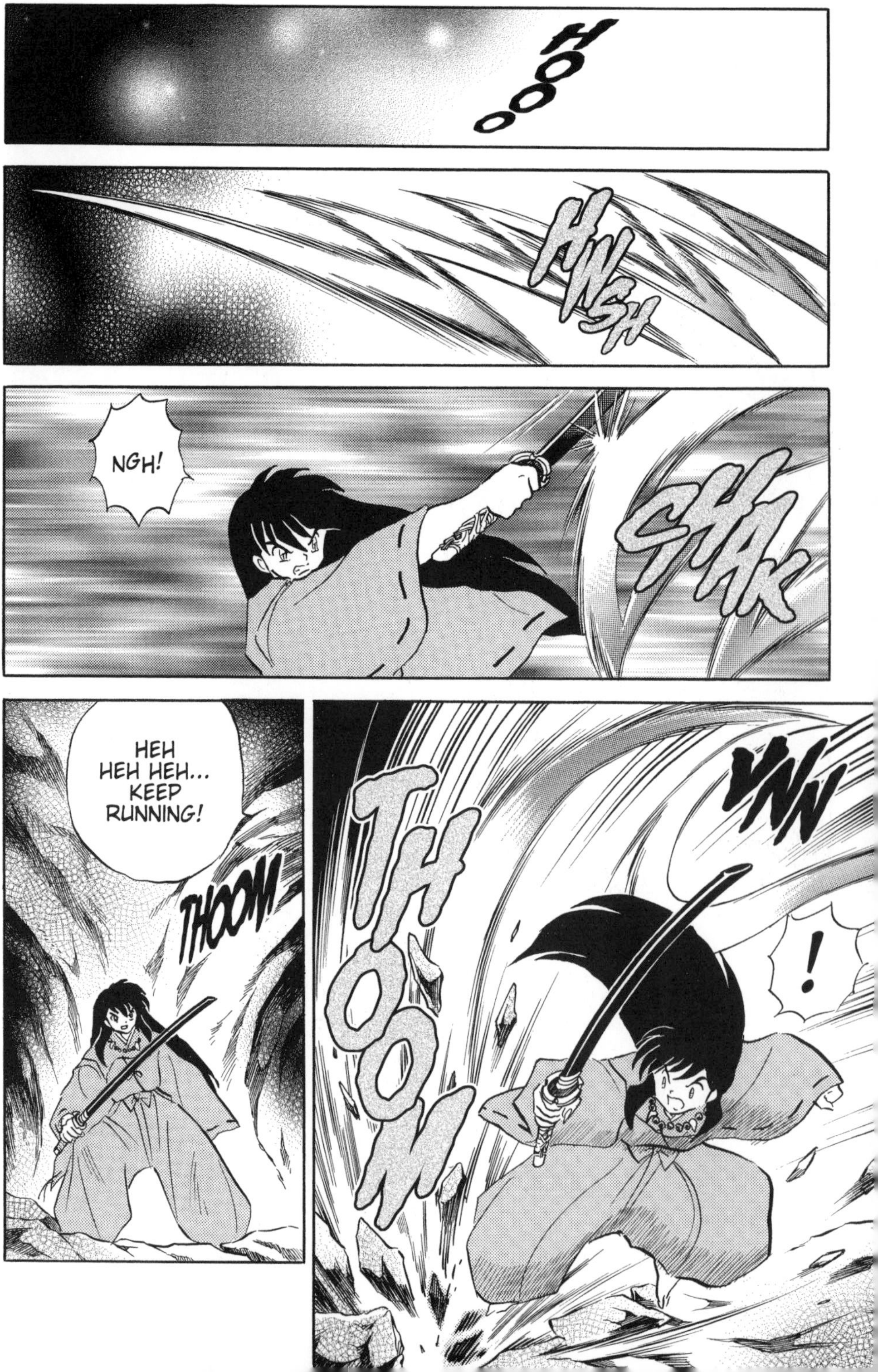
HOOOO
HWSH
NGH!
CHAK
THOOOM
VNN
!
HEH HEH HEH... KEEP RUNNING!
THOOM

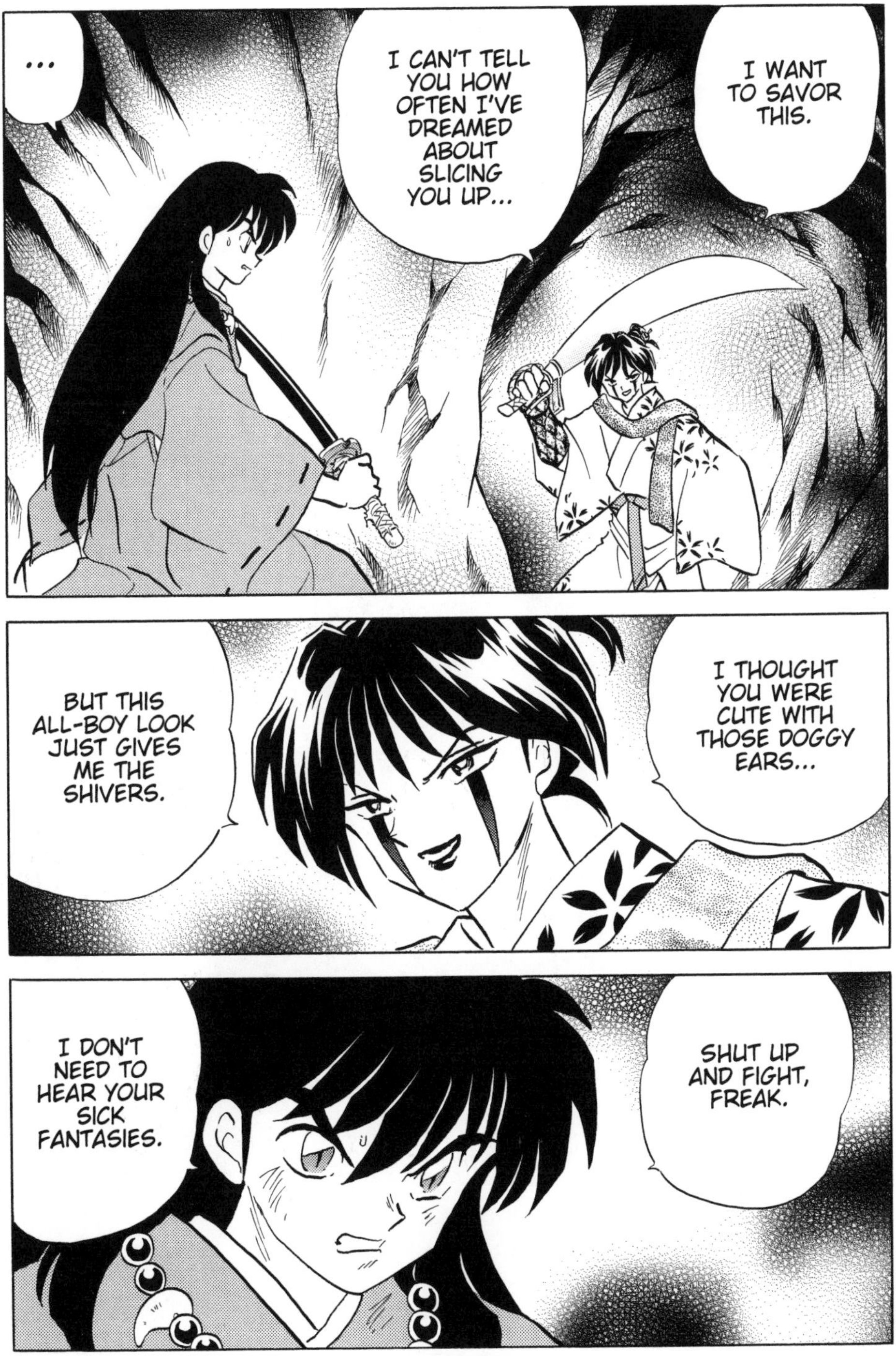
I WANT TO SAVOR THIS.
I CAN'T TELL YOU HOW OFTEN I'VE DREAMED ABOUT SLICING YOU UP...
...
I THOUGHT YOU WERE CUTE WITH THOSE DOGGY EARS...
BUT THIS ALL-BOY LOOK JUST GIVES ME THE SHIVERS.
SHUT UP AND FIGHT, FREAK.
I DON'T NEED TO HEAR YOUR SICK FANTASIES.

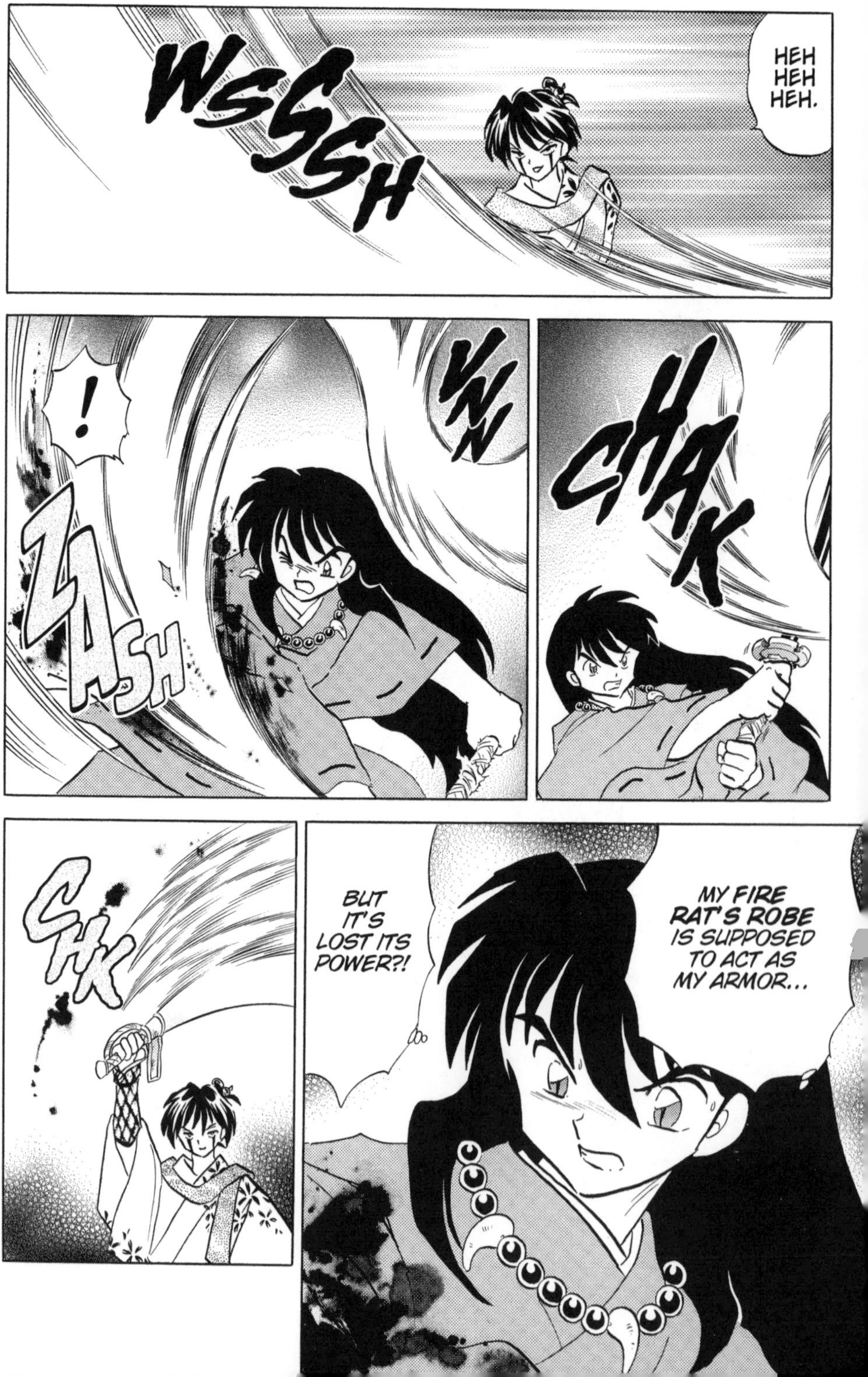
HEH HEH HEH.
WSSSH
CHAK
VNN
!
ZASH
MY FIRE RAT'S ROBE IS SUPPOSED TO ACT AS MY ARMOR...
BUT IT'S LOST ITS POWER?!
CHK

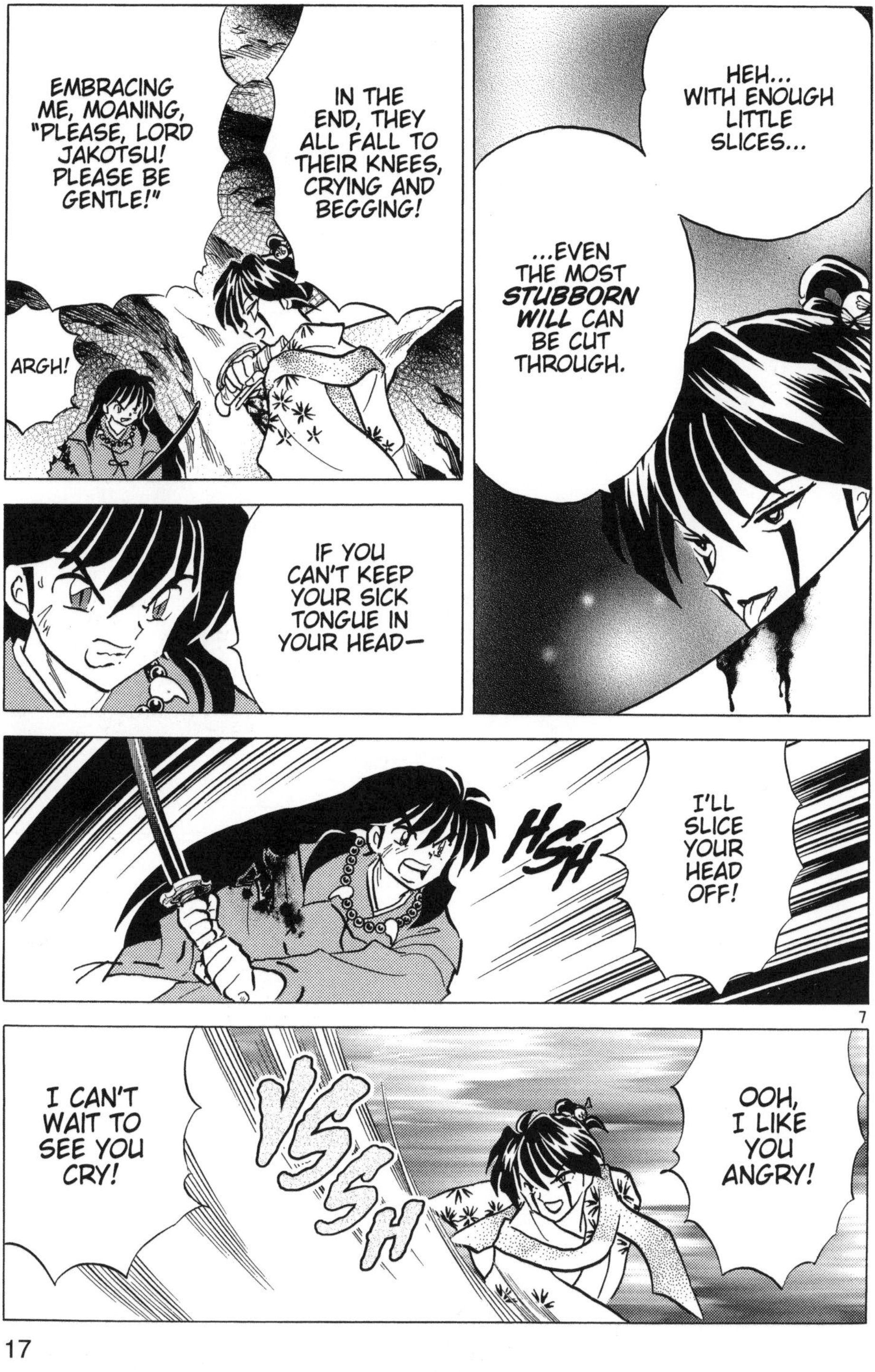
HEH... WITH ENOUGH LITTLE SLICES...
...EVEN THE MOST STUBBORN WILL CAN BE CUT THROUGH.
IN THE END, THEY ALL FALL TO THEIR KNEES, CRYING AND BEGGING!
EMBRACING ME, MOANING, "PLEASE, LORD JAKOTSU! PLEASE BE GENTLE!"
ARGH!
IF YOU CAN'T KEEP YOUR SICK TONGUE IN YOUR HEAD—
I'LL SLICE YOUR HEAD OFF!
HSH
7
OOH, I LIKE YOU ANGRY!
VSSH
I CAN'T WAIT TO SEE YOU CRY!

D...DAMN IT!

WOBBLE

SHAH

HWNNN

!

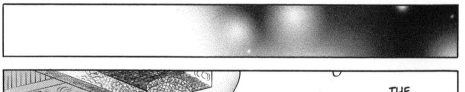

...

THE BARRIER YOU'VE RAISED IS PROTECTING NARAKU, PROTECTING *EVIL!*

HOW CAN YOU KNOWINGLY DO SUCH A THING?!

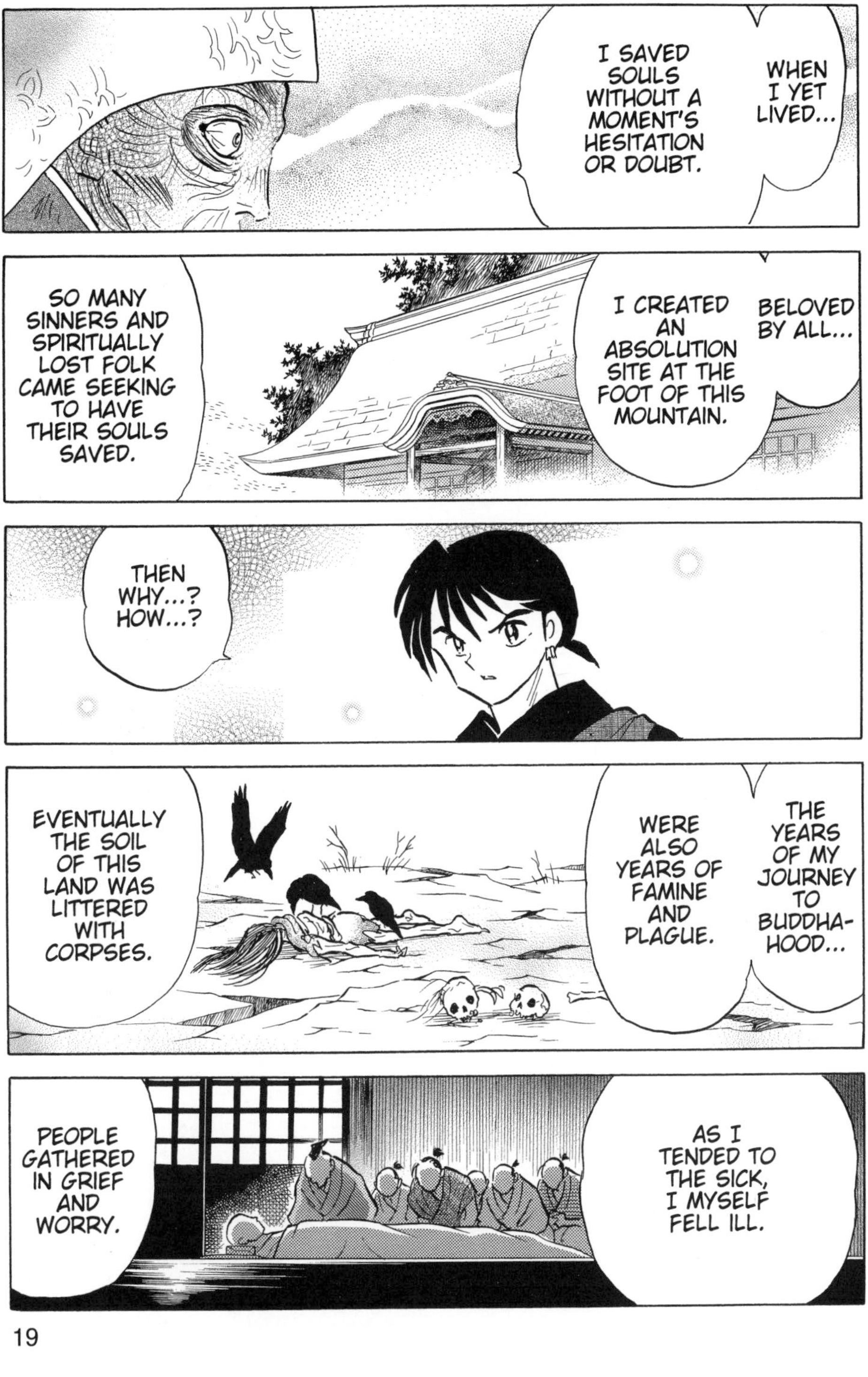
WHEN I YET LIVED...
I SAVED SOULS WITHOUT A MOMENT'S HESITATION OR DOUBT.
BELOVED BY ALL...
I CREATED AN ABSOLUTION SITE AT THE FOOT OF THIS MOUNTAIN.
SO MANY SINNERS AND SPIRITUALLY LOST FOLK CAME SEEKING TO HAVE THEIR SOULS SAVED.
THEN WHY...? HOW...?
THE YEARS OF MY JOURNEY TO BUDDHA-HOOD...
WERE ALSO YEARS OF FAMINE AND PLAGUE.
EVENTUALLY THE SOIL OF THIS LAND WAS LITTERED WITH CORPSES.
AS I TENDED TO THE SICK, I MYSELF FELL ILL.
PEOPLE GATHERED IN GRIEF AND WORRY.

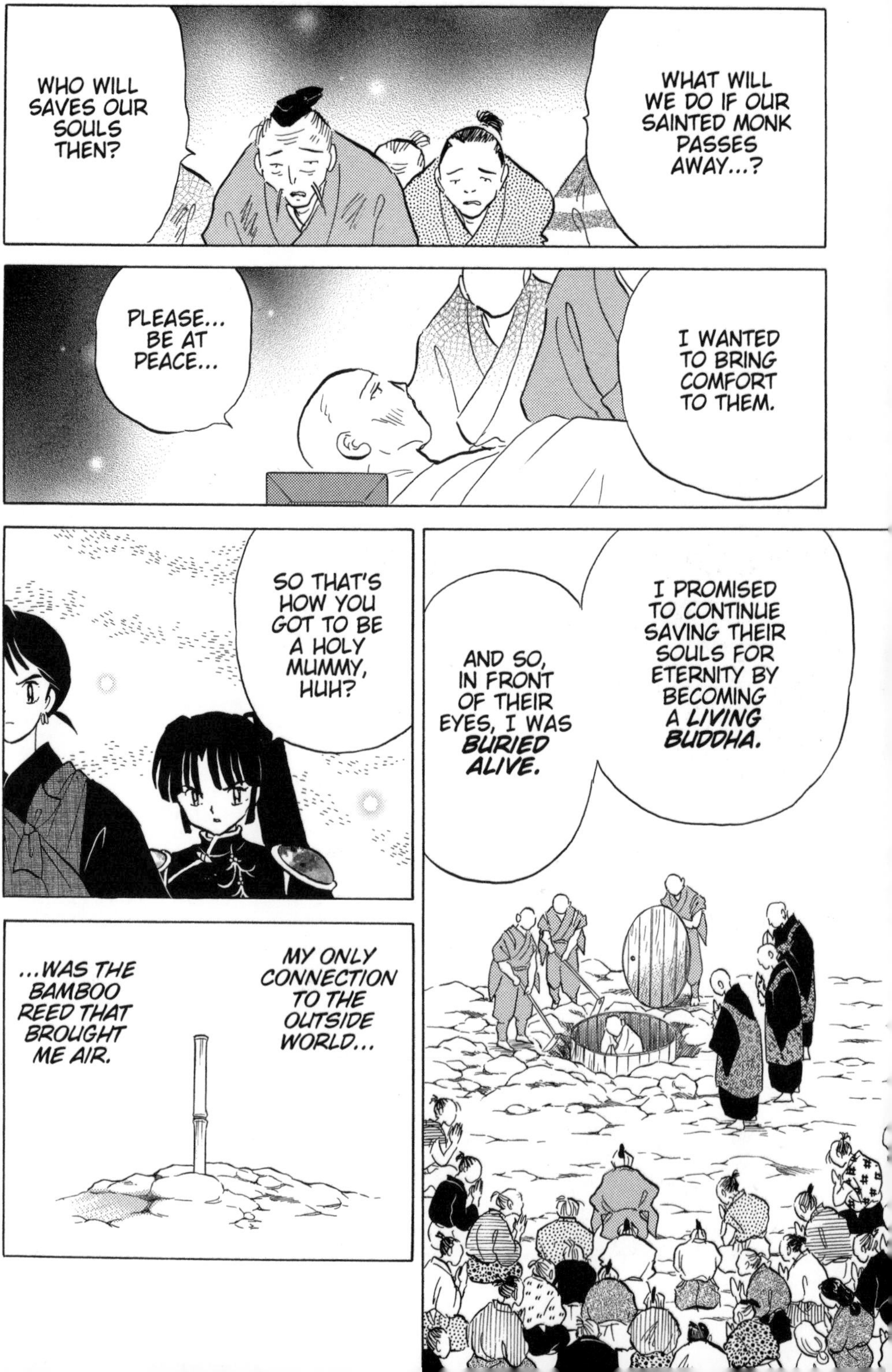
WHAT WILL WE DO IF OUR SAINTED MONK PASSES AWAY...?
WHO WILL SAVES OUR SOULS THEN?
I WANTED TO BRING COMFORT TO THEM.
PLEASE... BE AT PEACE...
I PROMISED TO CONTINUE SAVING THEIR SOULS FOR ETERNITY BY BECOMING A *LIVING BUDDHA.*
AND SO, IN FRONT OF THEIR EYES, I WAS *BURIED ALIVE.*
SO THAT'S HOW YOU GOT TO BE A HOLY MUMMY, HUH?
MY ONLY CONNECTION TO THE OUTSIDE WORLD...
...WAS THE BAMBOO REED THAT BROUGHT ME AIR.

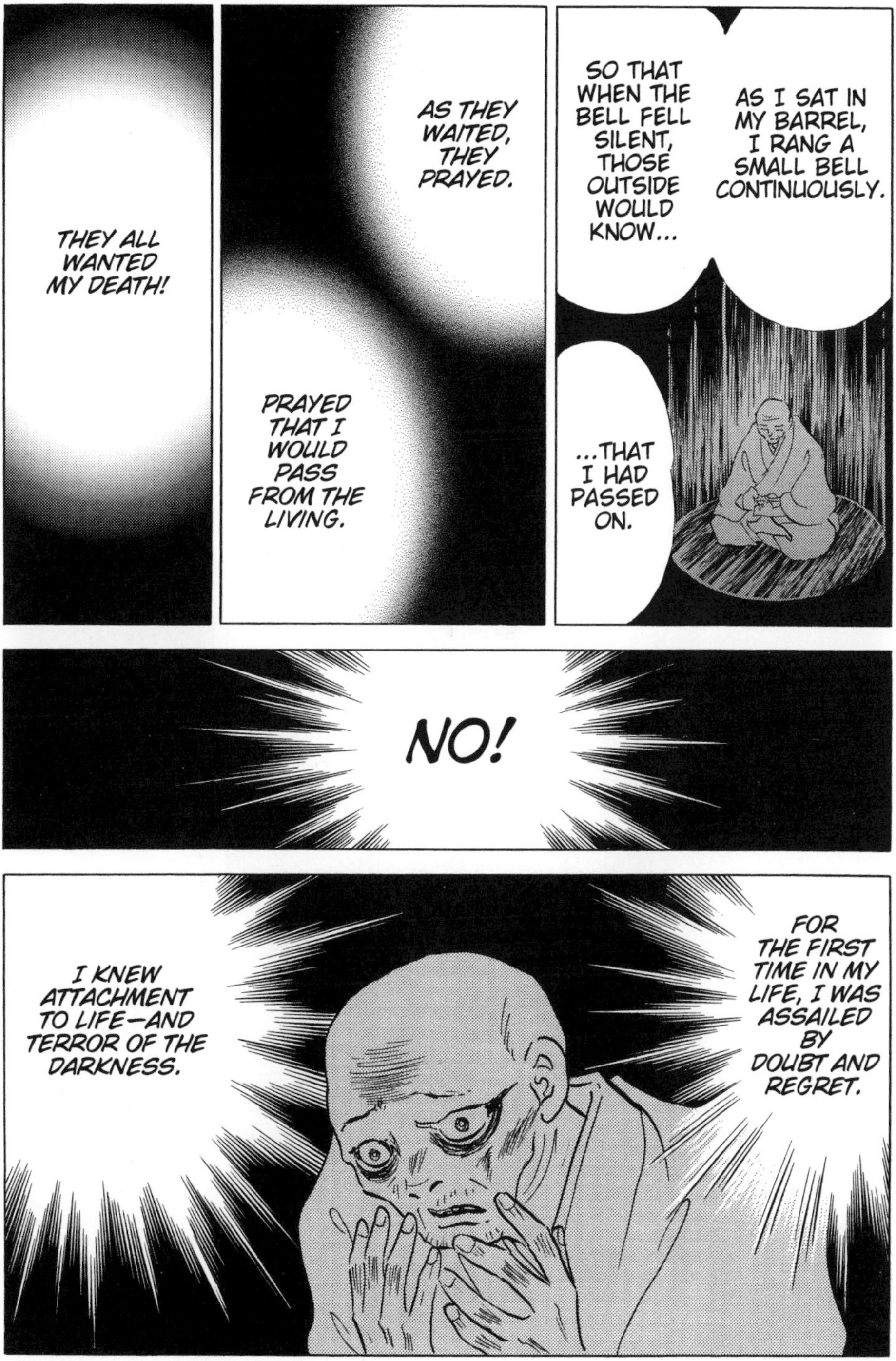
AS I SAT IN MY BARREL, I RANG A SMALL BELL CONTINUOUSLY.
SO THAT WHEN THE BELL FELL SILENT, THOSE OUTSIDE WOULD KNOW...
...THAT I HAD PASSED ON.
AS THEY WAITED, THEY PRAYED.
PRAYED THAT I WOULD PASS FROM THE LIVING.
THEY ALL WANTED MY DEATH!
NO!
FOR THE FIRST TIME IN MY LIFE, I WAS ASSAILED BY DOUBT AND REGRET.
I KNEW ATTACHMENT TO LIFE—AND TERROR OF THE DARKNESS.

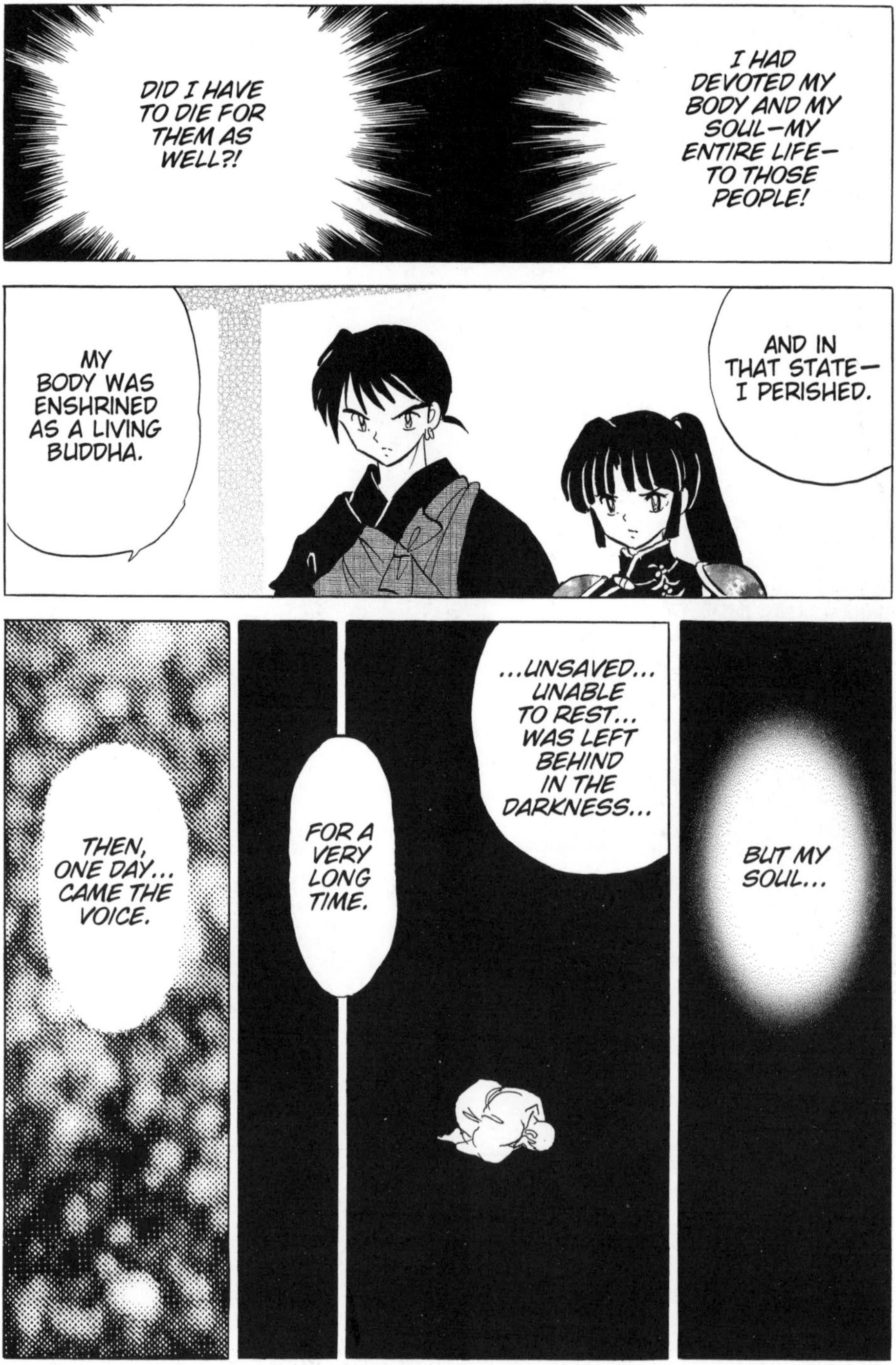
I HAD DEVOTED MY BODY AND MY SOUL—MY ENTIRE LIFE—TO THOSE PEOPLE!
DID I HAVE TO DIE FOR THEM AS WELL?!
AND IN THAT STATE—I PERISHED.
MY BODY WAS ENSHRINED AS A LIVING BUDDHA.
BUT MY SOUL...
...UNSAVED... UNABLE TO REST... WAS LEFT BEHIND IN THE DARKNESS...
FOR A VERY LONG TIME.
THEN, ONE DAY... CAME THE VOICE.

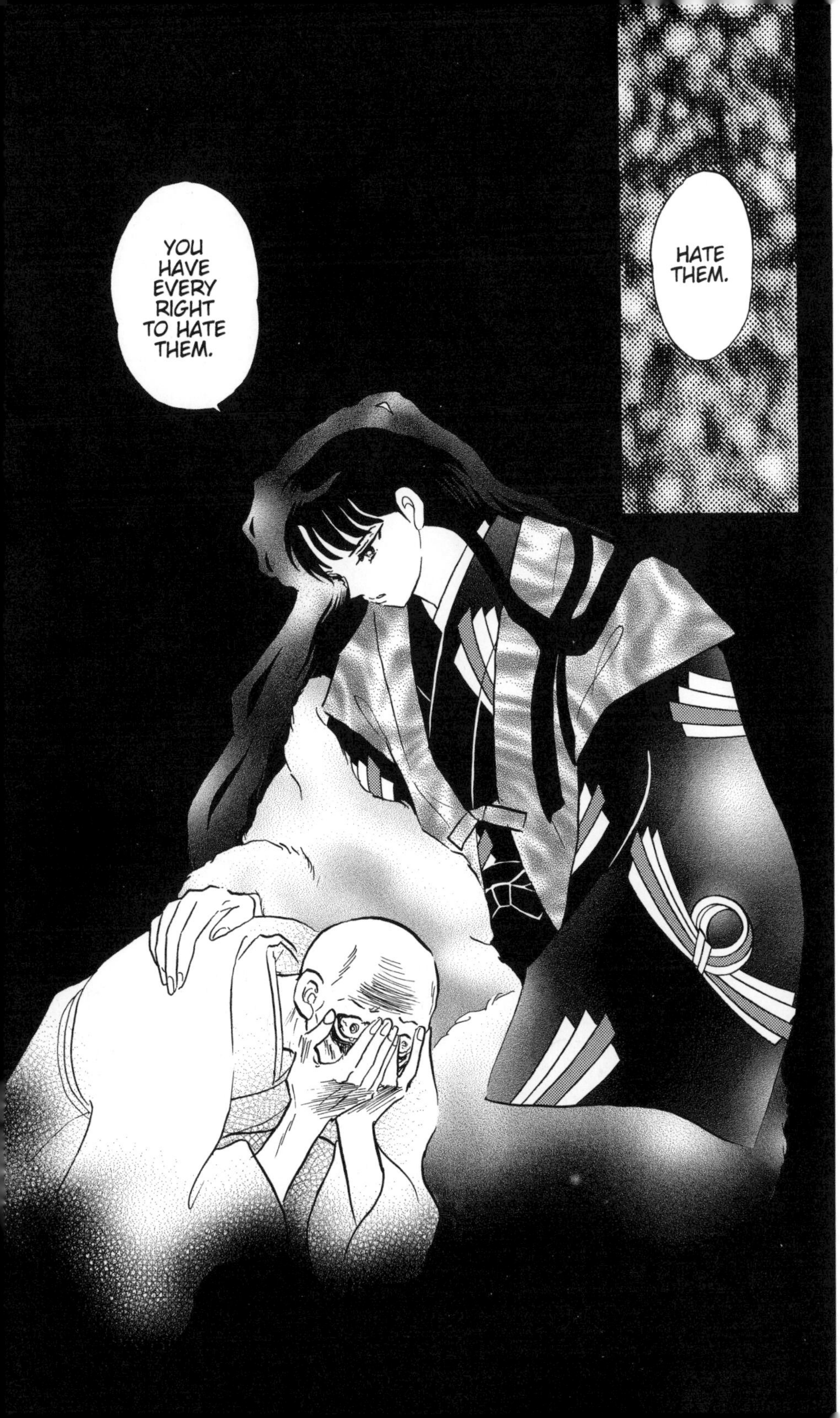
HATE THEM.
YOU HAVE EVERY RIGHT TO HATE THEM.

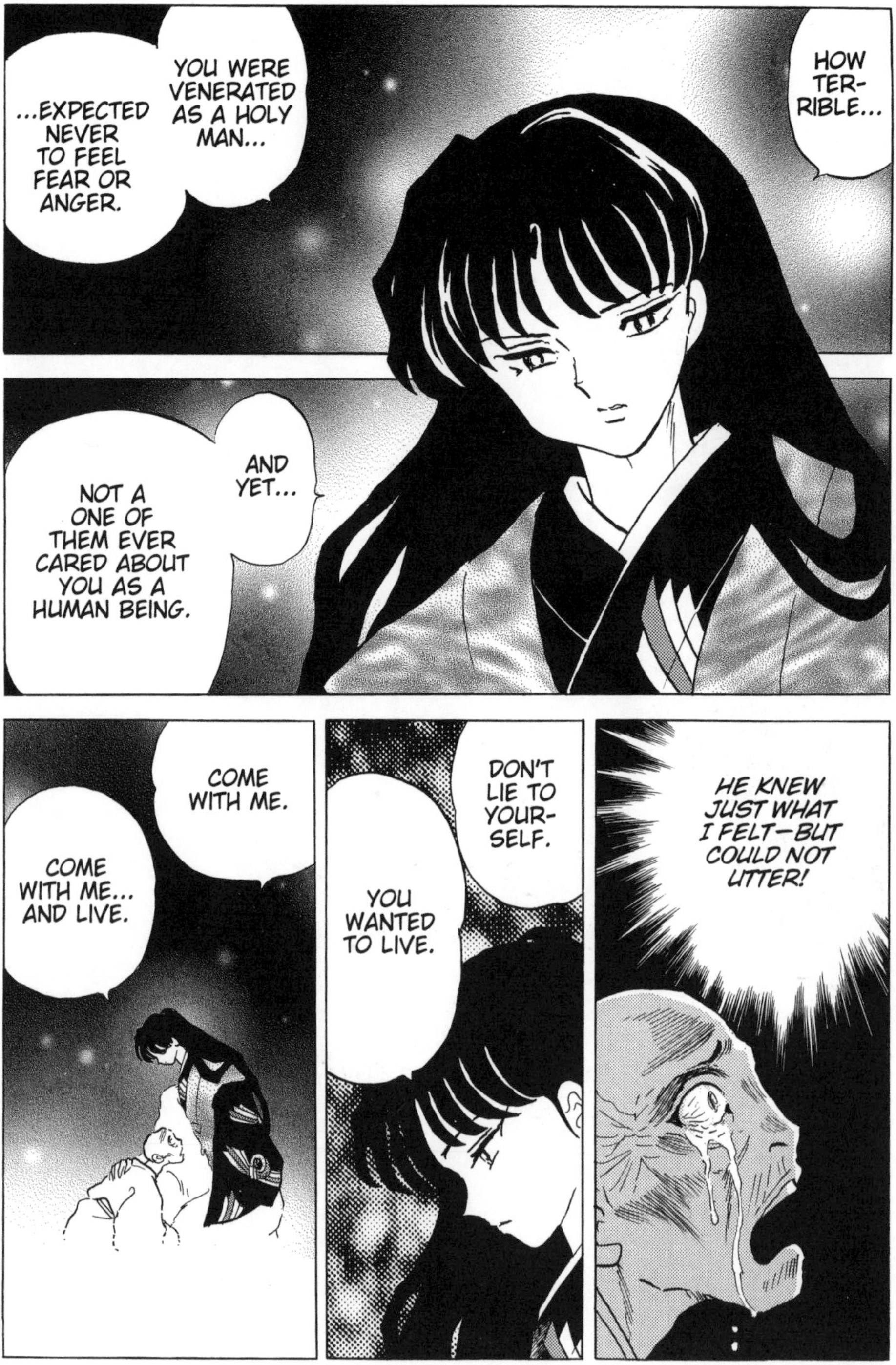
HOW TERRIBLE...
YOU WERE VENERATED AS A HOLY MAN...
...EXPECTED NEVER TO FEEL FEAR OR ANGER.
AND YET...
NOT A ONE OF THEM EVER CARED ABOUT YOU AS A HUMAN BEING.
HE KNEW JUST WHAT I FELT—BUT COULD NOT UTTER!
DON'T LIE TO YOURSELF.
YOU WANTED TO LIVE.
COME WITH ME.
COME WITH ME... AND LIVE.

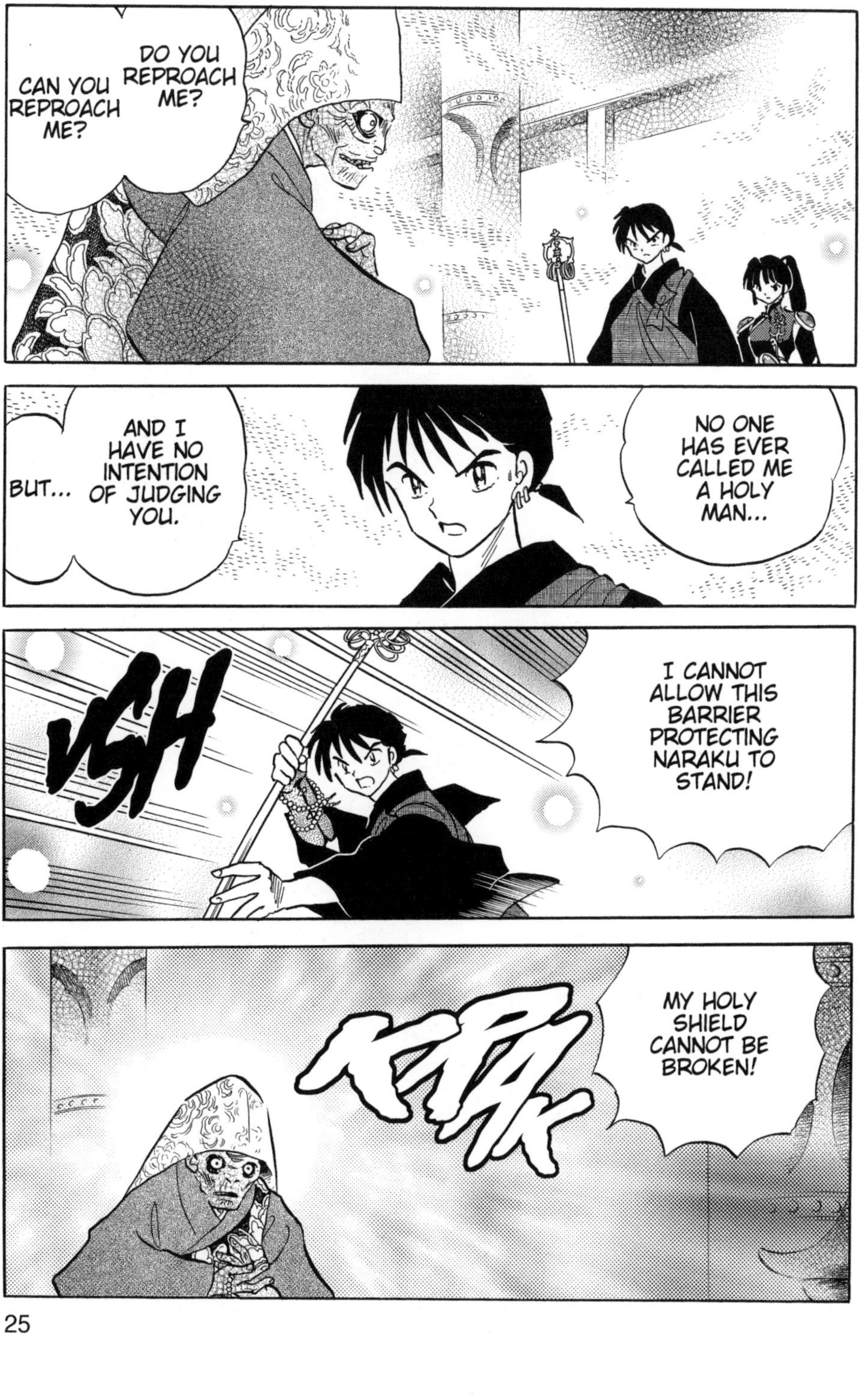
DO YOU REPROACH ME?
CAN YOU REPROACH ME?
NO ONE HAS EVER CALLED ME A HOLY MAN...
AND I HAVE NO INTENTION OF JUDGING YOU.
BUT...
I CANNOT ALLOW THIS BARRIER PROTECTING NARAKU TO STAND!
VSH
MY HOLY SHIELD CANNOT BE BROKEN!
KRAK

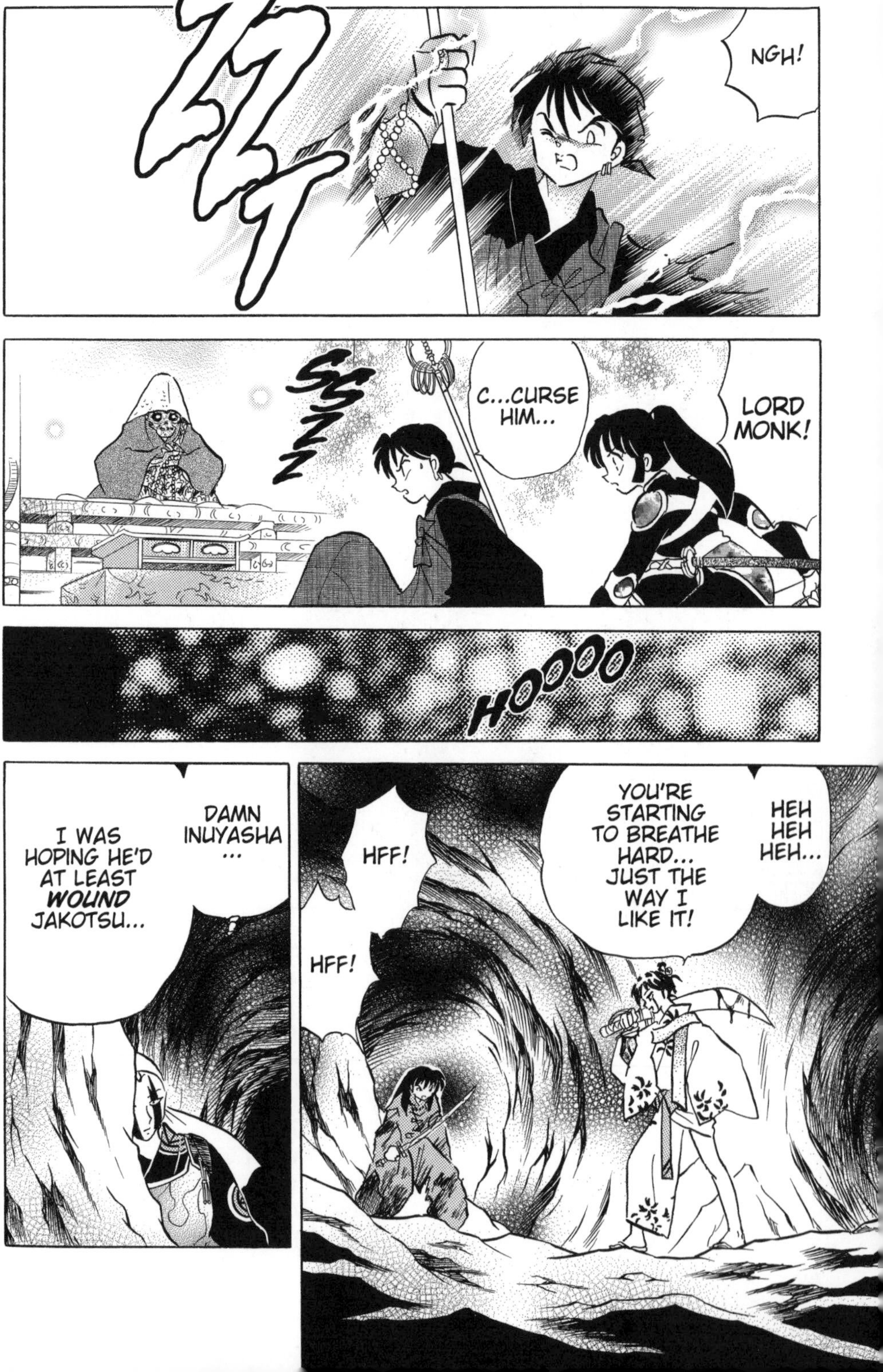

ZZT
NGH!
LORD MONK!
C...CURSE HIM...
SSZZZ
HOOOO
HEH HEH HEH...
YOU'RE STARTING TO BREATHE HARD... JUST THE WAY I LIKE IT!
HFF!
HFF!
DAMN INUYASHA...
I WAS HOPING HE'D AT LEAST **WOUND** JAKOTSU...

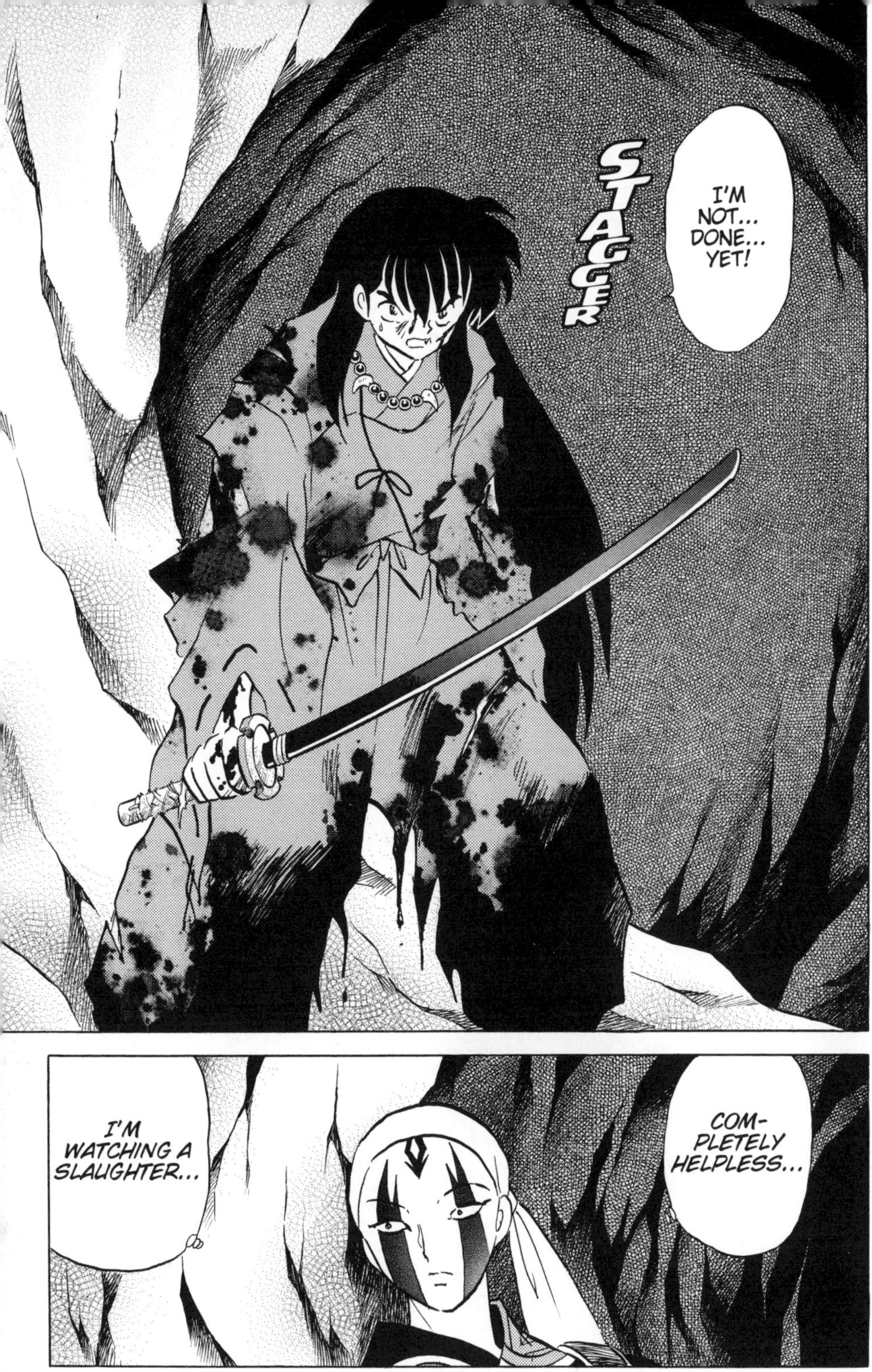
I'M NOT... DONE... YET!
STAGGER
COM-PLETELY HELPLESS...
I'M WATCHING A SLAUGHTER...

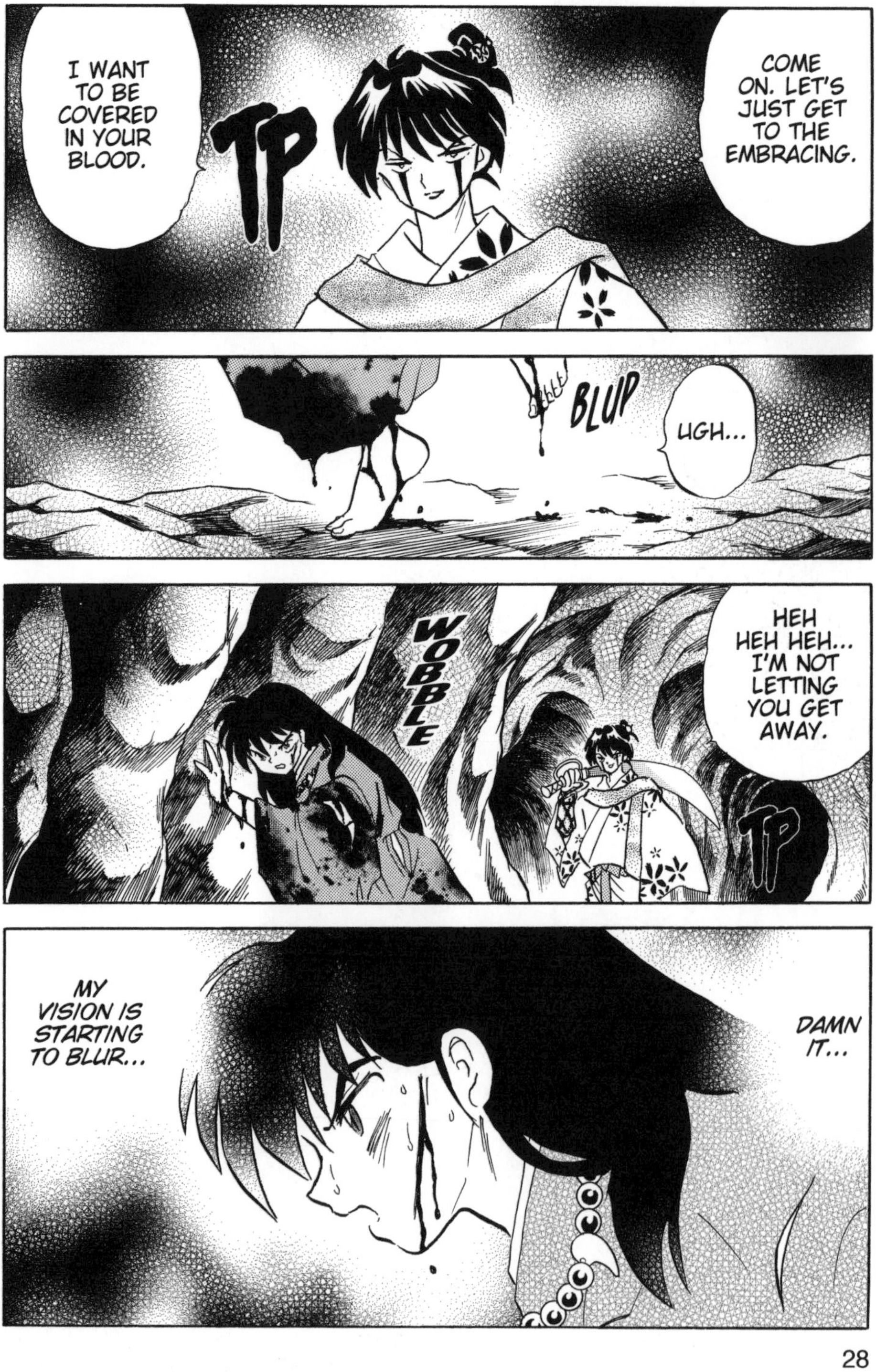
COME ON. LET'S JUST GET TO THE EMBRACING.
TP
I WANT TO BE COVERED IN YOUR BLOOD.
UGH...
BLUP
HEH HEH HEH... I'M NOT LETTING YOU GET AWAY.
TP
WOBBLE
DAMN IT...
MY VISION IS STARTING TO BLUR...

SCROLL TWO
MOUNT HAKUREI CHANGES

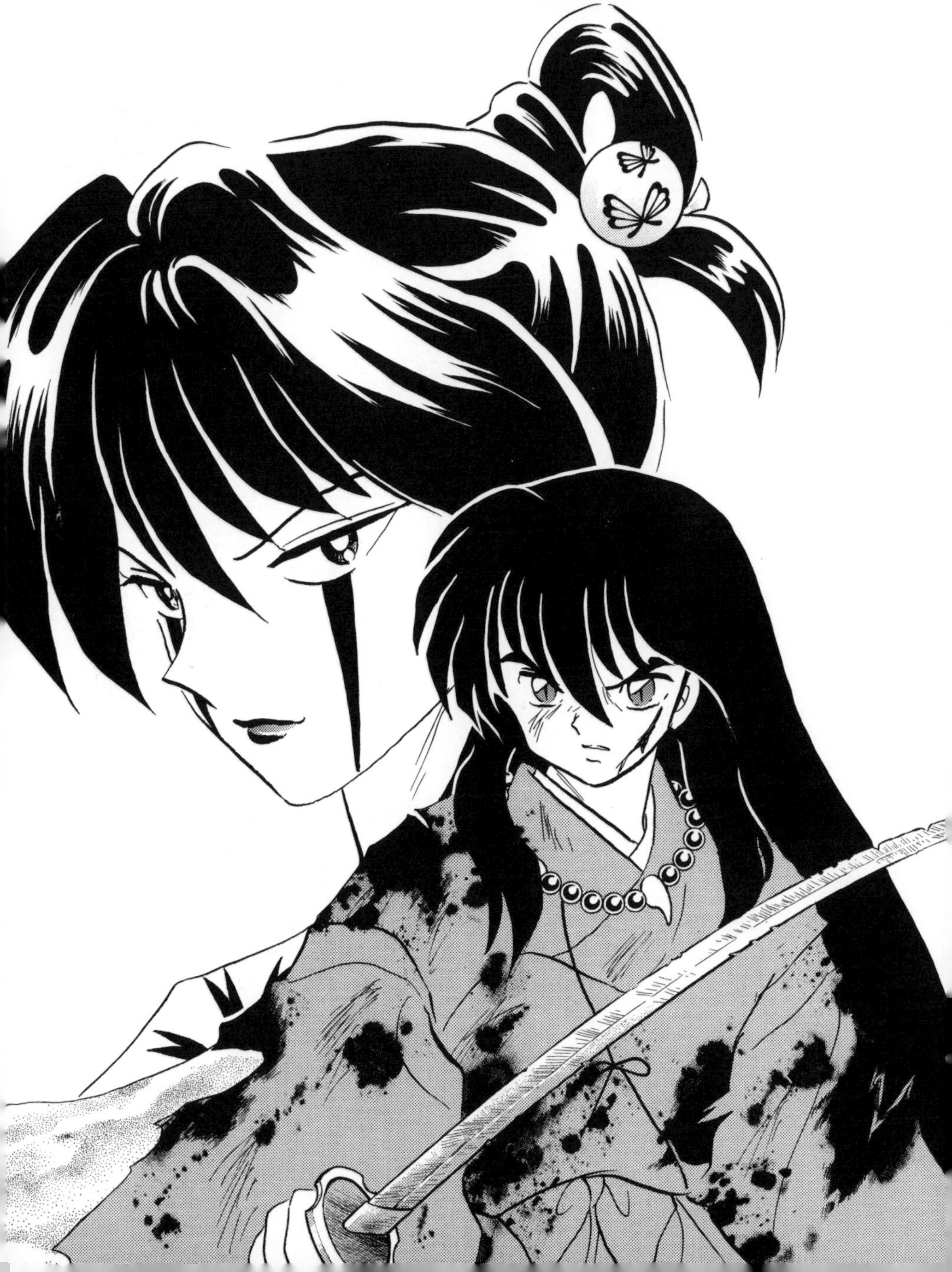

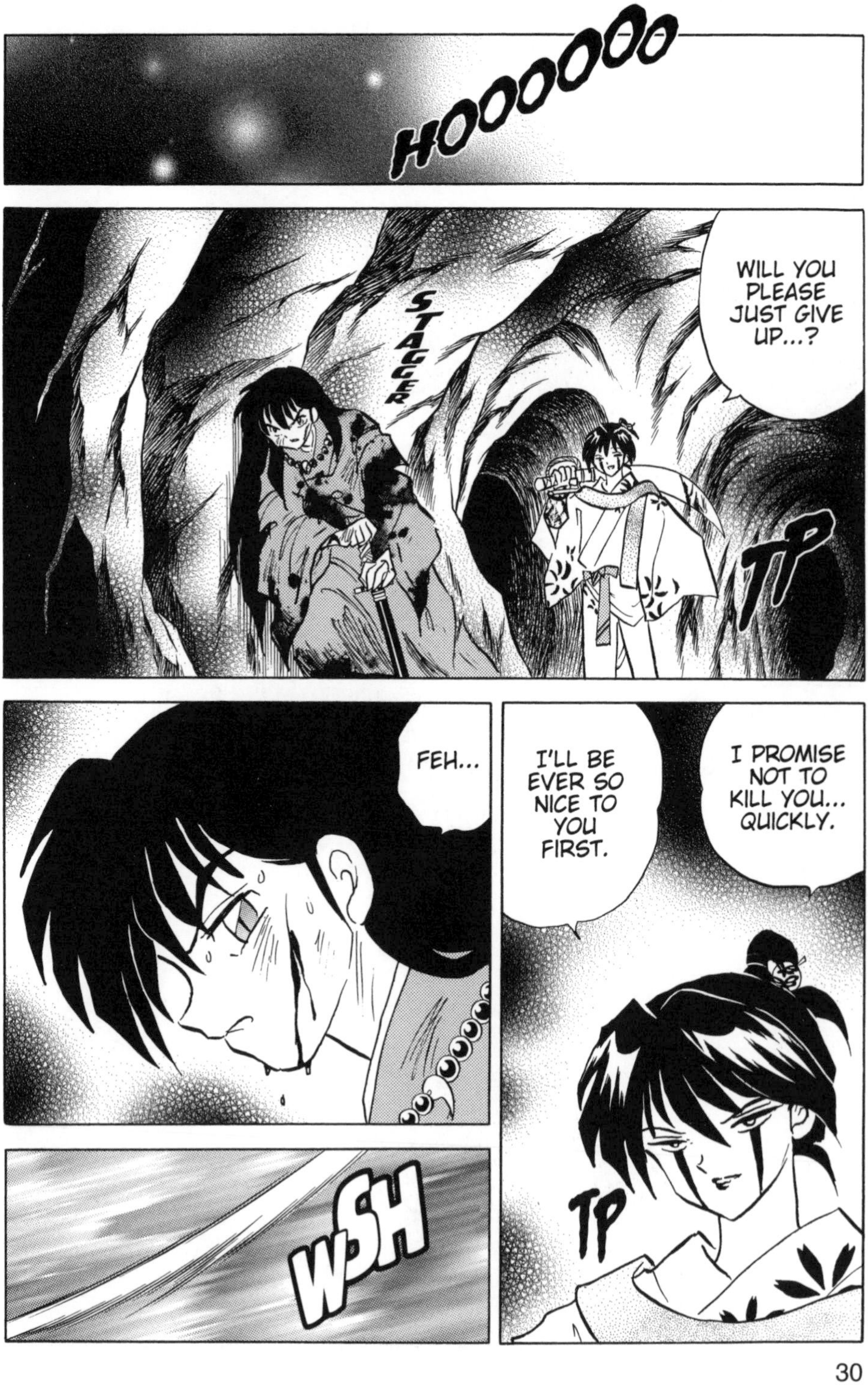
HOOOOOO
WILL YOU PLEASE JUST GIVE UP...?
STAGGER
TP
I PROMISE NOT TO KILL YOU... QUICKLY.
I'LL BE EVER SO NICE TO YOU FIRST.
TP
FEH...
WSH

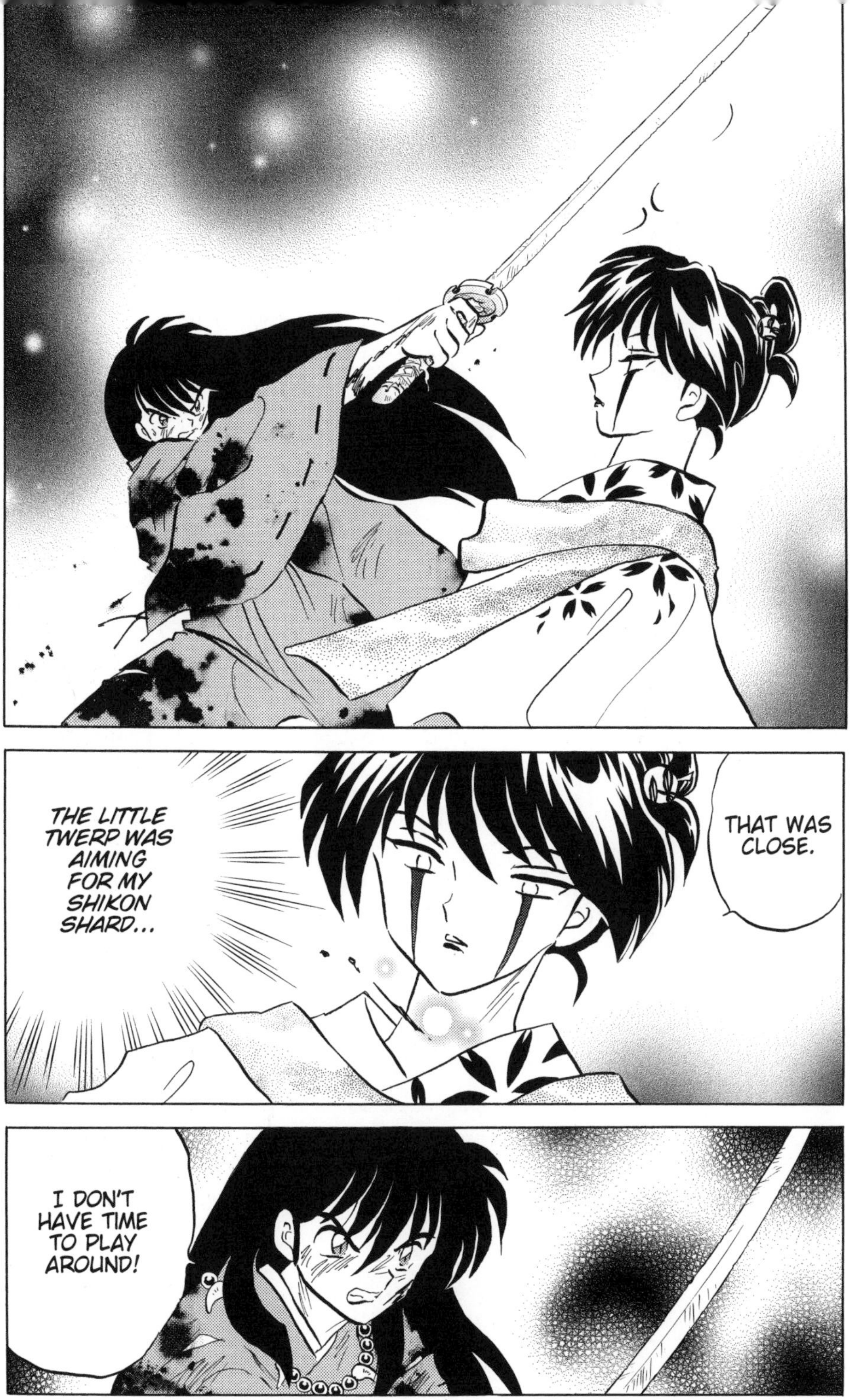
THAT WAS CLOSE.
THE LITTLE TWERP WAS AIMING FOR MY SHIKON SHARD...
I DON'T HAVE TIME TO PLAY AROUND!

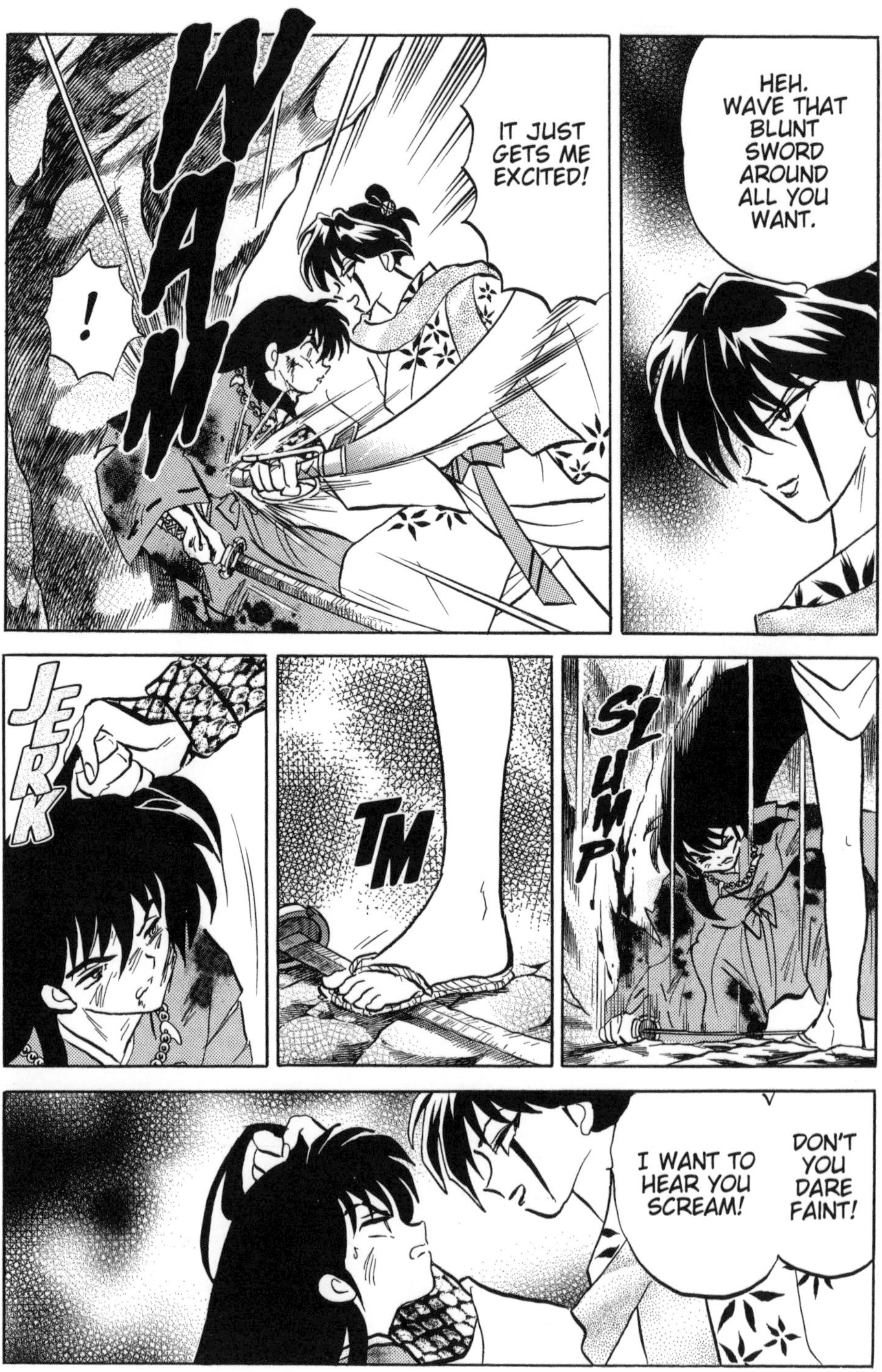
HEH. WAVE THAT BLUNT SWORD AROUND ALL YOU WANT.
IT JUST GETS ME EXCITED!
WAM
!
SLUMP
TM
JERK
DON'T YOU DARE FAINT!
I WANT TO HEAR YOU SCREAM!

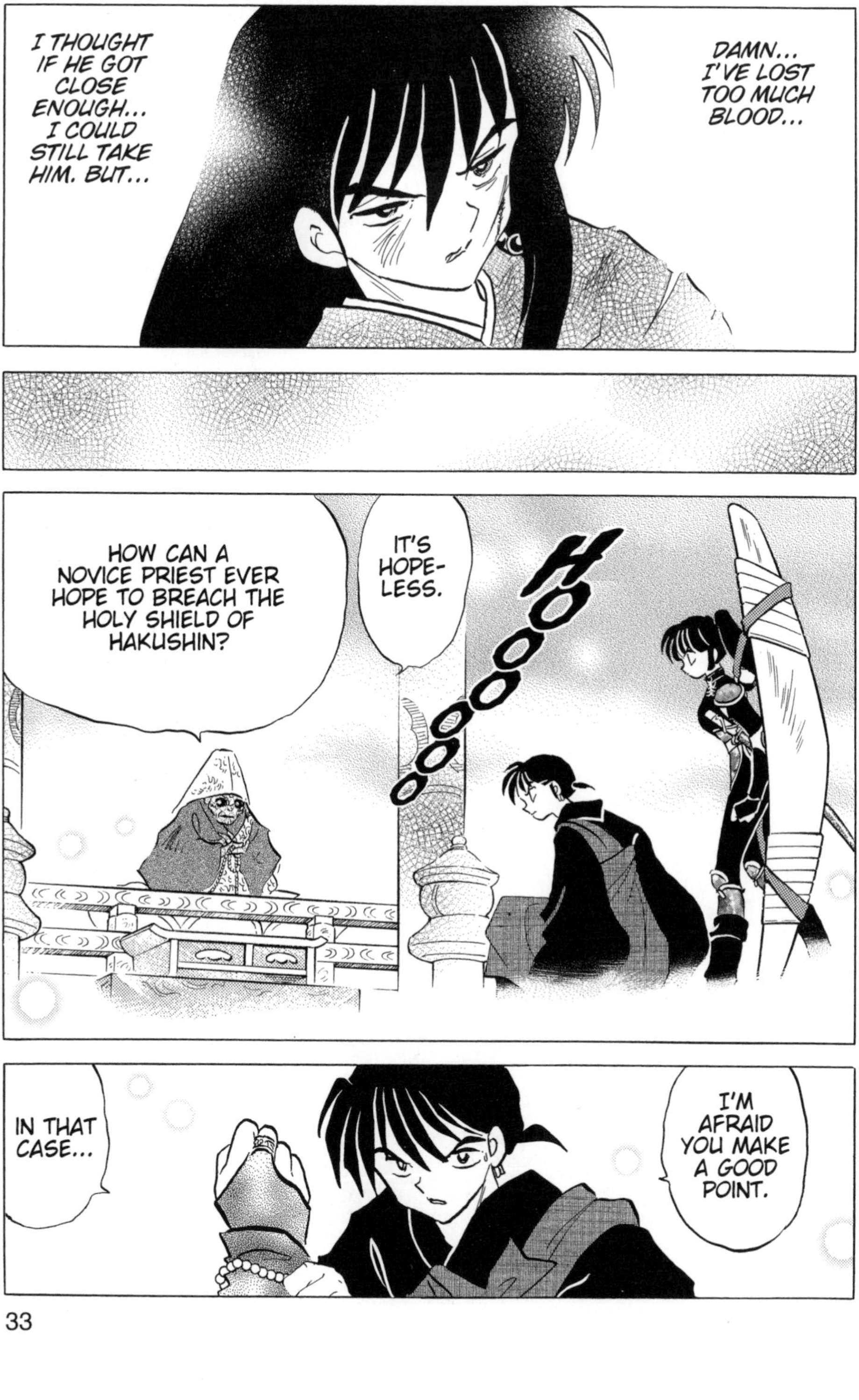
DAMN... I'VE LOST TOO MUCH BLOOD...
I THOUGHT IF HE GOT CLOSE ENOUGH... I COULD STILL TAKE HIM. BUT...
HOOOOOOOO
IT'S HOPE-LESS.
HOW CAN A NOVICE PRIEST EVER HOPE TO BREACH THE HOLY SHIELD OF HAKUSHIN?
I'M AFRAID YOU MAKE A GOOD POINT.
IN THAT CASE...

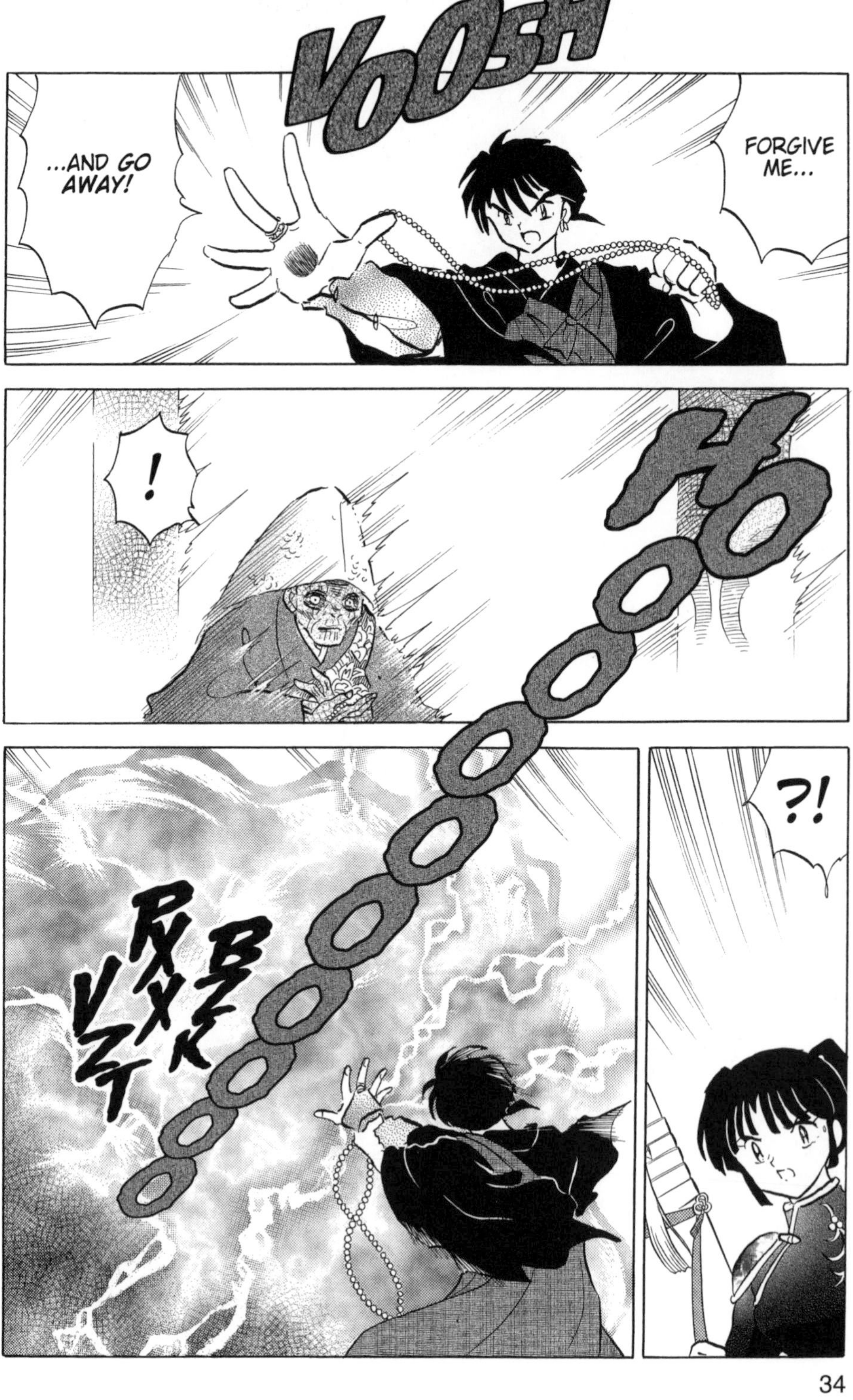
VOOSH
FORGIVE ME...
...AND GO AWAY!
!
HOOOOOOOOOOOOOO
?!
BZZK

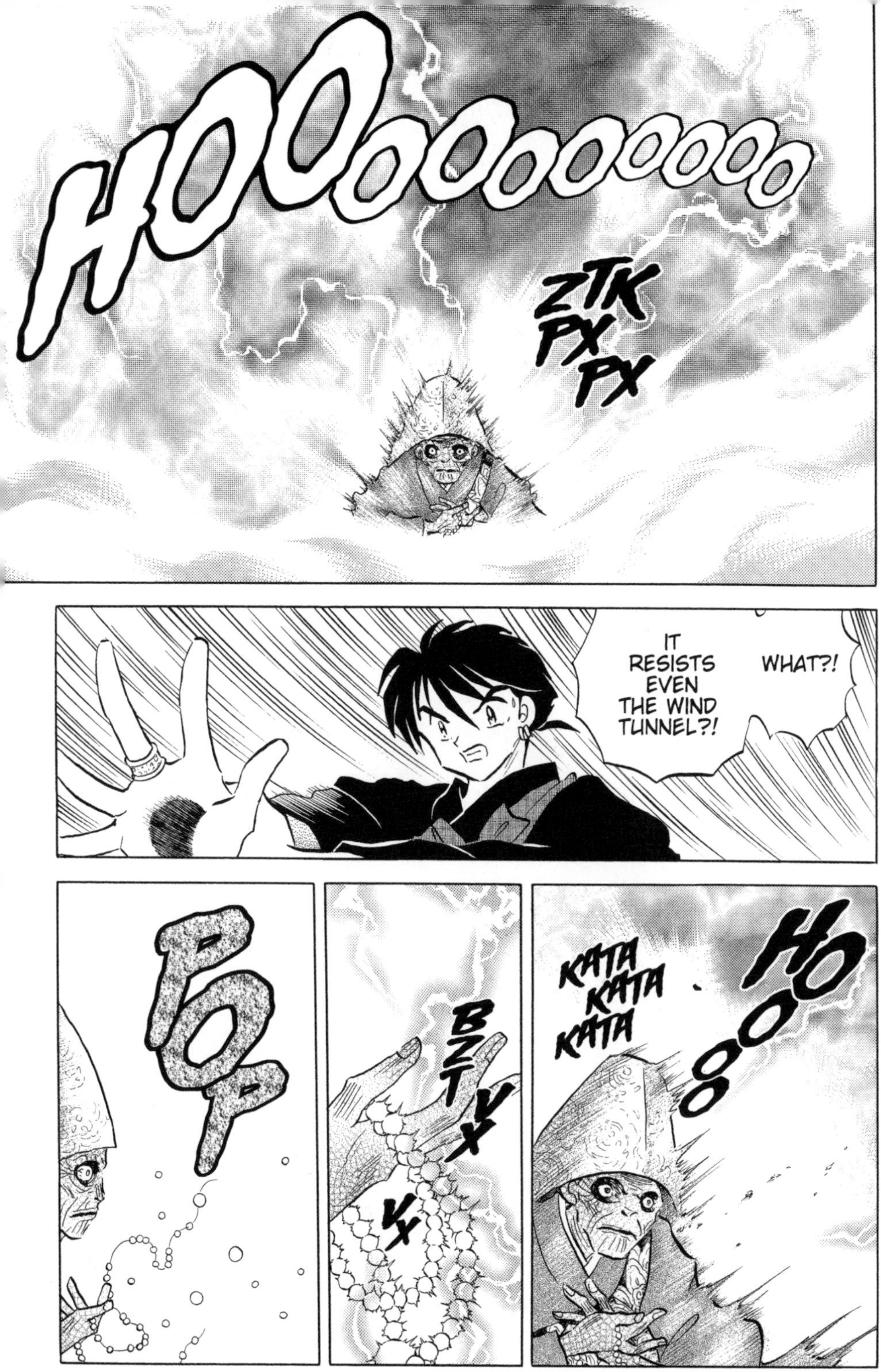
HOOOOOOOOOO
ZTK
PX PX
WHAT?!
IT RESISTS EVEN THE WIND TUNNEL?!
HOOOO
KATA KATA KATA
BZZT
VX VX
POP

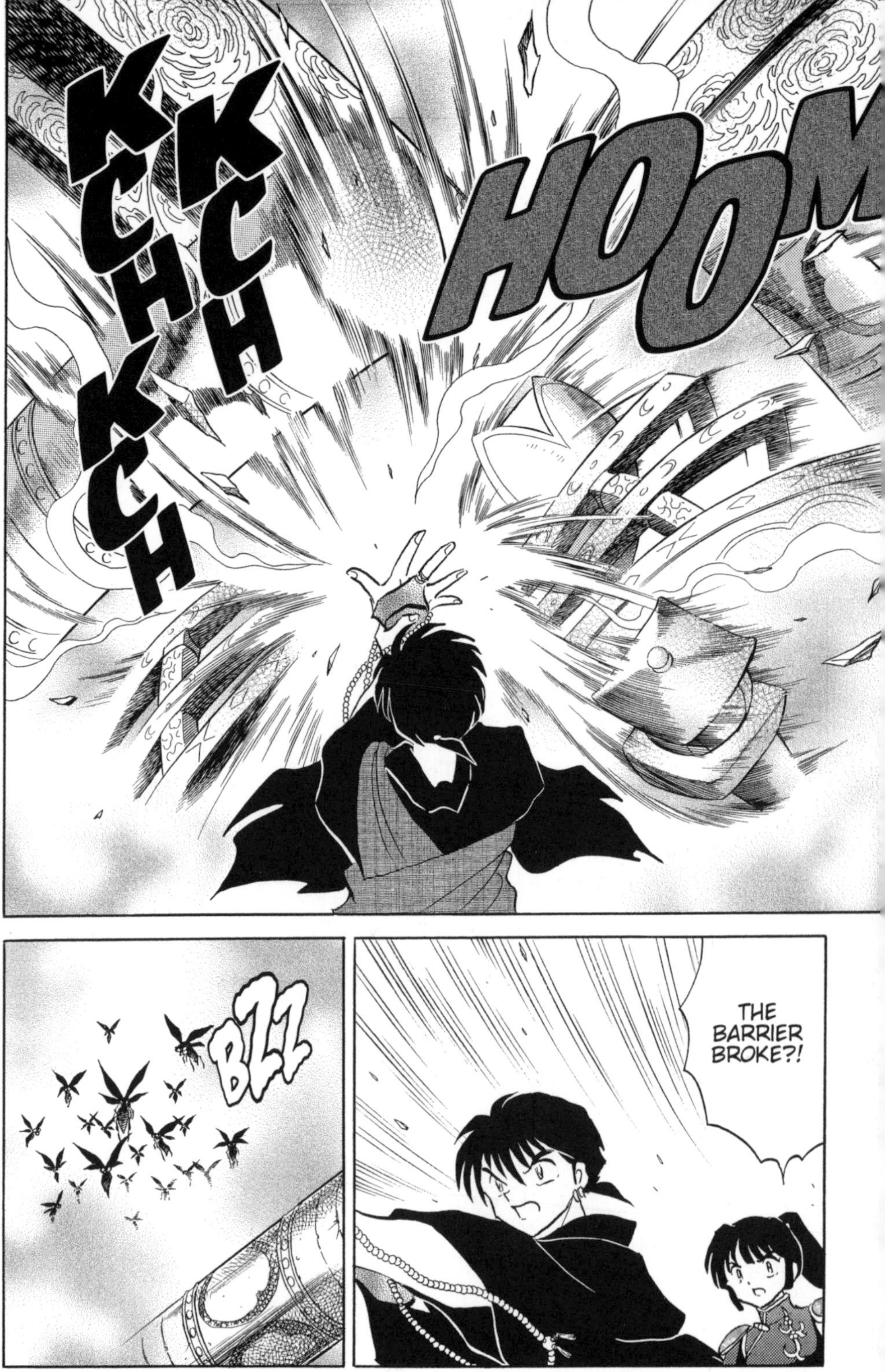
HOOM
KCH
KCHKCH
THE BARRIER BROKE?!
BZZ

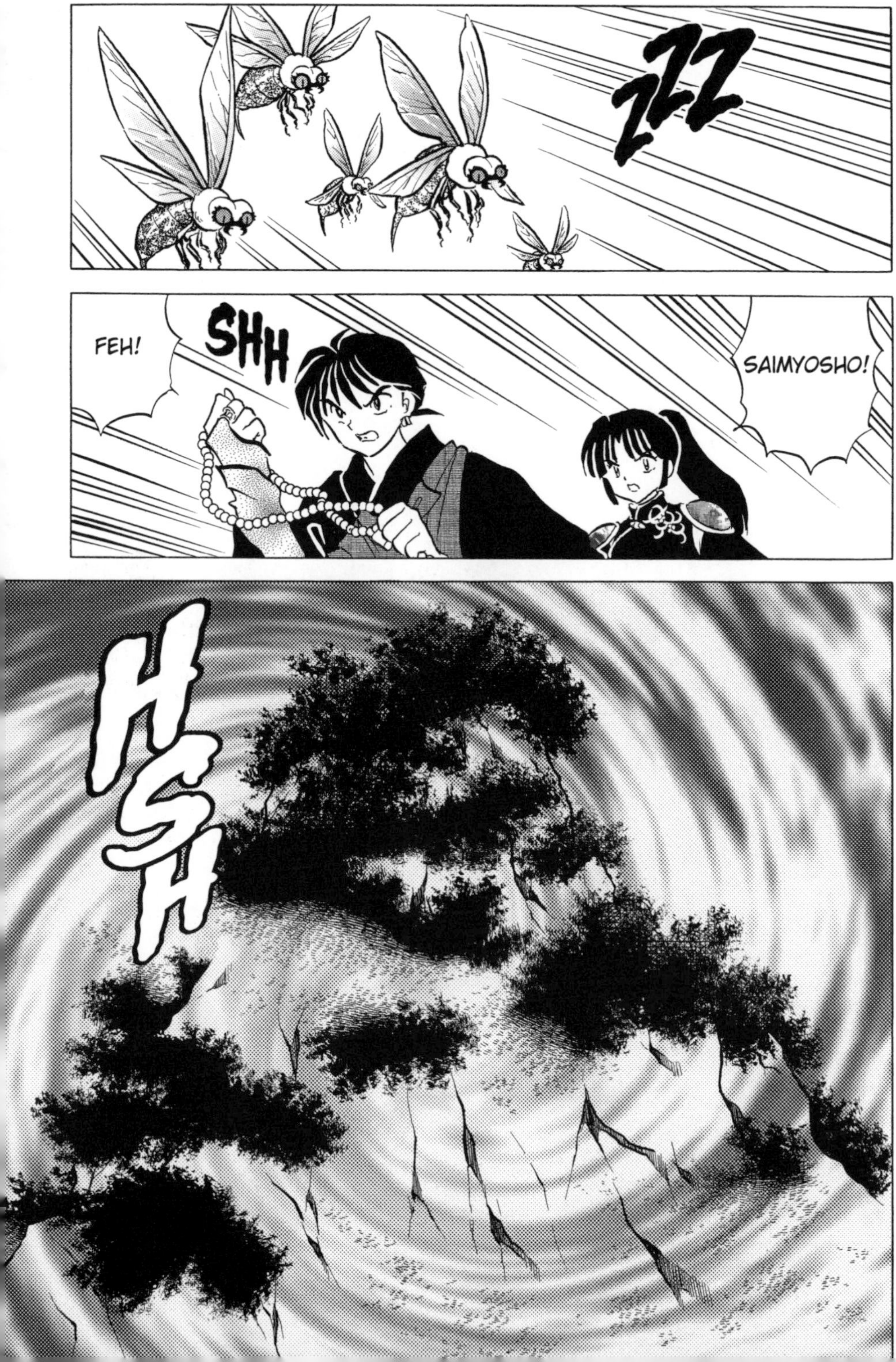
ZZZ
SAIMYOSHO!
SHH
FEH!
HSH

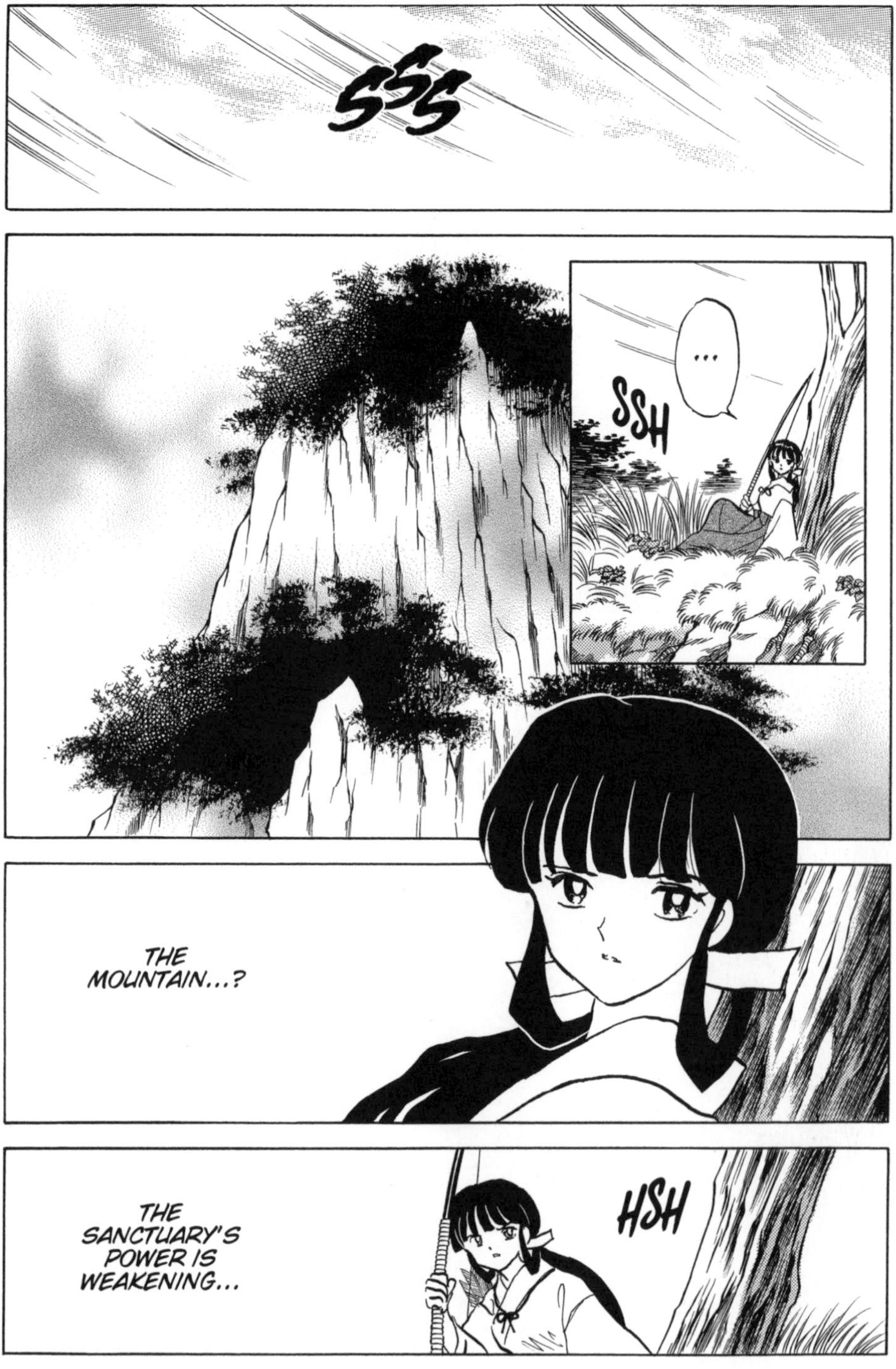
SSS
...
SSH
THE MOUNTAIN...?
HSH
THE SANCTUARY'S POWER IS WEAKENING...

SOMETHING
JUST
SLIPPED
OUT...

!

GLEEM

EH?

THE
HORDE...

SUDDENLY
SO
RESTLESS...

?!

39

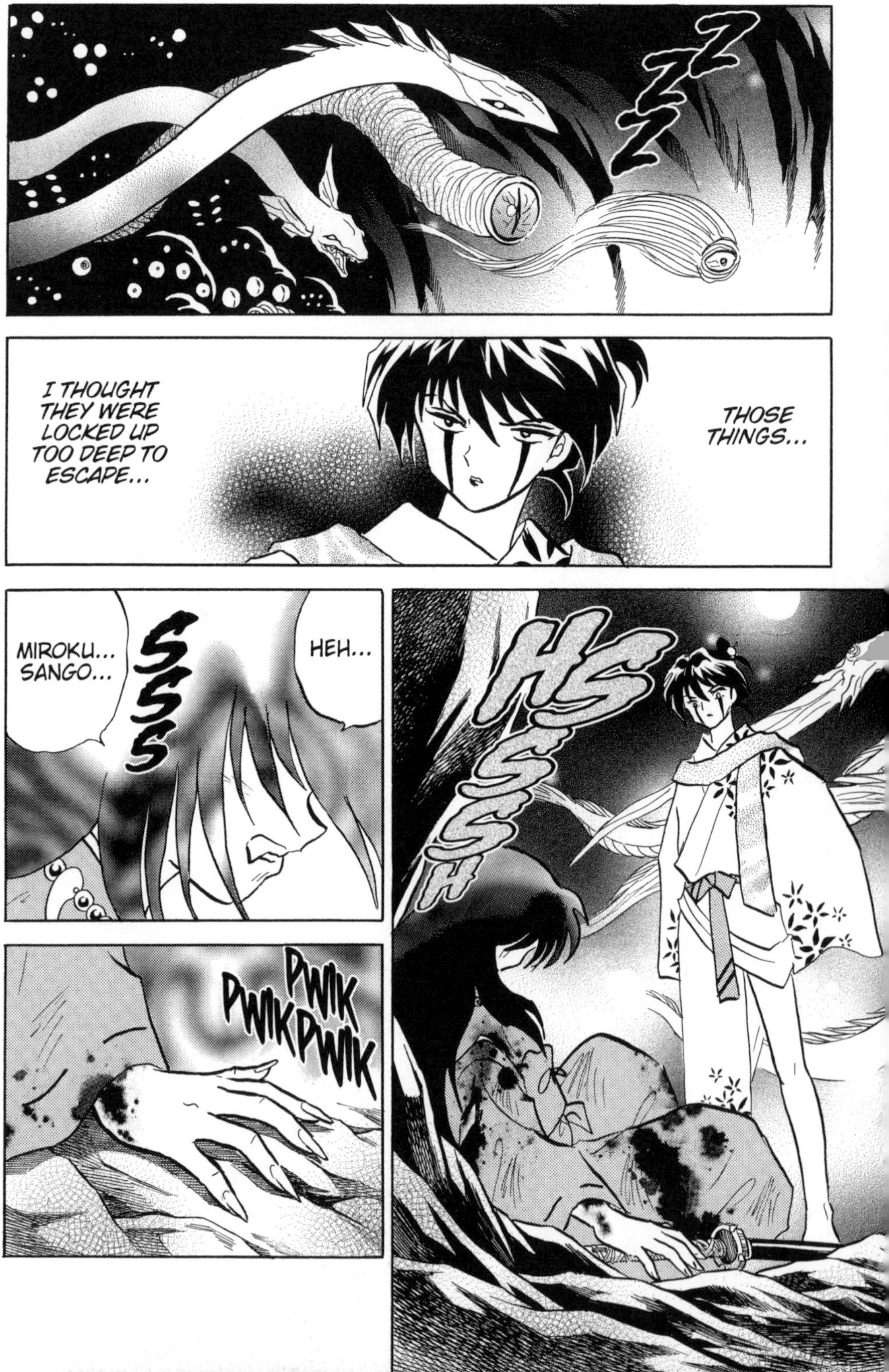
ZZZ
THOSE THINGS...
I THOUGHT THEY WERE LOCKED UP TOO DEEP TO ESCAPE...
HSSSSH
HEH...
SSSS
MIROKU... SANGO...
PWIK PWIK PWIK

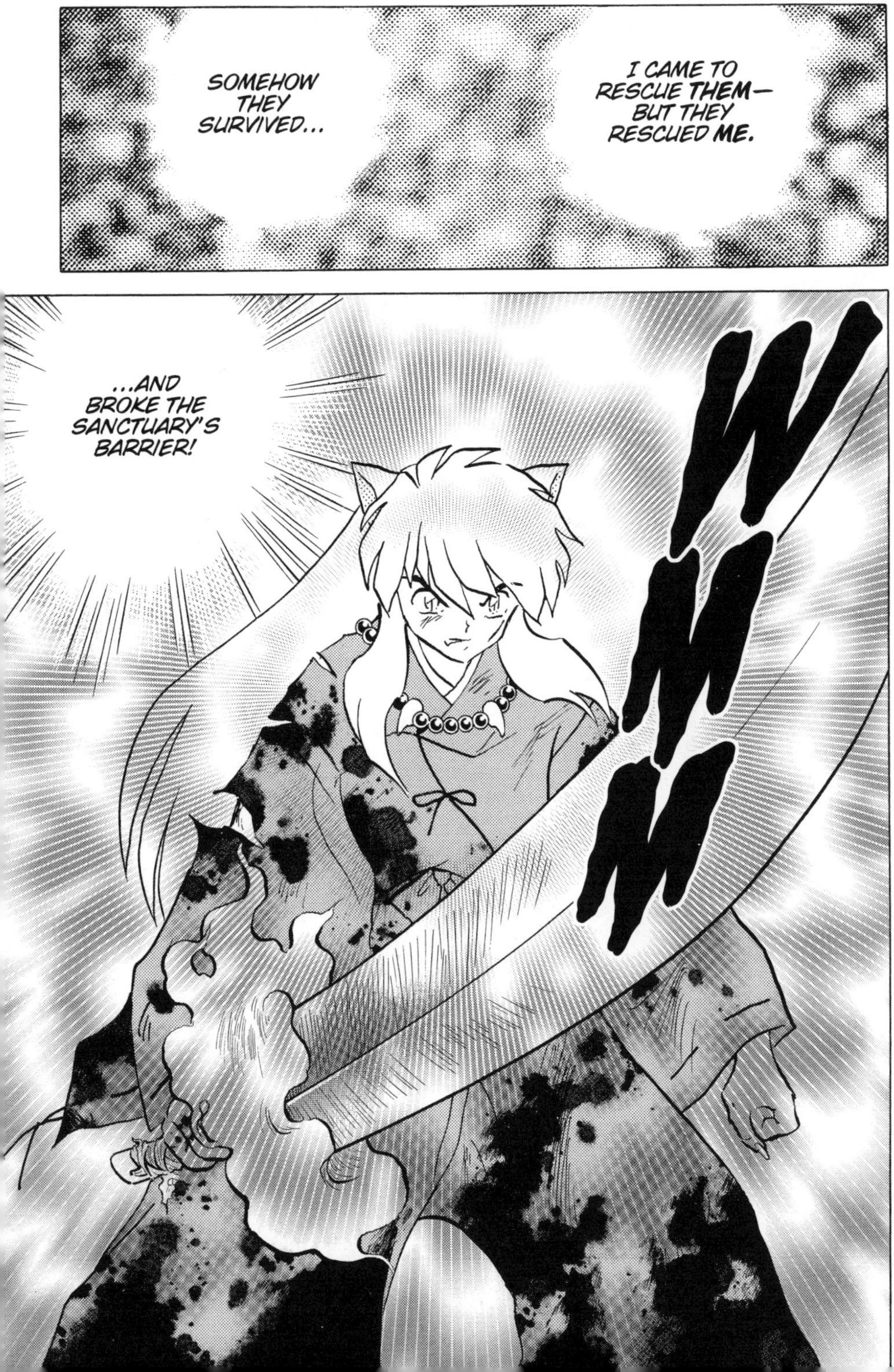
I CAME TO RESCUE THEM—BUT THEY RESCUED ME.
SOMEHOW THEY SURVIVED...
...AND BROKE THE SANCTUARY'S BARRIER!
WMMM

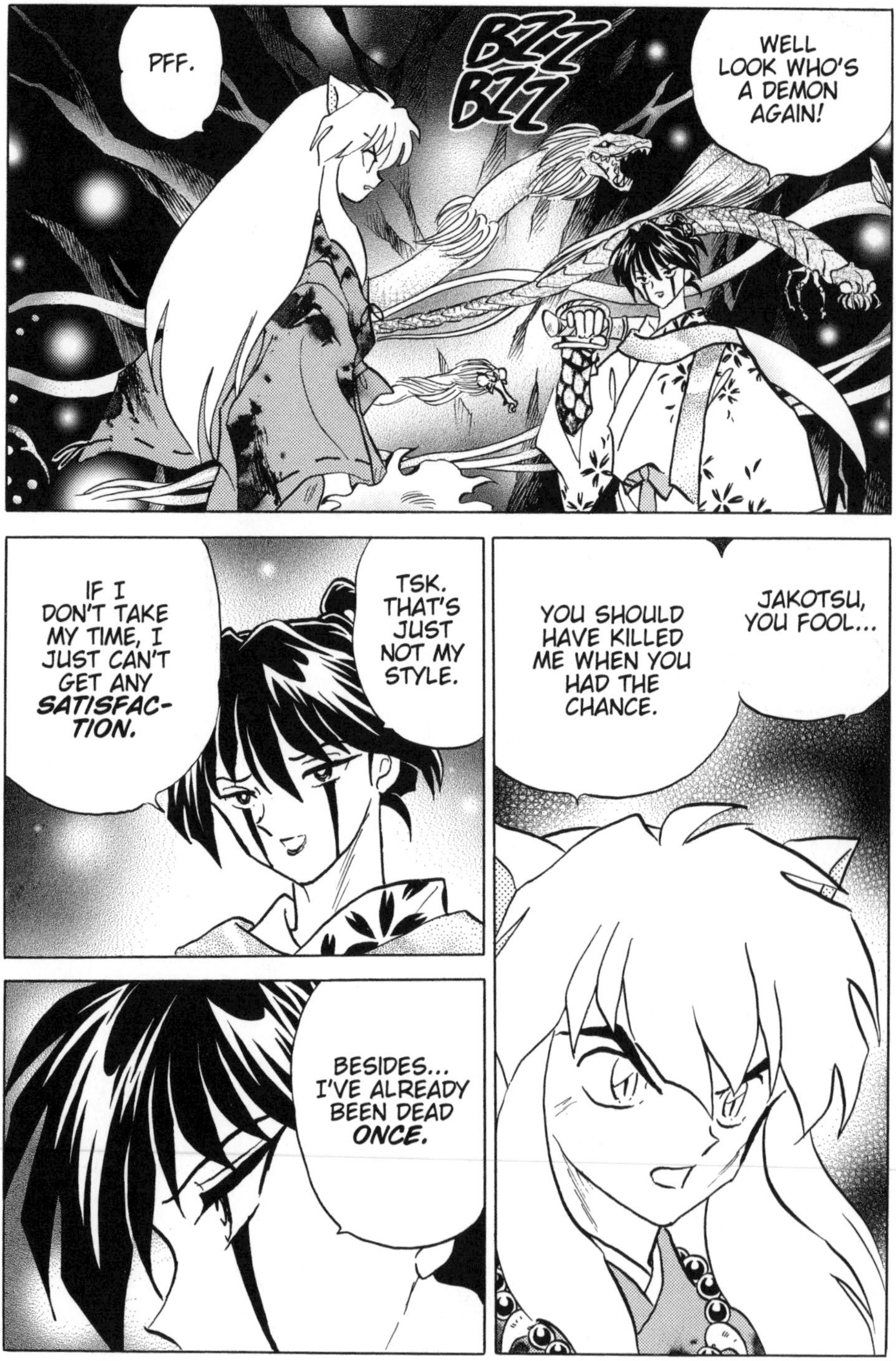
WELL LOOK WHO'S A DEMON AGAIN!
BZZZ BZZZ
PFF.
JAKOTSU, YOU FOOL...
YOU SHOULD HAVE KILLED ME WHEN YOU HAD THE CHANCE.
TSK. THAT'S JUST NOT MY STYLE.
IF I DON'T TAKE MY TIME, I JUST CAN'T GET ANY SATISFACTION.
BESIDES... I'VE ALREADY BEEN DEAD ONCE.

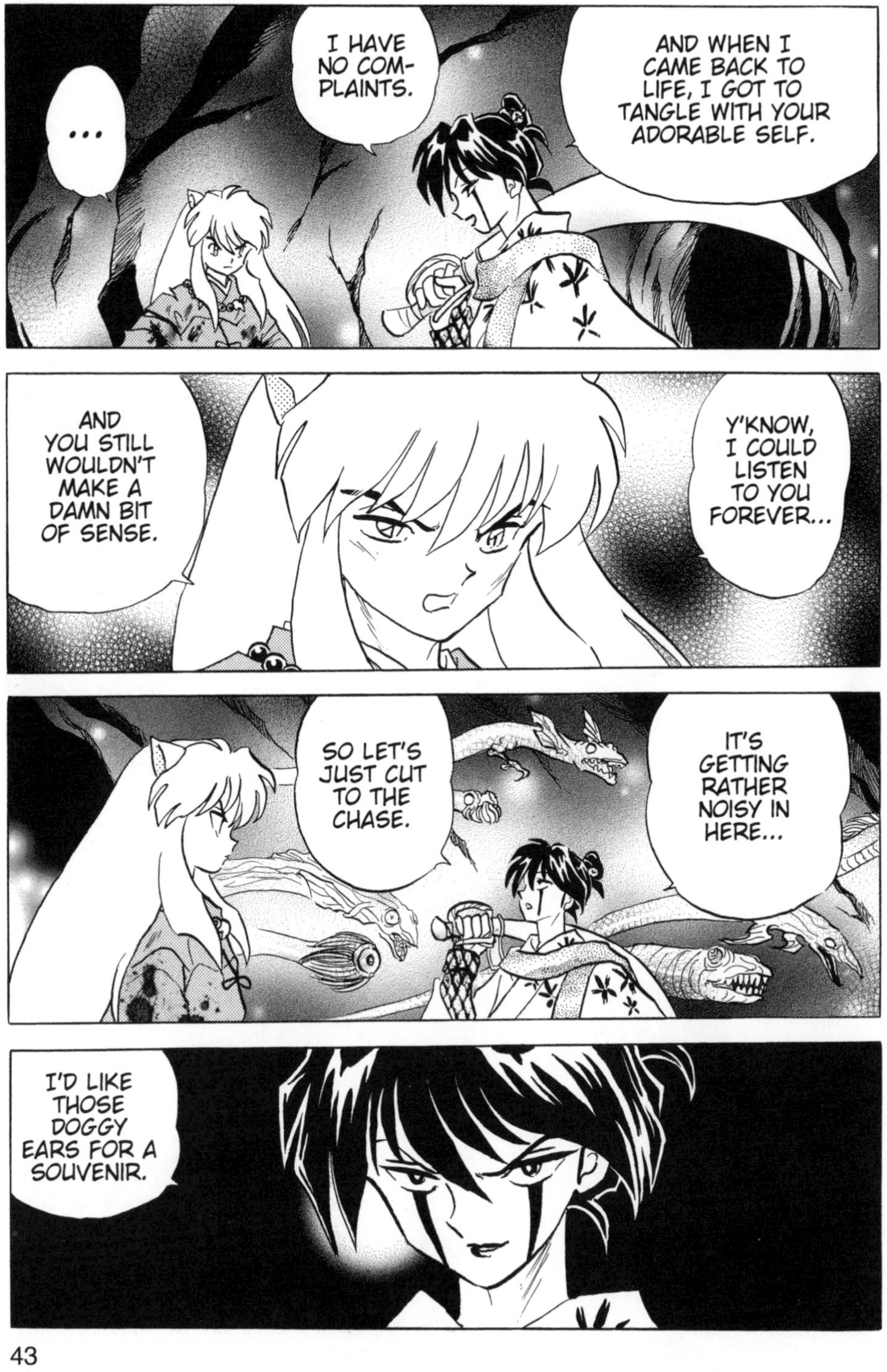
AND WHEN I CAME BACK TO LIFE, I GOT TO TANGLE WITH YOUR ADORABLE SELF.
I HAVE NO COM-PLAINTS.
...
Y'KNOW, I COULD LISTEN TO YOU FOREVER...
AND YOU STILL WOULDN'T MAKE A DAMN BIT OF SENSE.
IT'S GETTING RATHER NOISY IN HERE...
SO LET'S JUST CUT TO THE CHASE.
I'D LIKE THOSE DOGGY EARS FOR A SOUVENIR.

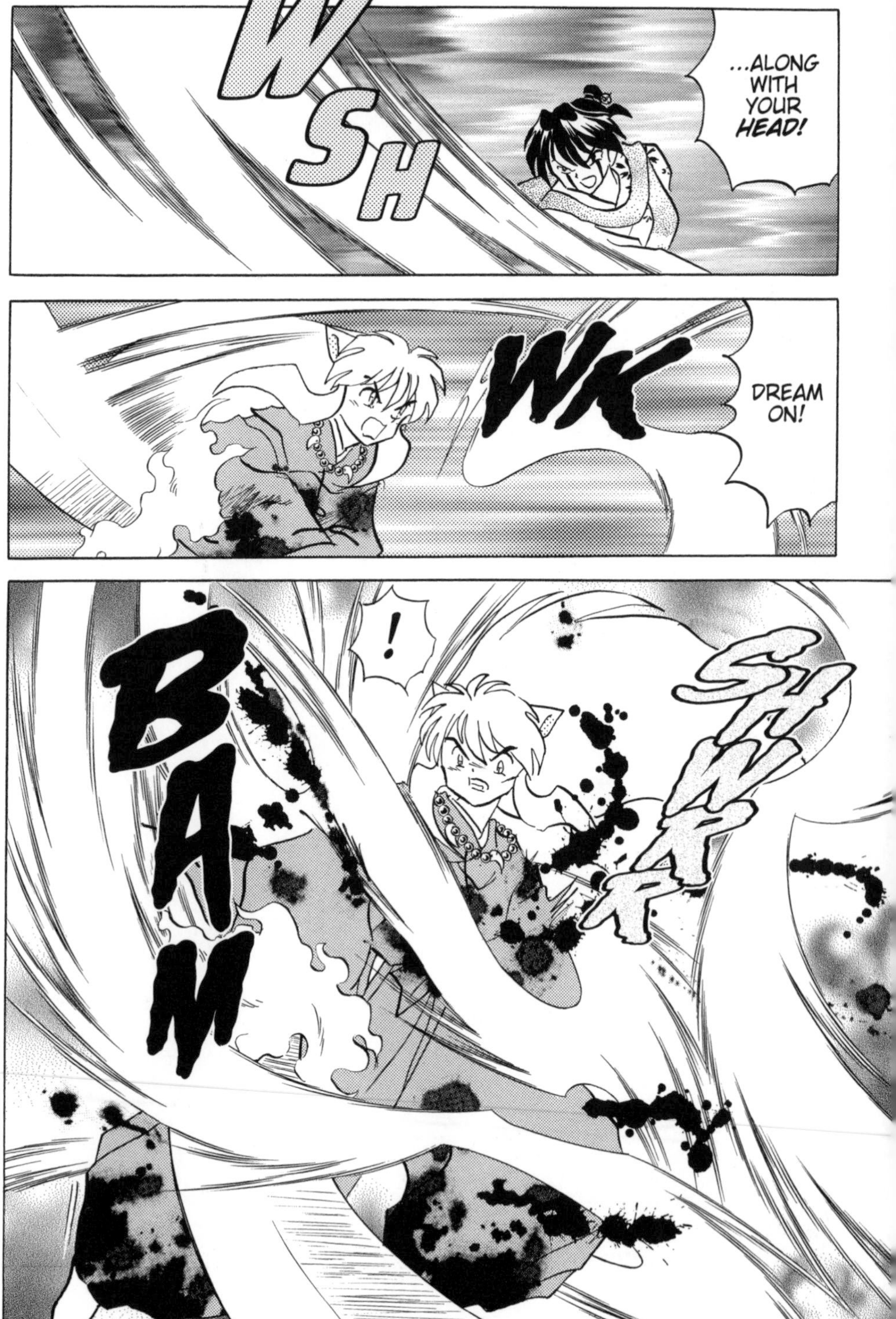
...ALONG WITH YOUR HEAD!
WSH
DREAM ON!
WK
!
SHWKK
BAM

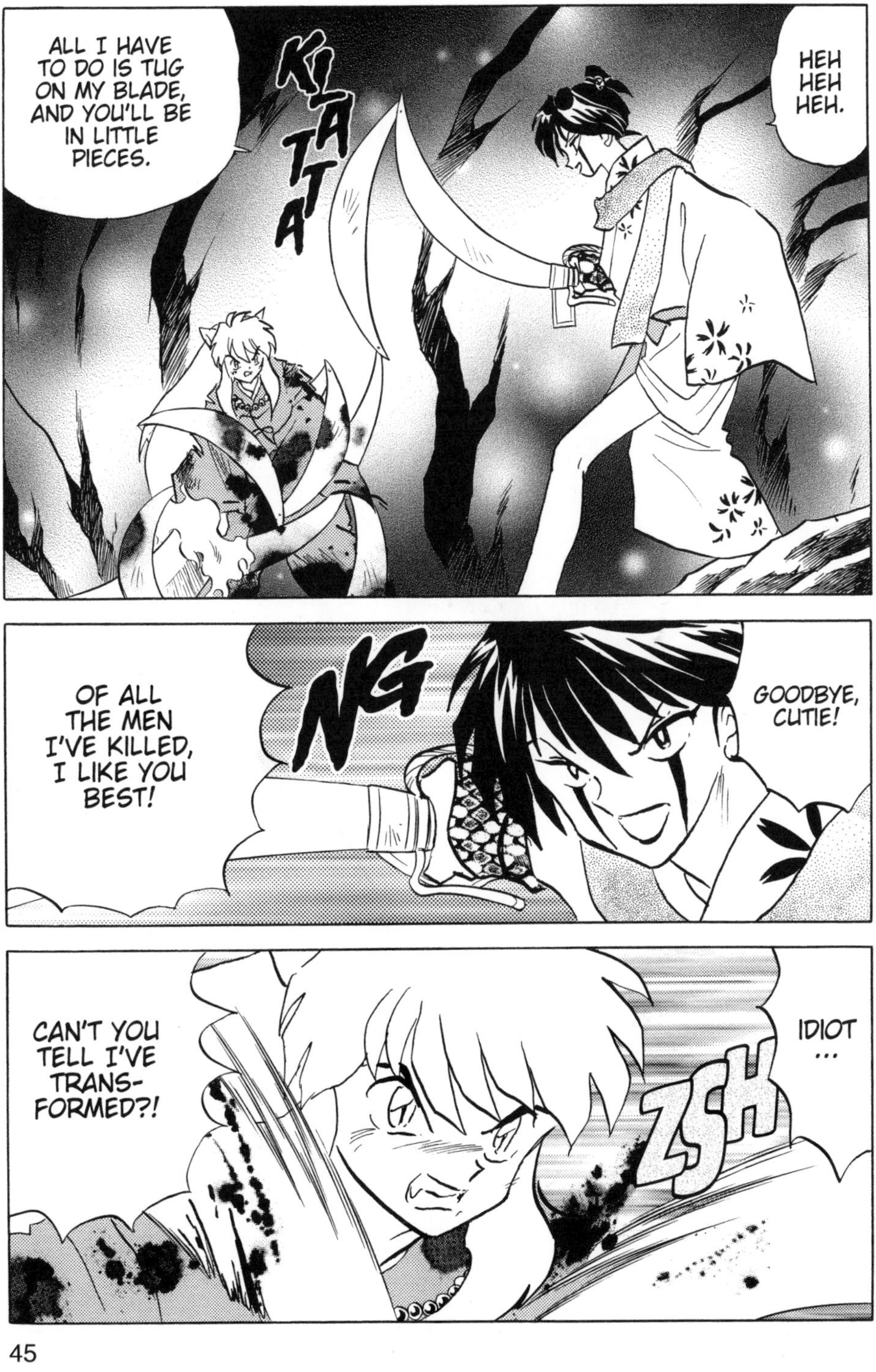
HEH HEH HEH.
KLATATA
ALL I HAVE TO DO IS TUG ON MY BLADE, AND YOU'LL BE IN LITTLE PIECES.
GOODBYE, CUTIE!
NG
OF ALL THE MEN I'VE KILLED, I LIKE YOU BEST!
IDIOT ...
ZSH
CAN'T YOU TELL I'VE TRANS-FORMED?!

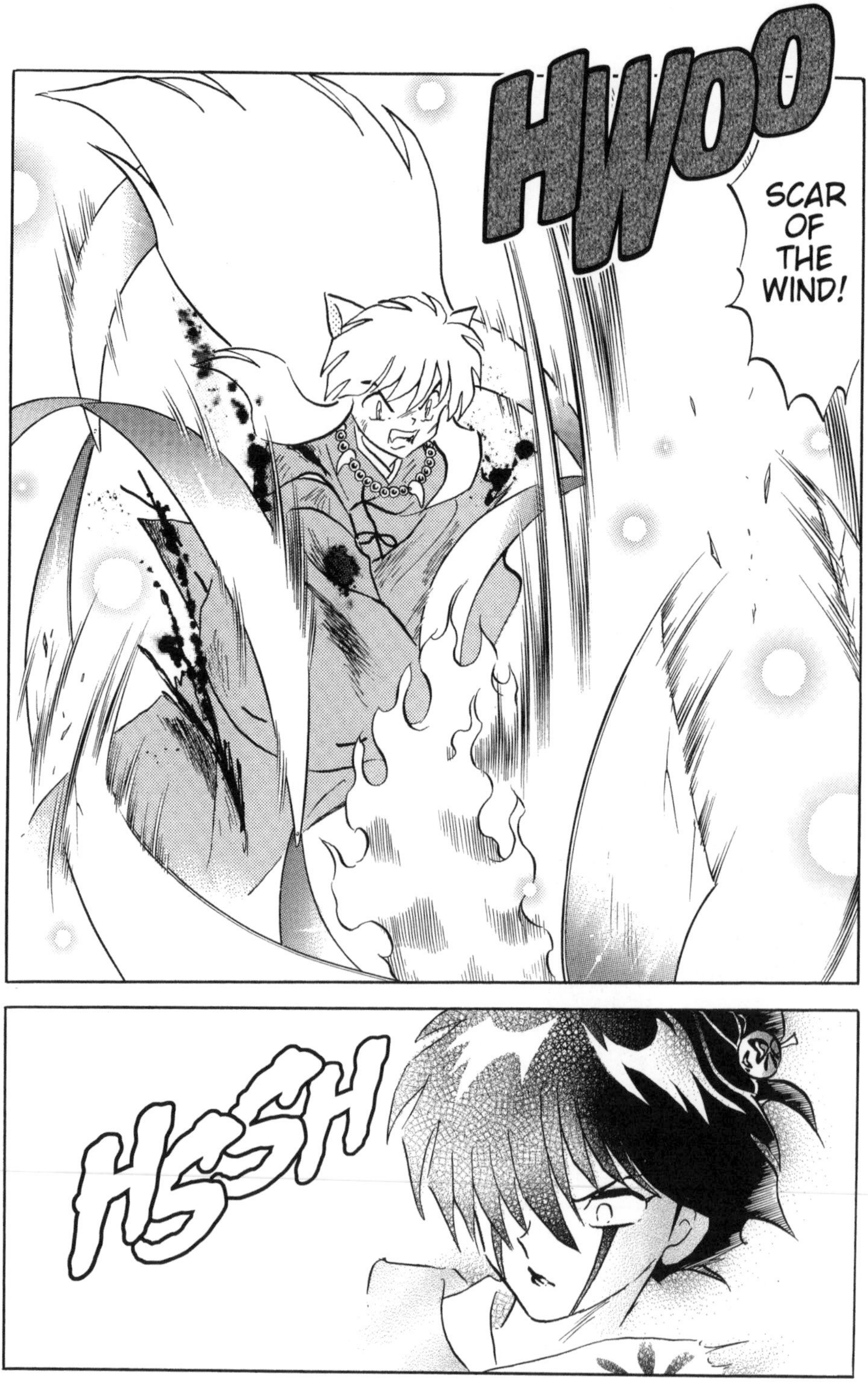
HWOO
SCAR OF THE WIND!
HSSH

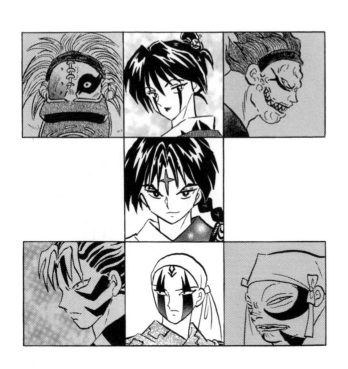

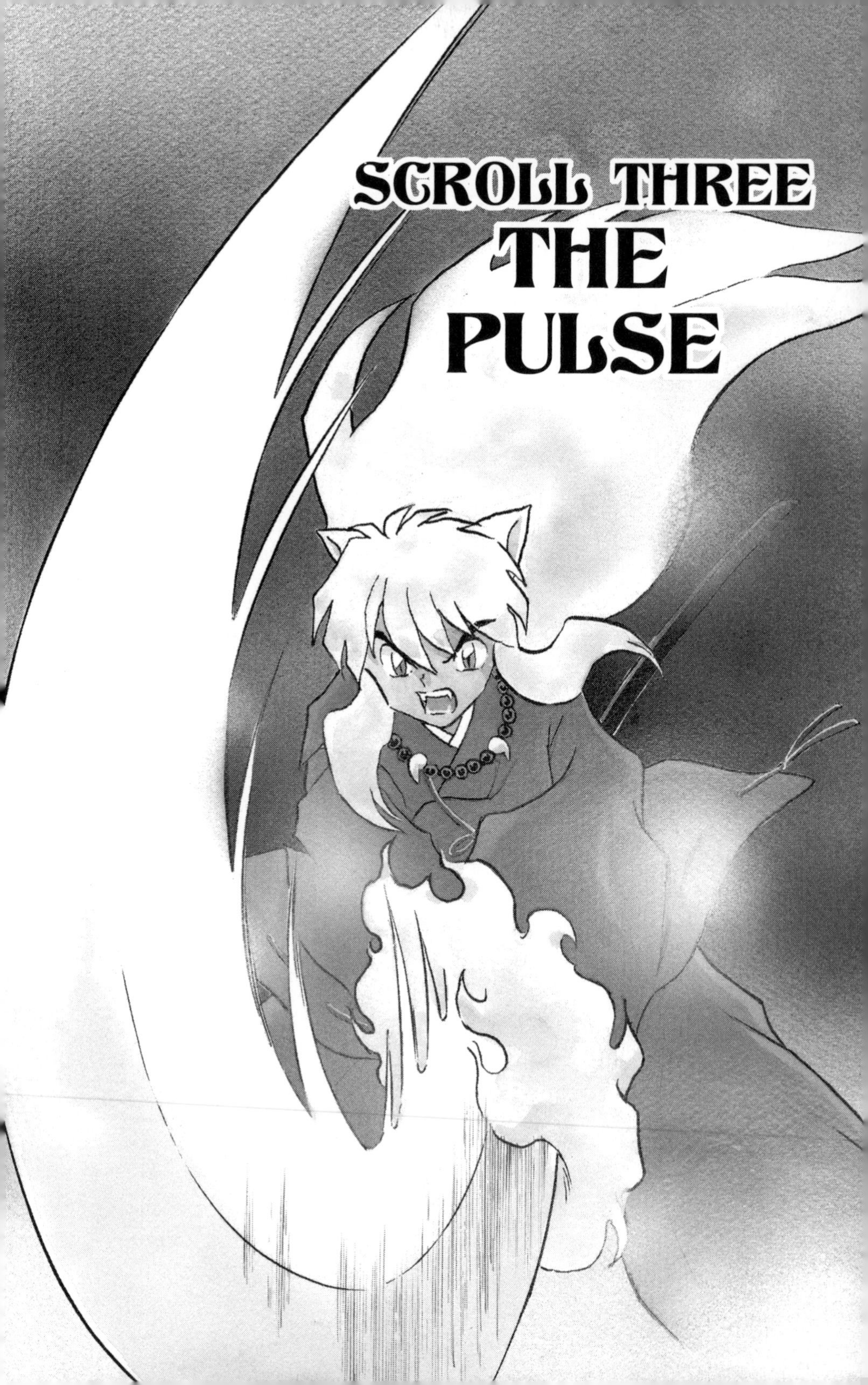
SCROLL THREE
THE PULSE

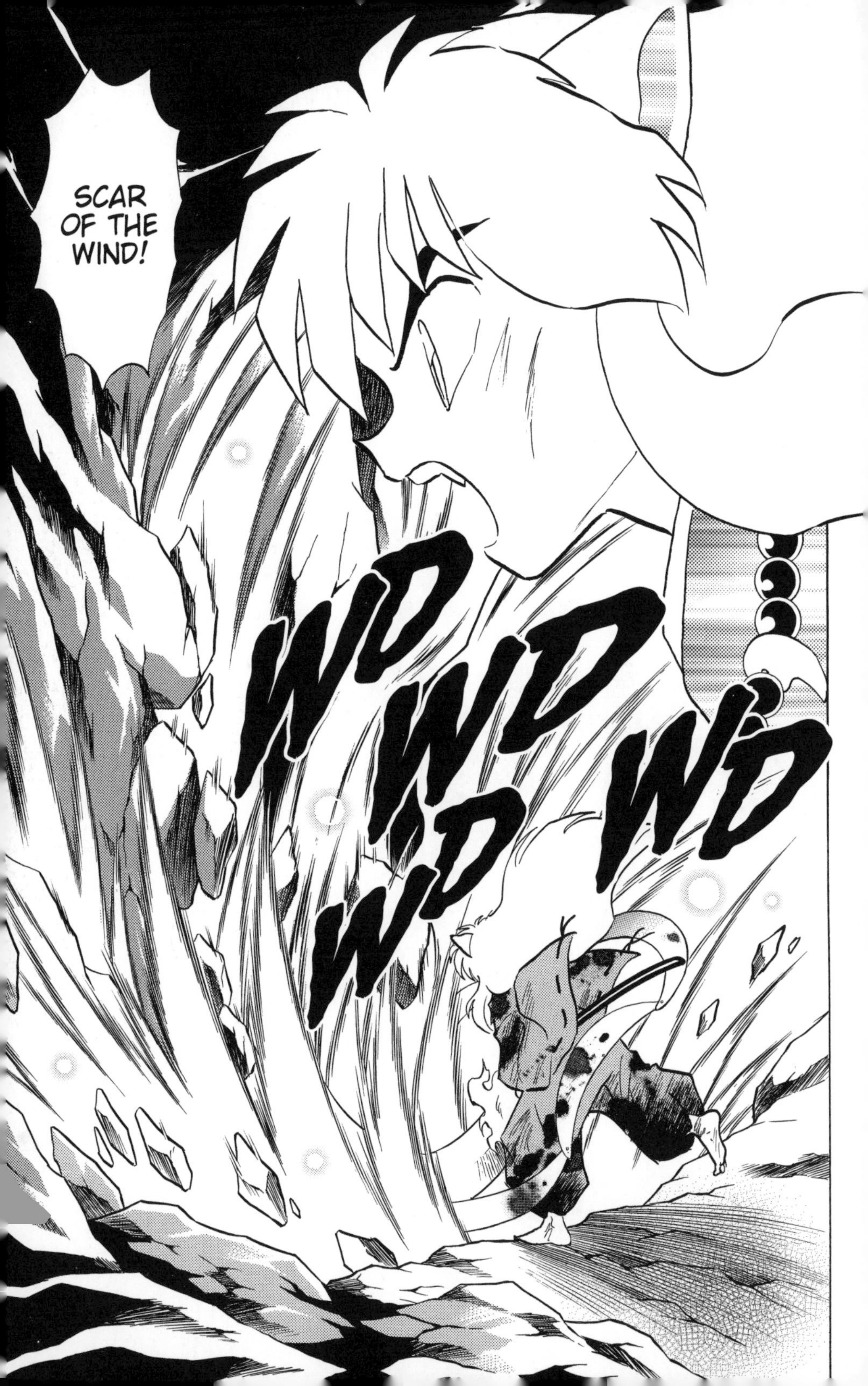
SCAR OF THE WIND!
WND
WND
WND
WND

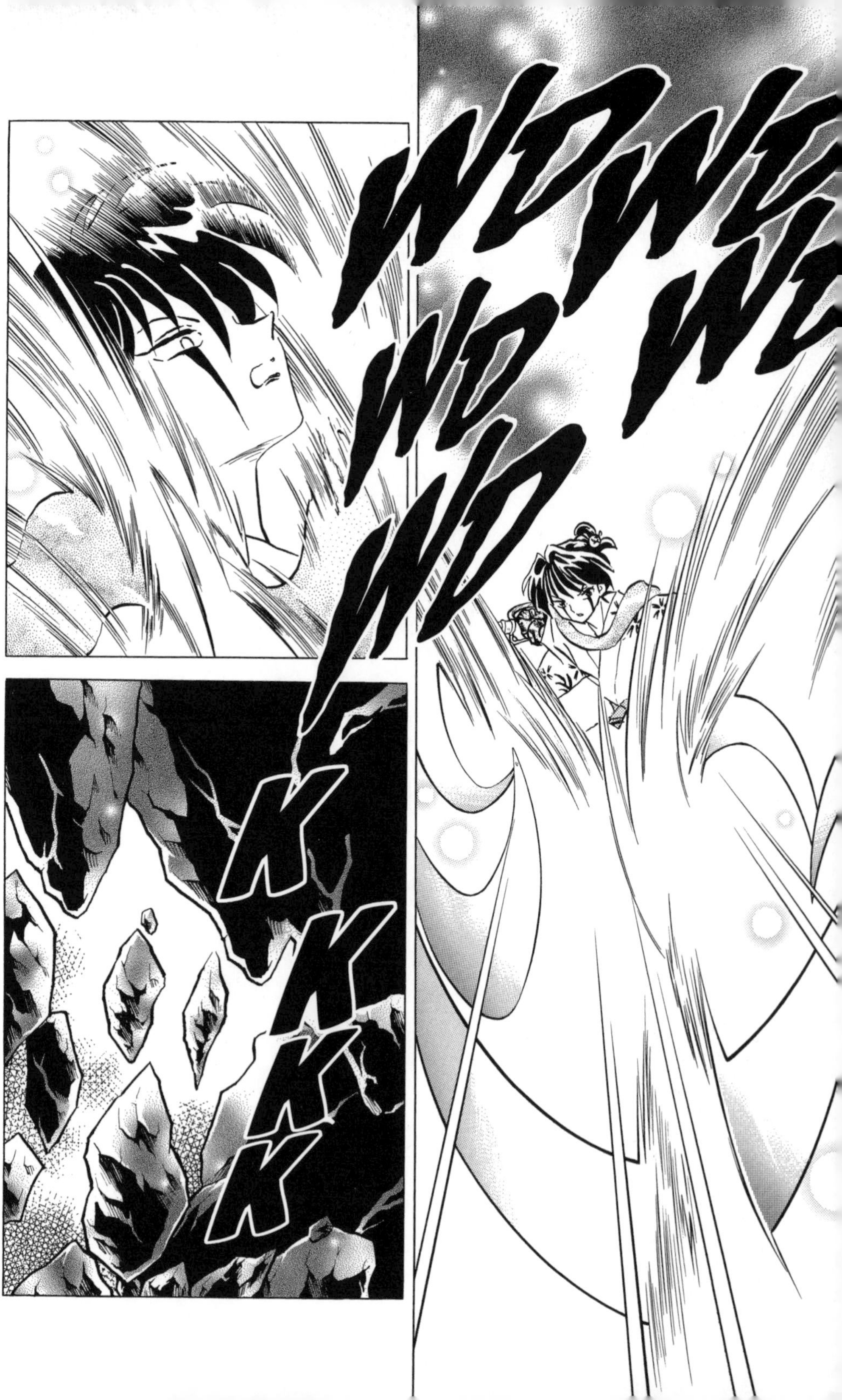
KKKKK

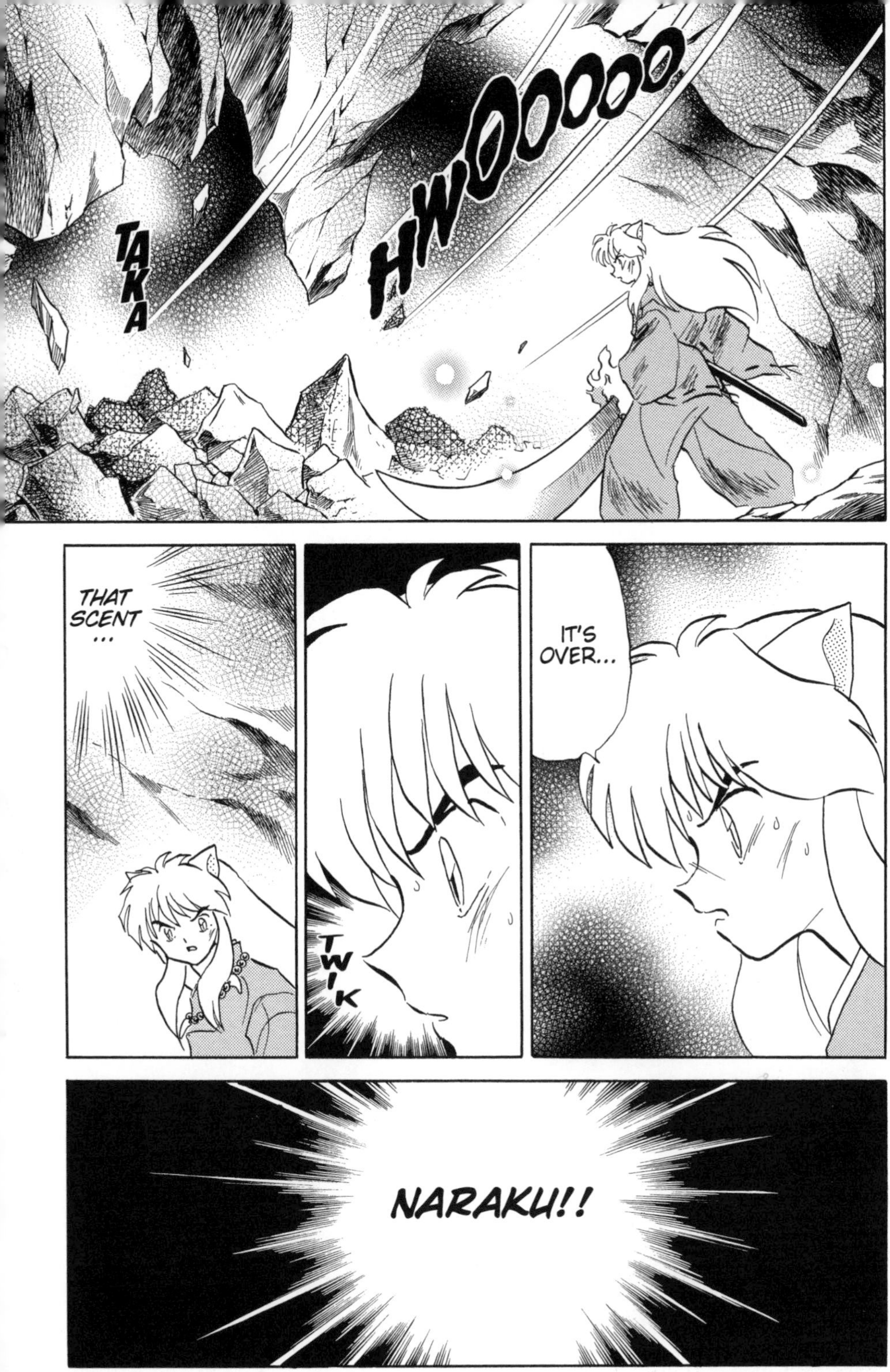
HWOOOOO
TAKA
IT'S OVER...
TWIK
THAT SCENT ...
NARAKU!!

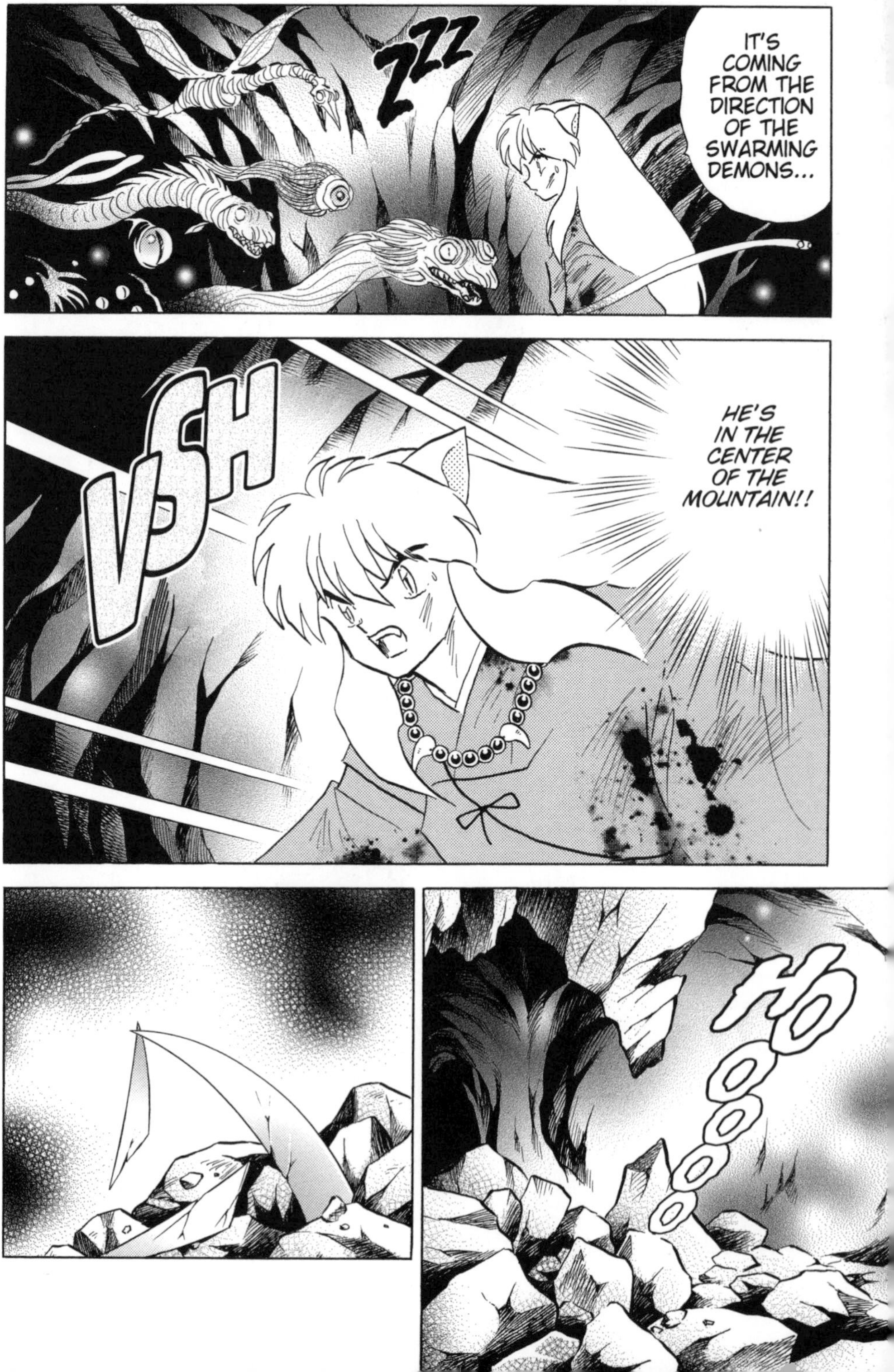
IT'S COMING FROM THE DIRECTION OF THE SWARMING DEMONS...
ZZZ
HE'S IN THE CENTER OF THE MOUNTAIN!!
VSH
HOOOOOOO

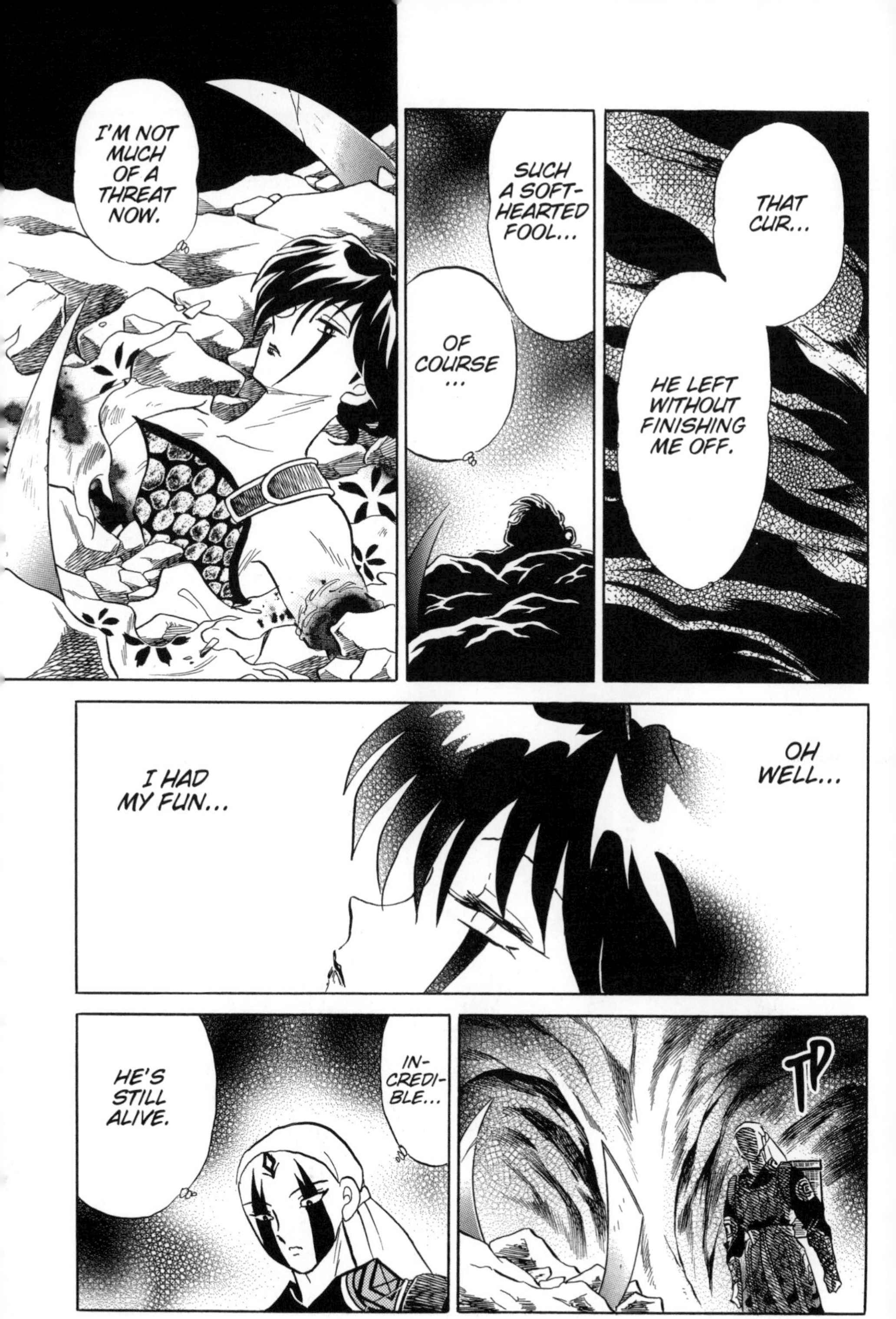
THAT CUR...
HE LEFT WITHOUT FINISHING ME OFF.
SUCH A SOFT-HEARTED FOOL...
OF COURSE...
I'M NOT MUCH OF A THREAT NOW.
OH WELL...
I HAD MY FUN...
TP
IN-CREDI-BLE...
HE'S STILL ALIVE.

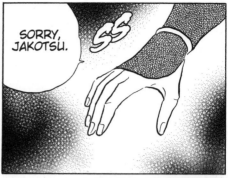

SORRY, JAKOTSU.

I NEED ALL THE SHIKON SHARDS I CAN GET!

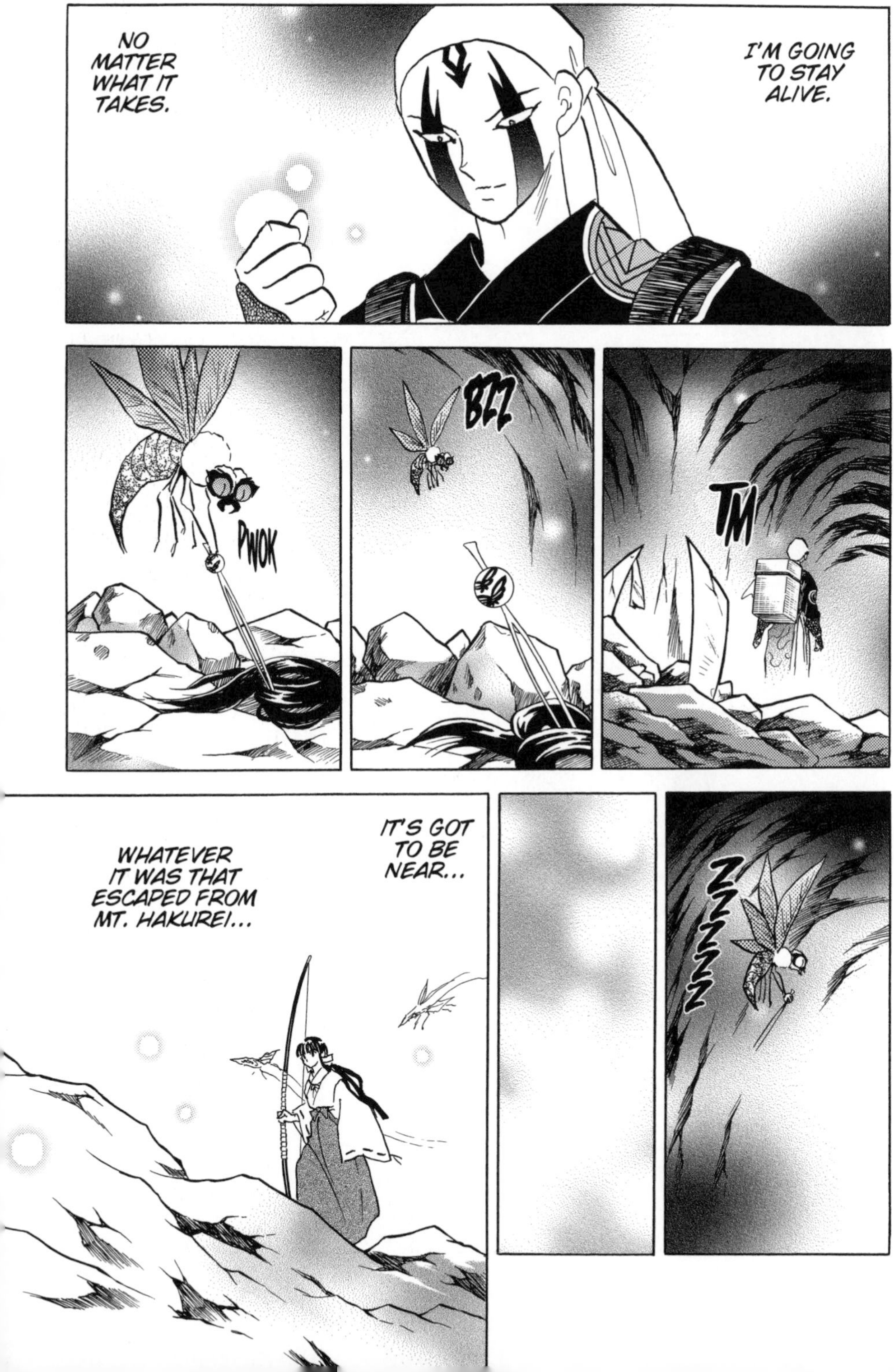
I'M GOING TO STAY ALIVE.
NO MATTER WHAT IT TAKES.
TM
BZZ
PWOK
ZZZZZZ
IT'S GOT TO BE NEAR...
WHATEVER IT WAS THAT ESCAPED FROM MT. HAKUREI...

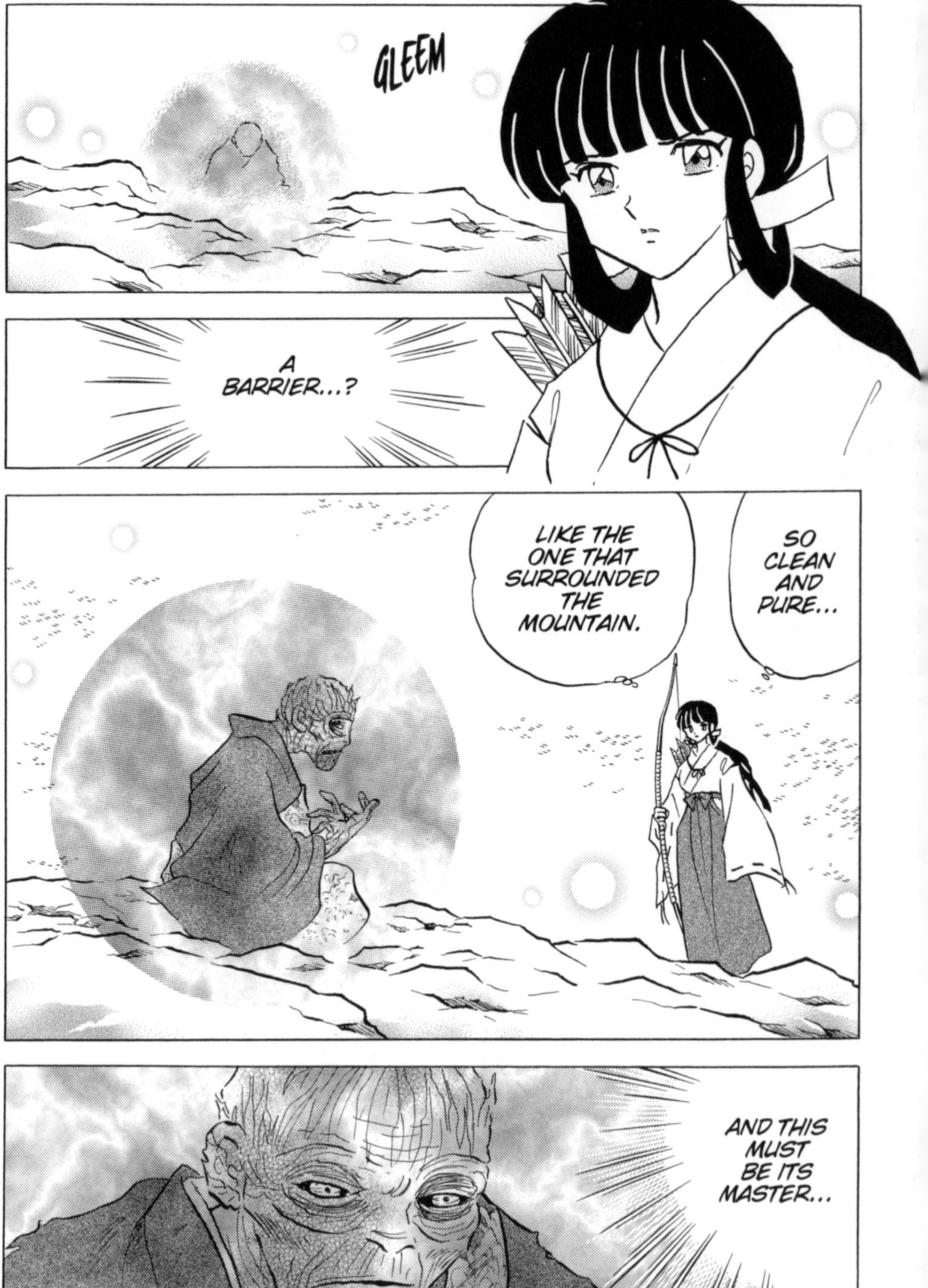
GLEEM
A BARRIER...?
SO CLEAN AND PURE...
LIKE THE ONE THAT SURROUNDED THE MOUNTAIN.
AND THIS MUST BE ITS MASTER...

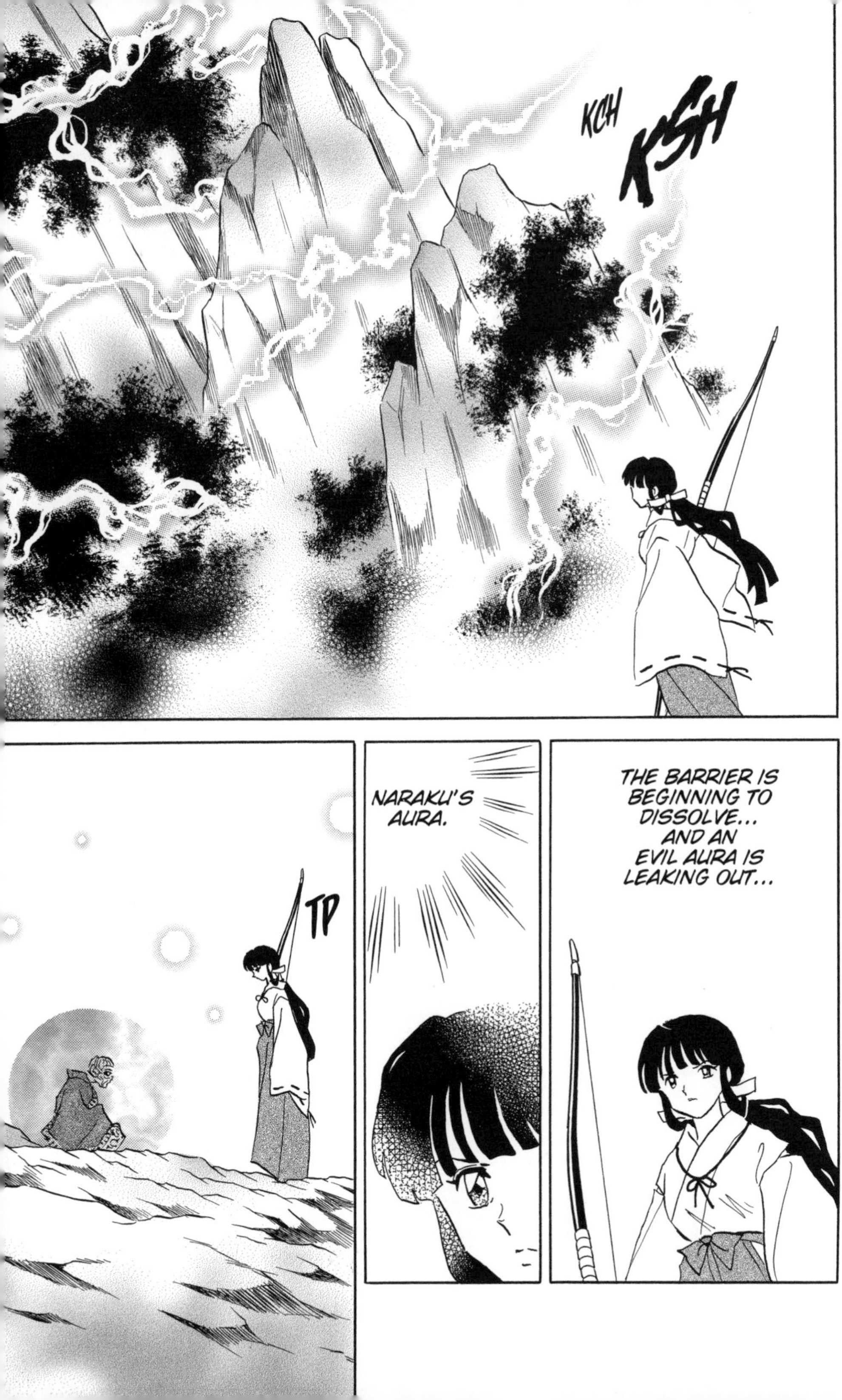
KCH
KSH
THE BARRIER IS BEGINNING TO DISSOLVE... AND AN EVIL AURA IS LEAKING OUT...
NARAKU'S AURA.
TP

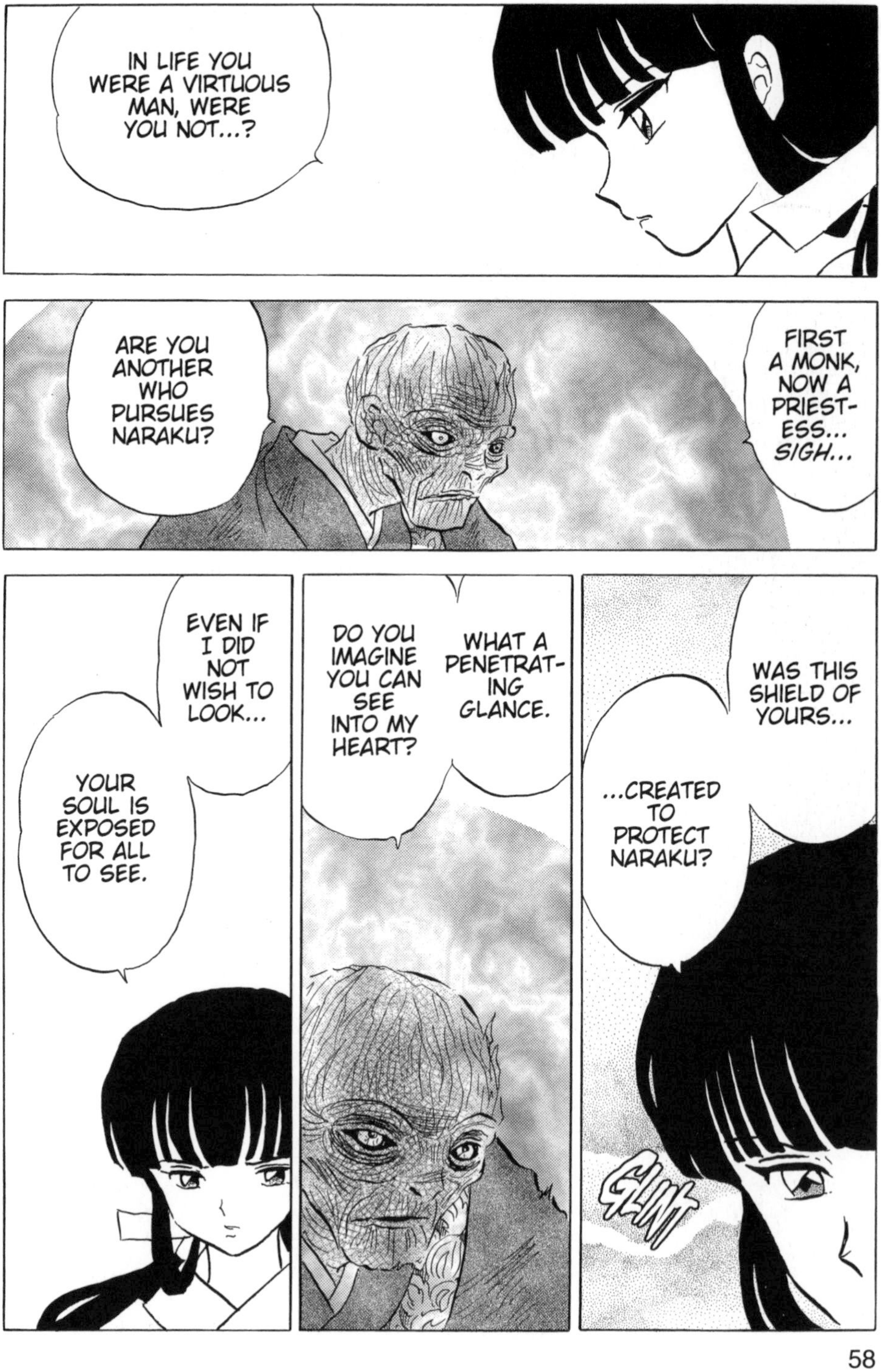

IN LIFE YOU WERE A VIRTUOUS MAN, WERE YOU NOT...?
FIRST A MONK, NOW A PRIEST-ESS... SIGH...
ARE YOU ANOTHER WHO PURSUES NARAKU?
WAS THIS SHIELD OF YOURS...
...CREATED TO PROTECT NARAKU?
GLINT
WHAT A PENETRAT-ING GLANCE.
DO YOU IMAGINE YOU CAN SEE INTO MY HEART?
EVEN IF I DID NOT WISH TO LOOK...
YOUR SOUL IS EXPOSED FOR ALL TO SEE.

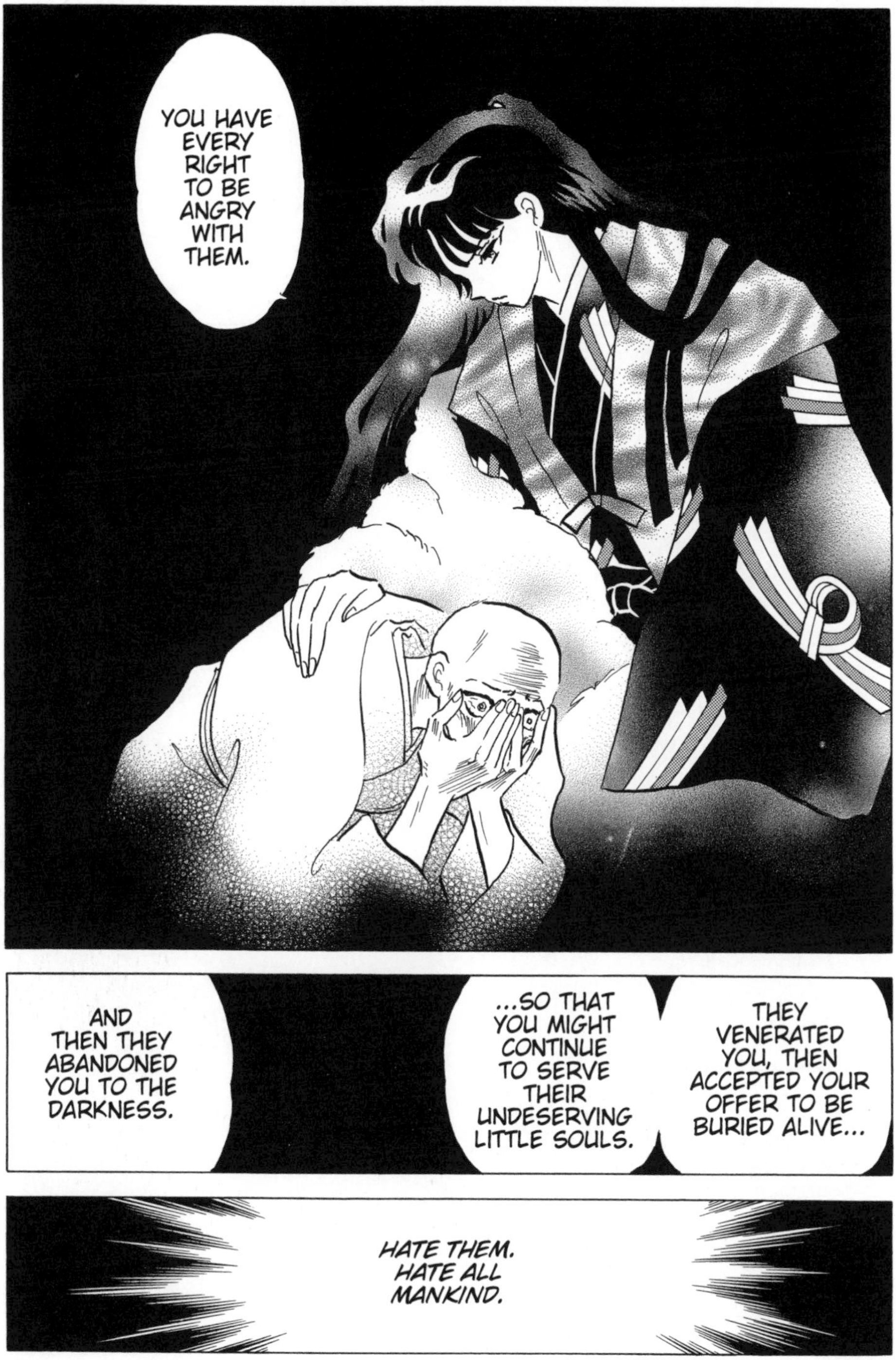
YOU HAVE EVERY RIGHT TO BE ANGRY WITH THEM.
THEY VENERATED YOU, THEN ACCEPTED YOUR OFFER TO BE BURIED ALIVE...
...SO THAT YOU MIGHT CONTINUE TO SERVE THEIR UNDESERVING LITTLE SOULS.
AND THEN THEY ABANDONED YOU TO THE DARKNESS.
HATE THEM. HATE ALL MANKIND.

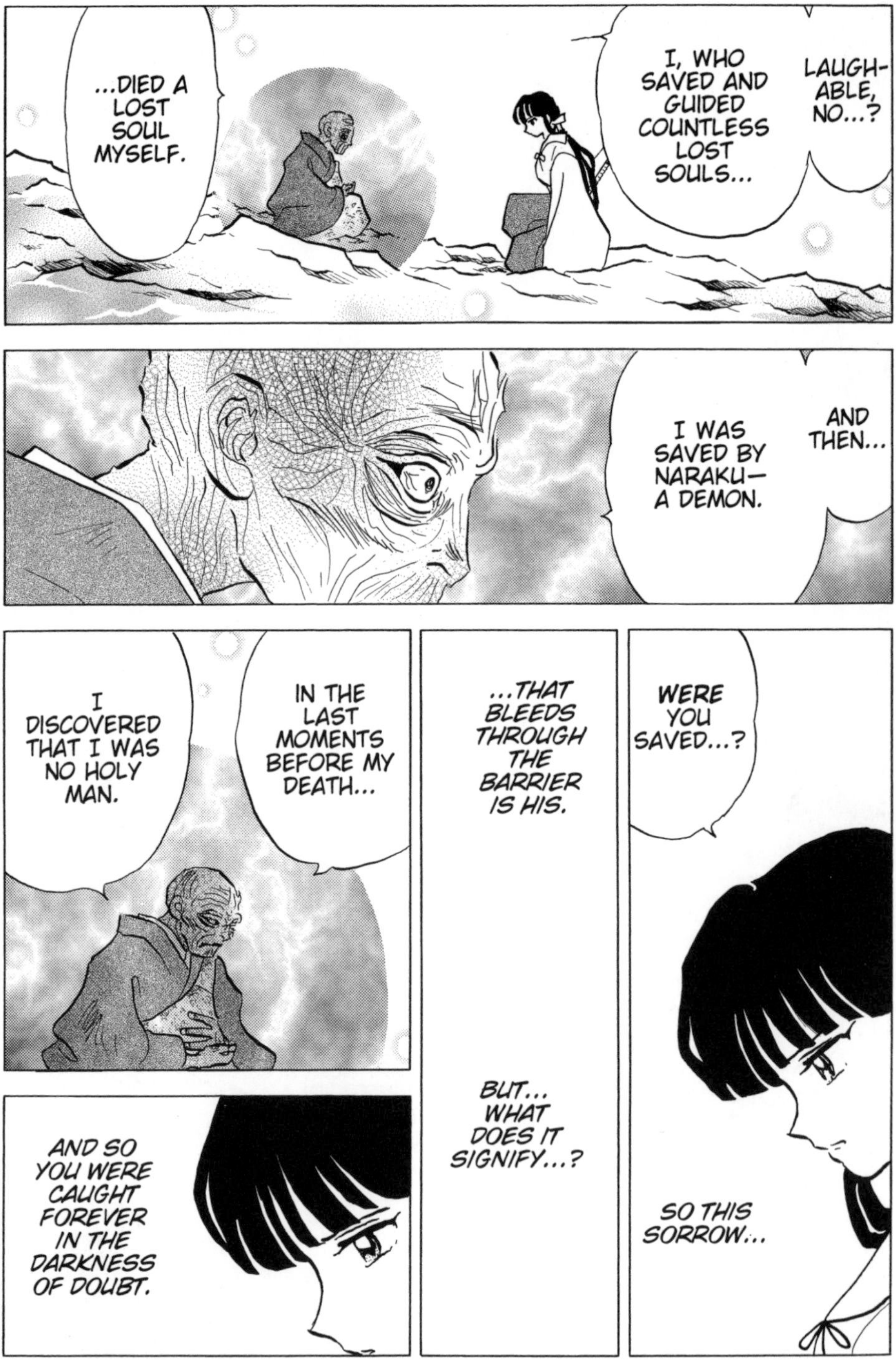
LAUGHABLE, NO...?
I, WHO SAVED AND GUIDED COUNTLESS LOST SOULS...
...DIED A LOST SOUL MYSELF.
AND THEN...
I WAS SAVED BY NARAKU—A DEMON.
WERE YOU SAVED...?
SO THIS SORROW...
...THAT BLEEDS THROUGH THE BARRIER IS HIS.
BUT... WHAT DOES IT SIGNIFY...?
IN THE LAST MOMENTS BEFORE MY DEATH...
I DISCOVERED THAT I WAS NO HOLY MAN.
AND SO YOU WERE CAUGHT FOREVER IN THE DARKNESS OF DOUBT.

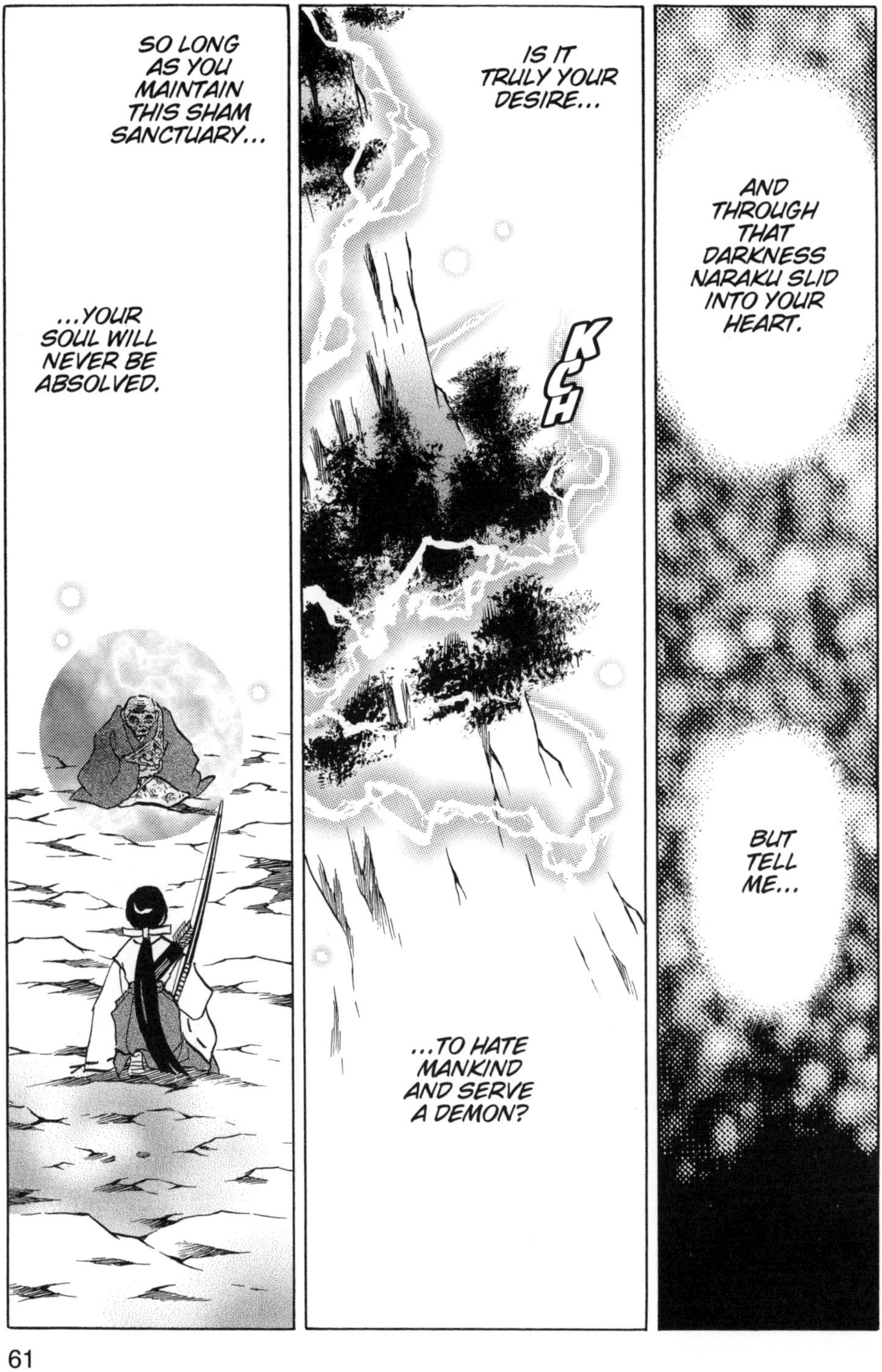
AND THROUGH THAT DARKNESS NARAKU SLID INTO YOUR HEART.
BUT TELL ME...
IS IT TRULY YOUR DESIRE...
KCH
...TO HATE MANKIND AND SERVE A DEMON?
SO LONG AS YOU MAINTAIN THIS SHAM SANCTUARY...
...YOUR SOUL WILL NEVER BE ABSOLVED.

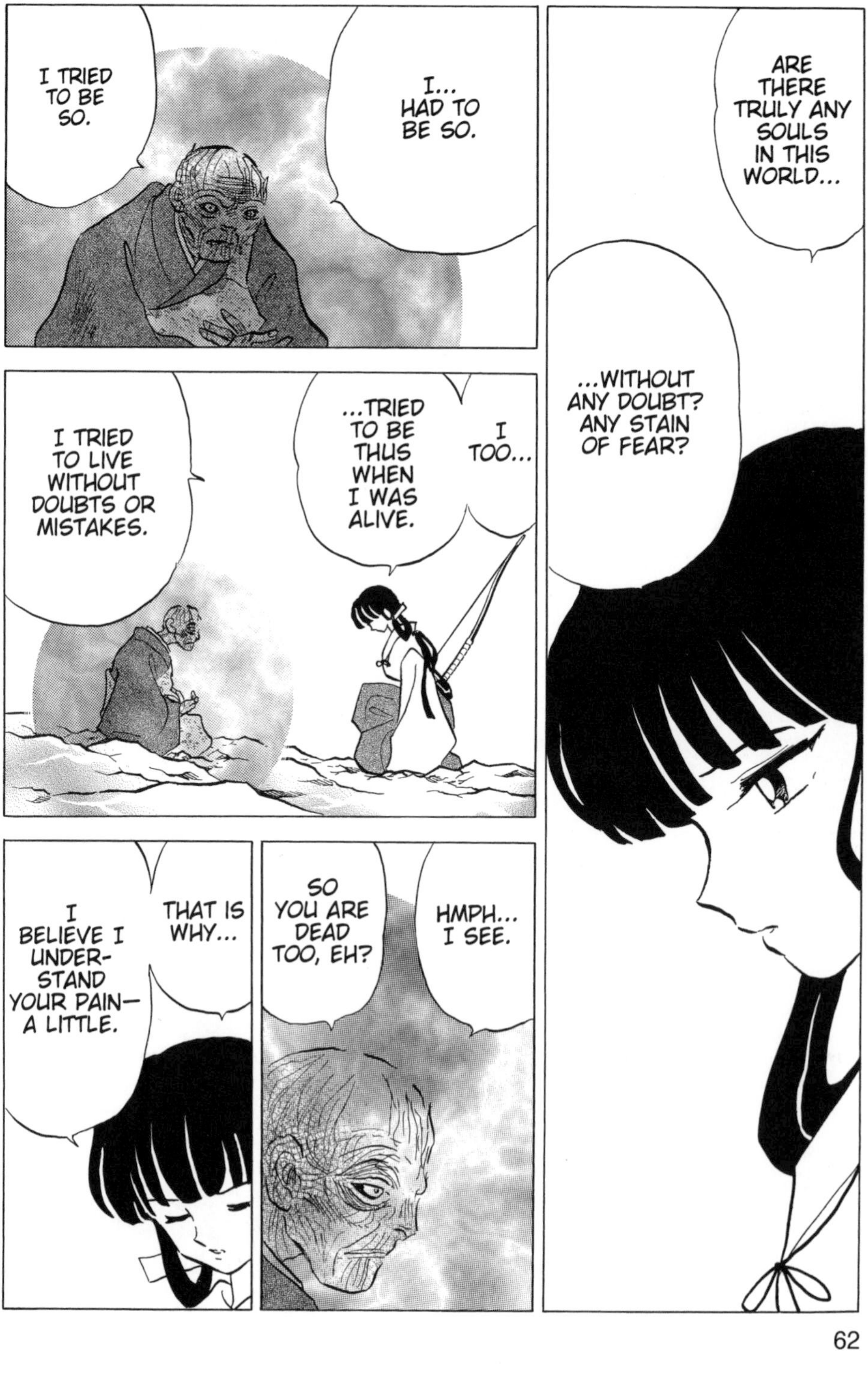
ARE THERE TRULY ANY SOULS IN THIS WORLD...
...WITHOUT ANY DOUBT? ANY STAIN OF FEAR?
I... HAD TO BE SO.
I TRIED TO BE SO.
I TOO...
...TRIED TO BE THUS WHEN I WAS ALIVE.
I TRIED TO LIVE WITHOUT DOUBTS OR MISTAKES.
HMPH... I SEE.
SO YOU ARE DEAD TOO, EH?
THAT IS WHY...
I BELIEVE I UNDER-STAND YOUR PAIN—A LITTLE.

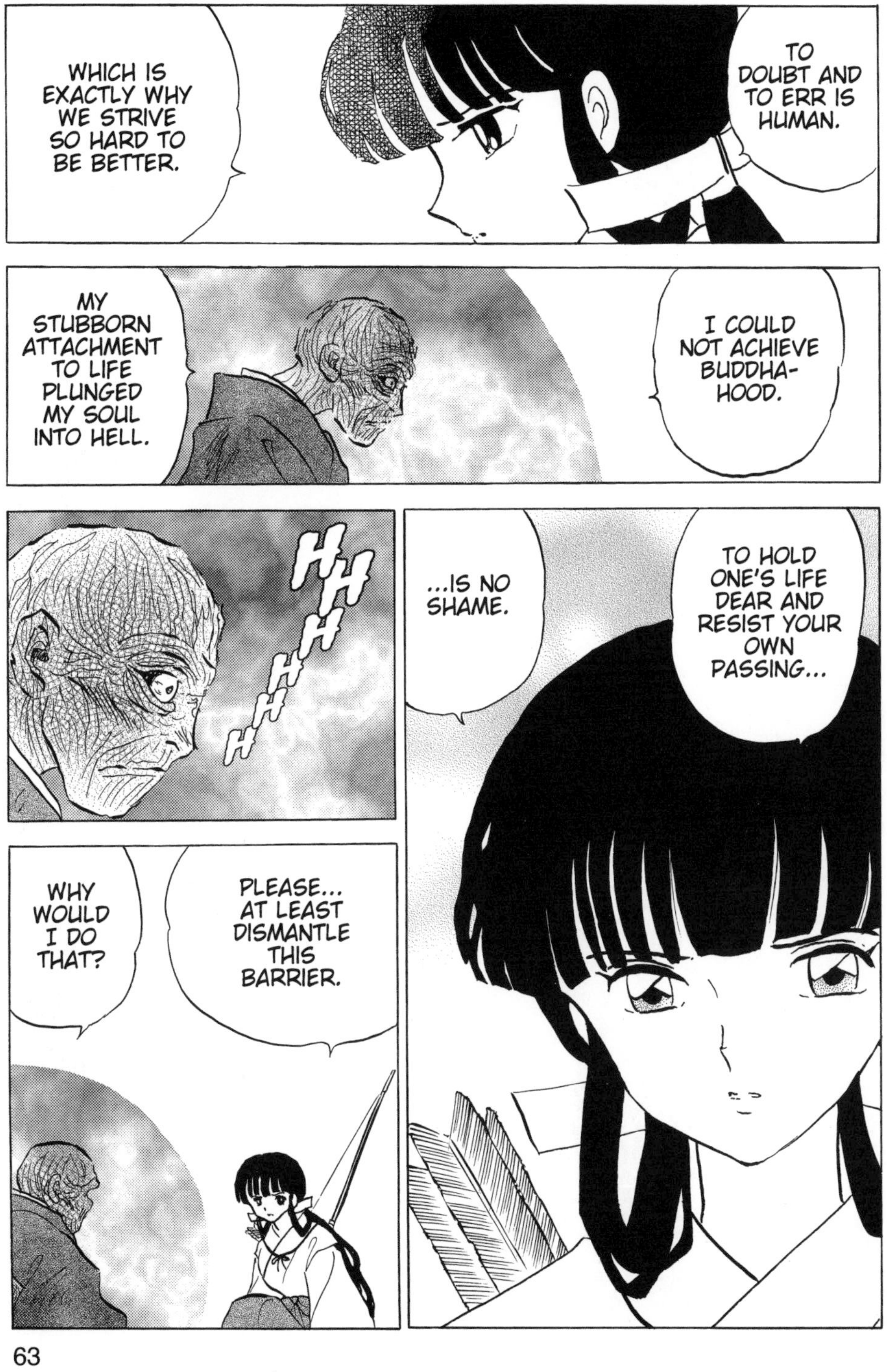
TO DOUBT AND TO ERR IS HUMAN.
WHICH IS EXACTLY WHY WE STRIVE SO HARD TO BE BETTER.
I COULD NOT ACHIEVE BUDDHA-HOOD.
MY STUBBORN ATTACHMENT TO LIFE PLUNGED MY SOUL INTO HELL.
TO HOLD ONE'S LIFE DEAR AND RESIST YOUR OWN PASSING...
...IS NO SHAME.
HHHHHHHH
PLEASE... AT LEAST DISMANTLE THIS BARRIER.
WHY WOULD I DO THAT?

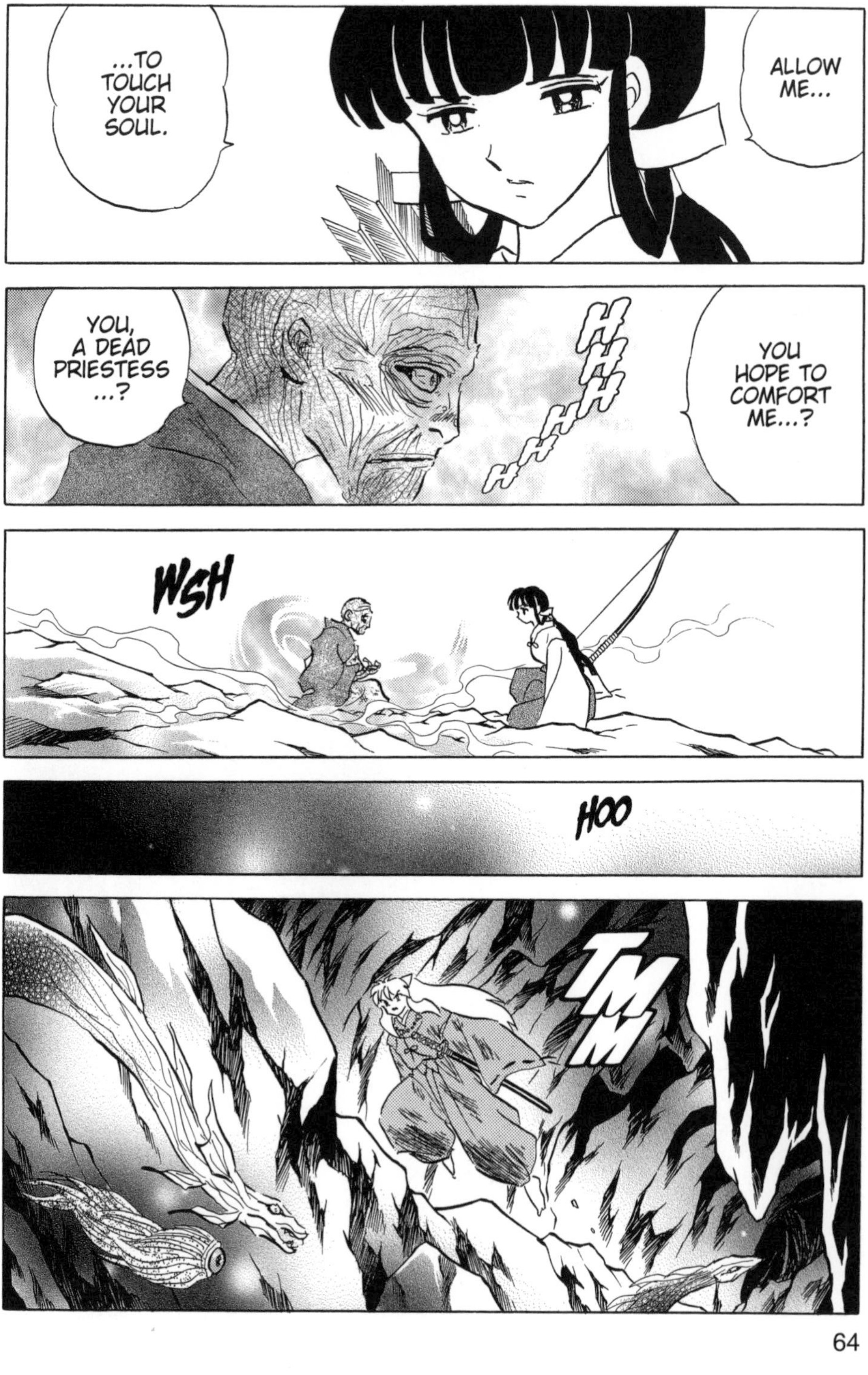
ALLOW ME...
...TO TOUCH YOUR SOUL.
YOU HOPE TO COMFORT ME...?
HHHHHHH
YOU, A DEAD PRIESTESS ...?
WSH
HOO
TMM

HUH? WHAT'S THAT RUMBLING SOUND?

IT'S LIKE...A HEARTBEAT.

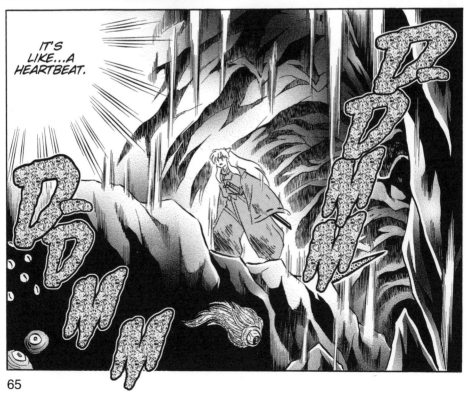

65

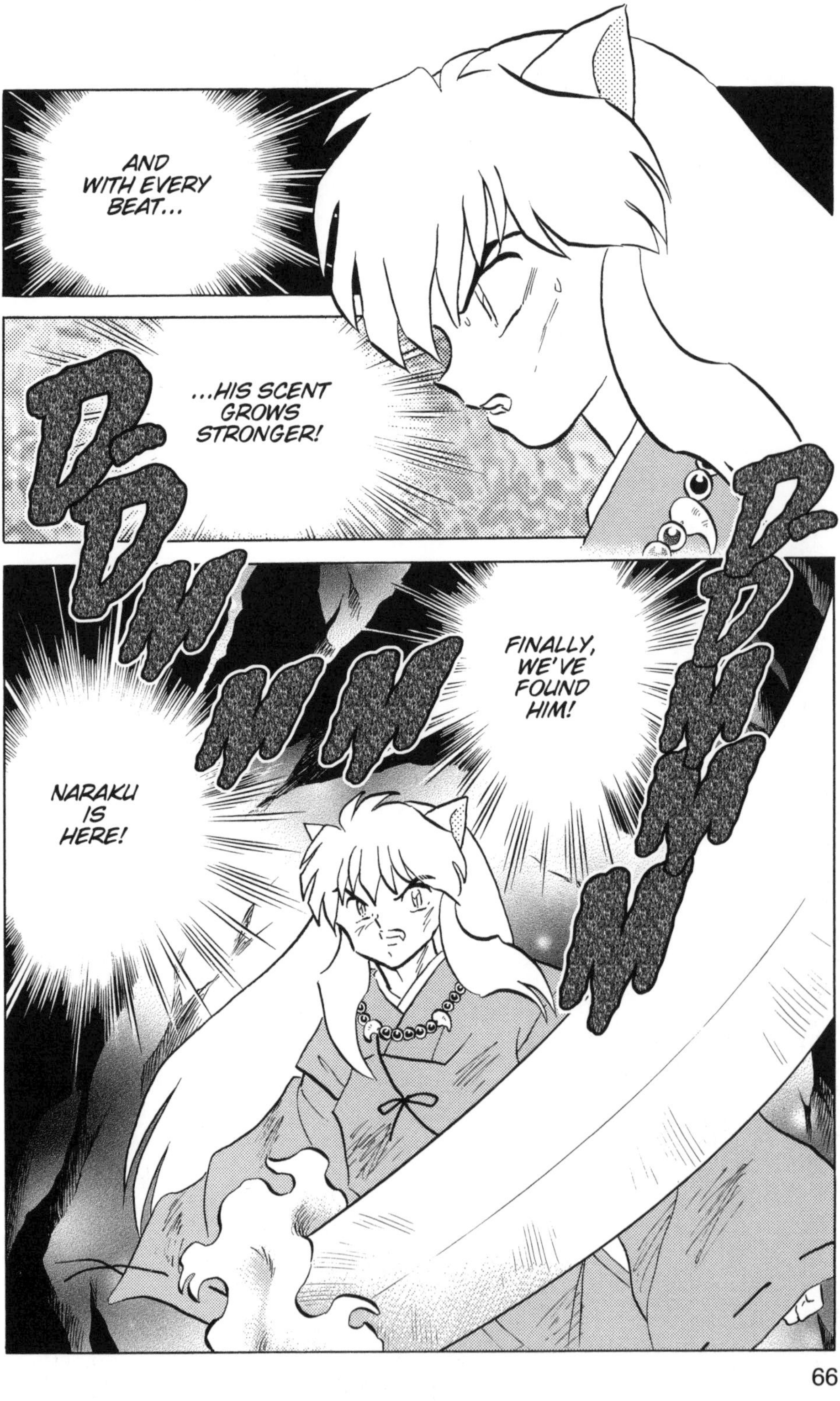
AND WITH EVERY BEAT...
...HIS SCENT GROWS STRONGER!
BDMMMM
BDMMMM
FINALLY, WE'VE FOUND HIM!
NARAKU IS HERE!

SCROLL FOUR
THE SANCTUARY DESTROYED

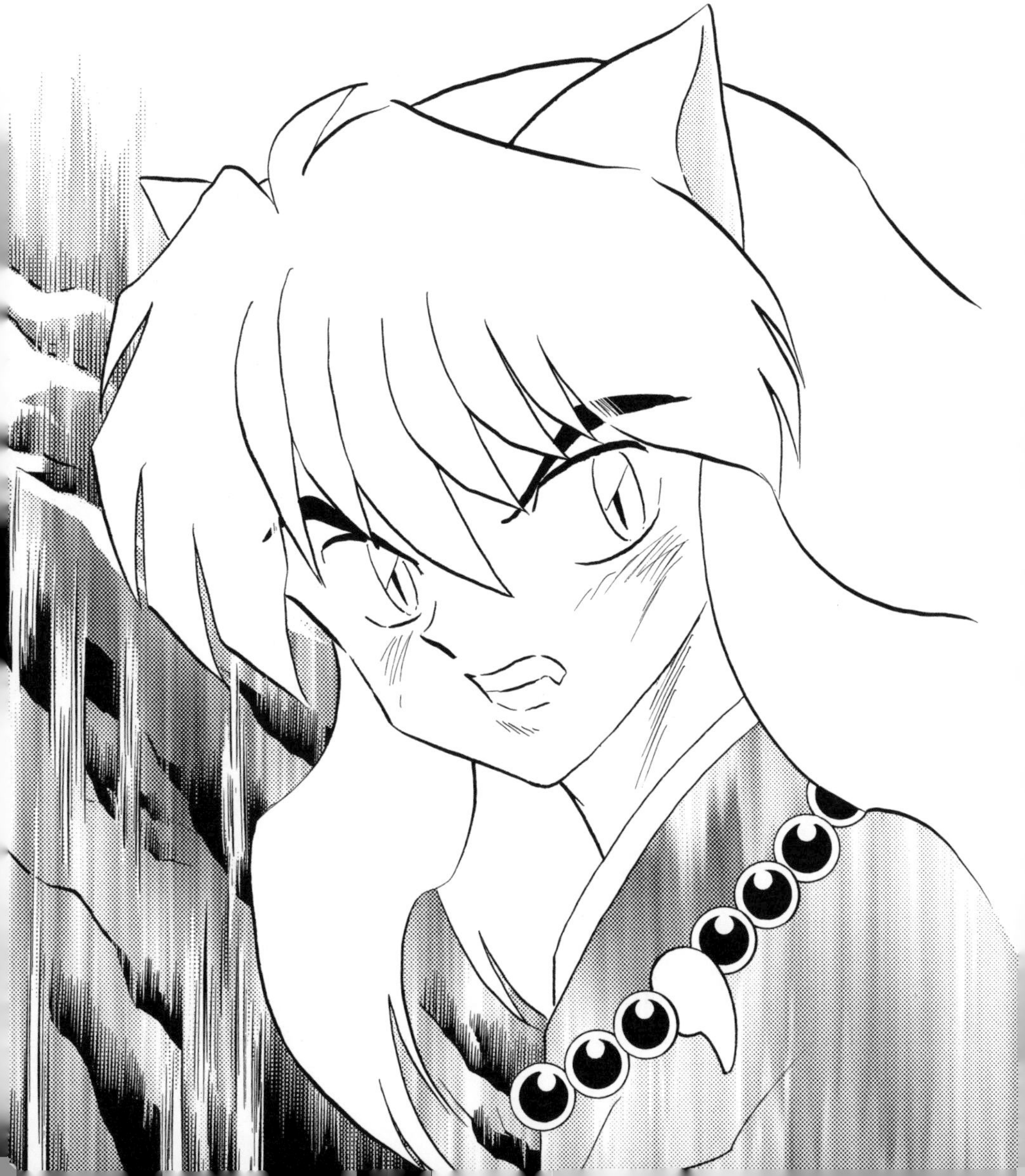

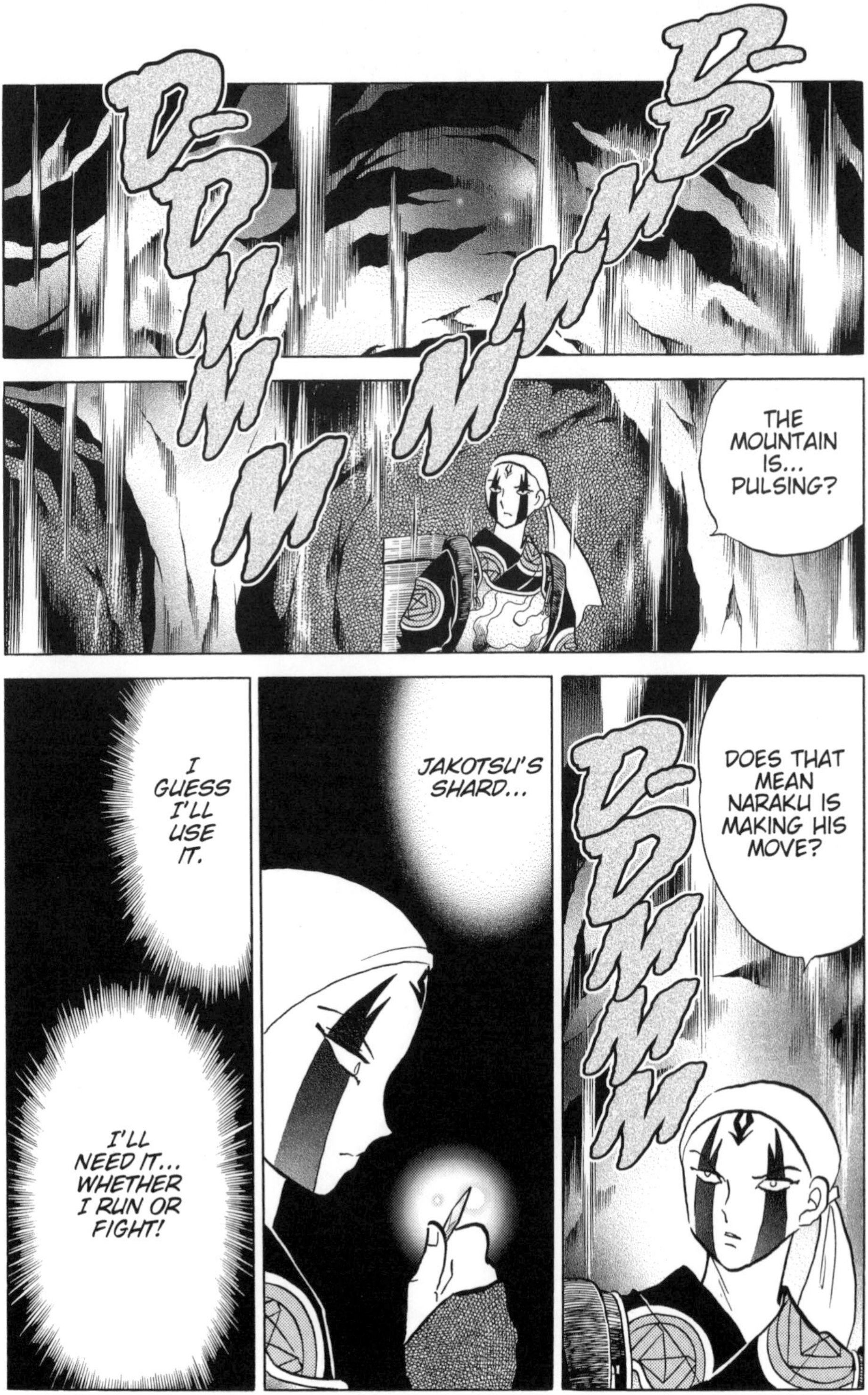
D-DOMMMMMMMB
THE MOUNTAIN IS... PULSING?
DOES THAT MEAN NARAKU IS MAKING HIS MOVE?
D-DOMMMM
JAKOTSU'S SHARD...
I GUESS I'LL USE IT.
I'LL NEED IT... WHETHER I RUN OR FIGHT!

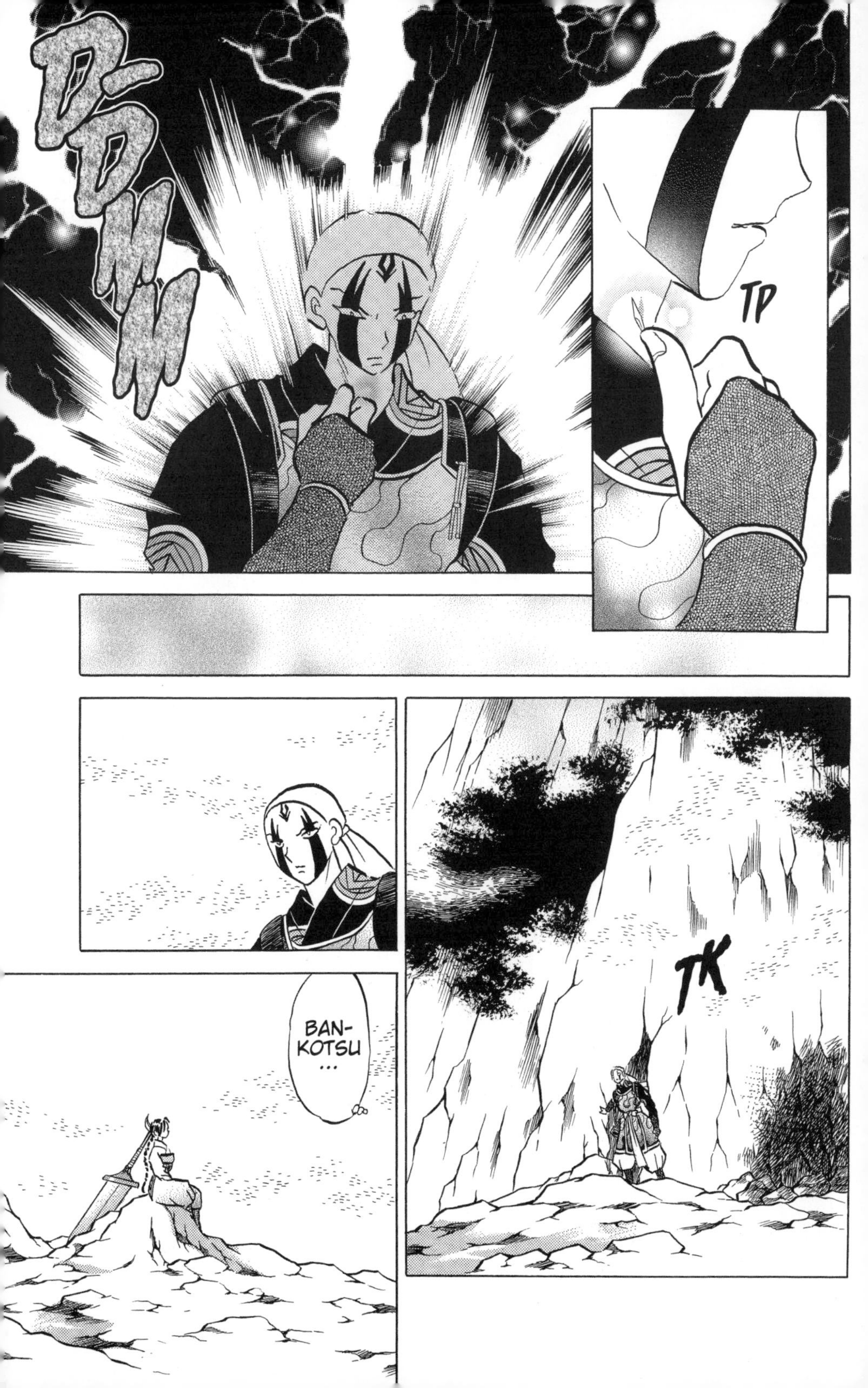
DOMM
TP
TK
BAN-
KOTSU
...

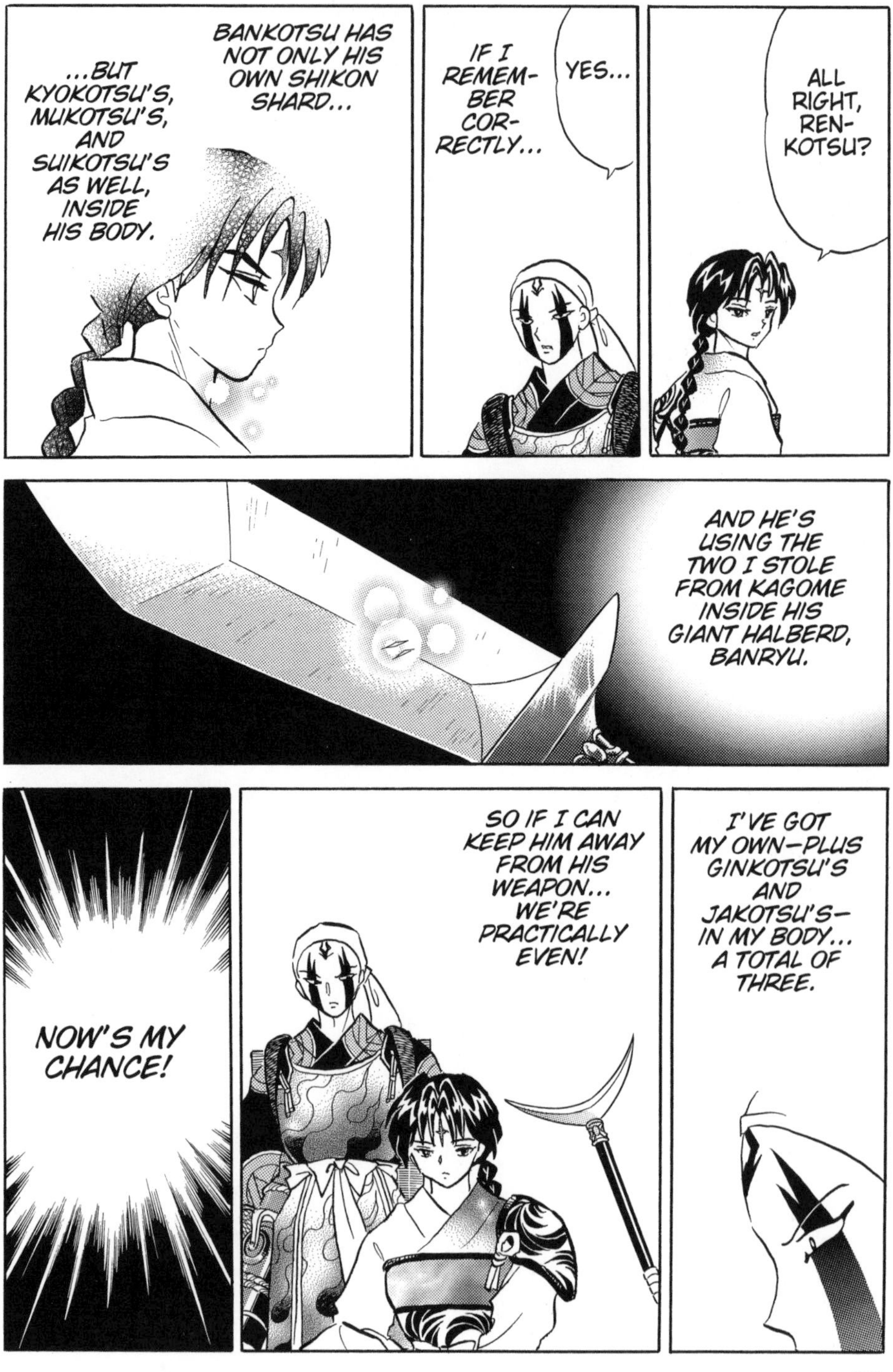
ALL RIGHT, REN-KOTSU?
YES...
IF I REMEM-BER COR-RECTLY...
BANKOTSU HAS NOT ONLY HIS OWN SHIKON SHARD...
...BUT KYOKOTSU'S, MUKOTSU'S, AND SUIKOTSU'S AS WELL, INSIDE HIS BODY.
AND HE'S USING THE TWO I STOLE FROM KAGOME INSIDE HIS GIANT HALBERD, BANRYU.
I'VE GOT MY OWN—PLUS GINKOTSU'S AND JAKOTSU'S—IN MY BODY... A TOTAL OF THREE.
SO IF I CAN KEEP HIM AWAY FROM HIS WEAPON... WE'RE PRACTICALLY EVEN!
NOW'S MY CHANCE!

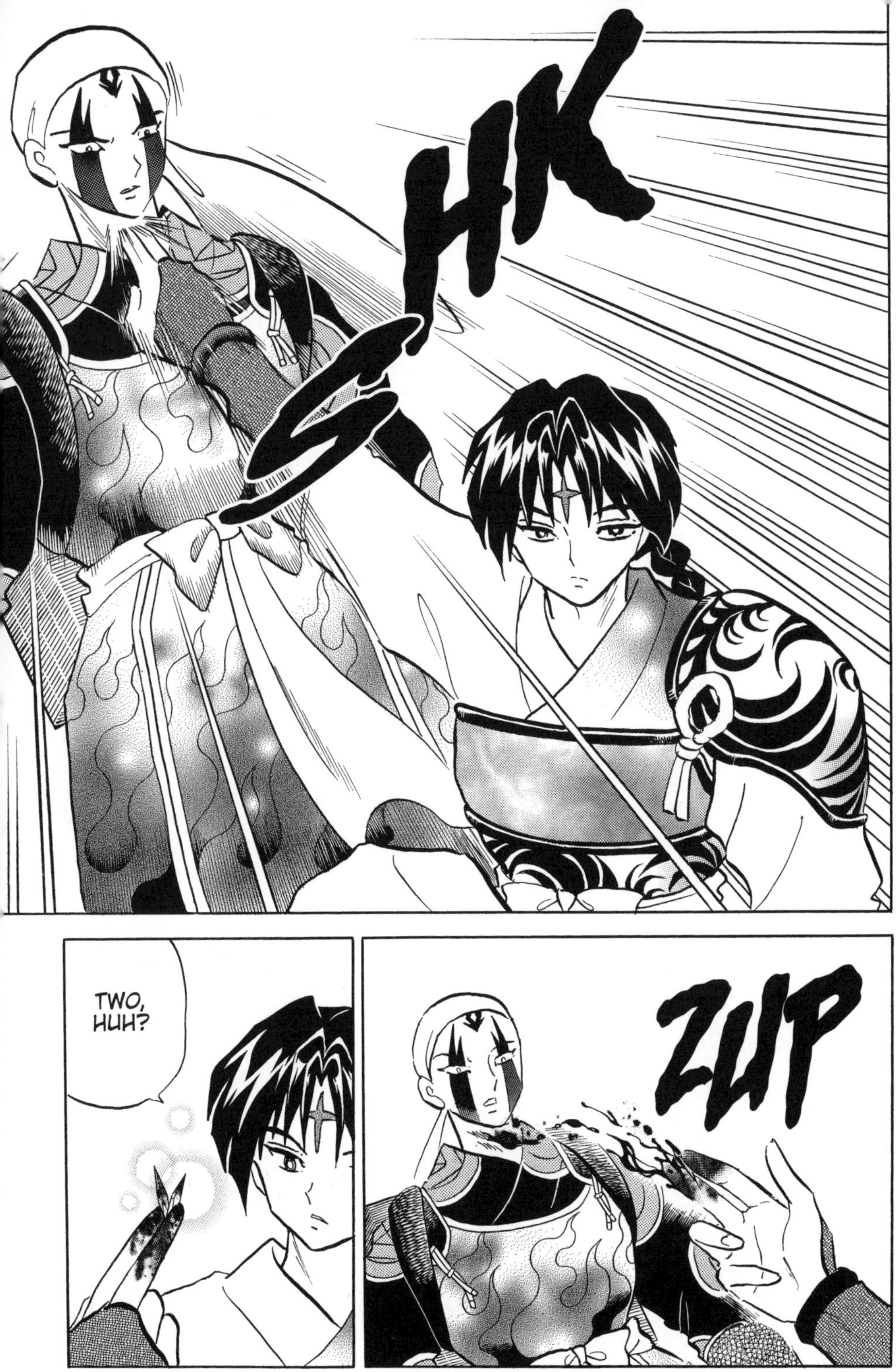
SHK
ZUP
TWO, HUH?

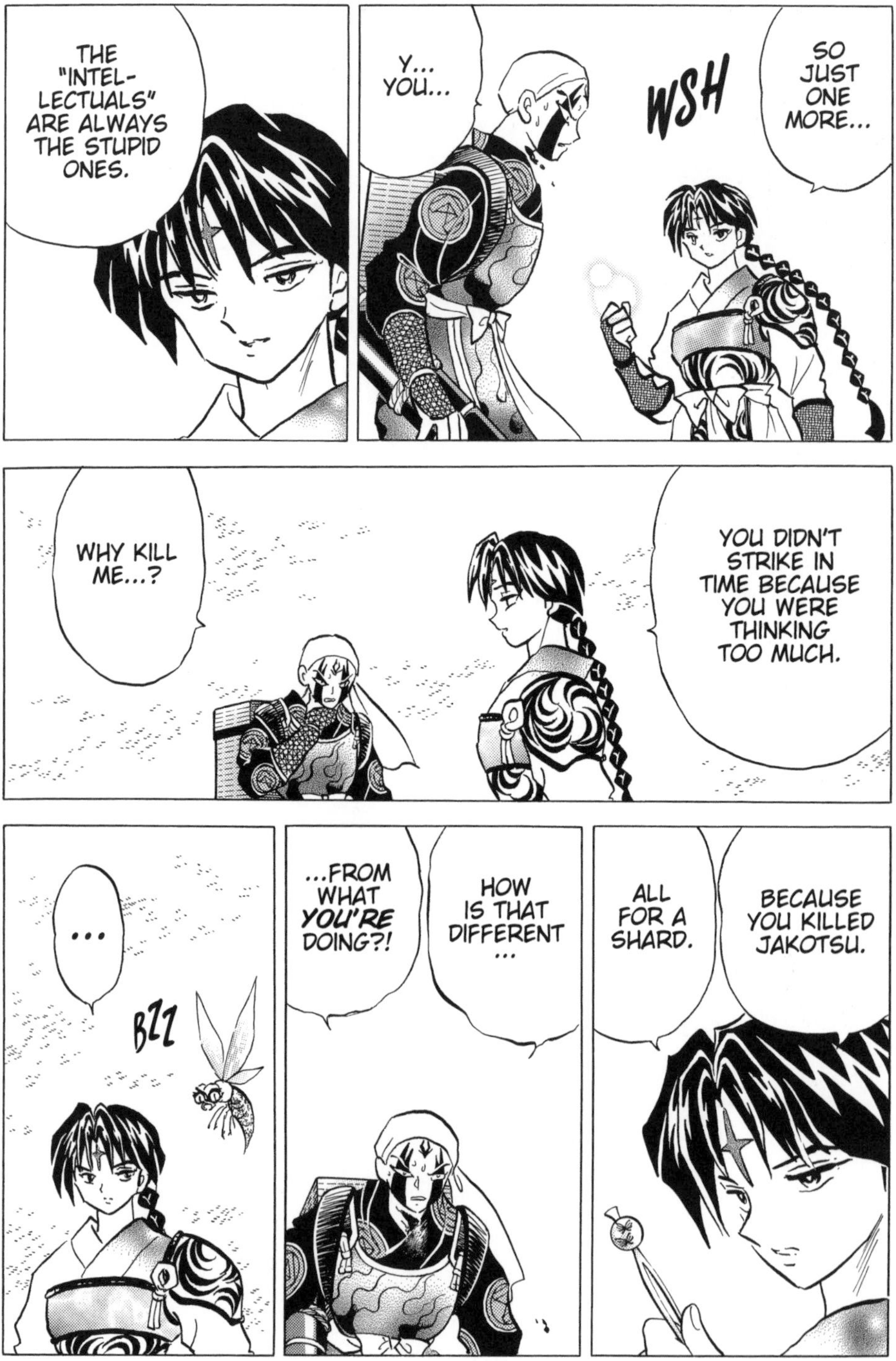
SO JUST ONE MORE...
WSH
Y... YOU...
THE "INTEL-LECTUALS" ARE ALWAYS THE STUPID ONES.
YOU DIDN'T STRIKE IN TIME BECAUSE YOU WERE THINKING TOO MUCH.
WHY KILL ME...?
BECAUSE YOU KILLED JAKOTSU.
ALL FOR A SHARD.
HOW IS THAT DIFFERENT ...
...FROM WHAT *YOU'RE* DOING?!
...
BZZ

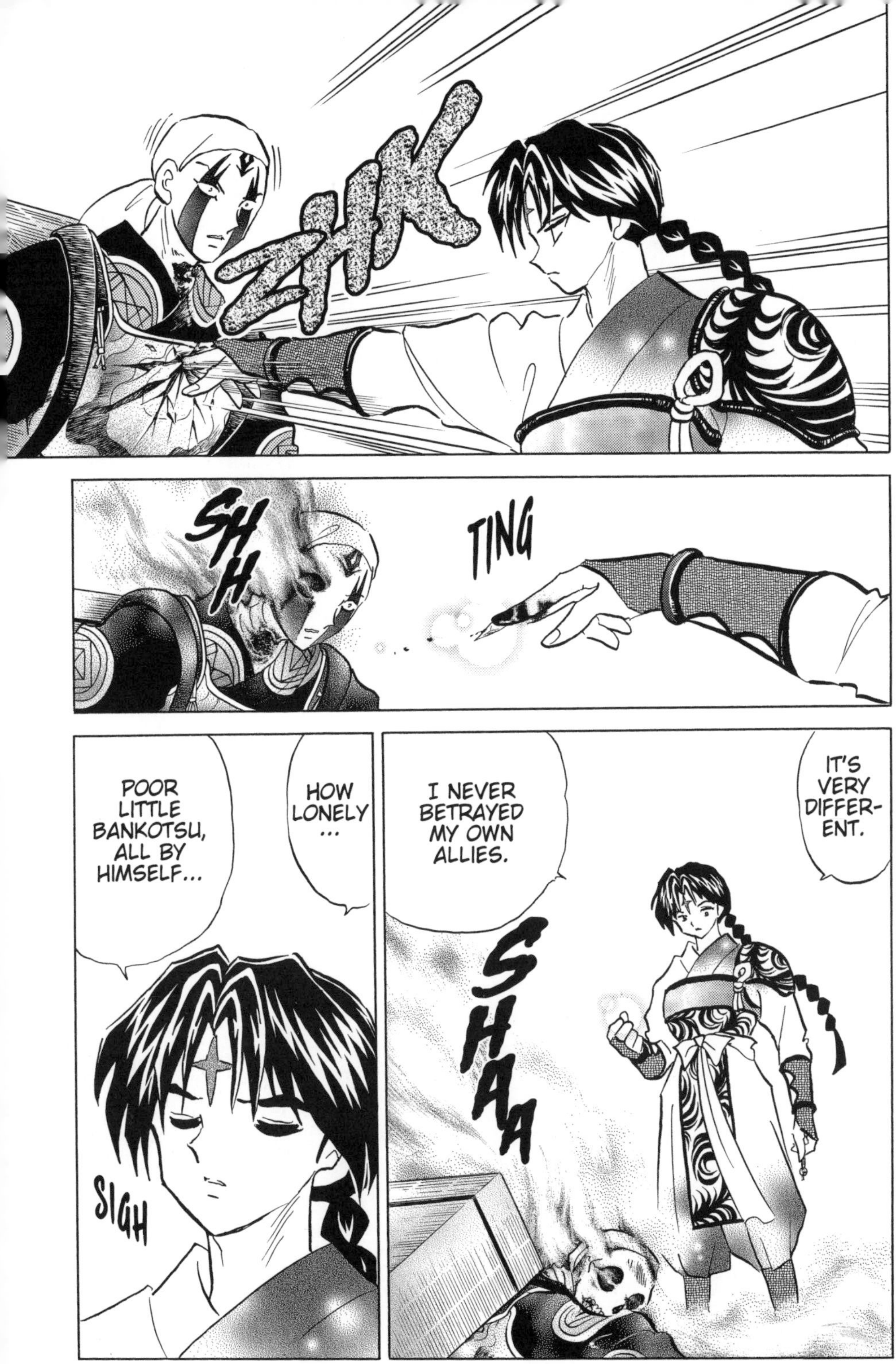
ZHK
TING
SHH
IT'S VERY DIFFER-ENT.
I NEVER BETRAYED MY OWN ALLIES.
SHAAA
HOW LONELY...
POOR LITTLE BANKOTSU, ALL BY HIMSELF...
SIGH

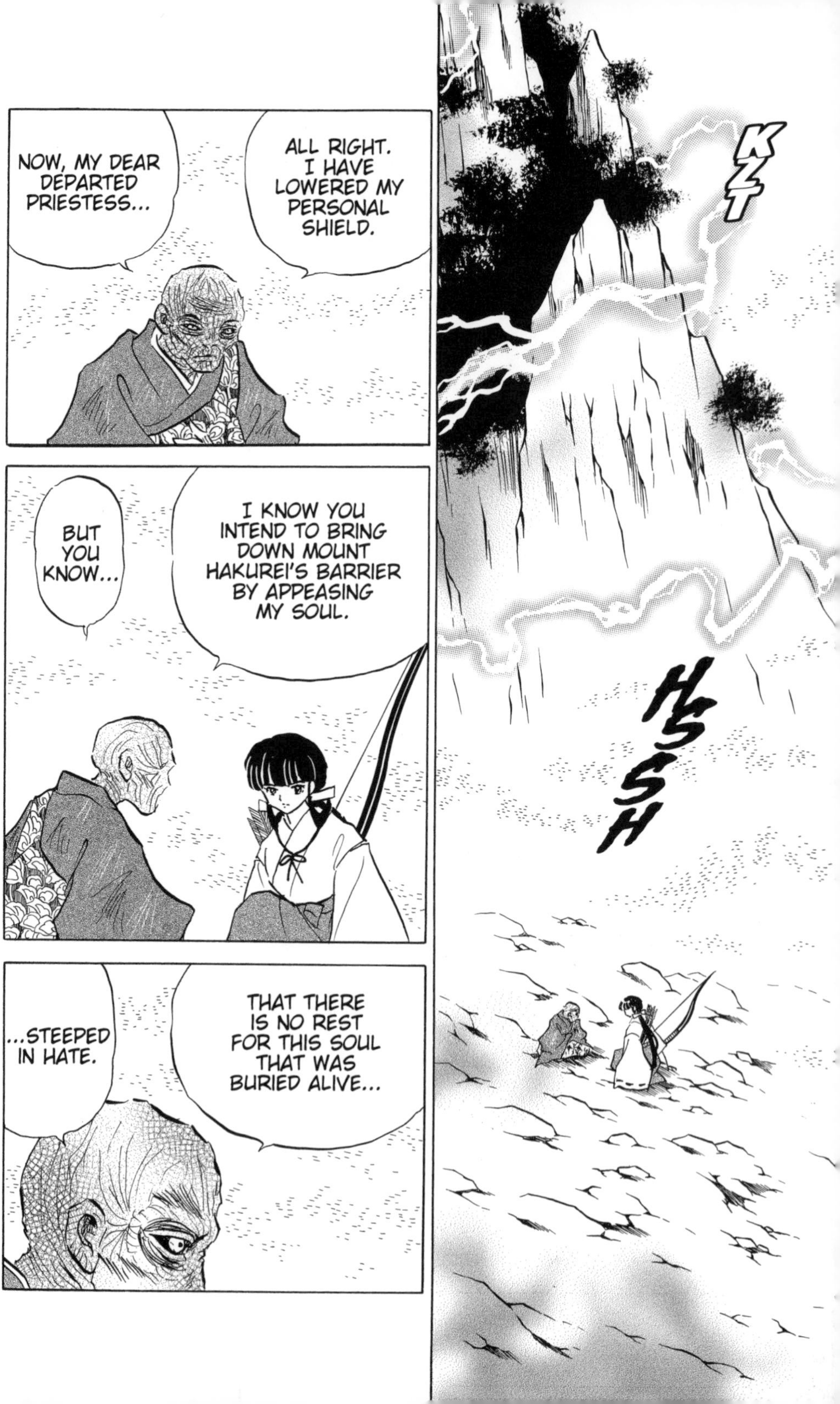
KZT
HSSH
ALL RIGHT. I HAVE LOWERED MY PERSONAL SHIELD.
NOW, MY DEAR DEPARTED PRIESTESS...
I KNOW YOU INTEND TO BRING DOWN MOUNT HAKUREI'S BARRIER BY APPEASING MY SOUL.
BUT YOU KNOW...
THAT THERE IS NO REST FOR THIS SOUL THAT WAS BURIED ALIVE...
...STEEPED IN HATE.

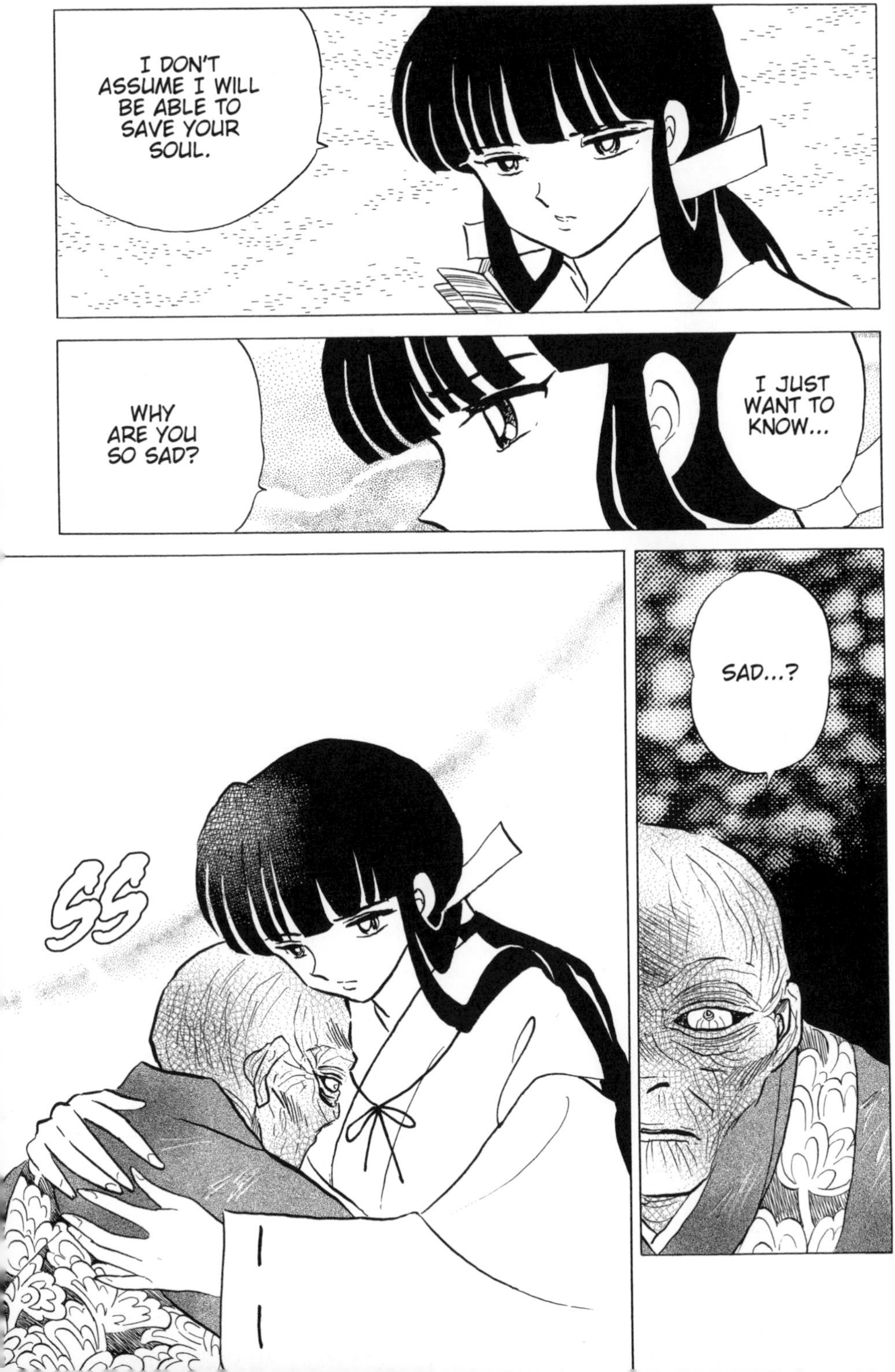
I DON'T ASSUME I WILL BE ABLE TO SAVE YOUR SOUL.
I JUST WANT TO KNOW...
WHY ARE YOU SO SAD?
SAD...?
SS

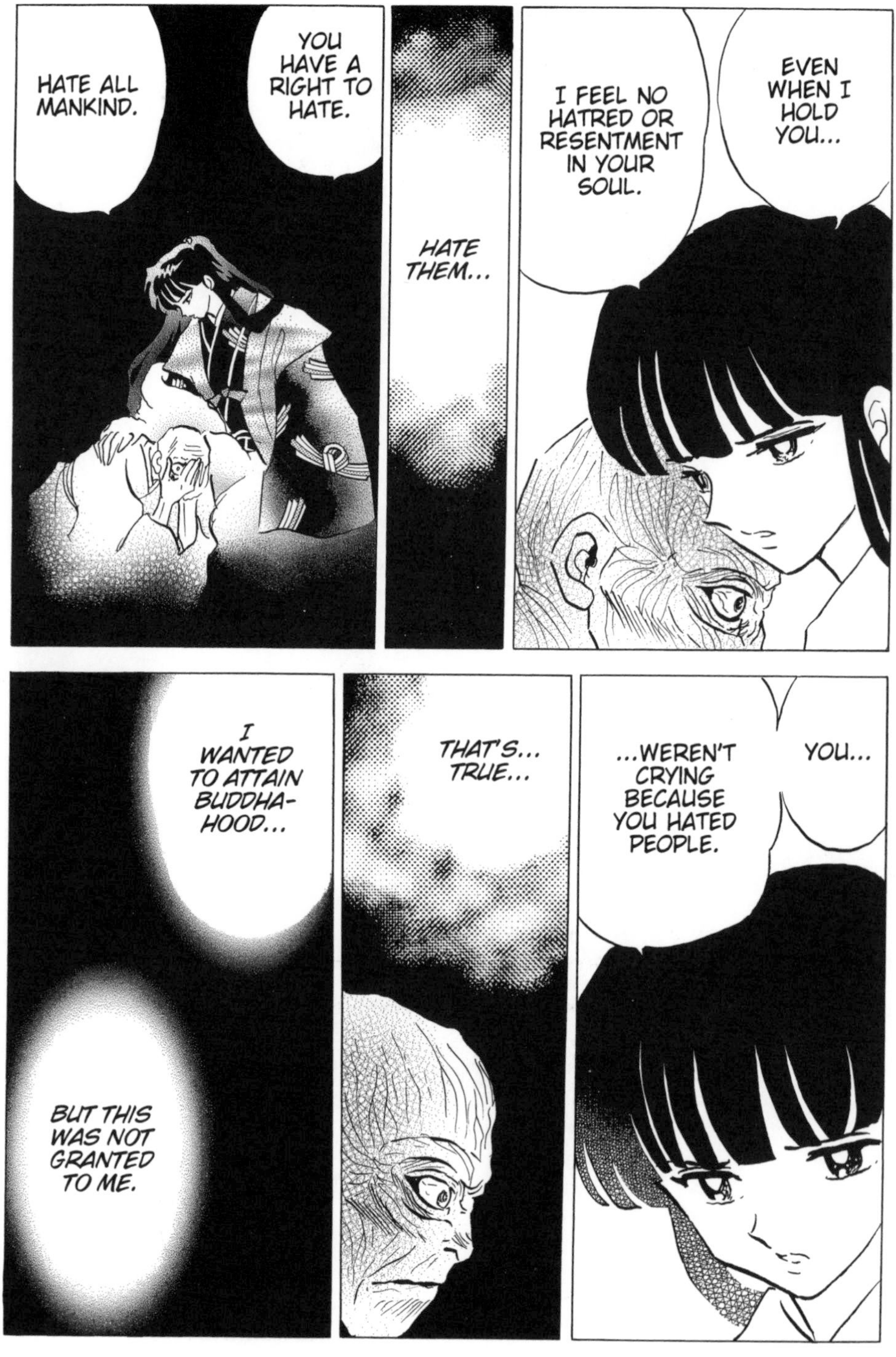
EVEN WHEN I HOLD YOU...
I FEEL NO HATRED OR RESENTMENT IN YOUR SOUL.
HATE THEM...
YOU HAVE A RIGHT TO HATE.
HATE ALL MANKIND.
YOU...
...WEREN'T CRYING BECAUSE YOU HATED PEOPLE.
THAT'S... TRUE...
I WANTED TO ATTAIN BUDDHA-HOOD...
BUT THIS WAS NOT GRANTED TO ME.

I DID NOT WANT TO KNOW THE TRUTH... THAT I WAS WEAK.
I PUNISHED MYSELF FOR THE WEAKNESS OF MY HEART.
YOU MUST HAVE FELT SUCH SORROW.
YES... SUCH SORROW...
YOU HAVE SERVED HUMANITY LONG ENOUGH.
NOW...
BE AT PEACE.
...

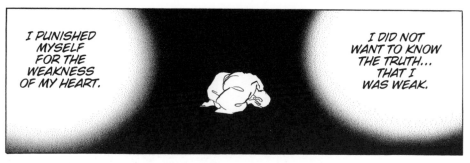

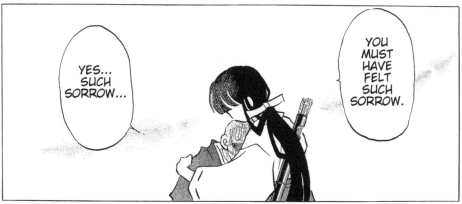

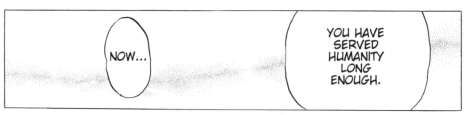

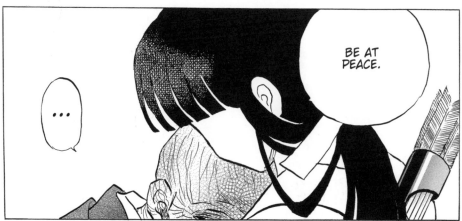

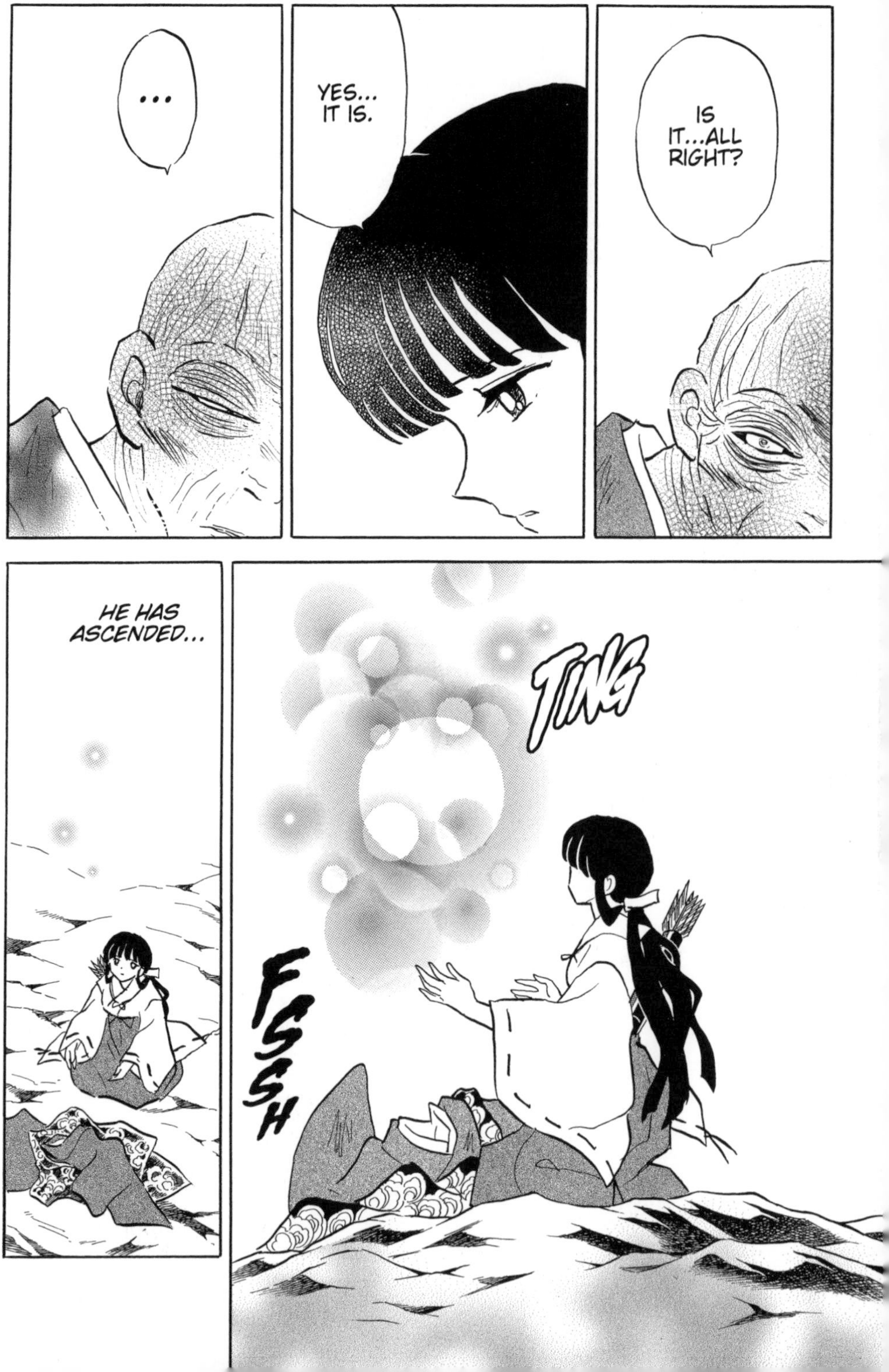
IS IT...ALL RIGHT?
YES... IT IS.
...
TING
FSSH
HE HAS ASCENDED...

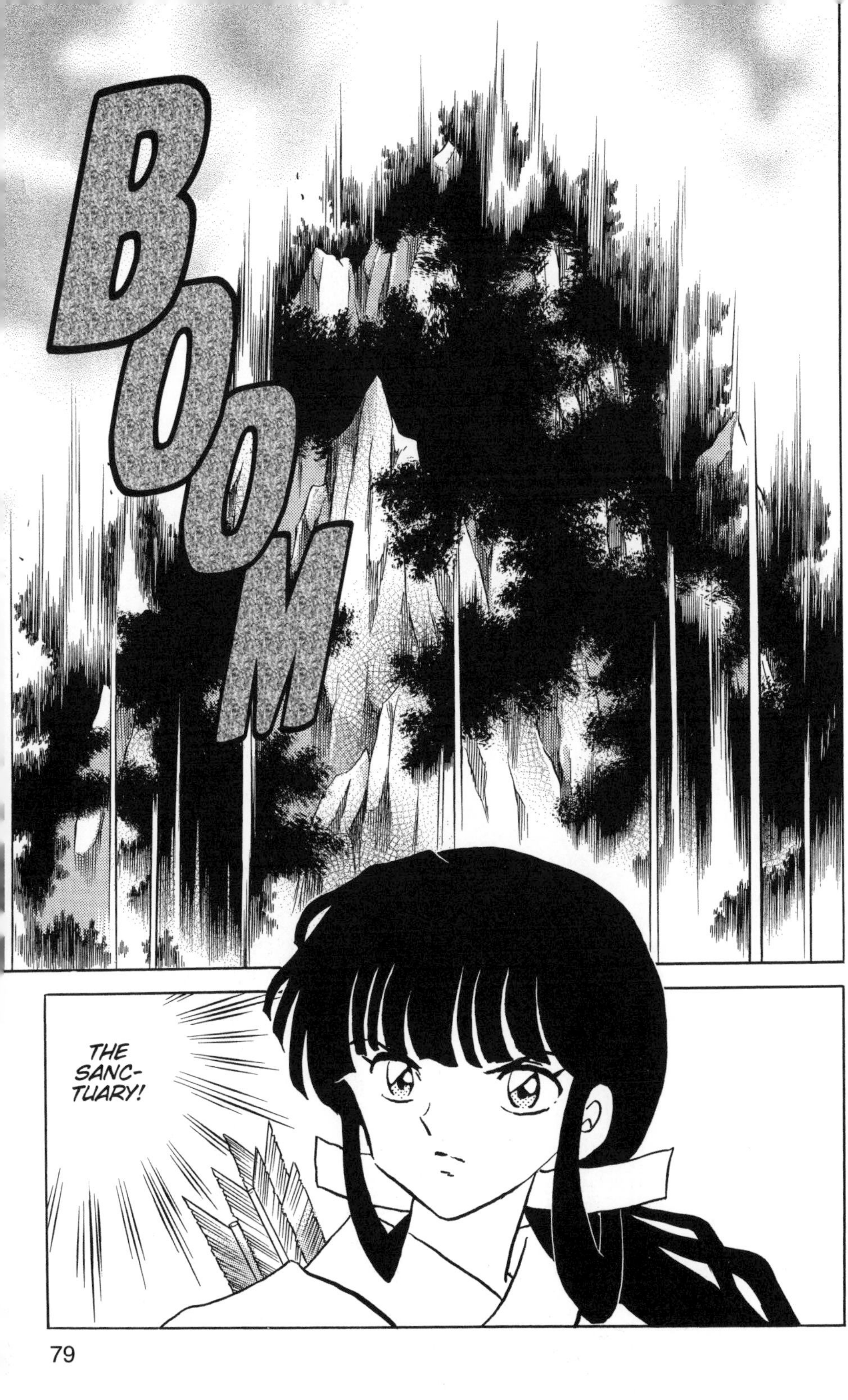
BOOOM
THE SANCTUARY!

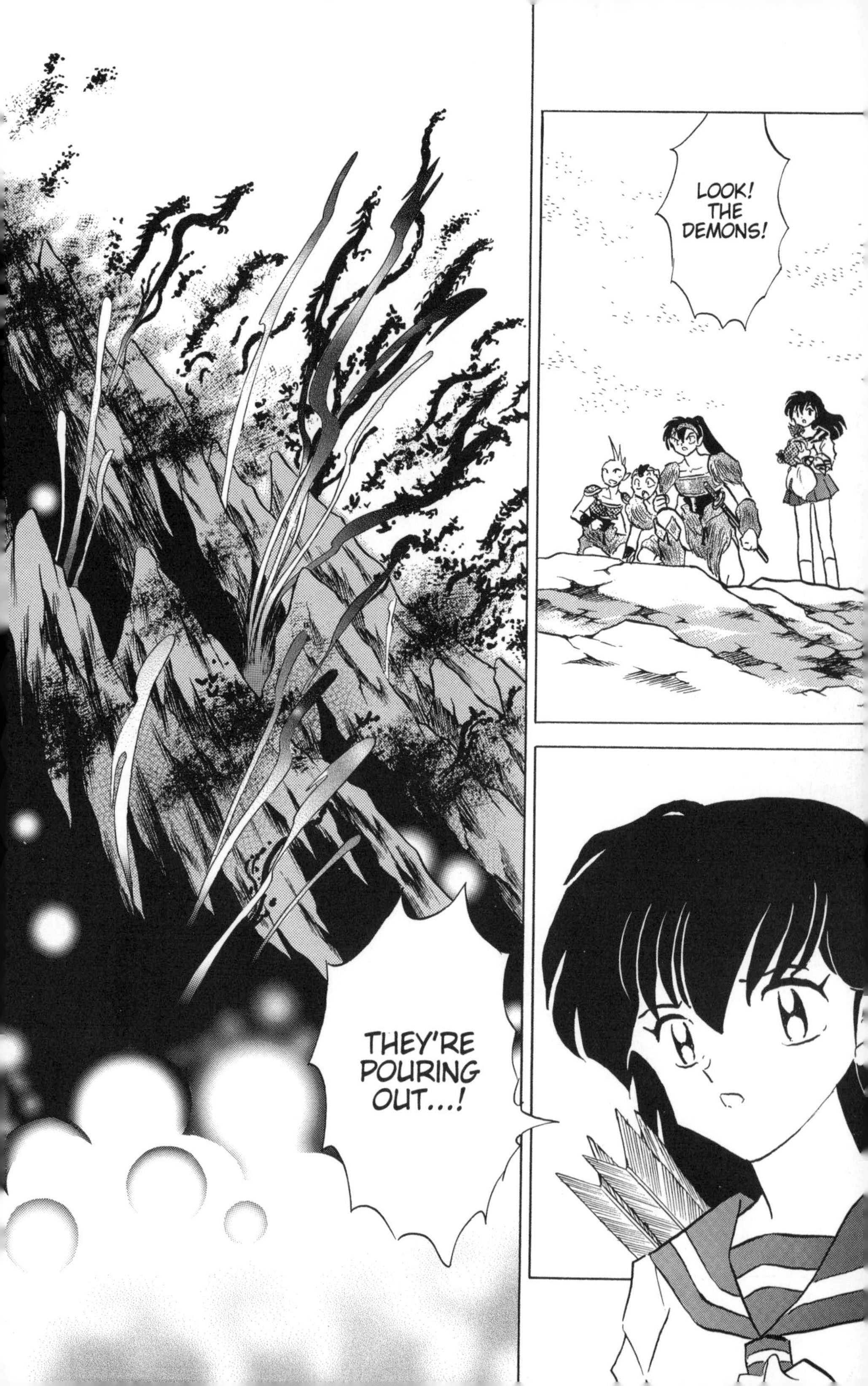
LOOK! THE DEMONS!
THEY'RE POURING OUT...!

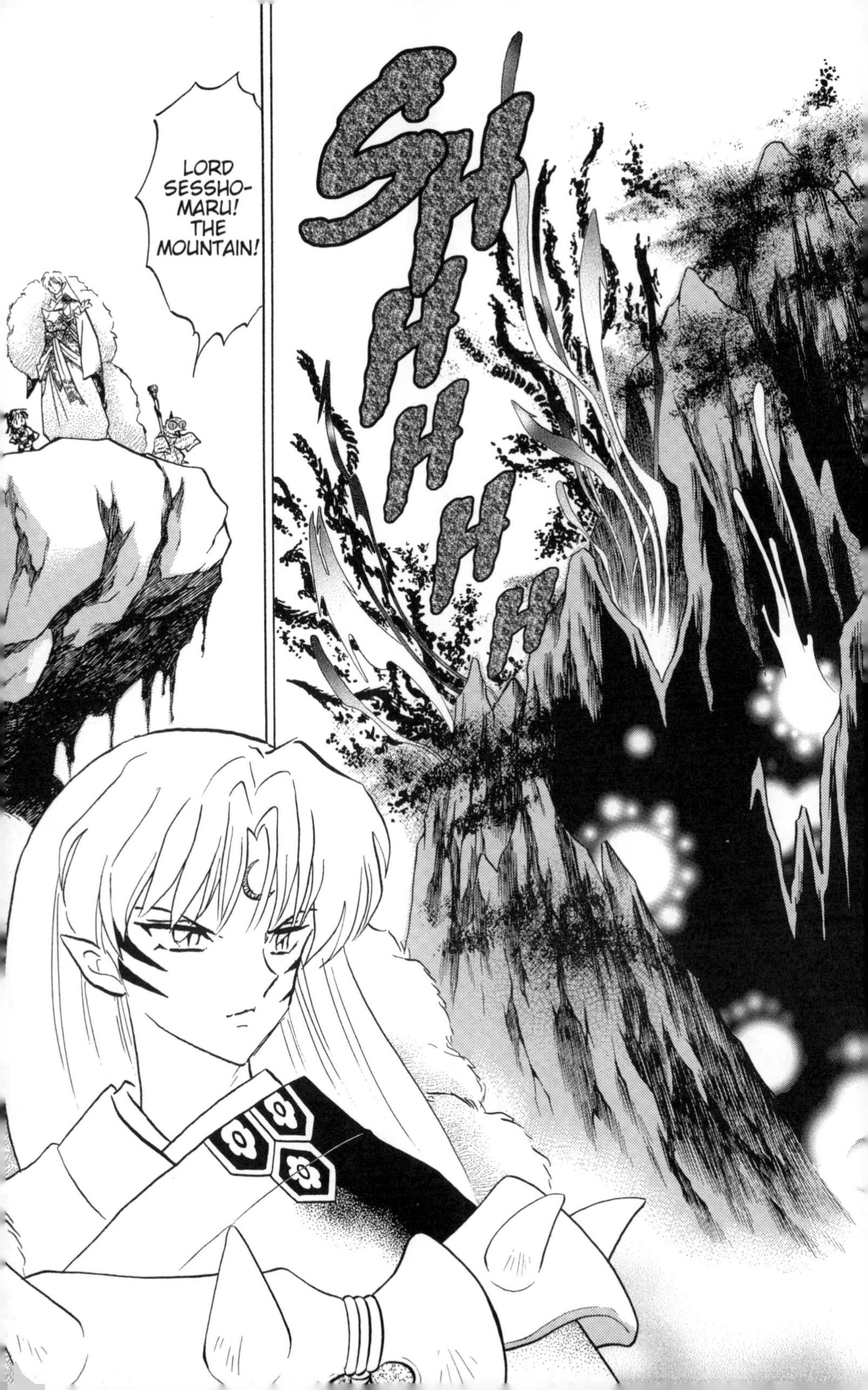
SHHHHHH
LORD SESSHO-MARU! THE MOUNTAIN!

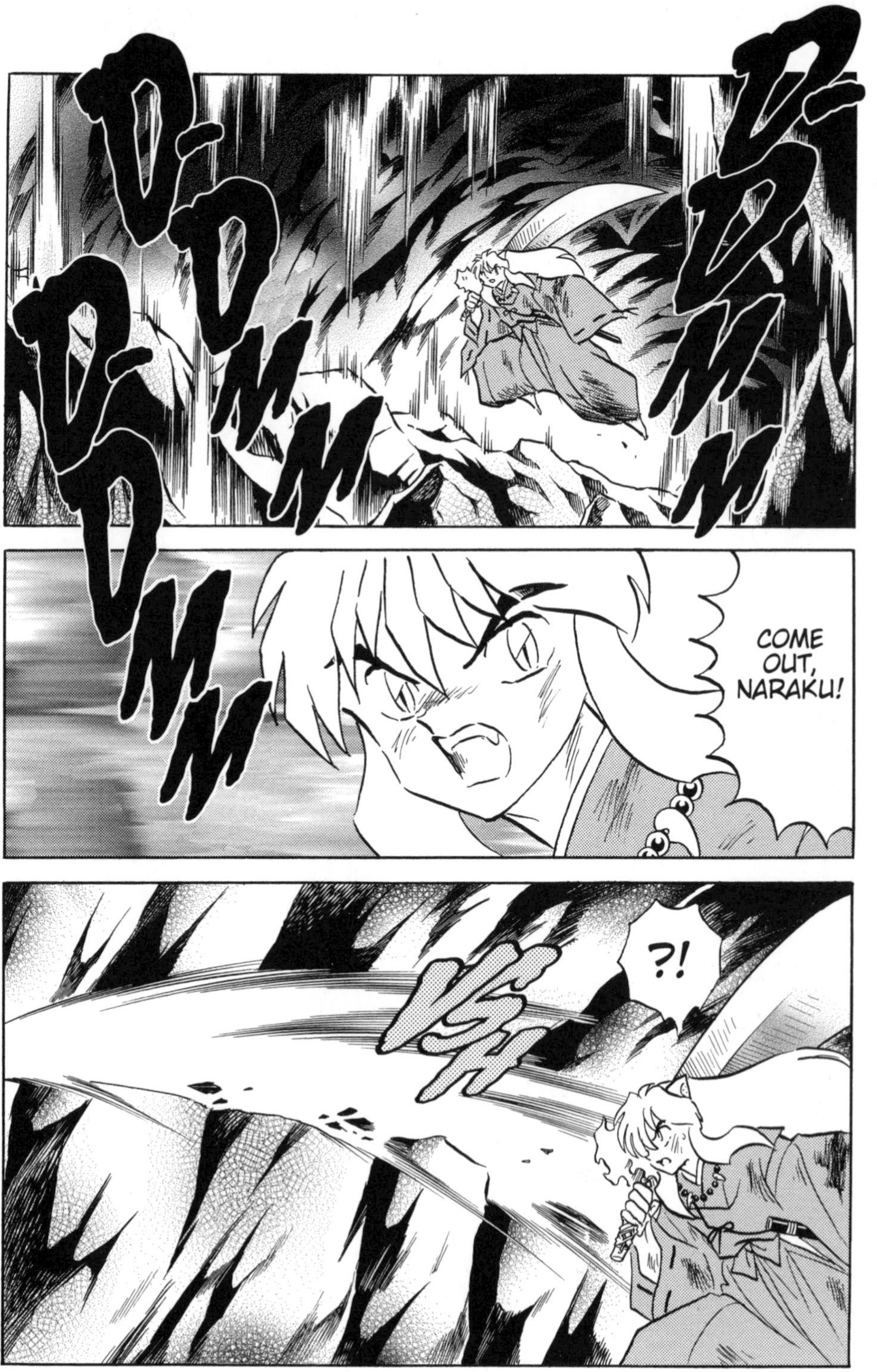
DOMMMM
D-D-DOMMM
D-D-DOMMMM
COME OUT, NARAKU!
?!
VSH

WHOA!

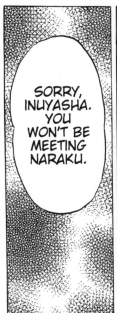

SORRY, INUYASHA. YOU WON'T BE MEETING NARAKU.

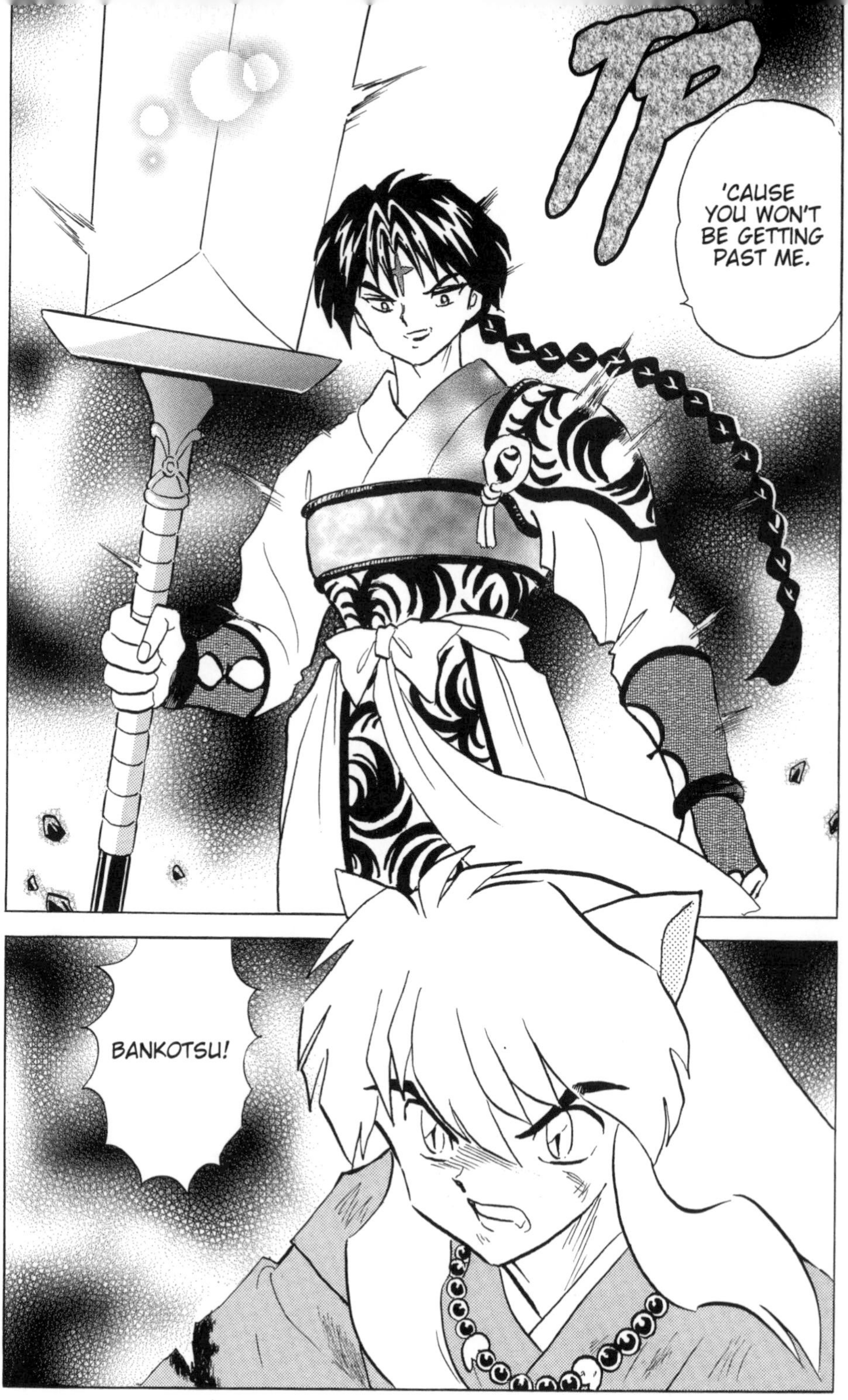
'CAUSE YOU WON'T BE GETTING PAST ME.
BANKOTSU!

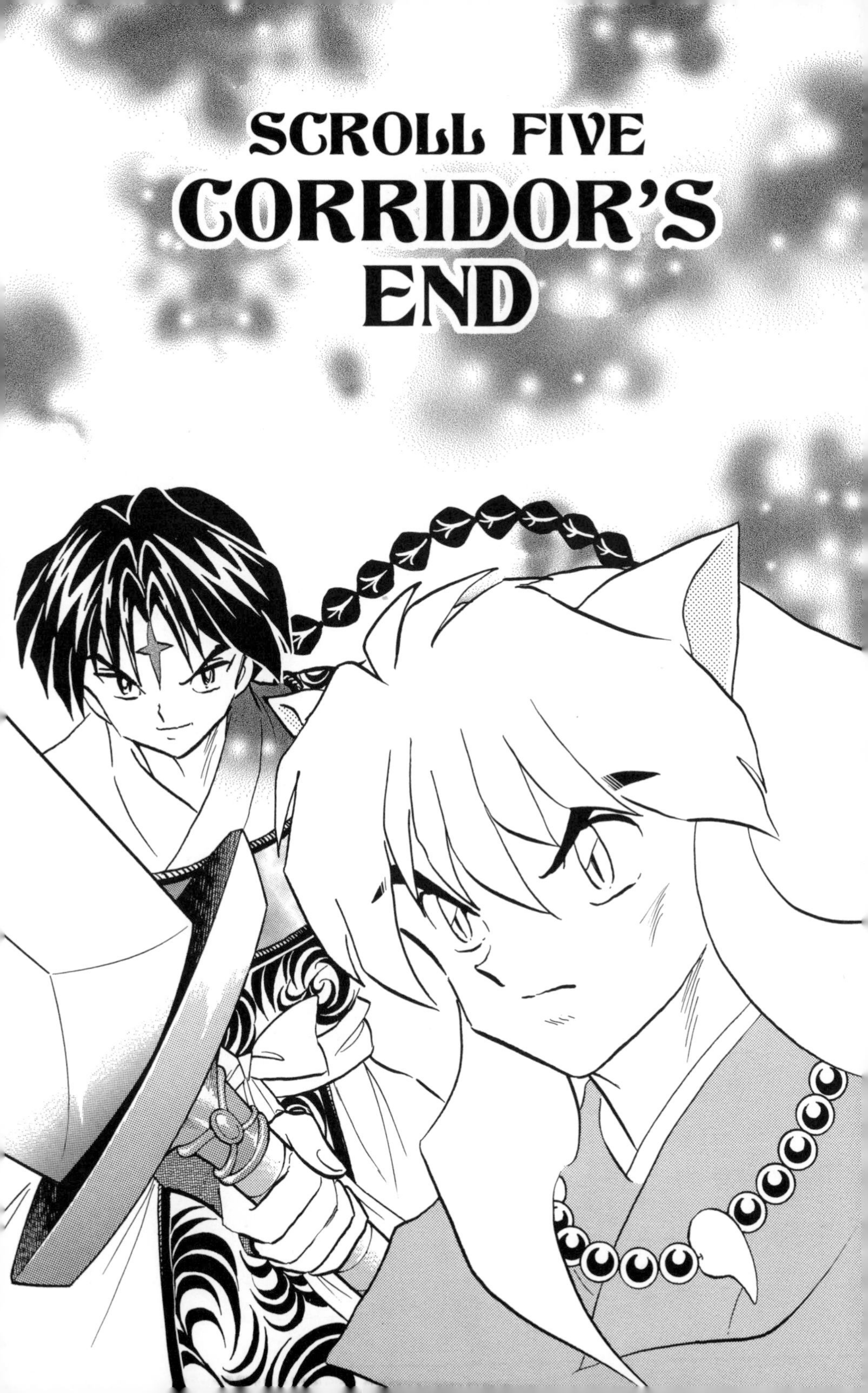
SCROLL FIVE
CORRIDOR'S END

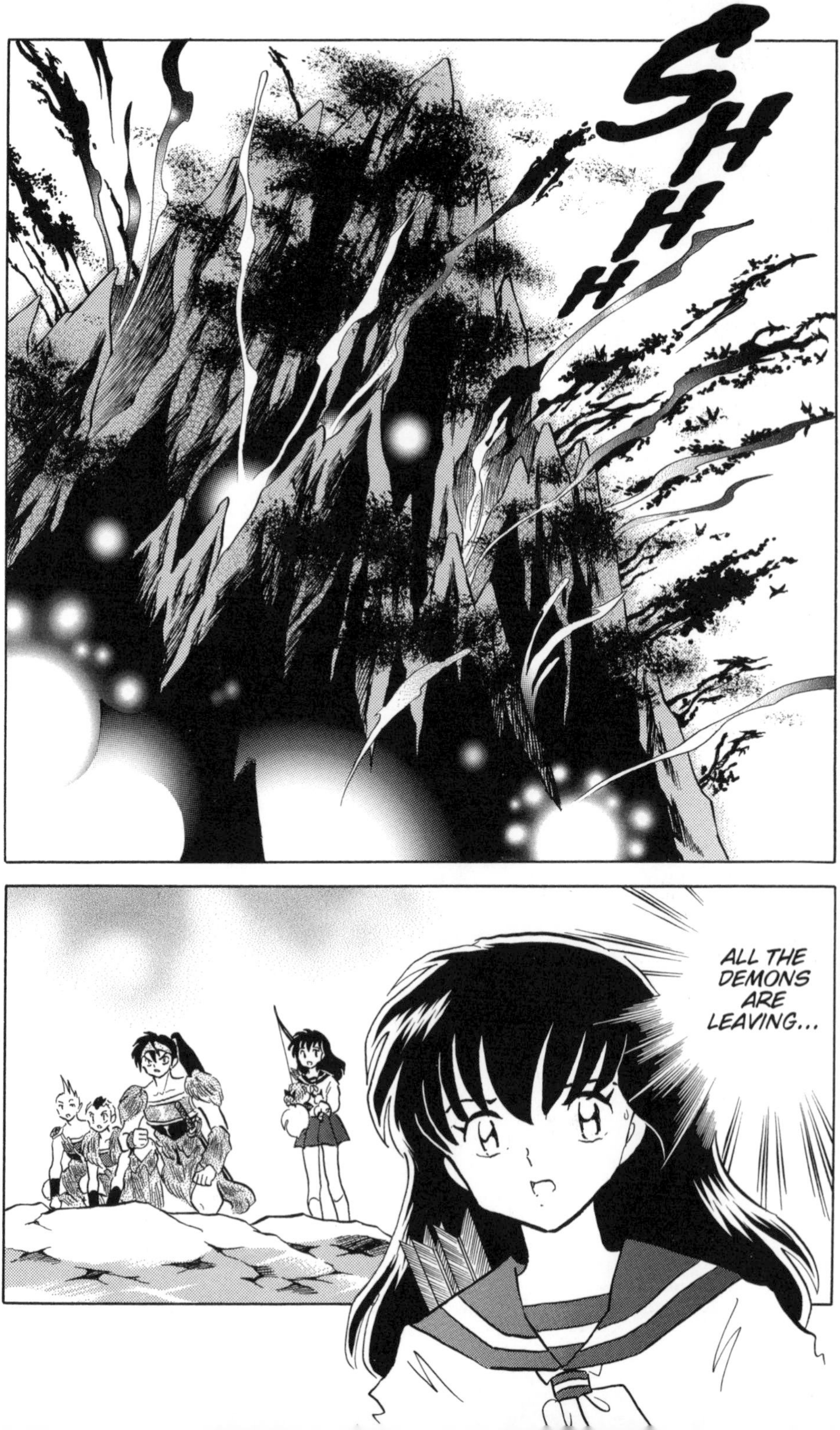
SHHHH
ALL THE DEMONS ARE LEAVING...

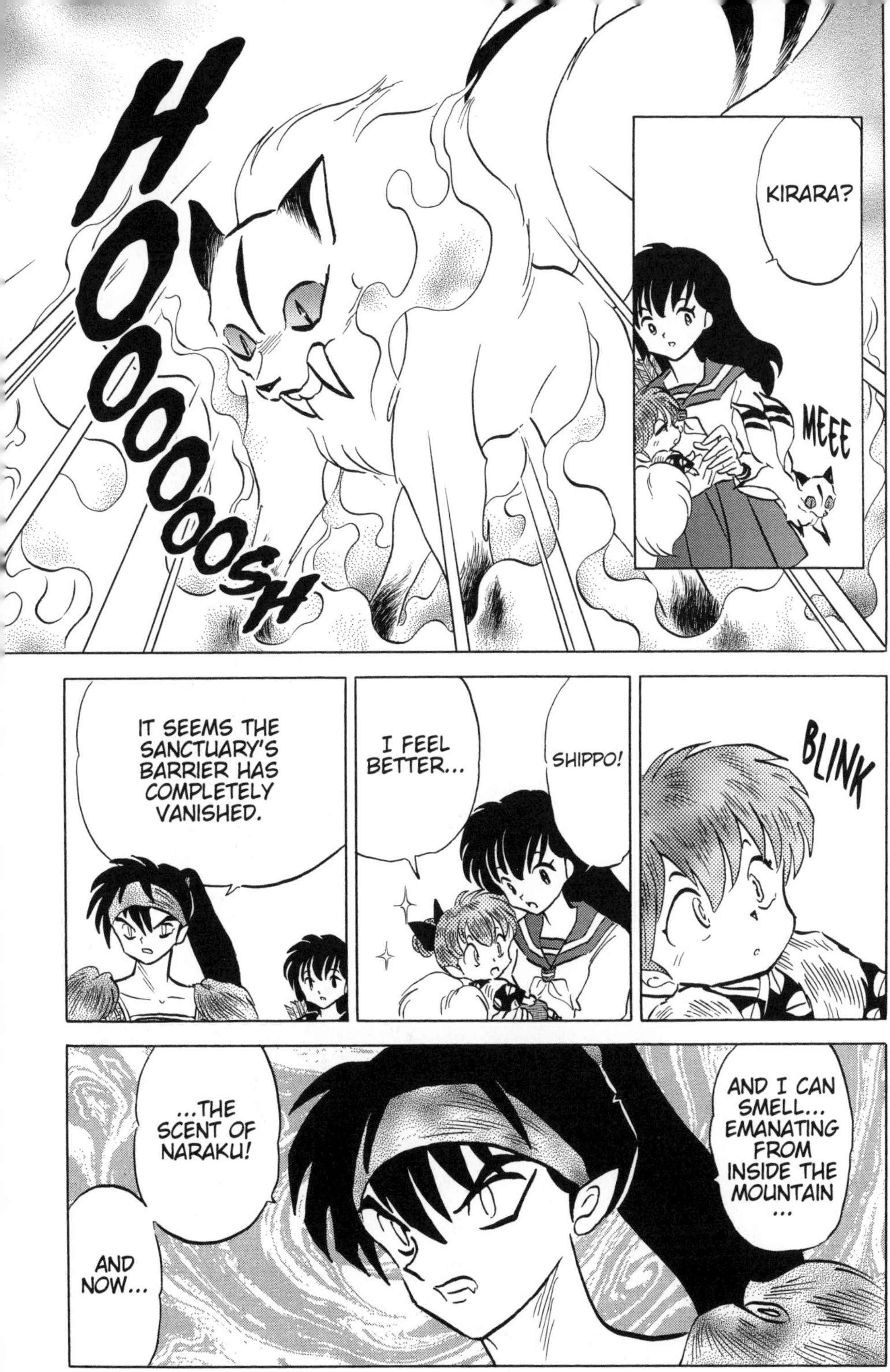
KIRARA?
MEEE
HOOOOOOSH
BLINK
SHIPPO!
I FEEL BETTER...
IT SEEMS THE SANCTUARY'S BARRIER HAS COMPLETELY VANISHED.
AND I CAN SMELL... EMANATING FROM INSIDE THE MOUNTAIN ...
...THE SCENT OF NARAKU!
AND NOW...

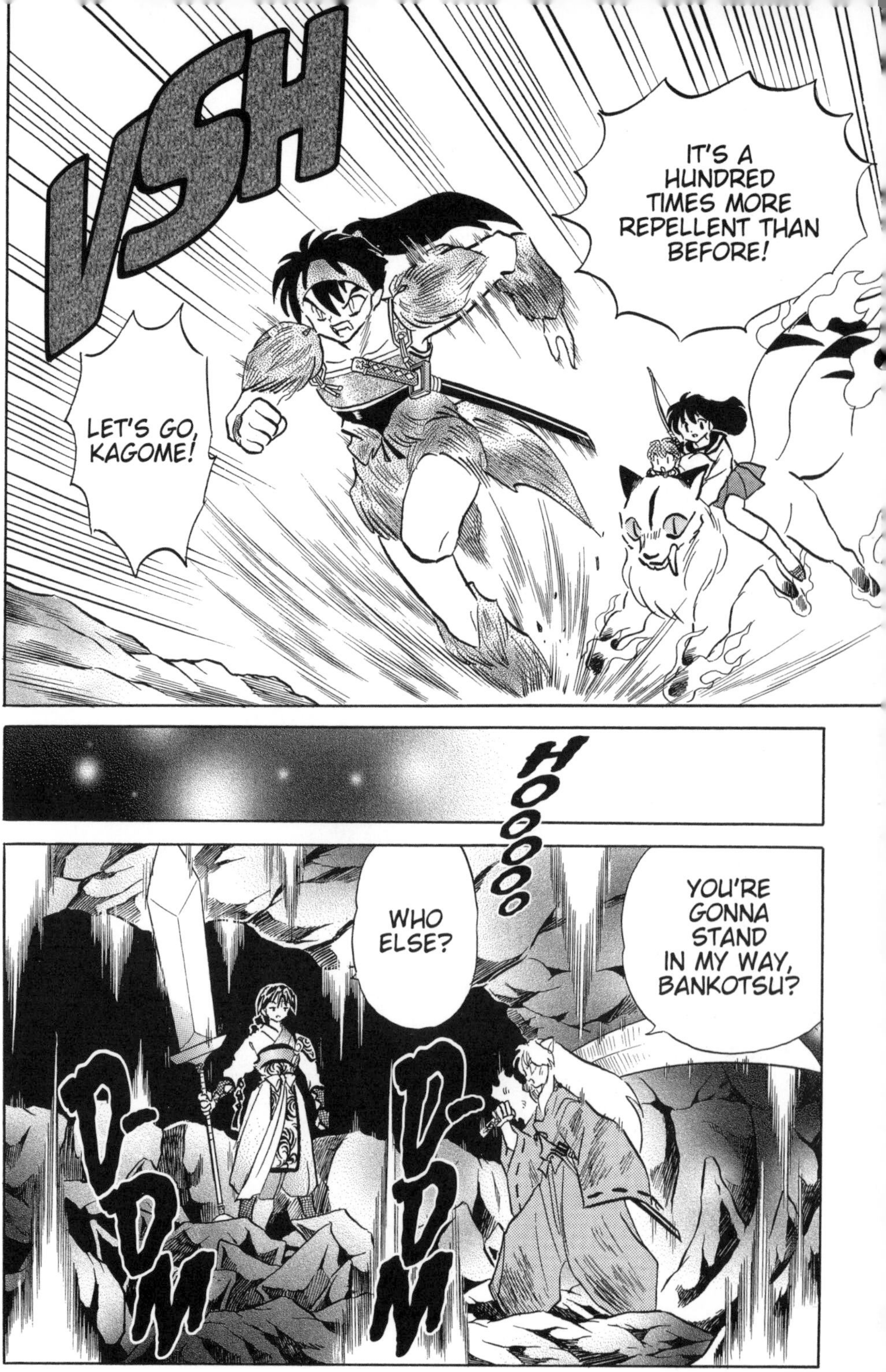
IT'S A HUNDRED TIMES MORE REPELLENT THAN BEFORE!
VSH
LET'S GO, KAGOME!
HOOOOOOO
YOU'RE GONNA STAND IN MY WAY, BANKOTSU?
WHO ELSE?
D-D-M
D-D-M

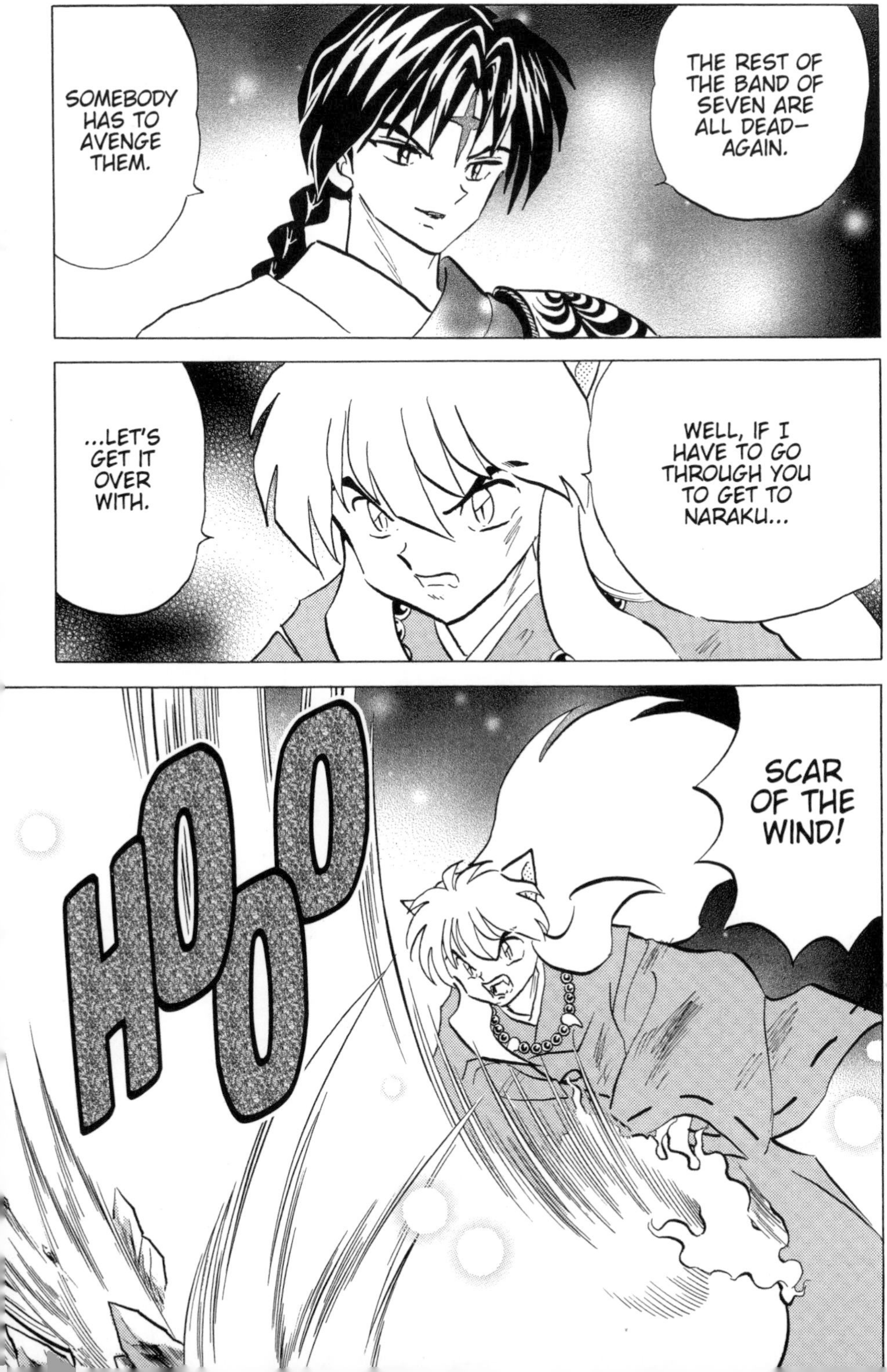
THE REST OF THE BAND OF SEVEN ARE ALL DEAD— AGAIN.
SOMEBODY HAS TO AVENGE THEM.
WELL, IF I HAVE TO GO THROUGH YOU TO GET TO NARAKU...
...LET'S GET IT OVER WITH.
SCAR OF THE WIND!
HOOOO

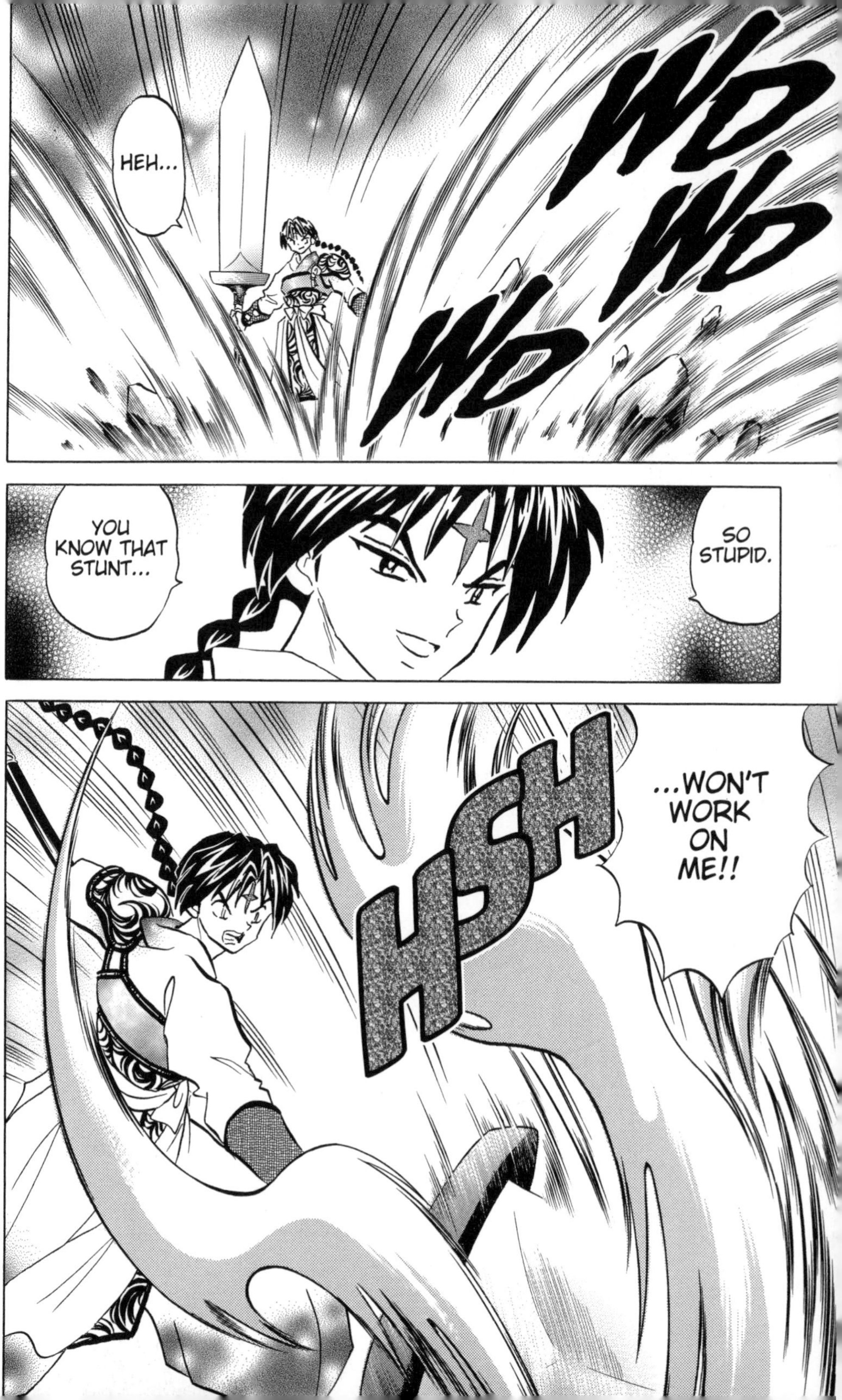
WO WO WO
HEH...
SO STUPID.
YOU KNOW THAT STUNT...
...WON'T WORK ON ME!!
HSH

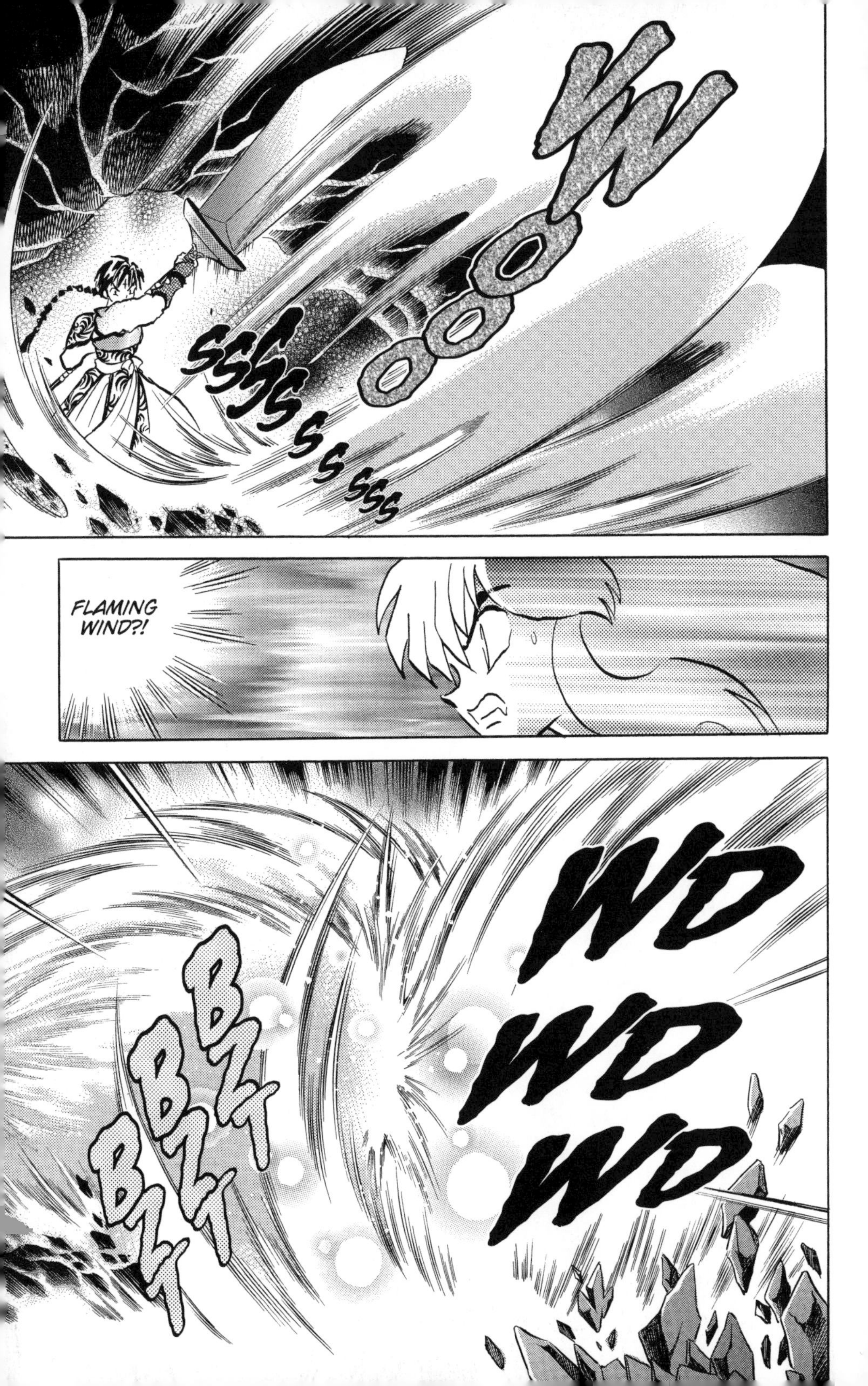
VWOOOOO
SSSSSSSSS
FLAMING WIND?!
WD WD WD
BZZT BZZT

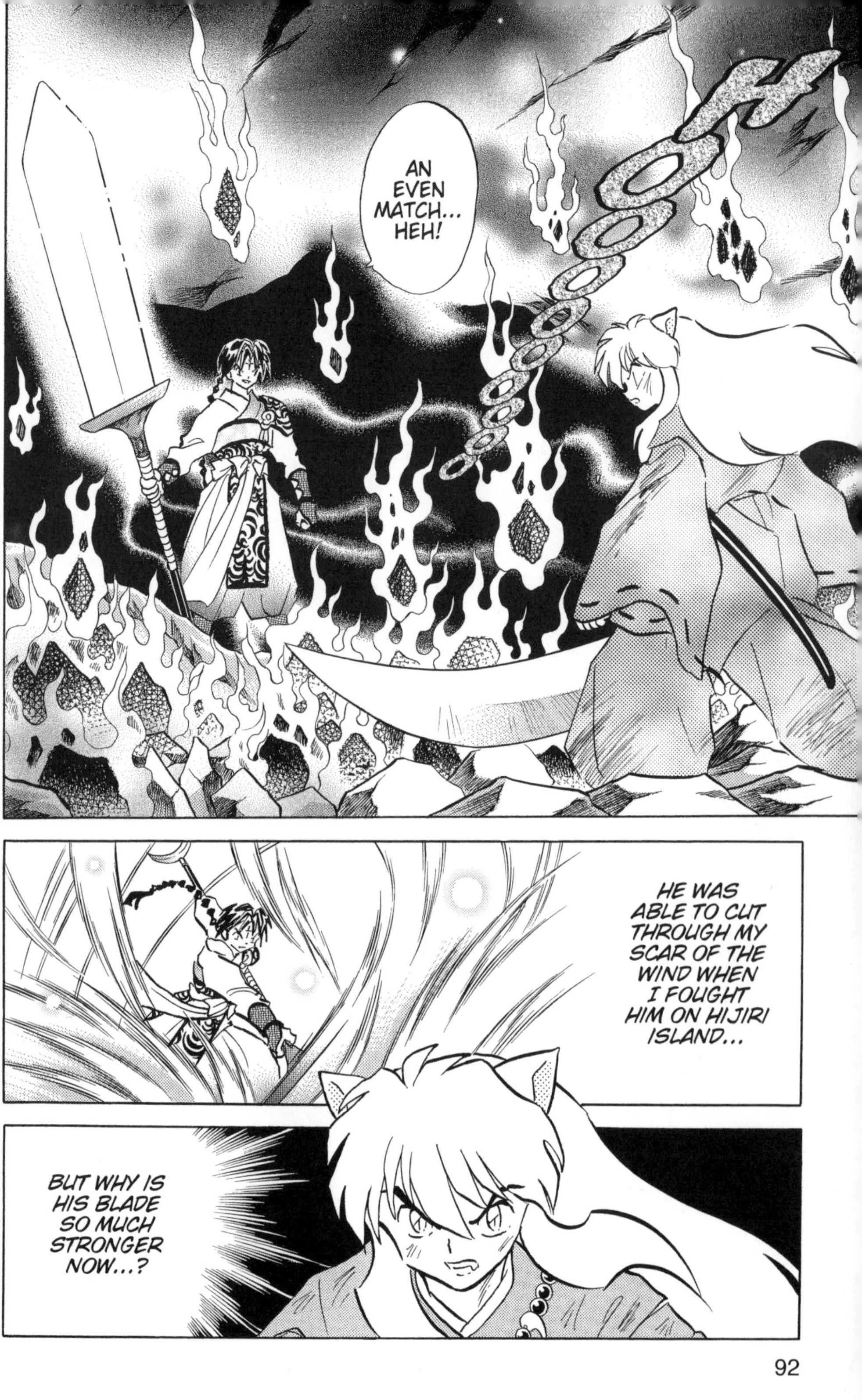
AN EVEN MATCH... HEH!
HE WAS ABLE TO CUT THROUGH MY SCAR OF THE WIND WHEN I FOUGHT HIM ON HIJIRI ISLAND...
BUT WHY IS HIS BLADE SO MUCH STRONGER NOW...?

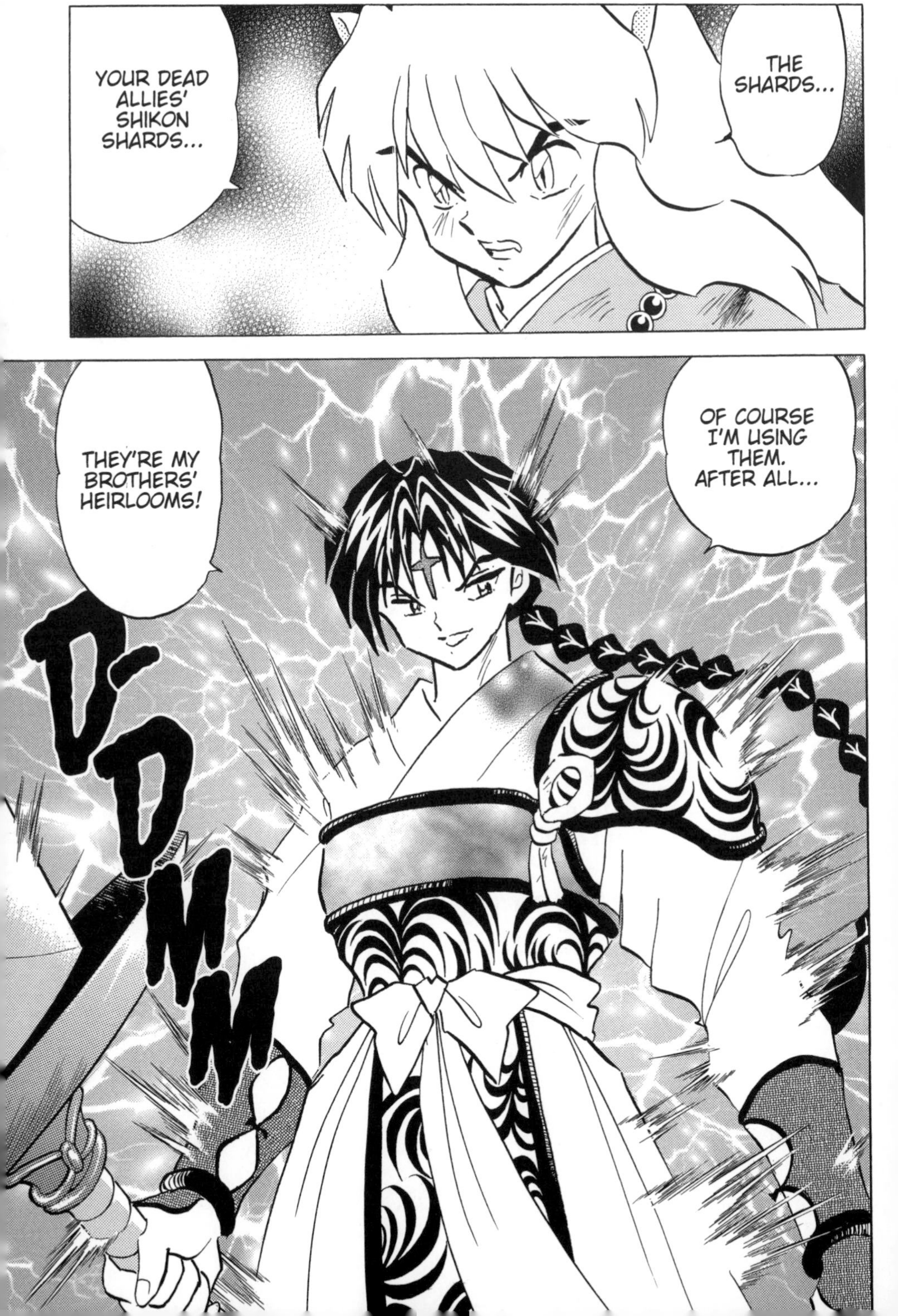
THE SHARDS...
YOUR DEAD ALLIES' SHIKON SHARDS...
OF COURSE I'M USING THEM. AFTER ALL...
THEY'RE MY BROTHERS' HEIRLOOMS!
D-DMMM

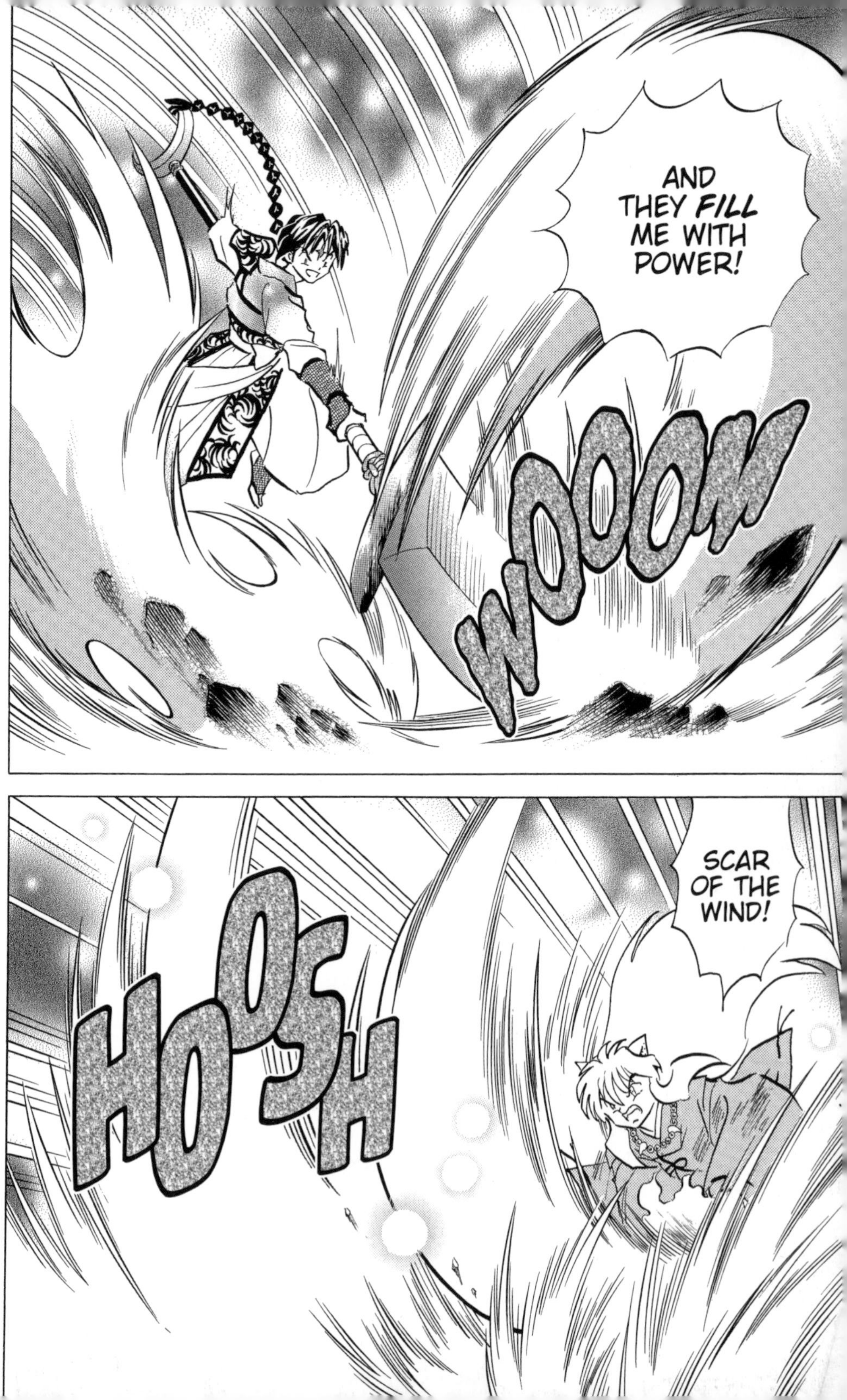
AND THEY FILL ME WITH POWER!
WOOOM
SCAR OF THE WIND!
HOOOSH

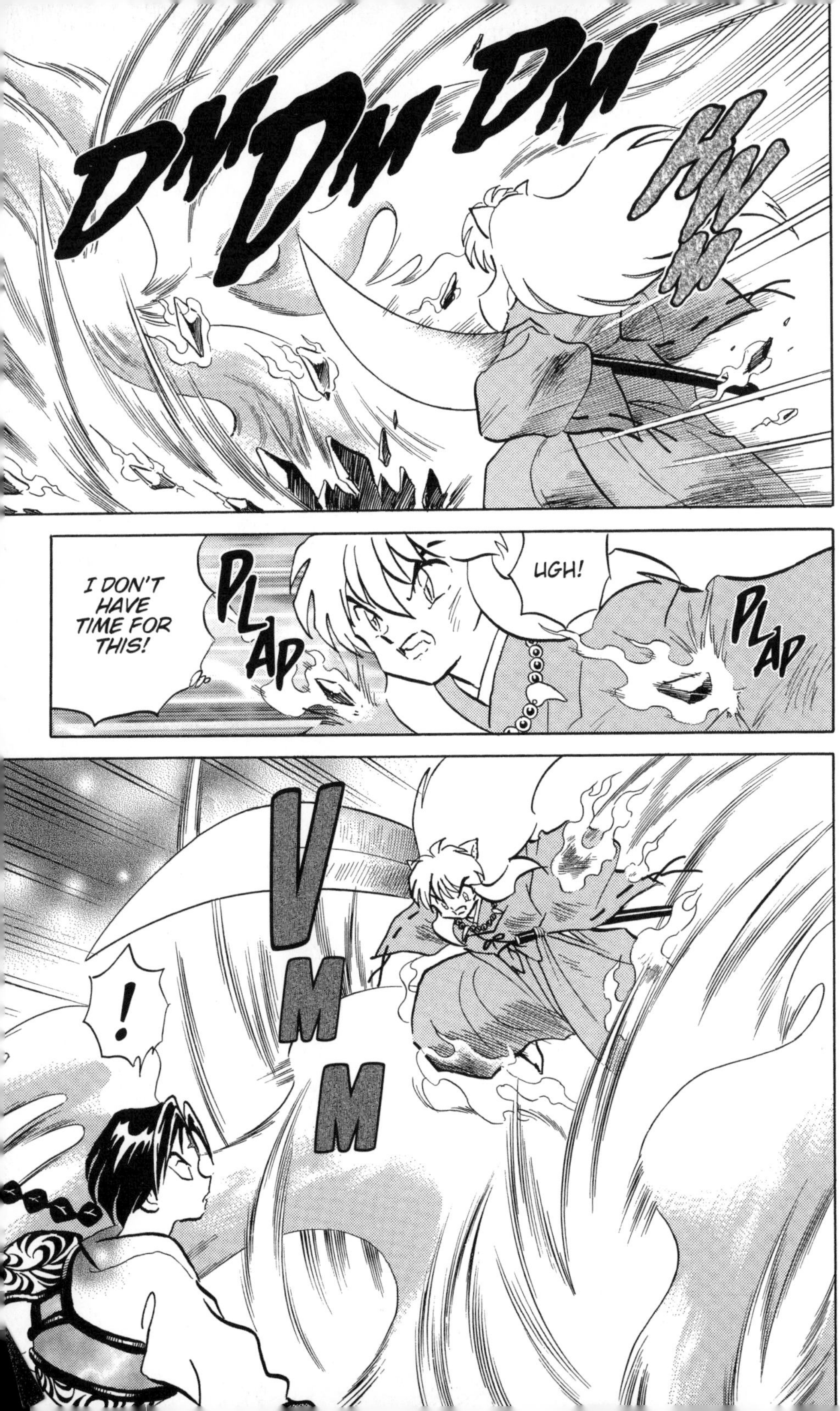
DMDMDM
HWMM
UGH!
PLAP
I DON'T HAVE TIME FOR THIS!
PLAP
VMMM
!

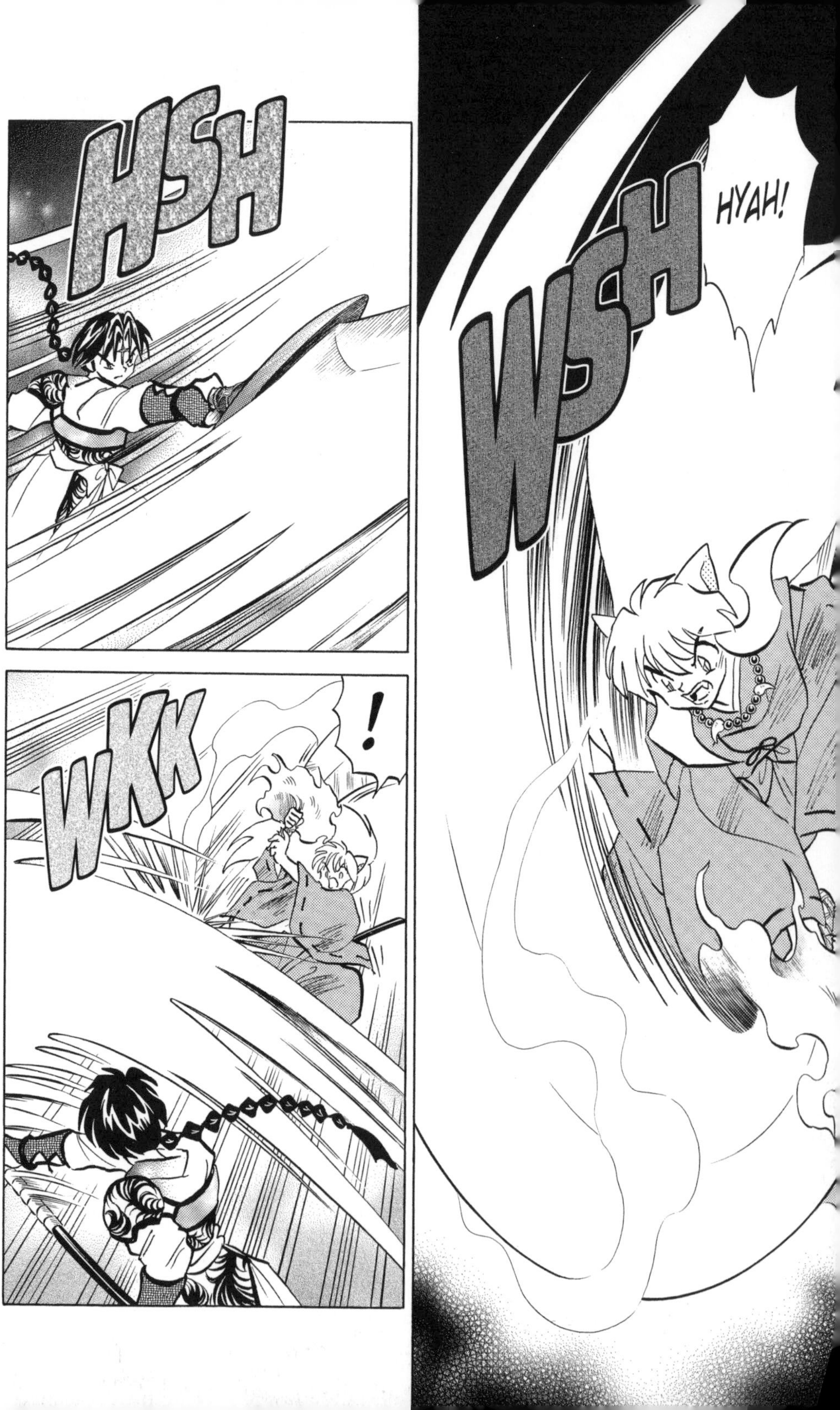
WSH
HYAH!
HSH
WKK
!

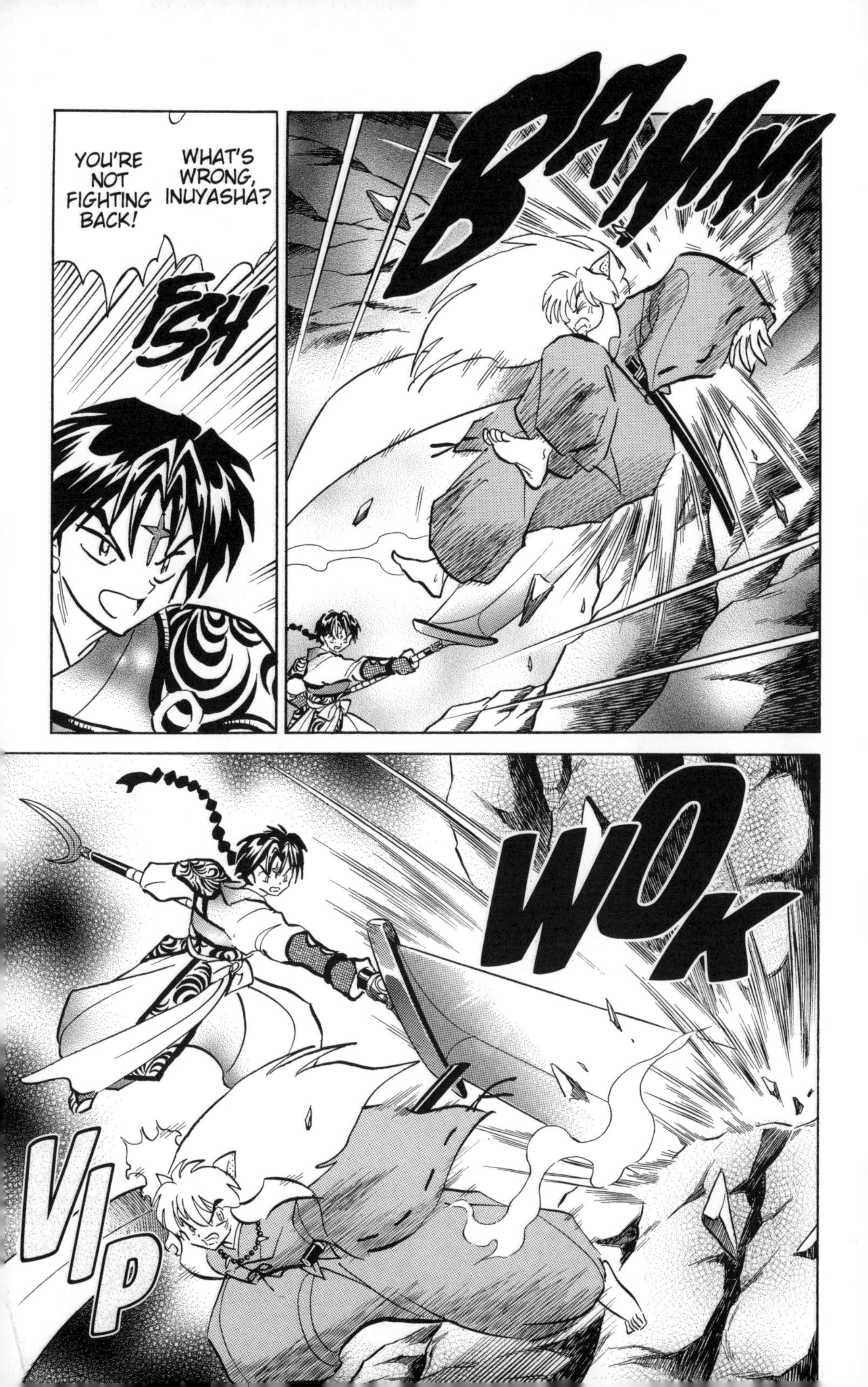
BAMM
WHAT'S WRONG, INUYASHA?
YOU'RE NOT FIGHTING BACK!
FSH
WOK
VIP

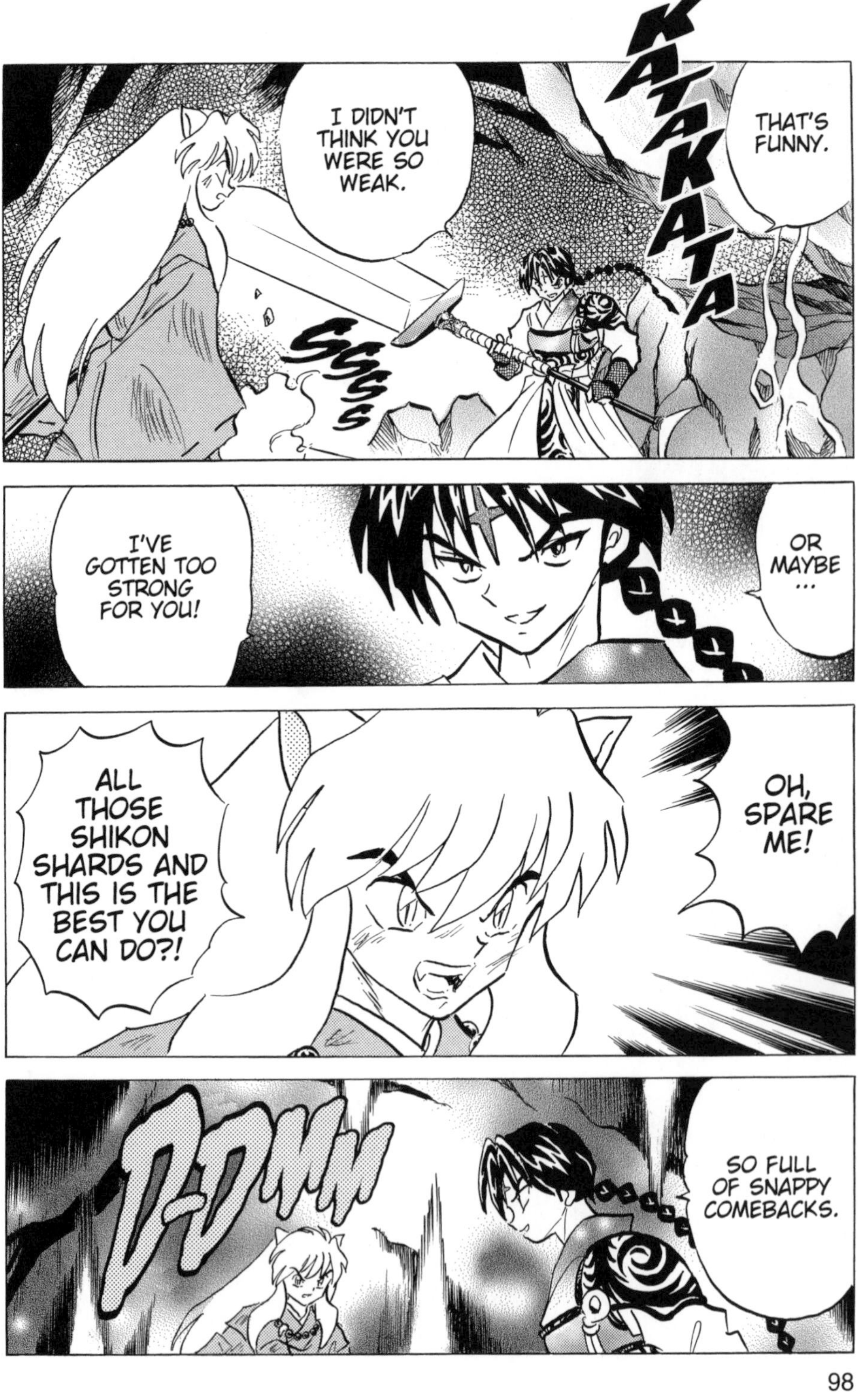
KATAKATA
THAT'S FUNNY.
I DIDN'T THINK YOU WERE SO WEAK.
SGSSS
OR MAYBE ...
I'VE GOTTEN TOO STRONG FOR YOU!
OH, SPARE ME!
ALL THOSE SHIKON SHARDS AND THIS IS THE BEST YOU CAN DO?!
SO FULL OF SNAPPY COMEBACKS.
DOMM

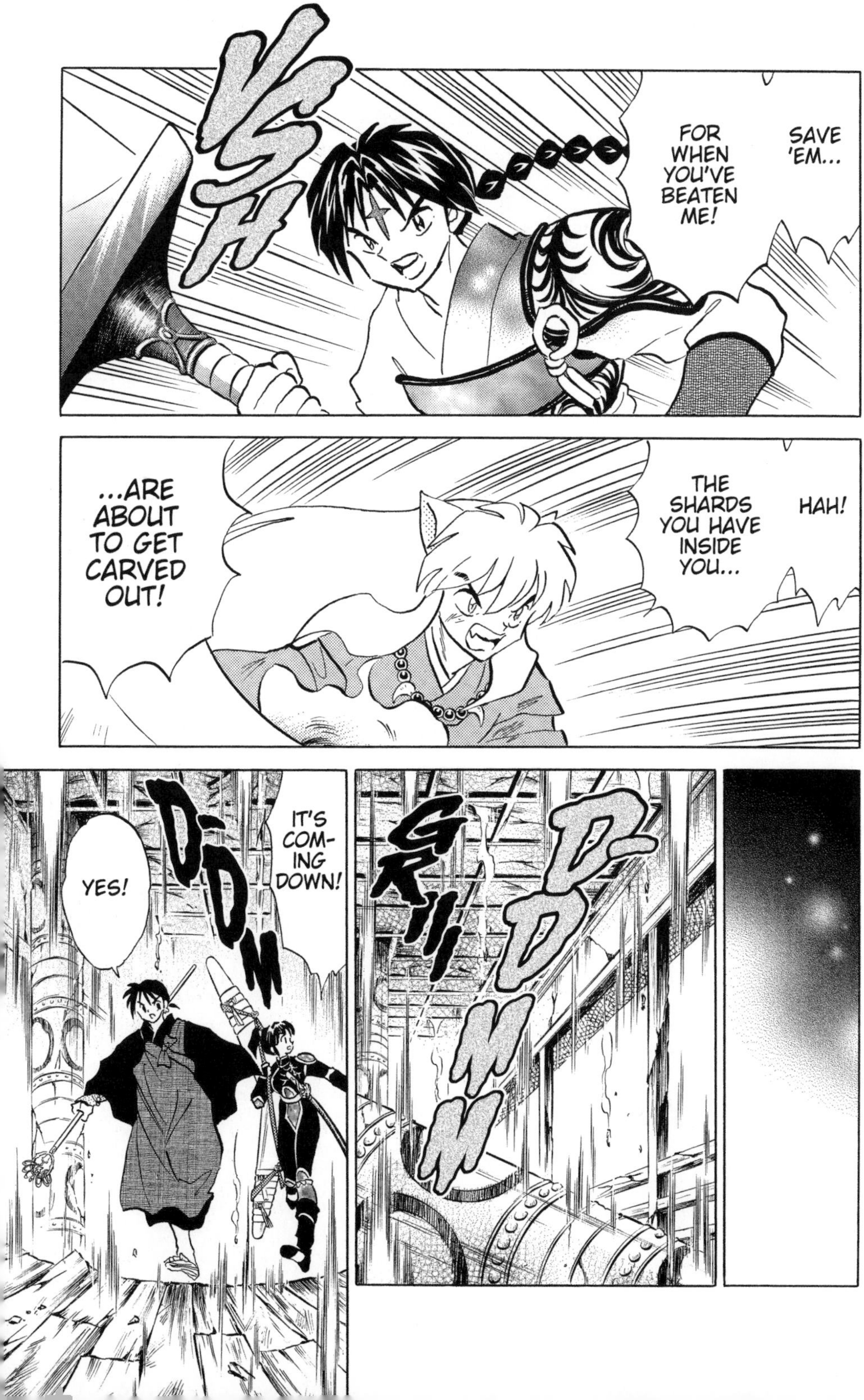
SAVE 'EM...
FOR WHEN YOU'VE BEATEN ME!
VSH
HAH!
THE SHARDS YOU HAVE INSIDE YOU...
...ARE ABOUT TO GET CARVED OUT!
D-DMMM
GRIII
IT'S COMING DOWN!
YES!
D-DM

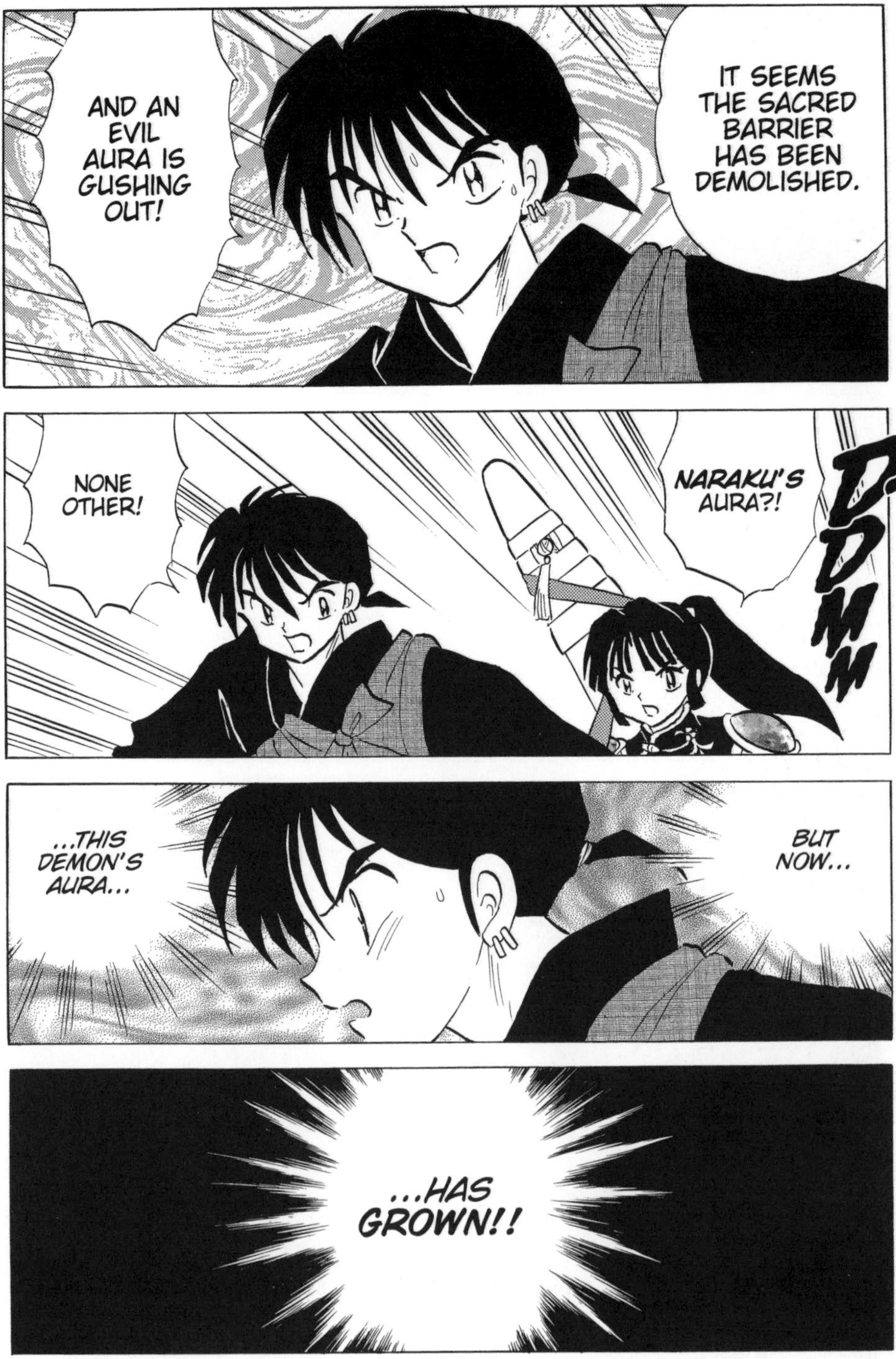
IT SEEMS THE SACRED BARRIER HAS BEEN DEMOLISHED.
AND AN EVIL AURA IS GUSHING OUT!
D-DMM
NARAKU'S AURA?!
NONE OTHER!
BUT NOW...
...THIS DEMON'S AURA...
...HAS GROWN!!

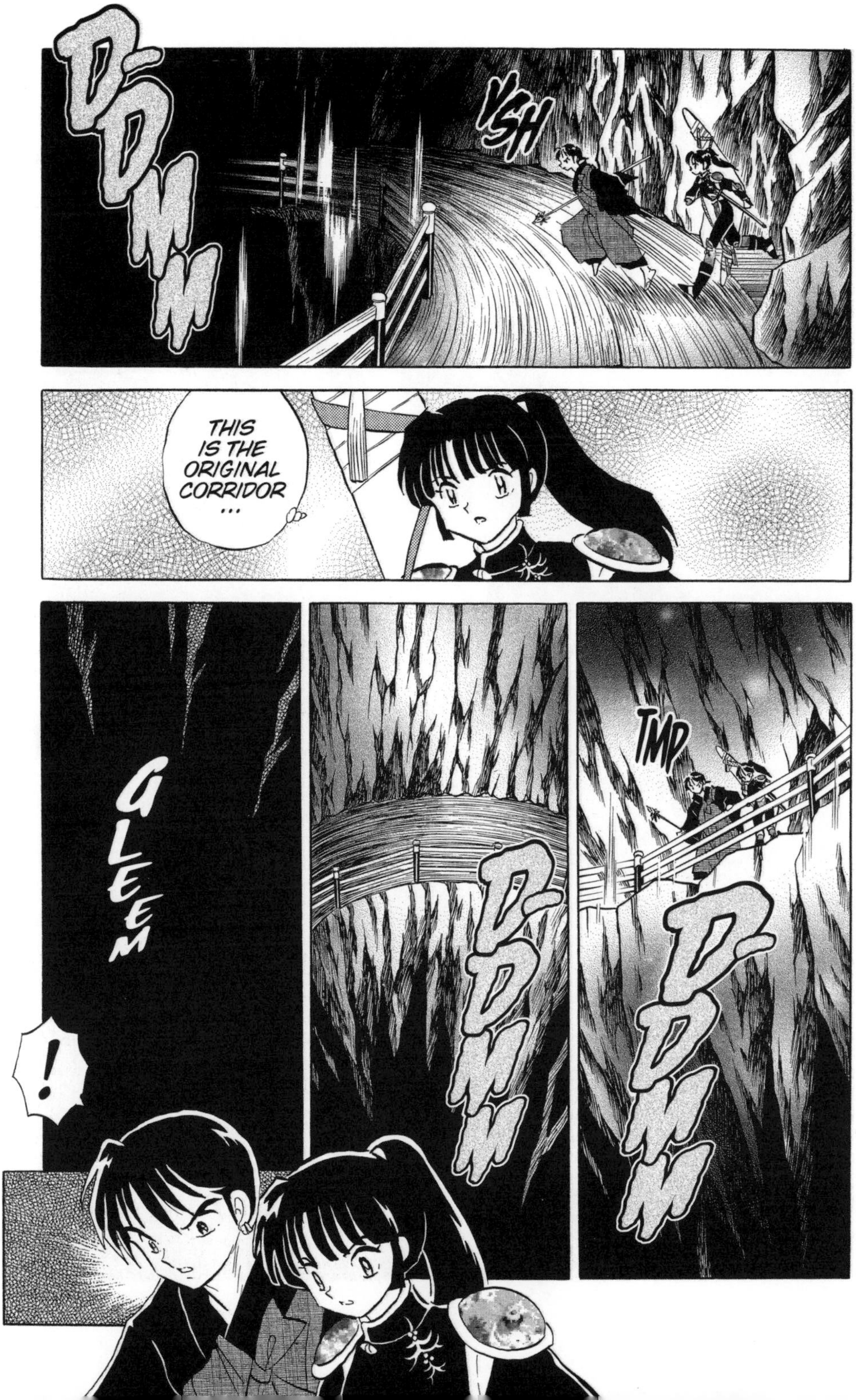
VSH
D-DMM
THIS IS THE ORIGINAL CORRIDOR ...
TMP
D-DMM
D-DMM
GLEEM
!

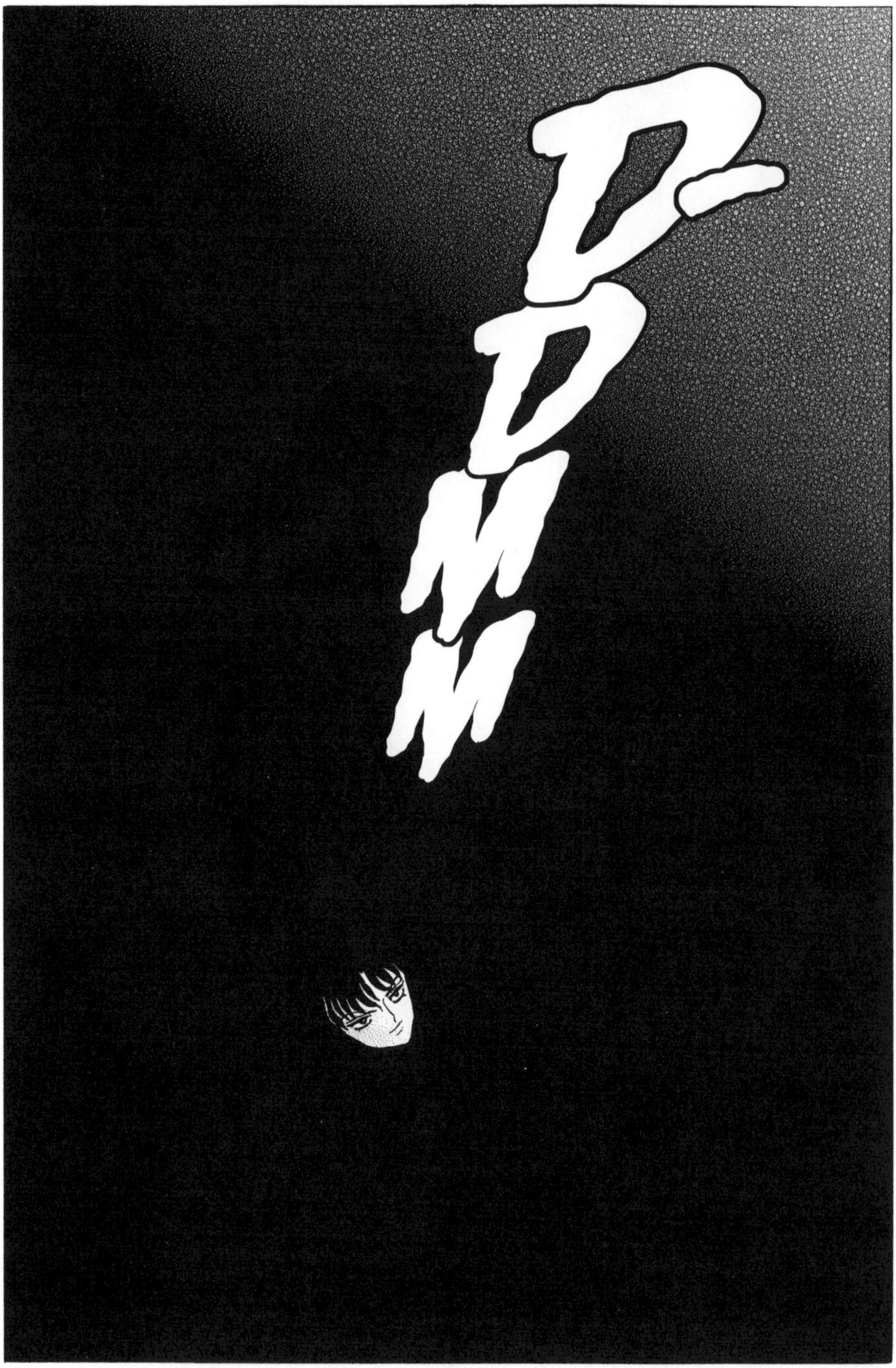
D-DMM

SCROLL SIX
THE TWO AURAS

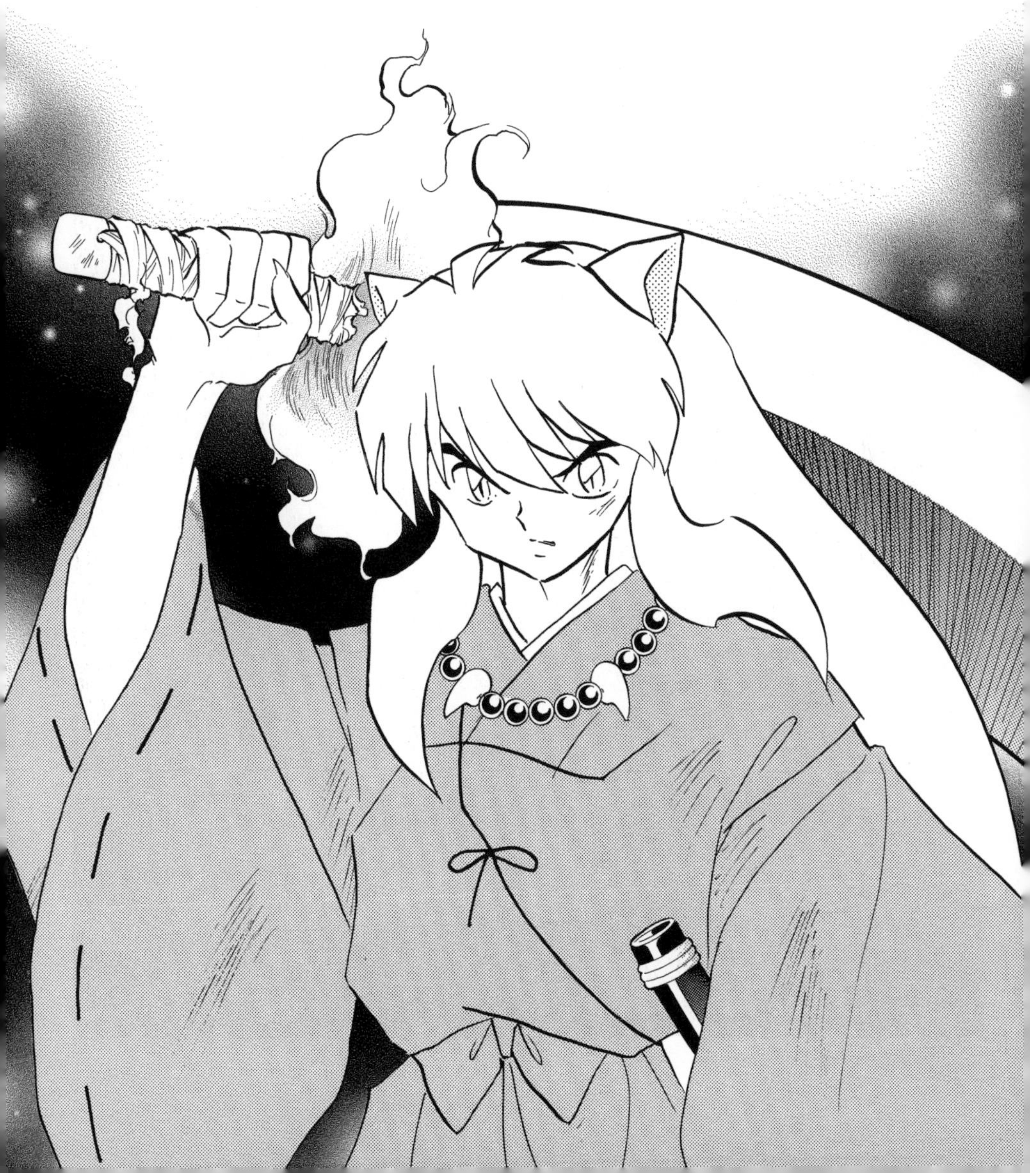

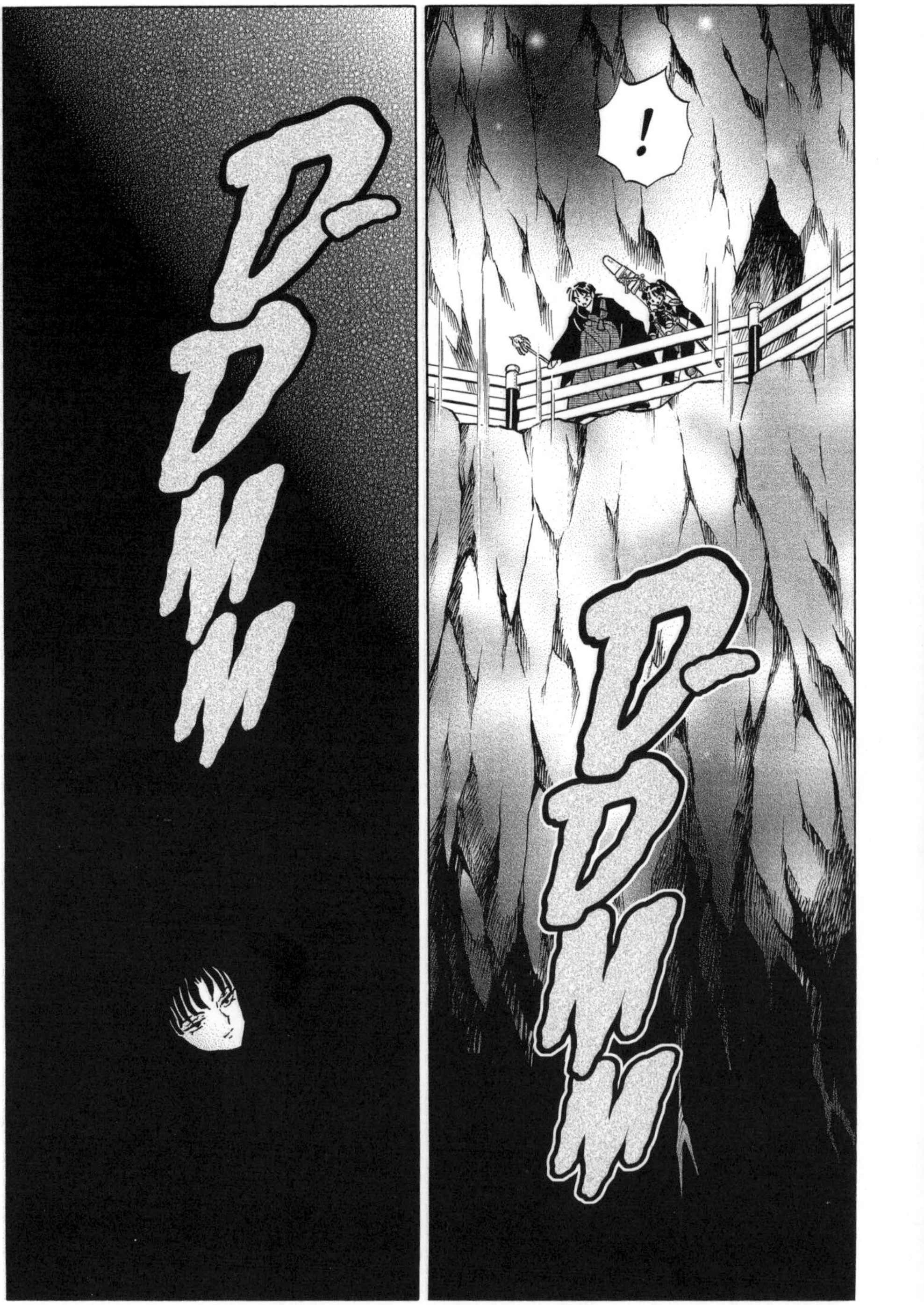
!
D-DUMM
D-DUMM

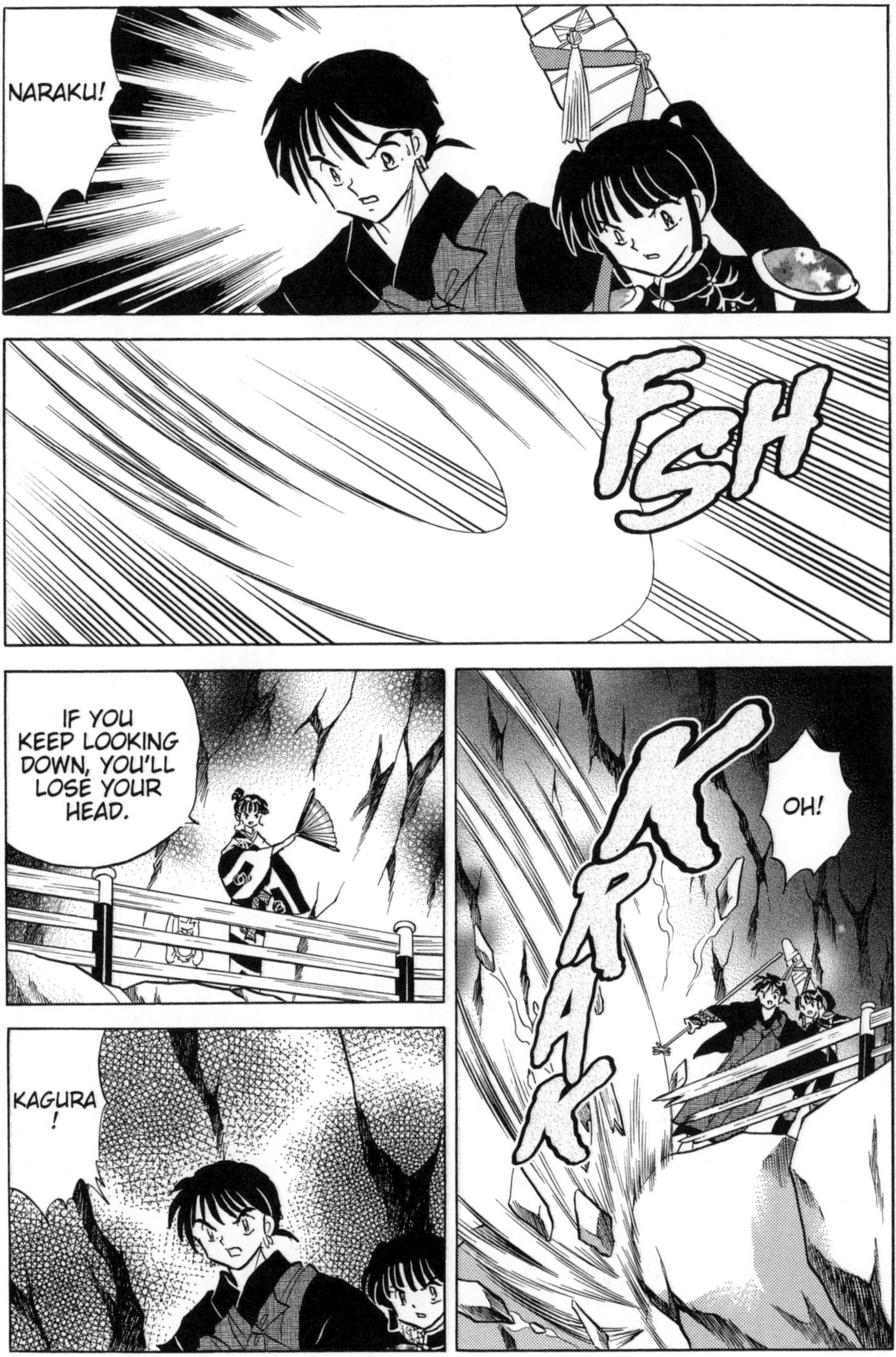
NARAKU!
FSH
KRAAK
OH!
IF YOU KEEP LOOKING DOWN, YOU'LL LOSE YOUR HEAD.
KAGURA!

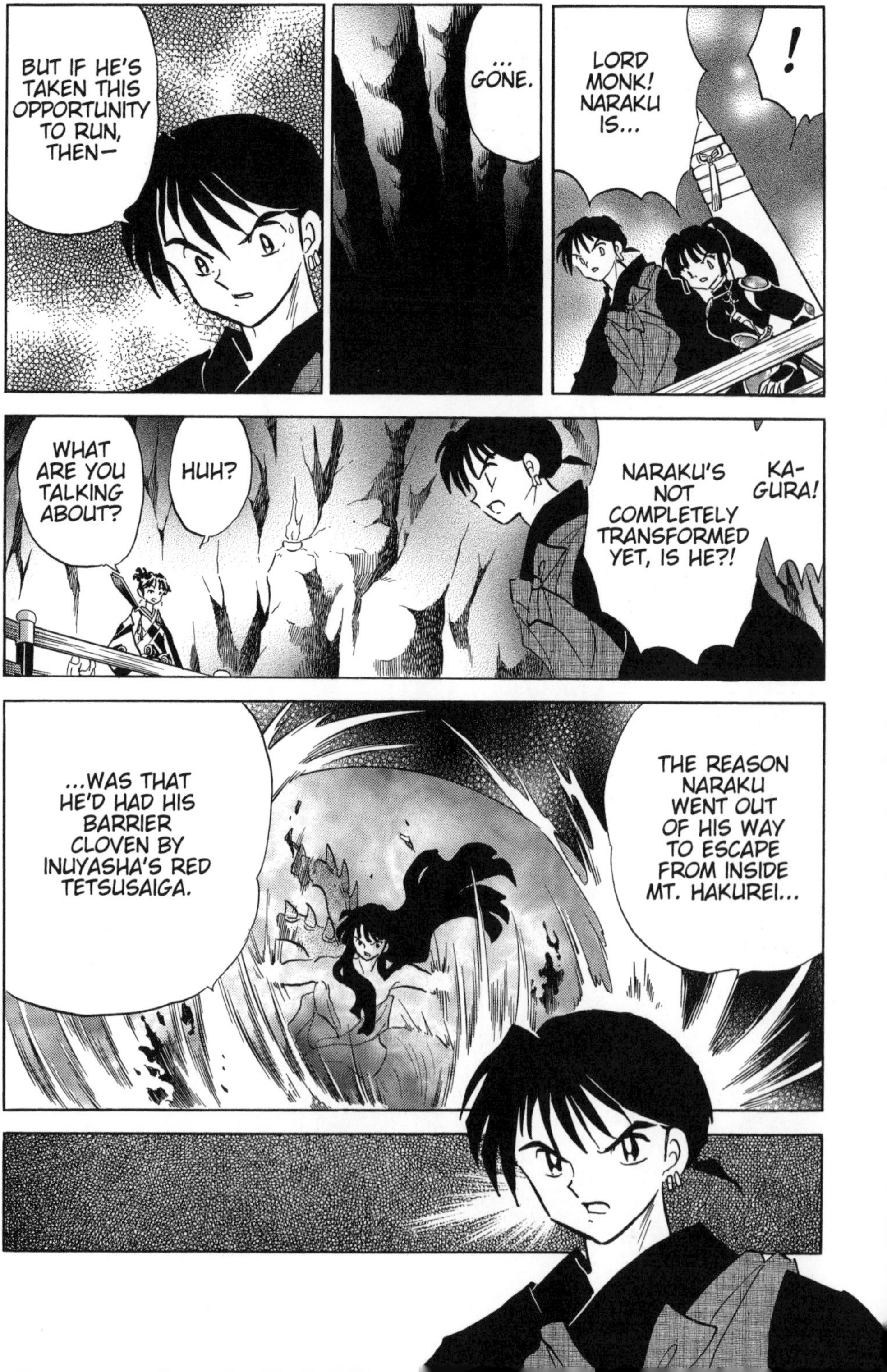
!
LORD MONK! NARAKU IS...
...GONE.
BUT IF HE'S TAKEN THIS OPPORTUNITY TO RUN, THEN—
KA-GURA!
NARAKU'S NOT COMPLETELY TRANSFORMED YET, IS HE?!
HUH?
WHAT ARE YOU TALKING ABOUT?
THE REASON NARAKU WENT OUT OF HIS WAY TO ESCAPE FROM INSIDE MT. HAKUREI...
...WAS THAT HE'D HAD HIS BARRIER CLOVEN BY INUYASHA'S RED TETSUSAIGA.

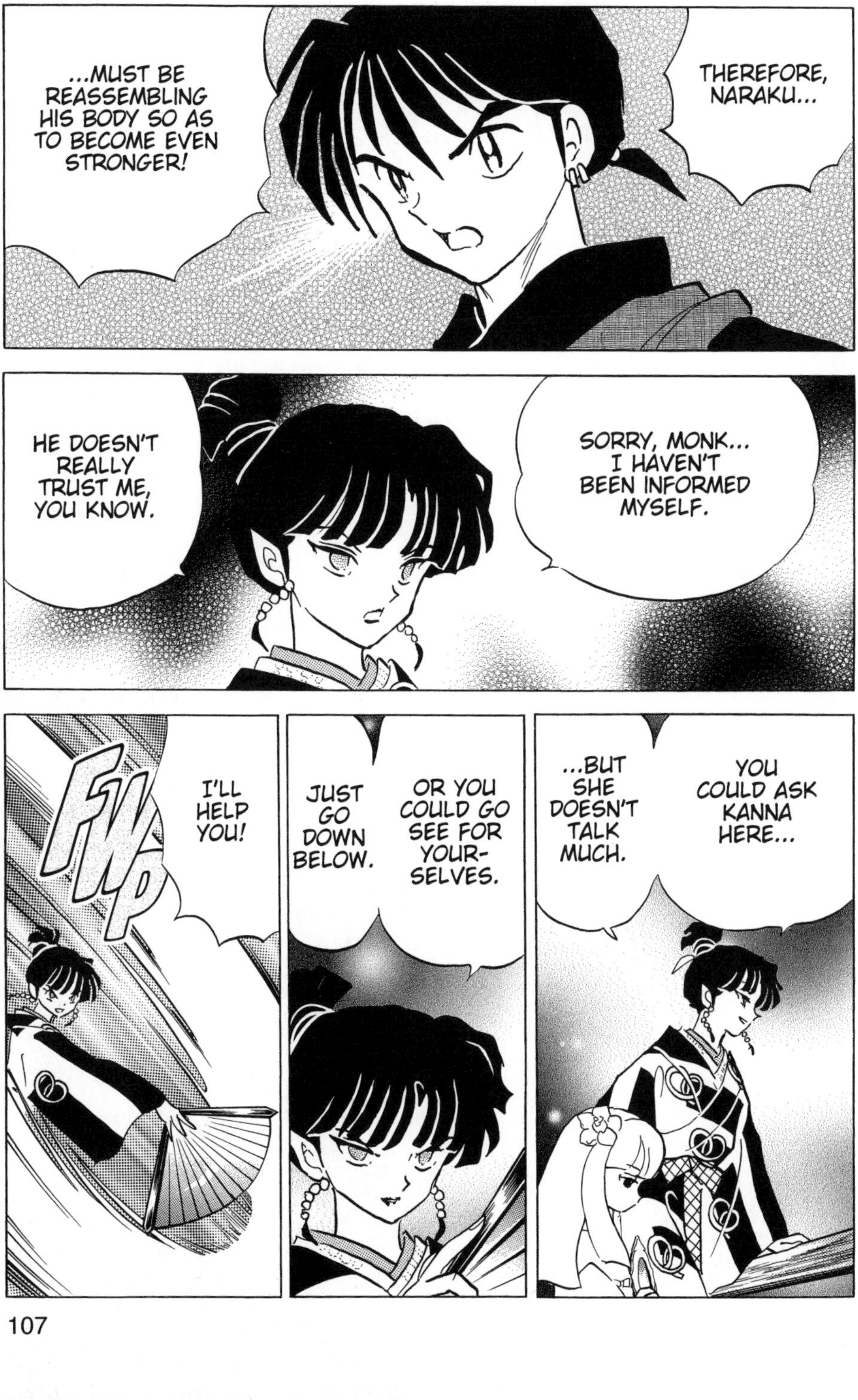
THEREFORE, NARAKU...
...MUST BE REASSEMBLING HIS BODY SO AS TO BECOME EVEN STRONGER!
SORRY, MONK... I HAVEN'T BEEN INFORMED MYSELF.
HE DOESN'T REALLY TRUST ME, YOU KNOW.
YOU COULD ASK KANNA HERE...
...BUT SHE DOESN'T TALK MUCH.
OR YOU COULD GO SEE FOR YOUR-SELVES.
JUST GO DOWN BELOW.
I'LL HELP YOU!
FWP

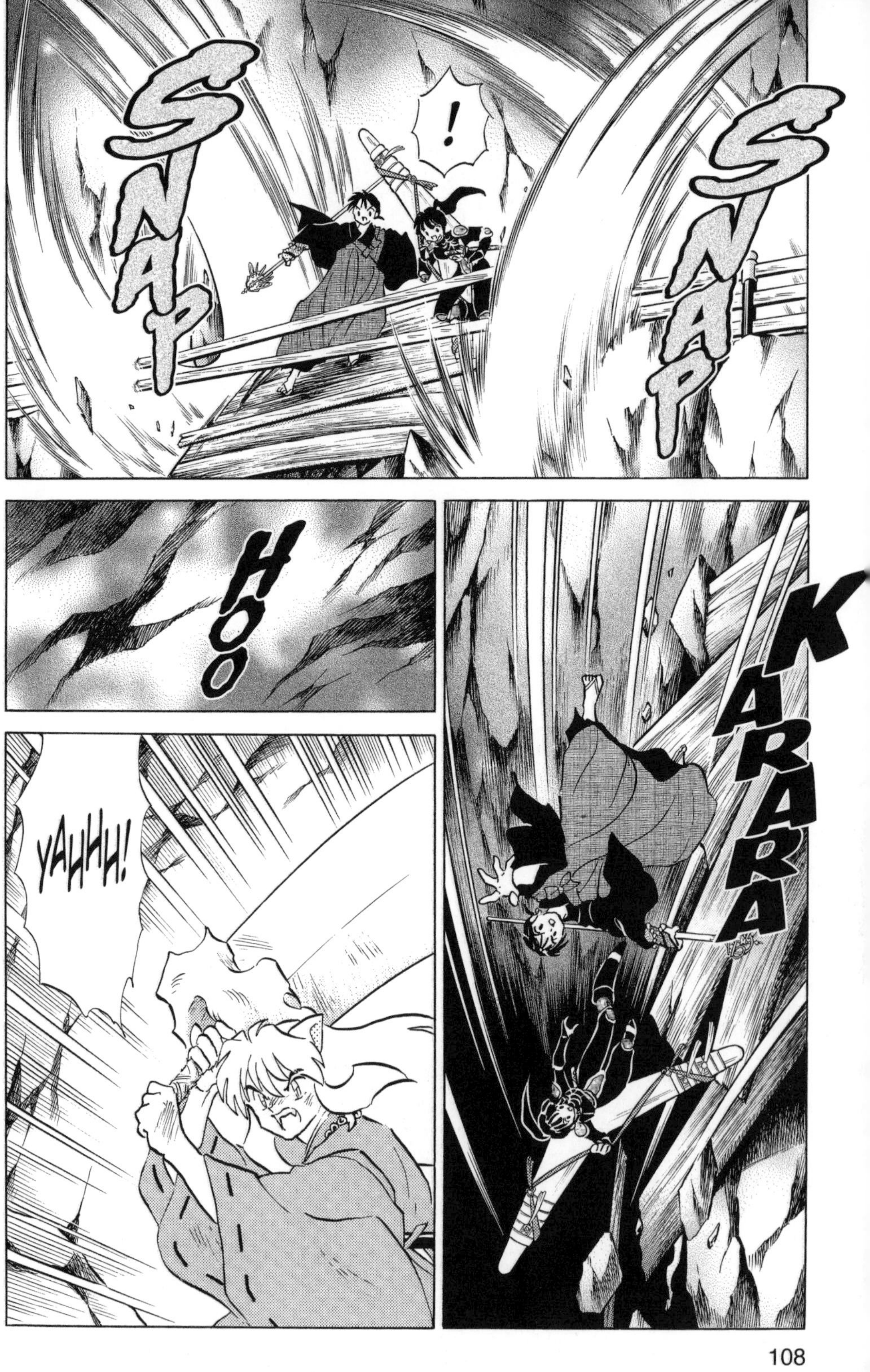

SNAP
!
SNAP
KARARA
HOO
YAHHH!

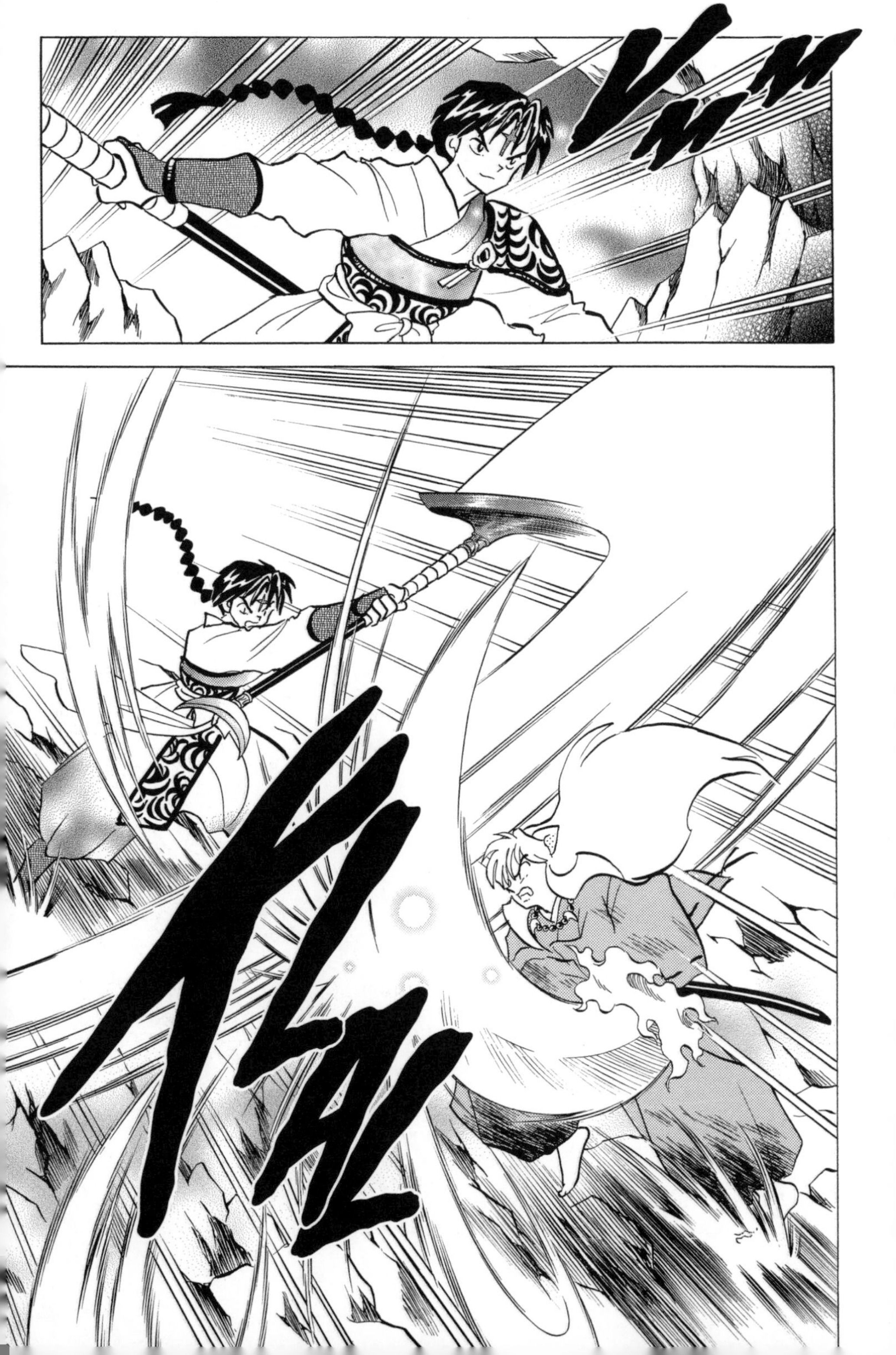
VMM

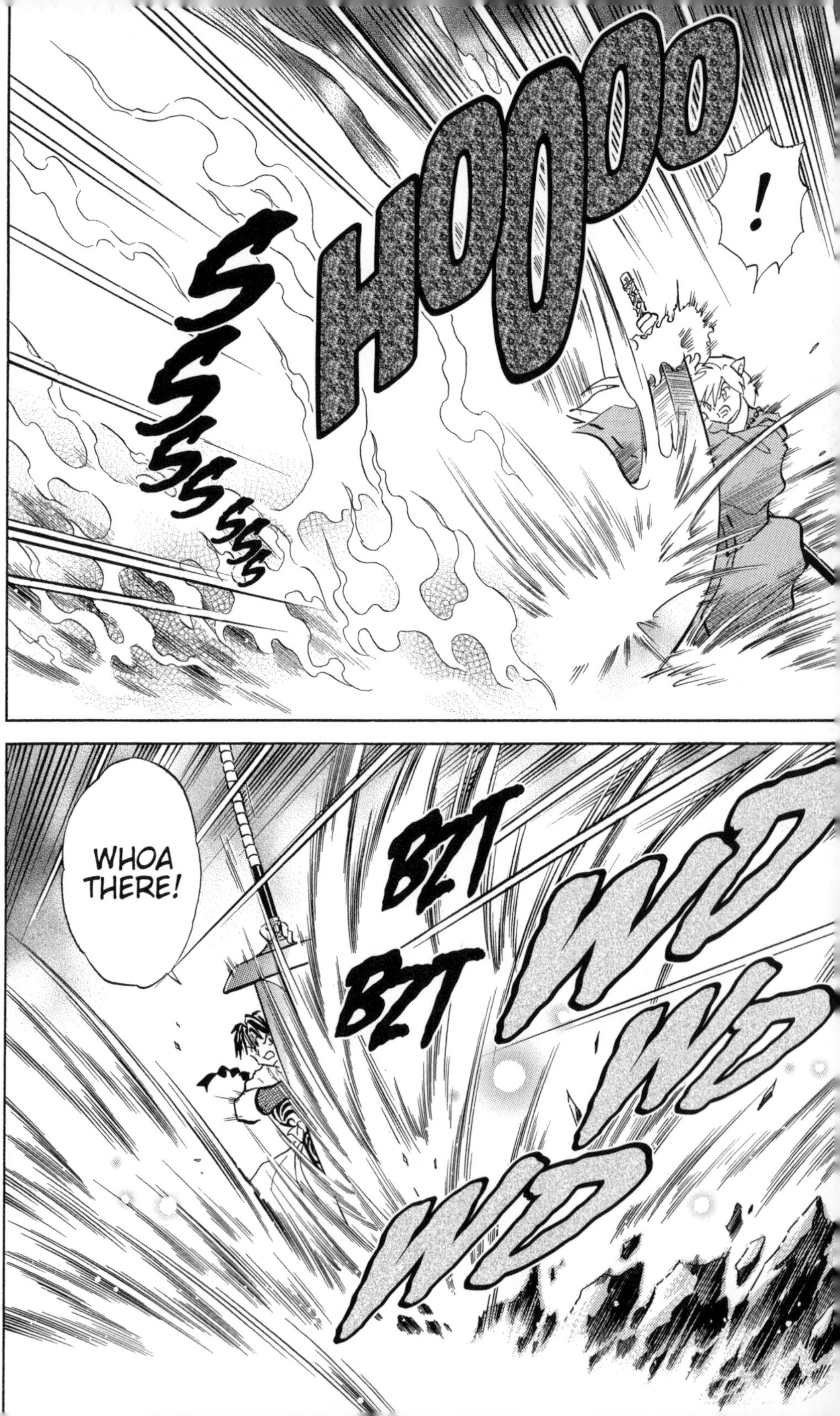
!
SSSSSSSHOOOO
WUD WUD WUD
BZT BZT
WHOA THERE!

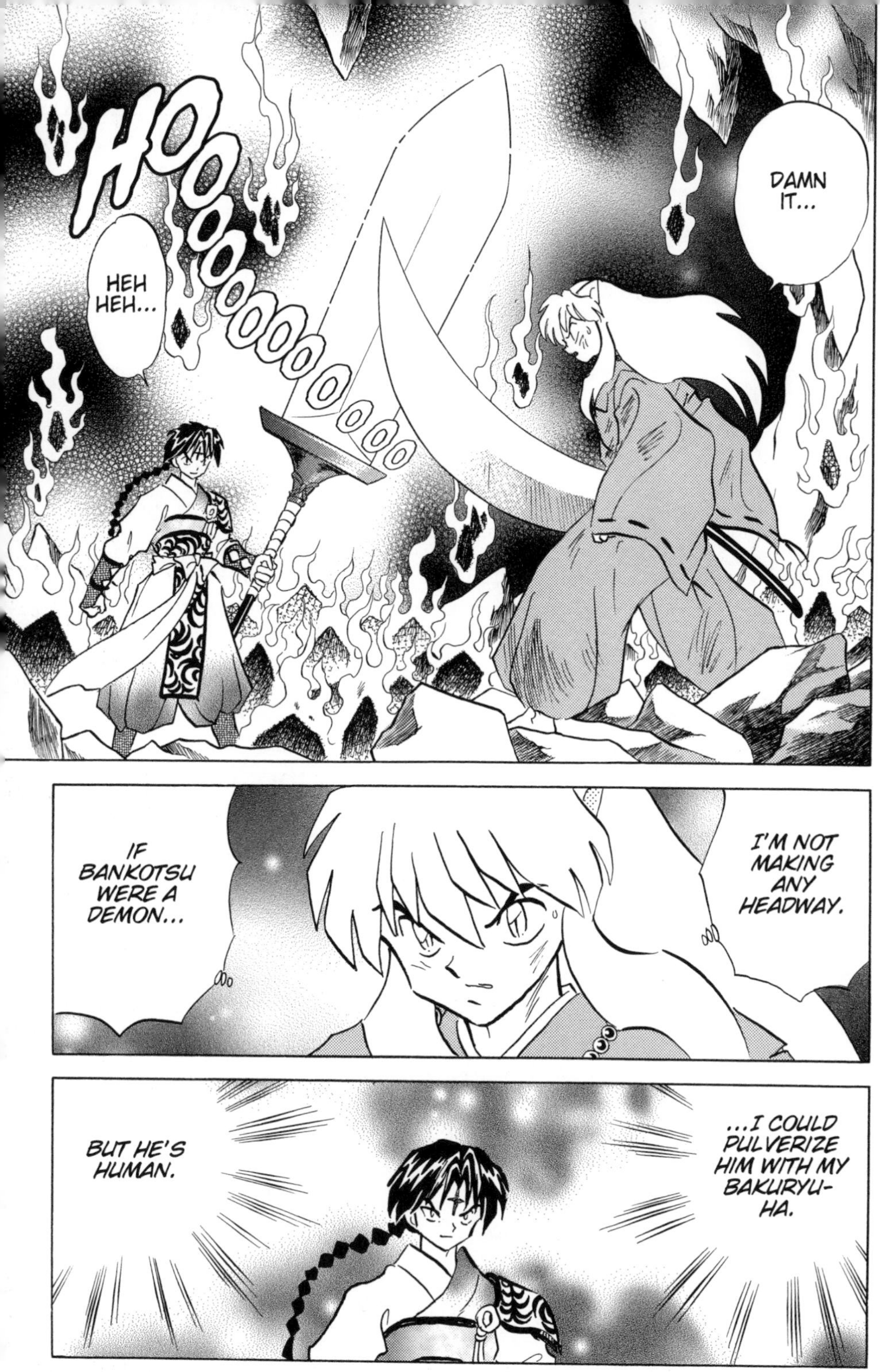

DAMN IT...
HOOOOOOOOOOOO
HEH HEH...
I'M NOT MAKING ANY HEADWAY.
IF BANKOTSU WERE A DEMON...
...I COULD PULVERIZE HIM WITH MY BAKURYU-HA.
BUT HE'S HUMAN.

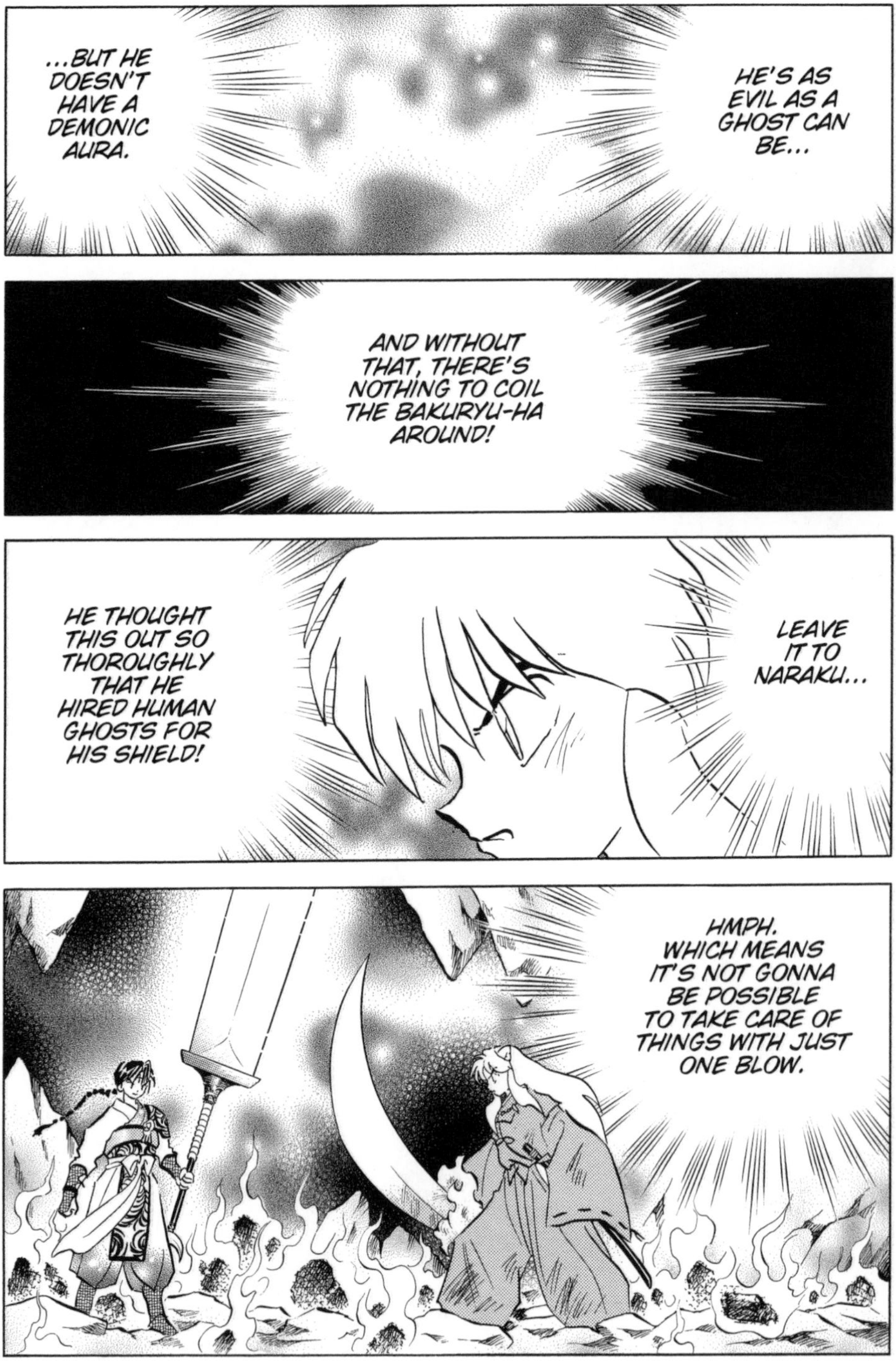
HE'S AS EVIL AS A GHOST CAN BE...
...BUT HE DOESN'T HAVE A DEMONIC AURA.
AND WITHOUT THAT, THERE'S NOTHING TO COIL THE BAKURYU-HA AROUND!
LEAVE IT TO NARAKU...
HE THOUGHT THIS OUT SO THOROUGHLY THAT HE HIRED HUMAN GHOSTS FOR HIS SHIELD!
HMPH. WHICH MEANS IT'S NOT GONNA BE POSSIBLE TO TAKE CARE OF THINGS WITH JUST ONE BLOW.

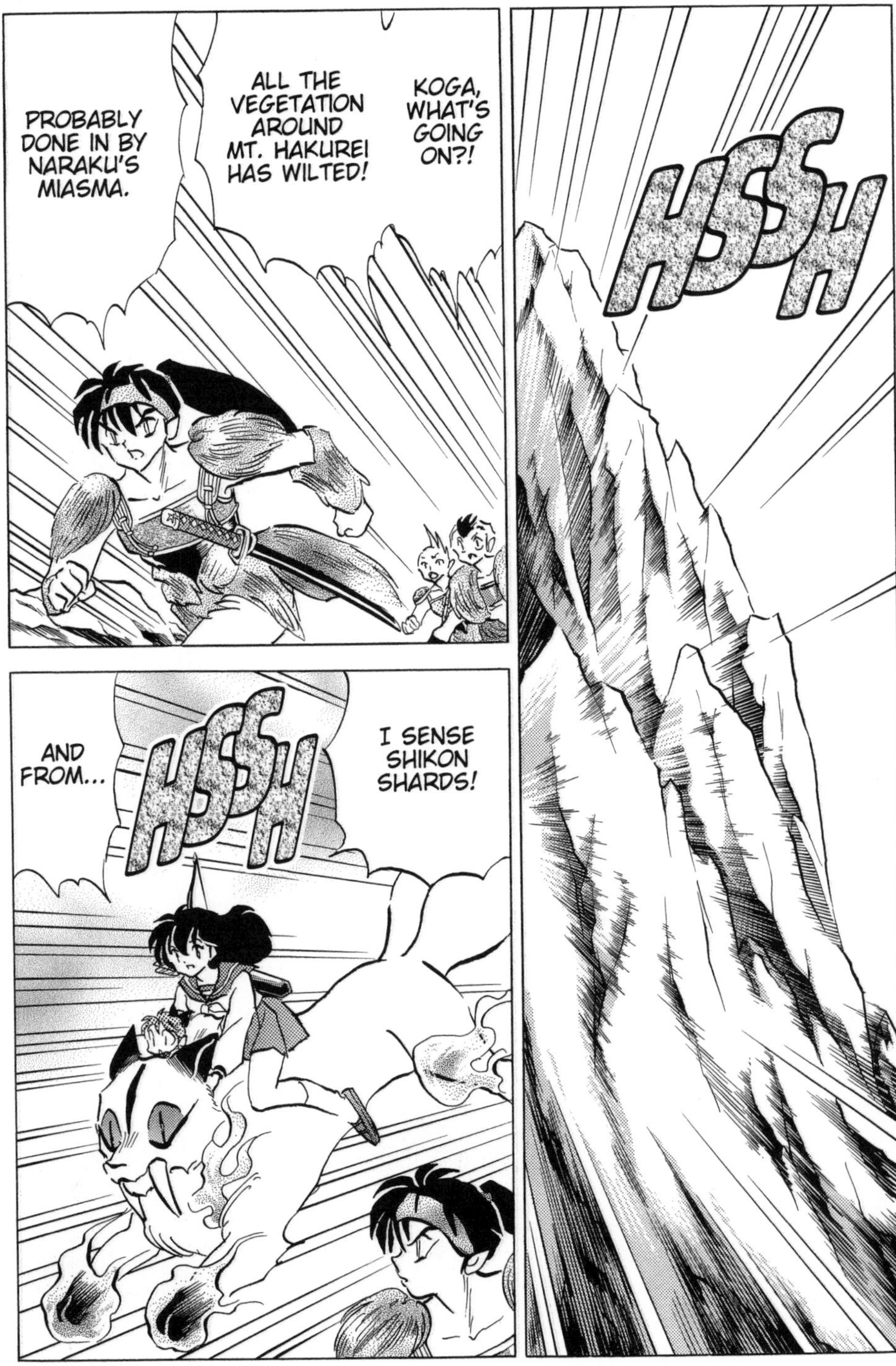
HSSH
KOGA, WHAT'S GOING ON?!
ALL THE VEGETATION AROUND MT. HAKUREI HAS WILTED!
PROBABLY DONE IN BY NARAKU'S MIASMA.
I SENSE SHIKON SHARDS!
HSSH
AND FROM...

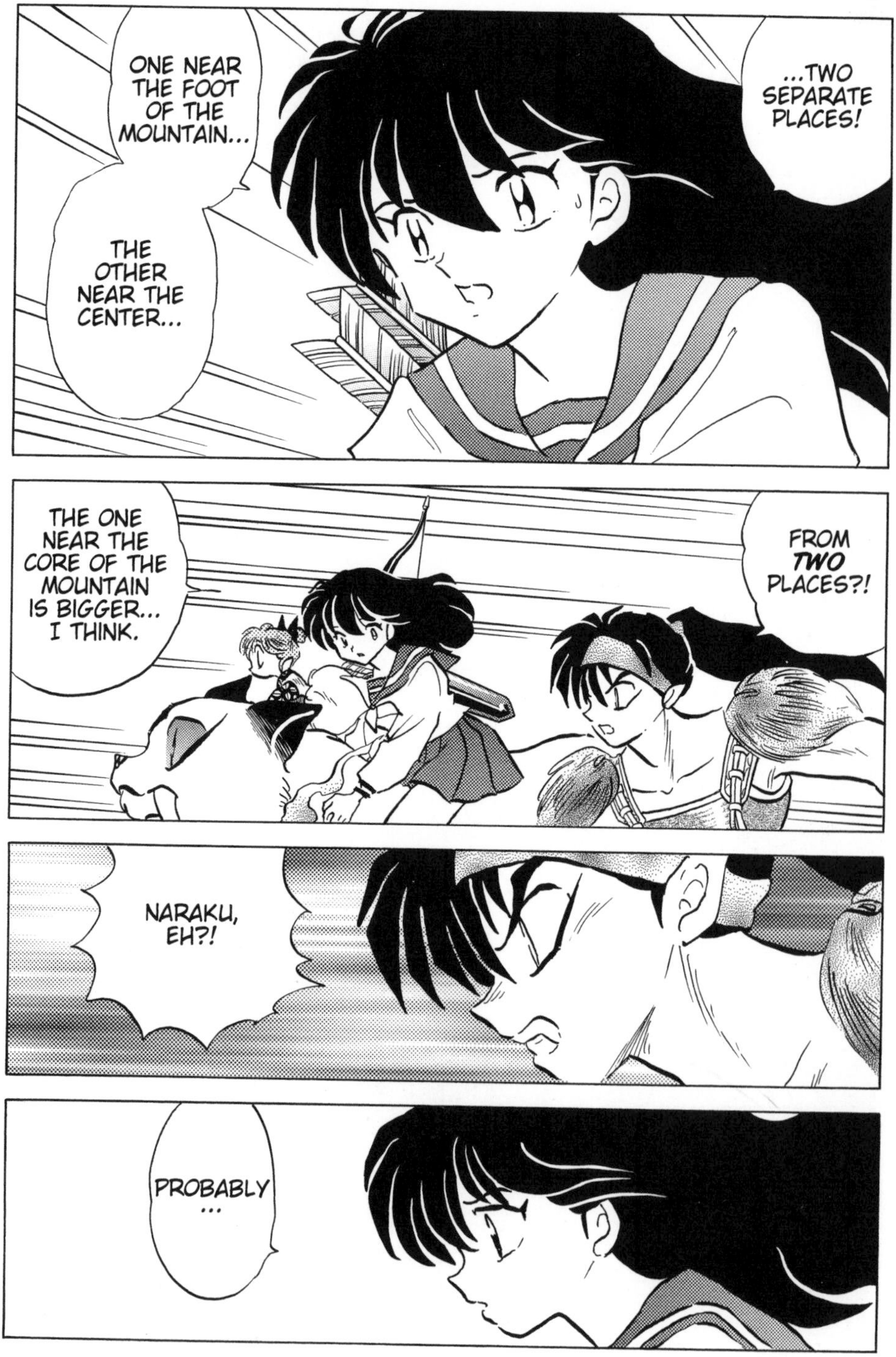
...TWO SEPARATE PLACES!
ONE NEAR THE FOOT OF THE MOUNTAIN...
THE OTHER NEAR THE CENTER...
FROM ***TWO*** PLACES?!
THE ONE NEAR THE CORE OF THE MOUNTAIN IS BIGGER... I THINK.
NARAKU, EH?!
PROBABLY...

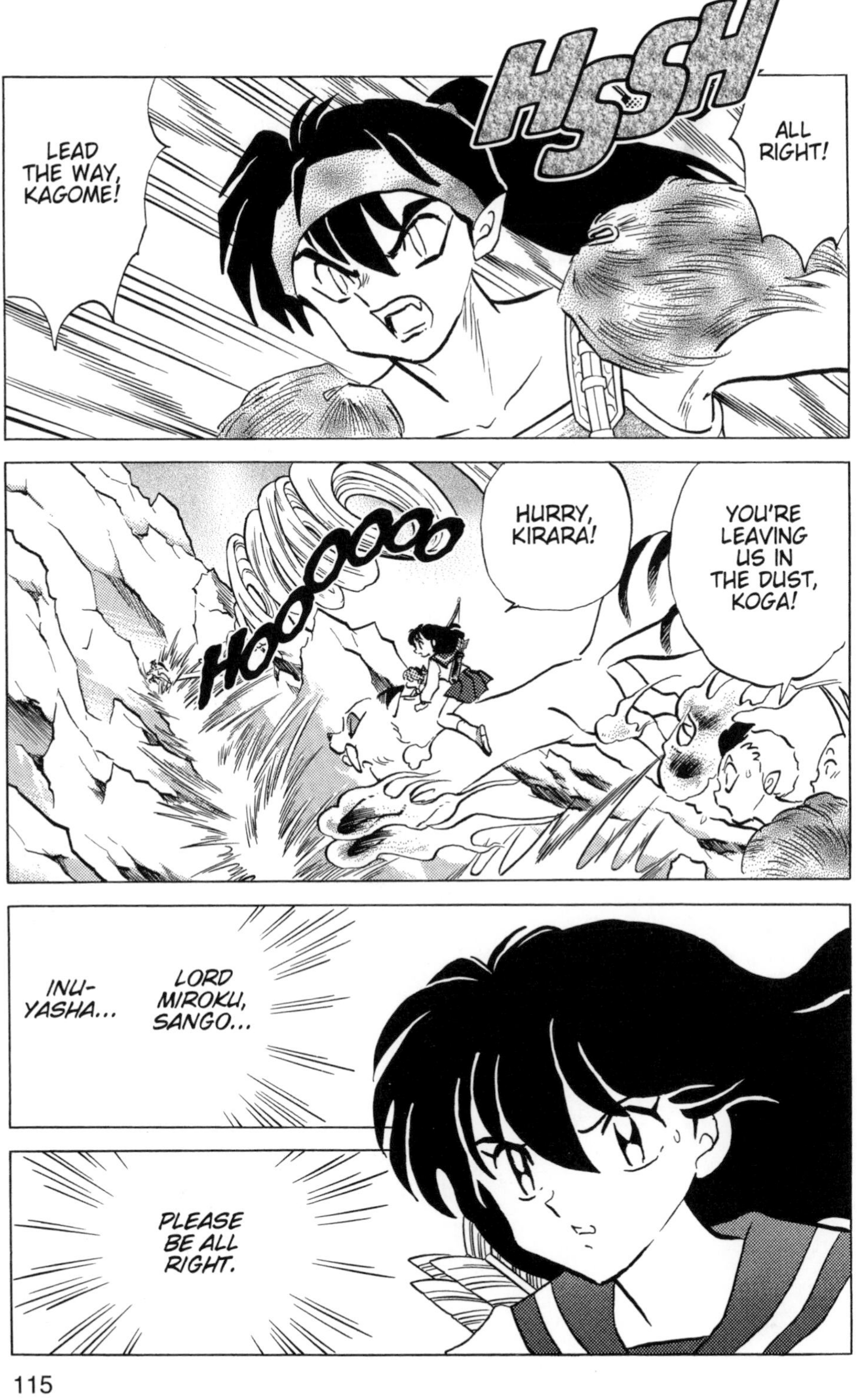
HSSH
ALL RIGHT!
LEAD THE WAY, KAGOME!
YOU'RE LEAVING US IN THE DUST, KOGA!
HURRY, KIRARA!
HOOOOOOO
LORD MIROKU, SANGO...
INU-YASHA...
PLEASE BE ALL RIGHT.

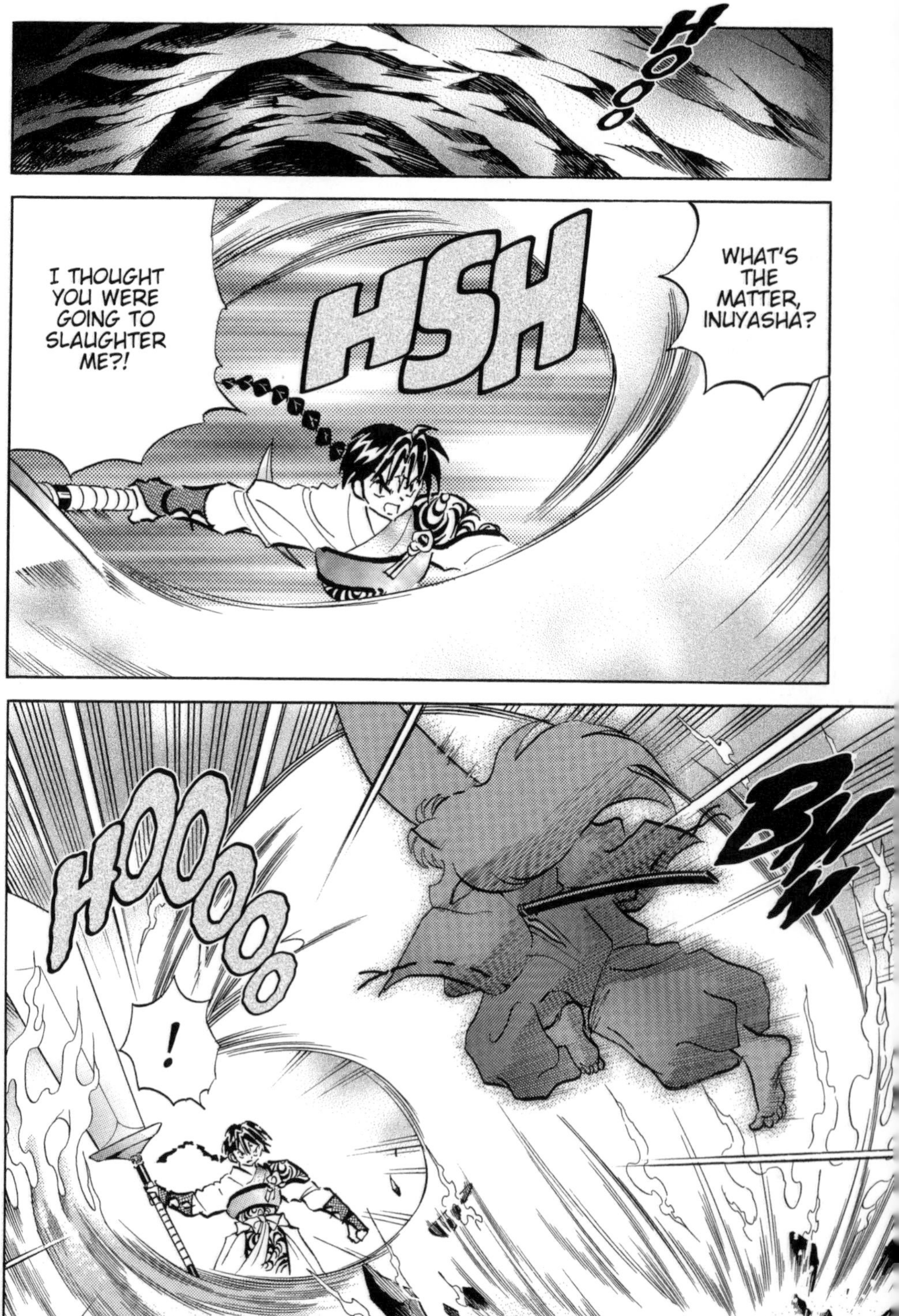
HOOO
WHAT'S THE MATTER, INUYASHA?
HSH
I THOUGHT YOU WERE GOING TO SLAUGHTER ME?!
BMM
HOOOOO
!

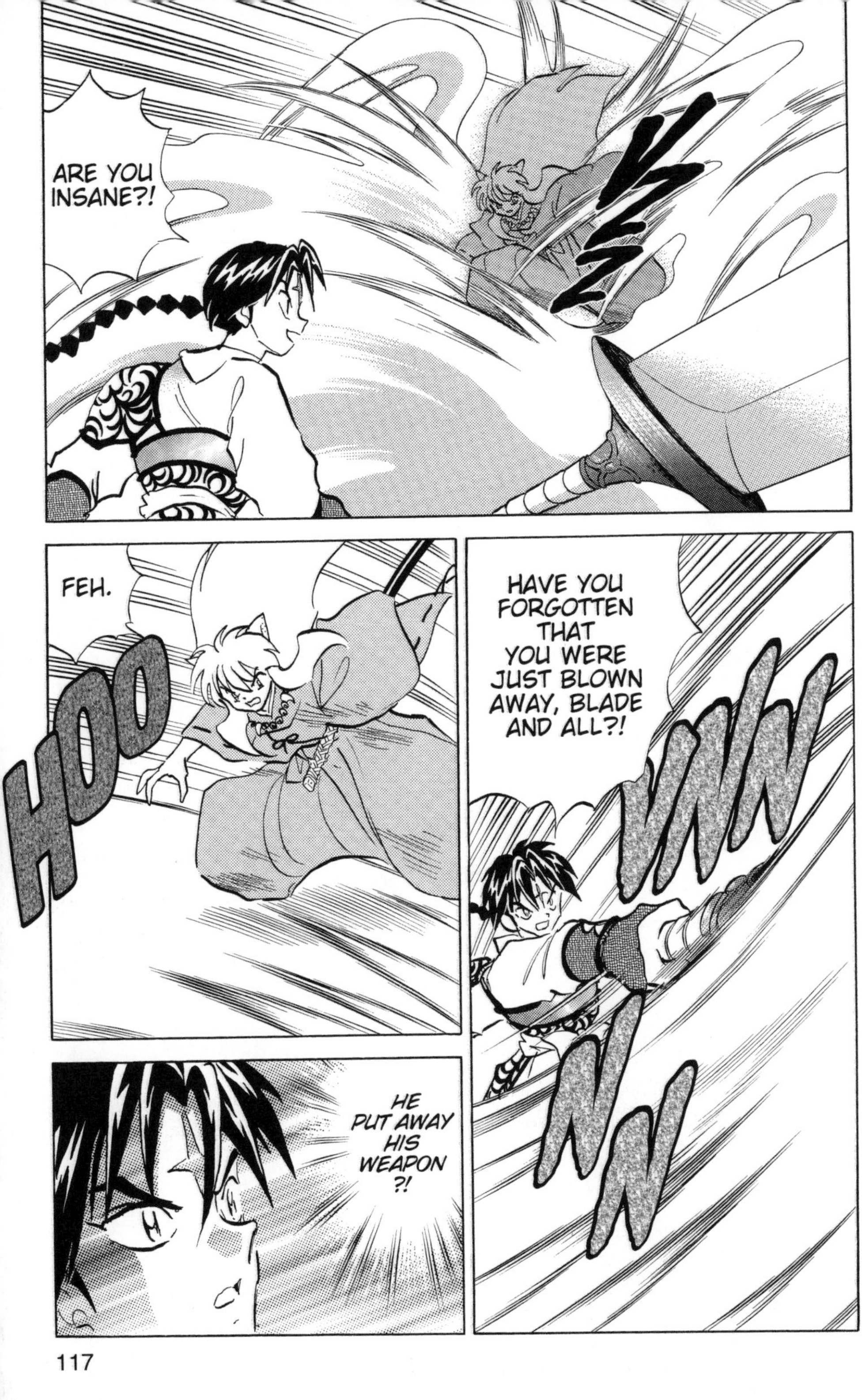
ARE YOU INSANE?!
HAVE YOU FORGOTTEN THAT YOU WERE JUST BLOWN AWAY, BLADE AND ALL?!
FEH.
HOO
HE PUT AWAY HIS WEAPON ?!

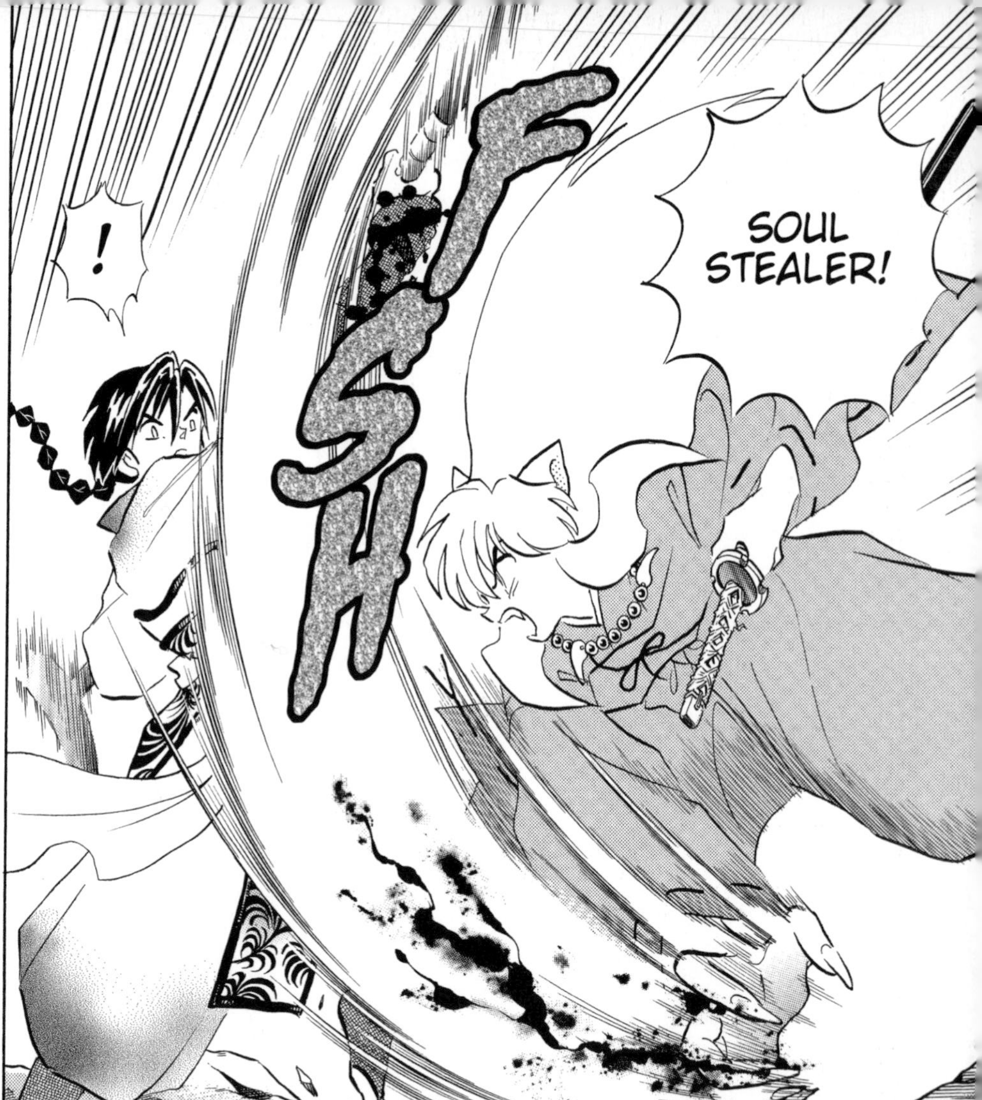
SOUL STEALER!
!
FSSH
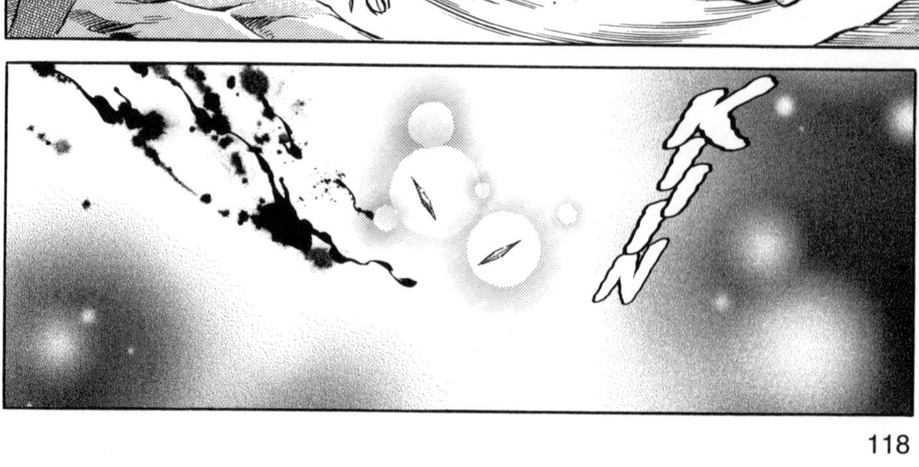
KSHNN

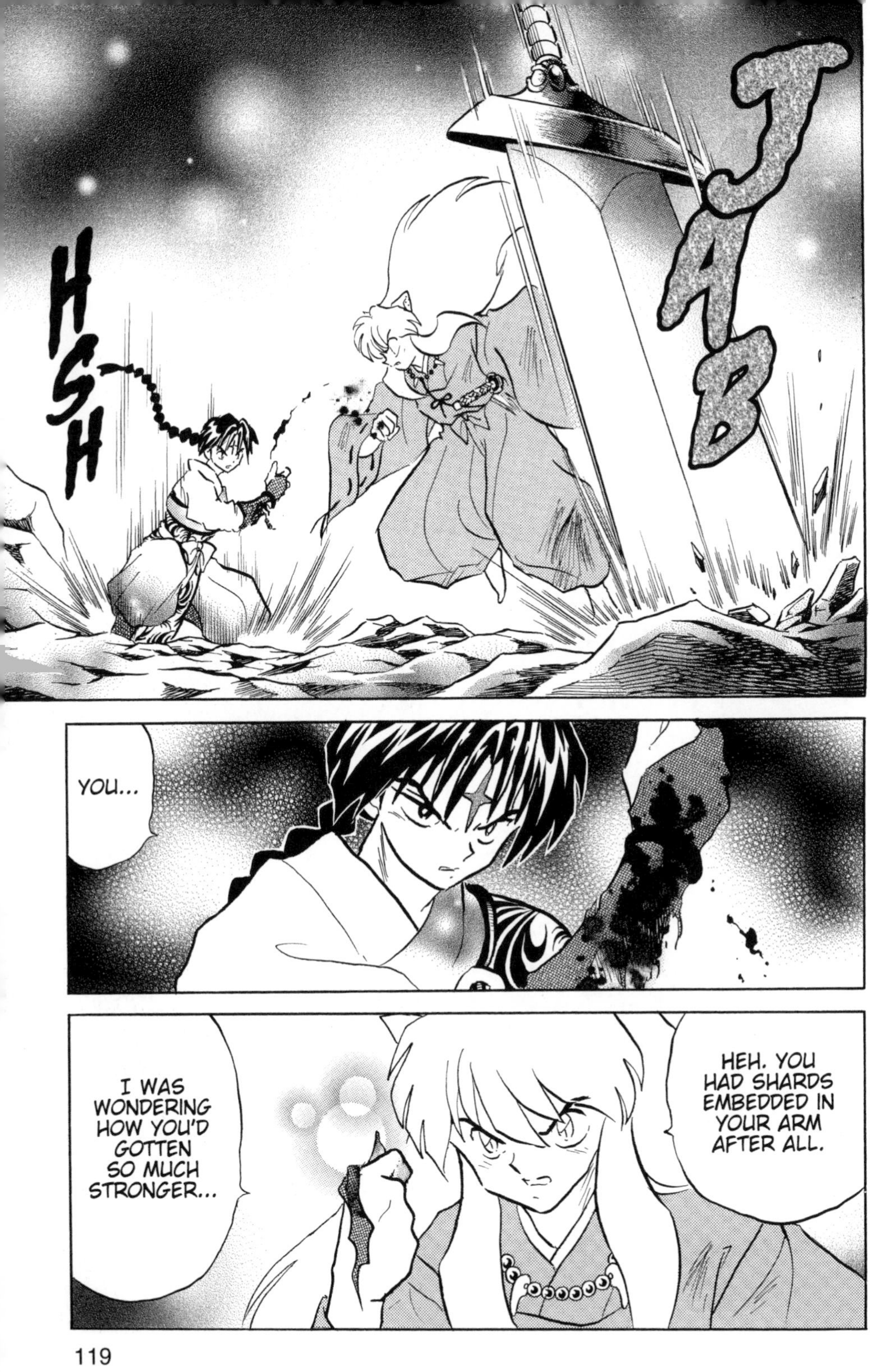
JAB
HSH
YOU...
HEH. YOU HAD SHARDS EMBEDDED IN YOUR ARM AFTER ALL.
I WAS WONDERING HOW YOU'D GOTTEN SO MUCH STRONGER...

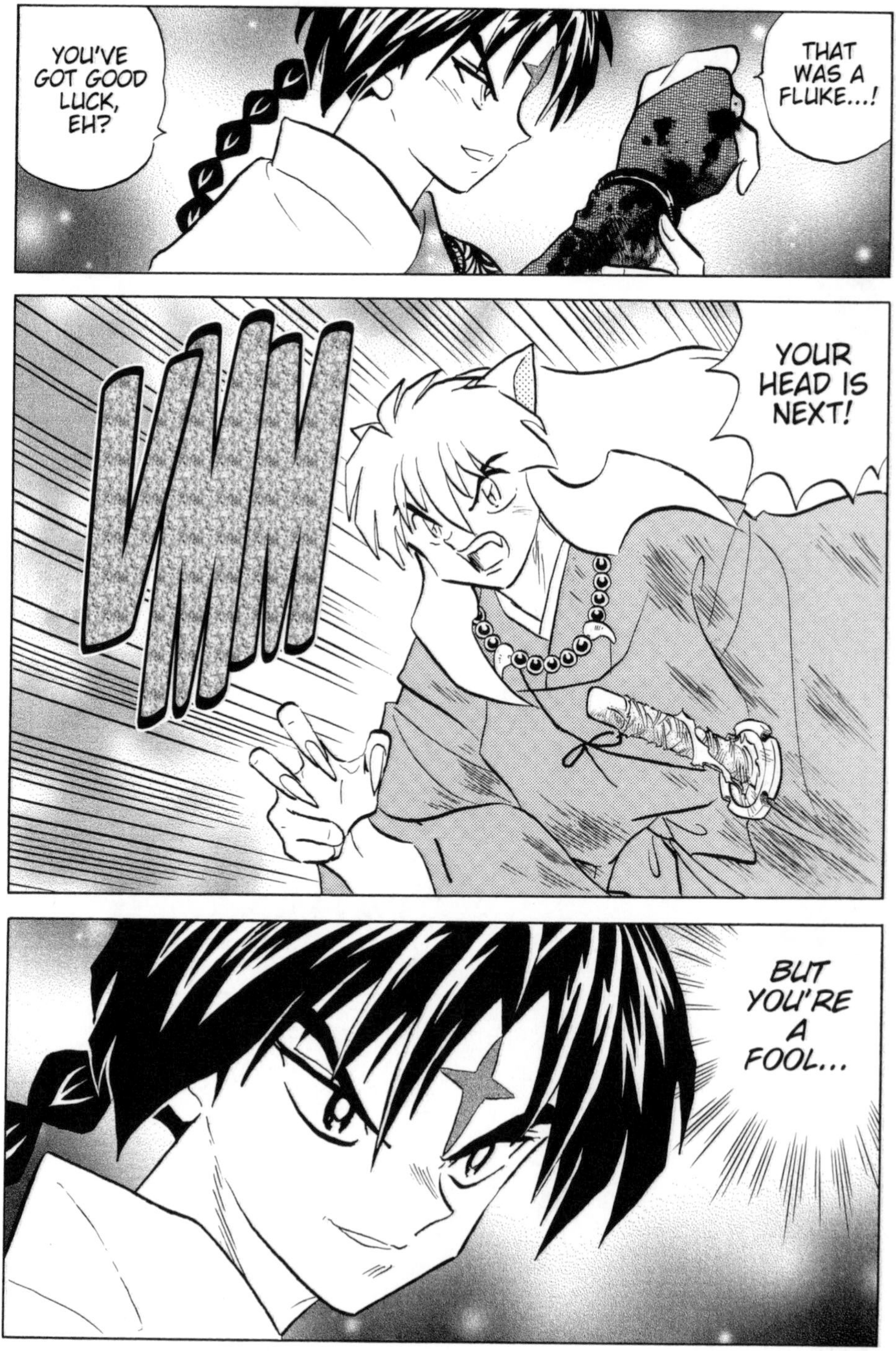
THAT WAS A FLUKE...!
YOU'VE GOT GOOD LUCK, EH?
YOUR HEAD IS NEXT!
VMM
BUT YOU'RE A FOOL...

SCROLL SEVEN
BANKOTSU'S STRENGTH

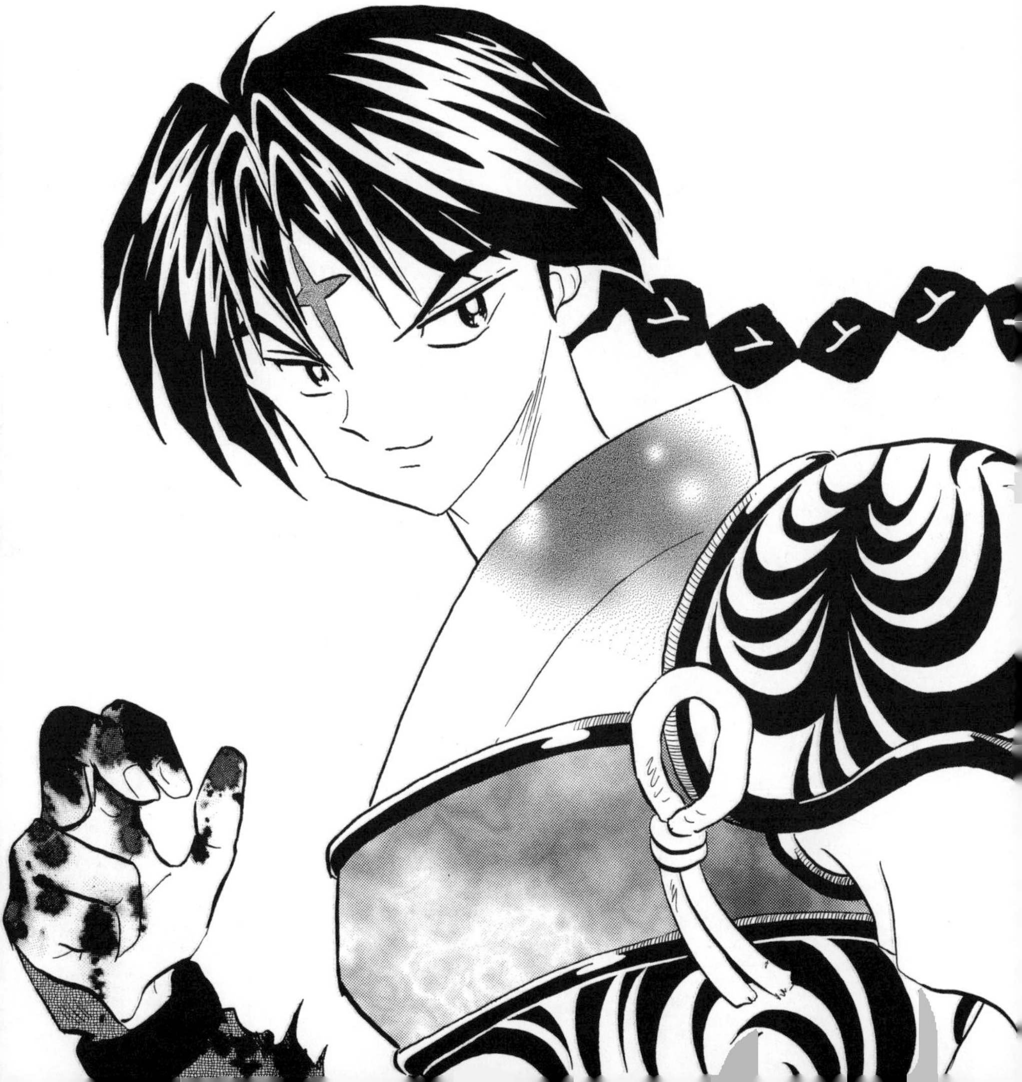

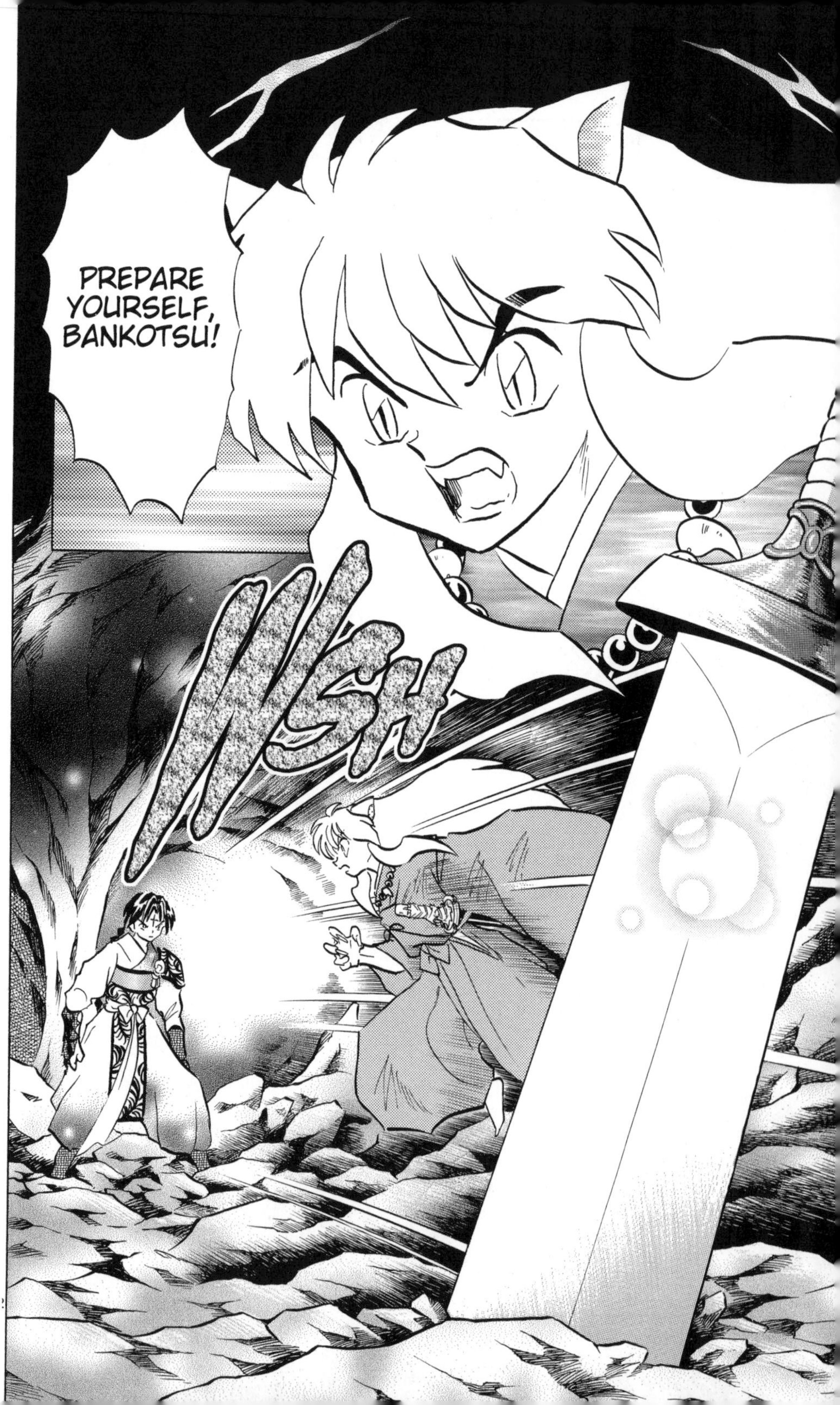
PREPARE YOURSELF, BANKOTSU!
WSH

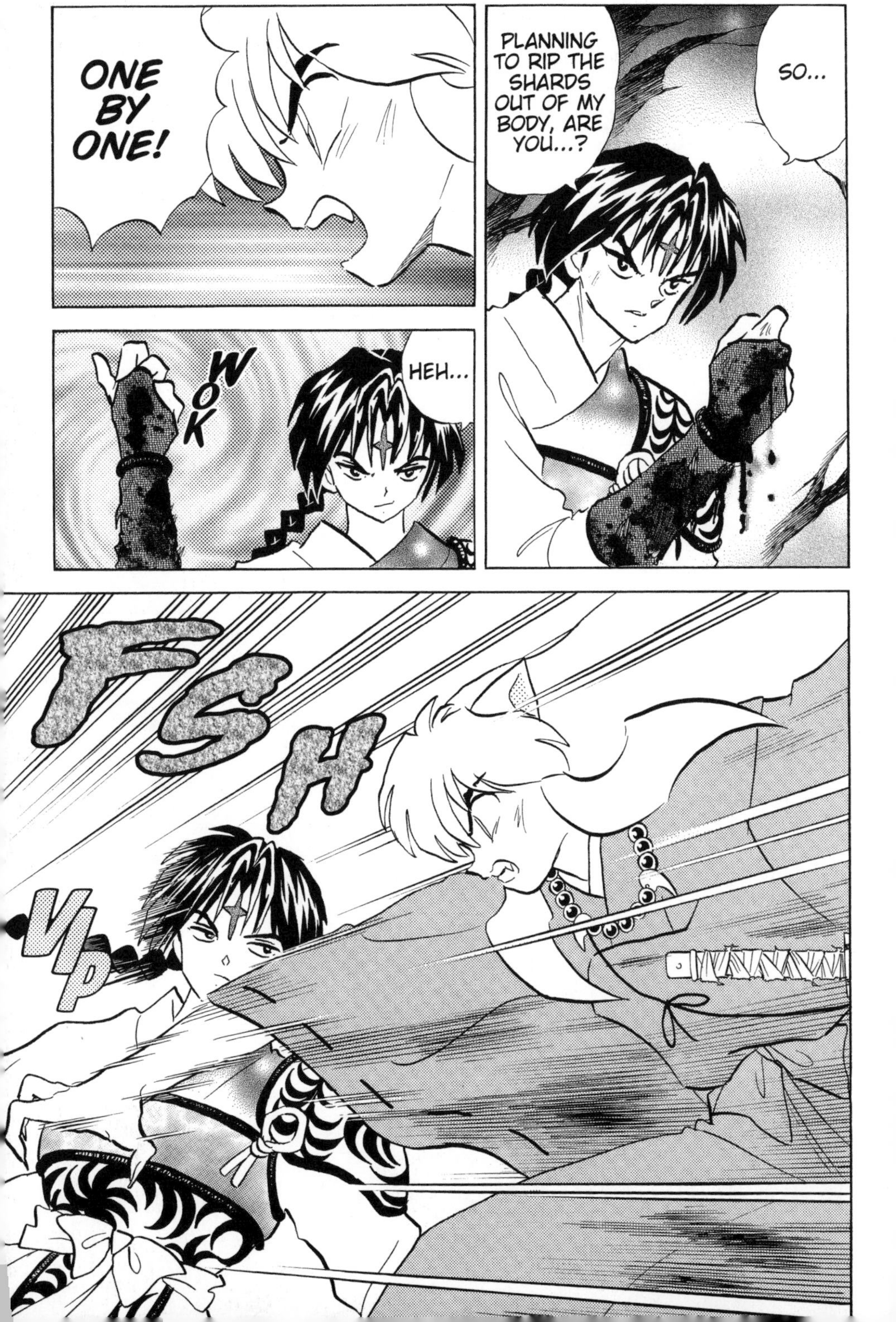
SO...
PLANNING TO RIP THE SHARDS OUT OF MY BODY, ARE YOU...?
ONE BY ONE!
HEH...
WOK
FSH
VIP

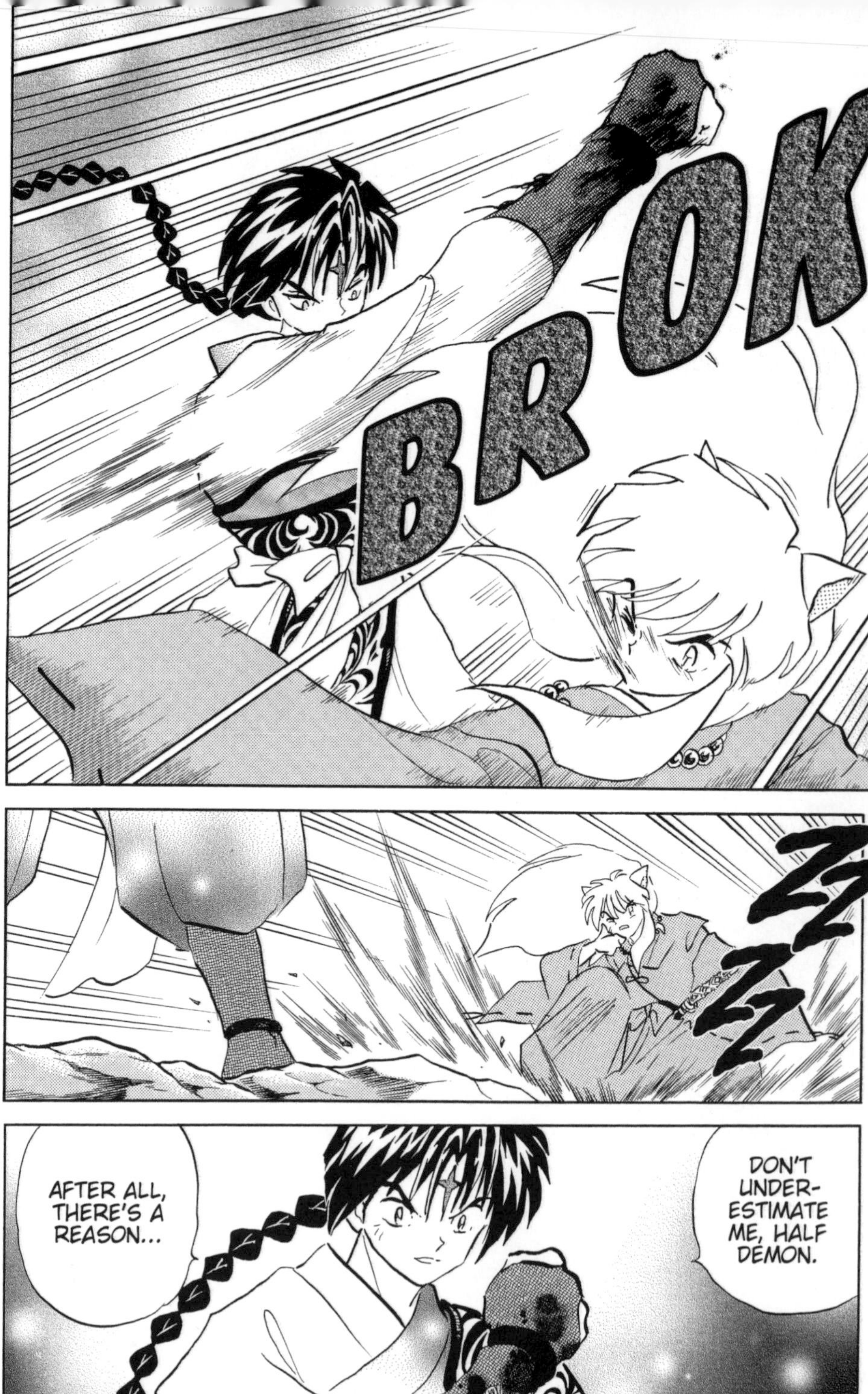
BROK
ZZZ
DON'T UNDER-ESTIMATE ME, HALF DEMON.
AFTER ALL, THERE'S A REASON...

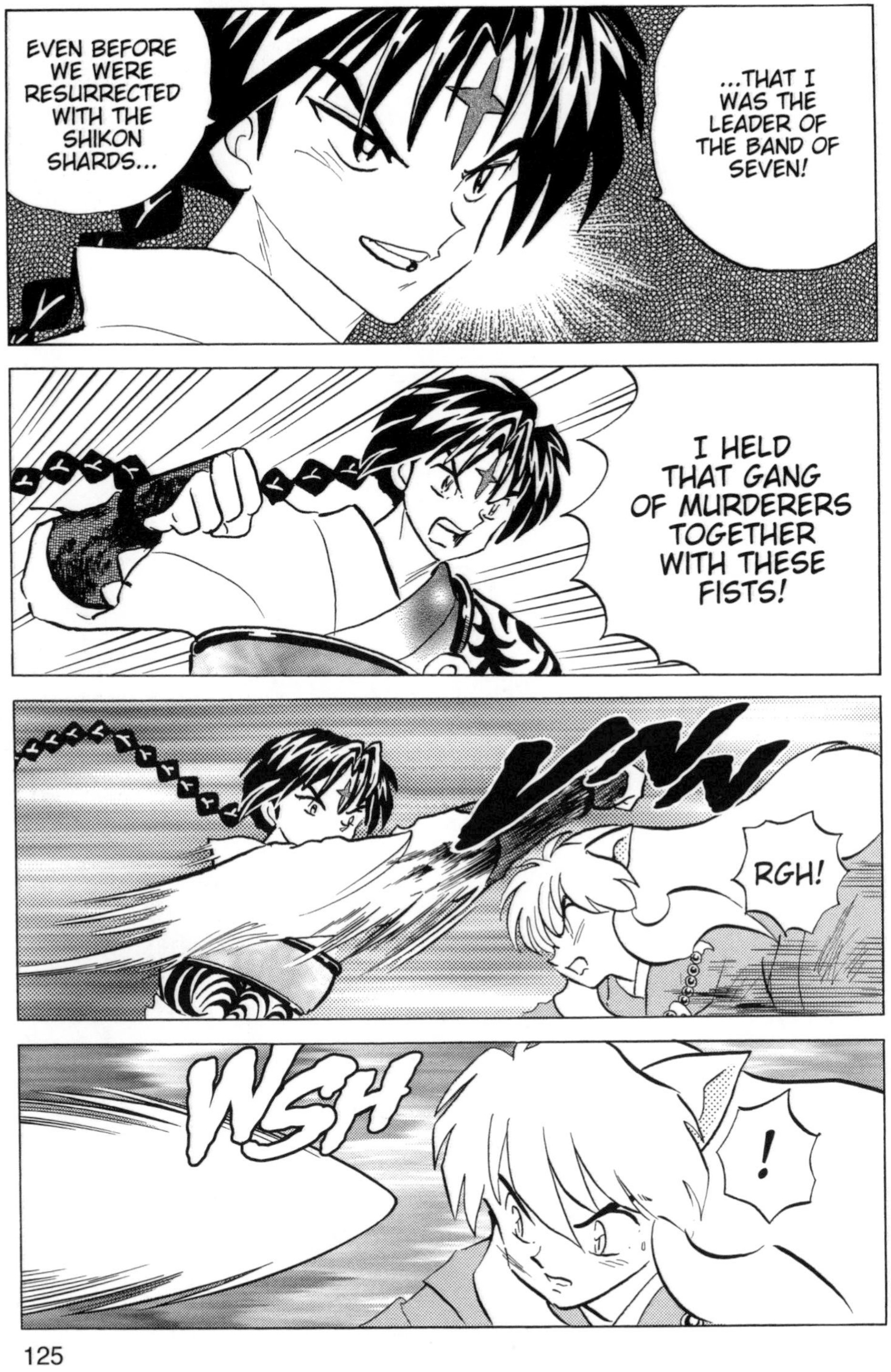
EVEN BEFORE WE WERE RESURRECTED WITH THE SHIKON SHARDS...
...THAT I WAS THE LEADER OF THE BAND OF SEVEN!
I HELD THAT GANG OF MURDERERS TOGETHER WITH THESE FISTS!
VVN
RGH!
WSH
!

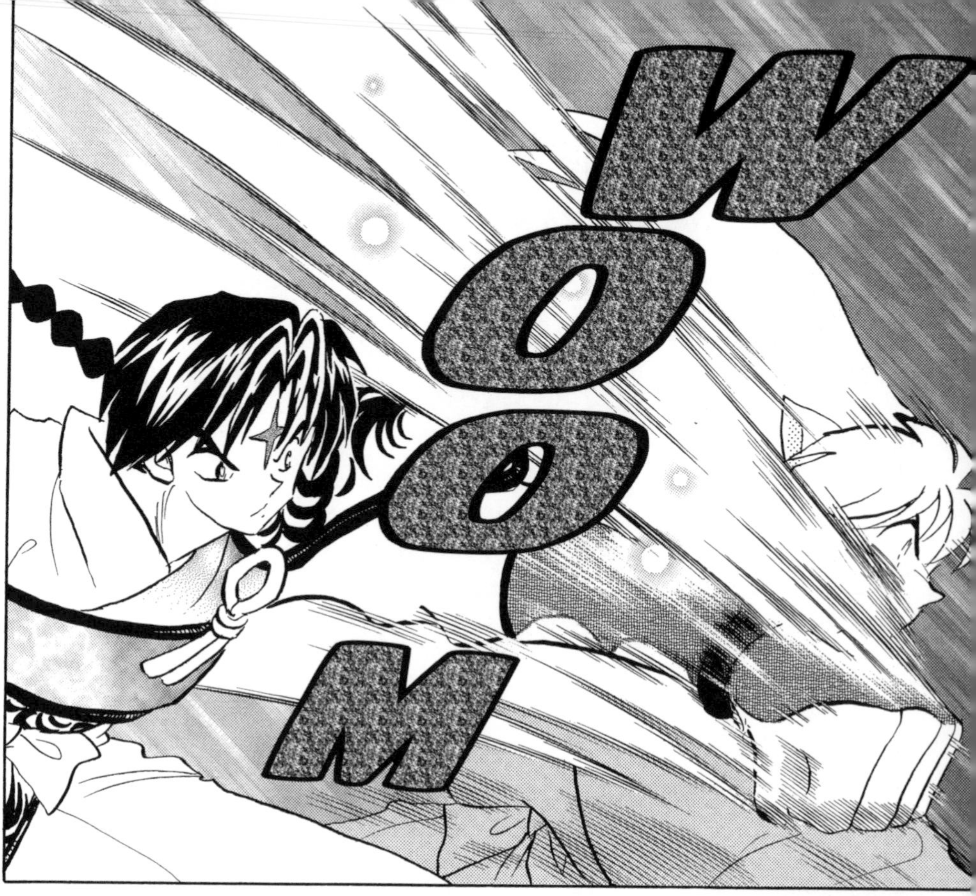
WOOM
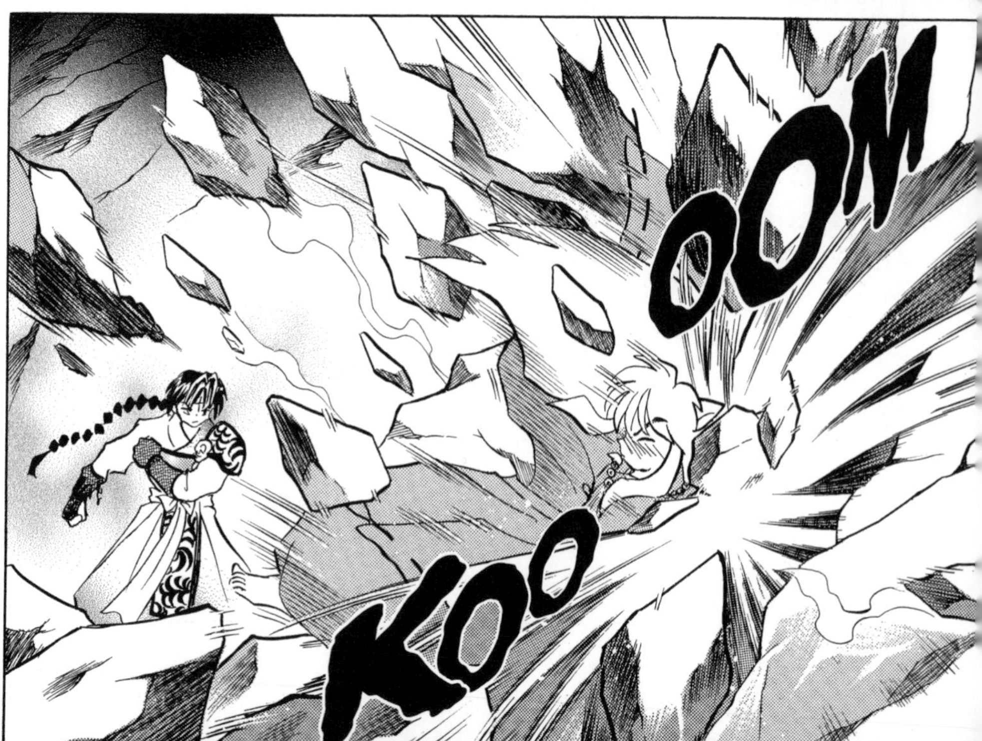
KOOOOM

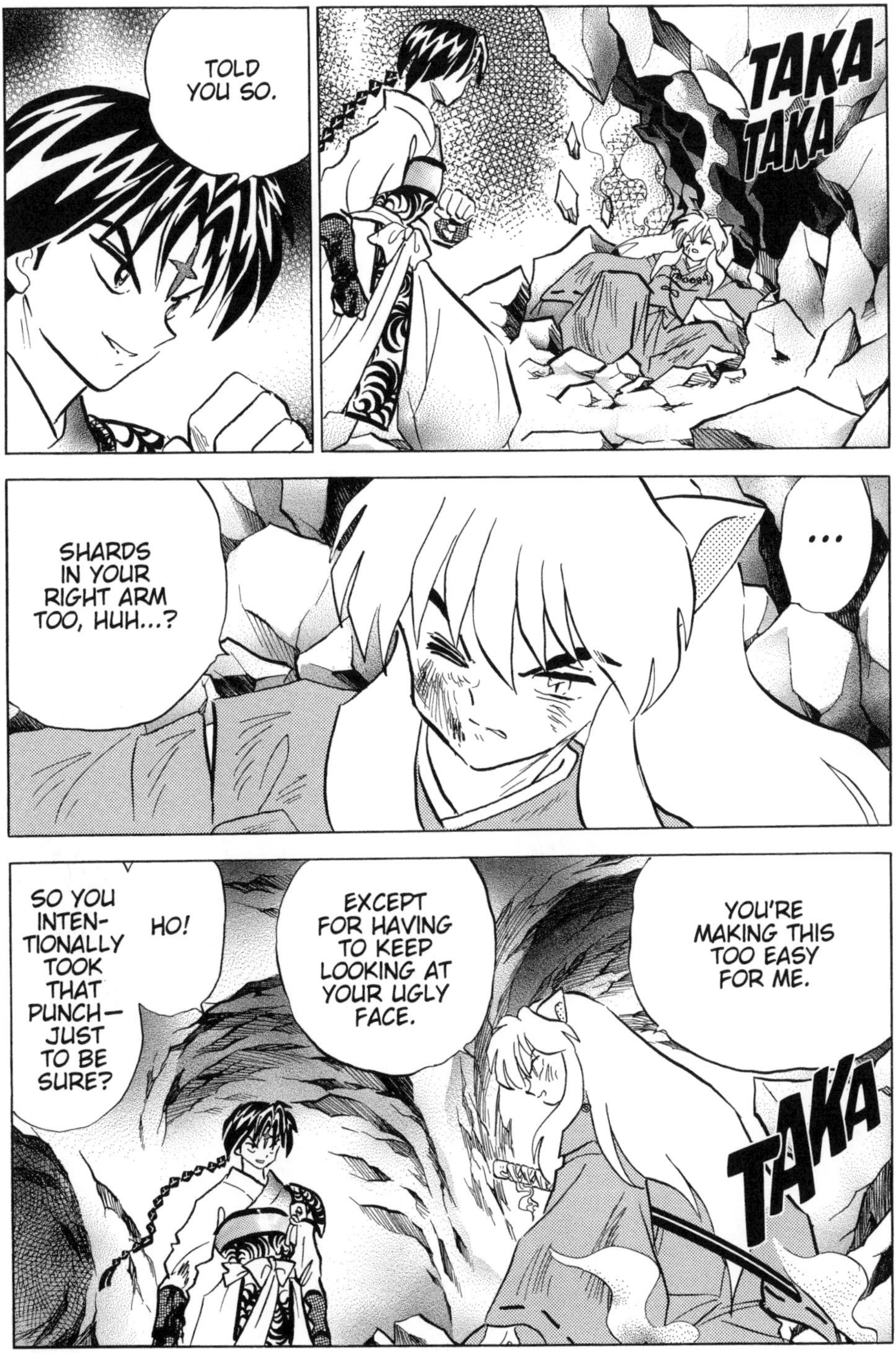
TAKA TAKA
TOLD YOU SO.
...
SHARDS IN YOUR RIGHT ARM TOO, HUH...?
YOU'RE MAKING THIS TOO EASY FOR ME.
TAKA
EXCEPT FOR HAVING TO KEEP LOOKING AT YOUR UGLY FACE.
HO!
SO YOU INTENTIONALLY TOOK THAT PUNCH— JUST TO BE SURE?

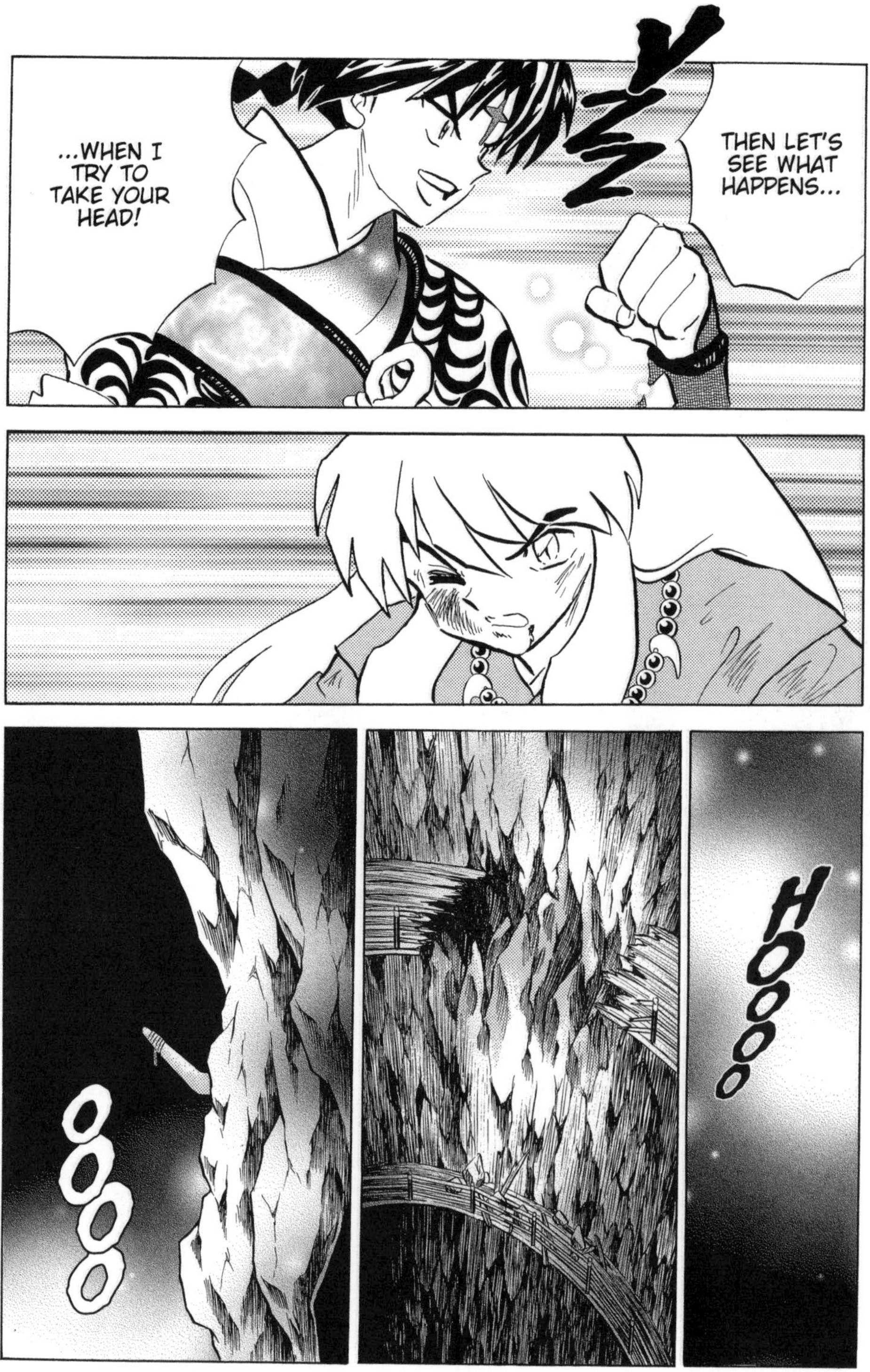
THEN LET'S SEE WHAT HAPPENS...
...WHEN I TRY TO TAKE YOUR HEAD!
HOOOO
OOOO

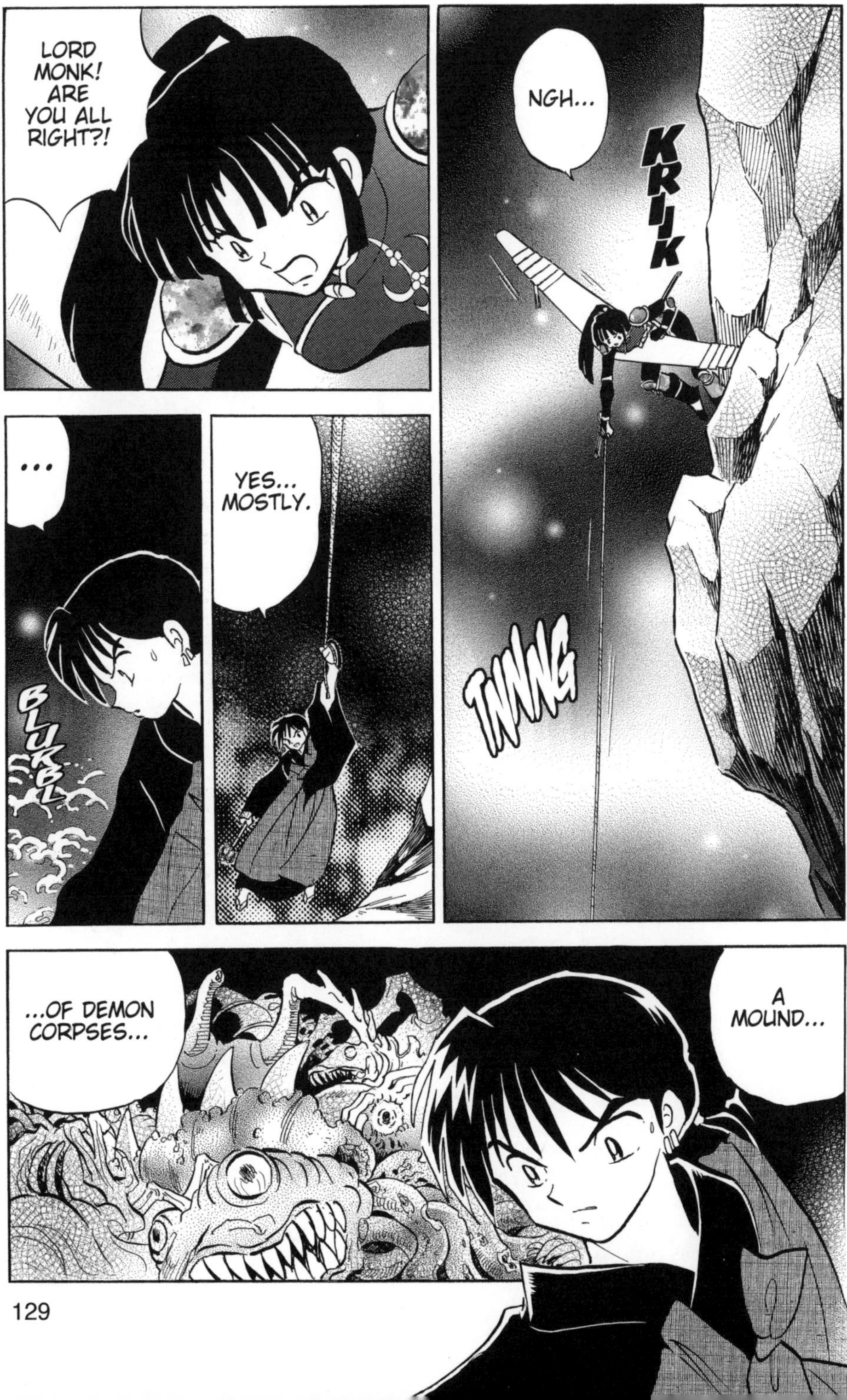
NGH...
KRIIK
TNNNG
LORD MONK! ARE YOU ALL RIGHT?!
YES... MOSTLY.
...
BLURBL
A MOUND...
...OF DEMON CORPSES...

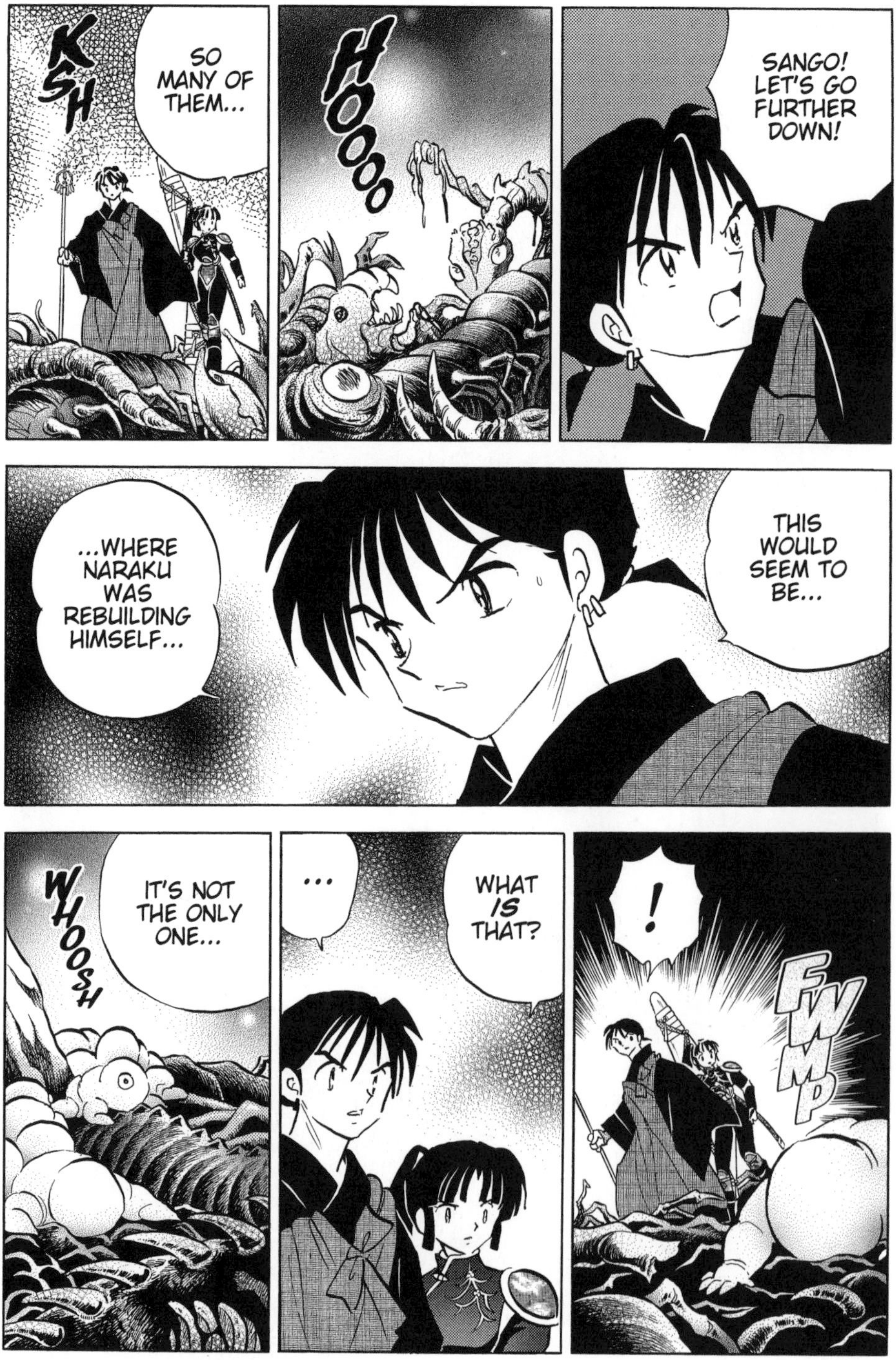
SANGO! LET'S GO FURTHER DOWN!
HOOOOO
KSH
SO MANY OF THEM...
THIS WOULD SEEM TO BE...
...WHERE NARAKU WAS REBUILDING HIMSELF...
!
FWMP
WHAT *IS* THAT?
...
IT'S NOT THE ONLY ONE...
WHOOSH

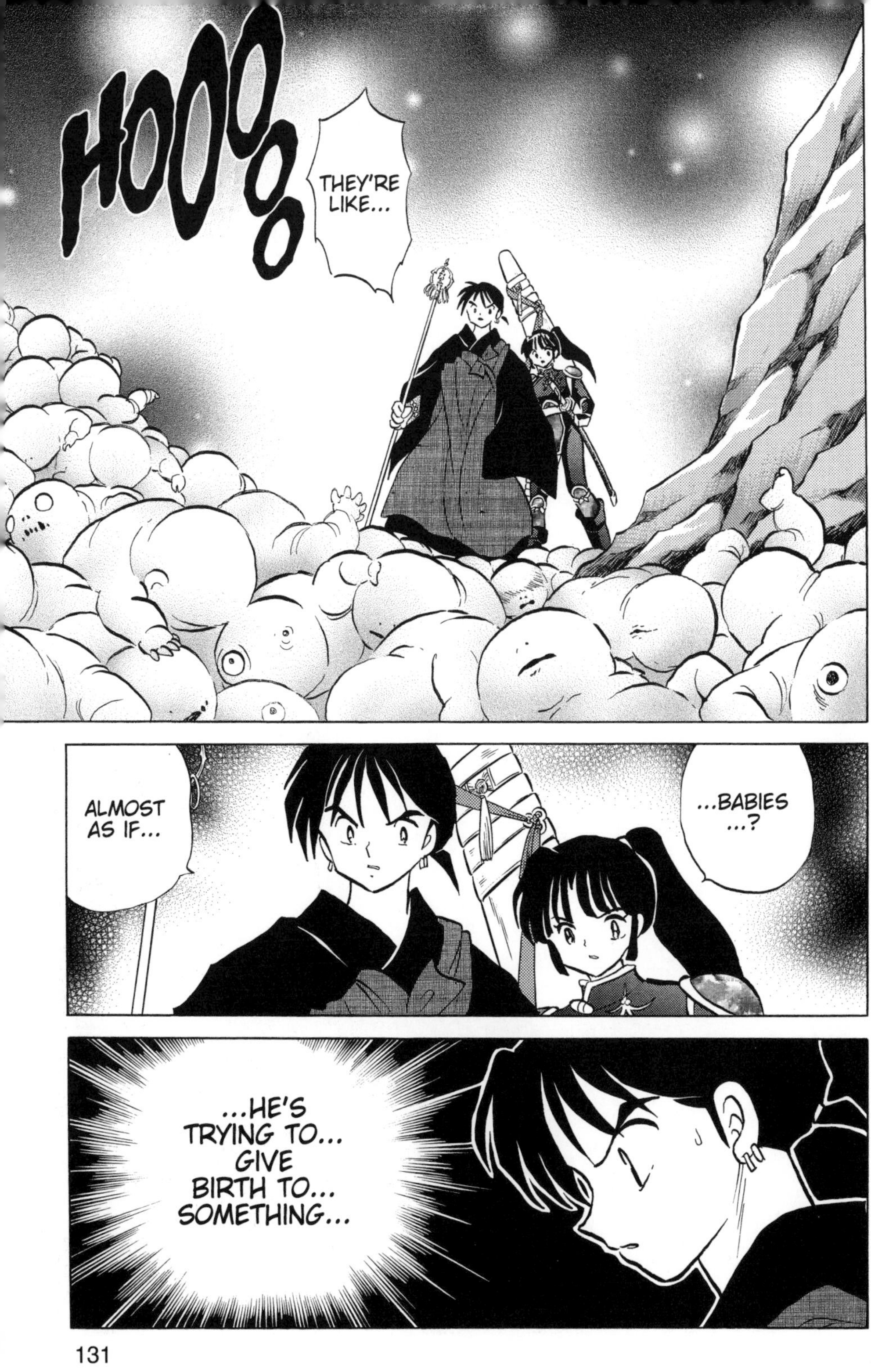
HOOOOO
THEY'RE LIKE...
...BABIES ...?
ALMOST AS IF...
...HE'S TRYING TO... GIVE BIRTH TO... SOMETHING...

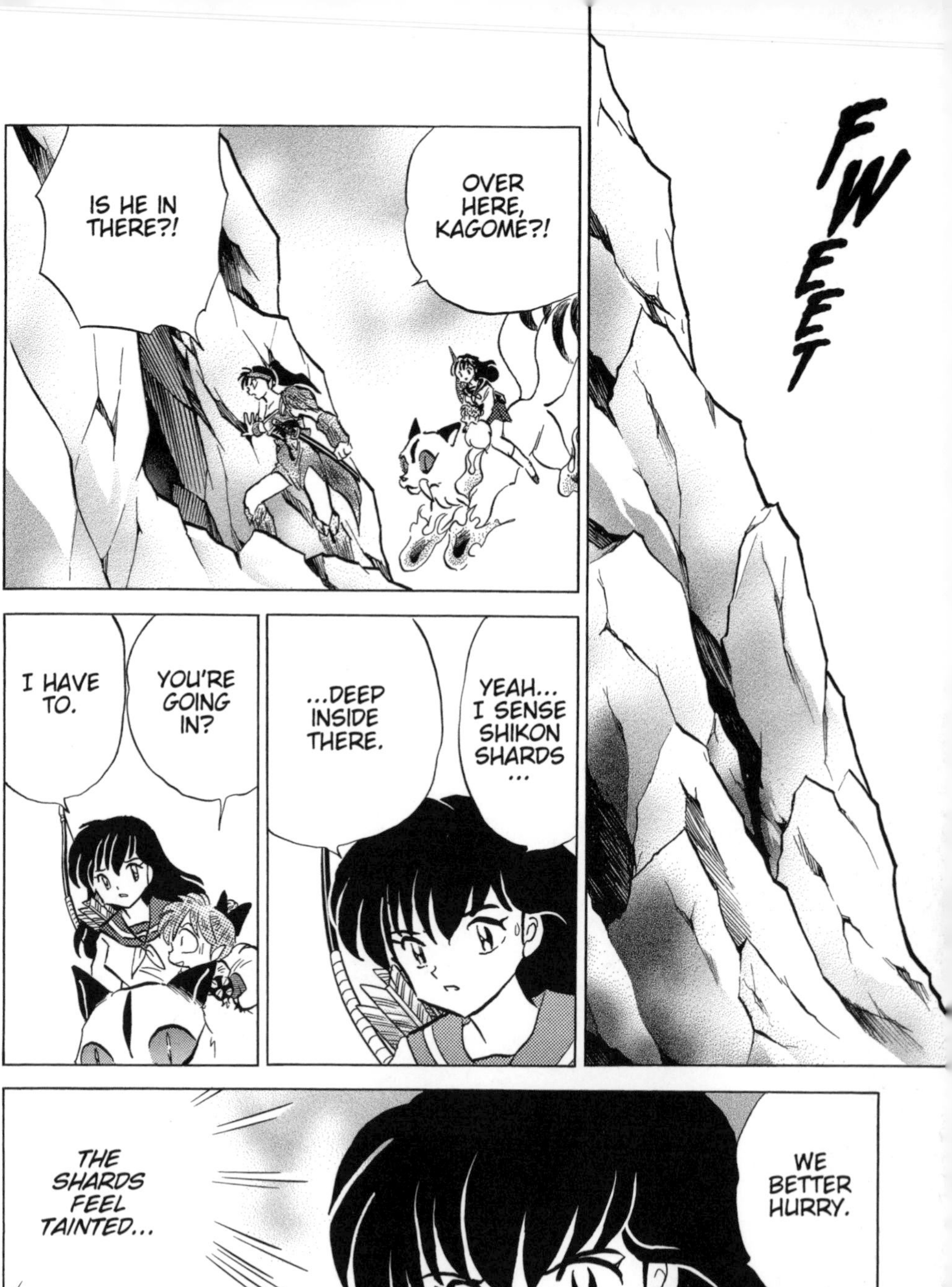
FWEET
OVER HERE, KAGOME?!
IS HE IN THERE?!
YEAH... I SENSE SHIKON SHARDS...
...DEEP INSIDE THERE.
YOU'RE GOING IN?
I HAVE TO.
WE BETTER HURRY.
THE SHARDS FEEL TAINTED...

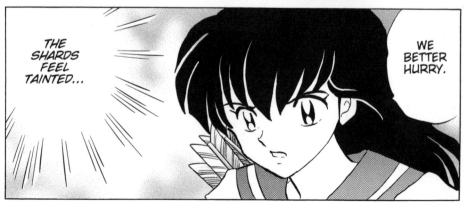

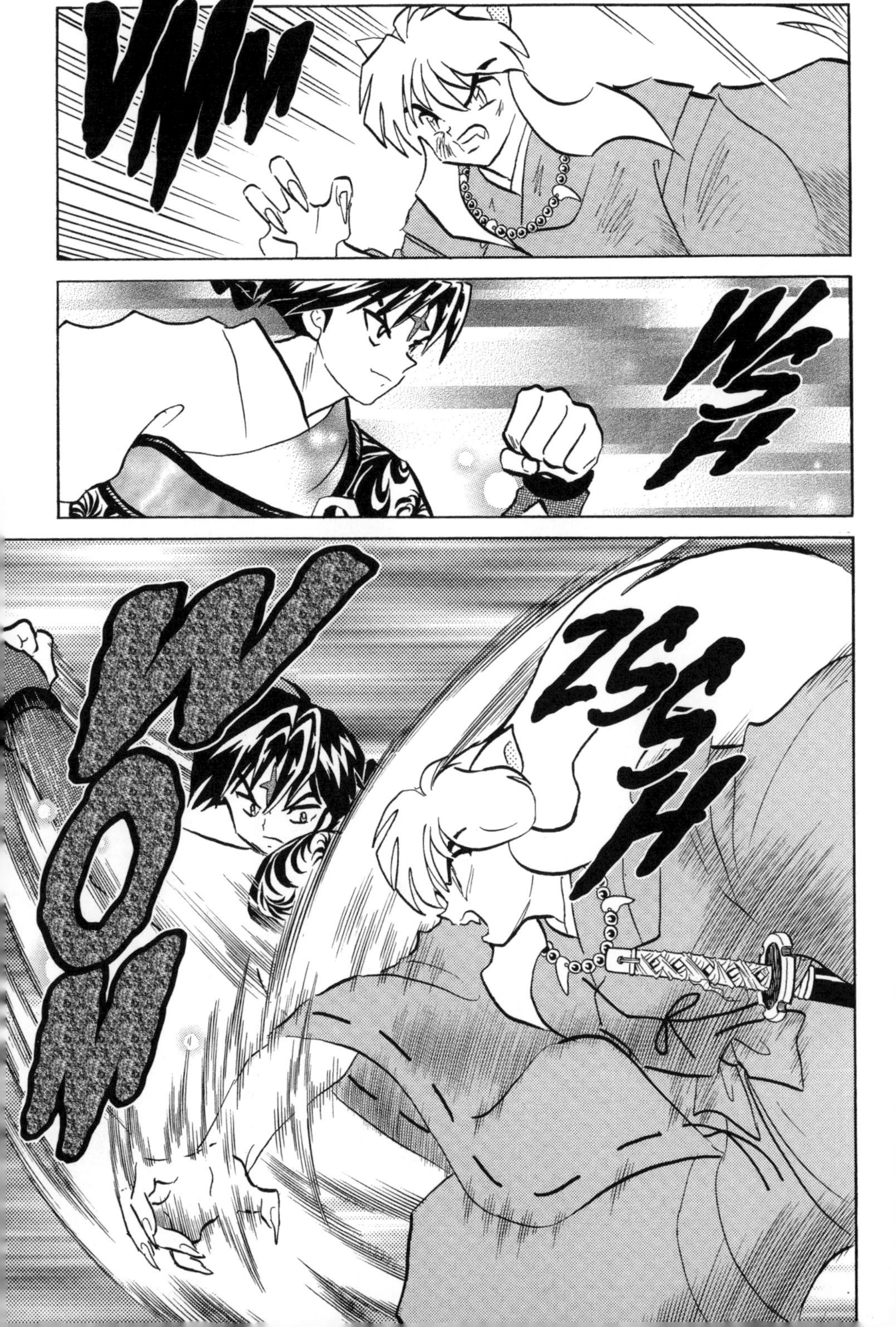
VMM
WSH
ZSCH
WOM

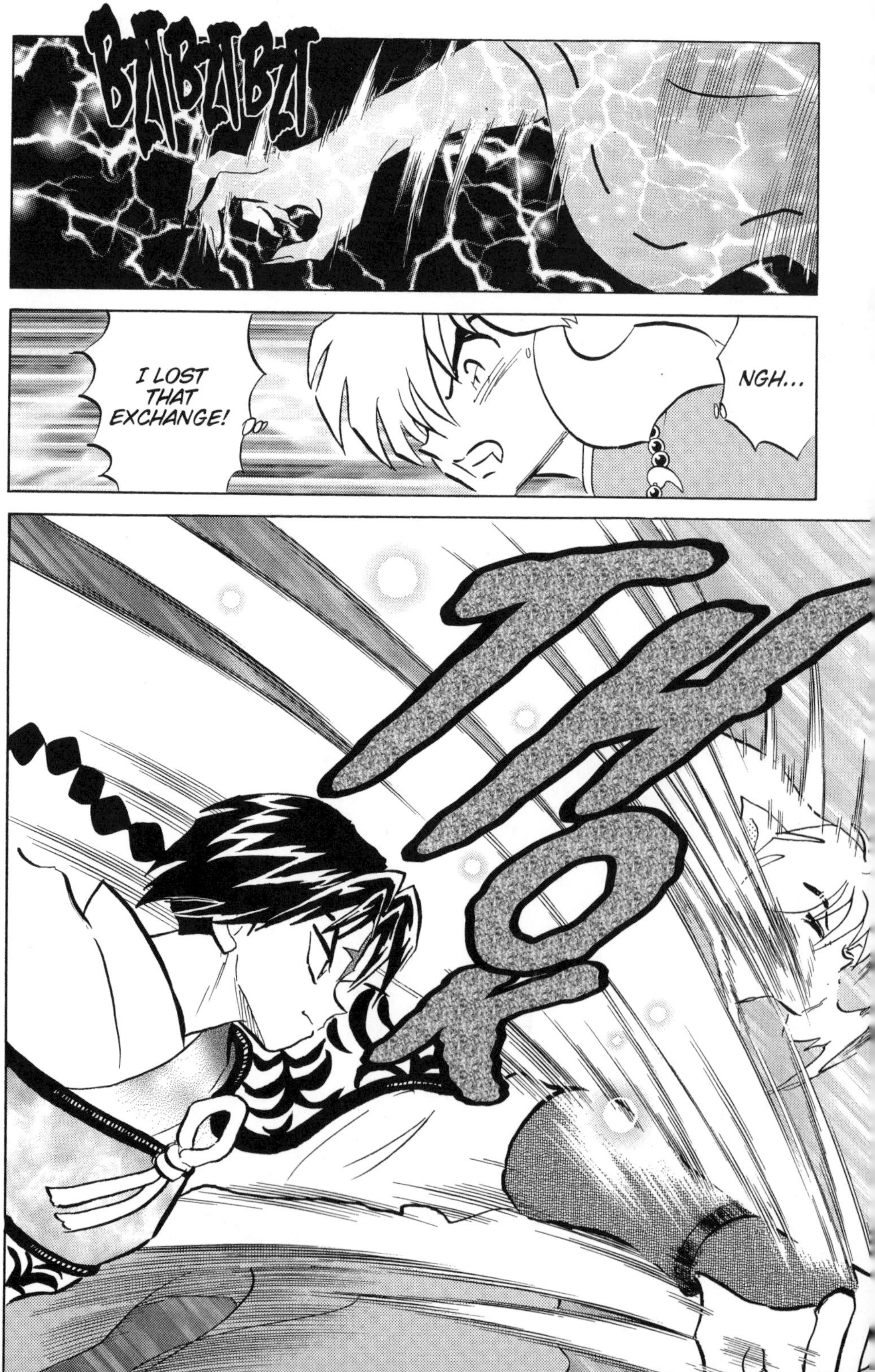
BZZTBZZTBZZT
NGH...
I LOST THAT EXCHANGE!
THWOK

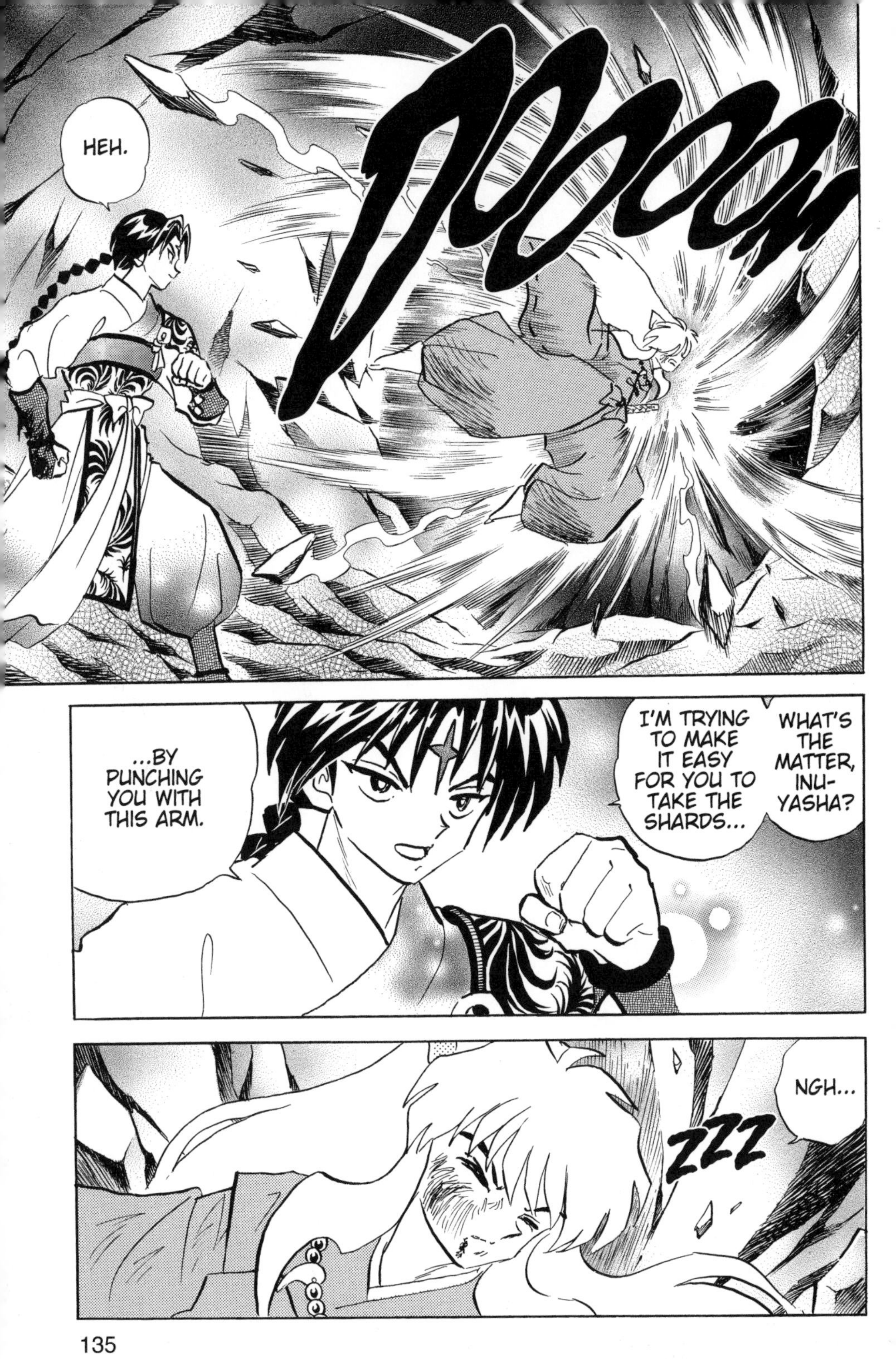
HEH.
WHAT'S THE MATTER, INU-YASHA?
I'M TRYING TO MAKE IT EASY FOR YOU TO TAKE THE SHARDS...
...BY PUNCHING YOU WITH THIS ARM.
NGH...
ZZZ

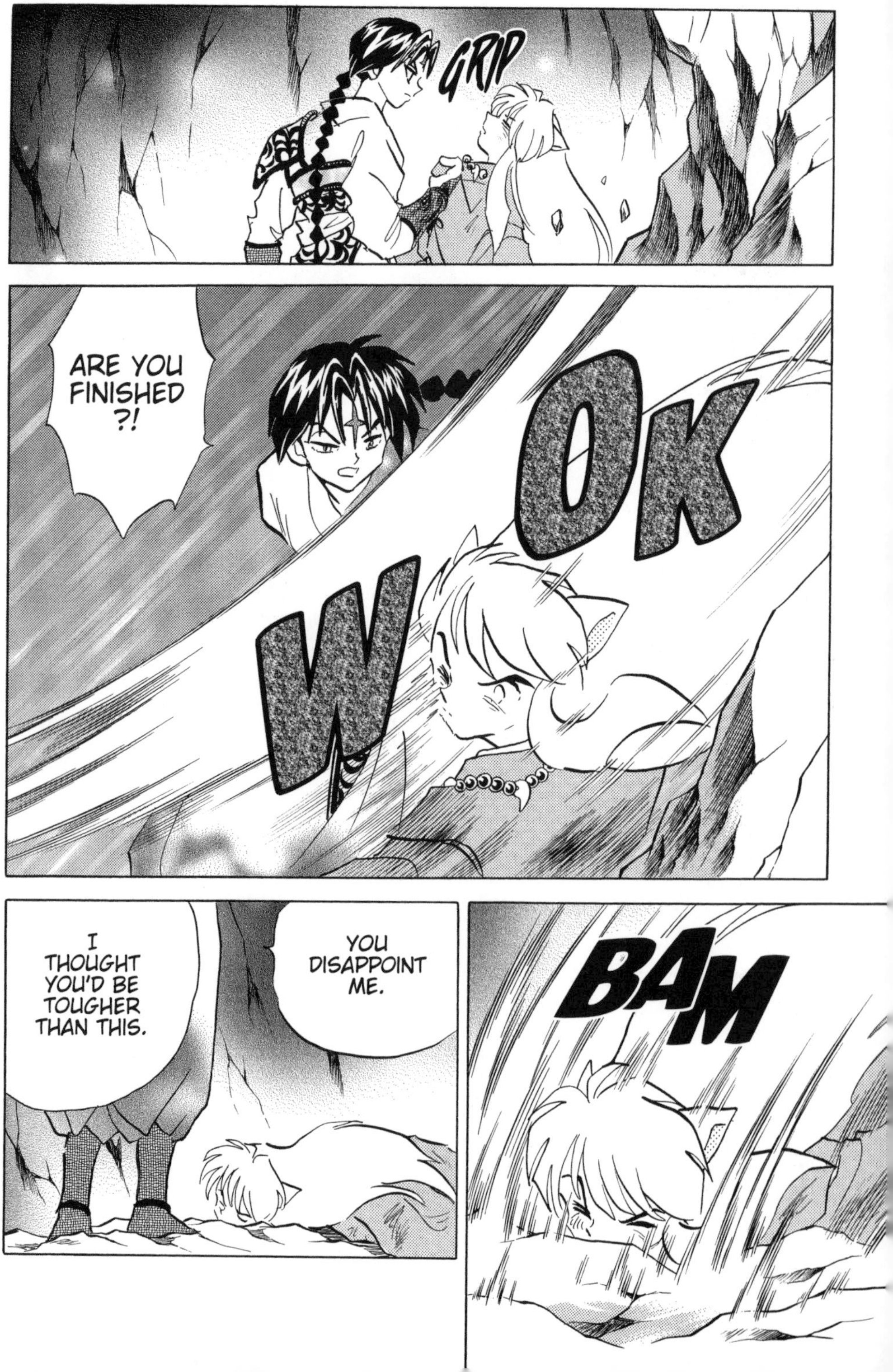
GRIP
ARE YOU FINISHED ?!
WOK
BAM
YOU DISAPPOINT ME.
I THOUGHT YOU'D BE TOUGHER THAN THIS.

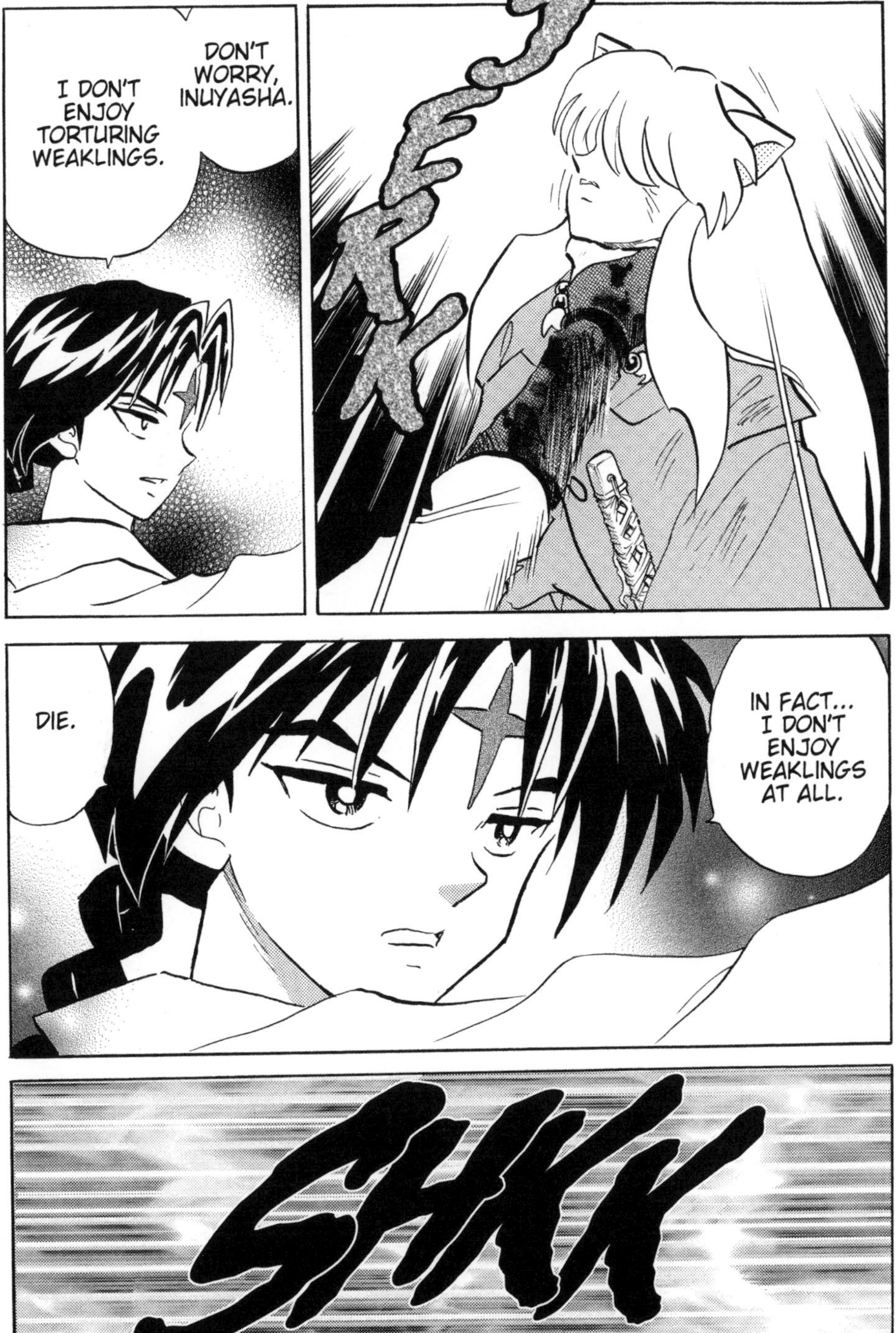
JERK
DON'T WORRY, INUYASHA.
I DON'T ENJOY TORTURING WEAKLINGS.
IN FACT... I DON'T ENJOY WEAKLINGS AT ALL.
DIE.
SHKK

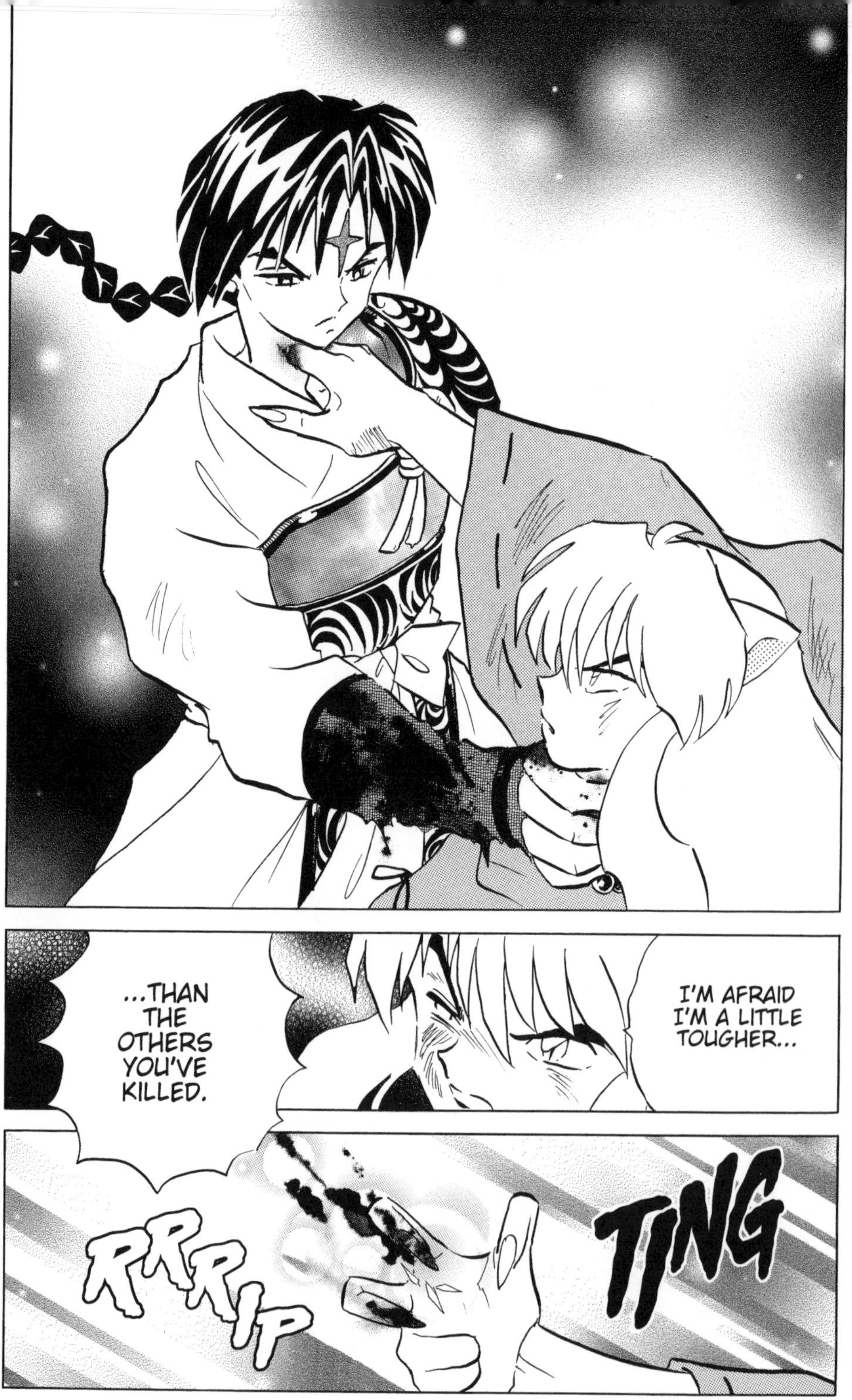
I'M AFRAID I'M A LITTLE TOUGHER...
...THAN THE OTHERS YOU'VE KILLED.
TING
RRRIP

SCROLL EIGHT
CUT IN TWO

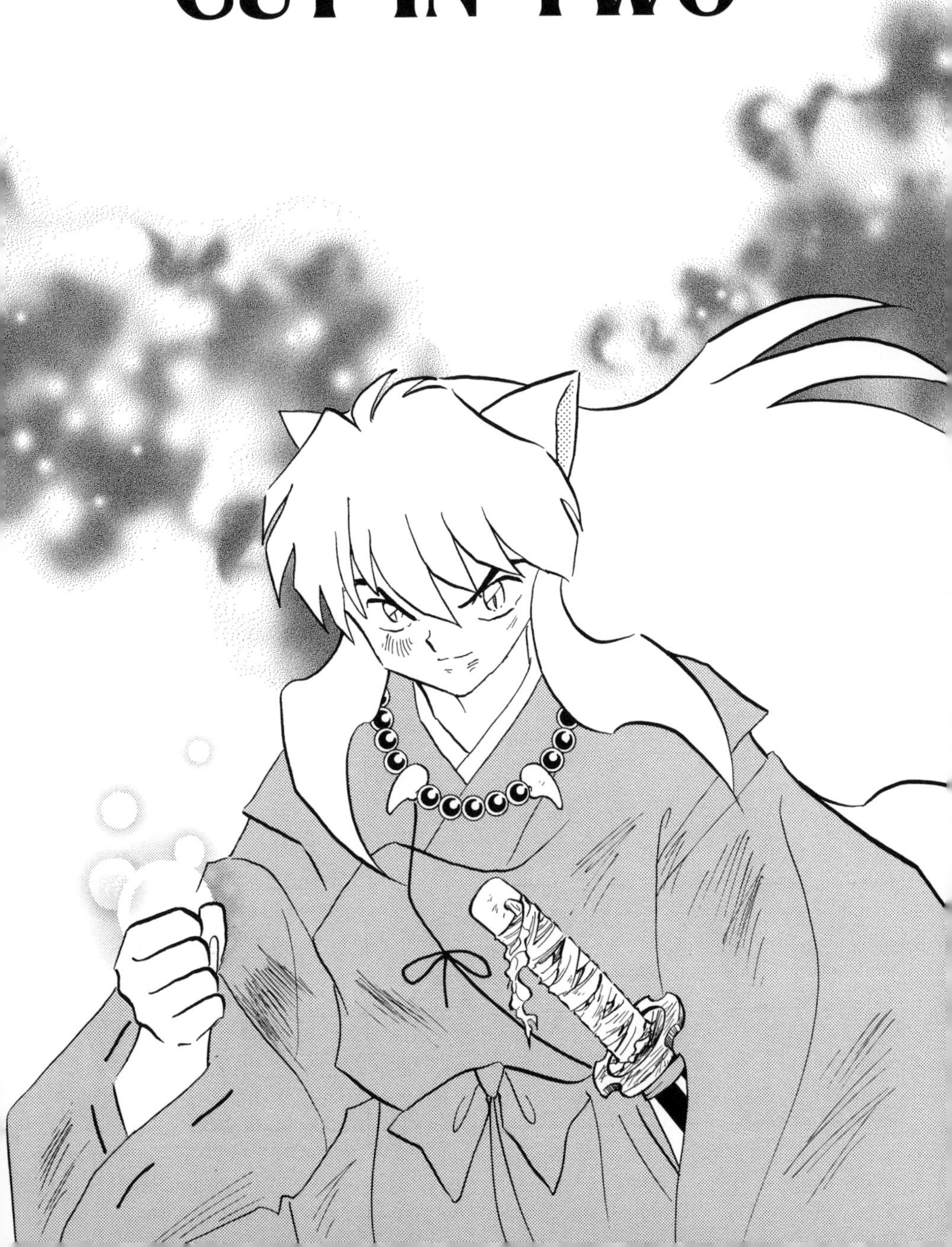

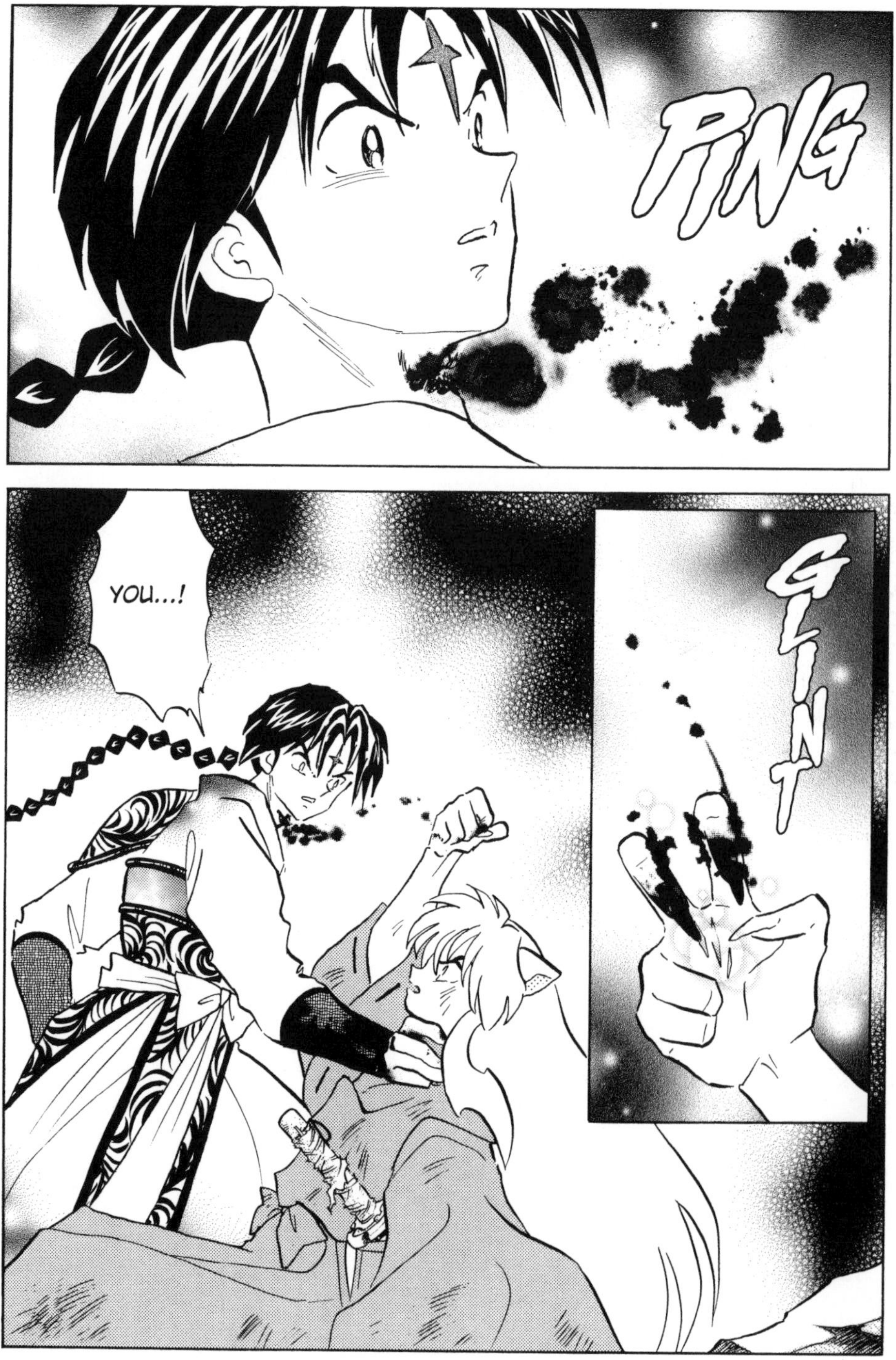
PING
GLINT
YOU...!

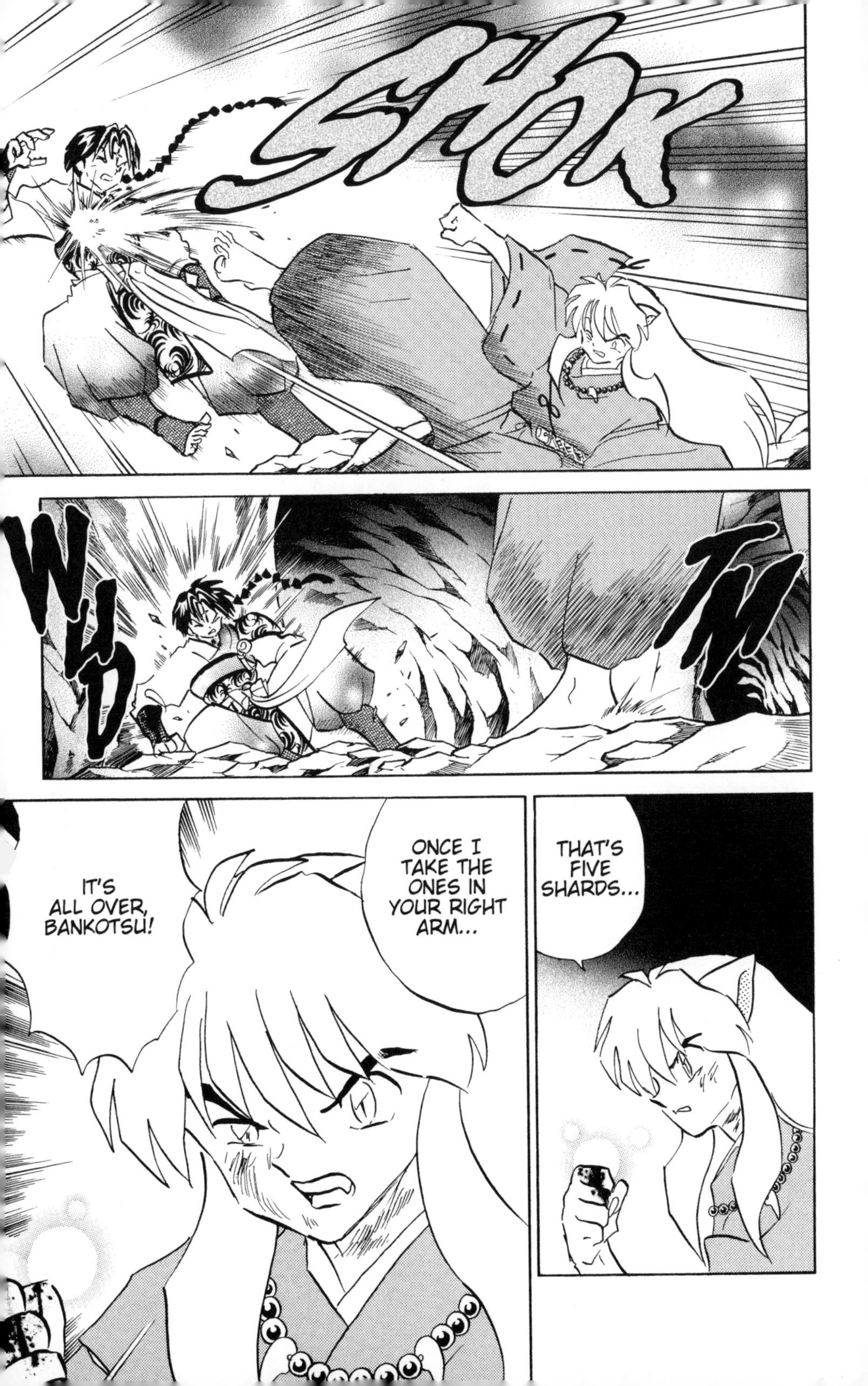
SHOK
THAT'S FIVE SHARDS...
ONCE I TAKE THE ONES IN YOUR RIGHT ARM...
IT'S ALL OVER, BANKOTSU!

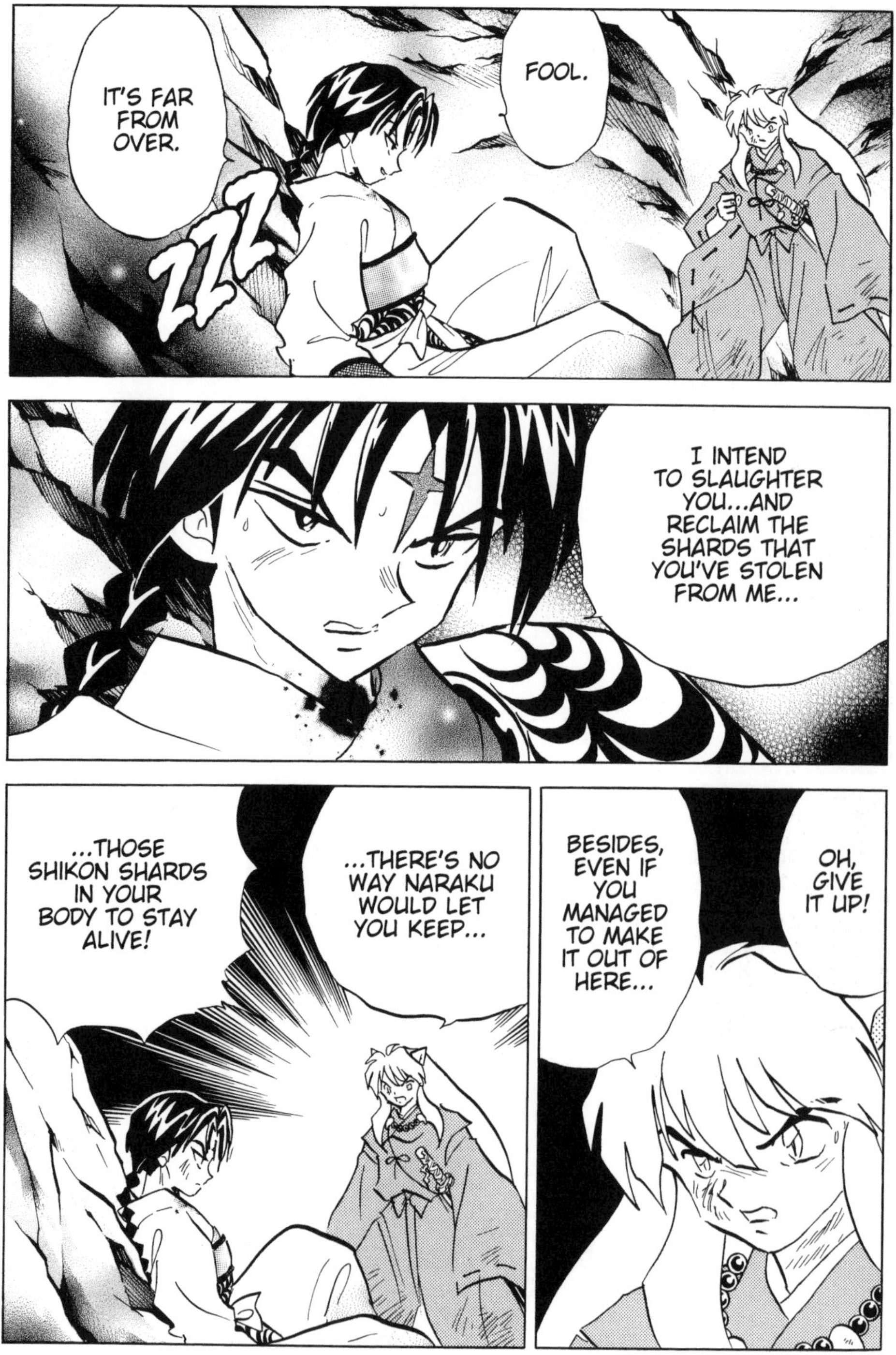
FOOL.
IT'S FAR FROM OVER.
ZZZ
I INTEND TO SLAUGHTER YOU...AND RECLAIM THE SHARDS THAT YOU'VE STOLEN FROM ME...
OH, GIVE IT UP!
BESIDES, EVEN IF YOU MANAGED TO MAKE IT OUT OF HERE...
...THERE'S NO WAY NARAKU WOULD LET YOU KEEP...
...THOSE SHIKON SHARDS IN YOUR BODY TO STAY ALIVE!

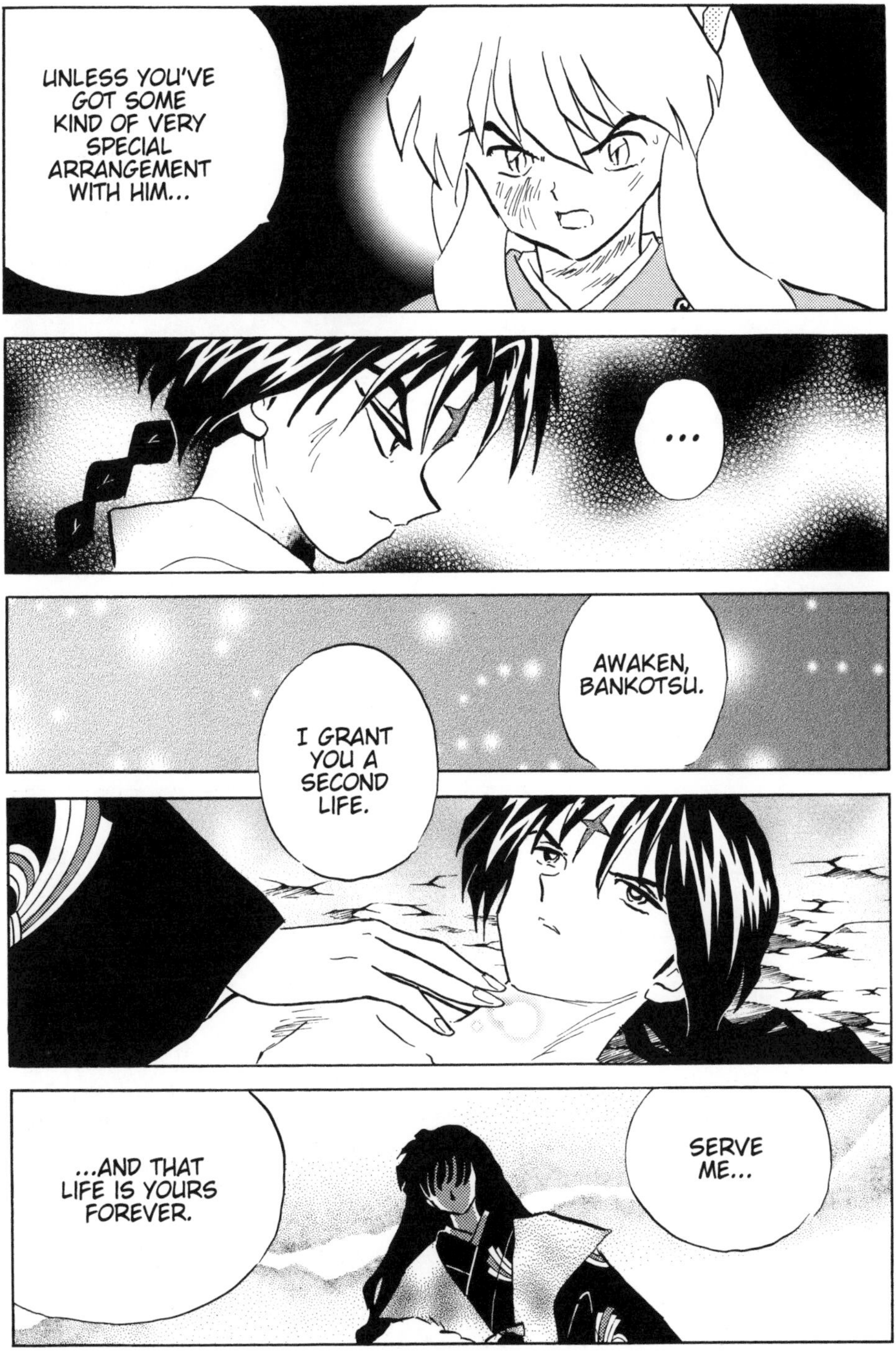
UNLESS YOU'VE GOT SOME KIND OF VERY SPECIAL ARRANGEMENT WITH HIM...
...
AWAKEN, BANKOTSU.
I GRANT YOU A SECOND LIFE.
SERVE ME...
...AND THAT LIFE IS YOURS FOREVER.

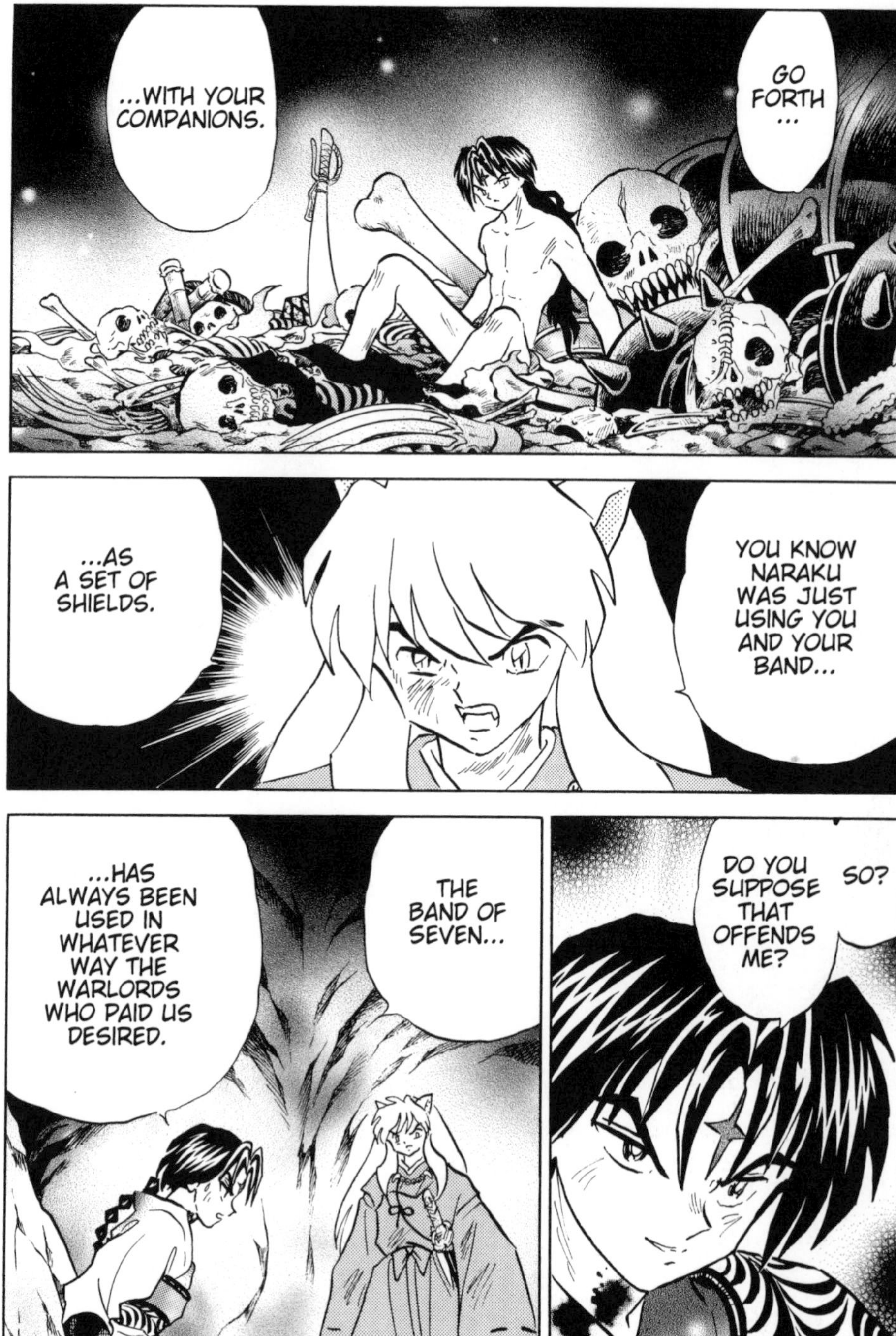
GO FORTH...
...WITH YOUR COMPANIONS.
YOU KNOW NARAKU WAS JUST USING YOU AND YOUR BAND...
...AS A SET OF SHIELDS.
SO?
DO YOU SUPPOSE THAT OFFENDS ME?
THE BAND OF SEVEN...
...HAS ALWAYS BEEN USED IN WHATEVER WAY THE WARLORDS WHO PAID US DESIRED.

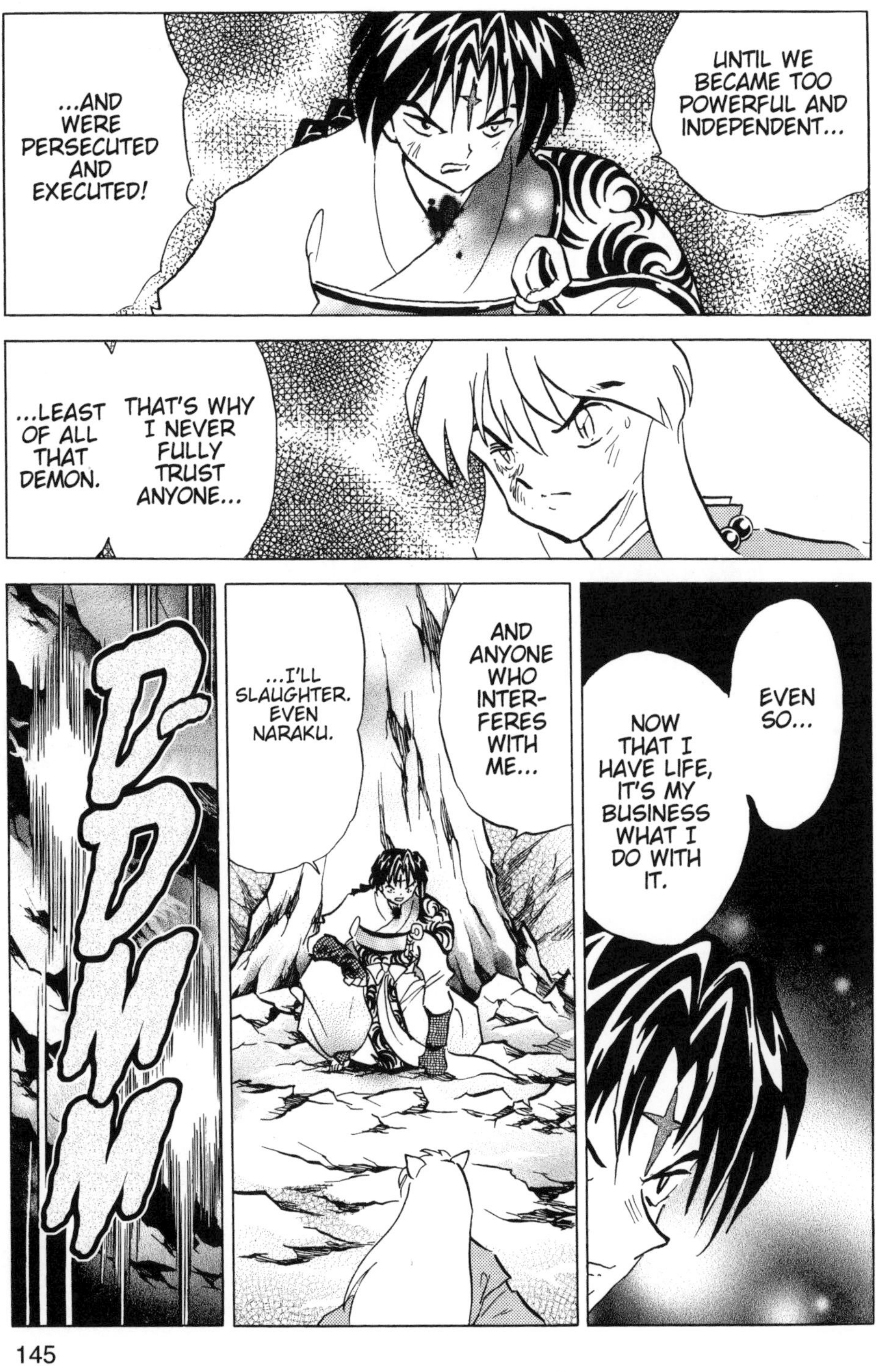
UNTIL WE BECAME TOO POWERFUL AND INDEPENDENT...
...AND WERE PERSECUTED AND EXECUTED!
THAT'S WHY I NEVER FULLY TRUST ANYONE...
...LEAST OF ALL THAT DEMON.
EVEN SO...
NOW THAT I HAVE LIFE, IT'S MY BUSINESS WHAT I DO WITH IT.
AND ANYONE WHO INTER-FERES WITH ME...
...I'LL SLAUGHTER. EVEN NARAKU.
D-DMM

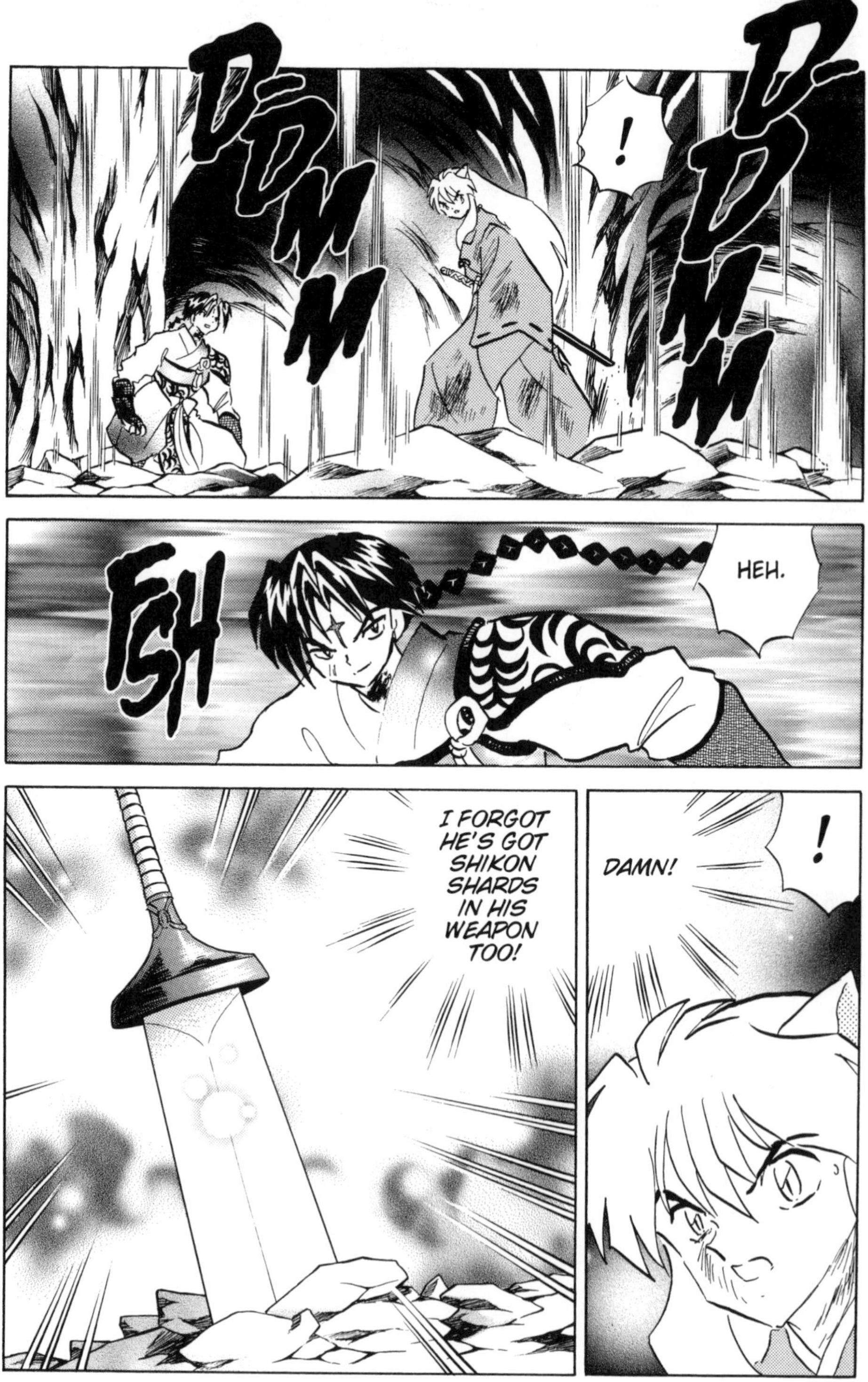
D-DDMMM
!
D-DMMM
HEH.
FSH
!
DAMN!
I FORGOT HE'S GOT SHIKON SHARDS IN HIS WEAPON TOO!

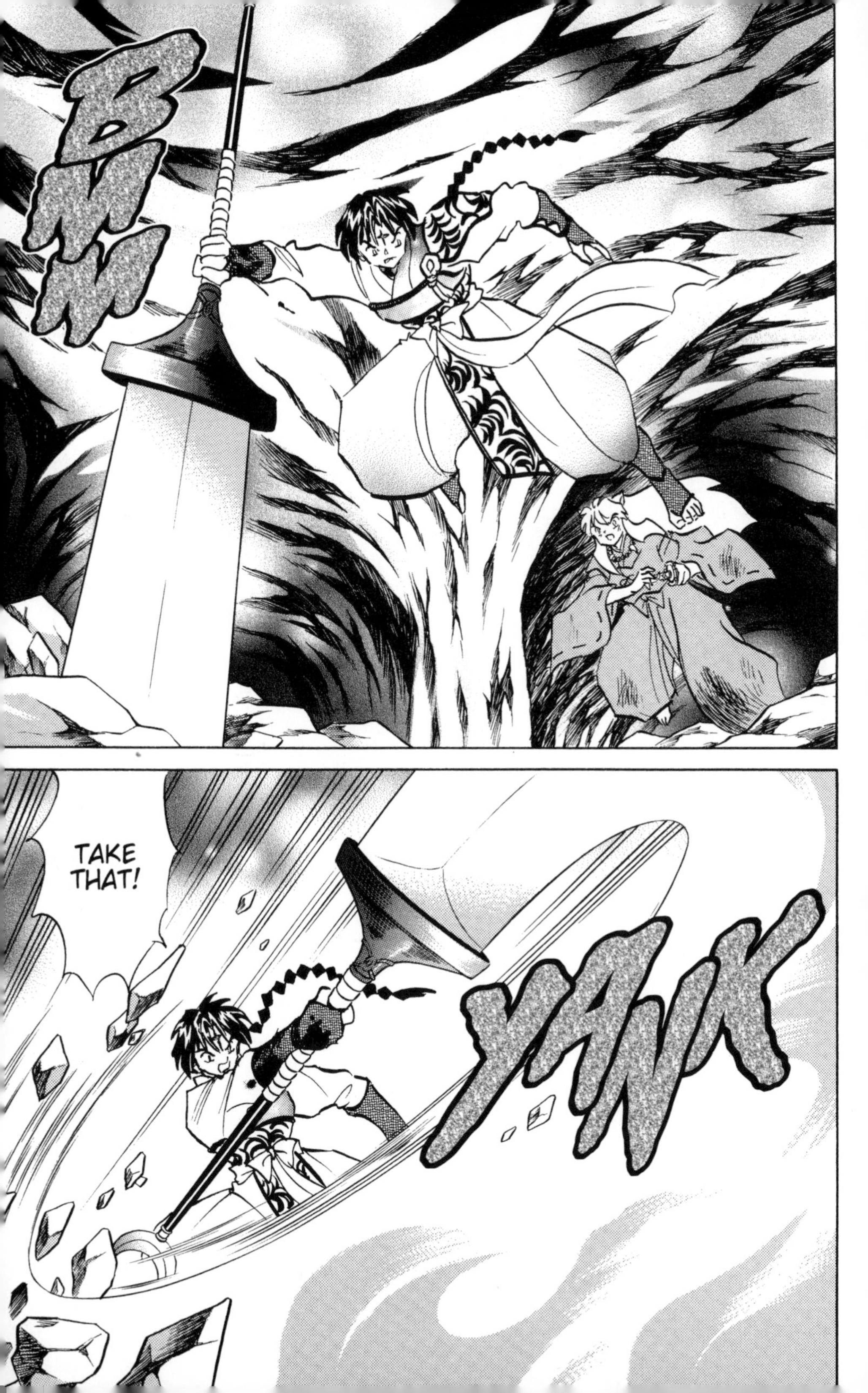
BMM
TAKE THAT!
YANK

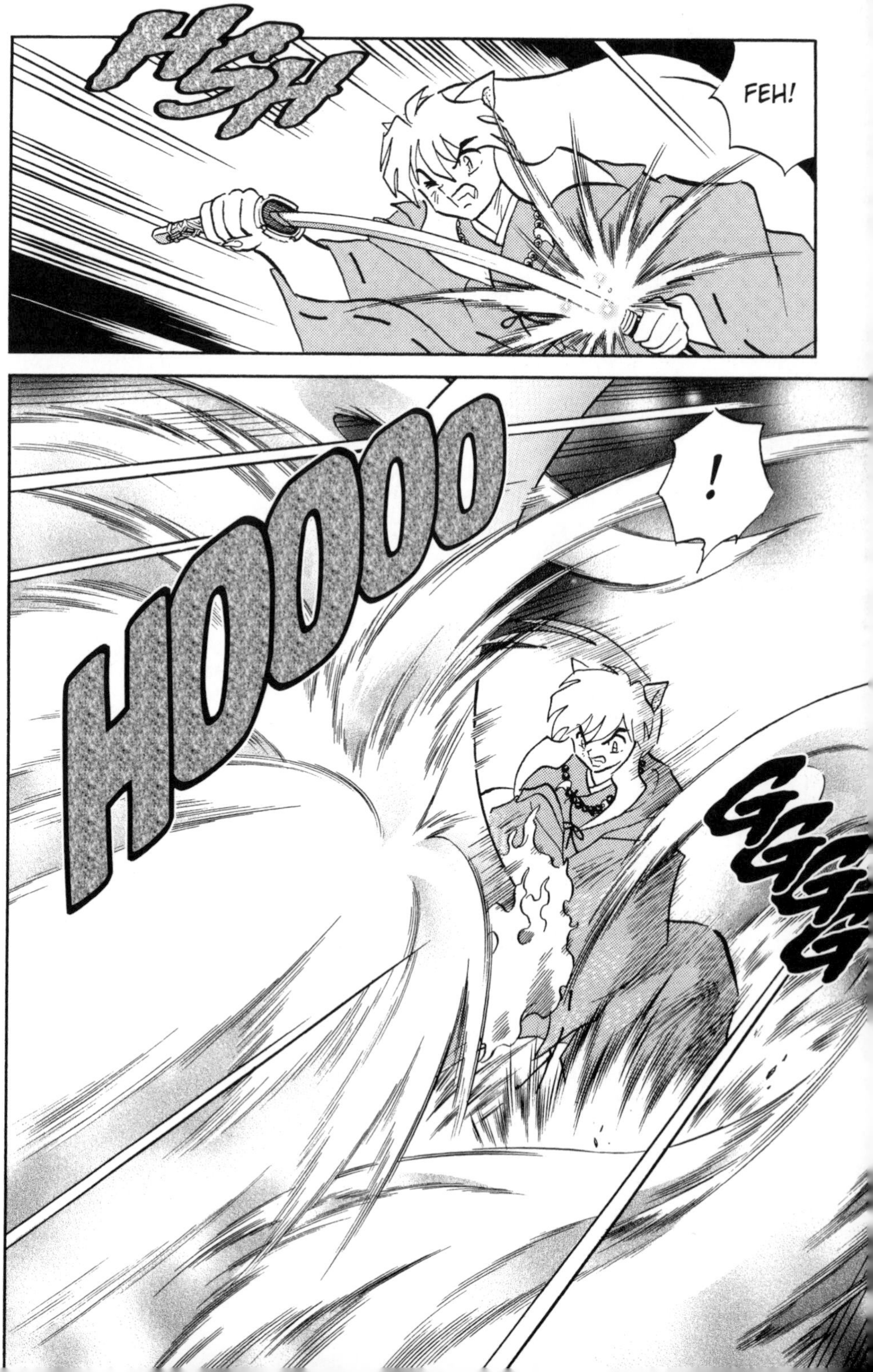
FEH!
HSH
!
HOOOO
GGGG

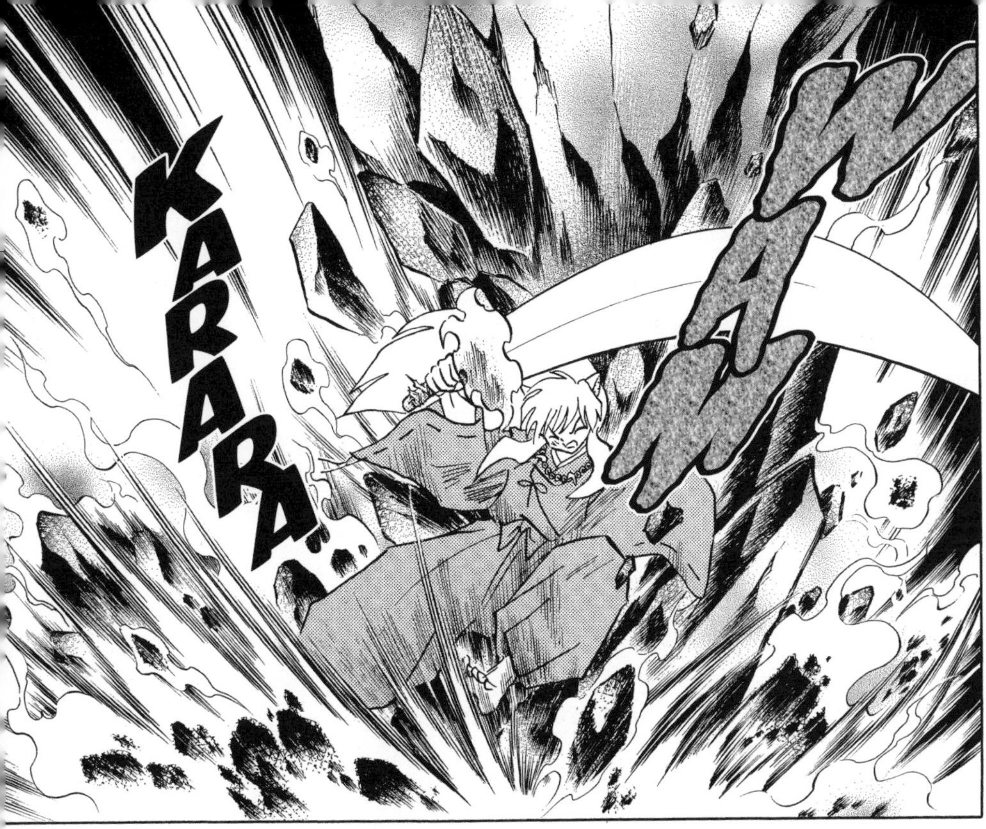
WAM
KARARA...

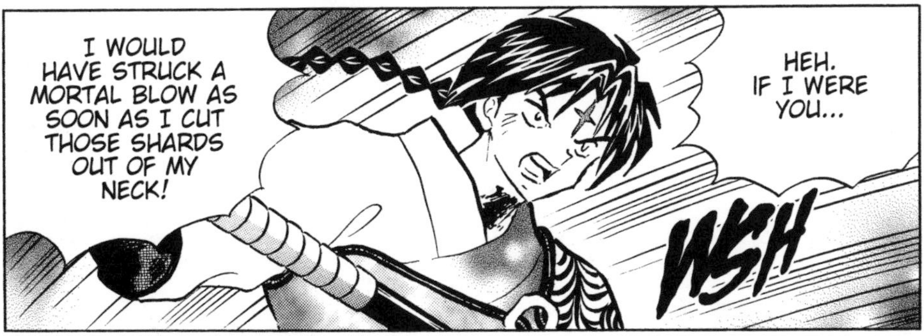
HEH. IF I WERE YOU...
I WOULD HAVE STRUCK A MORTAL BLOW AS SOON AS I CUT THOSE SHARDS OUT OF MY NECK!
WSH

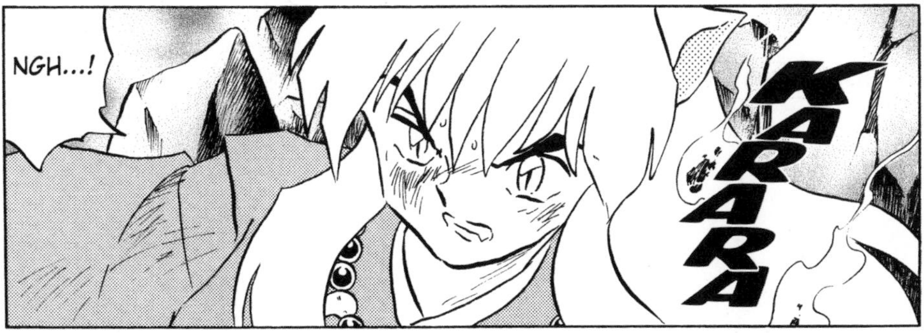
KARARA
NGH...!

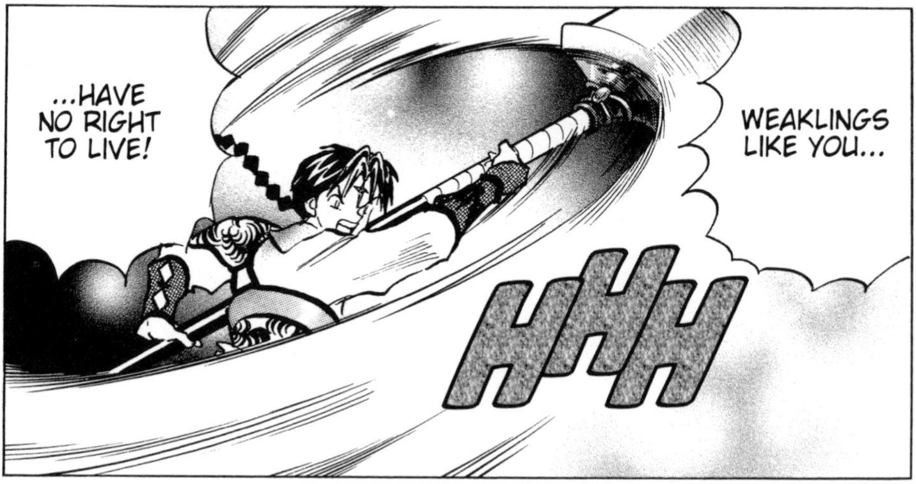
WEAKLINGS LIKE YOU...
...HAVE NO RIGHT TO LIVE!
HHH
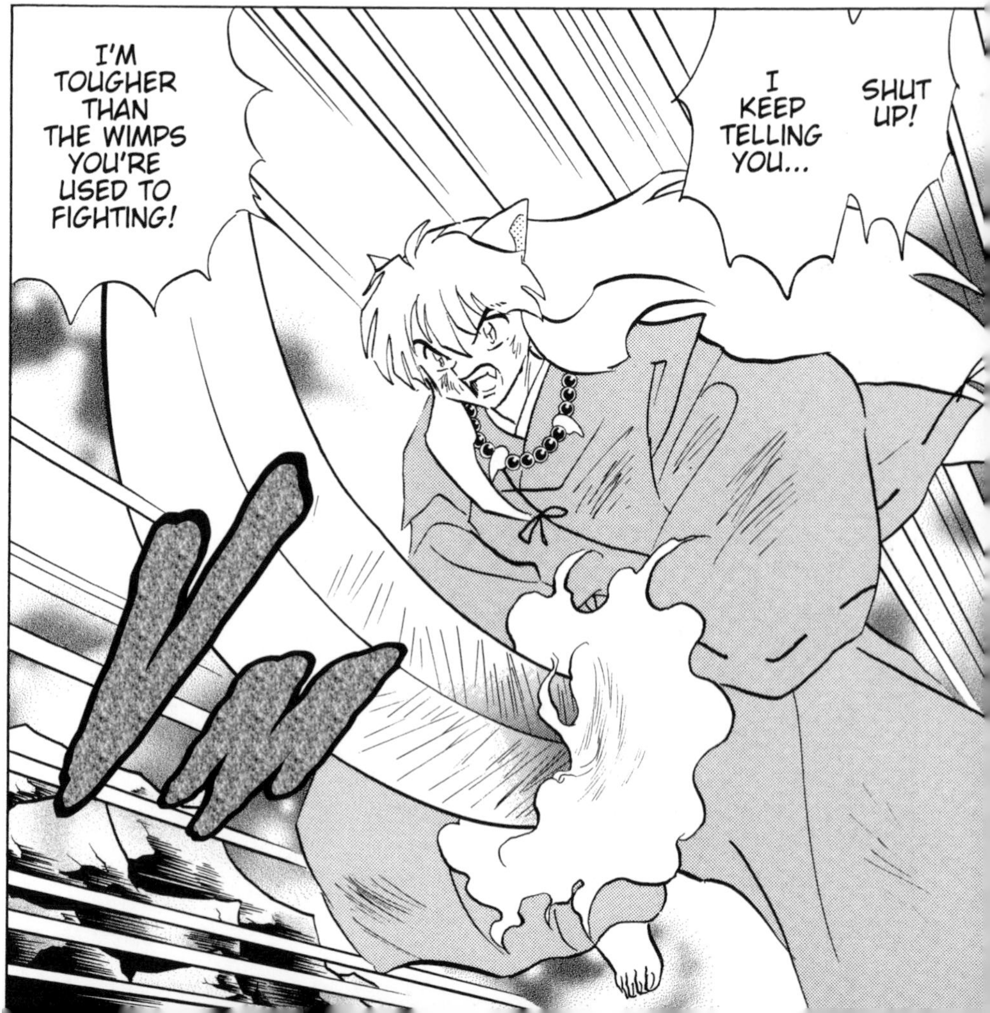
SHUT UP!
I KEEP TELLING YOU...
I'M TOUGHER THAN THE WIMPS YOU'RE USED TO FIGHTING!

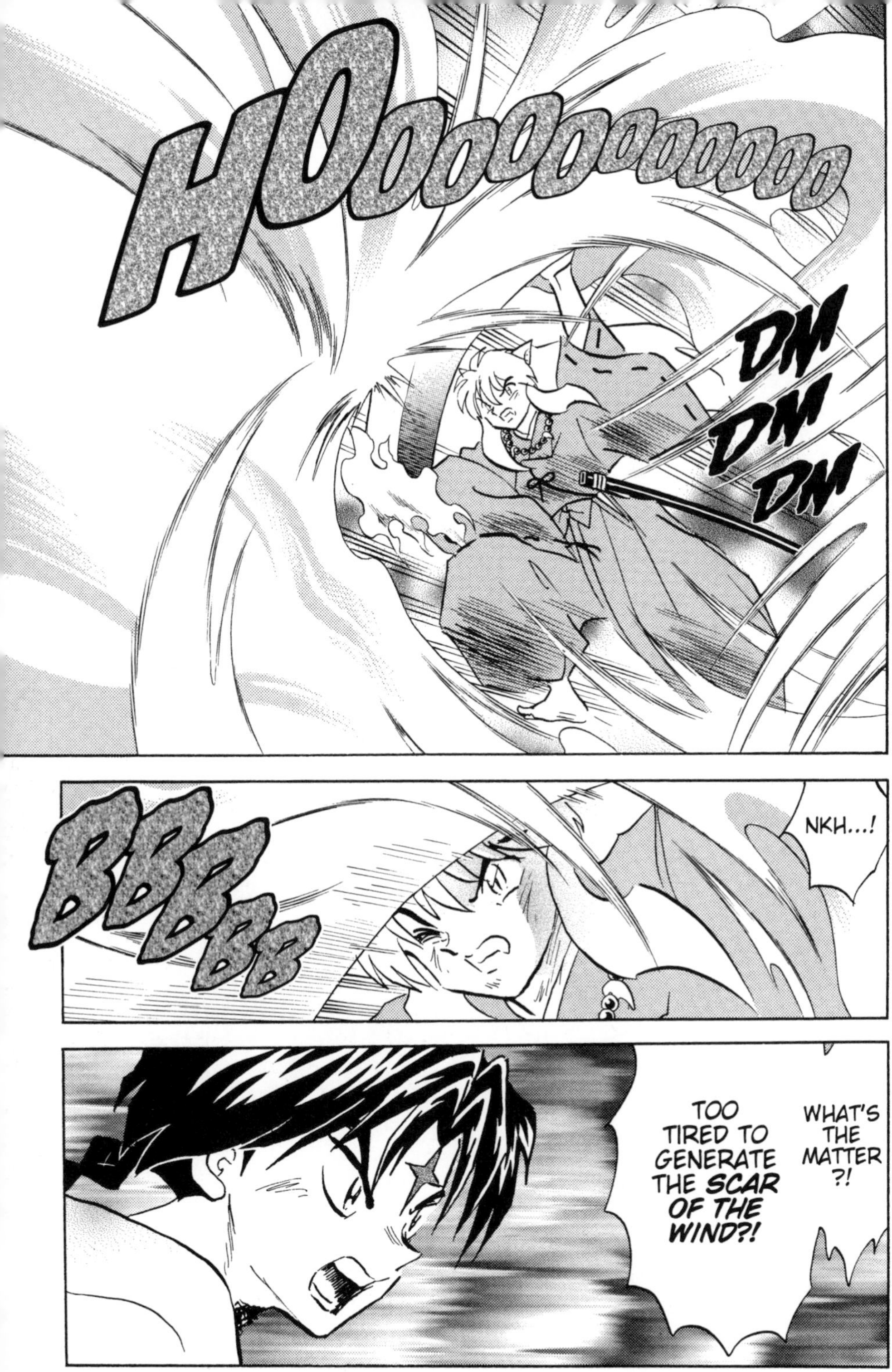
HOOOOOOOOOOO
DM DM DM
NKH...!
BBBBBB
WHAT'S THE MATTER ?!
TOO TIRED TO GENERATE THE SCAR OF THE WIND?!

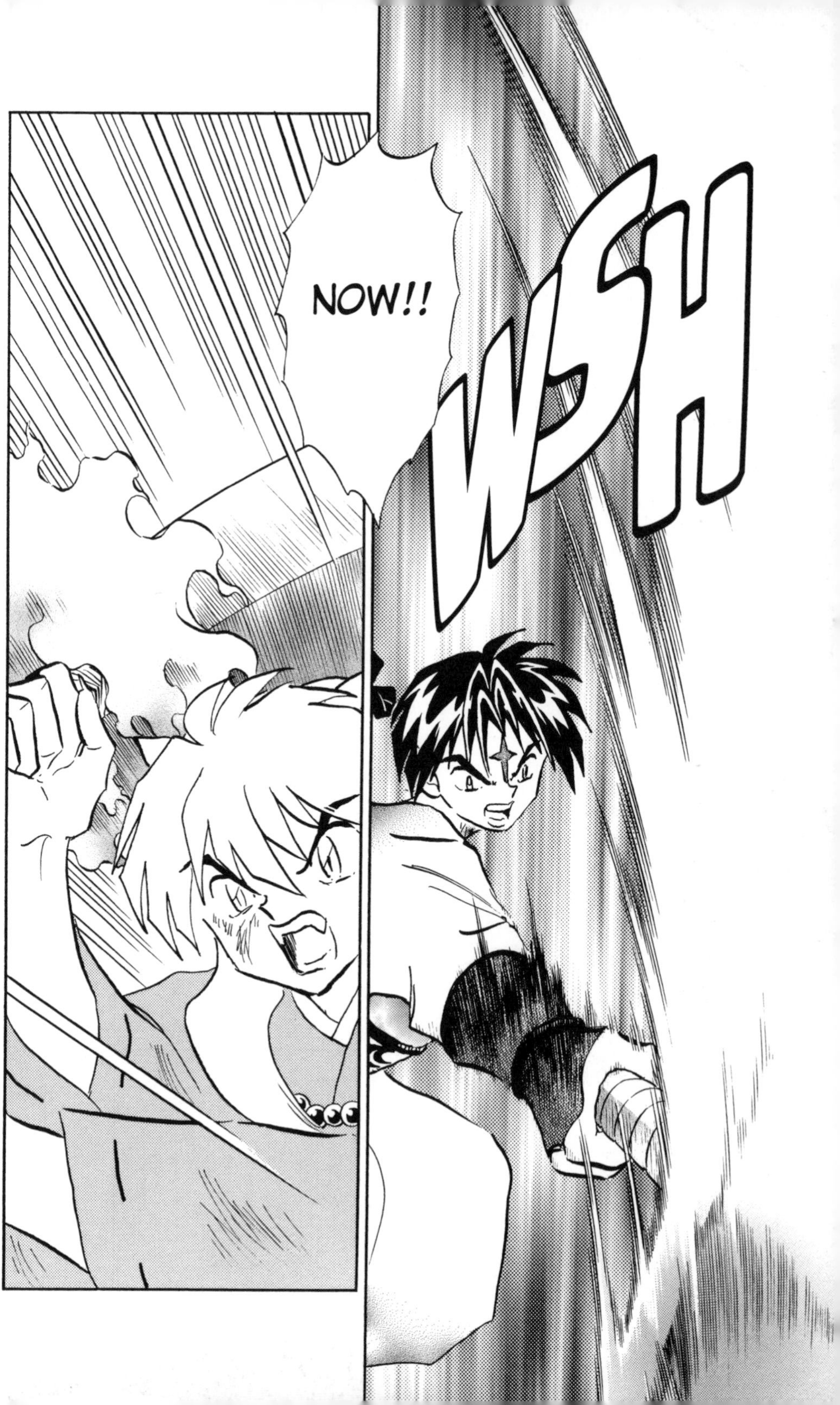
WSH
NOW!!

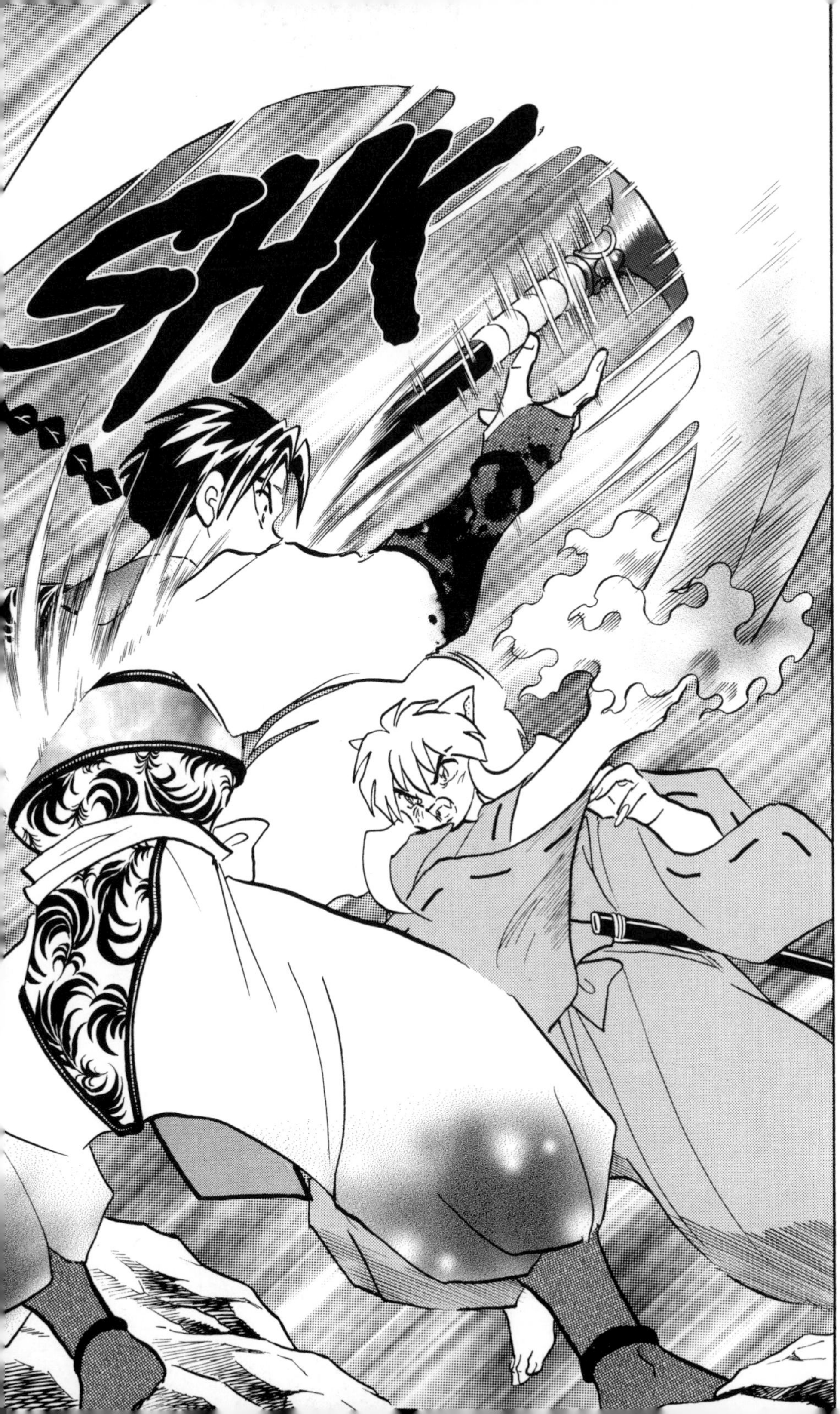
SHK

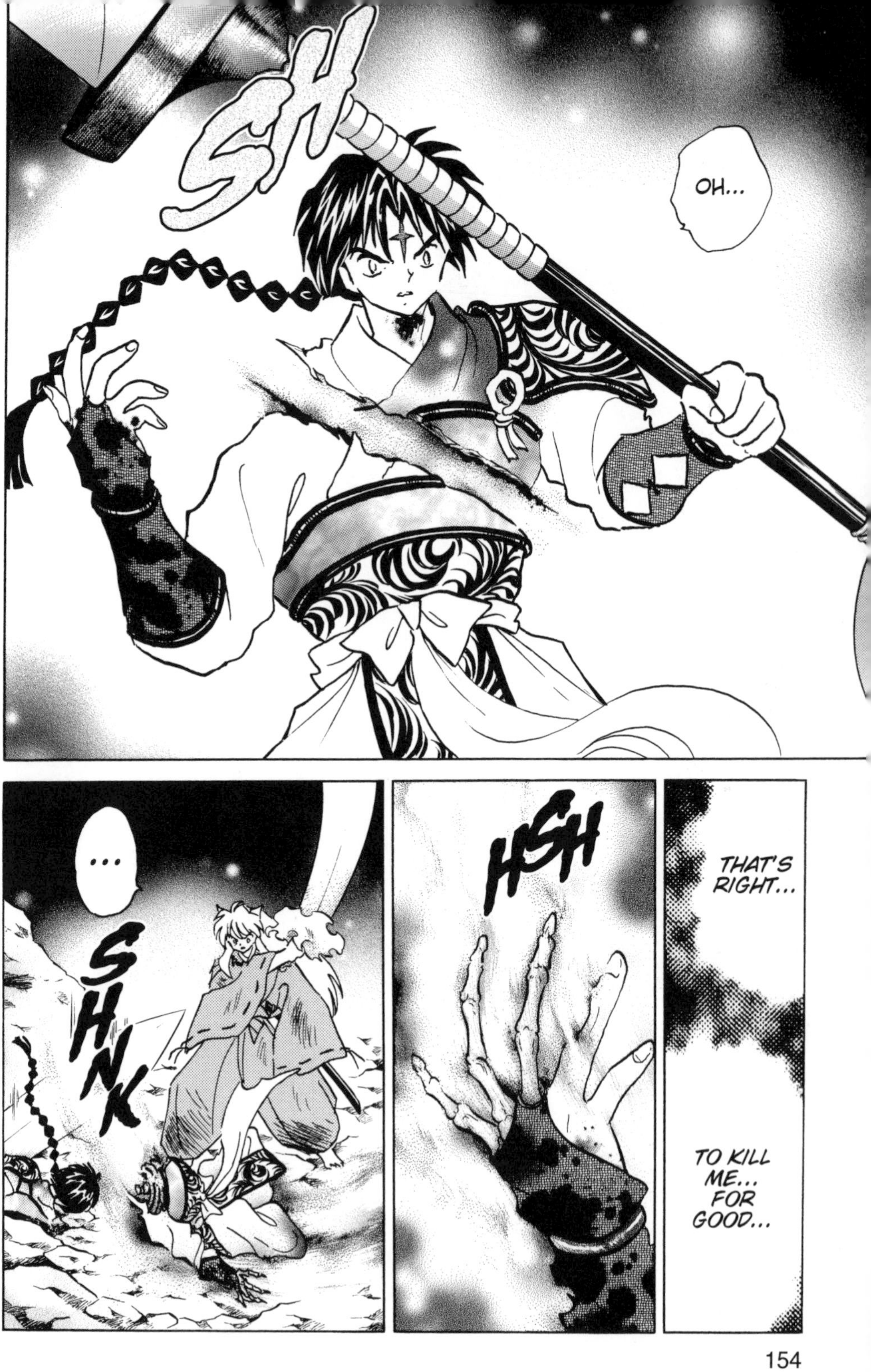
SH
OH...
THAT'S RIGHT...
TO KILL ME... FOR GOOD...
HSH
...
SHNK

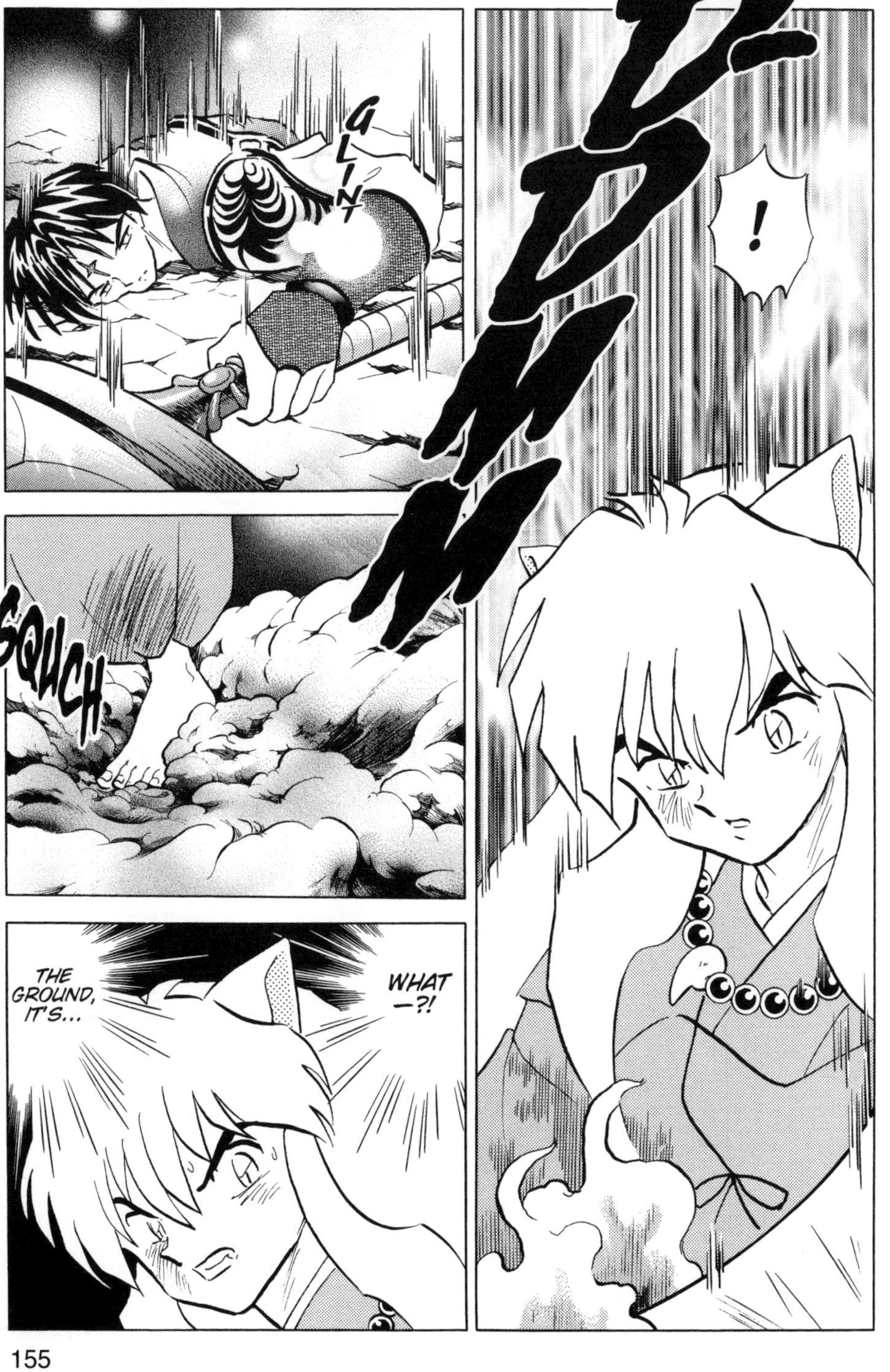
D-DMMM
!
GLINT
SQUCH
WHAT —?!
THE GROUND, IT'S...

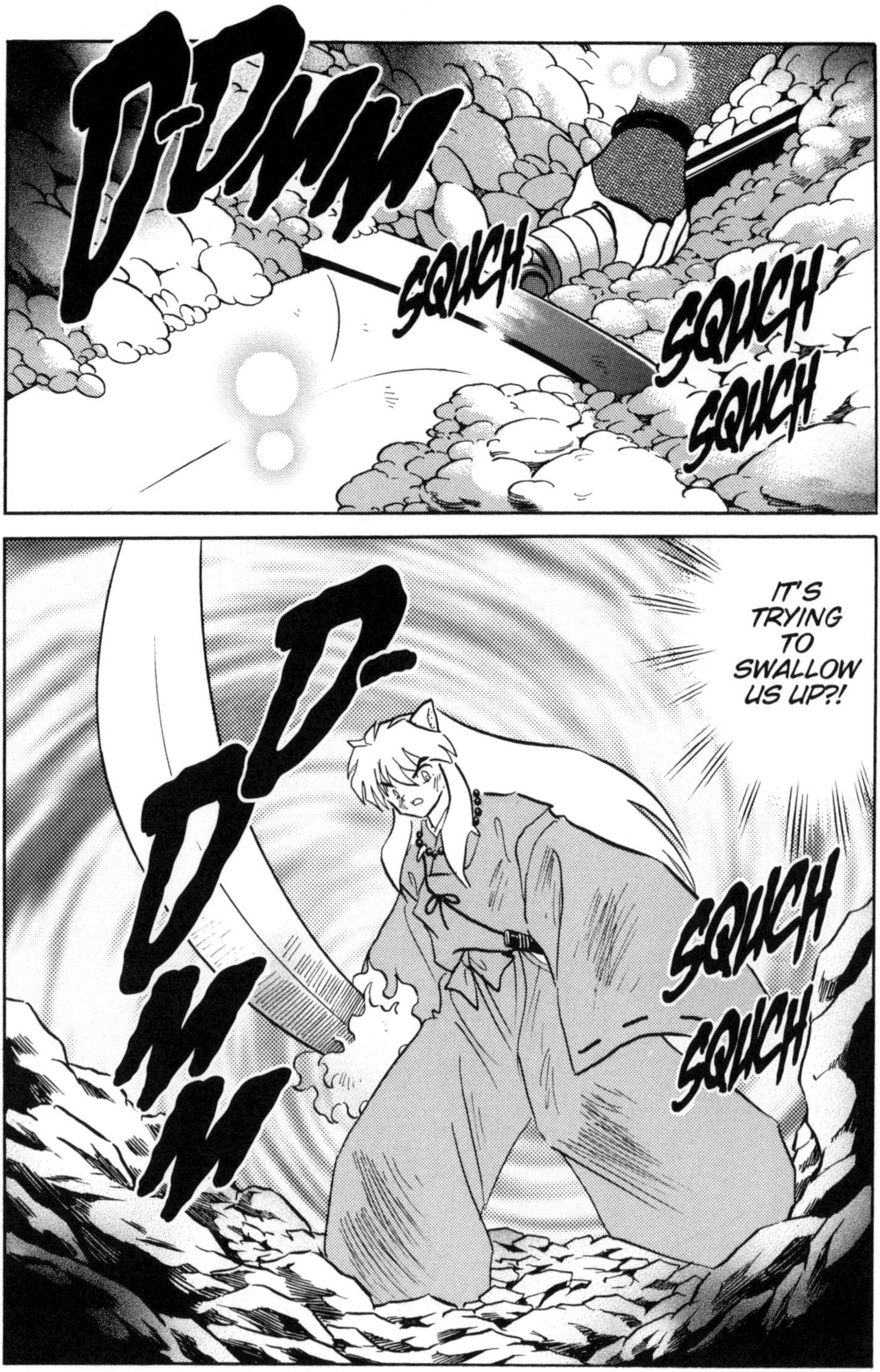
D-DMM
SQUCH
SQUCH
SQUCH
IT'S TRYING TO SWALLOW US UP?!
D-D-D-MMM
SQUCH
SQUCH

SCROLL NINE
THE WALL OF FLESH

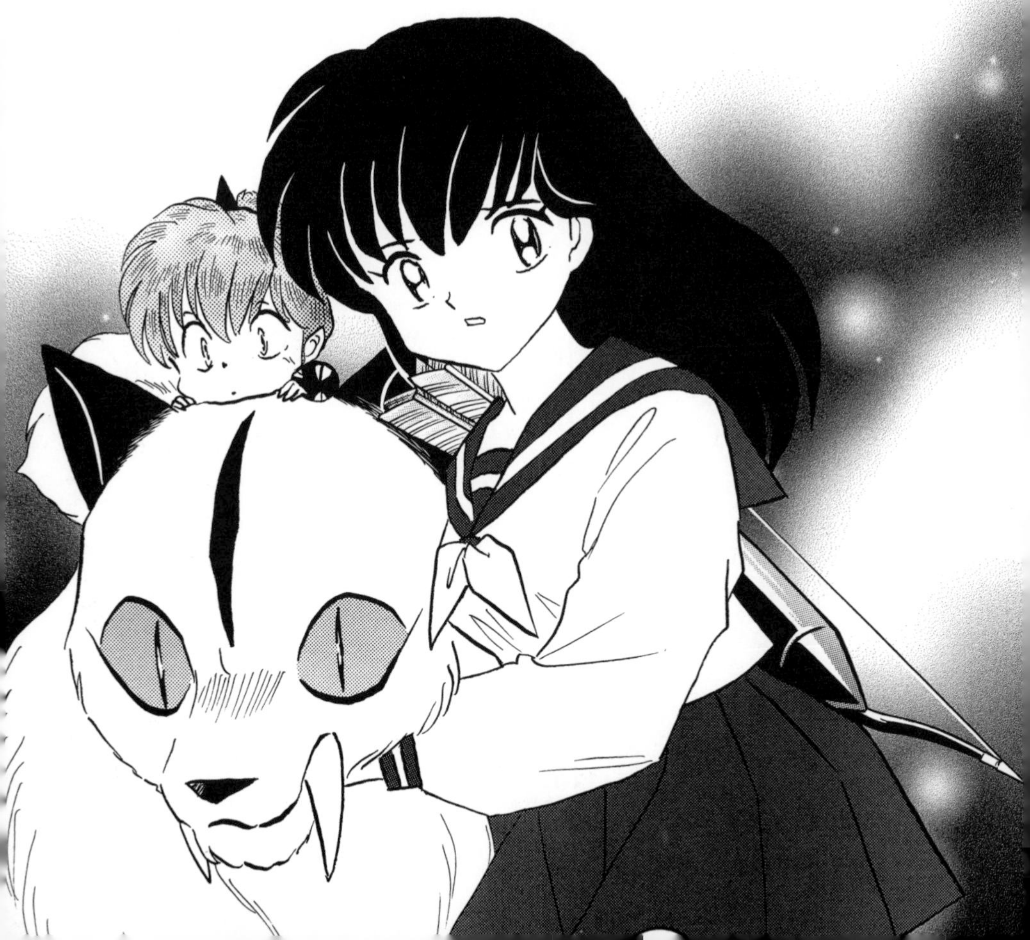

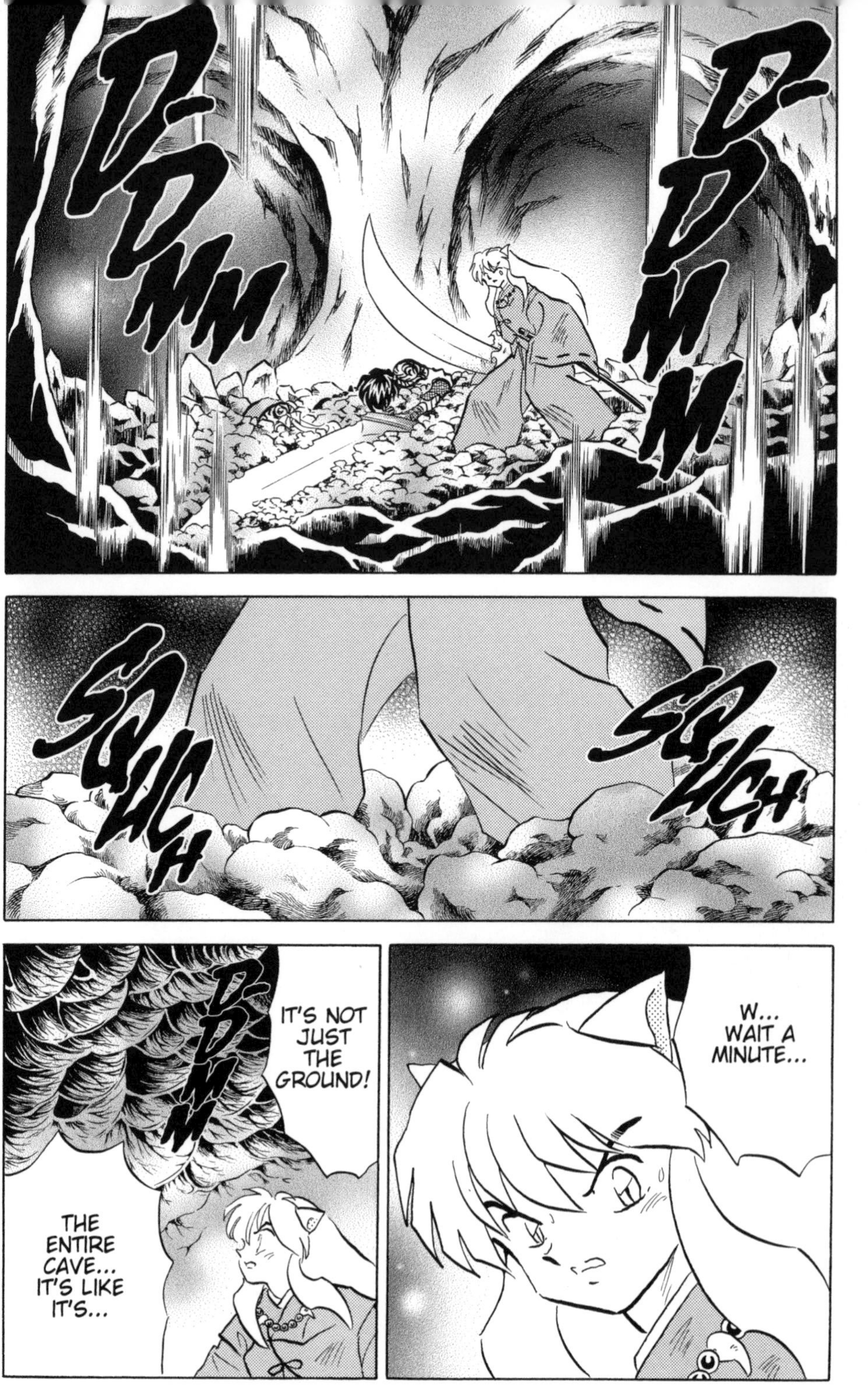
D-DUMMM
D-DUMM
SQUCH
SQUCH
W... WAIT A MINUTE...
D-DUMM
IT'S NOT JUST THE GROUND!
THE ENTIRE CAVE... IT'S LIKE IT'S...

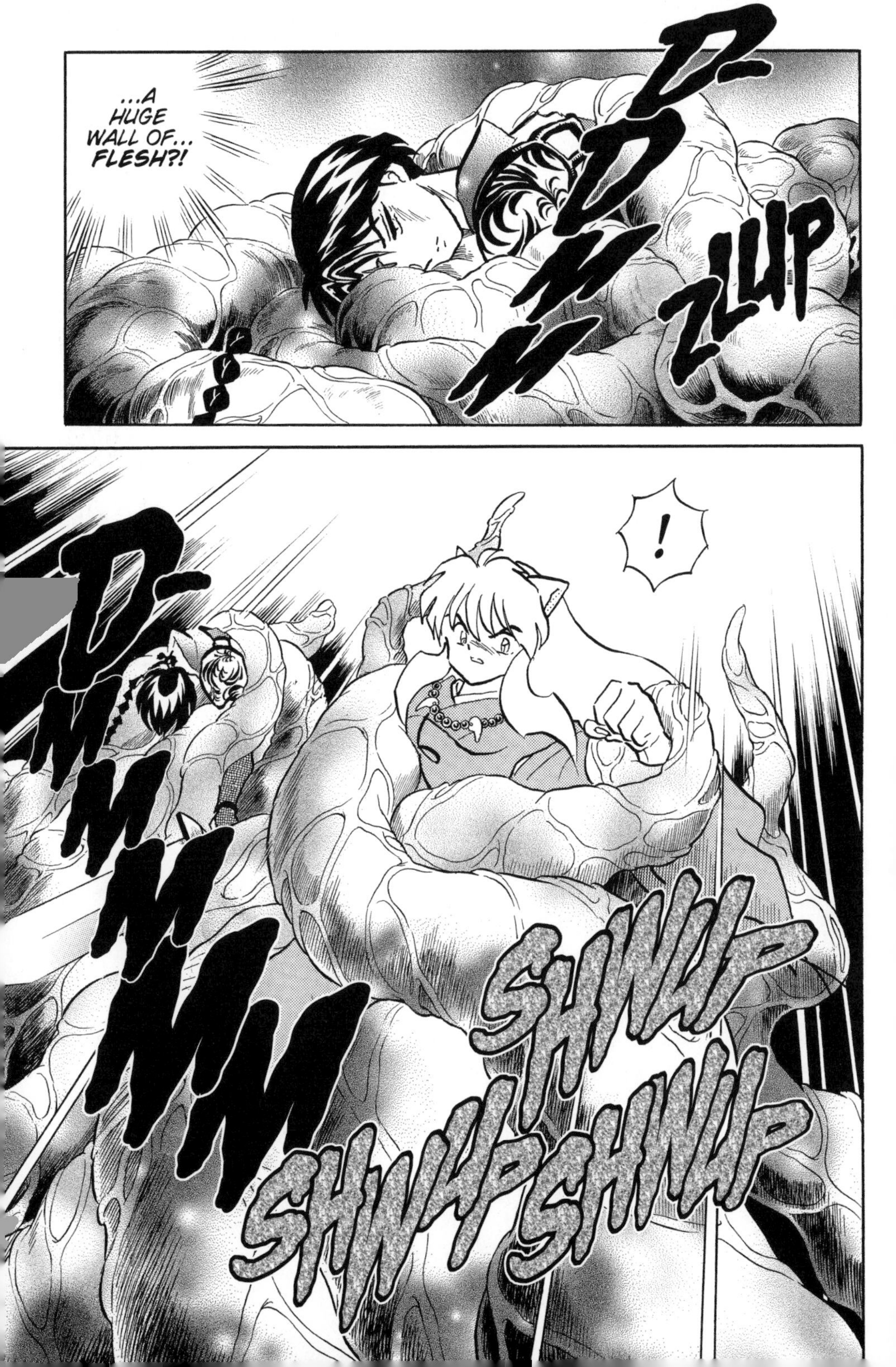
...A HUGE WALL OF... FLESH?!
D-DMM
ZLUP
!
D-MMMMM
SHWUP
SHWUP SHWUP

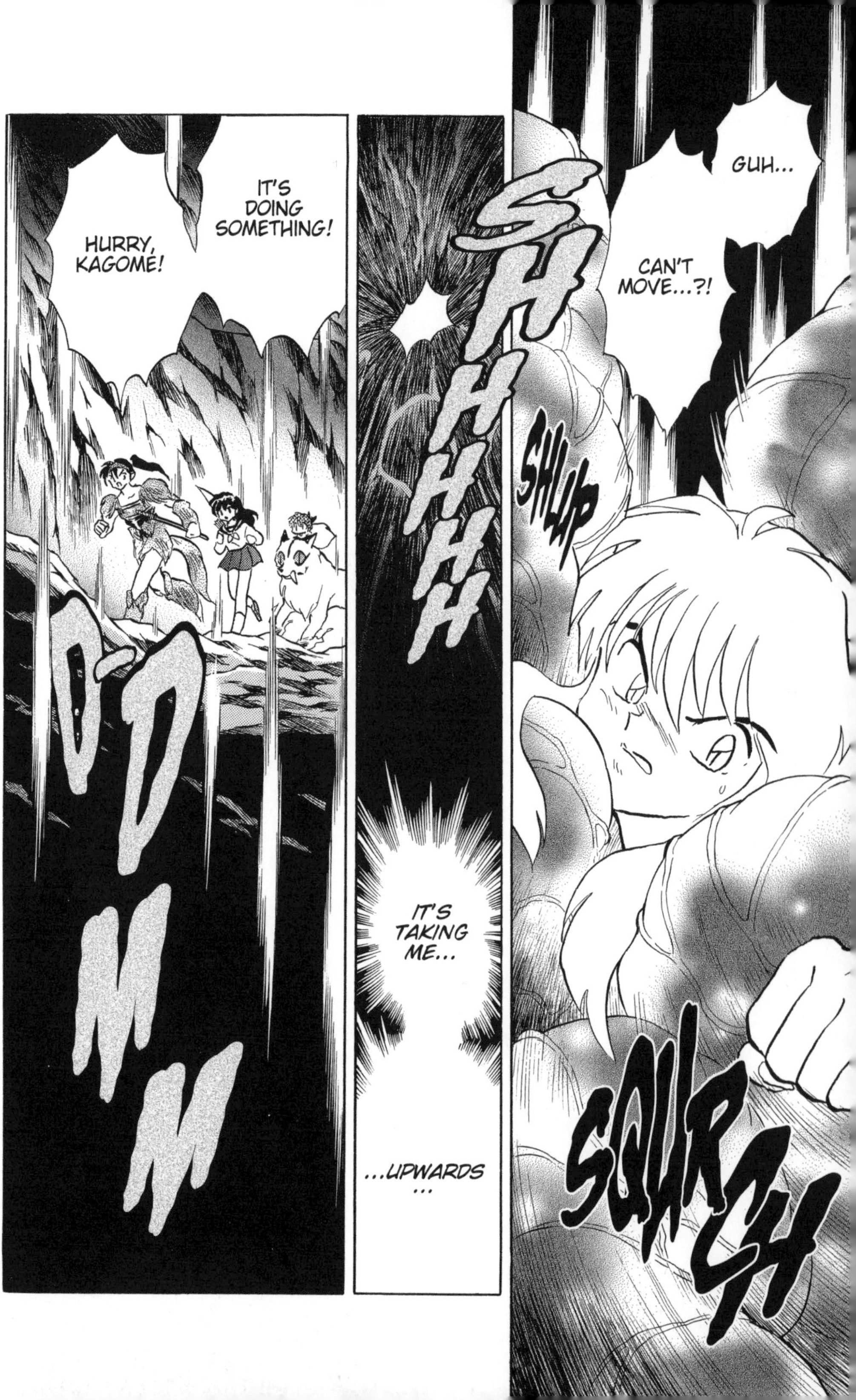
GUH...
CAN'T MOVE...?!
SHLUP
SQUIRCH
SHHHHH
IT'S TAKING ME...
...UPWARDS...
IT'S DOING SOMETHING!
HURRY, KAGOME!
D-DMMM

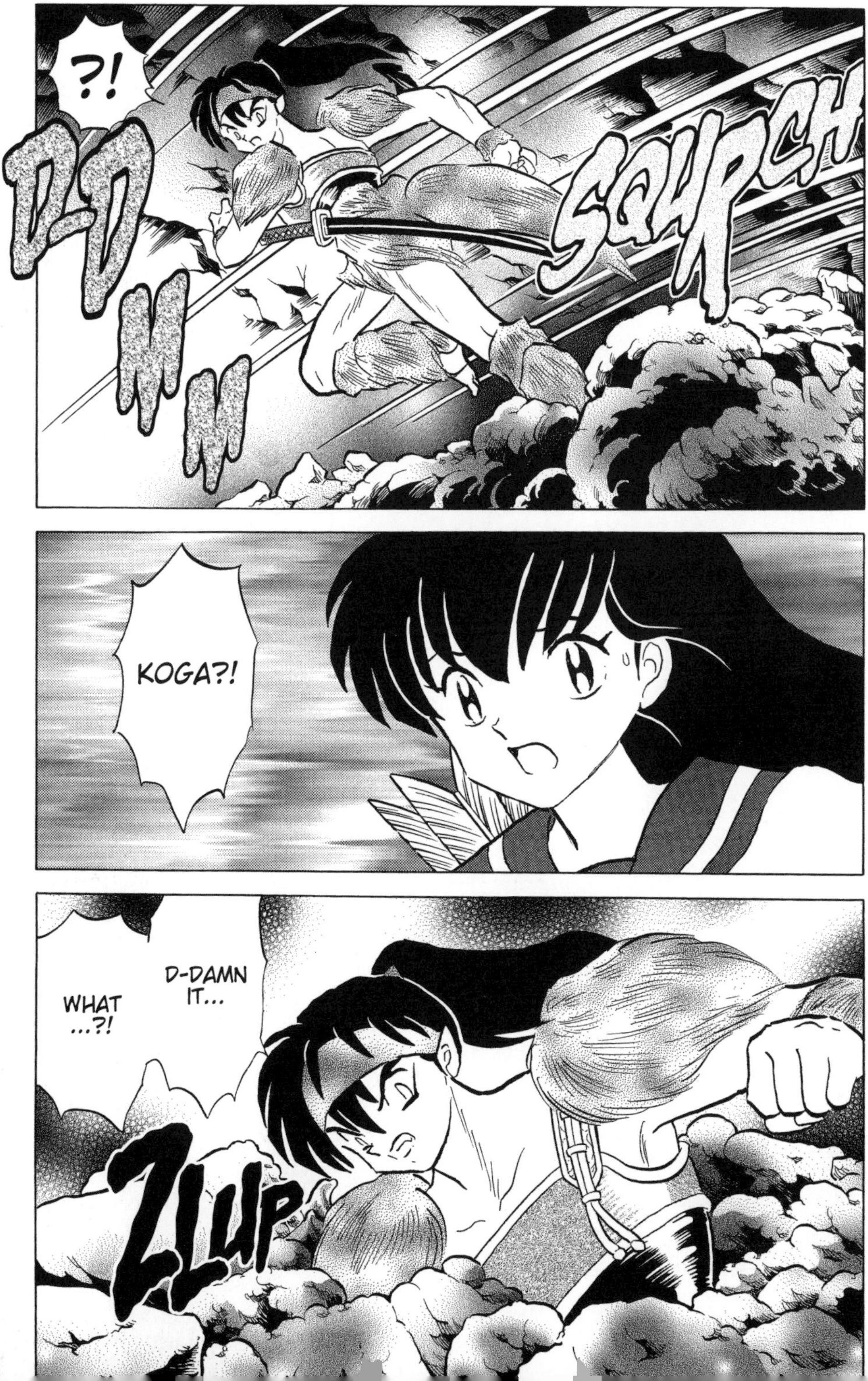
?!
D-D
MMM
SQUPCH
KOGA?!
D-DAMN IT...
WHAT ...?!
ZLUP

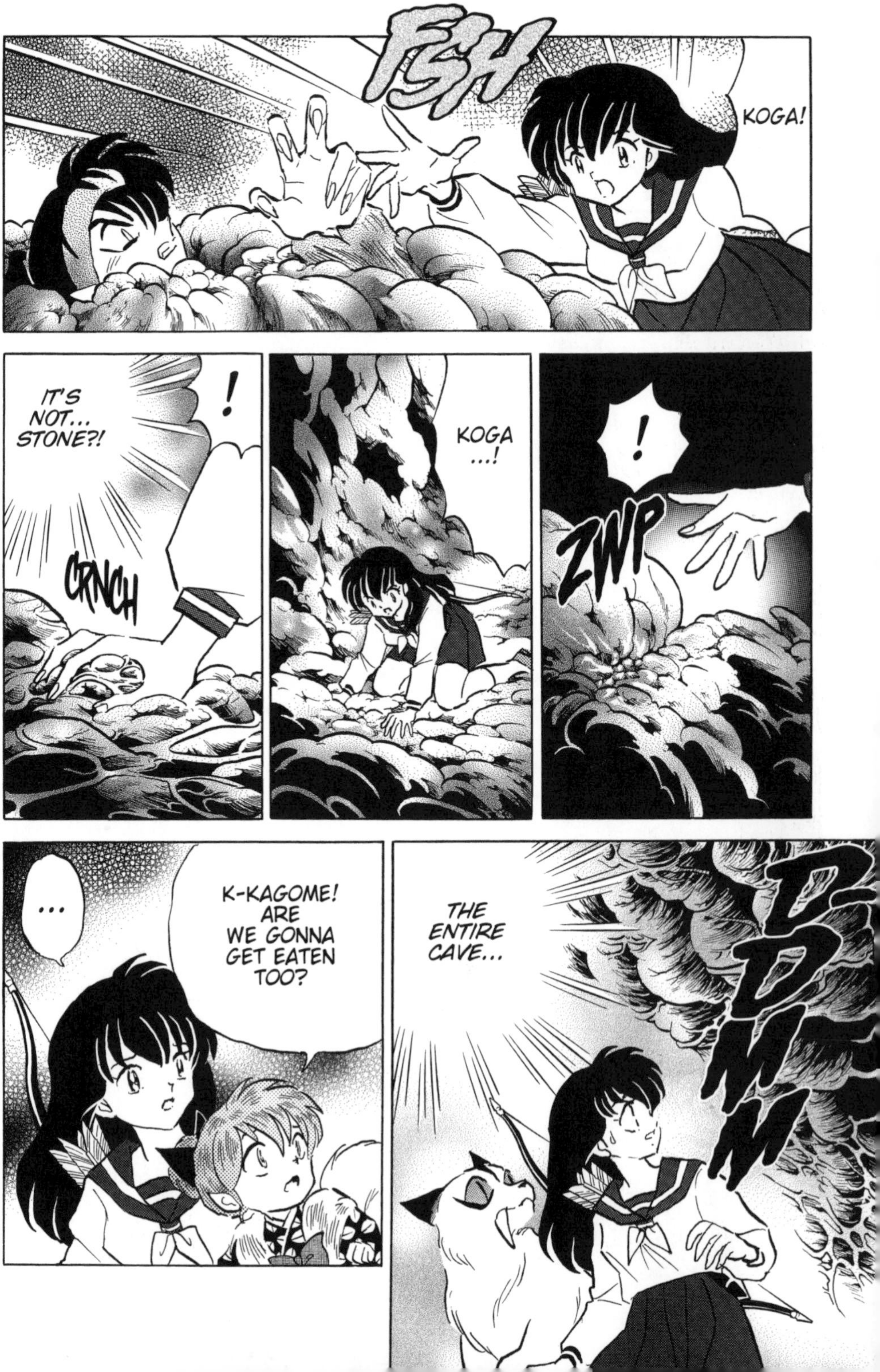
FSH
KOGA!
!
ZWP
KOGA ...!
!
IT'S NOT... STONE?!
CRNCH
THE ENTIRE CAVE...
K-KAGOME! ARE WE GONNA GET EATEN TOO?
...

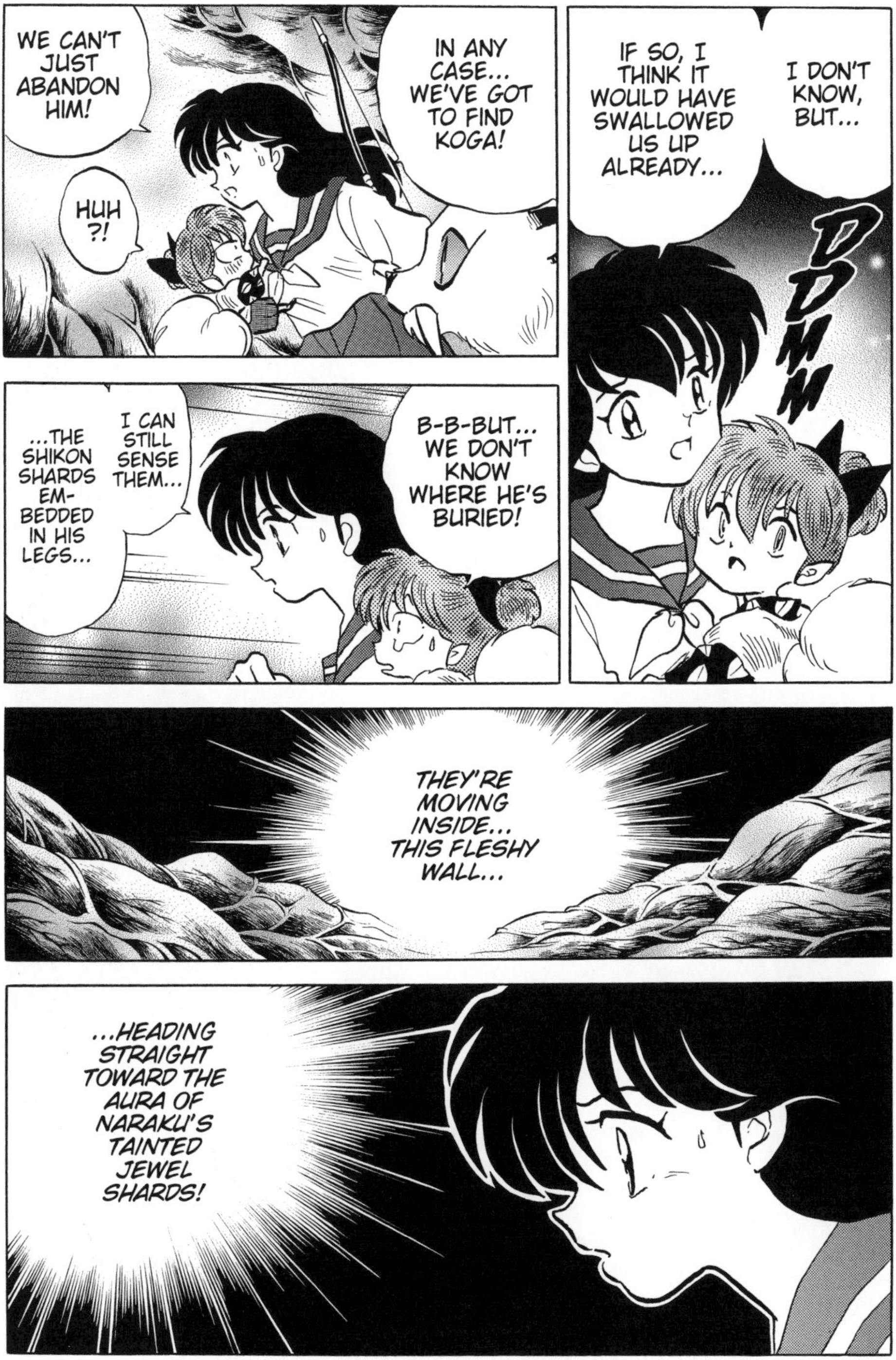
I DON'T KNOW, BUT...
IF SO, I THINK IT WOULD HAVE SWALLOWED US UP ALREADY...
DDMM
IN ANY CASE... WE'VE GOT TO FIND KOGA!
WE CAN'T JUST ABANDON HIM!
HUH?!
B-B-BUT... WE DON'T KNOW WHERE HE'S BURIED!
I CAN STILL SENSE THEM...
...THE SHIKON SHARDS EM-BEDDED IN HIS LEGS...
THEY'RE MOVING INSIDE... THIS FLESHY WALL...
...HEADING STRAIGHT TOWARD THE AURA OF NARAKU'S TAINTED JEWEL SHARDS!

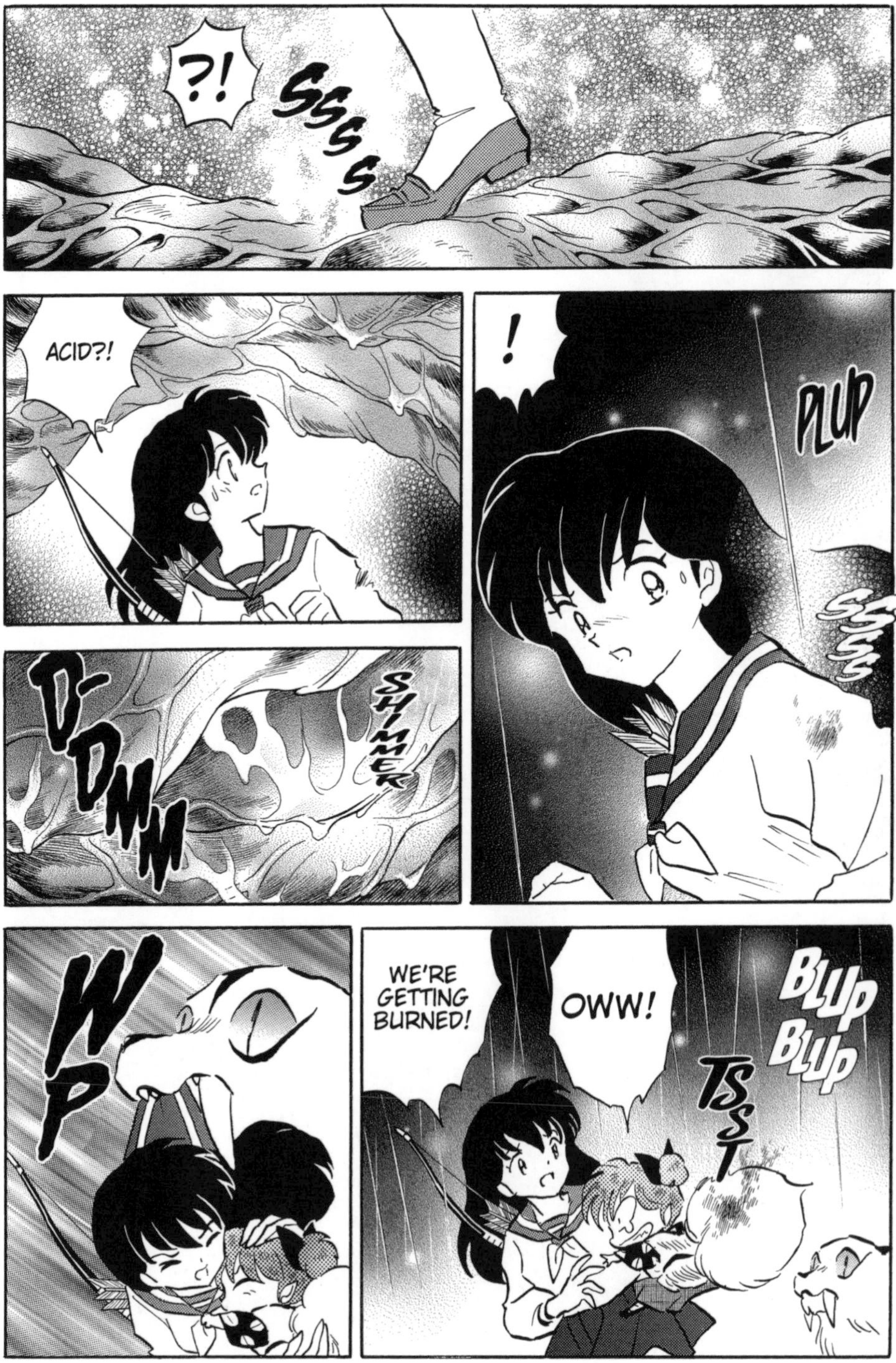
?!
SSSSS
!
PLUP
SSSSS
ACID?!
D-DMM
SHIMMER
BLUP BLUP
OWW!
TSST
WE'RE GETTING BURNED!
WP

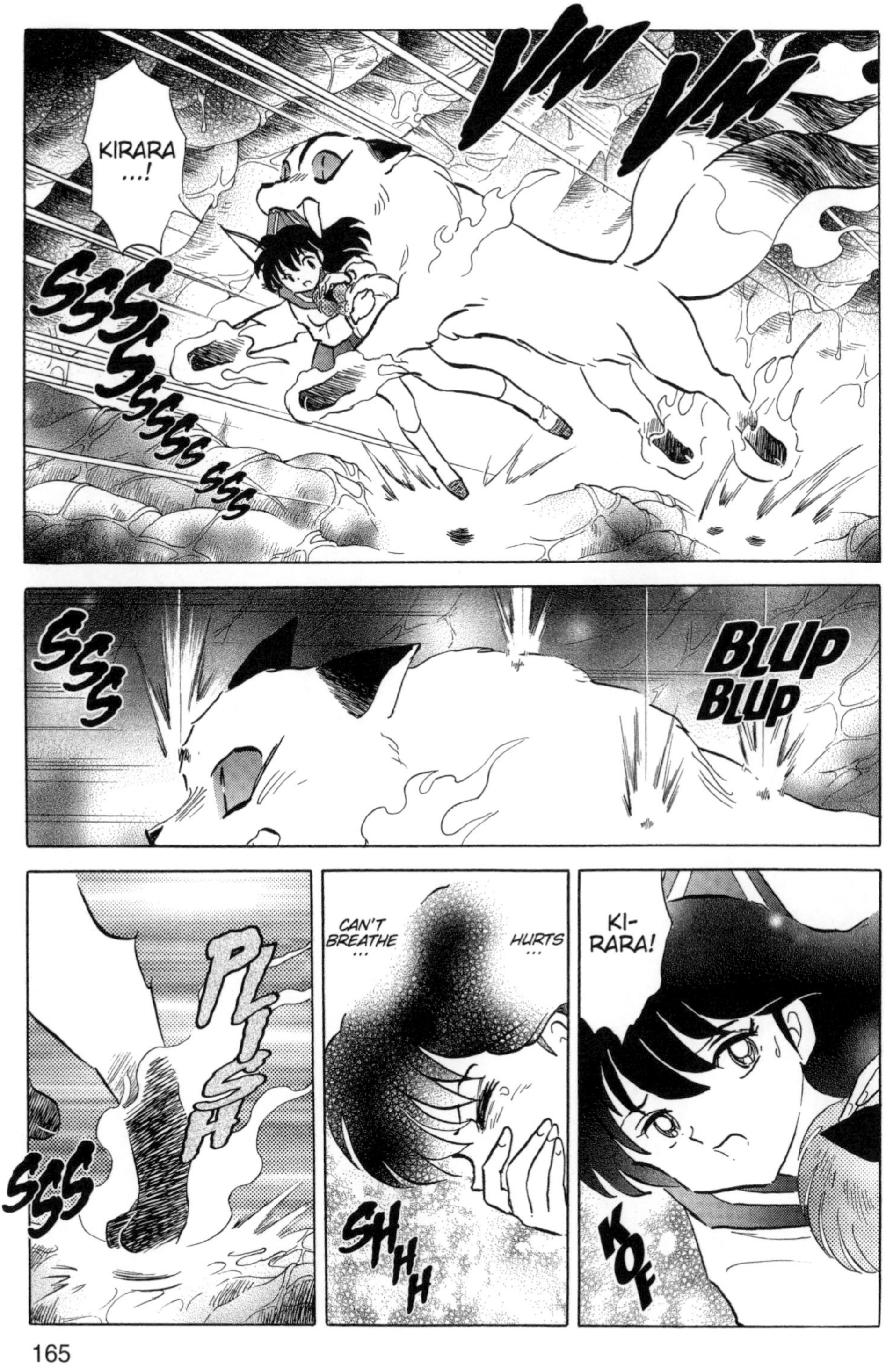
VM VM
KIRARA ...!
SSSSSSSSSSS SSS
BLUP BLUP
SSSS
KI-RARA!
KOF
HURTS ...
CAN'T BREATHE ...
SHHH
PLISH
SSS

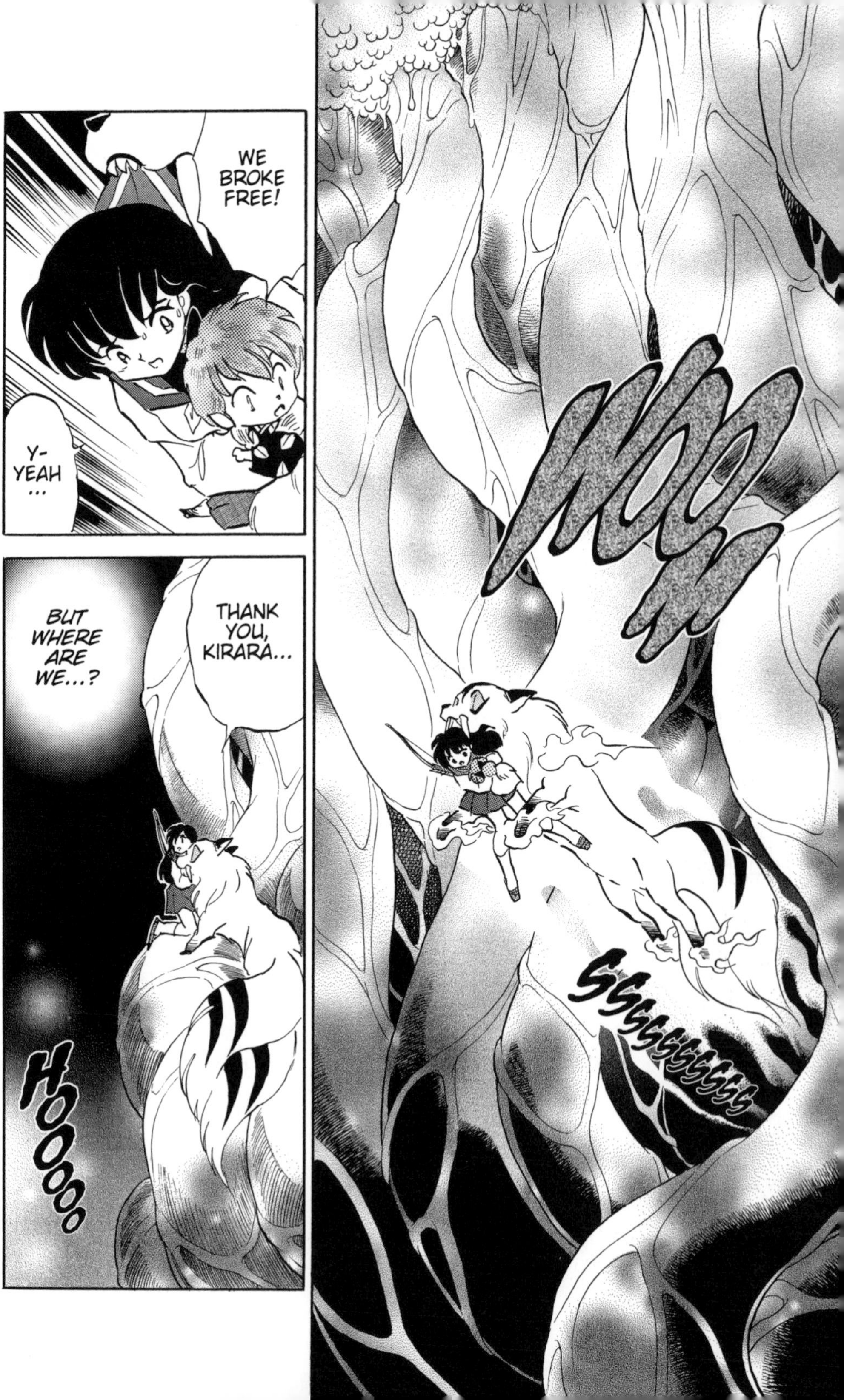
SSSSSSSSSSSS
WE BROKE FREE!
Y-YEAH...
THANK YOU, KIRARA...
BUT WHERE ARE WE...?
HOOOOOO

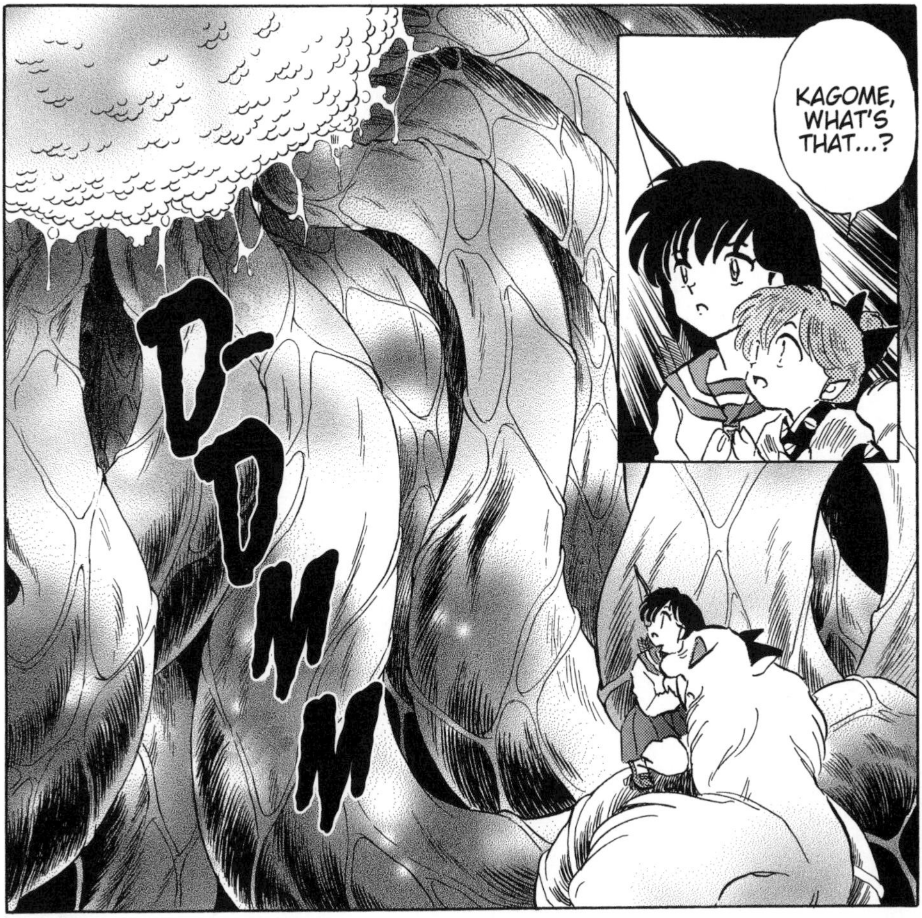
KAGOME, WHAT'S THAT...?
D-DMMM

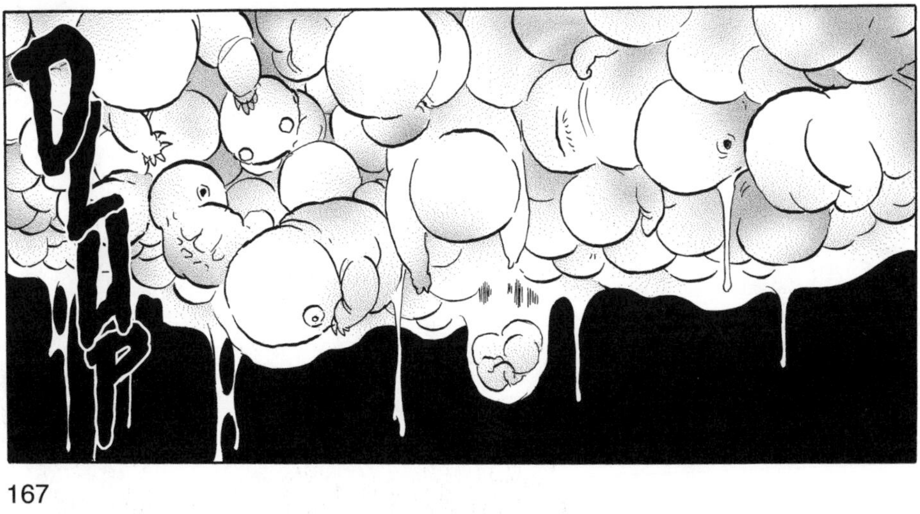
DLUP

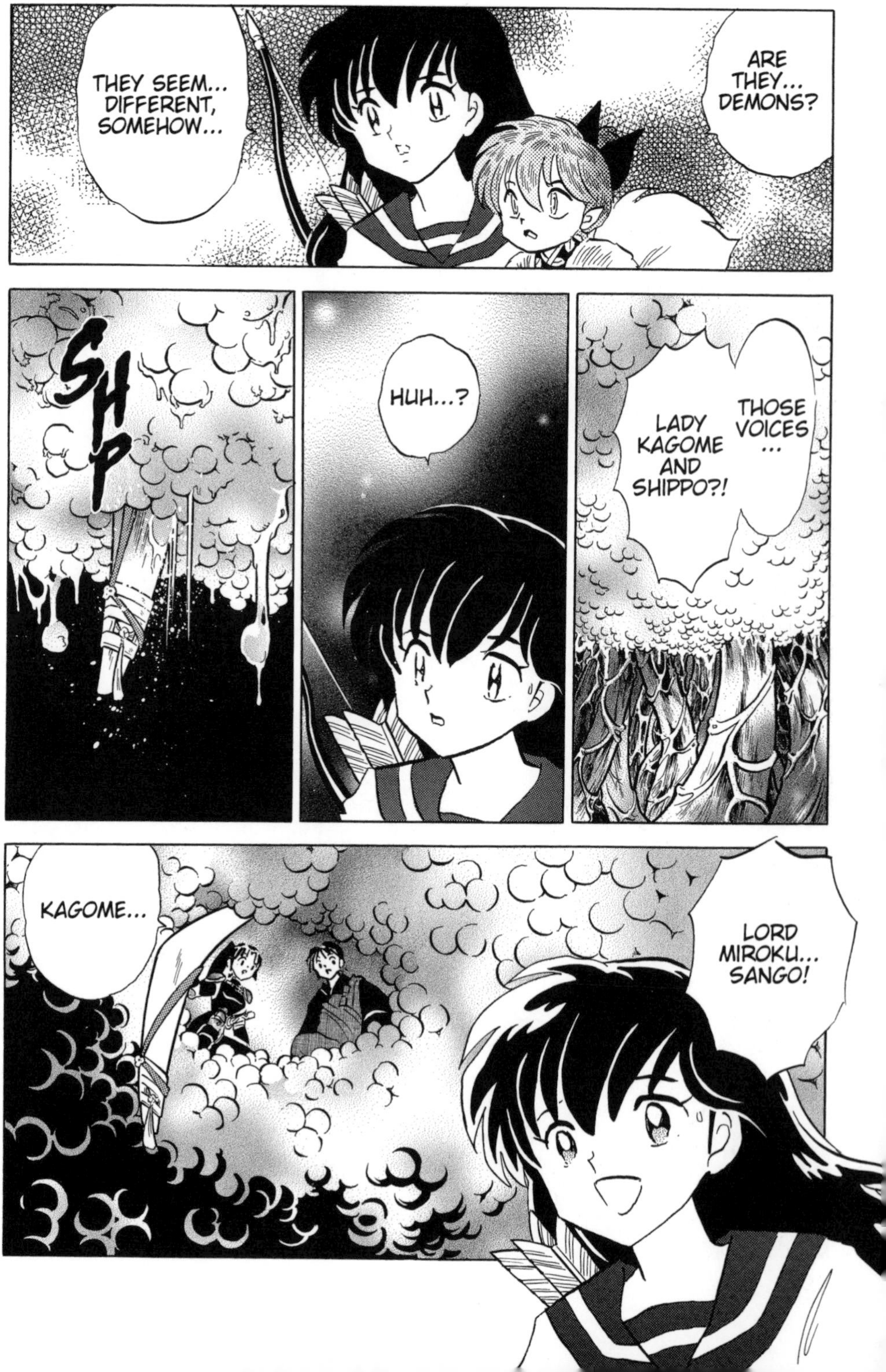
ARE THEY... DEMONS?
THEY SEEM... DIFFERENT, SOMEHOW...
THOSE VOICES ...
LADY KAGOME AND SHIPPO?!
HUH...?
SHP
LORD MIROKU... SANGO!
KAGOME...

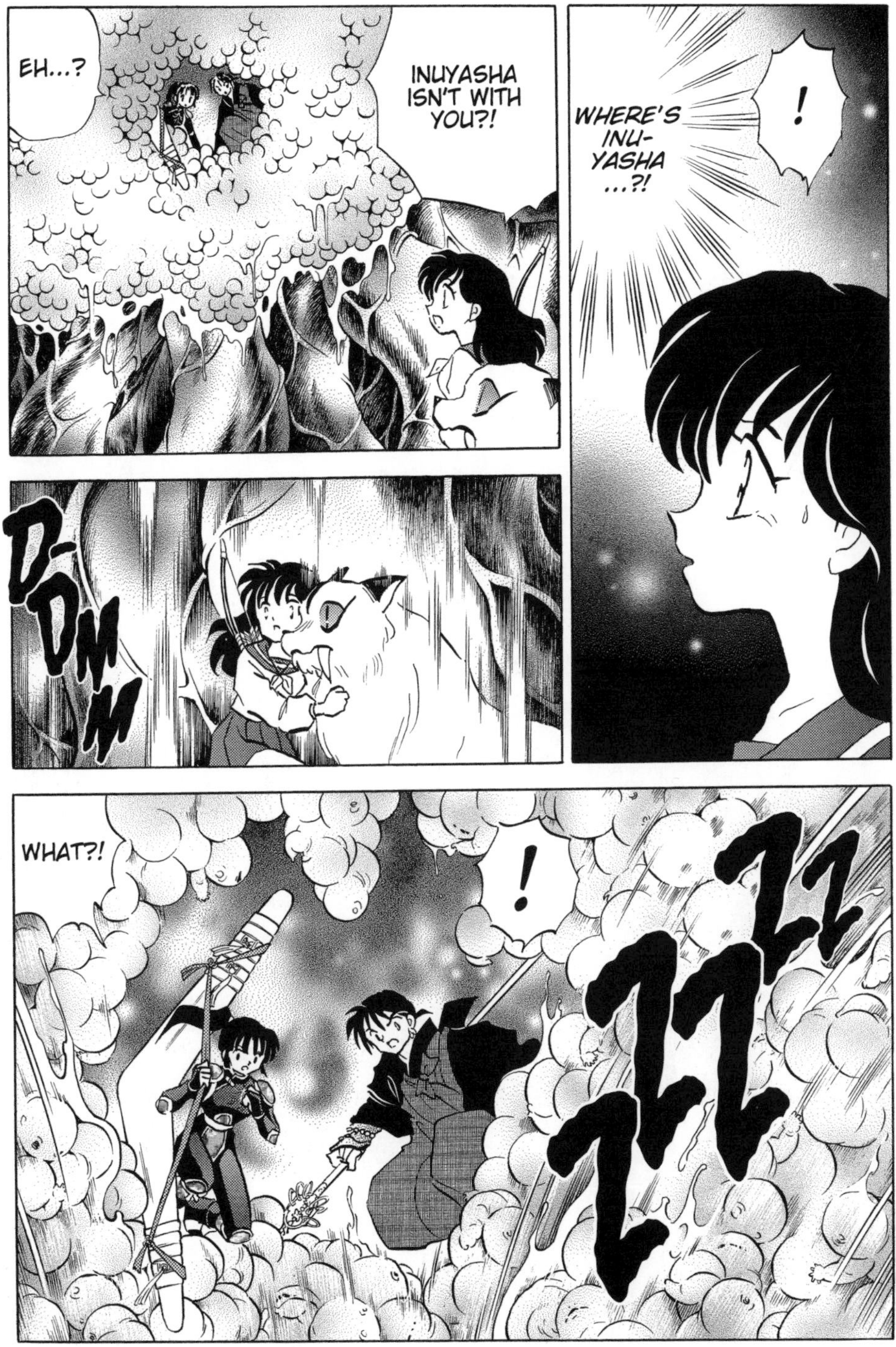
!
WHERE'S INU-YASHA ...?!
INUYASHA ISN'T WITH YOU?!
EH...?
D-DMMM
!
WHAT?!
ZZZZ

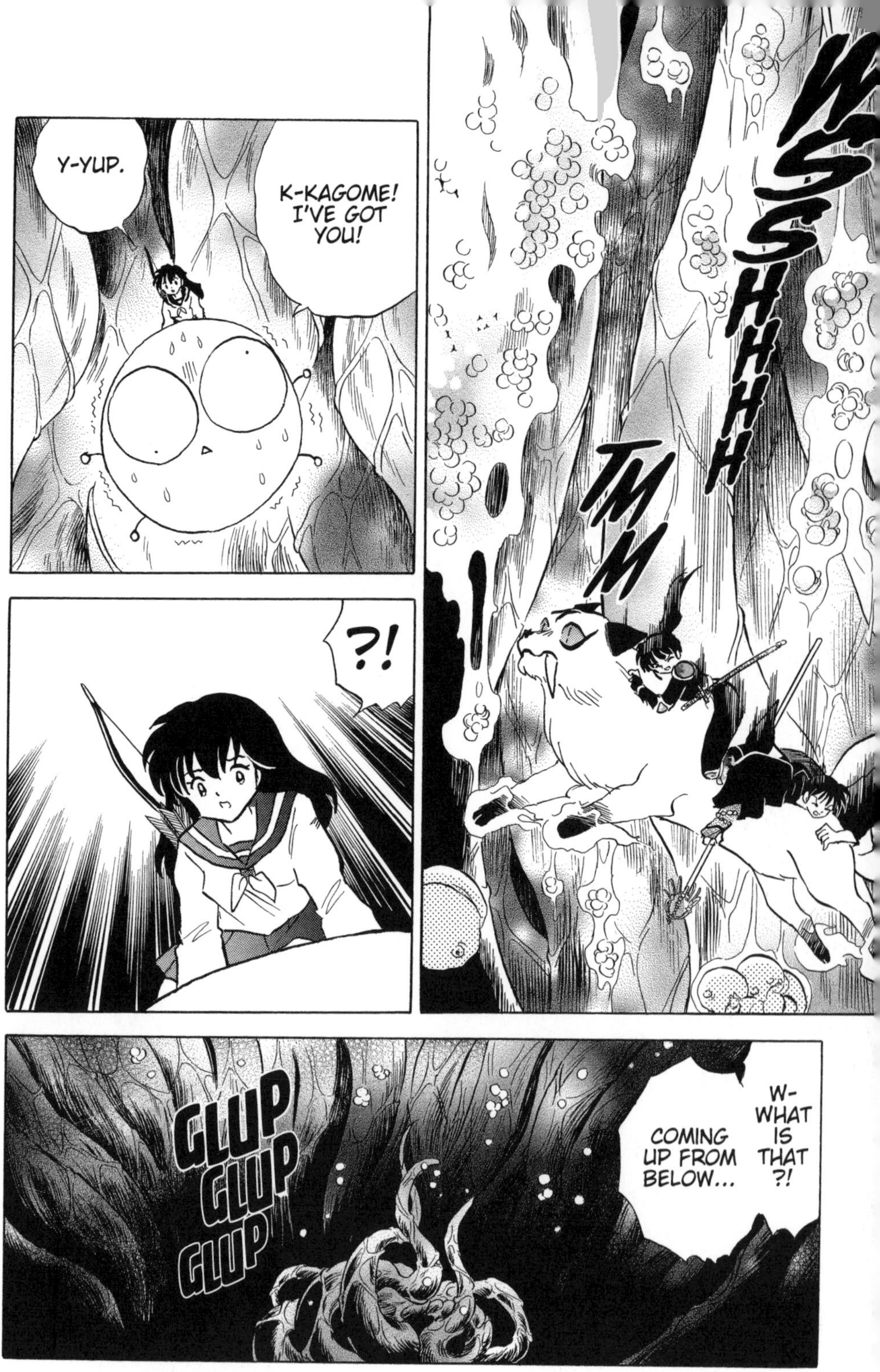
WSHHHHH
TMMM
K-KAGOME! I'VE GOT YOU!
Y-YUP.
?!
W-WHAT IS THAT?!
COMING UP FROM BELOW...
GLUP GLUP GLUP

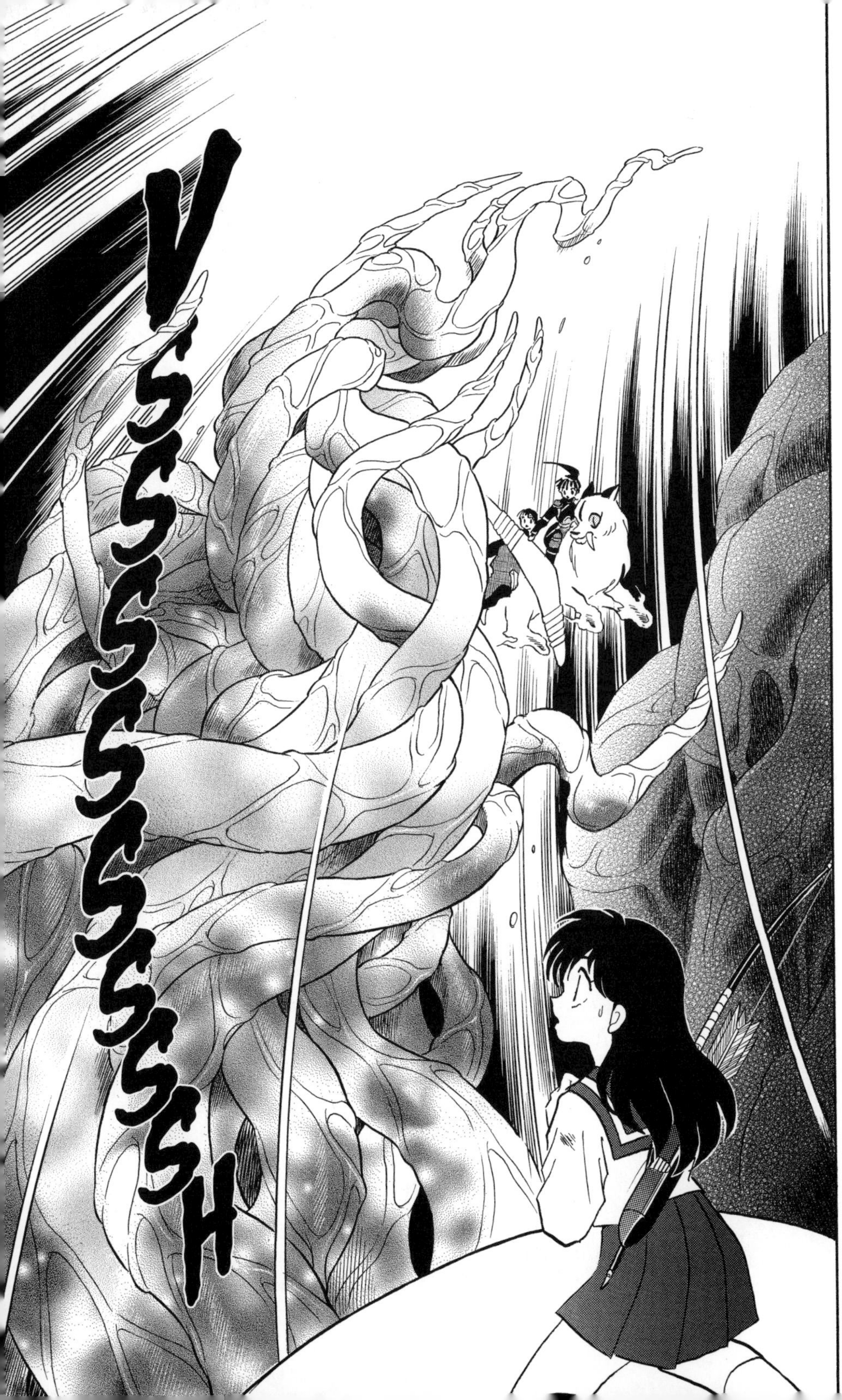
VSSSSSSSSH

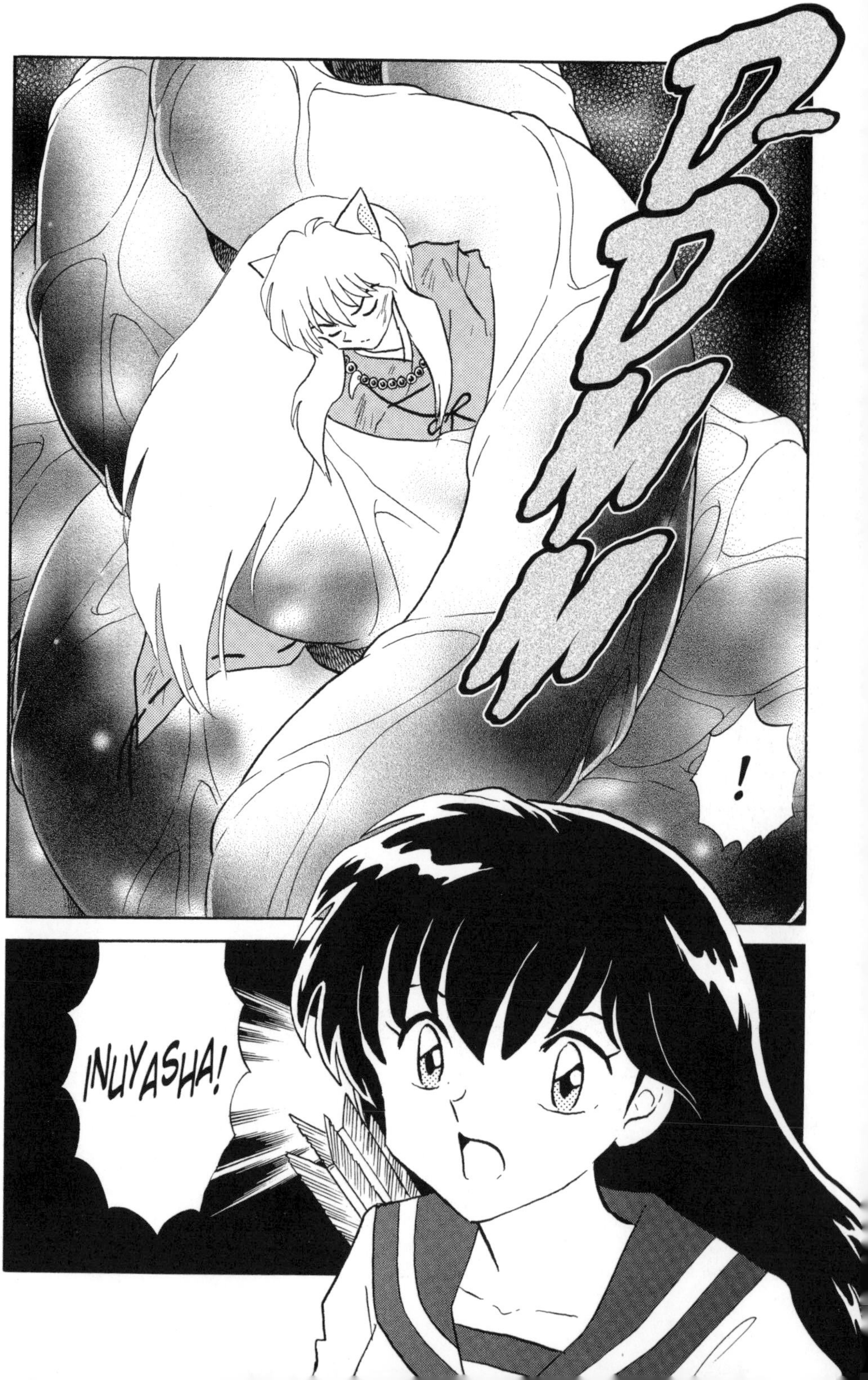
DOMMM
!
INUYASHA!

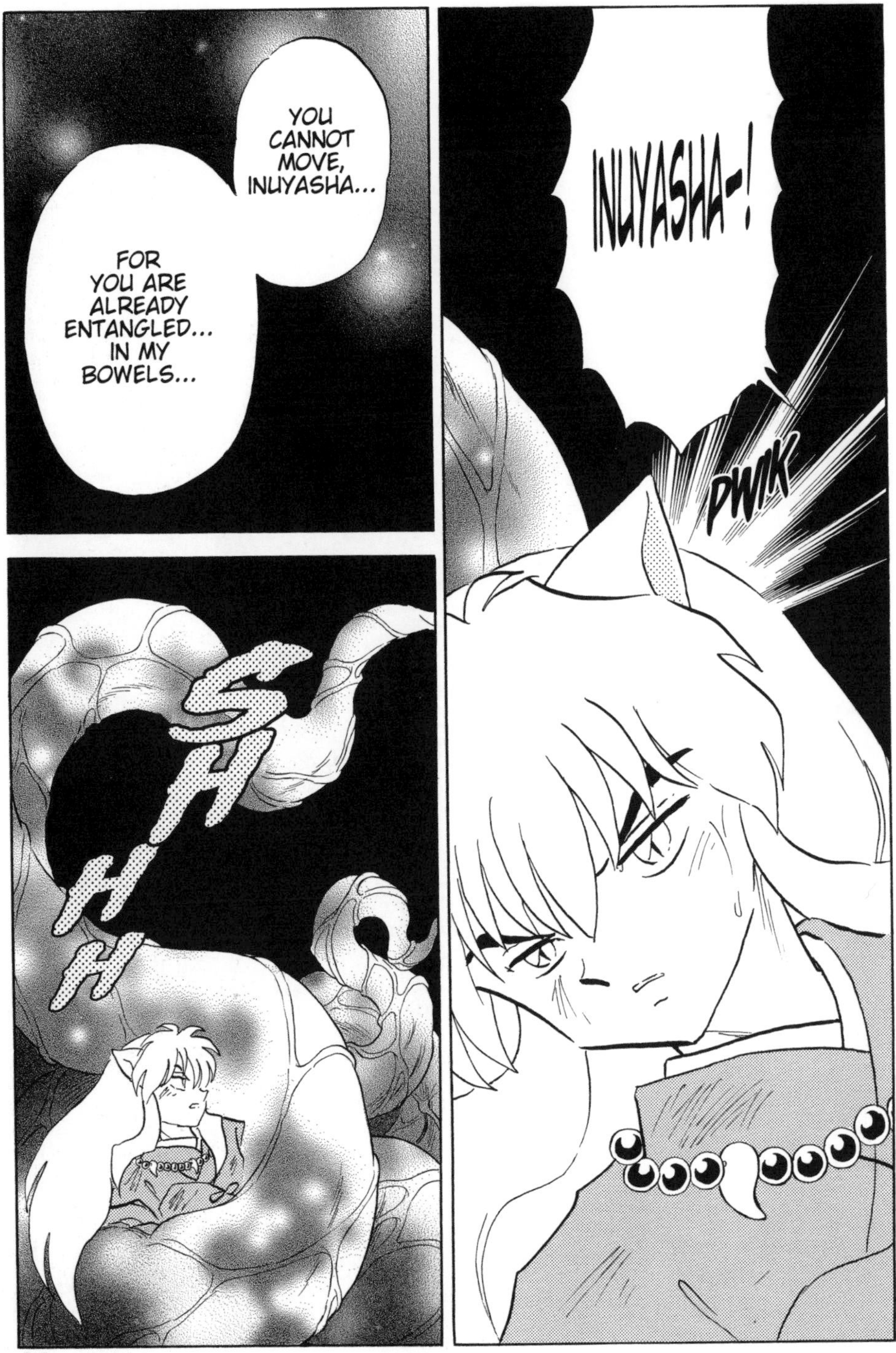
INUYASHA-!
PWIK
YOU CANNOT MOVE, INUYASHA...
FOR YOU ARE ALREADY ENTANGLED... IN MY BOWELS...
SHHHH

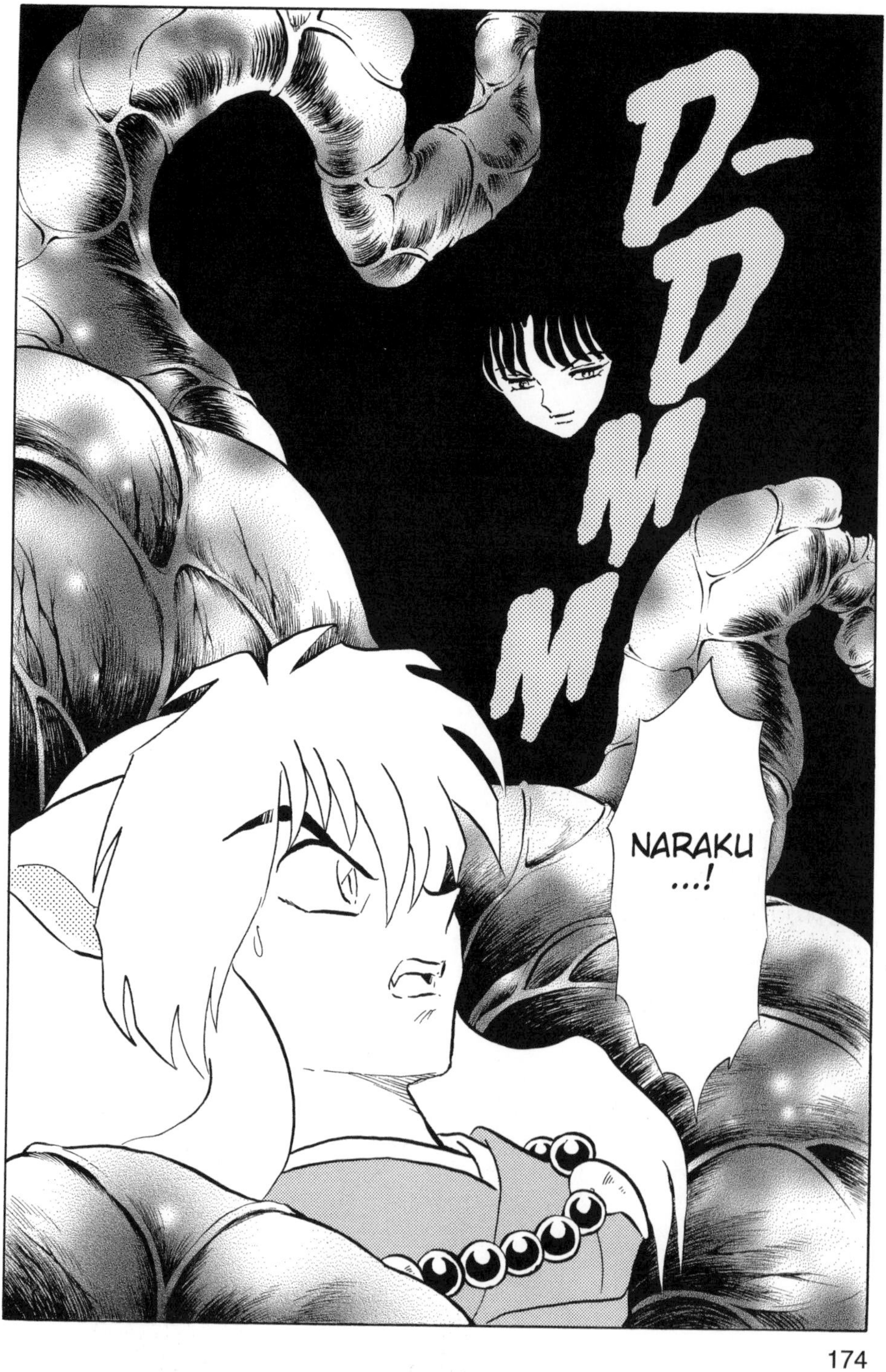
D-D-M-M-M
NARAKU ...!

SCROLL TEN
RESURRECTION

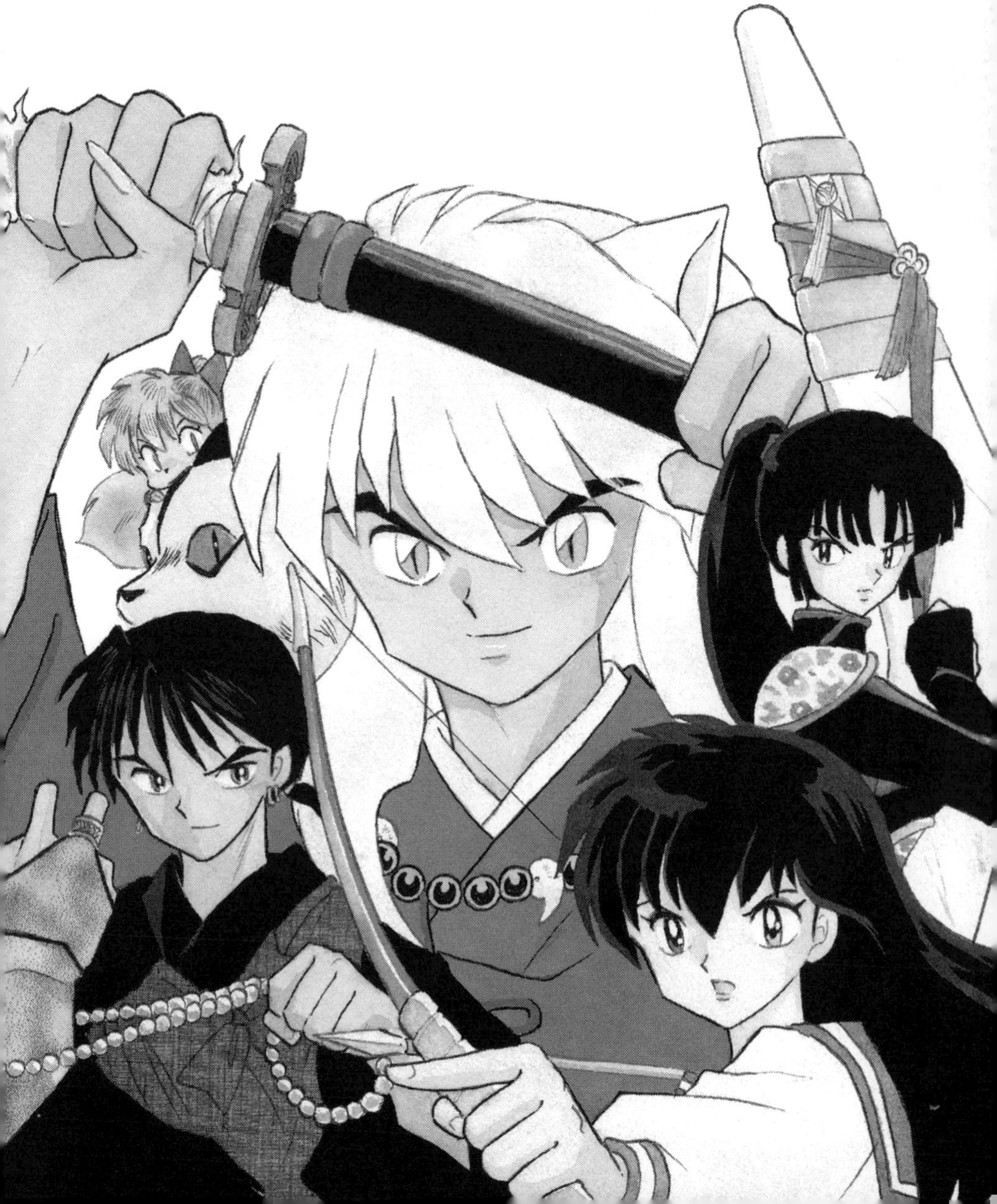

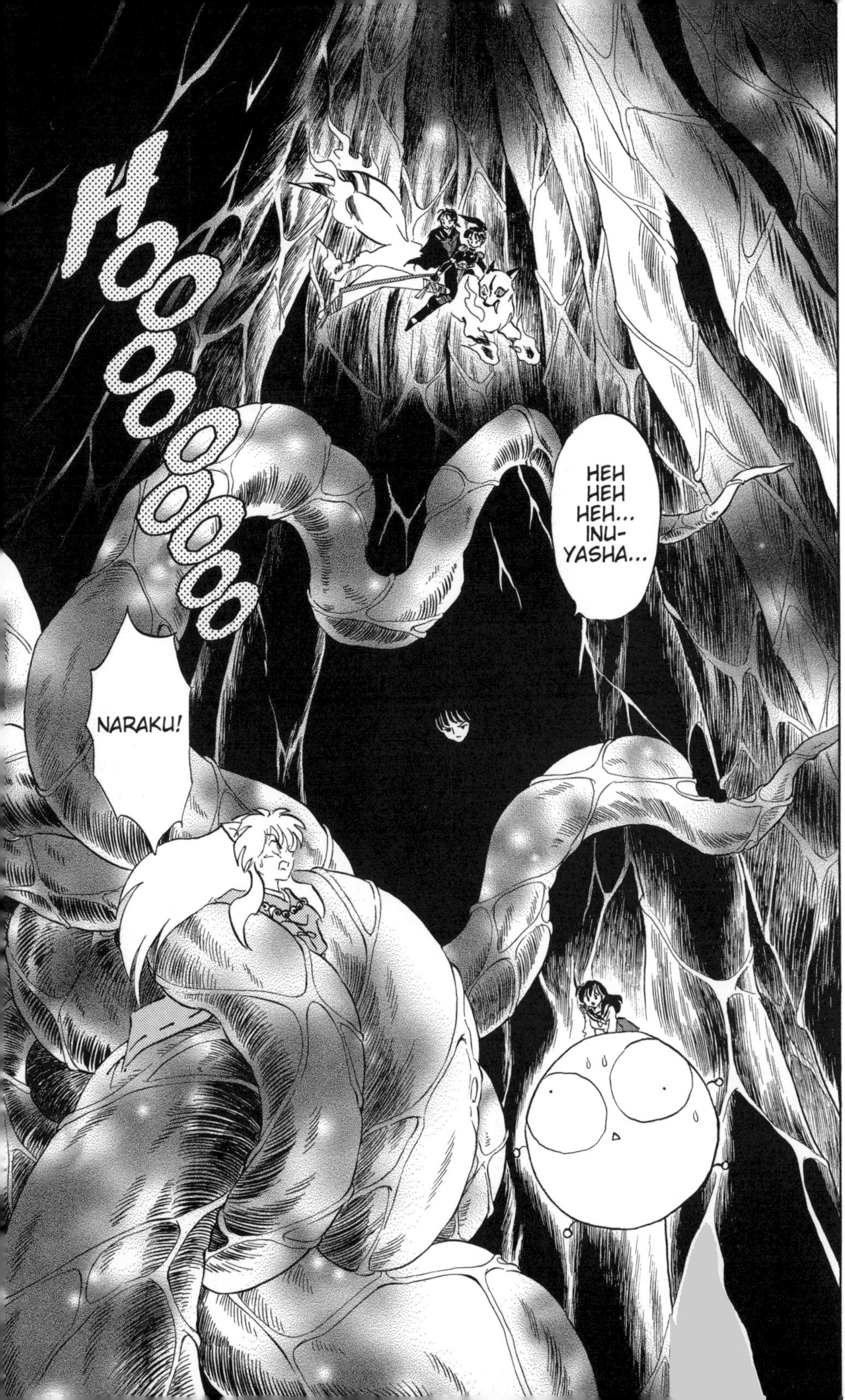
HEH
HEH
HEH... INU-YASHA...
HOOOOOOOOOO
NARAKU!

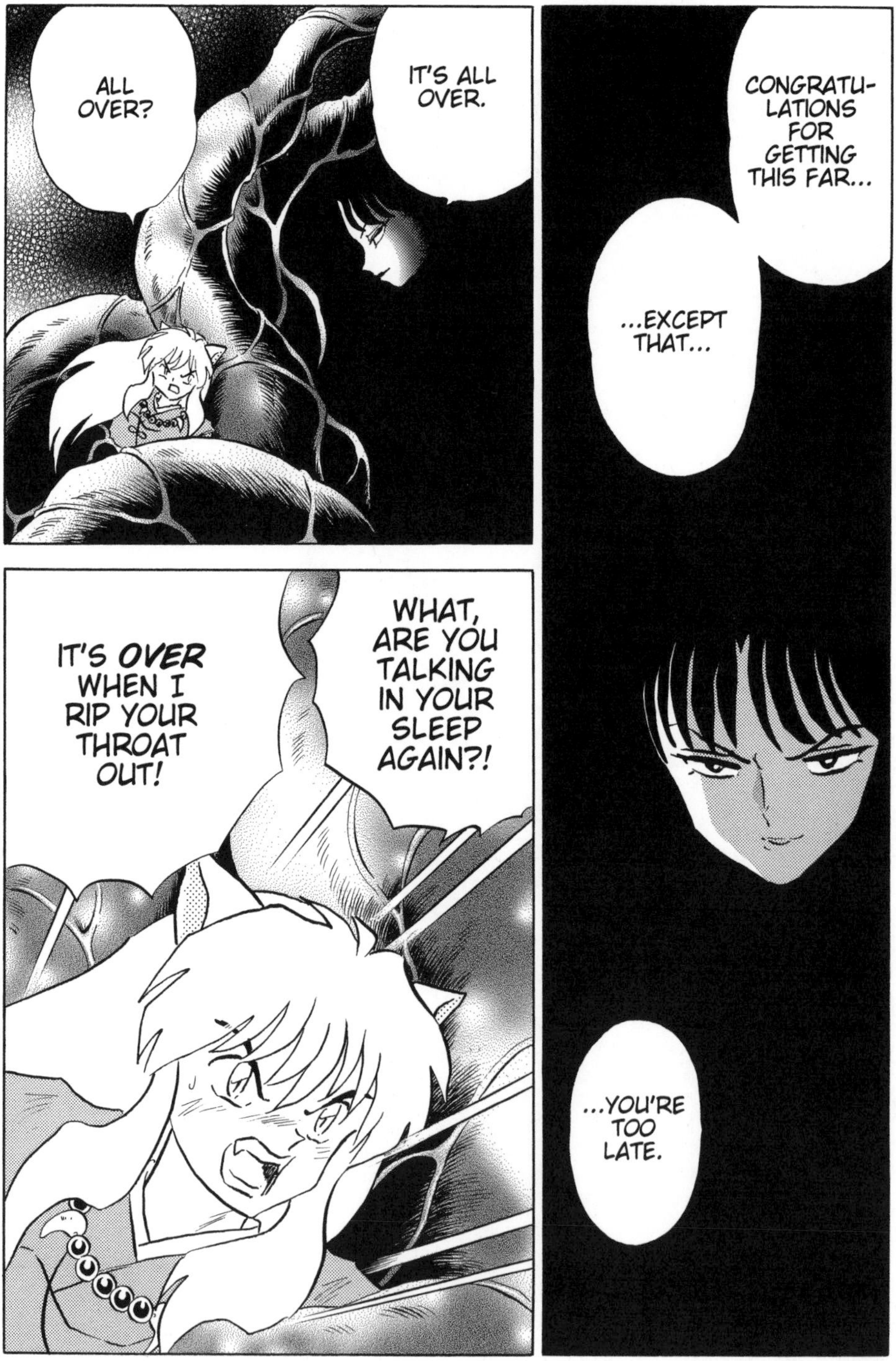
CONGRATU-LATIONS FOR GETTING THIS FAR...
...EXCEPT THAT...
...YOU'RE TOO LATE.
IT'S ALL OVER.
ALL OVER?
WHAT, ARE YOU TALKING IN YOUR SLEEP AGAIN?!
IT'S *OVER* WHEN I RIP YOUR THROAT OUT!

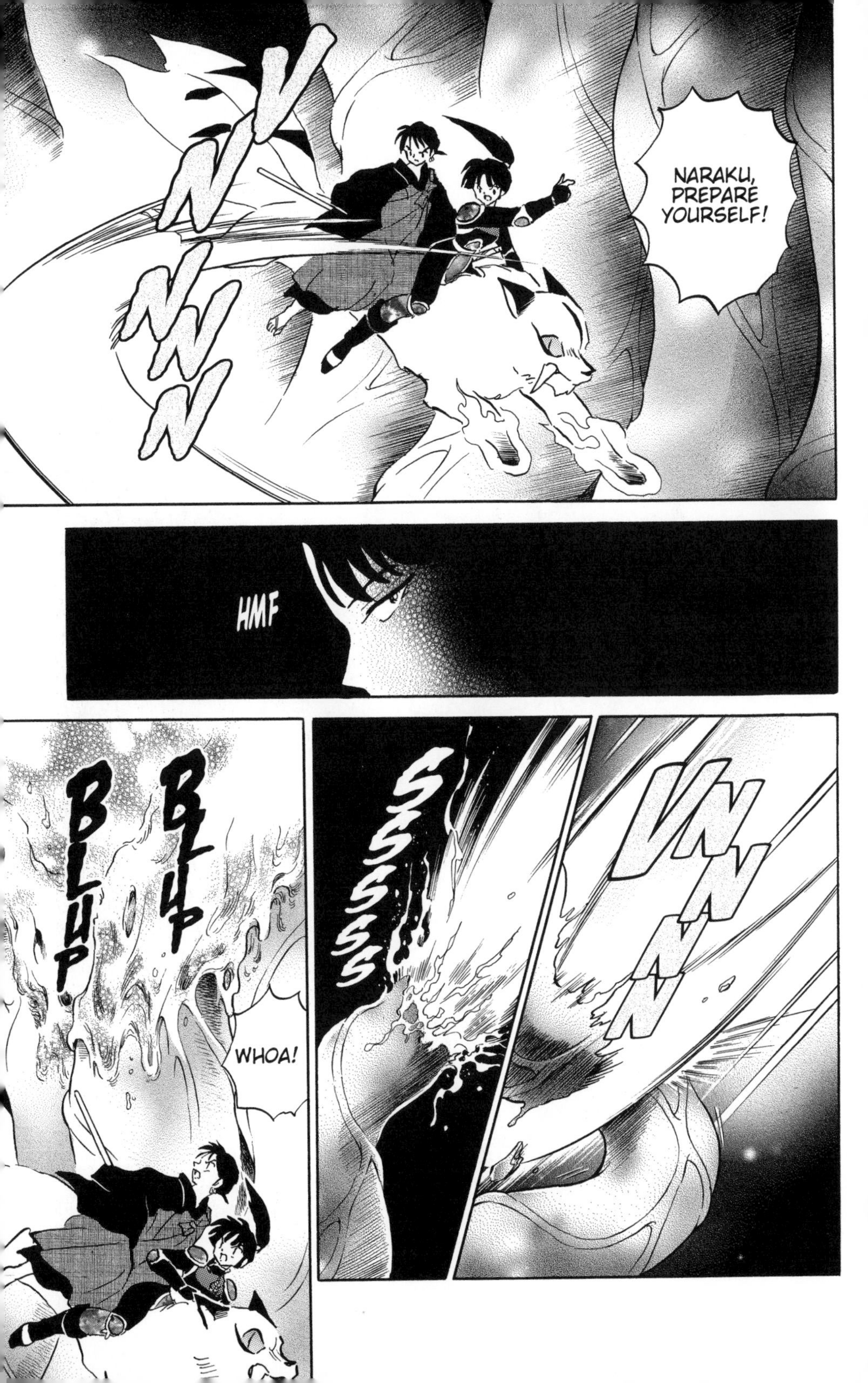
NARAKU, PREPARE YOURSELF!
HMF
SSSSSS
BLUP
BLUP
WHOA!

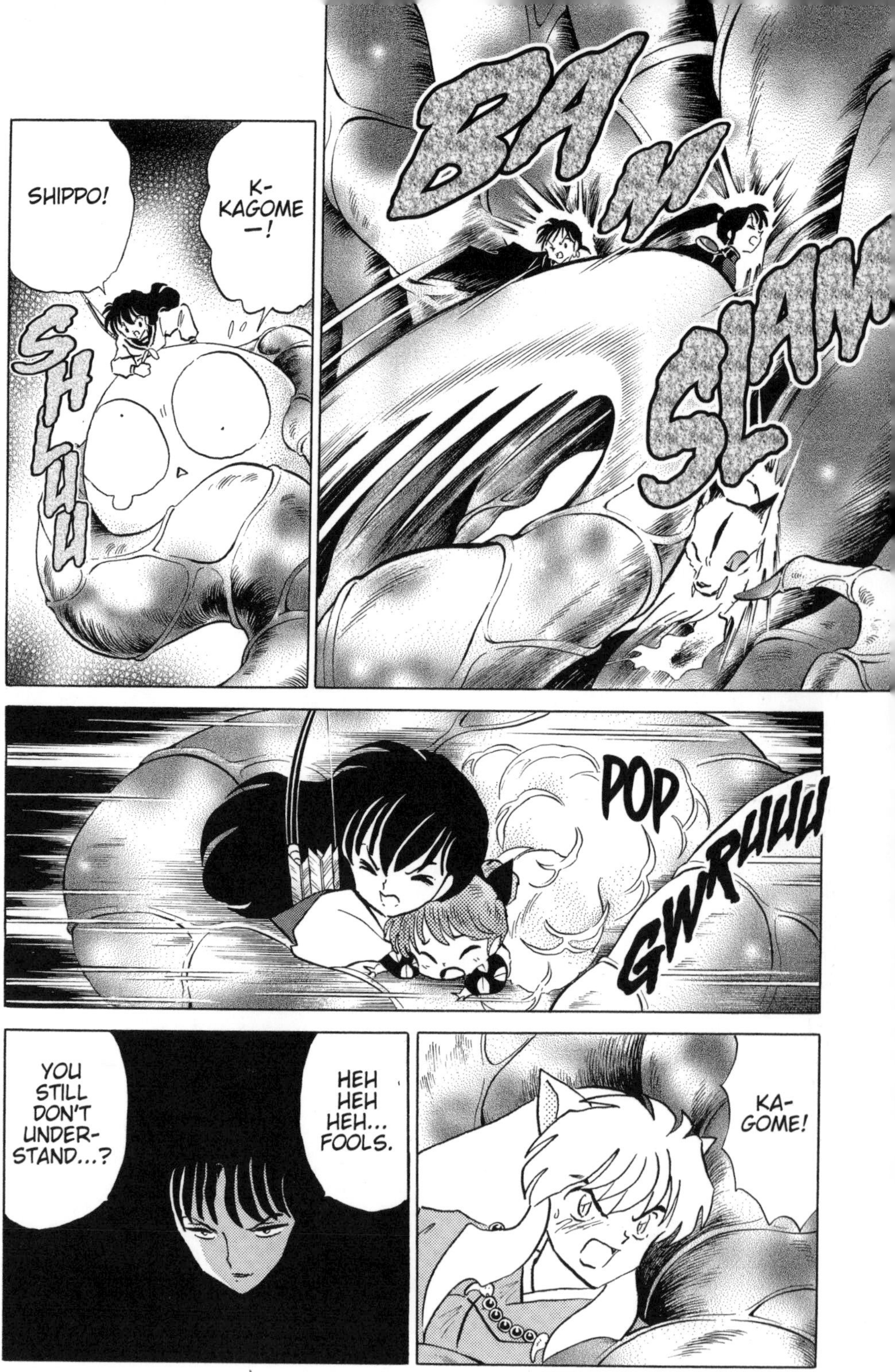
BAM
SLAM
K-KAGOME—!
SHIPPO!
SHLUUU
POP
GWRUUUU
KA-GOME!
HEH HEH HEH... FOOLS.
YOU STILL DON'T UNDER-STAND...?

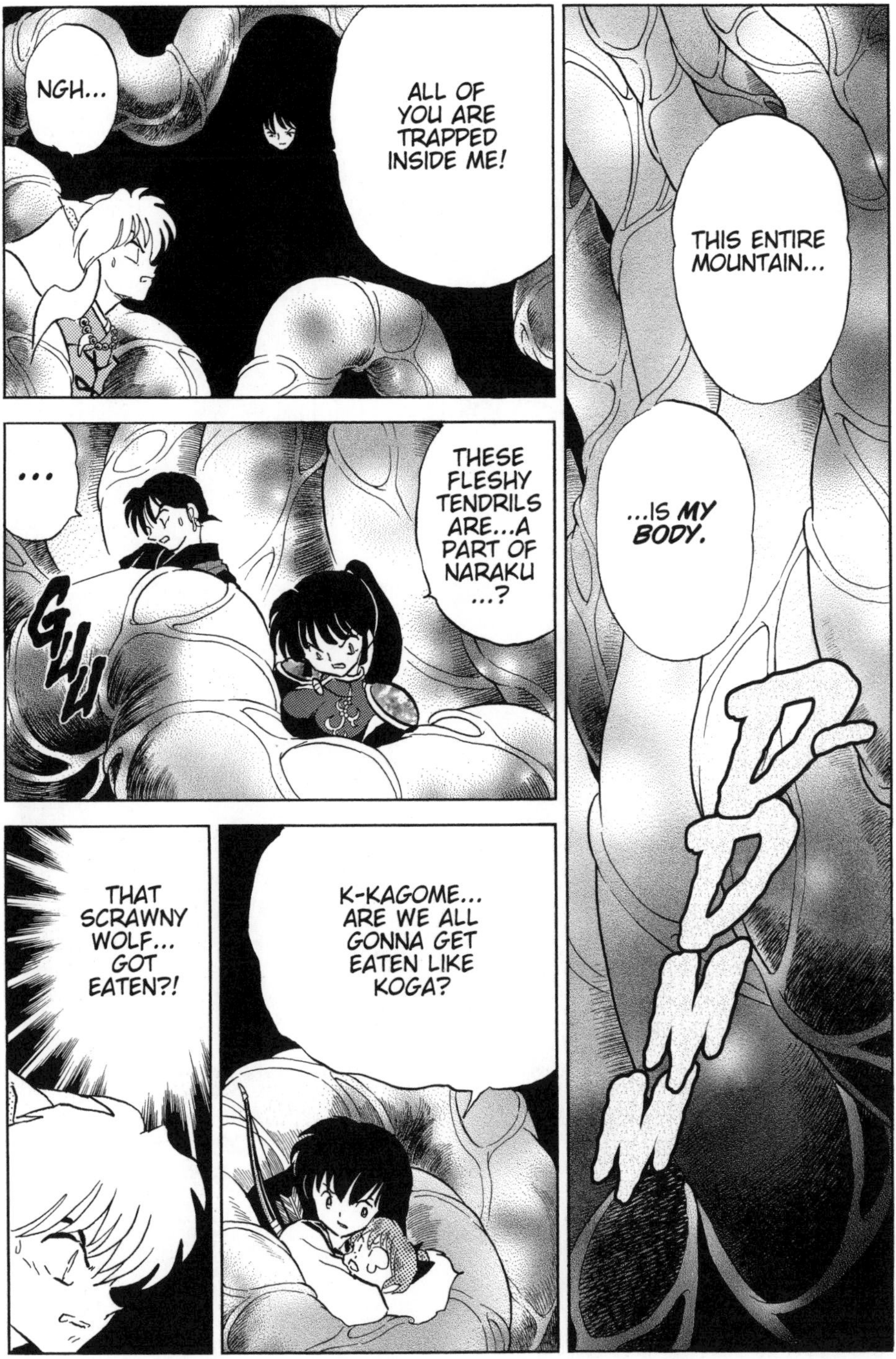

THIS ENTIRE MOUNTAIN...
...IS *MY BODY.*
DDMMM
ALL OF YOU ARE TRAPPED INSIDE ME!
NGH...
THESE FLESHY TENDRILS ARE...A PART OF NARAKU ...?
...
GWU
K-KAGOME... ARE WE ALL GONNA GET EATEN LIKE KOGA?
THAT SCRAWNY WOLF... GOT EATEN?!

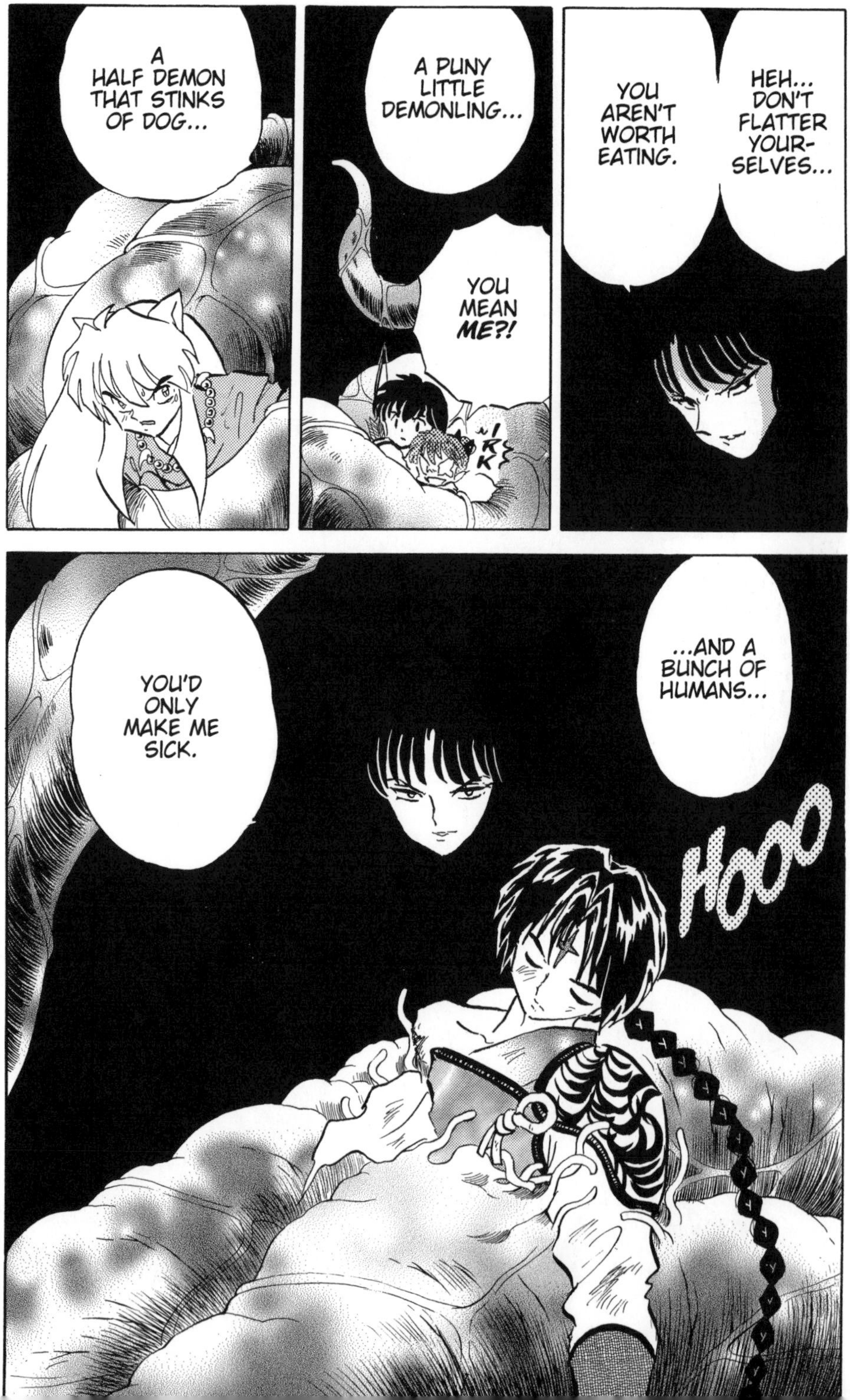
HEH... DON'T FLATTER YOUR-SELVES...
YOU AREN'T WORTH EATING.
A PUNY LITTLE DEMONLING...
YOU MEAN ME?!
A HALF DEMON THAT STINKS OF DOG...
...AND A BUNCH OF HUMANS...
HOOO
YOU'D ONLY MAKE ME SICK.

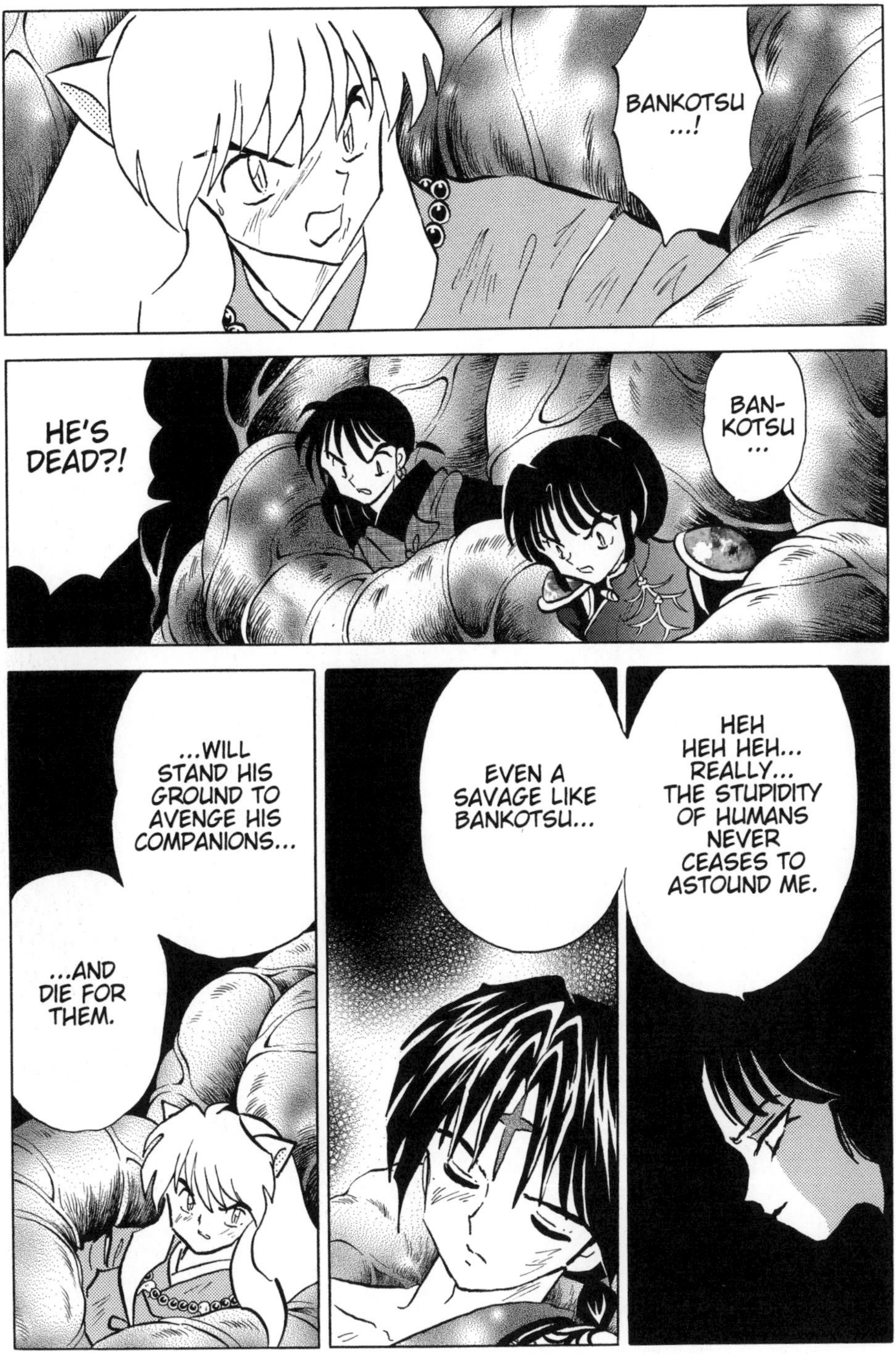
BANKOTSU ...!
BAN-KOTSU ...
HE'S DEAD?!
HEH HEH HEH... REALLY... THE STUPIDITY OF HUMANS NEVER CEASES TO ASTOUND ME.
EVEN A SAVAGE LIKE BANKOTSU...
...WILL STAND HIS GROUND TO AVENGE HIS COMPANIONS...
...AND DIE FOR THEM.

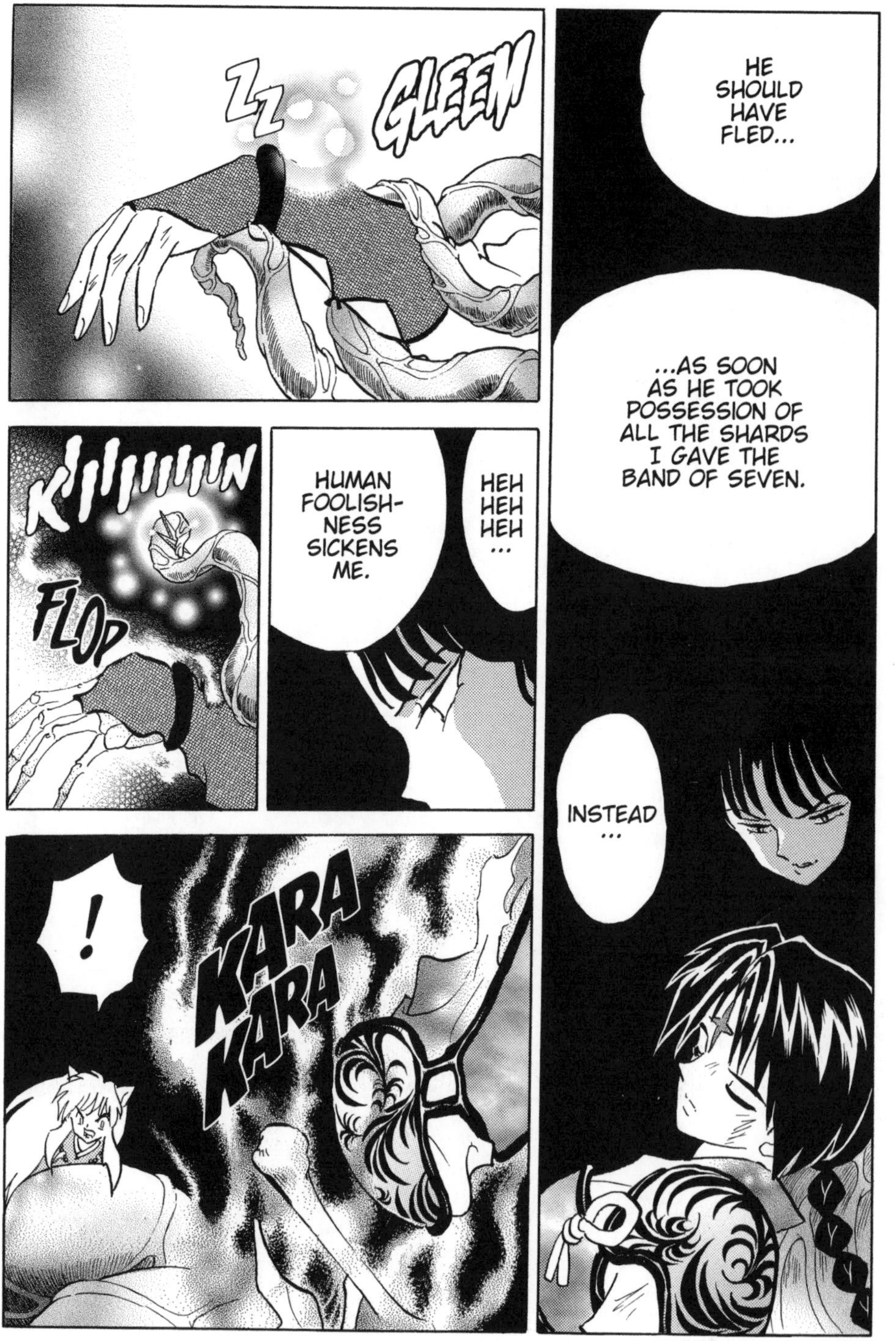
HE SHOULD HAVE FLED...
...AS SOON AS HE TOOK POSSESSION OF ALL THE SHARDS I GAVE THE BAND OF SEVEN.
INSTEAD...
ZZ
GLEEM
HEH HEH HEH...
HUMAN FOOLISH-NESS SICKENS ME.
KIIIIIIIIN
FLOP
!
KARA KARA

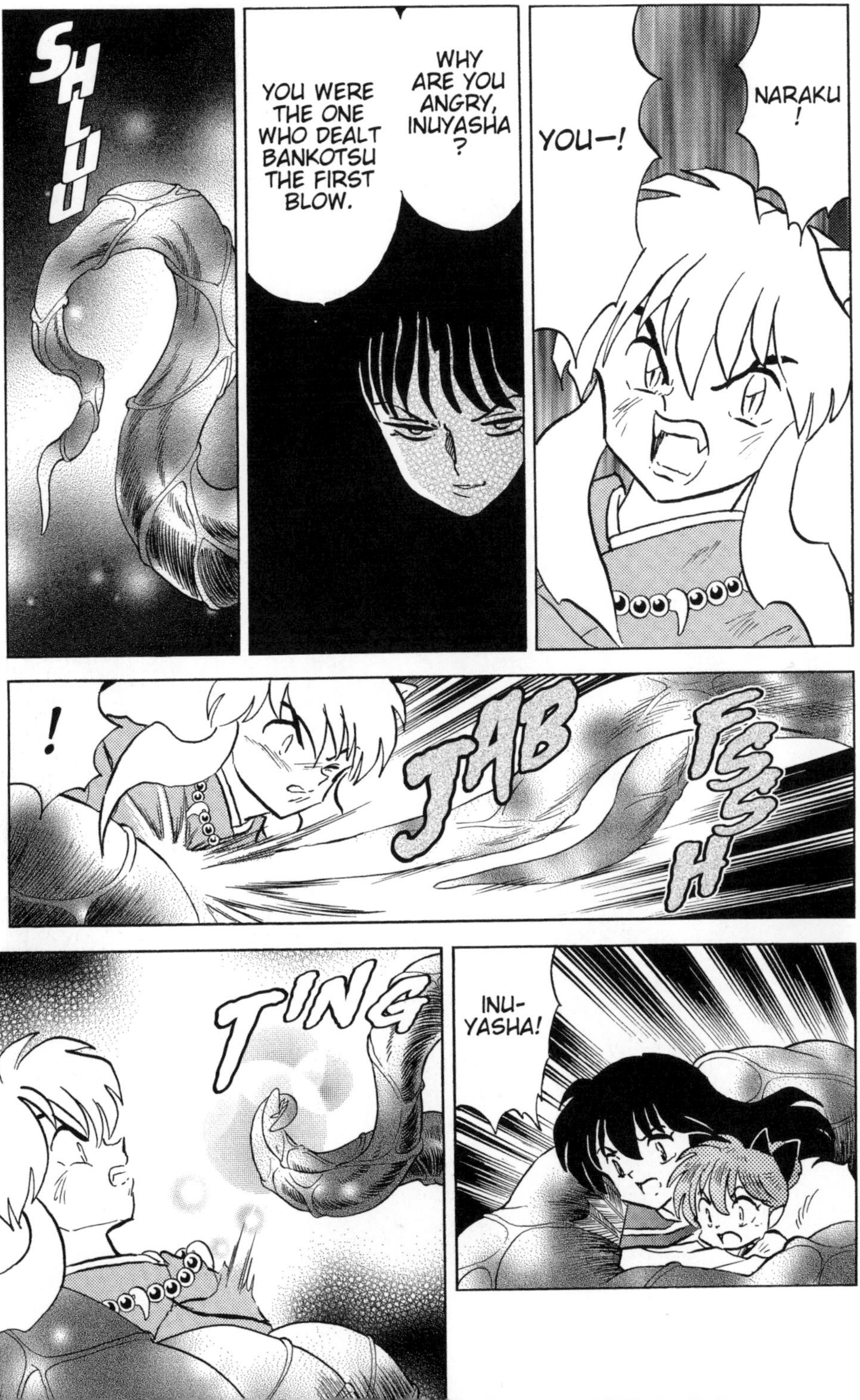
NARAKU!
YOU—!
WHY ARE YOU ANGRY, INUYASHA?
YOU WERE THE ONE WHO DEALT BANKOTSU THE FIRST BLOW.
SHLUU
FSSH
JAB
!
INU-YASHA!
TING

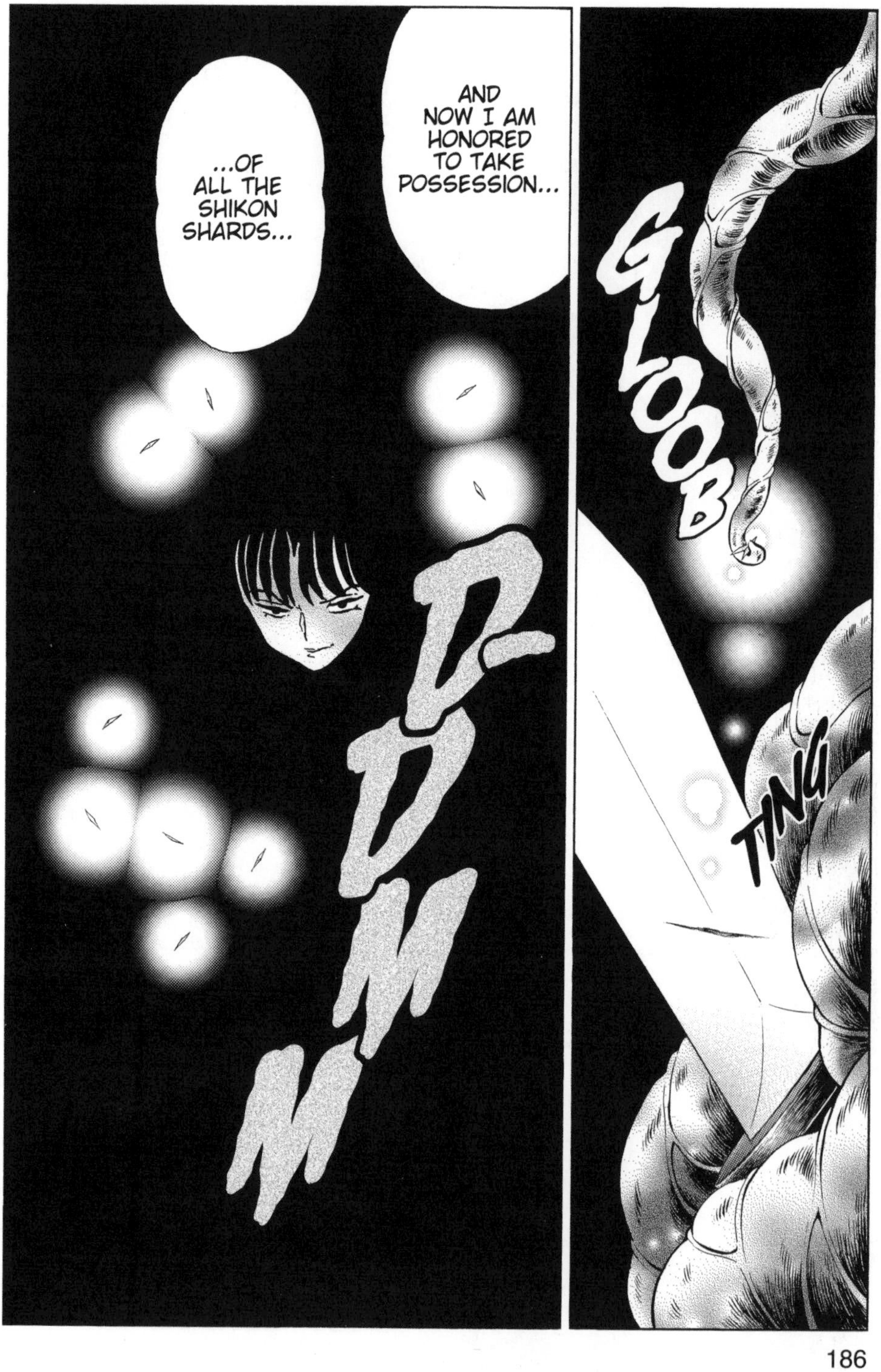
GLOOB
TING
AND NOW I AM HONORED TO TAKE POSSESSION...
...OF ALL THE SHIKON SHARDS...
D-DMM

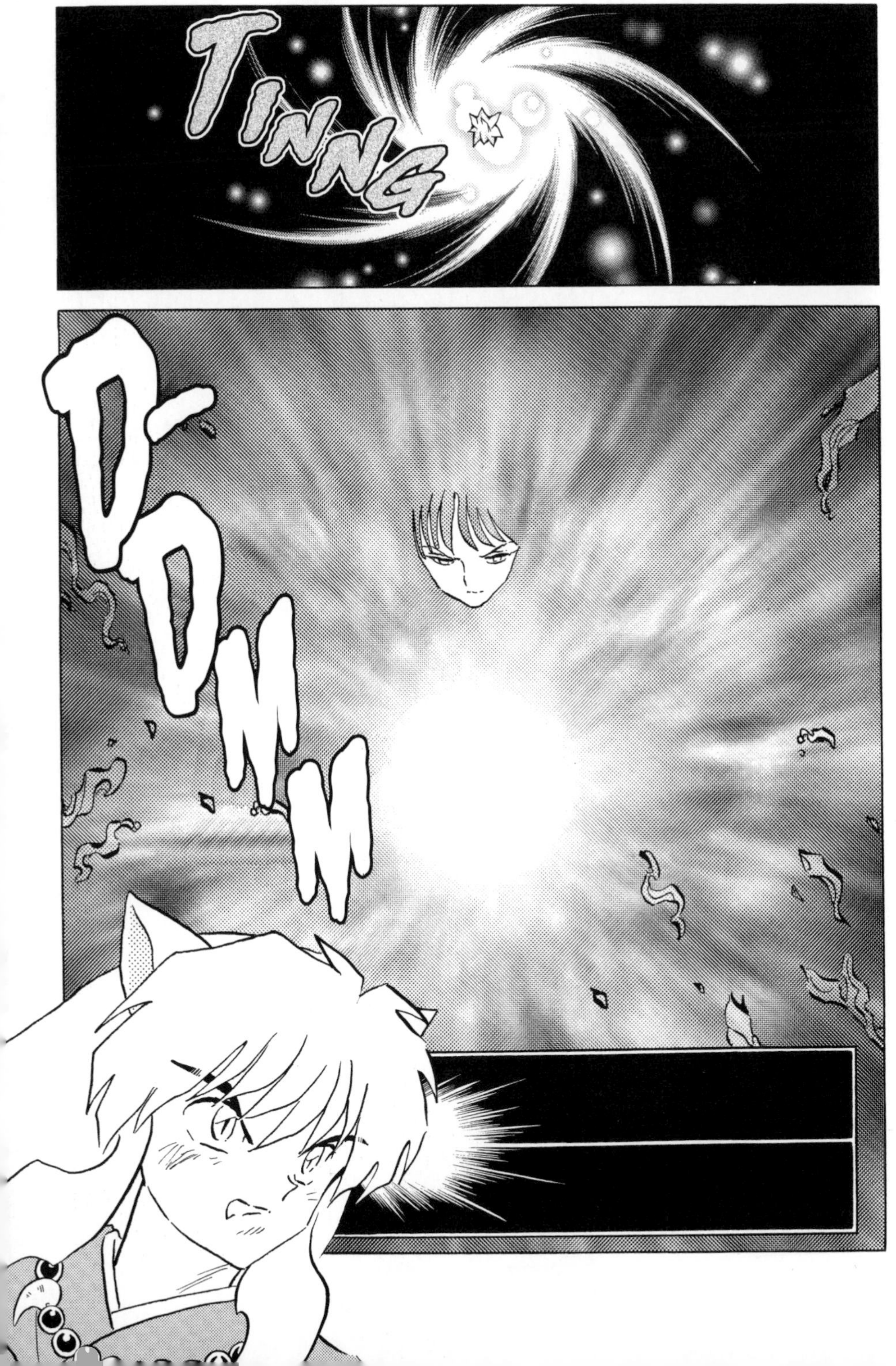
TINNG
D-DOMMM

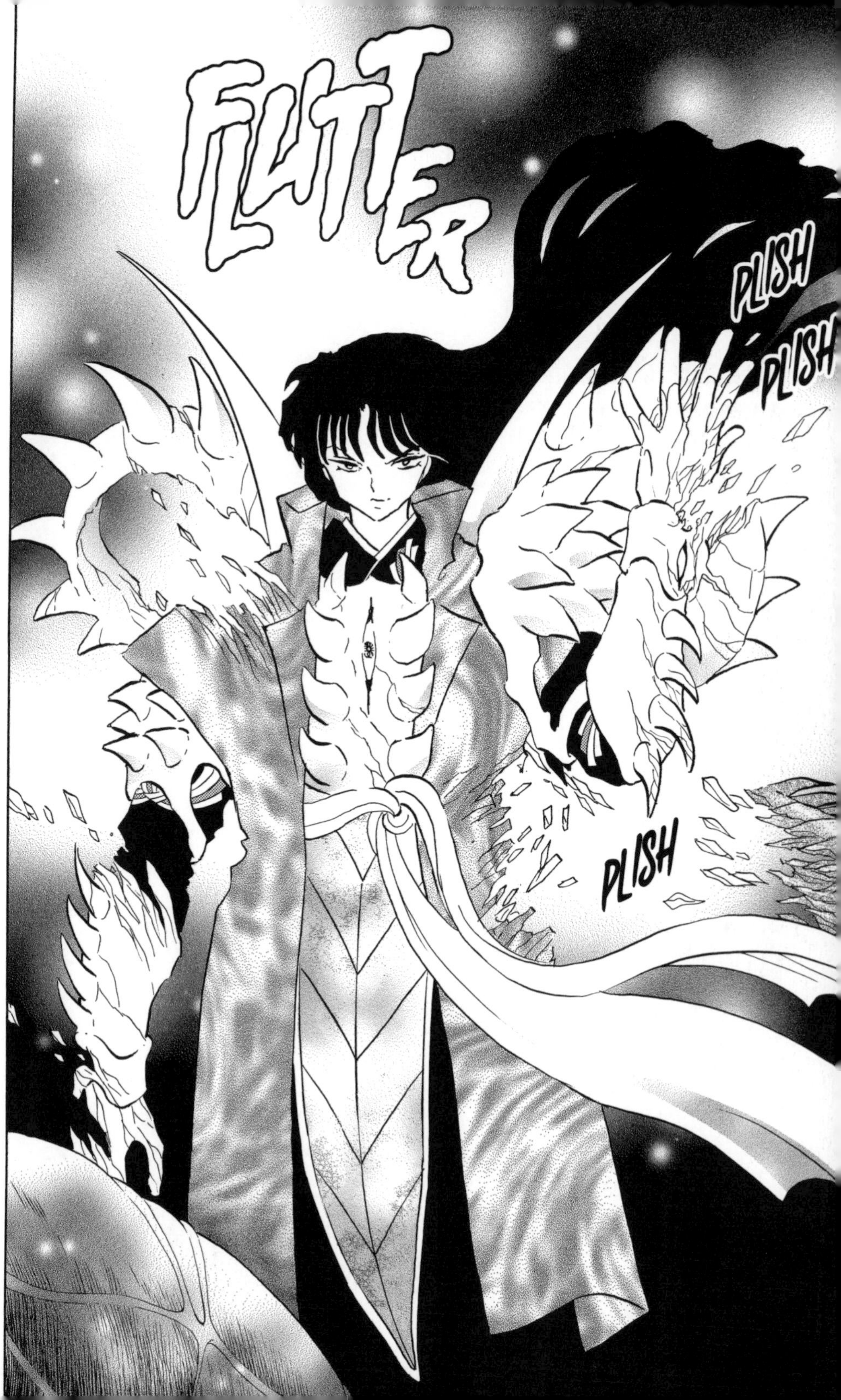
FLUTTER
PLISH
PLISH
PLISH

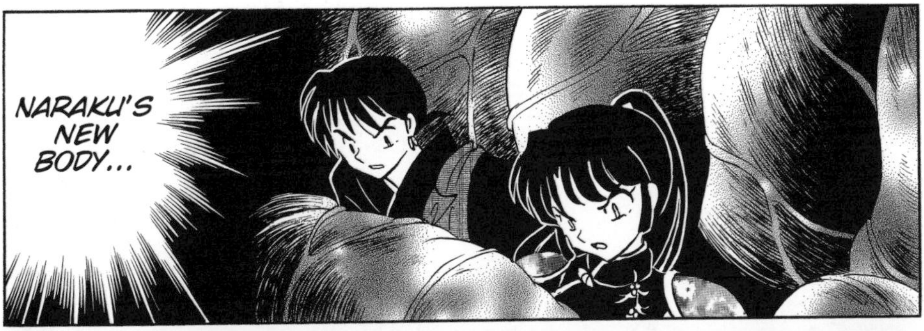
NARAKU'S NEW BODY...
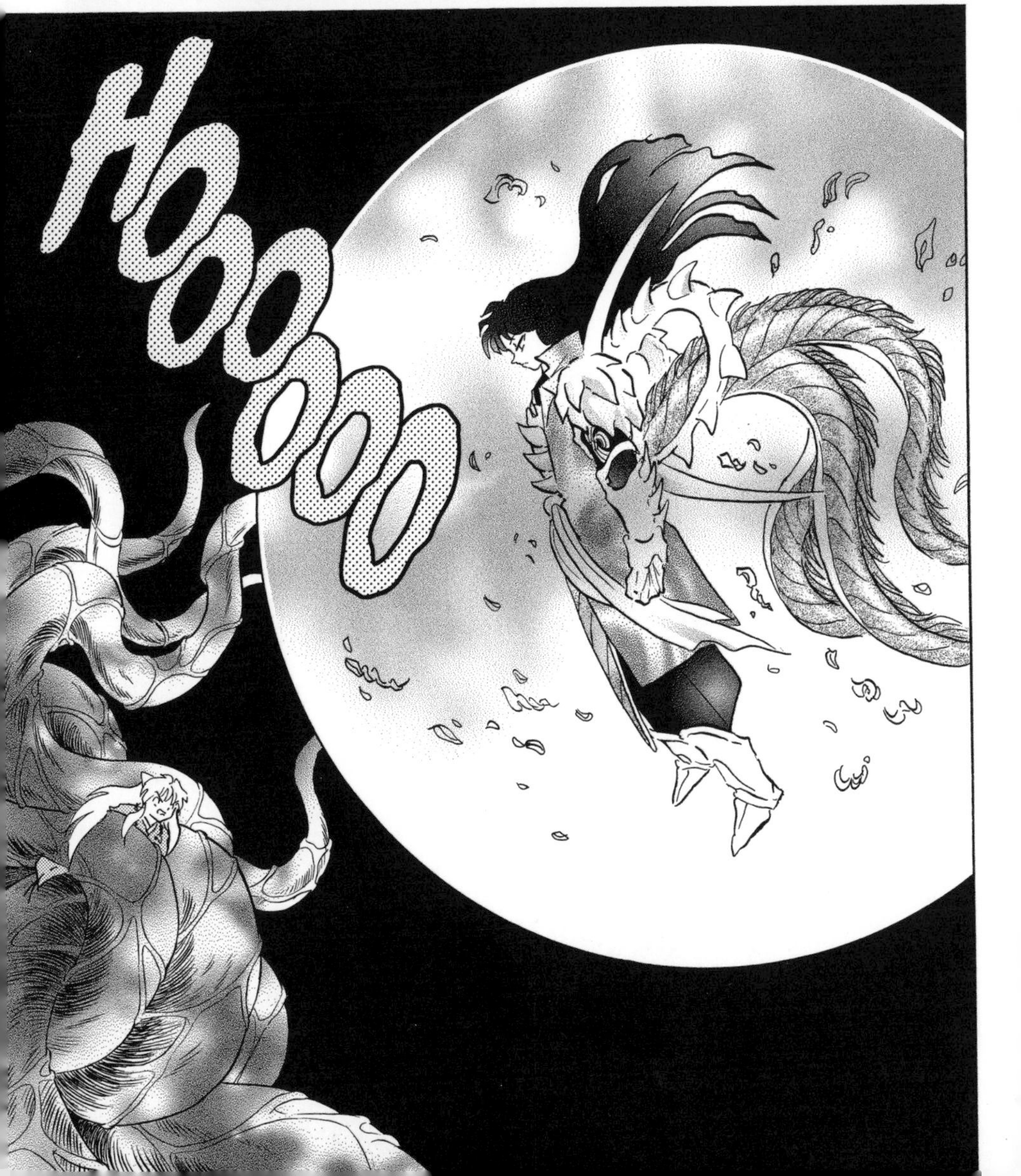
HOOOOOO

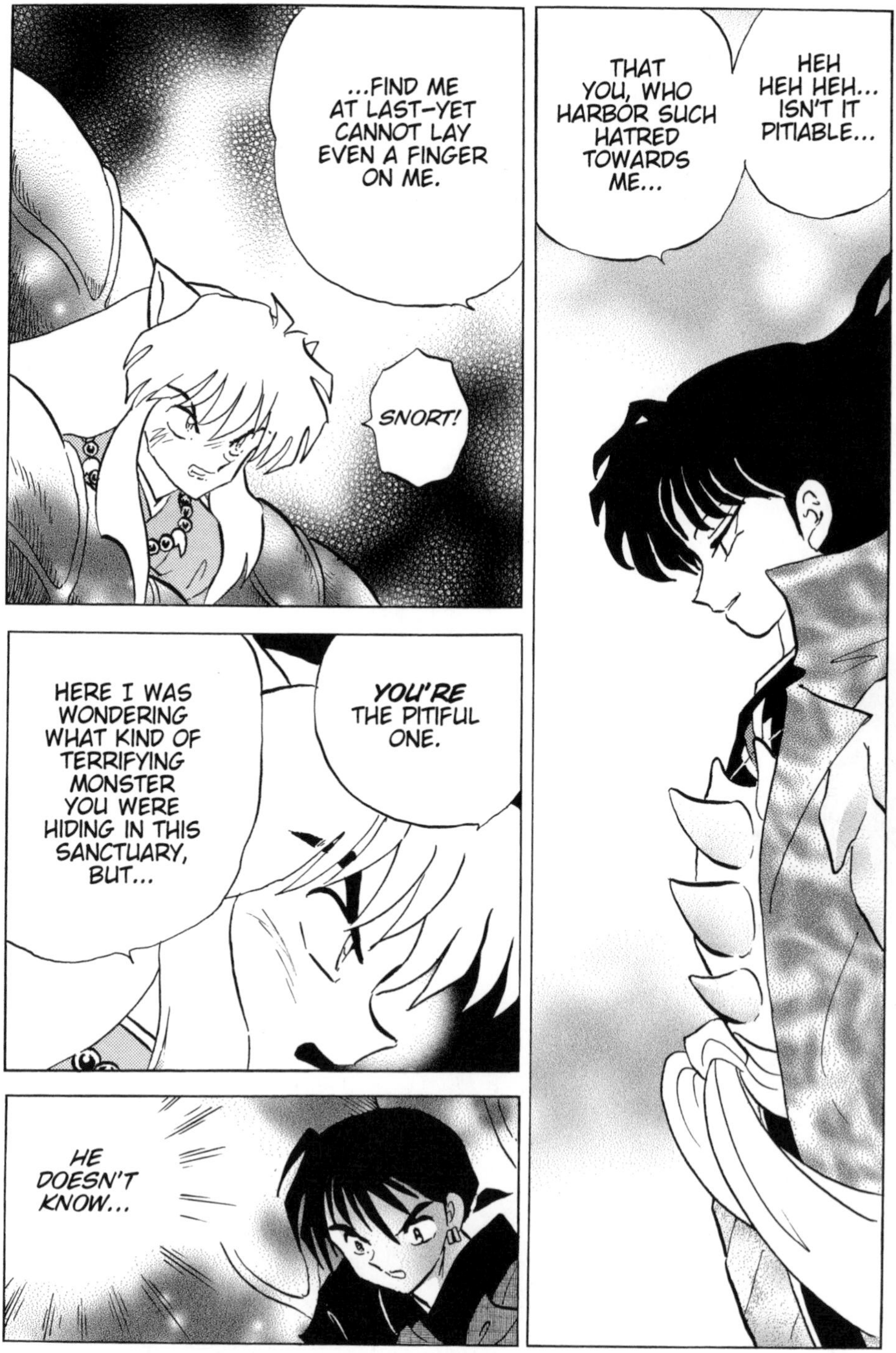
HEH HEH HEH... ISN'T IT PITIABLE...
THAT YOU, WHO HARBOR SUCH HATRED TOWARDS ME...
...FIND ME AT LAST—YET CANNOT LAY EVEN A FINGER ON ME.
SNORT!
YOU'RE THE PITIFUL ONE.
HERE I WAS WONDERING WHAT KIND OF TERRIFYING MONSTER YOU WERE HIDING IN THIS SANCTUARY, BUT...
HE DOESN'T KNOW...

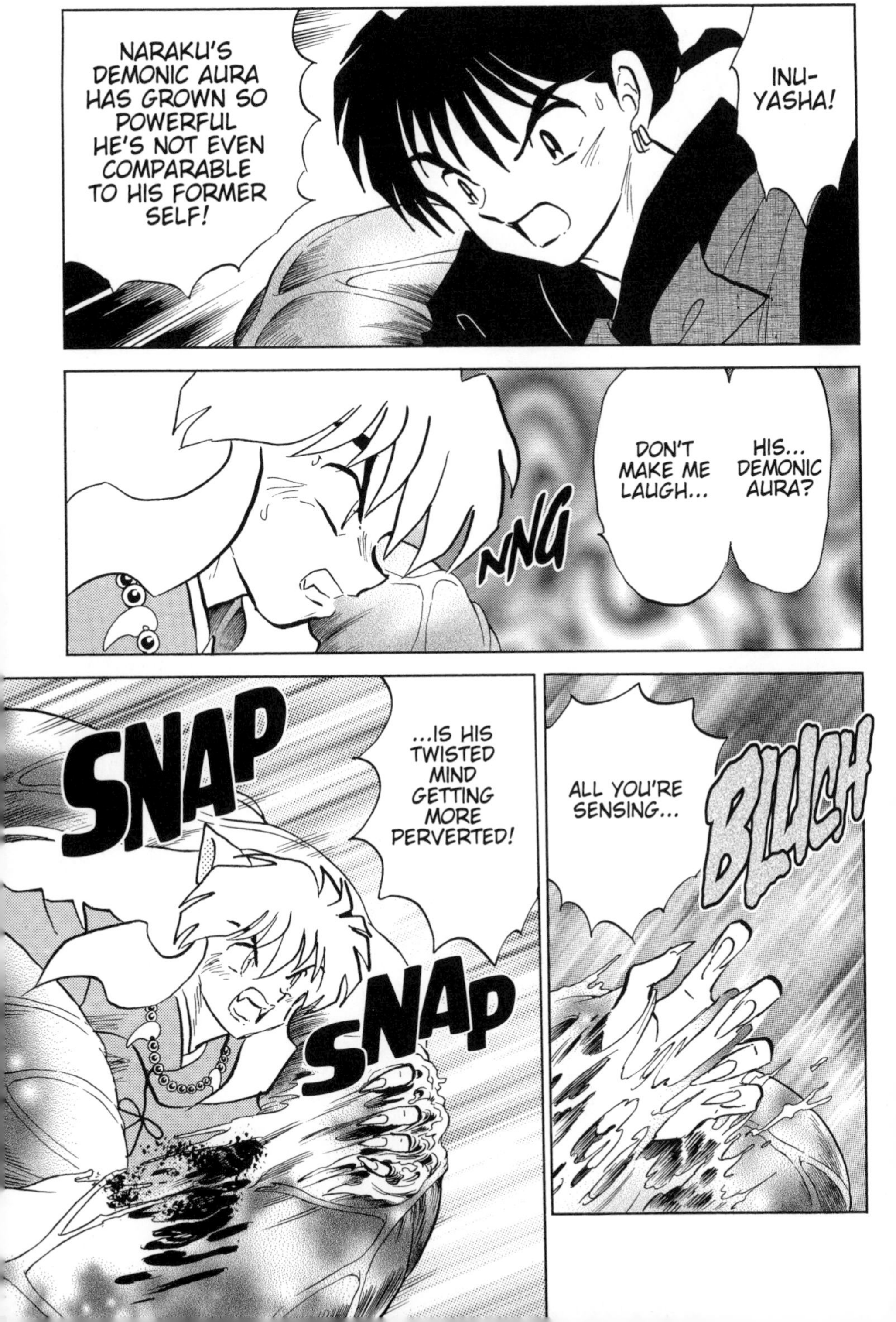
INU-YASHA!
NARAKU'S DEMONIC AURA HAS GROWN SO POWERFUL HE'S NOT EVEN COMPARABLE TO HIS FORMER SELF!
HIS... DEMONIC AURA?
DON'T MAKE ME LAUGH...
NNG
BLUCH
ALL YOU'RE SENSING...
...IS HIS TWISTED MIND GETTING MORE PERVERTED!
SNAP
SNAP

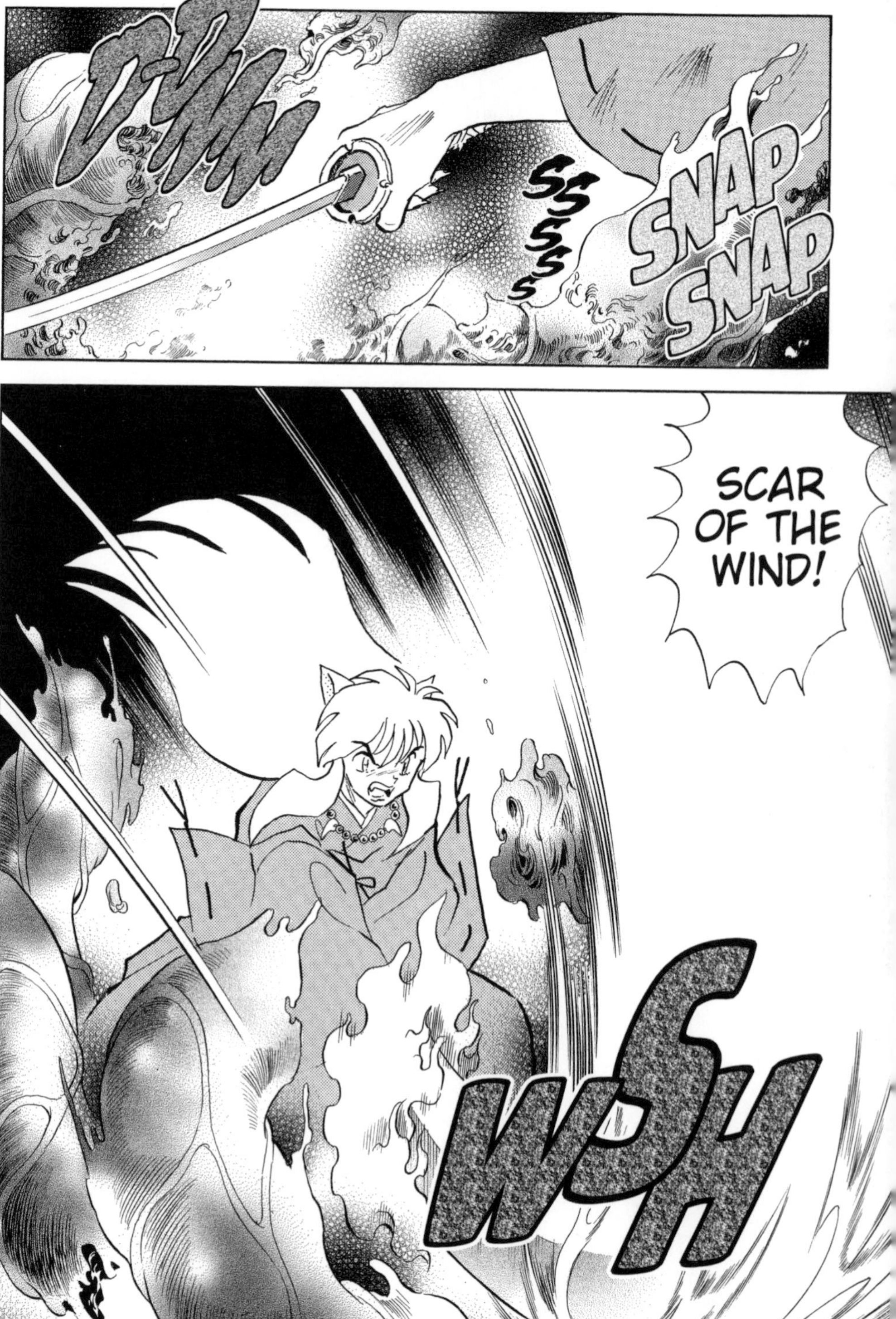
SNAP SNAP
SSSSSS
D-DMM
SCAR OF THE WIND!
WSH

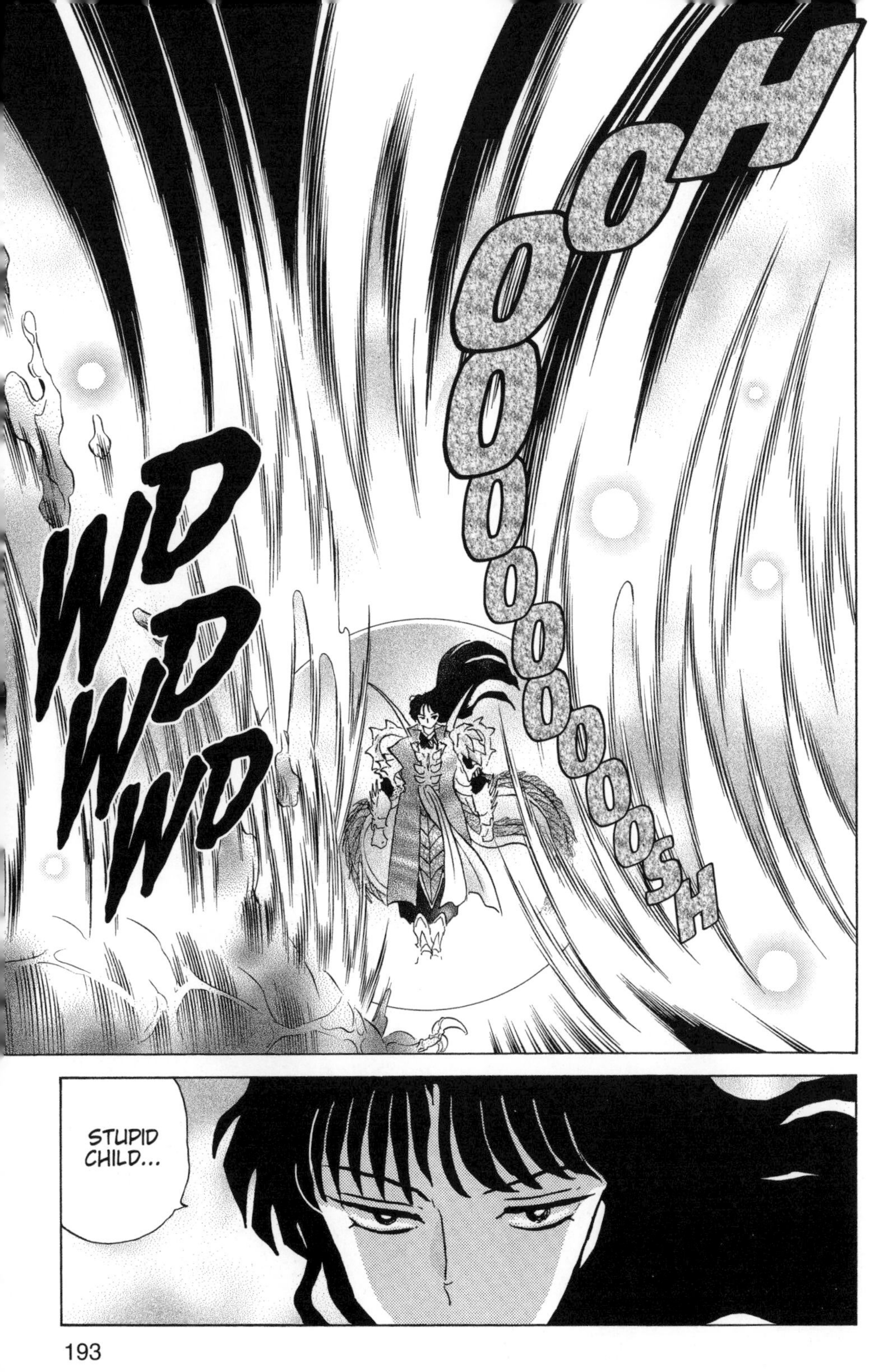
HOOOOOOOOOOOOSH
WD WD WD
STUPID CHILD...

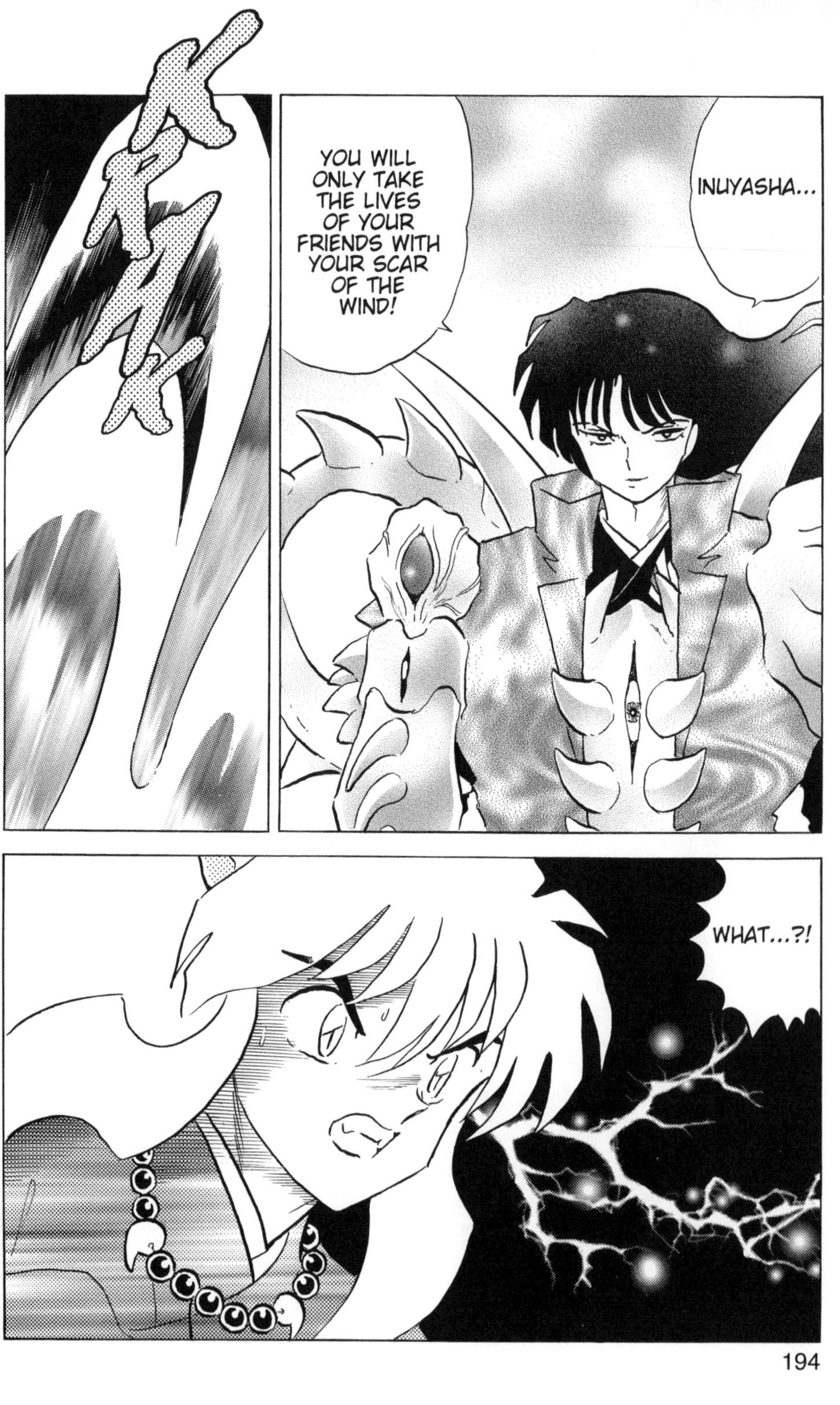
INUYASHA...
YOU WILL ONLY TAKE THE LIVES OF YOUR FRIENDS WITH YOUR SCAR OF THE WIND!
WHAT...?!

Volume 29
Inuyasha's True Feelings

SCROLL ONE
MAELSTROM OF EVIL

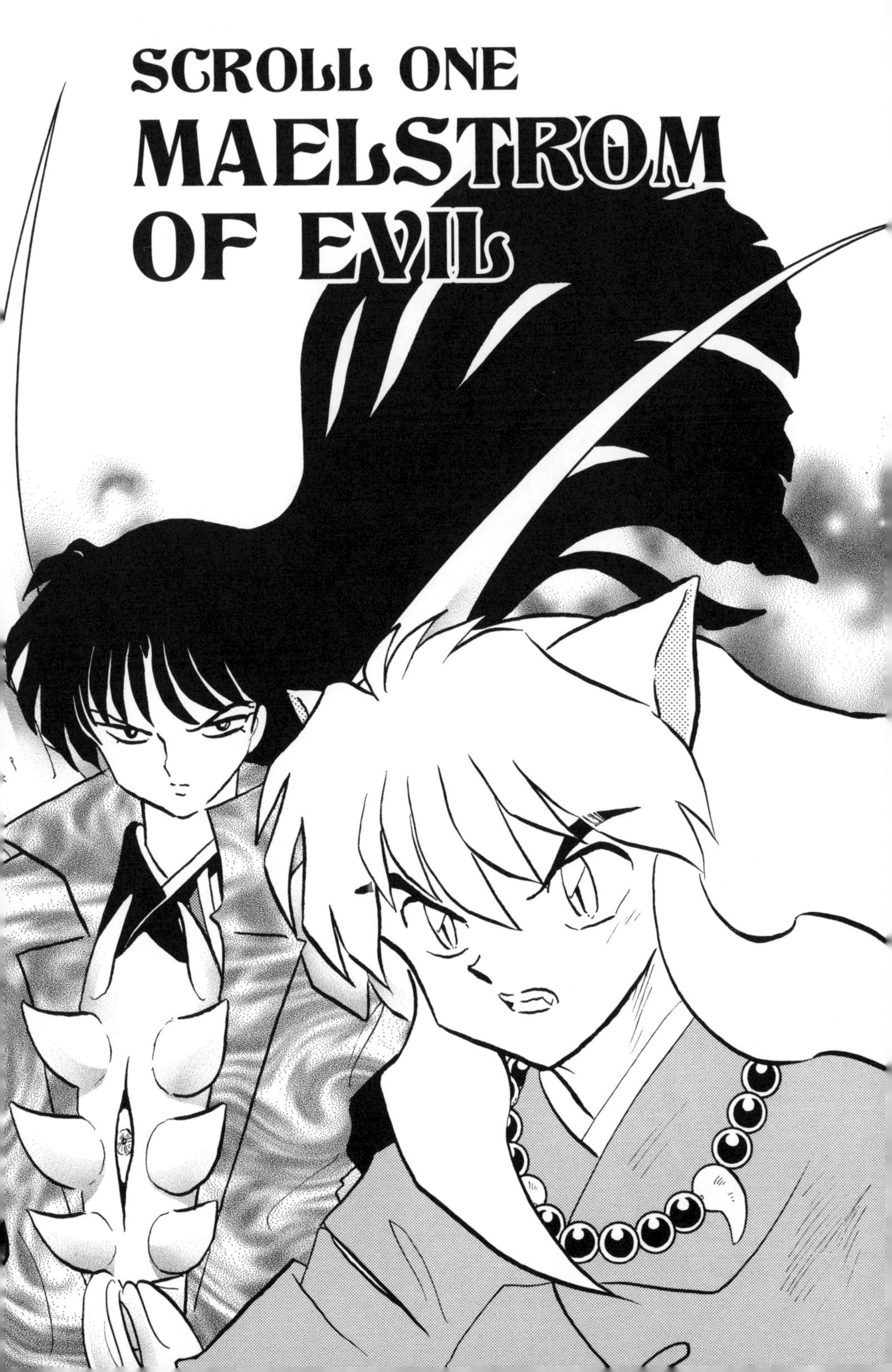

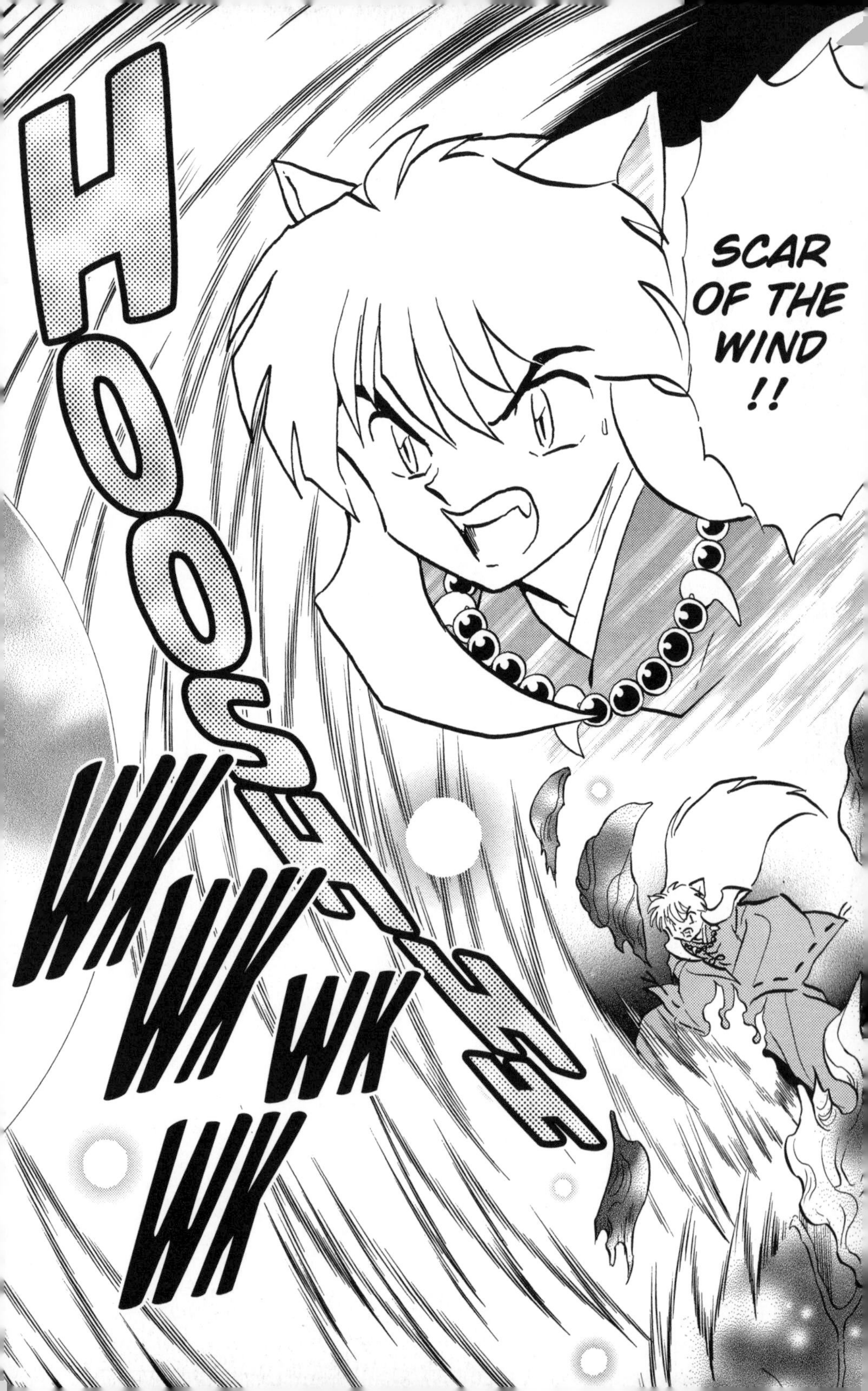
SCAR OF THE WIND !!

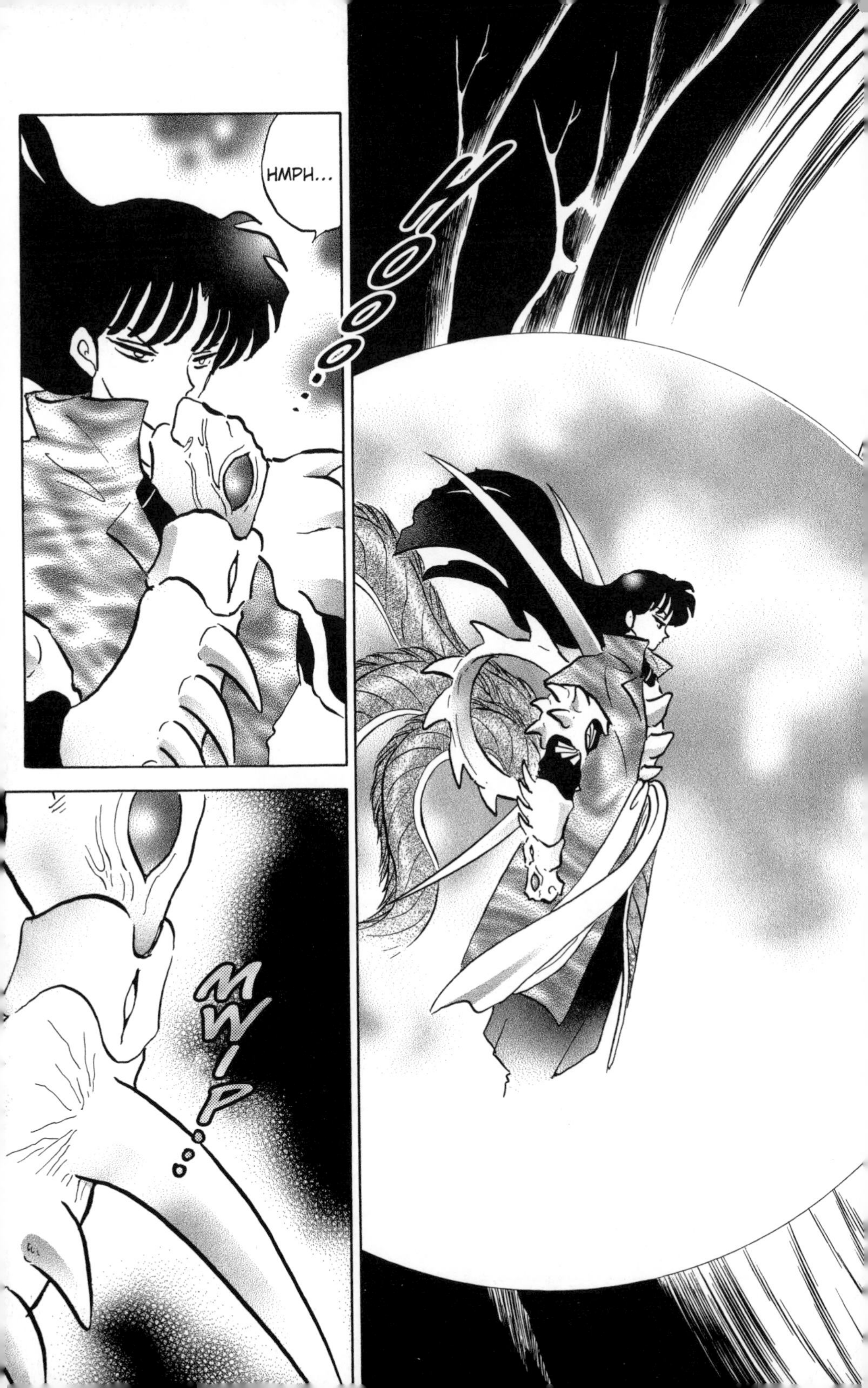
HOOO...
HMPH...
MWIP...

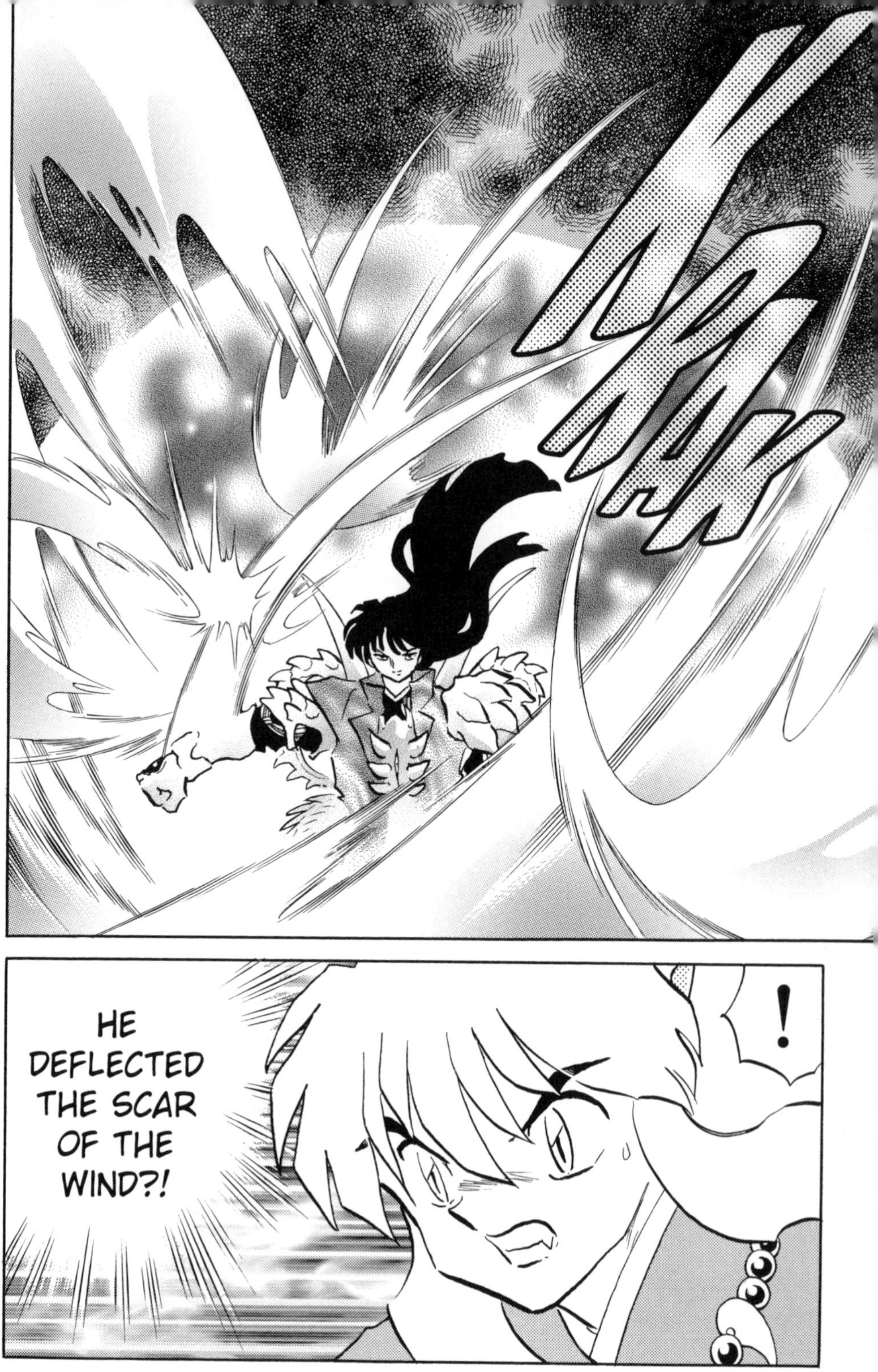
WHAK
!
HE DEFLECTED THE SCAR OF THE WIND?!

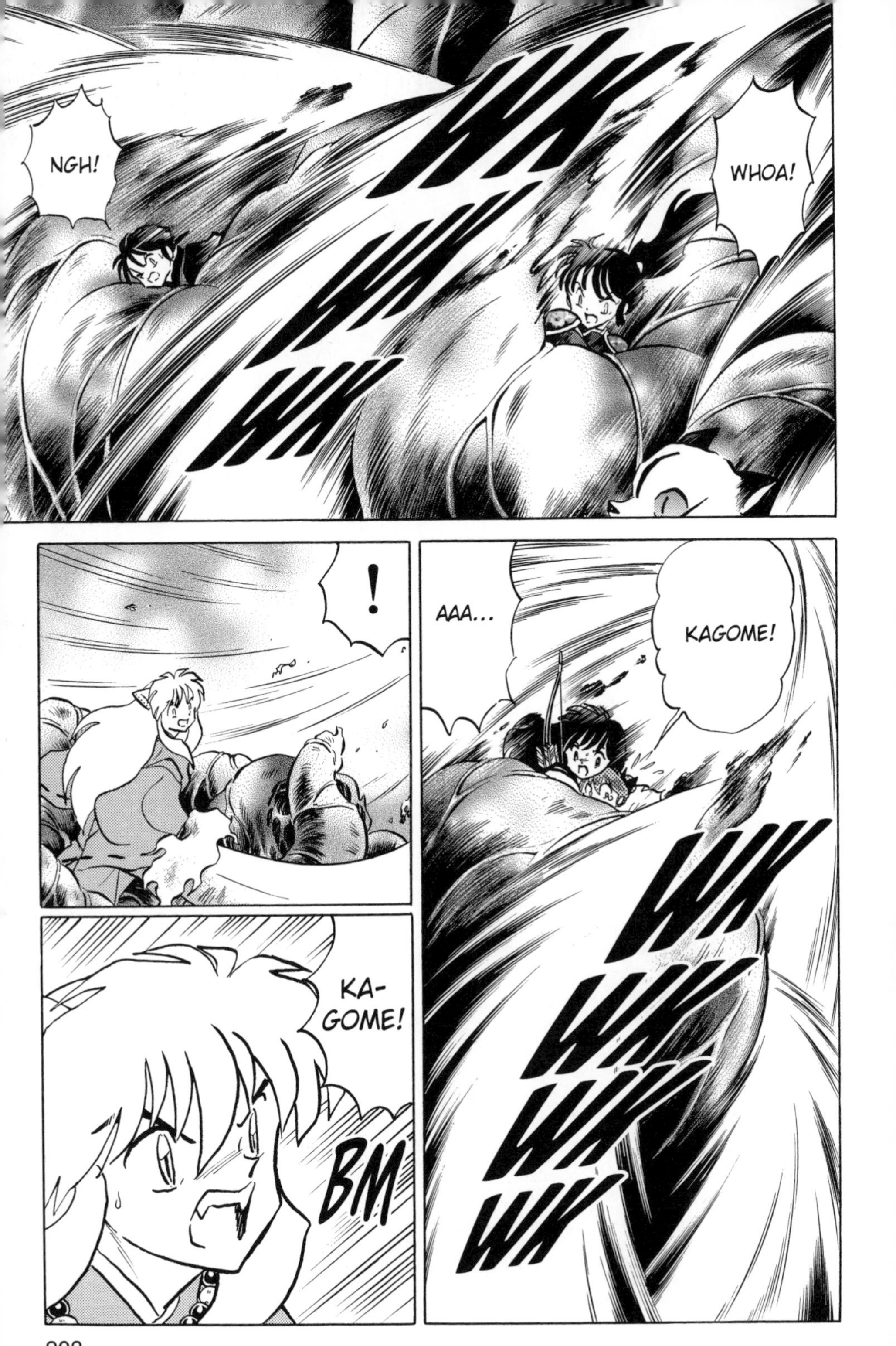
WHOA!
NGH!
WH
WH
WH
WH
KAGOME!
AAA...
WH
WH
WH
WH
WH
!
KA-GOME!
BM

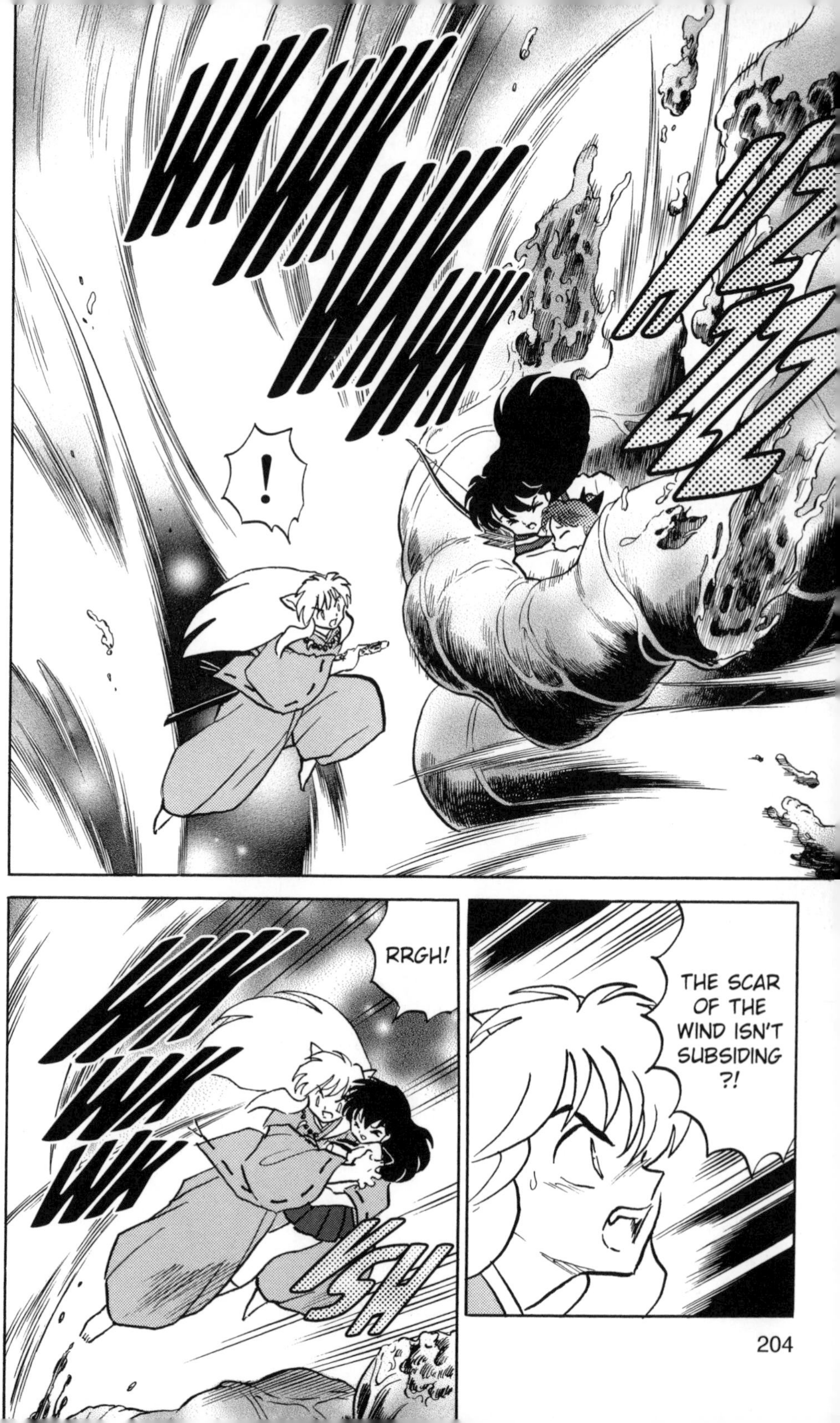
!
THE SCAR OF THE WIND ISN'T SUBSIDING ?!
RRGH!

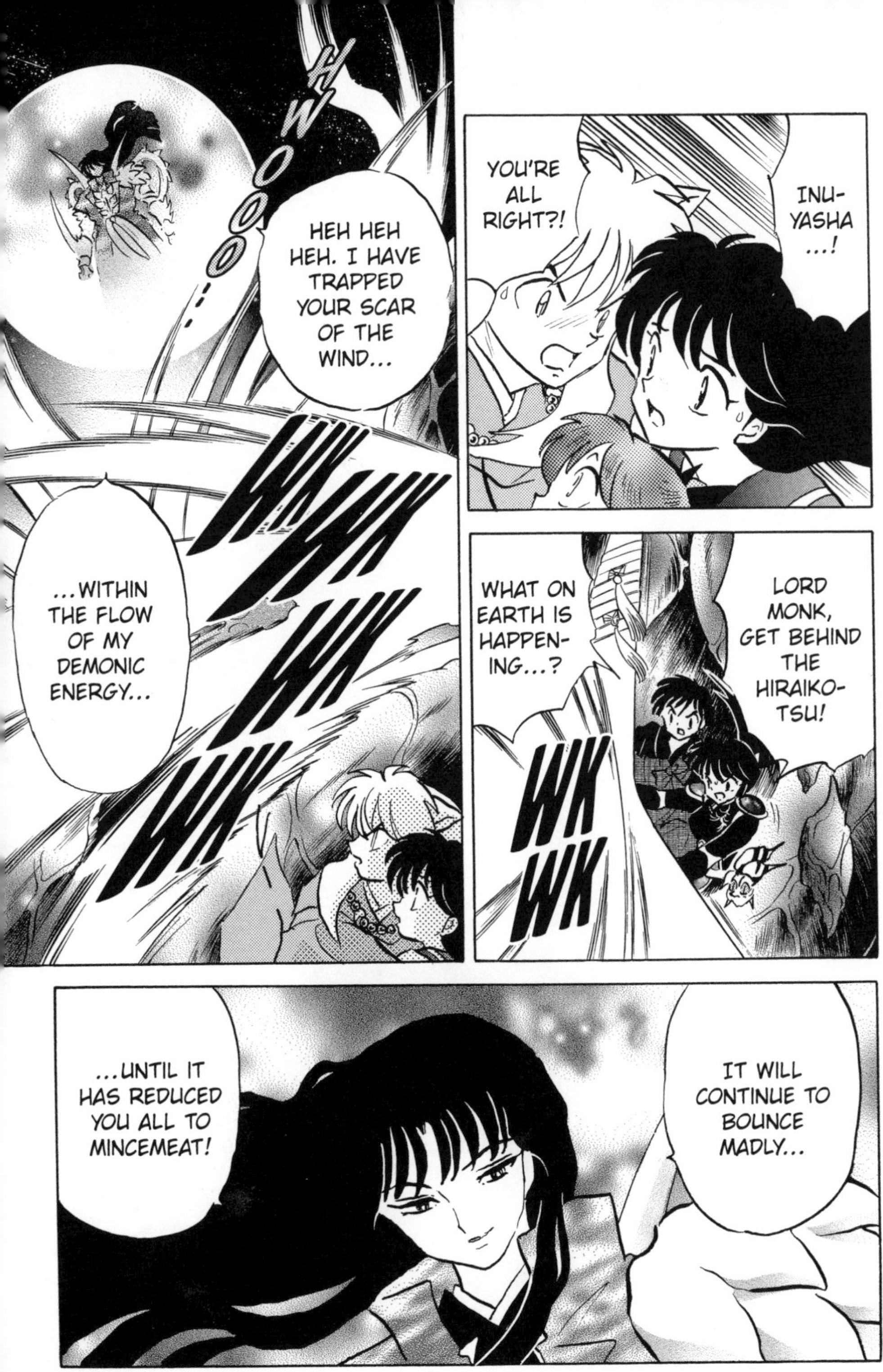
INU-YASHA...!
YOU'RE ALL RIGHT?!
LORD MONK, GET BEHIND THE HIRAIKOTSU!
WHAT ON EARTH IS HAPPENING...?
WK WK
HWOOOOO...
HEH HEH HEH. I HAVE TRAPPED YOUR SCAR OF THE WIND...
...WITHIN THE FLOW OF MY DEMONIC ENERGY...
WKWKWK
IT WILL CONTINUE TO BOUNCE MADLY...
...UNTIL IT HAS REDUCED YOU ALL TO MINCEMEAT!

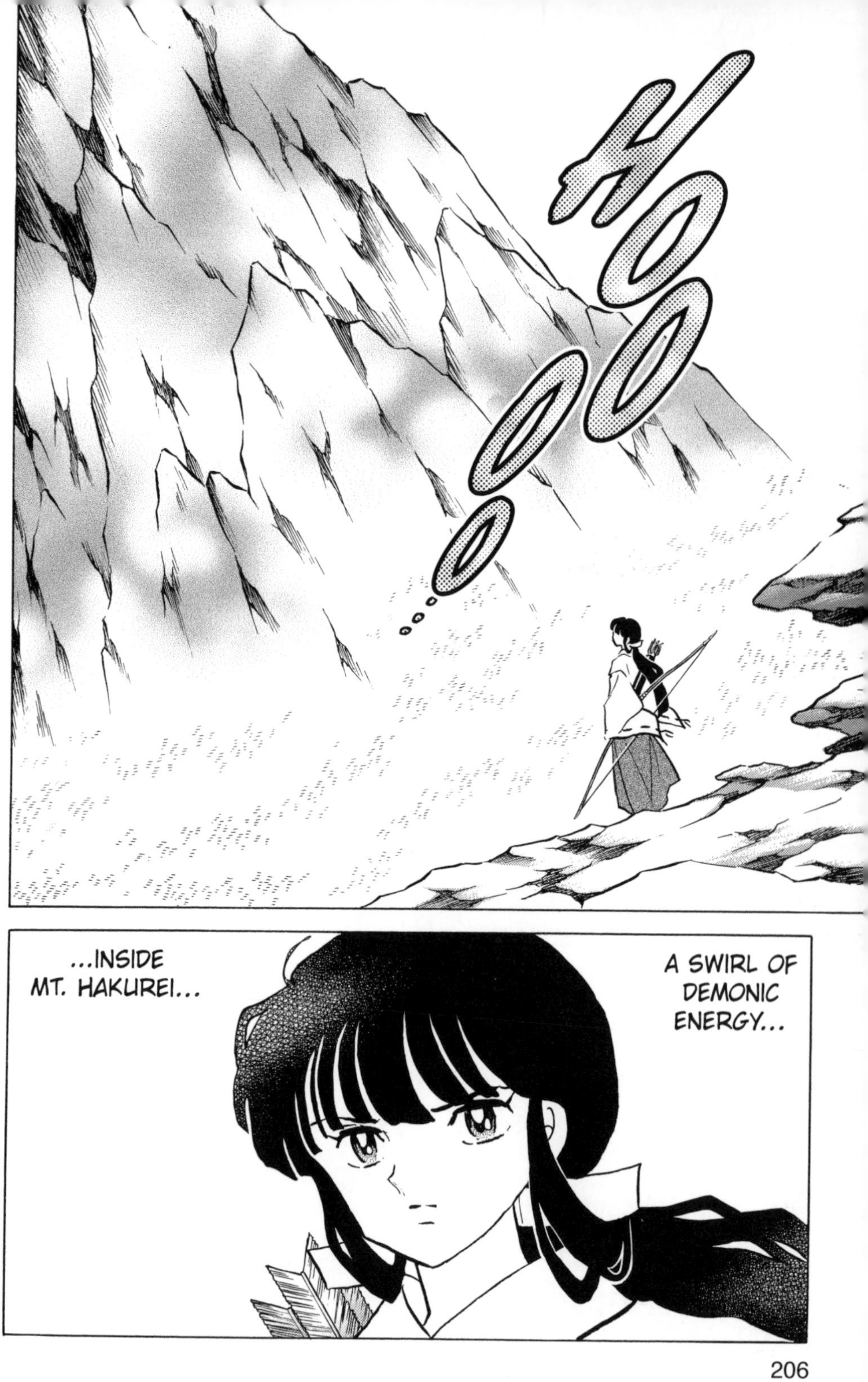
HOOOO...
A SWIRL OF DEMONIC ENERGY...
...INSIDE MT. HAKUREI...

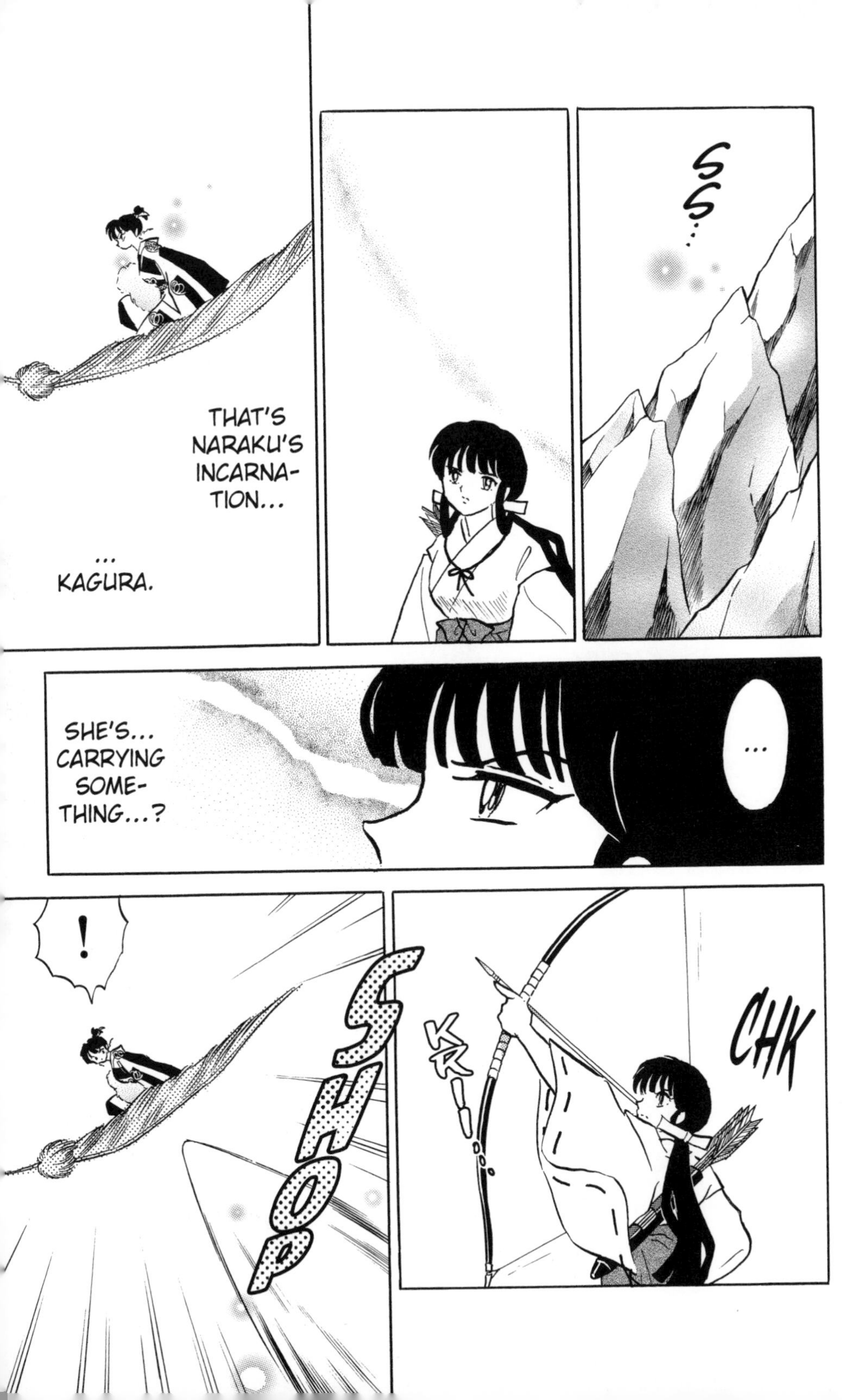
SS...
THAT'S NARAKU'S INCARNATION...
...KAGURA.
...
SHE'S... CARRYING SOMETHING...?
CHK
KRI...
!
SHOOP

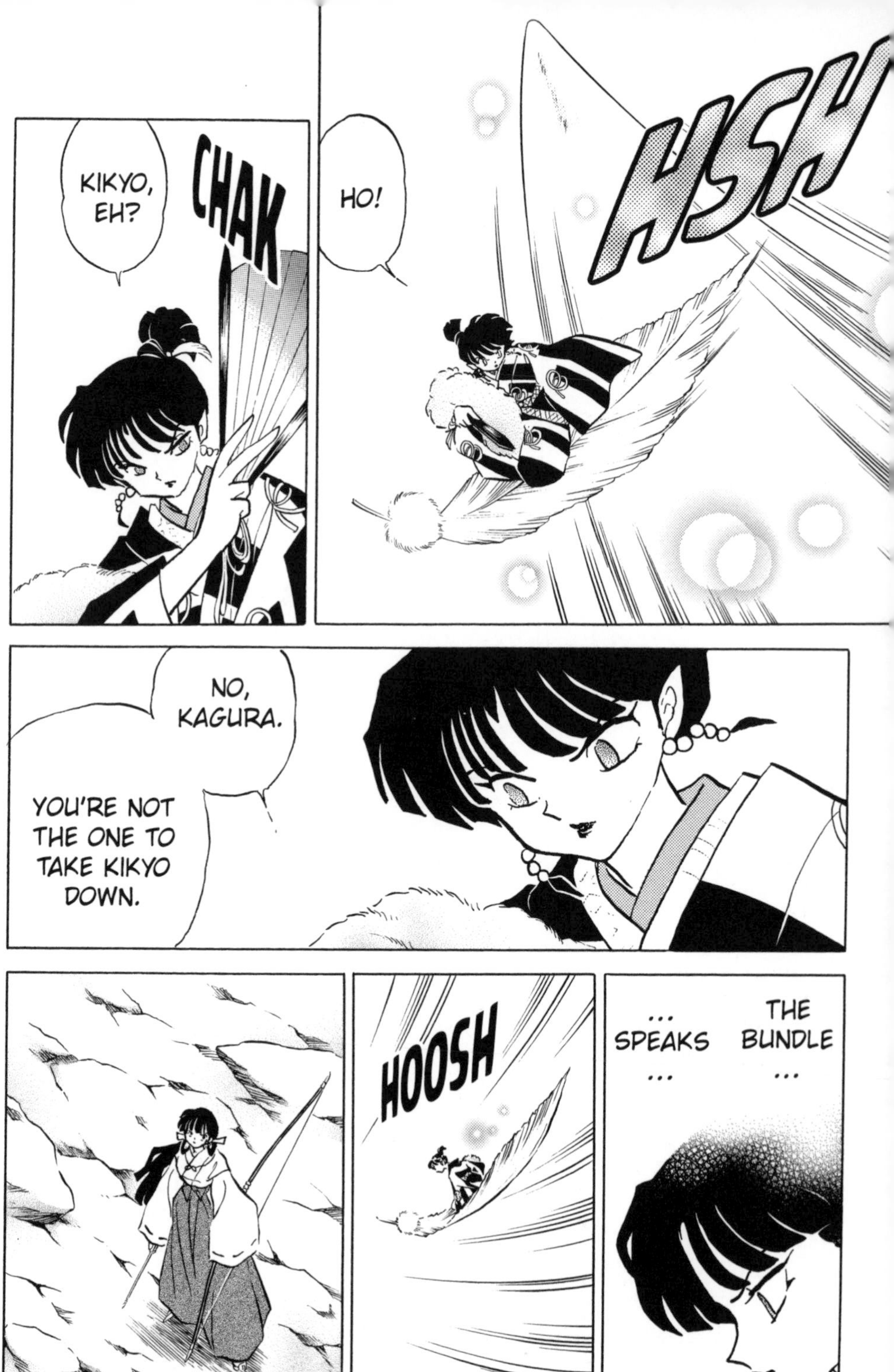
HSH
HO!
CHAK
KIKYO, EH?
NO, KAGURA.
YOU'RE NOT THE ONE TO TAKE KIKYO DOWN.
THE BUNDLE ...
... SPEAKS ...
HOOSH

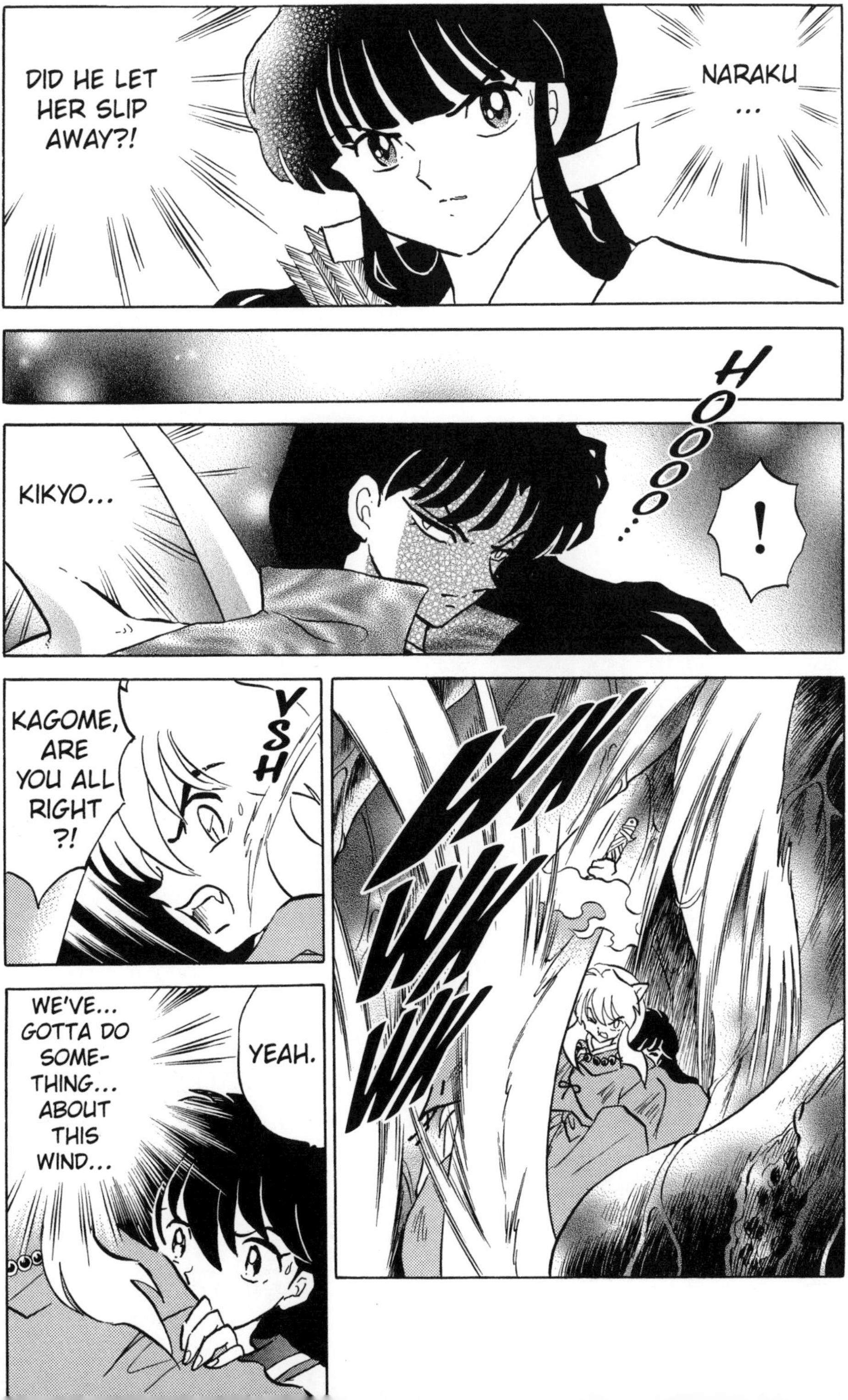
NARAKU ...
DID HE LET HER SLIP AWAY?!
HOOOOO...
!
KIKYO...
VSH
KAGOME, ARE YOU ALL RIGHT ?!
YEAH.
WE'VE... GOTTA DO SOME-THING... ABOUT THIS WIND...

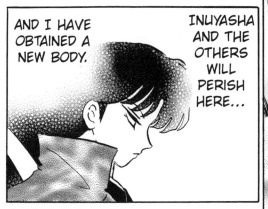

AND I HAVE OBTAINED A NEW BODY.

INUYASHA AND THE OTHERS WILL PERISH HERE...

ONLY ONE TASK REMAINS...

HEH.

DAMN YOU, NARAKU!

YOU THINK I'LL LET YOU ESCAPE?!

FF

!

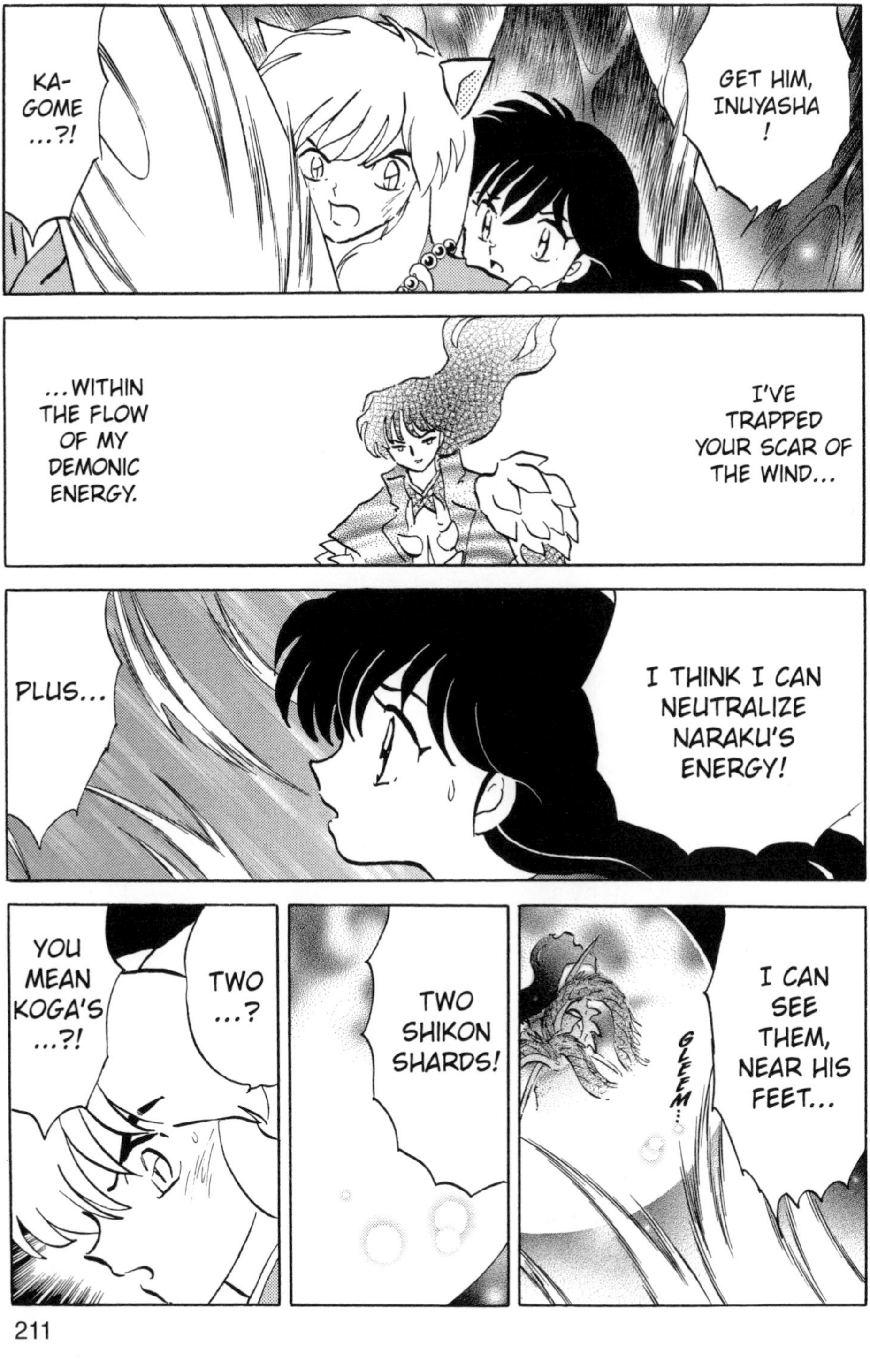
GET HIM, INUYASHA!
KA-GOME...?!
I'VE TRAPPED YOUR SCAR OF THE WIND...
...WITHIN THE FLOW OF MY DEMONIC ENERGY.
I THINK I CAN NEUTRALIZE NARAKU'S ENERGY!
PLUS...
I CAN SEE THEM, NEAR HIS FEET...
GLEEM...
TWO SHIKON SHARDS!
TWO...?
YOU MEAN KOGA'S...?!

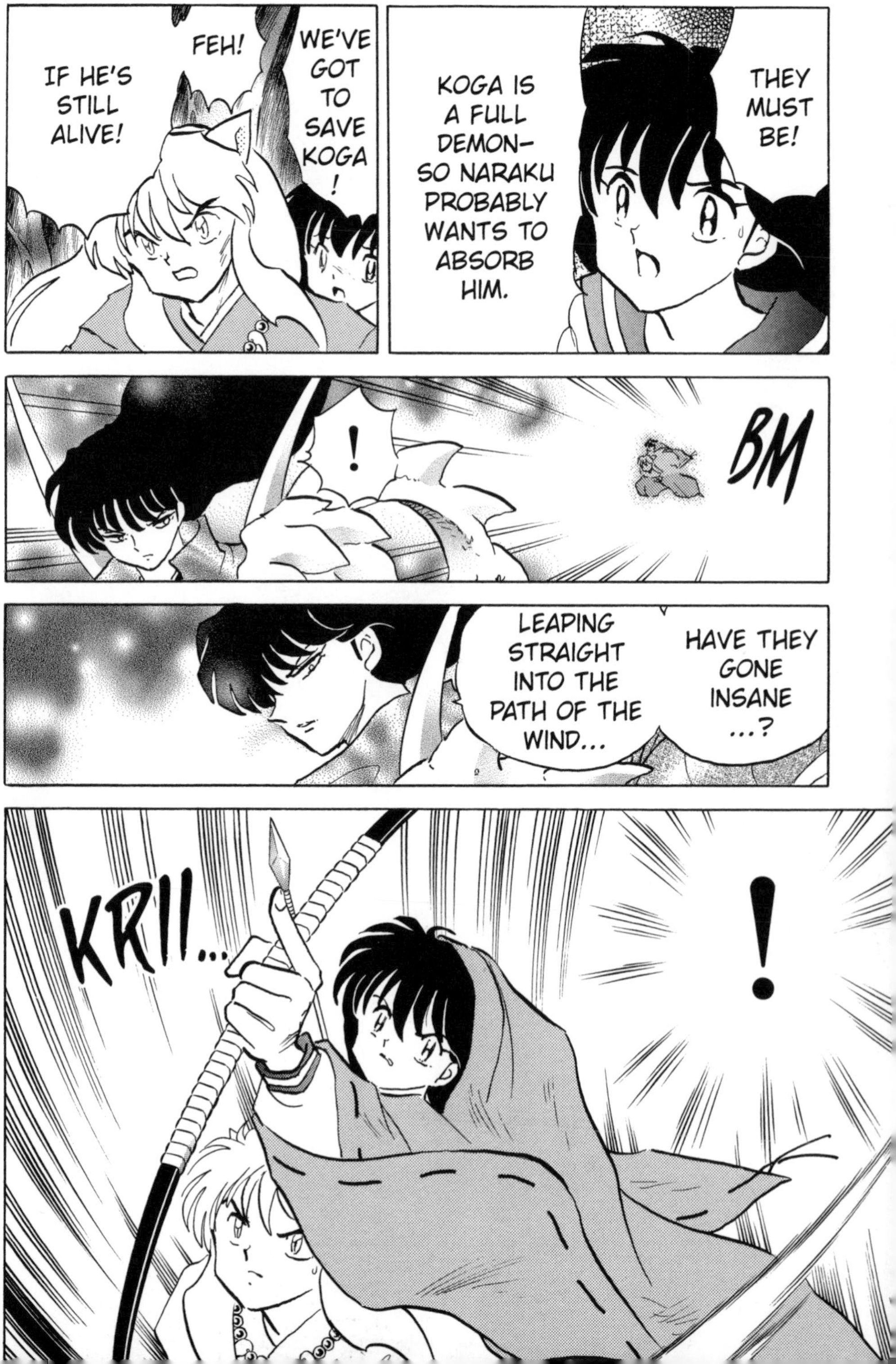
THEY MUST BE!
KOGA IS A FULL DEMON– SO NARAKU PROBABLY WANTS TO ABSORB HIM.
WE'VE GOT TO SAVE KOGA!
FEH!
IF HE'S STILL ALIVE!
BM
!
HAVE THEY GONE INSANE ...?
LEAPING STRAIGHT INTO THE PATH OF THE WIND...
!
KRII...

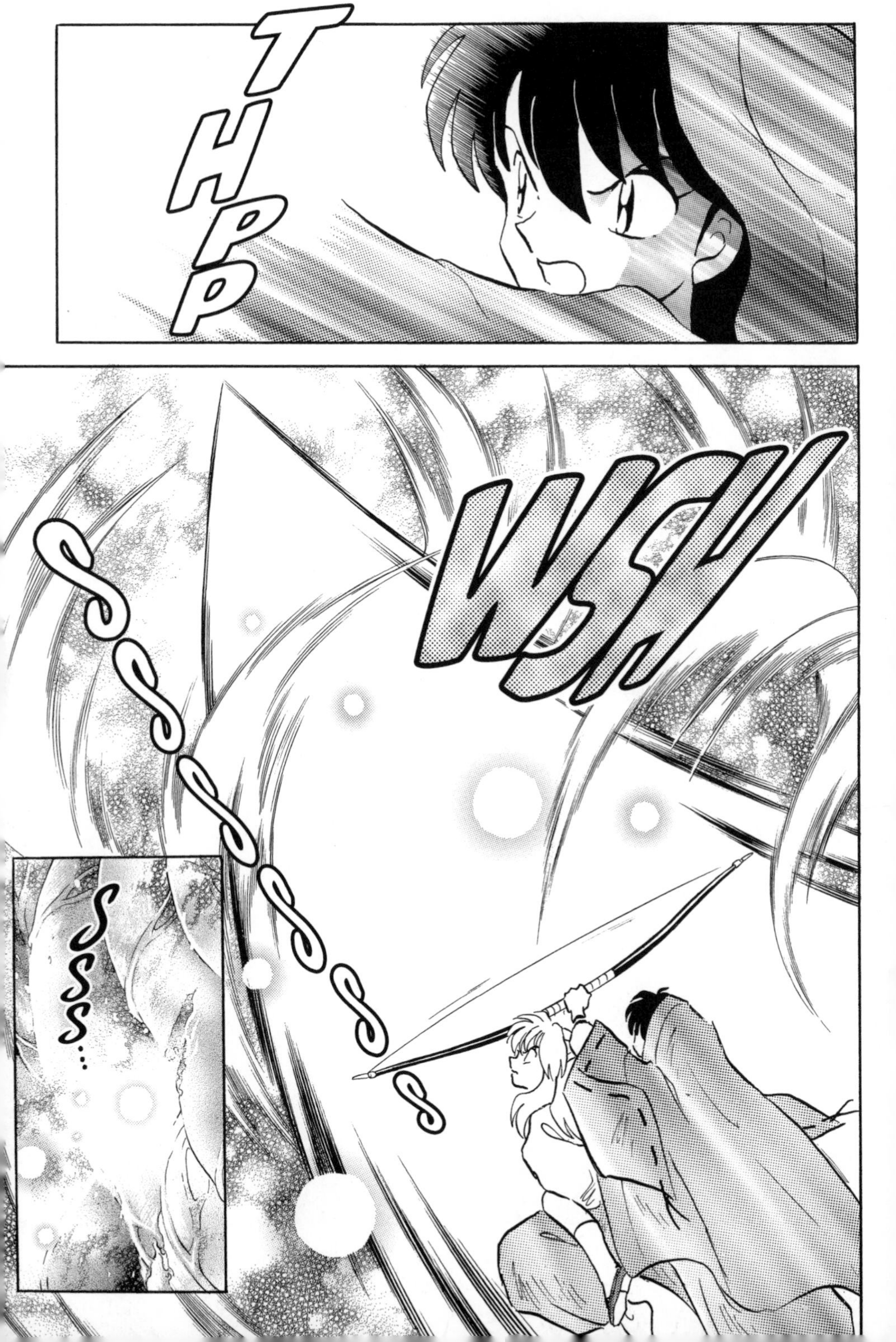
THPP
WSH
SSSSSSSS
SSS...

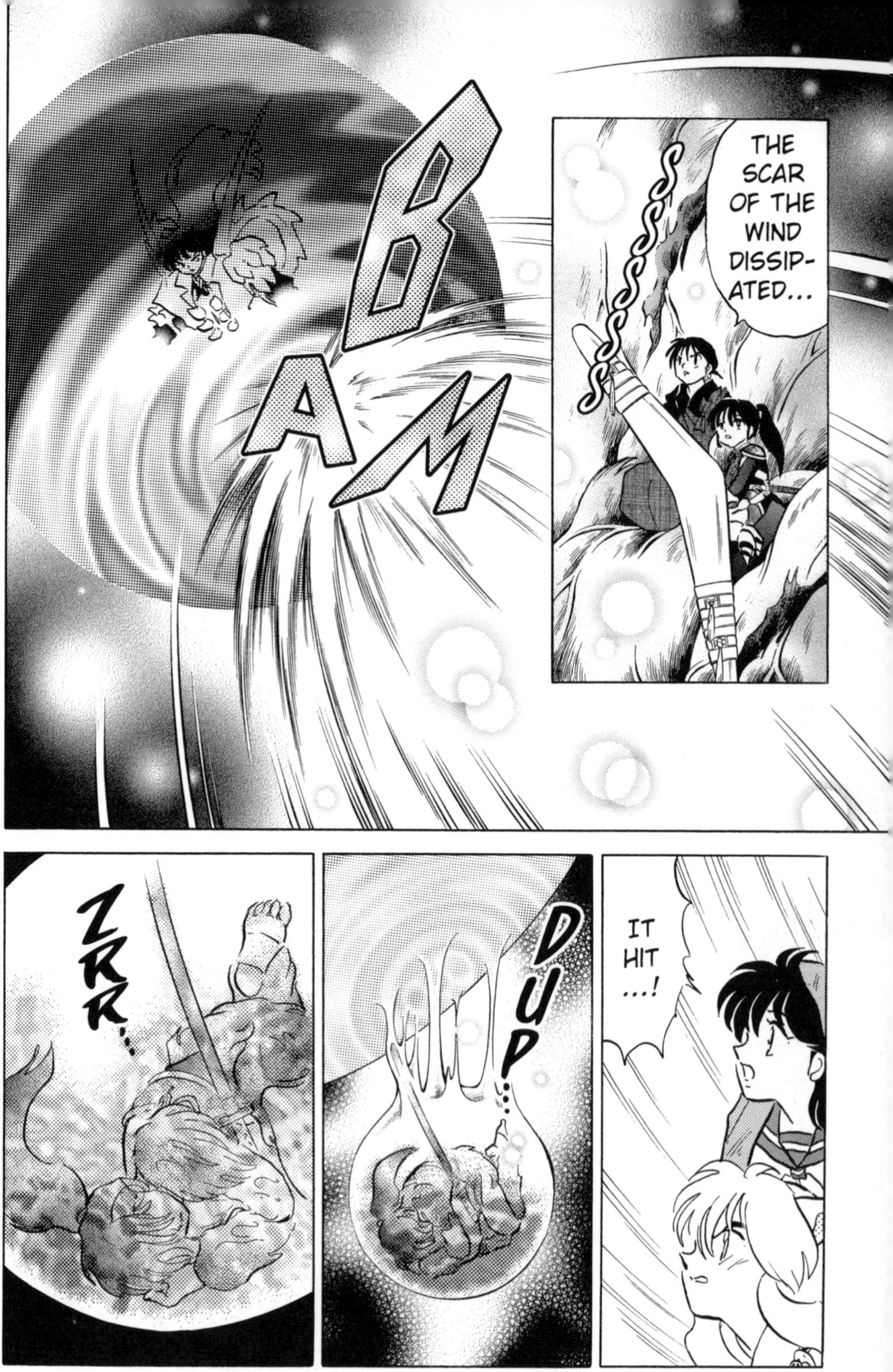
SSSSSS
THE SCAR OF THE WIND DISSIPATED...
BAM
IT HIT ...!
DUP...
ZRR...

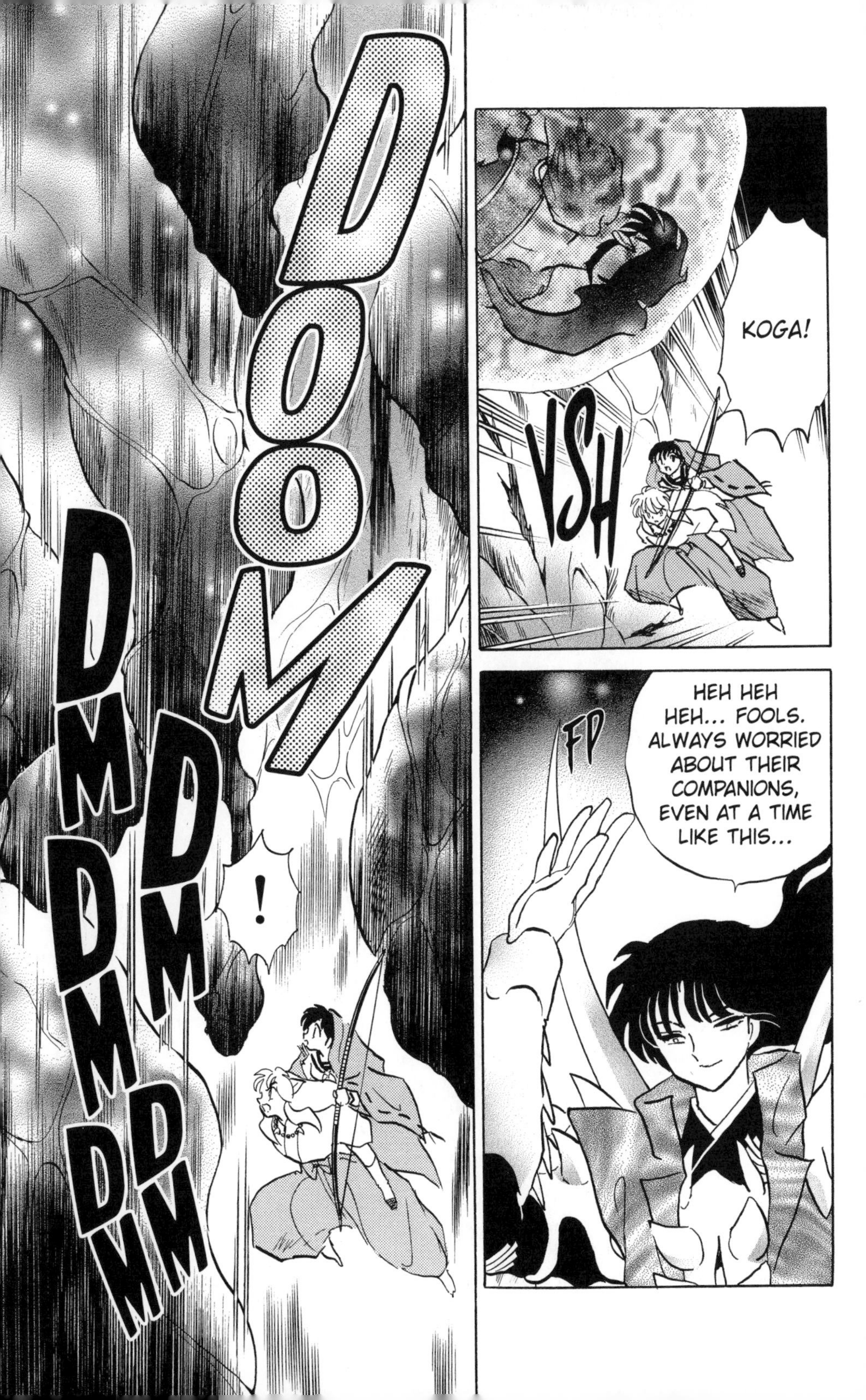
KOGA!
VSH
FP
HEH HEH HEH... FOOLS. ALWAYS WORRIED ABOUT THEIR COMPANIONS, EVEN AT A TIME LIKE THIS...
DOOM
!
DMDM
DMDMDM

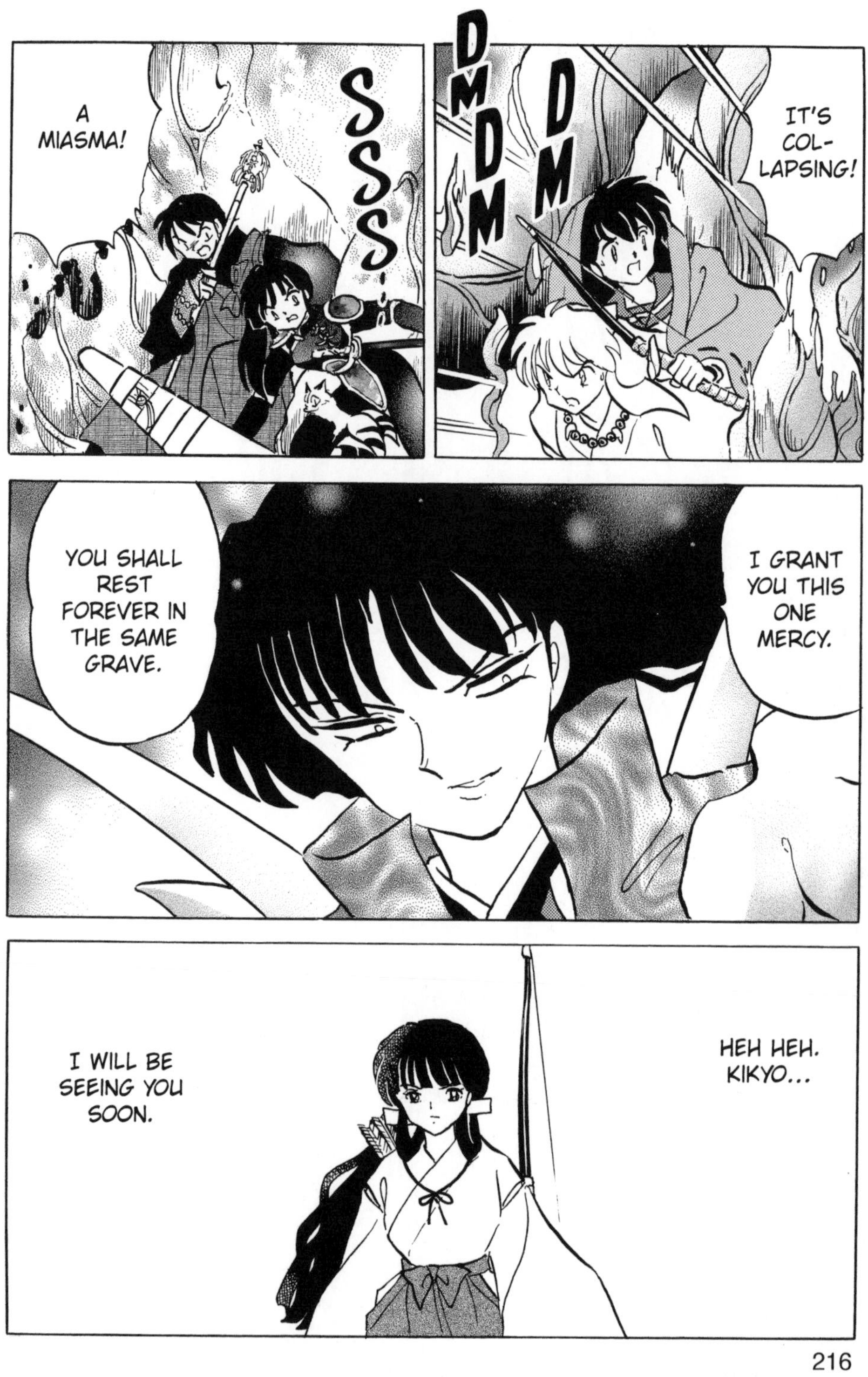
IT'S COL-LAPSING!
DM
DMDM
SSS
A MIASMA!
I GRANT YOU THIS ONE MERCY.
YOU SHALL REST FOREVER IN THE SAME GRAVE.
HEH HEH. KIKYO...
I WILL BE SEEING YOU SOON.

SCROLL TWO
HIS TRUE PURPOSE

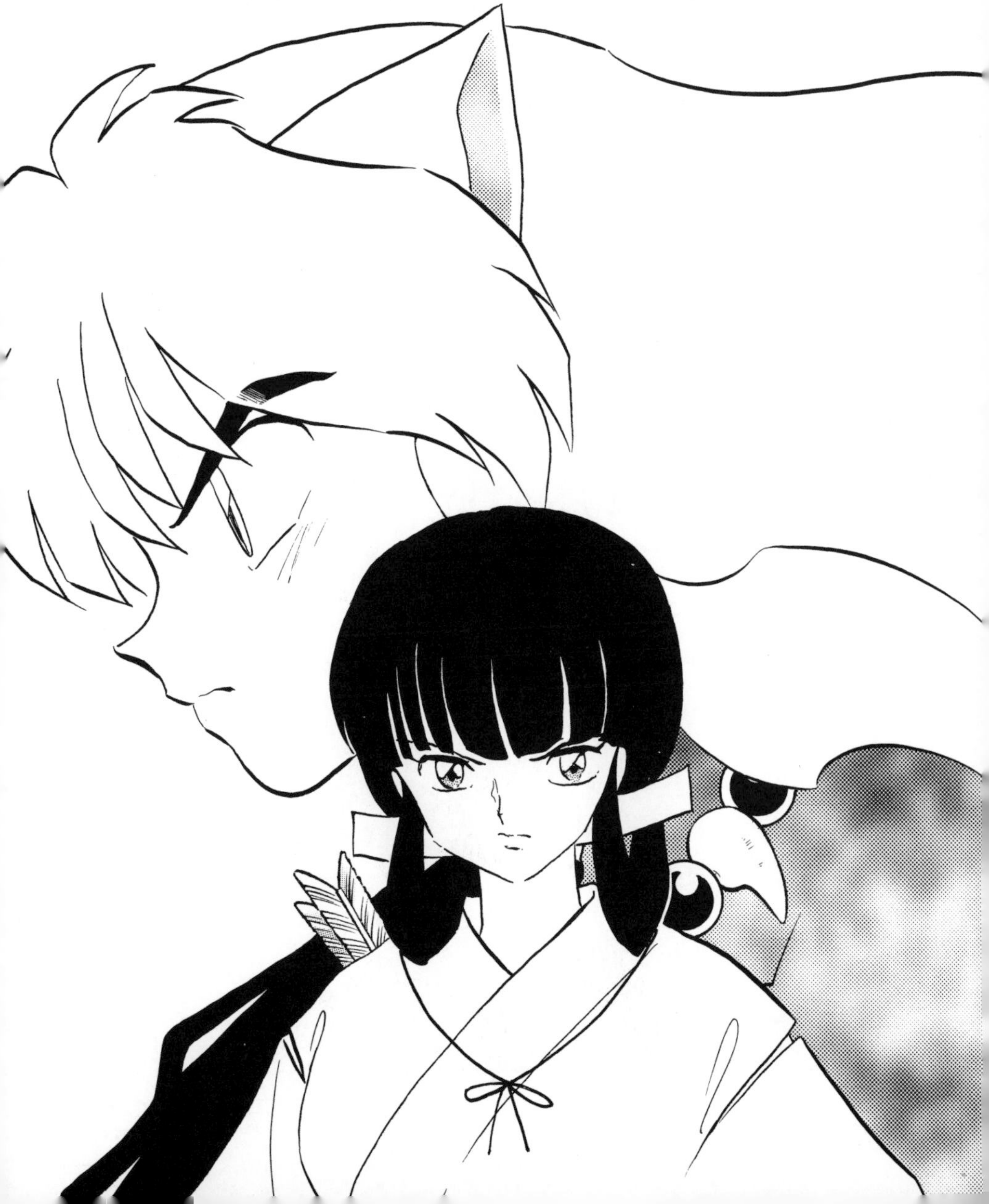

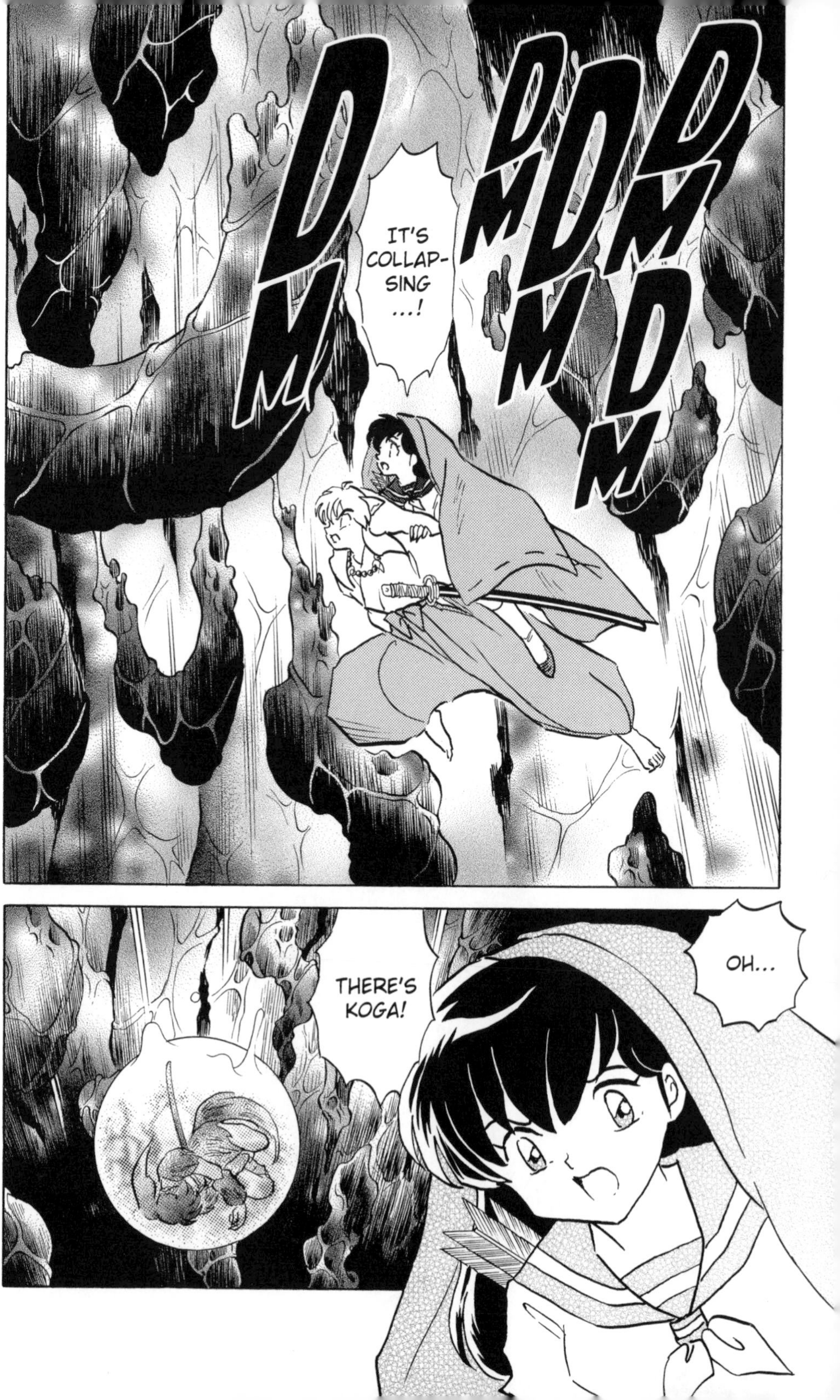
DMDMDMDM
IT'S COLLAP-SING ...!
DM
OH...
THERE'S KOGA!

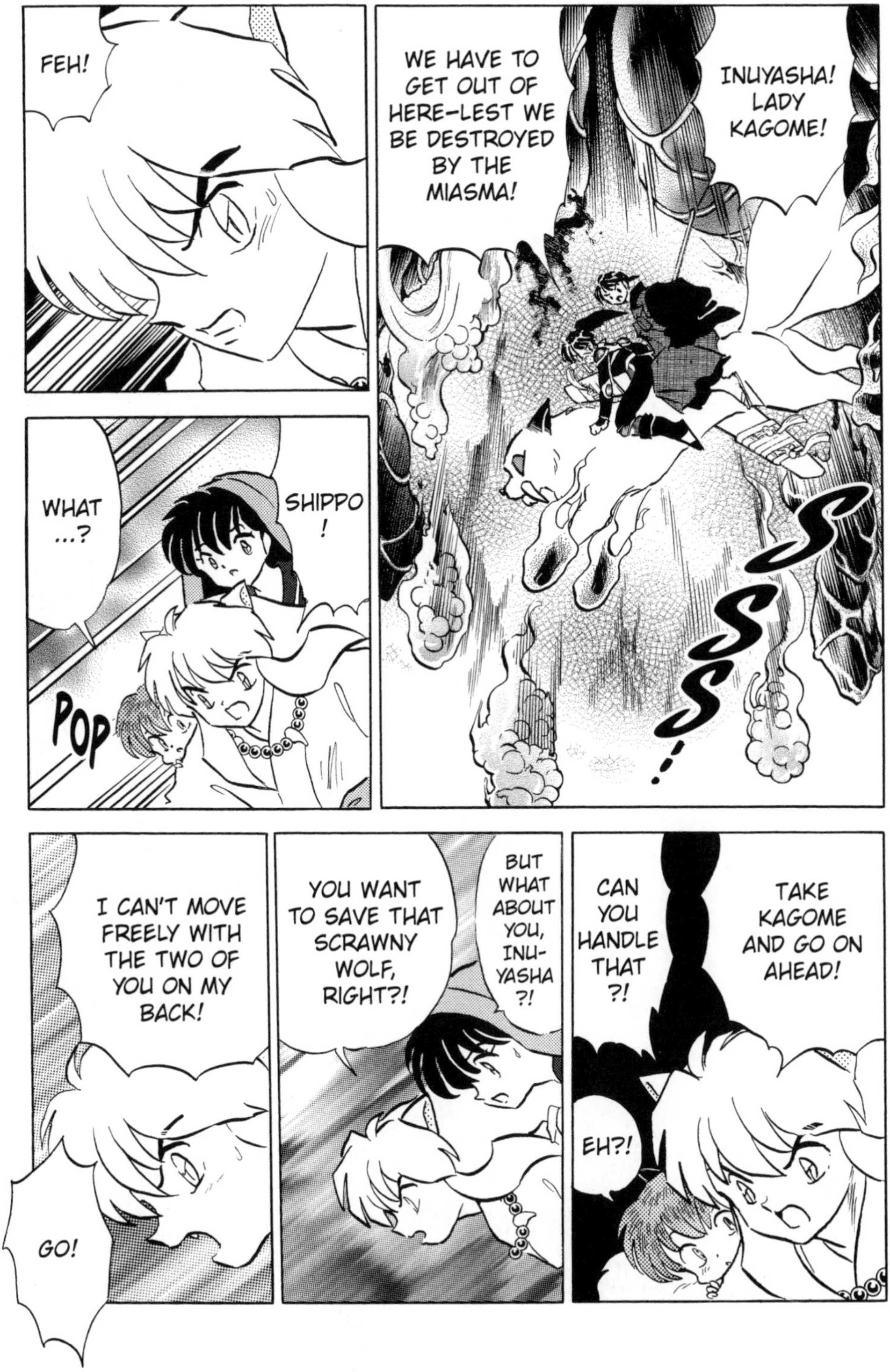
INUYASHA! LADY KAGOME!
WE HAVE TO GET OUT OF HERE–LEST WE BE DESTROYED BY THE MIASMA!
SSSS...
FEH!
SHIPPO!
WHAT ...?
POP
TAKE KAGOME AND GO ON AHEAD!
CAN YOU HANDLE THAT?!
EH?!
BUT WHAT ABOUT YOU, INU-YASHA?!
YOU WANT TO SAVE THAT SCRAWNY WOLF, RIGHT?!
I CAN'T MOVE FREELY WITH THE TWO OF YOU ON MY BACK!
GO!

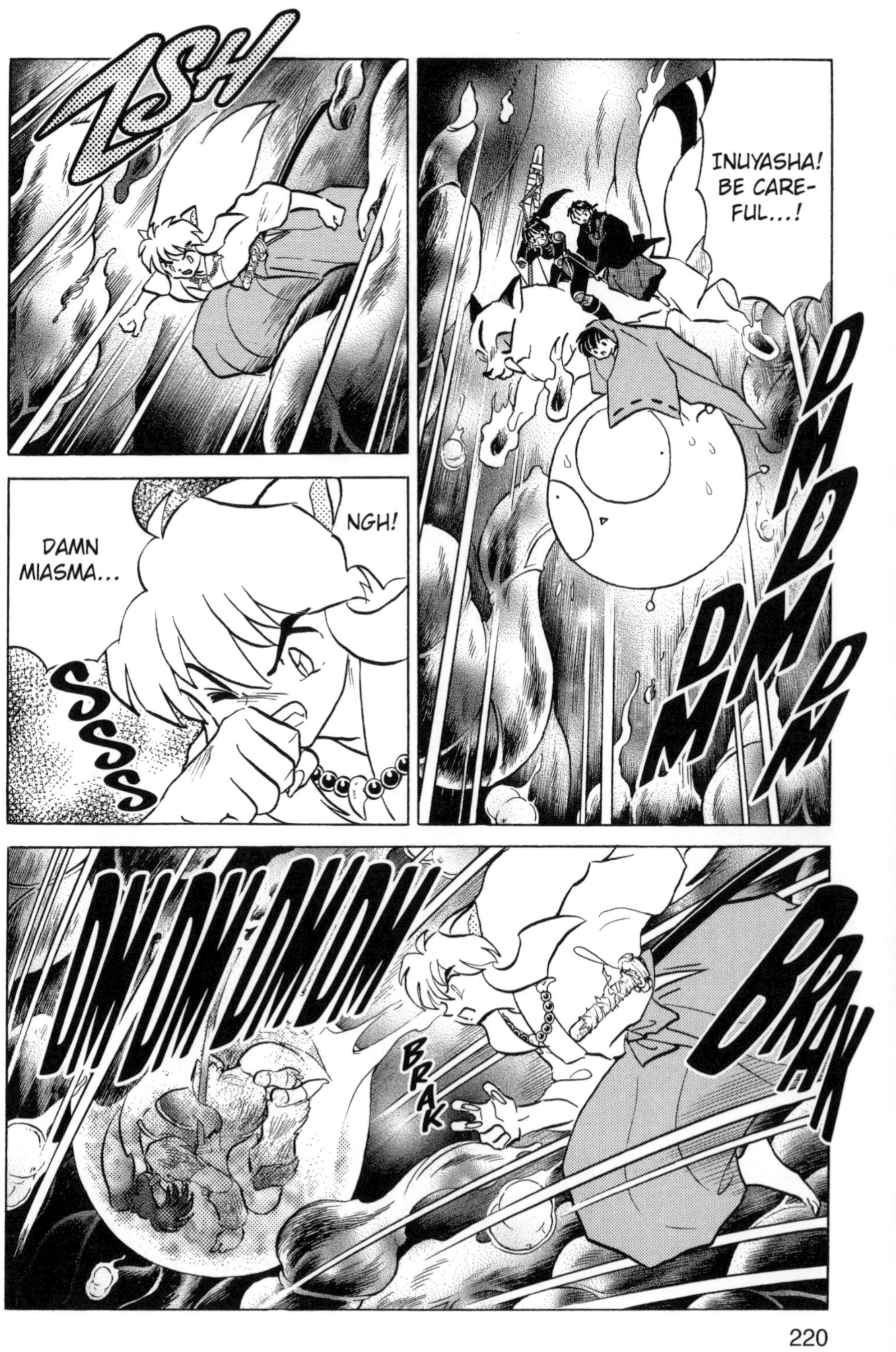
INUYASHA! BE CARE-FUL...!
DMDMDM
DMDM
ZSH
NGH!
DAMN MIASMA...
SSSS
BRAK
BRAK
DMDMDMDM

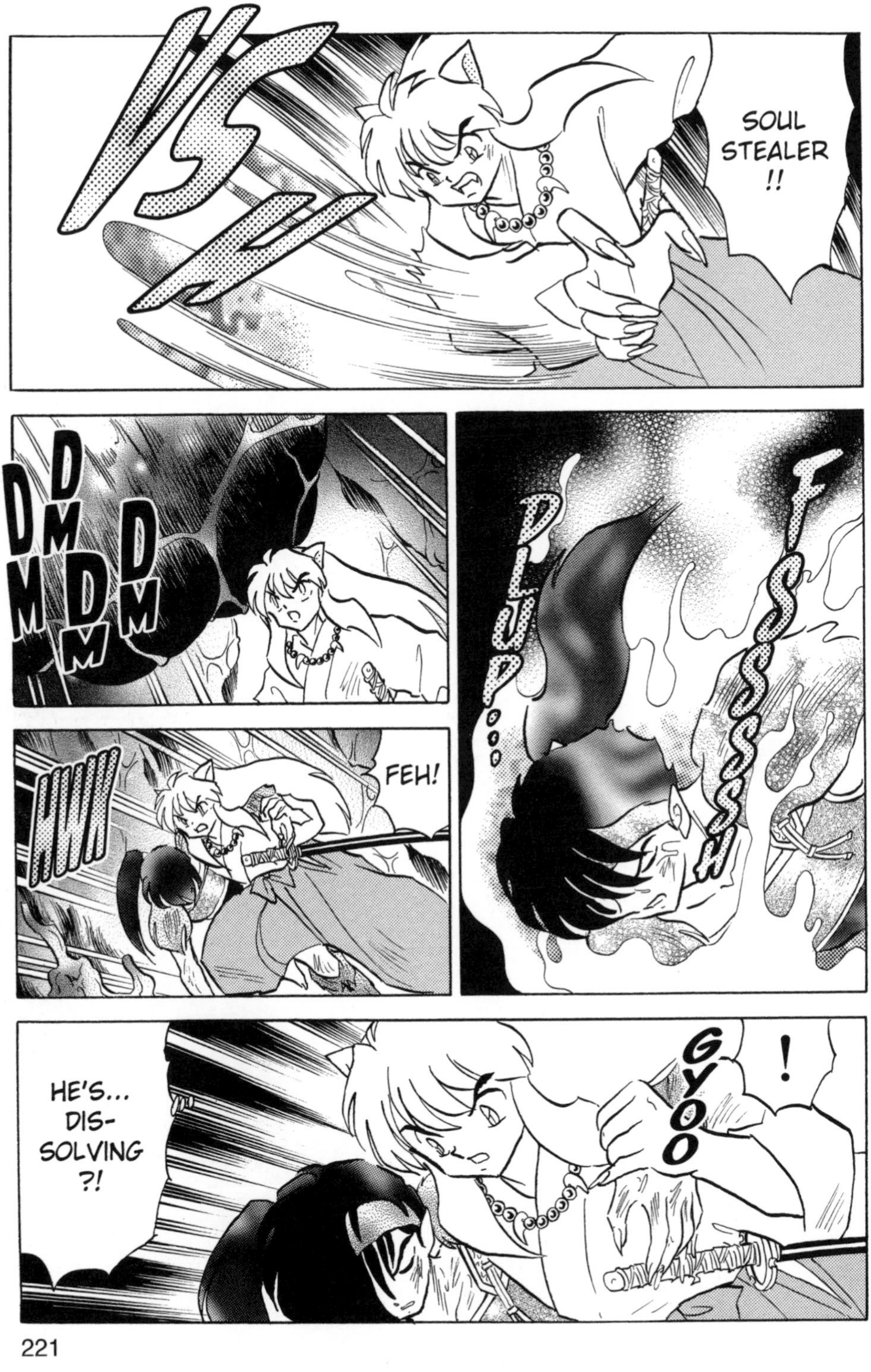
VSH
SOUL STEALER !!
FSSSSSSH
DLUP...
DMDMDMDM
FEH!
HWWW
!
GYOO
HE'S... DIS-SOLVING ?!

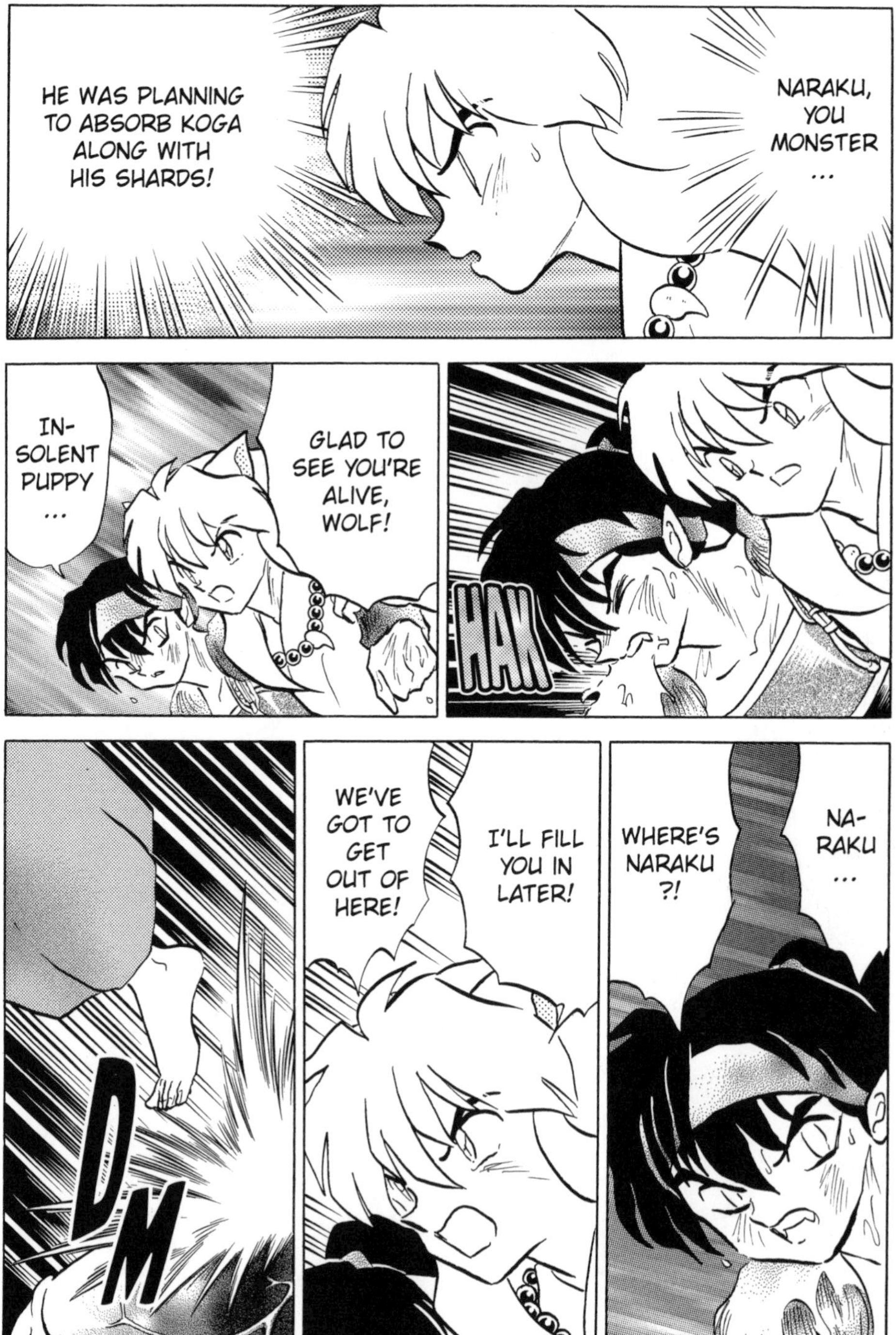
NARAKU, YOU MONSTER ...
HE WAS PLANNING TO ABSORB KOGA ALONG WITH HIS SHARDS!
HAK
GLAD TO SEE YOU'RE ALIVE, WOLF!
IN-SOLENT PUPPY ...
NA-RAKU ...
WHERE'S NARAKU ?!
I'LL FILL YOU IN LATER!
WE'VE GOT TO GET OUT OF HERE!
DM

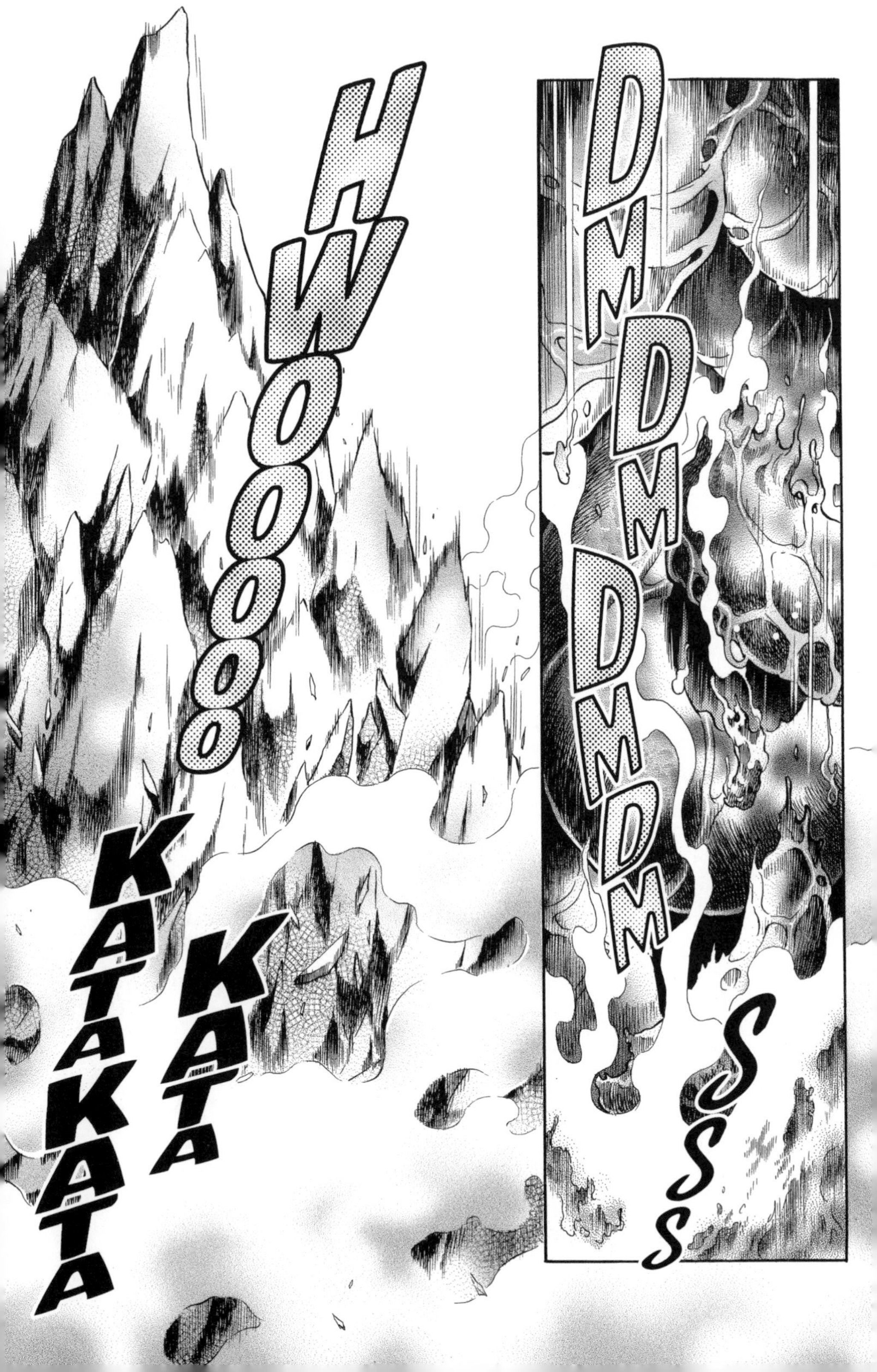
DMMDMMDMMDMM
SSSS
HWOOOOOO
KATAKATA
KATA

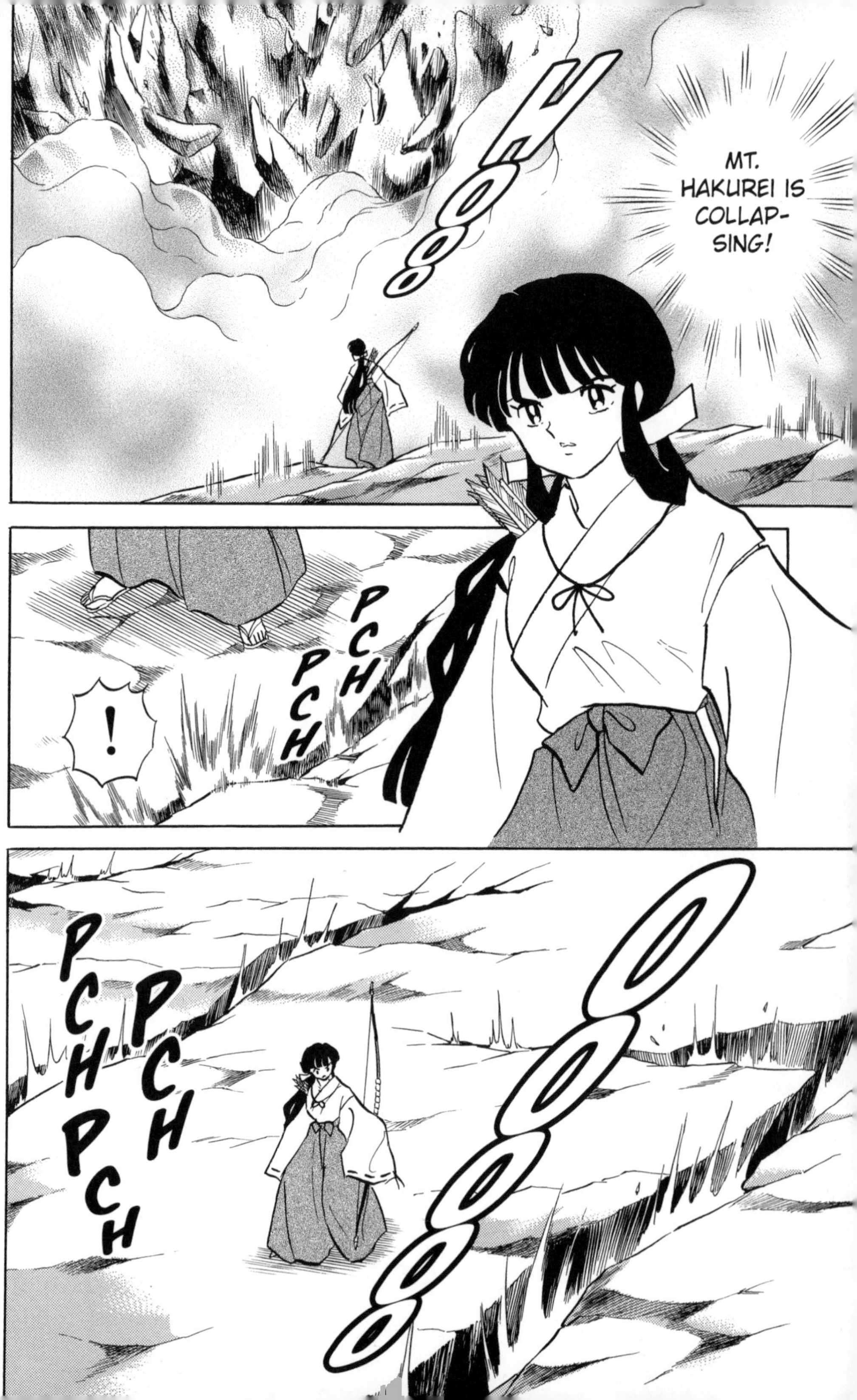
MT. HAKUREI IS COLLAP-SING!
HOOOOO
PCH PCH
!
OOOOOOO
PCH PCH
PCH PCH

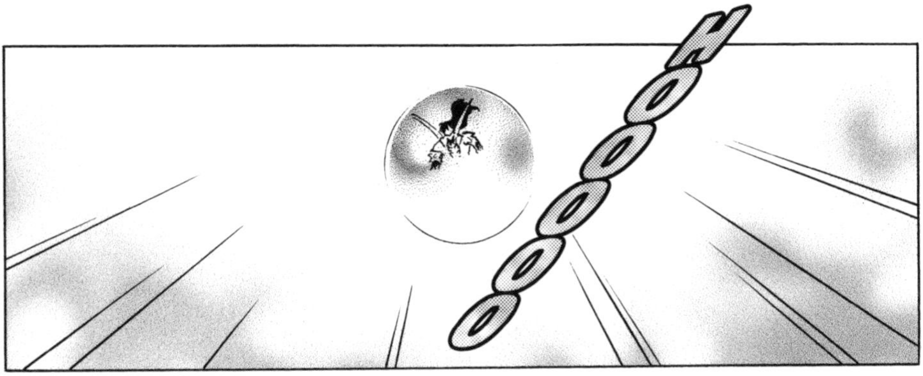
HOOOOO
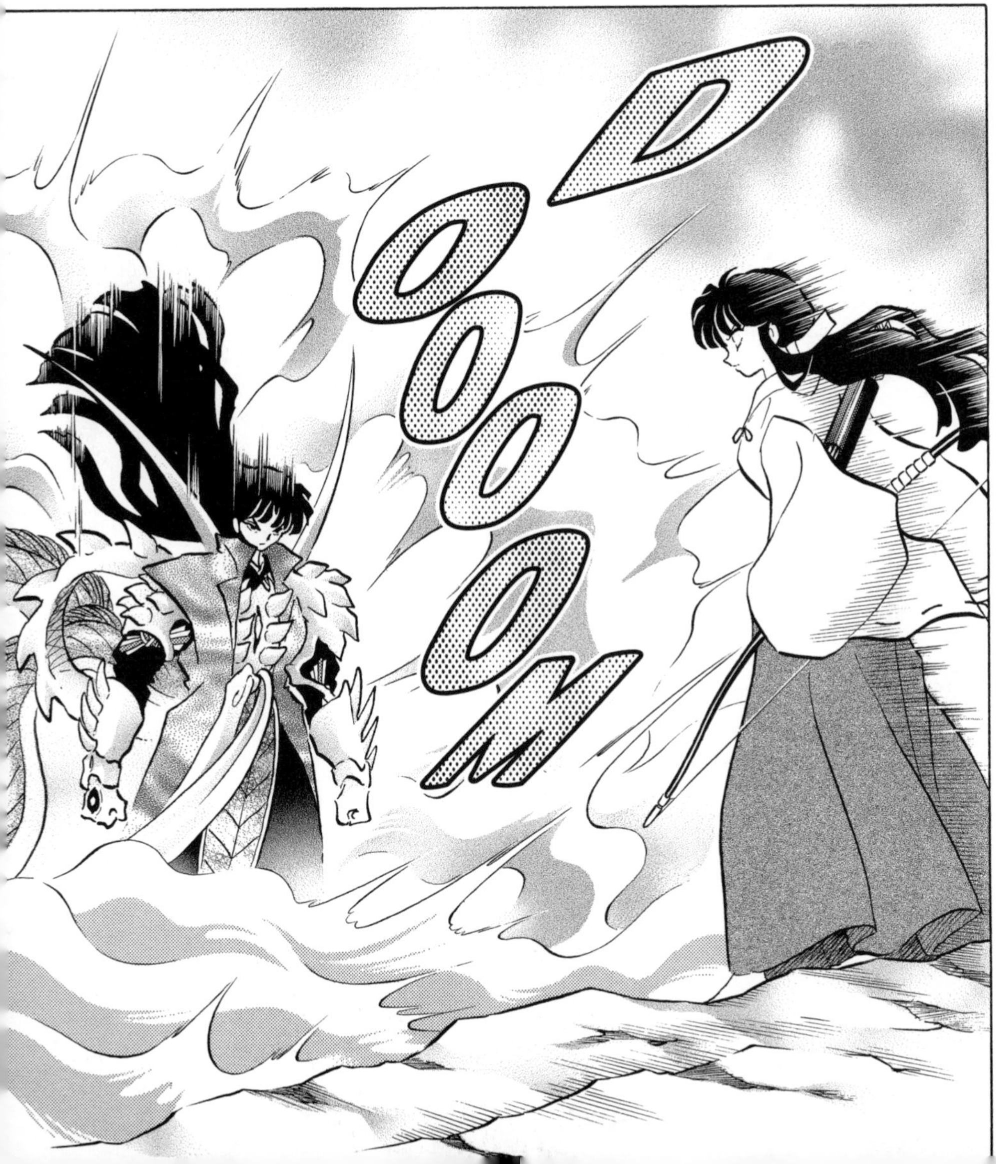
DOOOOM

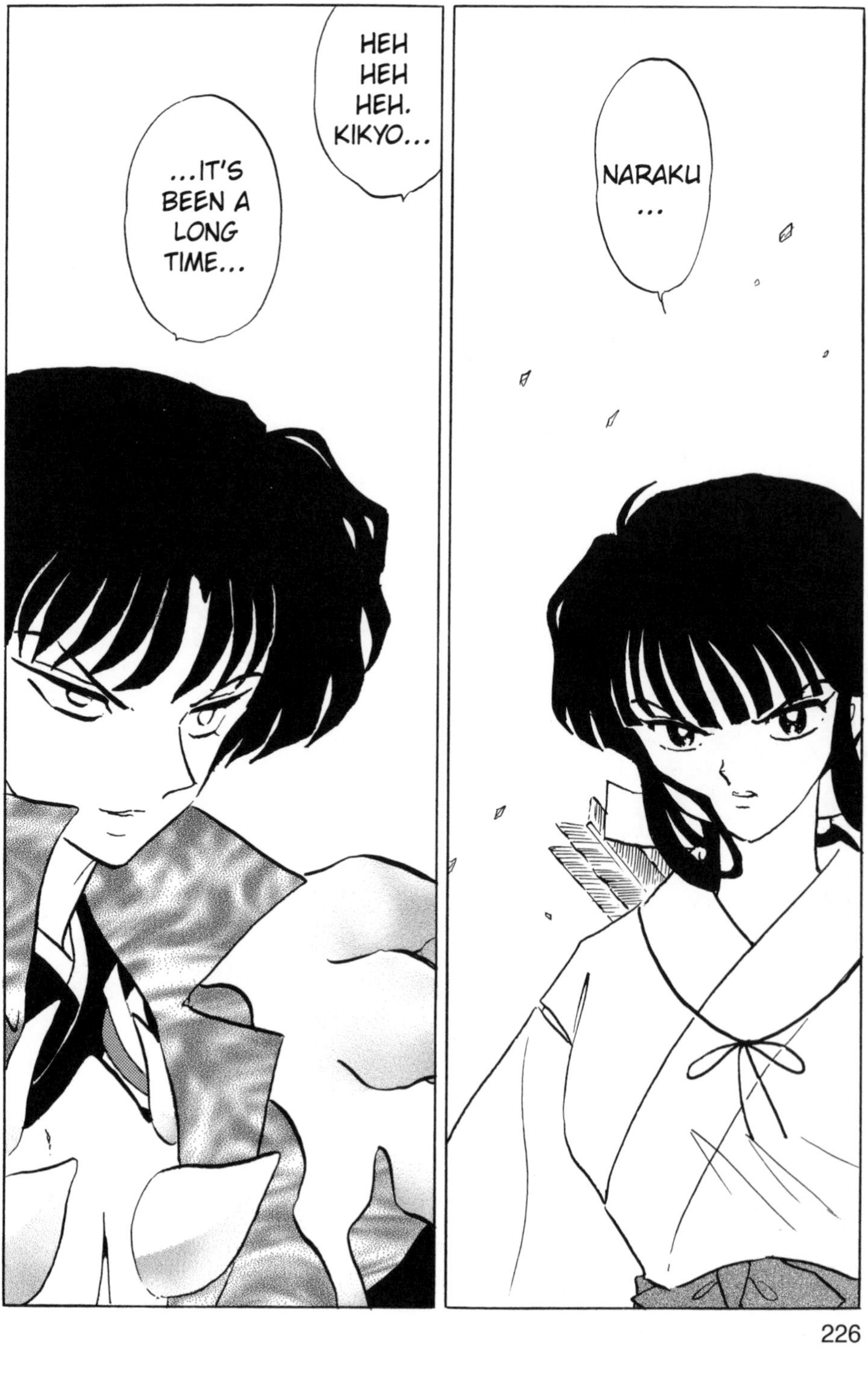
NARAKU ...
HEH HEH HEH. KIKYO...
...IT'S BEEN A LONG TIME...

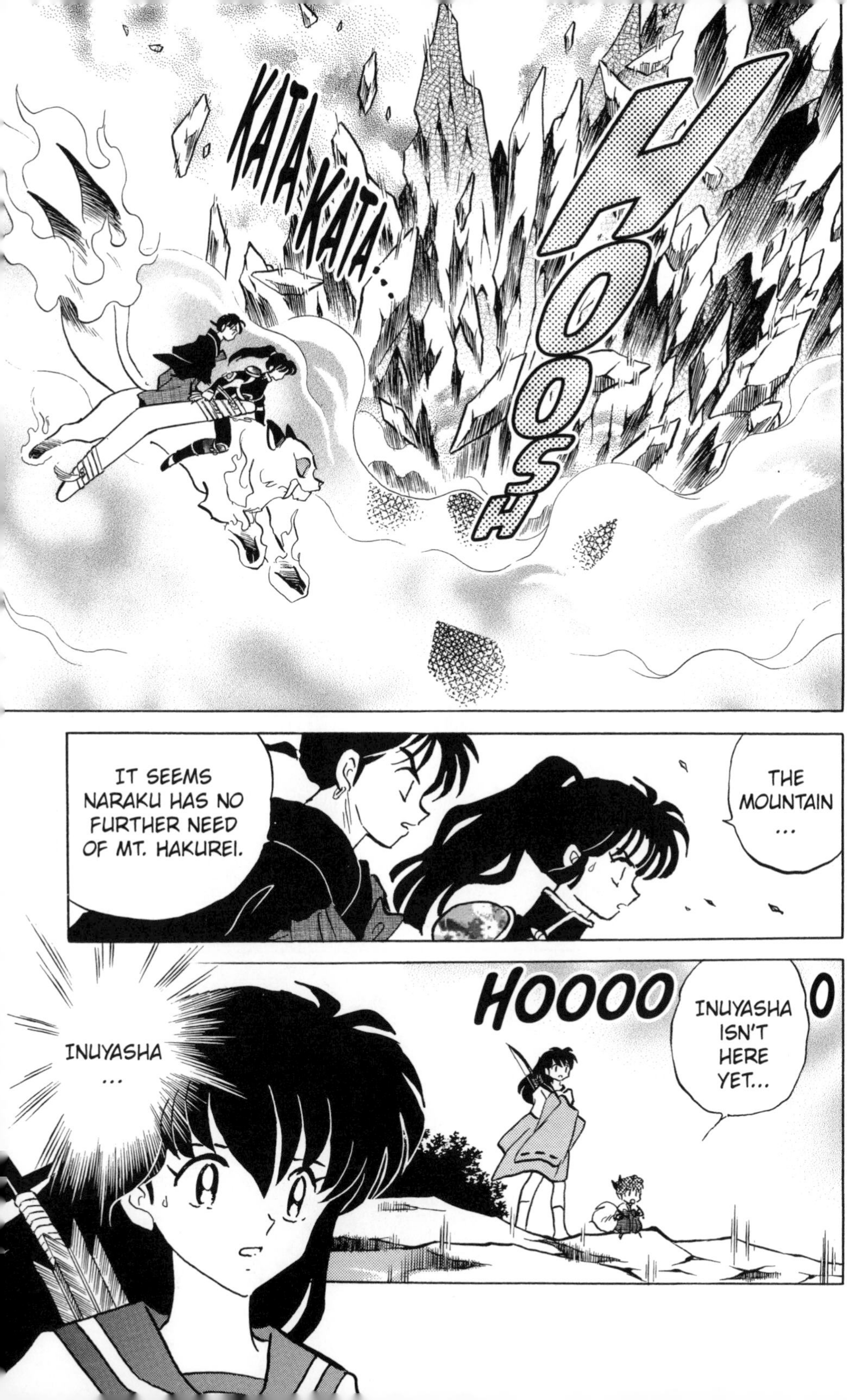
WHOOSH
KATA KATA KATA...
THE MOUNTAIN...
IT SEEMS NARAKU HAS NO FURTHER NEED OF MT. HAKUREI.
HOOOOO
INUYASHA ISN'T HERE YET...
INUYASHA...

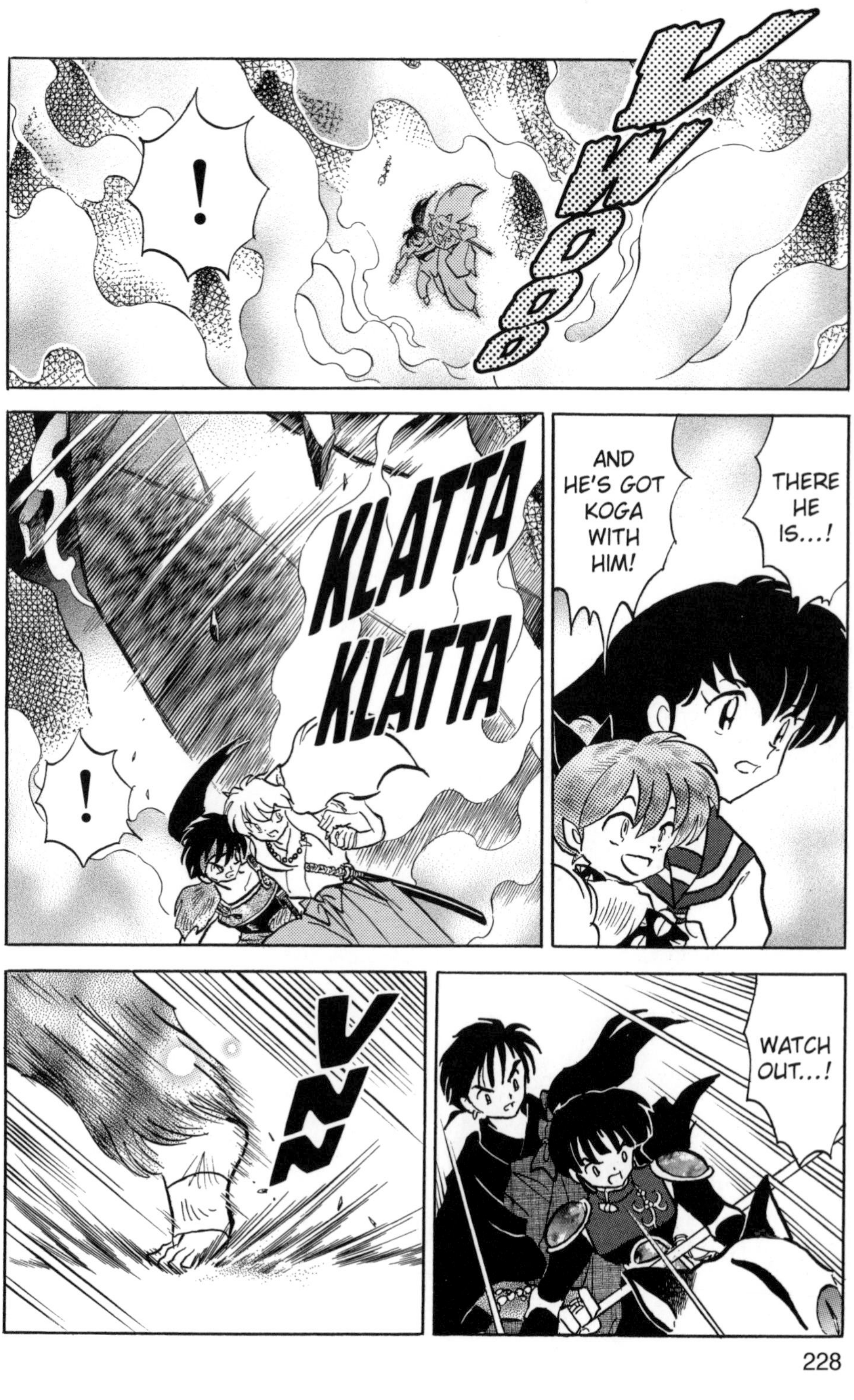
VWOOOOO
!
THERE HE IS...!
AND HE'S GOT KOGA WITH HIM!
KLATTA KLATTA
!
WATCH OUT...!
VNN

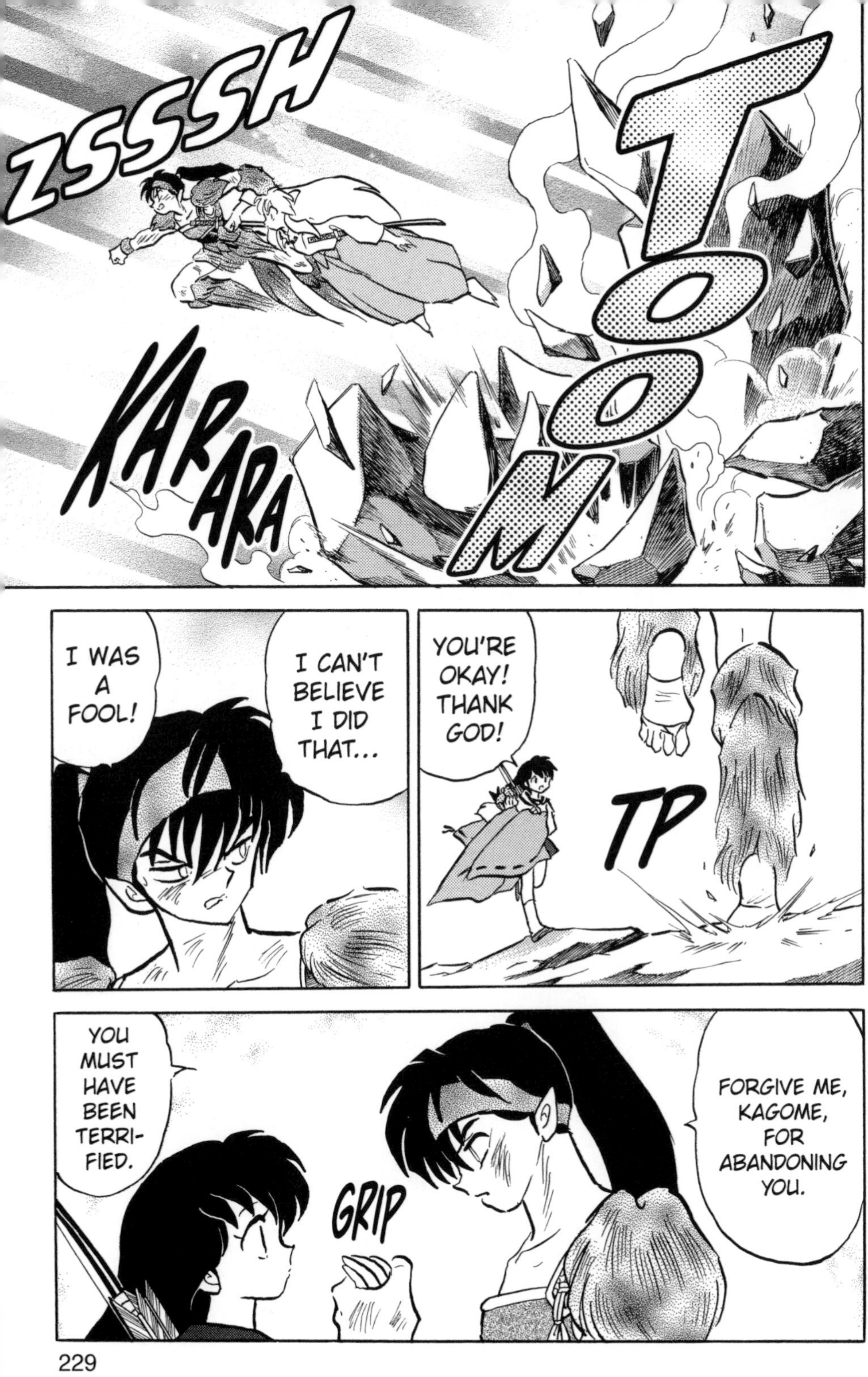
TOOM
ZSSSH
KARARA
YOU'RE OKAY! THANK GOD!
TP
I CAN'T BELIEVE I DID THAT...
I WAS A FOOL!
FORGIVE ME, KAGOME, FOR ABANDONING YOU.
GRIP
YOU MUST HAVE BEEN TERRI-FIED.

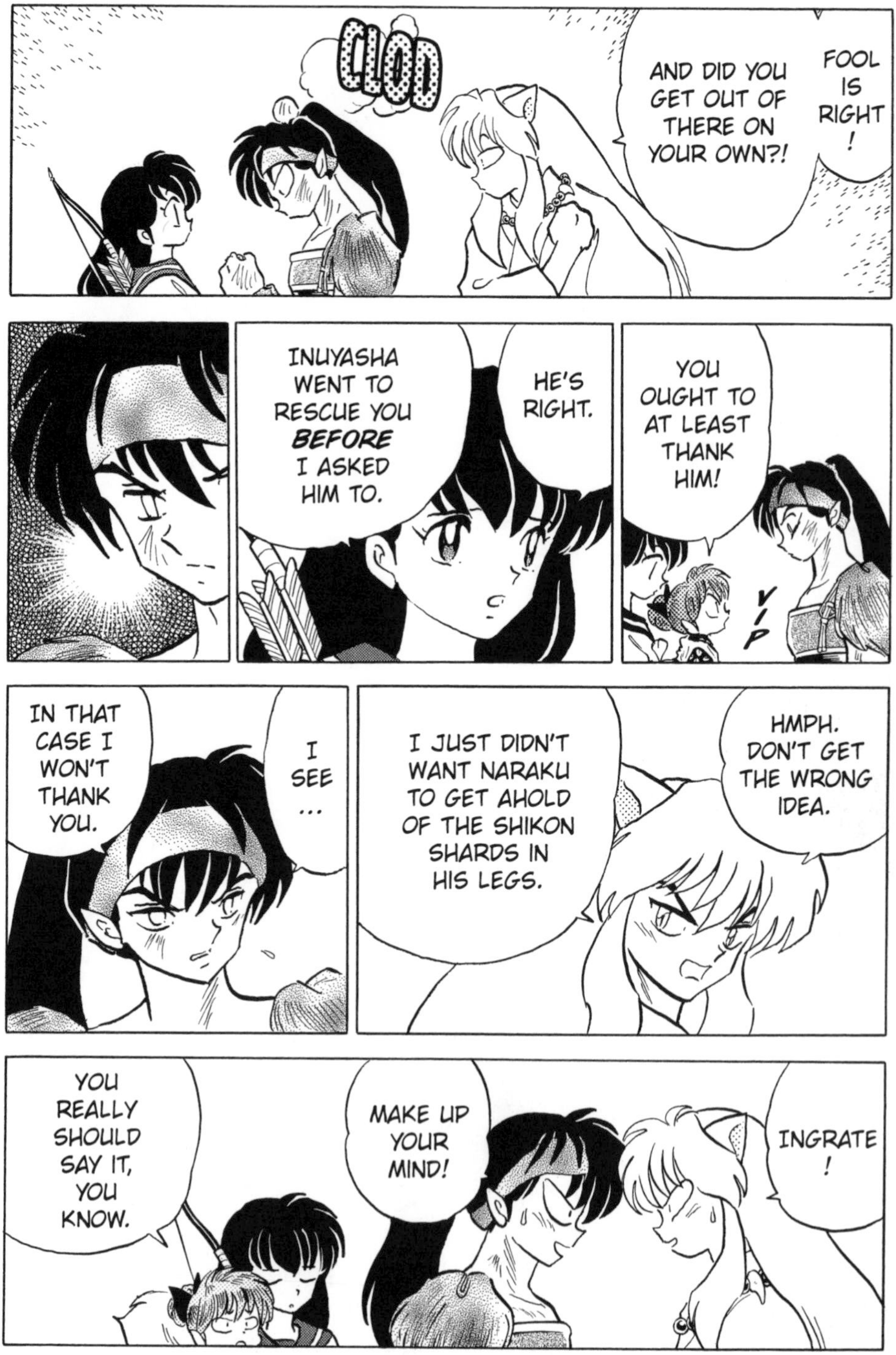
FOOL IS RIGHT!
AND DID YOU GET OUT OF THERE ON YOUR OWN?!
CLOD
YOU OUGHT TO AT LEAST THANK HIM!
HE'S RIGHT.
INUYASHA WENT TO RESCUE YOU BEFORE I ASKED HIM TO.
HMPH. DON'T GET THE WRONG IDEA.
I JUST DIDN'T WANT NARAKU TO GET AHOLD OF THE SHIKON SHARDS IN HIS LEGS.
I SEE...
IN THAT CASE I WON'T THANK YOU.
INGRATE!
MAKE UP YOUR MIND!
YOU REALLY SHOULD SAY IT, YOU KNOW.

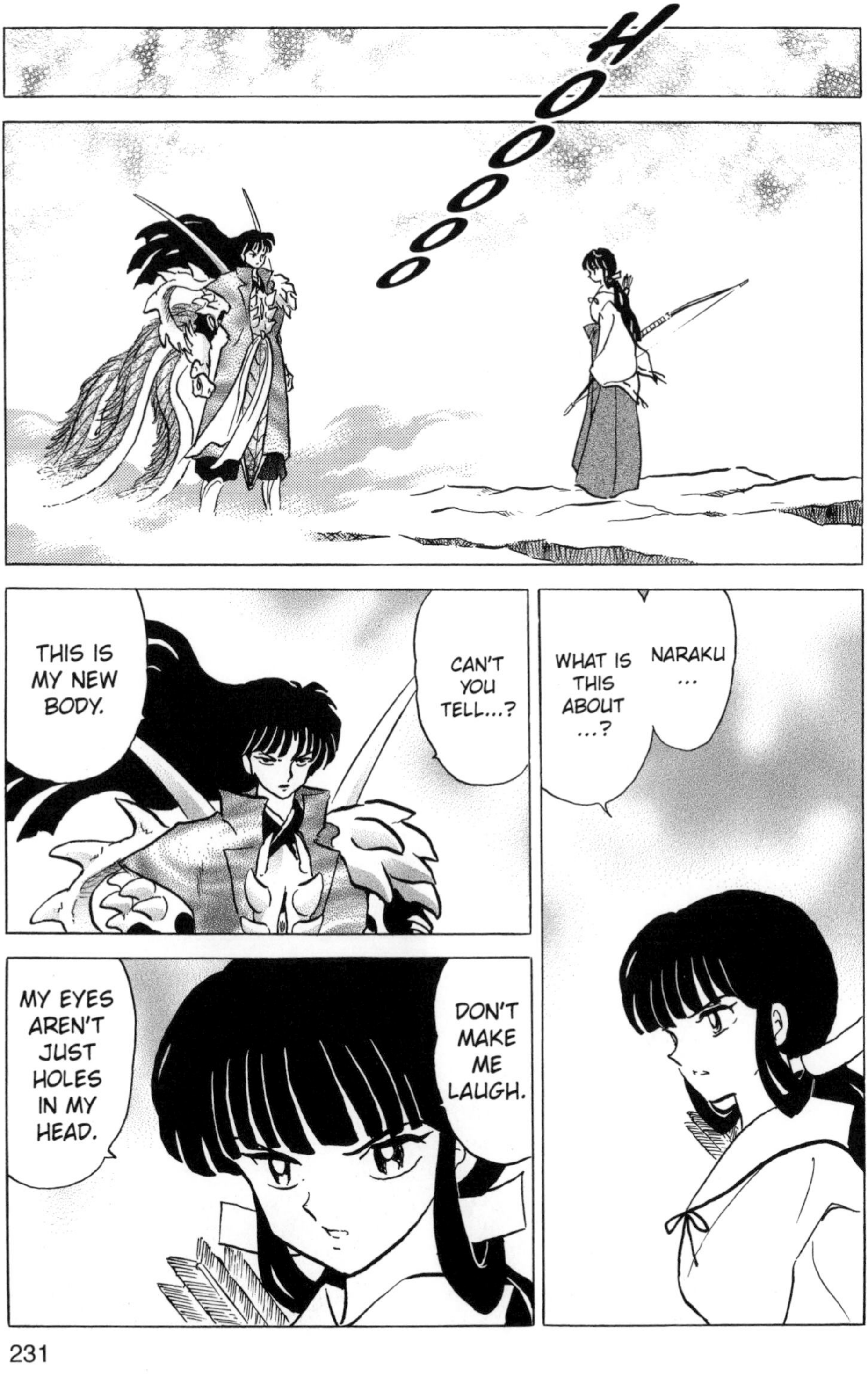
HOOOOO
NARAKU...
WHAT IS THIS ABOUT...?
CAN'T YOU TELL...?
THIS IS MY NEW BODY.
DON'T MAKE ME LAUGH.
MY EYES AREN'T JUST HOLES IN MY HEAD.

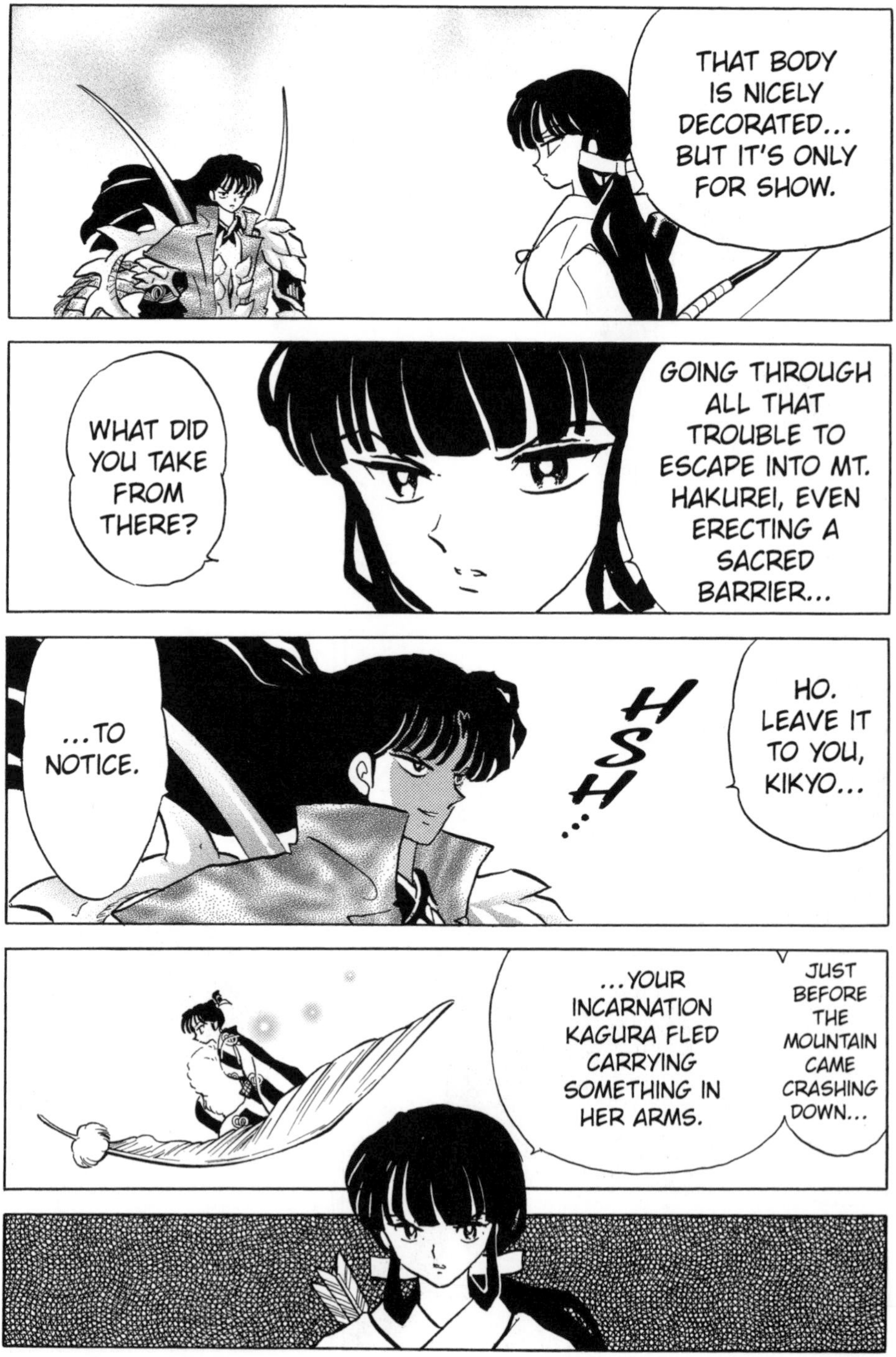
THAT BODY IS NICELY DECORATED... BUT IT'S ONLY FOR SHOW.
GOING THROUGH ALL THAT TROUBLE TO ESCAPE INTO MT. HAKUREI, EVEN ERECTING A SACRED BARRIER...
WHAT DID YOU TAKE FROM THERE?
HO. LEAVE IT TO YOU, KIKYO...
HSH...
...TO NOTICE.
JUST BEFORE THE MOUNTAIN CAME CRASHING DOWN...
...YOUR INCARNATION KAGURA FLED CARRYING SOMETHING IN HER ARMS.

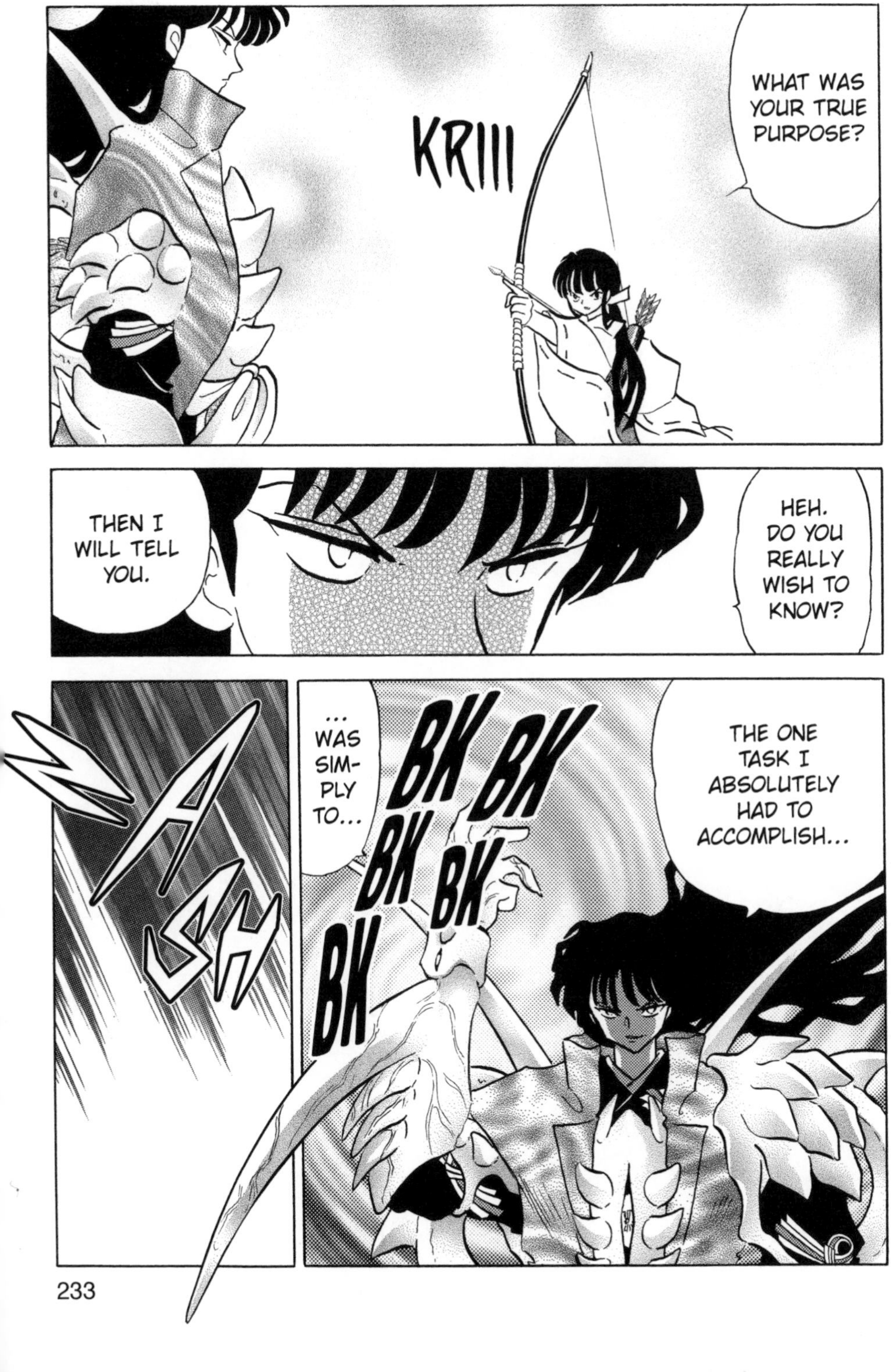
WHAT WAS YOUR TRUE PURPOSE?
KRIII
HEH. DO YOU REALLY WISH TO KNOW?
THEN I WILL TELL YOU.
THE ONE TASK I ABSOLUTELY HAD TO ACCOMPLISH...
...WAS SIMPLY TO...
BK BK BK BK BK
ZASH

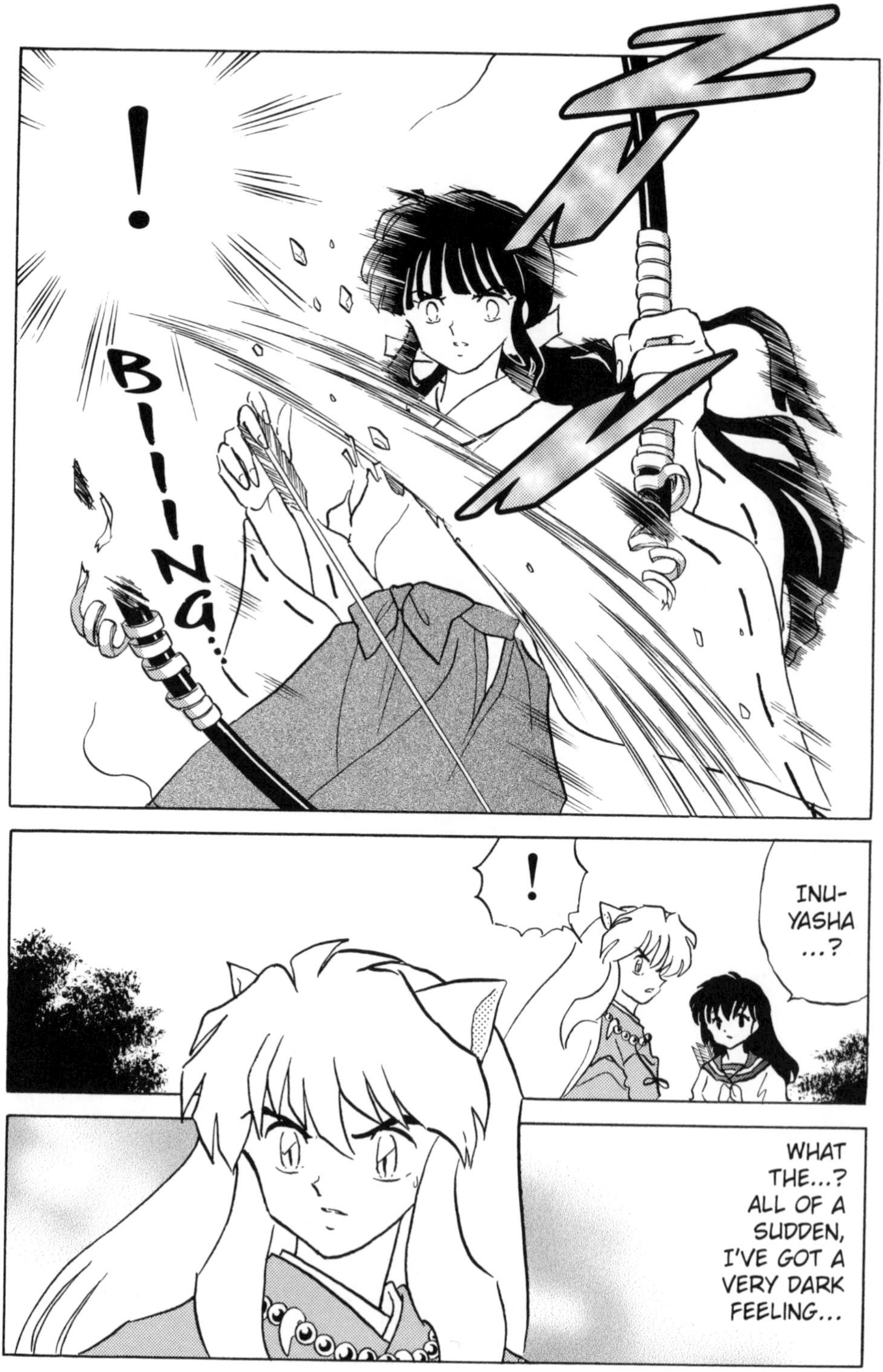
!
BIIING...
INU-YASHA...?
!
WHAT THE...? ALL OF A SUDDEN, I'VE GOT A VERY DARK FEELING...

SCROLL THREE
THE NEW BODY

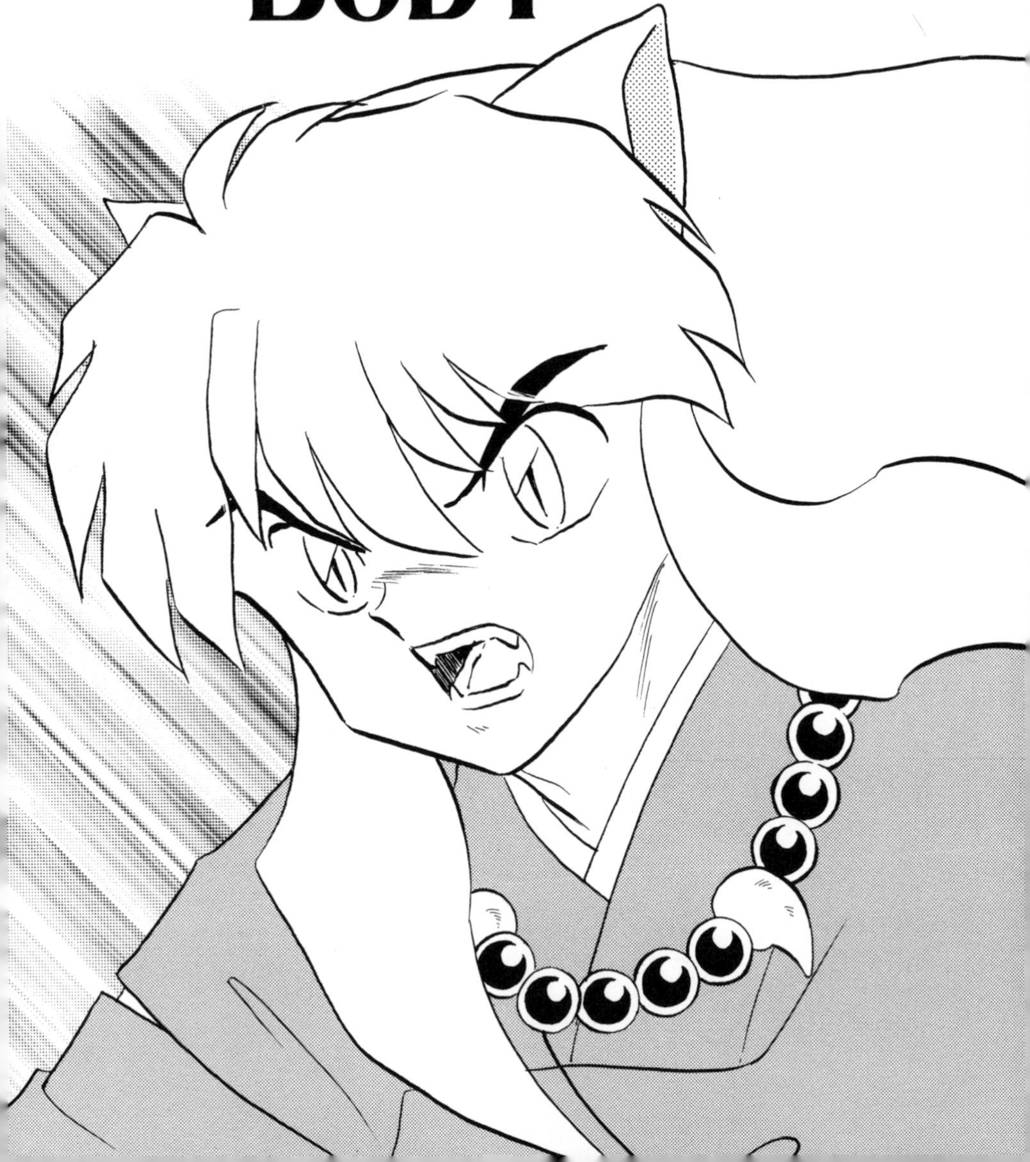

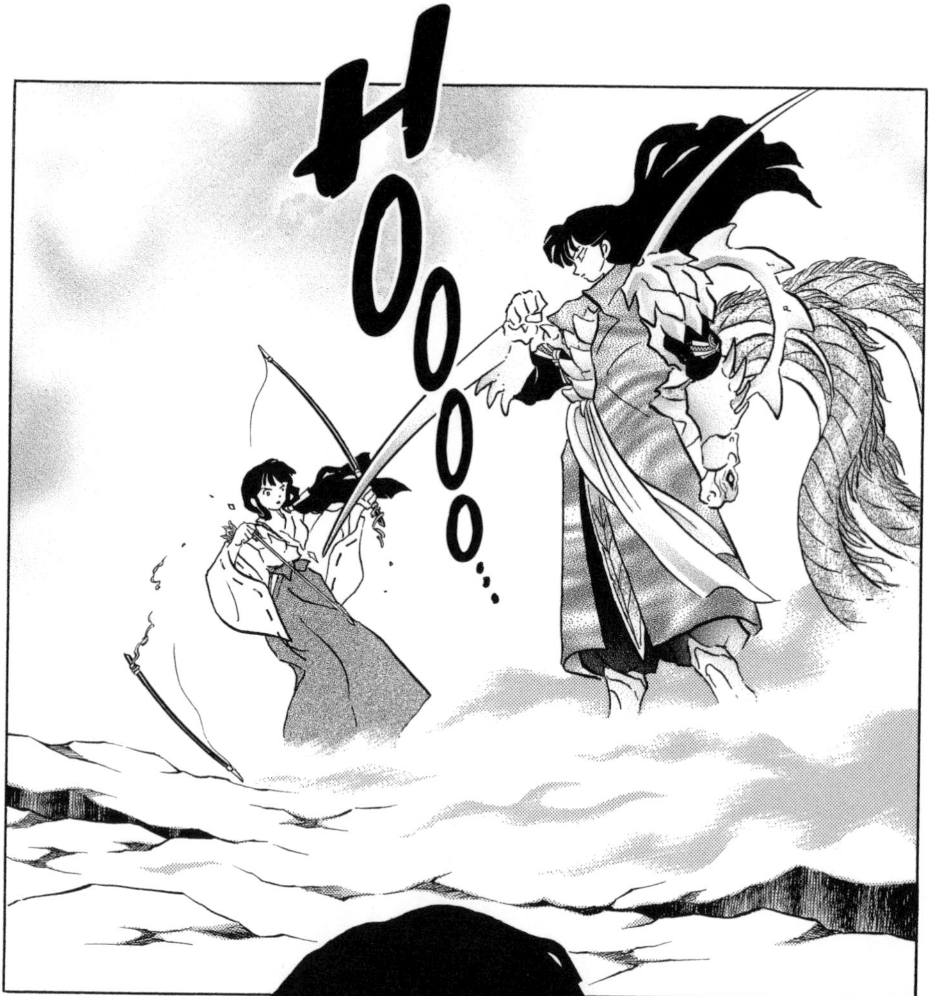
HOOOOOO...
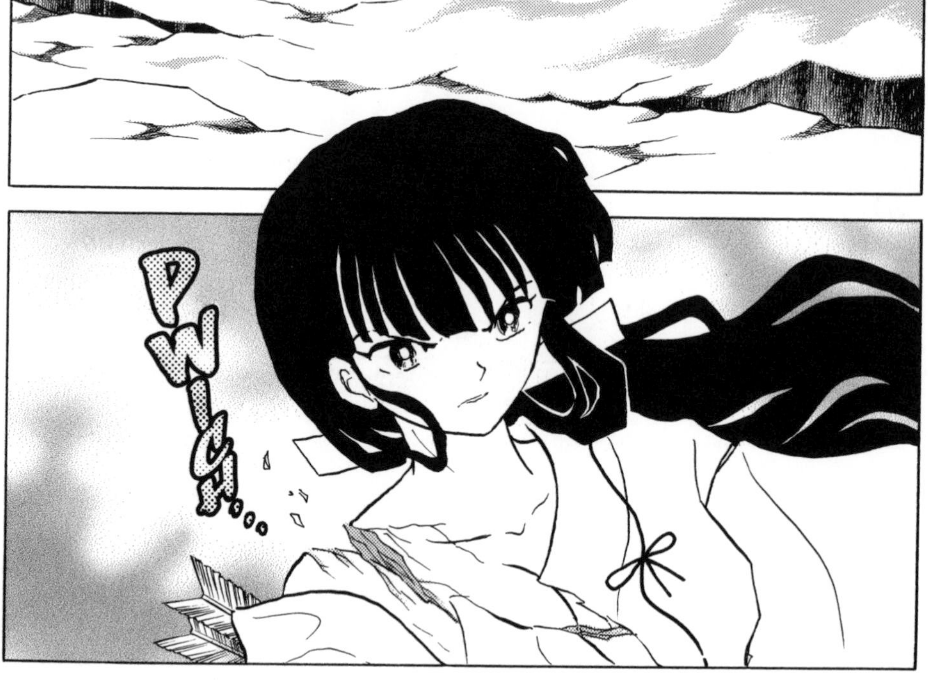
PWISH...

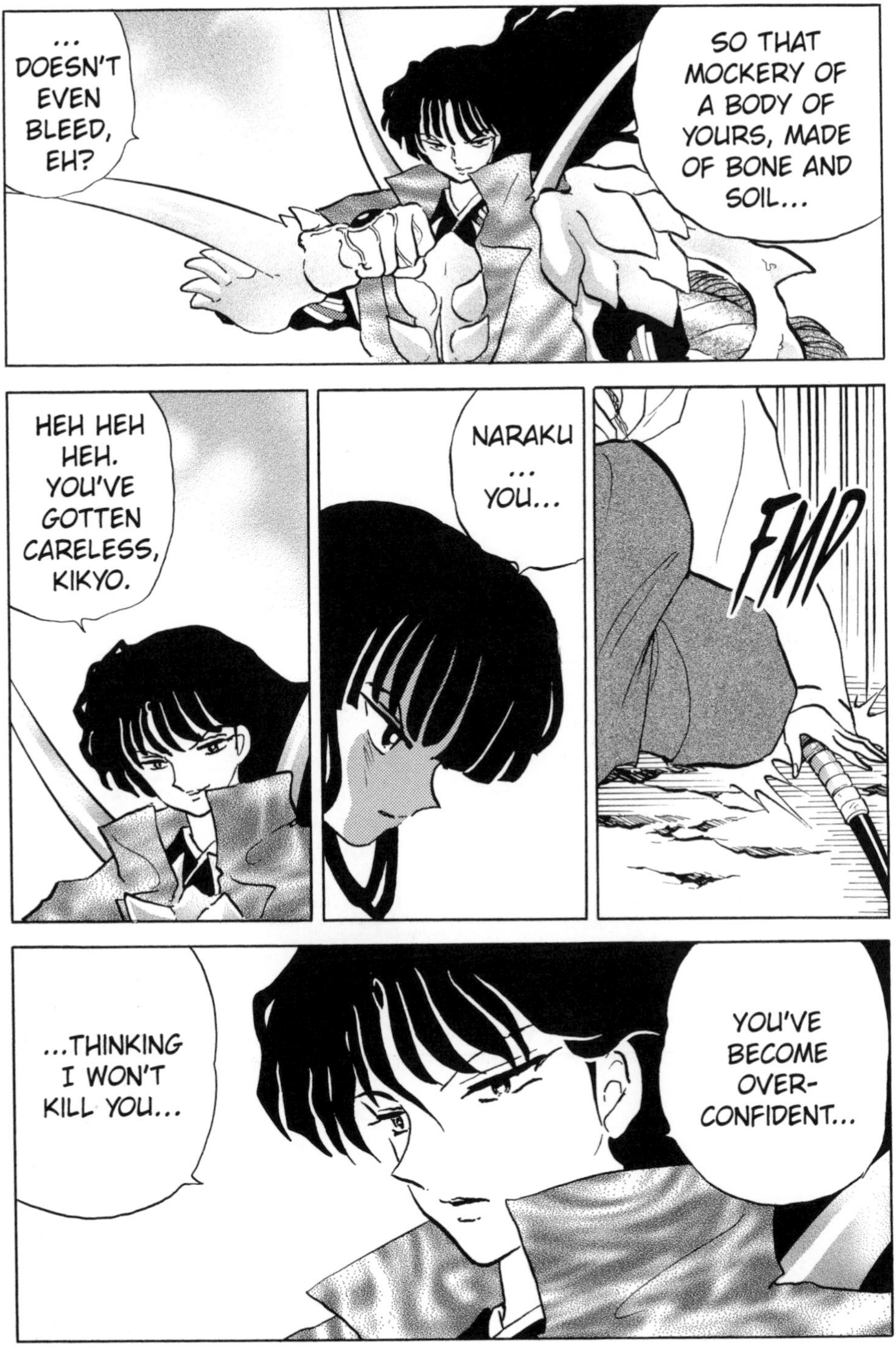
SO THAT MOCKERY OF A BODY OF YOURS, MADE OF BONE AND SOIL...
... DOESN'T EVEN BLEED, EH?
FMP
NARAKU ... YOU...
HEH HEH HEH. YOU'VE GOTTEN CARELESS, KIKYO.
YOU'VE BECOME OVER-CONFIDENT...
...THINKING I WON'T KILL YOU...

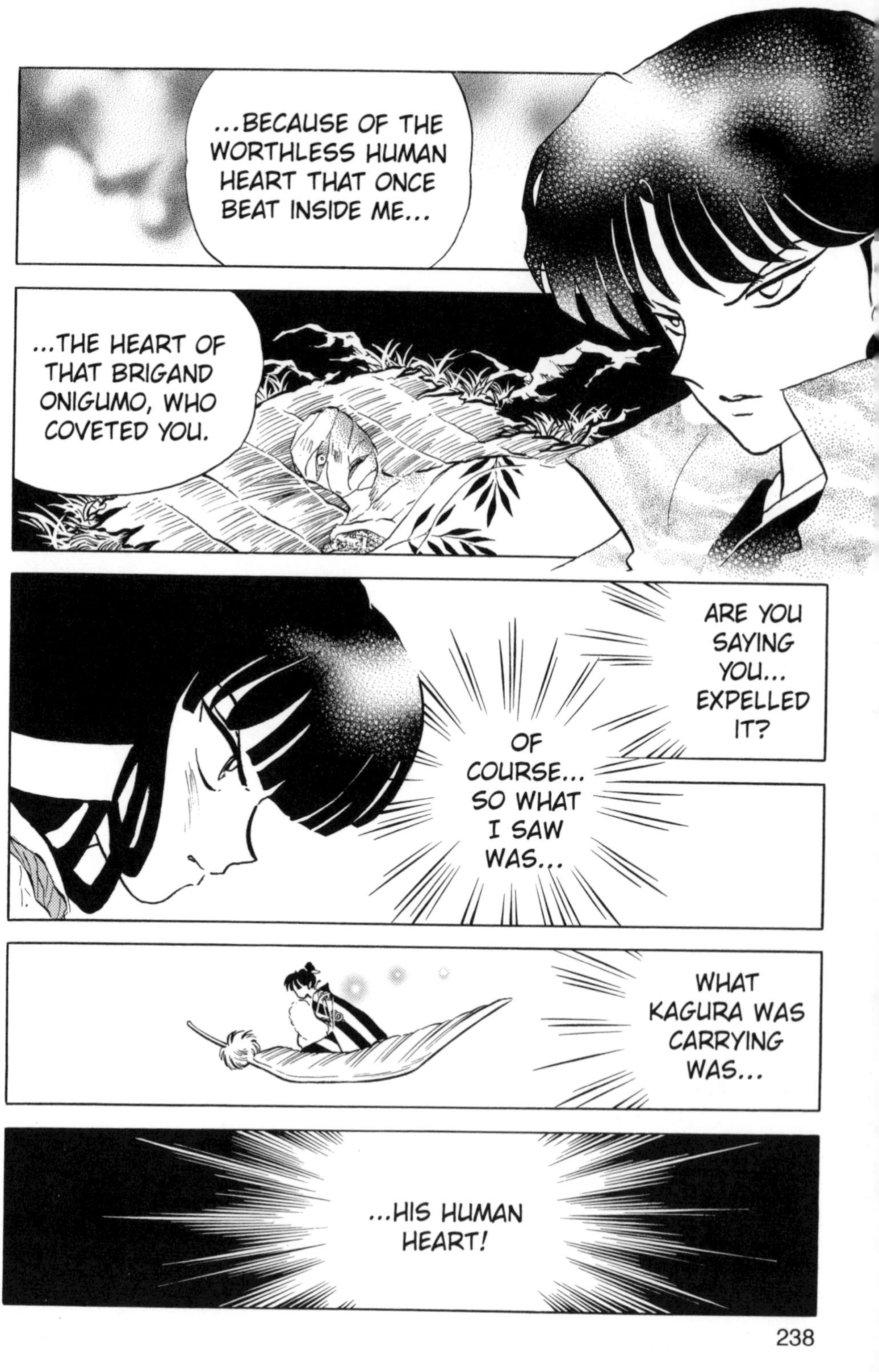
...BECAUSE OF THE WORTHLESS HUMAN HEART THAT ONCE BEAT INSIDE ME...
...THE HEART OF THAT BRIGAND ONIGUMO, WHO COVETED YOU.
ARE YOU SAYING YOU... EXPELLED IT?
OF COURSE... SO WHAT I SAW WAS...
WHAT KAGURA WAS CARRYING WAS...
...HIS HUMAN HEART!

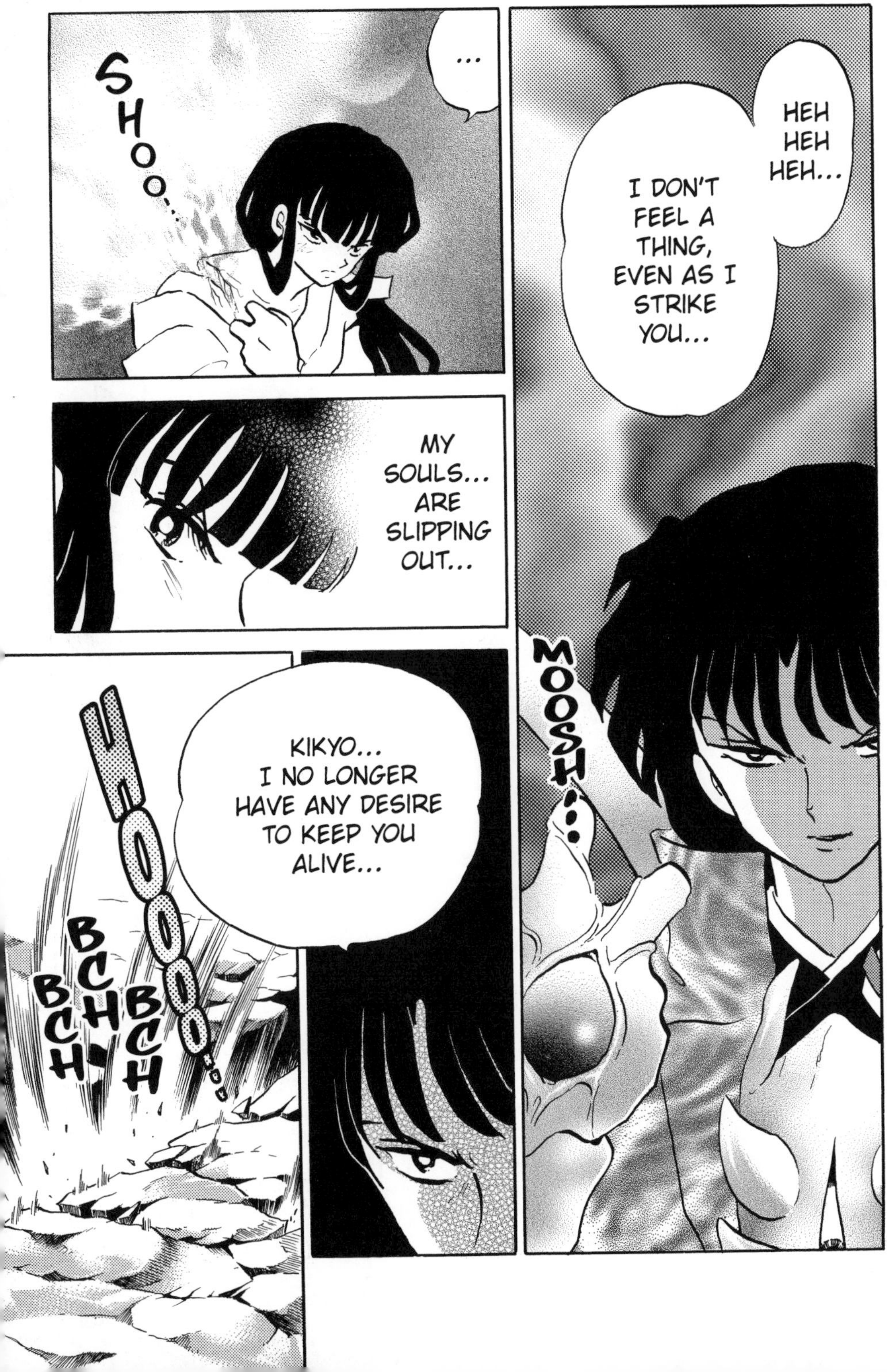
HEH HEH HEH...
I DON'T FEEL A THING, EVEN AS I STRIKE YOU...
MOOSH...
...
SHOO...
MY SOULS... ARE SLIPPING OUT...
KIKYO... I NO LONGER HAVE ANY DESIRE TO KEEP YOU ALIVE...
HOOOOO...
BCH BCH BCH

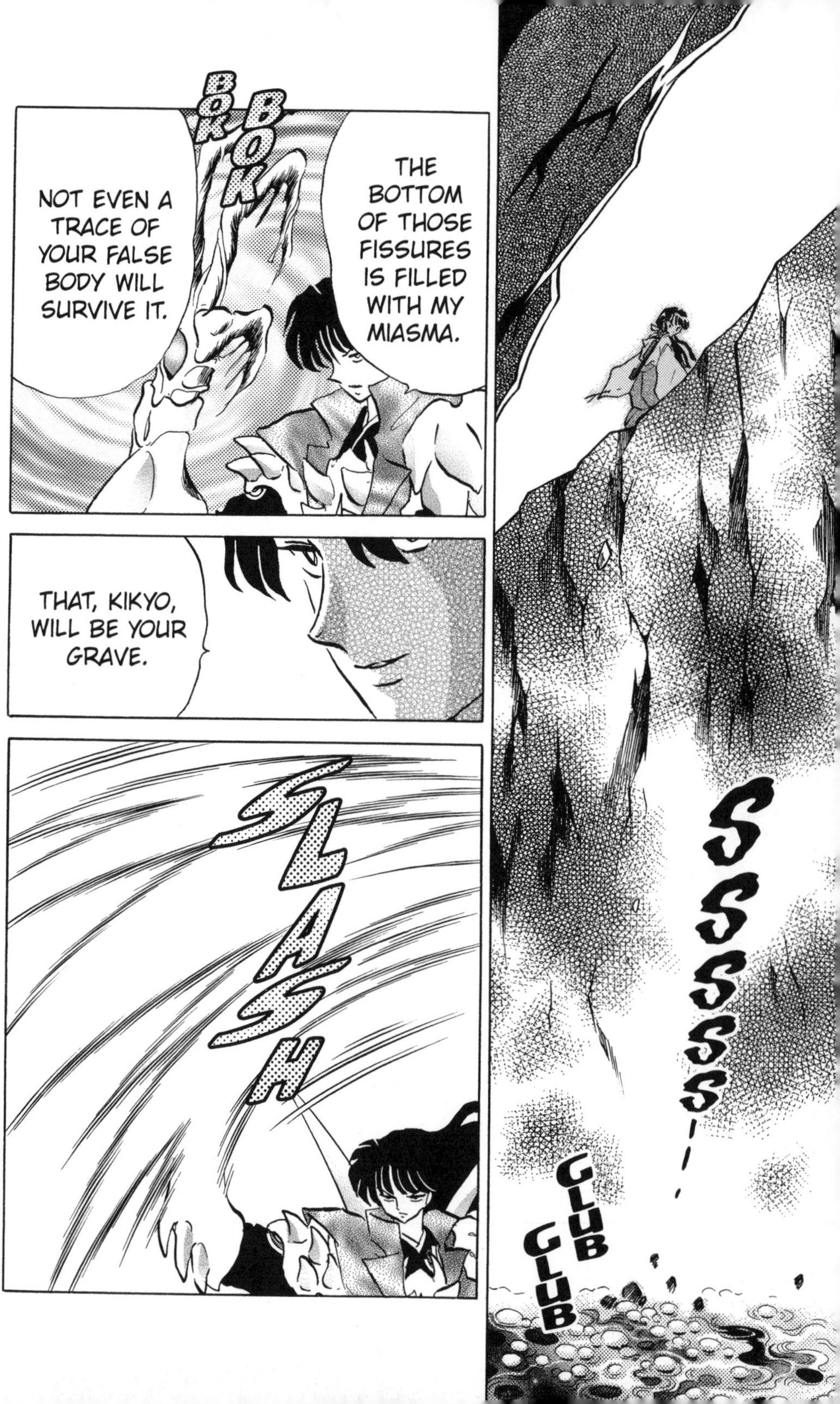
SSSSSS...
GLUB GLUB
BOK BOK
THE BOTTOM OF THOSE FISSURES IS FILLED WITH MY MIASMA.
NOT EVEN A TRACE OF YOUR FALSE BODY WILL SURVIVE IT.
THAT, KIKYO, WILL BE YOUR GRAVE.
SLASSH

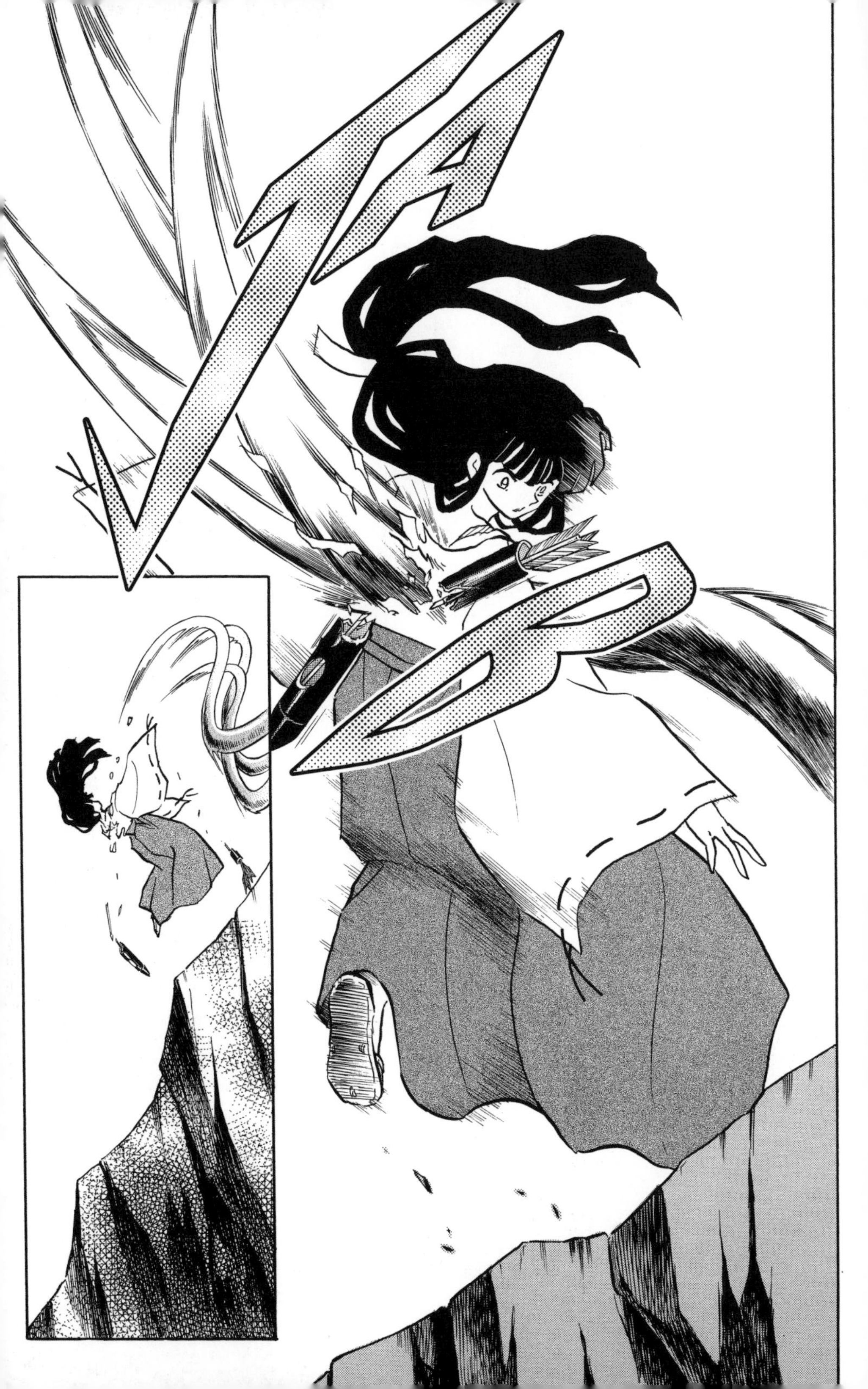

INUYASHA...
HYOOOOO
TP
DO YOU UNDER-STAND NOW, KIKYO...
...WHY THIS IS THE "NEW BODY"...
...THAT I SO DESIRED ?

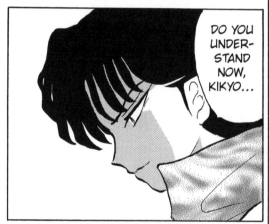

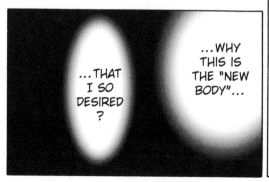

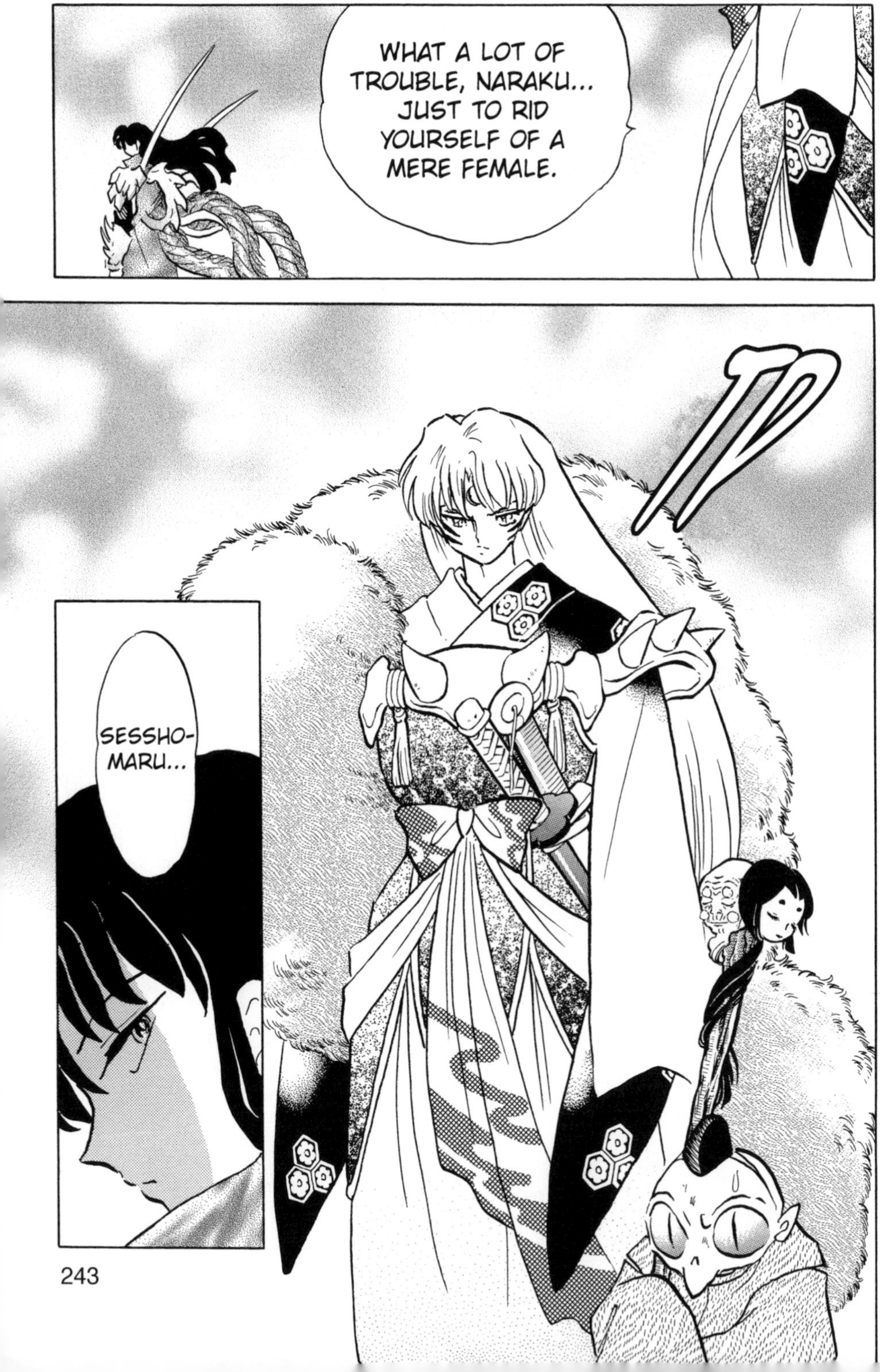
WHAT A LOT OF TROUBLE, NARAKU... JUST TO RID YOURSELF OF A MERE FEMALE.
SESSHO-MARU...

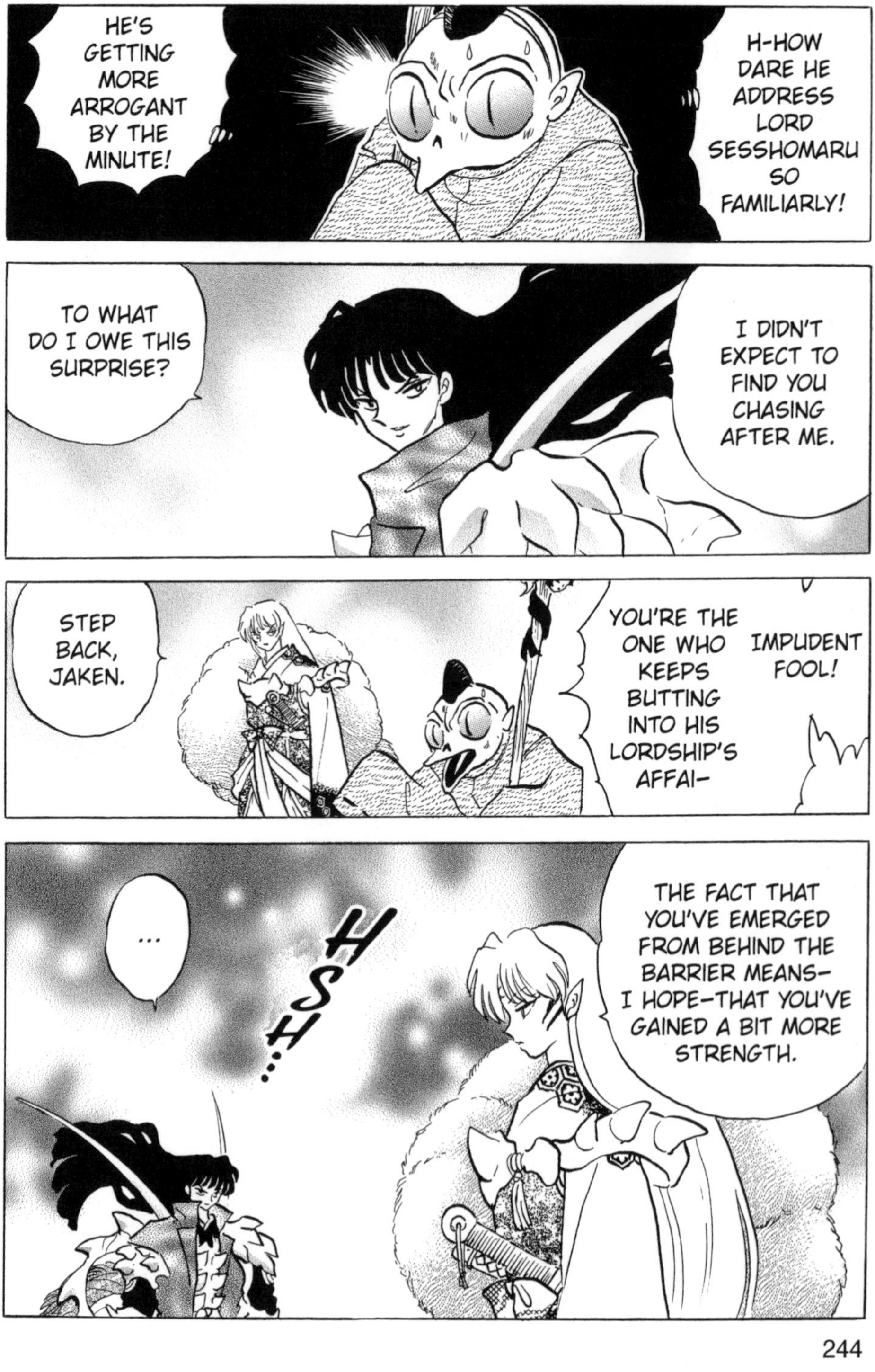
H-HOW DARE HE ADDRESS LORD SESSHOMARU SO FAMILIARLY!
HE'S GETTING MORE ARROGANT BY THE MINUTE!
I DIDN'T EXPECT TO FIND YOU CHASING AFTER ME.
TO WHAT DO I OWE THIS SURPRISE?
IMPUDENT FOOL!
YOU'RE THE ONE WHO KEEPS BUTTING INTO HIS LORDSHIP'S AFFAI–
STEP BACK, JAKEN.
THE FACT THAT YOU'VE EMERGED FROM BEHIND THE BARRIER MEANS– I HOPE–THAT YOU'VE GAINED A BIT MORE STRENGTH.
HSH...
...

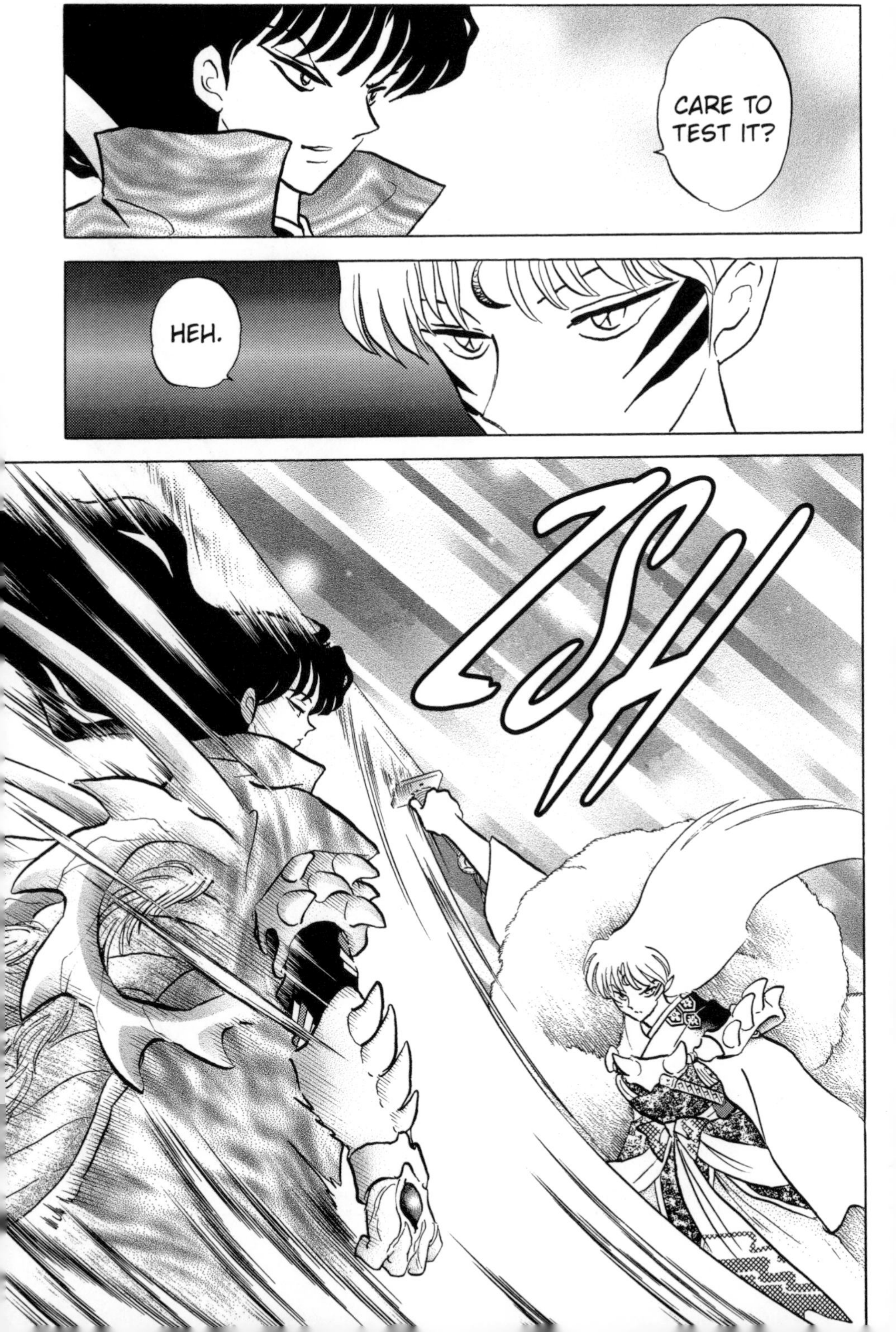
CARE TO TEST IT?
HEH.
ZSH

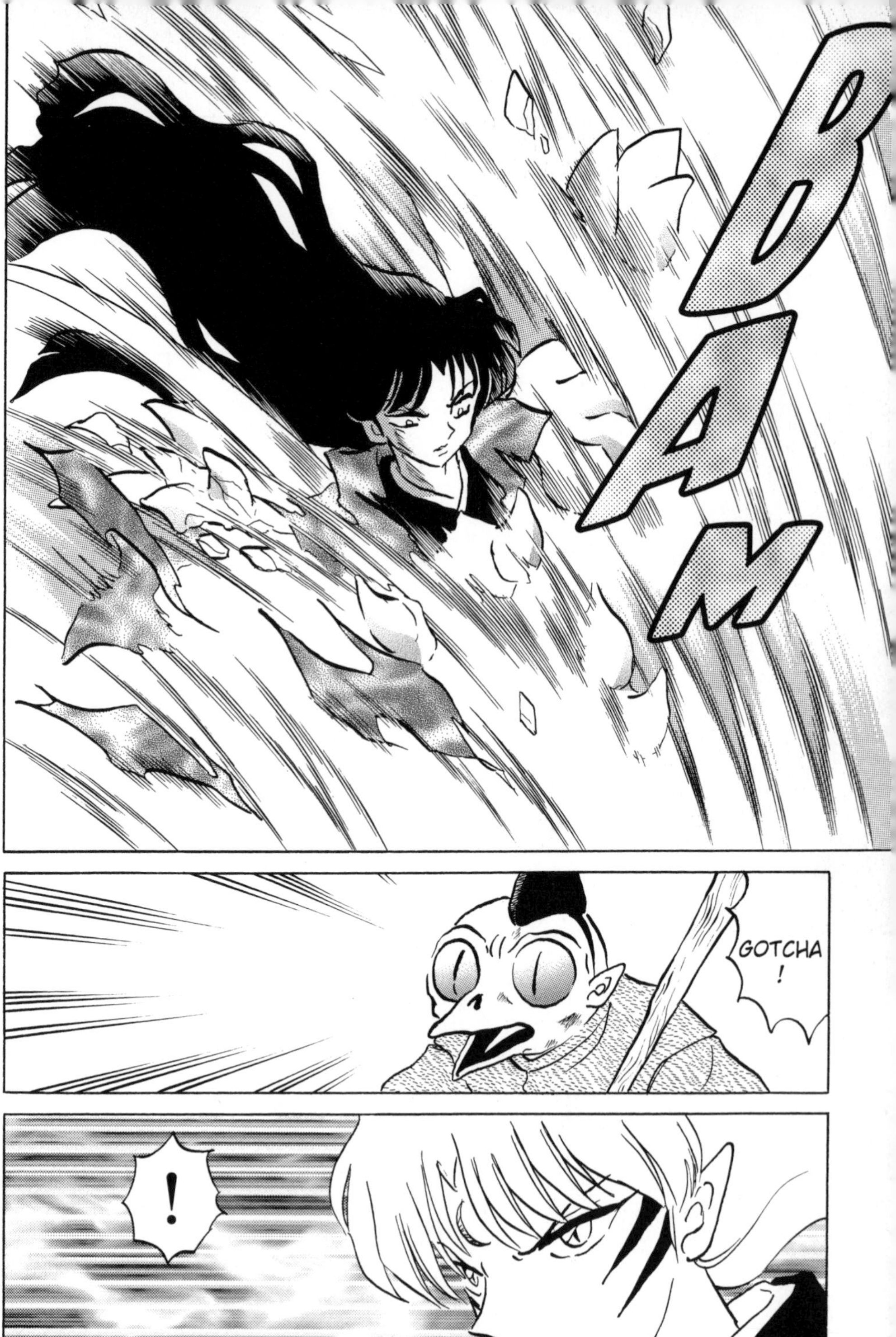
BAM
GOTCHA!
!

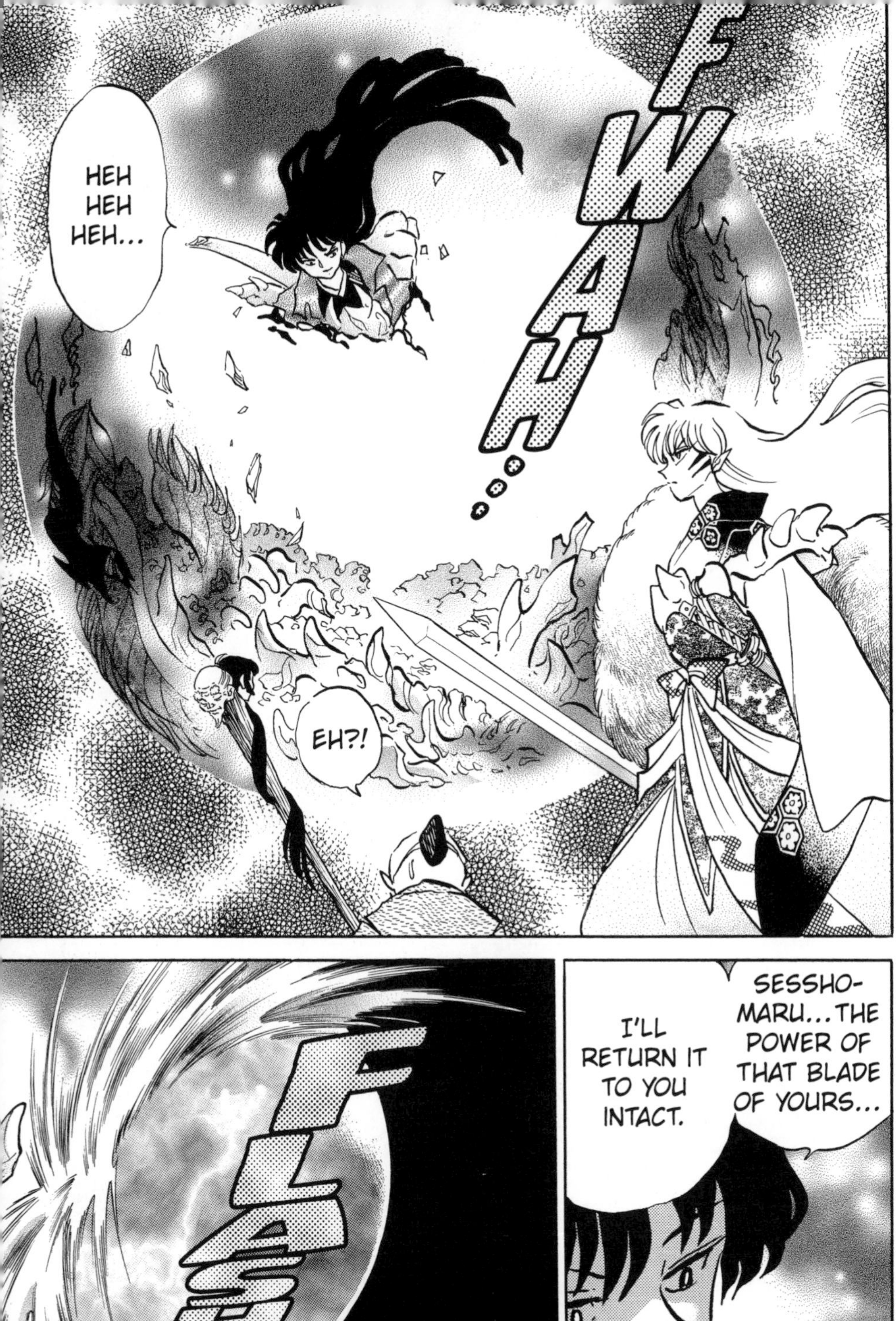
FWAHH...
HEH HEH HEH...
EH?!
SESSHO-MARU...THE POWER OF THAT BLADE OF YOURS...
I'LL RETURN IT TO YOU INTACT.
FLASH

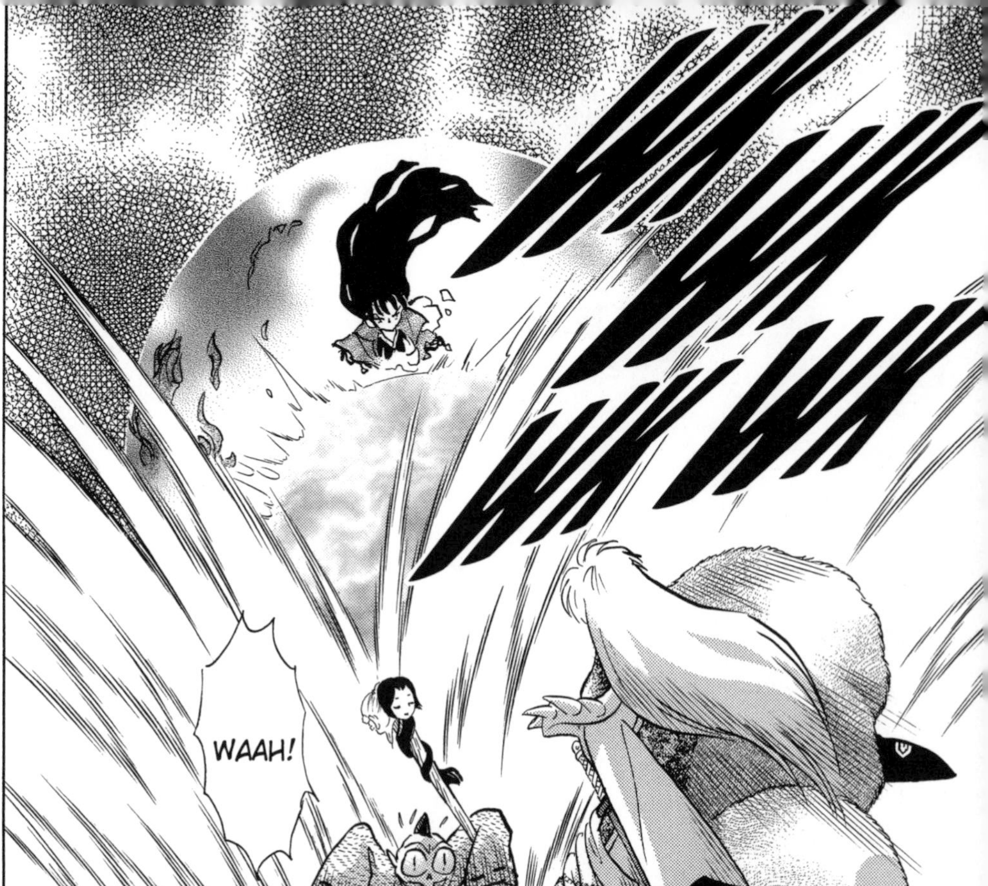
WAAH!

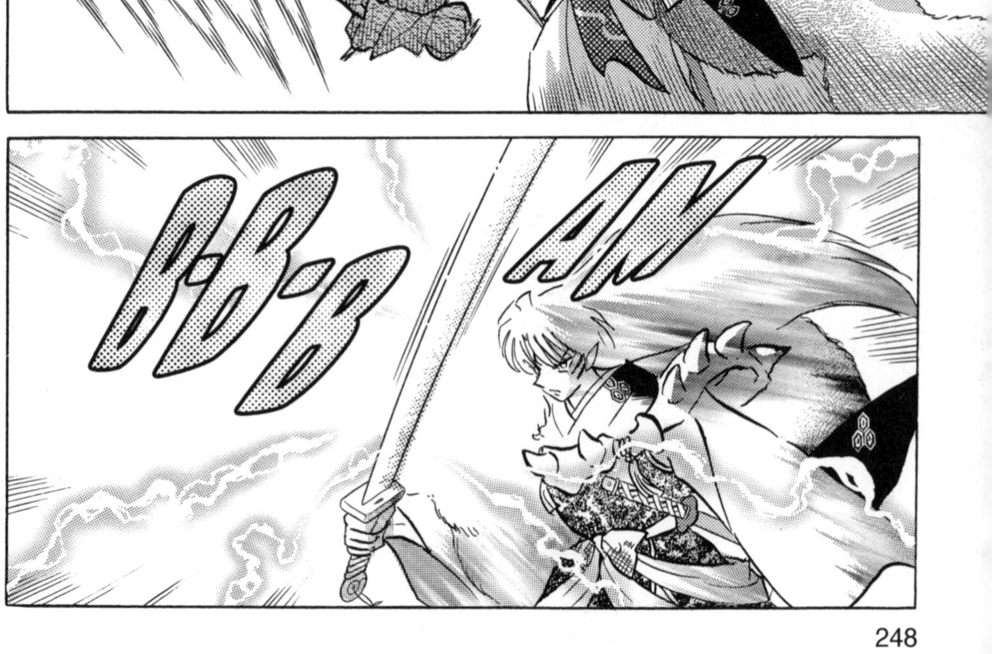
B-B-BAM

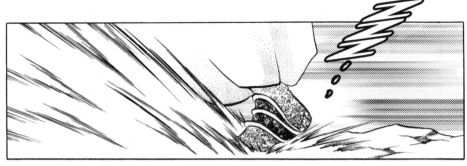

LORD SESSHO-MARU IS BEING PRESSED BACK?!

WHAT ...?

HEH HEH. IT'S USE-LESS ...

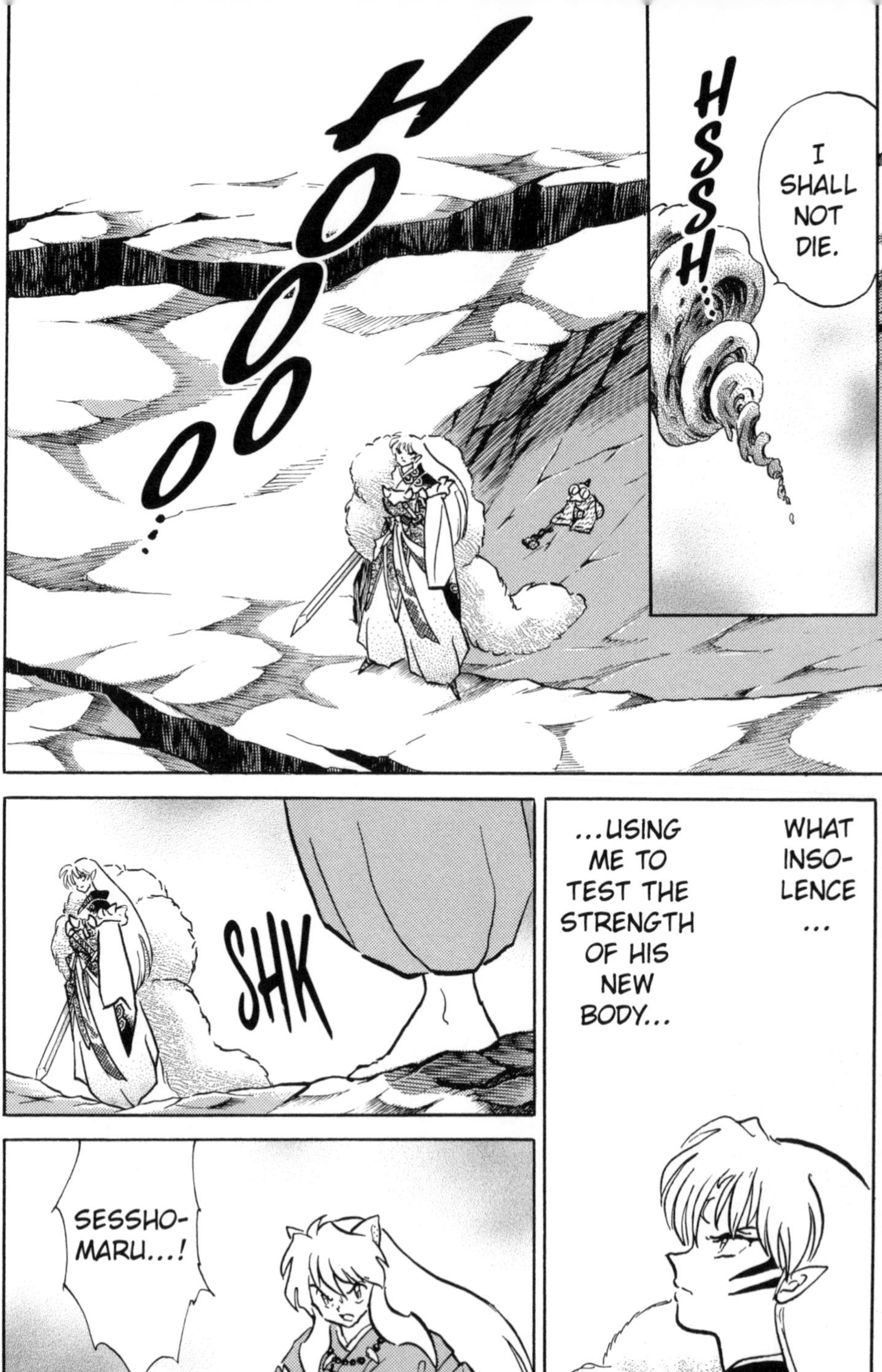
HSSH...
I SHALL NOT DIE.
HOOOOO...
WHAT INSO-LENCE...
...USING ME TO TEST THE STRENGTH OF HIS NEW BODY...
SHK
SESSHO-MARU...!

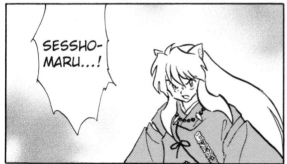

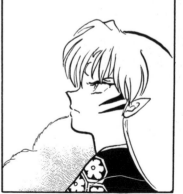

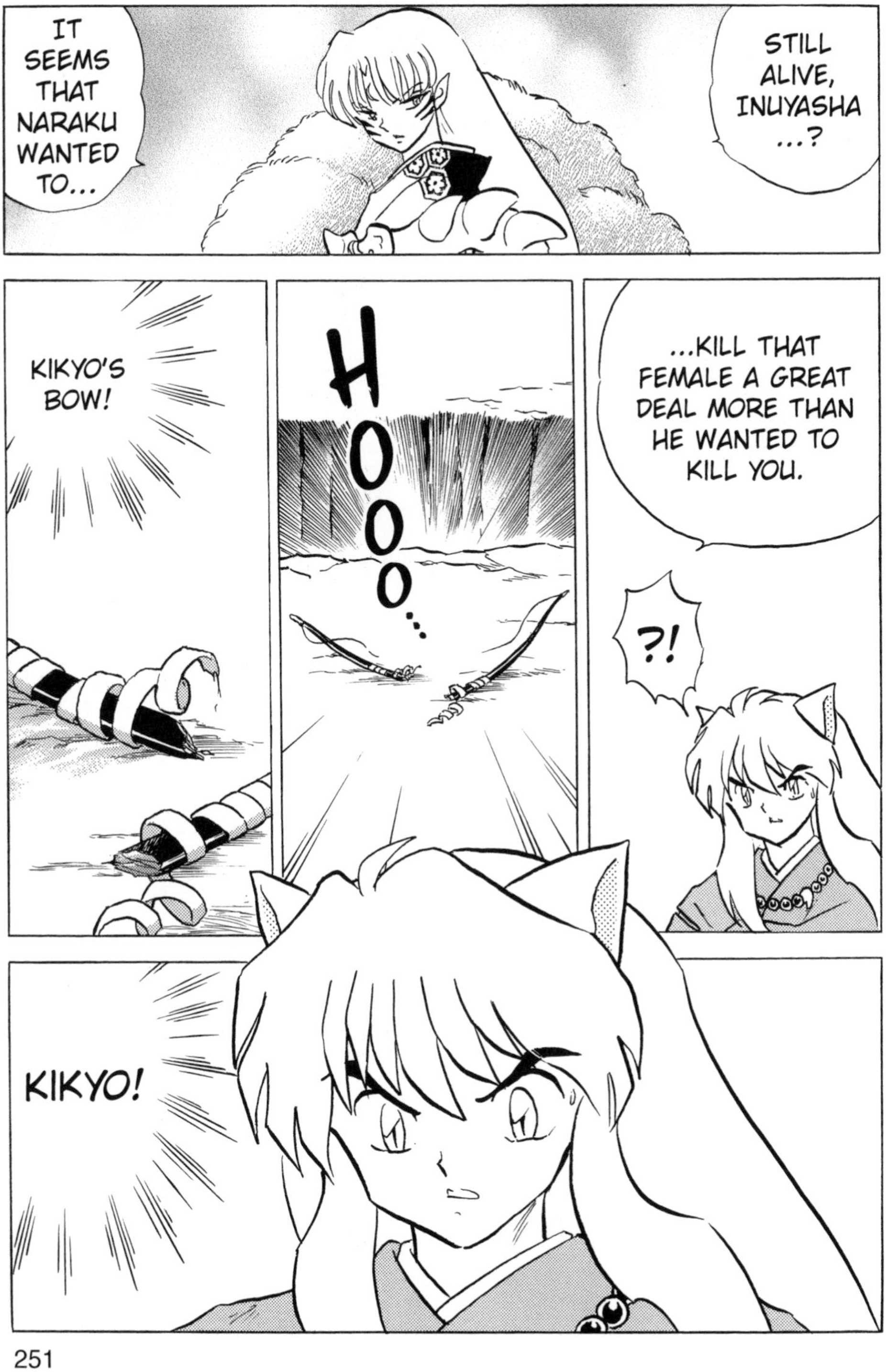
STILL ALIVE, INUYASHA...?
IT SEEMS THAT NARAKU WANTED TO...
...KILL THAT FEMALE A GREAT DEAL MORE THAN HE WANTED TO KILL YOU.
?!
HOOO...
KIKYO'S BOW!
KIKYO!

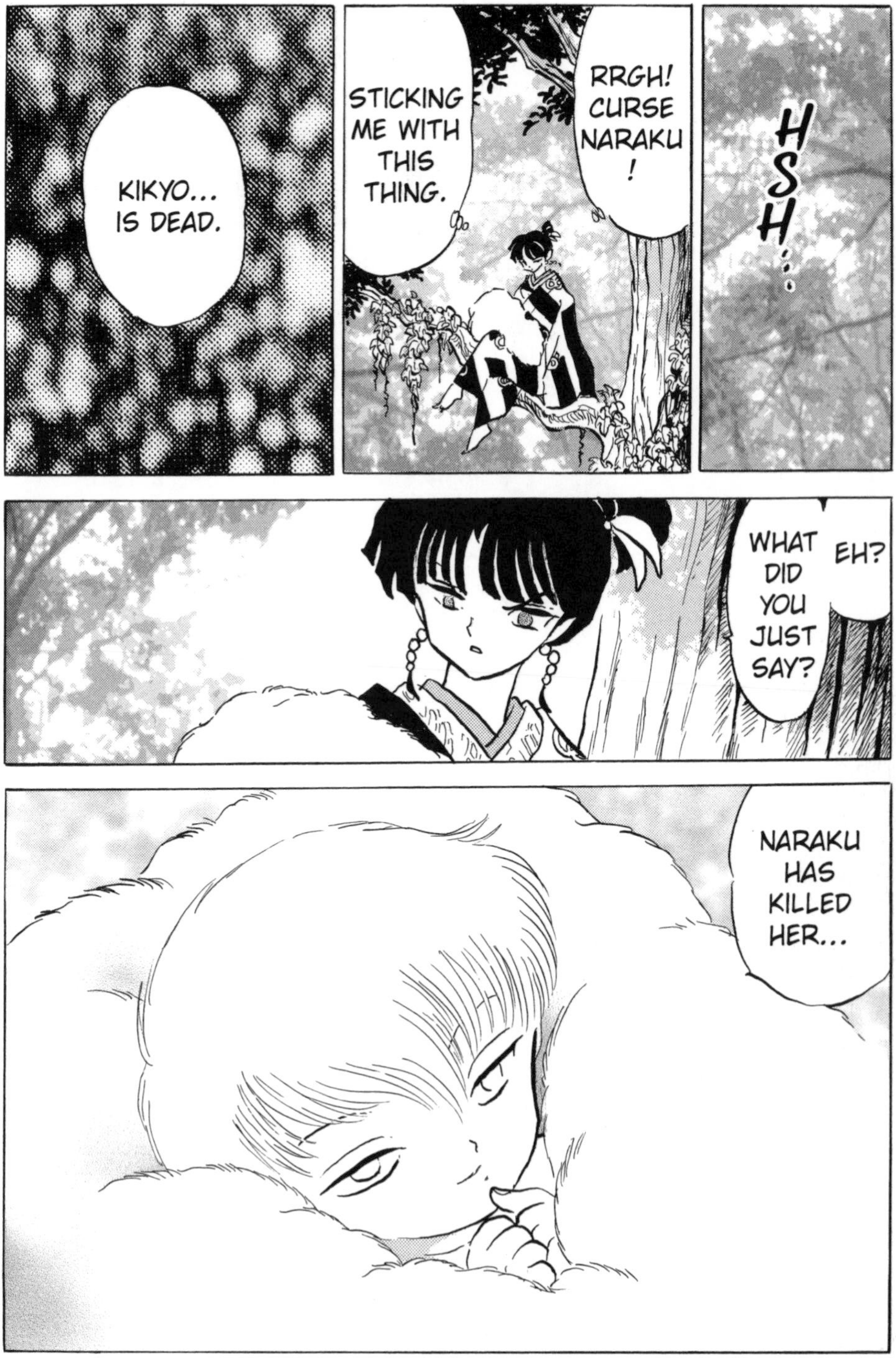
HSH...
RRGH! CURSE NARAKU!
STICKING ME WITH THIS THING.
KIKYO... IS DEAD.
EH?
WHAT DID YOU JUST SAY?
NARAKU HAS KILLED HER...

SCROLL FOUR
KIKYO'S LIFE

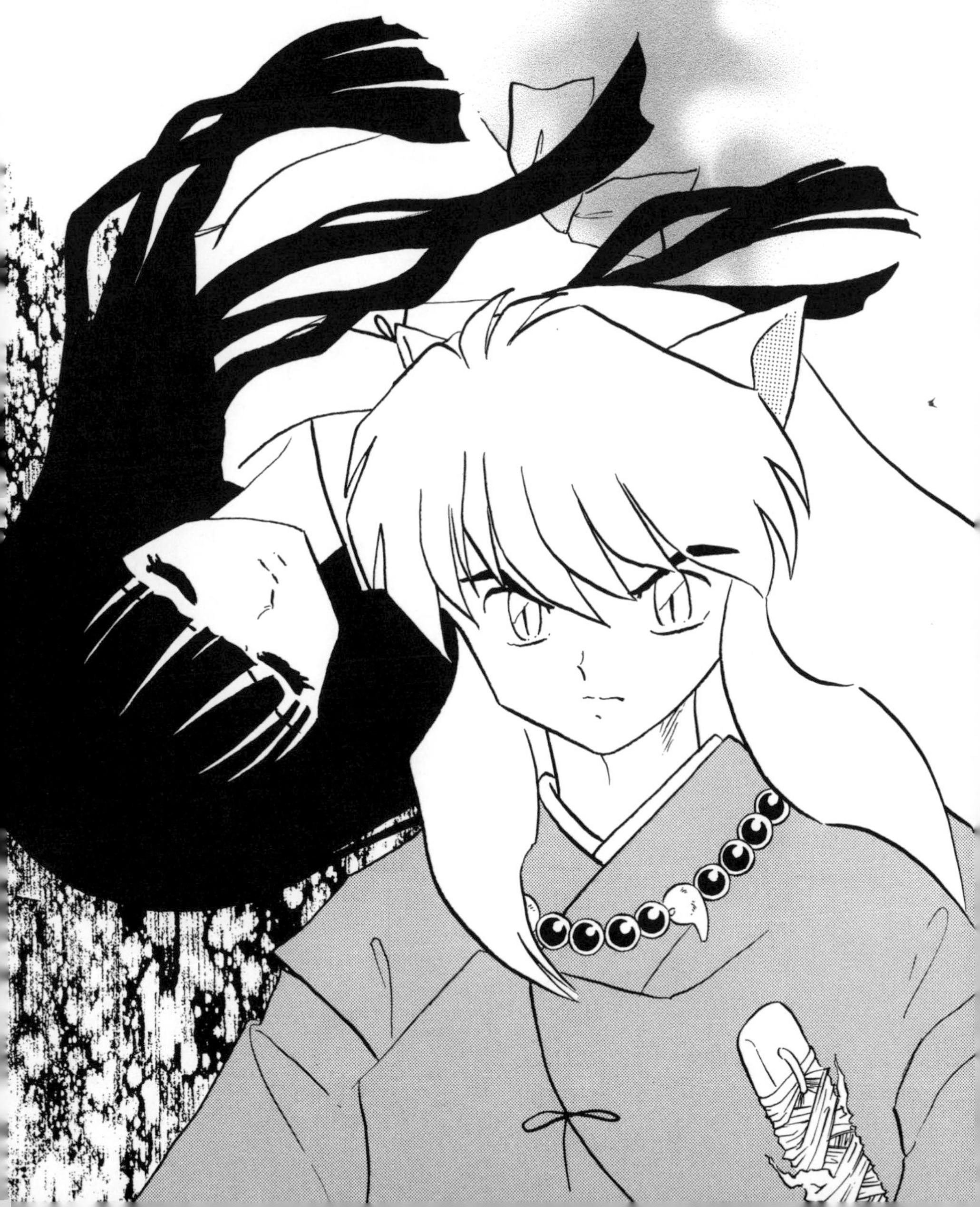

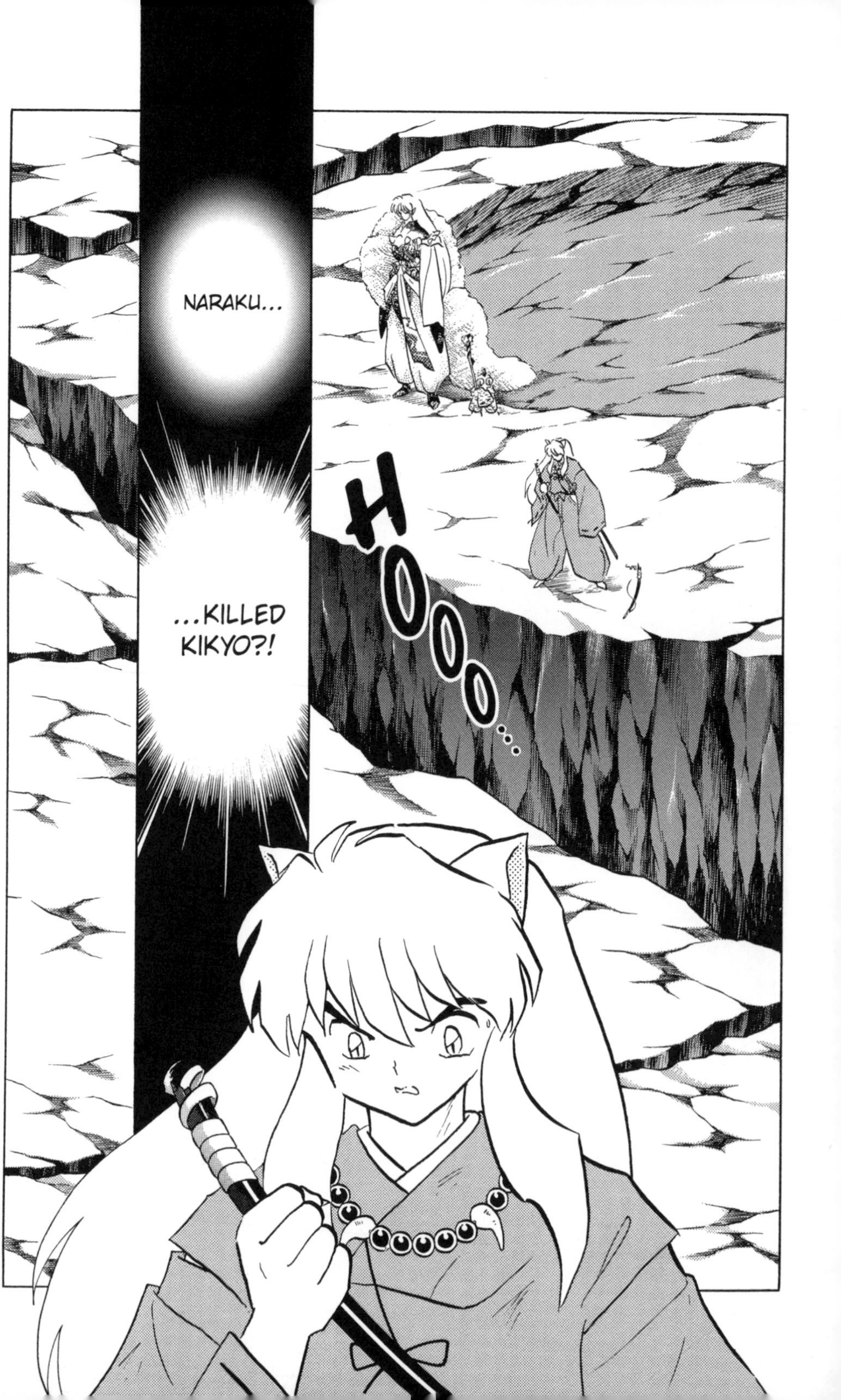
NARAKU...
...KILLED KIKYO?!
HOOOO...

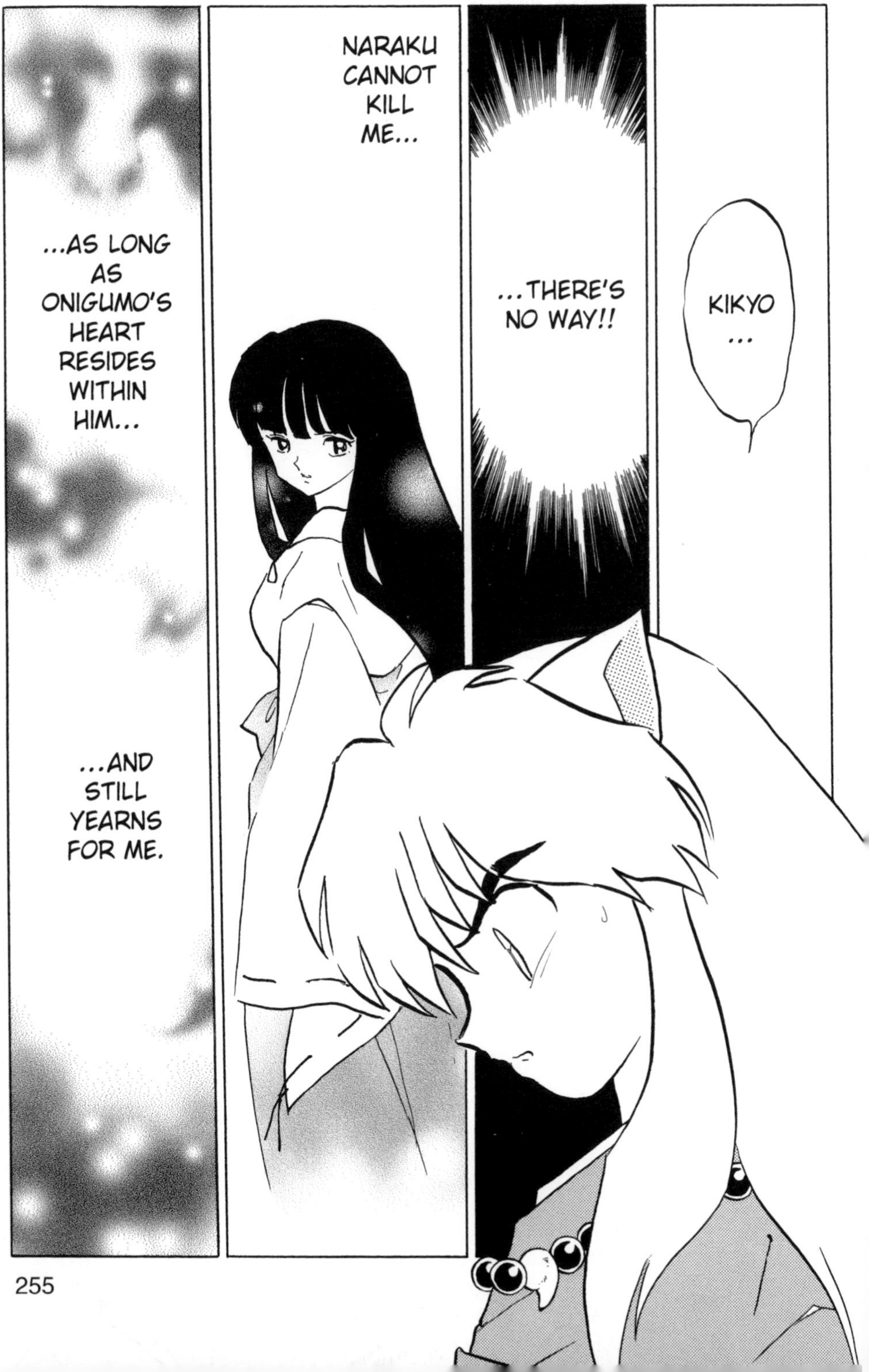
KIKYO ...
...THERE'S NO WAY!!
NARAKU CANNOT KILL ME...
...AS LONG AS ONIGUMO'S HEART RESIDES WITHIN HIM...
...AND STILL YEARNS FOR ME.

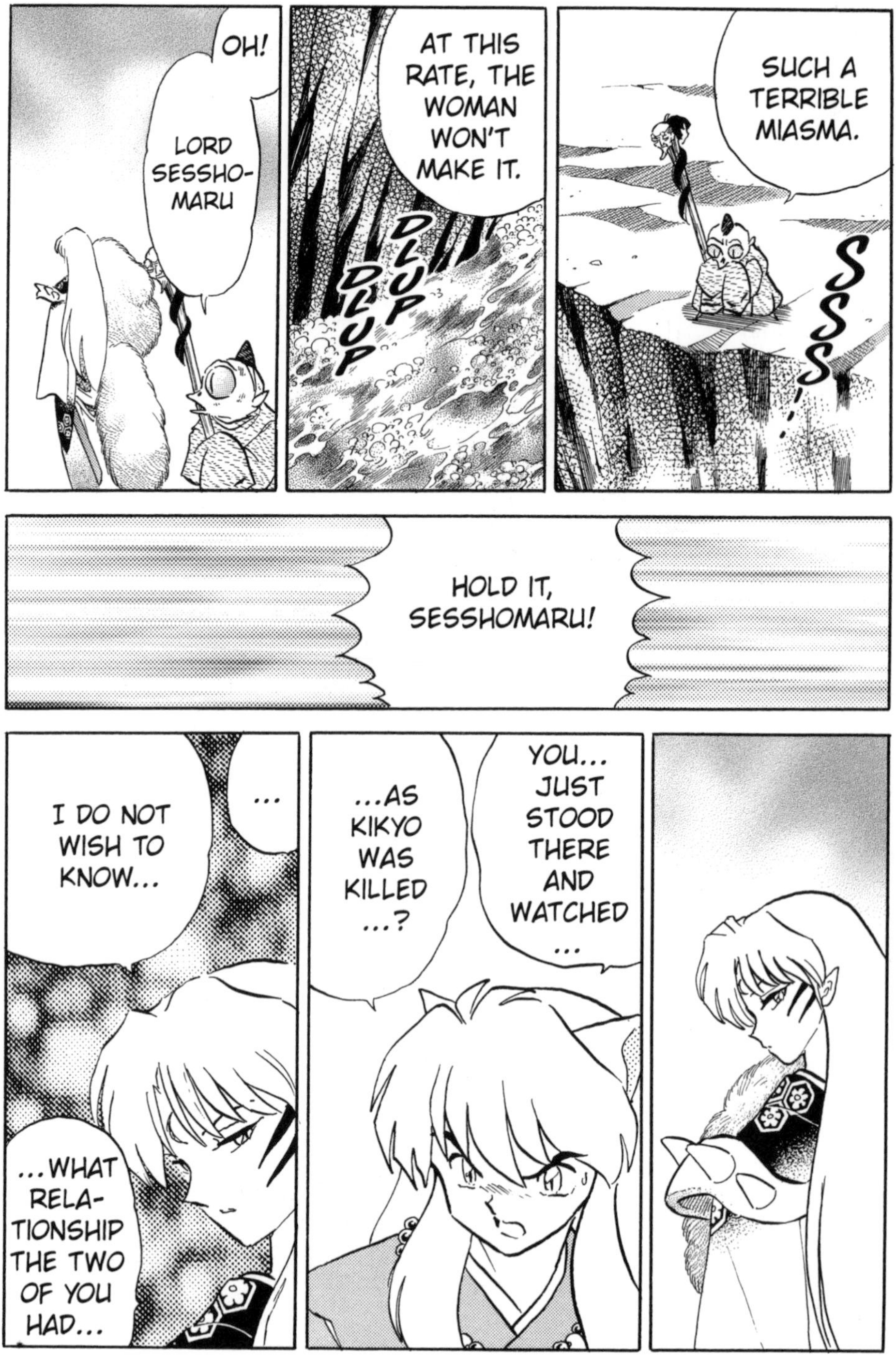
SUCH A TERRIBLE MIASMA.
SSS...
AT THIS RATE, THE WOMAN WON'T MAKE IT.
DLUP DLUP
OH!
LORD SESSHO-MARU
HOLD IT, SESSHOMARU!
YOU... JUST STOOD THERE AND WATCHED ...
...AS KIKYO WAS KILLED ...?
...
I DO NOT WISH TO KNOW...
...WHAT RELA-TIONSHIP THE TWO OF YOU HAD...

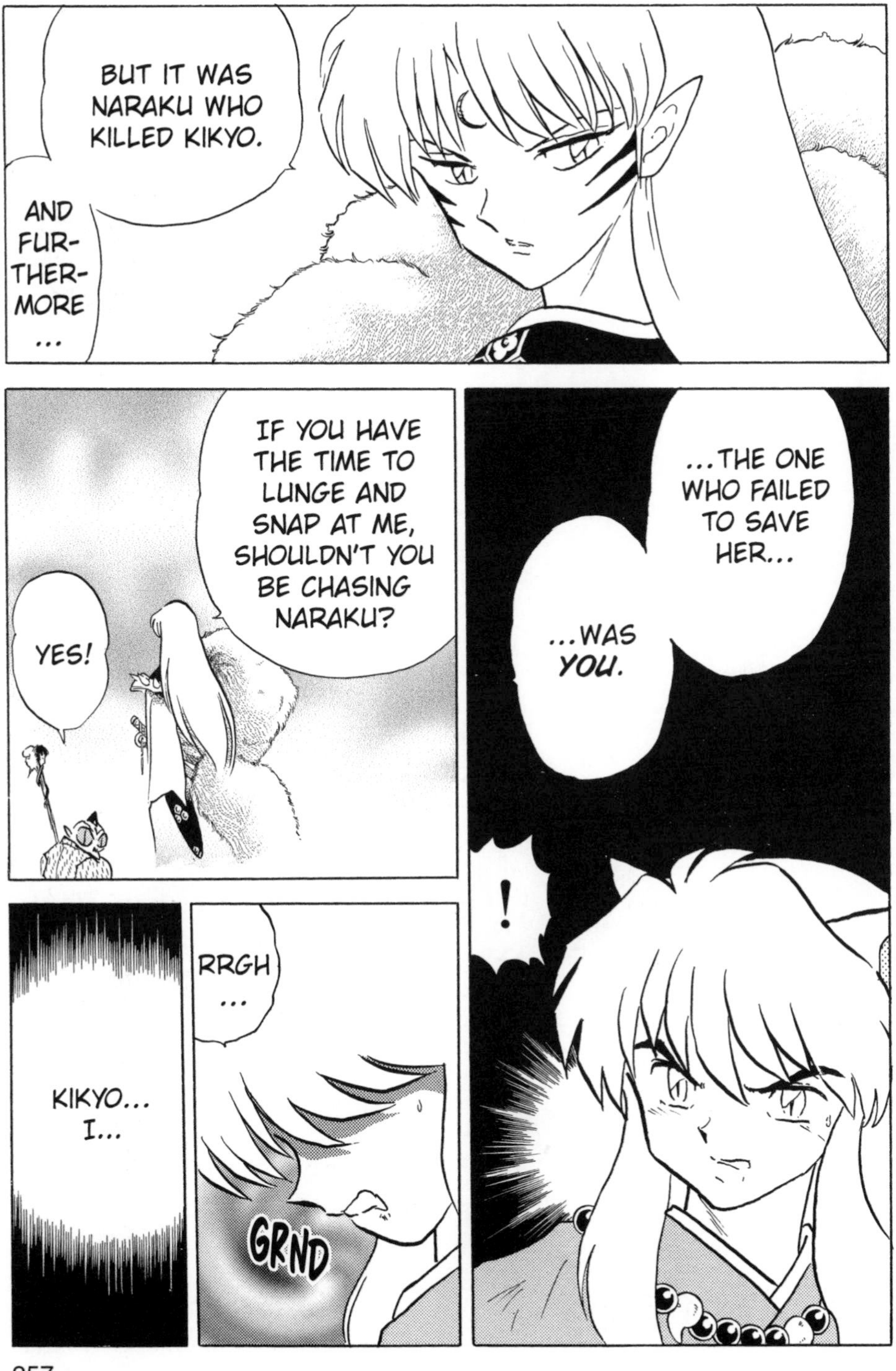
BUT IT WAS NARAKU WHO KILLED KIKYO.
AND FUR-THER-MORE ...
...THE ONE WHO FAILED TO SAVE HER...
...WAS *YOU.*
!
IF YOU HAVE THE TIME TO LUNGE AND SNAP AT ME, SHOULDN'T YOU BE CHASING NARAKU?
YES!
RRGH ...
GRND
KIKYO... I...

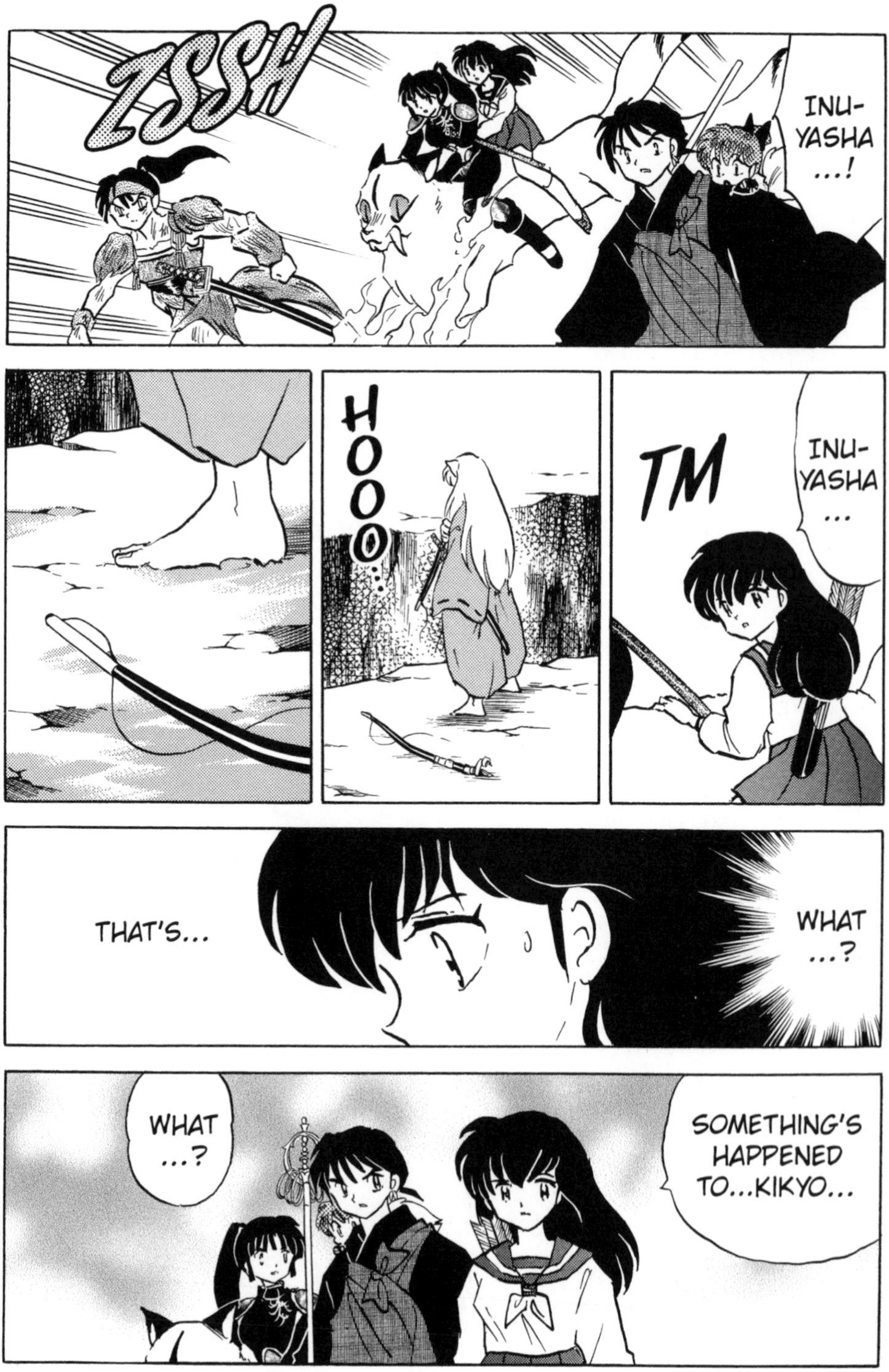

INU-YASHA ...!
ZSSH
INU-YASHA ...
TM
HOOO...
WHAT ...?
THAT'S...
SOMETHING'S HAPPENED TO...KIKYO...
WHAT ...?

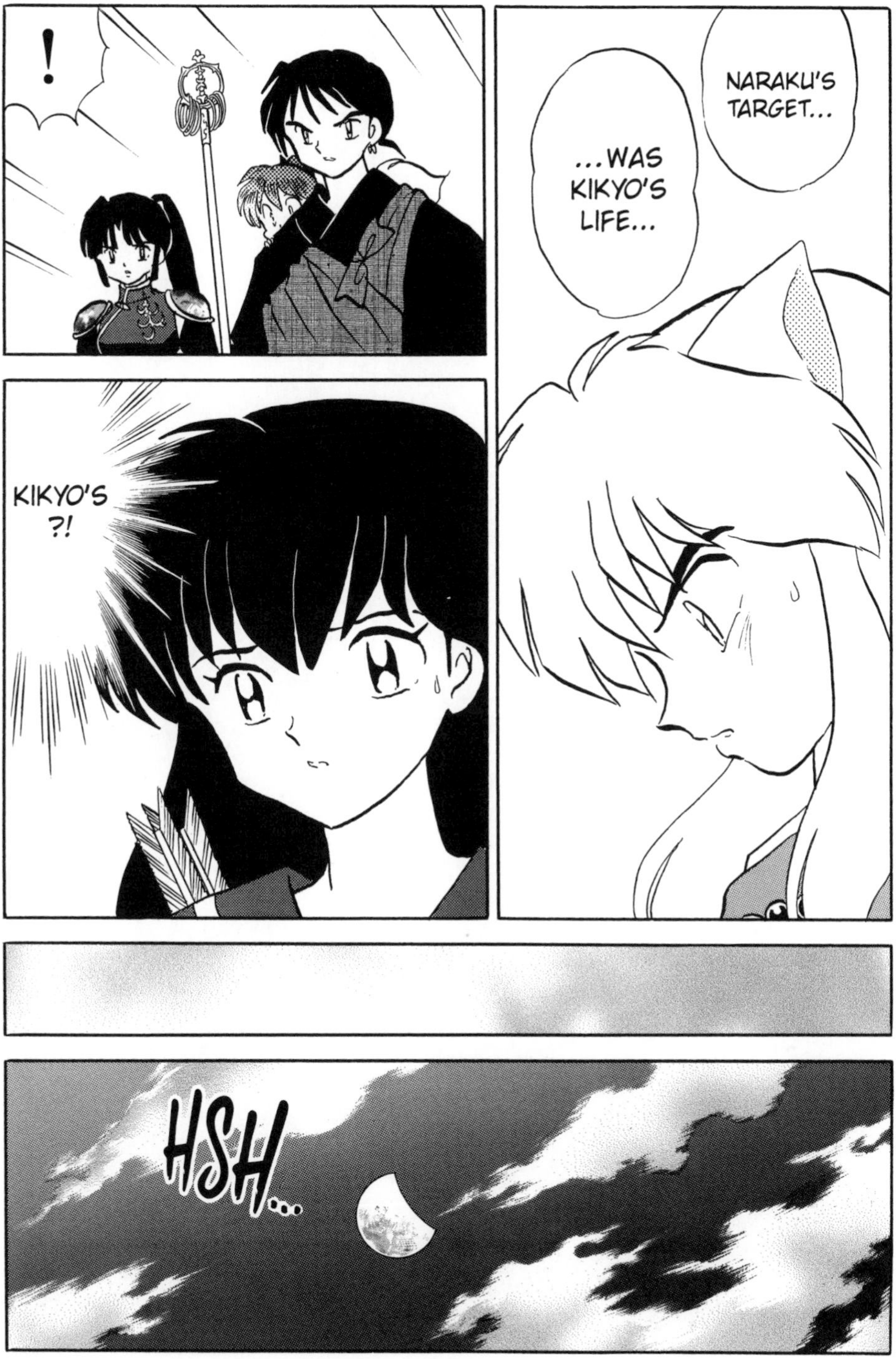
NARAKU'S TARGET...
...WAS KIKYO'S LIFE...
!
KIKYO'S ?!
HSH...

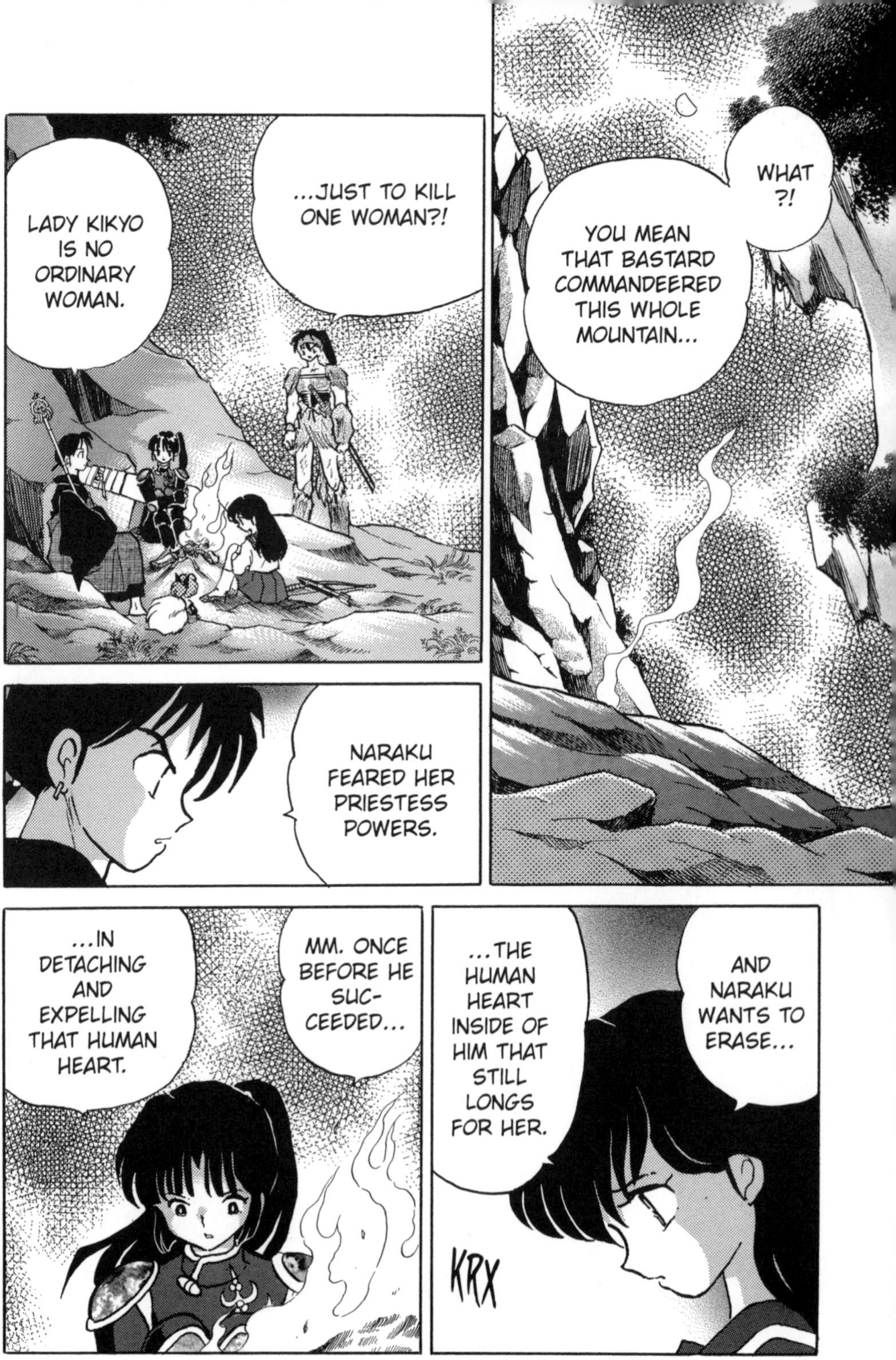
WHAT ?!
YOU MEAN THAT BASTARD COMMANDEERED THIS WHOLE MOUNTAIN...
...JUST TO KILL ONE WOMAN?!
LADY KIKYO IS NO ORDINARY WOMAN.
NARAKU FEARED HER PRIESTESS POWERS.
AND NARAKU WANTS TO ERASE...
...THE HUMAN HEART INSIDE OF HIM THAT STILL LONGS FOR HER.
KRX
MM. ONCE BEFORE HE SUC-CEEDED...
...IN DETACHING AND EXPELLING THAT HUMAN HEART.

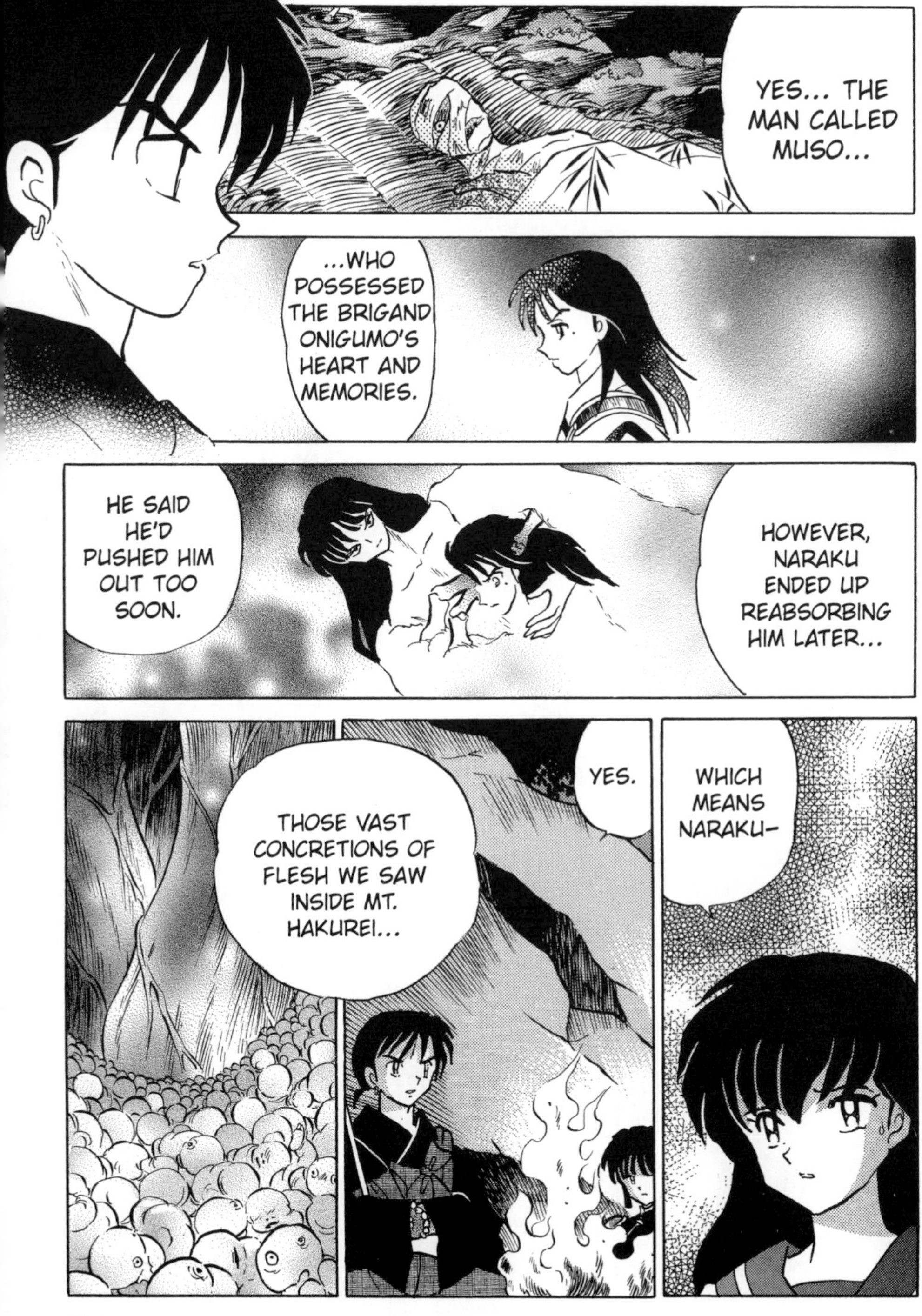
YES... THE MAN CALLED MUSO...
...WHO POSSESSED THE BRIGAND ONIGUMO'S HEART AND MEMORIES.
HOWEVER, NARAKU ENDED UP REABSORBING HIM LATER...
HE SAID HE'D PUSHED HIM OUT TOO SOON.
WHICH MEANS NARAKU-
YES.
THOSE VAST CONCRETIONS OF FLESH WE SAW INSIDE MT. HAKUREI...

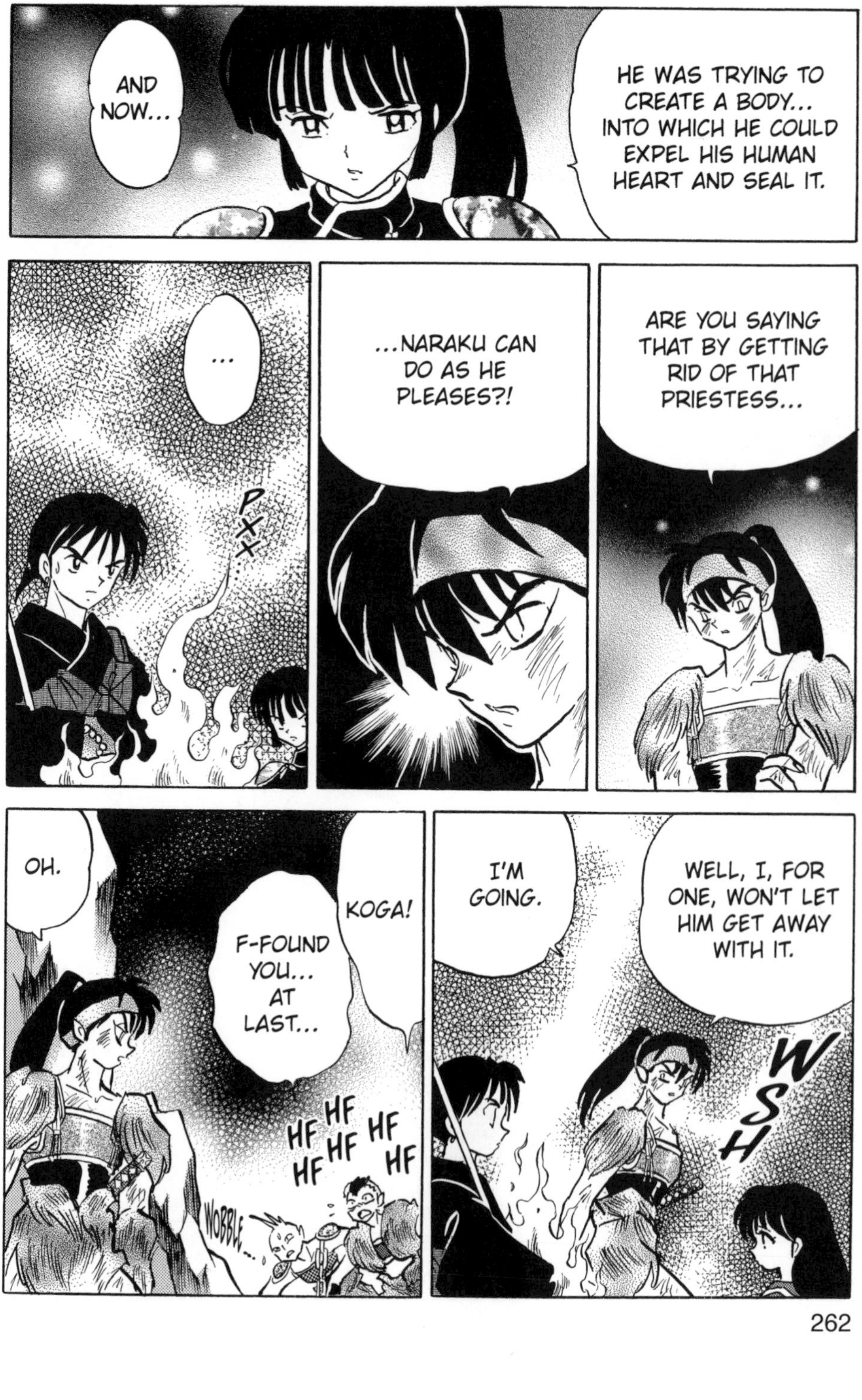
HE WAS TRYING TO CREATE A BODY... INTO WHICH HE COULD EXPEL HIS HUMAN HEART AND SEAL IT.
AND NOW...
ARE YOU SAYING THAT BY GETTING RID OF THAT PRIESTESS...
...NARAKU CAN DO AS HE PLEASES?!
...
WELL, I, FOR ONE, WON'T LET HIM GET AWAY WITH IT.
I'M GOING.
WSH
KOGA!
F-FOUND YOU... AT LAST...
HF HF HF HF HF HF
WOBBLE...
OH.

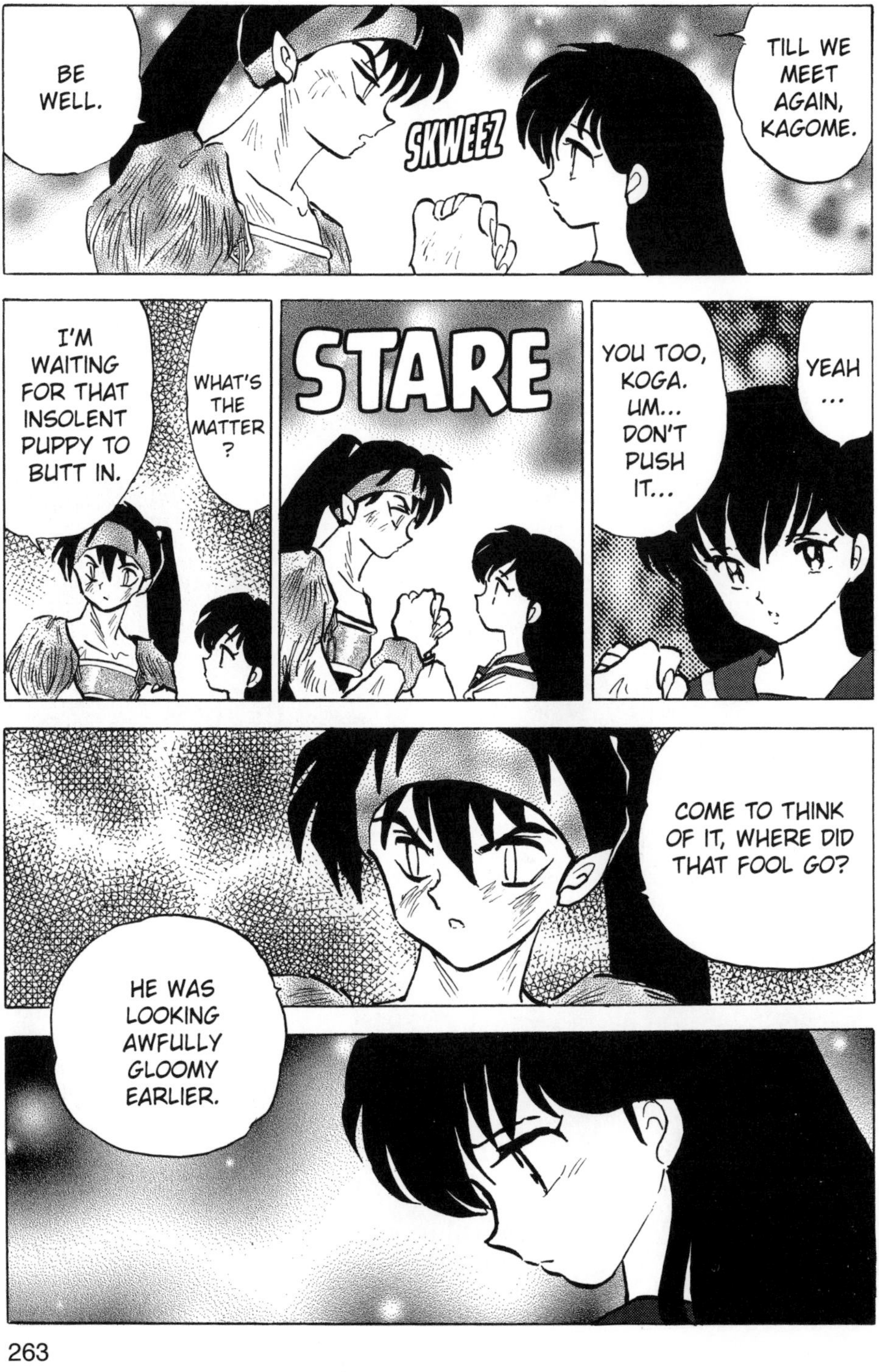
TILL WE MEET AGAIN, KAGOME.
SKWEEZ
BE WELL.
YEAH...
YOU TOO, KOGA. UM... DON'T PUSH IT...
STARE
WHAT'S THE MATTER?
I'M WAITING FOR THAT INSOLENT PUPPY TO BUTT IN.
COME TO THINK OF IT, WHERE DID THAT FOOL GO?
HE WAS LOOKING AWFULLY GLOOMY EARLIER.

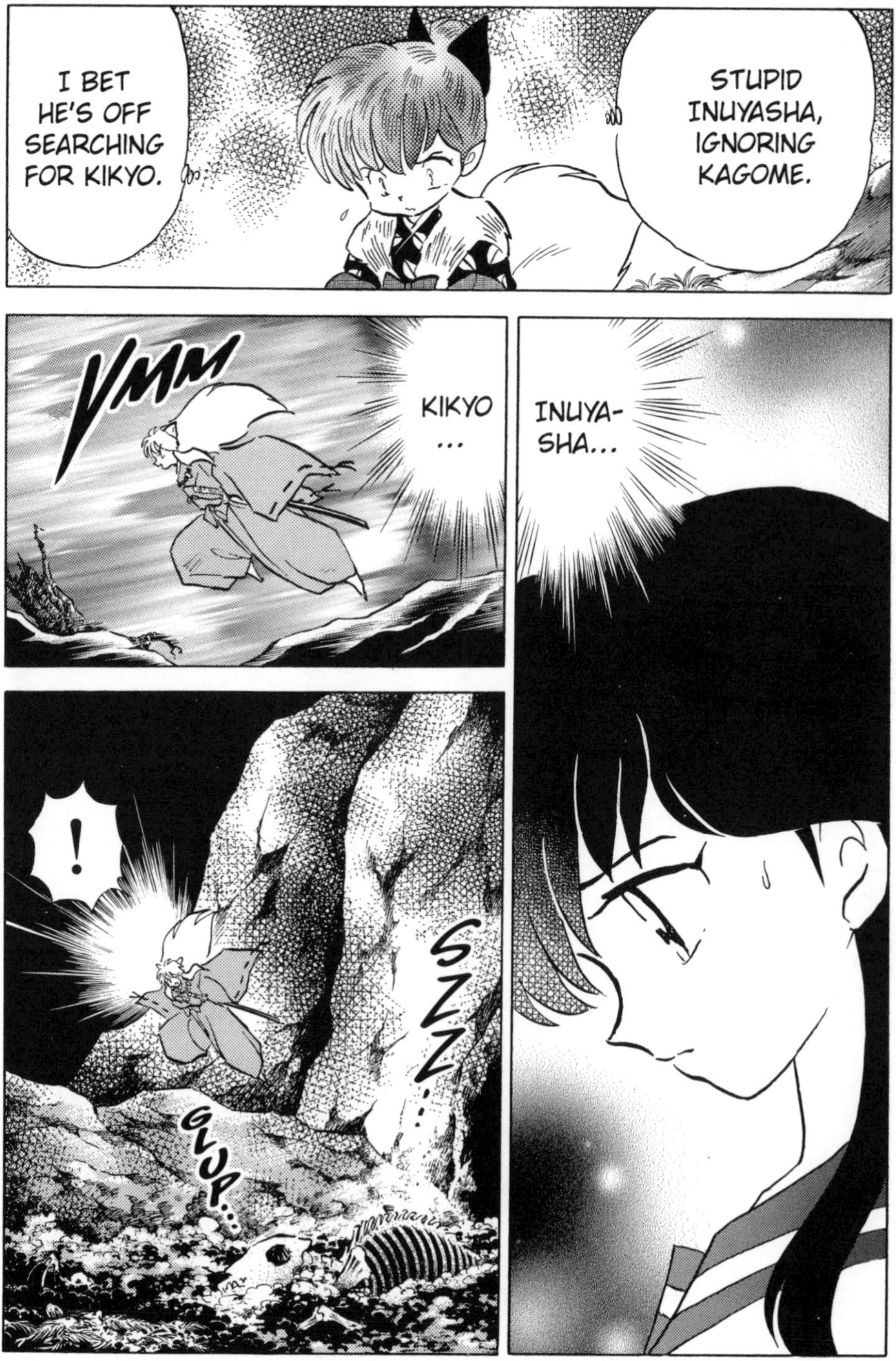
STUPID INUYASHA, IGNORING KAGOME.
I BET HE'S OFF SEARCHING FOR KIKYO.
INUYA-SHA...
VMM
KIKYO...
!
SZZ...
GLUP...

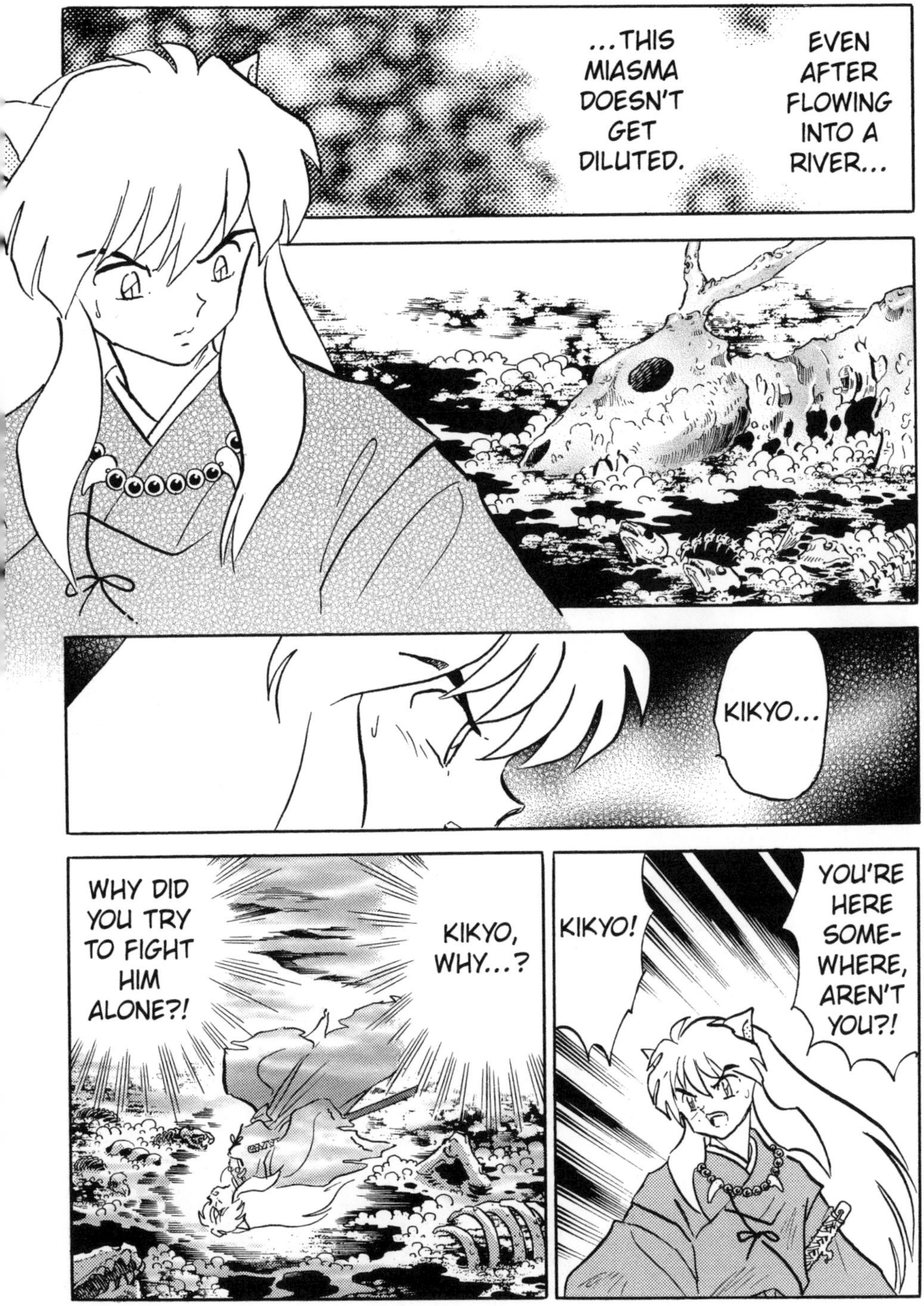
EVEN AFTER FLOWING INTO A RIVER...
...THIS MIASMA DOESN'T GET DILUTED.
KIKYO...
YOU'RE HERE SOMEWHERE, AREN'T YOU?!
KIKYO!
KIKYO, WHY...?
WHY DID YOU TRY TO FIGHT HIM ALONE?!

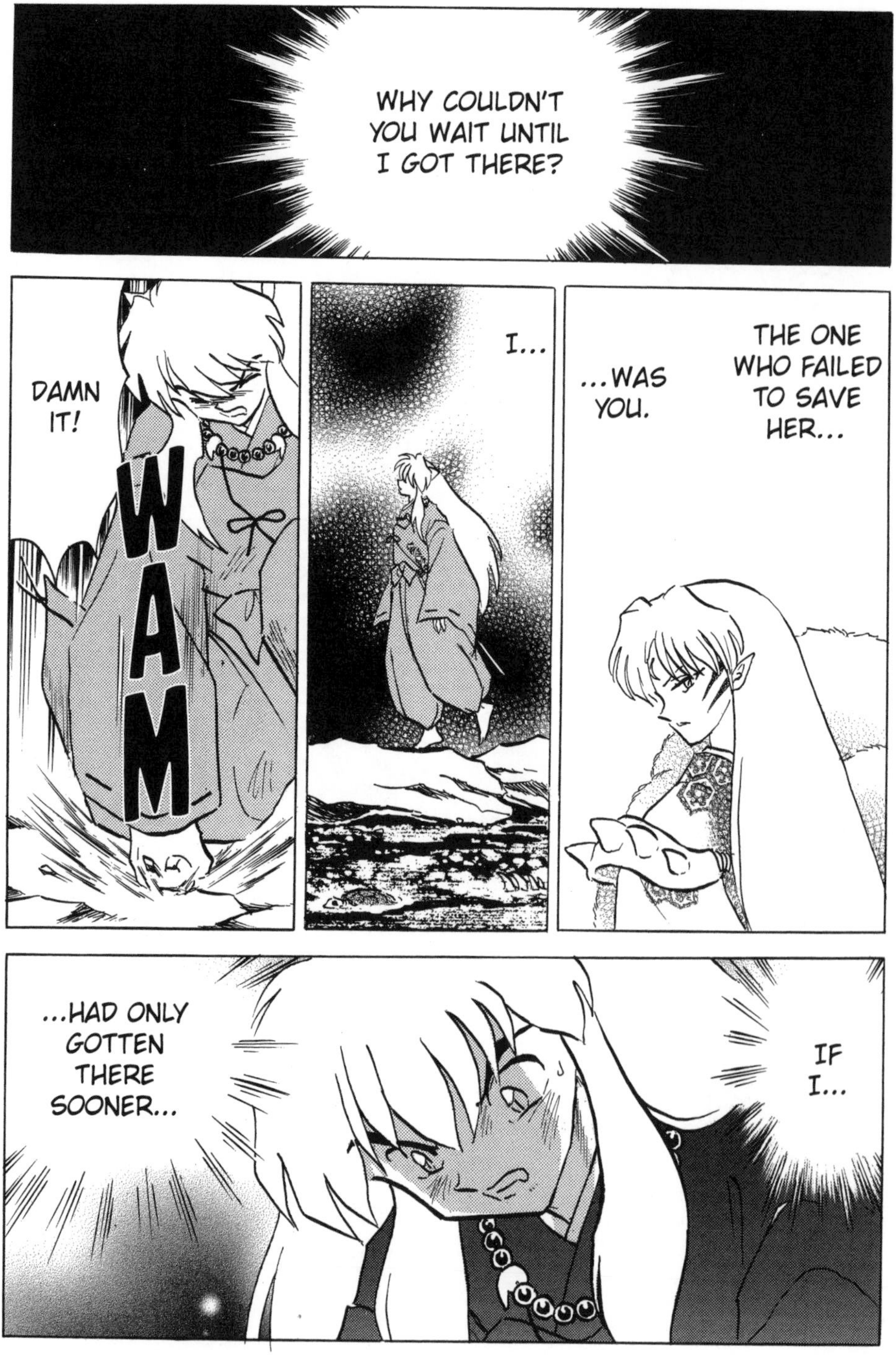
WHY COULDN'T YOU WAIT UNTIL I GOT THERE?
THE ONE WHO FAILED TO SAVE HER...
...WAS YOU.
I...
DAMN IT!
WAM
IF I...
...HAD ONLY GOTTEN THERE SOONER...

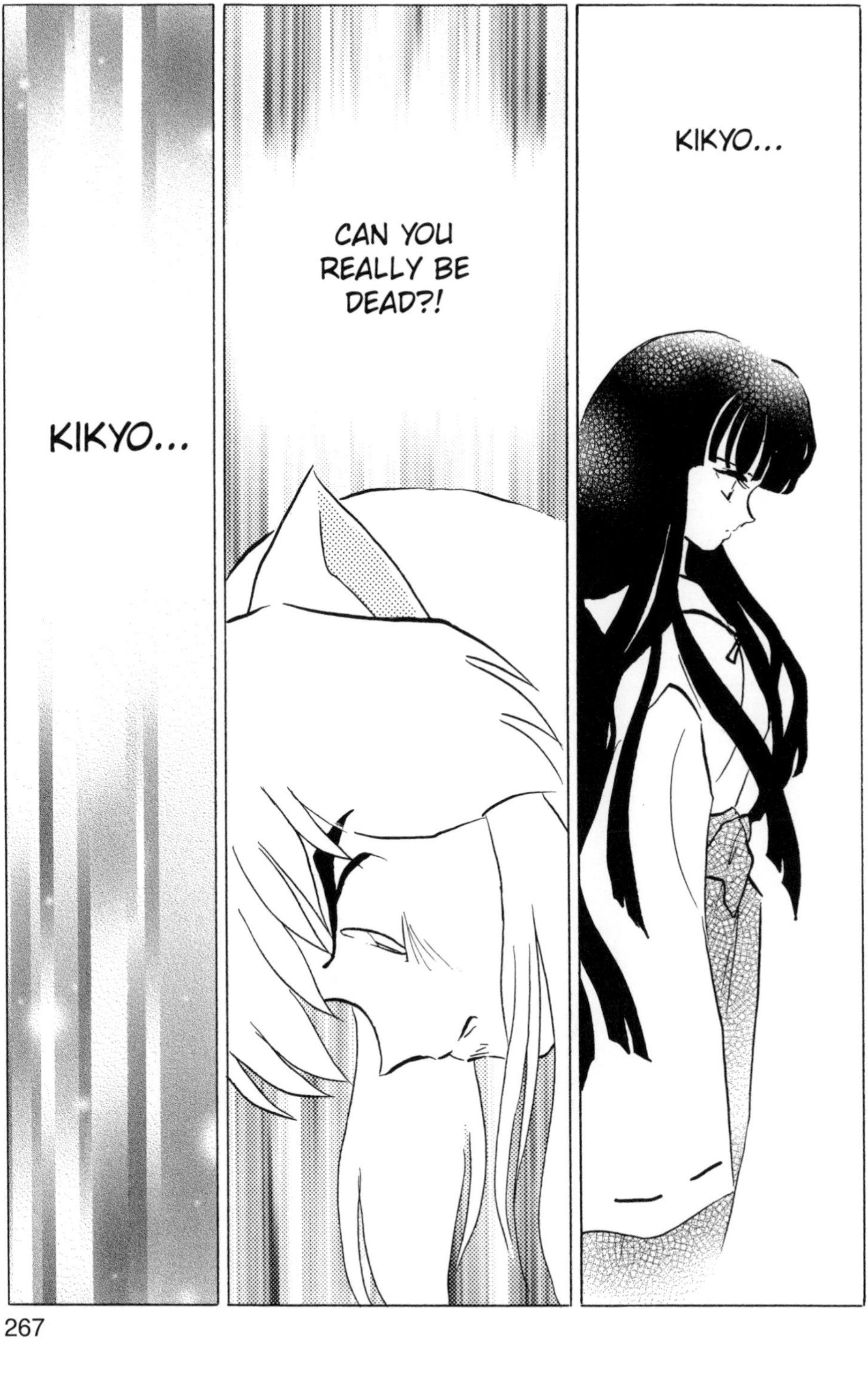
KIKYO...
CAN YOU REALLY BE DEAD?!
KIKYO...

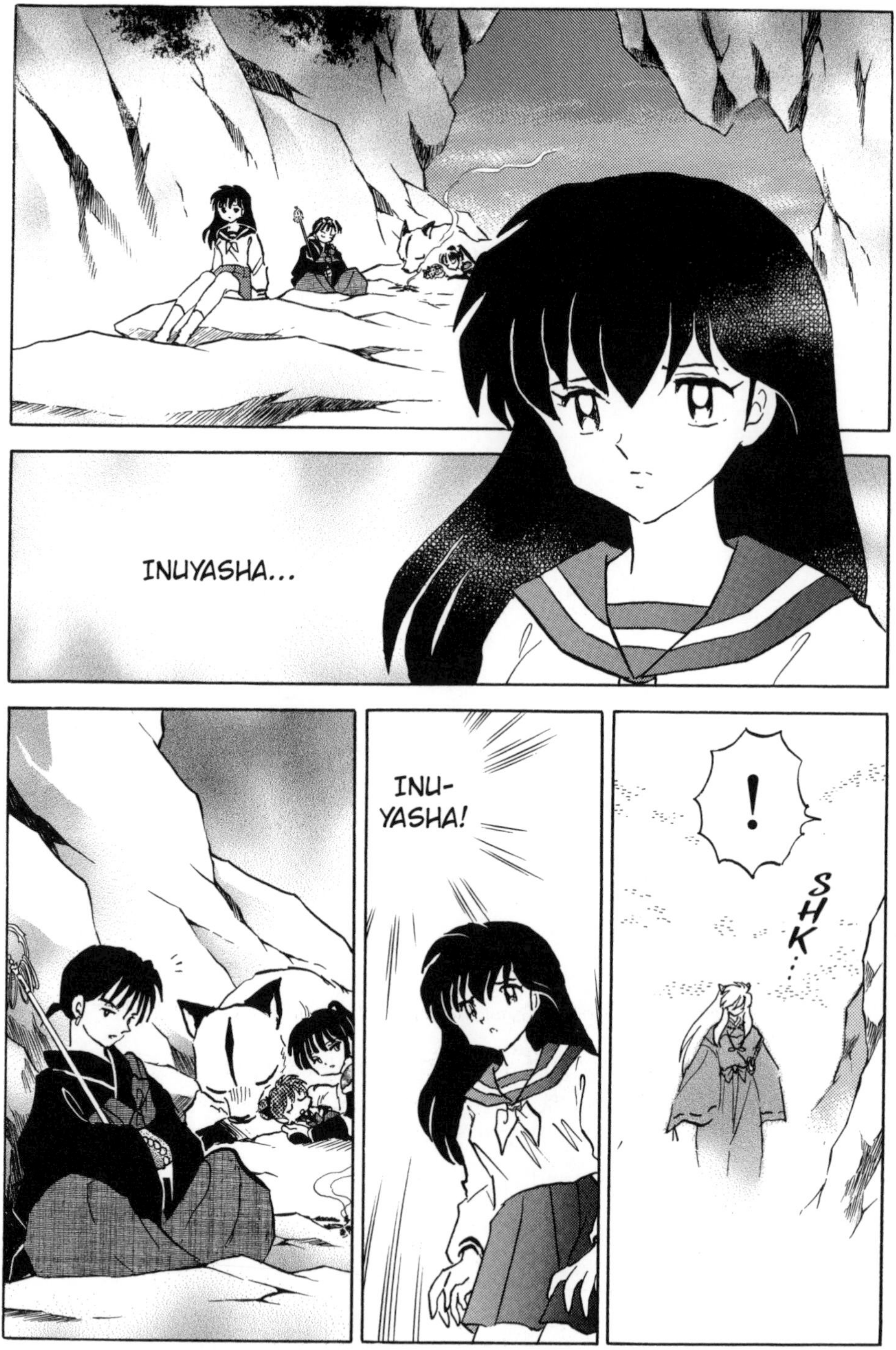
INUYASHA...
!
SHK...
INU-
YASHA!

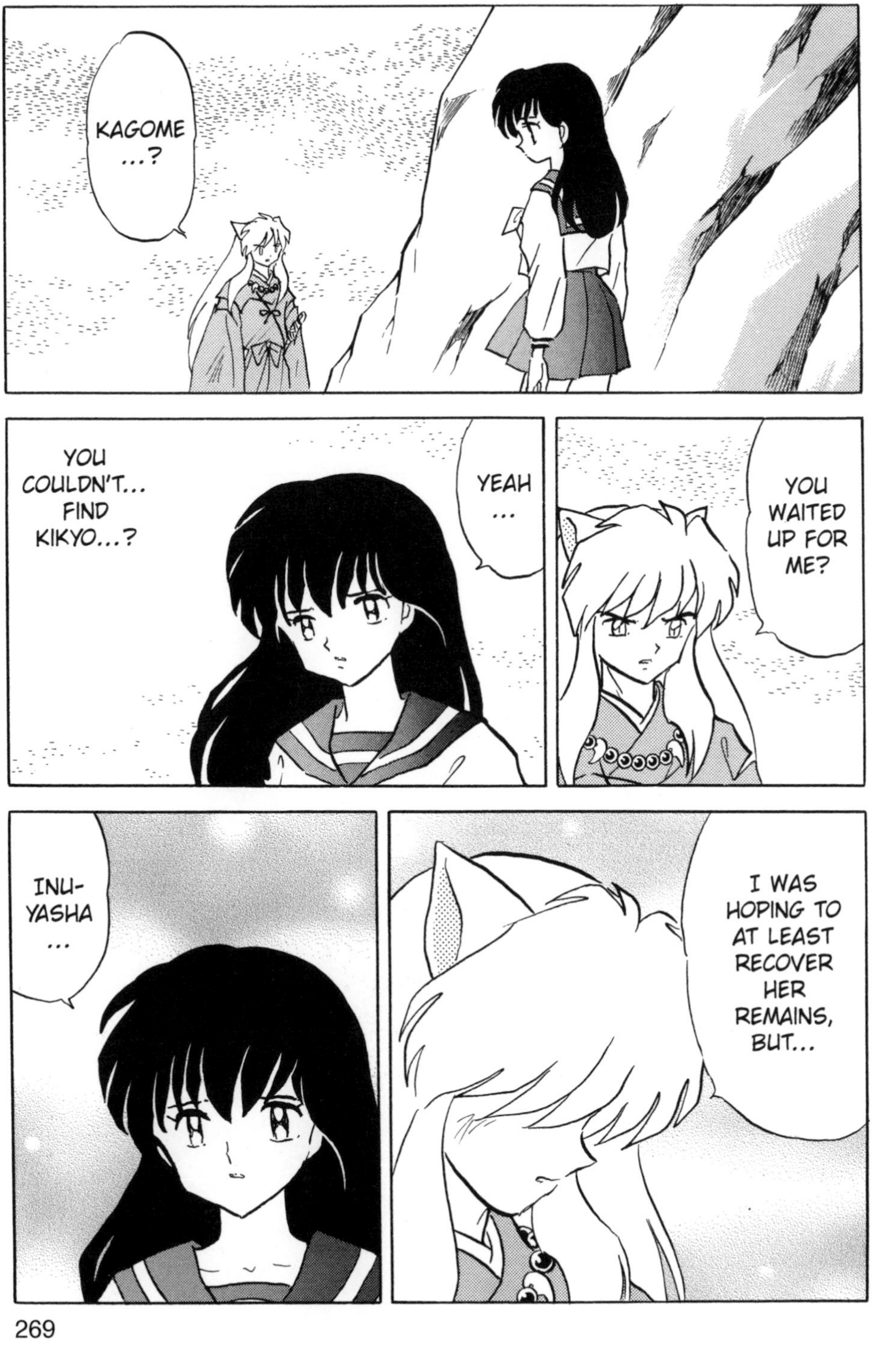
KAGOME ...?
YOU WAITED UP FOR ME?
YEAH ...
YOU COULDN'T... FIND KIKYO...?
I WAS HOPING TO AT LEAST RECOVER HER REMAINS, BUT...
INU-YASHA ...

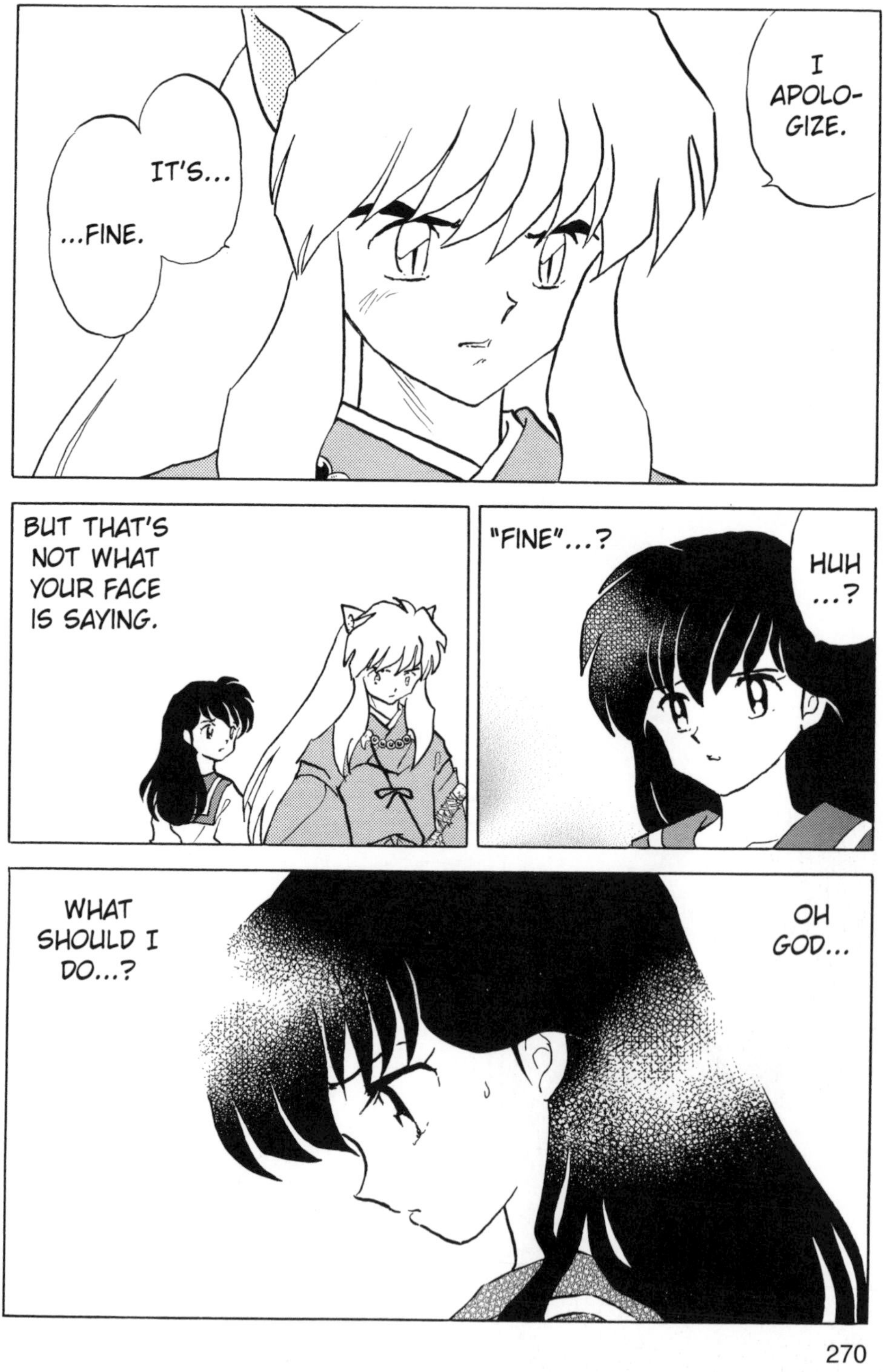
I APOLOGIZE.
IT'S... ...FINE.
HUH...?
"FINE"...?
BUT THAT'S NOT WHAT YOUR FACE IS SAYING.
OH GOD...
WHAT SHOULD I DO...?

SCROLL FIVE
INUYASHA'S TRUE FEELINGS

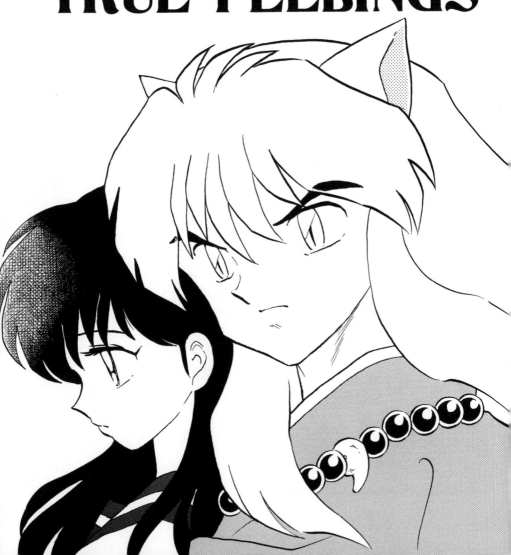

IMPOS-SIBLE!
HOOOO
COULD THE RUMORS BE TRUE?
THAT MT. HAKUREI CAME CRASHING DOWN AND DISAPPEARED OVERNIGHT...?
I ONLY HOPE NOTHING WORSE COMES OF THIS...!
ZZZ
ZZZ

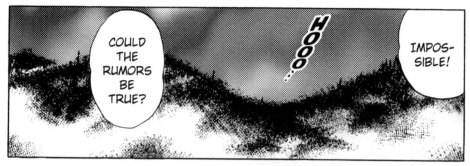

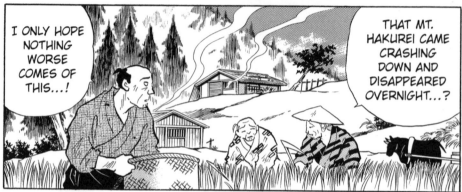

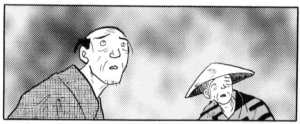

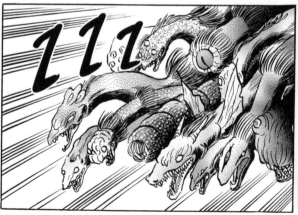

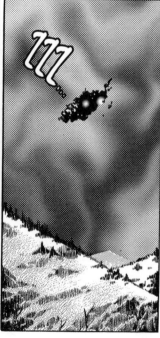

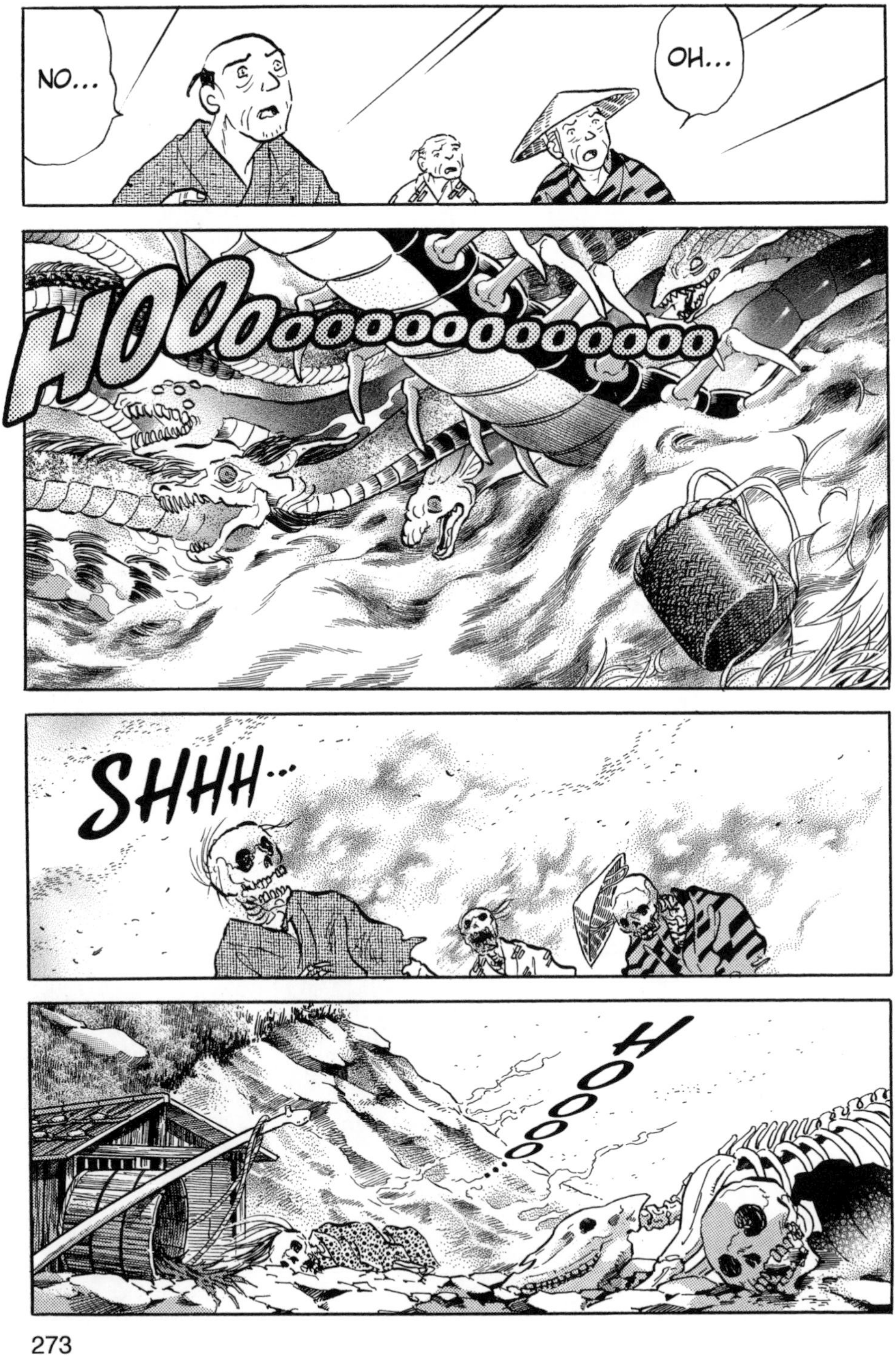
OH...
NO...
HOOOOOOOOOOOOOOOOO
SHHH...
HOOOOO...

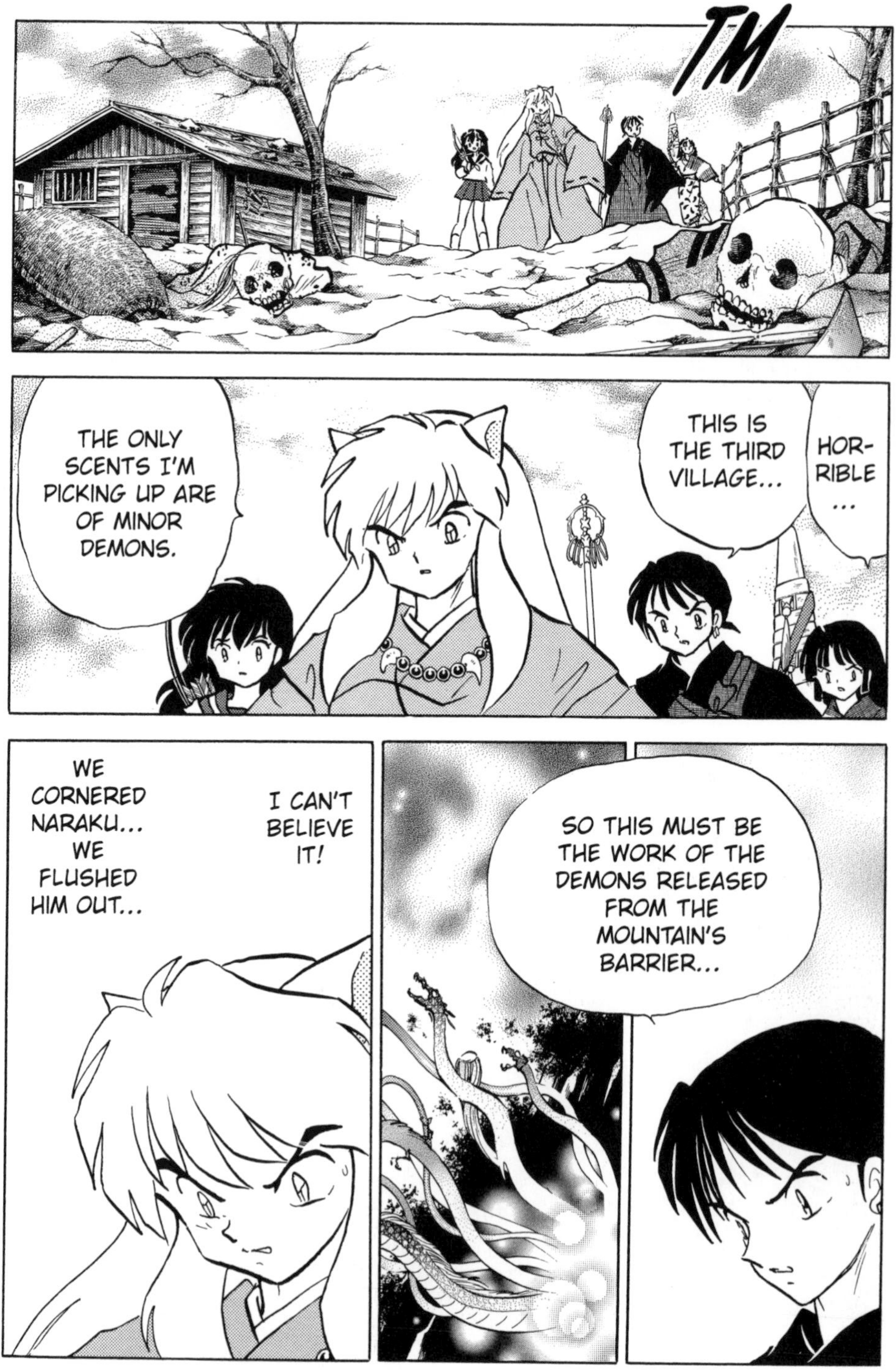
TM
HOR-RIBLE...
THIS IS THE THIRD VILLAGE...
THE ONLY SCENTS I'M PICKING UP ARE OF MINOR DEMONS.
SO THIS MUST BE THE WORK OF THE DEMONS RELEASED FROM THE MOUNTAIN'S BARRIER...
I CAN'T BELIEVE IT!
WE CORNERED NARAKU... WE FLUSHED HIM OUT...

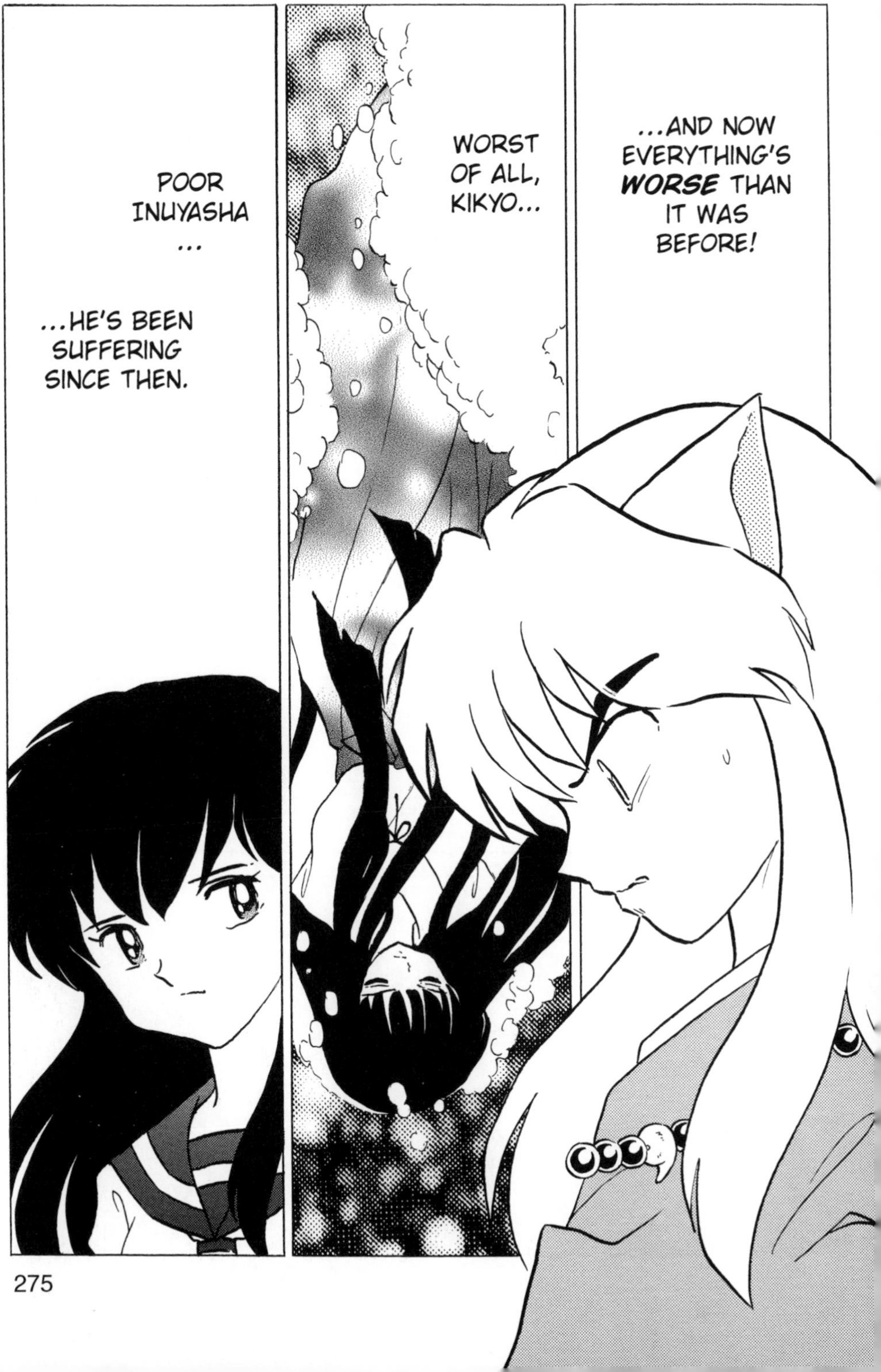
...AND NOW EVERYTHING'S **WORSE** THAN IT WAS BEFORE!
WORST OF ALL, KIKYO...
POOR INUYASHA...
...HE'S BEEN SUFFERING SINCE THEN.

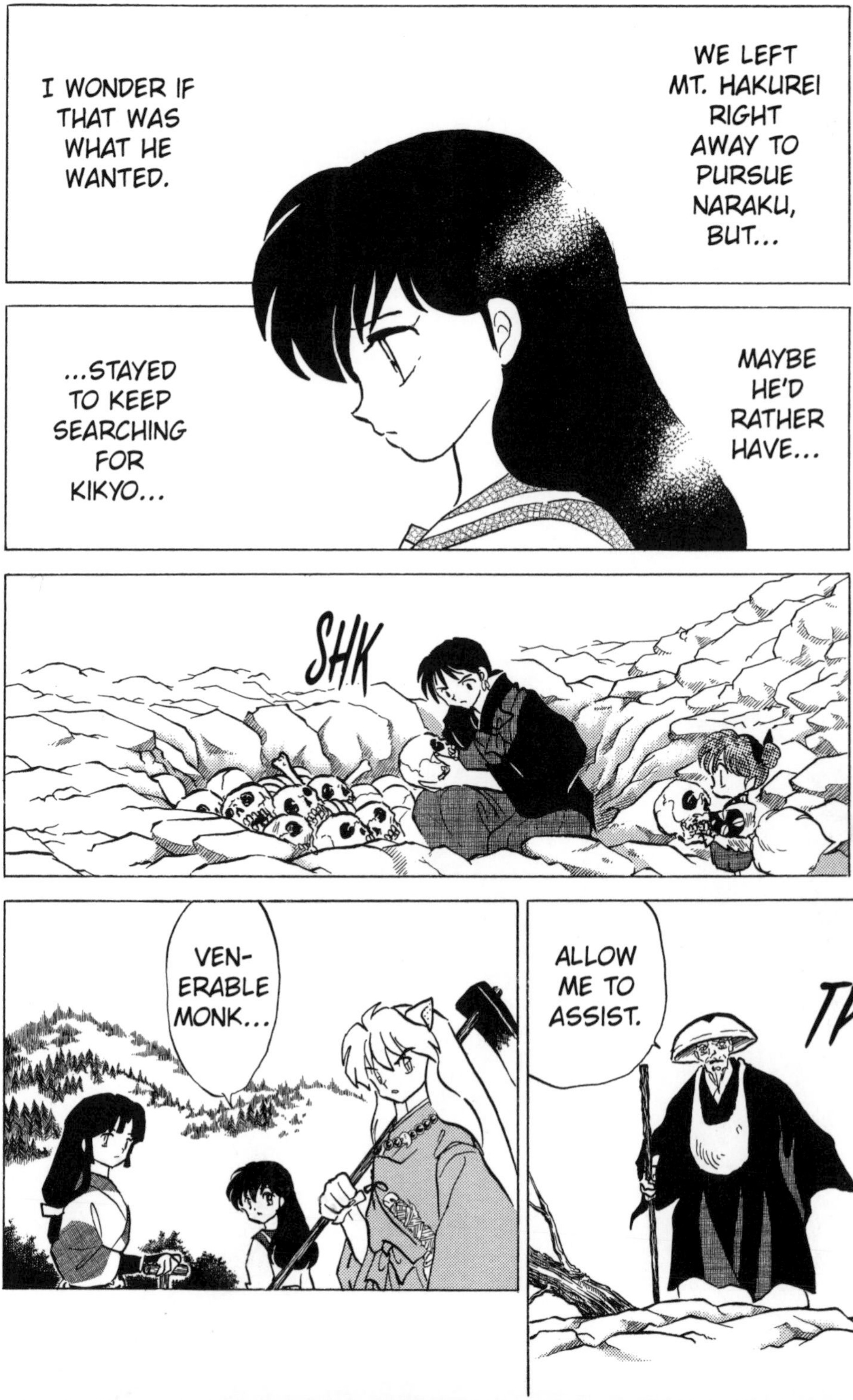
WE LEFT MT. HAKUREI RIGHT AWAY TO PURSUE NARAKU, BUT...
I WONDER IF THAT WAS WHAT HE WANTED.
MAYBE HE'D RATHER HAVE...
...STAYED TO KEEP SEARCHING FOR KIKYO...
SHK
TP
ALLOW ME TO ASSIST.
VEN-ERABLE MONK...

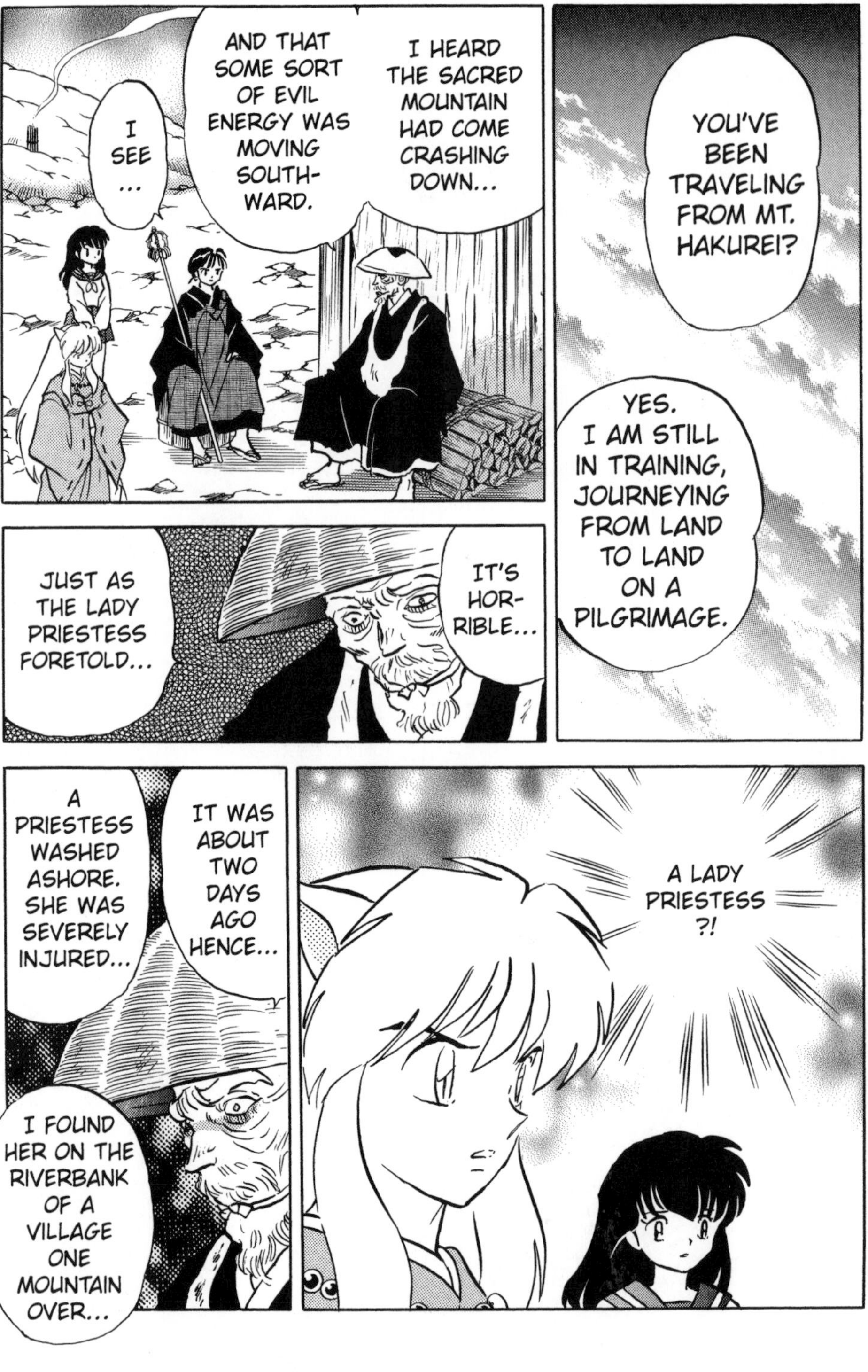
YOU'VE BEEN TRAVELING FROM MT. HAKUREI?
YES. I AM STILL IN TRAINING, JOURNEYING FROM LAND TO LAND ON A PILGRIMAGE.
I HEARD THE SACRED MOUNTAIN HAD COME CRASHING DOWN...
AND THAT SOME SORT OF EVIL ENERGY WAS MOVING SOUTH-WARD.
I SEE...
IT'S HOR-RIBLE...
JUST AS THE LADY PRIESTESS FORETOLD...
A LADY PRIESTESS ?!
IT WAS ABOUT TWO DAYS AGO HENCE...
A PRIESTESS WASHED ASHORE. SHE WAS SEVERELY INJURED...
I FOUND HER ON THE RIVERBANK OF A VILLAGE ONE MOUNTAIN OVER...

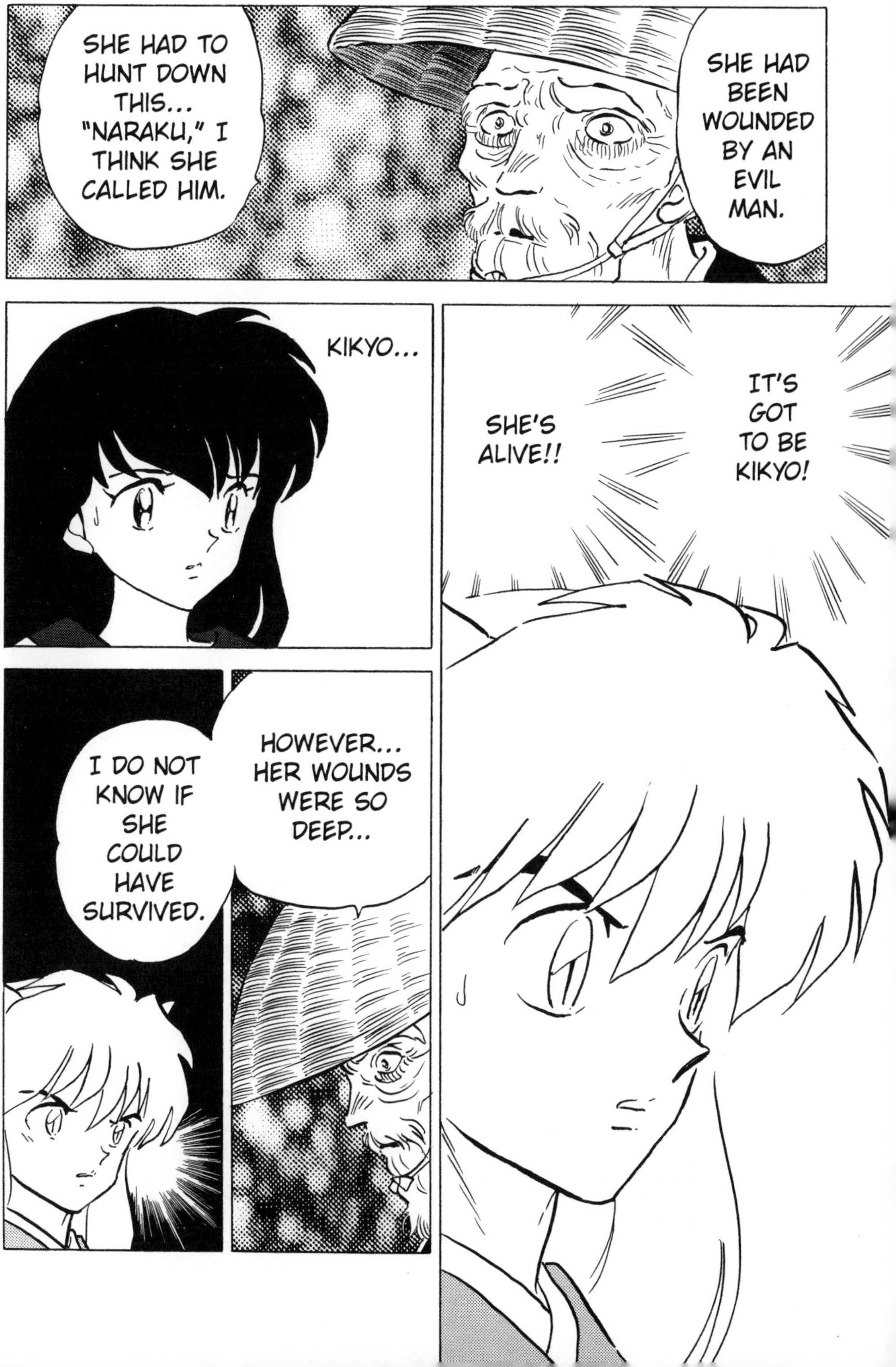
SHE HAD BEEN WOUNDED BY AN EVIL MAN.
SHE HAD TO HUNT DOWN THIS... "NARAKU," I THINK SHE CALLED HIM.
IT'S GOT TO BE KIKYO!
SHE'S ALIVE!!
KIKYO...
HOWEVER... HER WOUNDS WERE SO DEEP...
I DO NOT KNOW IF SHE COULD HAVE SURVIVED.

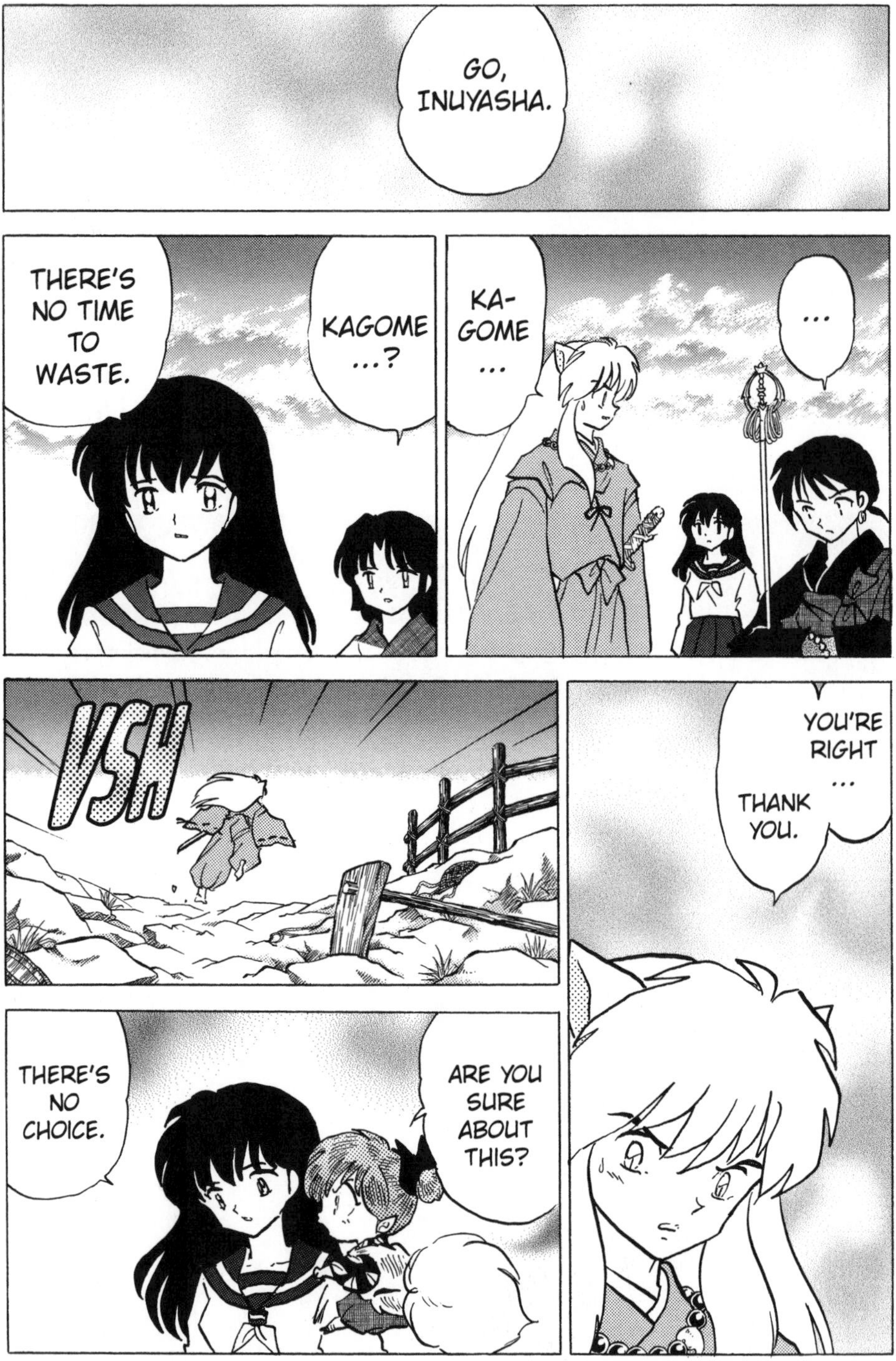
GO, INUYASHA.
...
KA-GOME ...
KAGOME ...?
THERE'S NO TIME TO WASTE.
YOU'RE RIGHT ...
THANK YOU.
VSH
ARE YOU SURE ABOUT THIS?
THERE'S NO CHOICE.

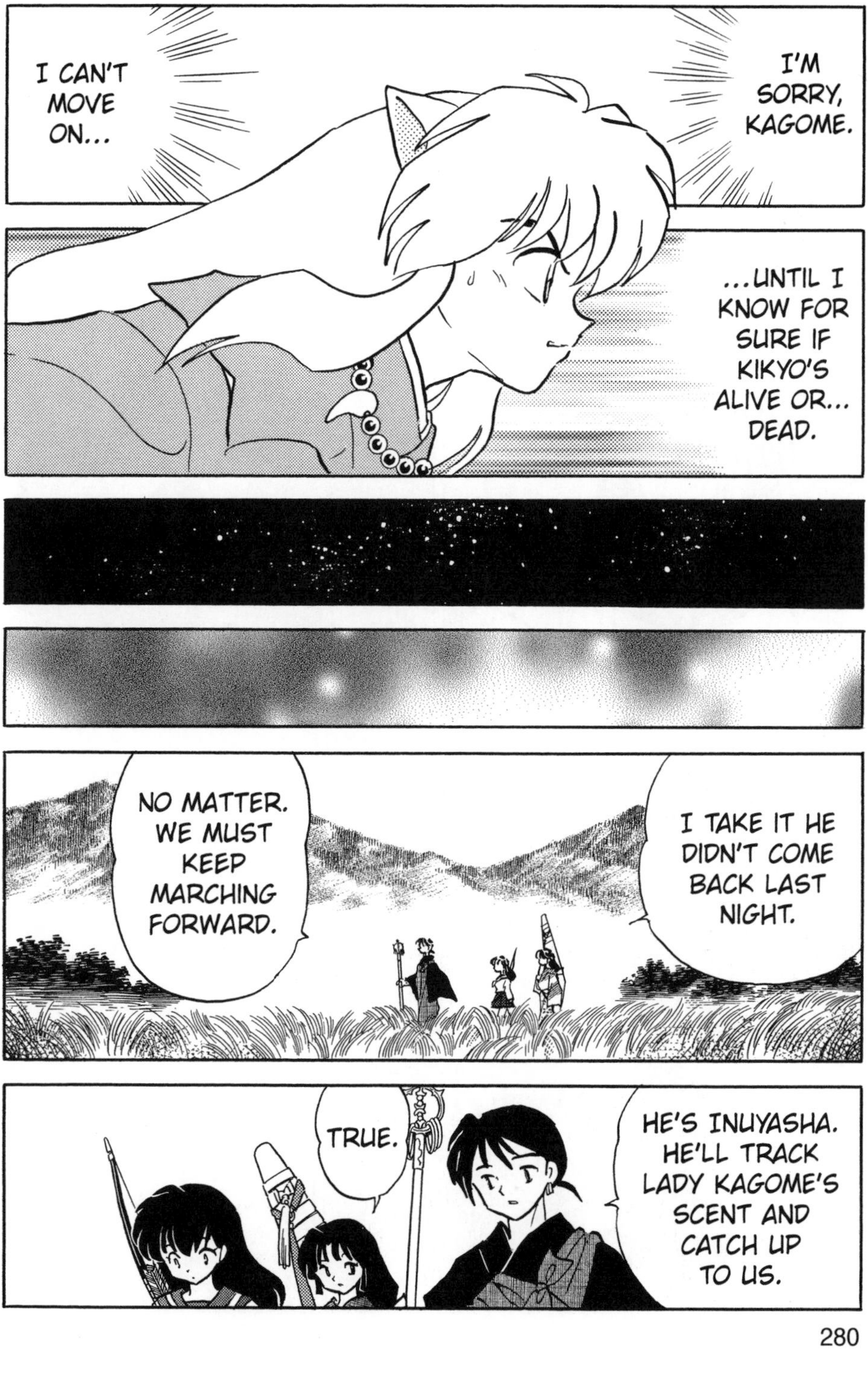
I'M SORRY, KAGOME.
I CAN'T MOVE ON...
...UNTIL I KNOW FOR SURE IF KIKYO'S ALIVE OR... DEAD.
I TAKE IT HE DIDN'T COME BACK LAST NIGHT.
NO MATTER. WE MUST KEEP MARCHING FORWARD.
HE'S INUYASHA. HE'LL TRACK LADY KAGOME'S SCENT AND CATCH UP TO US.
TRUE.

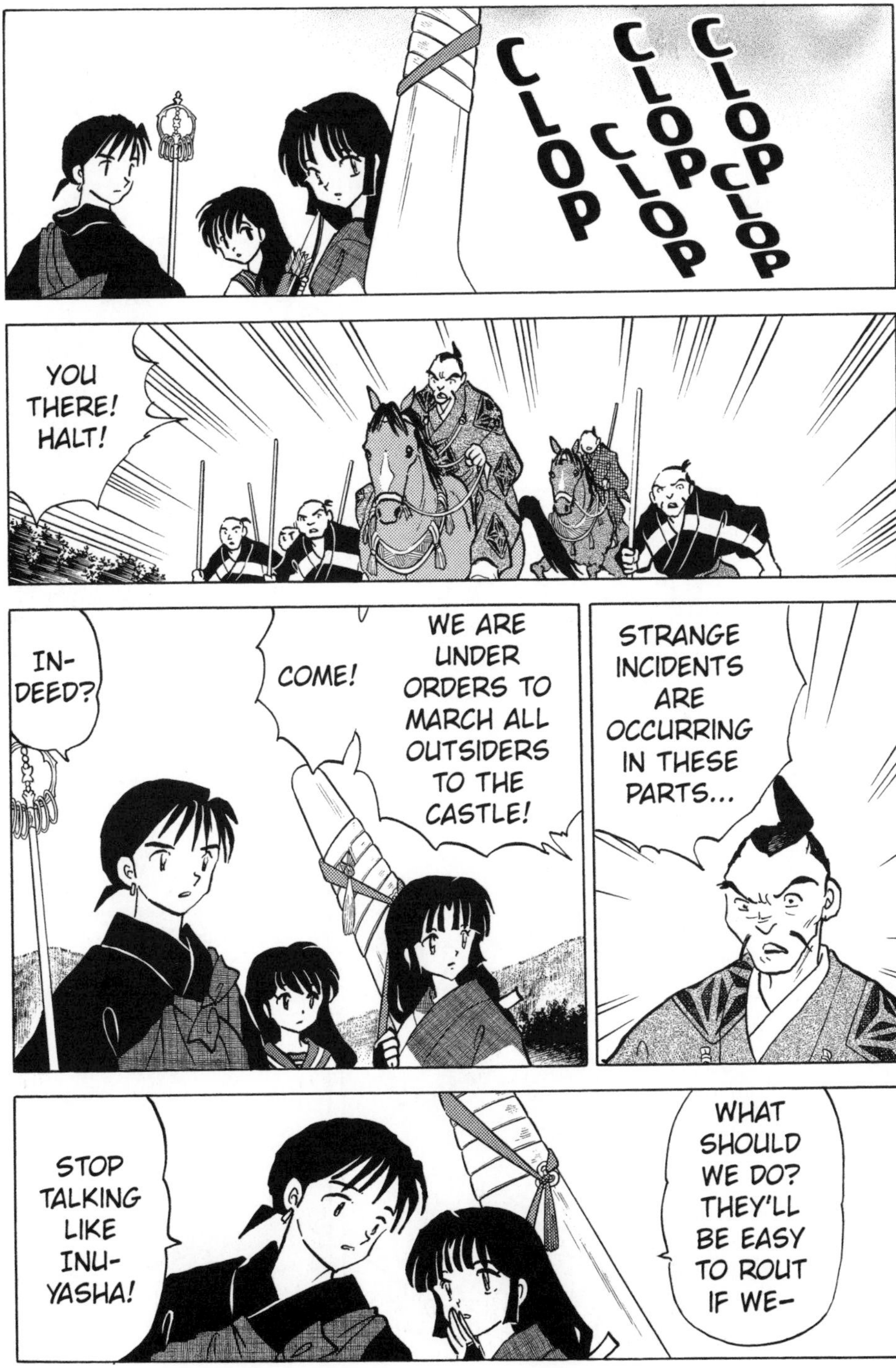
CLOP CLOP
CLOP CLOP
CLOP
YOU THERE! HALT!
STRANGE INCIDENTS ARE OCCURRING IN THESE PARTS...
WE ARE UNDER ORDERS TO MARCH ALL OUTSIDERS TO THE CASTLE!
COME!
IN-DEED?
WHAT SHOULD WE DO? THEY'LL BE EASY TO ROUT IF WE-
STOP TALKING LIKE INU-YASHA!

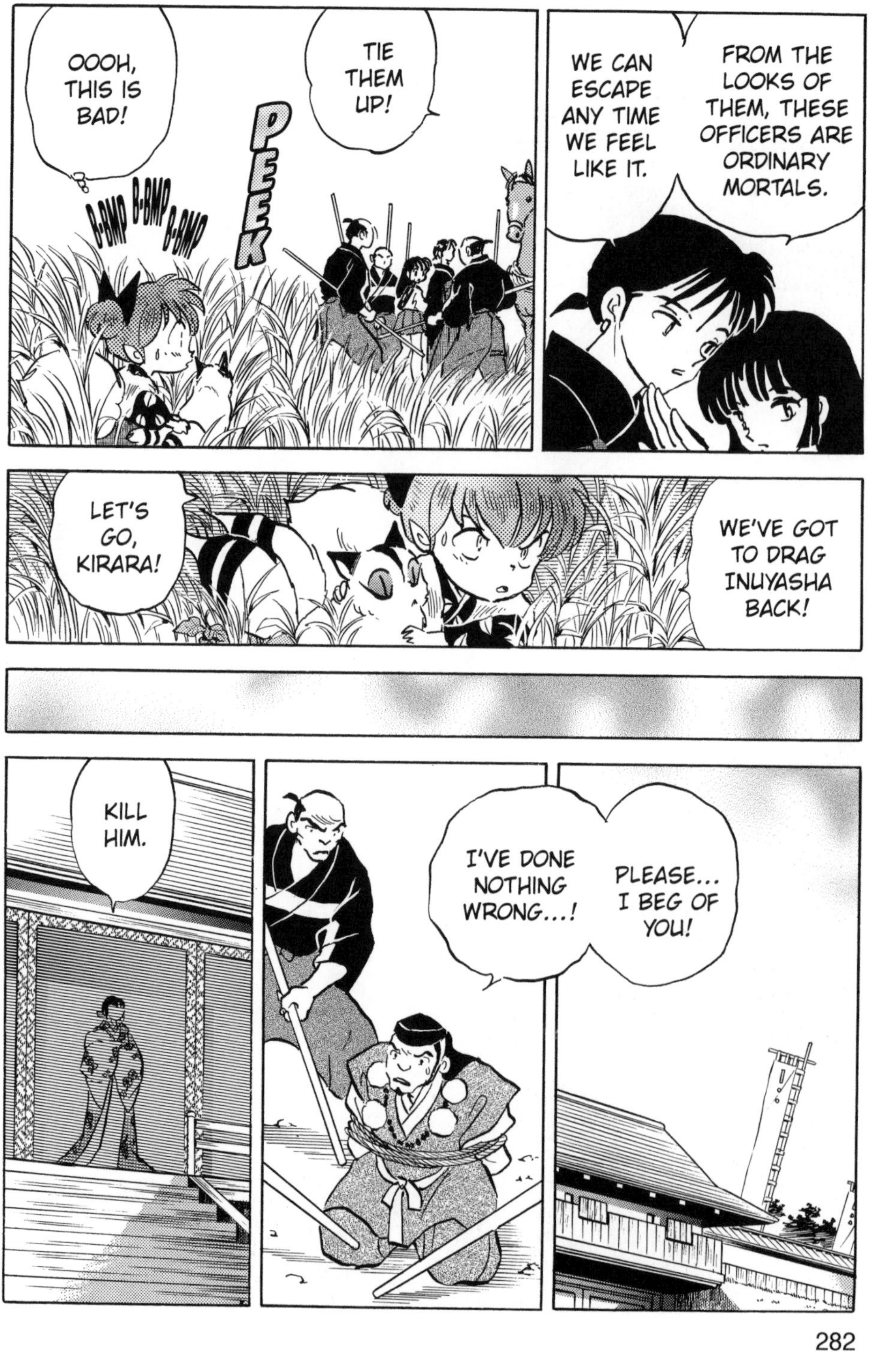
FROM THE LOOKS OF THEM, THESE OFFICERS ARE ORDINARY MORTALS.
WE CAN ESCAPE ANY TIME WE FEEL LIKE IT.
TIE THEM UP!
PEEK
OOOH, THIS IS BAD!
B-BMP B-BMP B-BMP
WE'VE GOT TO DRAG INUYASHA BACK!
LET'S GO, KIRARA!
PLEASE... I BEG OF YOU!
I'VE DONE NOTHING WRONG...!
KILL HIM.

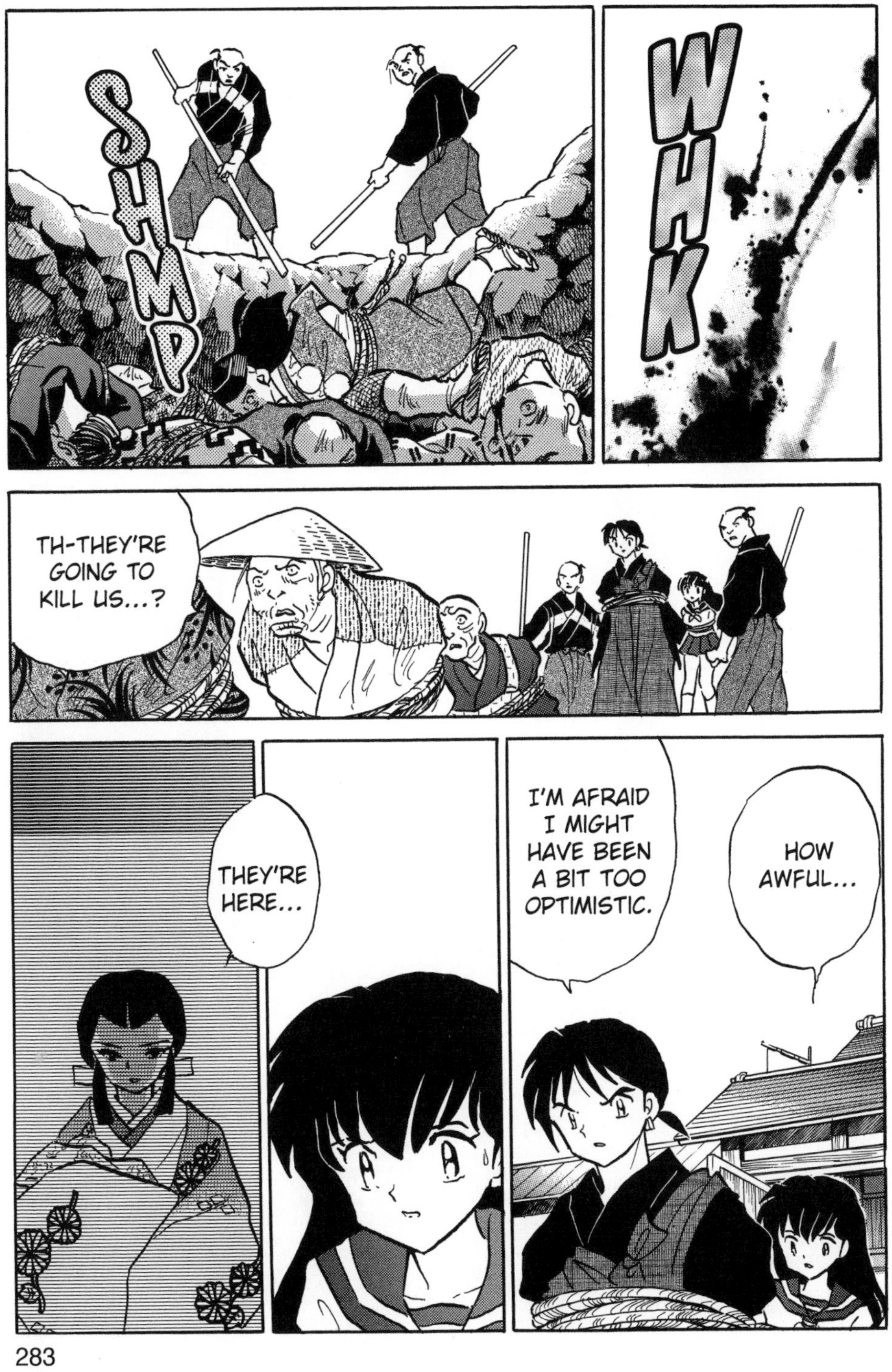
WHK
SHMP
TH-THEY'RE GOING TO KILL US...?
HOW AWFUL...
I'M AFRAID I MIGHT HAVE BEEN A BIT TOO OPTIMISTIC.
THEY'RE HERE...

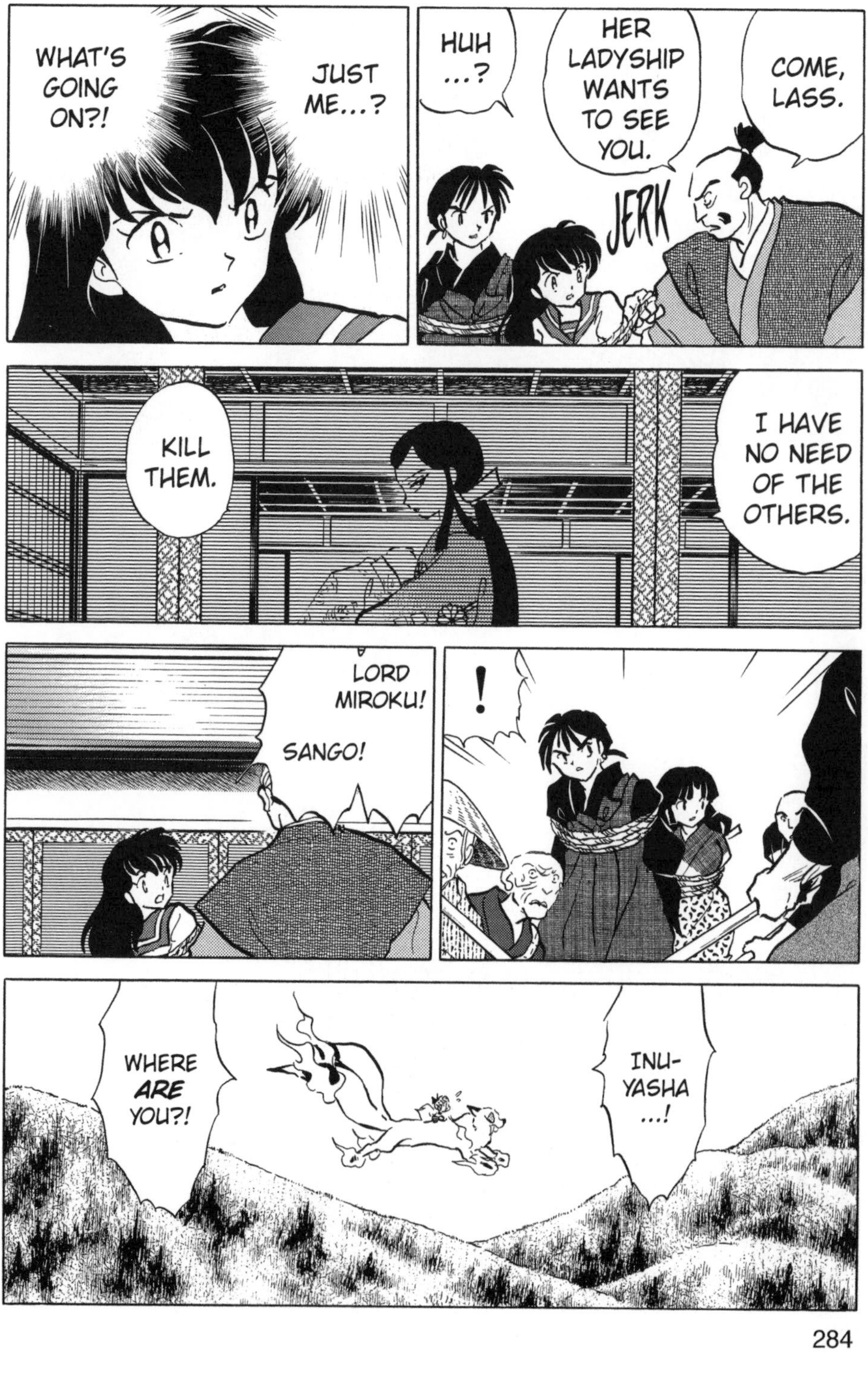
COME, LASS.
HER LADYSHIP WANTS TO SEE YOU.
HUH ...?
JERK
JUST ME...?
WHAT'S GOING ON?!
I HAVE NO NEED OF THE OTHERS.
KILL THEM.
!
LORD MIROKU!
SANGO!
INU-YASHA ...!
WHERE ARE YOU?!

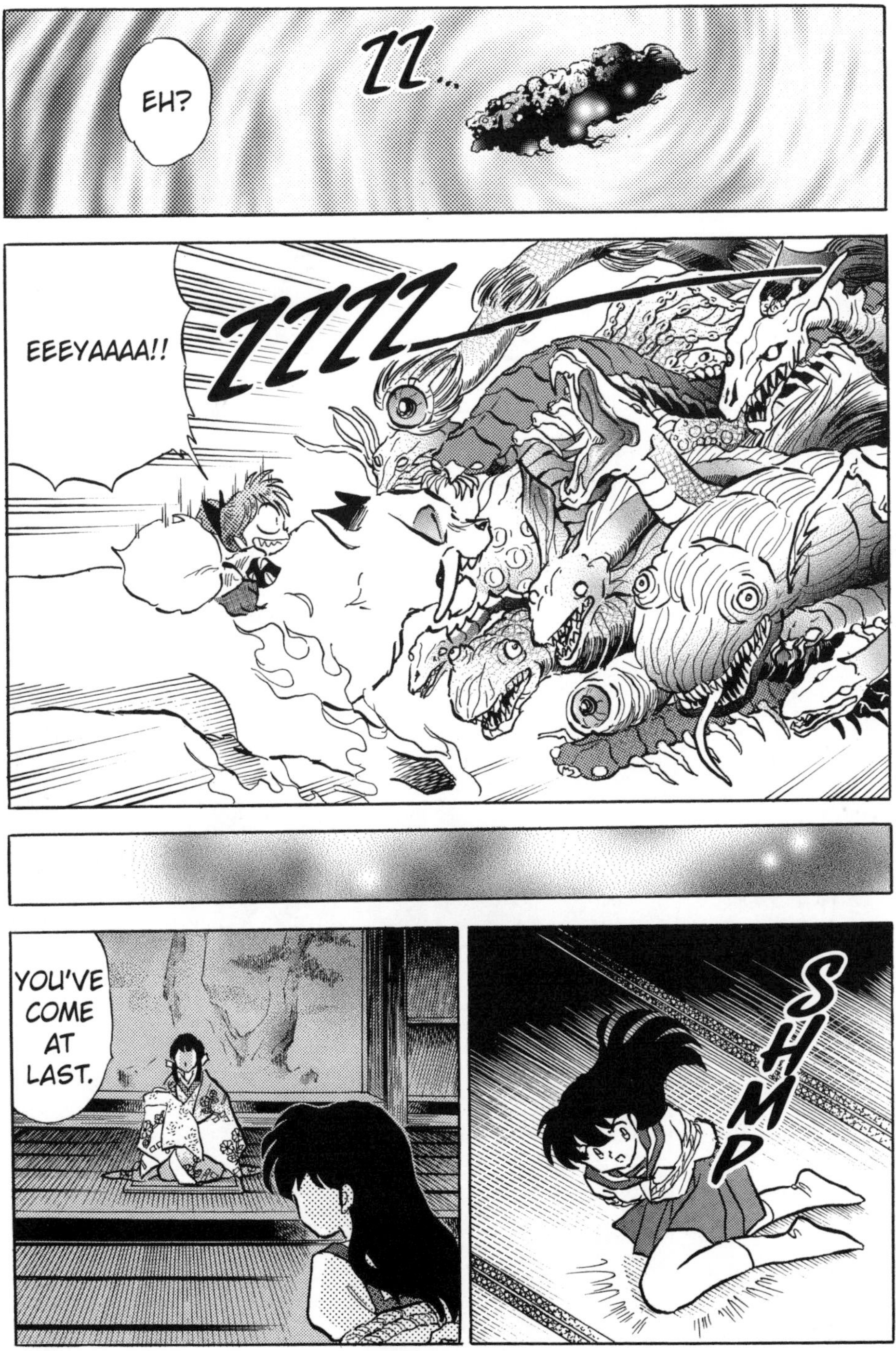
ZZ...
EH?
ZZZZ
EEEYAAAA!!
SHMP
YOU'VE COME AT LAST.

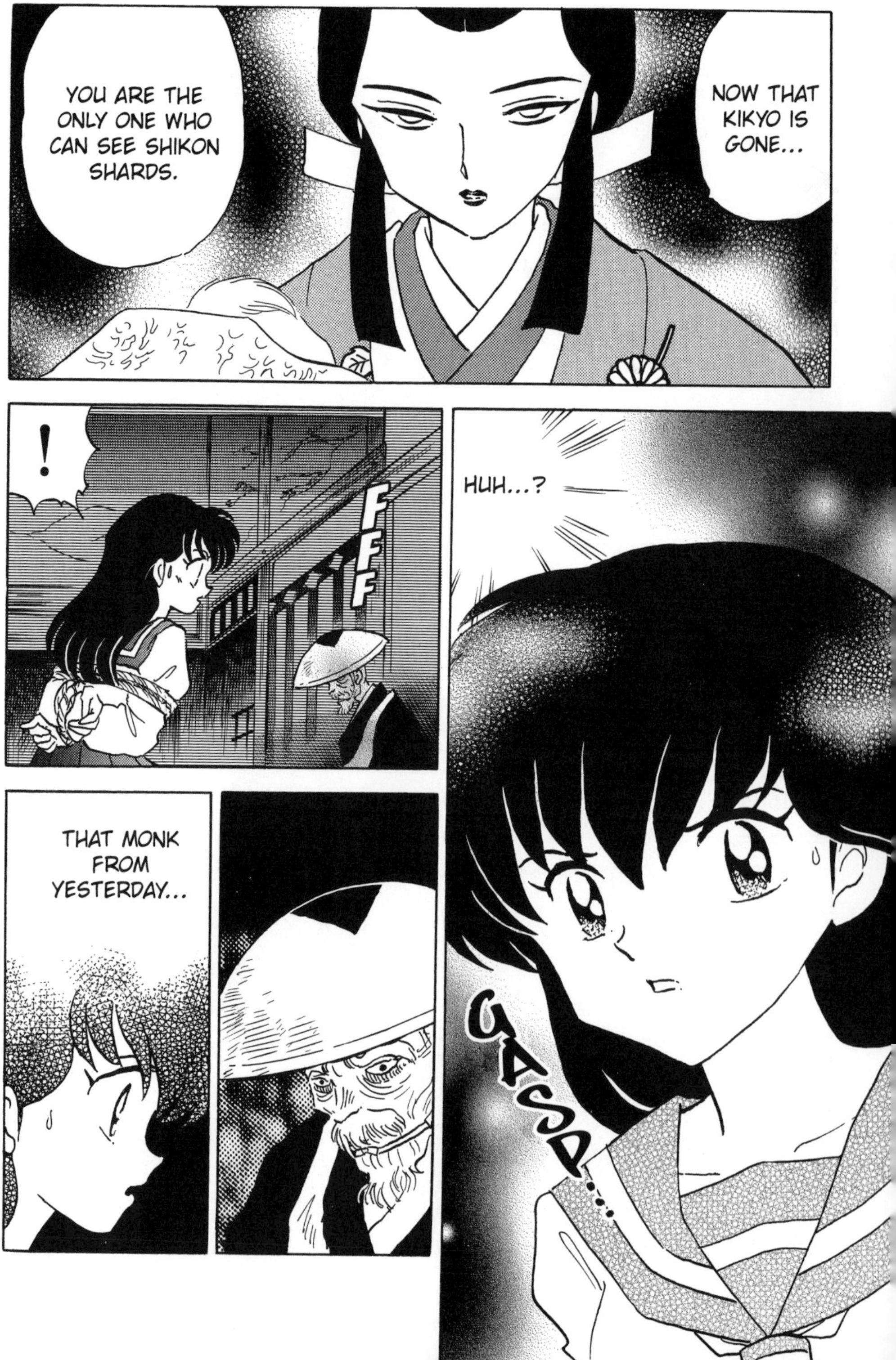
NOW THAT KIKYO IS GONE...
YOU ARE THE ONLY ONE WHO CAN SEE SHIKON SHARDS.
HUH...?
GASP...
!
FFF
THAT MONK FROM YESTERDAY...

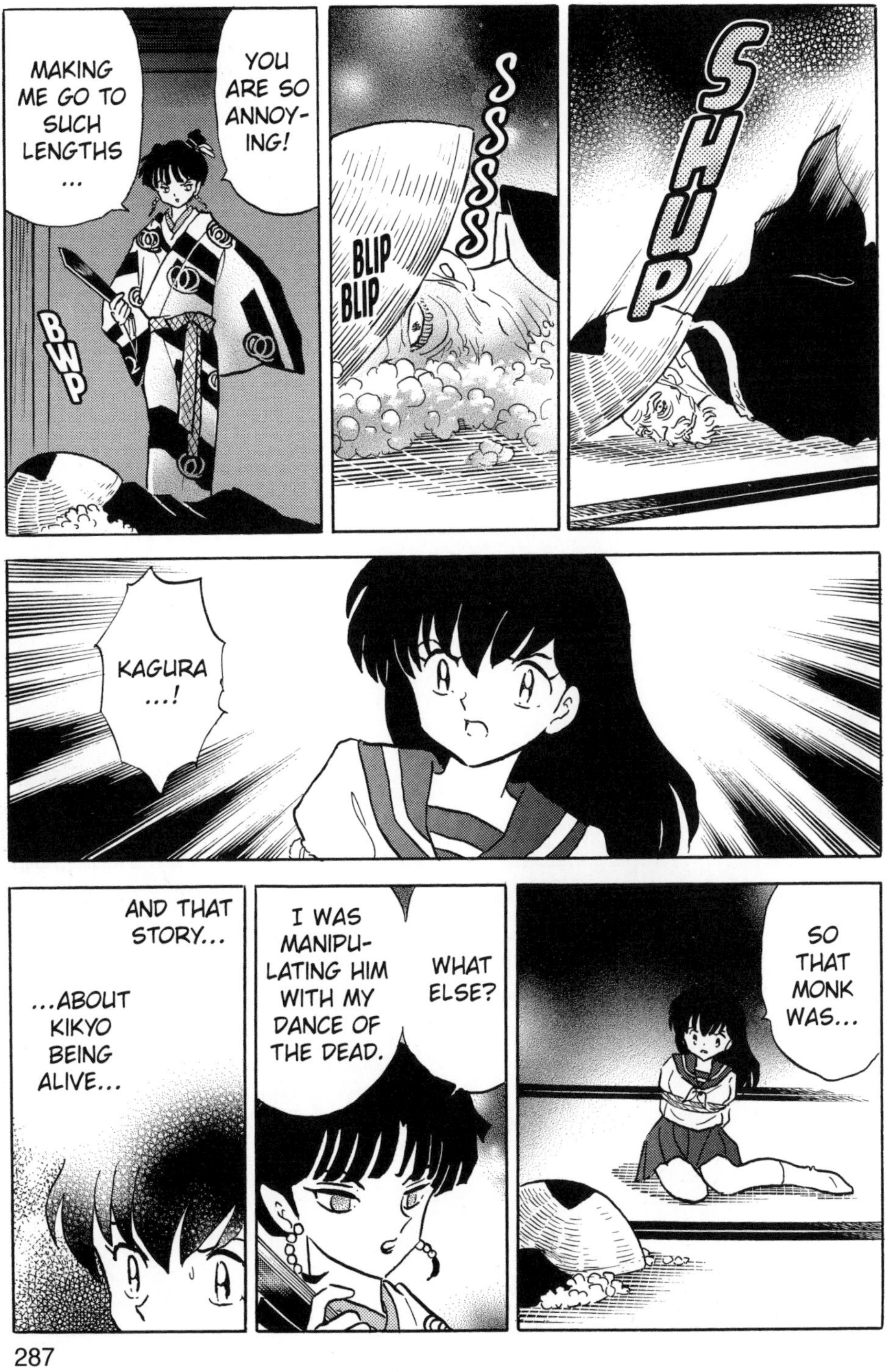
SHUP
SSSS
BLIP BLIP
YOU ARE SO ANNOY-ING!
MAKING ME GO TO SUCH LENGTHS ...
BWP
KAGURA ...!
SO THAT MONK WAS...
WHAT ELSE?
I WAS MANIPU-LATING HIM WITH MY DANCE OF THE DEAD.
AND THAT STORY...
...ABOUT KIKYO BEING ALIVE...

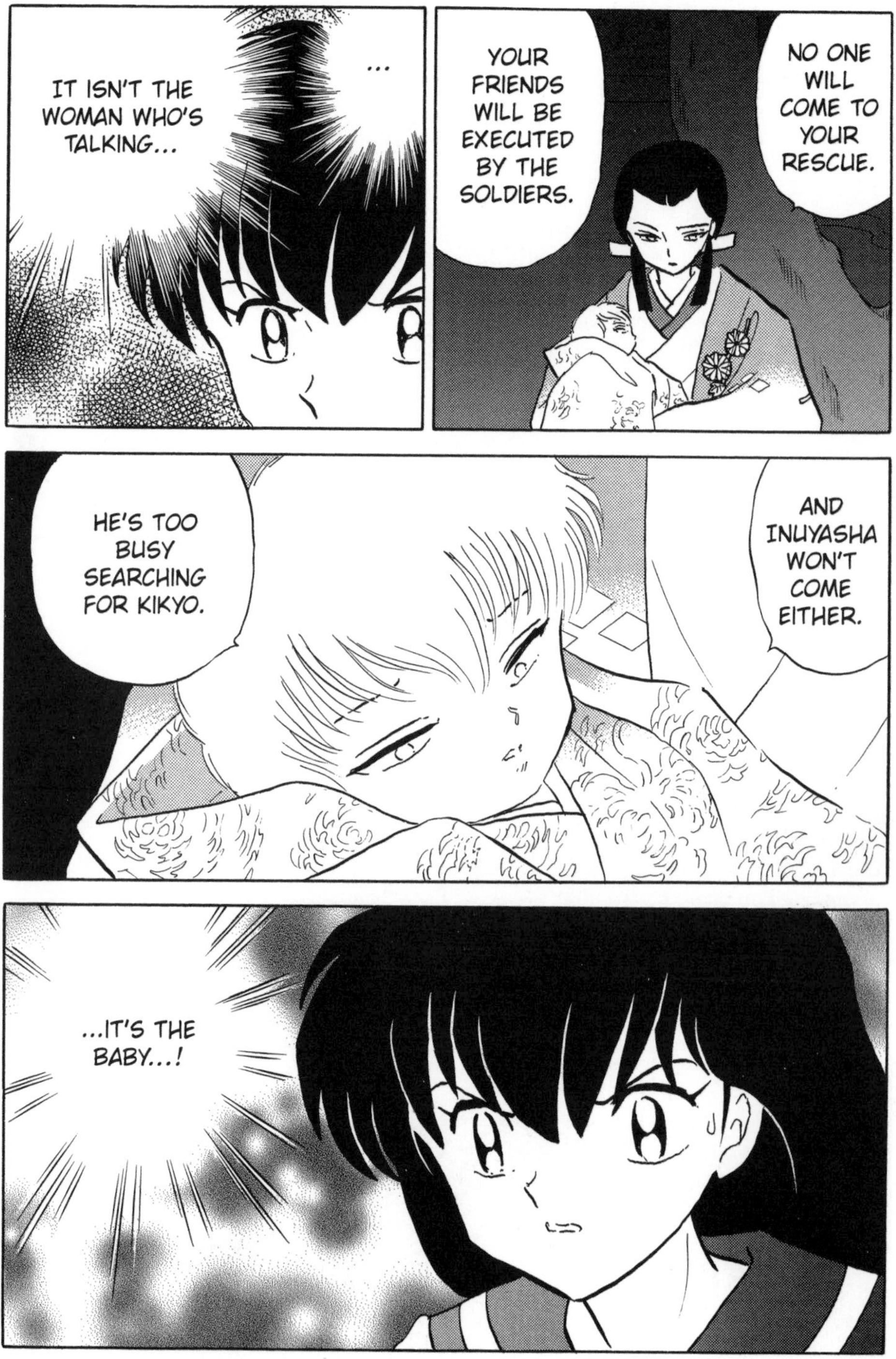
NO ONE WILL COME TO YOUR RESCUE.
YOUR FRIENDS WILL BE EXECUTED BY THE SOLDIERS.
...
IT ISN'T THE WOMAN WHO'S TALKING...
AND INUYASHA WON'T COME EITHER.
HE'S TOO BUSY SEARCHING FOR KIKYO.
...IT'S THE BABY...!

SCROLL SIX
DARKNESS IN THE HEART

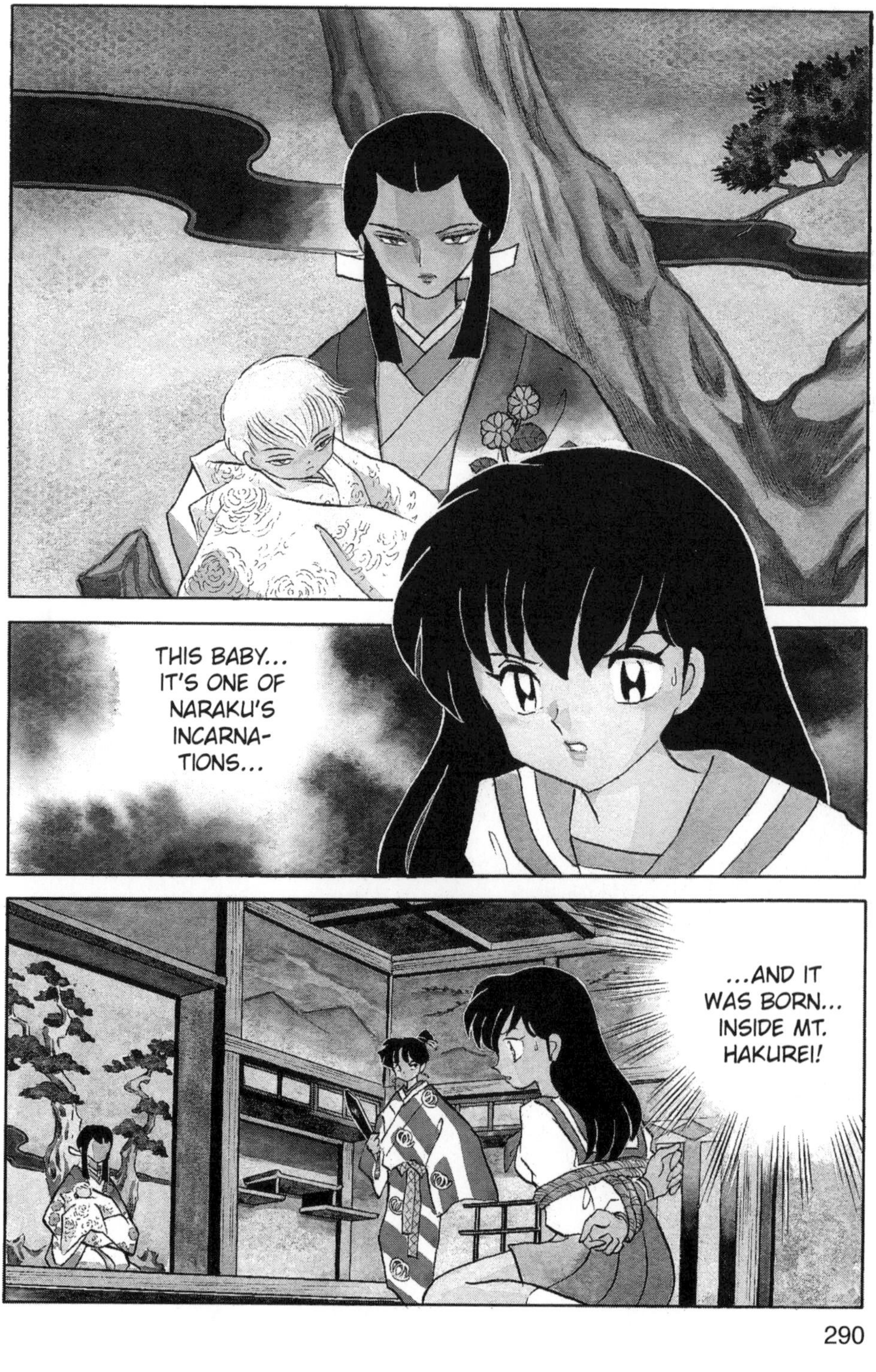
THIS BABY... IT'S ONE OF NARAKU'S INCARNA-TIONS...
...AND IT WAS BORN... INSIDE MT. HAKUREI!

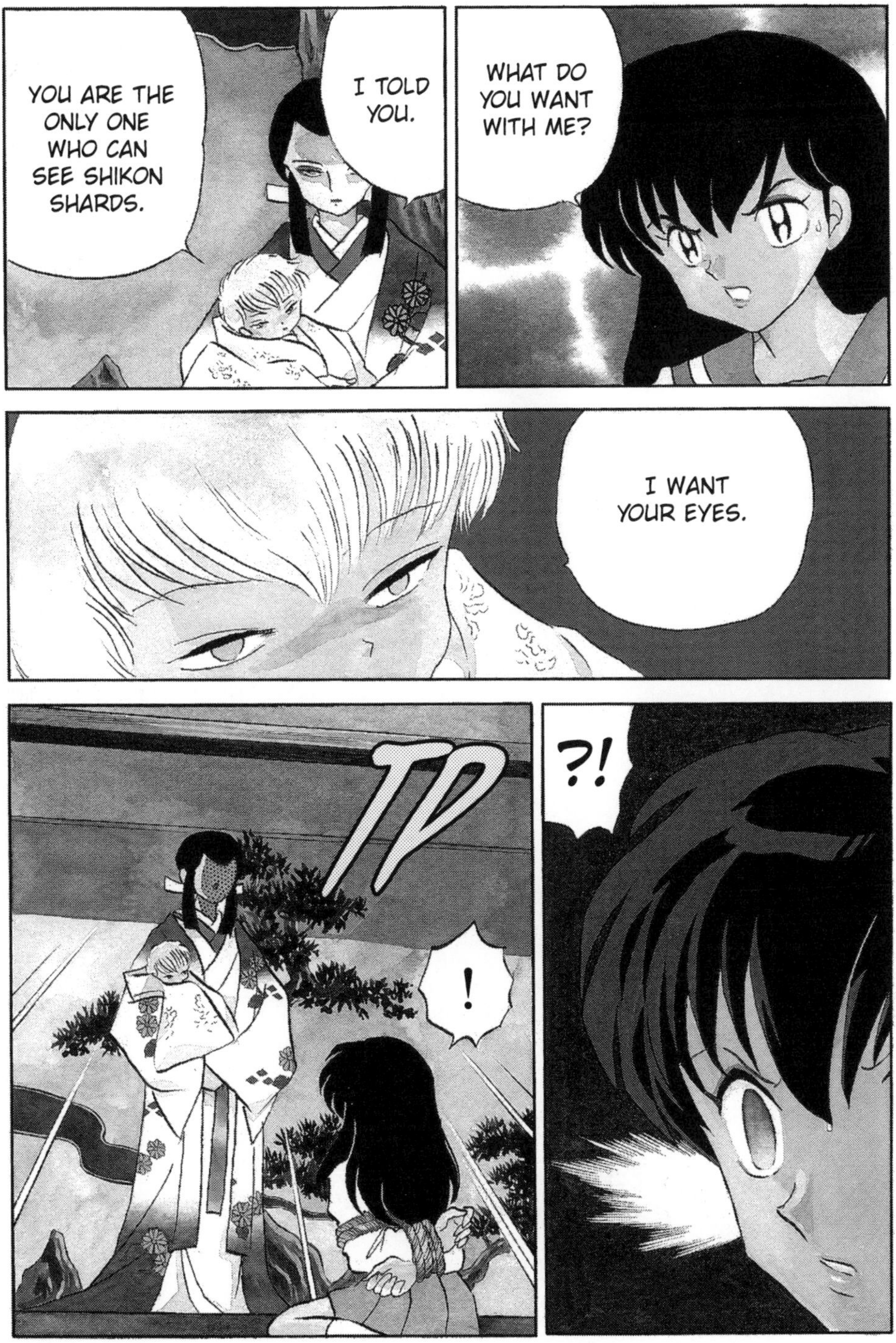
WHAT DO YOU WANT WITH ME?
I TOLD YOU.
YOU ARE THE ONLY ONE WHO CAN SEE SHIKON SHARDS.
I WANT YOUR EYES.
?!
TP
!

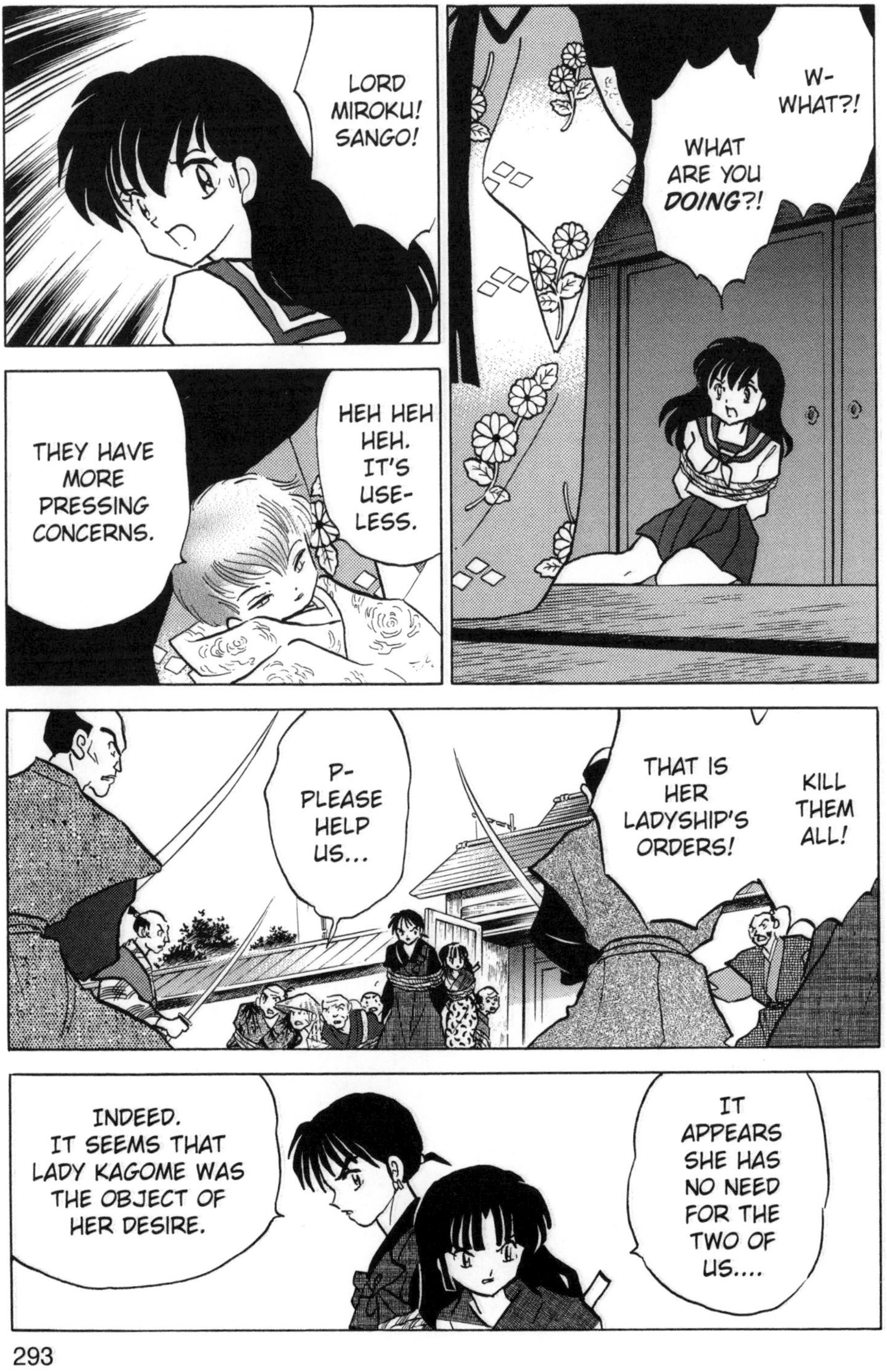
W-WHAT?!
WHAT ARE YOU *DOING*?!
LORD MIROKU! SANGO!
HEH HEH HEH. IT'S USELESS.
THEY HAVE MORE PRESSING CONCERNS.
KILL THEM ALL!
THAT IS HER LADYSHIP'S ORDERS!
P-PLEASE HELP US...
IT APPEARS SHE HAS NO NEED FOR THE TWO OF US....
INDEED. IT SEEMS THAT LADY KAGOME WAS THE OBJECT OF HER DESIRE.

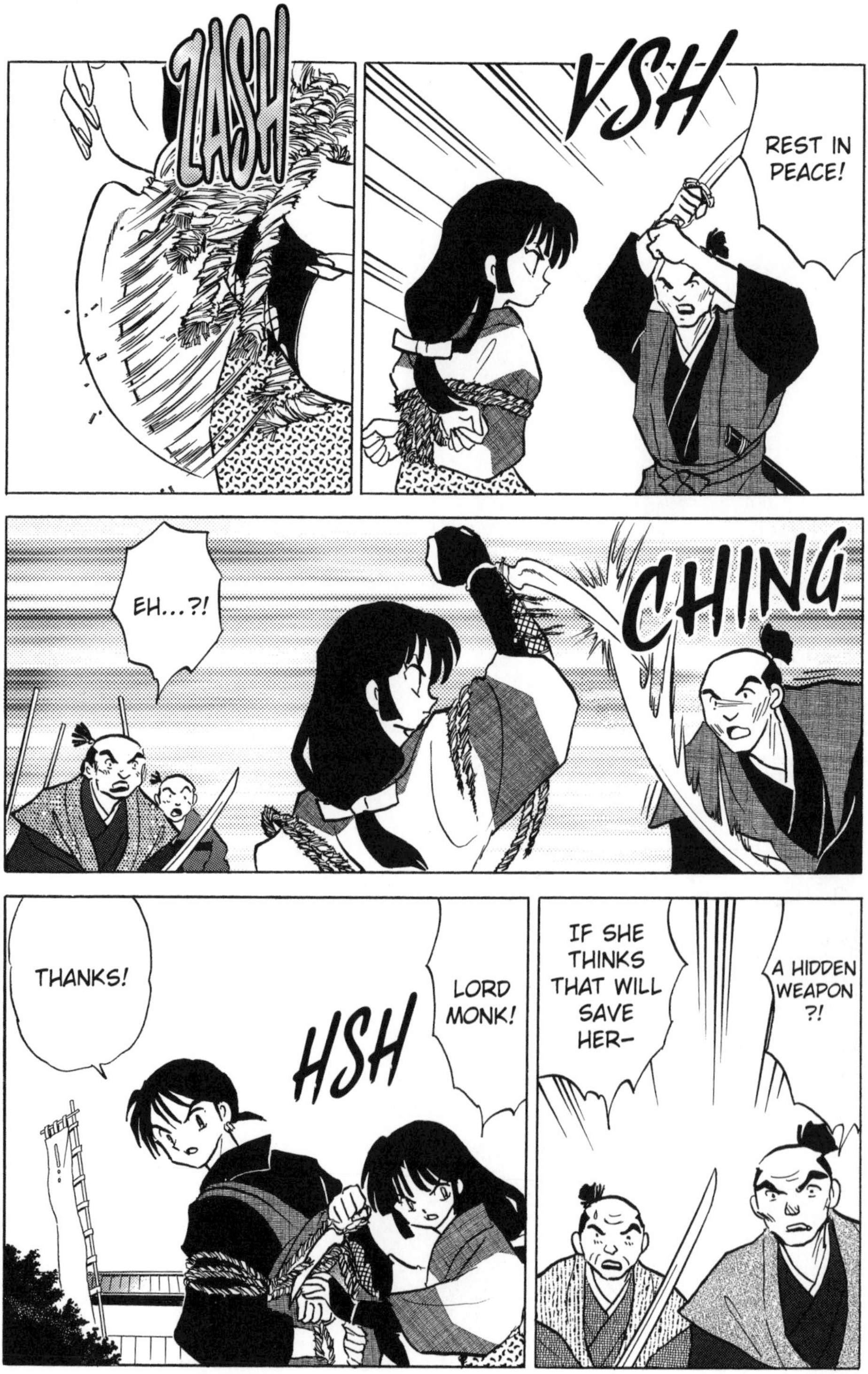
VSH
REST IN PEACE!
ZASH
CHING
EH...?!
A HIDDEN WEAPON ?!
IF SHE THINKS THAT WILL SAVE HER-
LORD MONK!
HSH
THANKS!

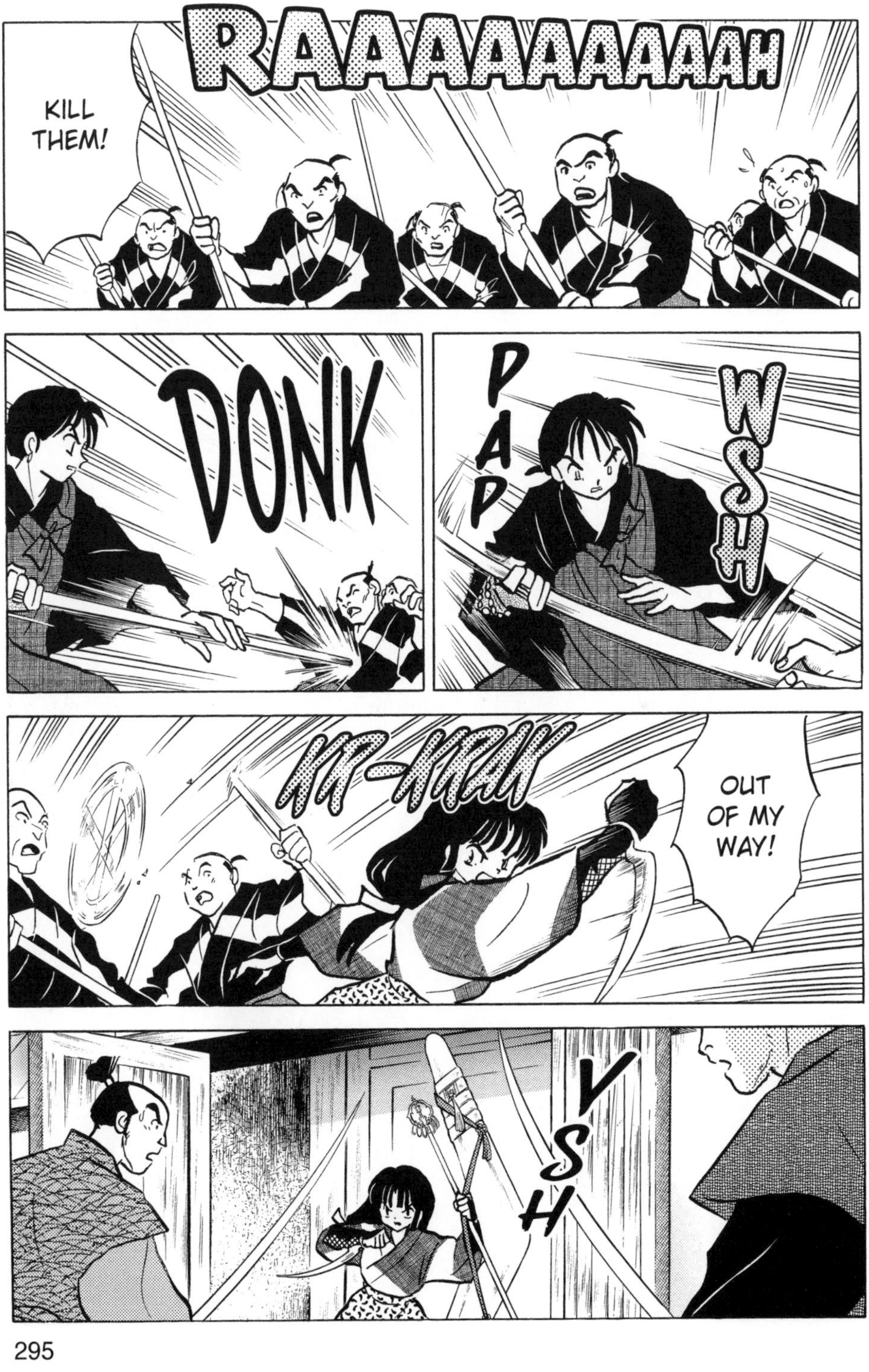
RAAAAAAAAAAH
KILL THEM!
WSH
PAP
DONK
OUT OF MY WAY!
KR-KRAK
VSH

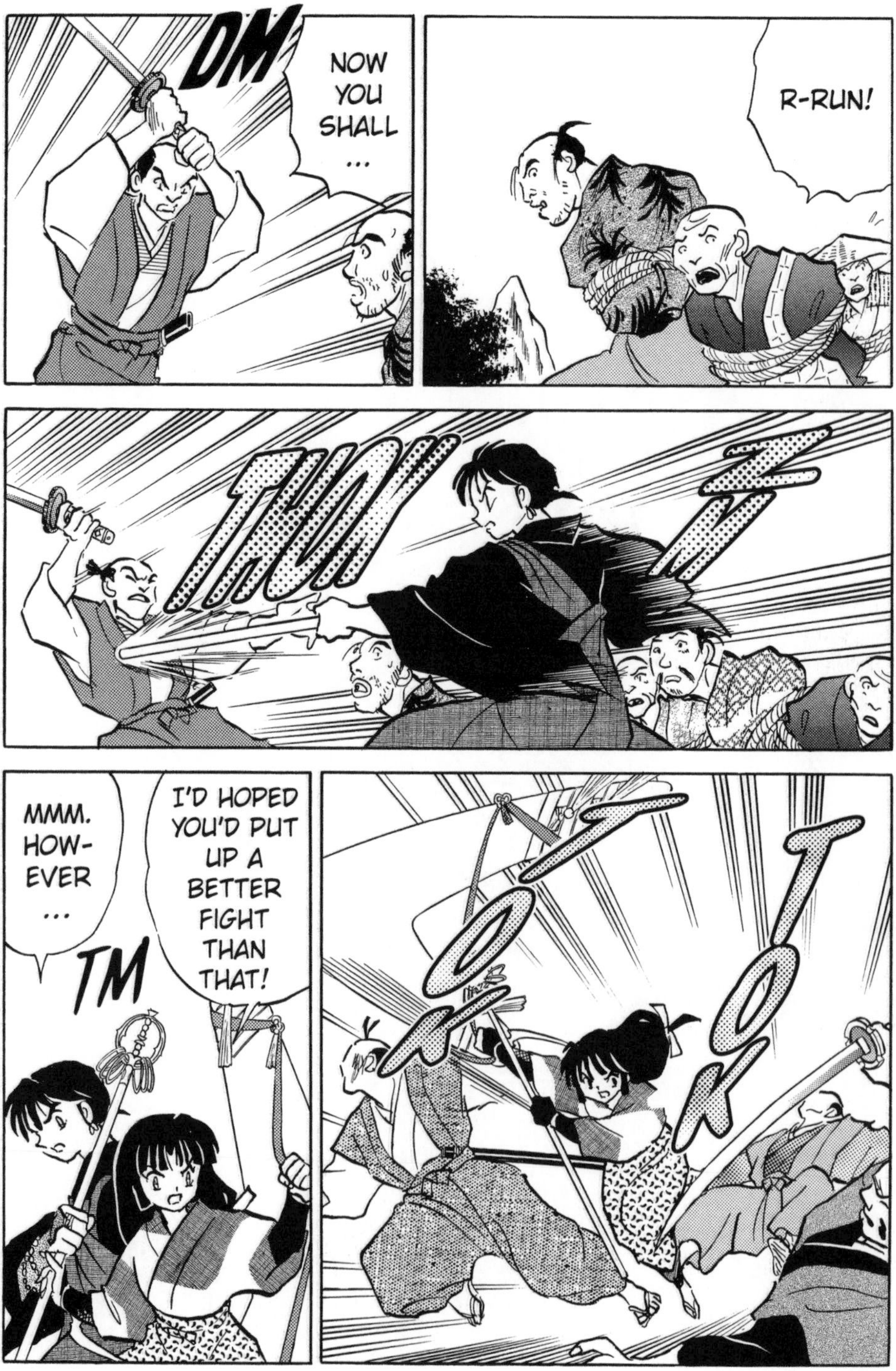
R-RUN!
DM
NOW YOU SHALL ...
TOK
TOK
I'D HOPED YOU'D PUT UP A BETTER FIGHT THAN THAT!
MMM. HOW-EVER ...
TM

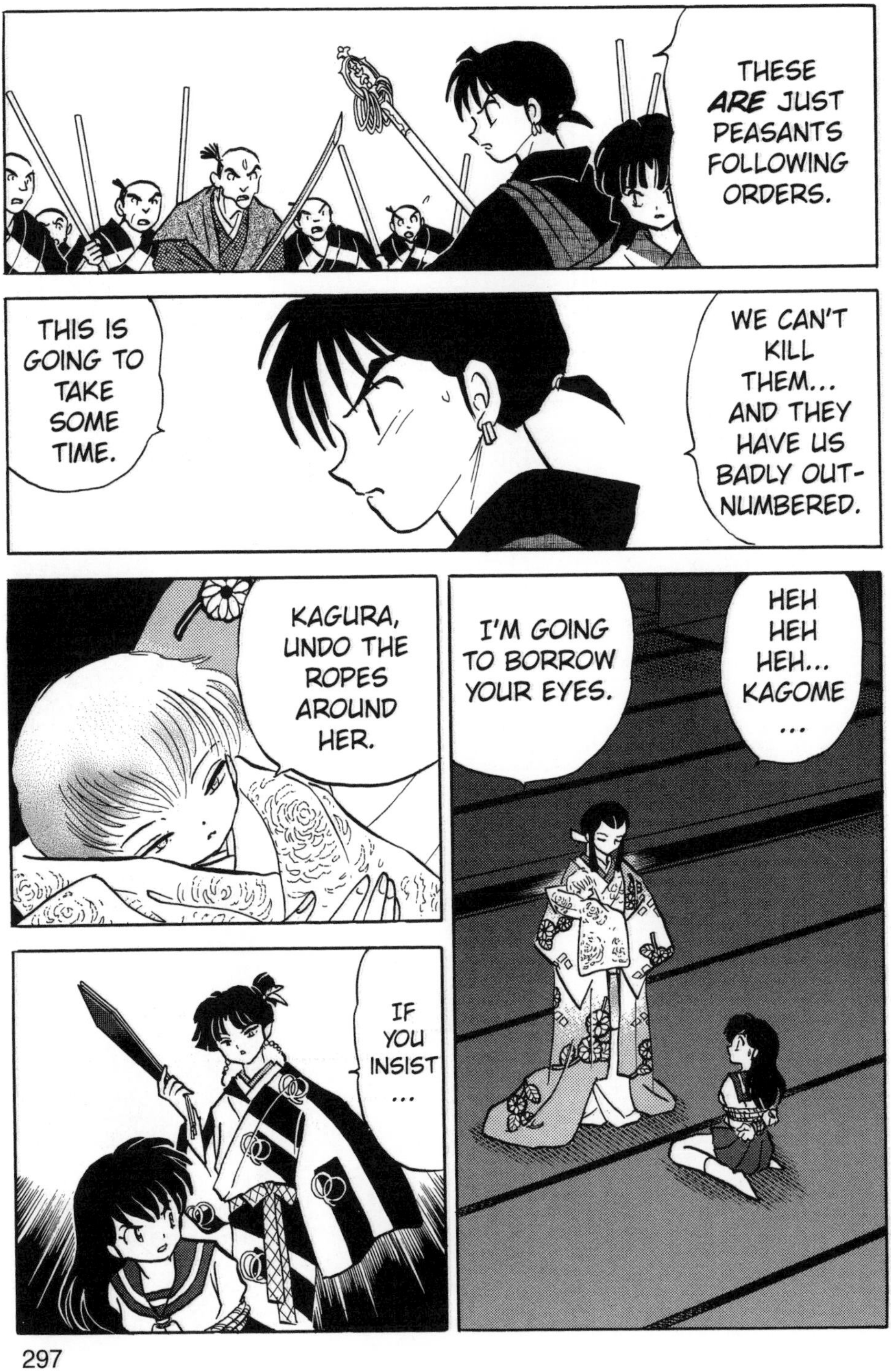
THESE ARE JUST PEASANTS FOLLOWING ORDERS.
WE CAN'T KILL THEM... AND THEY HAVE US BADLY OUT-NUMBERED.
THIS IS GOING TO TAKE SOME TIME.
HEH HEH HEH... KAGOME ...
I'M GOING TO BORROW YOUR EYES.
KAGURA, UNDO THE ROPES AROUND HER.
IF YOU INSIST ...

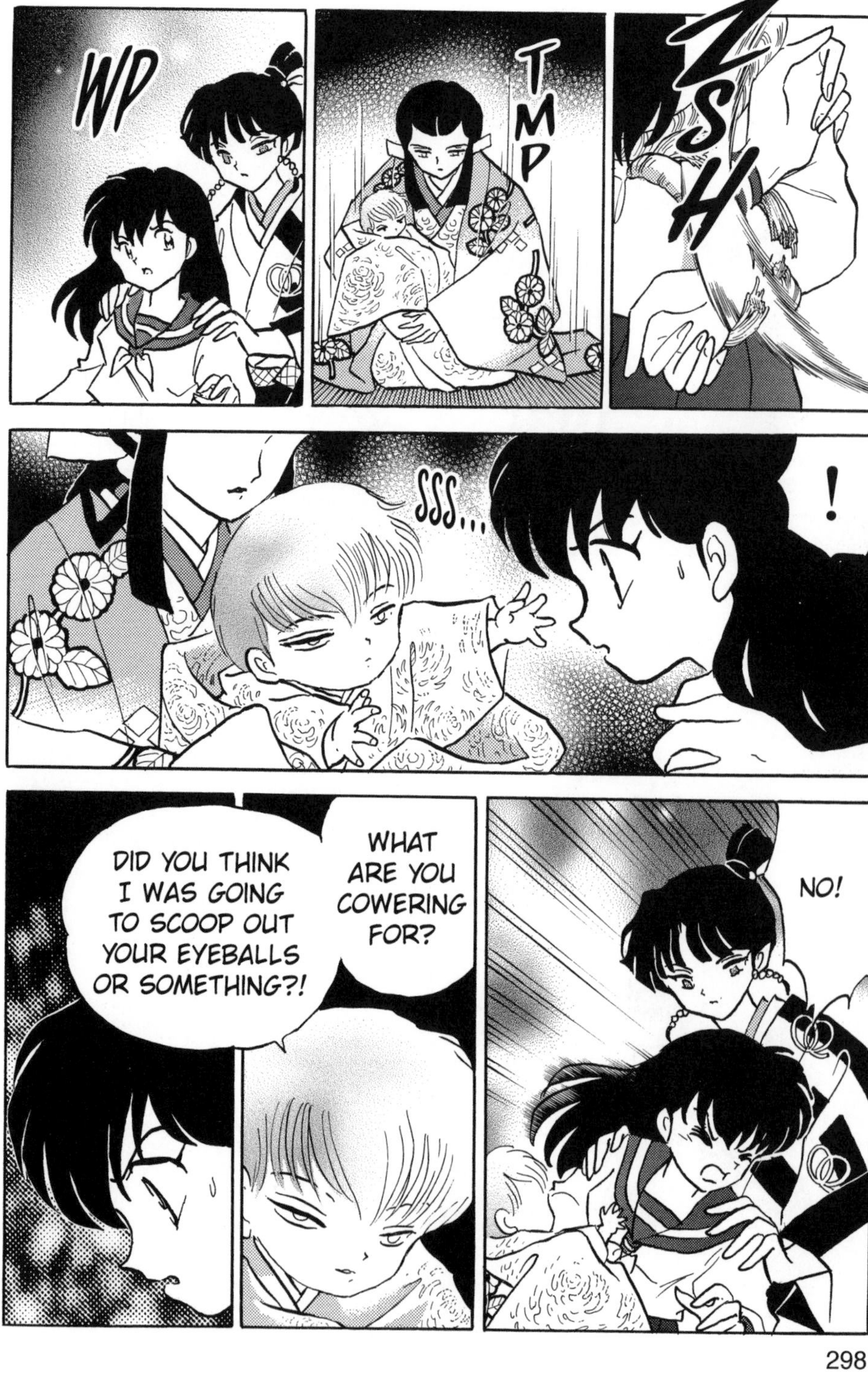
ZSH
TMP
WP
!
SSS...
NO!
WHAT ARE YOU COWERING FOR?
DID YOU THINK I WAS GOING TO SCOOP OUT YOUR EYEBALLS OR SOMETHING?!

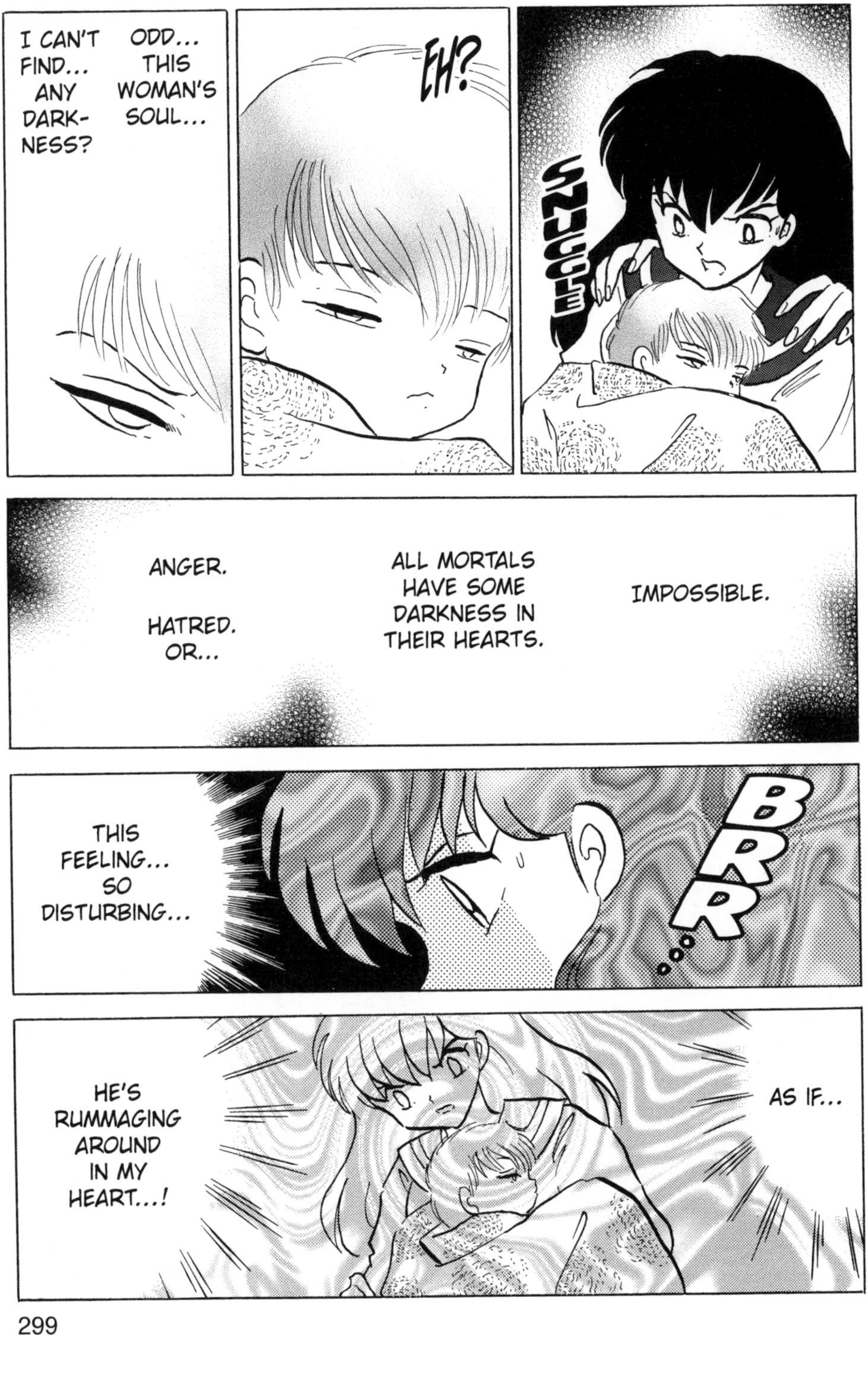
SNUGGLE
EH?
ODD... THIS WOMAN'S SOUL...
I CAN'T FIND... ANY DARKNESS?
IMPOSSIBLE.
ALL MORTALS HAVE SOME DARKNESS IN THEIR HEARTS.
ANGER.
HATRED. OR...
BRR
THIS FEELING... SO DISTURBING...
AS IF...
HE'S RUMMAGING AROUND IN MY HEART...!

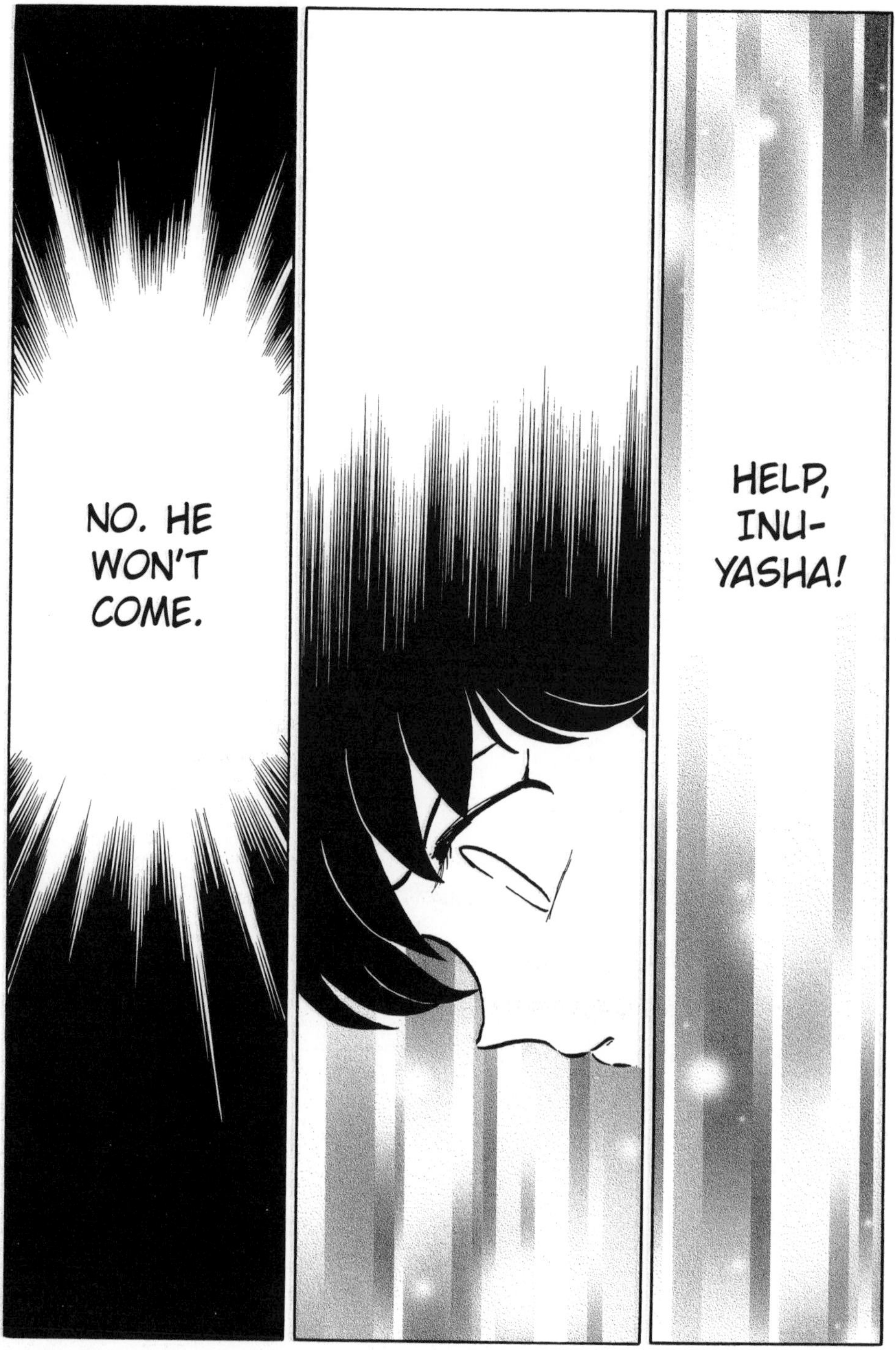
HELP, INU-YASHA!
NO. HE WON'T COME.

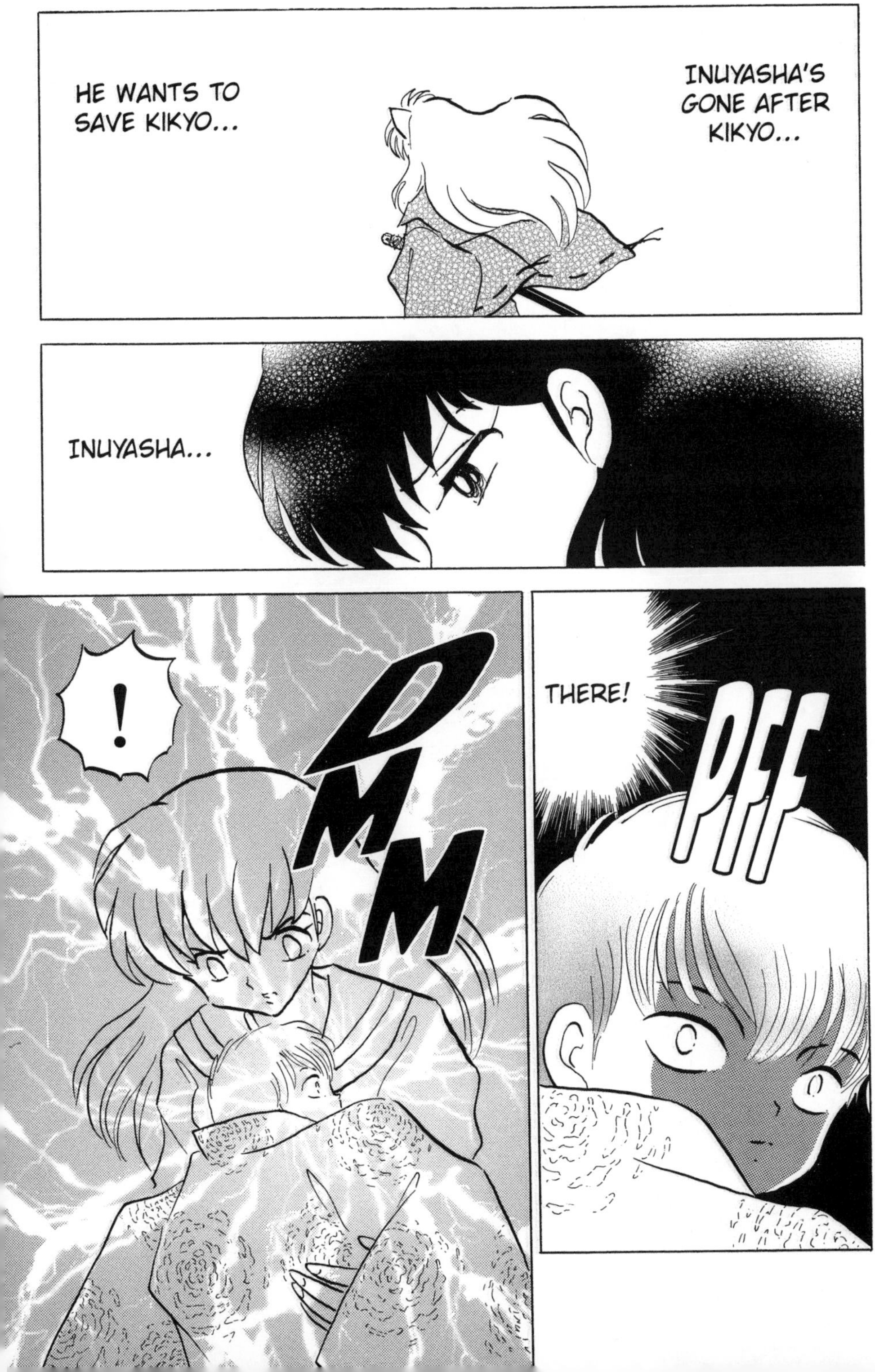

INUYASHA'S GONE AFTER KIKYO...
HE WANTS TO SAVE KIKYO...
INUYASHA...
THERE!
PFF
!
DMM

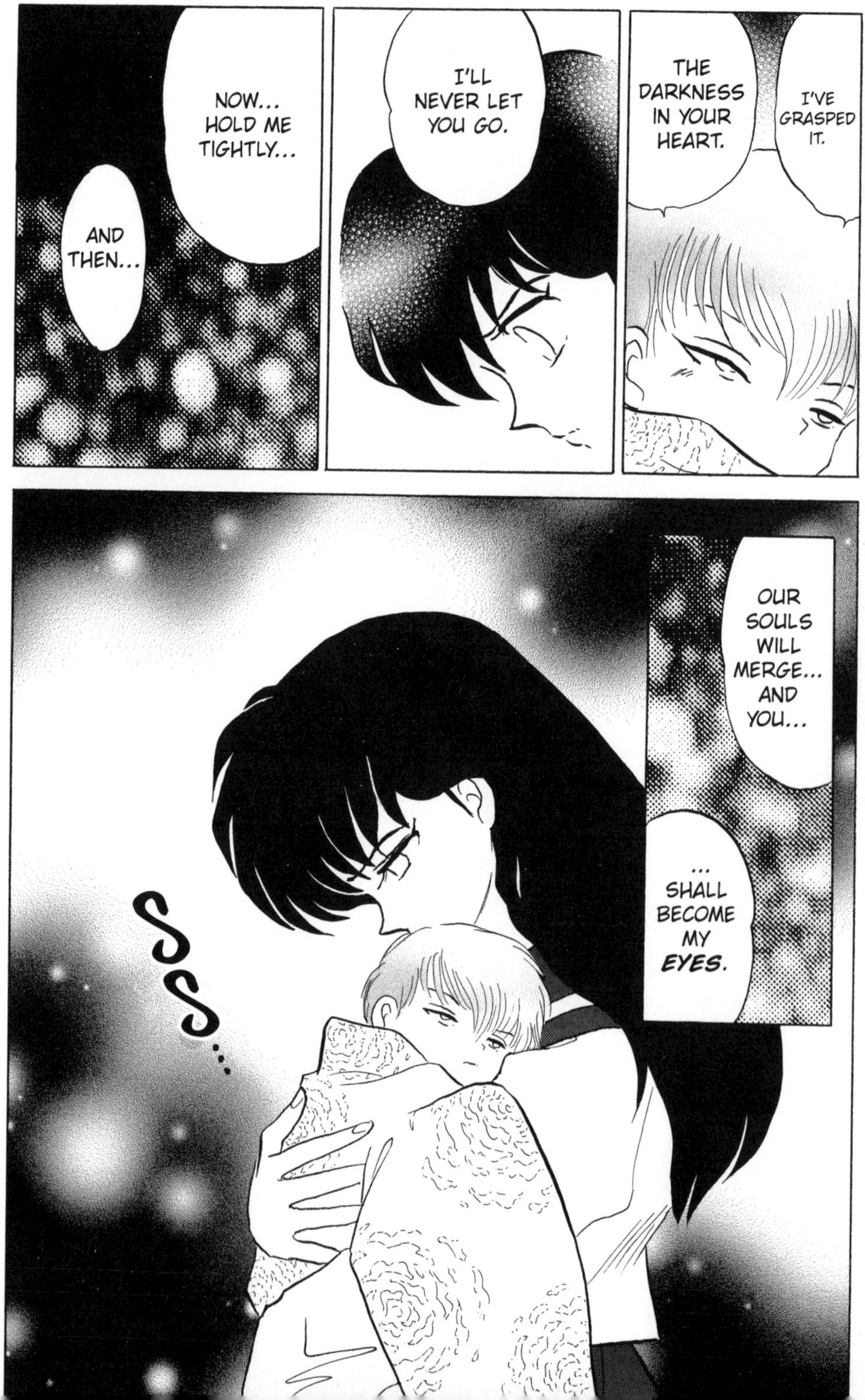
I'VE GRASPED IT.
THE DARKNESS IN YOUR HEART.
I'LL NEVER LET YOU GO.
NOW... HOLD ME TIGHTLY...
AND THEN...
OUR SOULS WILL MERGE... AND YOU...
... SHALL BECOME MY *EYES*.
SS...

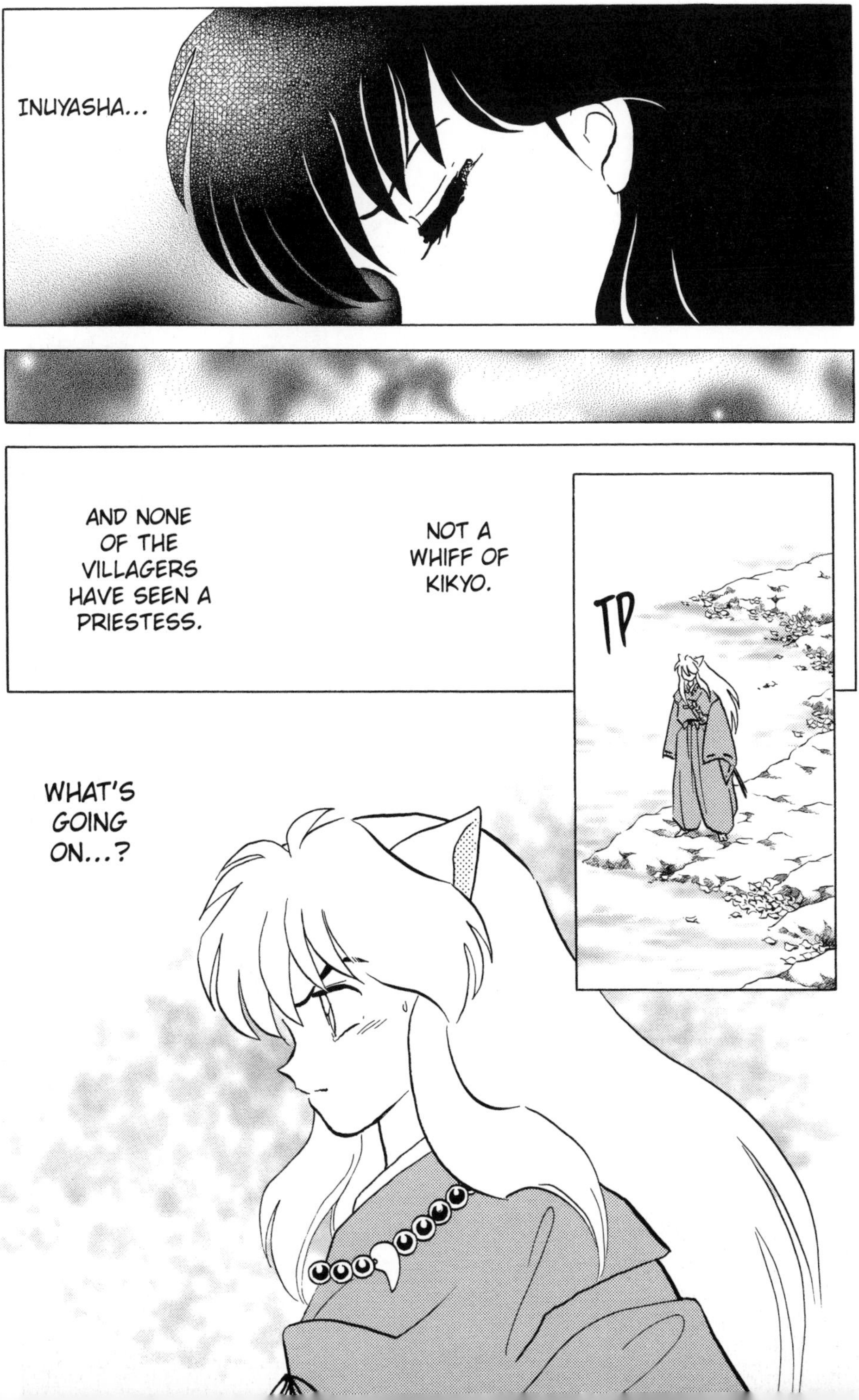
INUYASHA...
TP
NOT A WHIFF OF KIKYO.
AND NONE OF THE VILLAGERS HAVE SEEN A PRIESTESS.
WHAT'S GOING ON...?

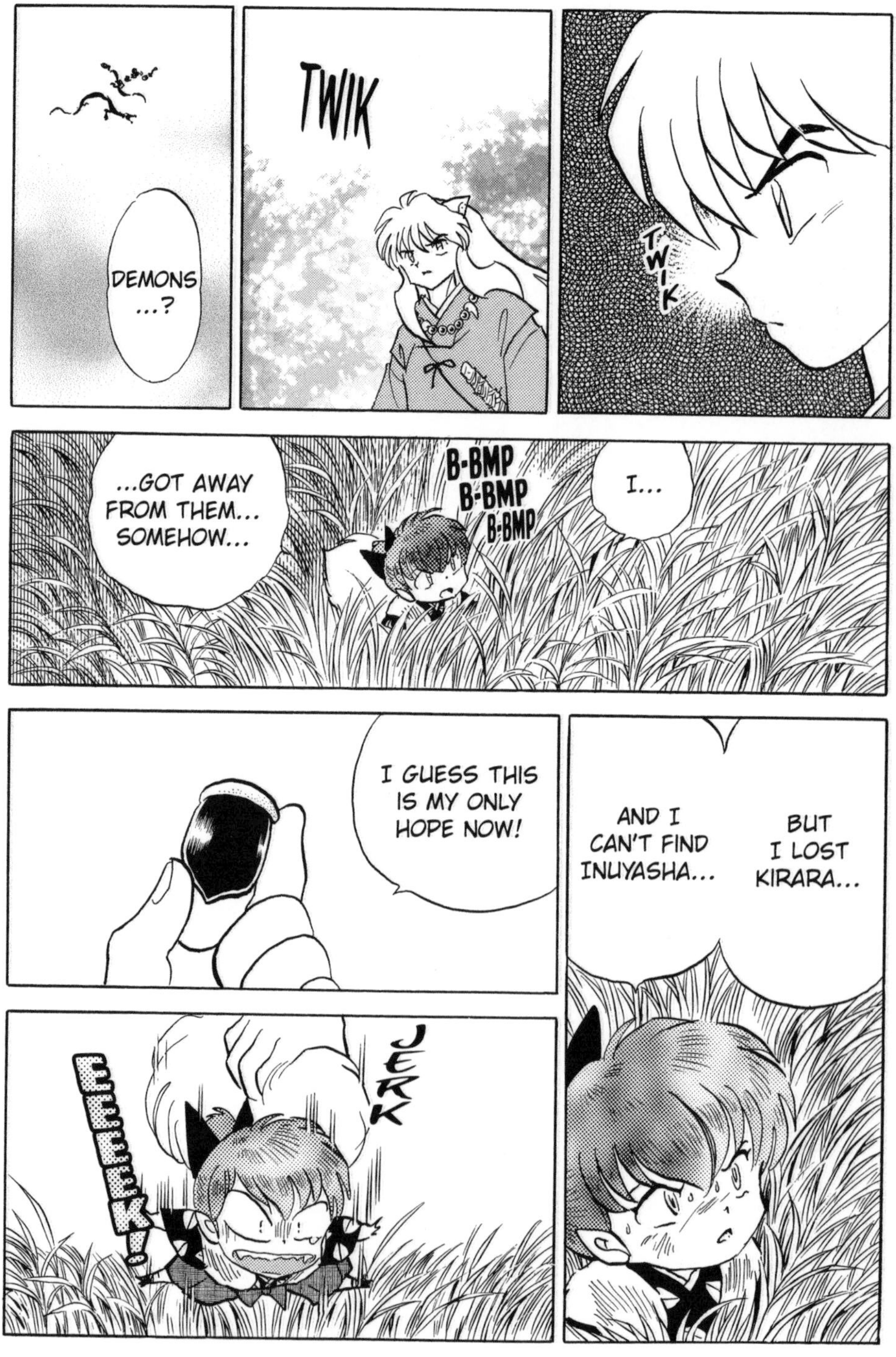
TWIK
TWIK
DEMONS ...?
I...
B-BMP B-BMP B-BMP
...GOT AWAY FROM THEM... SOMEHOW...
BUT I LOST KIRARA...
AND I CAN'T FIND INUYASHA...
I GUESS THIS IS MY ONLY HOPE NOW!
JERK
EEEEEK!

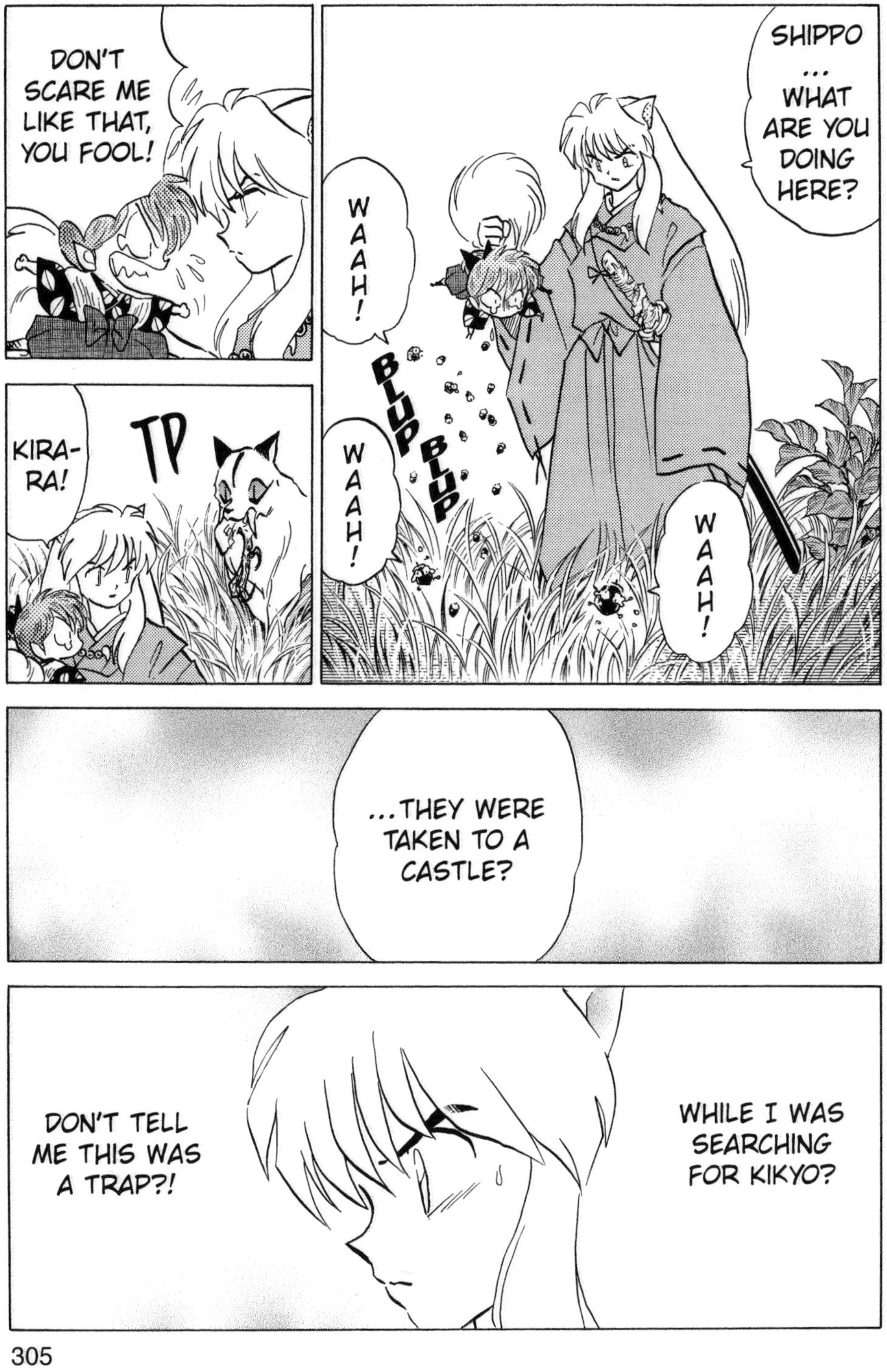
SHIPPO ... WHAT ARE YOU DOING HERE?
WAAH!
WAAH!
BLUP BLUP
WAAH!
DON'T SCARE ME LIKE THAT, YOU FOOL!
TP
KIRA-RA!
...THEY WERE TAKEN TO A CASTLE?
WHILE I WAS SEARCHING FOR KIKYO?
DON'T TELL ME THIS WAS A TRAP?!

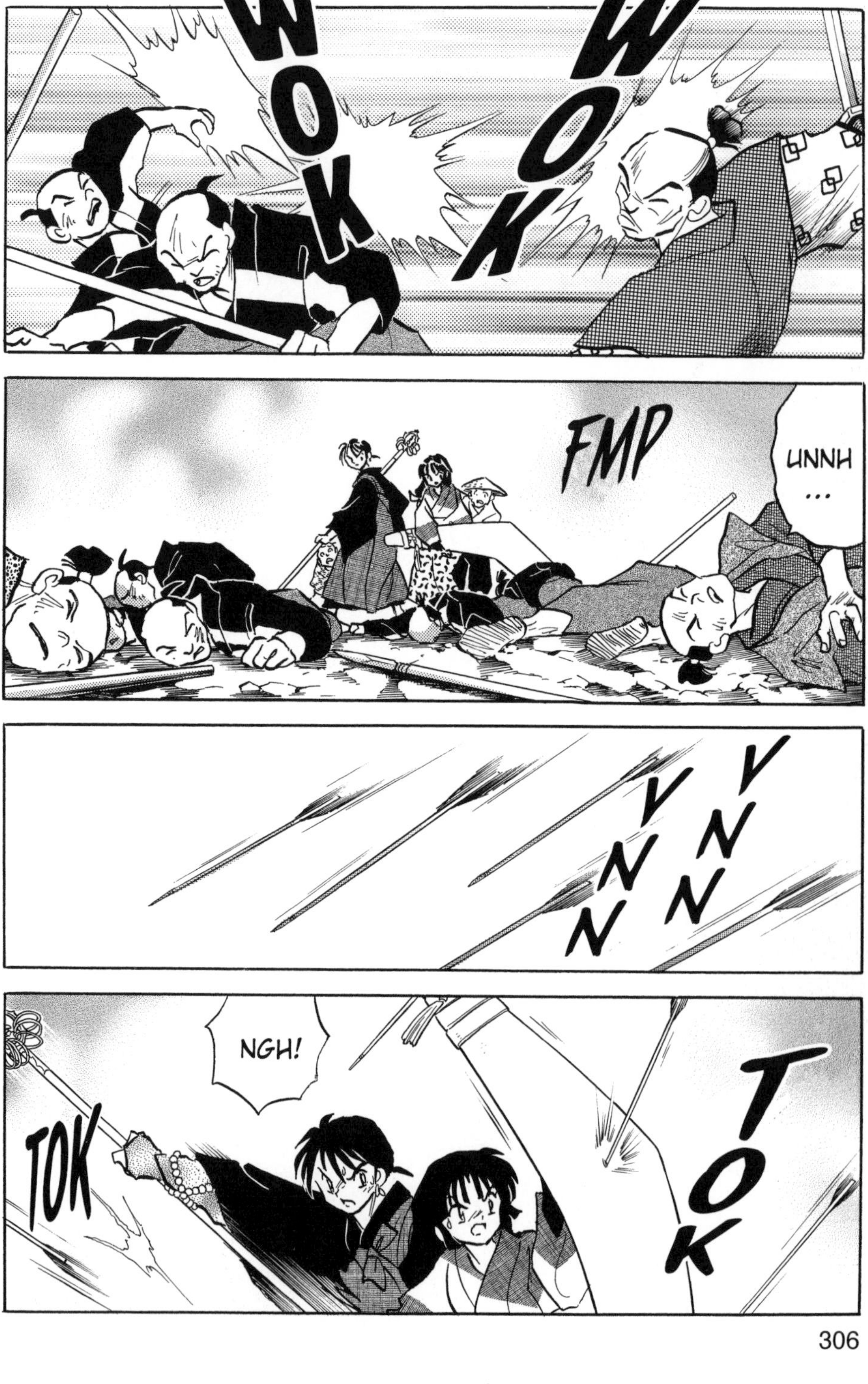
WOK
WOK
UNNH...
FMP
VNNN
VNNN
TOK
NGH!
TOK

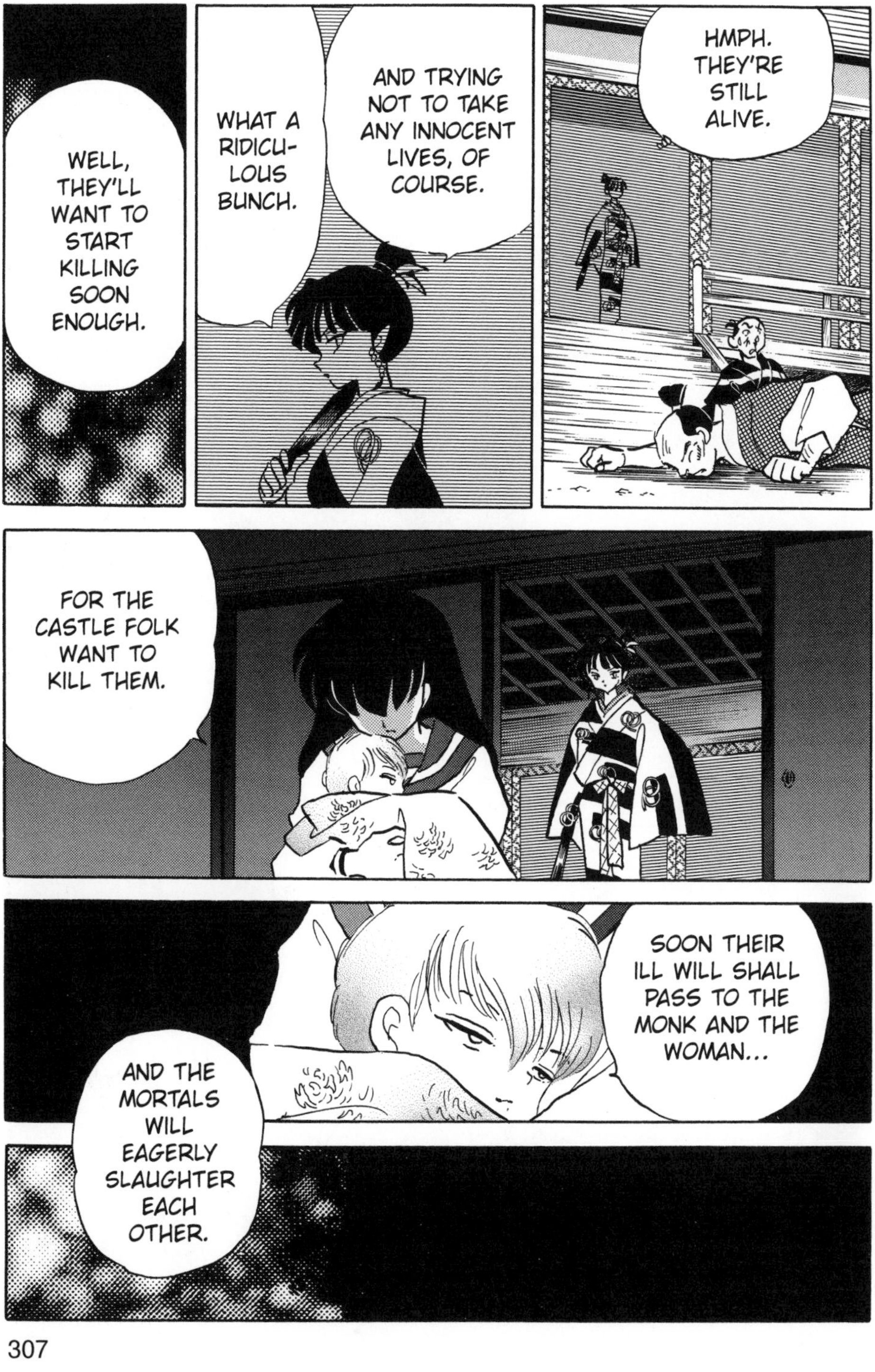
HMPH. THEY'RE STILL ALIVE.
AND TRYING NOT TO TAKE ANY INNOCENT LIVES, OF COURSE.
WHAT A RIDICULOUS BUNCH.
WELL, THEY'LL WANT TO START KILLING SOON ENOUGH.
FOR THE CASTLE FOLK WANT TO KILL THEM.
SOON THEIR ILL WILL SHALL PASS TO THE MONK AND THE WOMAN...
AND THE MORTALS WILL EAGERLY SLAUGHTER EACH OTHER.

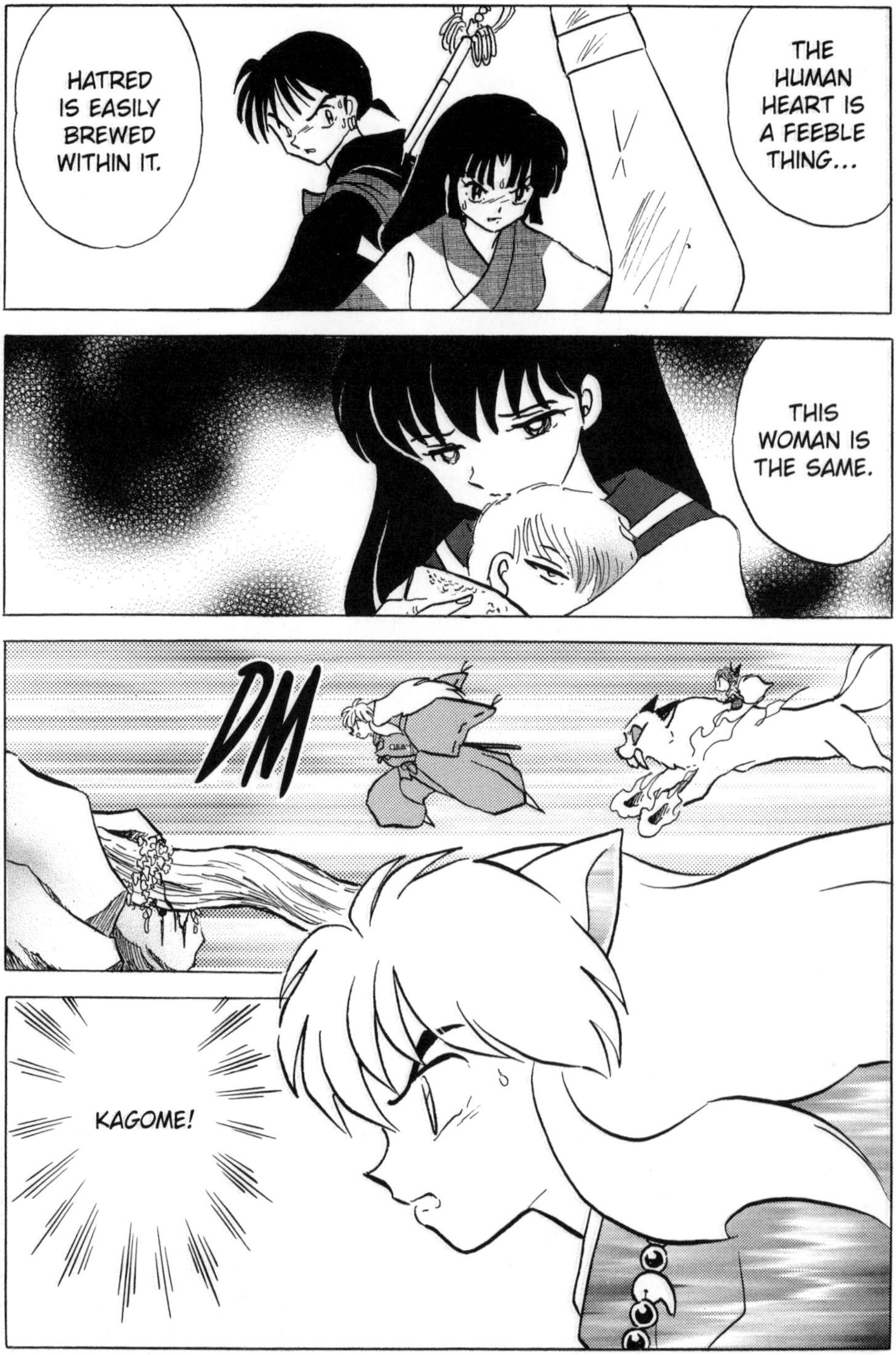
THE HUMAN HEART IS A FEEBLE THING...
HATRED IS EASILY BREWED WITHIN IT.
THIS WOMAN IS THE SAME.
DM
KAGOME!

SCROLL SEVEN
SUGGESTION

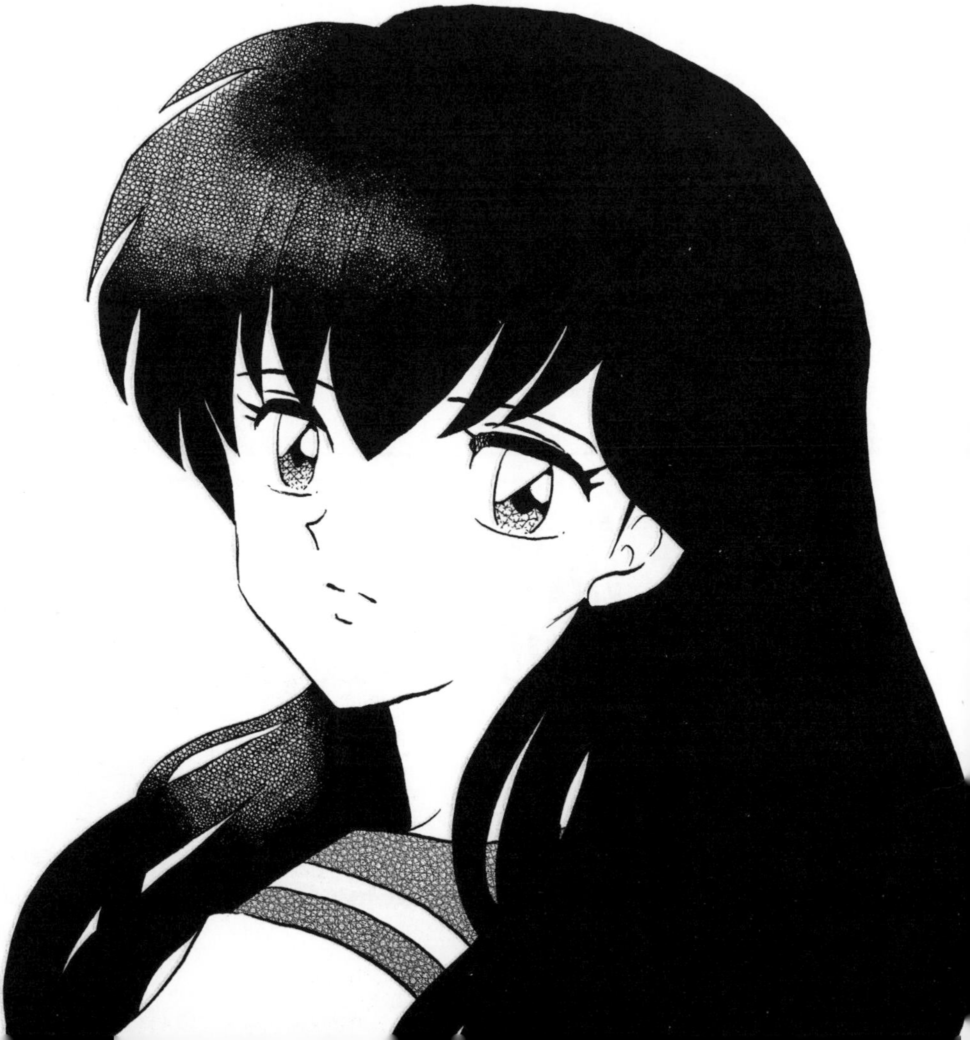

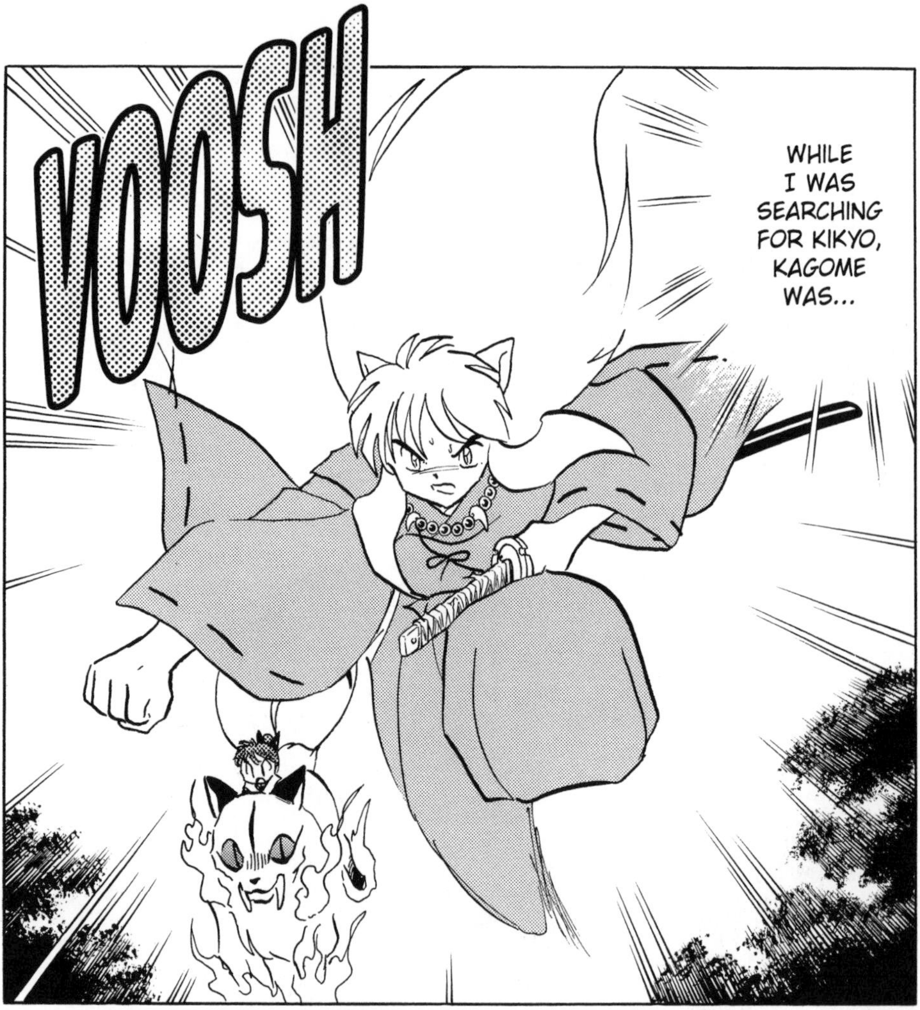
VOOSH
WHILE I WAS SEARCHING FOR KIKYO, KAGOME WAS...
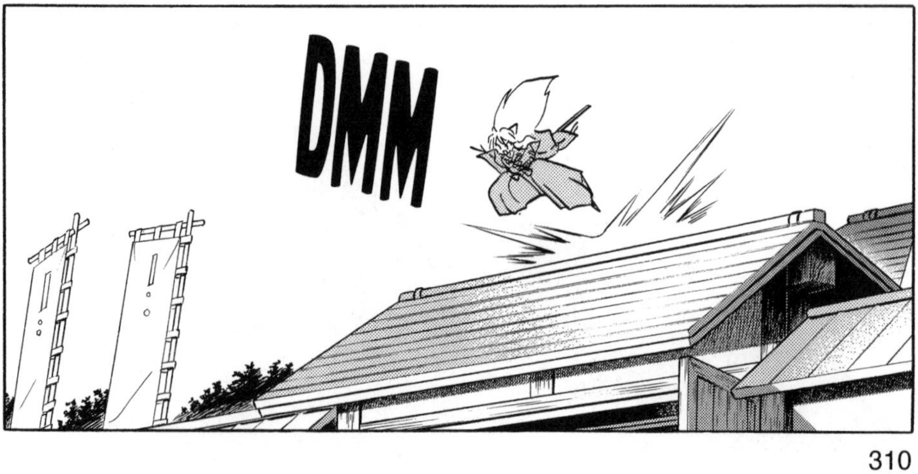
DMM

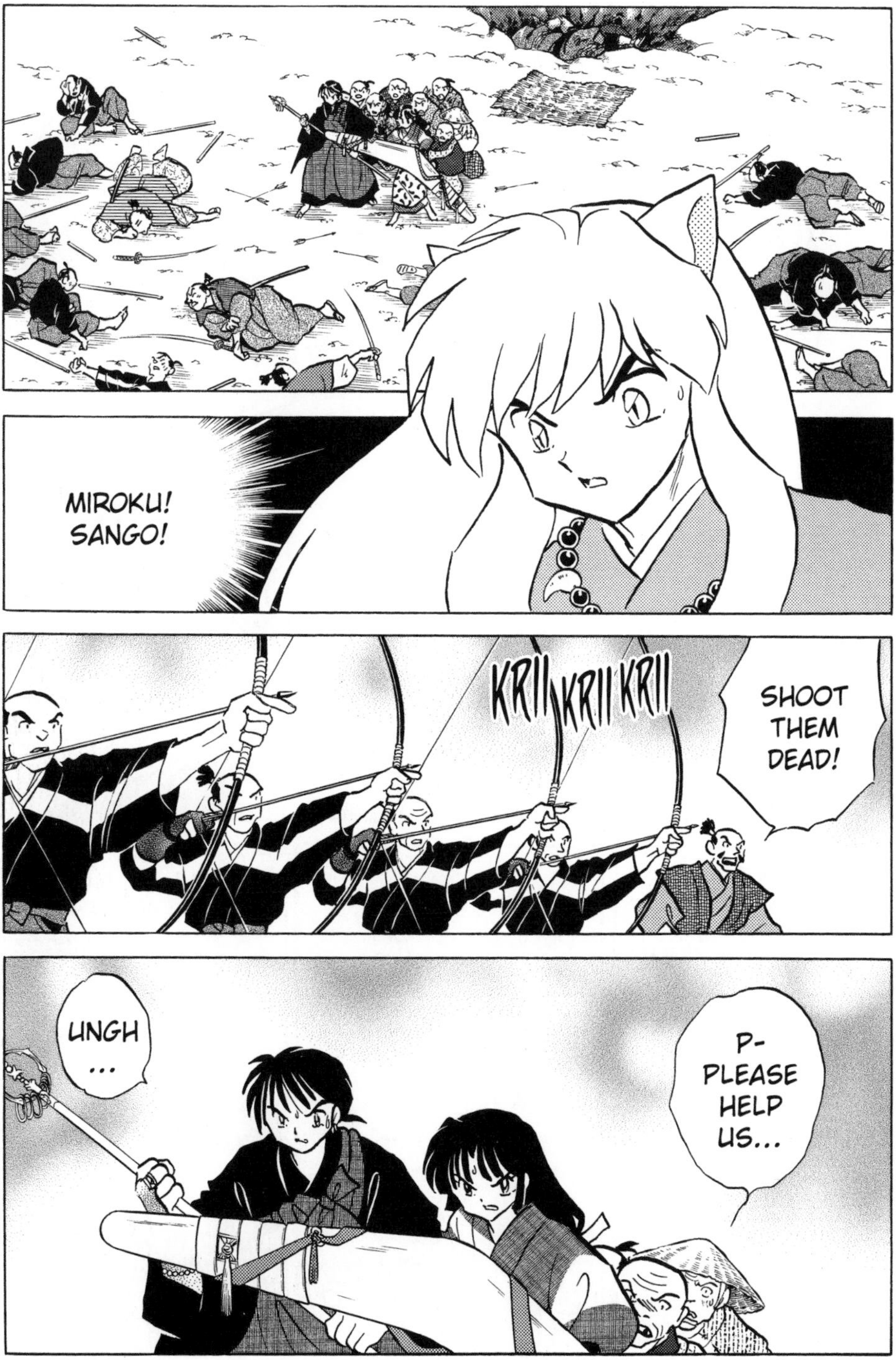
MIROKU! SANGO!
SHOOT THEM DEAD!
KRII KRII KRII
P- PLEASE HELP US...
UNGH ...

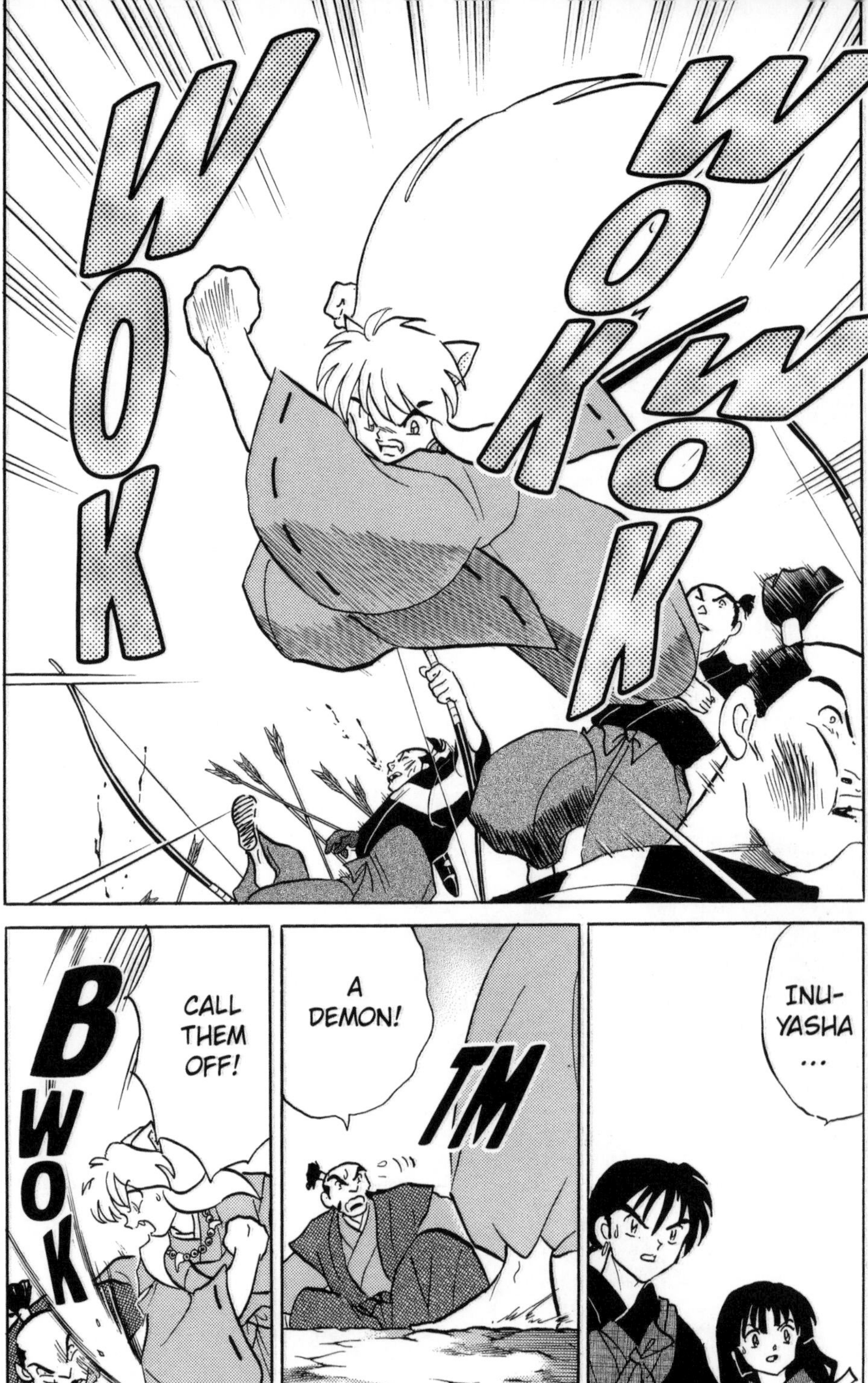
WOK
WOK
WOK
INU-YASHA...
A DEMON!
TM
CALL THEM OFF!
BWOK

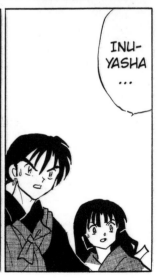

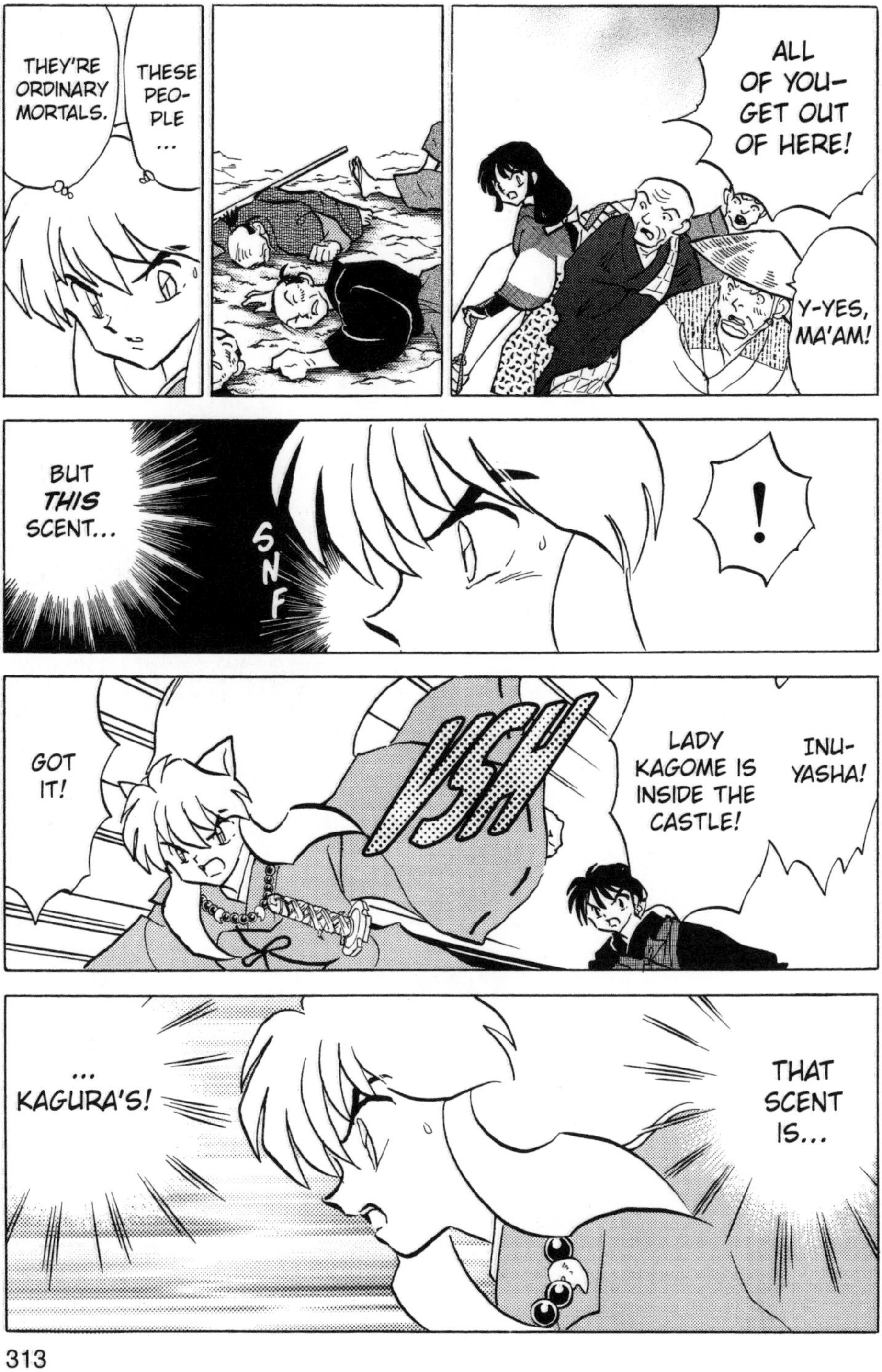
ALL OF YOU-- GET OUT OF HERE!
Y-YES, MA'AM!
THESE PEO-PLE ...
THEY'RE ORDINARY MORTALS.
!
SNF
BUT *THIS* SCENT...
INU-YASHA!
LADY KAGOME IS INSIDE THE CASTLE!
VSH
GOT IT!
THAT SCENT IS...
... KAGURA'S!

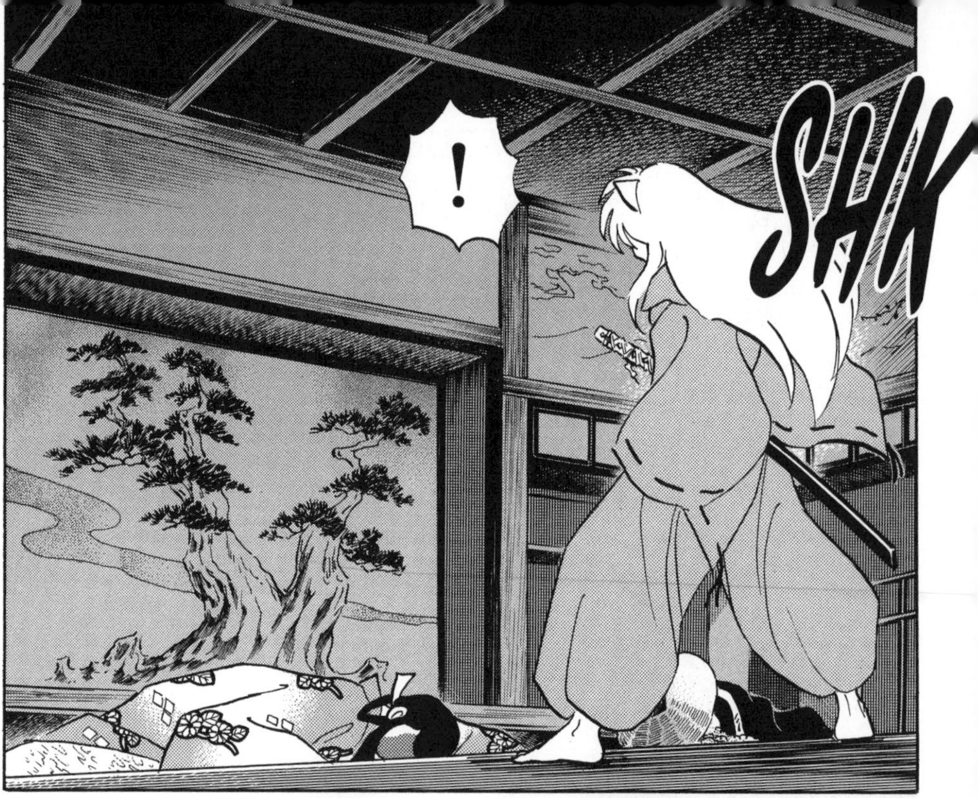
SHK
!

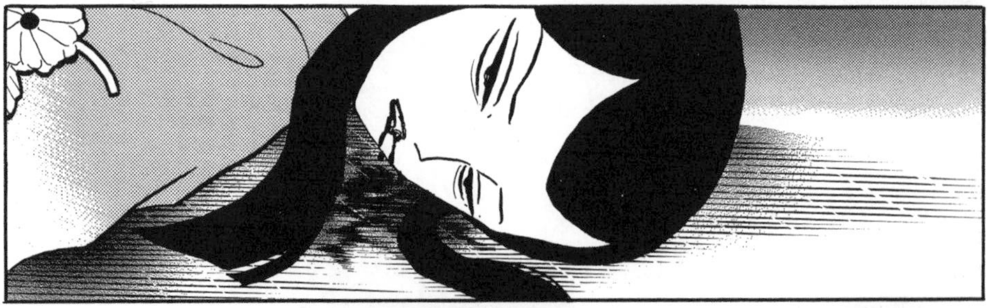

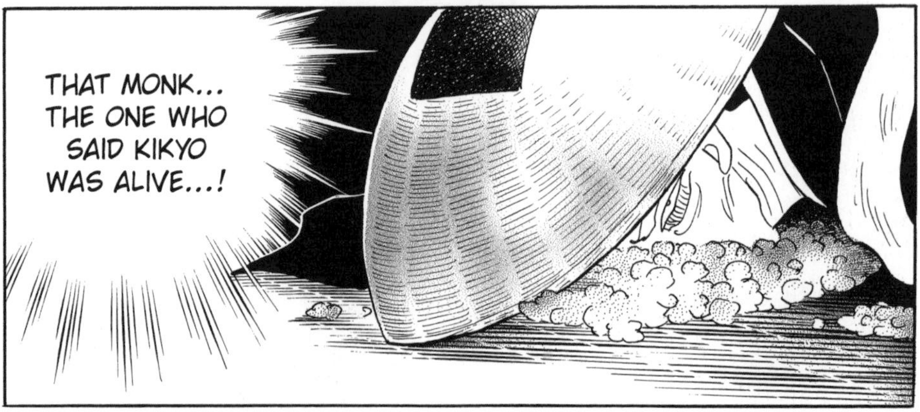
THAT MONK... THE ONE WHO SAID KIKYO WAS ALIVE...!

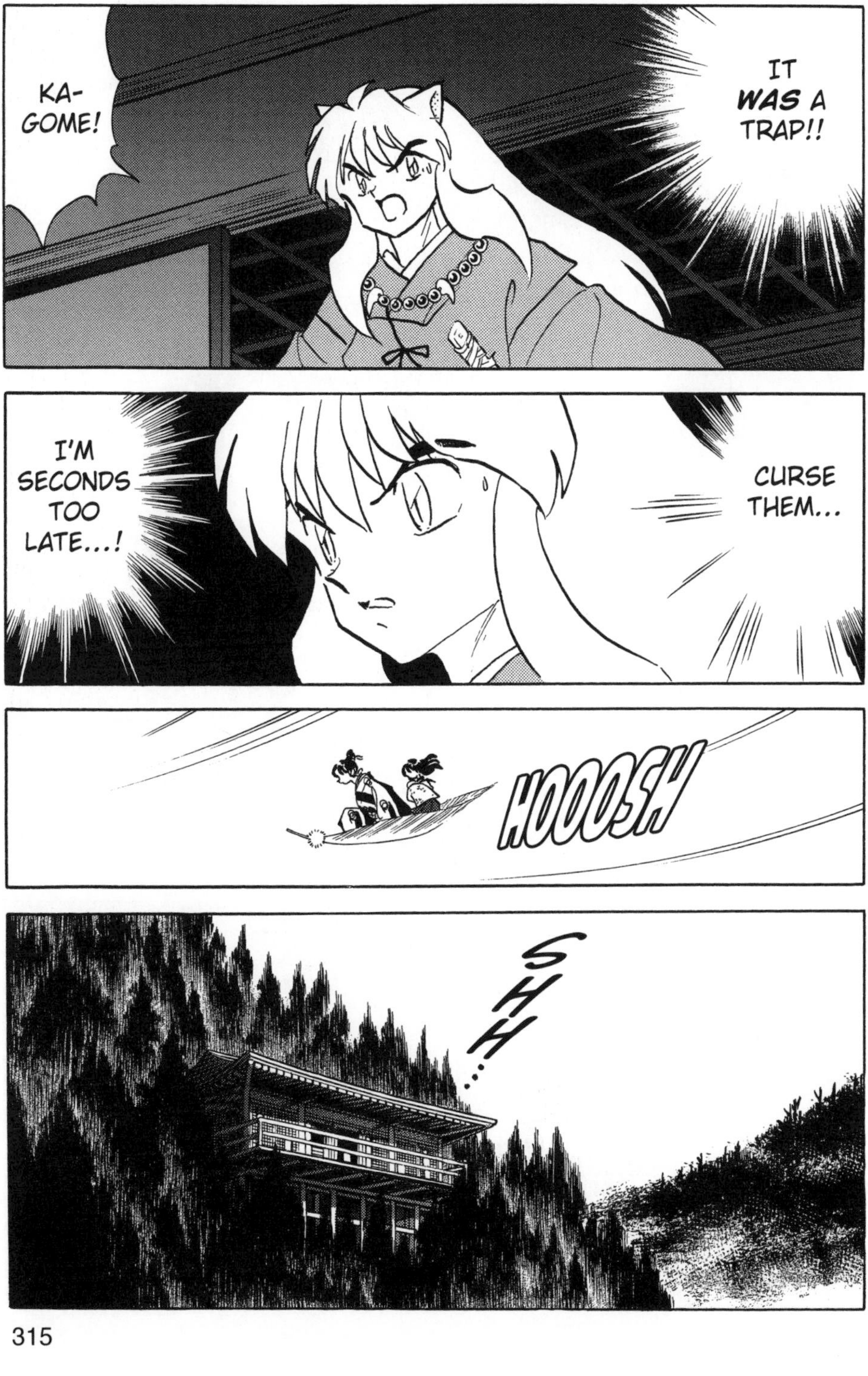
IT WAS A TRAP!!
KA-GOME!
CURSE THEM...
I'M SECONDS TOO LATE...!
HOOOSH
SHH...

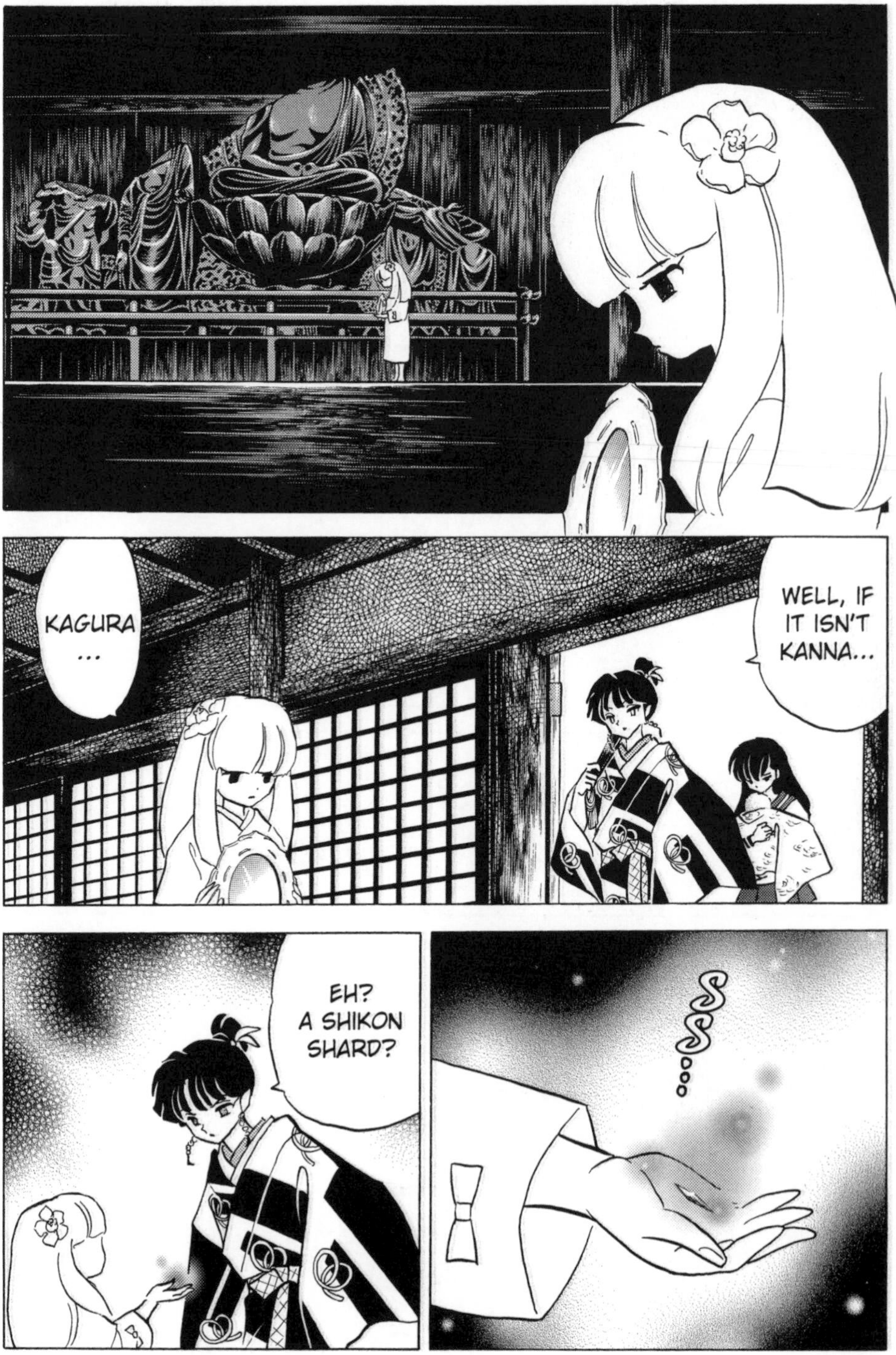
WELL, IF IT ISN'T KANNA...
KAGURA ...
SSooo
EH? A SHIKON SHARD?

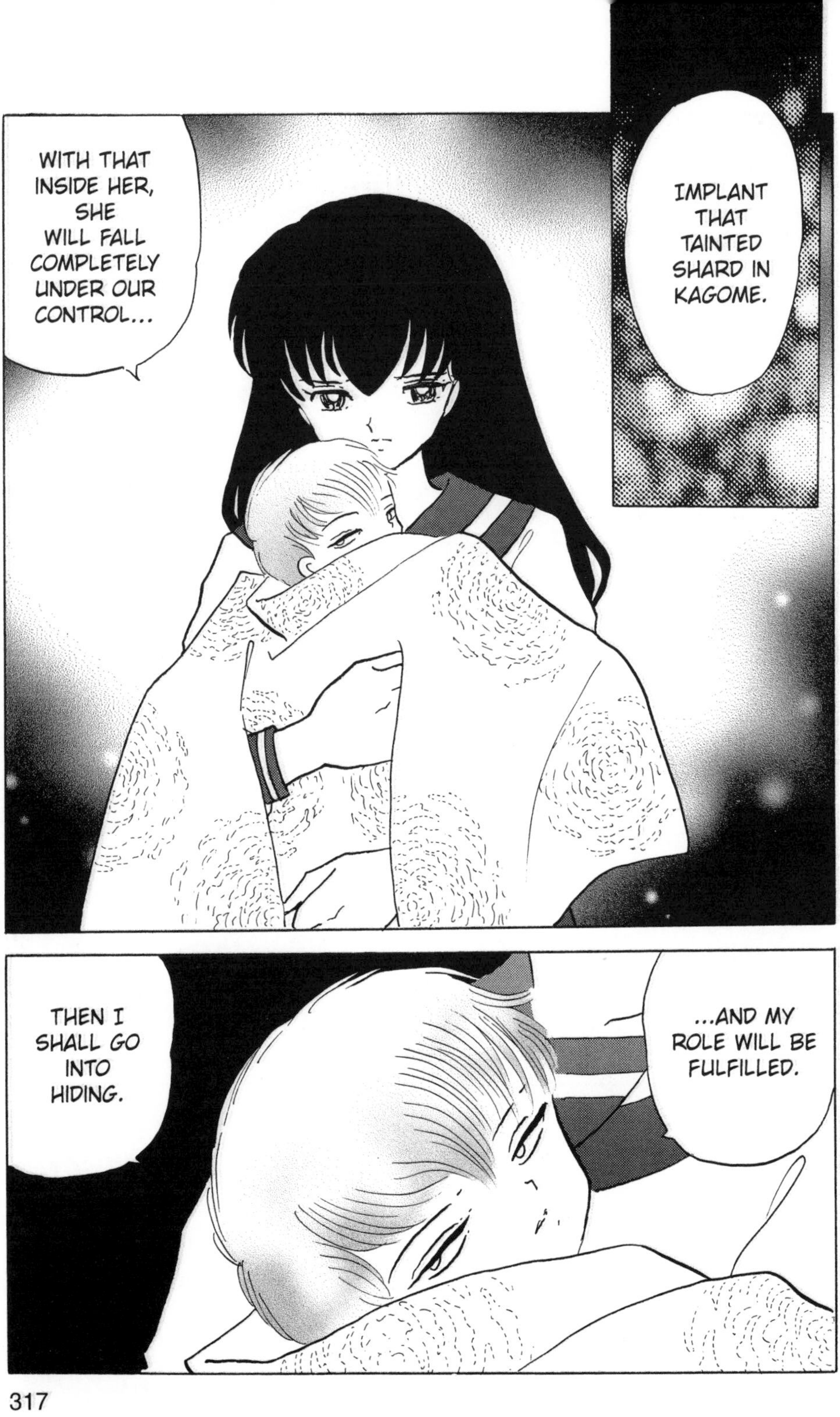
IMPLANT THAT TAINTED SHARD IN KAGOME.
WITH THAT INSIDE HER, SHE WILL FALL COMPLETELY UNDER OUR CONTROL...
...AND MY ROLE WILL BE FULFILLED.
THEN I SHALL GO INTO HIDING.

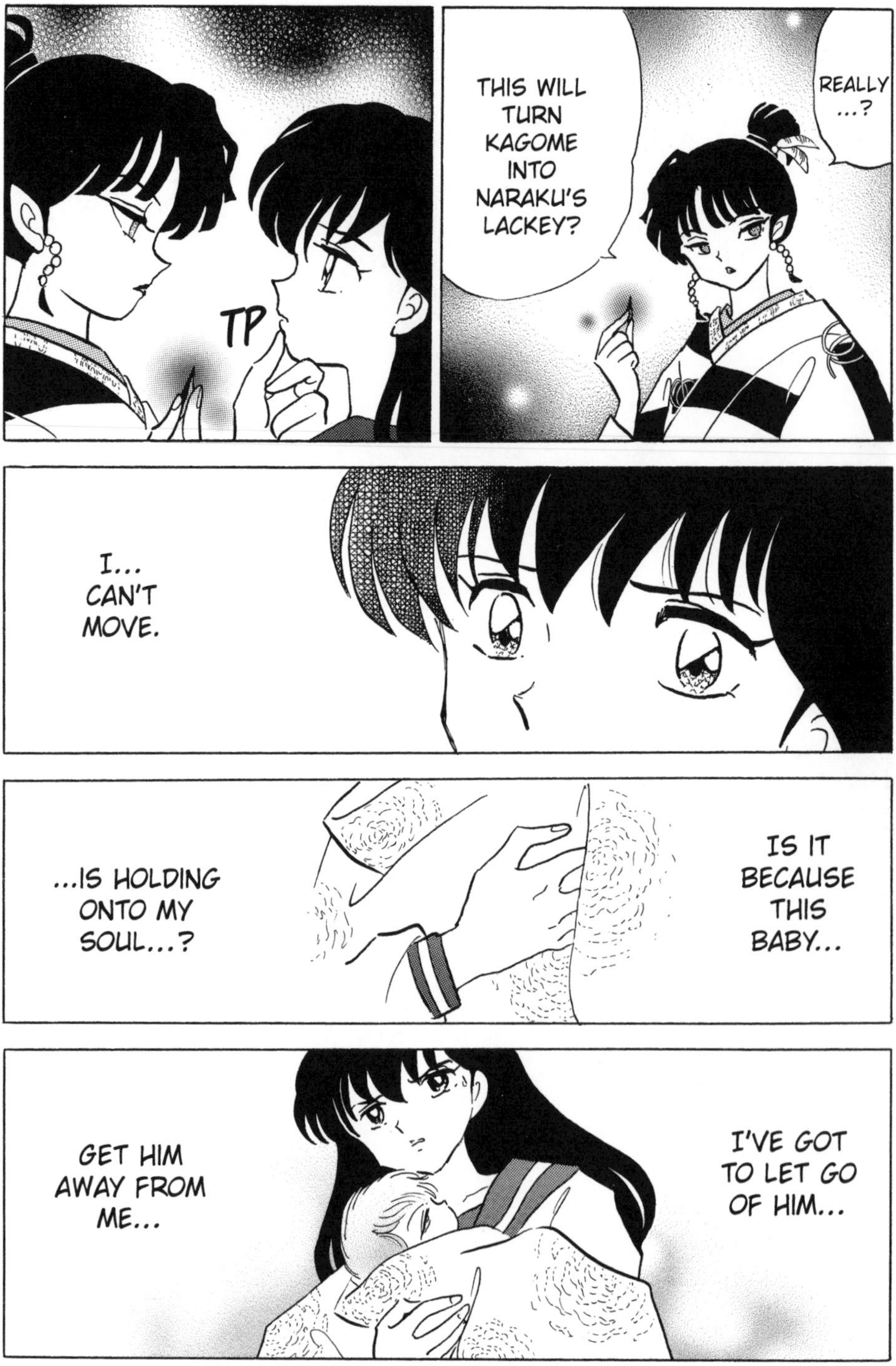
REALLY ...?
THIS WILL TURN KAGOME INTO NARAKU'S LACKEY?
TP
I... CAN'T MOVE.
IS IT BECAUSE THIS BABY...
...IS HOLDING ONTO MY SOUL...?
I'VE GOT TO LET GO OF HIM...
GET HIM AWAY FROM ME...

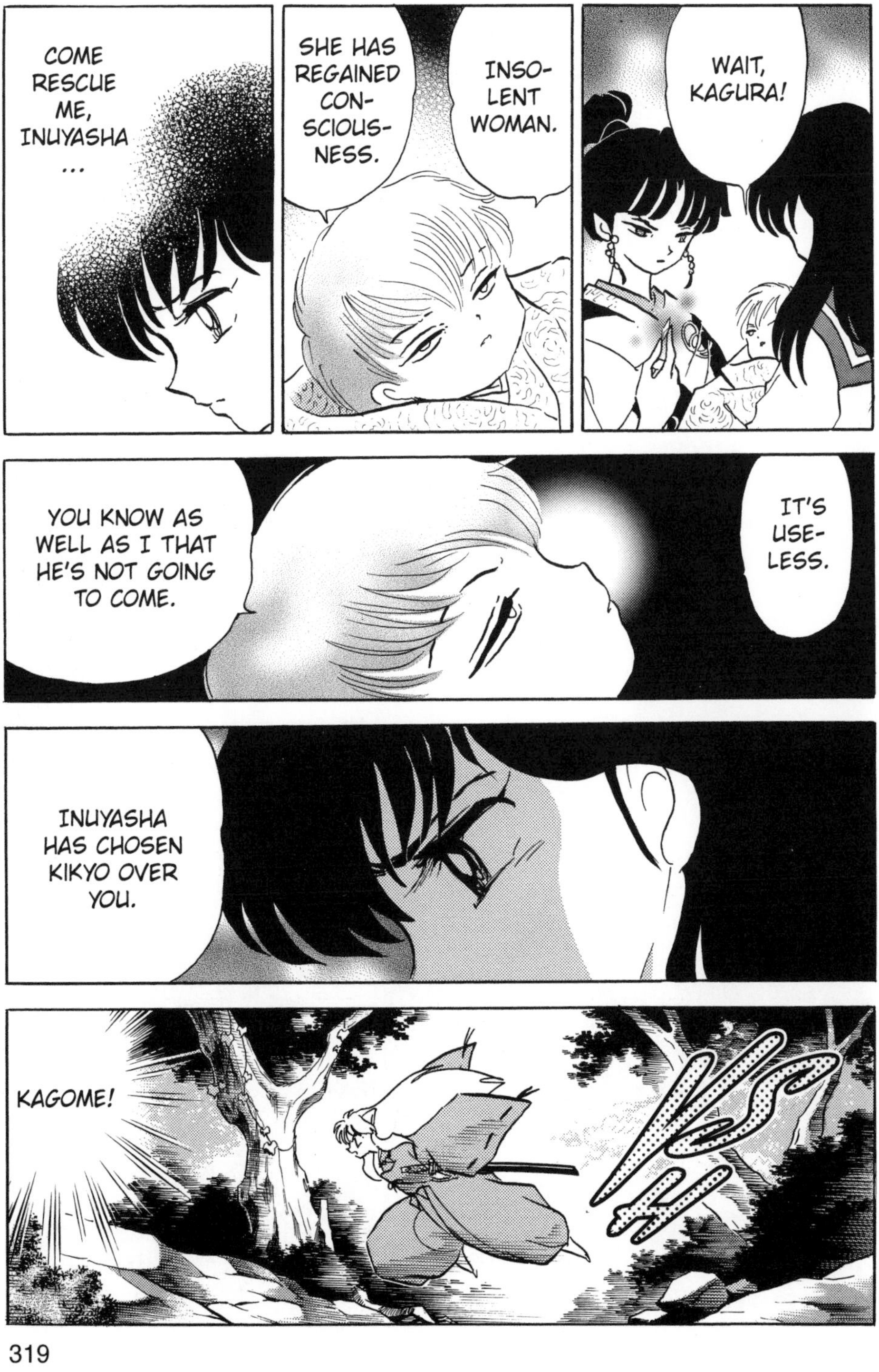
WAIT, KAGURA!
INSOLENT WOMAN.
SHE HAS REGAINED CONSCIOUSNESS.
COME RESCUE ME, INUYASHA ...
IT'S USELESS.
YOU KNOW AS WELL AS I THAT HE'S NOT GOING TO COME.
INUYASHA HAS CHOSEN KIKYO OVER YOU.
KAGOME!

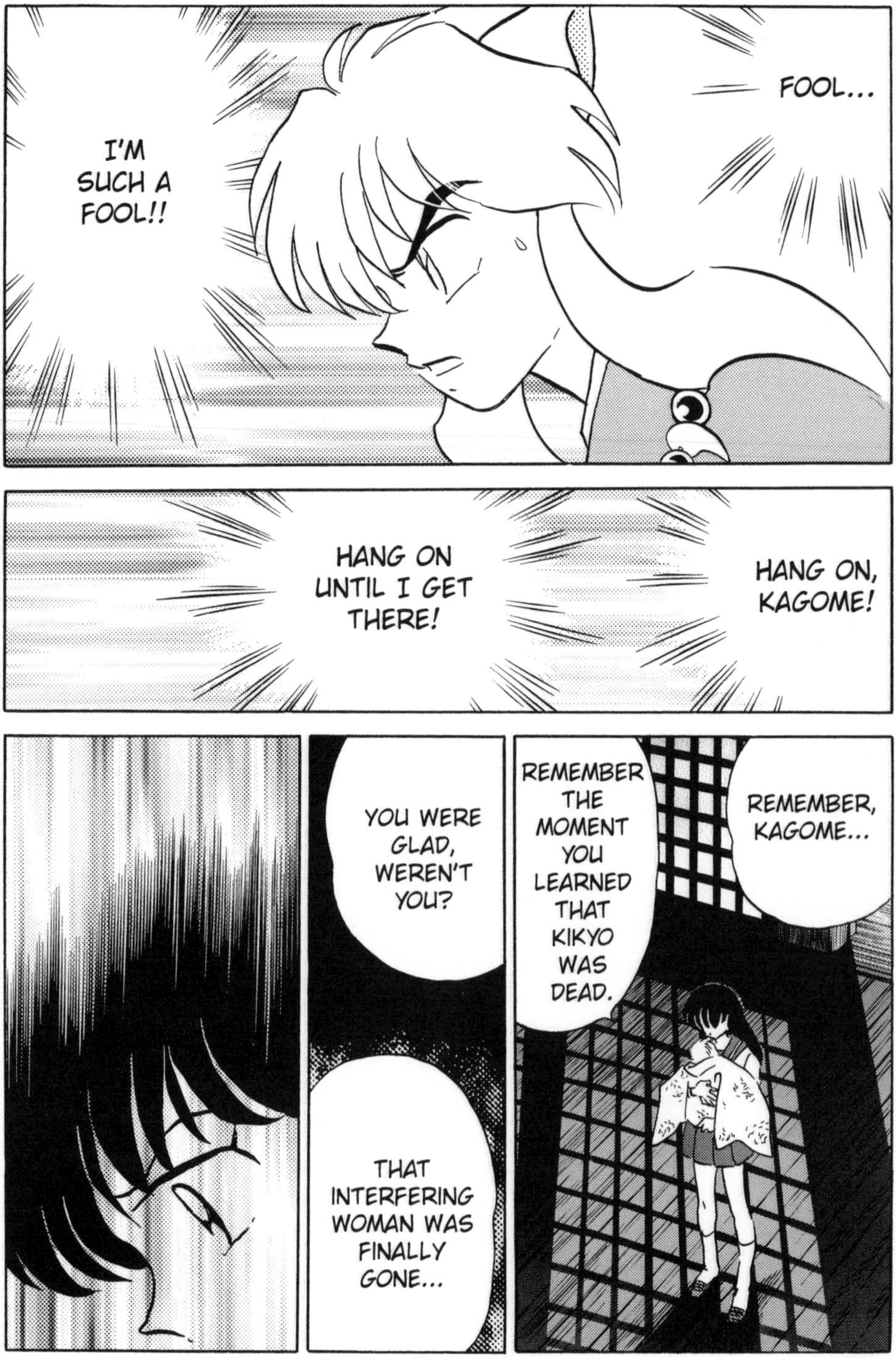
FOOL...
I'M SUCH A FOOL!!
HANG ON, KAGOME!
HANG ON UNTIL I GET THERE!
REMEMBER, KAGOME...
REMEMBER THE MOMENT YOU LEARNED THAT KIKYO WAS DEAD.
YOU WERE GLAD, WEREN'T YOU?
THAT INTERFERING WOMAN WAS FINALLY GONE...

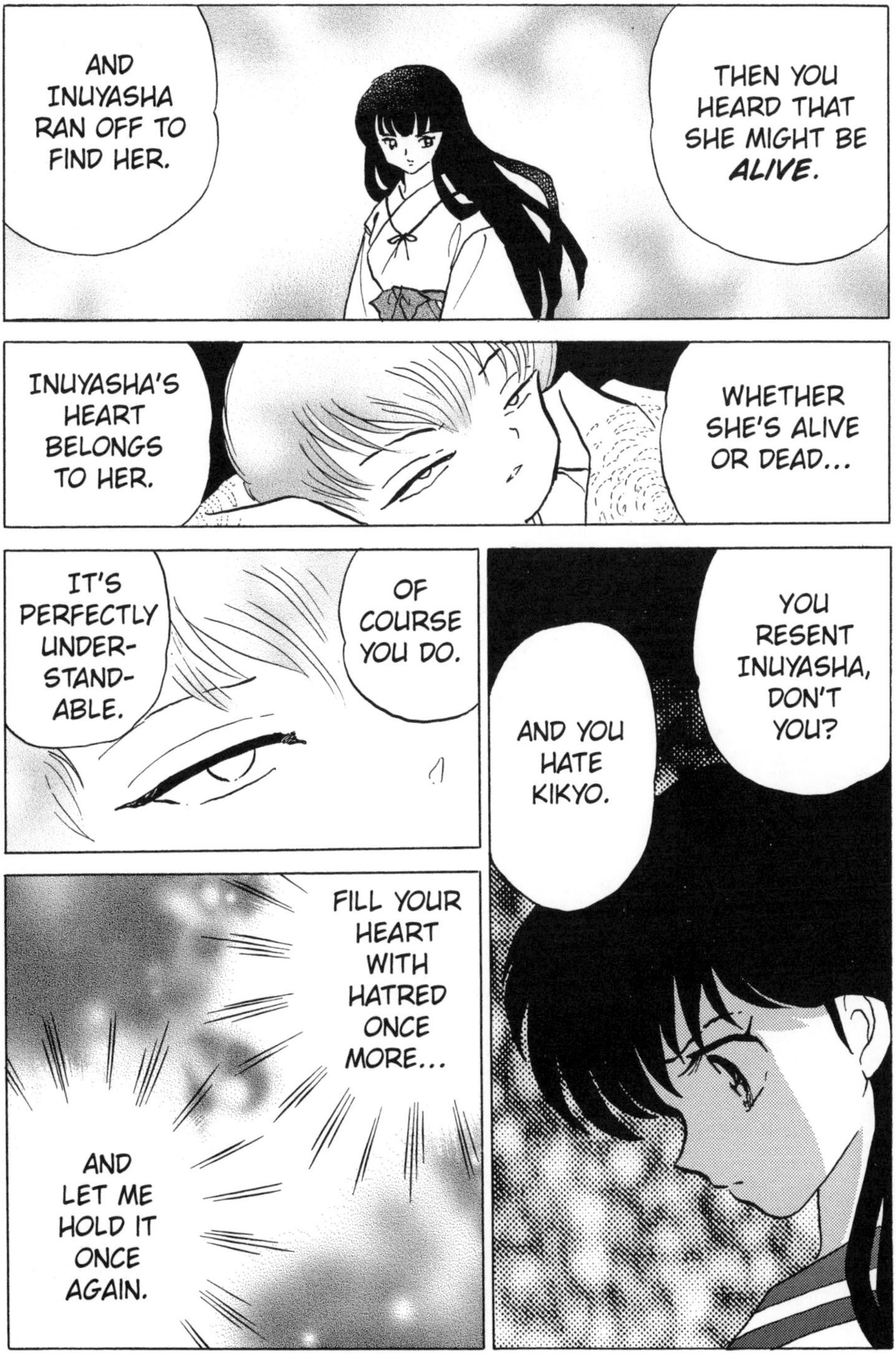
THEN YOU HEARD THAT SHE MIGHT BE ***ALIVE.***
AND INUYASHA RAN OFF TO FIND HER.
WHETHER SHE'S ALIVE OR DEAD...
INUYASHA'S HEART BELONGS TO HER.
YOU RESENT INUYASHA, DON'T YOU?
AND YOU HATE KIKYO.
OF COURSE YOU DO.
IT'S PERFECTLY UNDER-STAND-ABLE.
FILL YOUR HEART WITH HATRED ONCE MORE...
AND LET ME HOLD IT ONCE AGAIN.

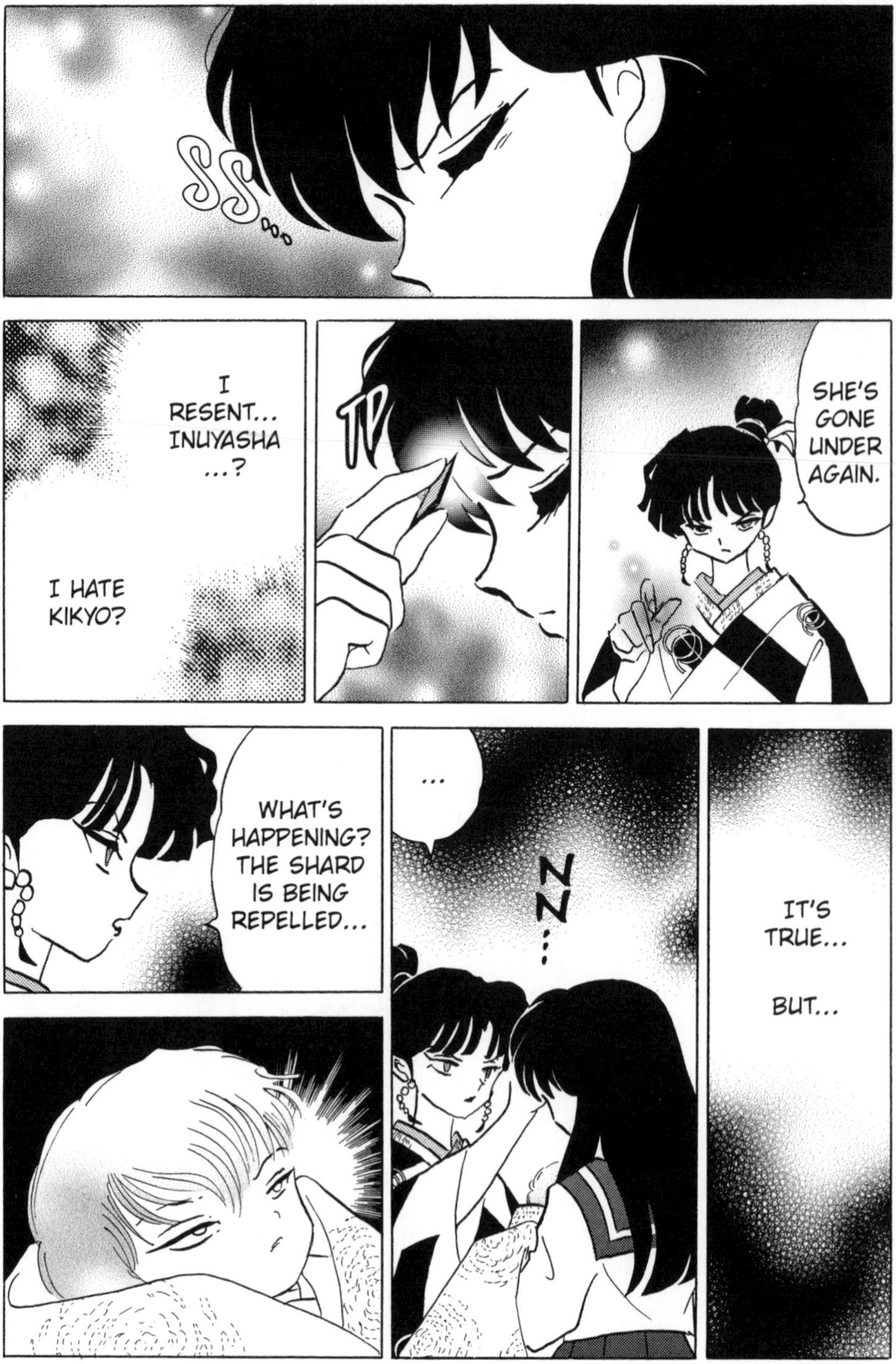
SS...
SHE'S GONE UNDER AGAIN.
TP
I RESENT... INUYASHA...?
I HATE KIKYO?
IT'S TRUE...
BUT...
...
NN...
WHAT'S HAPPENING? THE SHARD IS BEING REPELLED...

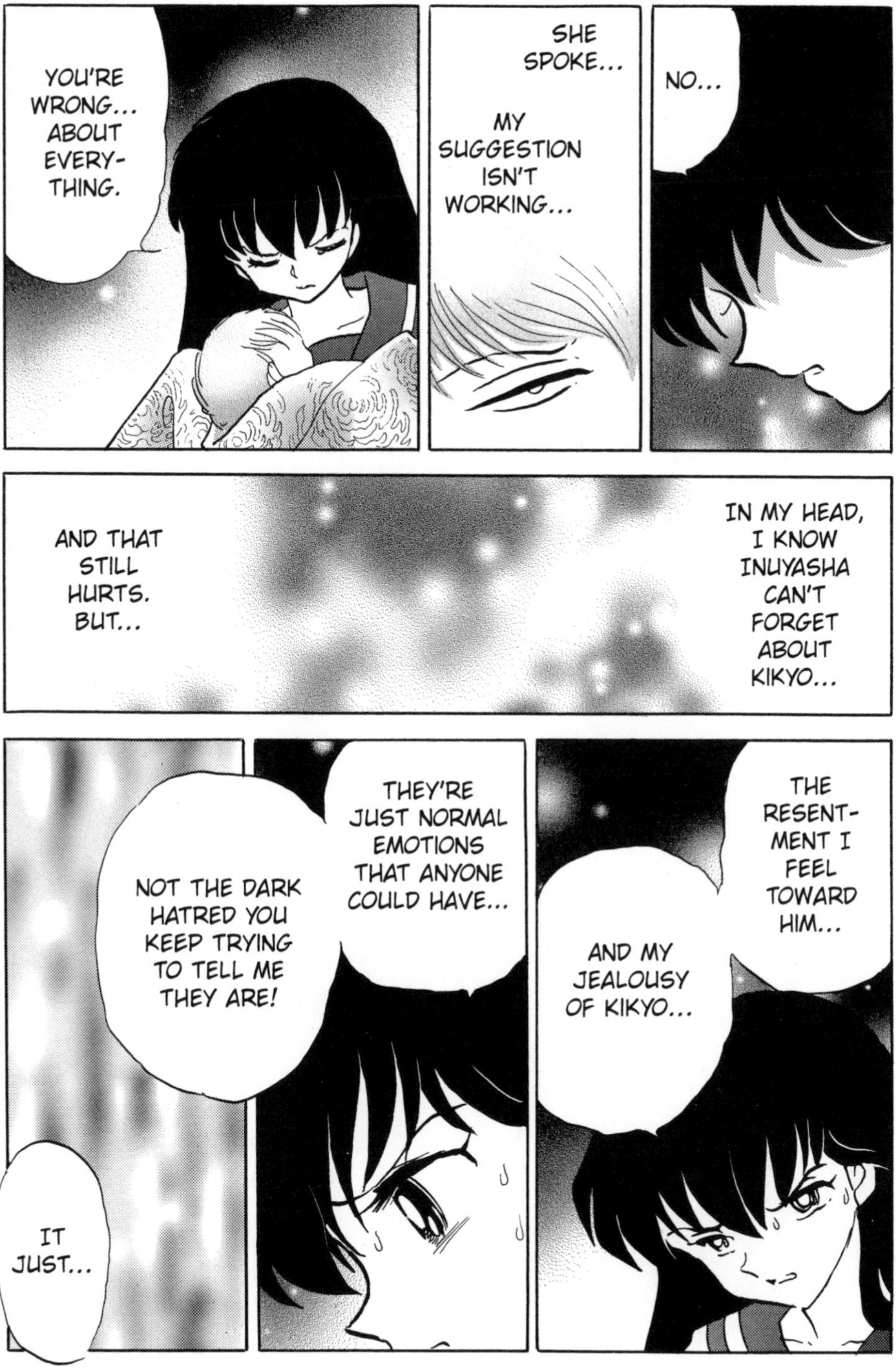
NO...
SHE SPOKE...
MY SUGGESTION ISN'T WORKING...
YOU'RE WRONG... ABOUT EVERYTHING.
IN MY HEAD, I KNOW INUYASHA CAN'T FORGET ABOUT KIKYO...
AND THAT STILL HURTS. BUT...
THE RESENTMENT I FEEL TOWARD HIM...
AND MY JEALOUSY OF KIKYO...
THEY'RE JUST NORMAL EMOTIONS THAT ANYONE COULD HAVE...
NOT THE DARK HATRED YOU KEEP TRYING TO TELL ME THEY ARE!
IT JUST...

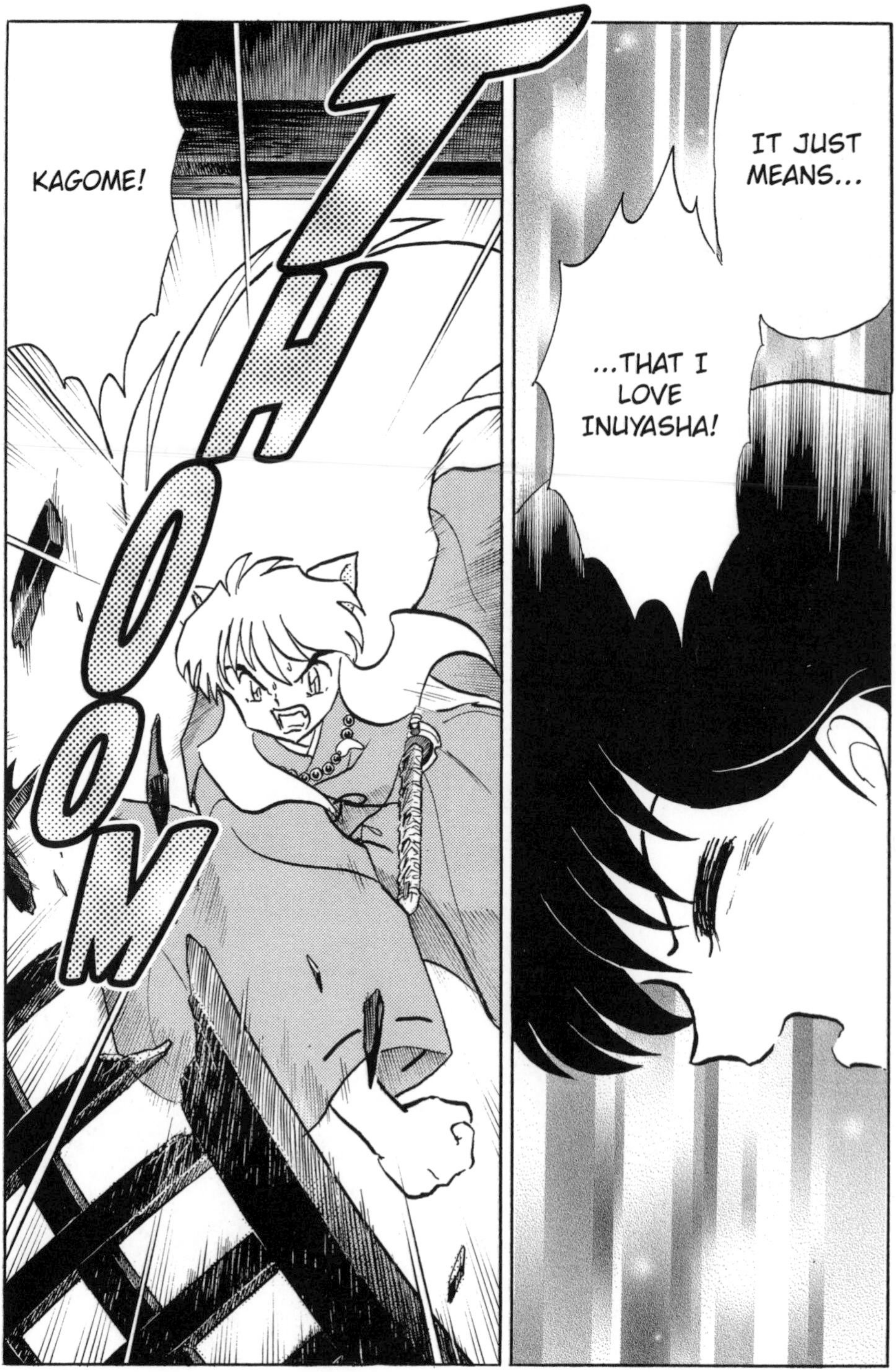
IT JUST MEANS...
...THAT I LOVE INUYASHA!
KAGOME!
THOOOOM

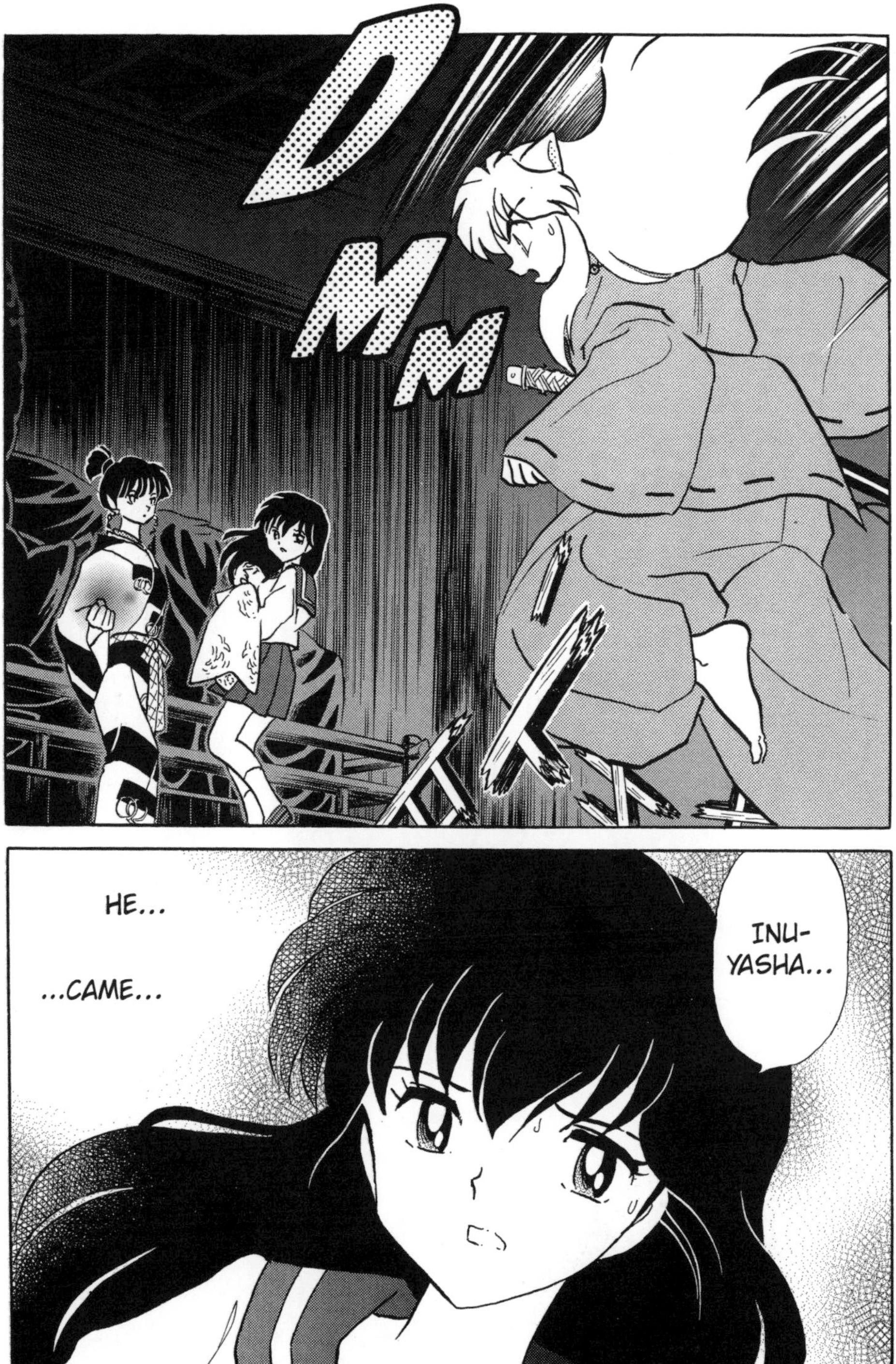
DMMM
INU-YASHA...
HE...
...CAME...

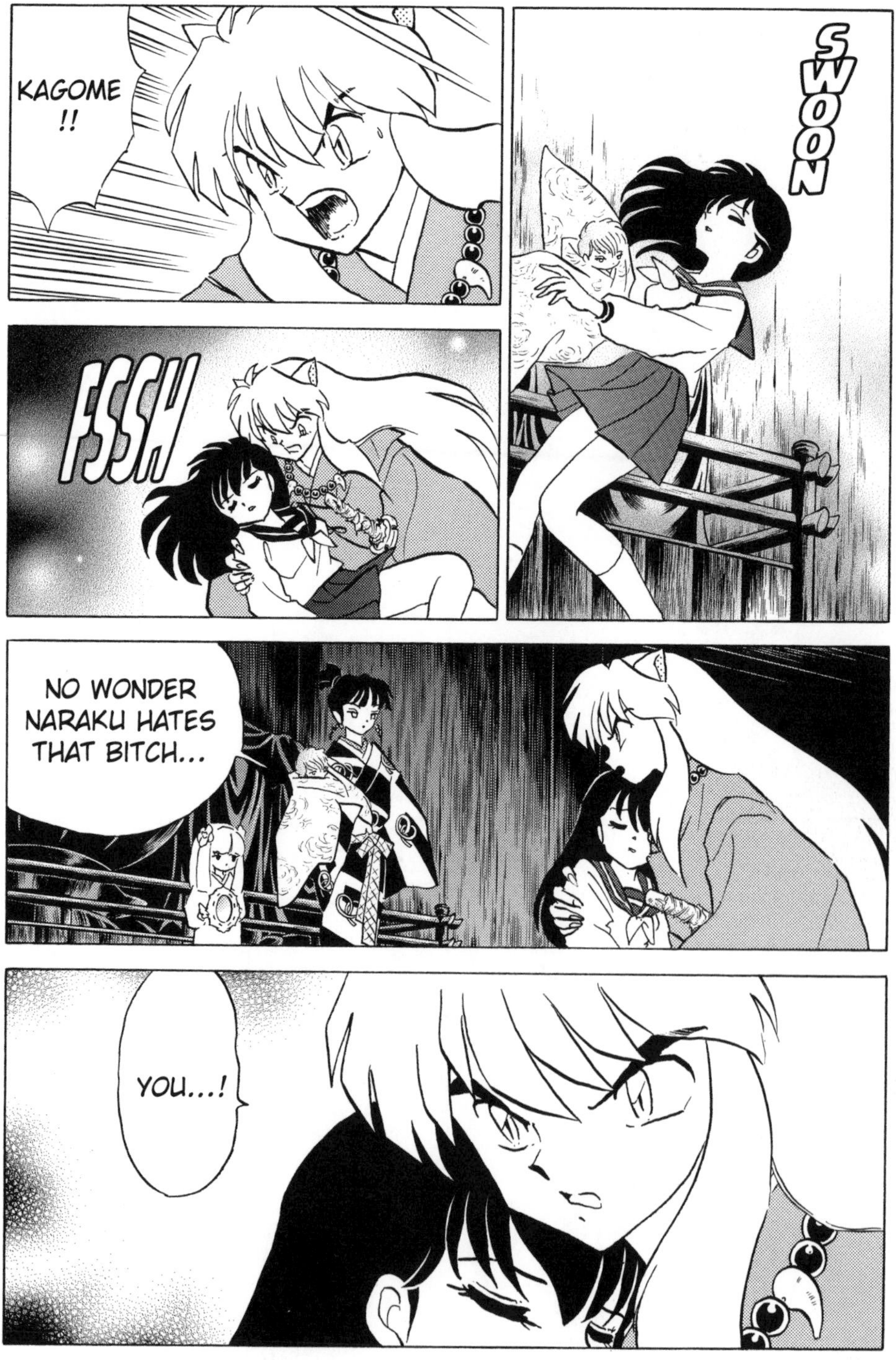
SWOON
KAGOME !!
FSSH
NO WONDER NARAKU HATES THAT BITCH...
YOU...!

SCROLL EIGHT
THE DISCARDED HEART

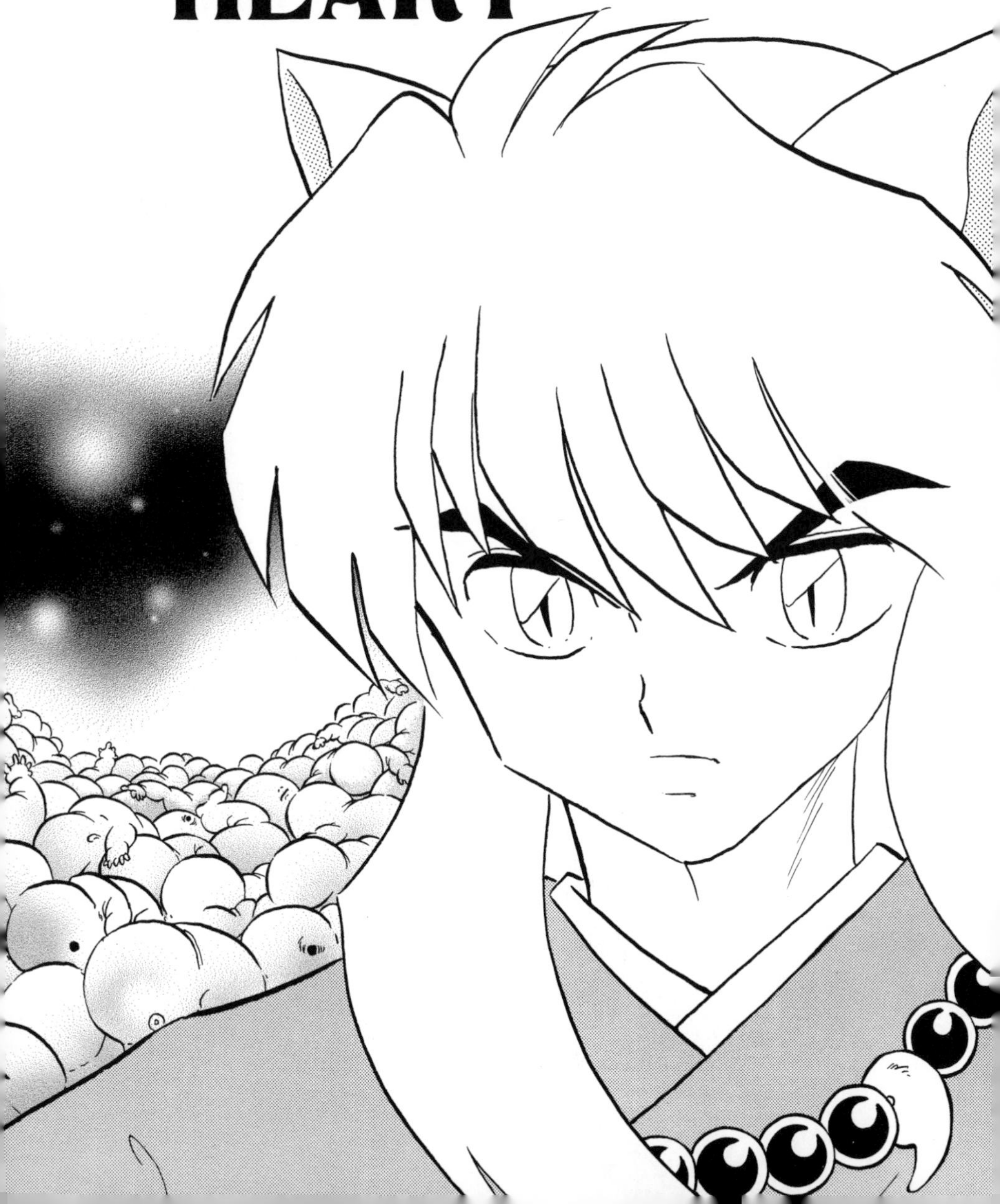

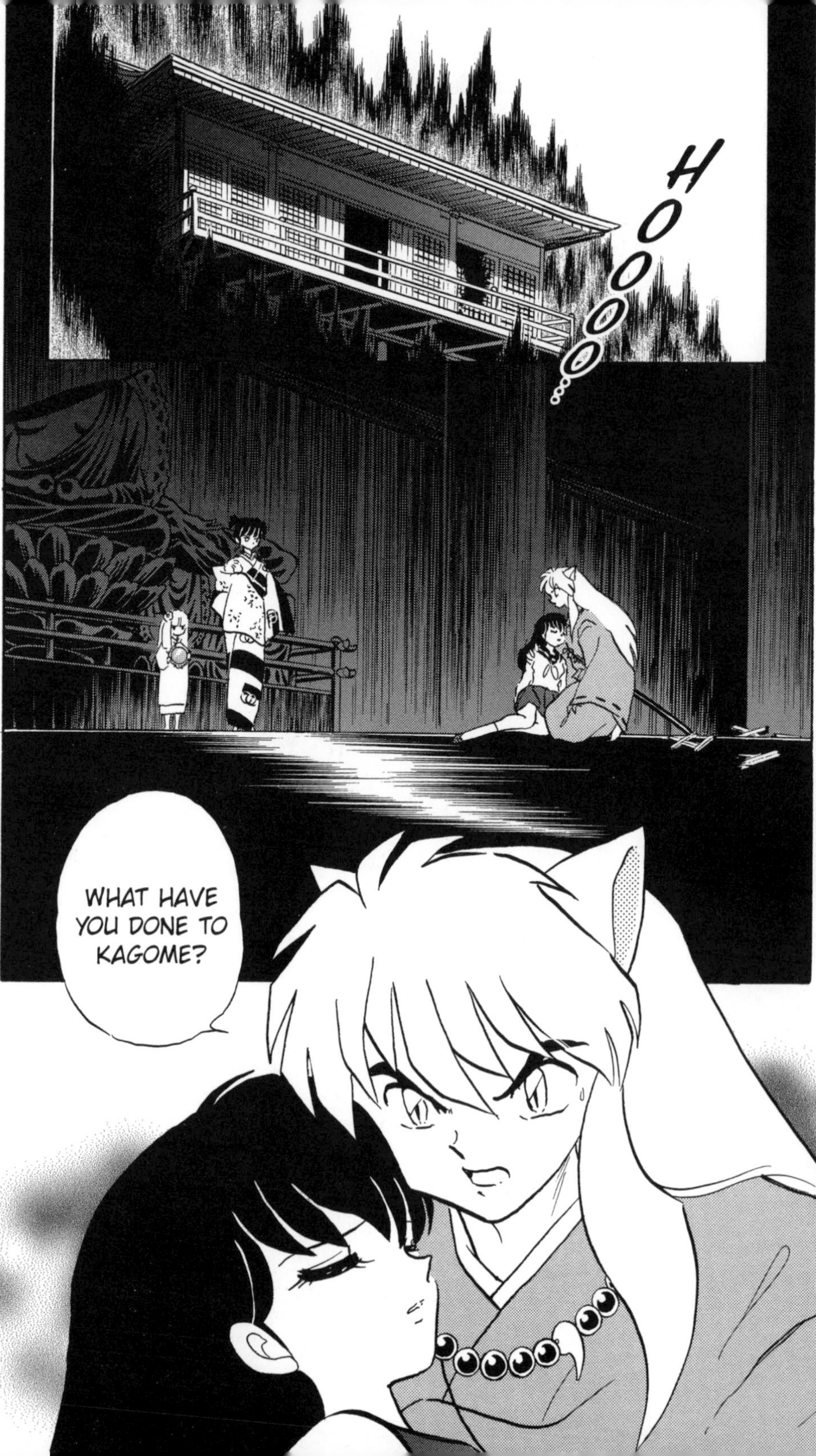
HOOOOO...
WHAT HAVE YOU DONE TO KAGOME?

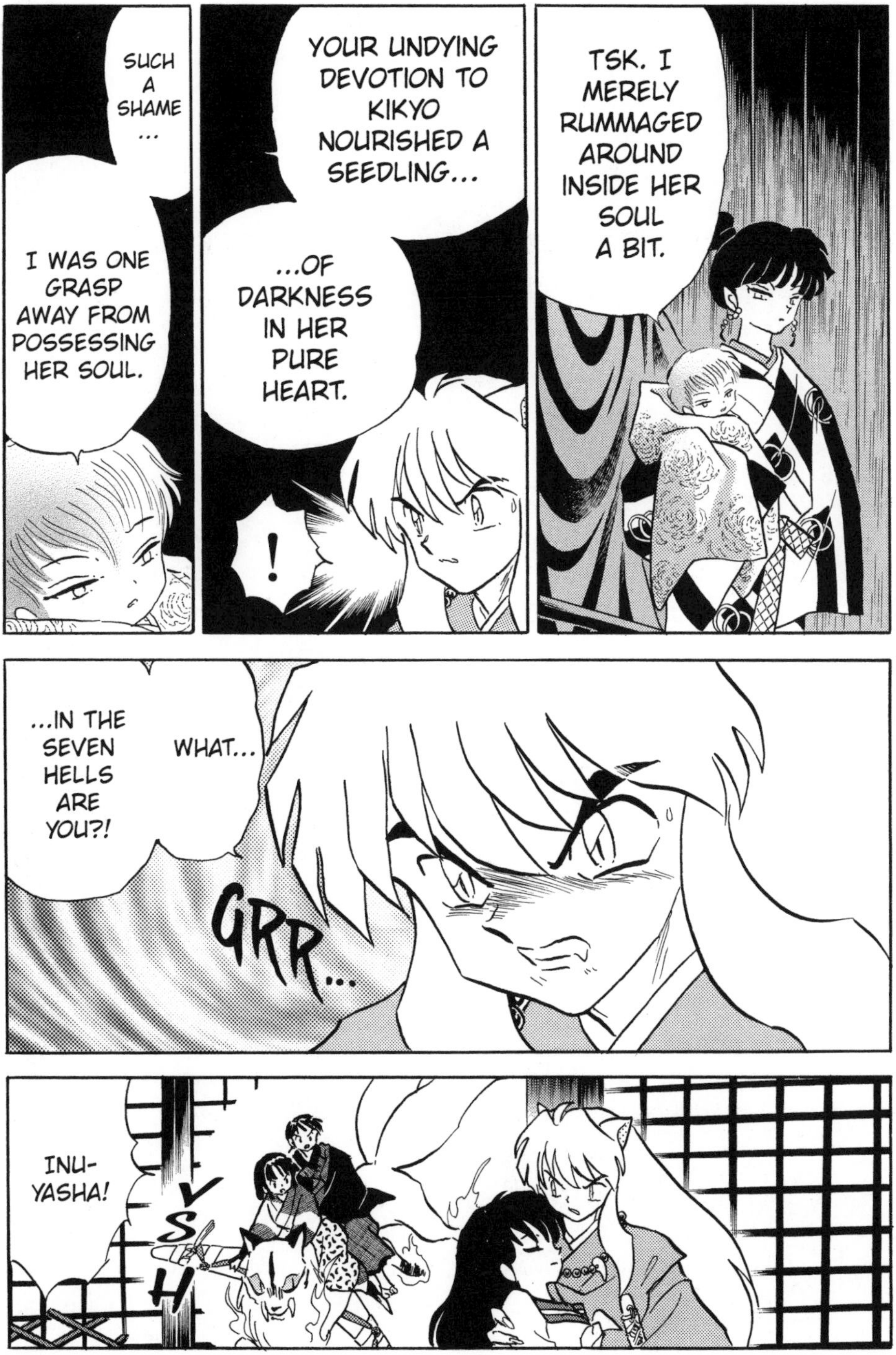
TSK. I MERELY RUMMAGED AROUND INSIDE HER SOUL A BIT.
YOUR UNDYING DEVOTION TO KIKYO NOURISHED A SEEDLING...
...OF DARKNESS IN HER PURE HEART.
!
SUCH A SHAME...
I WAS ONE GRASP AWAY FROM POSSESSING HER SOUL.
WHAT...
...IN THE SEVEN HELLS ARE YOU?!
GRR...
VSSH
INU-YASHA!

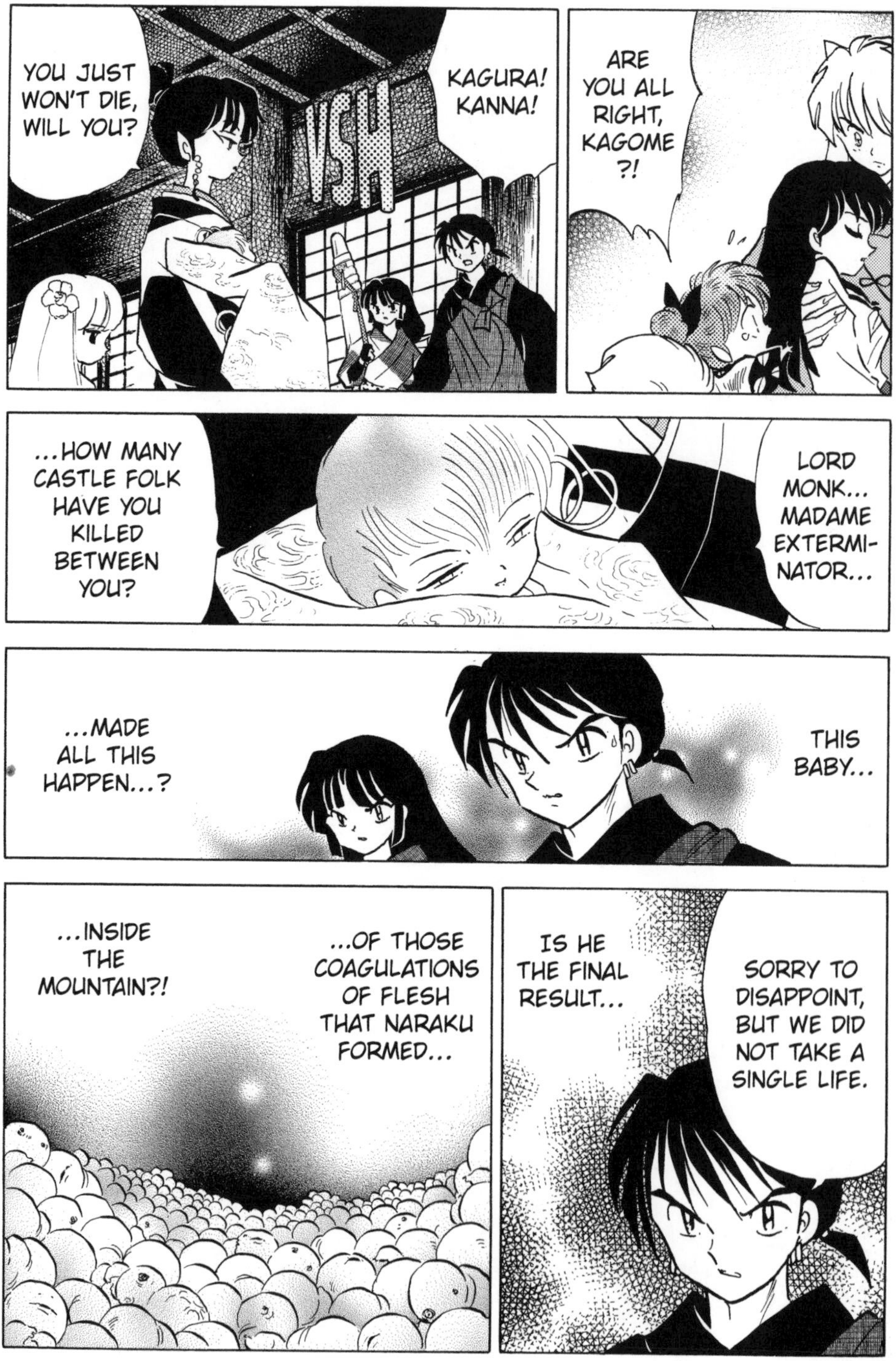
ARE YOU ALL RIGHT, KAGOME ?!
KAGURA! KANNA!
VSH
YOU JUST WON'T DIE, WILL YOU?
LORD MONK... MADAME EXTERMI-NATOR...
...HOW MANY CASTLE FOLK HAVE YOU KILLED BETWEEN YOU?
THIS BABY...
...MADE ALL THIS HAPPEN...?
SORRY TO DISAPPOINT, BUT WE DID NOT TAKE A SINGLE LIFE.
IS HE THE FINAL RESULT...
...OF THOSE COAGULATIONS OF FLESH THAT NARAKU FORMED...
...INSIDE THE MOUNTAIN?!

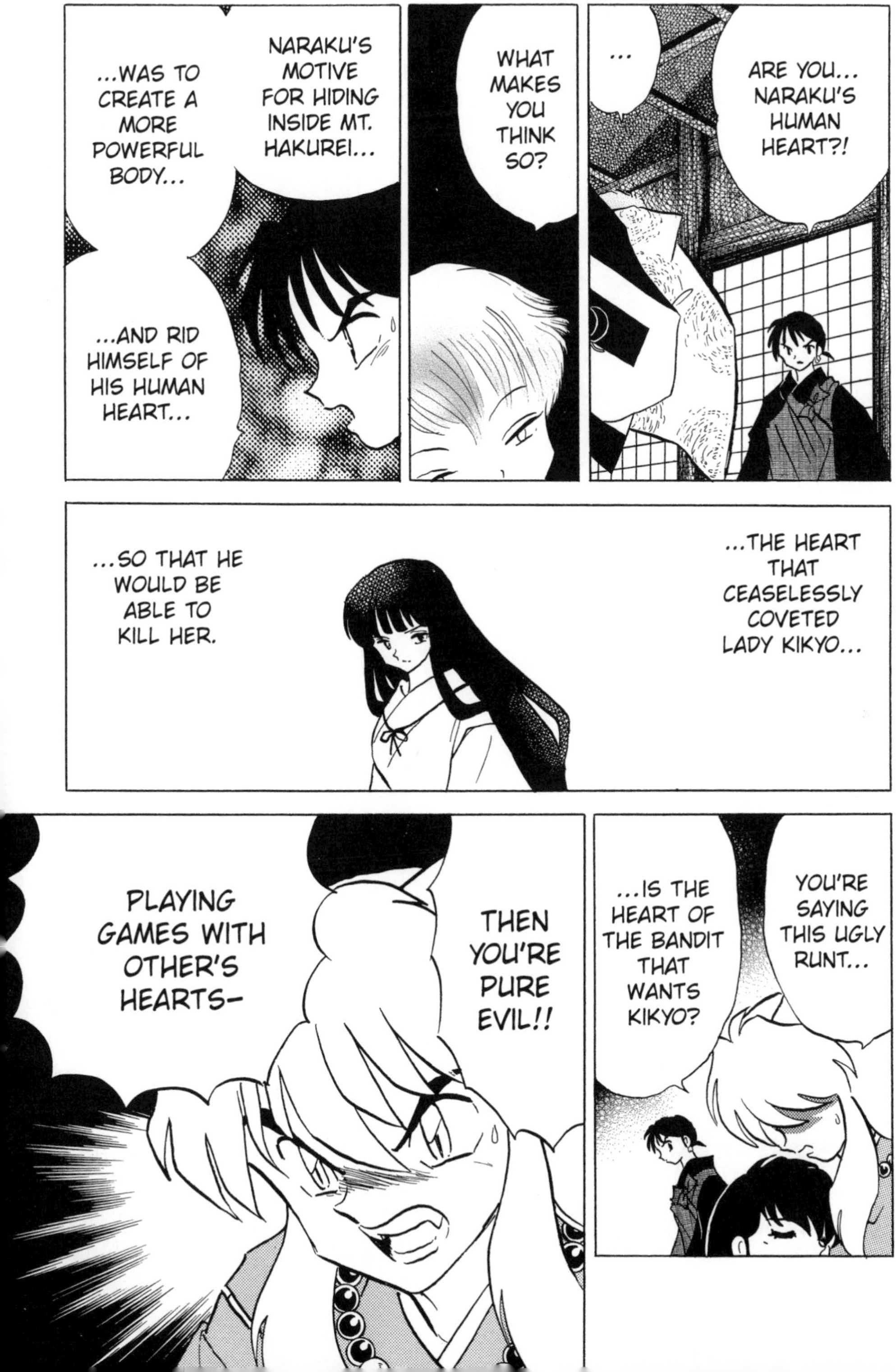
ARE YOU... NARAKU'S HUMAN HEART?!
...
WHAT MAKES YOU THINK SO?
NARAKU'S MOTIVE FOR HIDING INSIDE MT. HAKUREI...
...WAS TO CREATE A MORE POWERFUL BODY...
...AND RID HIMSELF OF HIS HUMAN HEART...
...THE HEART THAT CEASELESSLY COVETED LADY KIKYO...
...SO THAT HE WOULD BE ABLE TO KILL HER.
YOU'RE SAYING THIS UGLY RUNT...
...IS THE HEART OF THE BANDIT THAT WANTS KIKYO?
THEN YOU'RE PURE EVIL!!
PLAYING GAMES WITH OTHER'S HEARTS-

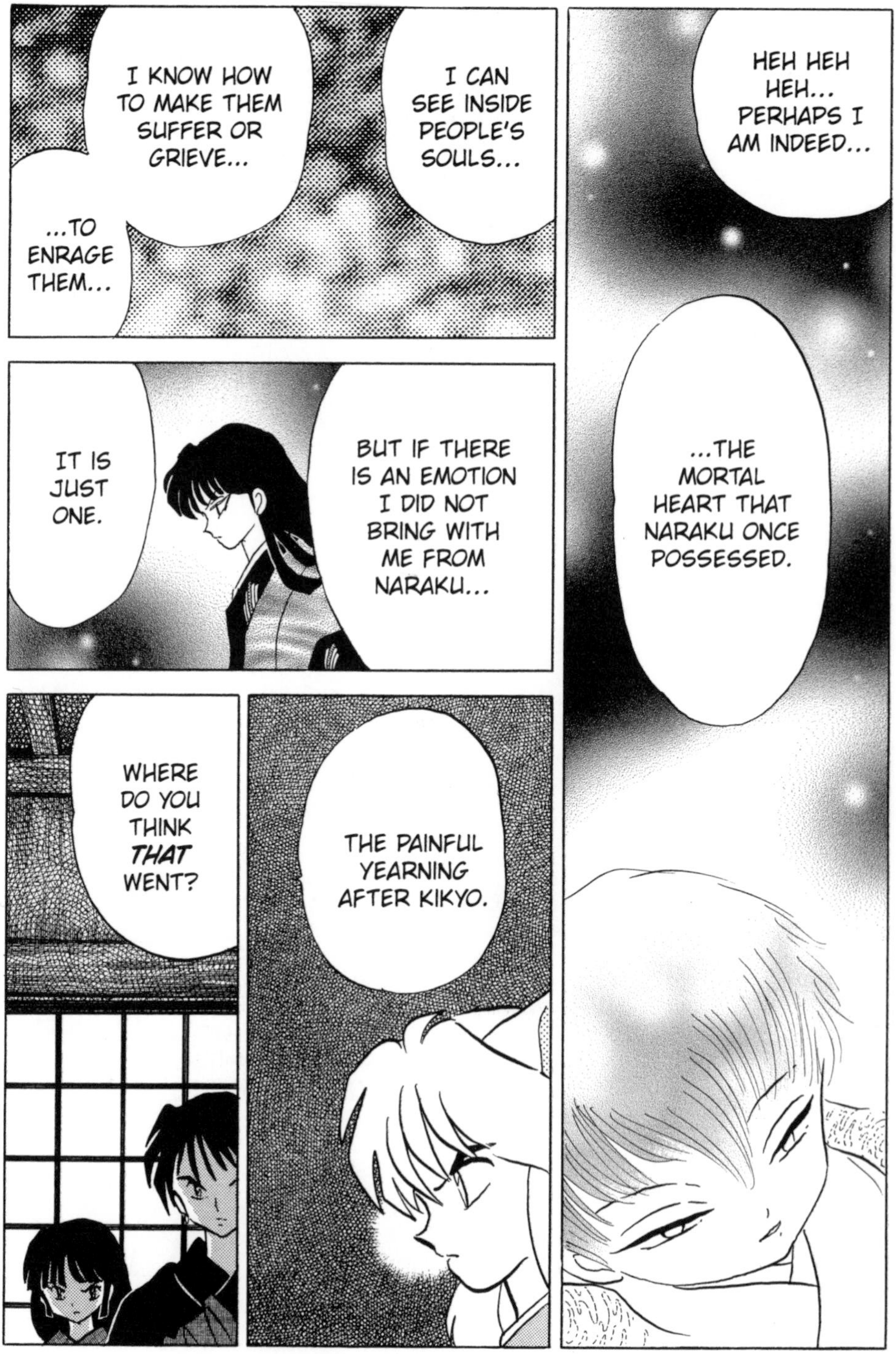
HEH HEH HEH... PERHAPS I AM INDEED...
...THE MORTAL HEART THAT NARAKU ONCE POSSESSED.
I CAN SEE INSIDE PEOPLE'S SOULS...
I KNOW HOW TO MAKE THEM SUFFER OR GRIEVE...
...TO ENRAGE THEM...
BUT IF THERE IS AN EMOTION I DID NOT BRING WITH ME FROM NARAKU...
IT IS JUST ONE.
THE PAINFUL YEARNING AFTER KIKYO.
WHERE DO YOU THINK ***THAT*** WENT?

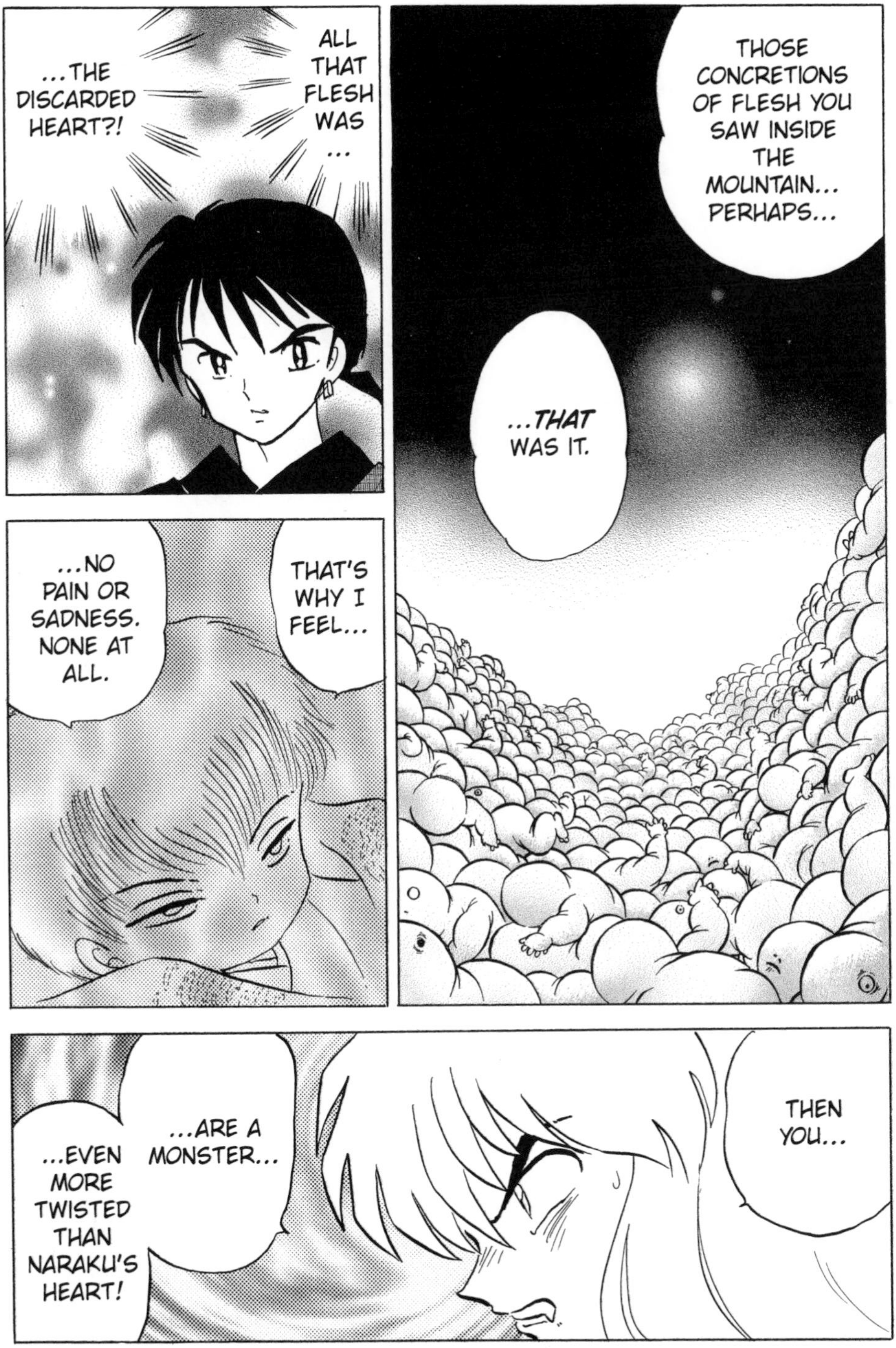
THOSE CONCRETIONS OF FLESH YOU SAW INSIDE THE MOUNTAIN... PERHAPS...
...*THAT* WAS IT.
ALL THAT FLESH WAS...
...THE DISCARDED HEART?!
THAT'S WHY I FEEL...
...NO PAIN OR SADNESS. NONE AT ALL.
THEN YOU...
...ARE A MONSTER...
...EVEN MORE TWISTED THAN NARAKU'S HEART!

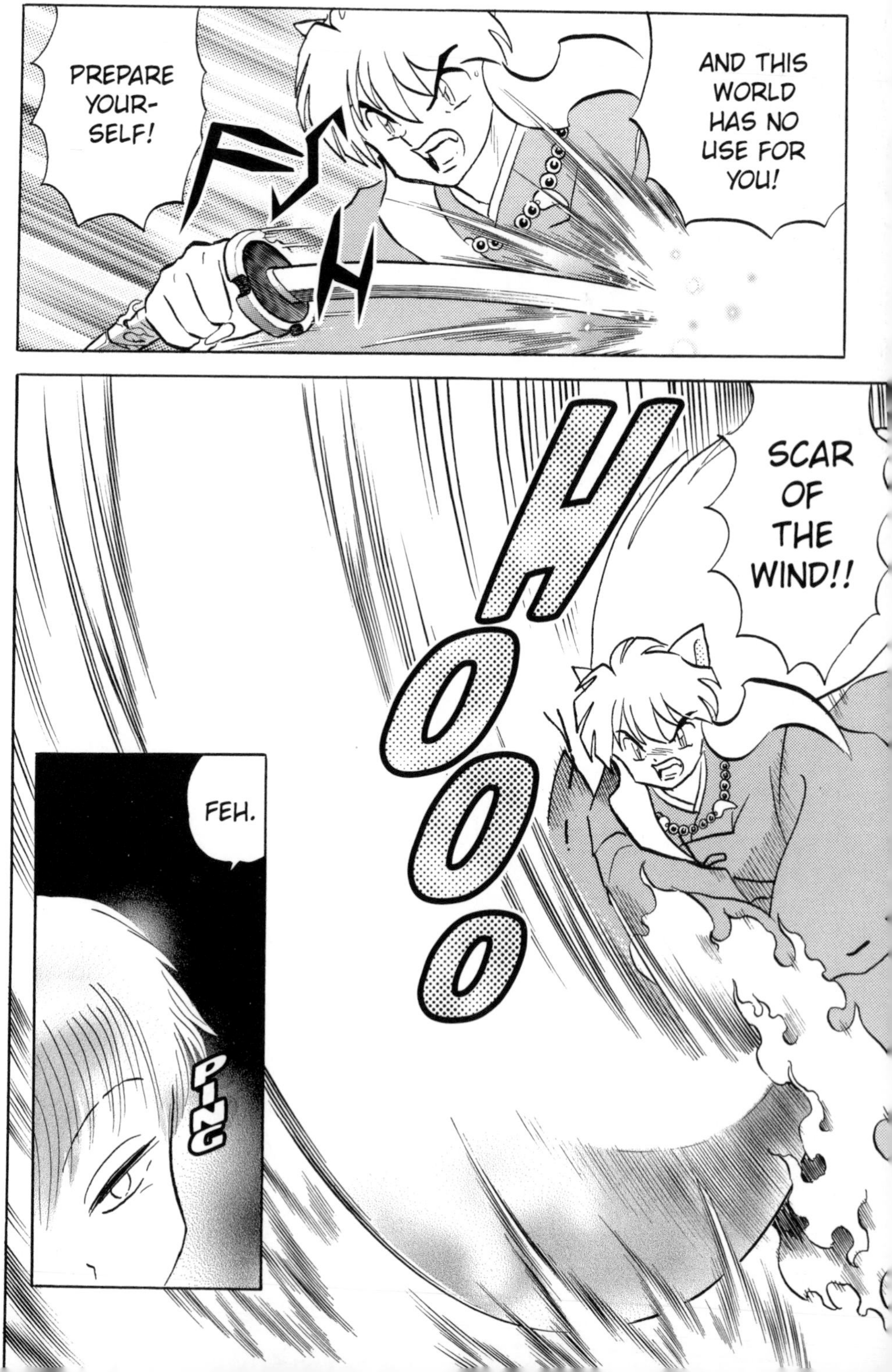
AND THIS WORLD HAS NO USE FOR YOU!
PREPARE YOUR-SELF!
SCAR OF THE WIND!!
HOOOO
FEH.
PING

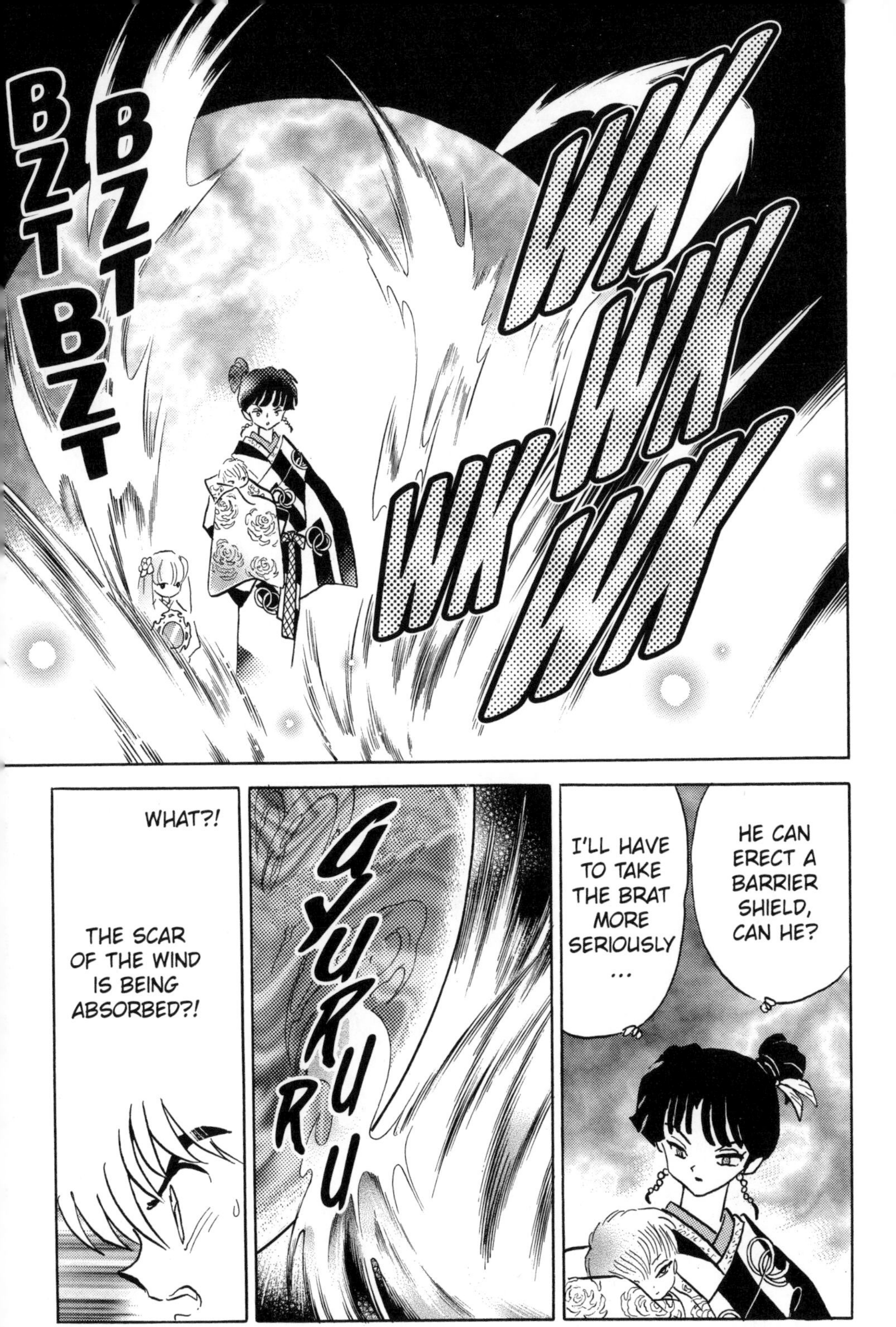
BZT
BZT
BZT
HE CAN ERECT A BARRIER SHIELD, CAN HE?
I'LL HAVE TO TAKE THE BRAT MORE SERIOUSLY...
WHAT?!
THE SCAR OF THE WIND IS BEING ABSORBED?!

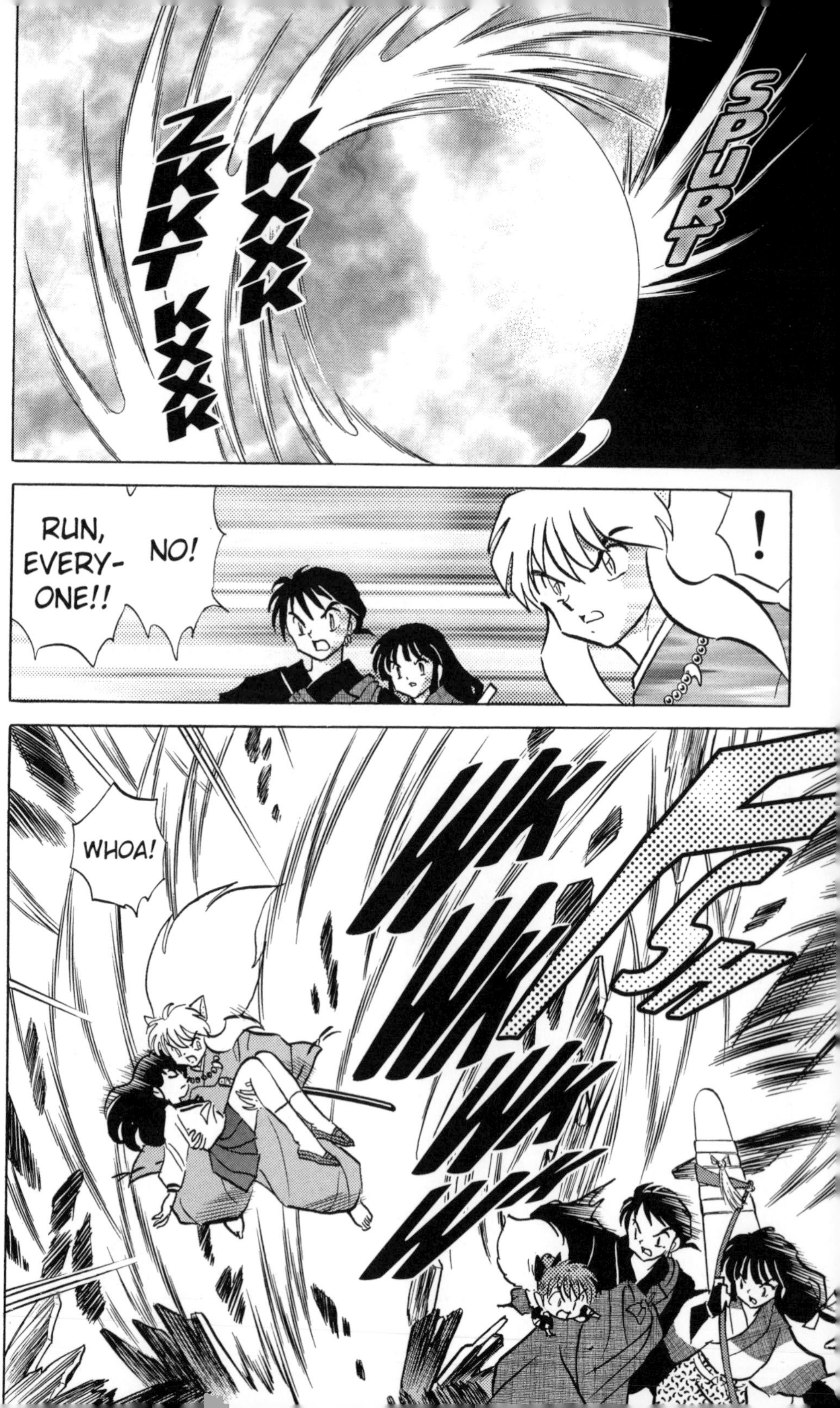
SPURT
!
NO!
RUN, EVERY-ONE!!
WHOA!

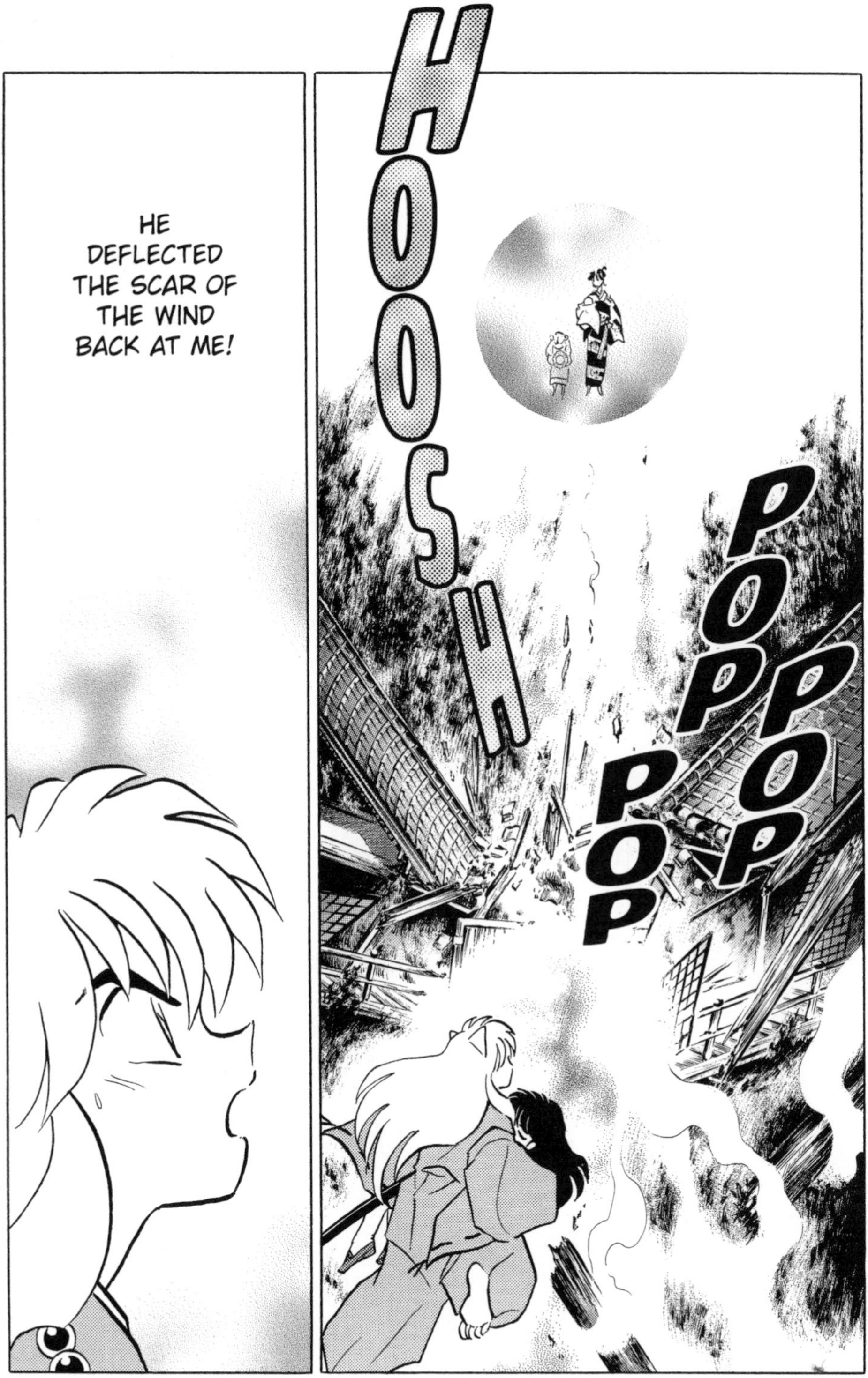
HOOOSH
POP
POP
POP
HE DEFLECTED THE SCAR OF THE WIND BACK AT ME!

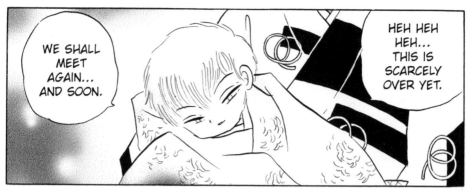

HEH HEH HEH... THIS IS SCARCELY OVER YET.
WE SHALL MEET AGAIN... AND SOON.
SHUT UP!
IF YOU TRY TO HURT KAGOME EVER AGAIN...
I'M EVER SO SORRY. I CAN'T PROMISE YOU I WON'T.
FOR SHE IS THE ONLY ONE IN THIS WORLD NOW WHO CAN FIND SHIKON SHARDS.
WHAT?!
THERE ARE ONLY A FEW LEFT TO FIND.

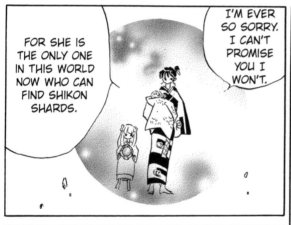

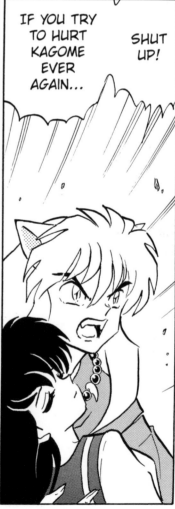

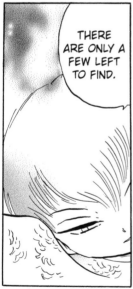

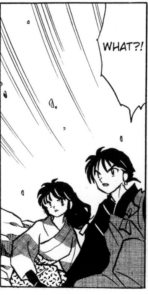

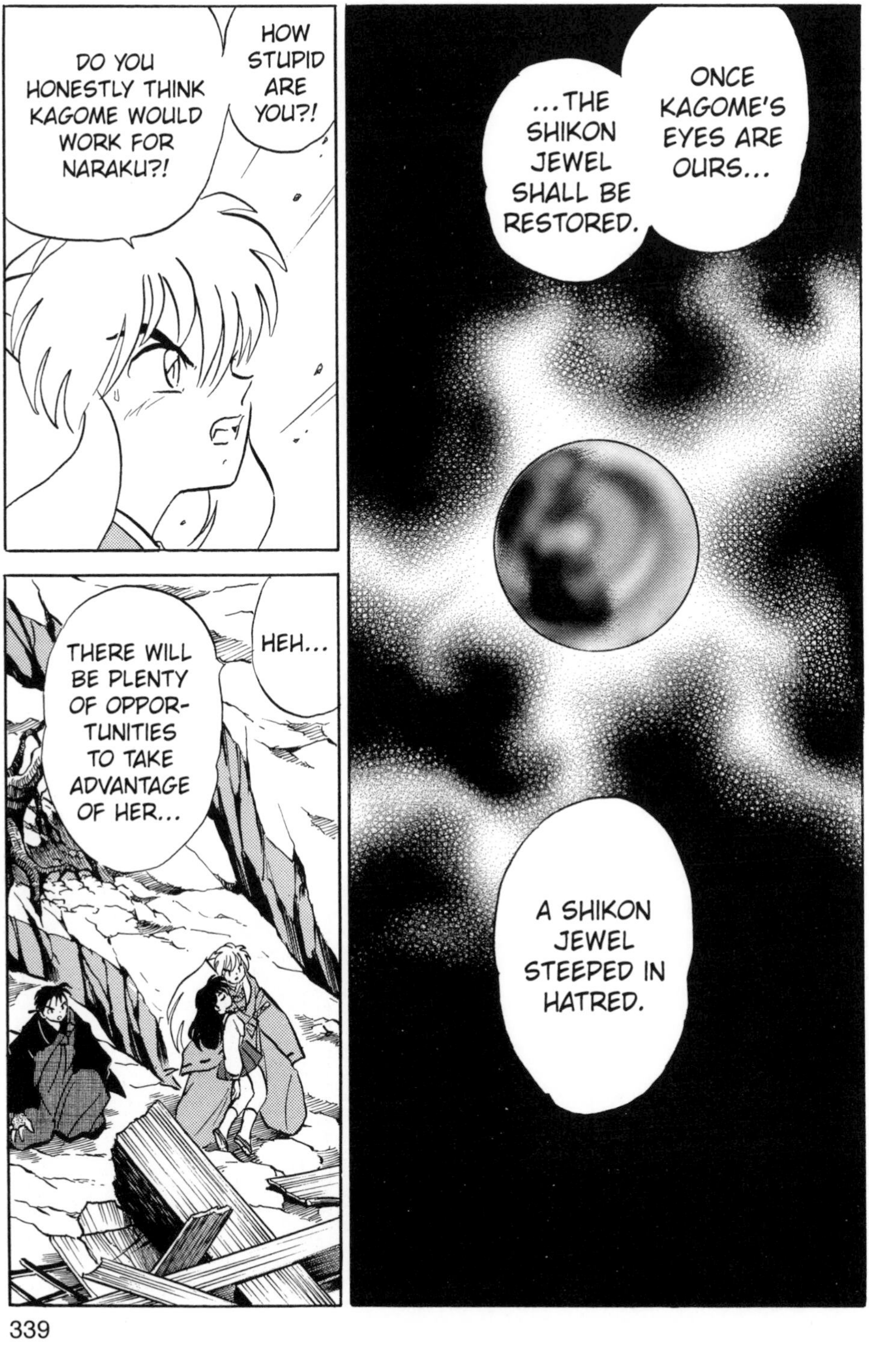
ONCE KAGOME'S EYES ARE OURS...
...THE SHIKON JEWEL SHALL BE RESTORED.
A SHIKON JEWEL STEEPED IN HATRED.
HOW STUPID ARE YOU?!
DO YOU HONESTLY THINK KAGOME WOULD WORK FOR NARAKU?!
HEH...
THERE WILL BE PLENTY OF OPPOR-TUNITIES TO TAKE ADVANTAGE OF HER...

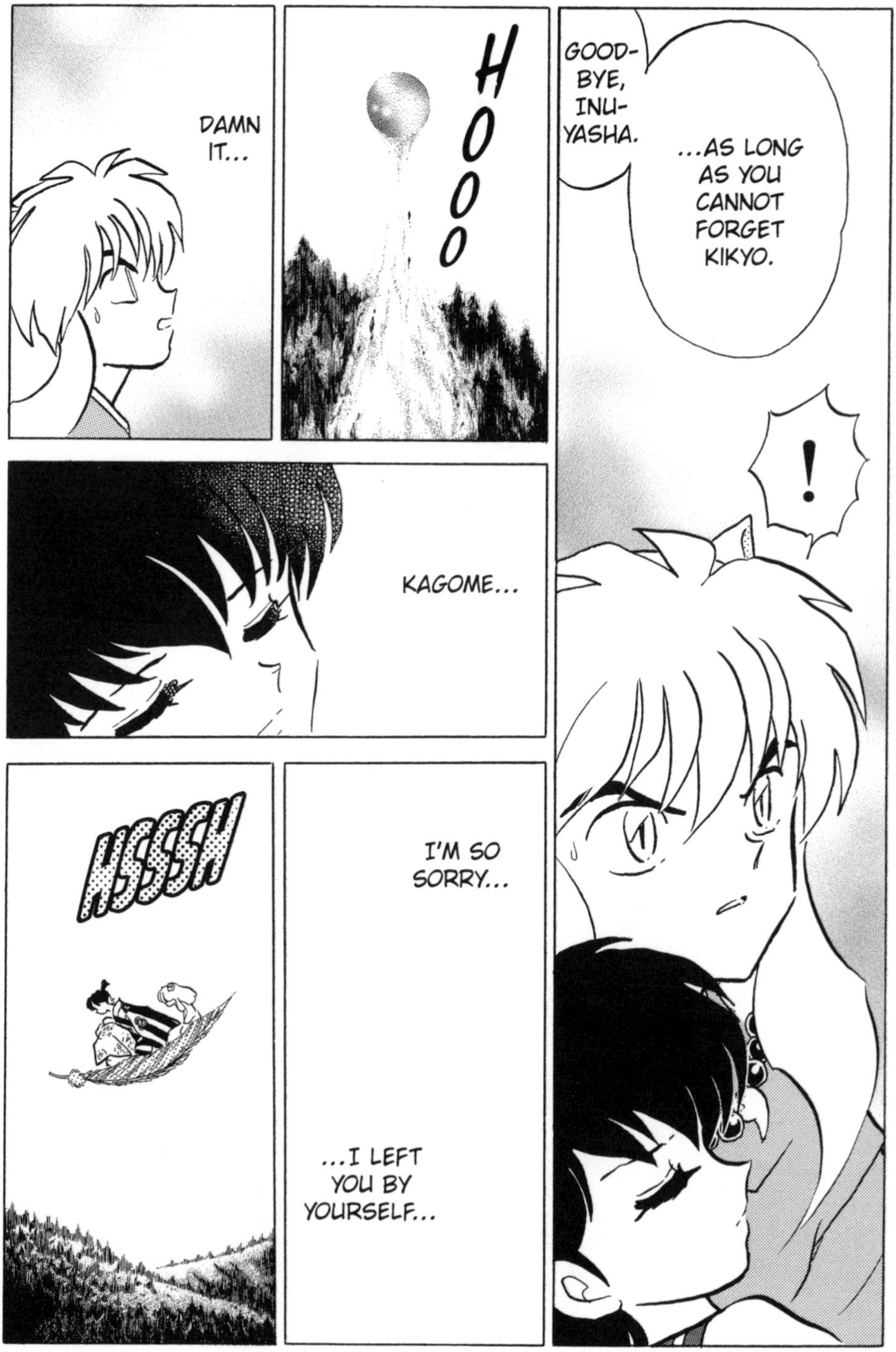
...AS LONG AS YOU CANNOT FORGET KIKYO.
GOOD-BYE, INU-YASHA.
!
HOOOO
DAMN IT...
KAGOME...
I'M SO SORRY...
...I LEFT YOU BY YOURSELF...
HSSSH

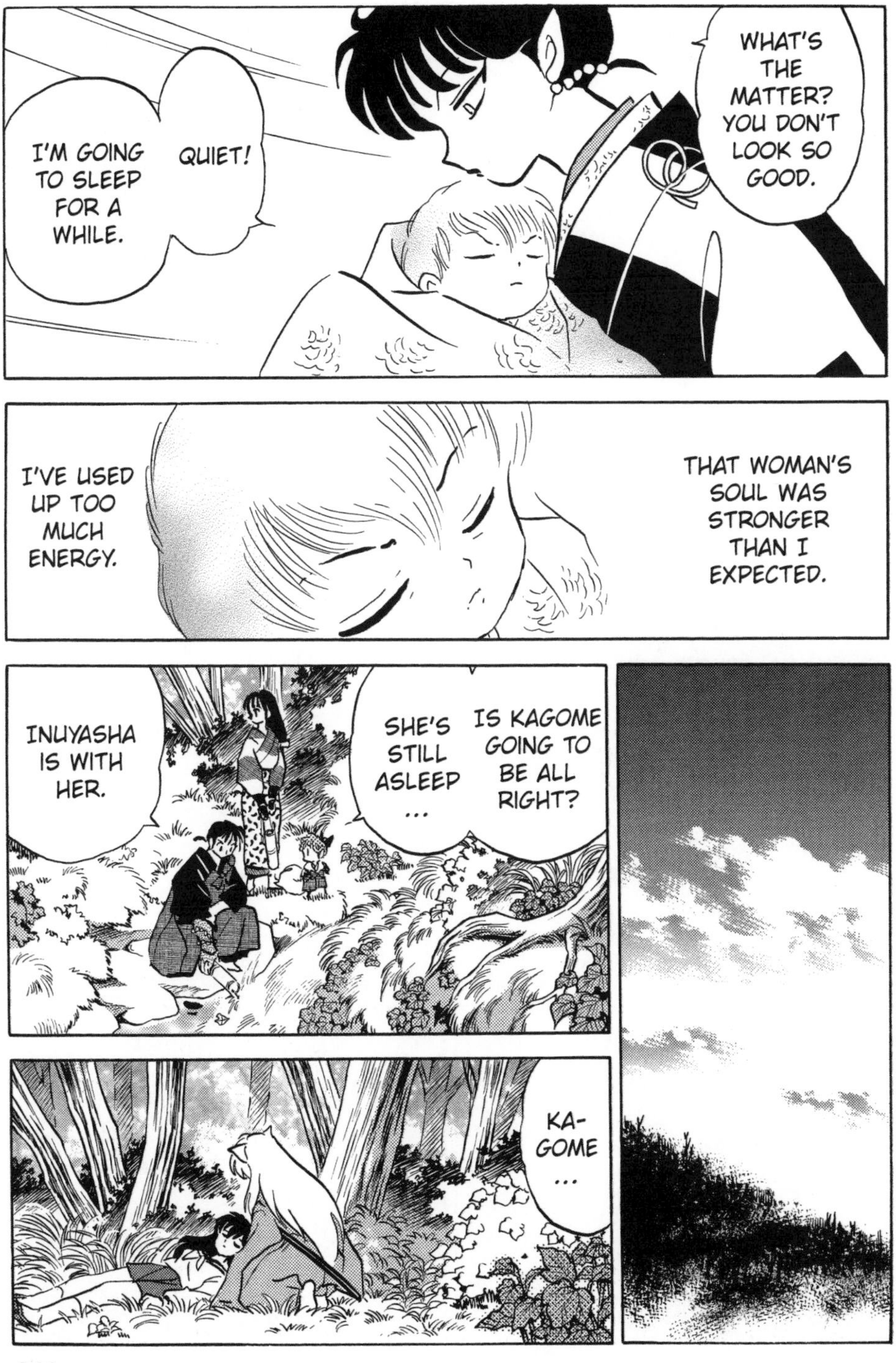
WHAT'S THE MATTER? YOU DON'T LOOK SO GOOD.
QUIET!
I'M GOING TO SLEEP FOR A WHILE.
THAT WOMAN'S SOUL WAS STRONGER THAN I EXPECTED.
I'VE USED UP TOO MUCH ENERGY.
IS KAGOME GOING TO BE ALL RIGHT?
SHE'S STILL ASLEEP...
INUYASHA IS WITH HER.
KA-GOME...

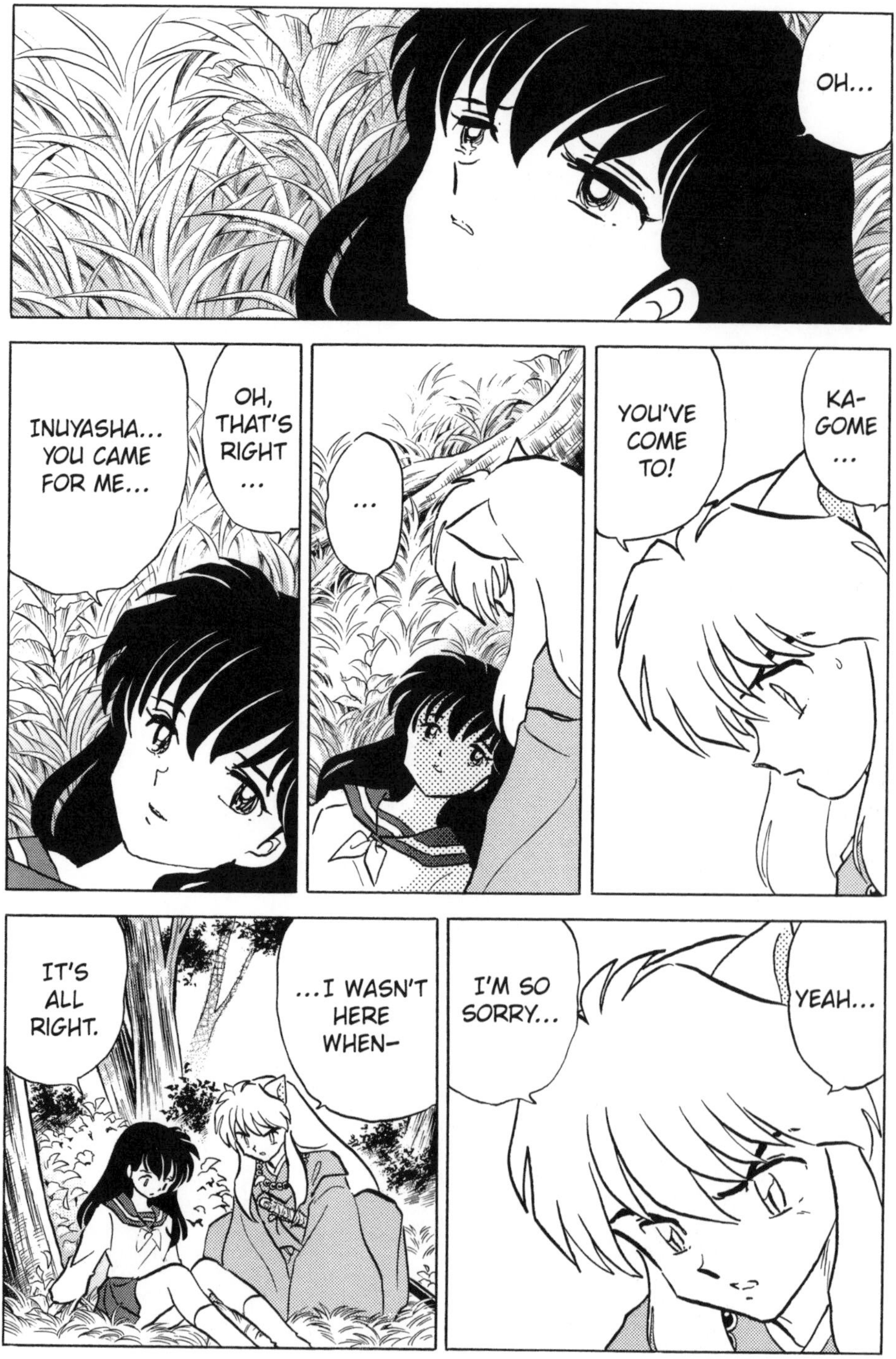
OH...
KA-GOME...
YOU'VE COME TO!
...
OH, THAT'S RIGHT...
INUYASHA... YOU CAME FOR ME...
YEAH...
I'M SO SORRY...
...I WASN'T HERE WHEN-
IT'S ALL RIGHT.

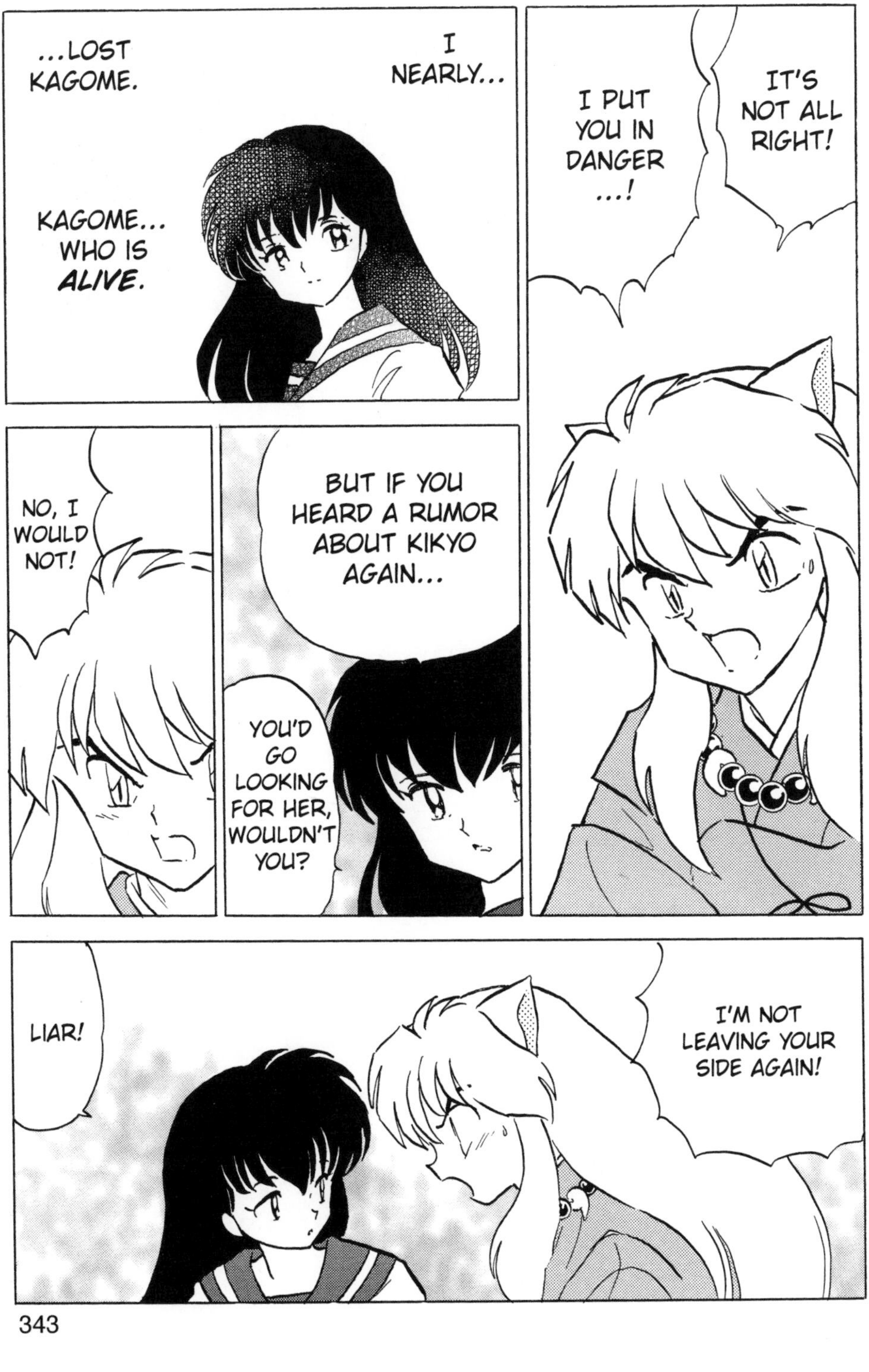
IT'S NOT ALL RIGHT!
I PUT YOU IN DANGER ...!
I NEARLY...
...LOST KAGOME.
KAGOME... WHO IS ALIVE.
BUT IF YOU HEARD A RUMOR ABOUT KIKYO AGAIN...
YOU'D GO LOOKING FOR HER, WOULDN'T YOU?
NO, I WOULD NOT!
I'M NOT LEAVING YOUR SIDE AGAIN!
LIAR!

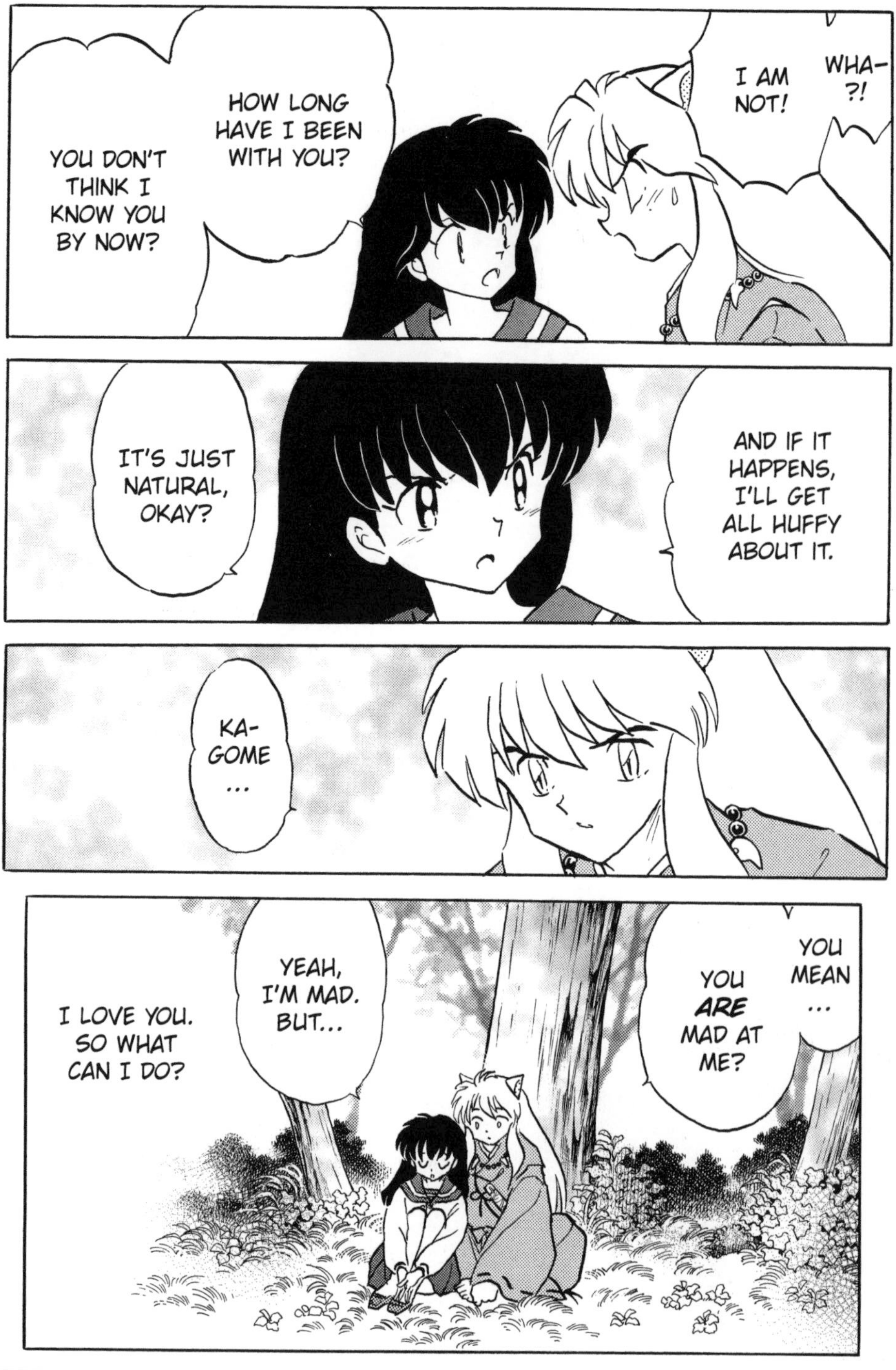
WHA- ?!
I AM NOT!
HOW LONG HAVE I BEEN WITH YOU?
YOU DON'T THINK I KNOW YOU BY NOW?
AND IF IT HAPPENS, I'LL GET ALL HUFFY ABOUT IT.
IT'S JUST NATURAL, OKAY?
KA-GOME ...
YOU MEAN ...
YOU **ARE** MAD AT ME?
YEAH, I'M MAD. BUT...
I LOVE YOU. SO WHAT CAN I DO?

SCROLL NINE
MIMISENRI

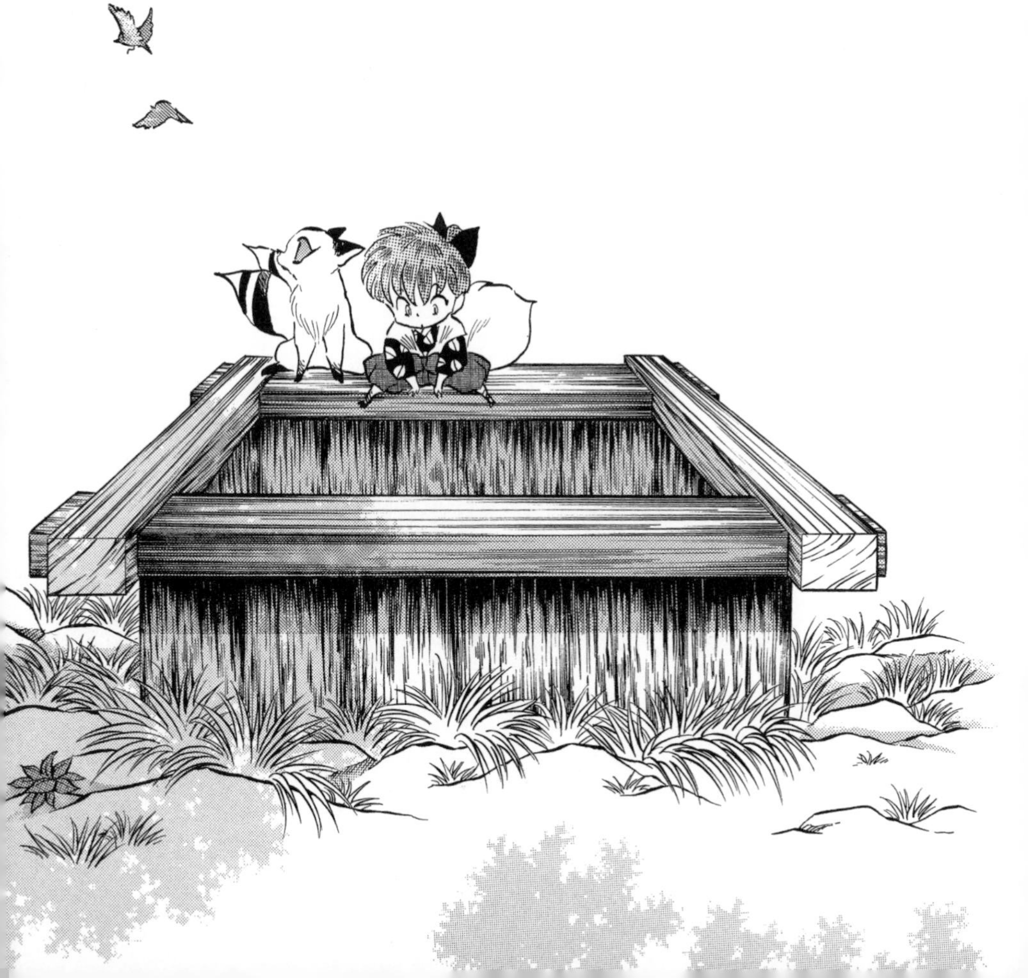

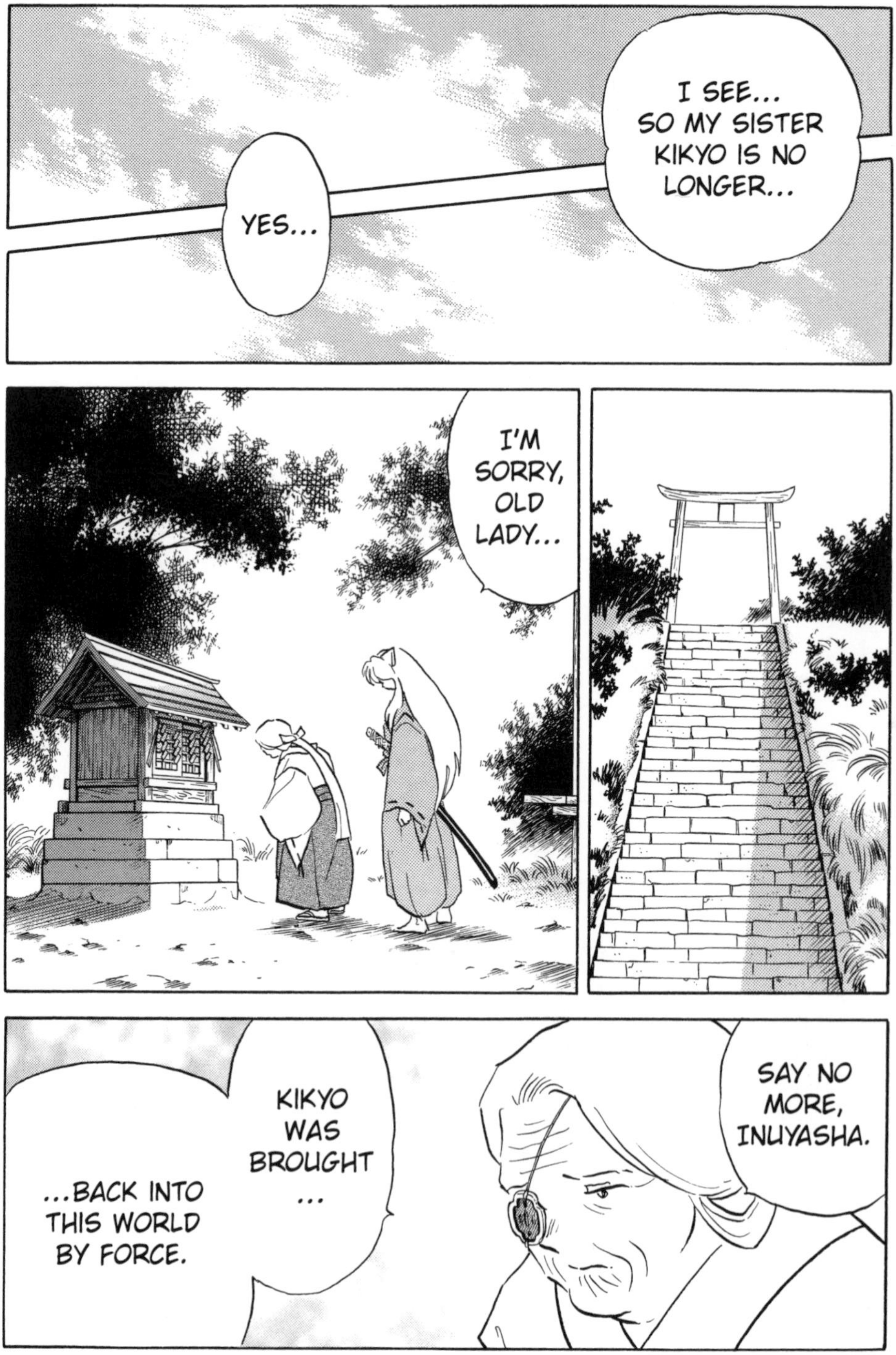
I SEE... SO MY SISTER KIKYO IS NO LONGER...
YES...
I'M SORRY, OLD LADY...
SAY NO MORE, INUYASHA.
KIKYO WAS BROUGHT ...
...BACK INTO THIS WORLD BY FORCE.

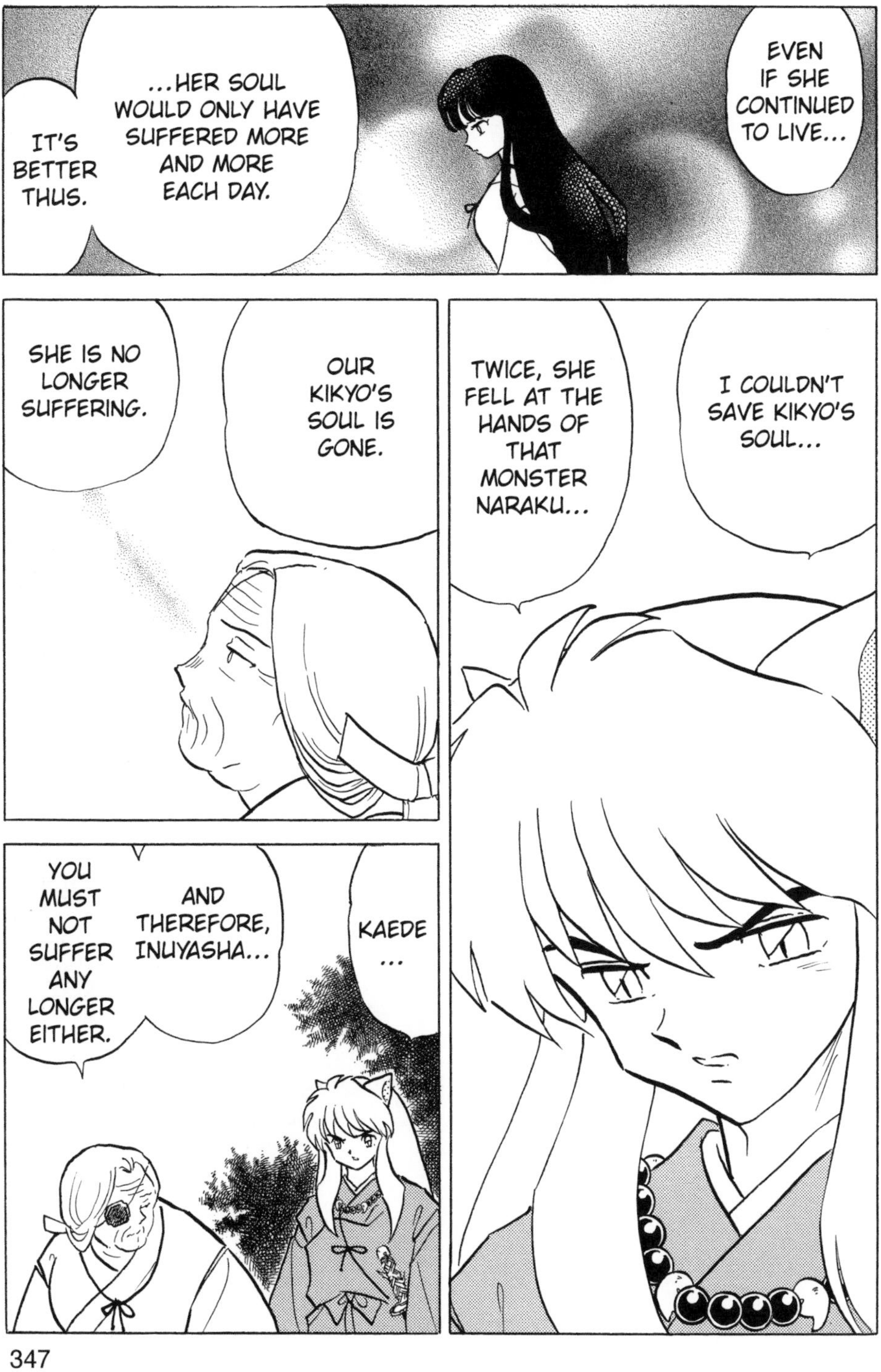
EVEN IF SHE CONTINUED TO LIVE...
...HER SOUL WOULD ONLY HAVE SUFFERED MORE AND MORE EACH DAY.
IT'S BETTER THUS.
I COULDN'T SAVE KIKYO'S SOUL...
TWICE, SHE FELL AT THE HANDS OF THAT MONSTER NARAKU...
OUR KIKYO'S SOUL IS GONE.
SHE IS NO LONGER SUFFERING.
KAEDE ...
AND THEREFORE, INUYASHA...
YOU MUST NOT SUFFER ANY LONGER EITHER.

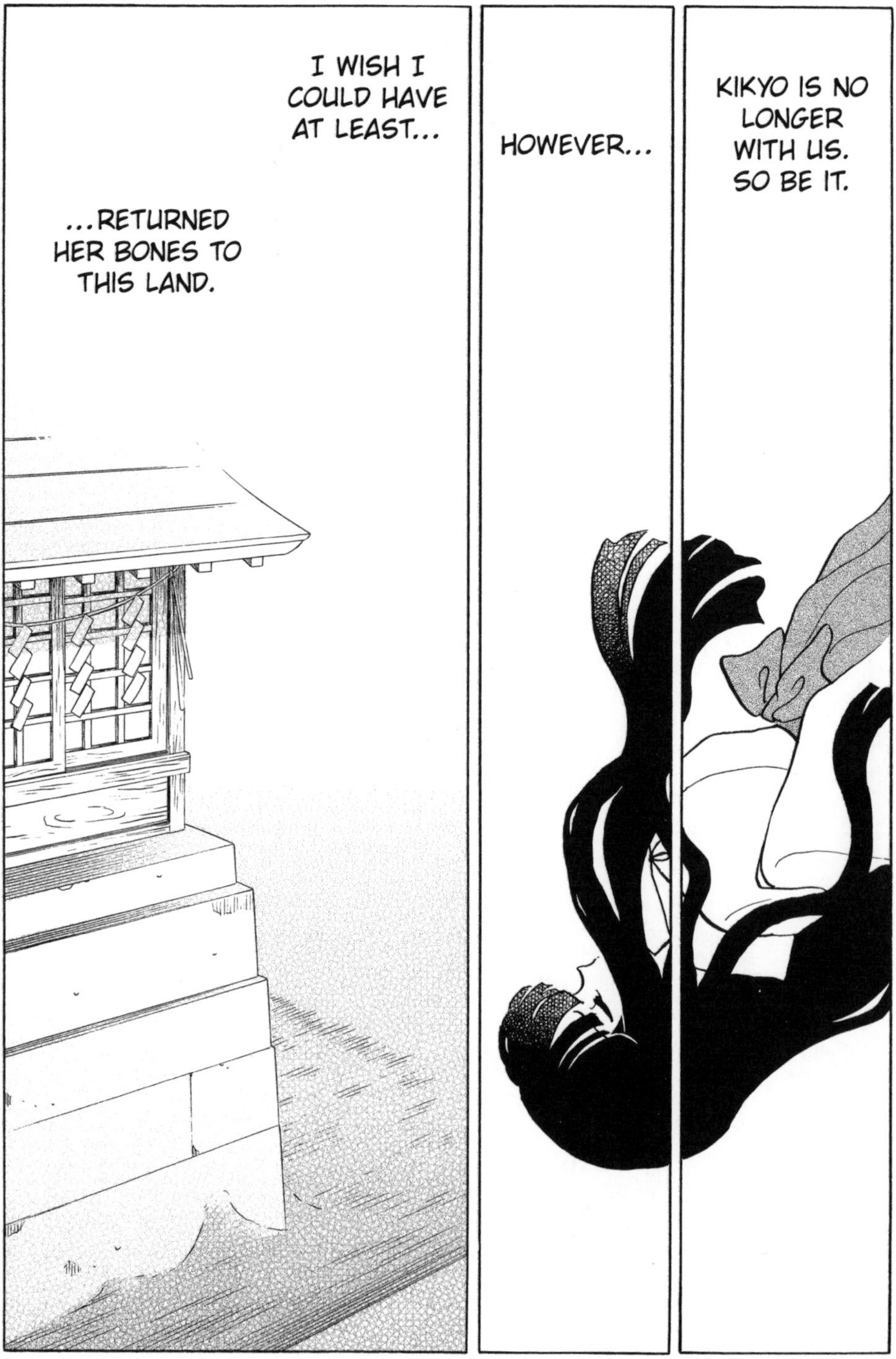
KIKYO IS NO LONGER WITH US. SO BE IT.
HOWEVER...
I WISH I COULD HAVE AT LEAST...
...RETURNED HER BONES TO THIS LAND.

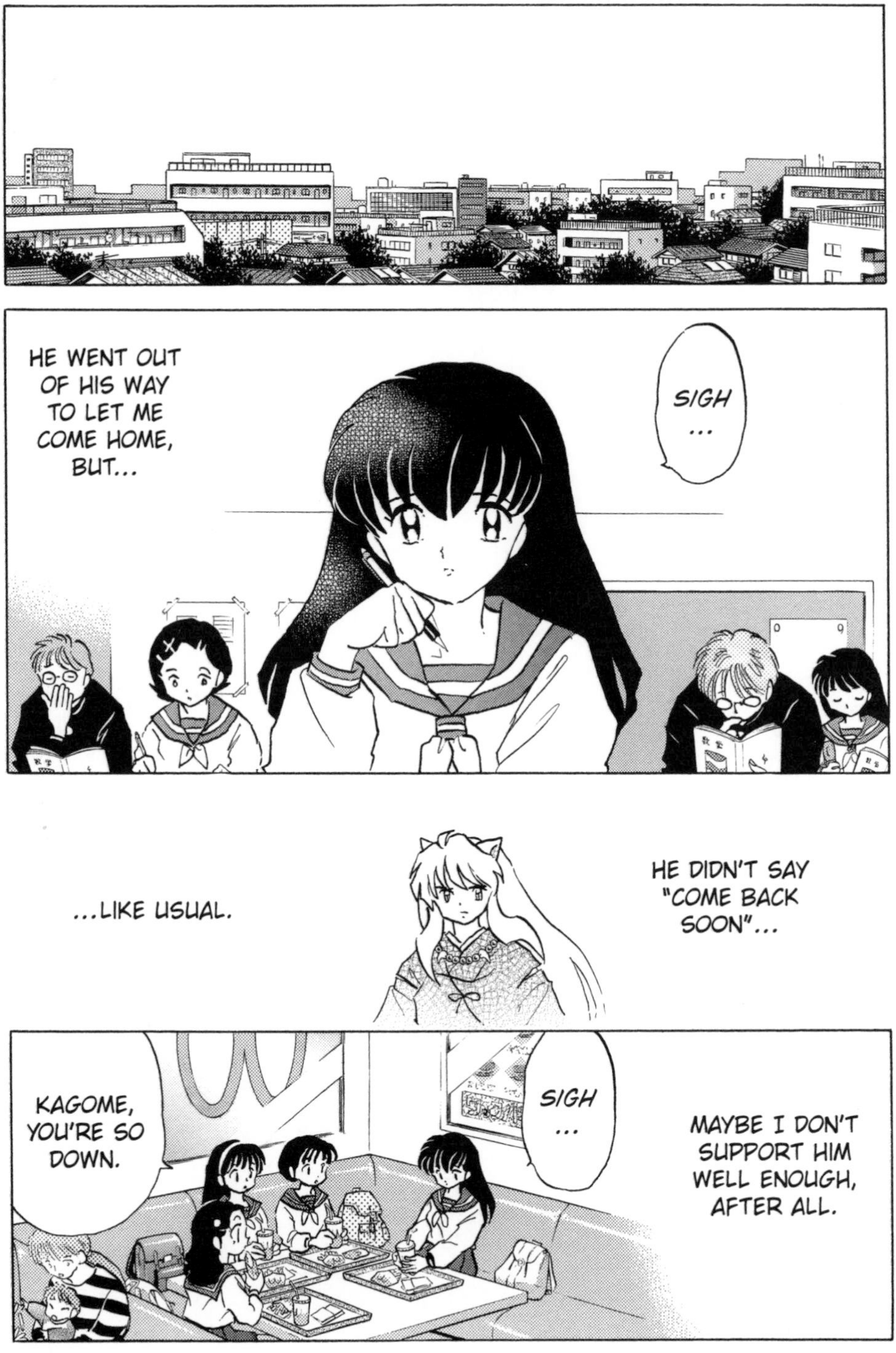
SIGH...
HE WENT OUT OF HIS WAY TO LET ME COME HOME, BUT...
HE DIDN'T SAY "COME BACK SOON"...
...LIKE USUAL.
MAYBE I DON'T SUPPORT HIM WELL ENOUGH, AFTER ALL.
SIGH...
KAGOME, YOU'RE SO DOWN.

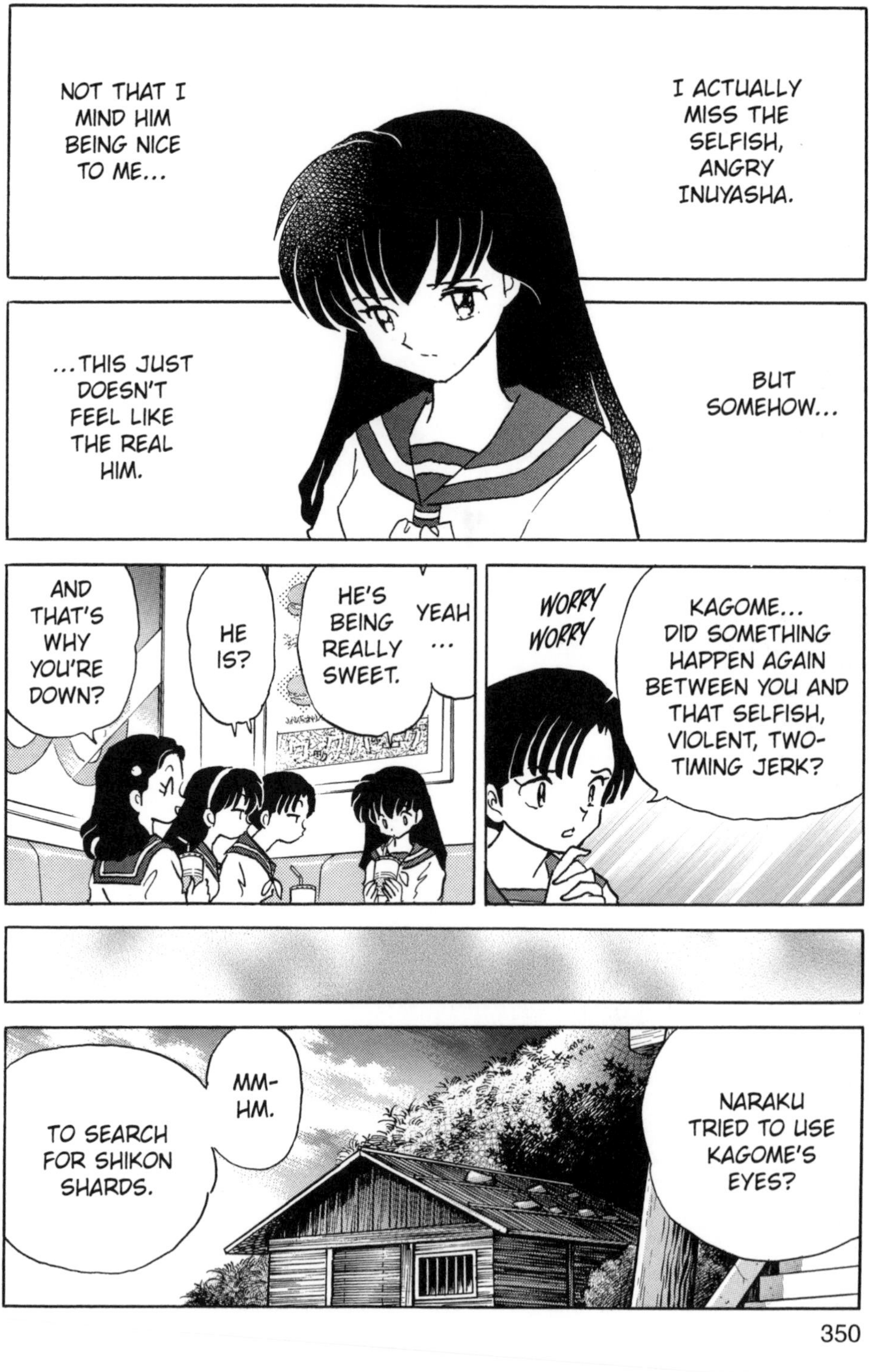
I ACTUALLY MISS THE SELFISH, ANGRY INUYASHA.
NOT THAT I MIND HIM BEING NICE TO ME...
BUT SOMEHOW...
...THIS JUST DOESN'T FEEL LIKE THE REAL HIM.
WORRY WORRY
KAGOME... DID SOMETHING HAPPEN AGAIN BETWEEN YOU AND THAT SELFISH, VIOLENT, TWO-TIMING JERK?
YEAH...
HE'S BEING REALLY SWEET.
HE IS?
AND THAT'S WHY YOU'RE DOWN?
NARAKU TRIED TO USE KAGOME'S EYES?
MM-HM.
TO SEARCH FOR SHIKON SHARDS.

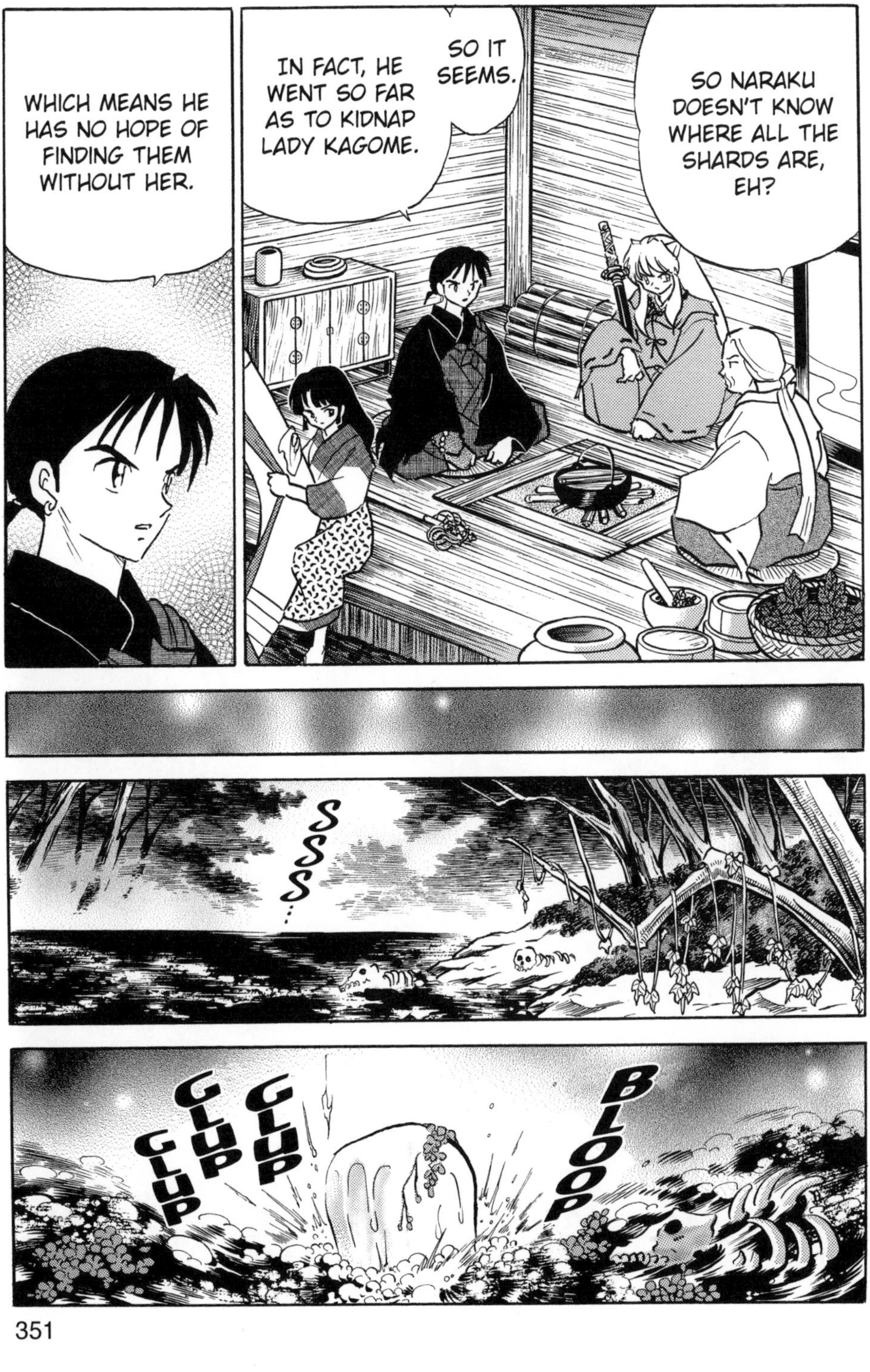
SO NARAKU DOESN'T KNOW WHERE ALL THE SHARDS ARE, EH?
SO IT SEEMS.
IN FACT, HE WENT SO FAR AS TO KIDNAP LADY KAGOME.
WHICH MEANS HE HAS NO HOPE OF FINDING THEM WITHOUT HER.
SSS...
BLOOP
GLUP
GLUP
GLUP

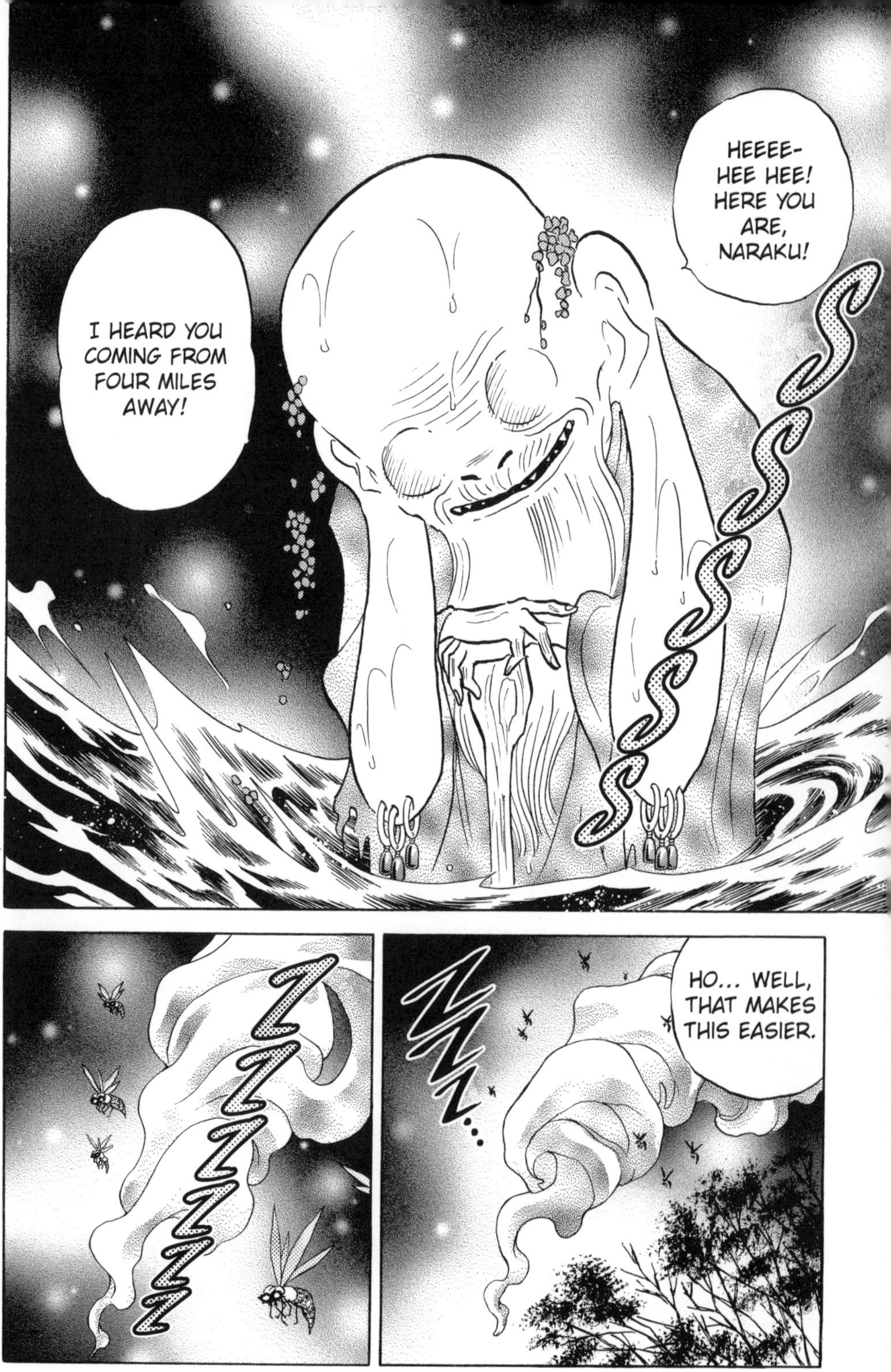
HEEEE-HEE HEE! HERE YOU ARE, NARAKU!
I HEARD YOU COMING FROM FOUR MILES AWAY!
HO... WELL, THAT MAKES THIS EASIER.

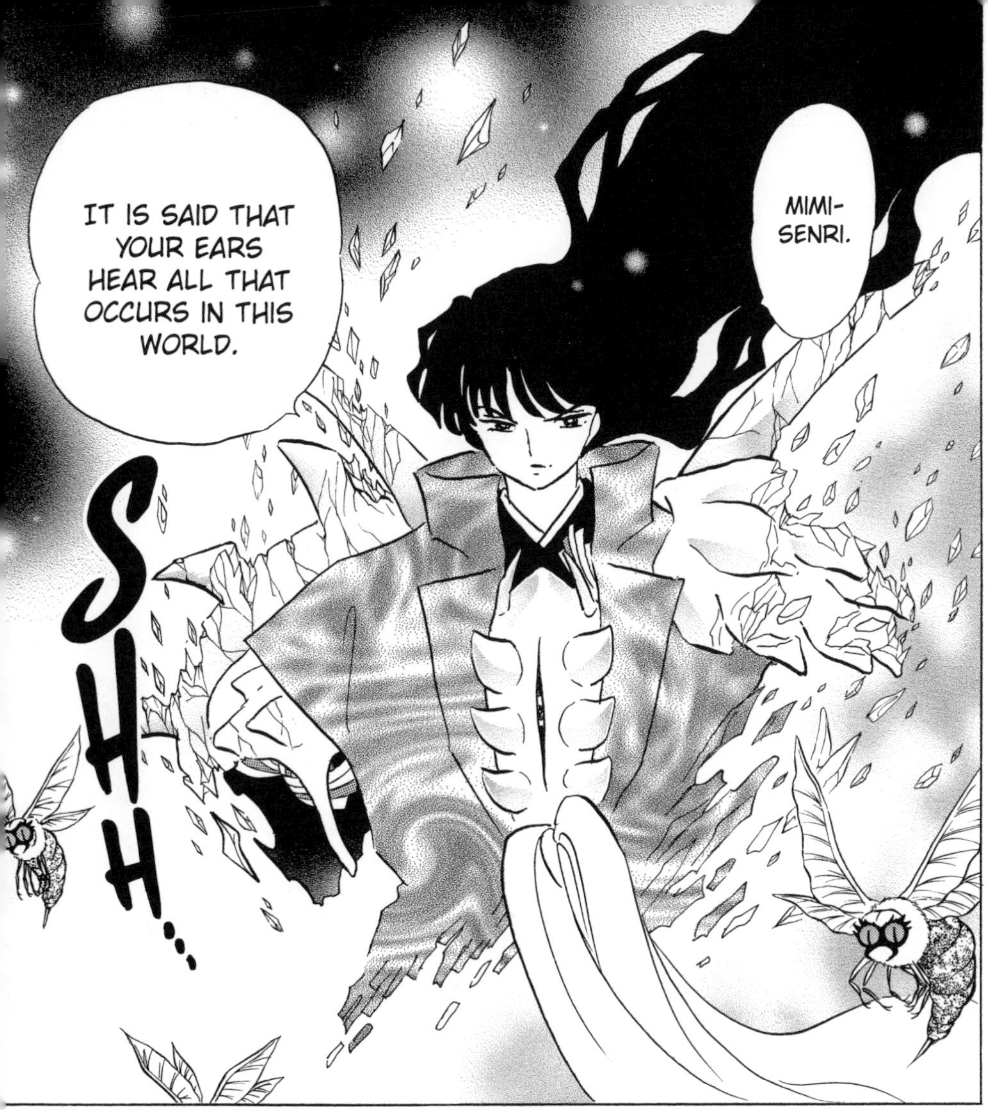
MIMI-SENRI.
IT IS SAID THAT YOUR EARS HEAR ALL THAT OCCURS IN THIS WORLD.
SHHH...

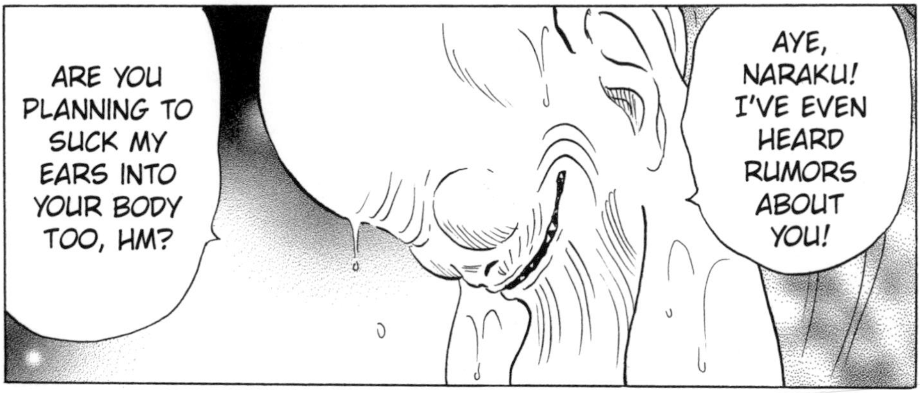
AYE, NARAKU! I'VE EVEN HEARD RUMORS ABOUT YOU!
ARE YOU PLANNING TO SUCK MY EARS INTO YOUR BODY TOO, HM?

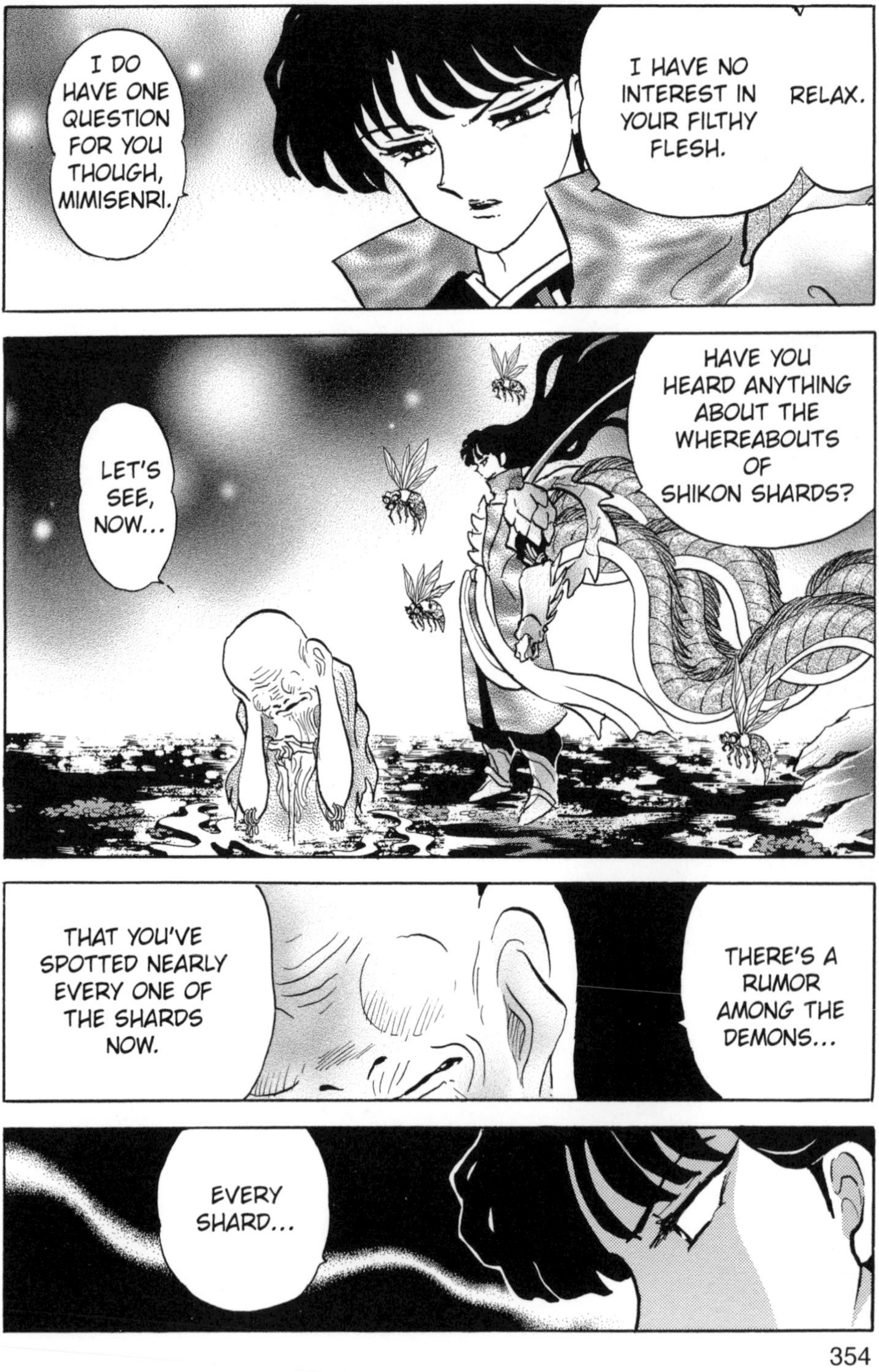
RELAX.
I HAVE NO INTEREST IN YOUR FILTHY FLESH.
I DO HAVE ONE QUESTION FOR YOU THOUGH, MIMISENRI.
HAVE YOU HEARD ANYTHING ABOUT THE WHEREABOUTS OF SHIKON SHARDS?
LET'S SEE, NOW...
THERE'S A RUMOR AMONG THE DEMONS...
THAT YOU'VE SPOTTED NEARLY EVERY ONE OF THE SHARDS NOW.
EVERY SHARD...

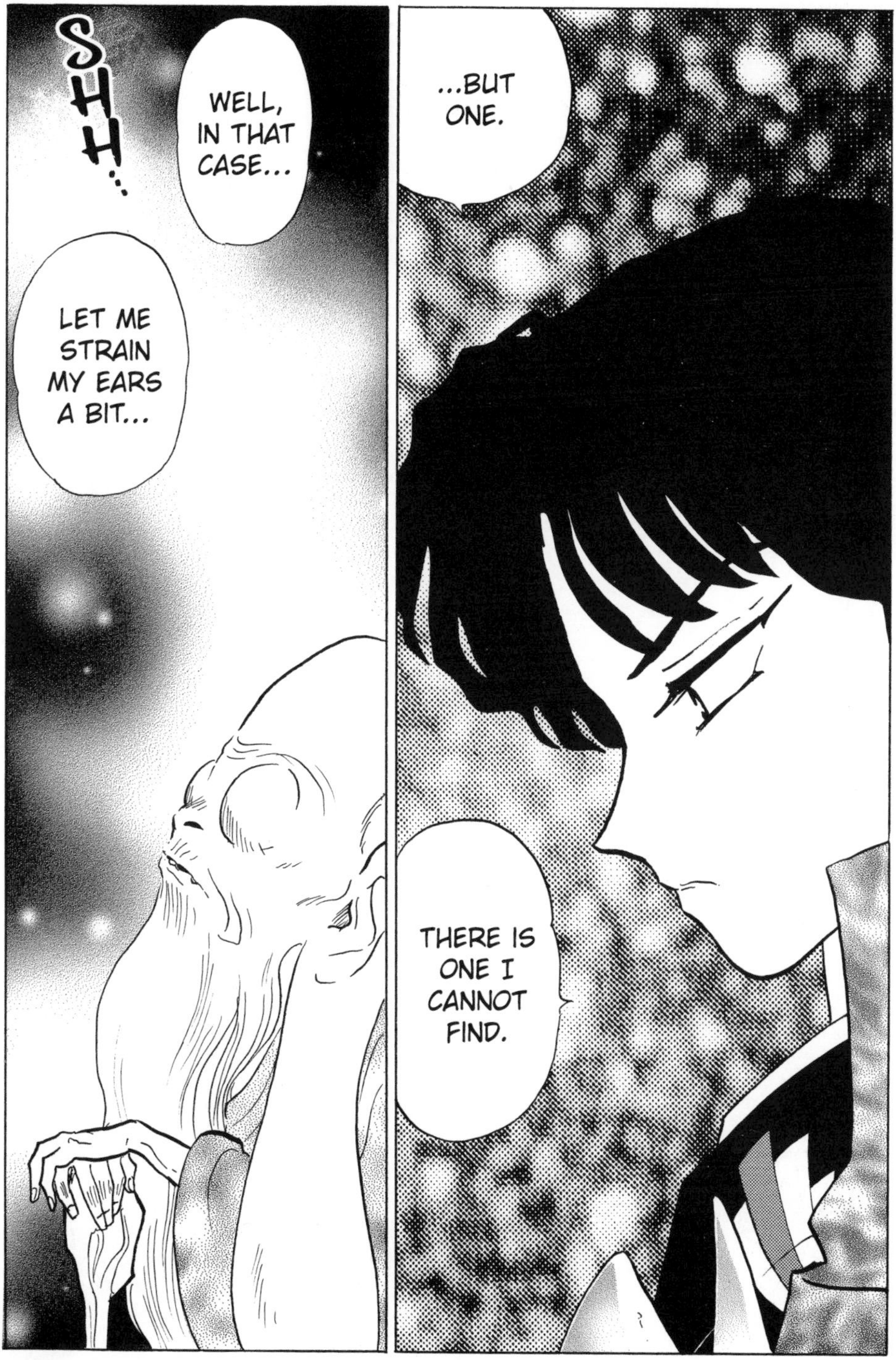
...BUT ONE.
THERE IS ONE I CANNOT FIND.
WELL, IN THAT CASE...
SHH...
LET ME STRAIN MY EARS A BIT...

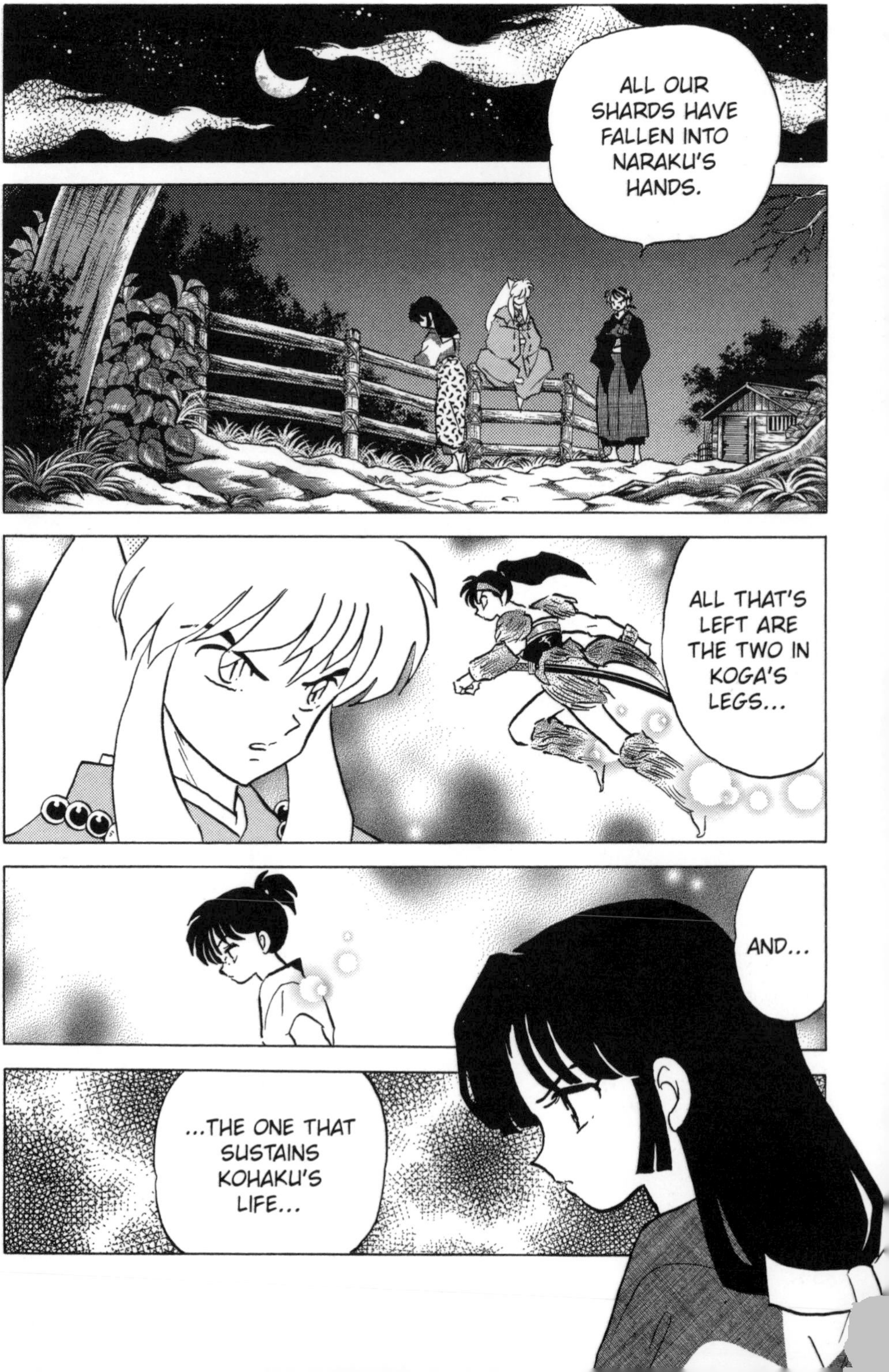
ALL OUR SHARDS HAVE FALLEN INTO NARAKU'S HANDS.
ALL THAT'S LEFT ARE THE TWO IN KOGA'S LEGS...
AND...
...THE ONE THAT SUSTAINS KOHAKU'S LIFE...

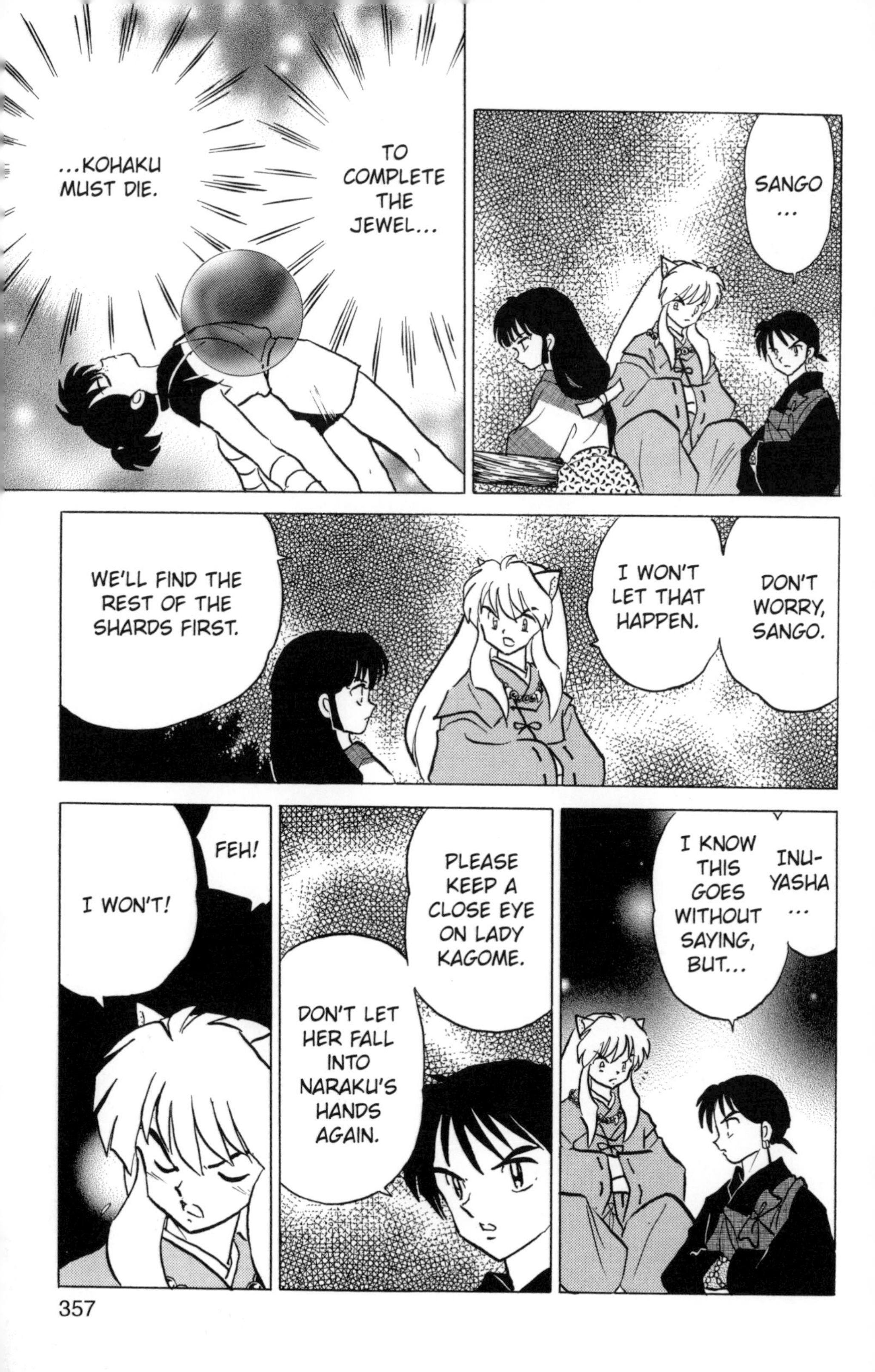
SANGO...
TO COMPLETE THE JEWEL...
...KOHAKU MUST DIE.
DON'T WORRY, SANGO.
I WON'T LET THAT HAPPEN.
WE'LL FIND THE REST OF THE SHARDS FIRST.
INU-YASHA...
I KNOW THIS GOES WITHOUT SAYING, BUT...
PLEASE KEEP A CLOSE EYE ON LADY KAGOME.
DON'T LET HER FALL INTO NARAKU'S HANDS AGAIN.
FEH!
I WON'T!

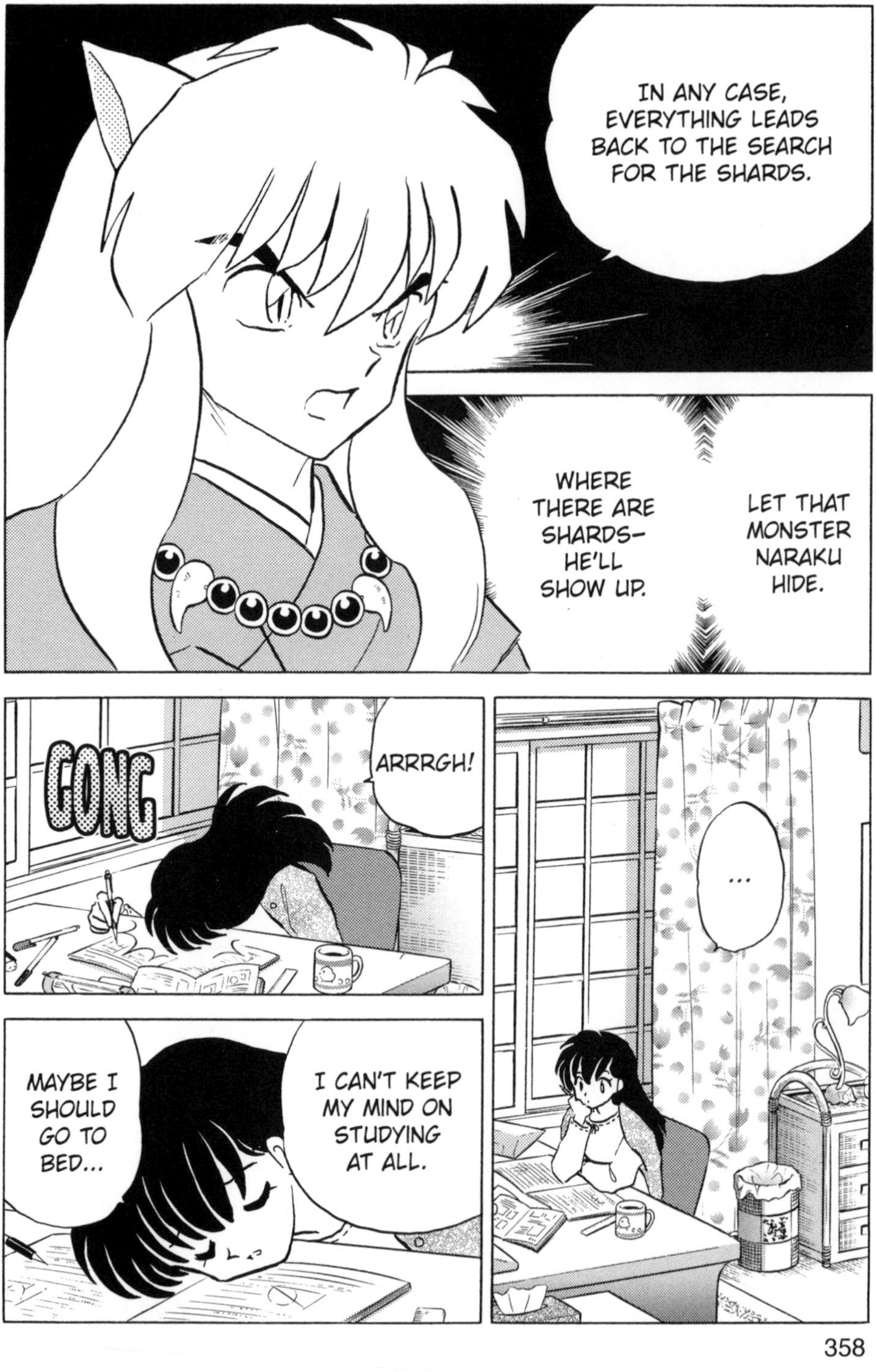
IN ANY CASE, EVERYTHING LEADS BACK TO THE SEARCH FOR THE SHARDS.
LET THAT MONSTER NARAKU HIDE.
WHERE THERE ARE SHARDS— HE'LL SHOW UP.
...
ARRRGH!
GONG
I CAN'T KEEP MY MIND ON STUDYING AT ALL.
MAYBE I SHOULD GO TO BED...

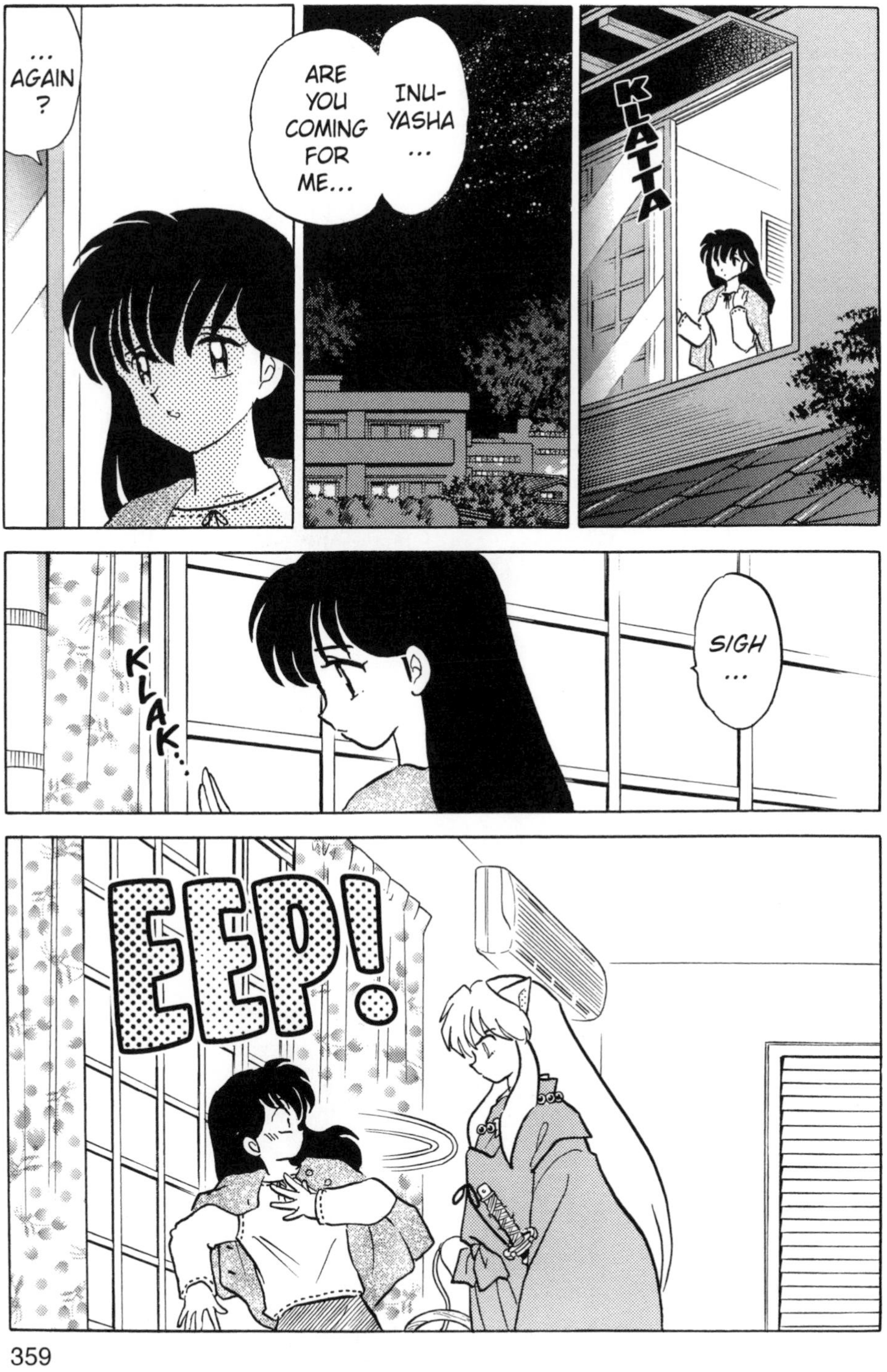
KLATTA
INU-YASHA...
ARE YOU COMING FOR ME...
...AGAIN?
SIGH...
KLAK...
EEP!

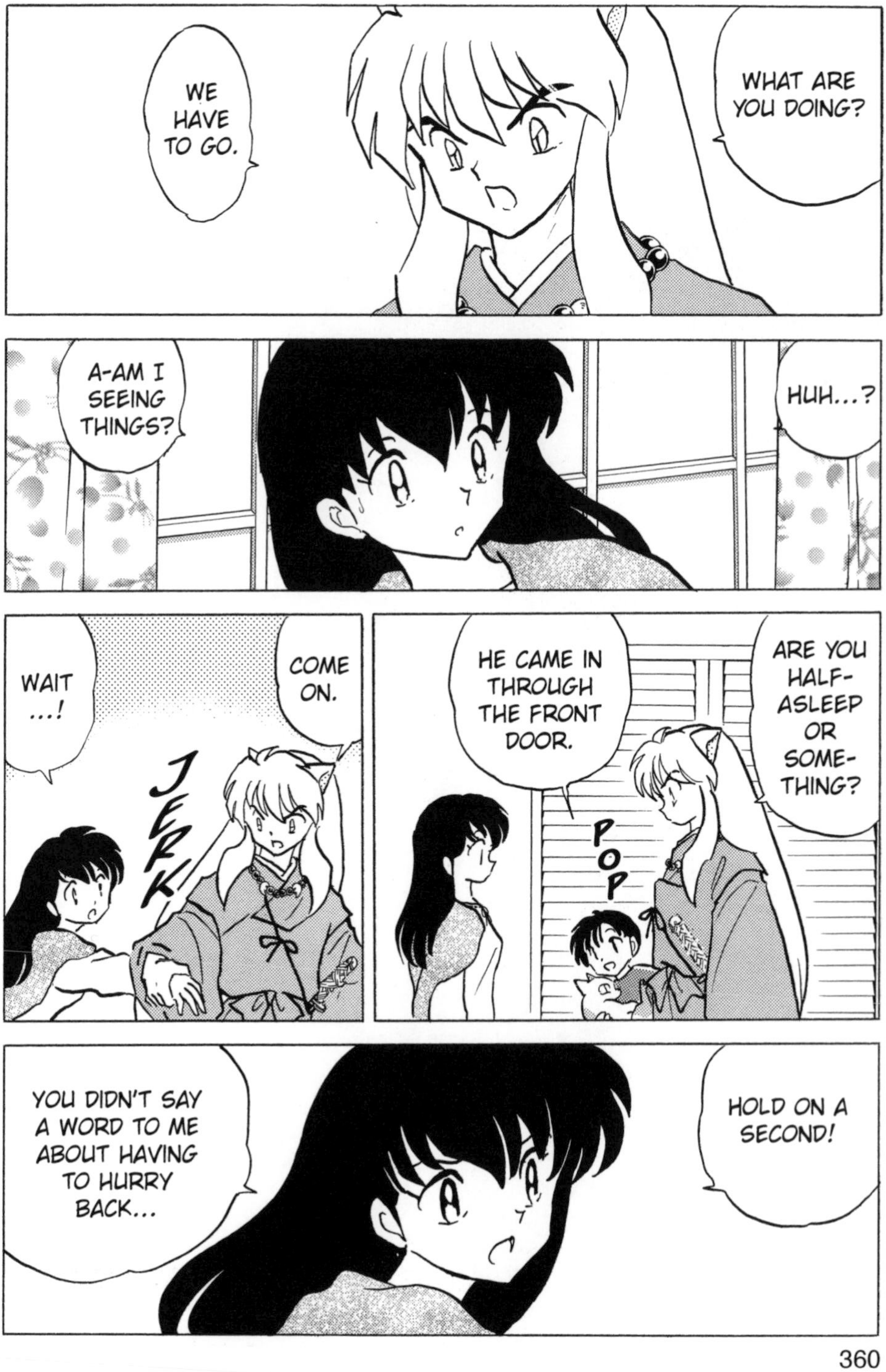
WHAT ARE YOU DOING?
WE HAVE TO GO.
HUH...?
A-AM I SEEING THINGS?
ARE YOU HALF-ASLEEP OR SOMETHING?
HE CAME IN THROUGH THE FRONT DOOR.
POP
COME ON.
JERK
WAIT...!
HOLD ON A SECOND!
YOU DIDN'T SAY A WORD TO ME ABOUT HAVING TO HURRY BACK...

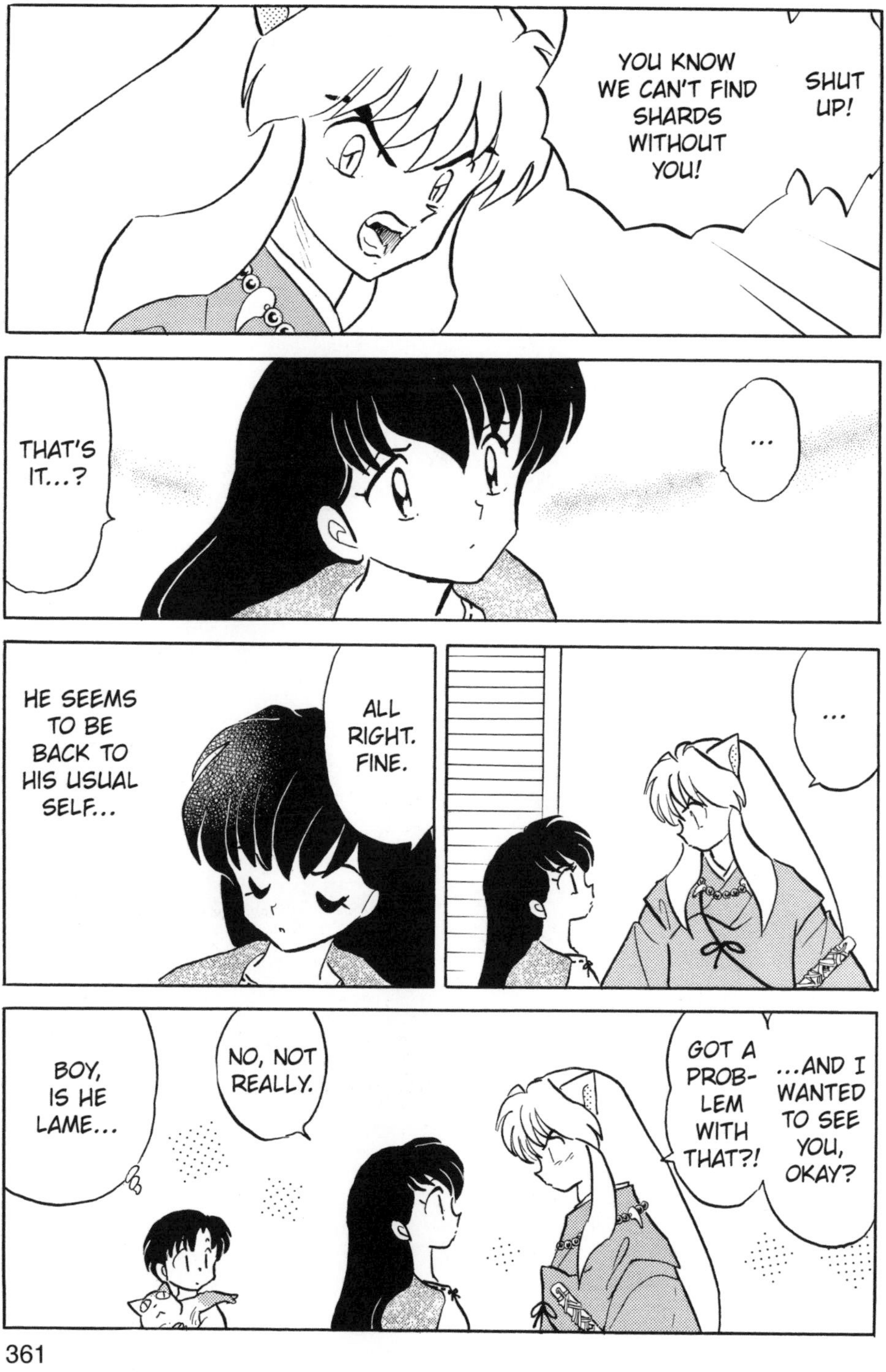
SHUT UP!
YOU KNOW WE CAN'T FIND SHARDS WITHOUT YOU!
...
THAT'S IT...?
...
ALL RIGHT. FINE.
HE SEEMS TO BE BACK TO HIS USUAL SELF...
...AND I WANTED TO SEE YOU, OKAY?
GOT A PROB-LEM WITH THAT?!
NO, NOT REALLY.
BOY, IS HE LAME...

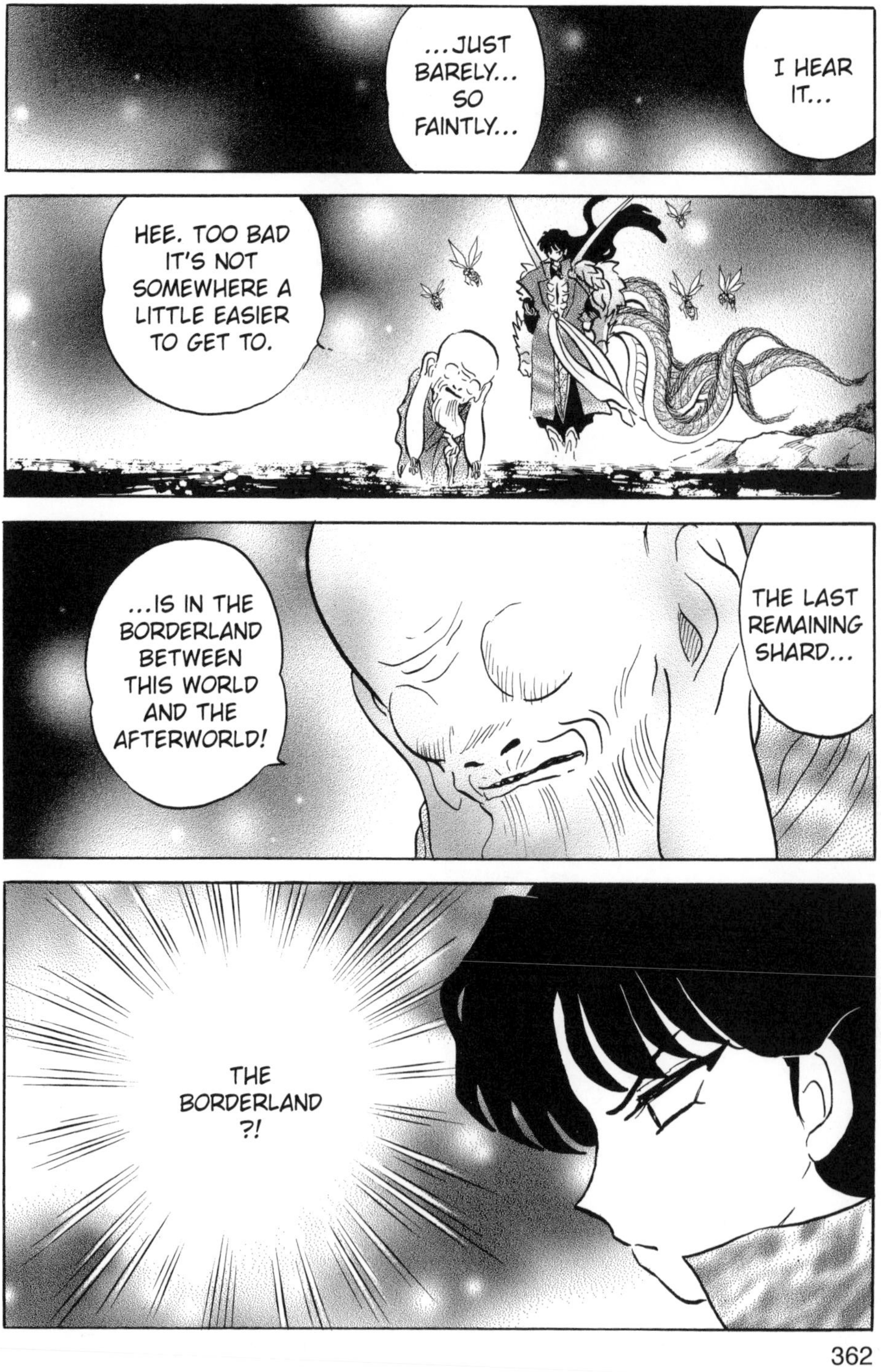
I HEAR IT...
...JUST BARELY... SO FAINTLY...
HEE. TOO BAD IT'S NOT SOMEWHERE A LITTLE EASIER TO GET TO.
THE LAST REMAINING SHARD...
...IS IN THE BORDERLAND BETWEEN THIS WORLD AND THE AFTERWORLD!
THE BORDERLAND ?!

SCROLL TEN

THE COLONY OF OGRE WOMEN

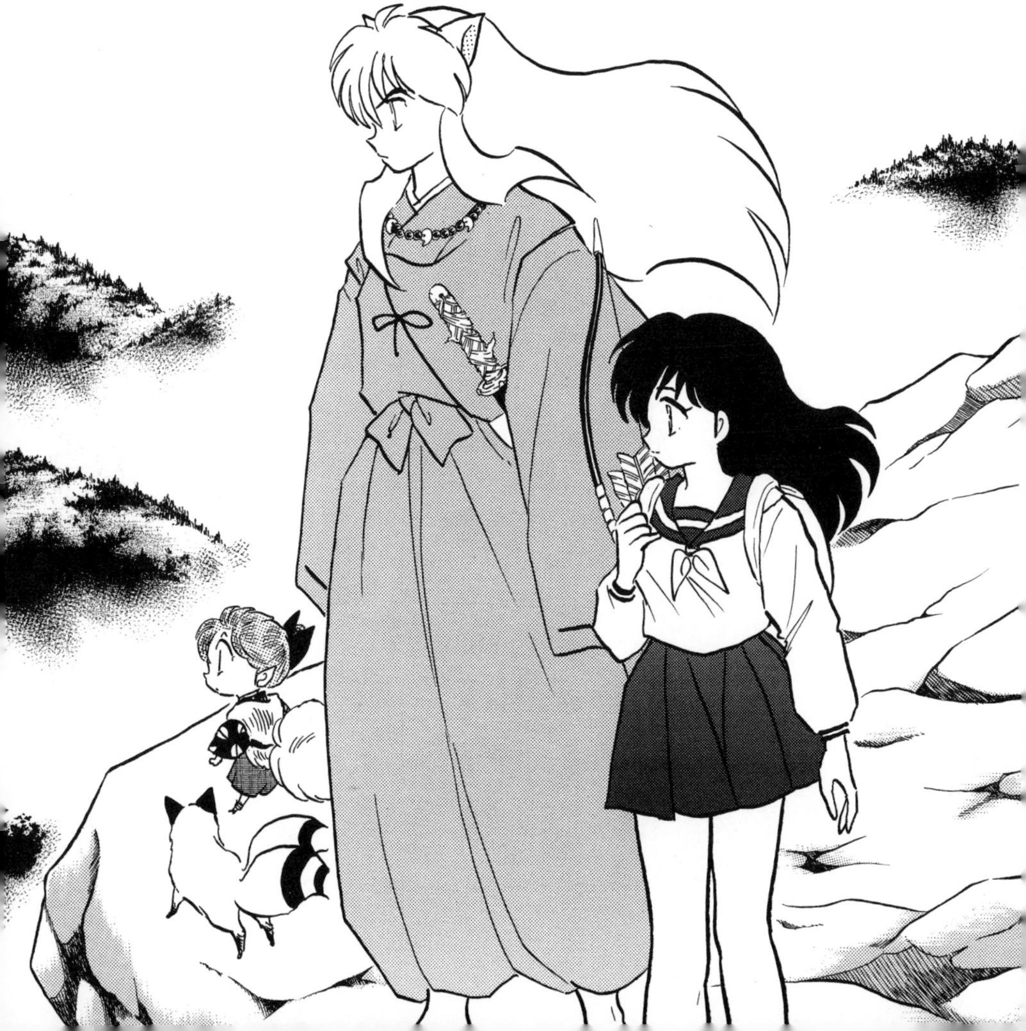

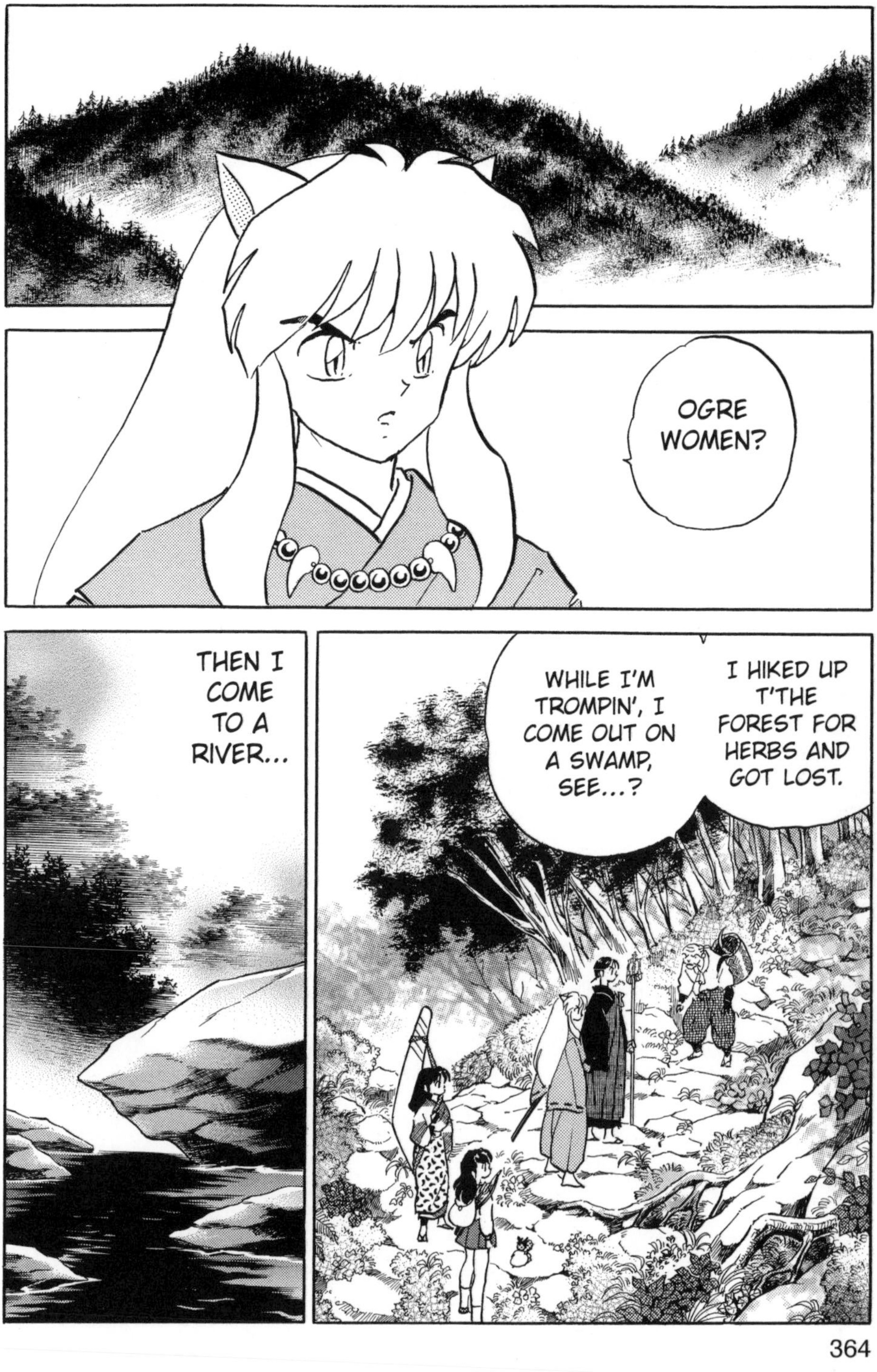
OGRE WOMEN?
I HIKED UP T'THE FOREST FOR HERBS AND GOT LOST.
WHILE I'M TROMPIN', I COME OUT ON A SWAMP, SEE...?
THEN I COME TO A RIVER...

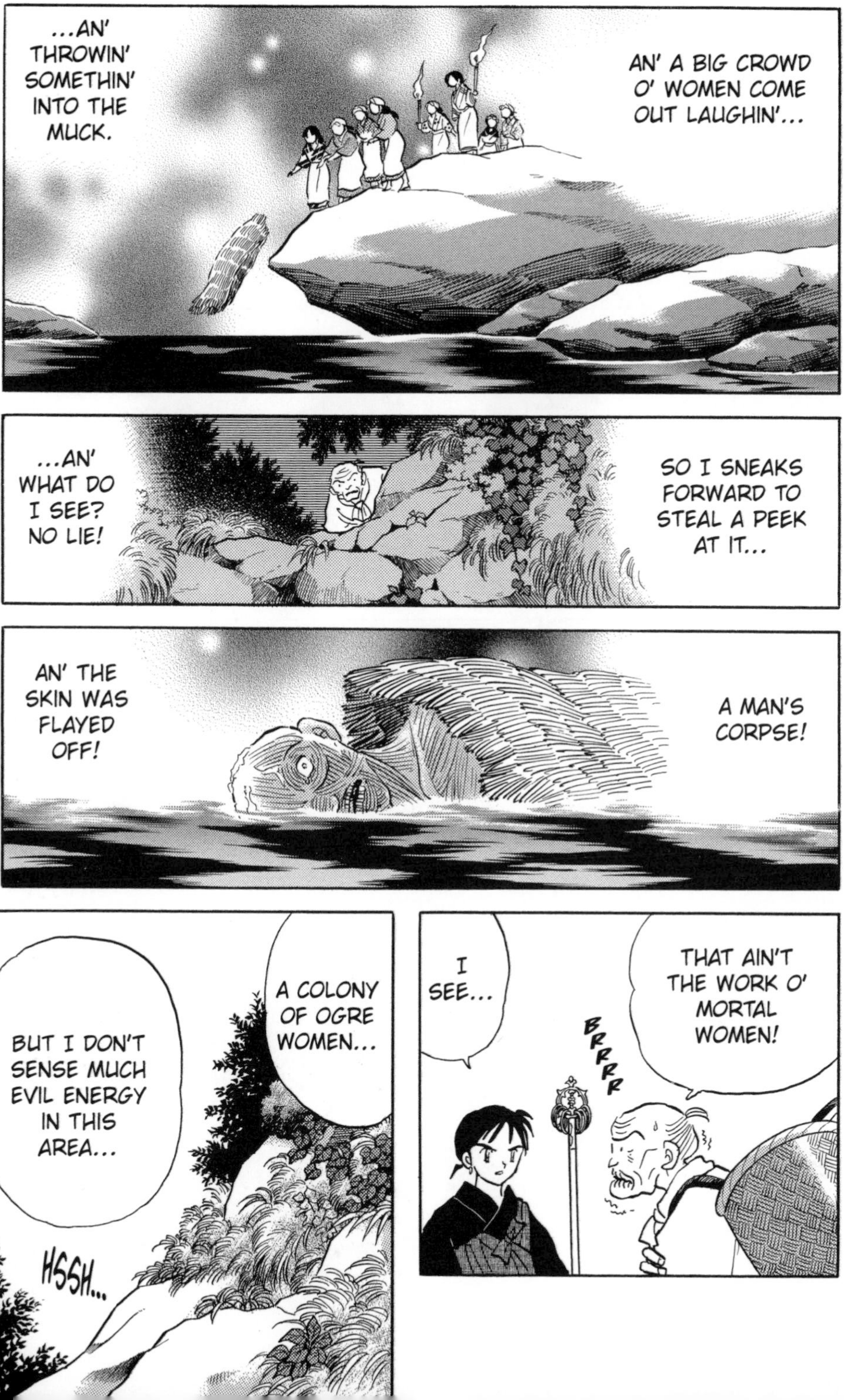
AN' A BIG CROWD O' WOMEN COME OUT LAUGHIN'...
...AN' THROWIN' SOMETHIN' INTO THE MUCK.
SO I SNEAKS FORWARD TO STEAL A PEEK AT IT...
...AN' WHAT DO I SEE? NO LIE!
A MAN'S CORPSE!
AN' THE SKIN WAS FLAYED OFF!
THAT AIN'T THE WORK O' MORTAL WOMEN!
BRRRR
I SEE...
A COLONY OF OGRE WOMEN...
BUT I DON'T SENSE MUCH EVIL ENERGY IN THIS AREA...
HSSH...

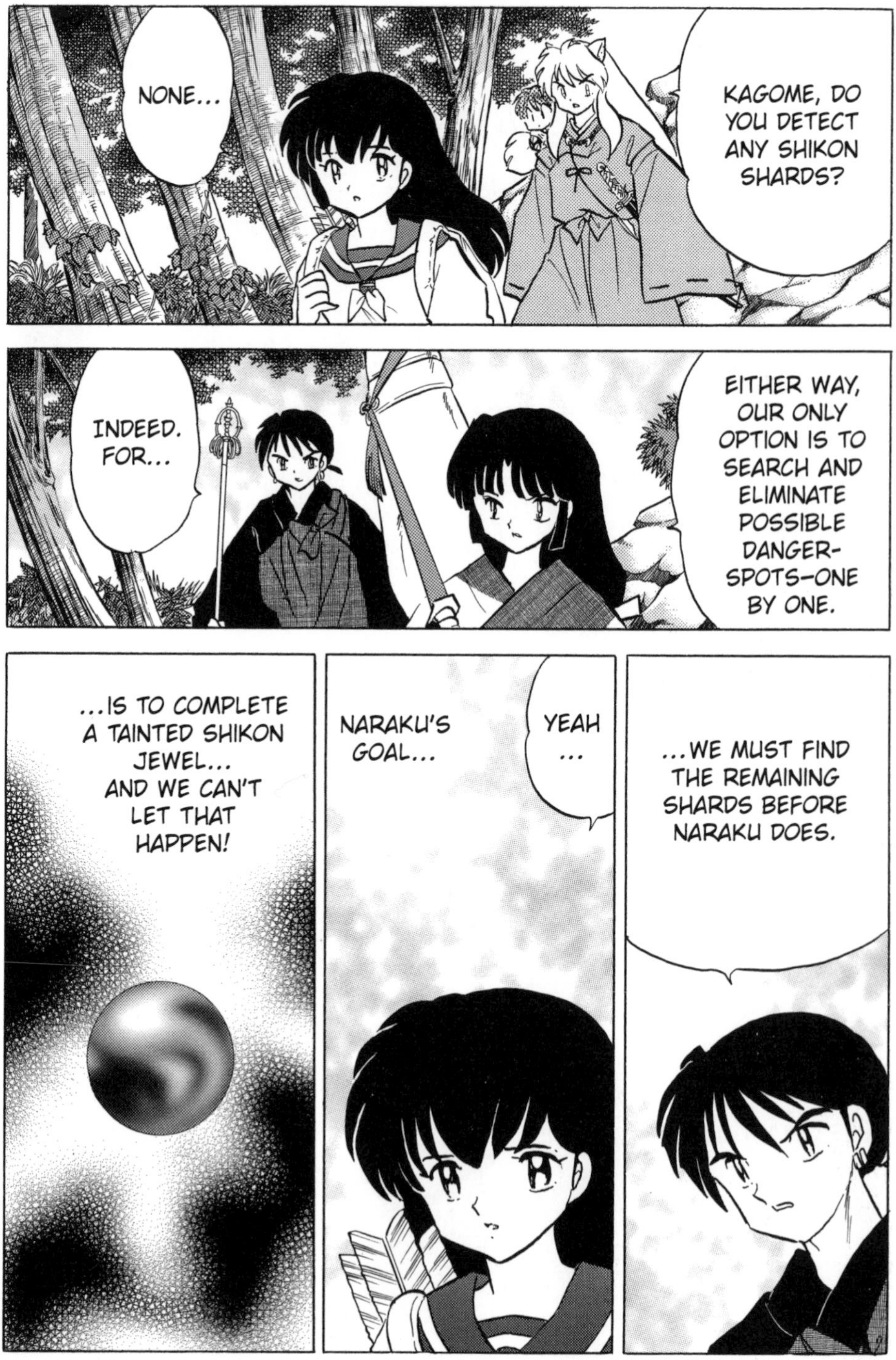
KAGOME, DO YOU DETECT ANY SHIKON SHARDS?
NONE...
EITHER WAY, OUR ONLY OPTION IS TO SEARCH AND ELIMINATE POSSIBLE DANGER-SPOTS—ONE BY ONE.
INDEED. FOR...
...WE MUST FIND THE REMAINING SHARDS BEFORE NARAKU DOES.
YEAH ...
NARAKU'S GOAL...
...IS TO COMPLETE A TAINTED SHIKON JEWEL... AND WE CAN'T LET THAT HAPPEN!

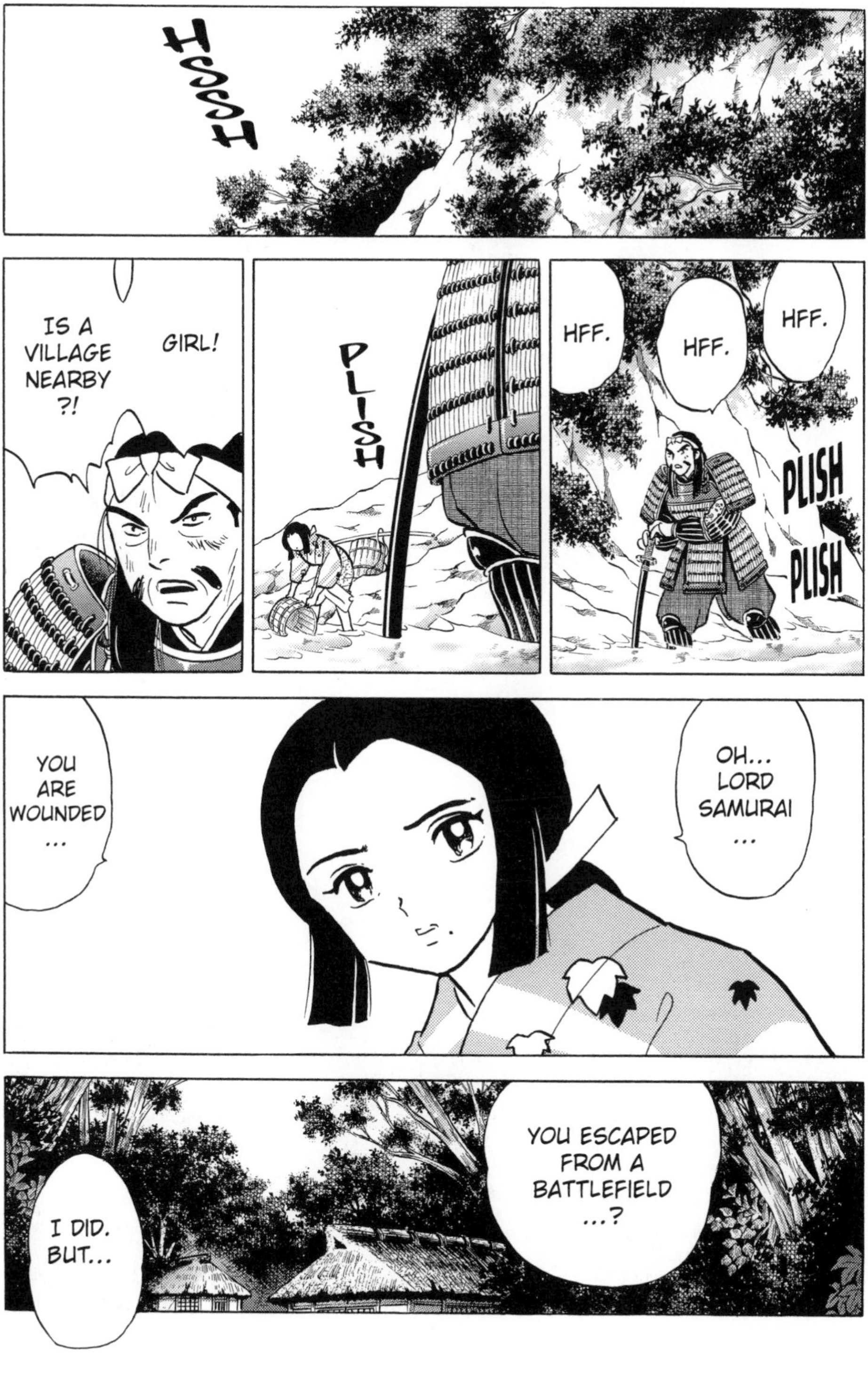
HSSSH
HFF.
HFF.
HFF.
PLISH
PLISH
PLISH
GIRL!
IS A VILLAGE NEARBY ?!
OH... LORD SAMURAI ...
YOU ARE WOUNDED ...
YOU ESCAPED FROM A BATTLEFIELD ...?
I DID. BUT...

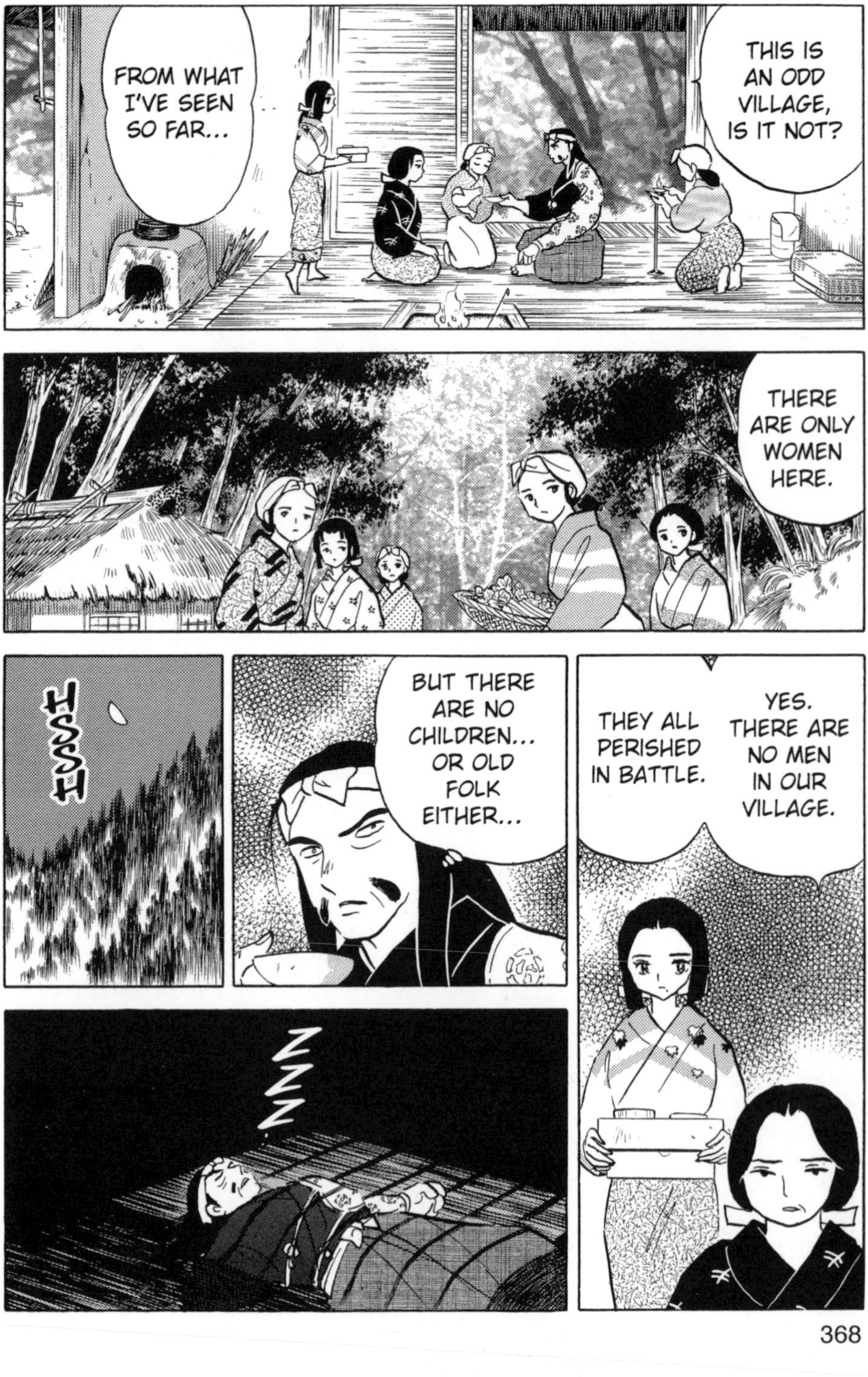
THIS IS AN ODD VILLAGE, IS IT NOT?
FROM WHAT I'VE SEEN SO FAR...
THERE ARE ONLY WOMEN HERE.
YES. THERE ARE NO MEN IN OUR VILLAGE.
THEY ALL PERISHED IN BATTLE.
BUT THERE ARE NO CHILDREN... OR OLD FOLK EITHER...
HSSH
ZZZ

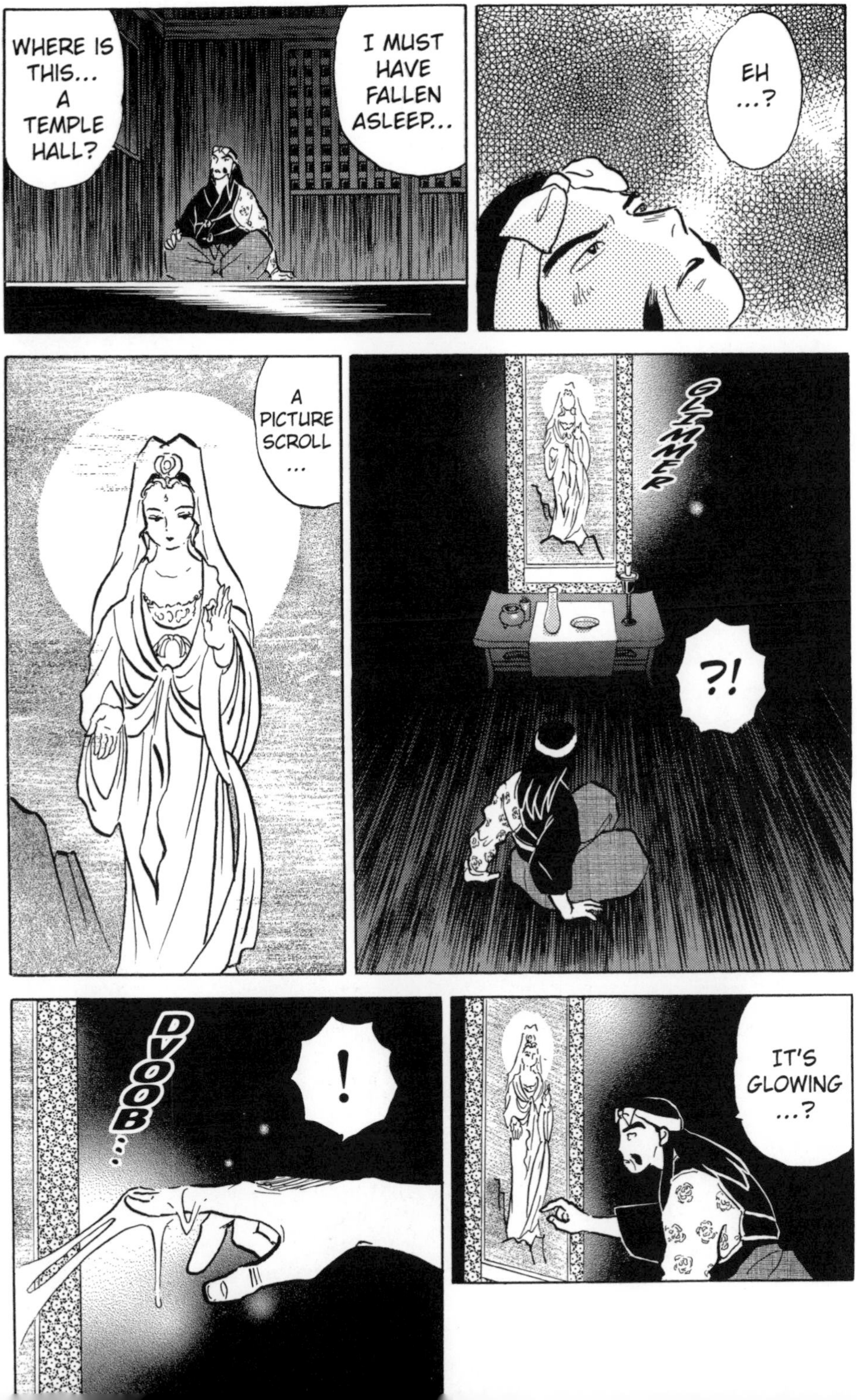
EH ...?
I MUST HAVE FALLEN ASLEEP...
WHERE IS THIS... A TEMPLE HALL?
GLIMMER
?!
A PICTURE SCROLL ...
IT'S GLOWING ...?
!
DVOOB...

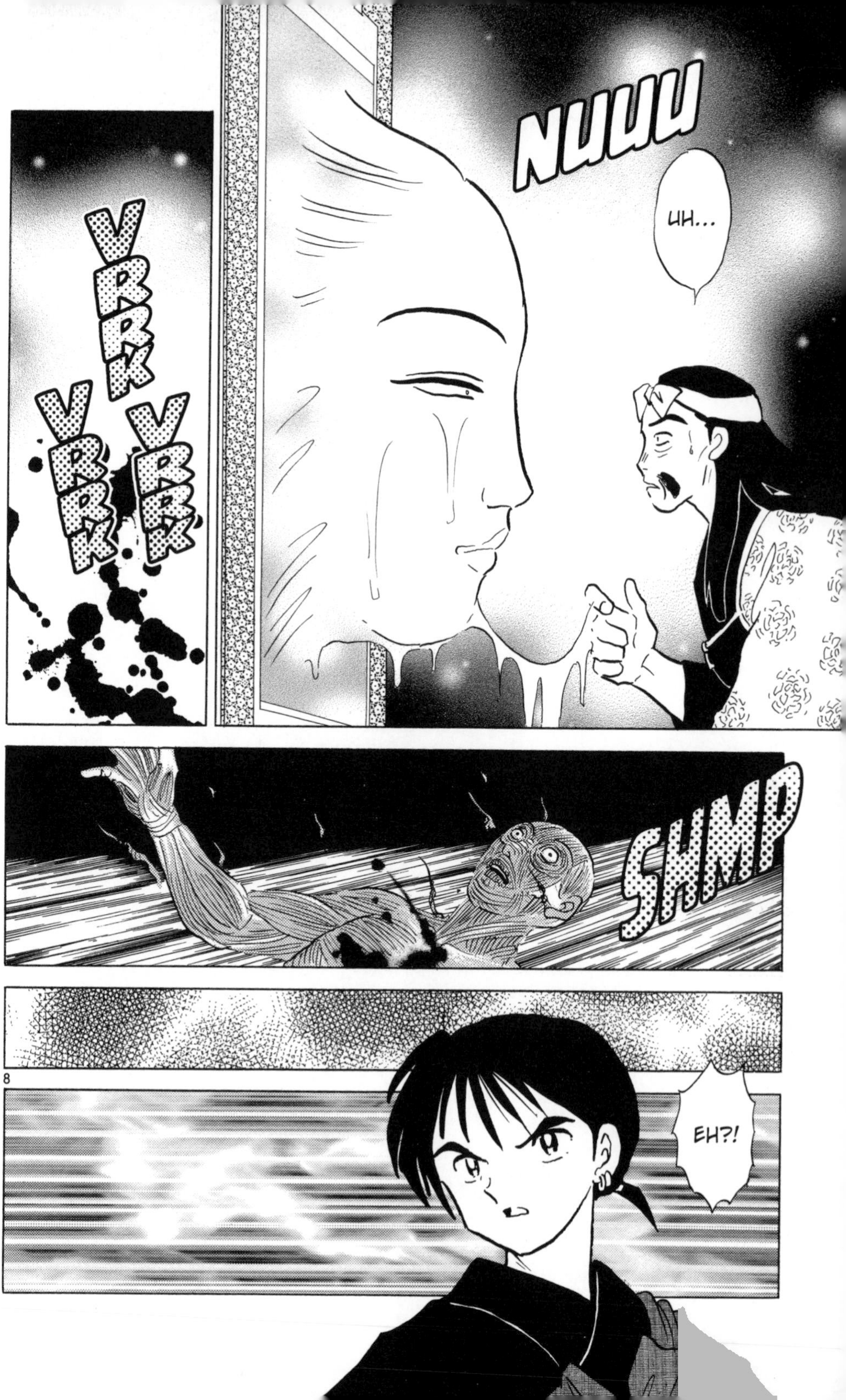
NUUU
UH...
VRRK
VRRK
VRRK
SHMP
EH?!
8

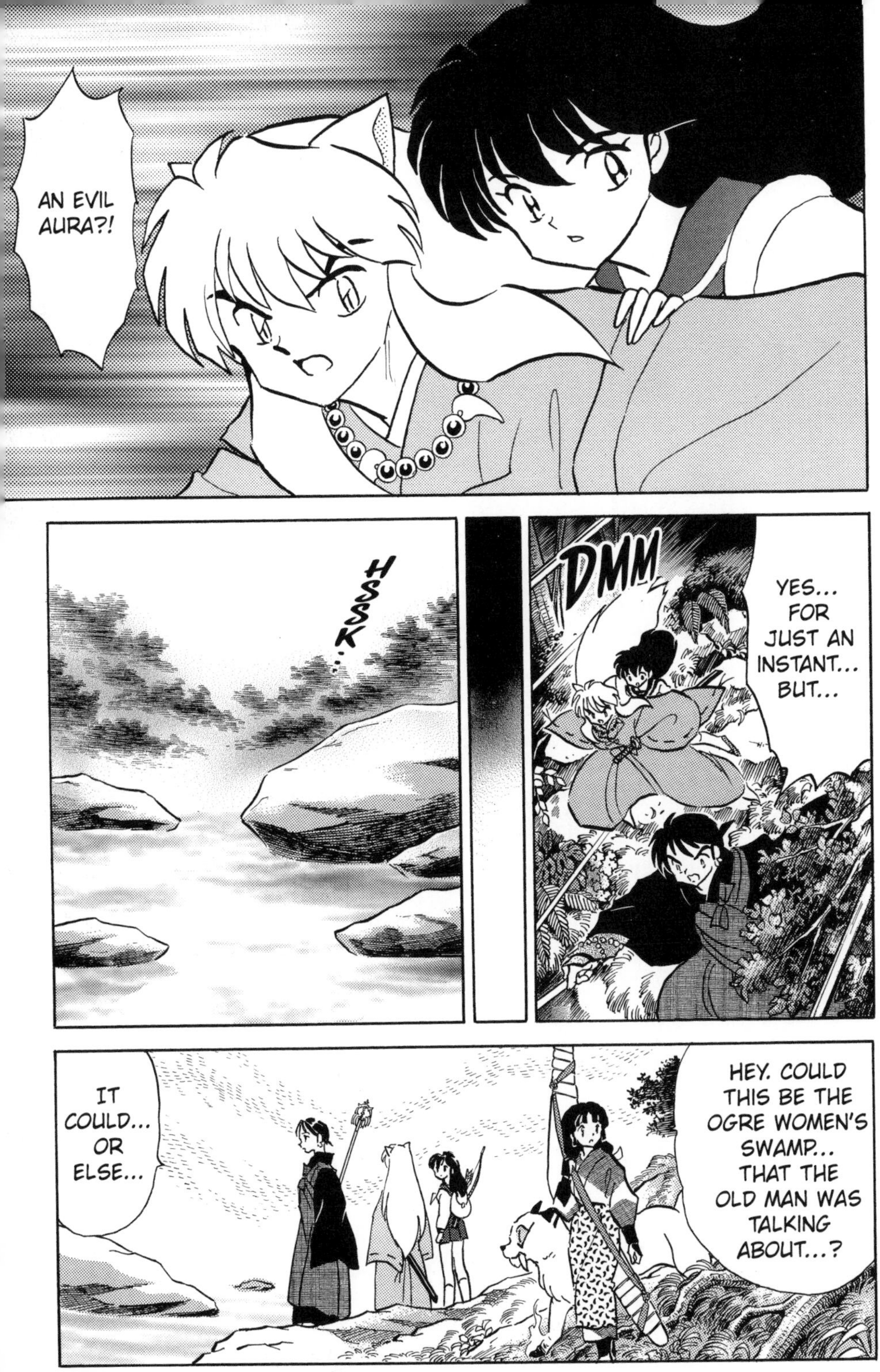
AN EVIL AURA?!
YES... FOR JUST AN INSTANT... BUT...
DMM
HSSK...
HEY. COULD THIS BE THE OGRE WOMEN'S SWAMP... THAT THE OLD MAN WAS TALKING ABOUT...?
IT COULD... OR ELSE...

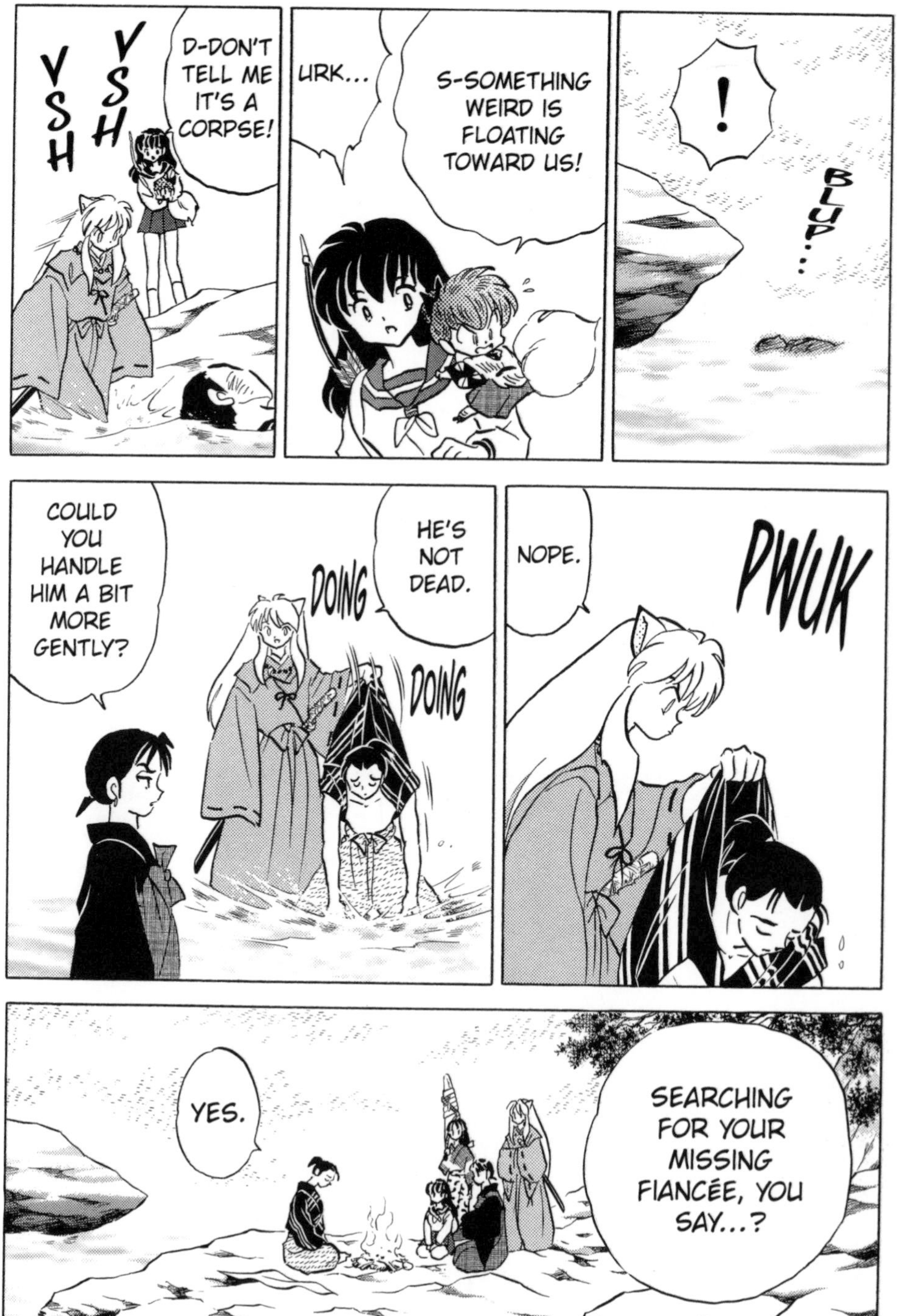
!
BLUP...
URK...
S-SOMETHING WEIRD IS FLOATING TOWARD US!
VSH VSH
D-DON'T TELL ME IT'S A CORPSE!
PWUK
NOPE.
HE'S NOT DEAD.
DOING DOING
COULD YOU HANDLE HIM A BIT MORE GENTLY?
SEARCHING FOR YOUR MISSING FIANCÉE, YOU SAY...?
YES.

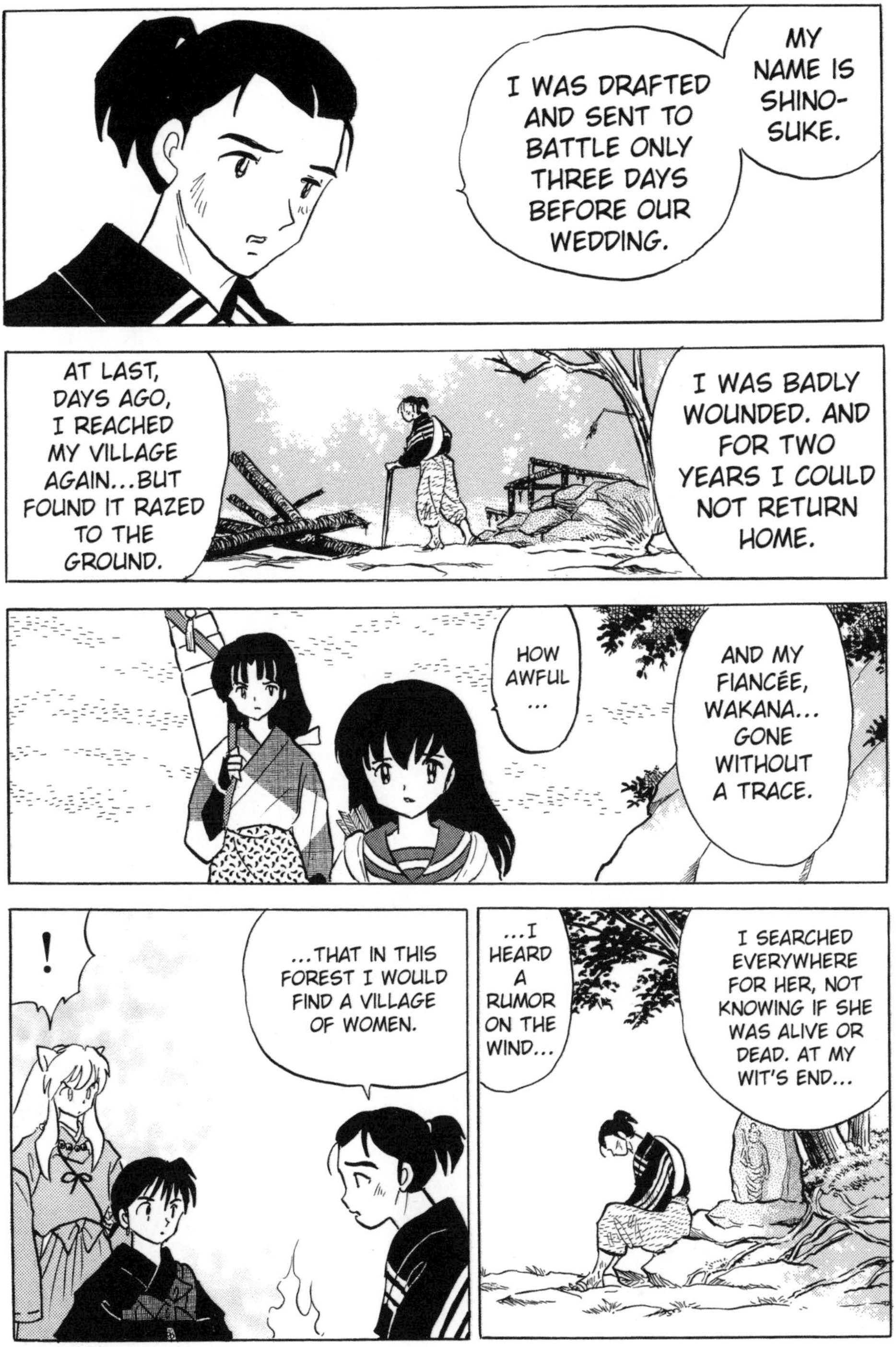
MY NAME IS SHINO-SUKE.
I WAS DRAFTED AND SENT TO BATTLE ONLY THREE DAYS BEFORE OUR WEDDING.
I WAS BADLY WOUNDED. AND FOR TWO YEARS I COULD NOT RETURN HOME.
AT LAST, DAYS AGO, I REACHED MY VILLAGE AGAIN...BUT FOUND IT RAZED TO THE GROUND.
AND MY FIANCÉE, WAKANA... GONE WITHOUT A TRACE.
HOW AWFUL ...
I SEARCHED EVERYWHERE FOR HER, NOT KNOWING IF SHE WAS ALIVE OR DEAD. AT MY WIT'S END...
...I HEARD A RUMOR ON THE WIND...
...THAT IN THIS FOREST I WOULD FIND A VILLAGE OF WOMEN.
!

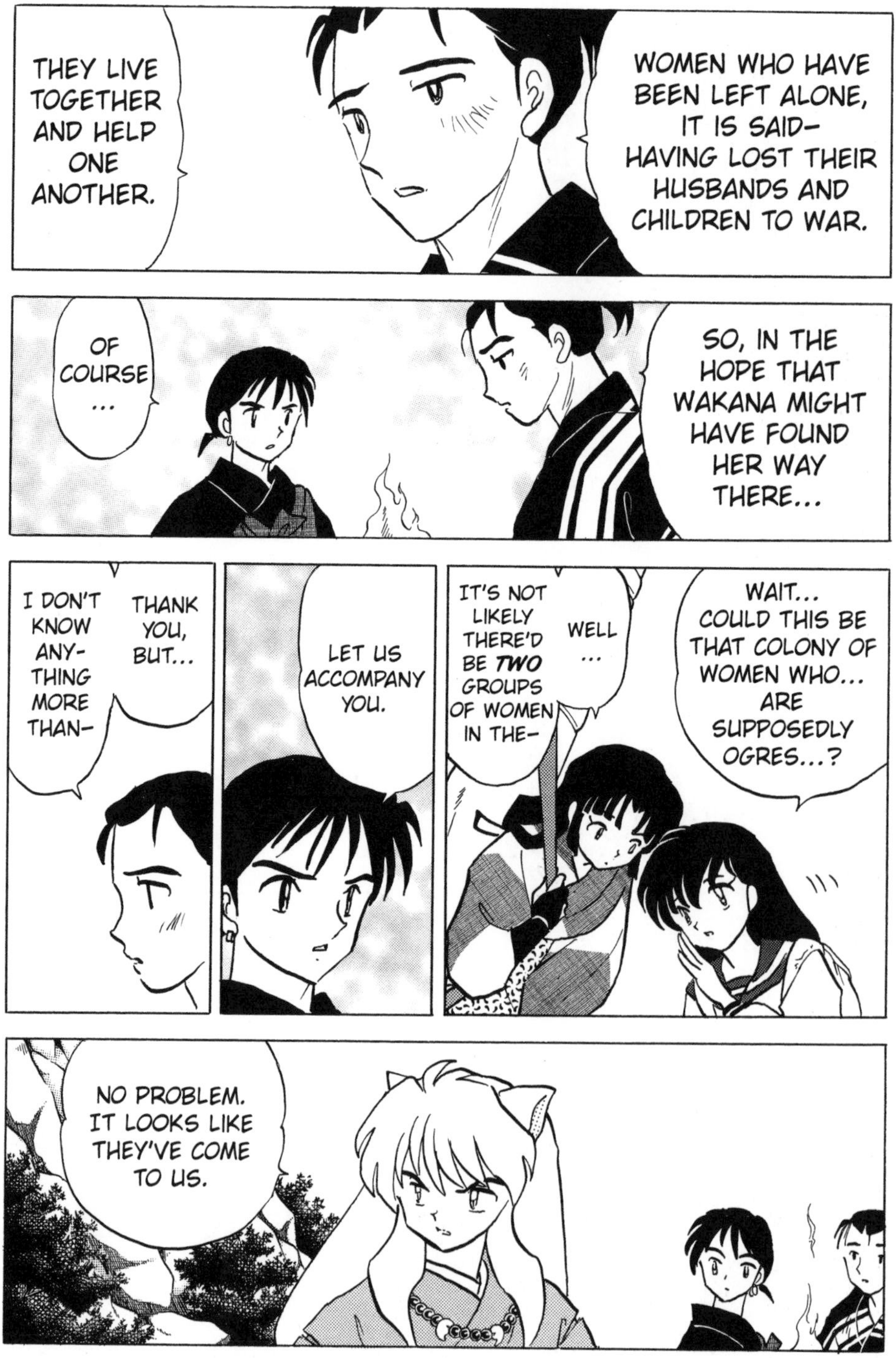
WOMEN WHO HAVE BEEN LEFT ALONE, IT IS SAID— HAVING LOST THEIR HUSBANDS AND CHILDREN TO WAR.
THEY LIVE TOGETHER AND HELP ONE ANOTHER.
SO, IN THE HOPE THAT WAKANA MIGHT HAVE FOUND HER WAY THERE...
OF COURSE ...
WAIT... COULD THIS BE THAT COLONY OF WOMEN WHO... ARE SUPPOSEDLY OGRES...?
WELL ...
IT'S NOT LIKELY THERE'D BE **TWO** GROUPS OF WOMEN IN THE—
LET US ACCOMPANY YOU.
THANK YOU, BUT...
I DON'T KNOW ANY-THING MORE THAN—
NO PROBLEM. IT LOOKS LIKE THEY'VE COME TO US.

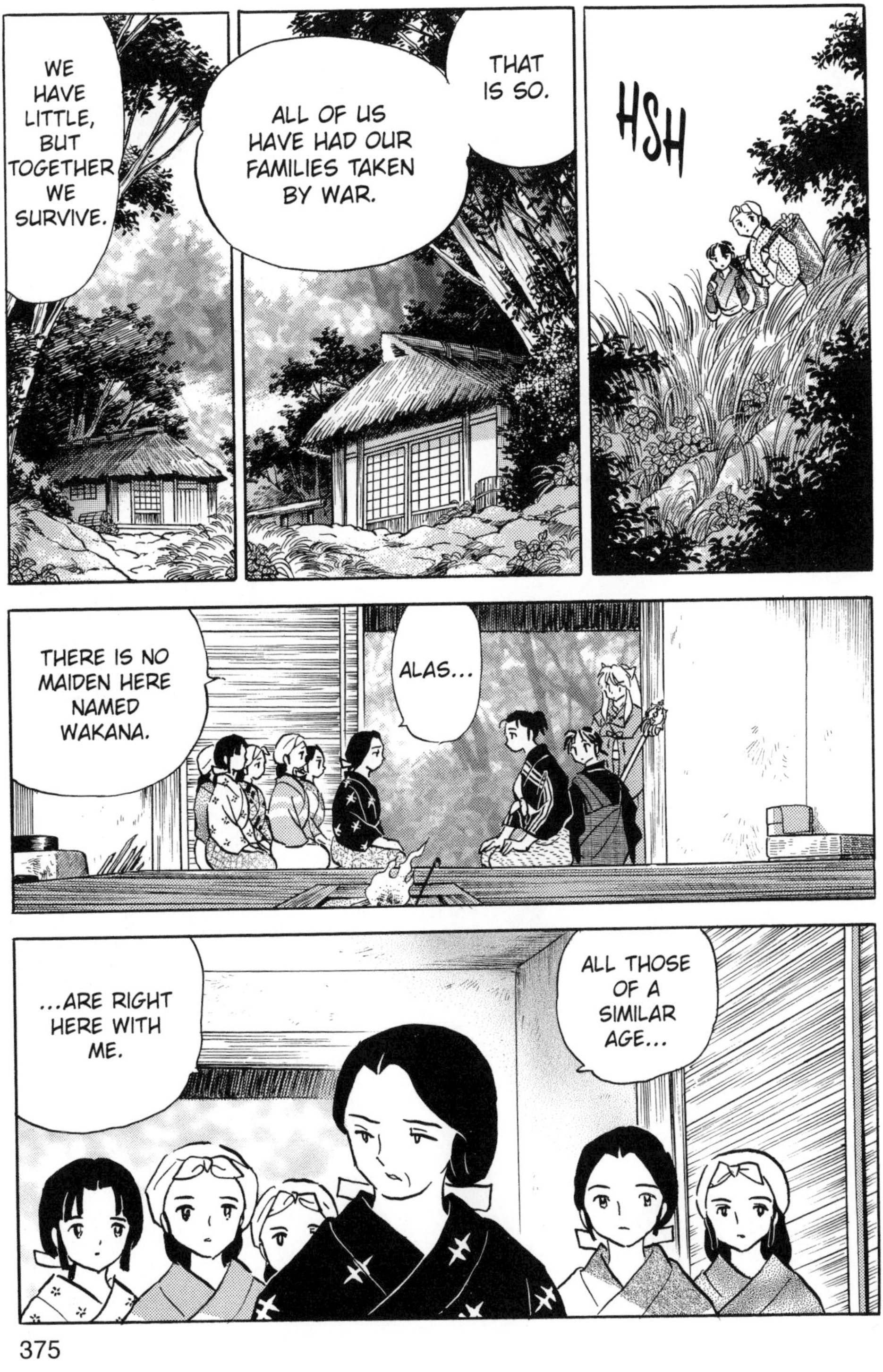
HSH
THAT IS SO.
ALL OF US HAVE HAD OUR FAMILIES TAKEN BY WAR.
WE HAVE LITTLE, BUT TOGETHER WE SURVIVE.
ALAS...
THERE IS NO MAIDEN HERE NAMED WAKANA.
ALL THOSE OF A SIMILAR AGE...
...ARE RIGHT HERE WITH ME.

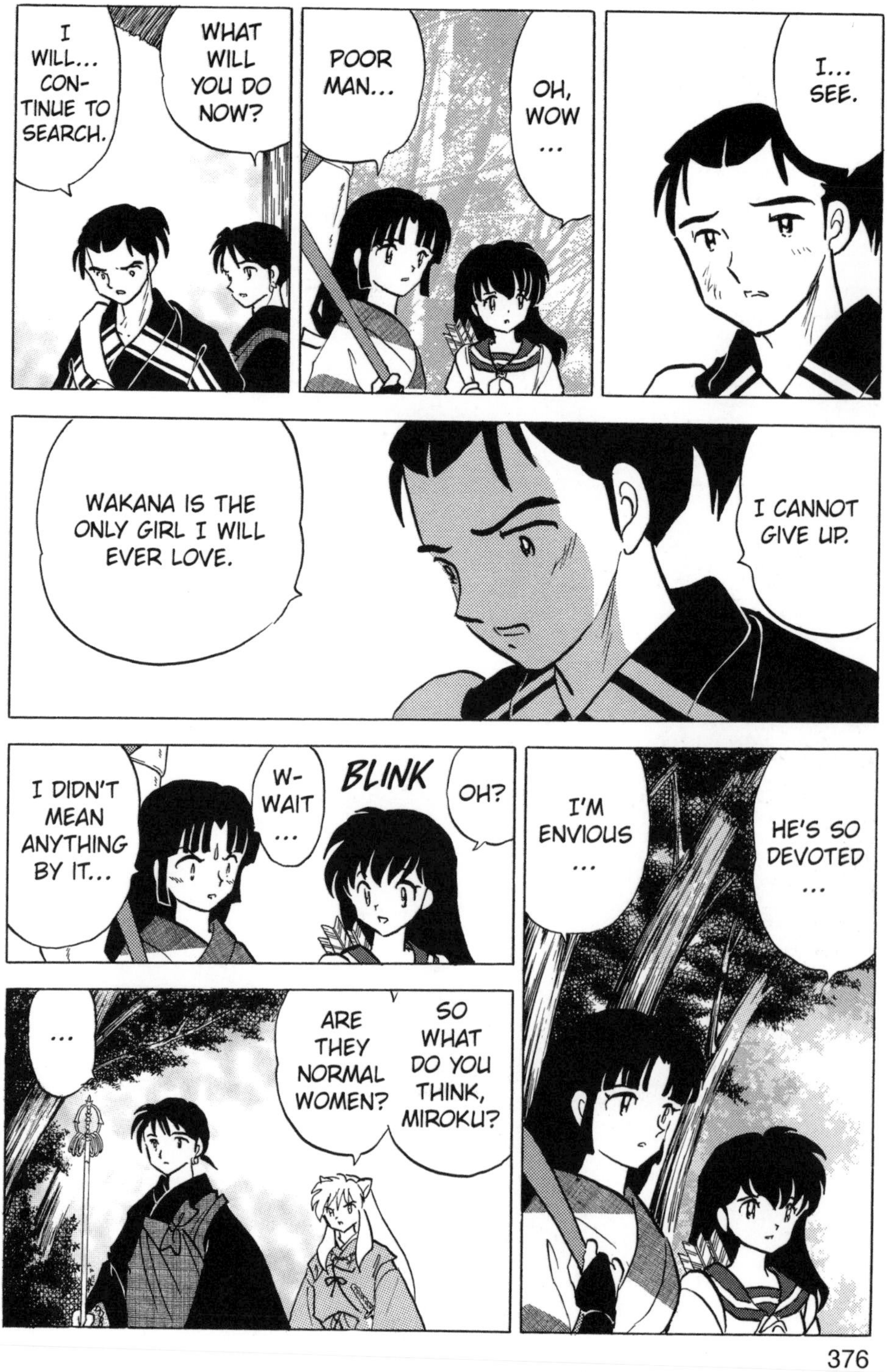
I... SEE.
OH, WOW...
POOR MAN...
WHAT WILL YOU DO NOW?
I WILL... CON-TINUE TO SEARCH.
I CANNOT GIVE UP.
WAKANA IS THE ONLY GIRL I WILL EVER LOVE.
HE'S SO DEVOTED...
I'M ENVIOUS...
OH?
BLINK
W-WAIT...
I DIDN'T MEAN ANYTHING BY IT...
SO WHAT DO YOU THINK, MIROKU?
ARE THEY NORMAL WOMEN?
...

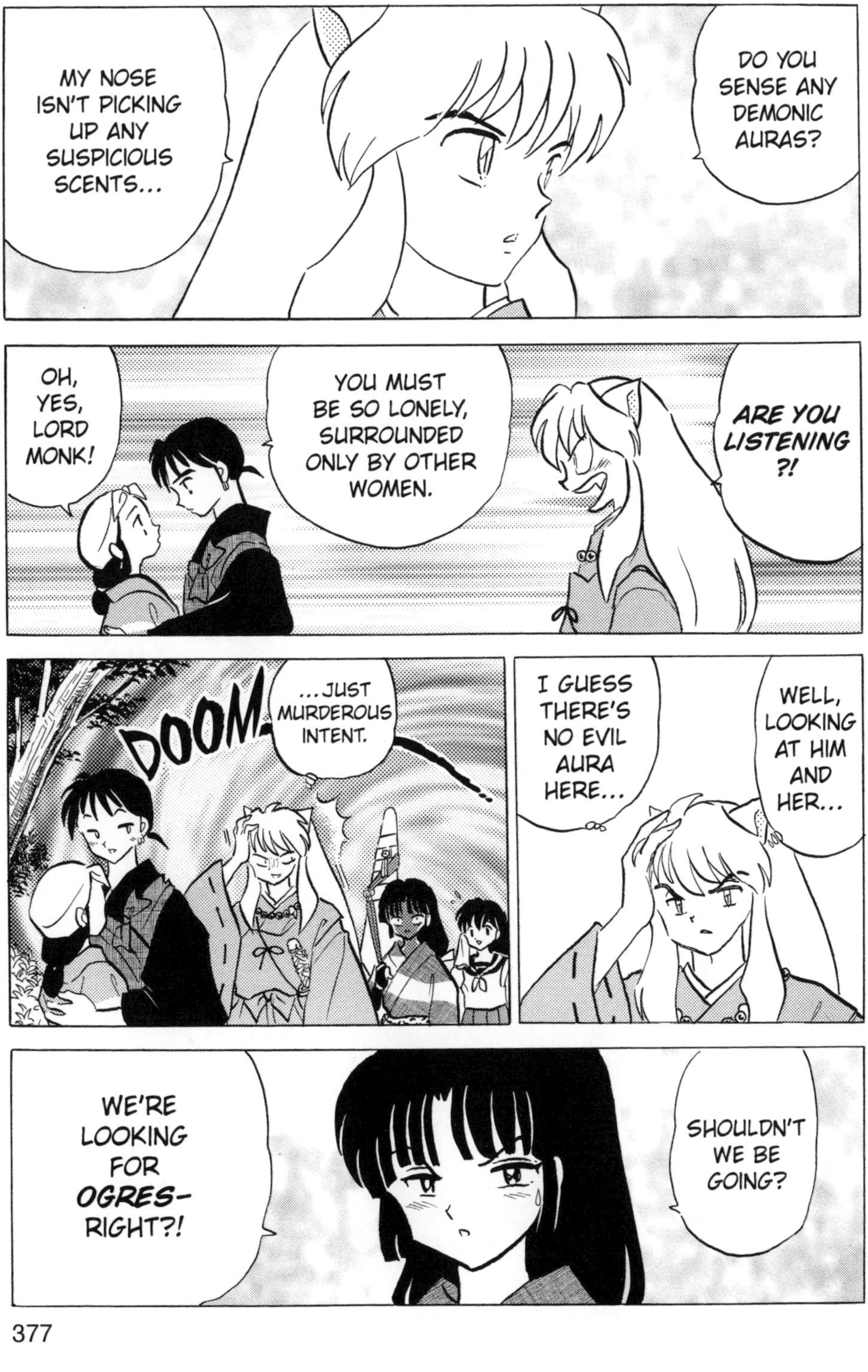
DO YOU SENSE ANY DEMONIC AURAS?
MY NOSE ISN'T PICKING UP ANY SUSPICIOUS SCENTS...
ARE YOU LISTENING?!
YOU MUST BE SO LONELY, SURROUNDED ONLY BY OTHER WOMEN.
OH, YES, LORD MONK!
WELL, LOOKING AT HIM AND HER...
I GUESS THERE'S NO EVIL AURA HERE...
...JUST MURDEROUS INTENT.
DOOM
SHOULDN'T WE BE GOING?
WE'RE LOOKING FOR *OGRES*-RIGHT?!

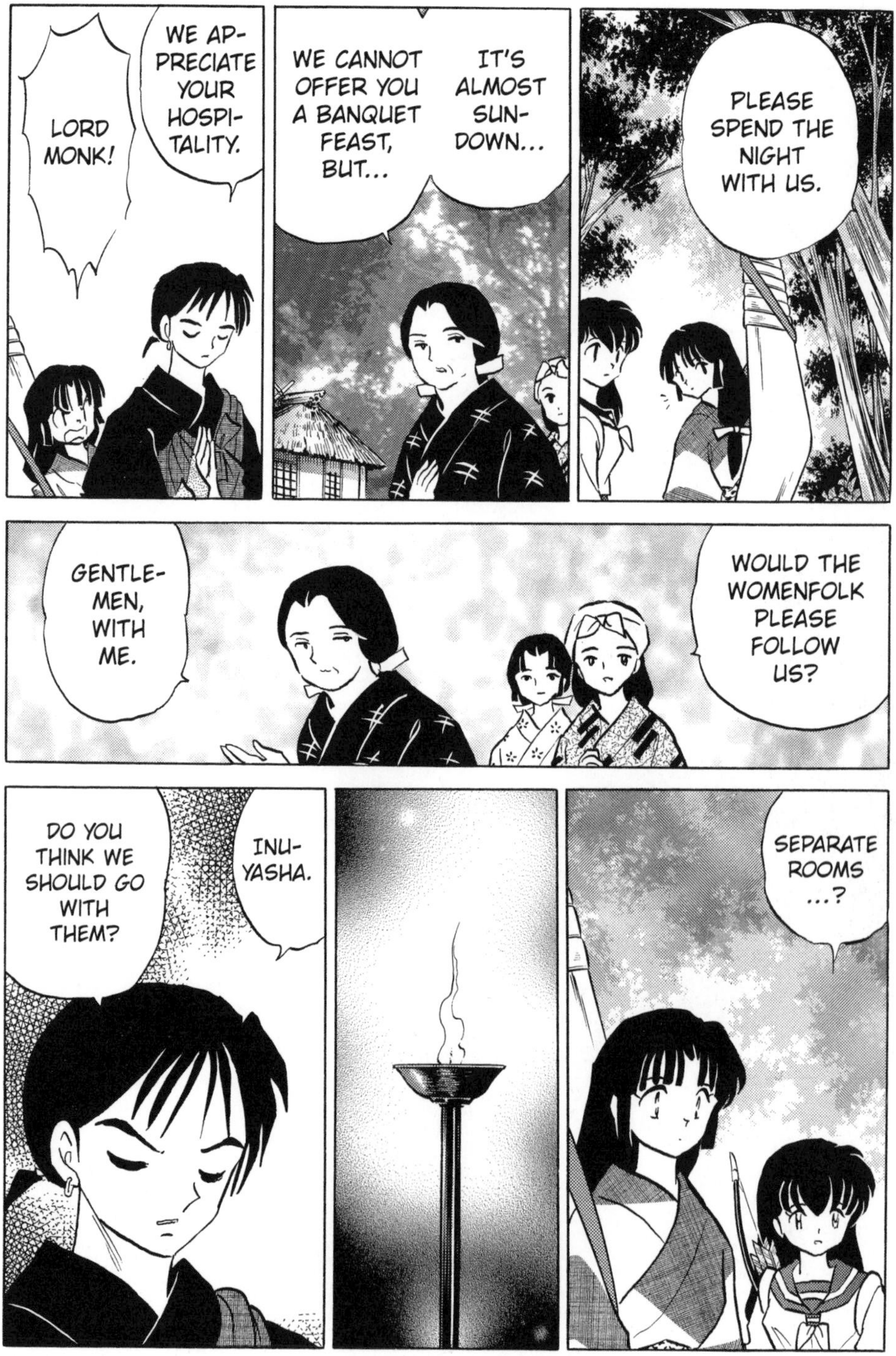
PLEASE SPEND THE NIGHT WITH US.
IT'S ALMOST SUN-DOWN...
WE CANNOT OFFER YOU A BANQUET FEAST, BUT...
WE AP-PRECIATE YOUR HOSPI-TALITY.
LORD MONK!
WOULD THE WOMENFOLK PLEASE FOLLOW US?
GENTLE-MEN, WITH ME.
SEPARATE ROOMS ...?
INU-YASHA.
DO YOU THINK WE SHOULD GO WITH THEM?

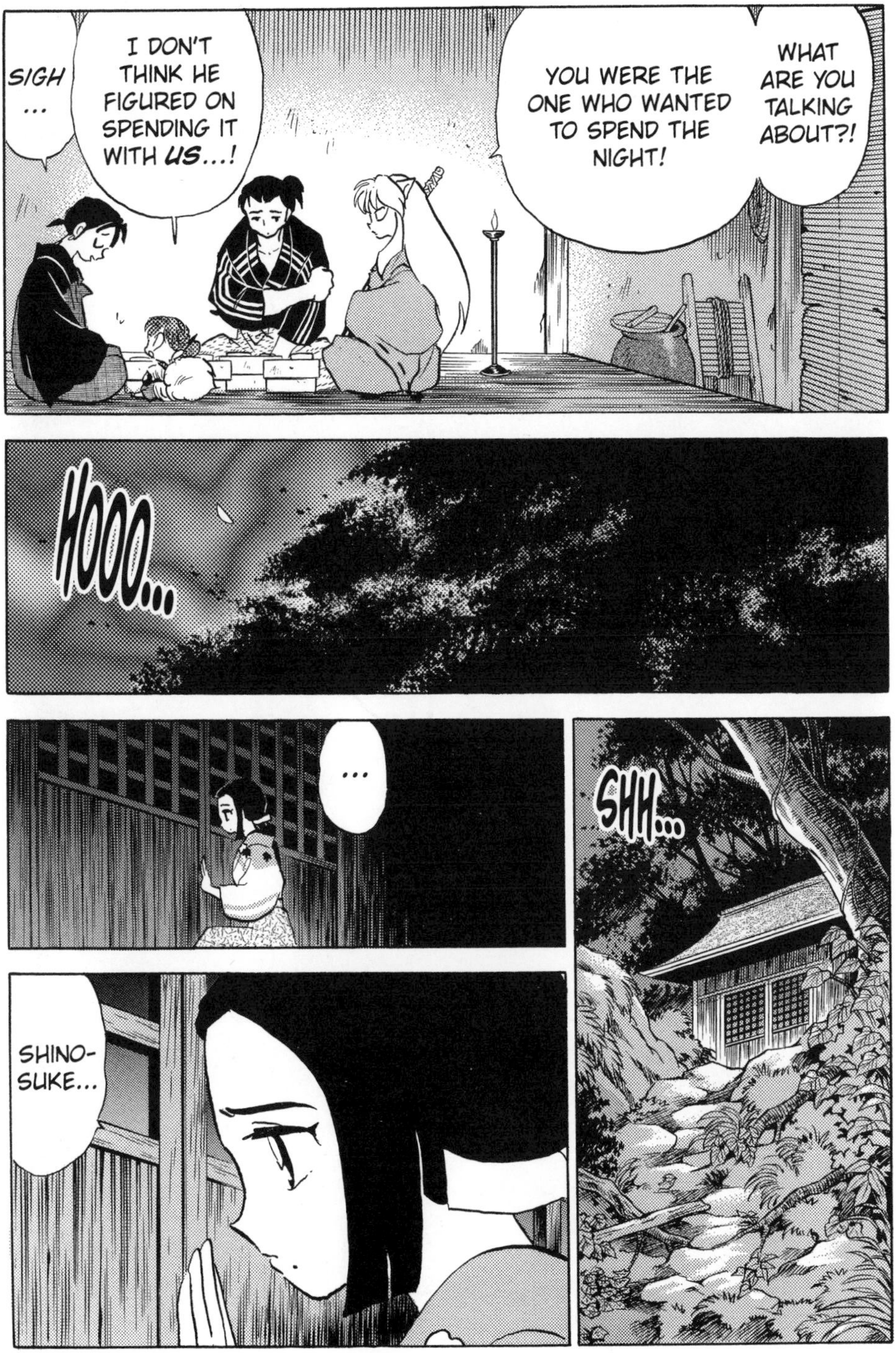
WHAT ARE YOU TALKING ABOUT?!
YOU WERE THE ONE WHO WANTED TO SPEND THE NIGHT!
I DON'T THINK HE FIGURED ON SPENDING IT WITH US...!
SIGH...
HOOO...
SHH...
...
SHINO-SUKE...

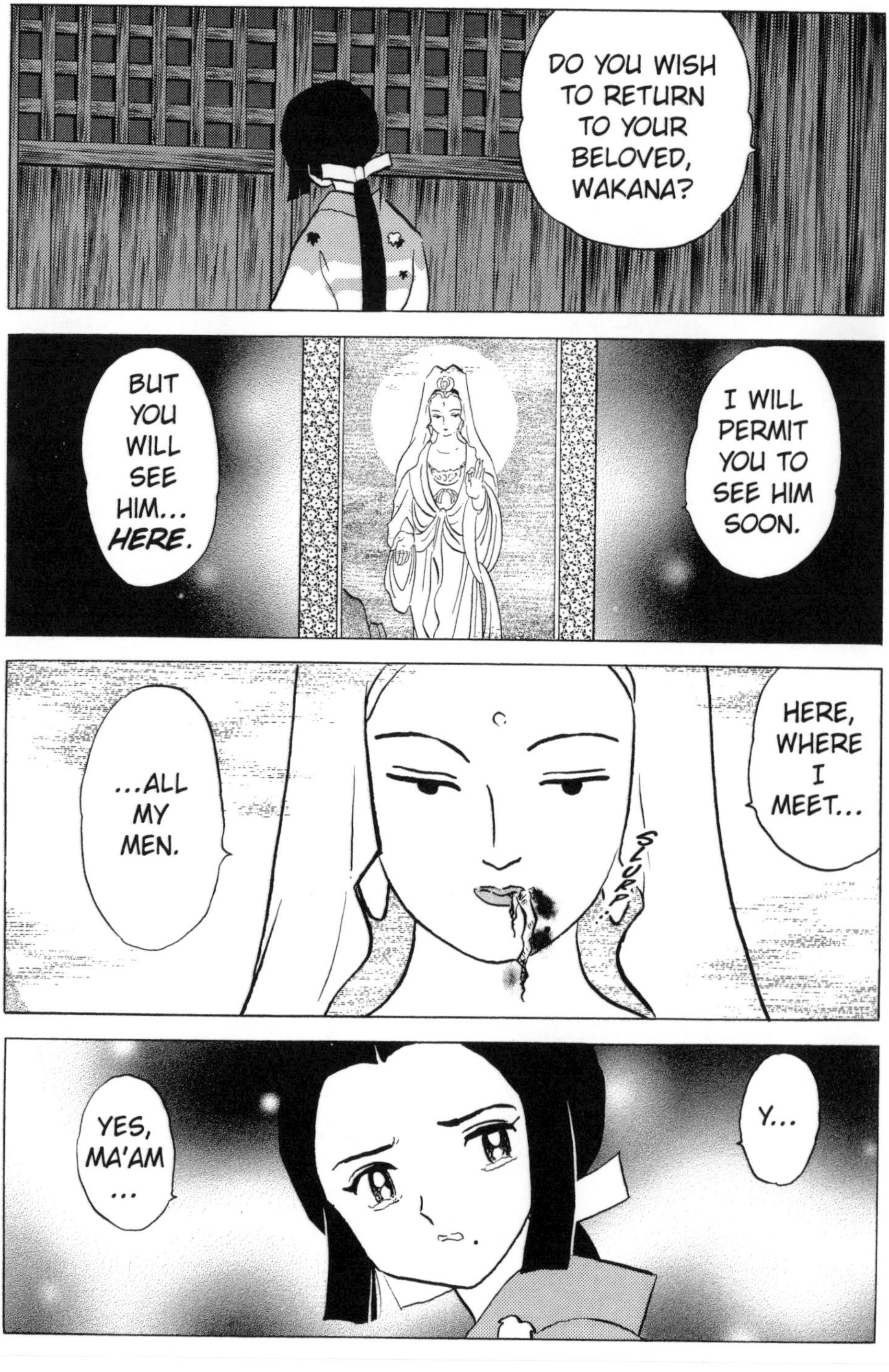
DO YOU WISH TO RETURN TO YOUR BELOVED, WAKANA?
I WILL PERMIT YOU TO SEE HIM SOON.
BUT YOU WILL SEE HIM... *HERE*.
HERE, WHERE I MEET...
SLURP...
...ALL MY MEN.
Y...
YES, MA'AM ...

Volume 30
Unique Among Women

SCROLL ONE
HALL OF THE BODHISATTVA

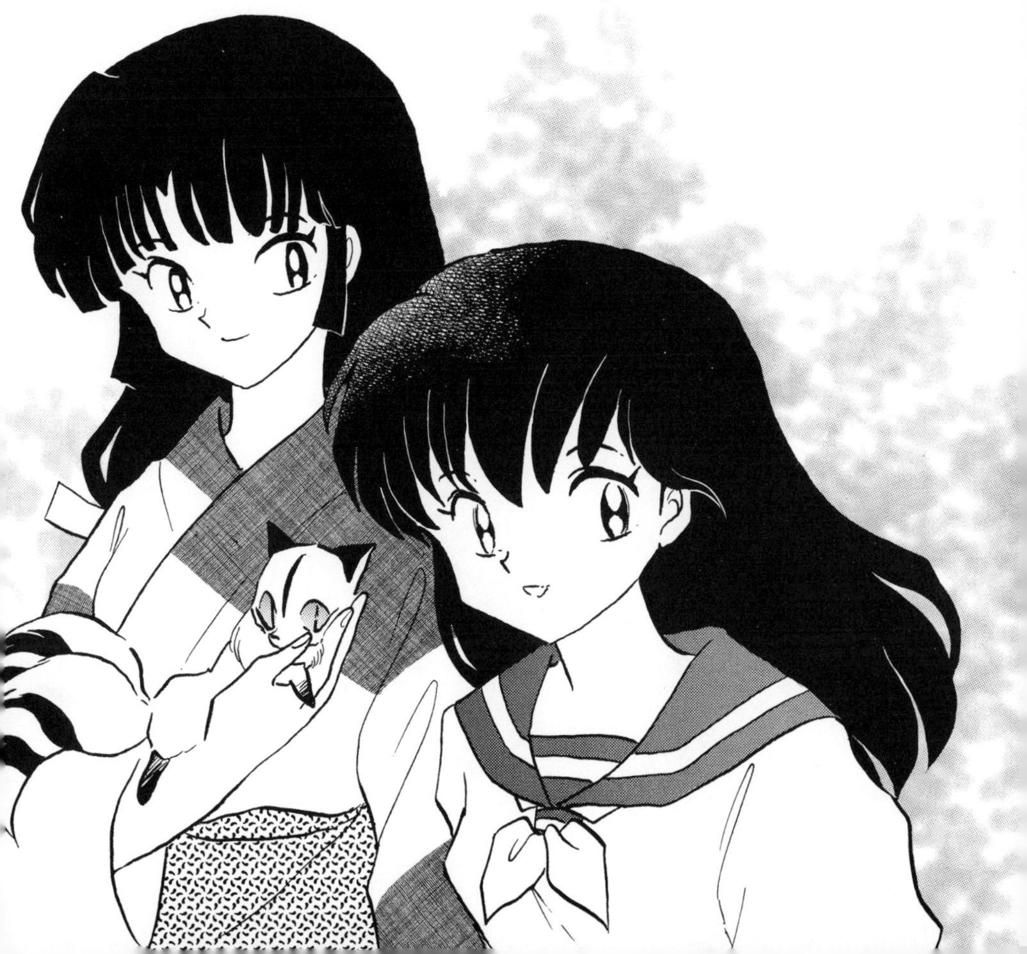

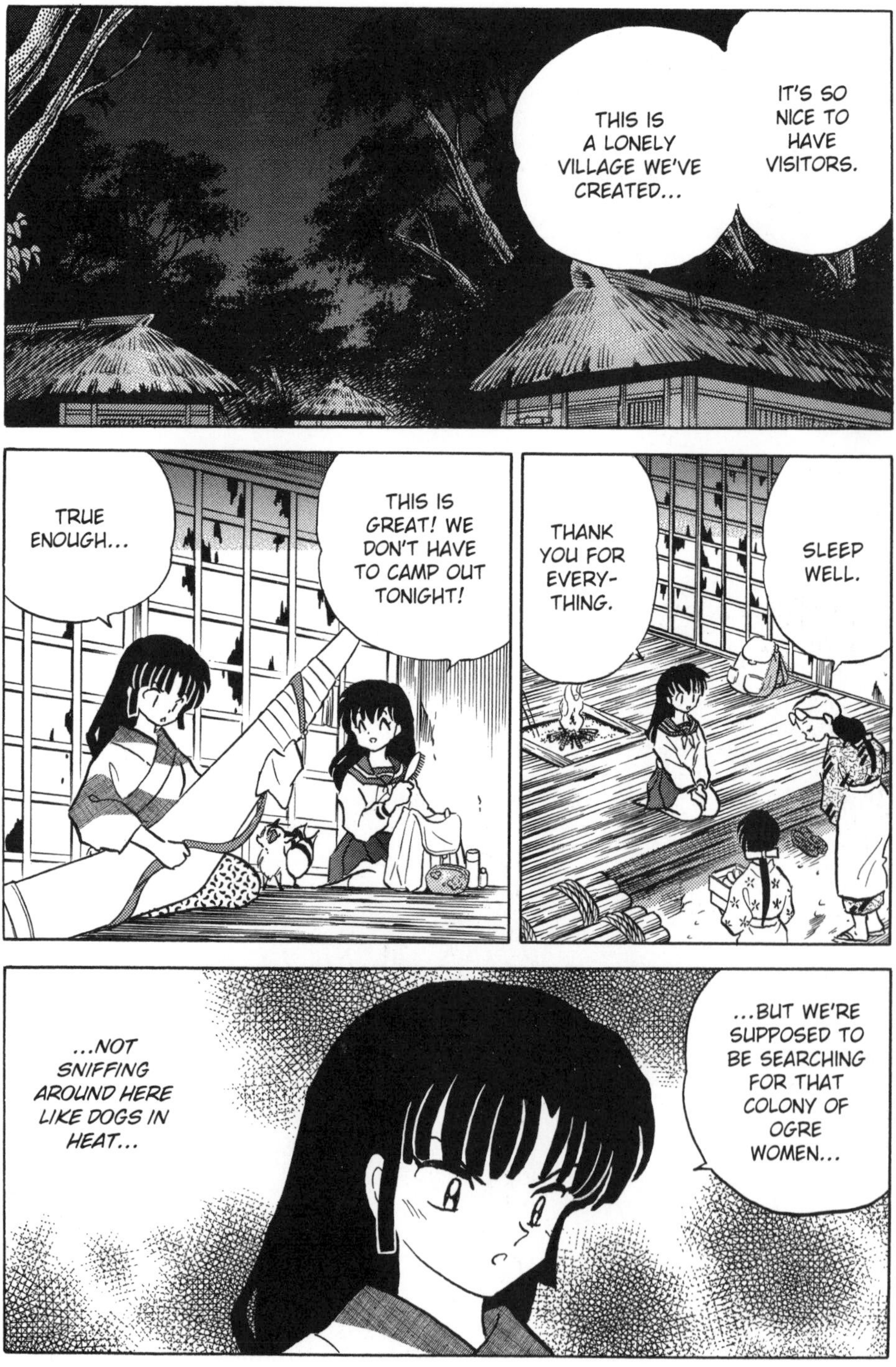
IT'S SO NICE TO HAVE VISITORS.
THIS IS A LONELY VILLAGE WE'VE CREATED...
SLEEP WELL.
THANK YOU FOR EVERY-THING.
THIS IS GREAT! WE DON'T HAVE TO CAMP OUT TONIGHT!
TRUE ENOUGH...
...BUT WE'RE SUPPOSED TO BE SEARCHING FOR THAT COLONY OF OGRE WOMEN...
...NOT SNIFFING AROUND HERE LIKE DOGS IN HEAT...

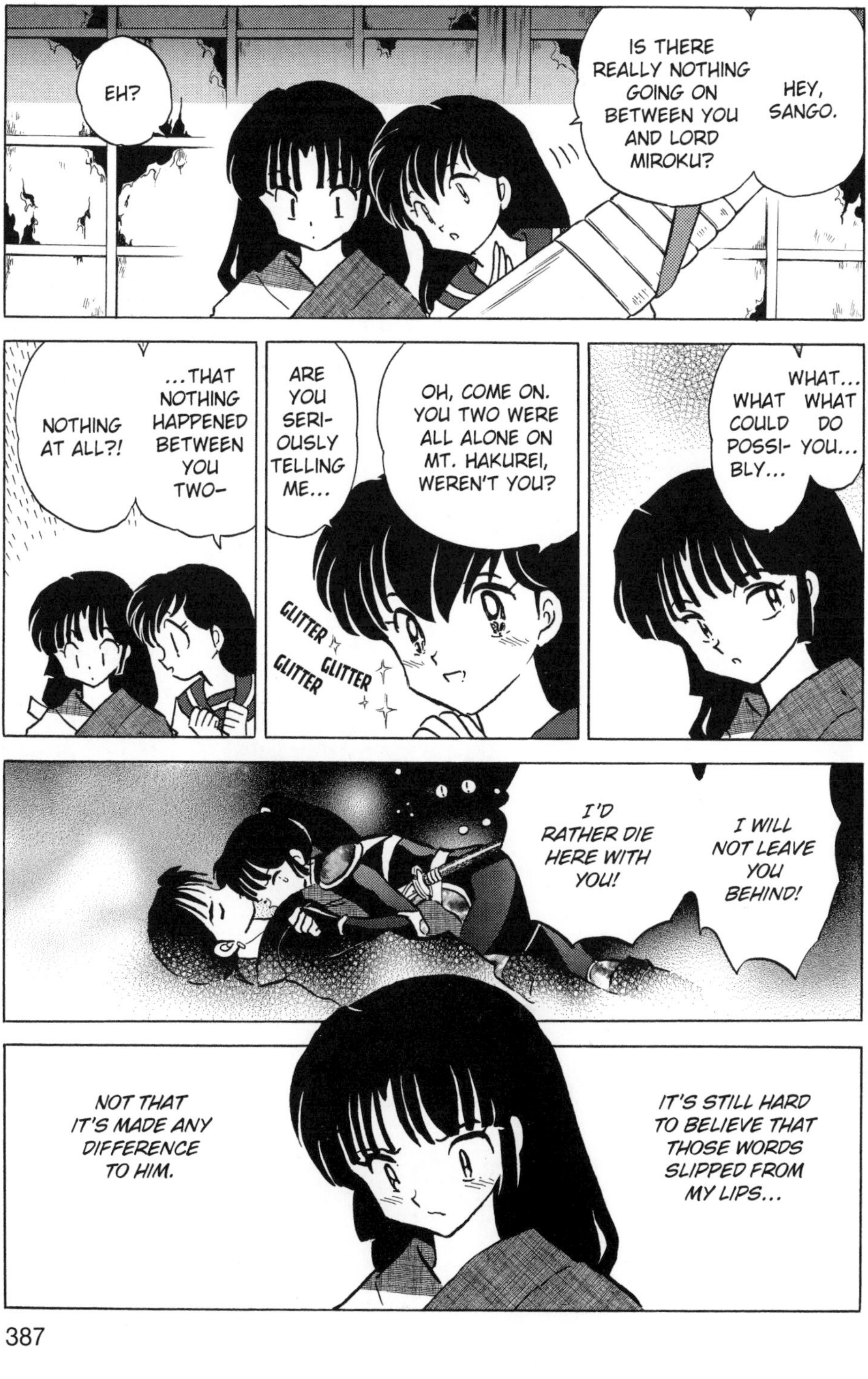
HEY, SANGO.
IS THERE REALLY NOTHING GOING ON BETWEEN YOU AND LORD MIROKU?
EH?
WHAT... WHAT DO YOU... WHAT COULD POSSIBLY...
OH, COME ON. YOU TWO WERE ALL ALONE ON MT. HAKUREI, WEREN'T YOU?
ARE YOU SERIOUSLY TELLING ME...
GLITTER GLITTER GLITTER
...THAT NOTHING HAPPENED BETWEEN YOU TWO-
NOTHING AT ALL?!
I WILL NOT LEAVE YOU BEHIND!
I'D RATHER DIE HERE WITH YOU!
IT'S STILL HARD TO BELIEVE THAT THOSE WORDS SLIPPED FROM MY LIPS...
NOT THAT IT'S MADE ANY DIFFERENCE TO HIM.

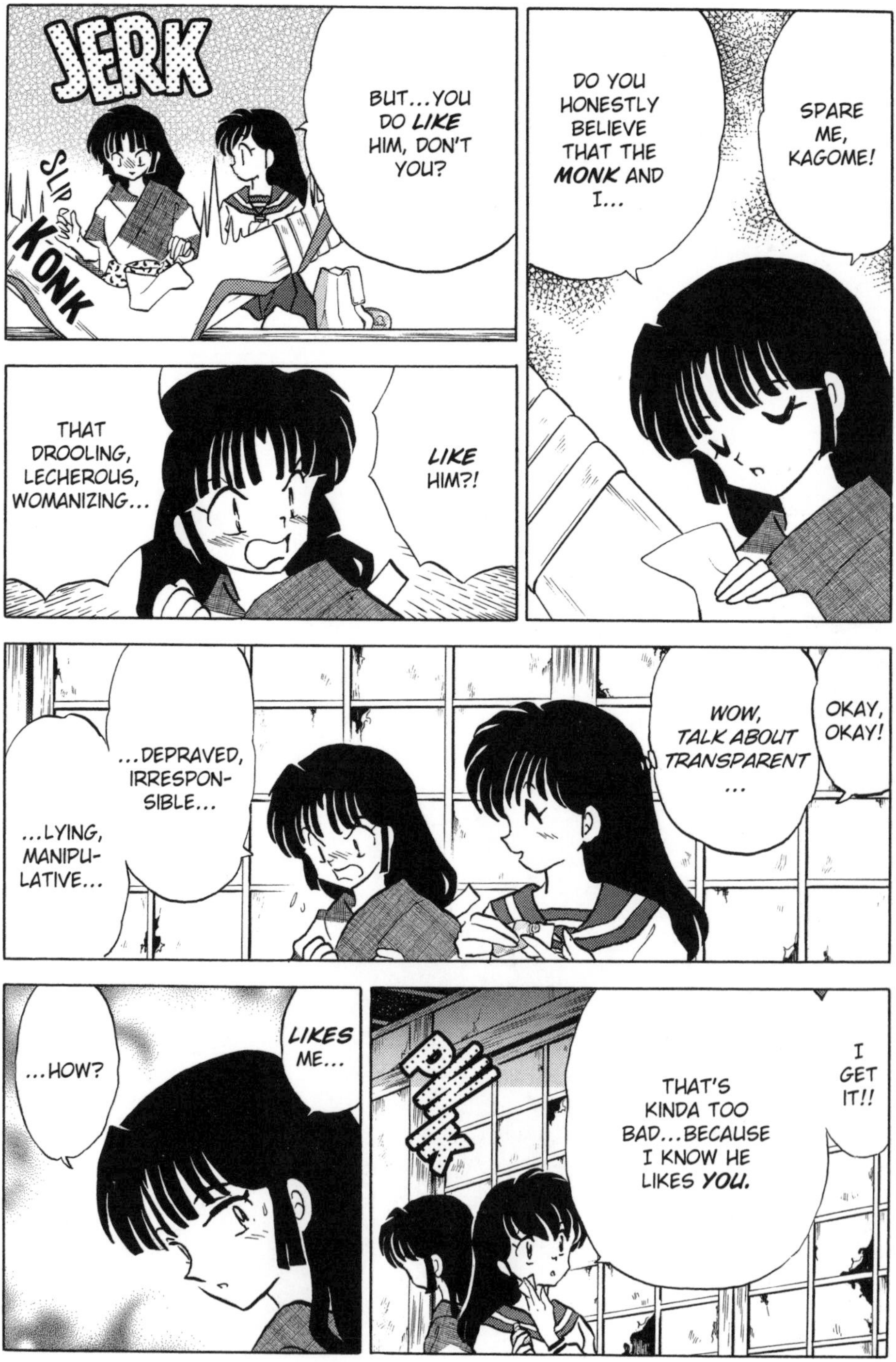
SPARE ME, KAGOME!
DO YOU HONESTLY BELIEVE THAT THE MONK AND I...
BUT...YOU DO LIKE HIM, DON'T YOU?
JERK
SLIP
KONK
LIKE HIM?!
THAT DROOLING, LECHEROUS, WOMANIZING...
OKAY, OKAY!
WOW, TALK ABOUT TRANSPARENT...
...DEPRAVED, IRRESPONSIBLE...
...LYING, MANIPULATIVE...
I GET IT!!
THAT'S KINDA TOO BAD...BECAUSE I KNOW HE LIKES YOU.
PINK
LIKES ME...
...HOW?

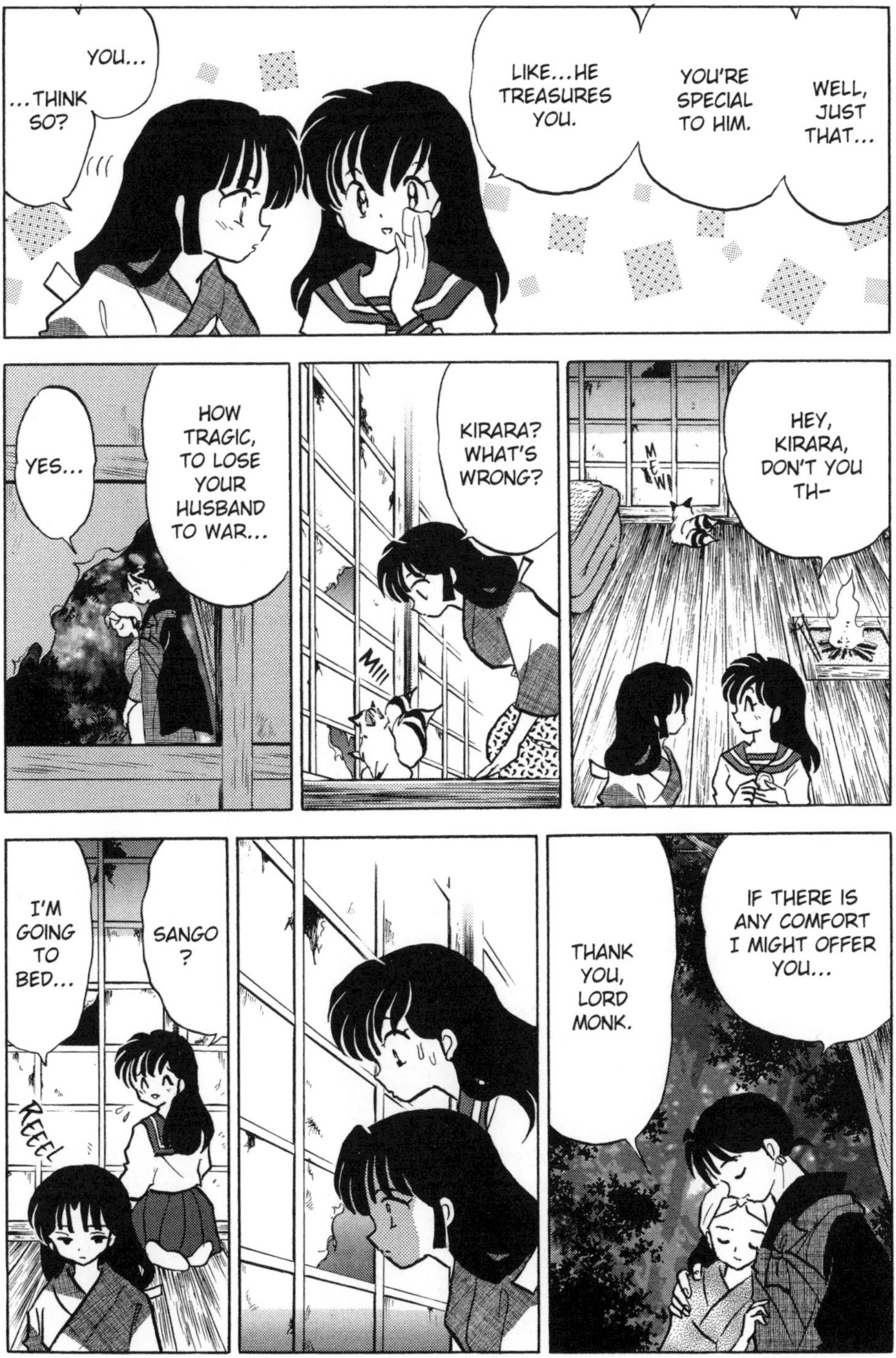
WELL, JUST THAT...
YOU'RE SPECIAL TO HIM.
LIKE...HE TREASURES YOU.
YOU... ...THINK SO?
HEY, KIRARA, DON'T YOU TH-
MEW
KIRARA? WHAT'S WRONG?
MII
HOW TRAGIC, TO LOSE YOUR HUSBAND TO WAR...
YES...
IF THERE IS ANY COMFORT I MIGHT OFFER YOU...
THANK YOU, LORD MONK.
SANGO?
I'M GOING TO BED...
REEEL

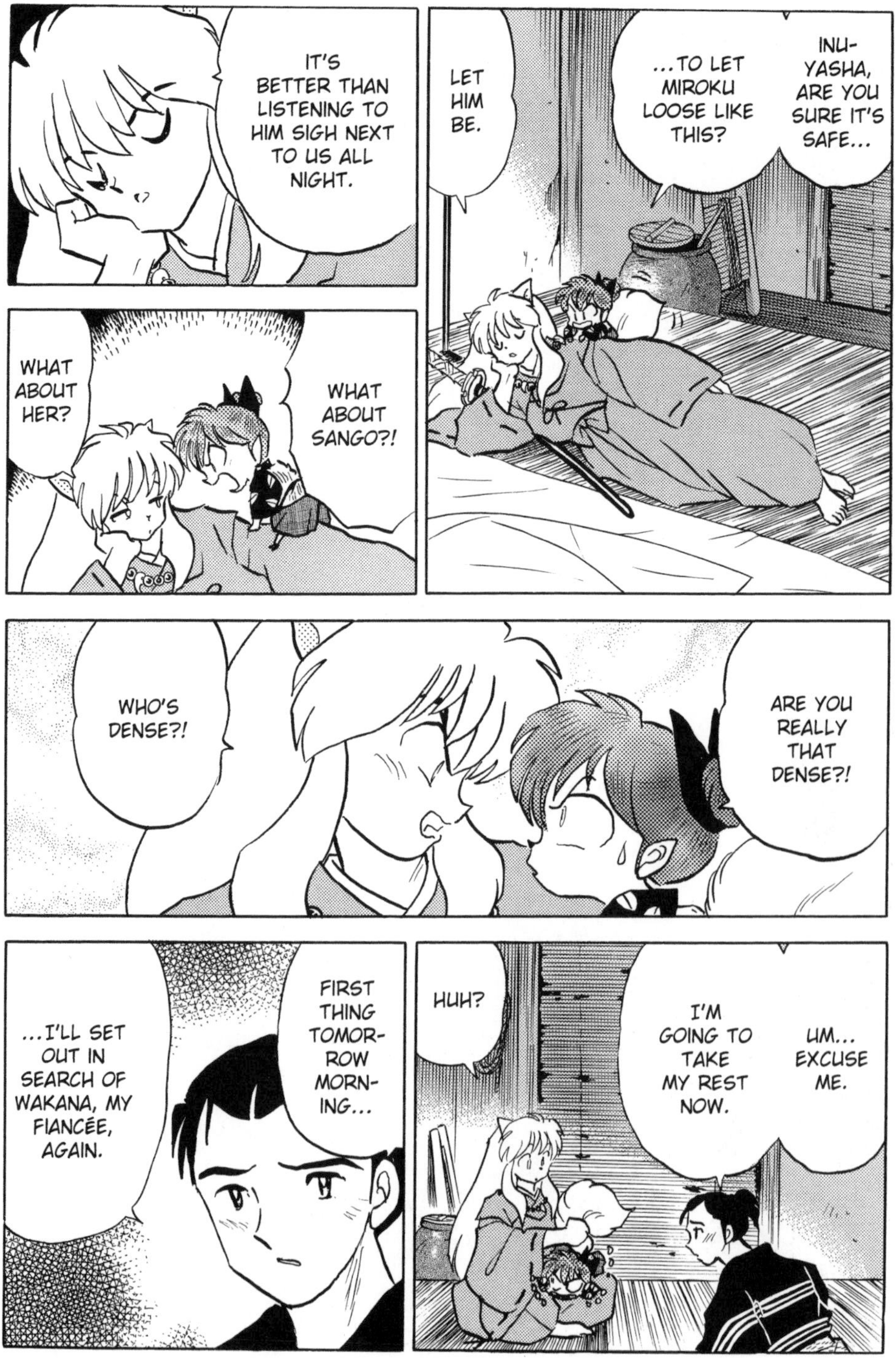
INU-YASHA, ARE YOU SURE IT'S SAFE...
...TO LET MIROKU LOOSE LIKE THIS?
LET HIM BE.
IT'S BETTER THAN LISTENING TO HIM SIGH NEXT TO US ALL NIGHT.
WHAT ABOUT SANGO?!
WHAT ABOUT HER?
ARE YOU REALLY THAT DENSE?!
WHO'S DENSE?!
UM... EXCUSE ME.
I'M GOING TO TAKE MY REST NOW.
HUH?
FIRST THING TOMORROW MORNING...
...I'LL SET OUT IN SEARCH OF WAKANA, MY FIANCÉE, AGAIN.

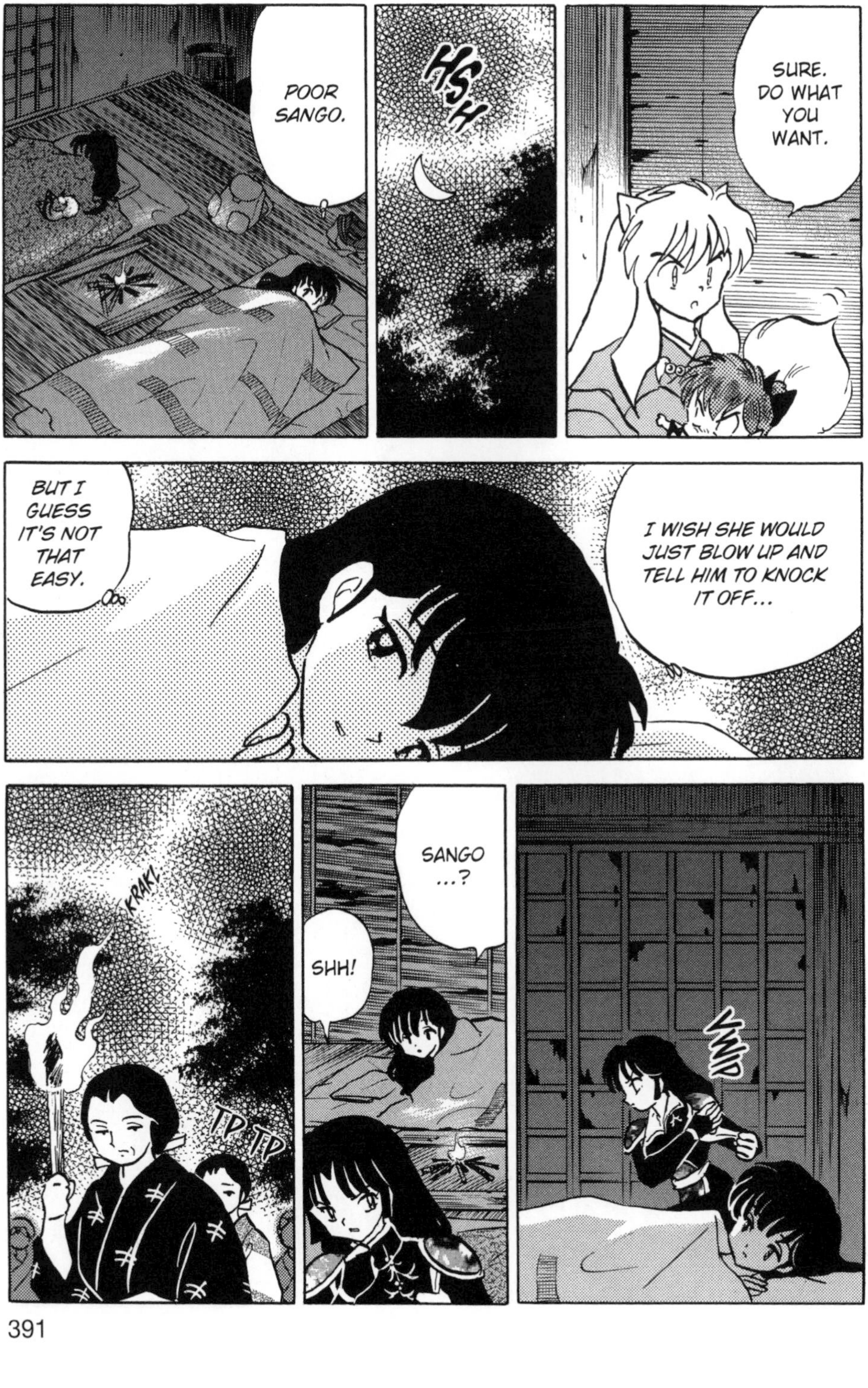
SURE. DO WHAT YOU WANT.
HSH
POOR SANGO.
I WISH SHE WOULD JUST BLOW UP AND TELL HIM TO KNOCK IT OFF...
BUT I GUESS IT'S NOT THAT EASY.
VWIP
SANGO ...?
SHH!
KRAK!
TP TP

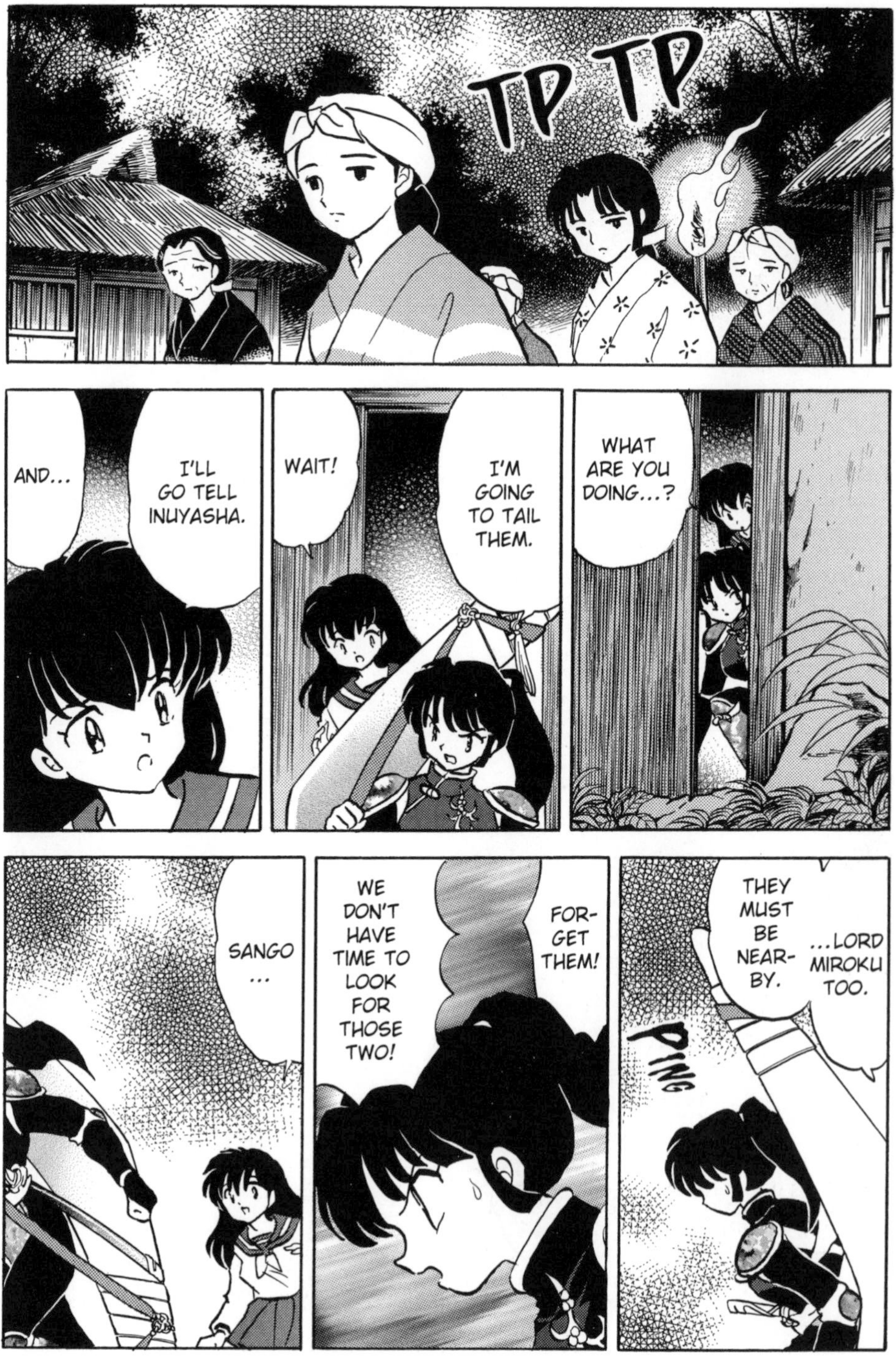
TP TP
WHAT ARE YOU DOING...?
I'M GOING TO TAIL THEM.
WAIT!
I'LL GO TELL INUYASHA.
AND...
...LORD MIROKU TOO.
THEY MUST BE NEARBY.
PING
FOR-GET THEM!
WE DON'T HAVE TIME TO LOOK FOR THOSE TWO!
SANGO...

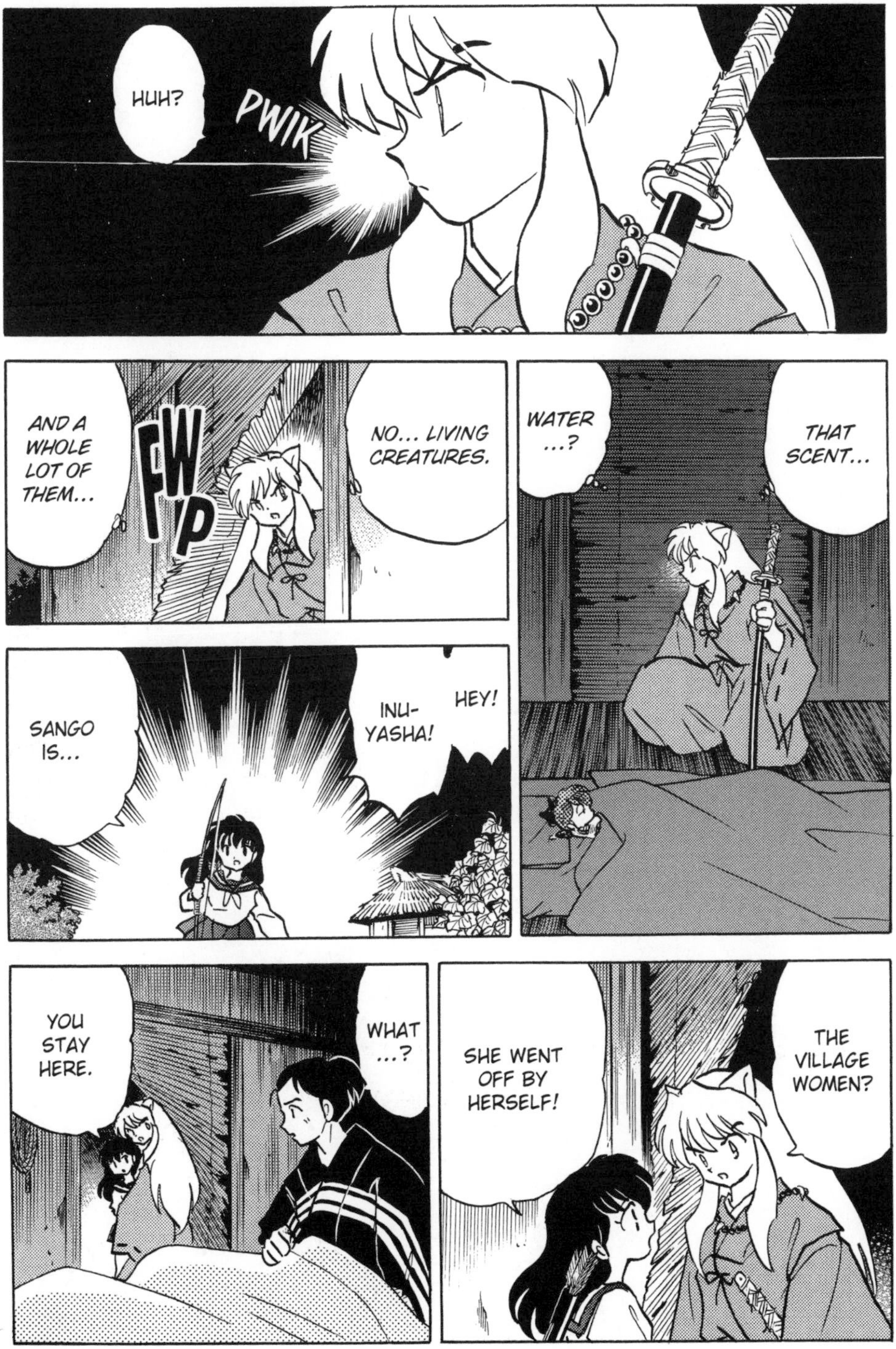
HUH?
PWIK
THAT SCENT...
WATER ...?
NO... LIVING CREATURES.
FWP
AND A WHOLE LOT OF THEM...
HEY!
INU-YASHA!
SANGO IS...
THE VILLAGE WOMEN?
SHE WENT OFF BY HERSELF!
WHAT ...?
YOU STAY HERE.

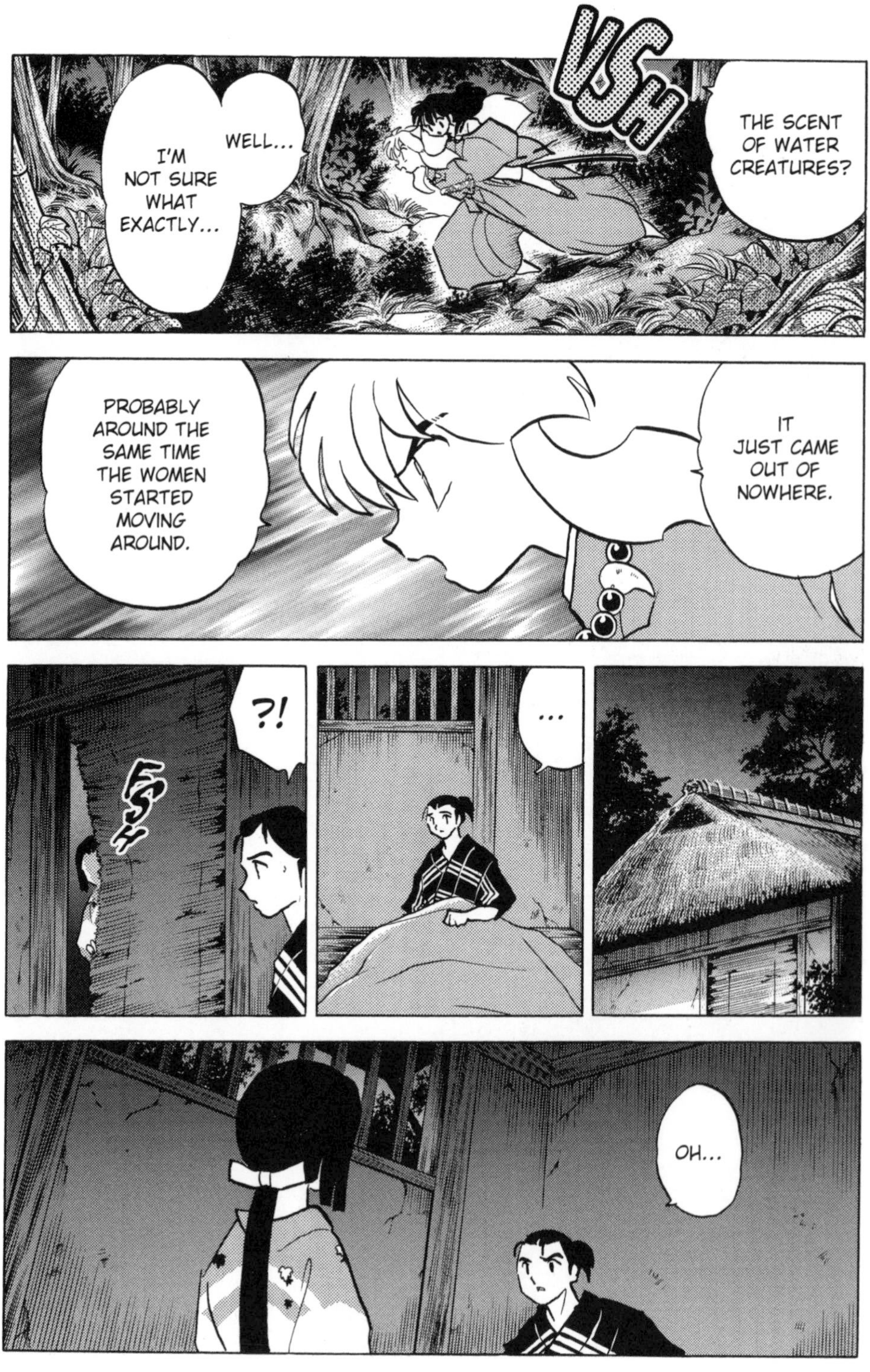
VSH
THE SCENT OF WATER CREATURES?
WELL...
I'M NOT SURE WHAT EXACTLY...
IT JUST CAME OUT OF NOWHERE.
PROBABLY AROUND THE SAME TIME THE WOMEN STARTED MOVING AROUND.
...
?!
FSH
OH...

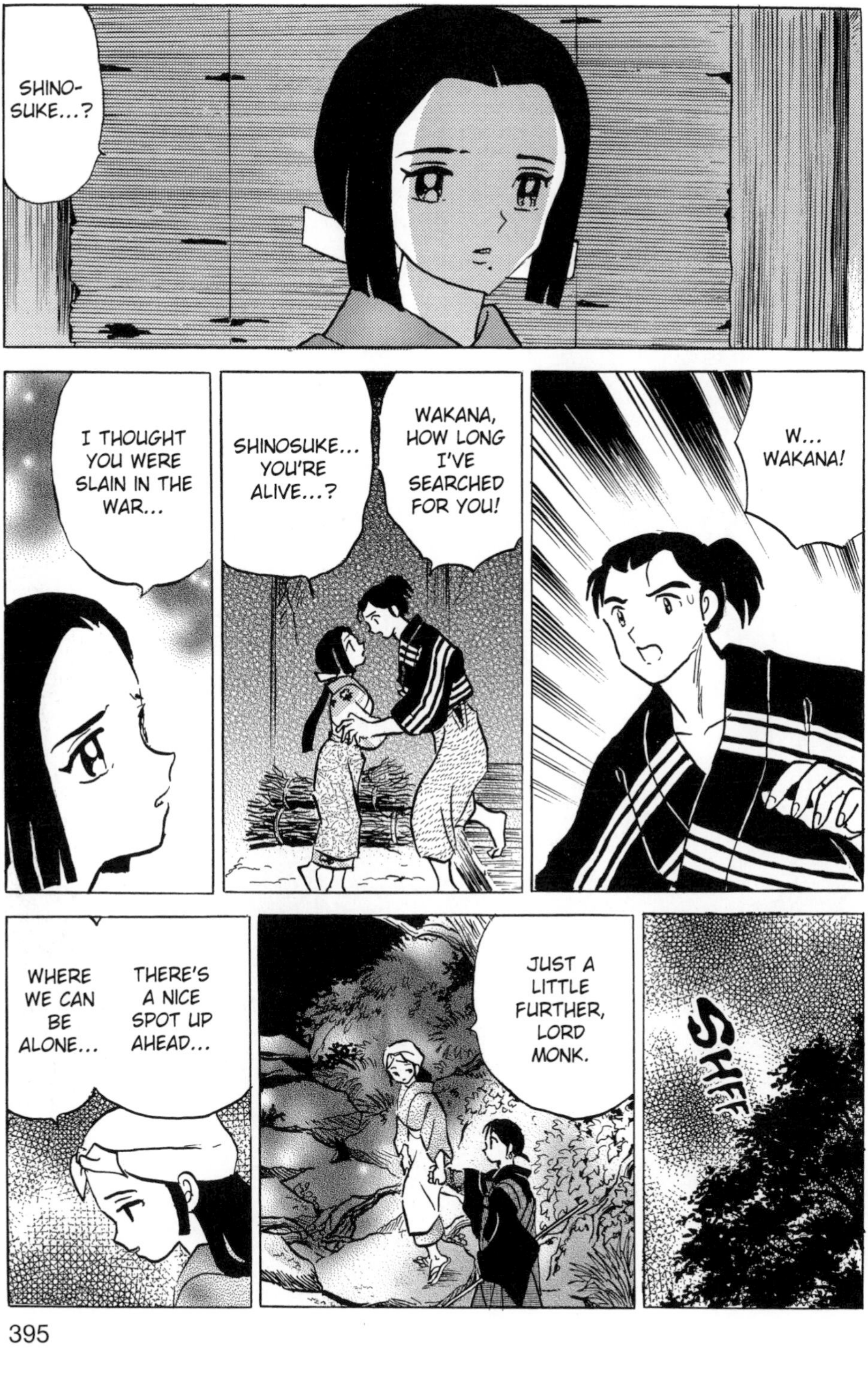
SHINO-SUKE...?
W... WAKANA!
WAKANA, HOW LONG I'VE SEARCHED FOR YOU!
SHINOSUKE... YOU'RE ALIVE...?
I THOUGHT YOU WERE SLAIN IN THE WAR...
SHFF
JUST A LITTLE FURTHER, LORD MONK.
THERE'S A NICE SPOT UP AHEAD...
WHERE WE CAN BE ALONE...

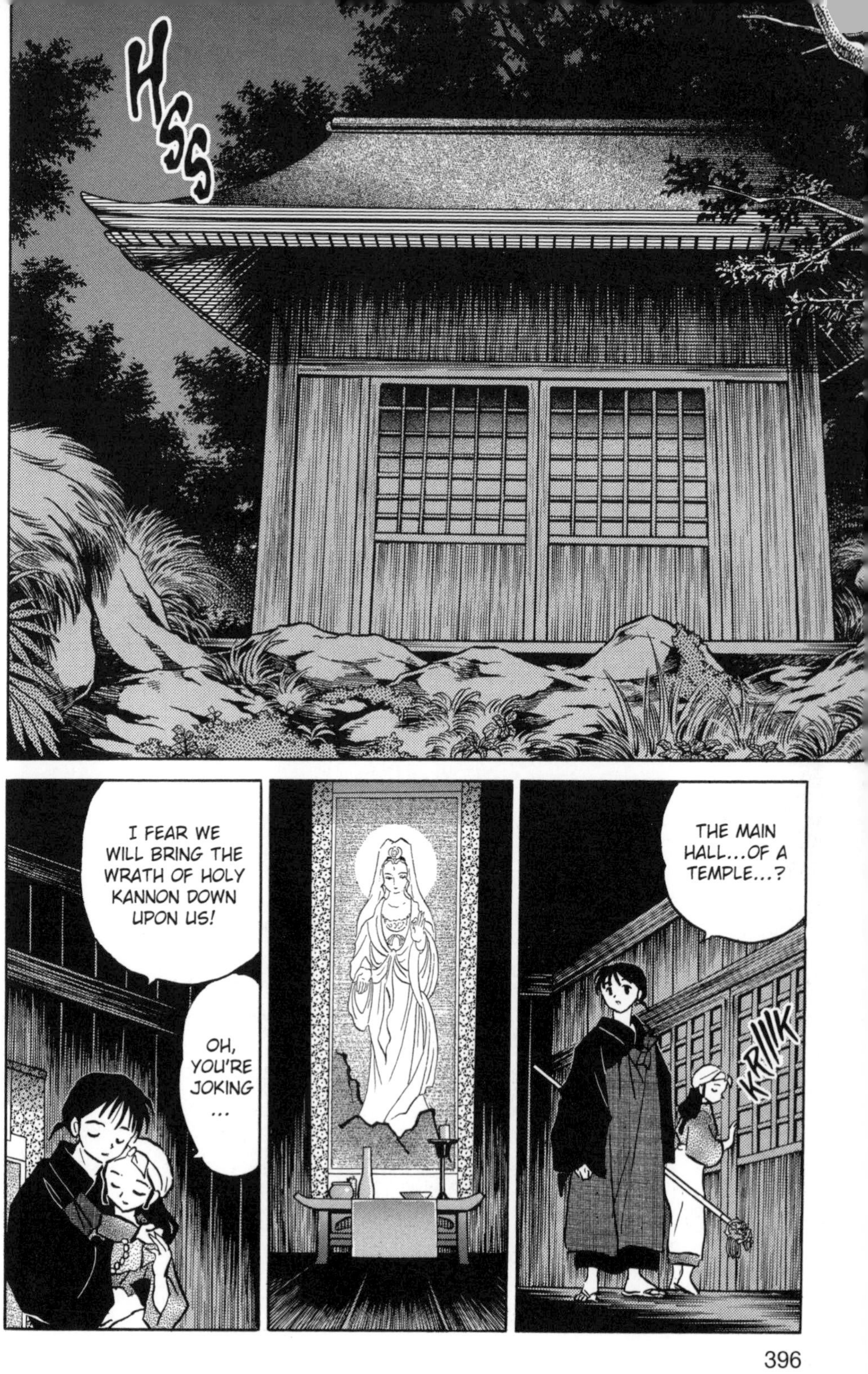
HSS
THE MAIN HALL...OF A TEMPLE...?
KRIIK
I FEAR WE WILL BRING THE WRATH OF HOLY KANNON DOWN UPON US!
OH, YOU'RE JOKING ...

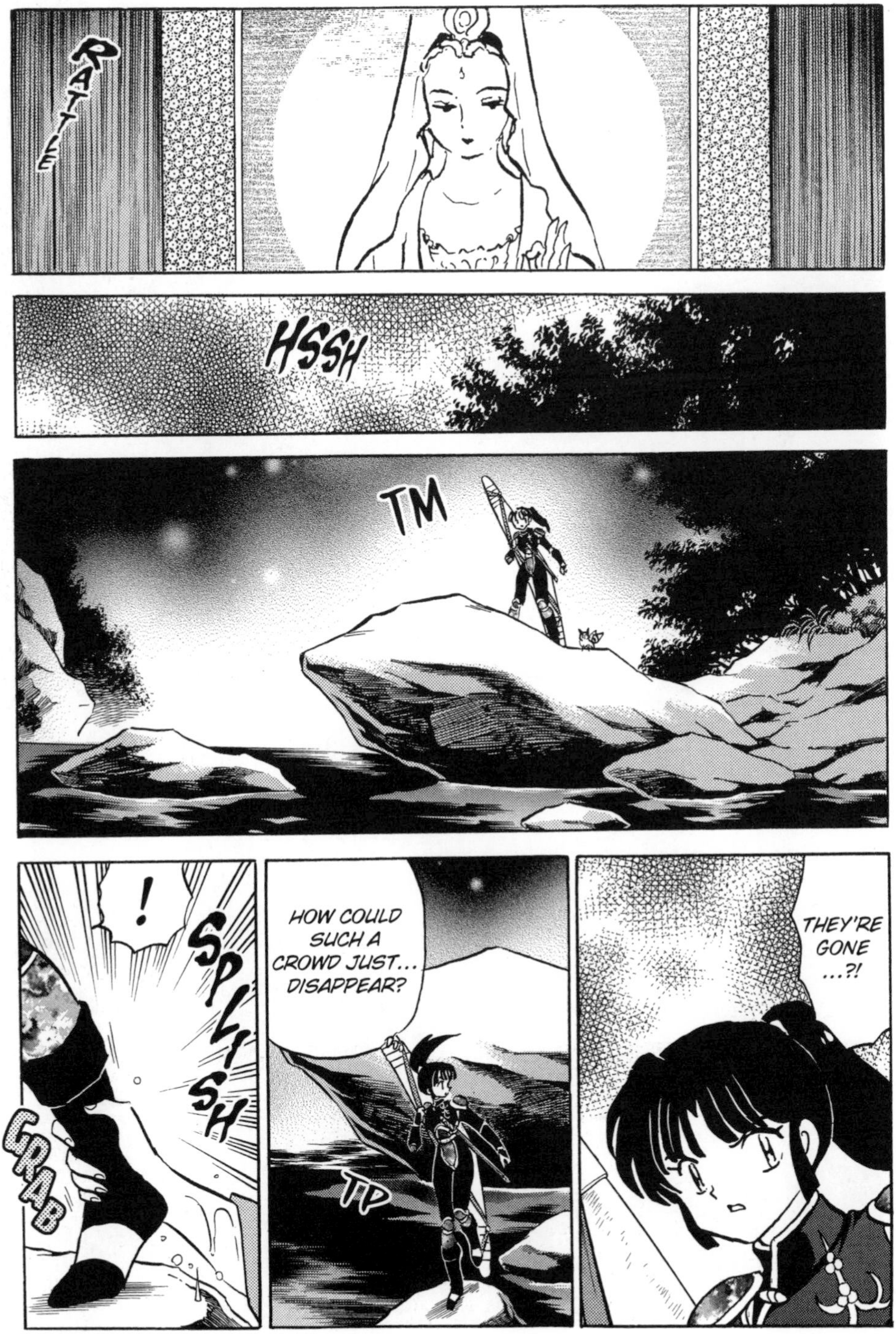
RATTLE
HSSH
TM
THEY'RE GONE ...?!
HOW COULD SUCH A CROWD JUST... DISAPPEAR?
TP
!
SPLISH
GRAB

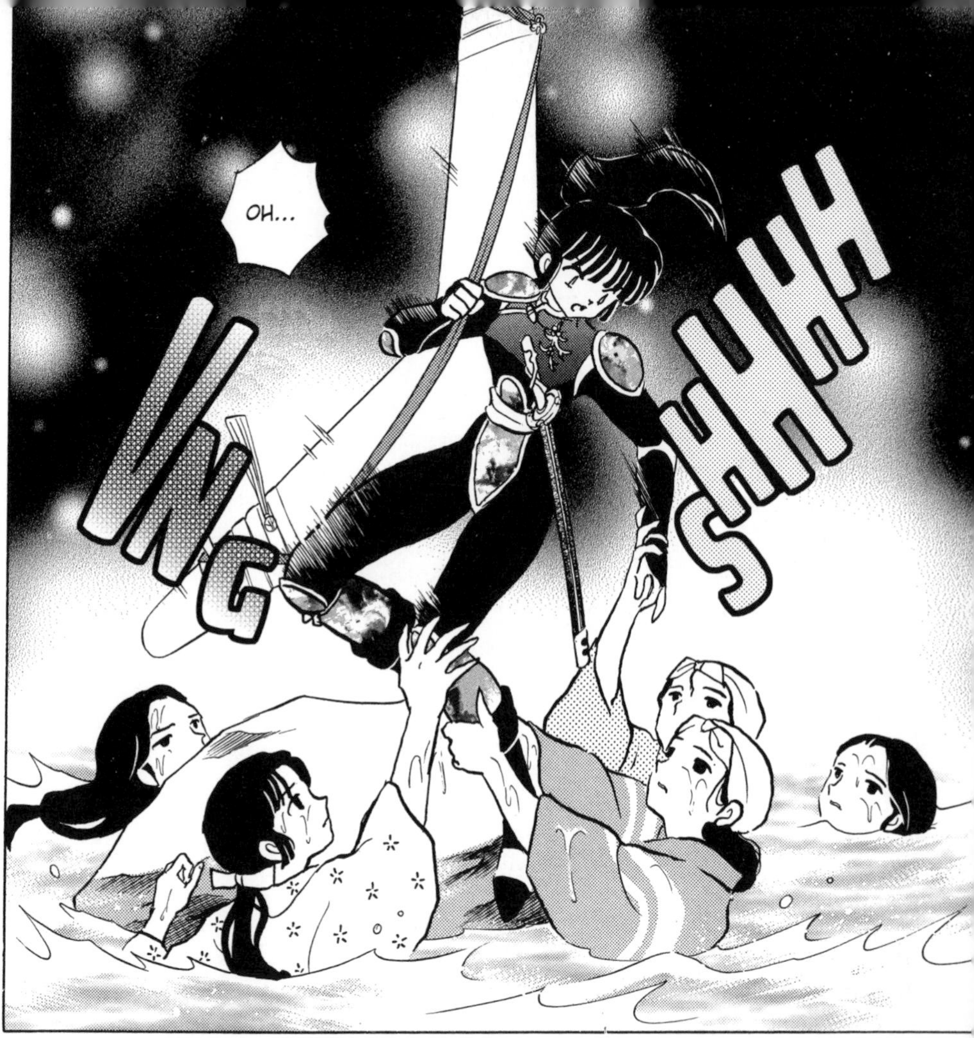
OH...
SHHHH
VNG
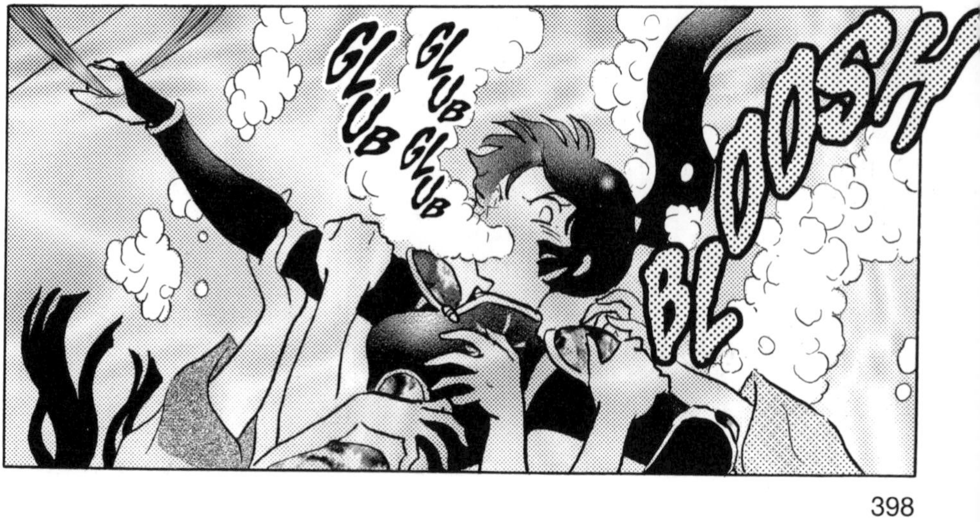
BLOOSH
GLUB GLUB
GLUB GLUB

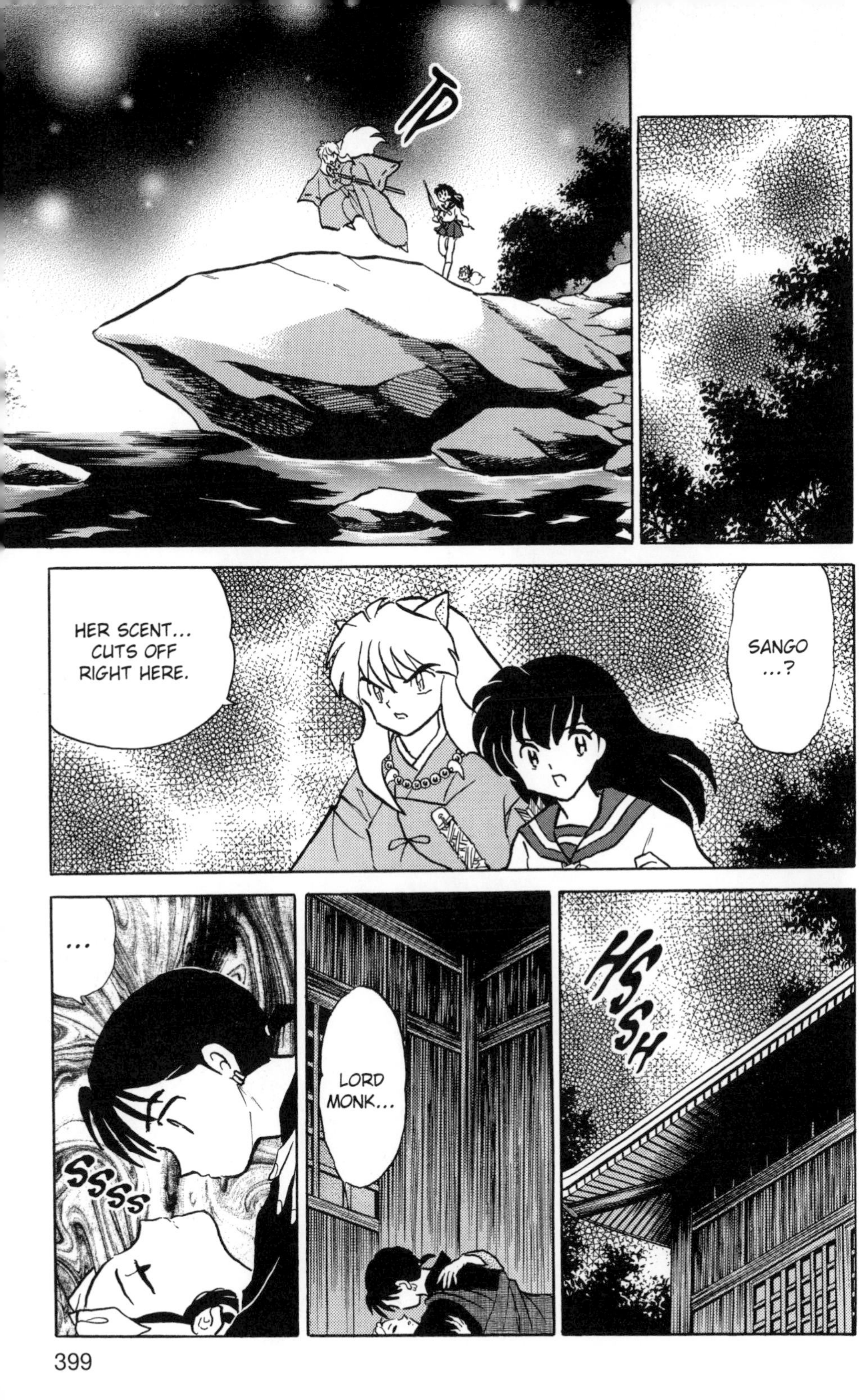
TP
SANGO
...?
HER SCENT...
CUTS OFF
RIGHT HERE.
HSSH
LORD
MONK...
...
SSSS

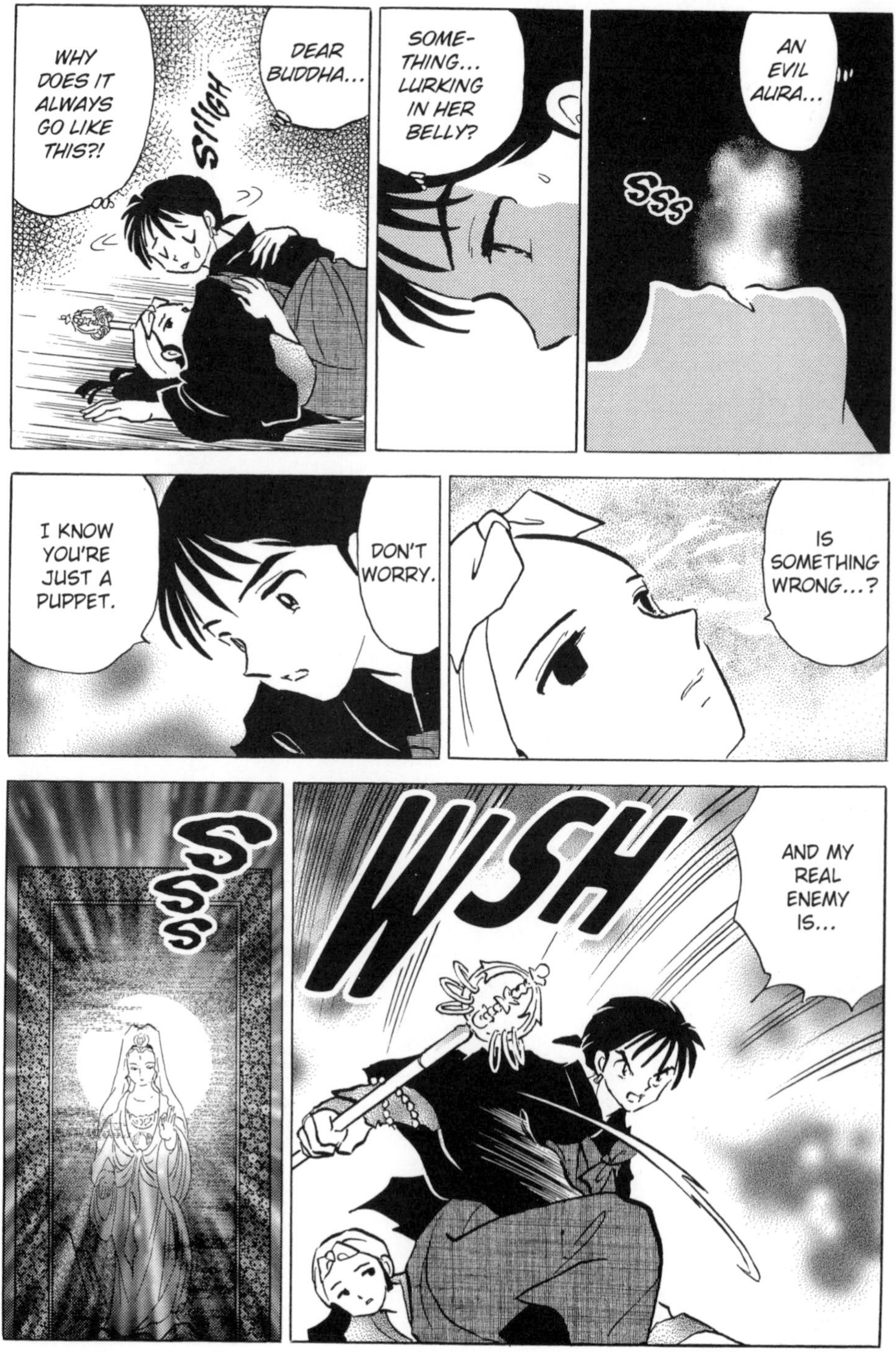
AN EVIL AURA...
SSS
SOMETHING... LURKING IN HER BELLY?
DEAR BUDDHA...
SIIIGH
WHY DOES IT ALWAYS GO LIKE THIS?!
IS SOMETHING WRONG...?
DON'T WORRY.
I KNOW YOU'RE JUST A PUPPET.
AND MY REAL ENEMY IS...
WISH
SSSS

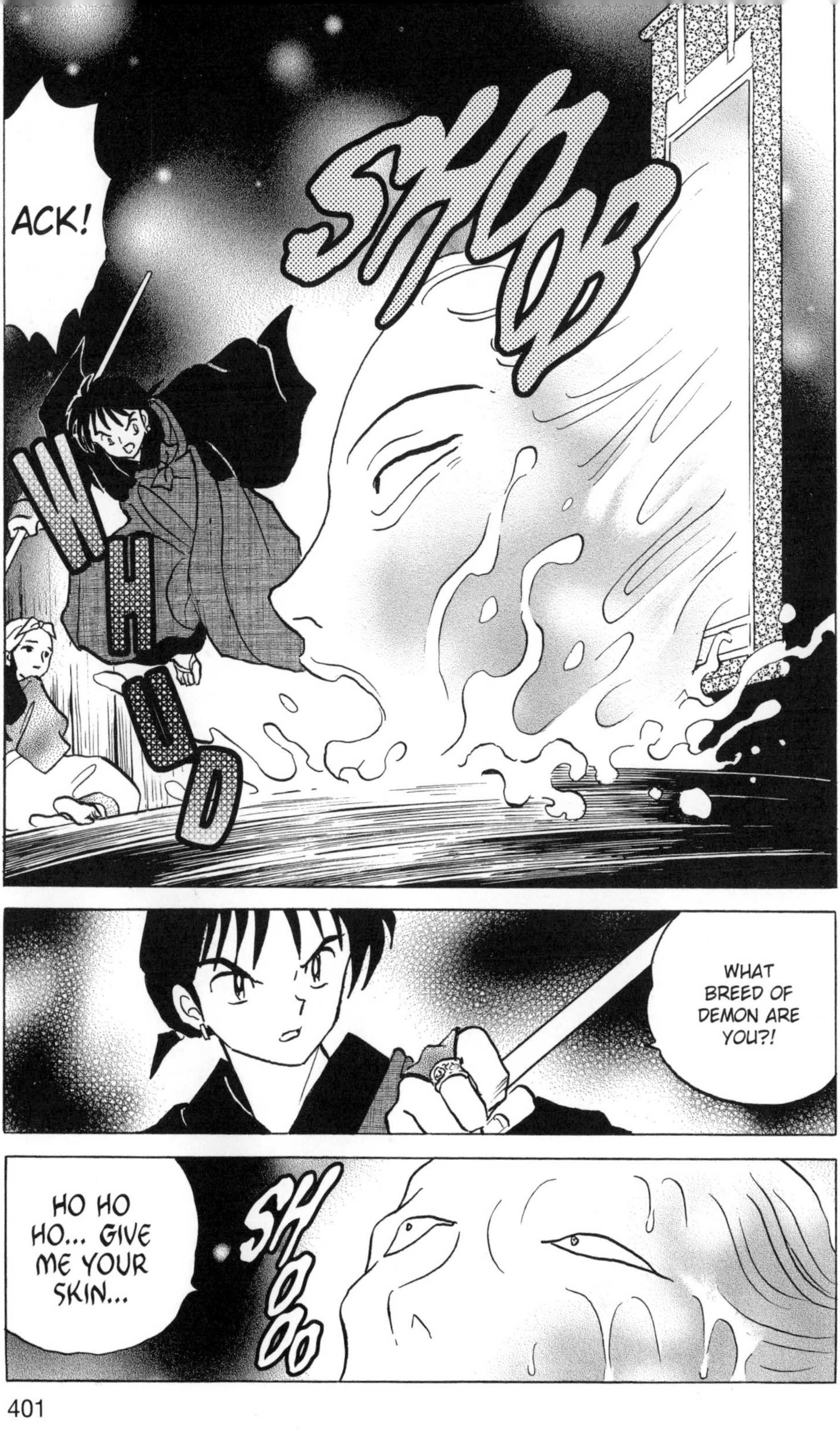
SHLOB
ACK!
WHUD
WHAT BREED OF DEMON ARE YOU?!
SHOOOO
HO HO HO... GIVE ME YOUR SKIN...

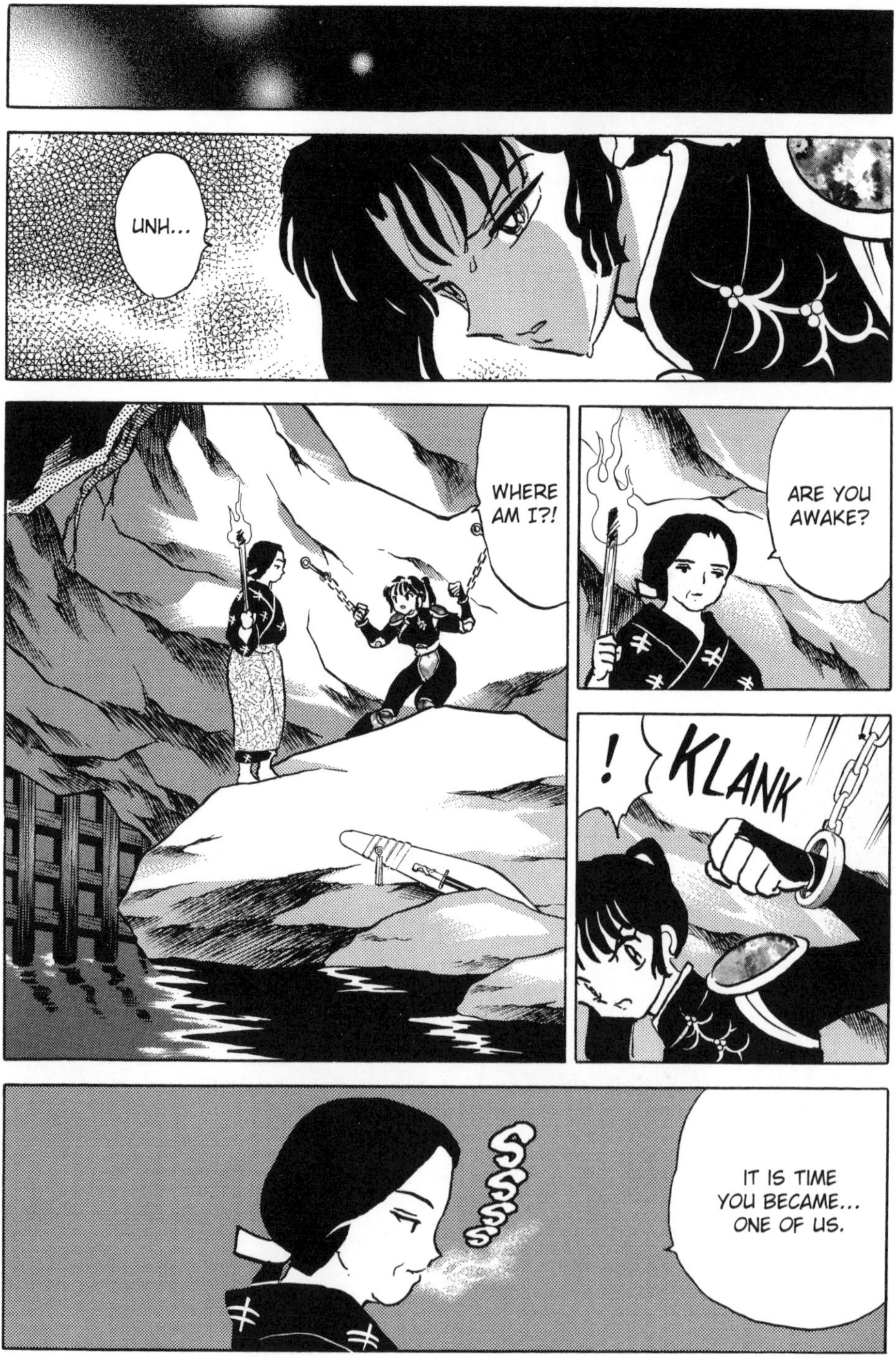
UNH...
ARE YOU AWAKE?
!
KLANK
WHERE AM I?!
SSSSSS
IT IS TIME YOU BECAME... ONE OF US.

SCROLL TWO
A DEMON IN THE BELLY

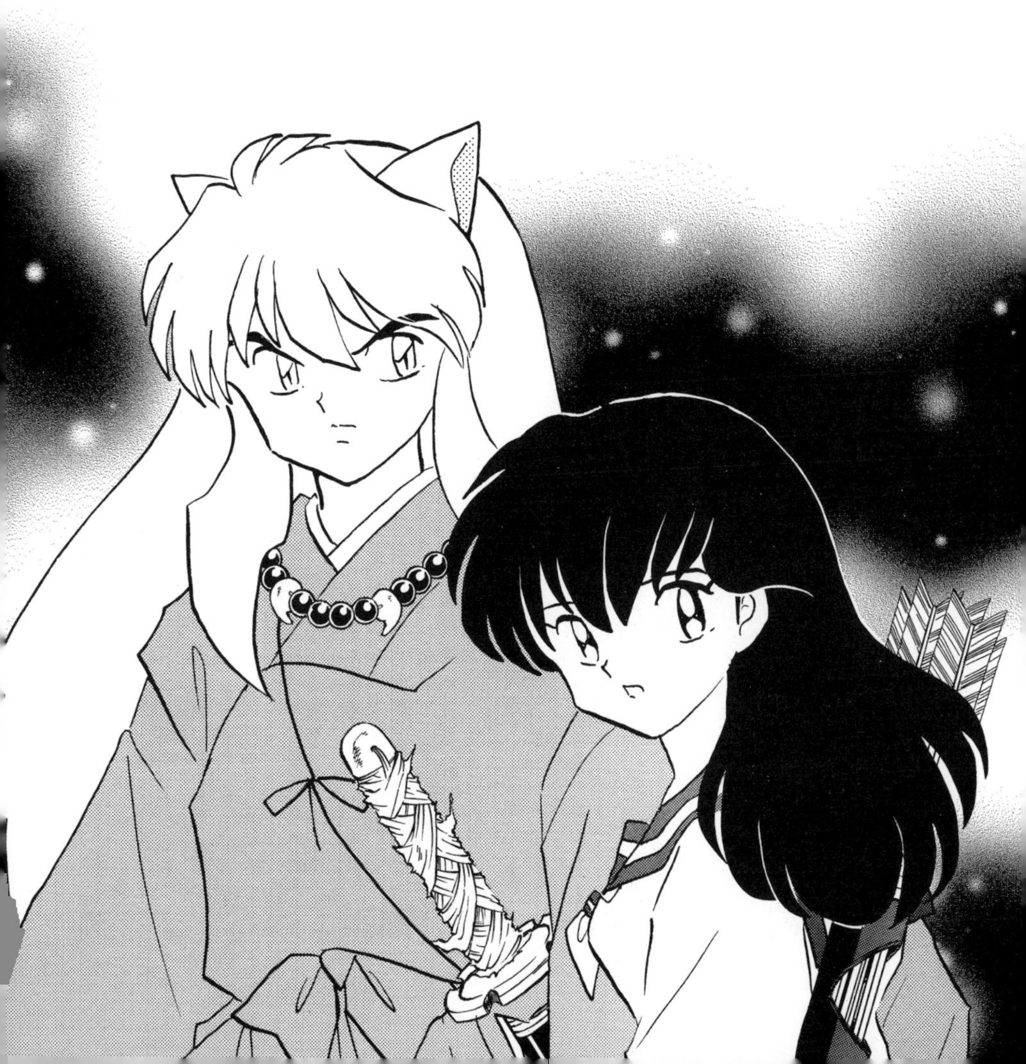

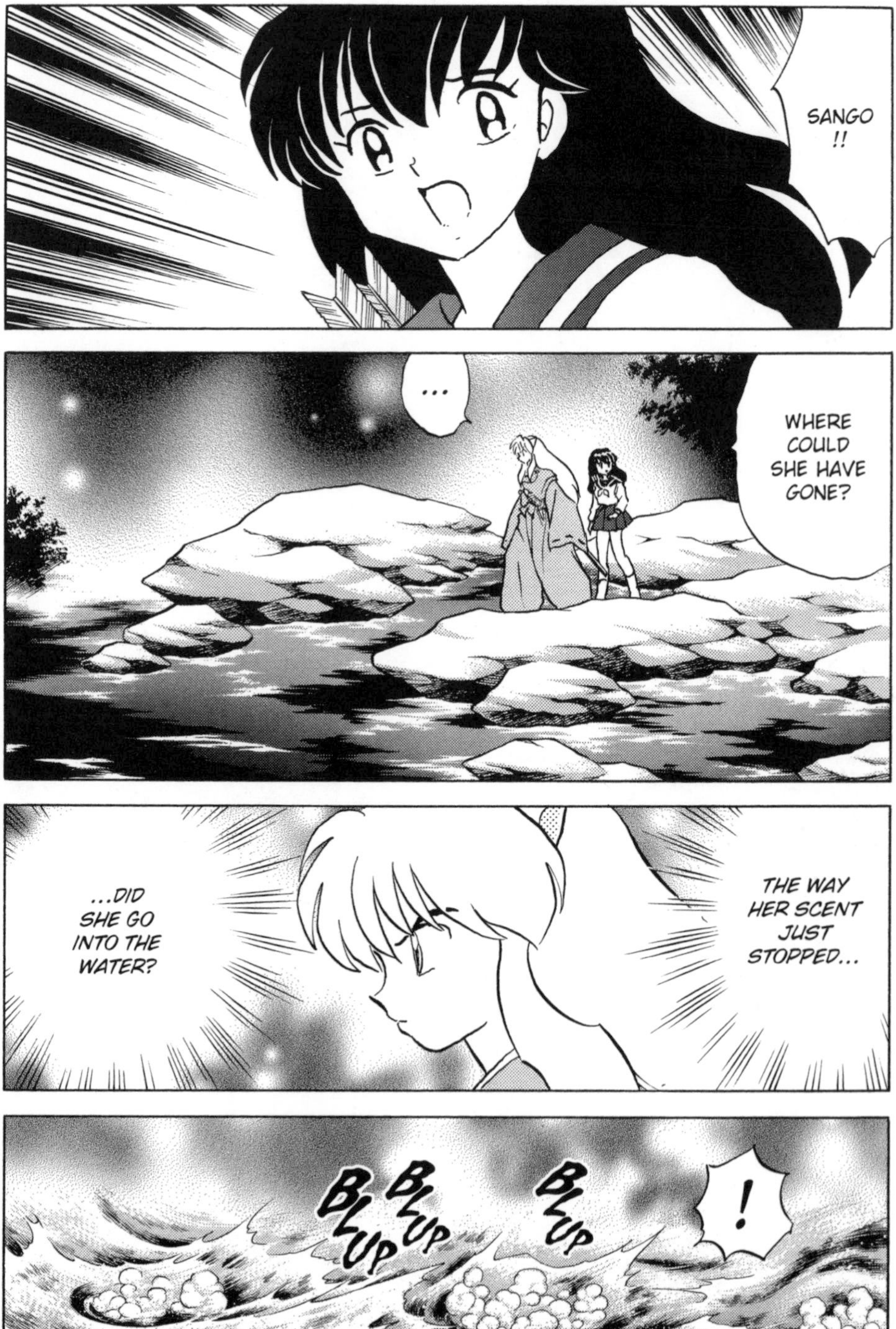
SANGO !!
WHERE COULD SHE HAVE GONE?
...
THE WAY HER SCENT JUST STOPPED...
...DID SHE GO INTO THE WATER?
!
BLUP
BLUP
BLUP

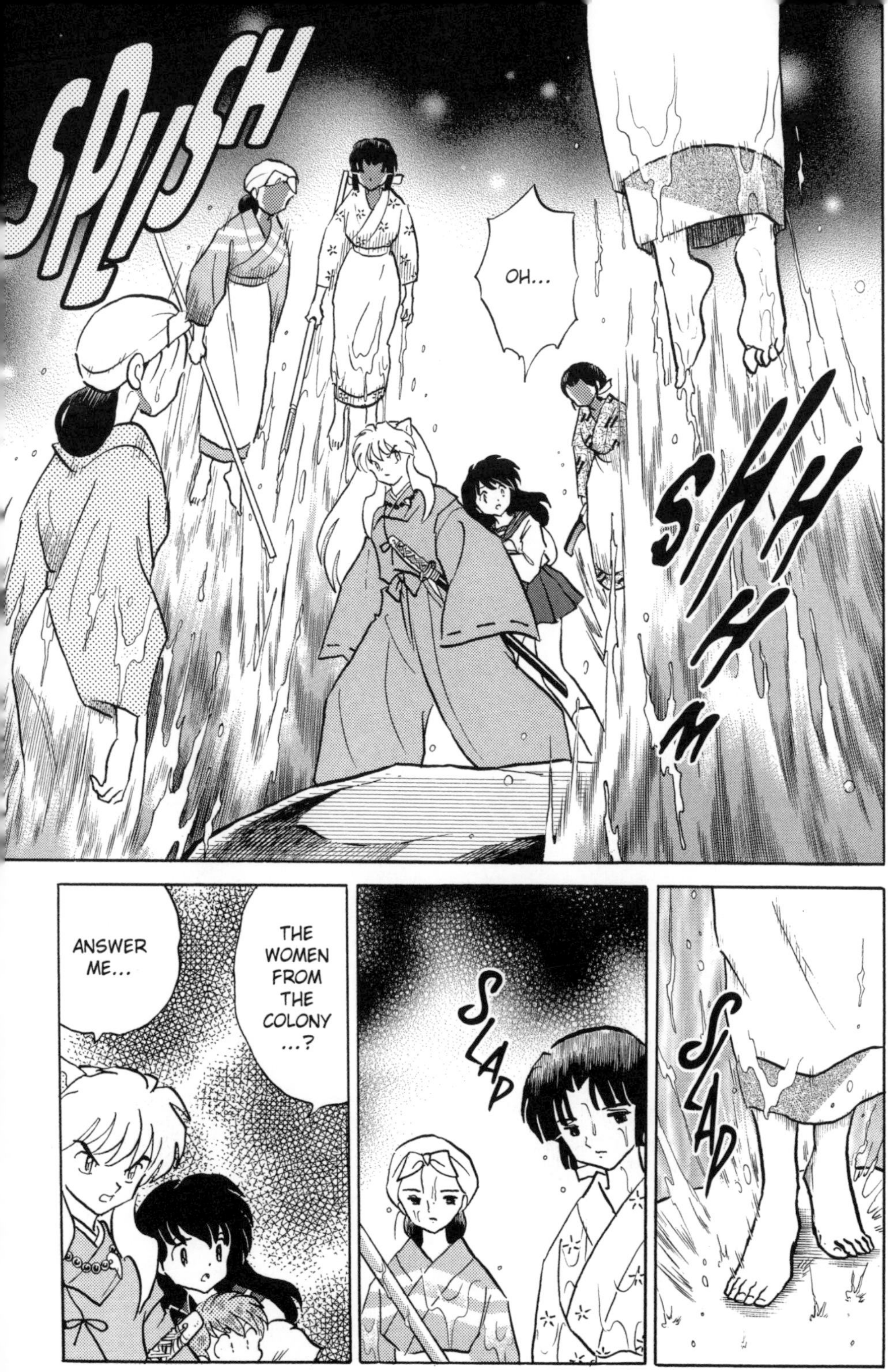
OH...
SHHHM
SPLISH
SLAP
SLAP
THE WOMEN FROM THE COLONY ...?
ANSWER ME...

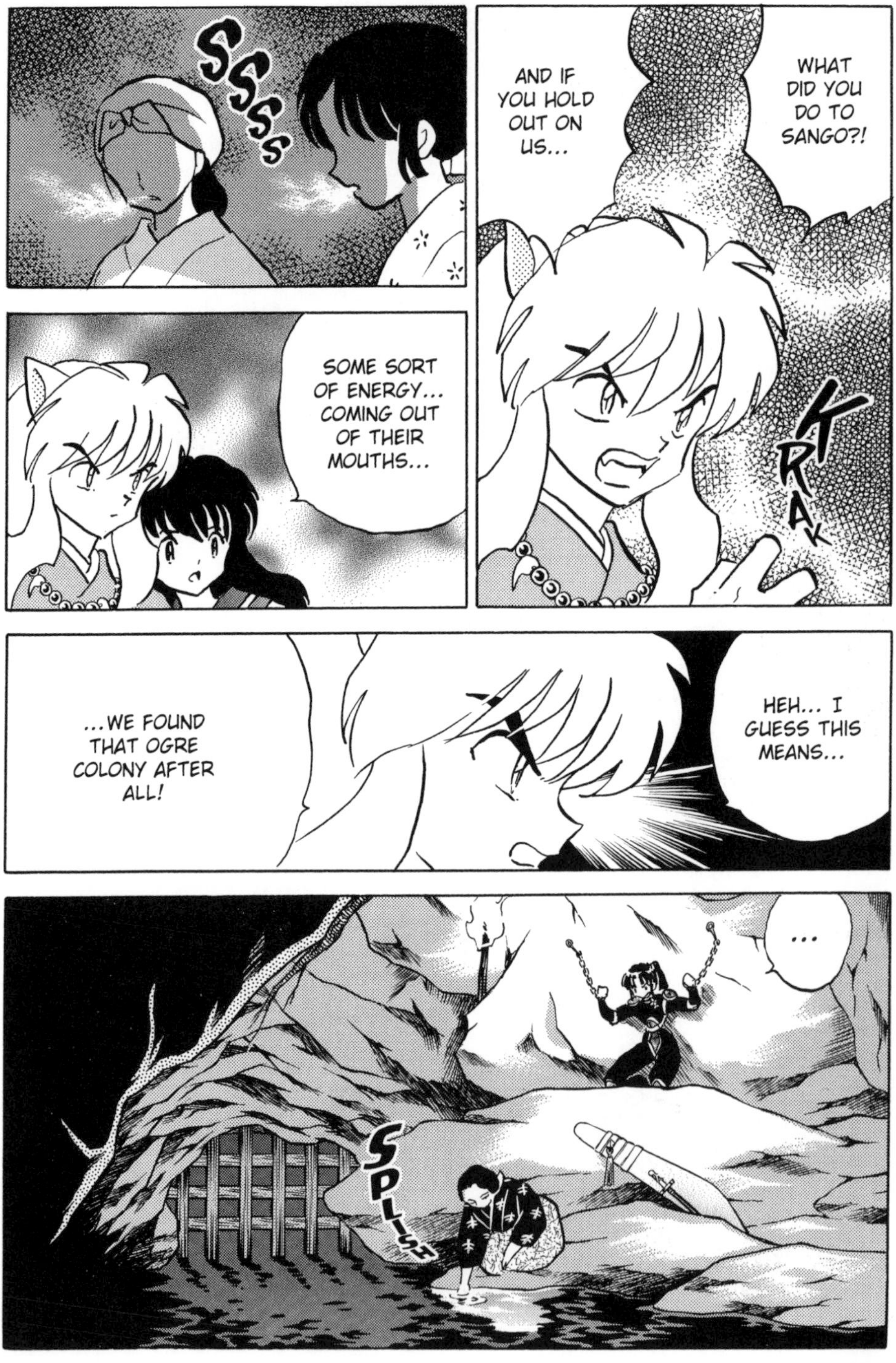
WHAT DID YOU DO TO SANGO?!
AND IF YOU HOLD OUT ON US...
KRAK
SSSS
SOME SORT OF ENERGY... COMING OUT OF THEIR MOUTHS...
HEH... I GUESS THIS MEANS...
...WE FOUND THAT OGRE COLONY AFTER ALL!
...
SPLISH

SOME CREA- TURE'S EGGS?!

WHAT IS THAT?!

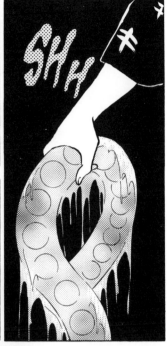

HATCH IT WITHIN YOUR BELLY...

SWALLOW IT.

...AND BECOME ONE OF US.

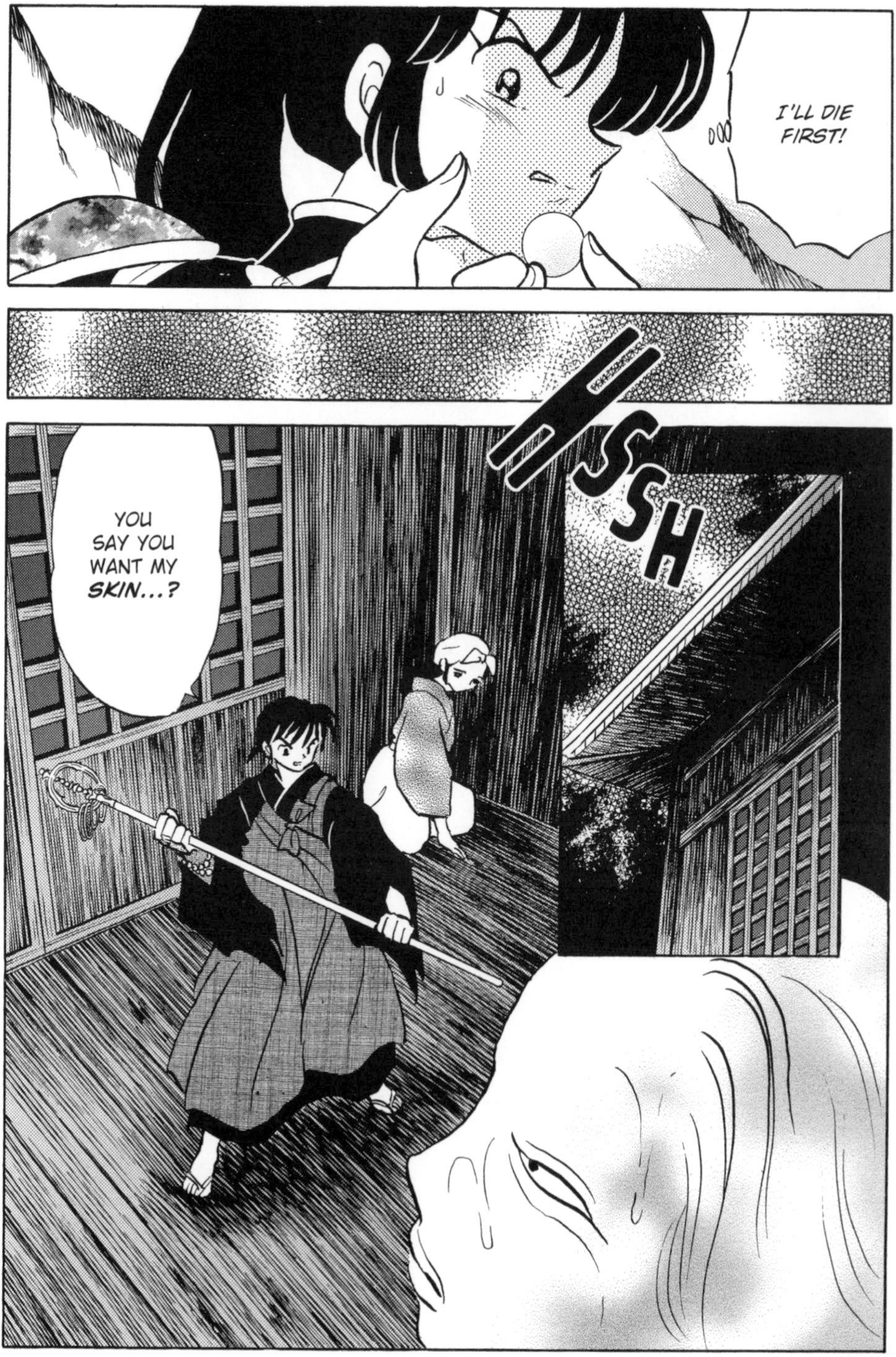
I'LL DIE FIRST!
HSSH
YOU SAY YOU WANT MY SKIN...?

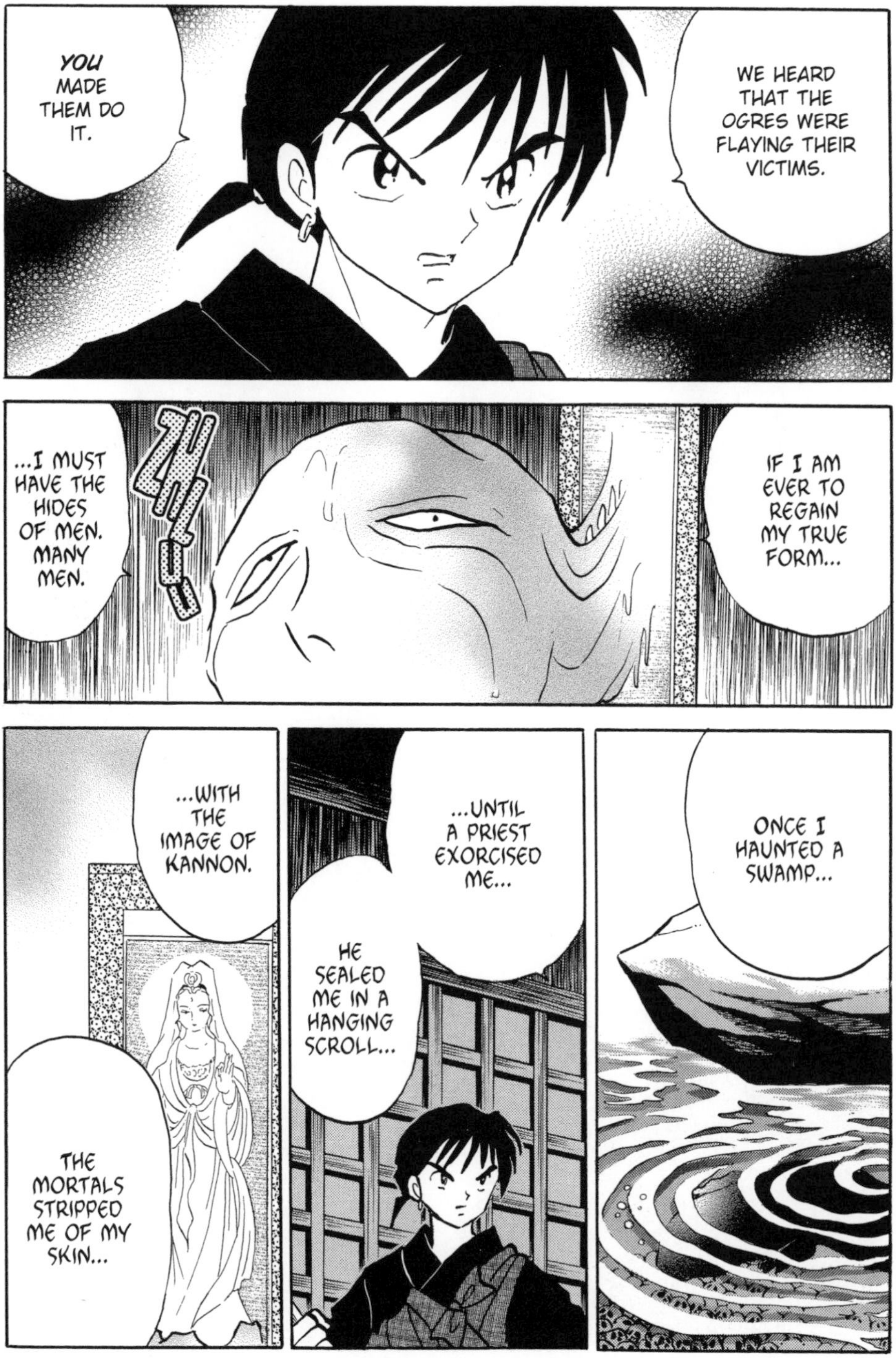
WE HEARD THAT THE OGRES WERE FLAYING THEIR VICTIMS.
YOU MADE THEM DO IT.
IF I AM EVER TO REGAIN MY TRUE FORM...
...I MUST HAVE THE HIDES OF MEN. MANY MEN.
ONCE I HAUNTED A SWAMP...
...UNTIL A PRIEST EXORCISED ME...
HE SEALED ME IN A HANGING SCROLL...
...WITH THE IMAGE OF KANNON.
THE MORTALS STRIPPED ME OF MY SKIN...

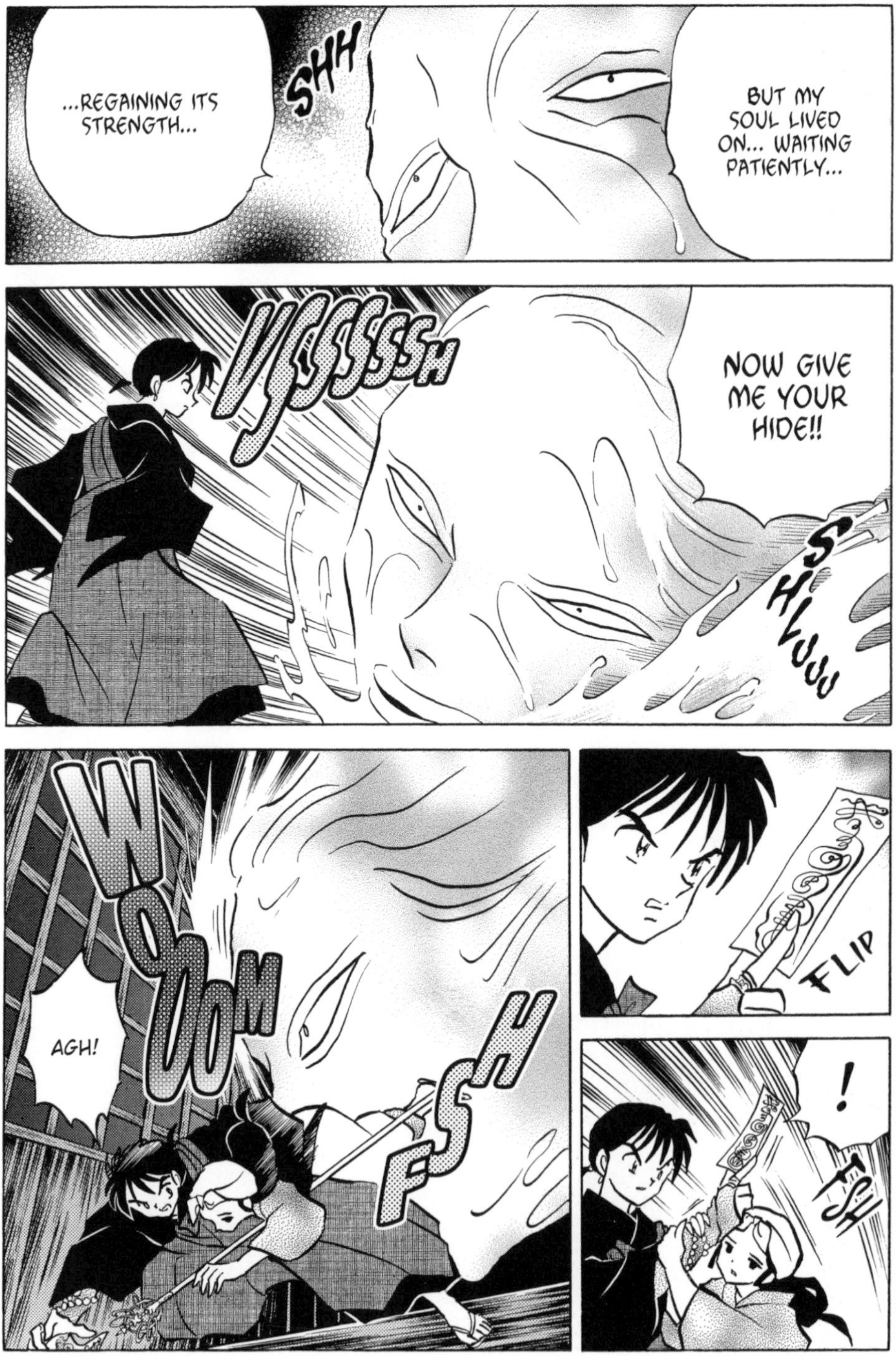
BUT MY SOUL LIVED ON... WAITING PATIENTLY...
SHH
...REGAINING ITS STRENGTH...
NOW GIVE ME YOUR HIDE!!
SHUUU
VSSSSSSH
FLIP
!
FSH
WOOOM
AGH!
FSSH

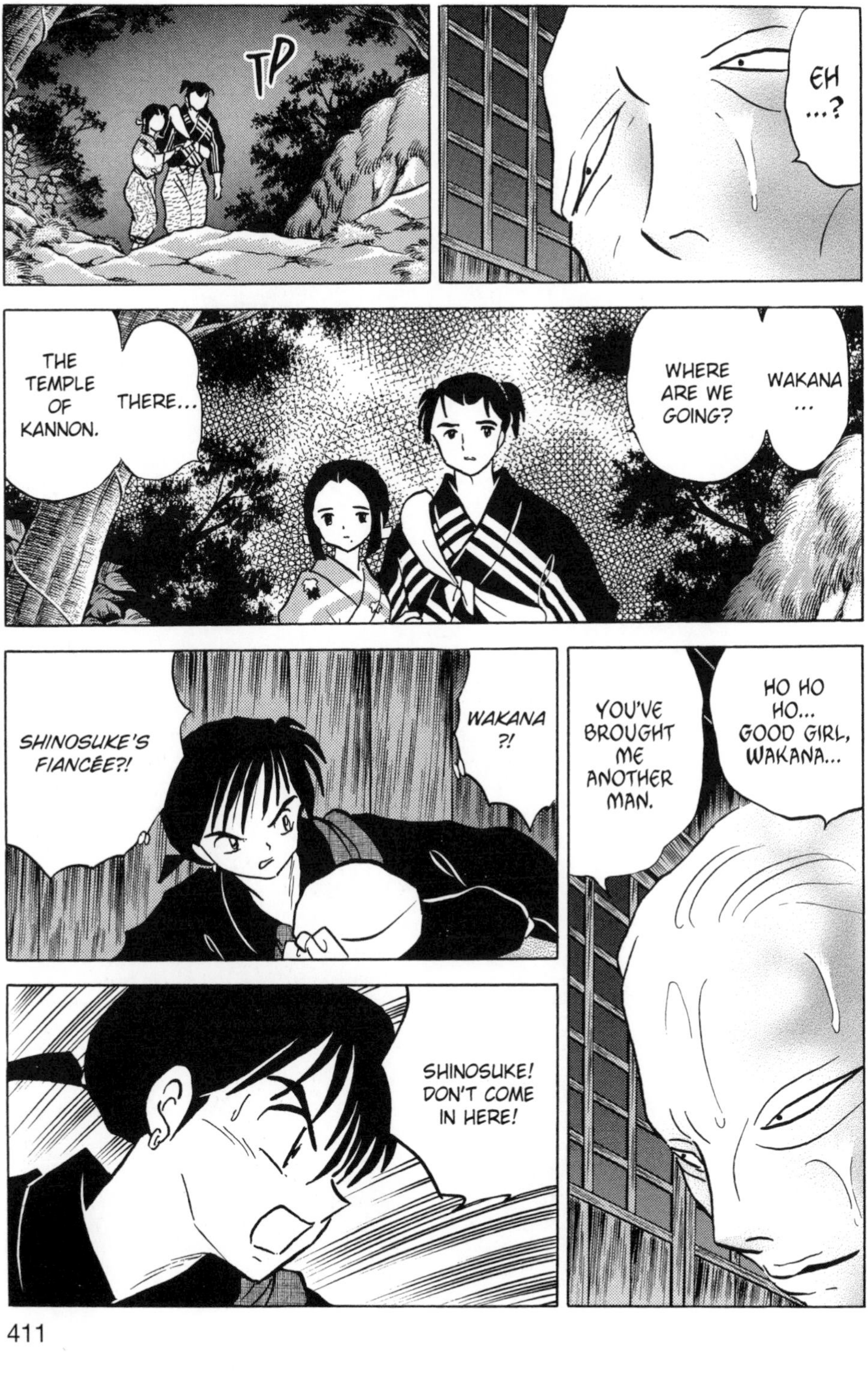
EH ...?
TP
WAKANA ...
WHERE ARE WE GOING?
THERE...
THE TEMPLE OF KANNON.
HO HO HO... GOOD GIRL, WAKANA...
YOU'VE BROUGHT ME ANOTHER MAN.
WAKANA ?!
SHINOSUKE'S FIANCÉE?!
SHINOSUKE! DON'T COME IN HERE!

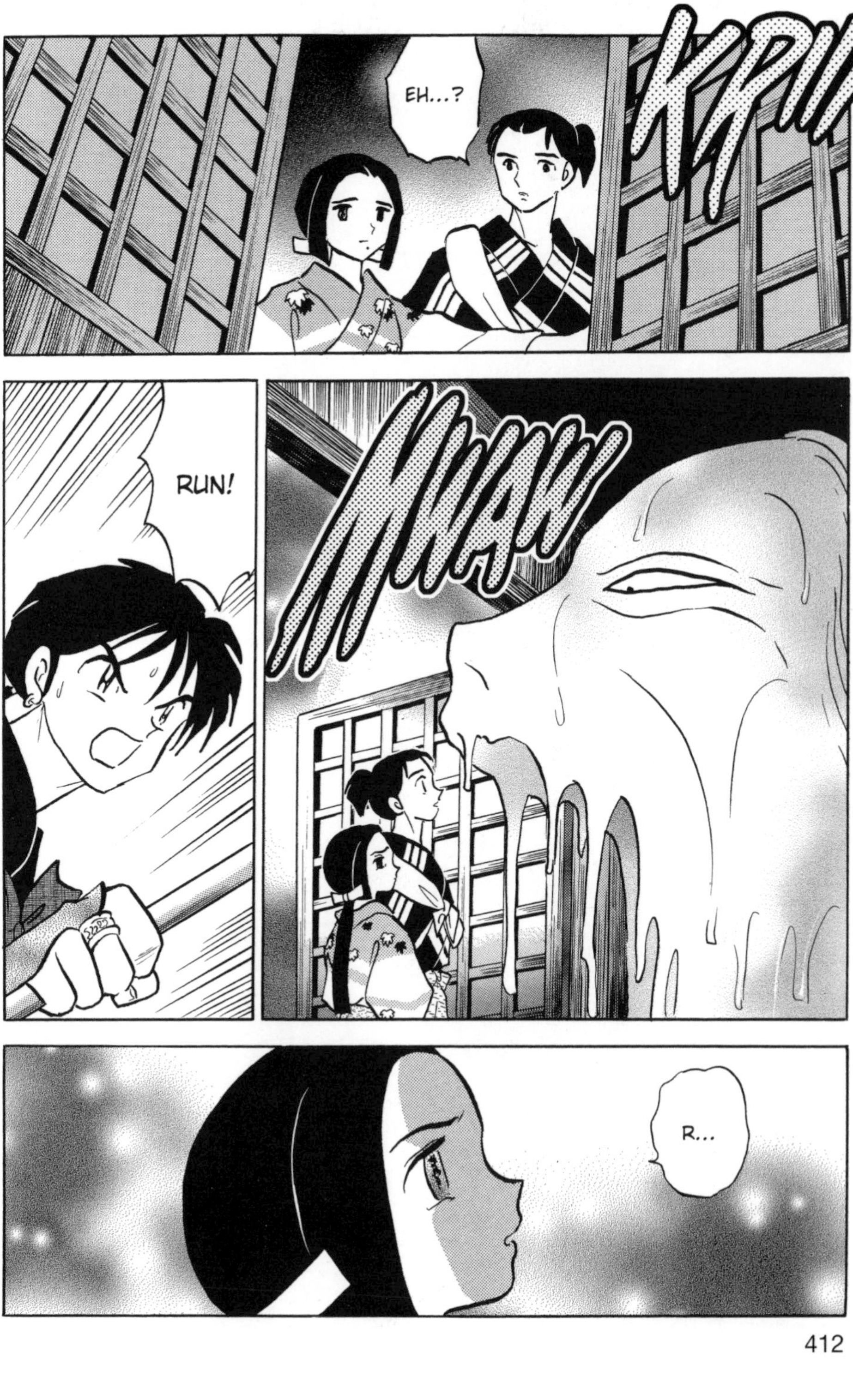
EH...?
RUN!
R...

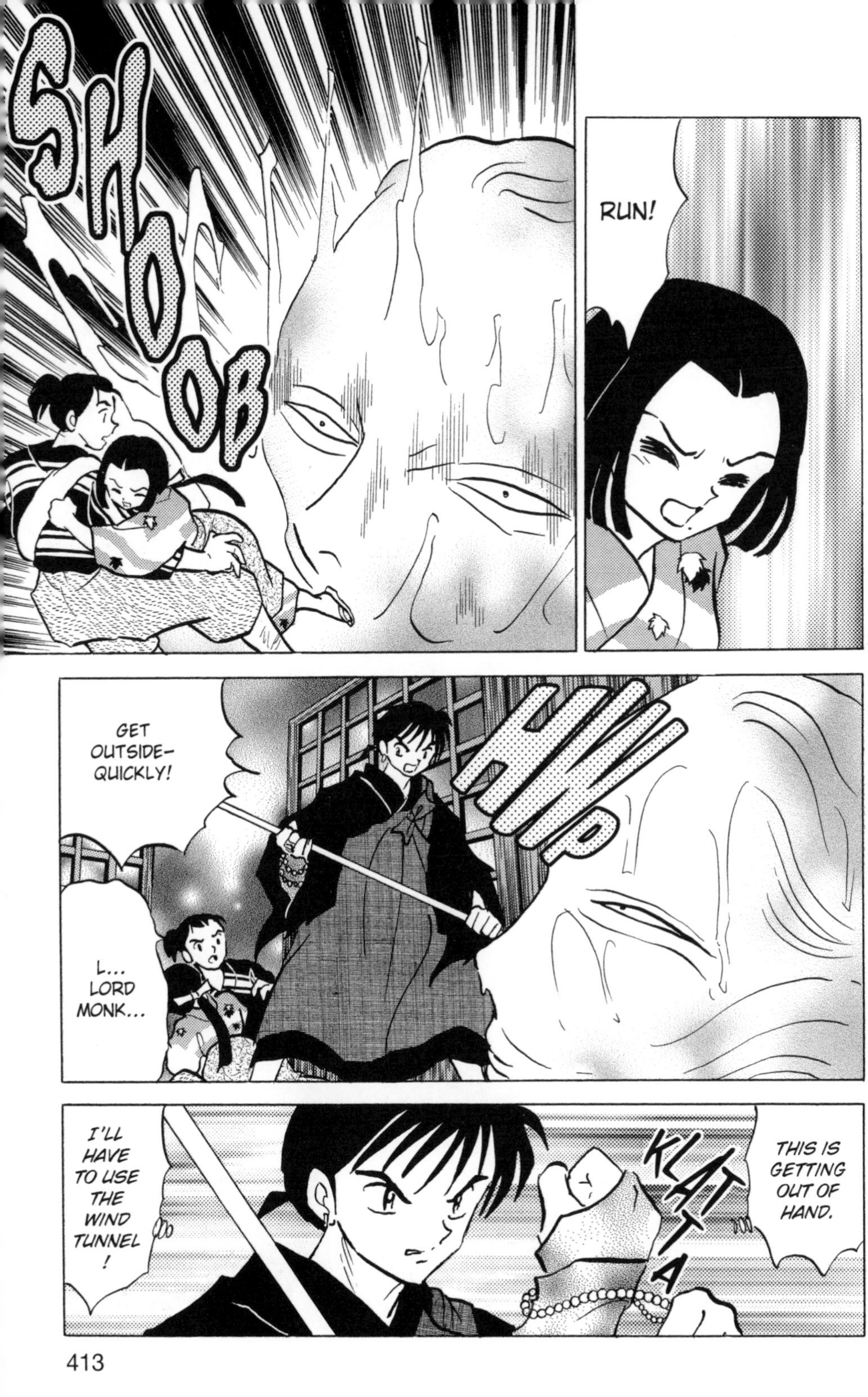
RUN!
SHOOOB
HWIP
GET OUTSIDE- QUICKLY!
L... LORD MONK...
THIS IS GETTING OUT OF HAND.
KLATTA
I'LL HAVE TO USE THE WIND TUNNEL!

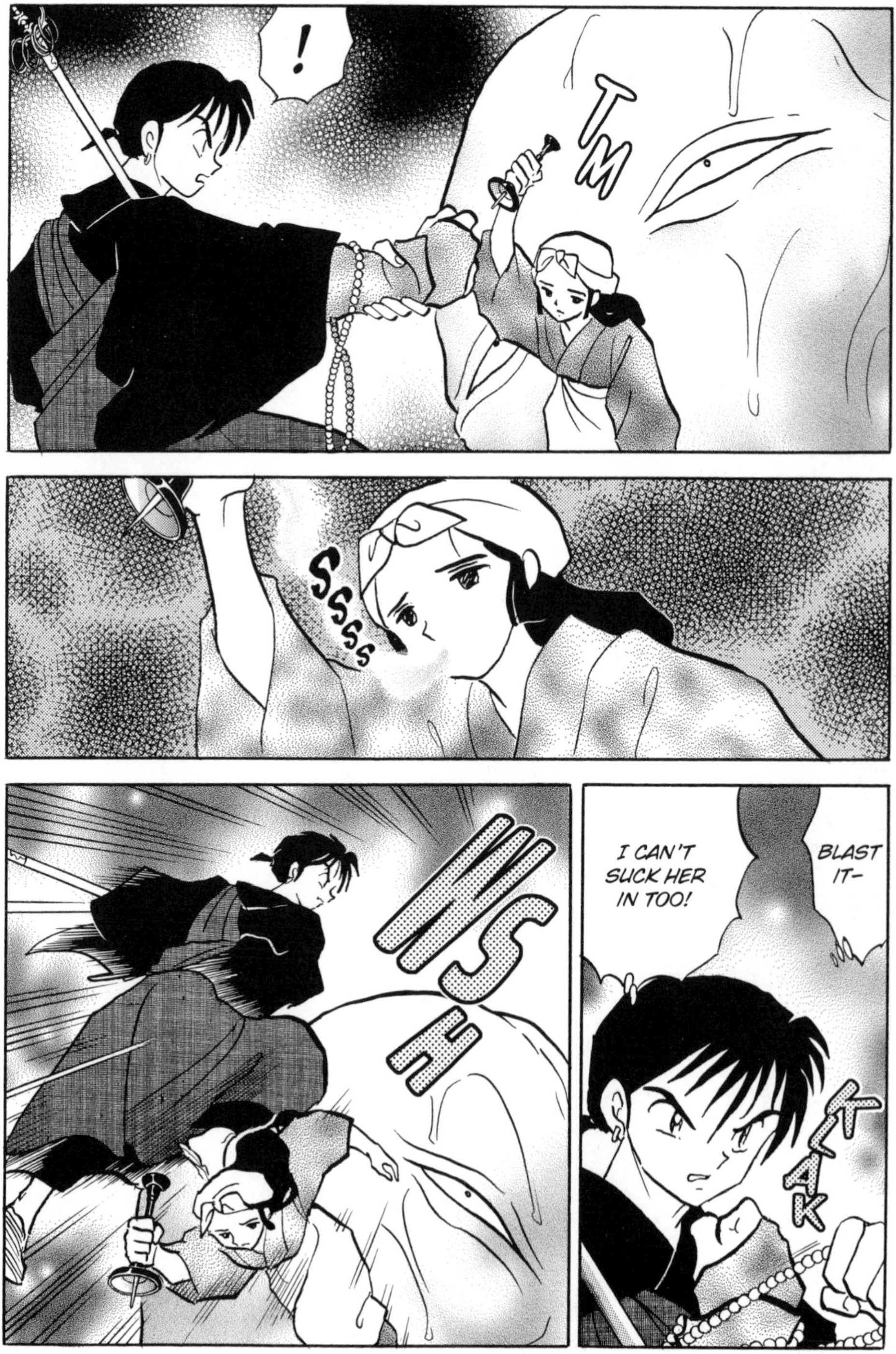
!
TM
SSSSS
BLAST IT-
I CAN'T SUCK HER IN TOO!
KLAK
WSH

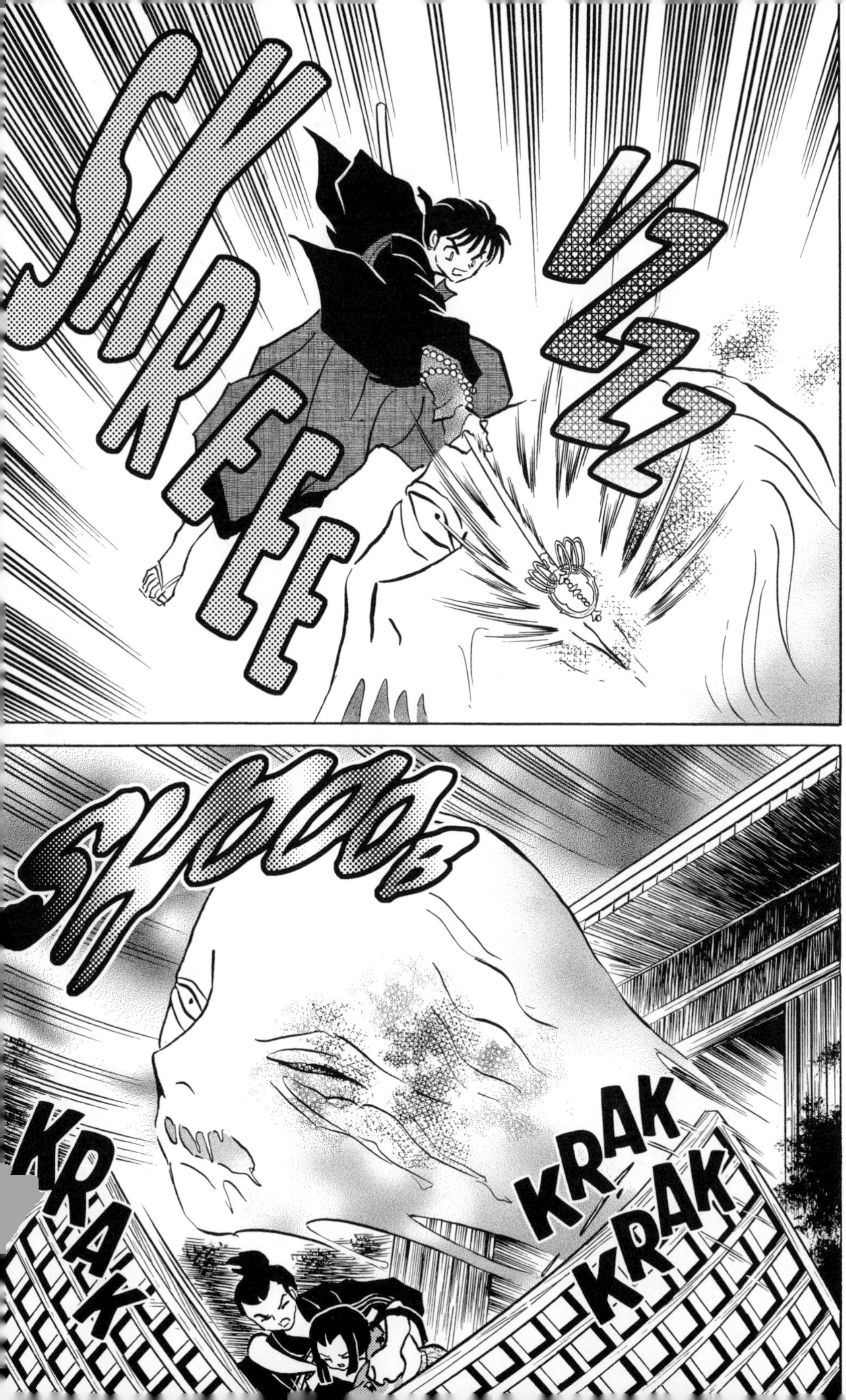
VZZZ
SHREEE
SHOOOB
KRAK KRAK
KRAK KRAK

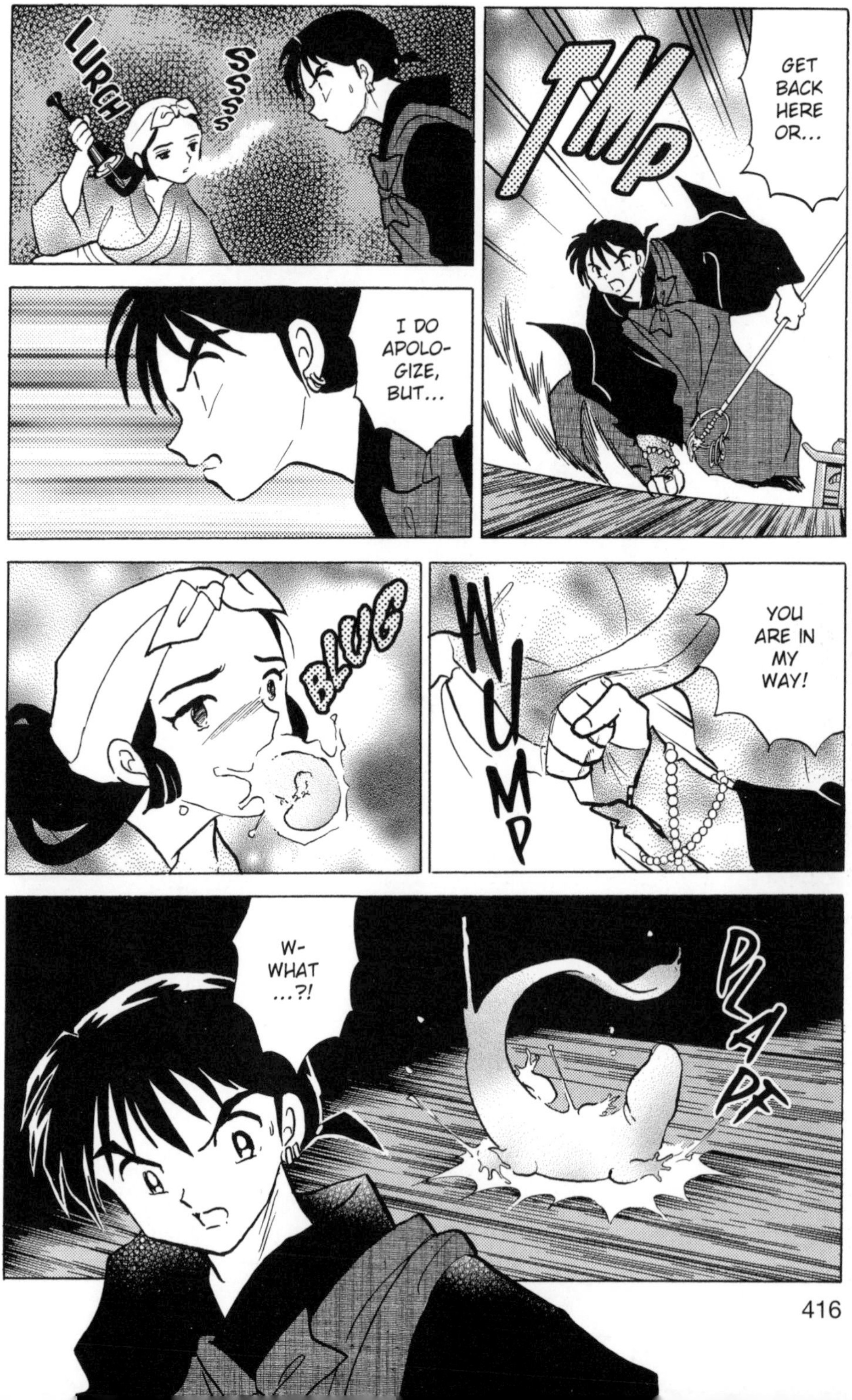
TMP
GET BACK HERE OR...
LURCH
SSSSS
I DO APOLOGIZE, BUT...
WUMP
YOU ARE IN MY WAY!
BLUG
W-WHAT ...?!
PLADF

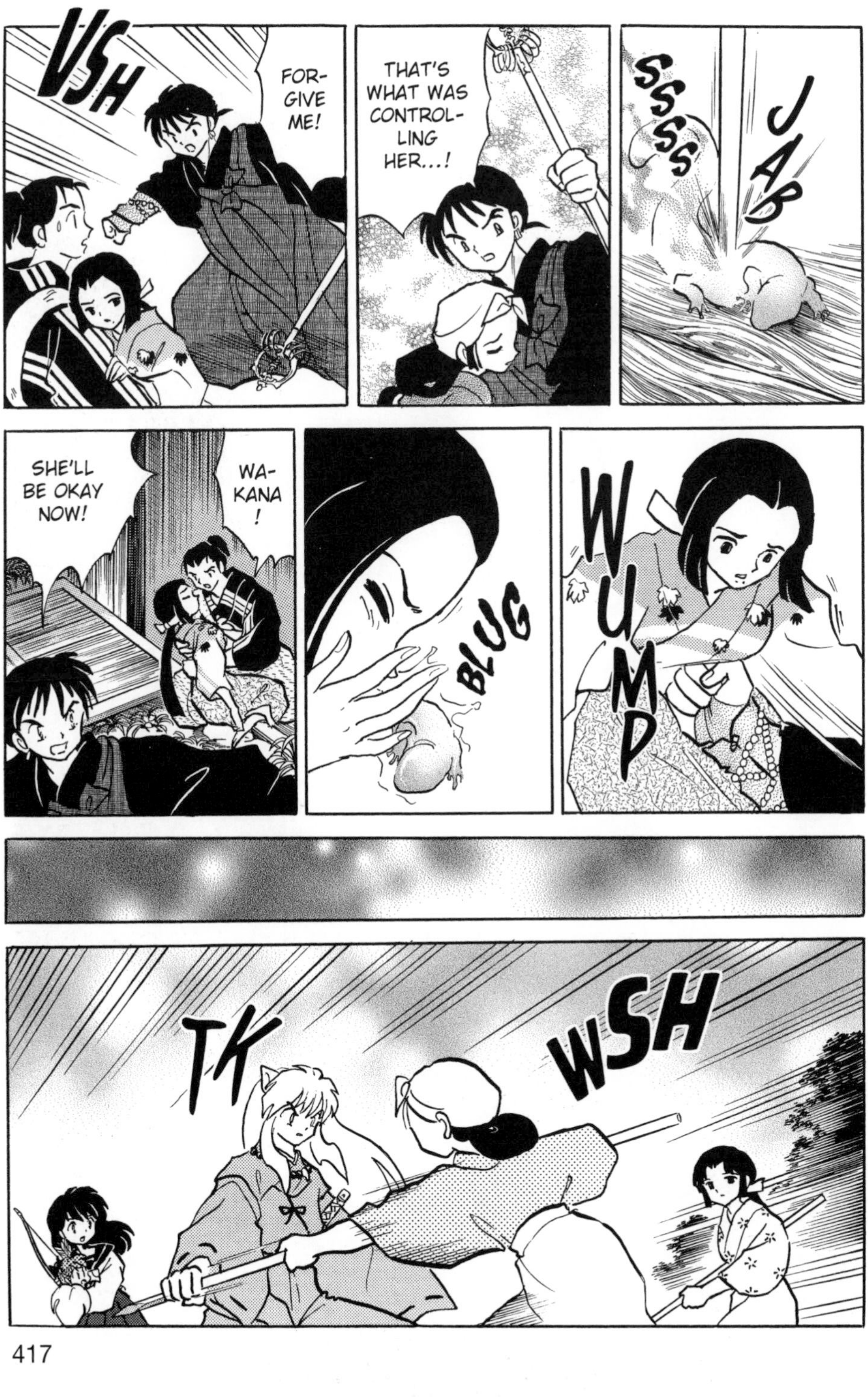

JAB
SSSS
THAT'S WHAT WAS CONTROLLING HER...!
VSH
FORGIVE ME!
WUMP
BLUG
WAKANA!
SHE'LL BE OKAY NOW!
WSH
TK

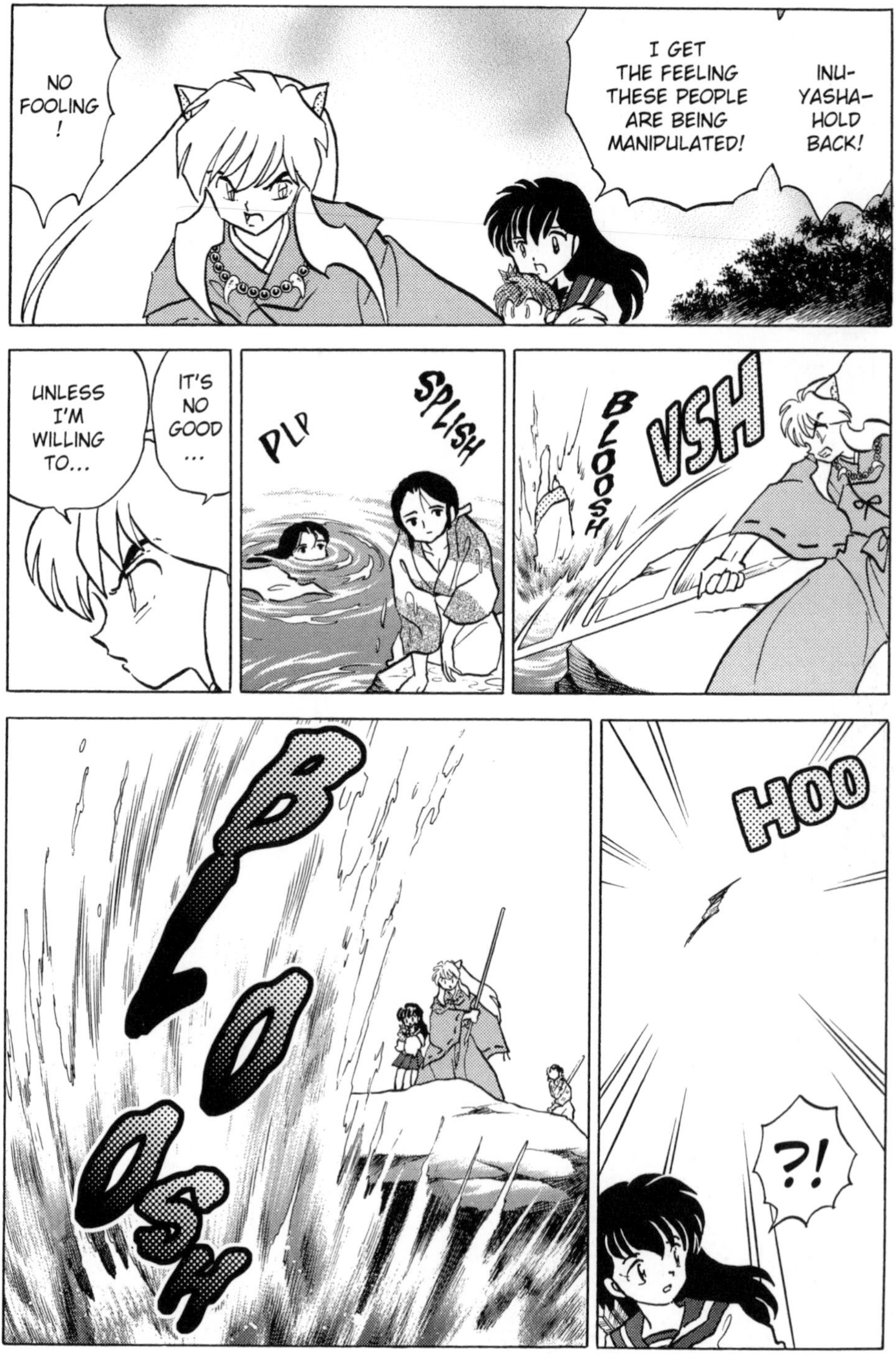
INU-YASHA—HOLD BACK!
I GET THE FEELING THESE PEOPLE ARE BEING MANIPULATED!
NO FOOLING!
VSH
BLOOSH
SPLISH
PLP
IT'S NO GOOD...
UNLESS I'M WILLING TO...
HOO
?!
BLOOSH

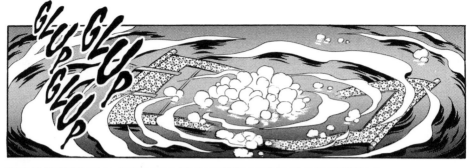

GLUP·GLUP·GLUP

A HANGING SCROLL ?!

SHOOOO!

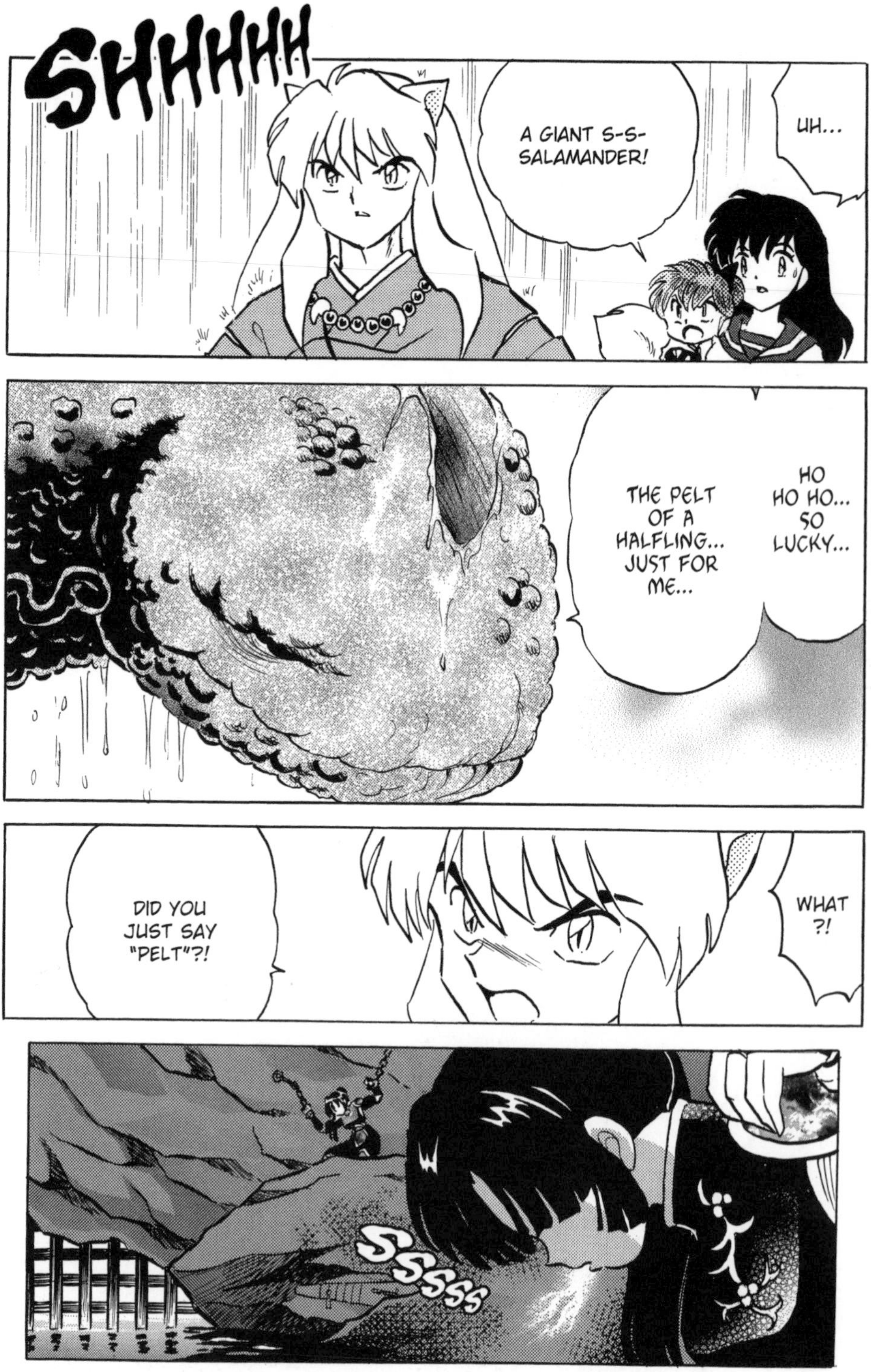
SHHHHH
UH...
A GIANT S-S-SALAMANDER!
HO HO HO... SO LUCKY...
THE PELT OF A HALFLING... JUST FOR ME...
WHAT?!
DID YOU JUST SAY "PELT"?!
SSSSS

SCROLL THREE
SANGO'S WHEREABOUTS

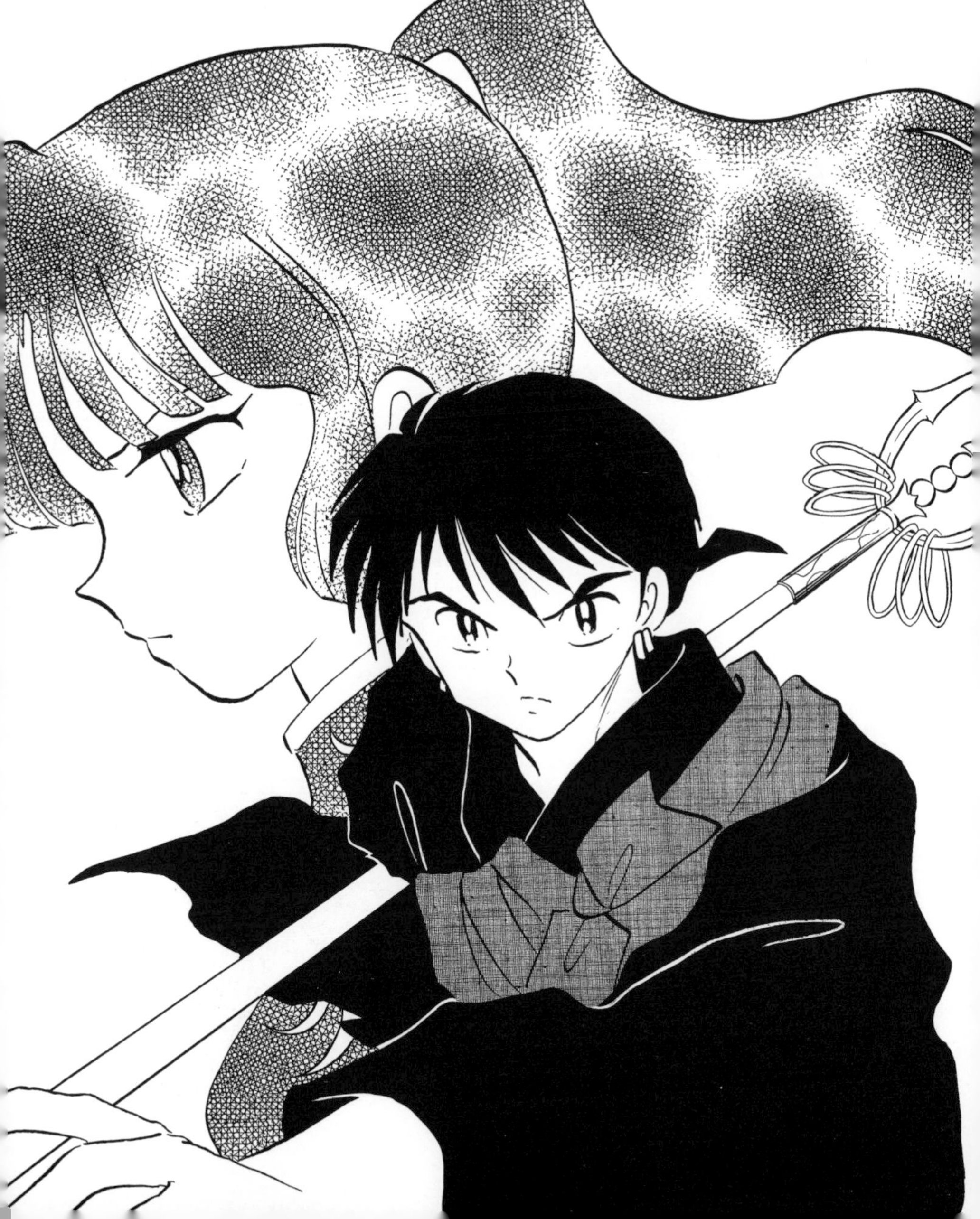

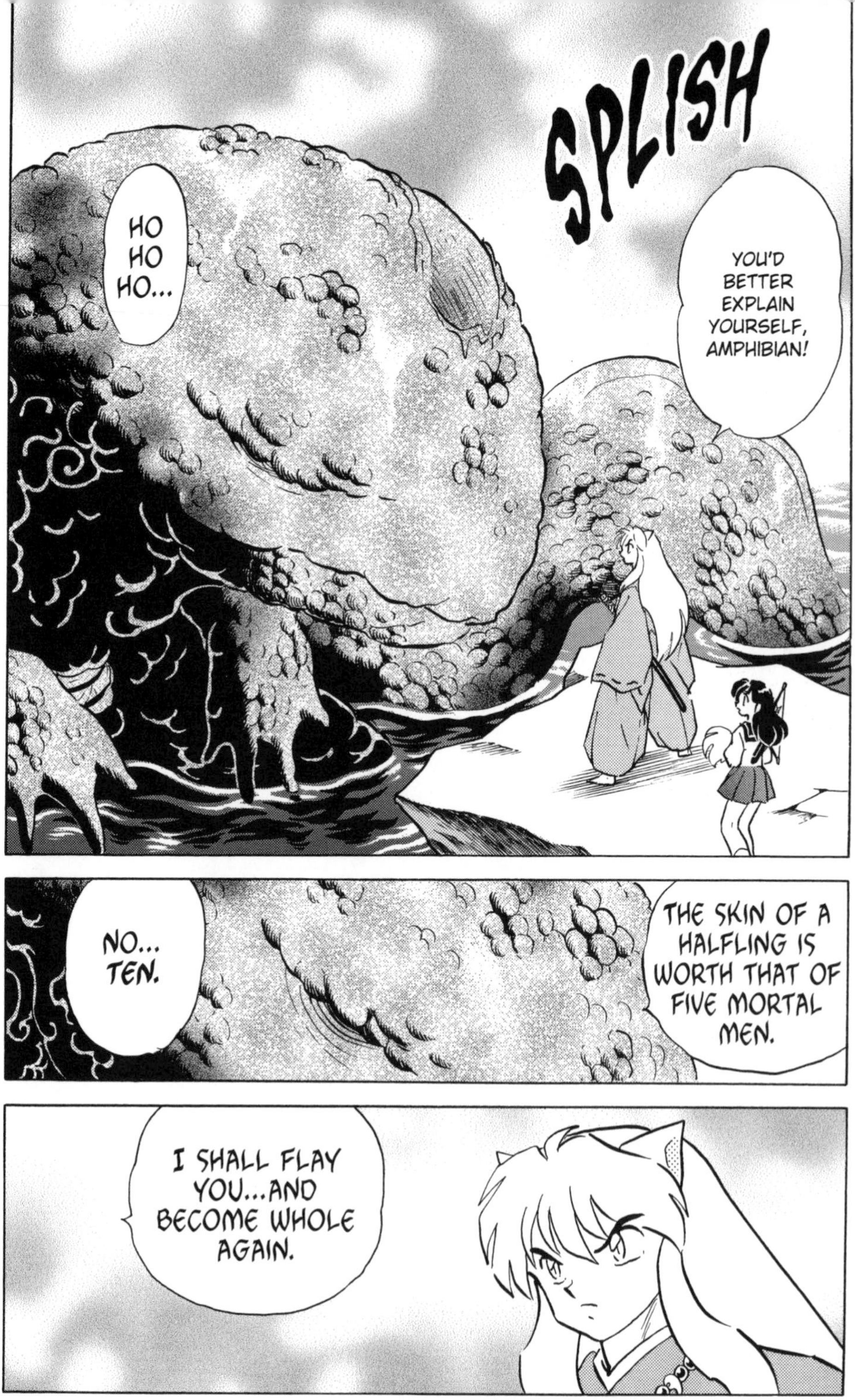
SPLISH
YOU'D BETTER EXPLAIN YOURSELF, AMPHIBIAN!
HO HO HO...
THE SKIN OF A HALFLING IS WORTH THAT OF FIVE MORTAL MEN.
NO... TEN.
I SHALL FLAY YOU...AND BECOME WHOLE AGAIN.

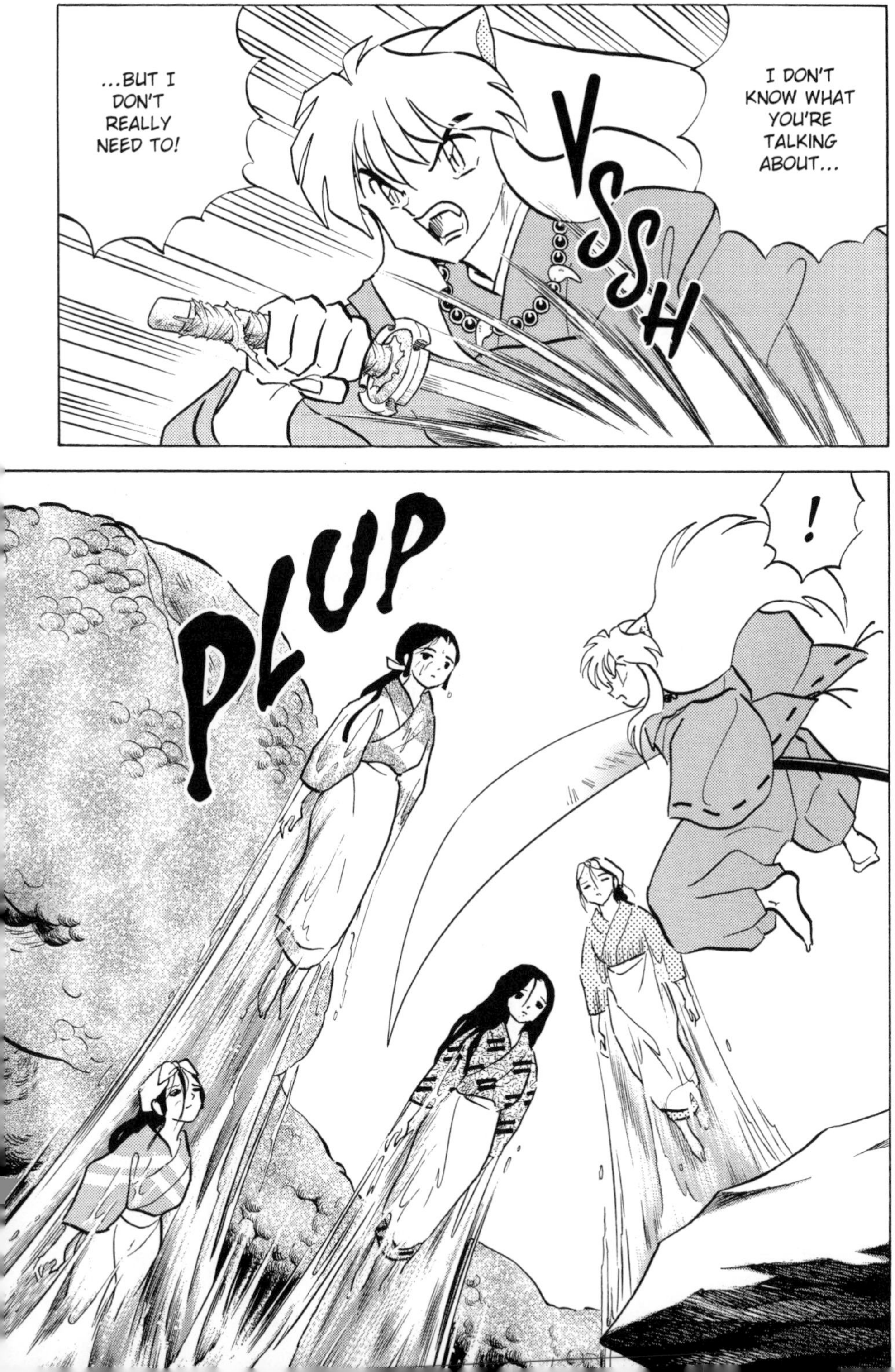
I DON'T KNOW WHAT YOU'RE TALKING ABOUT...
VSSH
...BUT I DON'T REALLY NEED TO!
!
PLUP

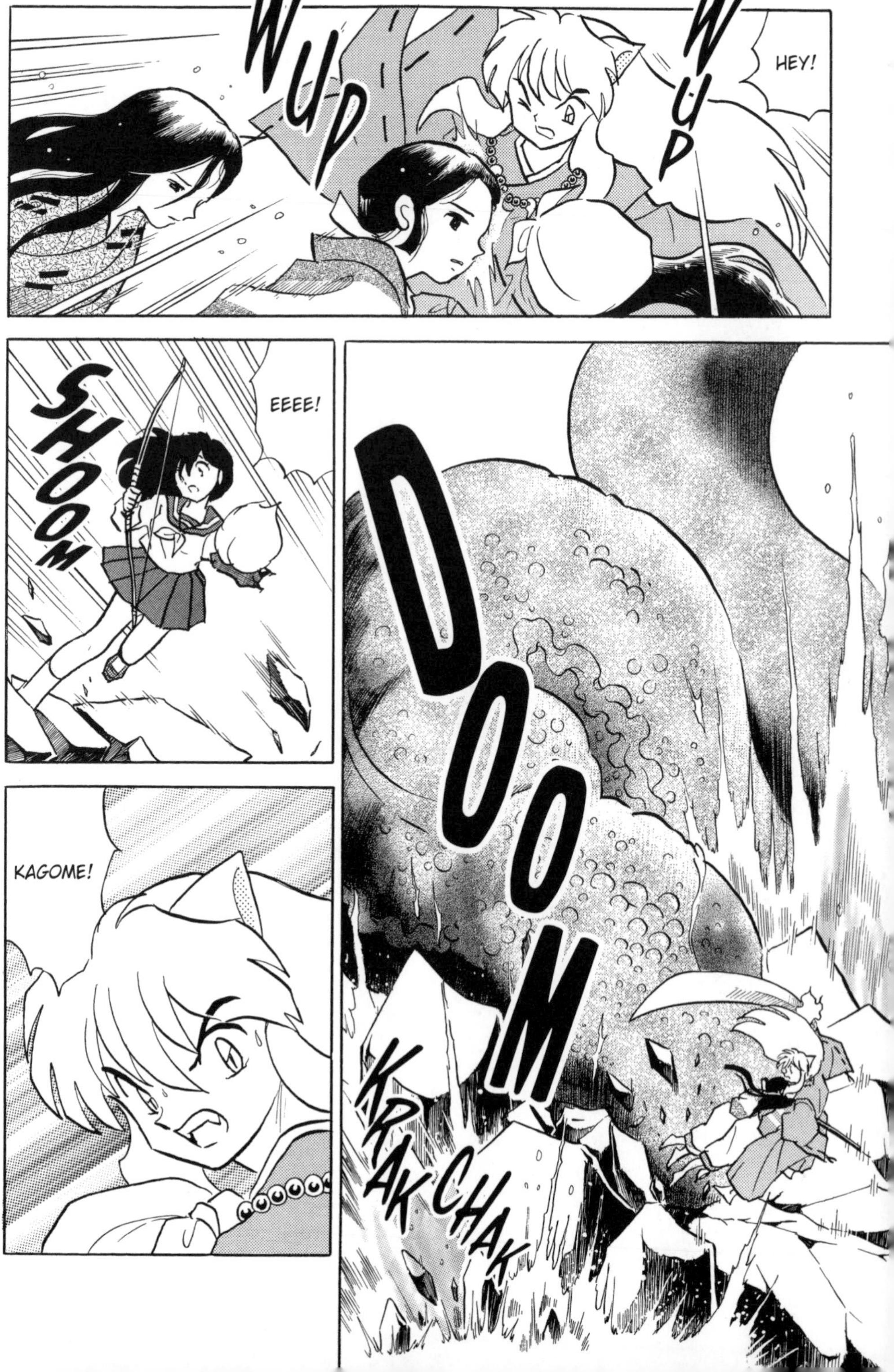
HEY!
WUP
WUP
DOOOM
KRAK
CHAK
EEEE!
SHOOOM
KAGOME!

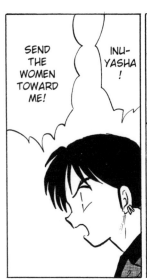

WMP
AT LAST IT SHOWS ITSELF!
LORD MIROKU...
INU-YASHA!
SEND THE WOMEN TOWARD ME!
OKAY...
BUT IF THIS IS JUST MORE OF YOUR CRAP...
WHMMM
WUP
FORGIVE ME!
WUP

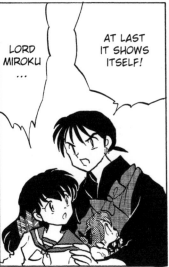

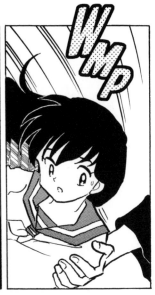

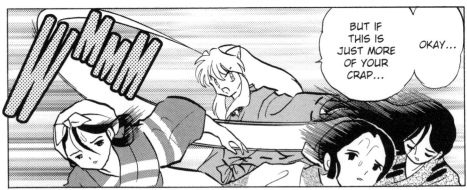

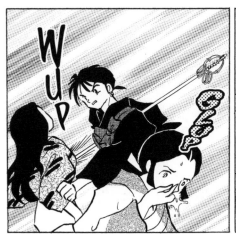

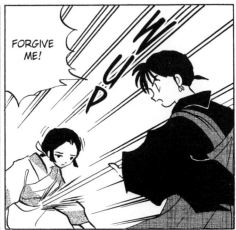

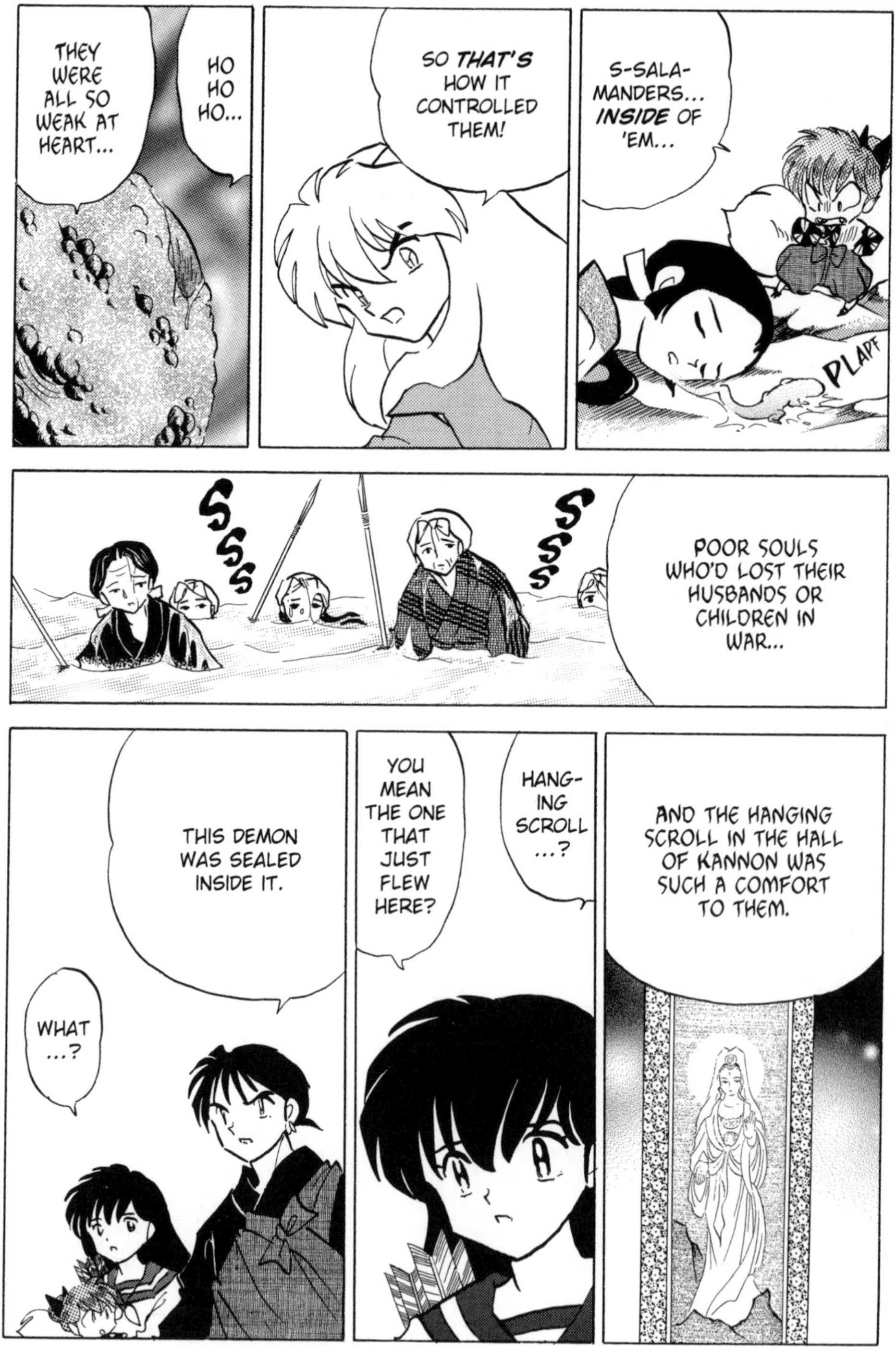
S-SALA-MANDERS... *INSIDE* OF 'EM...
PLAPF
SO *THAT'S* HOW IT CONTROLLED THEM!
HO HO HO...
THEY WERE ALL SO WEAK AT HEART...
POOR SOULS WHO'D LOST THEIR HUSBANDS OR CHILDREN IN WAR...
SSS
SSS
AND THE HANGING SCROLL IN THE HALL OF KANNON WAS SUCH A COMFORT TO THEM.
HANG-ING SCROLL ...?
YOU MEAN THE ONE THAT JUST FLEW HERE?
THIS DEMON WAS SEALED INSIDE IT.
WHAT ...?

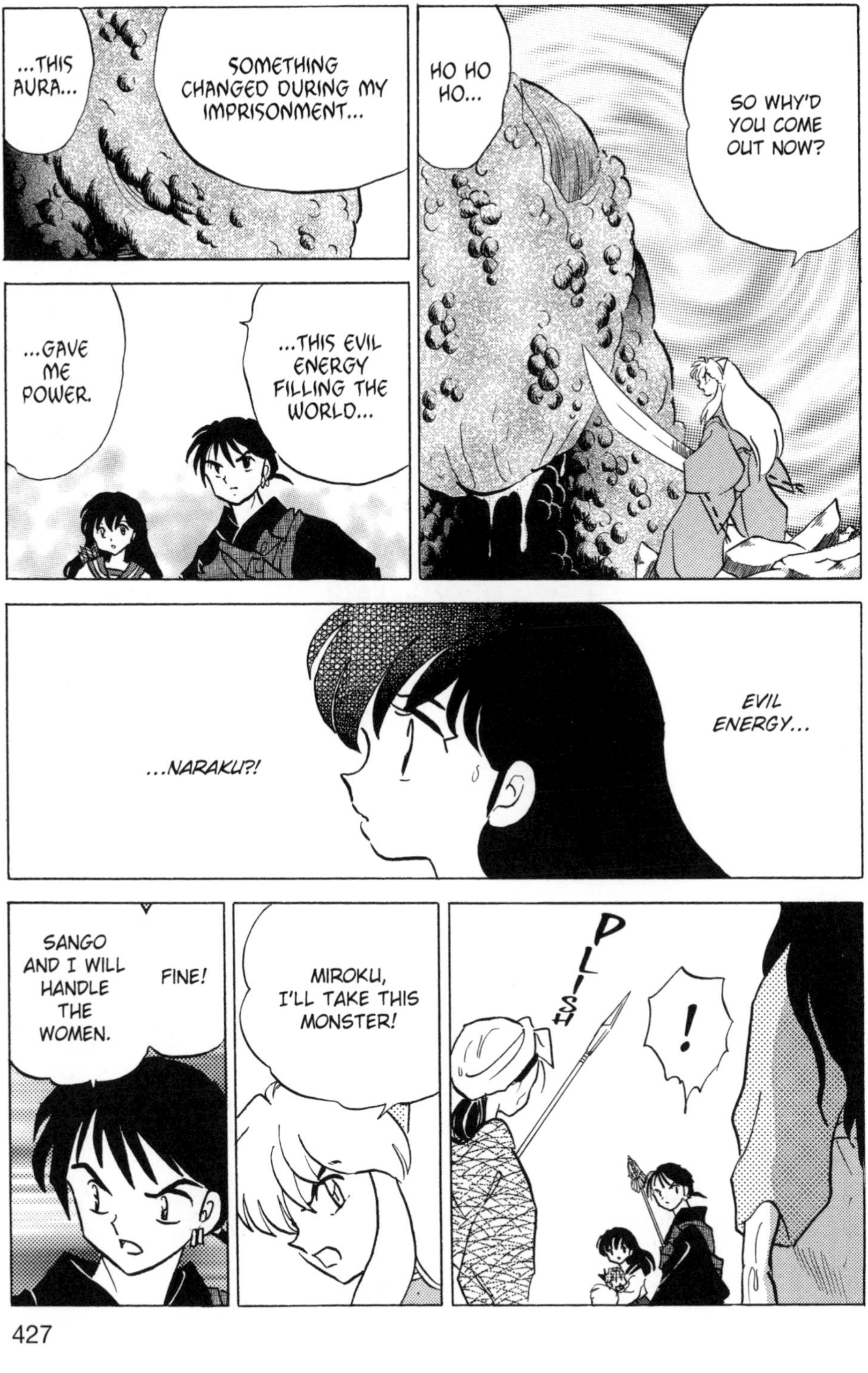
SO WHY'D YOU COME OUT NOW?
HO HO HO...
SOMETHING CHANGED DURING MY IMPRISONMENT...
...THIS AURA...
...THIS EVIL ENERGY FILLING THE WORLD...
...GAVE ME POWER.
EVIL ENERGY...
...NARAKU?!
PLISH
!
MIROKU, I'LL TAKE THIS MONSTER!
FINE!
SANGO AND I WILL HANDLE THE WOMEN.

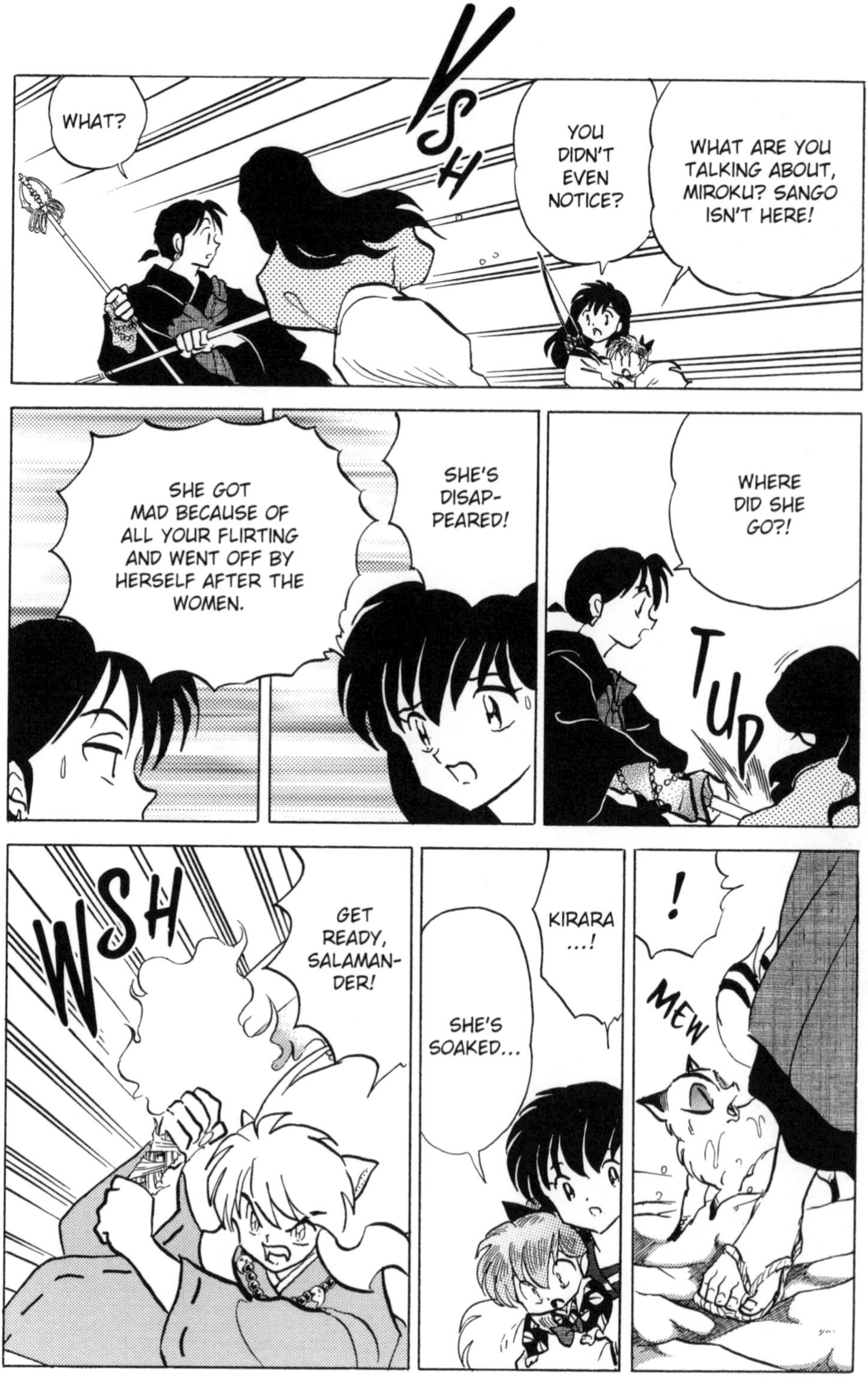
WHAT ARE YOU TALKING ABOUT, MIROKU? SANGO ISN'T HERE!
YOU DIDN'T EVEN NOTICE?
VSH
WHAT?
WHERE DID SHE GO?!
TUP
SHE'S DISAP-PEARED!
SHE GOT MAD BECAUSE OF ALL YOUR FLIRTING AND WENT OFF BY HERSELF AFTER THE WOMEN.
!
MEW
KIRARA ...!
SHE'S SOAKED...
GET READY, SALAMAN-DER!
WSH

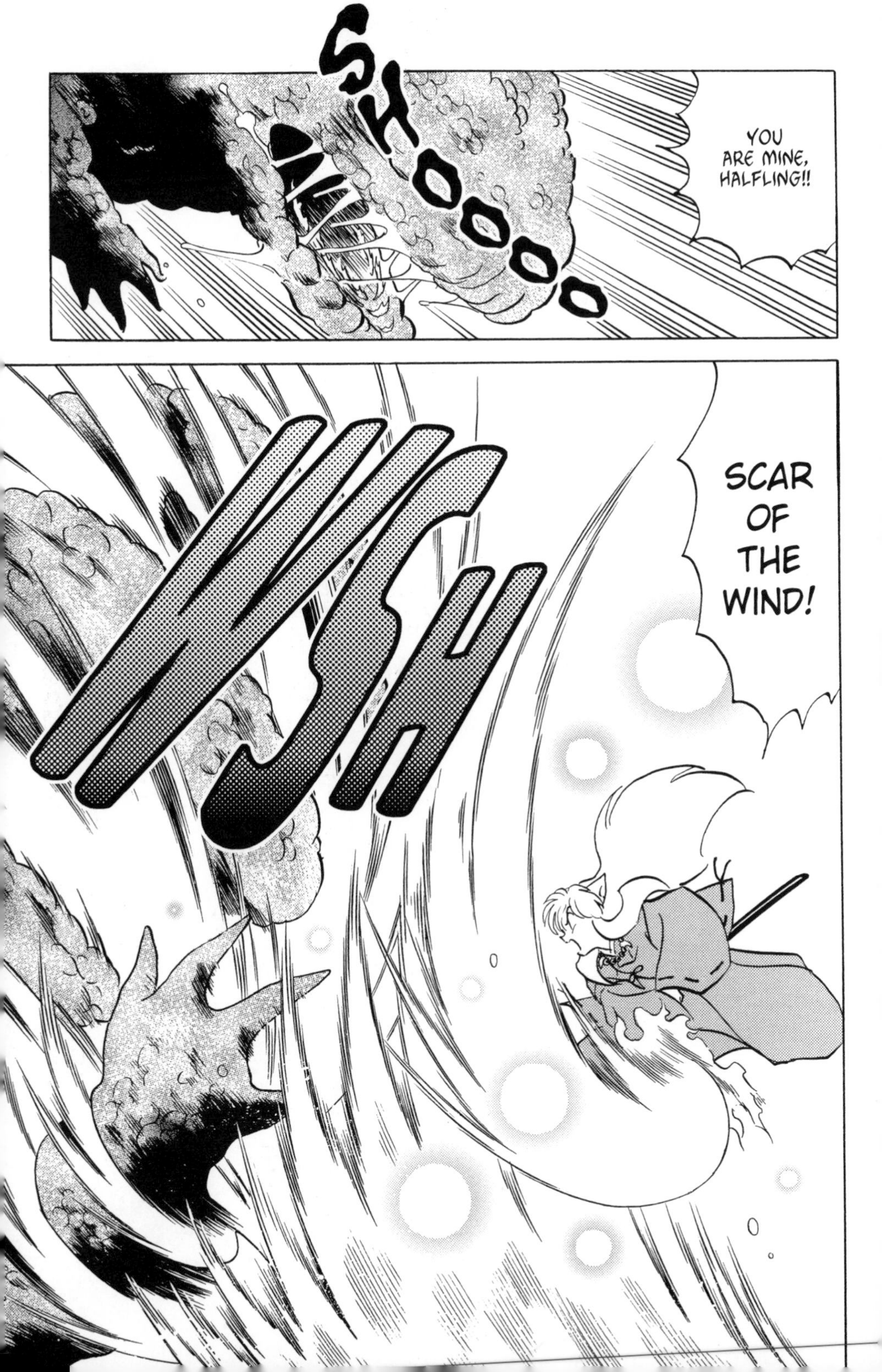
YOU ARE MINE, HALFLING!!
SHOOOOO
SCAR OF THE WIND!
WSH

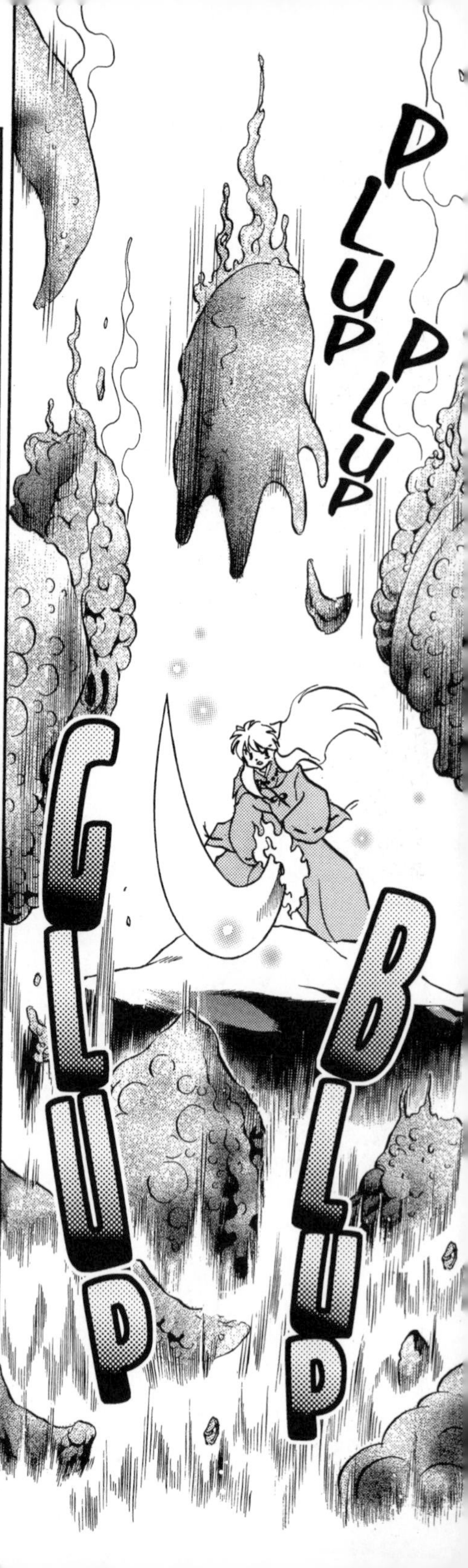
PLUP
PLUP
BLUP
CLUP

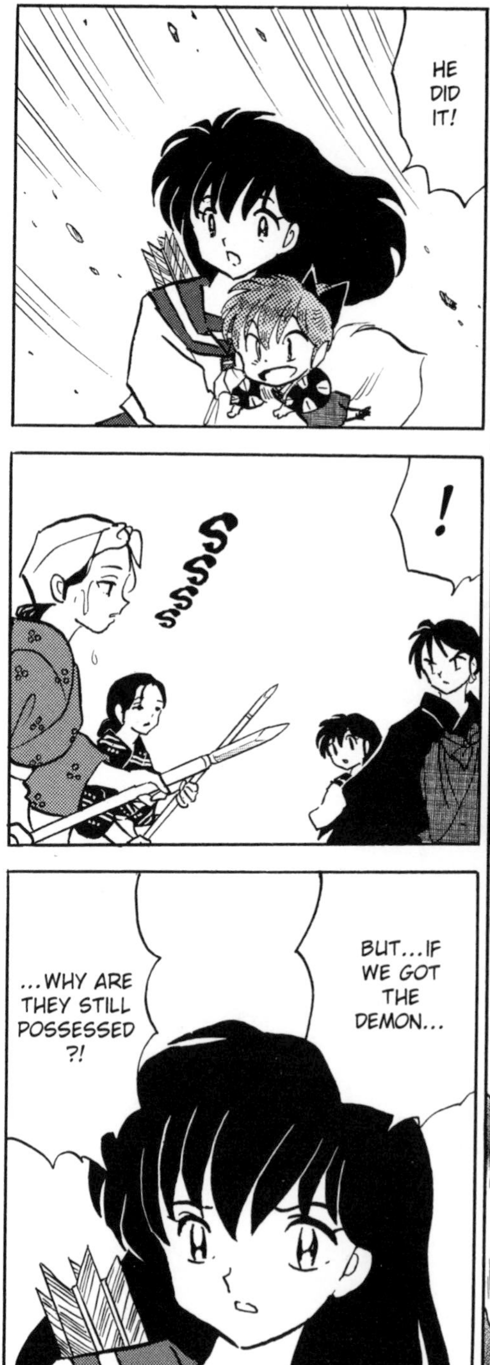
HE DID IT!
!
SSSSSS
BUT...IF WE GOT THE DEMON...
...WHY ARE THEY STILL POSSESSED ?!

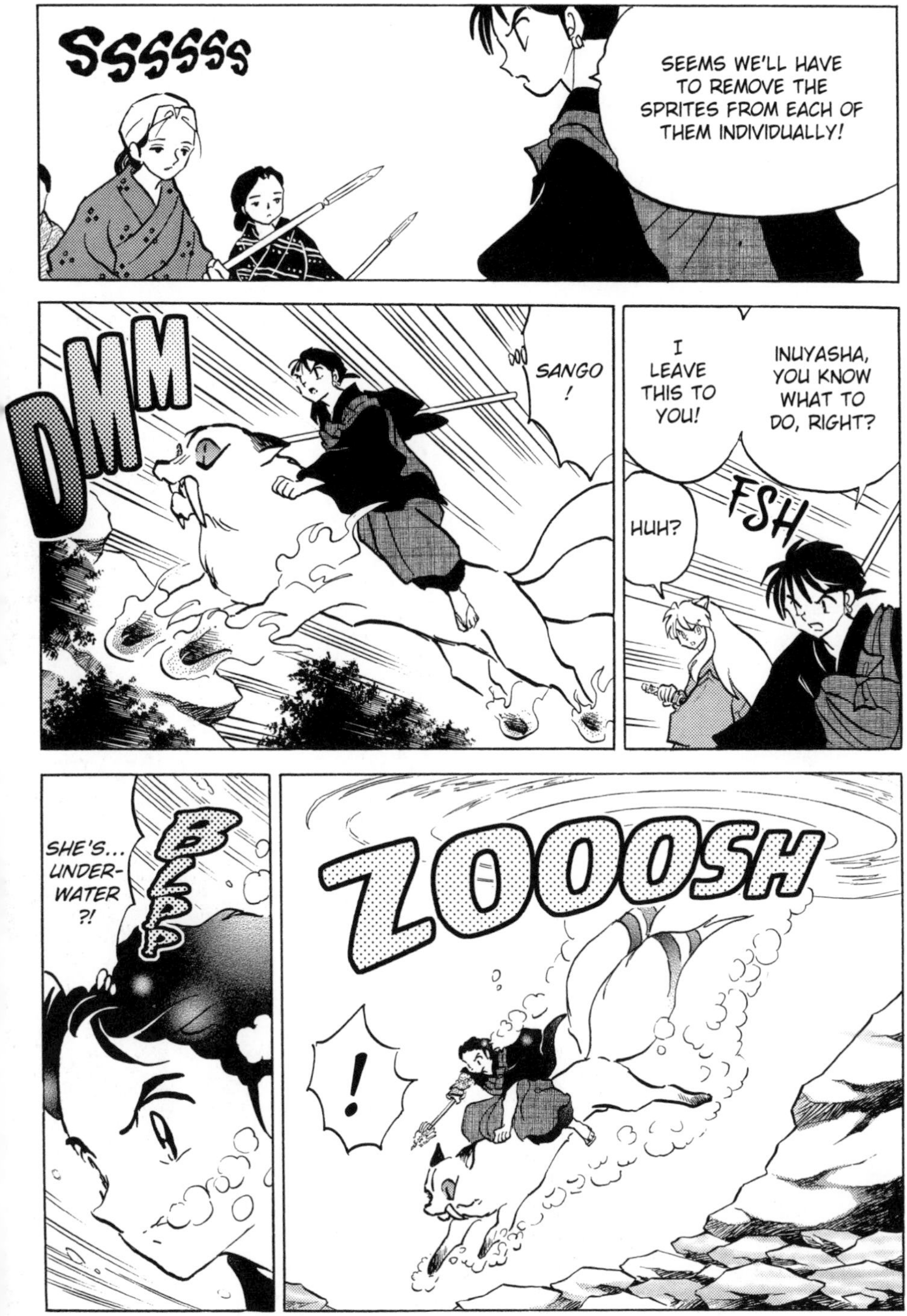
SEEMS WE'LL HAVE TO REMOVE THE SPRITES FROM EACH OF THEM INDIVIDUALLY!
SSSSSS
INUYASHA, YOU KNOW WHAT TO DO, RIGHT?
I LEAVE THIS TO YOU!
FSH
HUH?
SANGO!
DMM
ZOOOSH
!
BLPP
SHE'S... UNDER-WATER?!

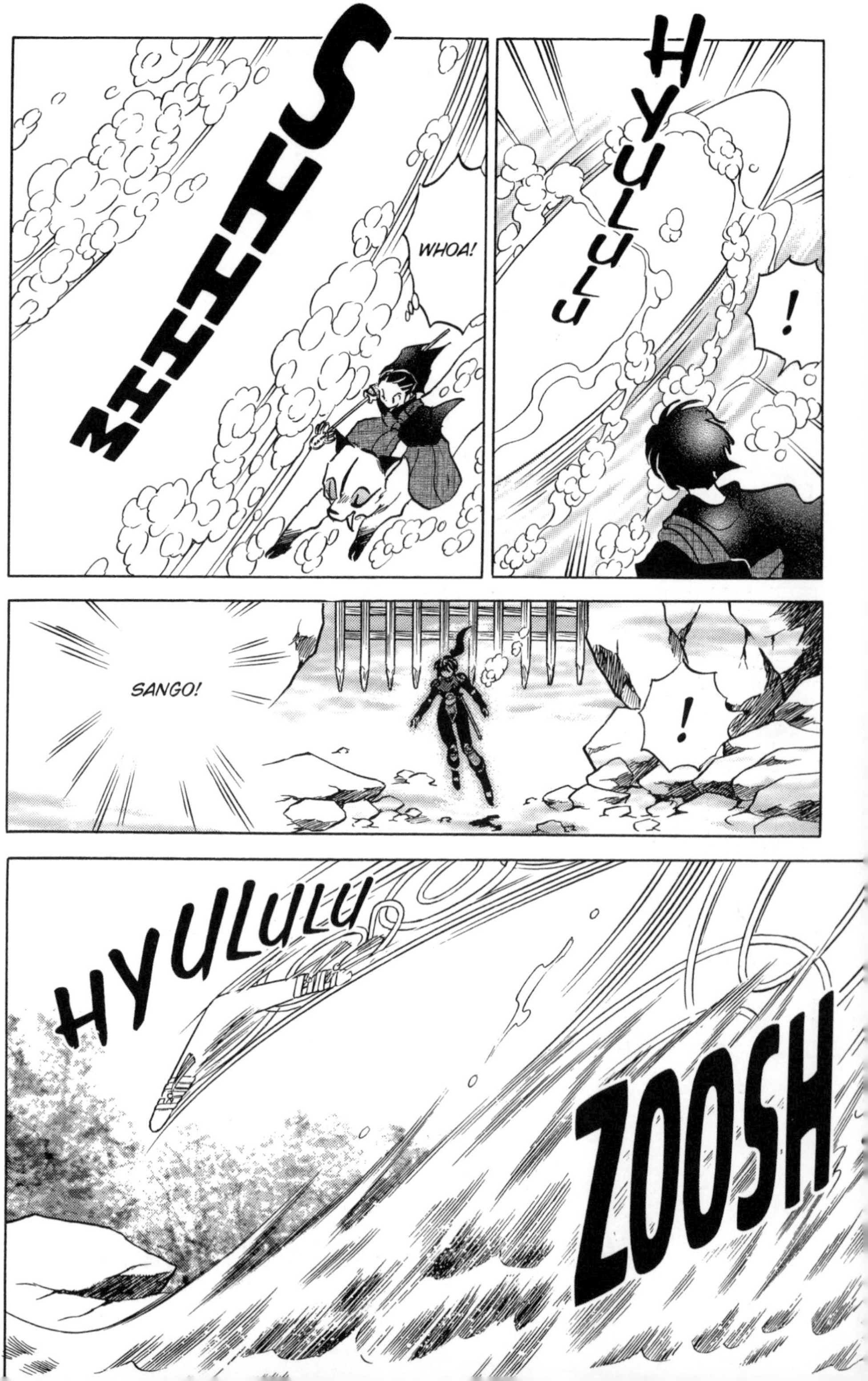
HYULULU
!
WHOA!
!
SANGO!
HYULULU
ZOOSH

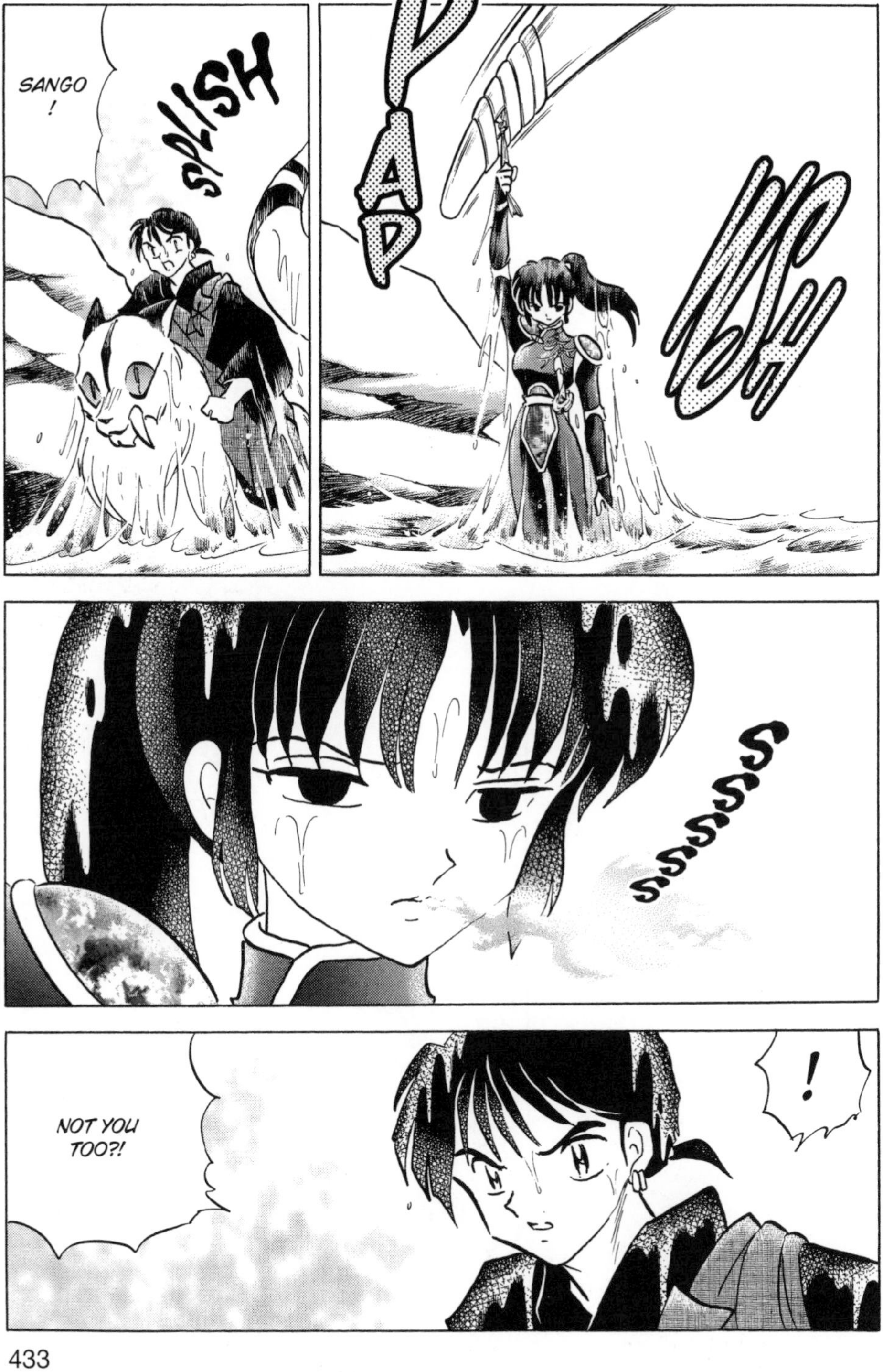
WOOSH
PAD
SPLISH
SANGO!
SSSSSSS
!
NOT YOU TOO?!

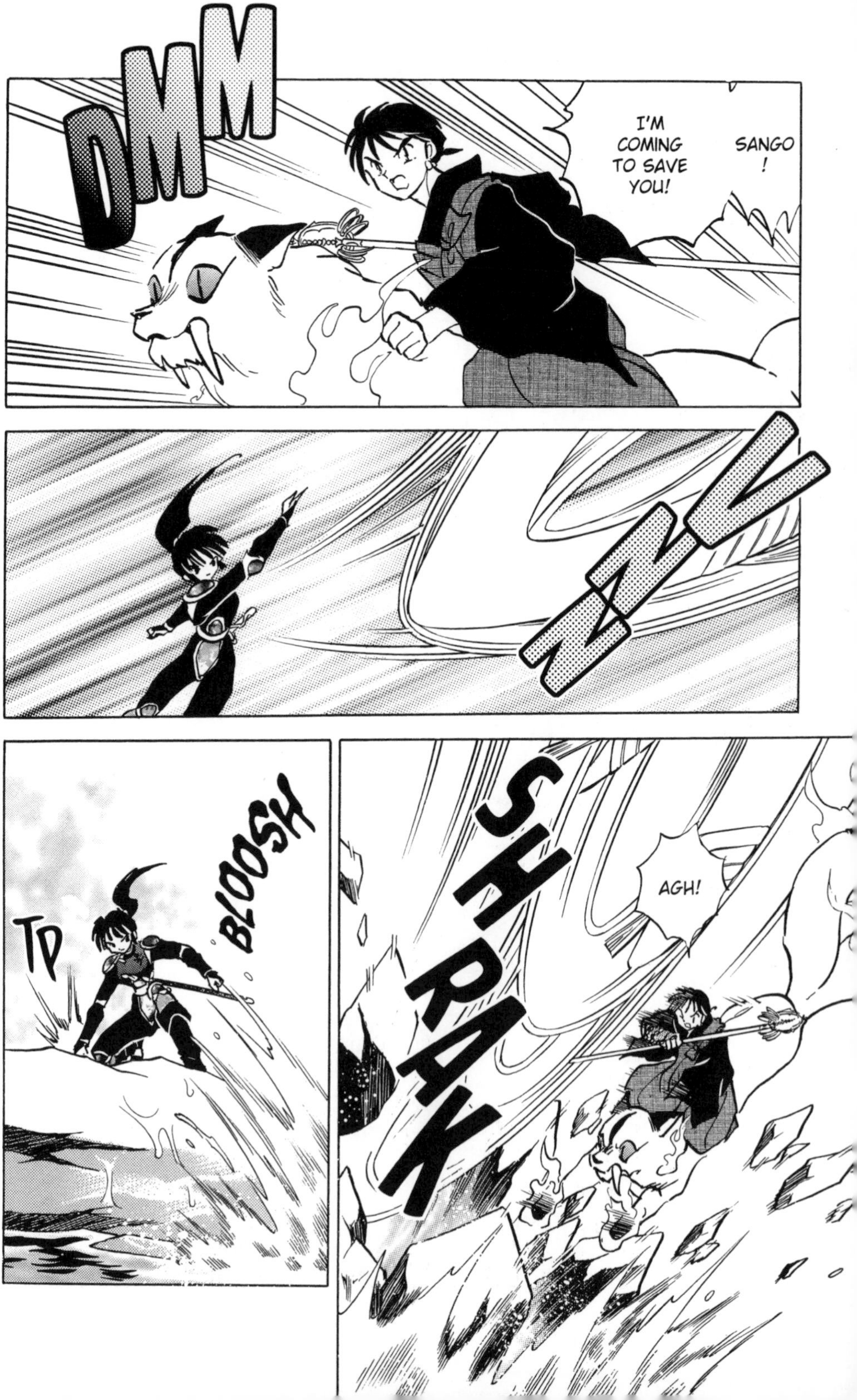
DMM
SANGO!
I'M COMING TO SAVE YOU!
SHRAK
AGH!
BLOOSH
TD

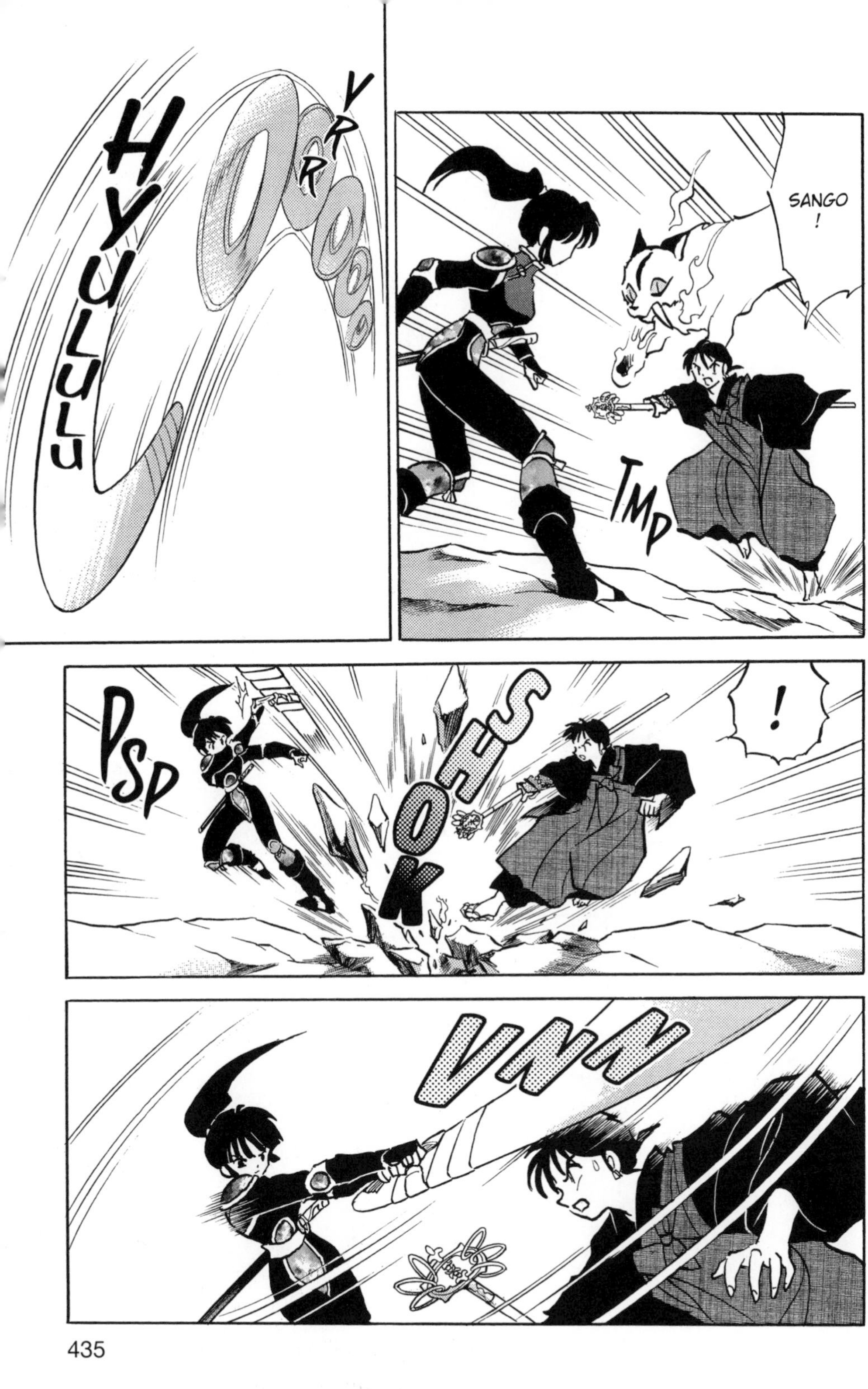
SANGO!
TMP
HYULULU
VRR
!
SHOK
PSP
VNN

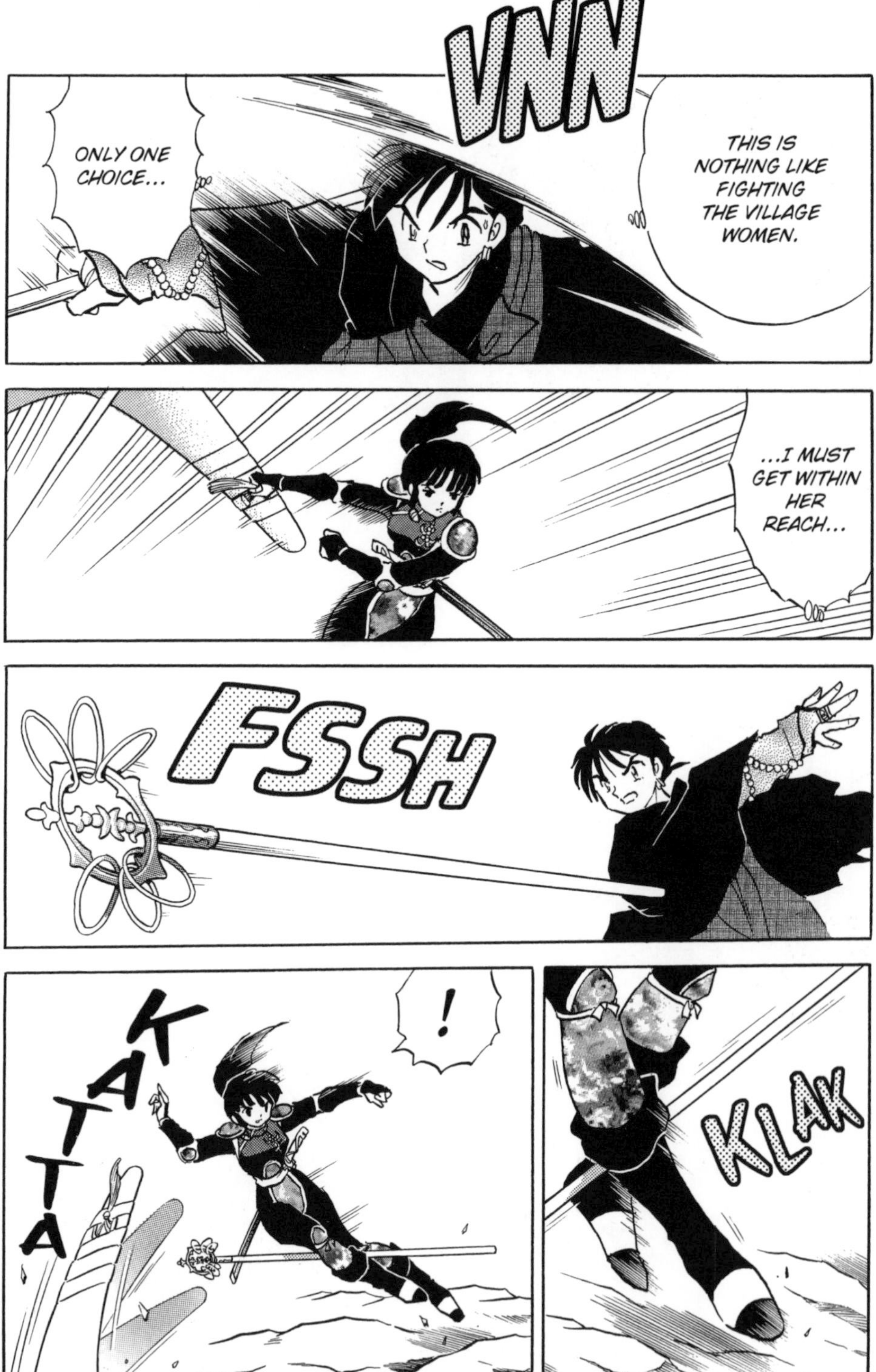
VNN
THIS IS NOTHING LIKE FIGHTING THE VILLAGE WOMEN.
ONLY ONE CHOICE...
...I MUST GET WITHIN HER REACH...
FSSH
KLAK
!
KATTA

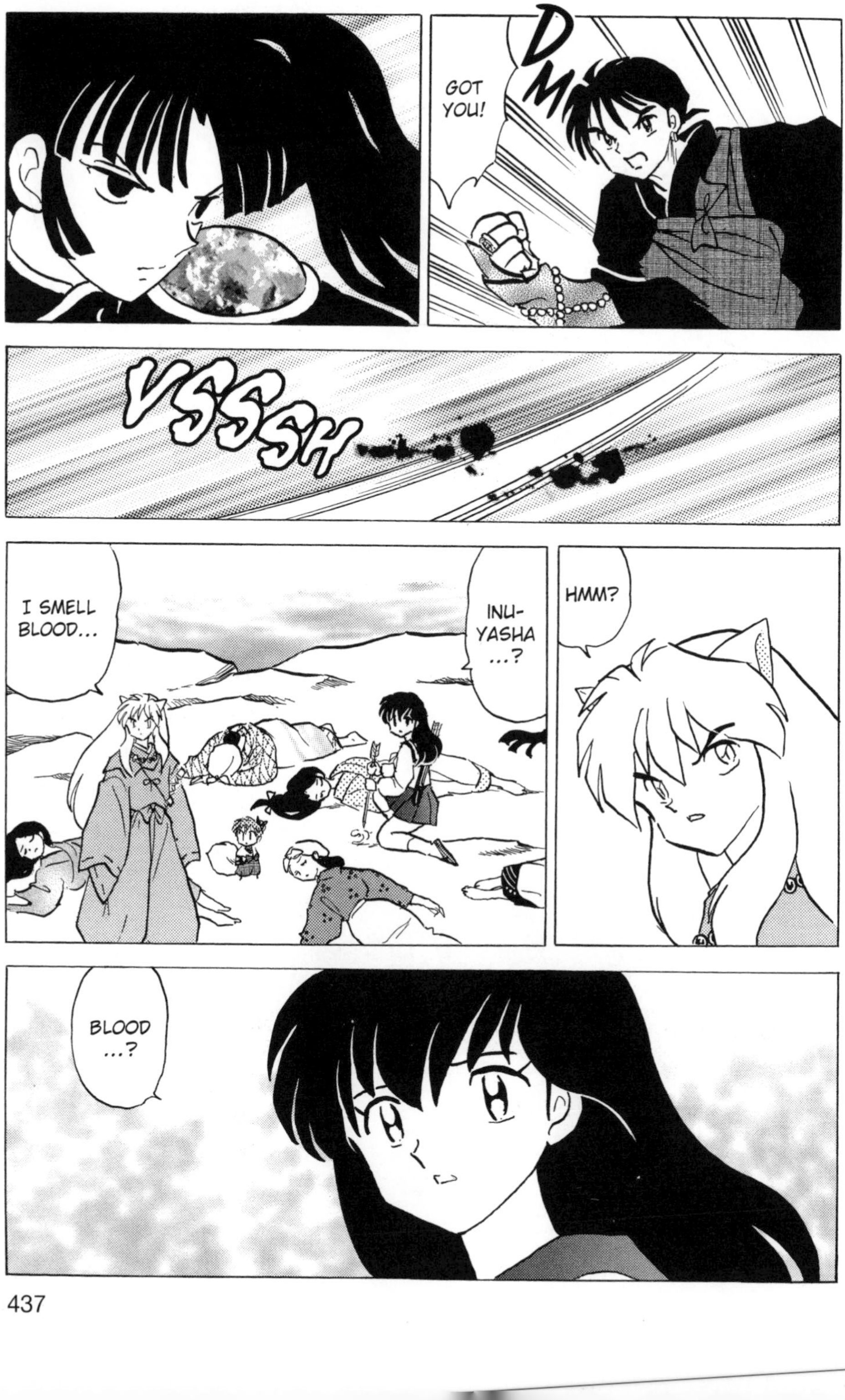
DM
GOT YOU!
VSSSH
HMM?
INU-YASHA...?
I SMELL BLOOD...
BLOOD...?

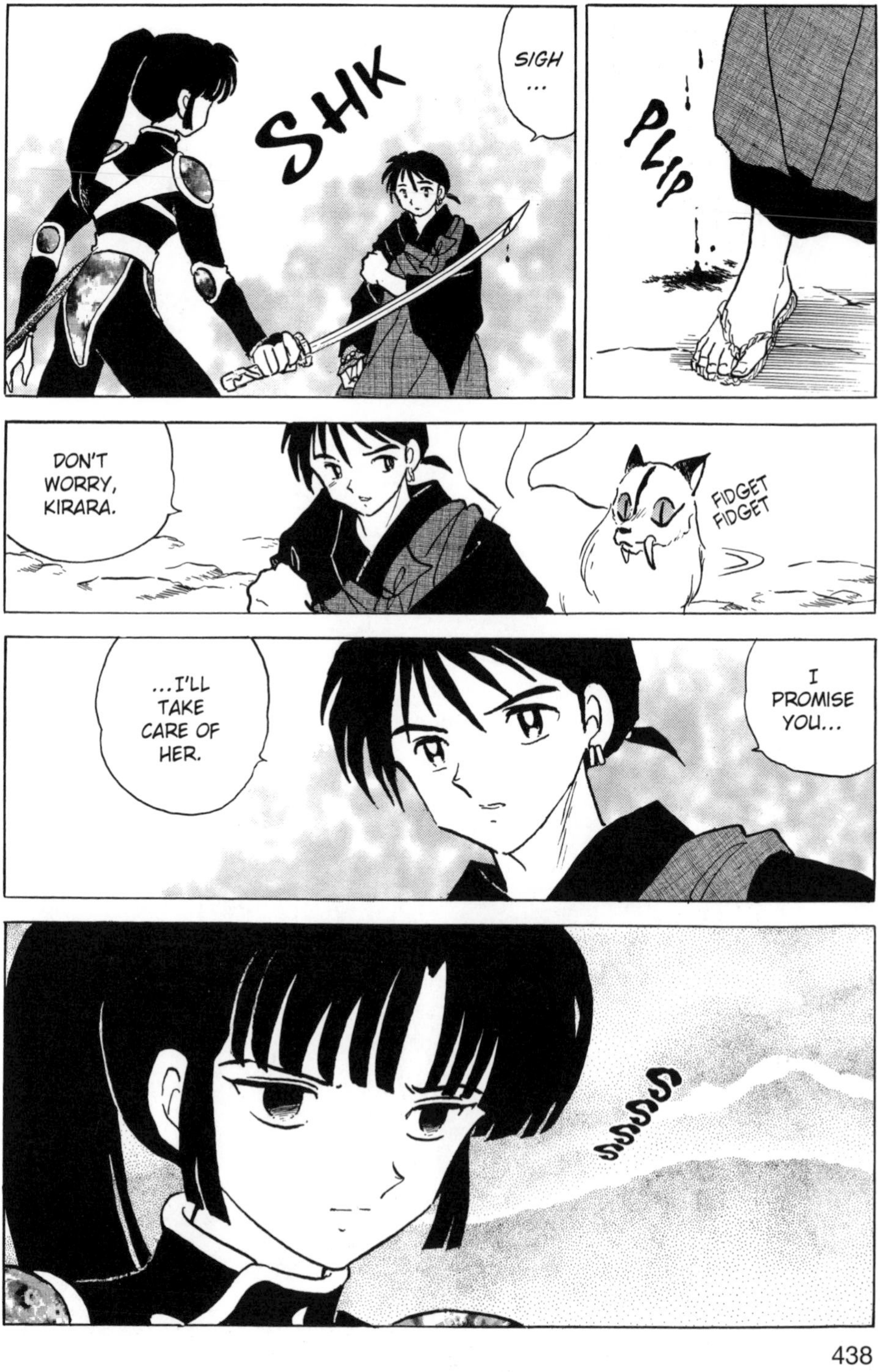
PLIP
SIGH ...
SHK
FIDGET FIDGET
DON'T WORRY, KIRARA.
I PROMISE YOU...
...I'LL TAKE CARE OF HER.

SCROLL FOUR
UNIQUE AMONG WOMEN

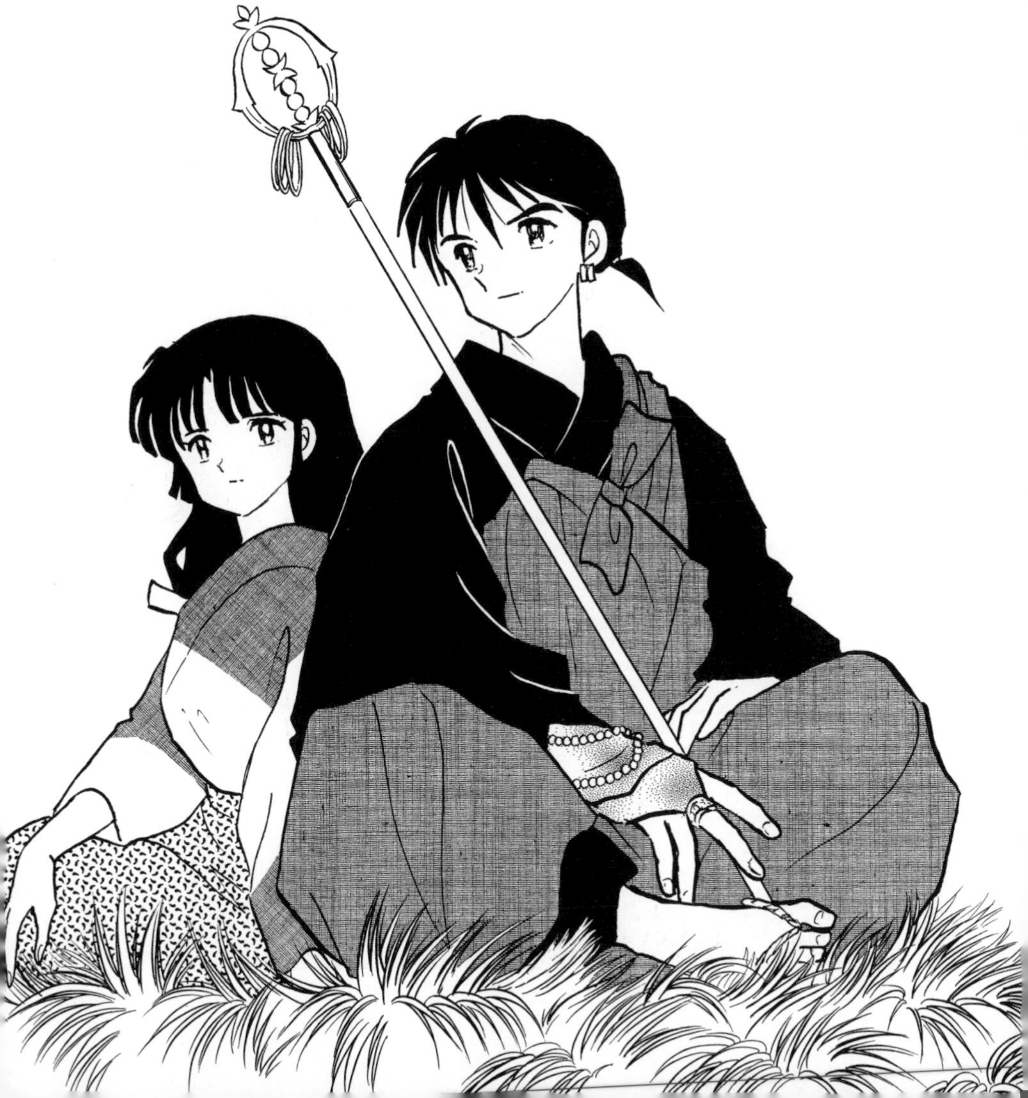

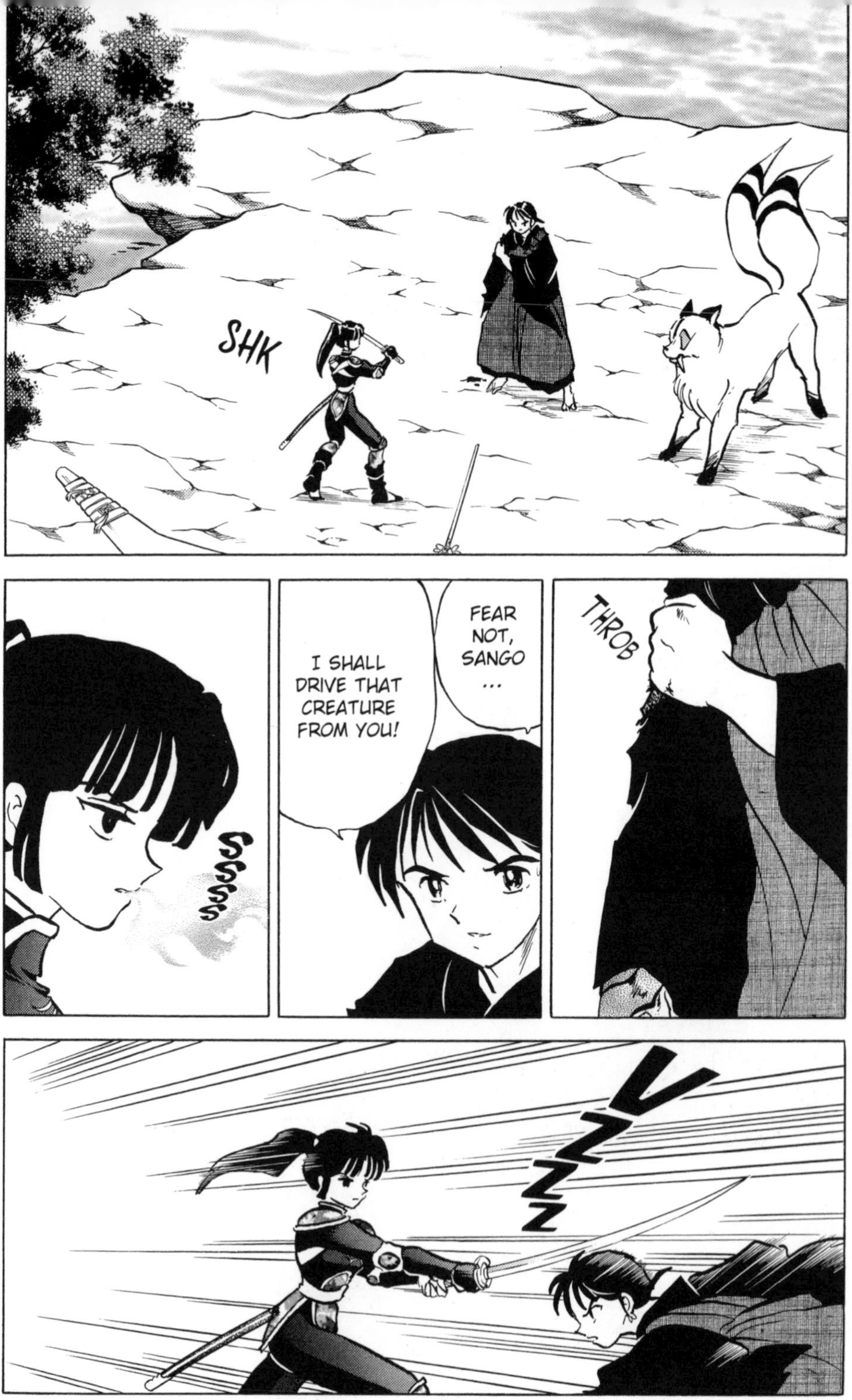
SHK
THROB
FEAR NOT, SANGO...
I SHALL DRIVE THAT CREATURE FROM YOU!
SSSSSS
VZZZZ

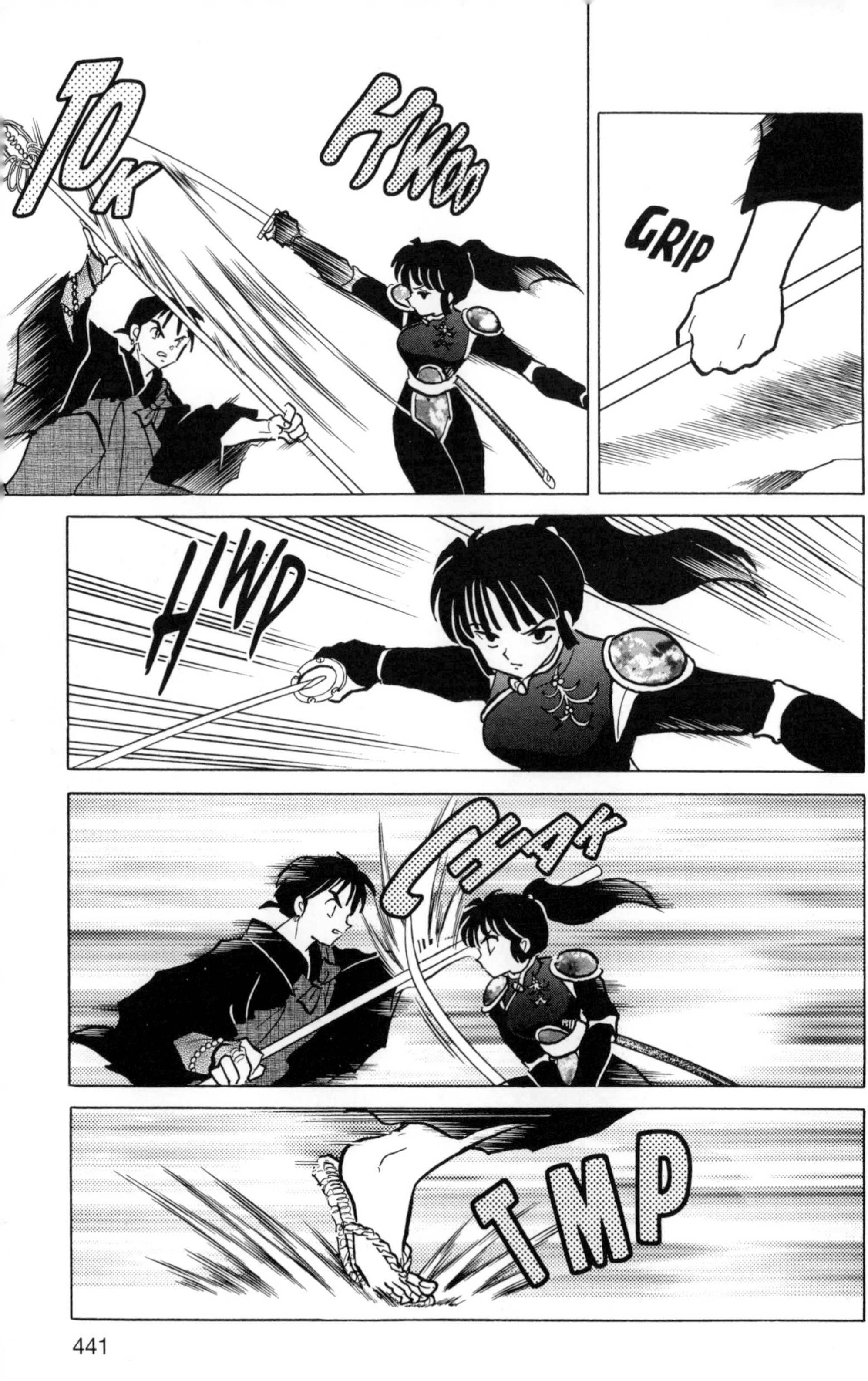
GRIP
HWOO
TOK
HWP
CHAK
TMP

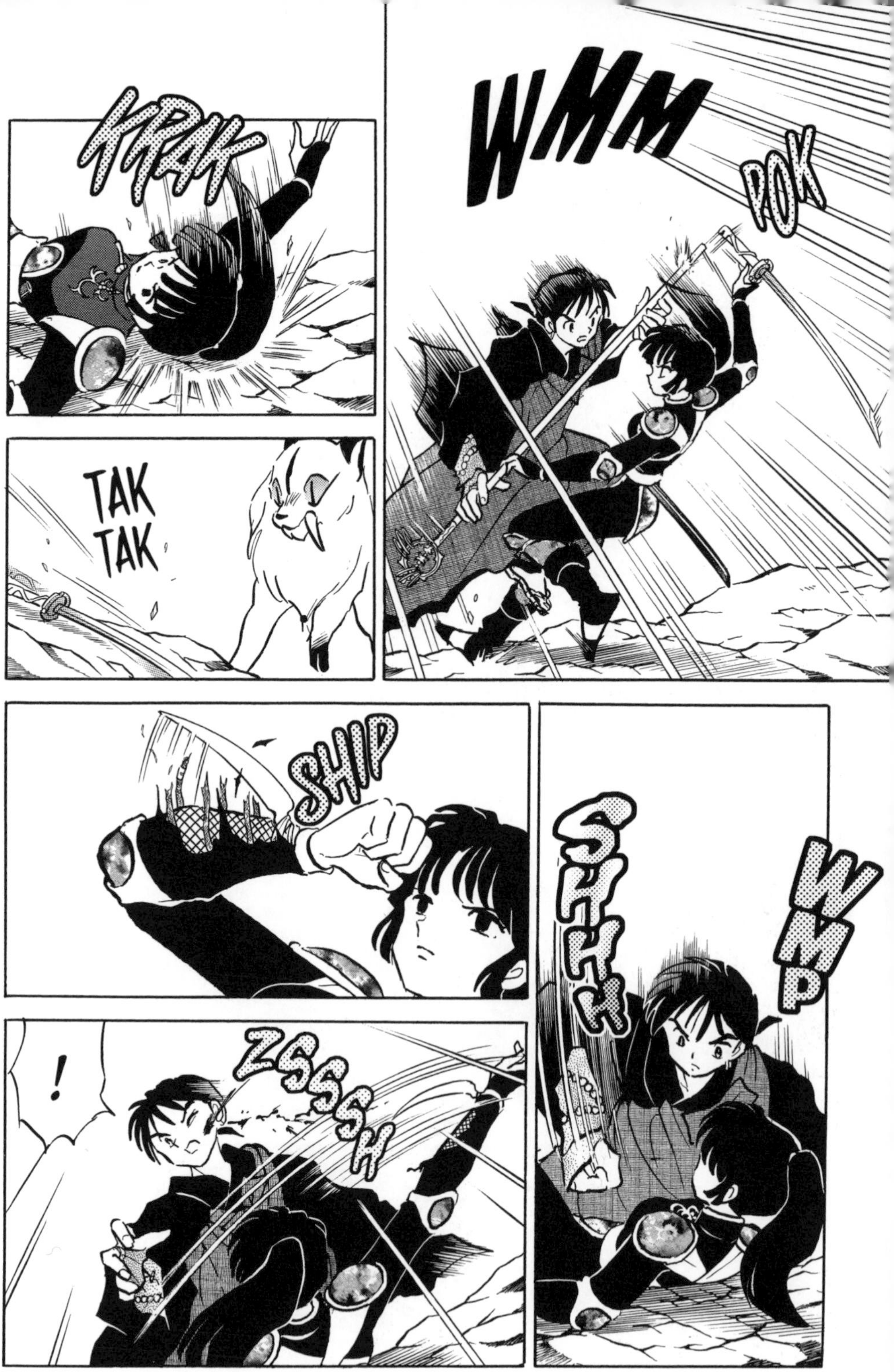
WMM
POK
KRAK
TAK TAK
SHHH
WMP
SHIP
ZSSSH
!

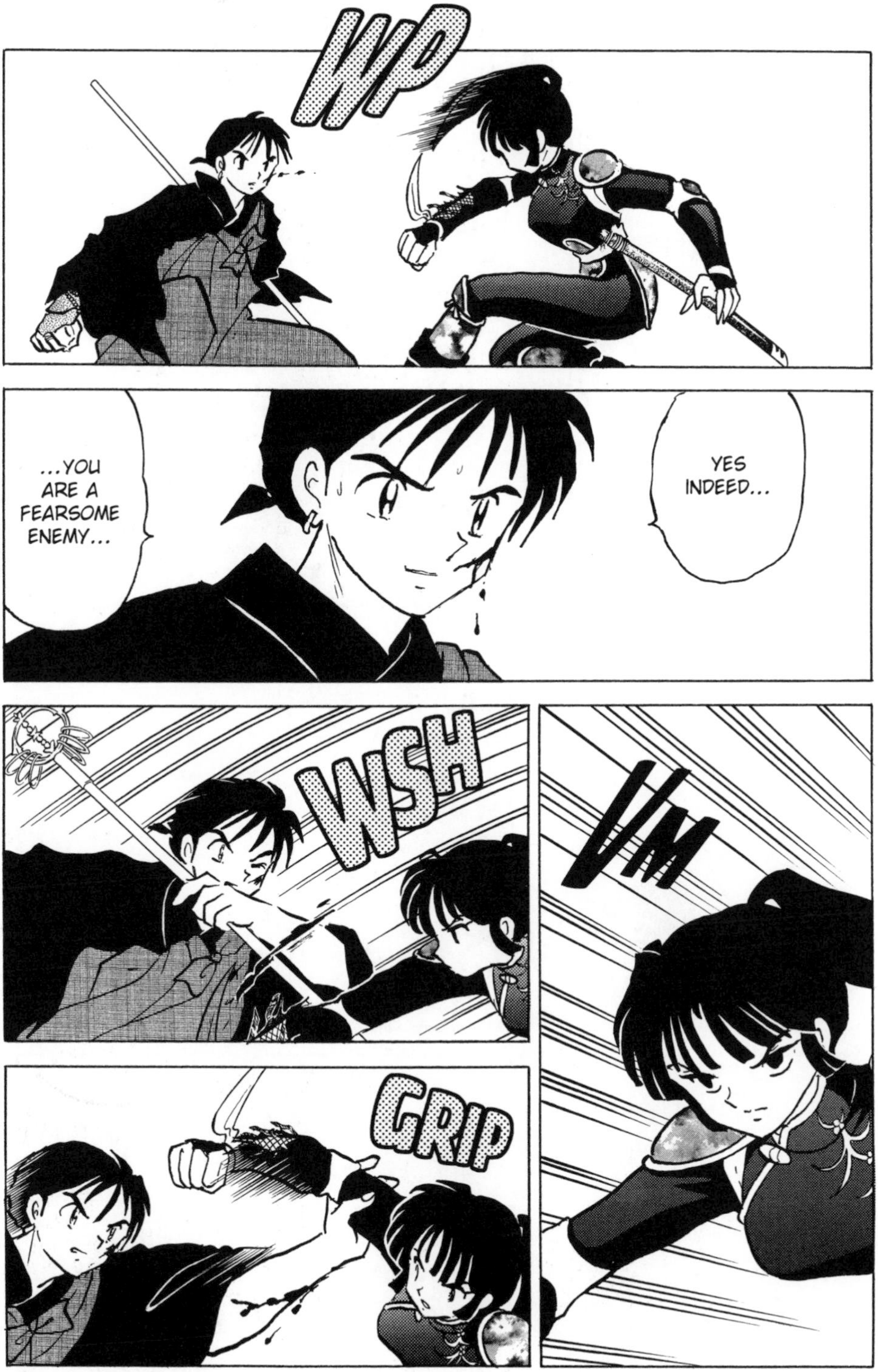
WP
YES INDEED...
...YOU ARE A FEARSOME ENEMY...
VM
WSH
GRIP

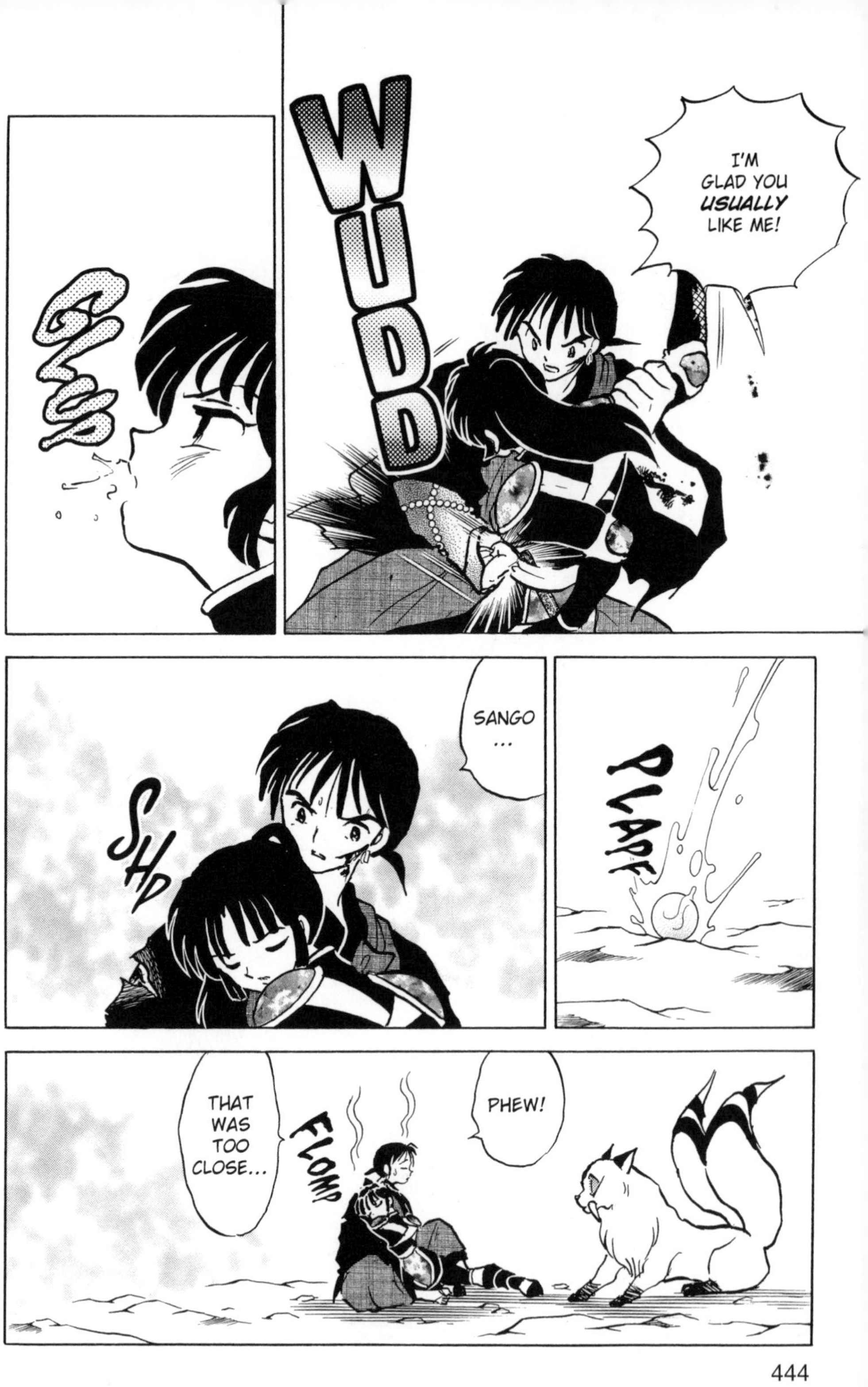
I'M GLAD YOU USUALLY LIKE ME!
WUDD
GLUP
PLAPF
SANGO ...
SHP
PHEW!
THAT WAS TOO CLOSE...
FLOMP

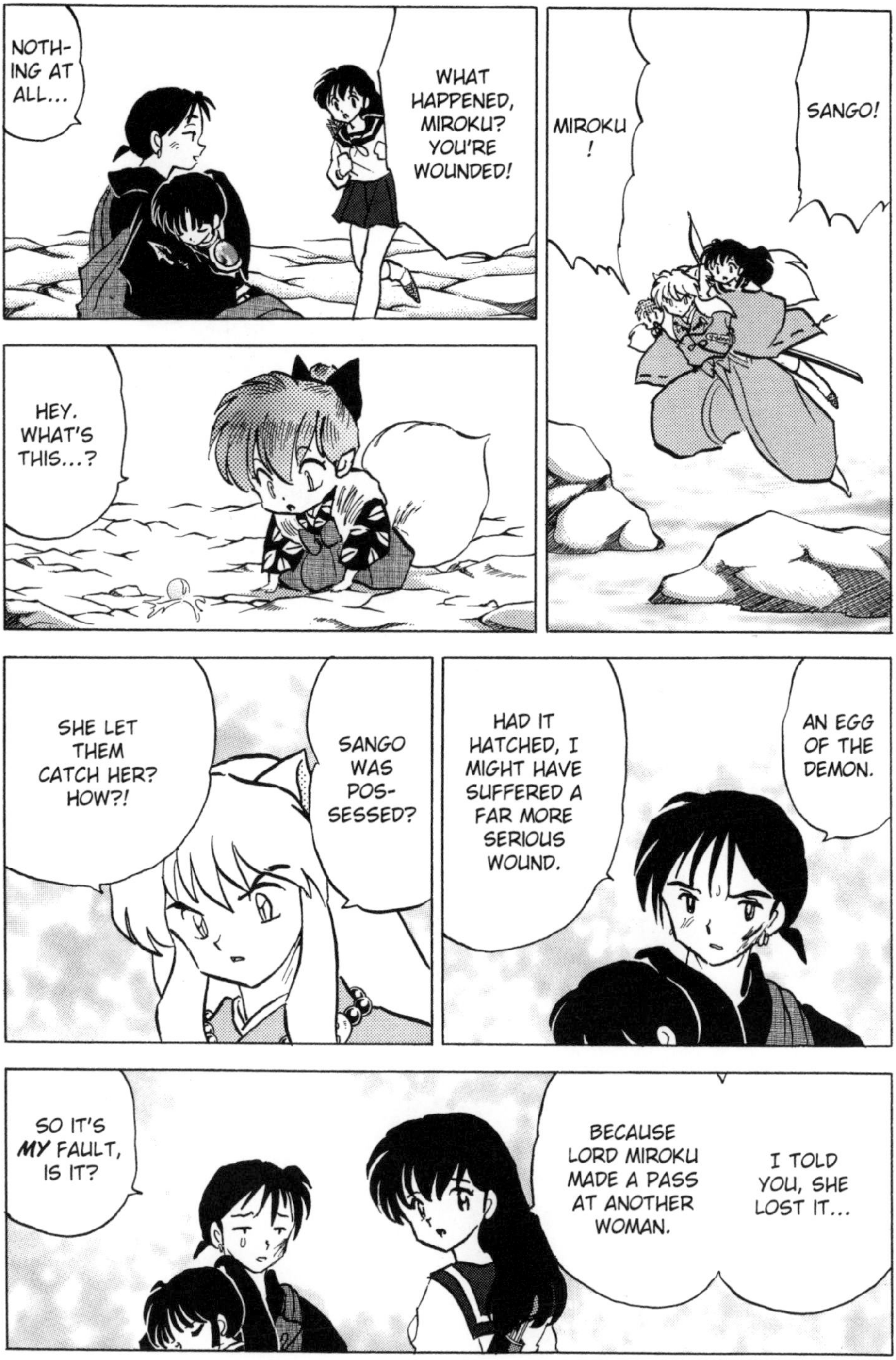
SANGO!
MIROKU!
WHAT HAPPENED, MIROKU? YOU'RE WOUNDED!
NOTHING AT ALL...
HEY. WHAT'S THIS...?
AN EGG OF THE DEMON.
HAD IT HATCHED, I MIGHT HAVE SUFFERED A FAR MORE SERIOUS WOUND.
SANGO WAS POSSESSED?
SHE LET THEM CATCH HER? HOW?!
I TOLD YOU, SHE LOST IT...
BECAUSE LORD MIROKU MADE A PASS AT ANOTHER WOMAN.
SO IT'S *MY* FAULT, IS IT?

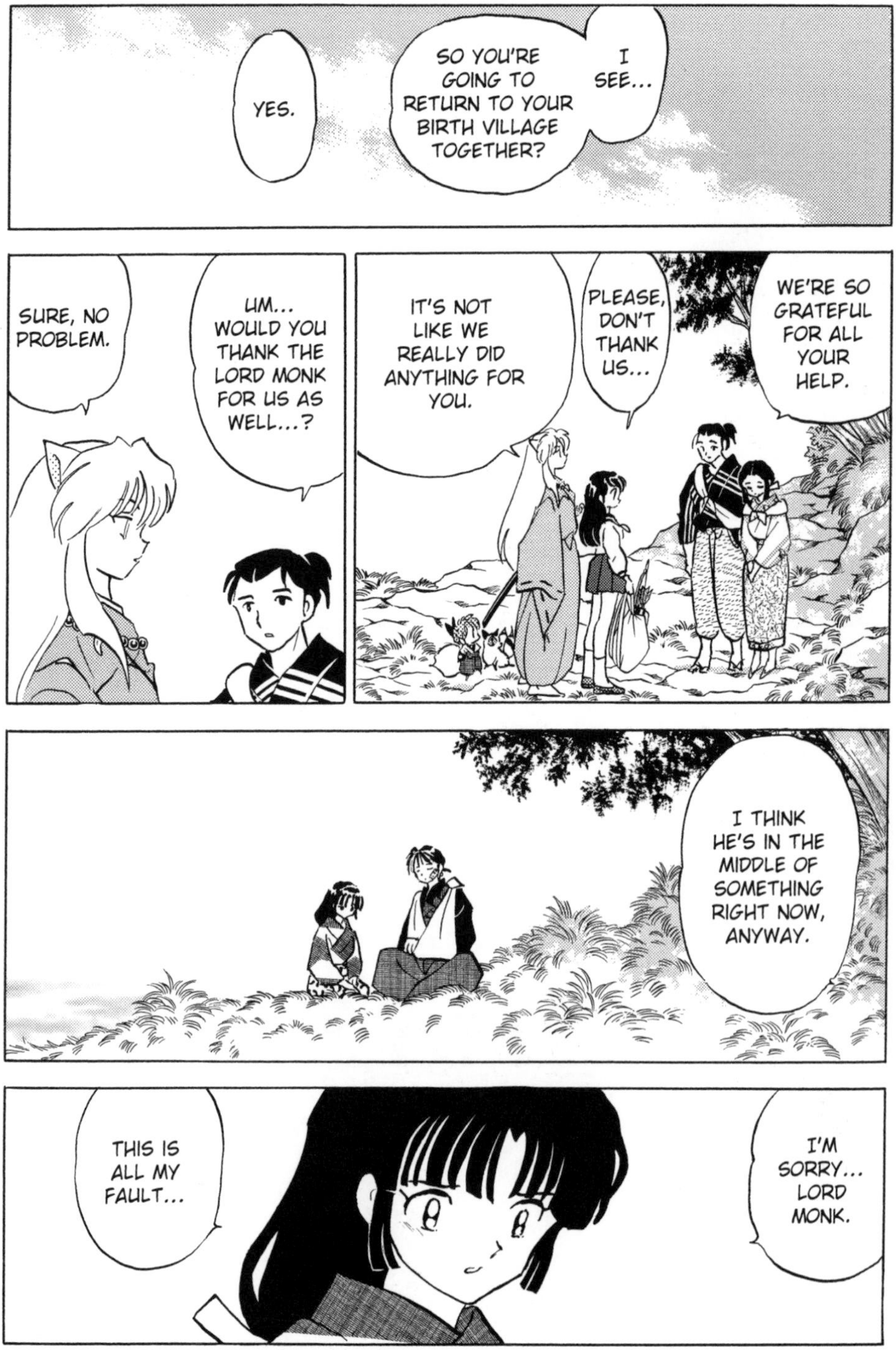
I SEE...
SO YOU'RE GOING TO RETURN TO YOUR BIRTH VILLAGE TOGETHER?
YES.
WE'RE SO GRATEFUL FOR ALL YOUR HELP.
PLEASE, DON'T THANK US...
IT'S NOT LIKE WE REALLY DID ANYTHING FOR YOU.
UM... WOULD YOU THANK THE LORD MONK FOR US AS WELL...?
SURE, NO PROBLEM.
I THINK HE'S IN THE MIDDLE OF SOMETHING RIGHT NOW, ANYWAY.
I'M SORRY... LORD MONK.
THIS IS ALL MY FAULT...

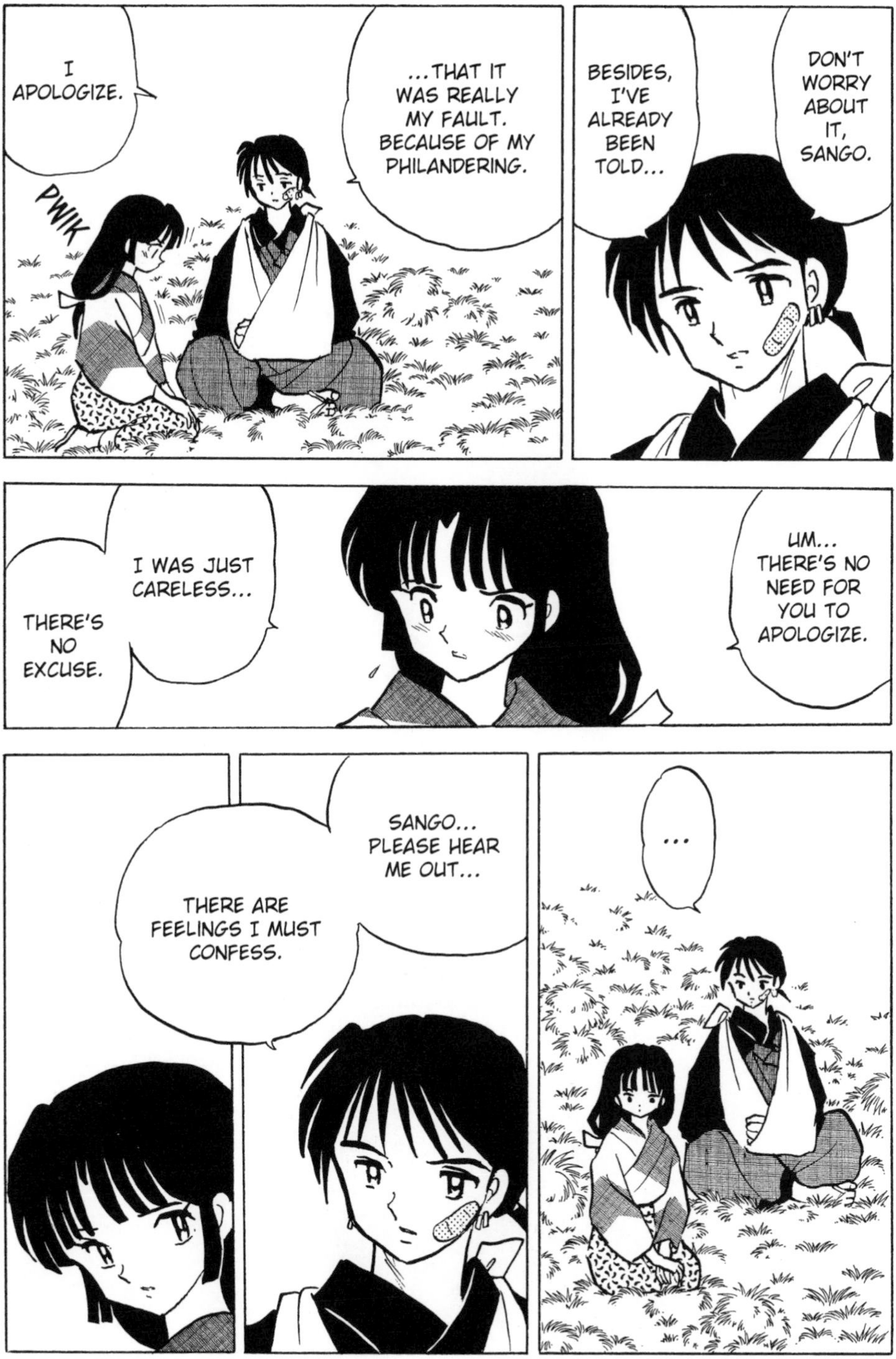
DON'T WORRY ABOUT IT, SANGO.
BESIDES, I'VE ALREADY BEEN TOLD...
...THAT IT WAS REALLY MY FAULT. BECAUSE OF MY PHILANDERING.
I APOLOGIZE.
PWIK
UM... THERE'S NO NEED FOR YOU TO APOLOGIZE.
I WAS JUST CARELESS...
THERE'S NO EXCUSE.
...
SANGO... PLEASE HEAR ME OUT...
THERE ARE FEELINGS I MUST CONFESS.

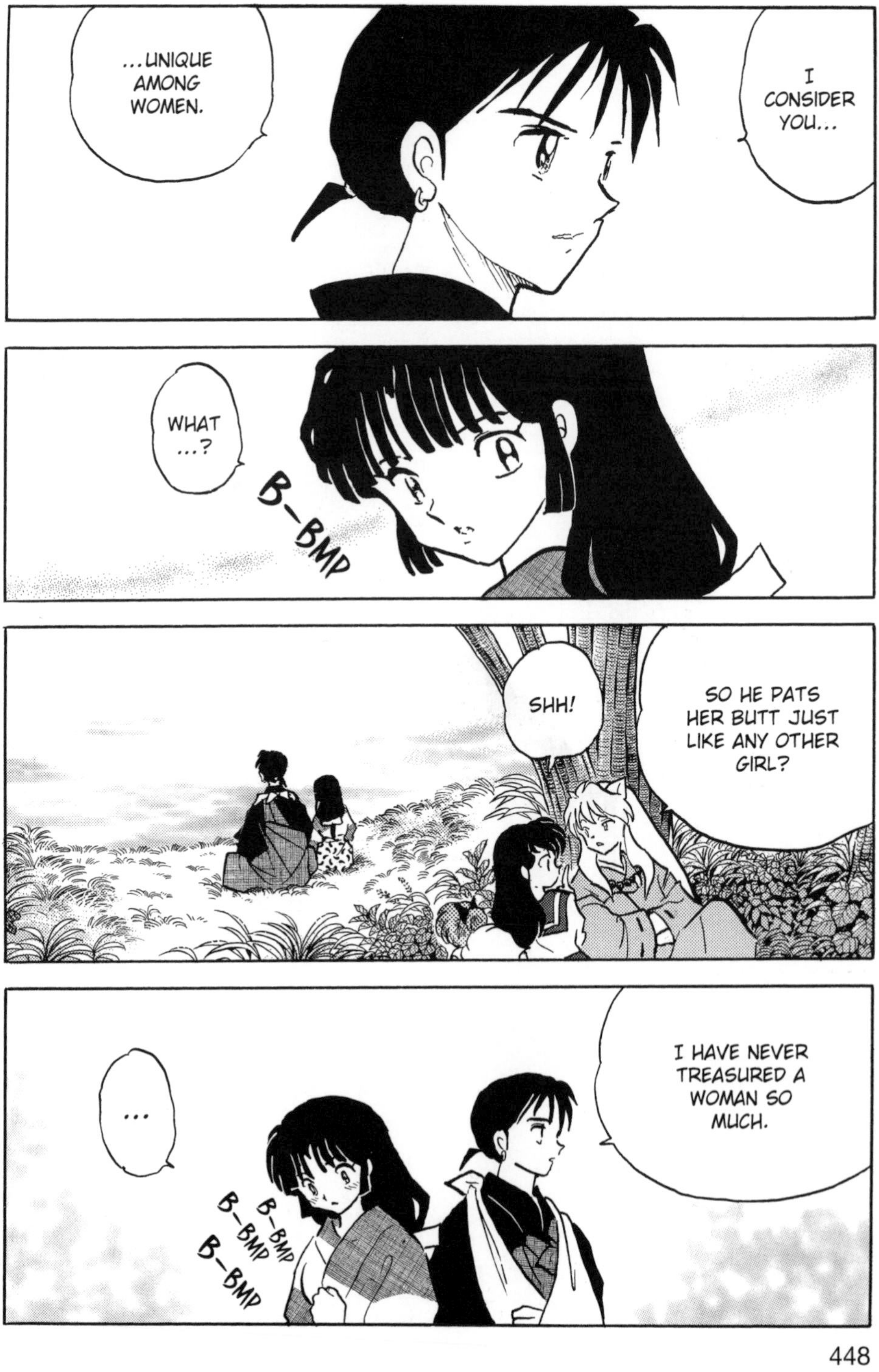
I CONSIDER YOU...
...UNIQUE AMONG WOMEN.
WHAT ...?
B-BMP
SO HE PATS HER BUTT JUST LIKE ANY OTHER GIRL?
SHH!
I HAVE NEVER TREASURED A WOMAN SO MUCH.
...
B-BMP
B-BMP
B-BMP

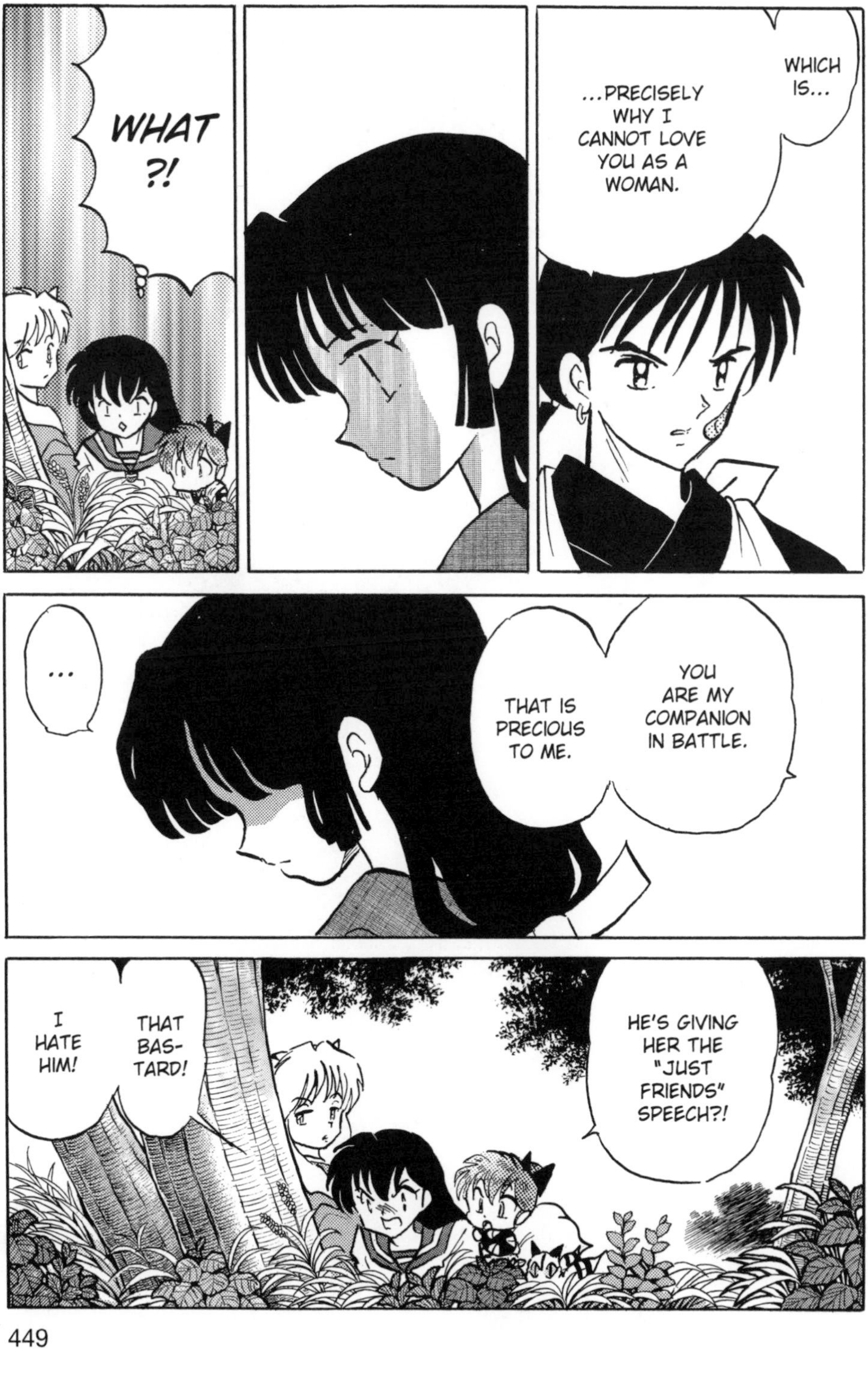
WHICH IS...
...PRECISELY WHY I CANNOT LOVE YOU AS A WOMAN.
WHAT ?!
YOU ARE MY COMPANION IN BATTLE.
THAT IS PRECIOUS TO ME.
...
HE'S GIVING HER THE "JUST FRIENDS" SPEECH?!
THAT BAS-TARD!
I HATE HIM!

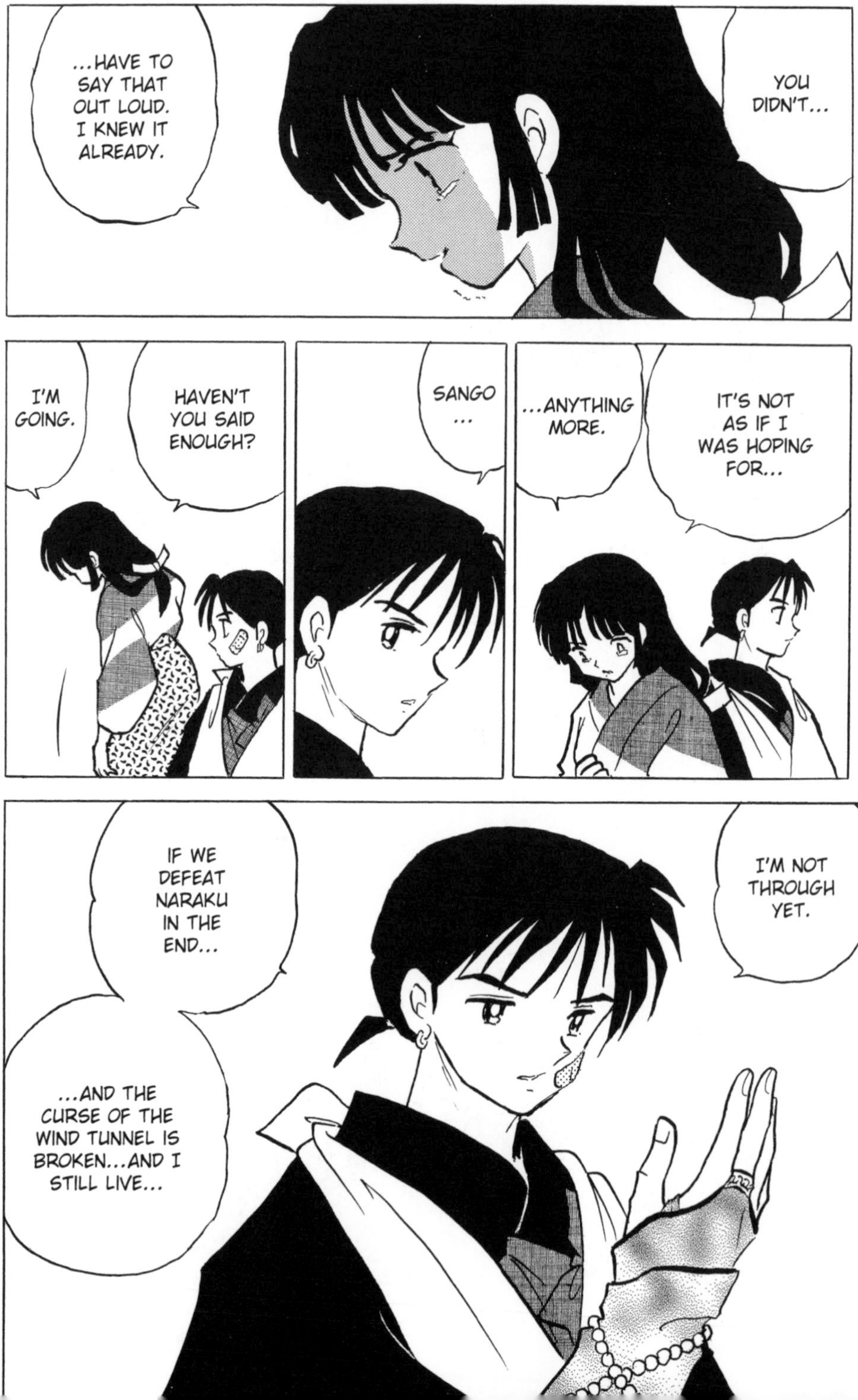
YOU DIDN'T...
...HAVE TO SAY THAT OUT LOUD. I KNEW IT ALREADY.
IT'S NOT AS IF I WAS HOPING FOR...
...ANYTHING MORE.
SANGO ...
HAVEN'T YOU SAID ENOUGH?
I'M GOING.
I'M NOT THROUGH YET.
IF WE DEFEAT NARAKU IN THE END...
...AND THE CURSE OF THE WIND TUNNEL IS BROKEN...AND I STILL LIVE...

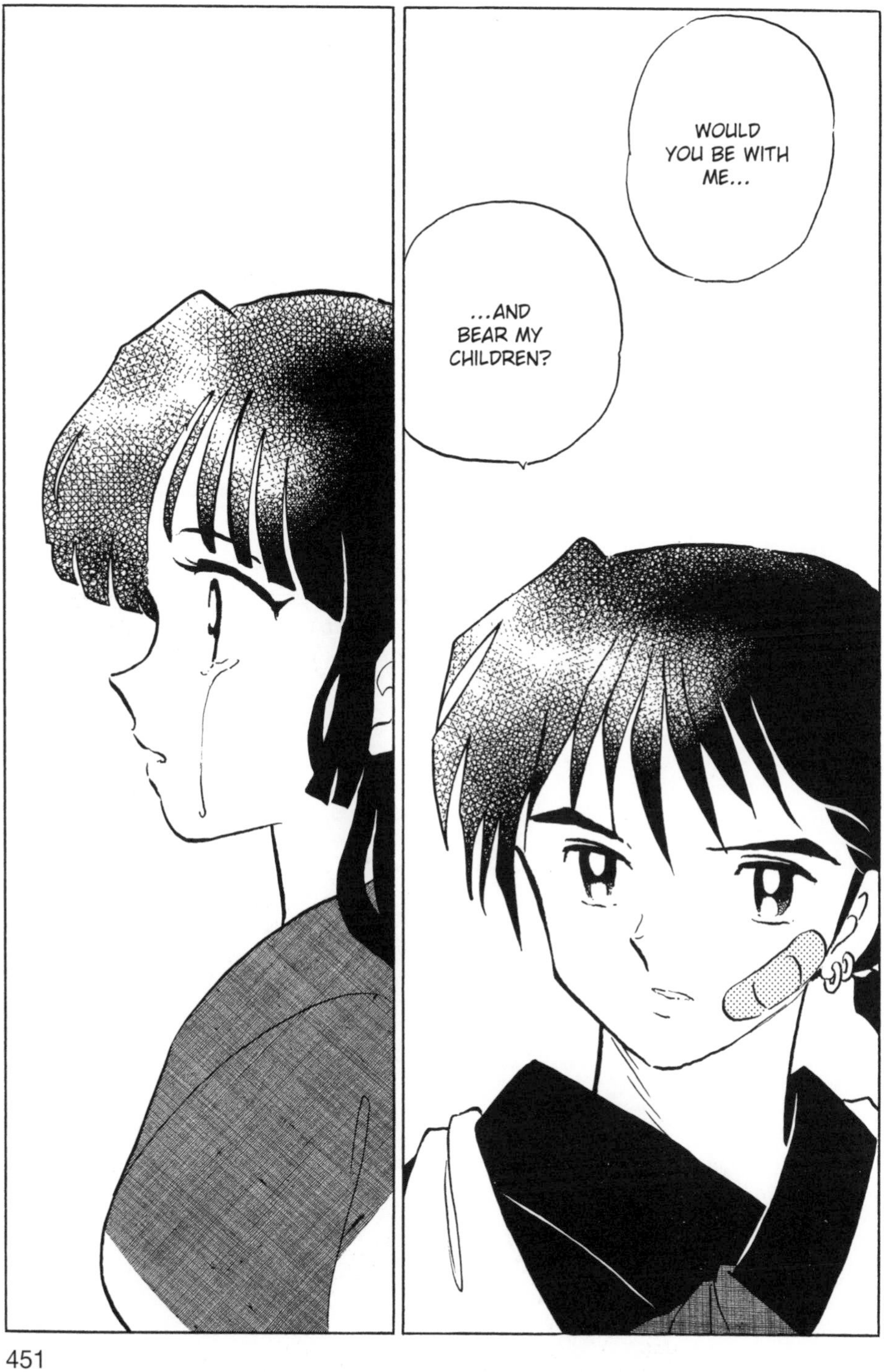
WOULD YOU BE WITH ME...
...AND BEAR MY CHILDREN?

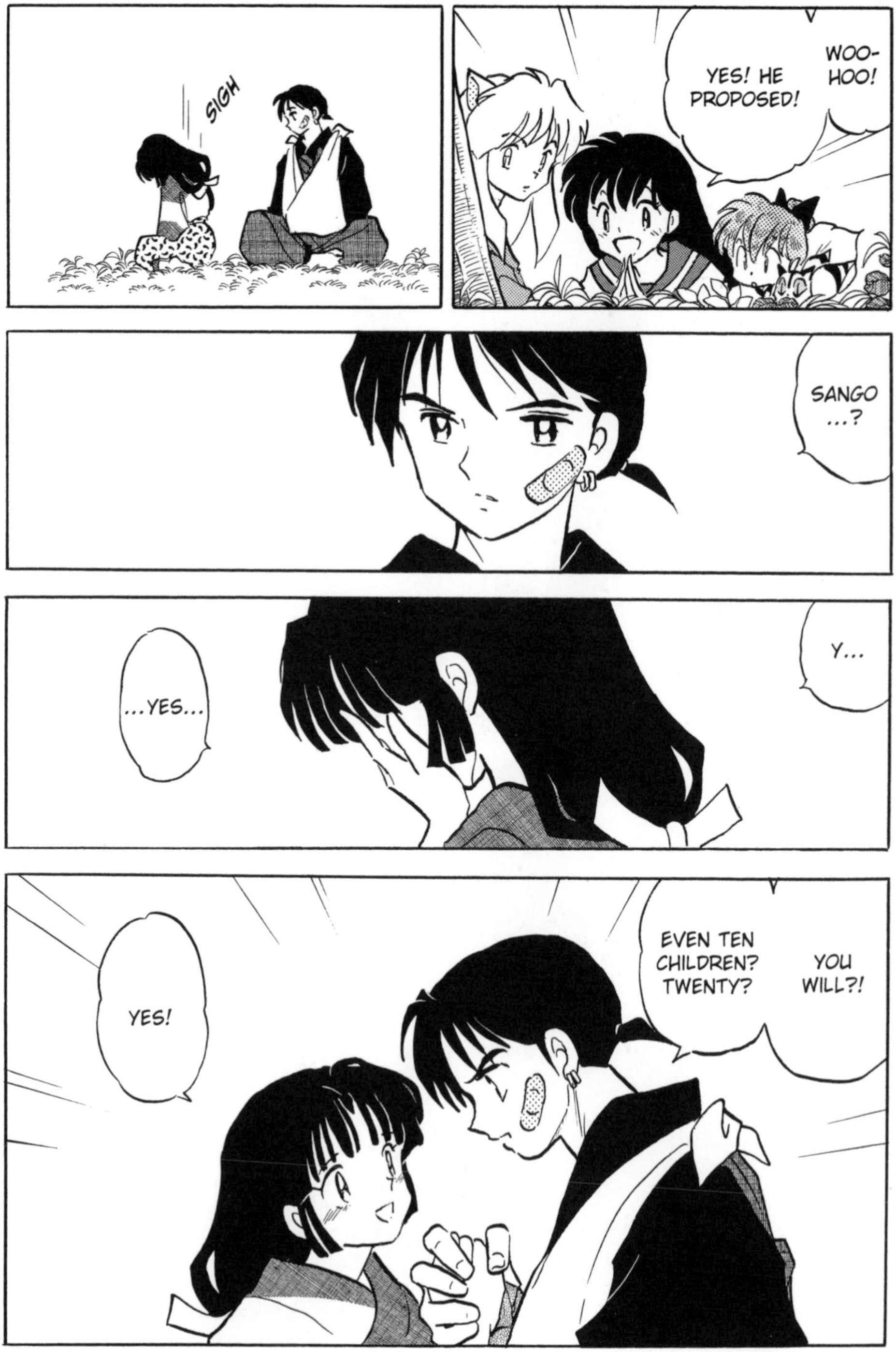
WOO-HOO!
YES! HE PROPOSED!
SIGH
SANGO ...?
Y...
...YES...
YOU WILL?!
EVEN TEN CHILDREN? TWENTY?
YES!

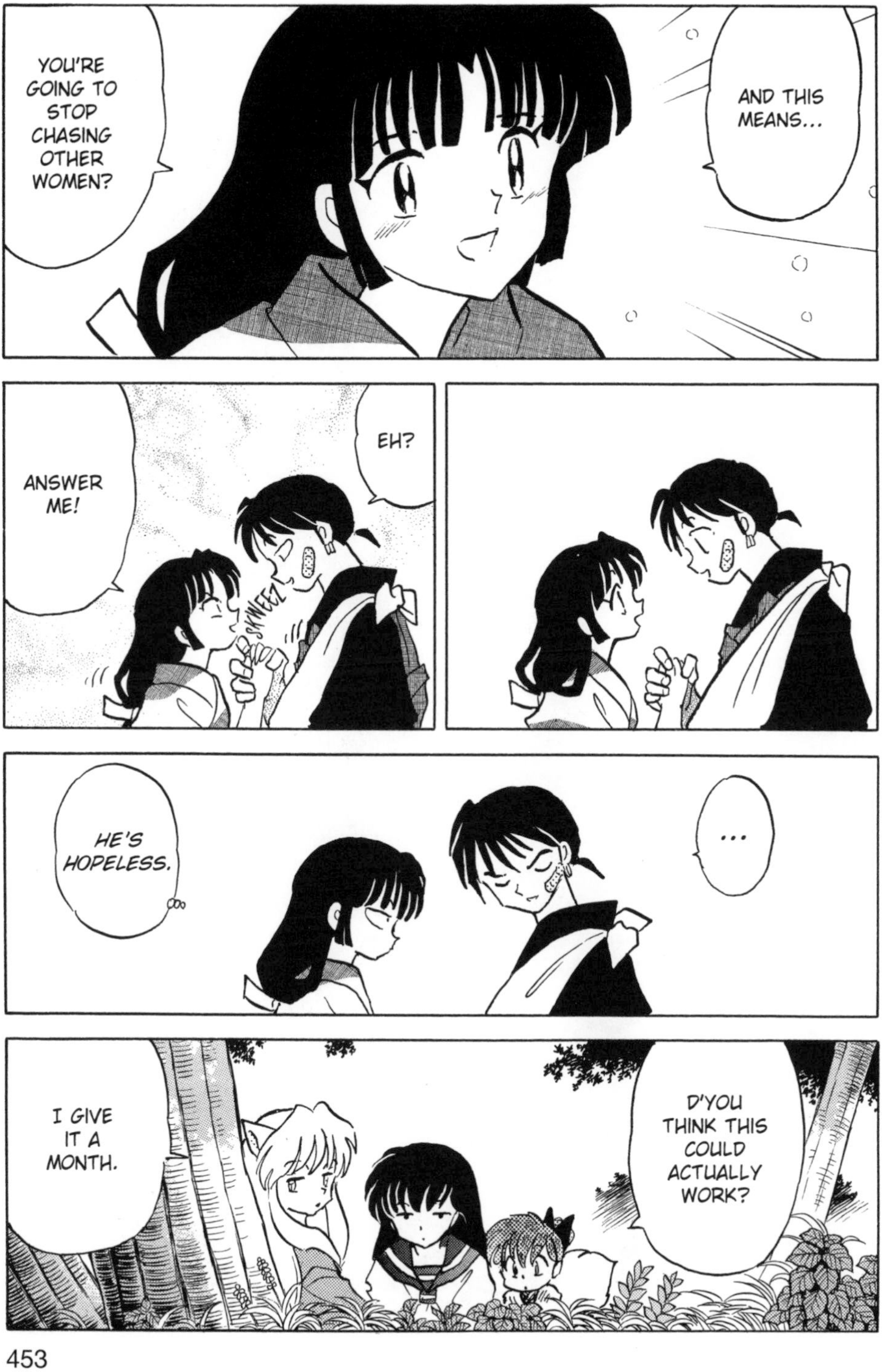
AND THIS MEANS...
YOU'RE GOING TO STOP CHASING OTHER WOMEN?
EH?
ANSWER ME!
SKWEEZ
...
HE'S HOPELESS.
D'YOU THINK THIS COULD ACTUALLY WORK?
I GIVE IT A MONTH.

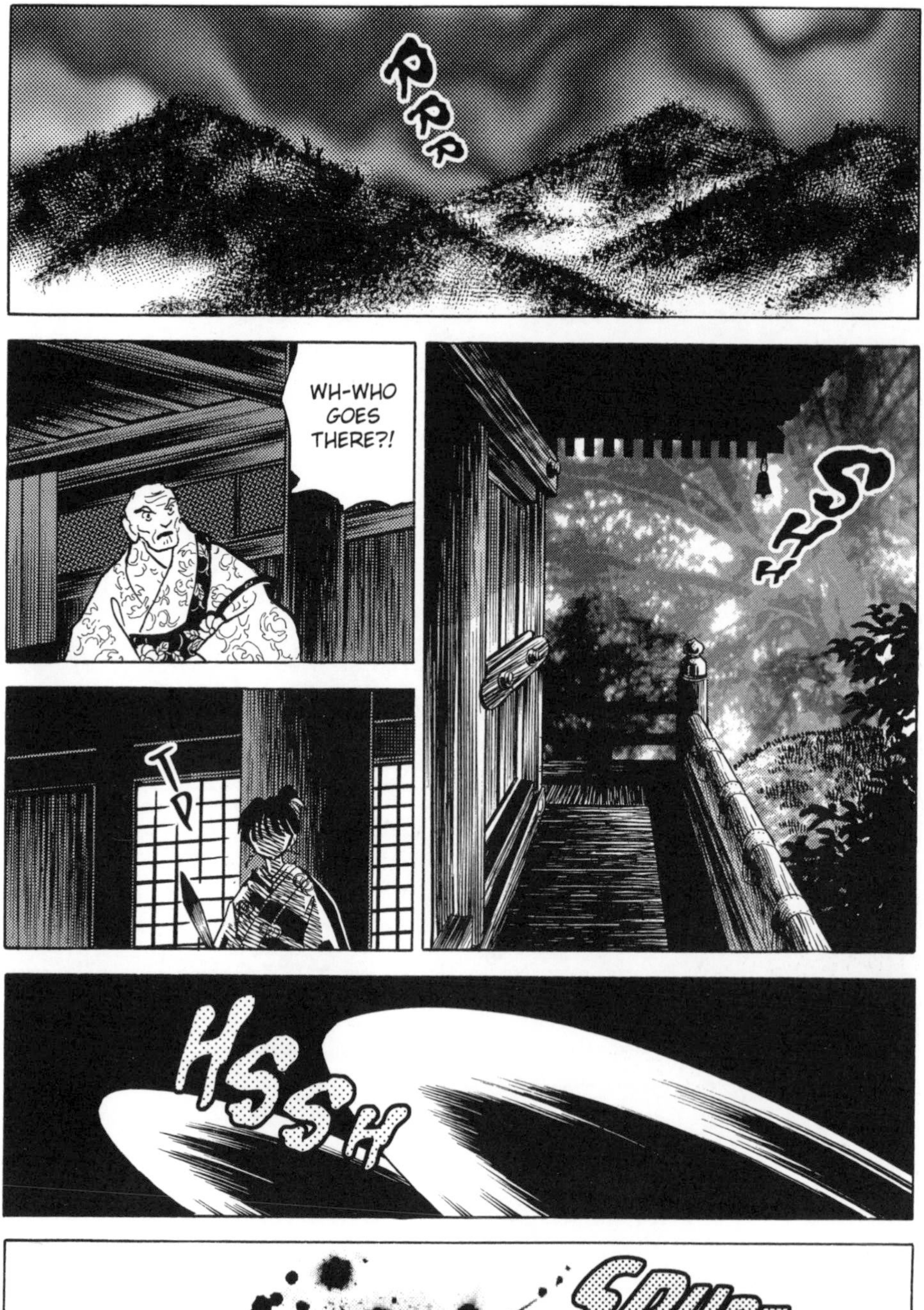
RRR
SHH
WH-WHO GOES THERE?!
TP
HSSH
SPURT

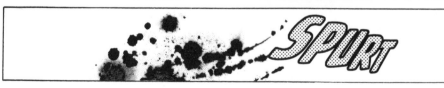

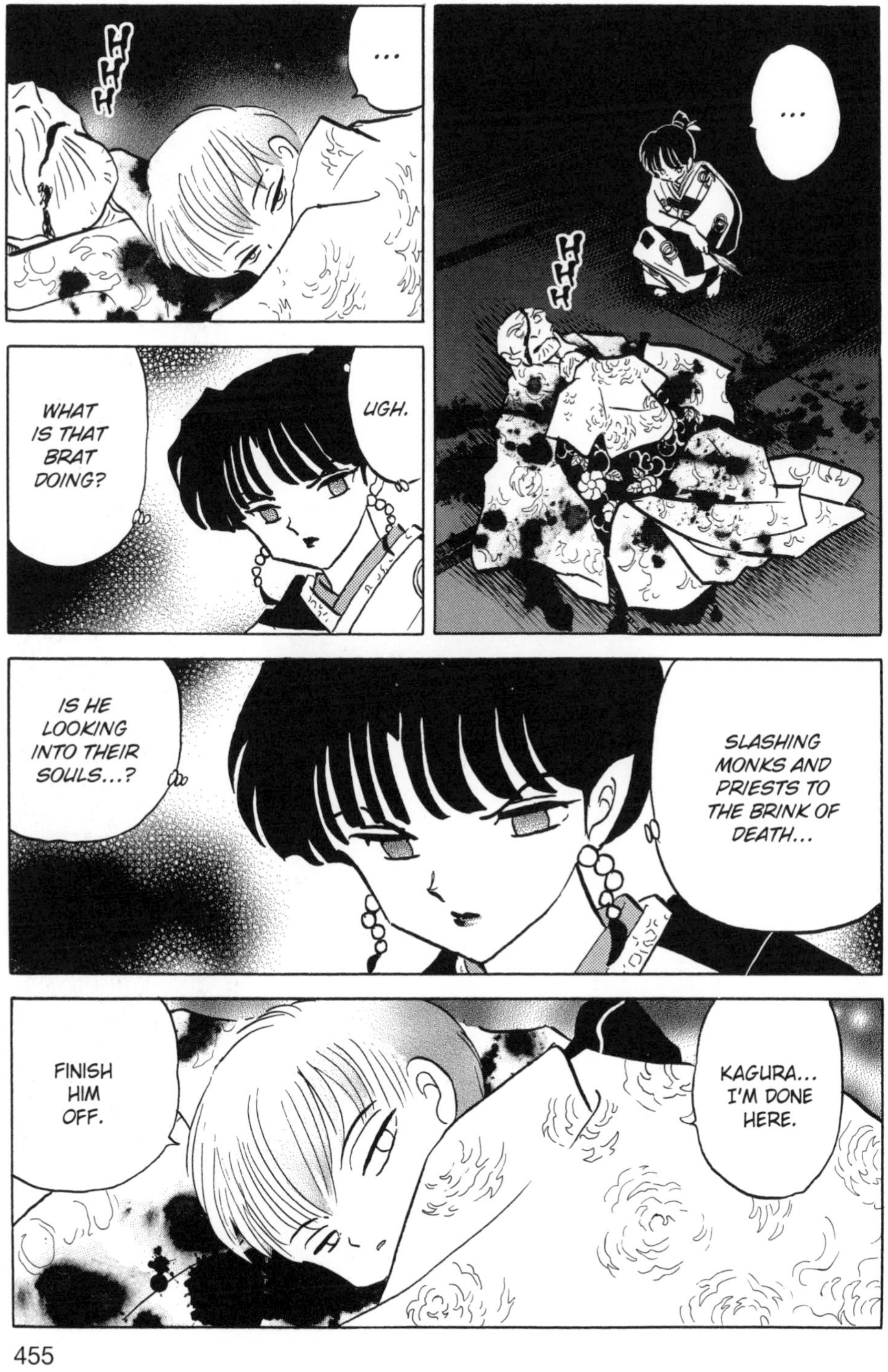
...
HHH
...
HHH
UGH.
WHAT IS THAT BRAT DOING?
SLASHING MONKS AND PRIESTS TO THE BRINK OF DEATH...
IS HE LOOKING INTO THEIR SOULS...?
KAGURA... I'M DONE HERE.
FINISH HIM OFF.

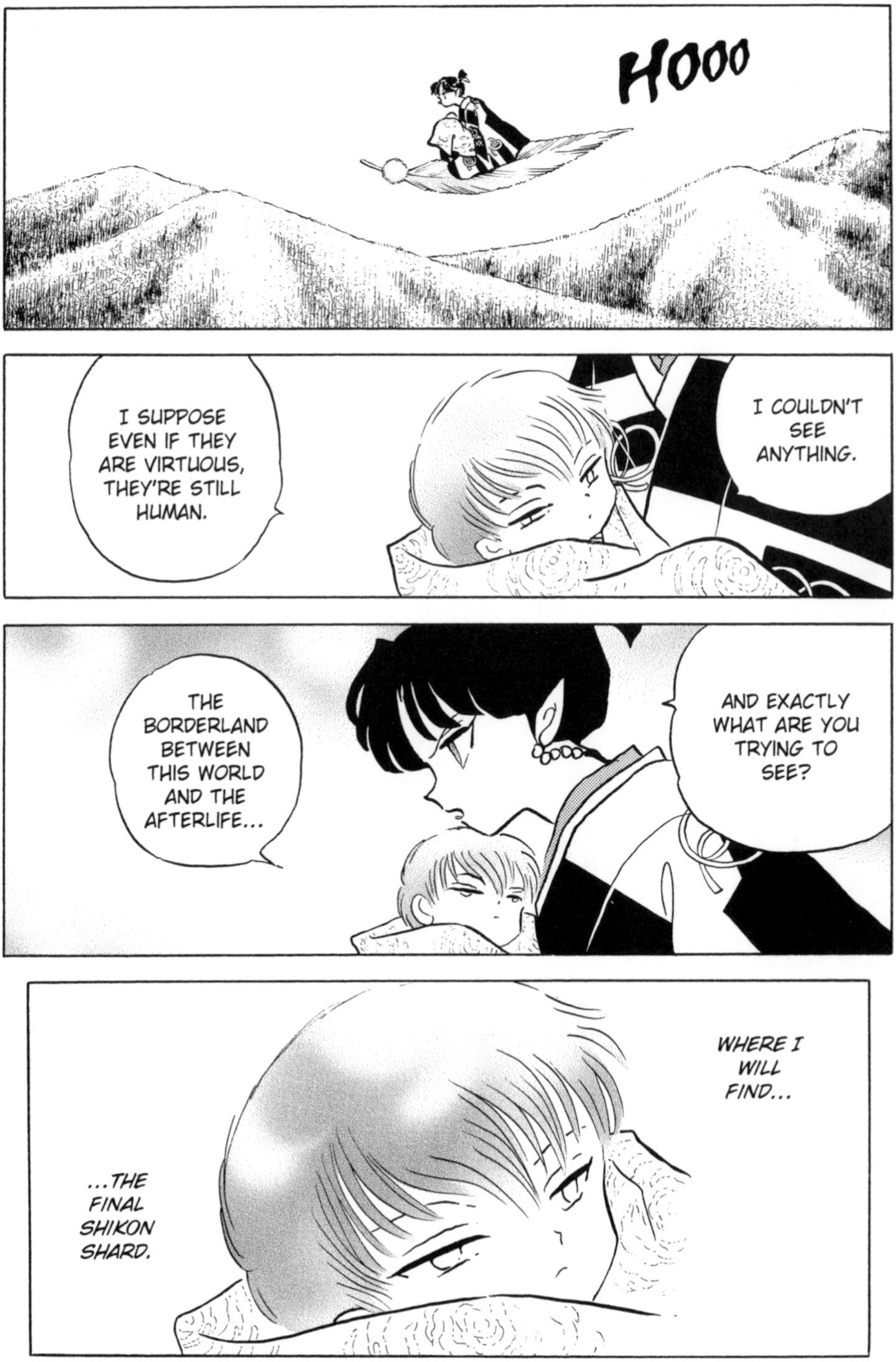
HOOO
I COULDN'T SEE ANYTHING.
I SUPPOSE EVEN IF THEY ARE VIRTUOUS, THEY'RE STILL HUMAN.
AND EXACTLY WHAT ARE YOU TRYING TO SEE?
THE BORDERLAND BETWEEN THIS WORLD AND THE AFTERLIFE...
WHERE I WILL FIND...
...THE FINAL SHIKON SHARD.

SCROLL FIVE
SPLIT IN HALF

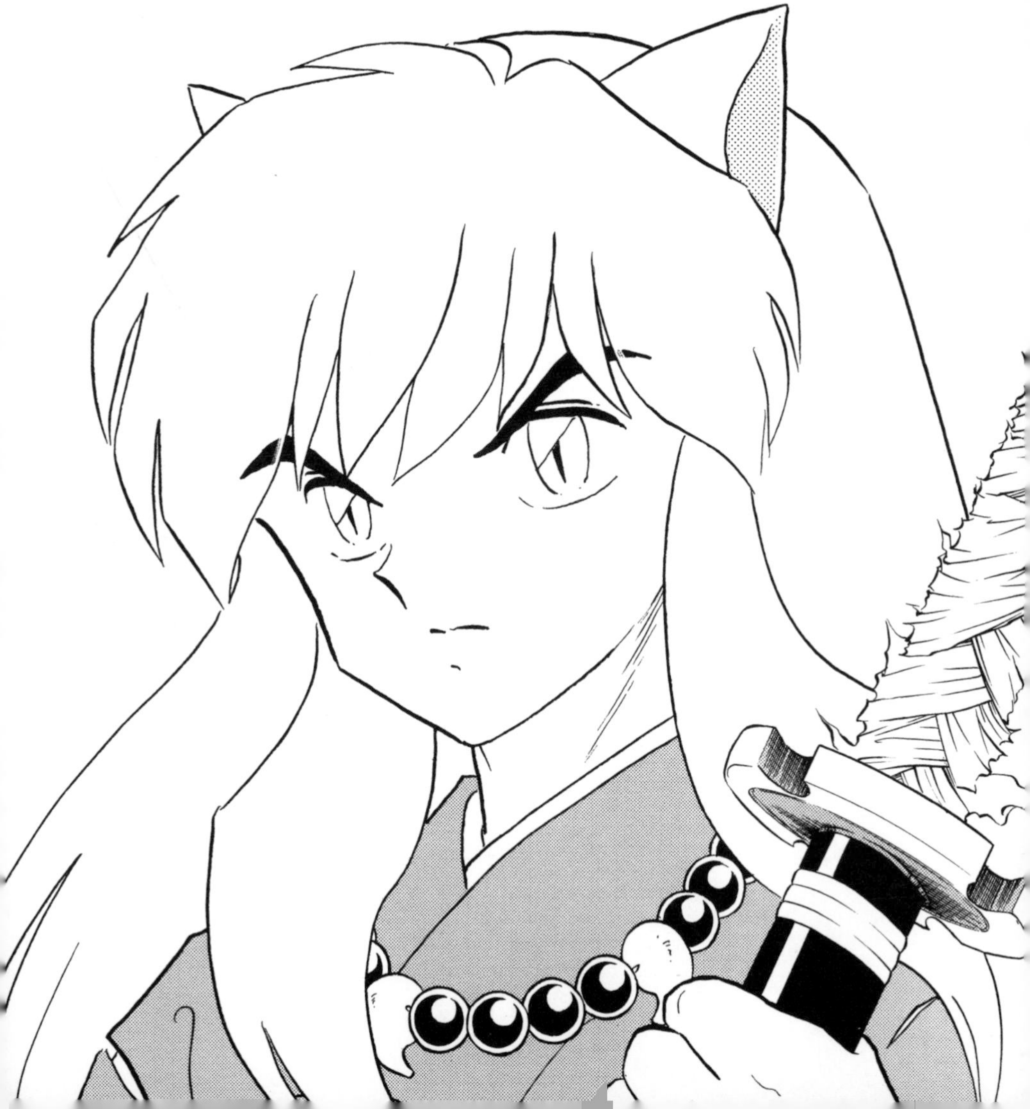

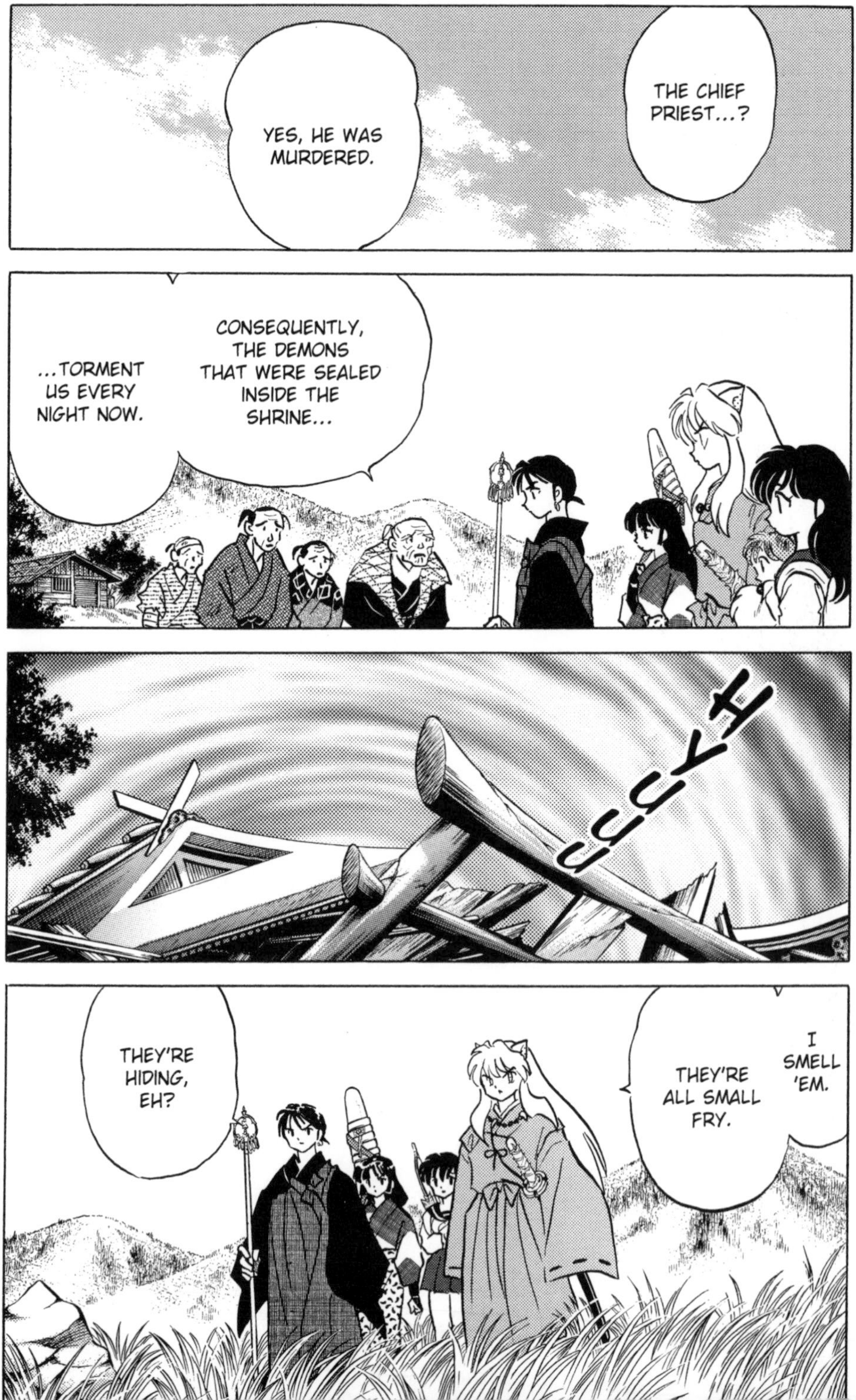
THE CHIEF PRIEST...?
YES, HE WAS MURDERED.
CONSEQUENTLY, THE DEMONS THAT WERE SEALED INSIDE THE SHRINE...
...TORMENT US EVERY NIGHT NOW.
HYUUU
I SMELL 'EM.
THEY'RE ALL SMALL FRY.
THEY'RE HIDING, EH?

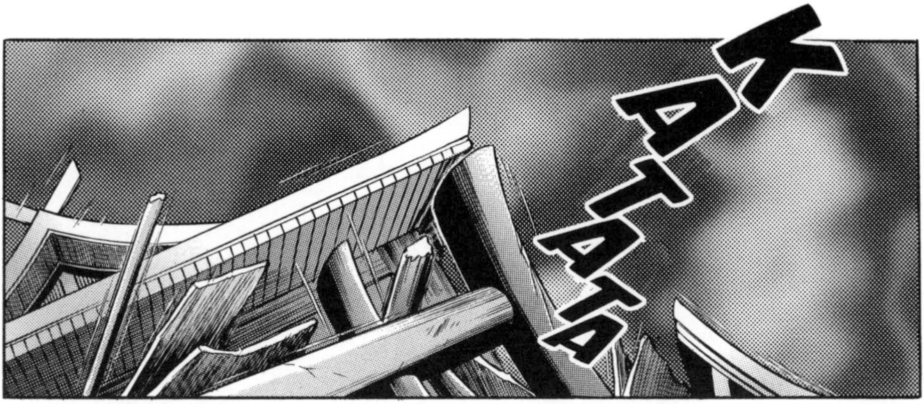
KATATA
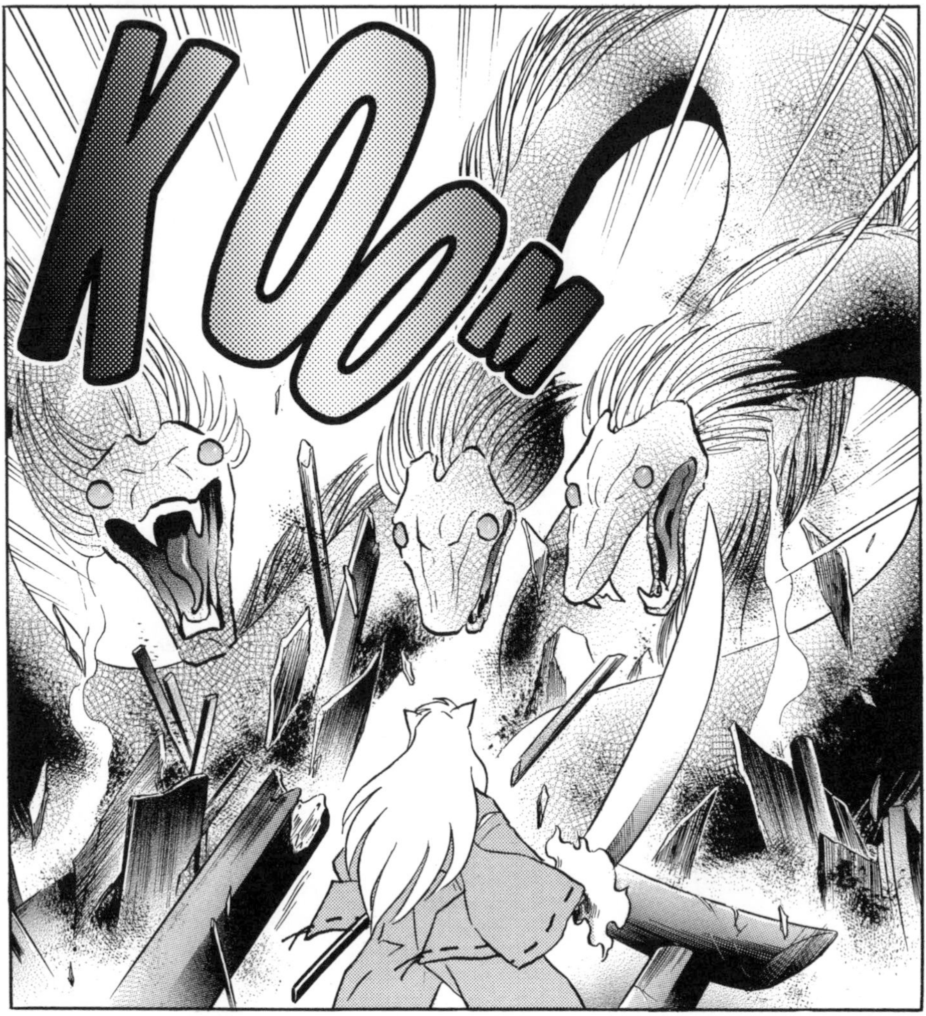
KOOM

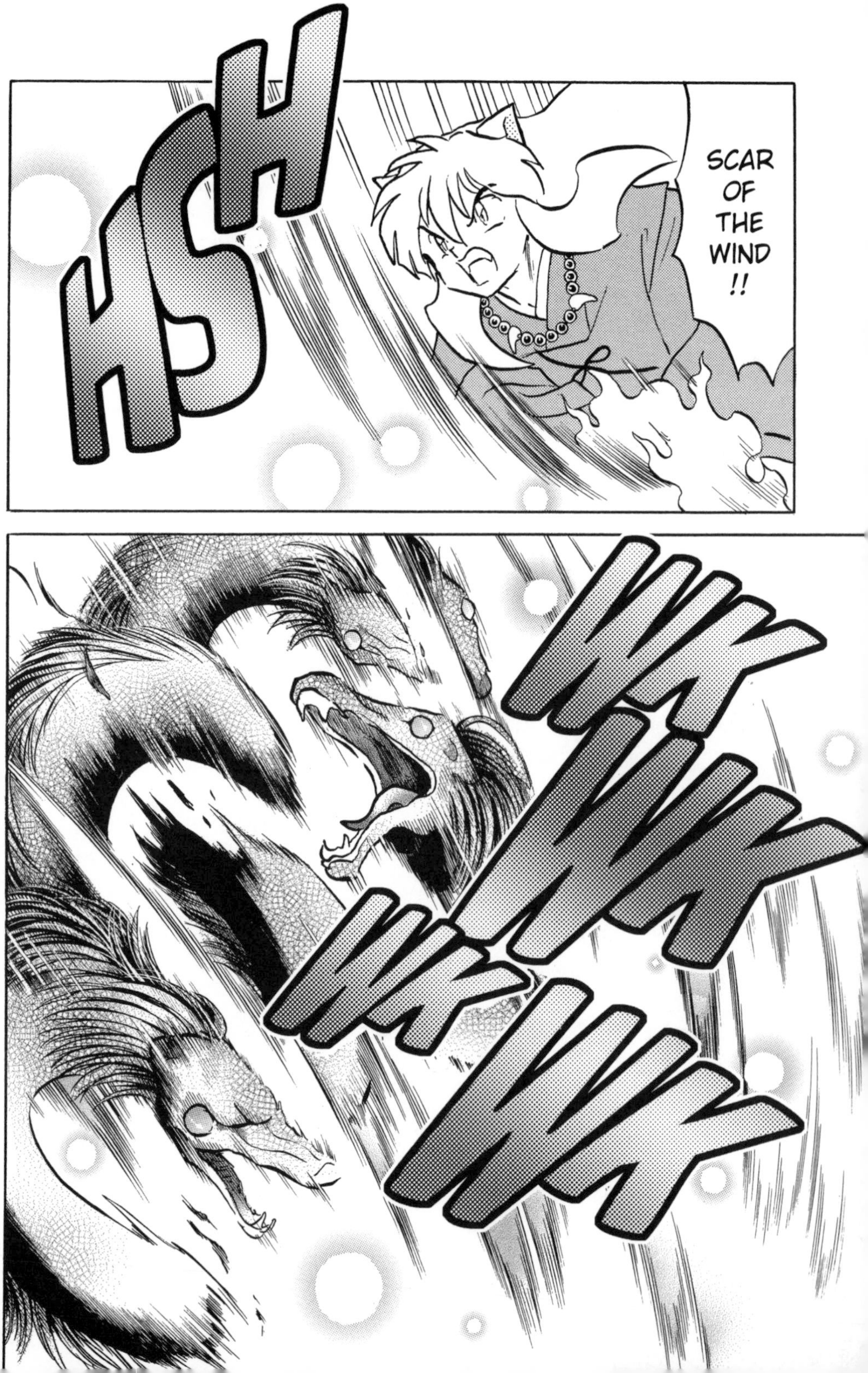
SCAR OF THE WIND !!
HSH
WK WK WK WK

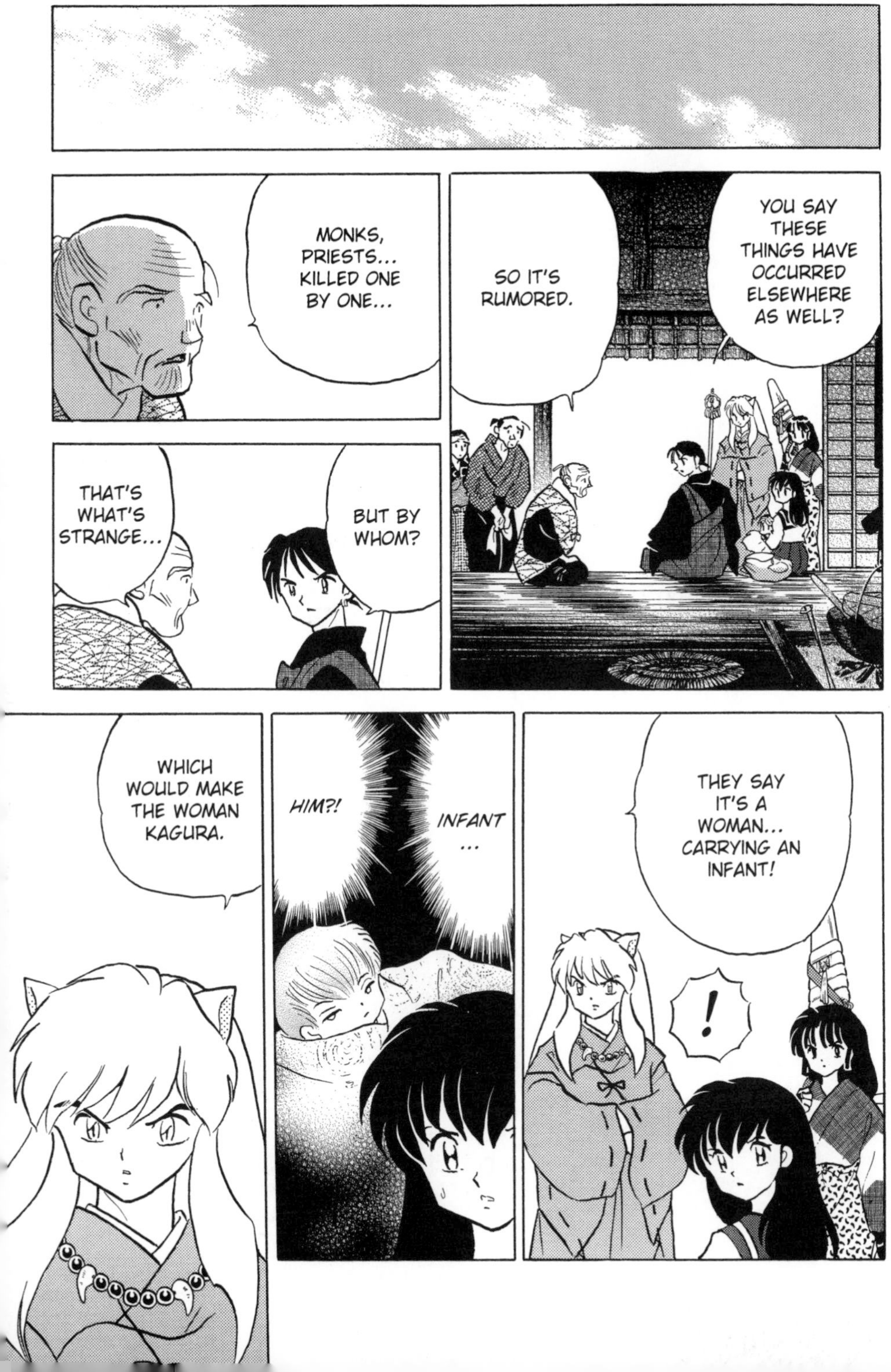
YOU SAY THESE THINGS HAVE OCCURRED ELSEWHERE AS WELL?
SO IT'S RUMORED.
MONKS, PRIESTS... KILLED ONE BY ONE...
BUT BY WHOM?
THAT'S WHAT'S STRANGE...
THEY SAY IT'S A WOMAN... CARRYING AN INFANT!
!
INFANT...
HIM?!
WHICH WOULD MAKE THE WOMAN KAGURA.

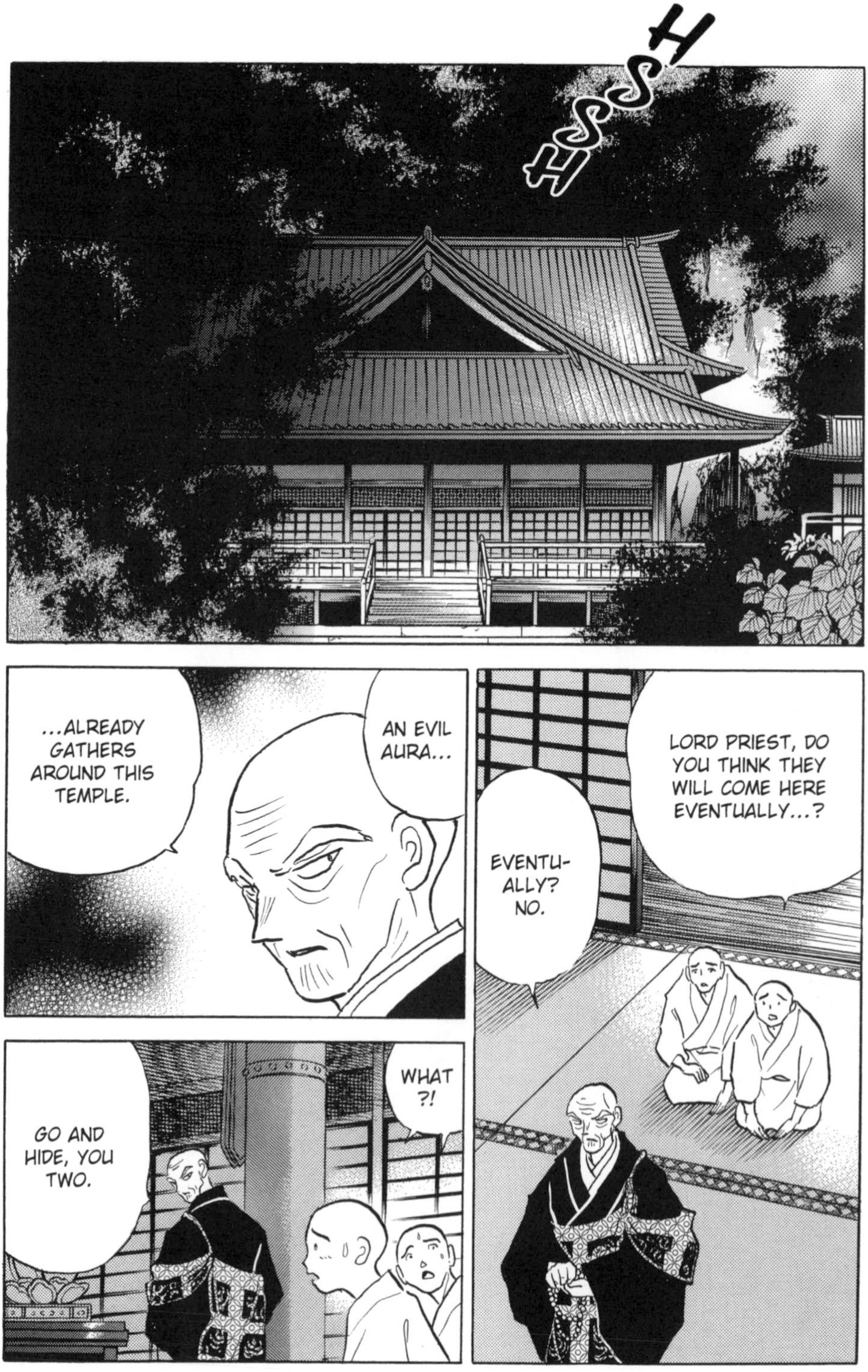
HSSH
LORD PRIEST, DO YOU THINK THEY WILL COME HERE EVENTUALLY...?
EVENTU-ALLY? NO.
AN EVIL AURA...
...ALREADY GATHERS AROUND THIS TEMPLE.
WHAT?!
GO AND HIDE, YOU TWO.

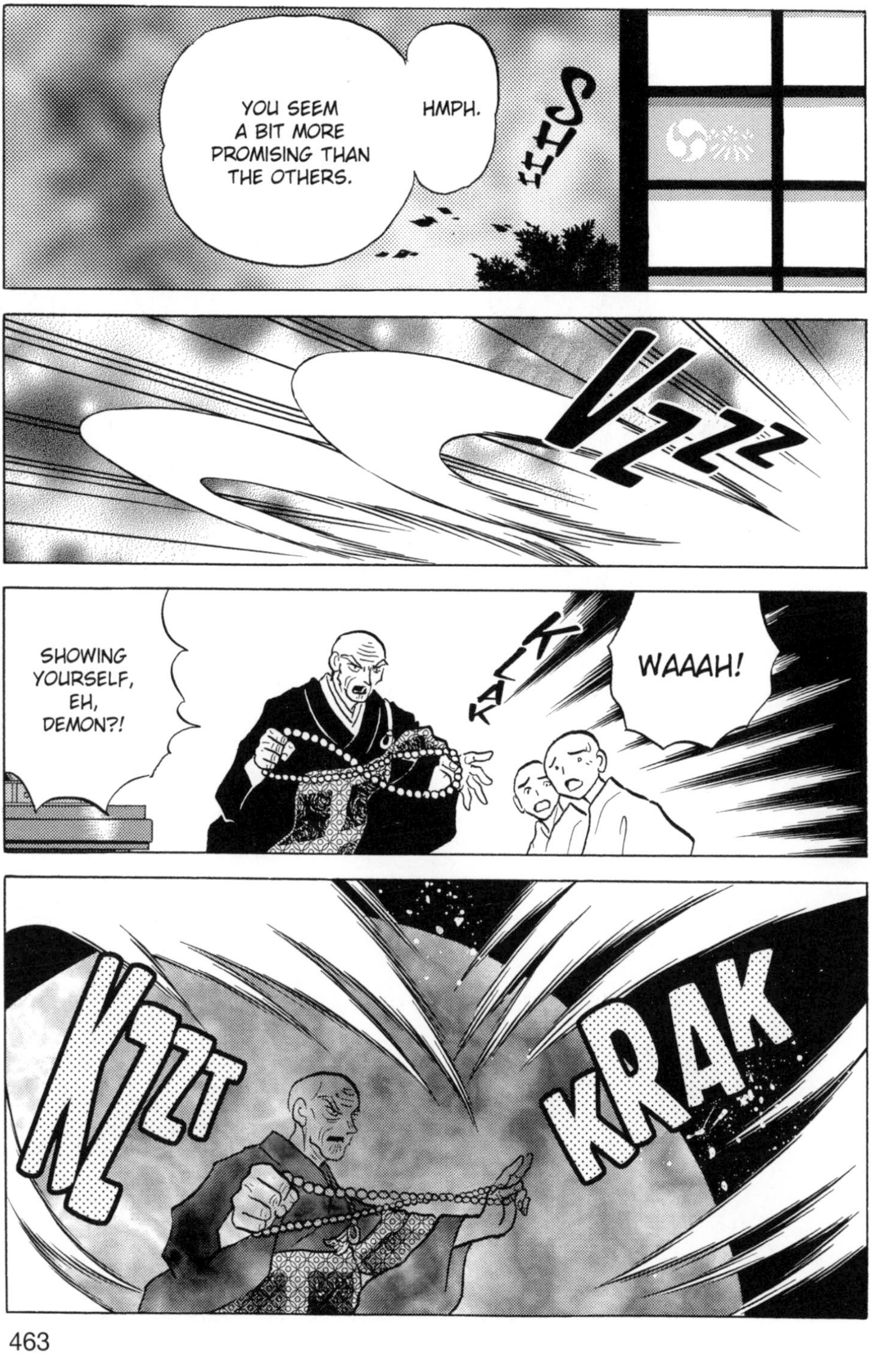
SHHH
HMPH.
YOU SEEM A BIT MORE PROMISING THAN THE OTHERS.
VZZZ
WAAAH!
KLAK
SHOWING YOURSELF, EH, DEMON?!
KRAK
KZZZT

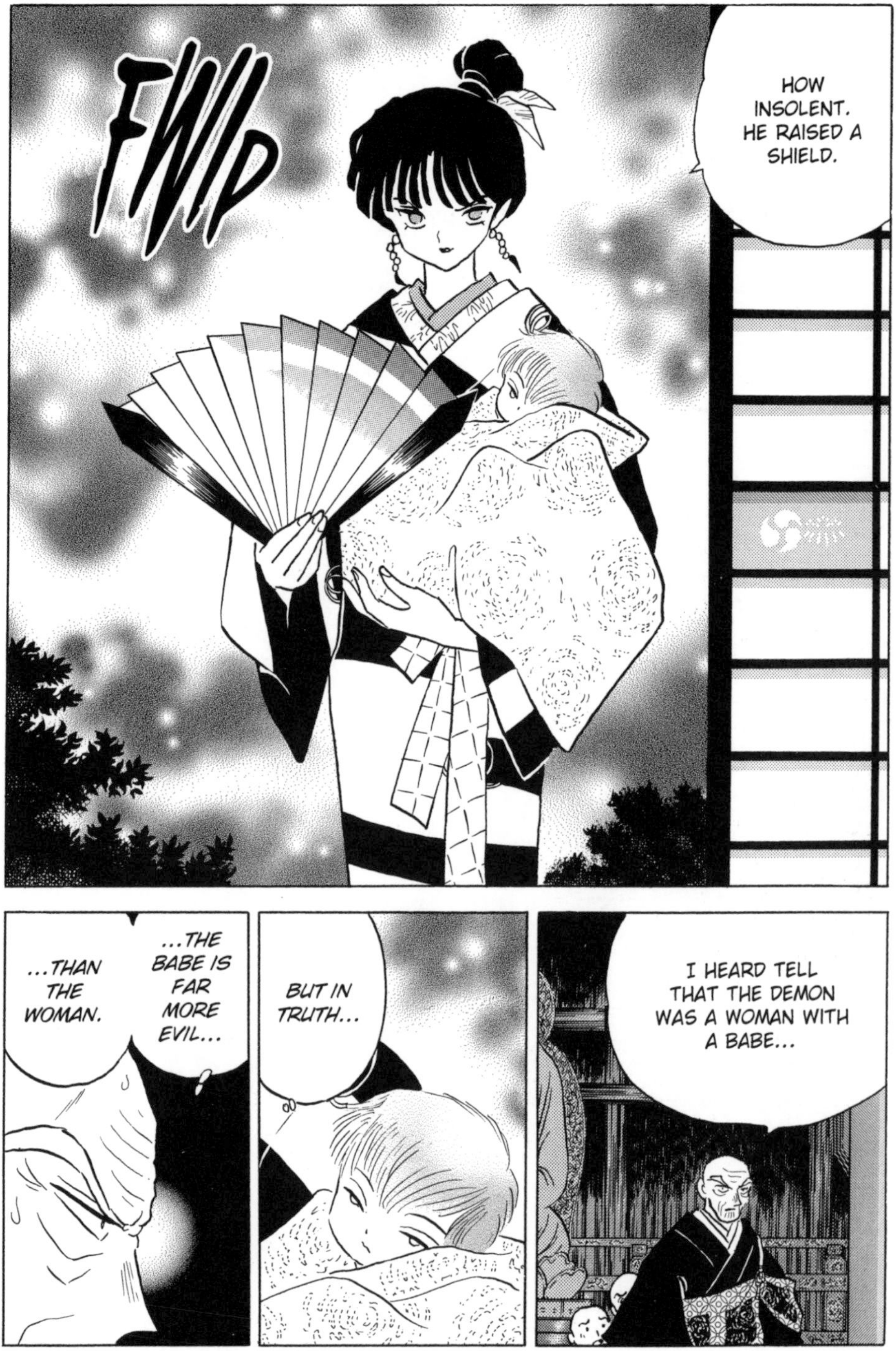
HOW INSOLENT. HE RAISED A SHIELD.
I HEARD TELL THAT THE DEMON WAS A WOMAN WITH A BABE...
BUT IN TRUTH...
...THE BABE IS FAR MORE EVIL...
...THAN THE WOMAN.

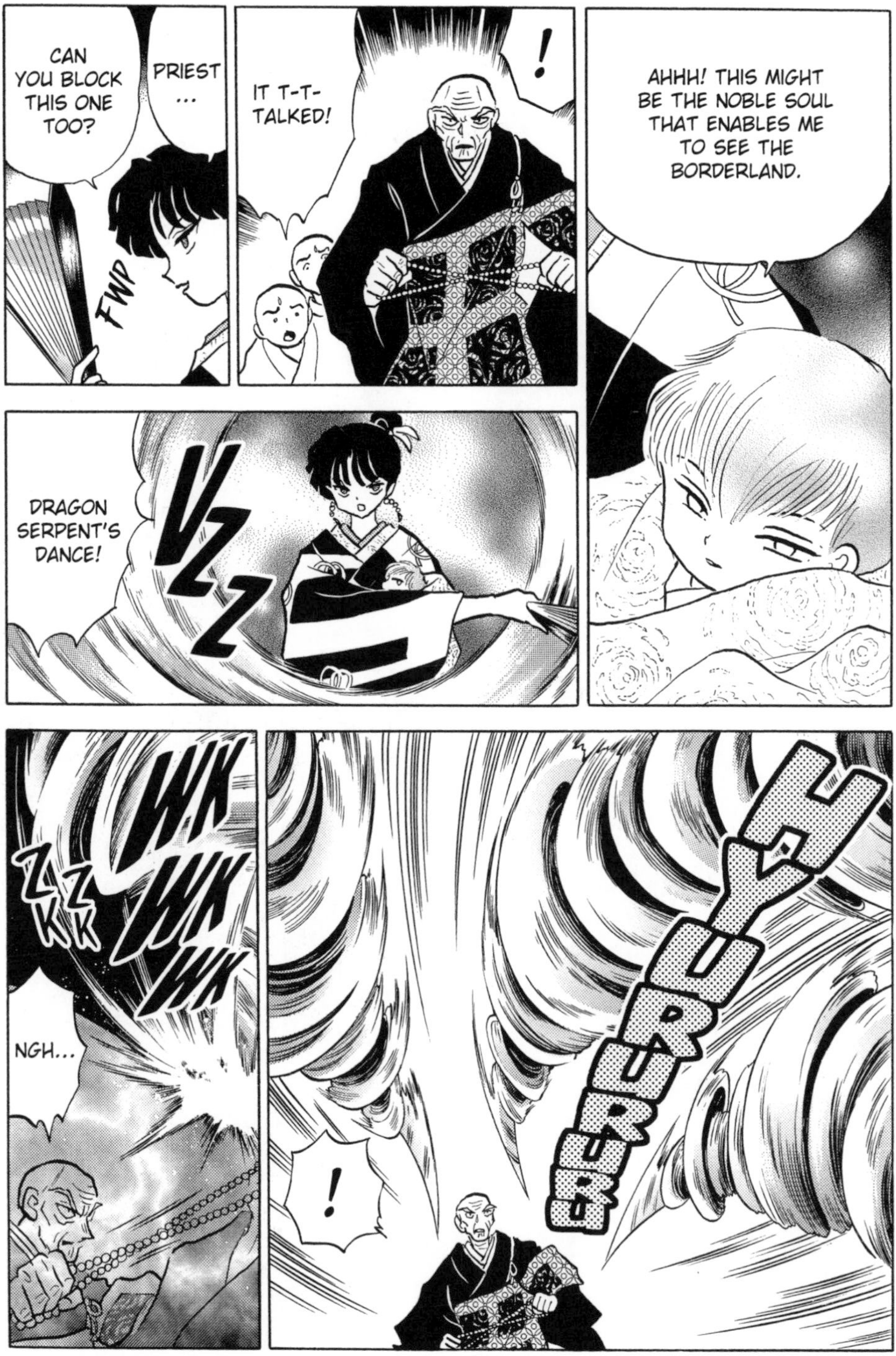
AHHH! THIS MIGHT BE THE NOBLE SOUL THAT ENABLES ME TO SEE THE BORDERLAND.
!
IT T-T-TALKED!
PRIEST...
CAN YOU BLOCK THIS ONE TOO?
FWP
DRAGON SERPENT'S DANCE!
VZZ
HYURURURURB
!
WK WK WK
ZK ZK
NGH...

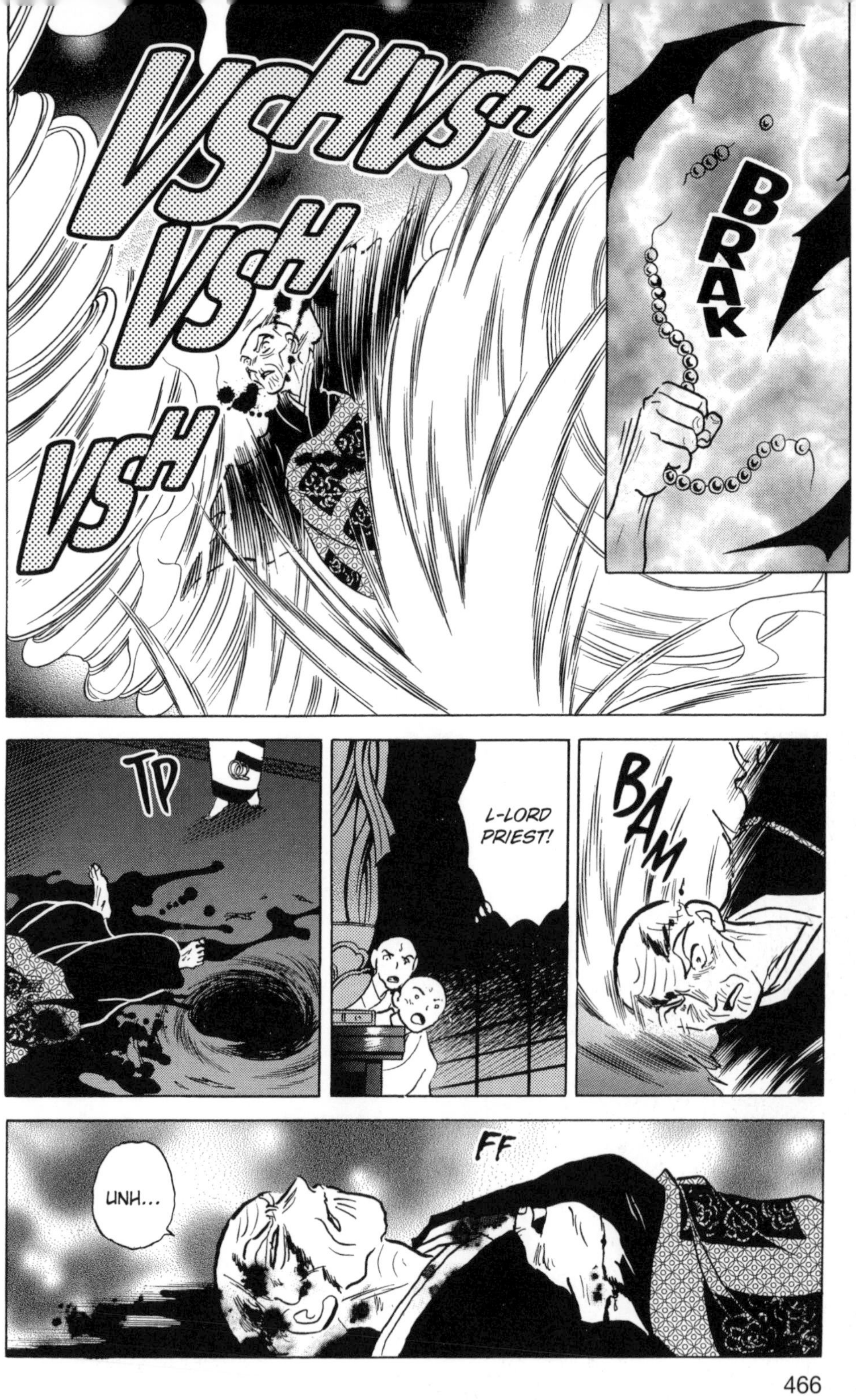
BRAK
VSHUSH
VSH
VSH
BAM
L-LORD PRIEST!
TP
FF
UNH...

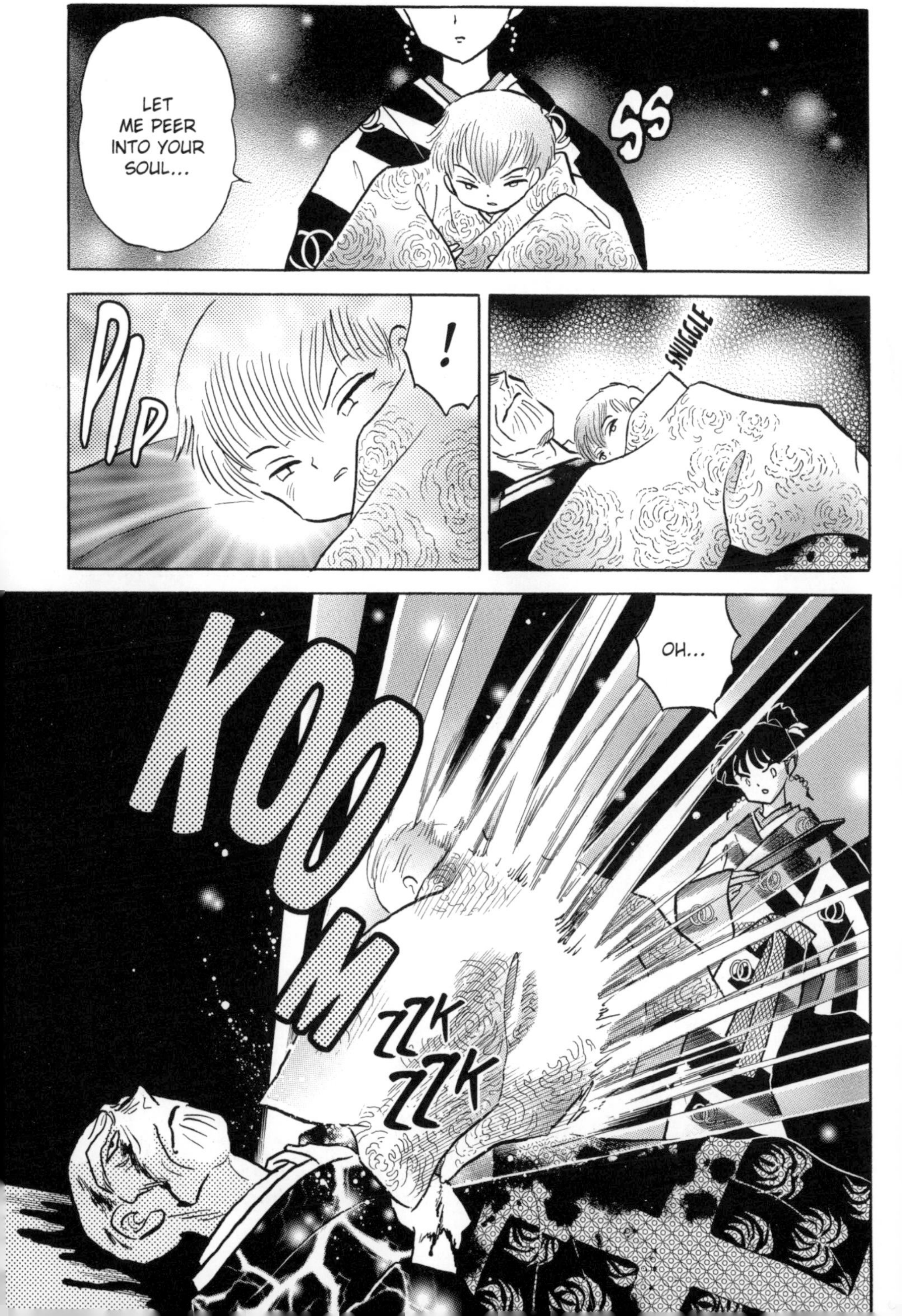
LET ME PEER INTO YOUR SOUL...
SS
SNUGGLE
!
PIP
OH...
KOOM
ZZK
ZZK

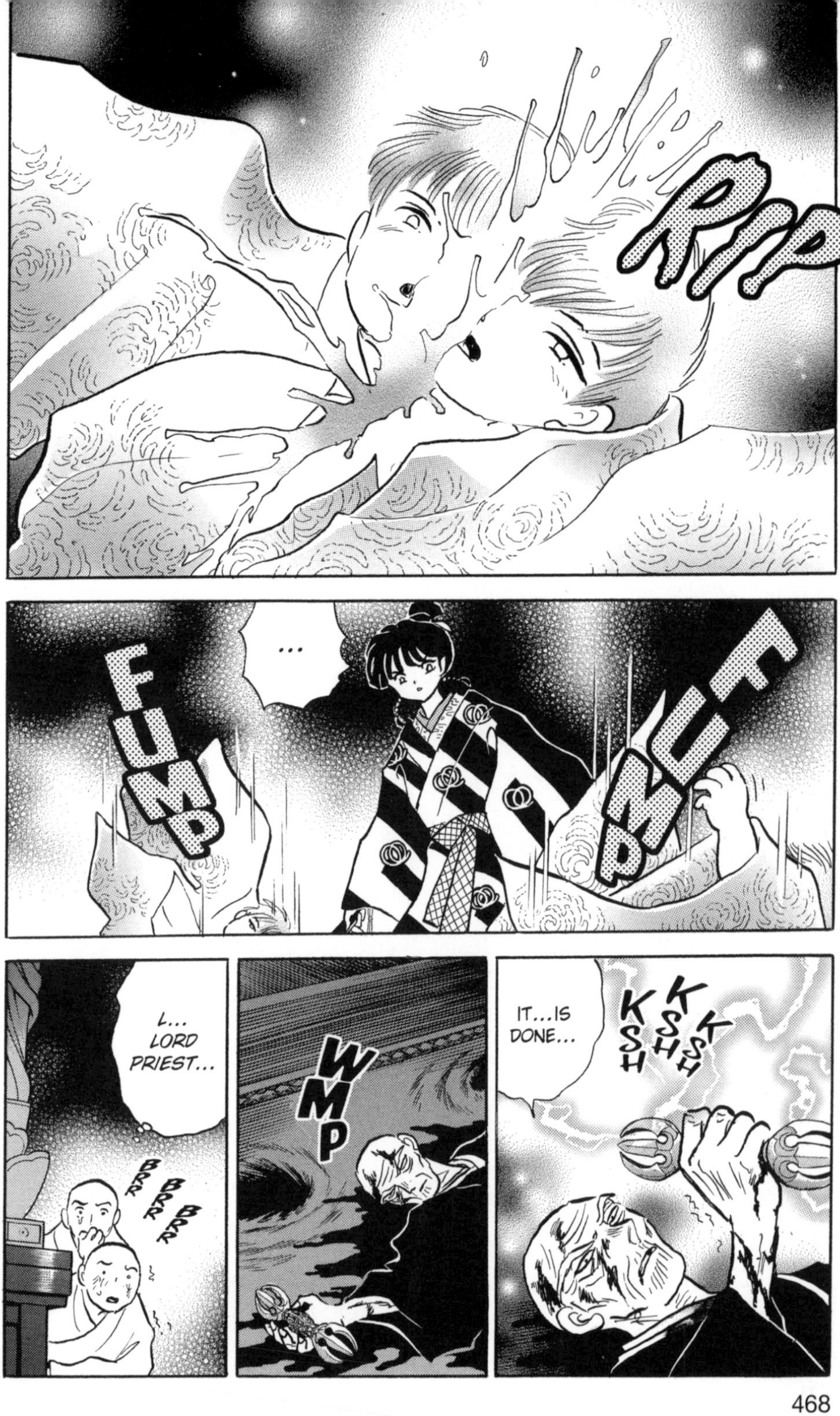
RIP
FUMP
...
FUMP
IT...IS DONE...
KSH KSH KSH
WMP
L... LORD PRIEST...
BRR BRR BRR

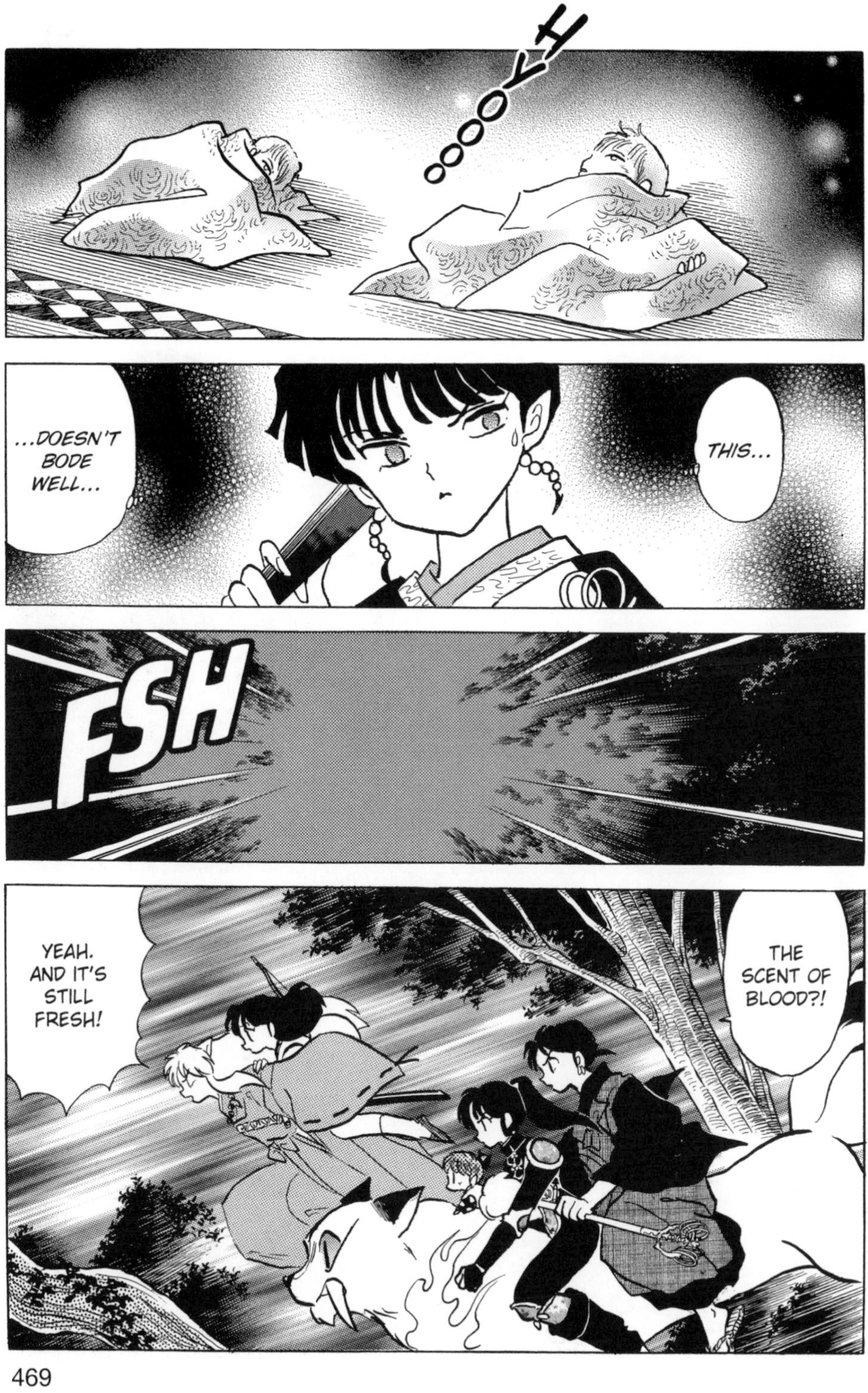
HYOOOO
THIS...
...DOESN'T BODE WELL...
FSH
THE SCENT OF BLOOD?!
YEAH. AND IT'S STILL FRESH!

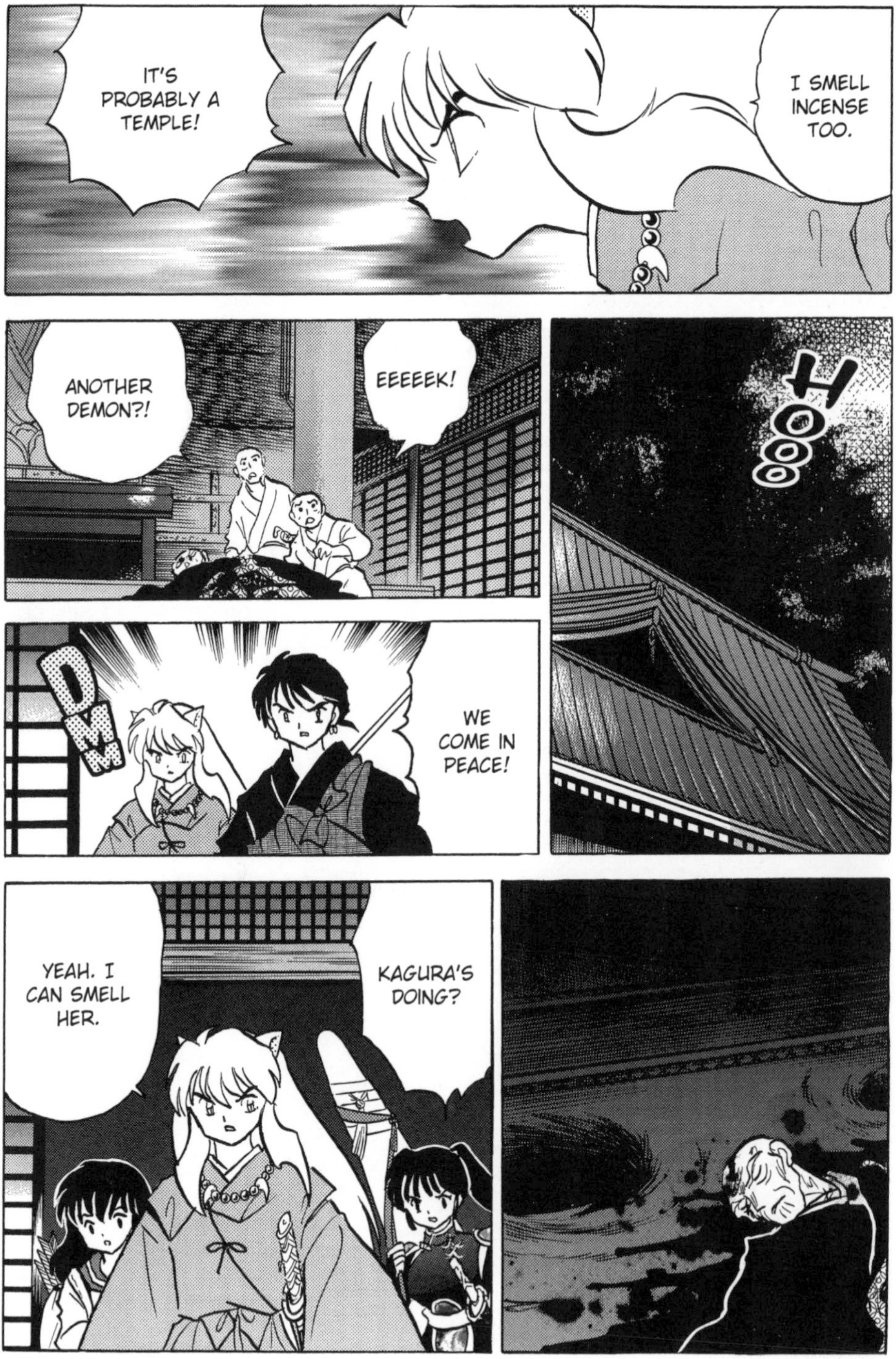
I SMELL INCENSE TOO.
IT'S PROBABLY A TEMPLE!
HOOO
EEEEEK!
ANOTHER DEMON?!
WE COME IN PEACE!
DMM
KAGURA'S DOING?
YEAH. I CAN SMELL HER.

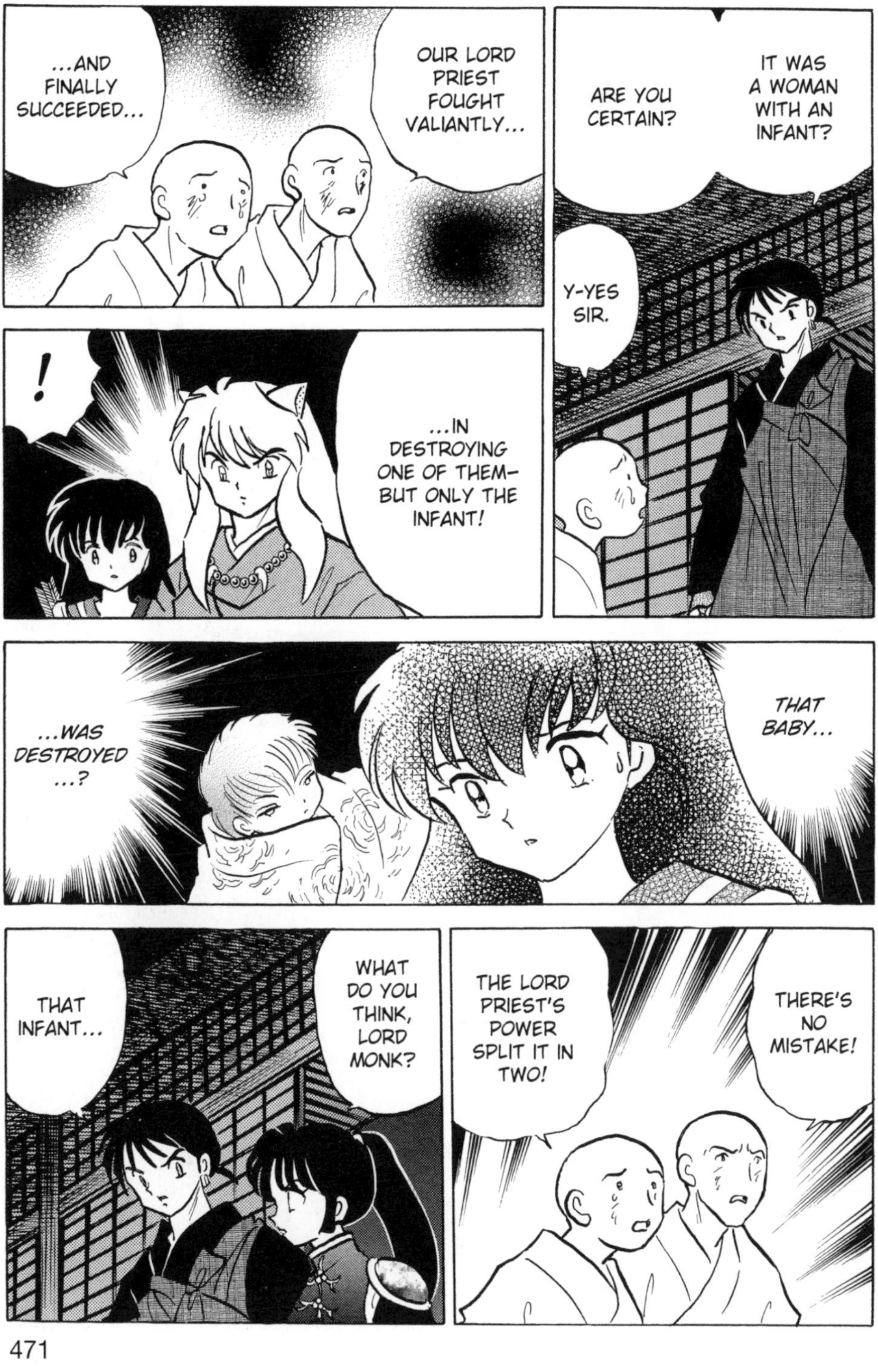
IT WAS A WOMAN WITH AN INFANT?
ARE YOU CERTAIN?
Y-YES SIR.
OUR LORD PRIEST FOUGHT VALIANTLY...
...AND FINALLY SUCCEEDED...
...IN DESTROYING ONE OF THEM-BUT ONLY THE INFANT!
!
THAT BABY...
...WAS DESTROYED ...?
THERE'S NO MISTAKE!
THE LORD PRIEST'S POWER SPLIT IT IN TWO!
WHAT DO YOU THINK, LORD MONK?
THAT INFANT...

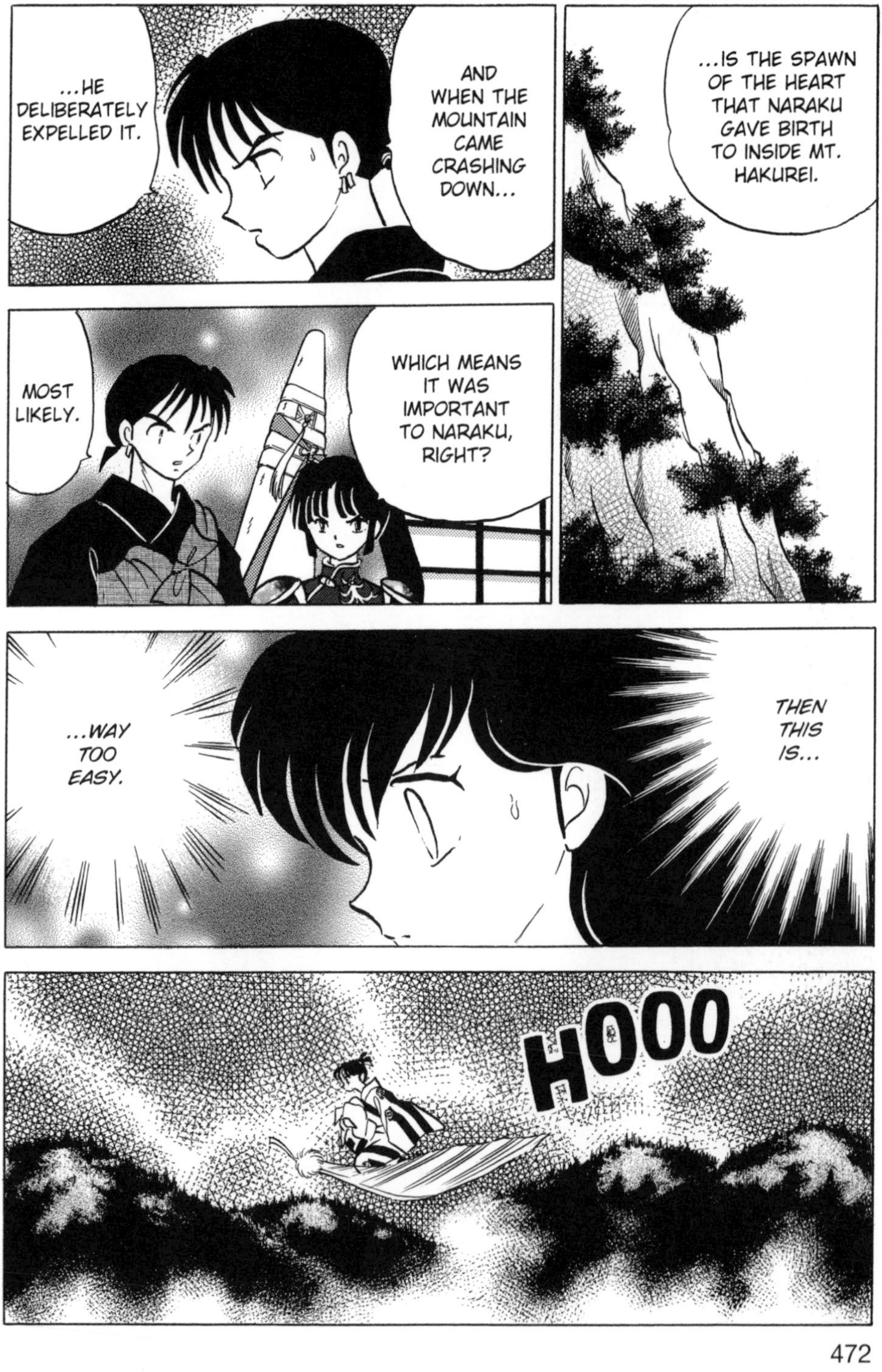
...IS THE SPAWN OF THE HEART THAT NARAKU GAVE BIRTH TO INSIDE MT. HAKUREI.
AND WHEN THE MOUNTAIN CAME CRASHING DOWN...
...HE DELIBERATELY EXPELLED IT.
WHICH MEANS IT WAS IMPORTANT TO NARAKU, RIGHT?
MOST LIKELY.
THEN THIS IS...
...WAY TOO EASY.
HOOO

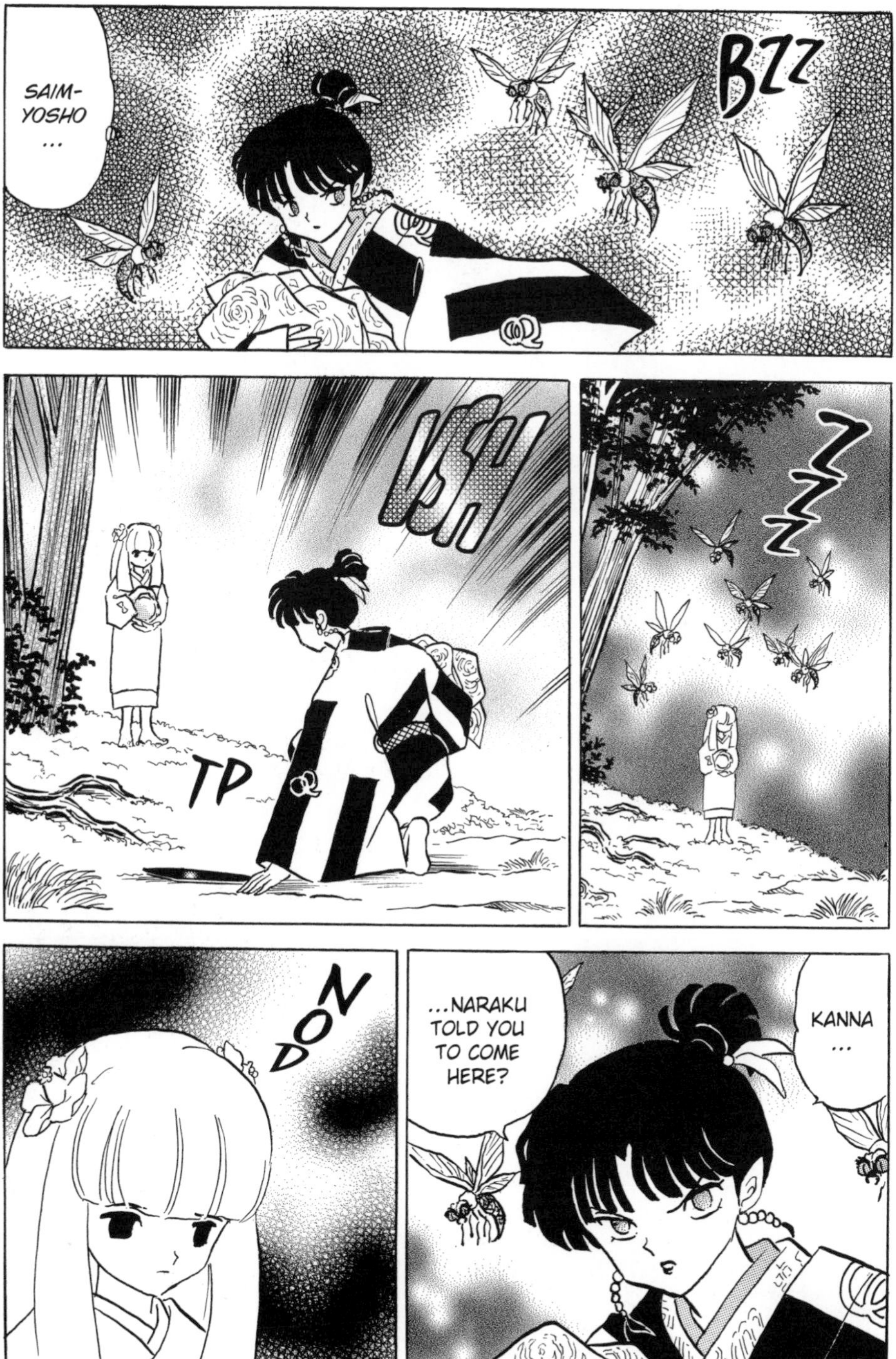
BZZ
SAIM-YOSHO ...
ZZZZ
VSH
TP
KANNA ...
...NARAKU TOLD YOU TO COME HERE?
NOD

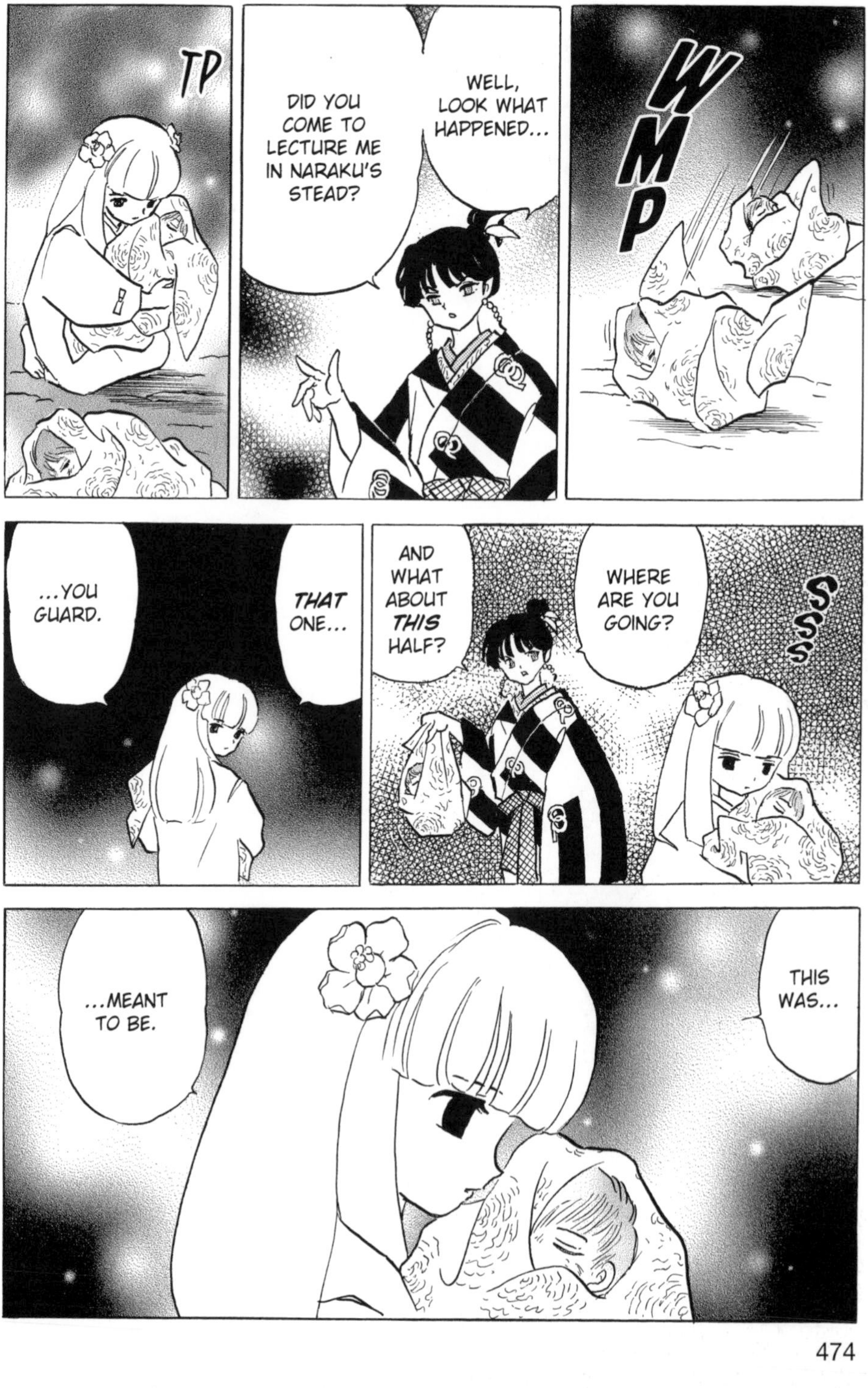
WMP
WELL, LOOK WHAT HAPPENED...
DID YOU COME TO LECTURE ME IN NARAKU'S STEAD?
TP
SSS
WHERE ARE YOU GOING?
AND WHAT ABOUT *THIS* HALF?
THAT ONE...
...YOU GUARD.
THIS WAS...
...MEANT TO BE.

SCROLL SIX
ENTEI

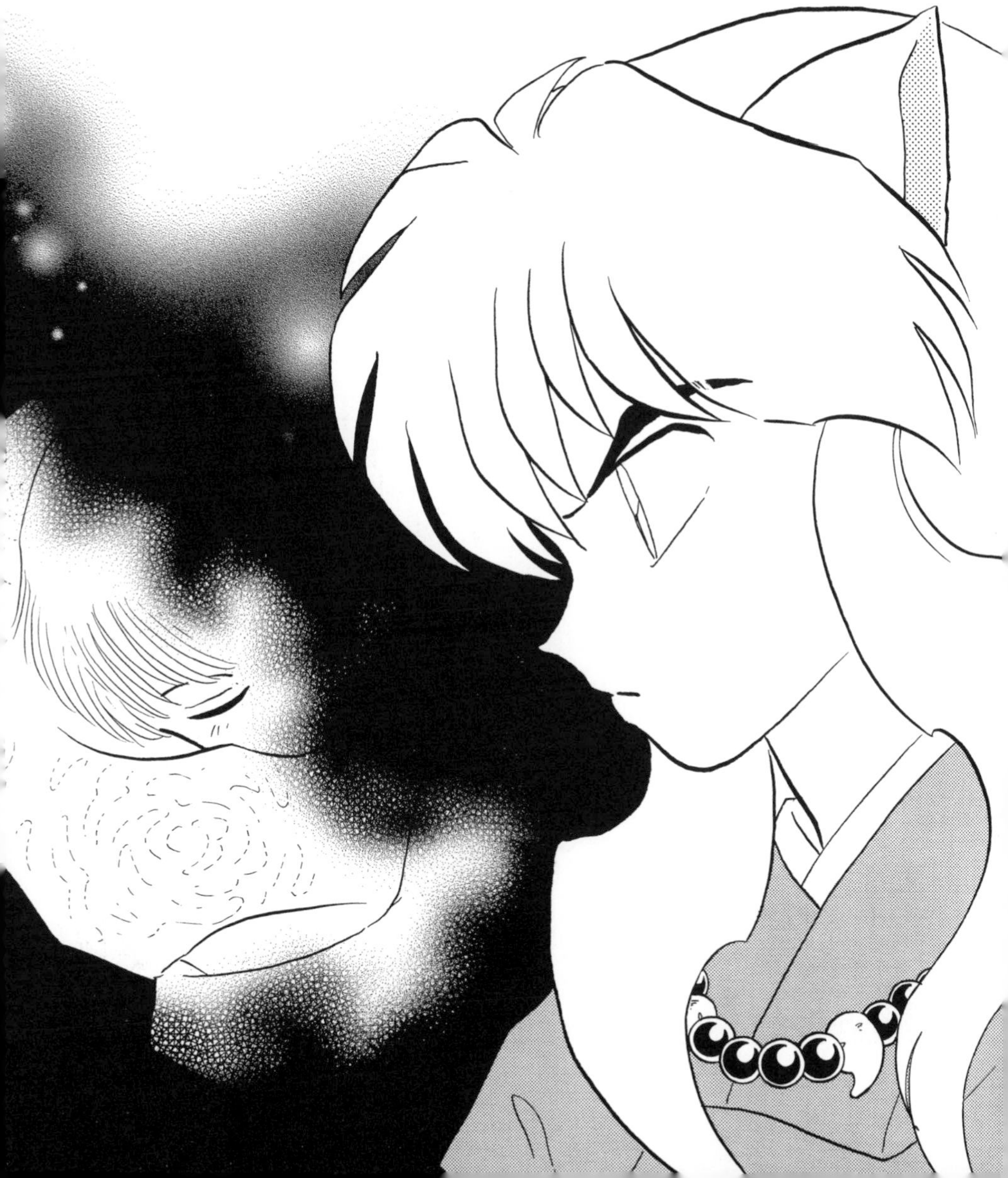

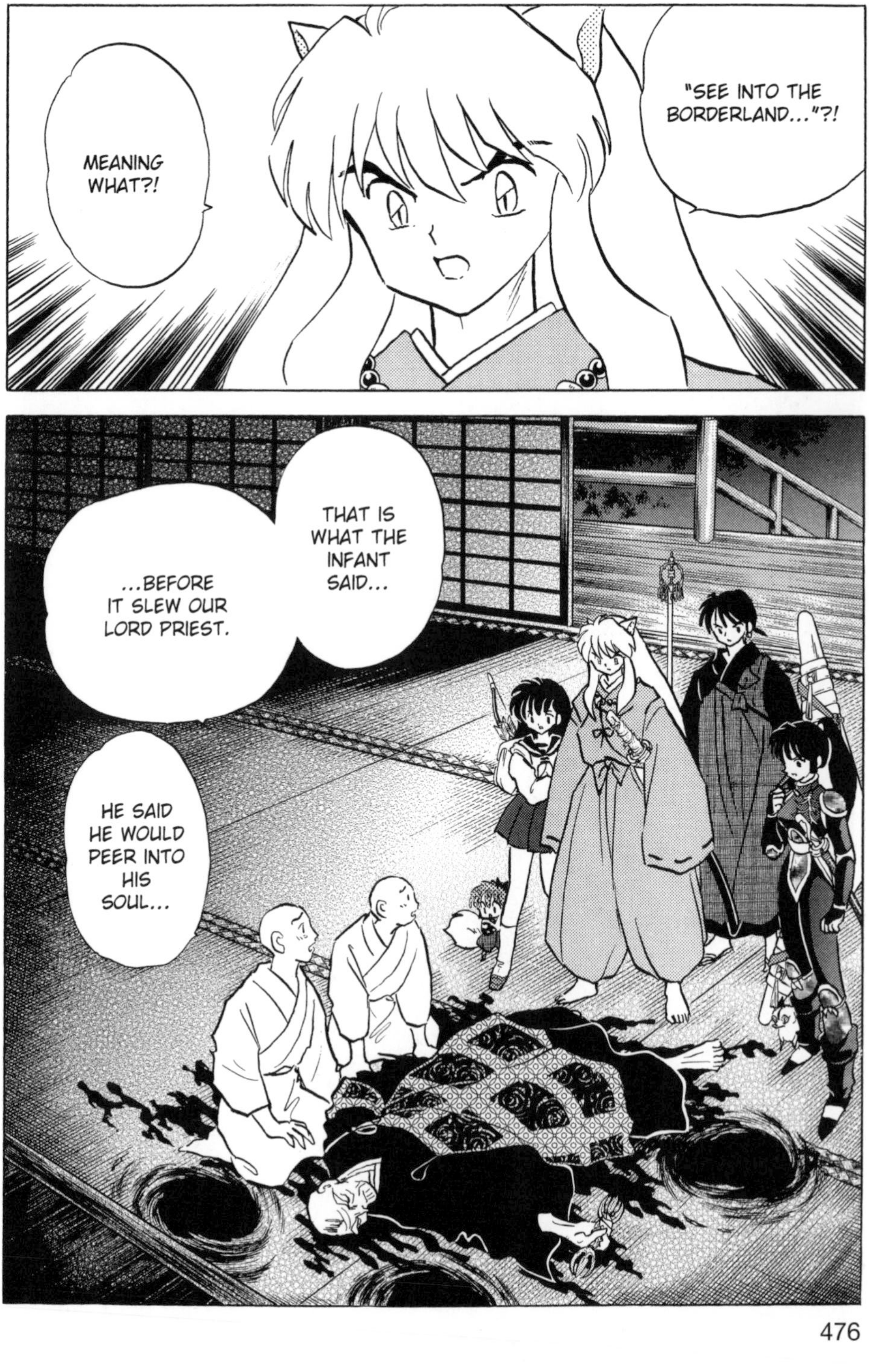
"SEE INTO THE BORDERLAND..."?!
MEANING WHAT?!
THAT IS WHAT THE INFANT SAID...
...BEFORE IT SLEW OUR LORD PRIEST.
HE SAID HE WOULD PEER INTO HIS SOUL...

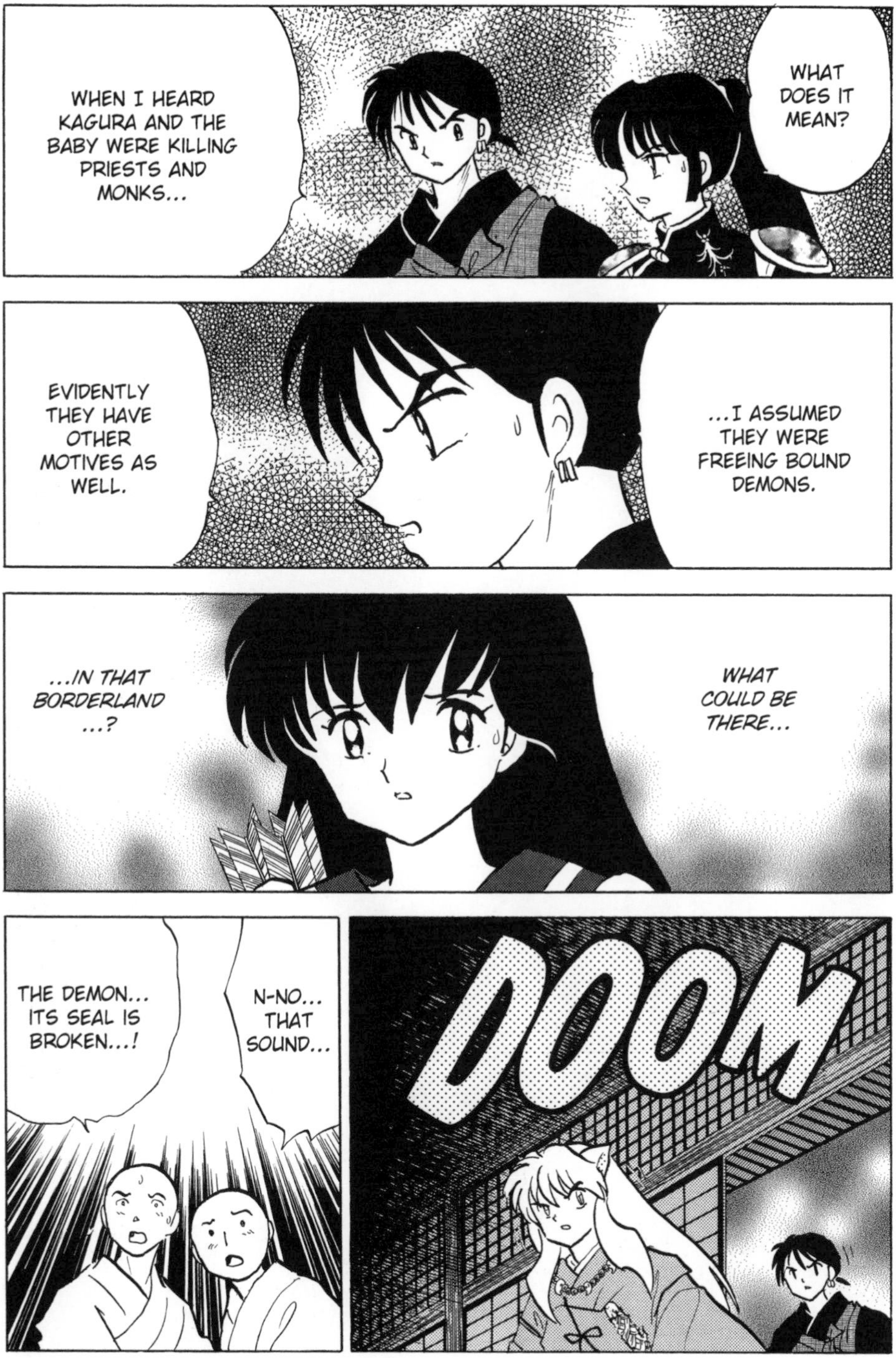
WHAT DOES IT MEAN?
WHEN I HEARD KAGURA AND THE BABY WERE KILLING PRIESTS AND MONKS...
...I ASSUMED THEY WERE FREEING BOUND DEMONS.
EVIDENTLY THEY HAVE OTHER MOTIVES AS WELL.
WHAT COULD BE THERE...
...IN THAT BORDERLAND...?
DOOM
N-NO... THAT SOUND...
THE DEMON... ITS SEAL IS BROKEN...!

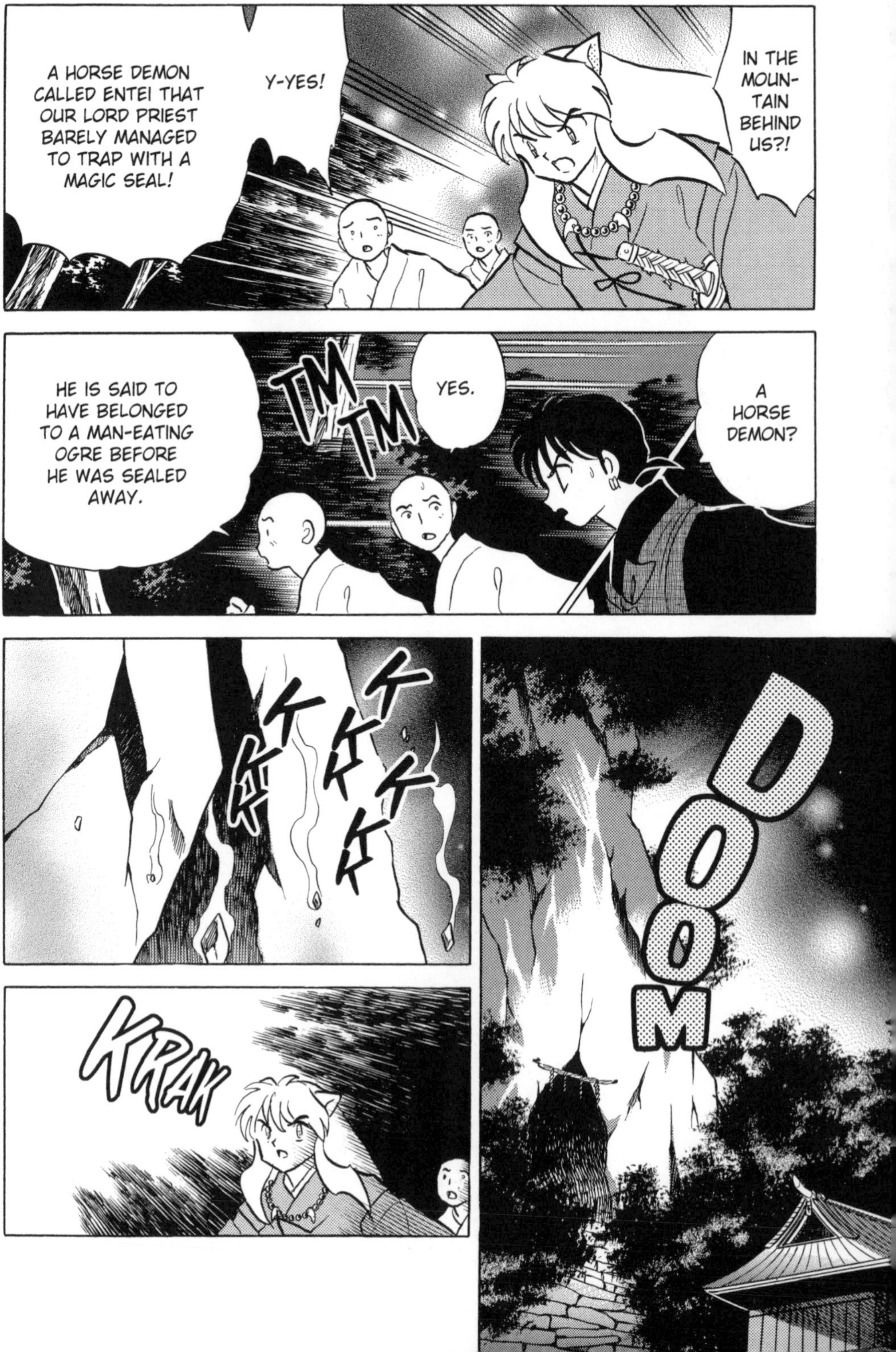

IN THE MOUNTAIN BEHIND US?!
Y-YES!
A HORSE DEMON CALLED ENTEI THAT OUR LORD PRIEST BARELY MANAGED TO TRAP WITH A MAGIC SEAL!
A HORSE DEMON?
YES.
TM TM
HE IS SAID TO HAVE BELONGED TO A MAN-EATING OGRE BEFORE HE WAS SEALED AWAY.
DOOOM
KKKK
KKK
KRAK

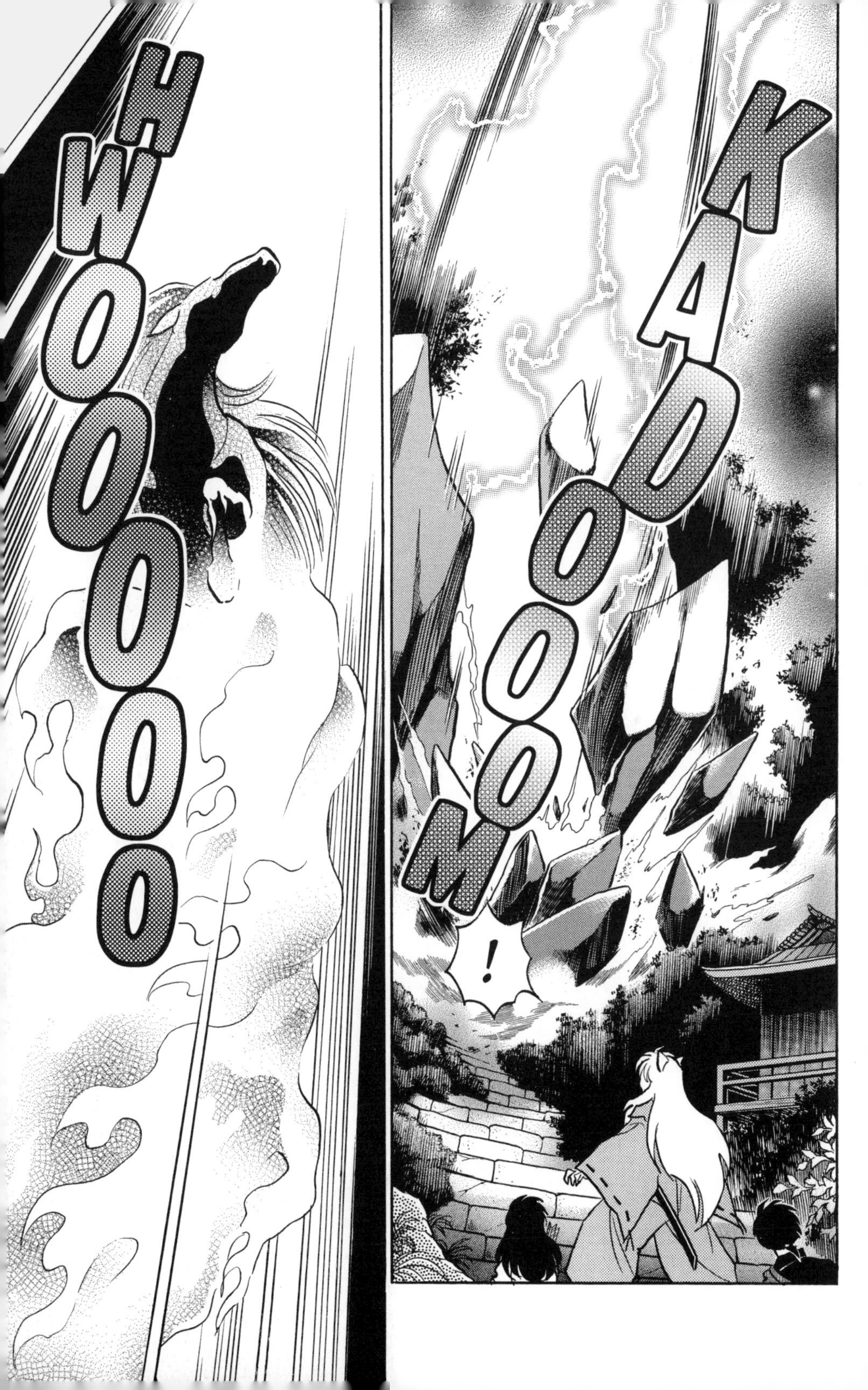
KADOOOOM
!
HWOOOOOOO

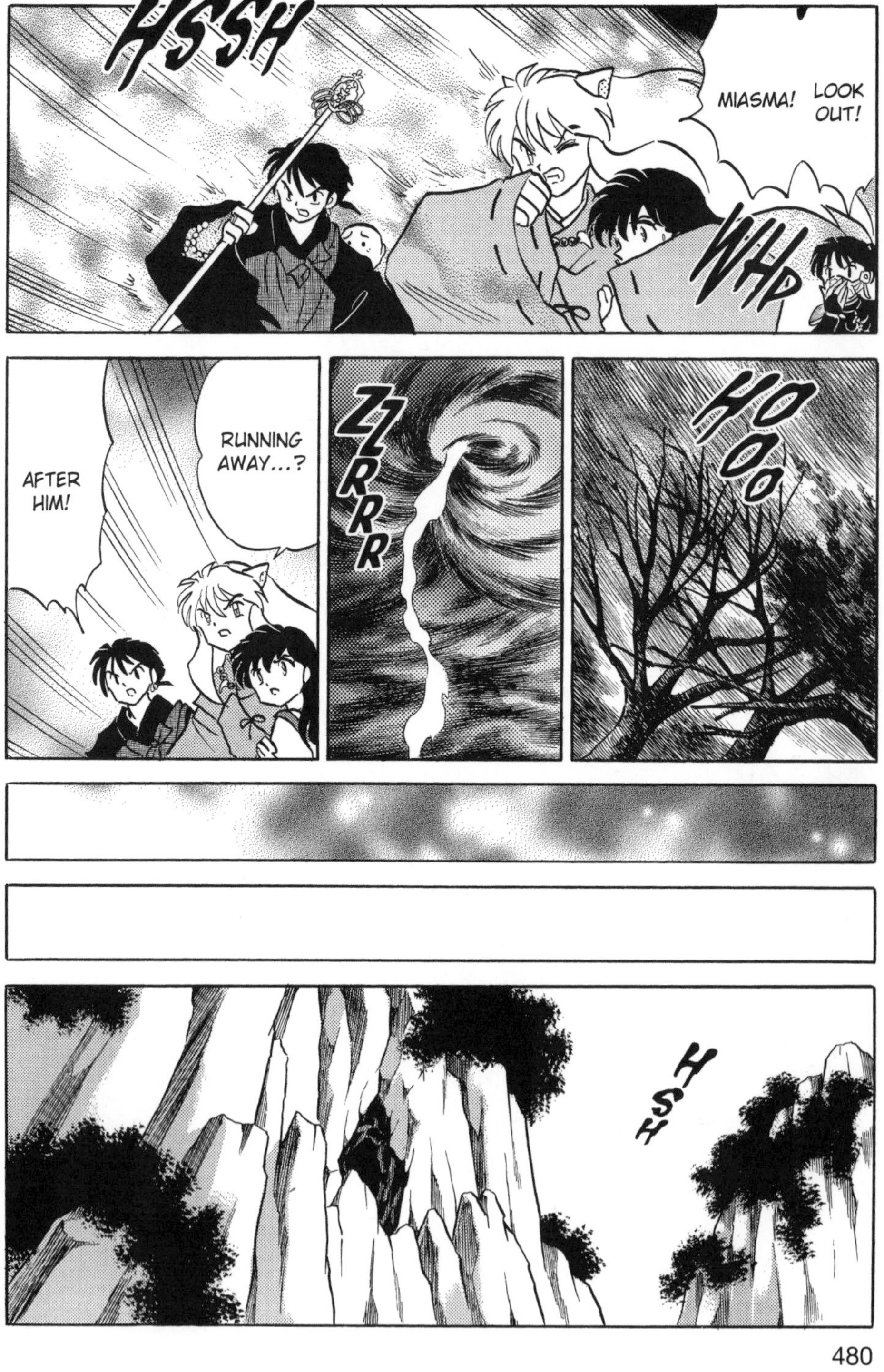
LOOK OUT!
MIASMA!
HSSH
WHP
HOOO
ZZRRRR
RUNNING AWAY...?
AFTER HIM!
HSSH

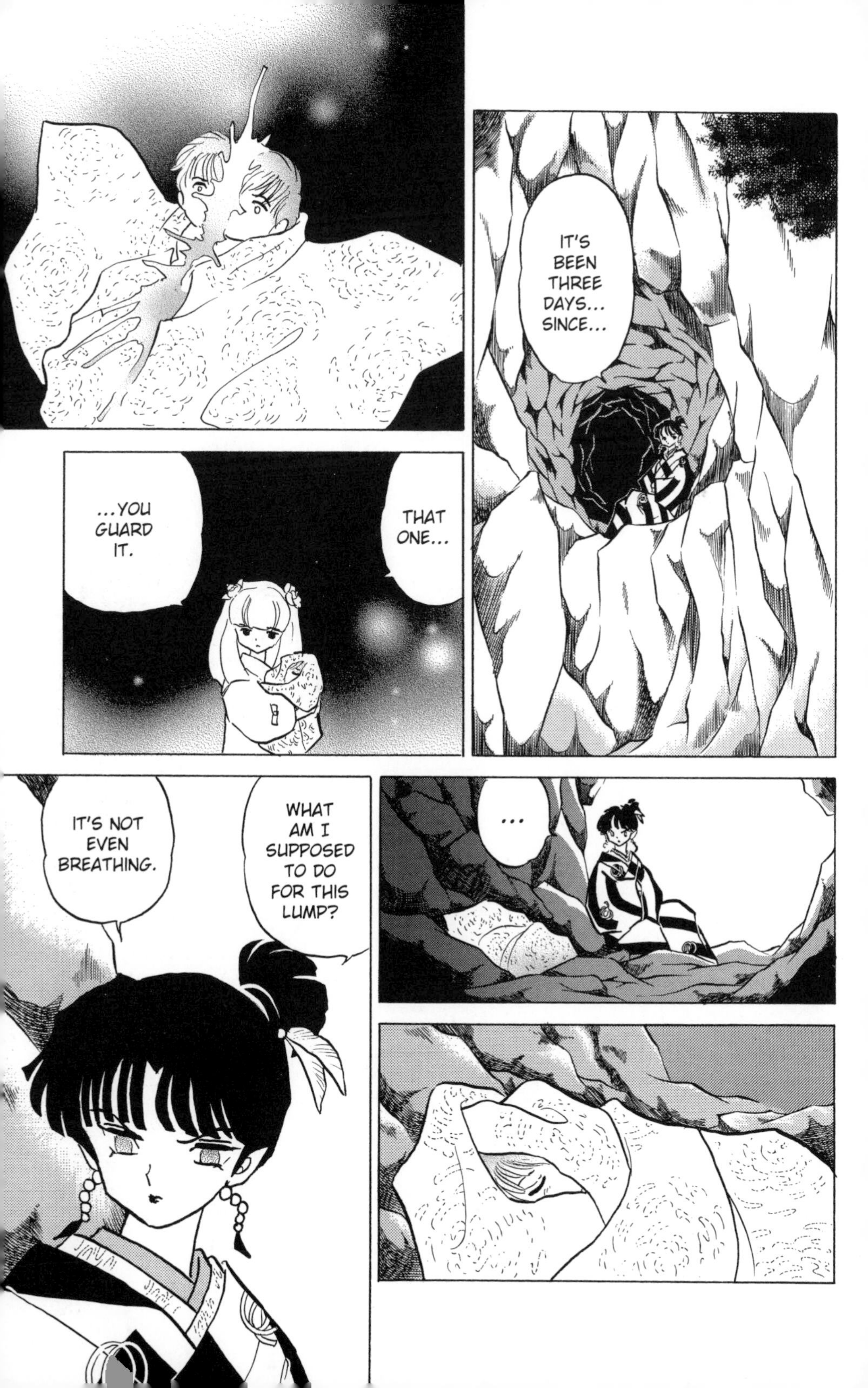
IT'S BEEN THREE DAYS... SINCE...
THAT ONE...
...YOU GUARD IT.
...
WHAT AM I SUPPOSED TO DO FOR THIS LUMP?
IT'S NOT EVEN BREATHING.

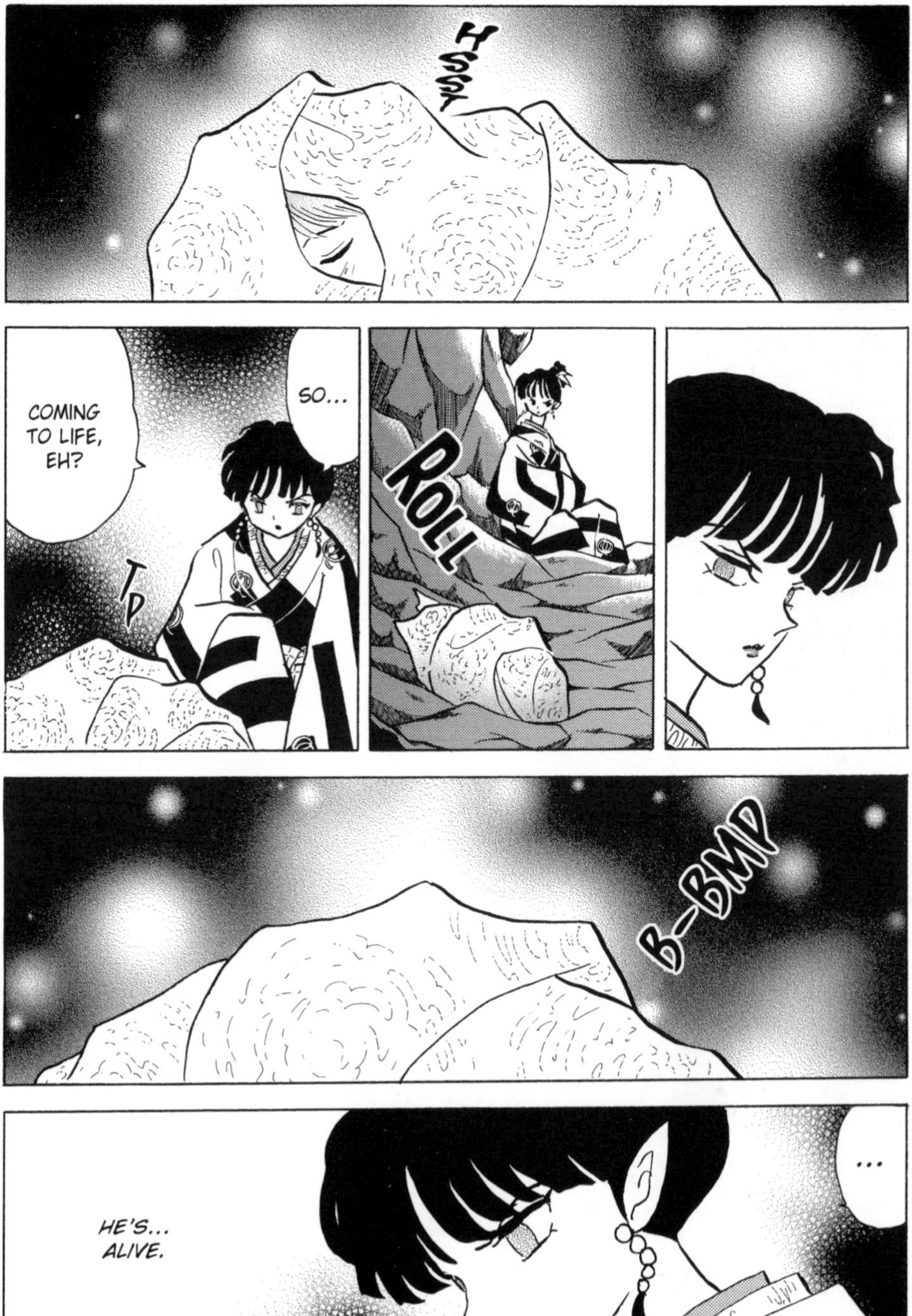
HSSST
ROLL
SO...
COMING TO LIFE, EH?
TP
B-BMP
...
HE'S... ALIVE.

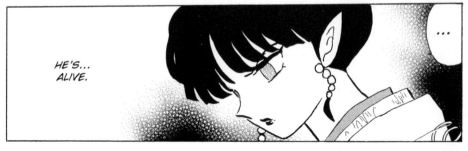

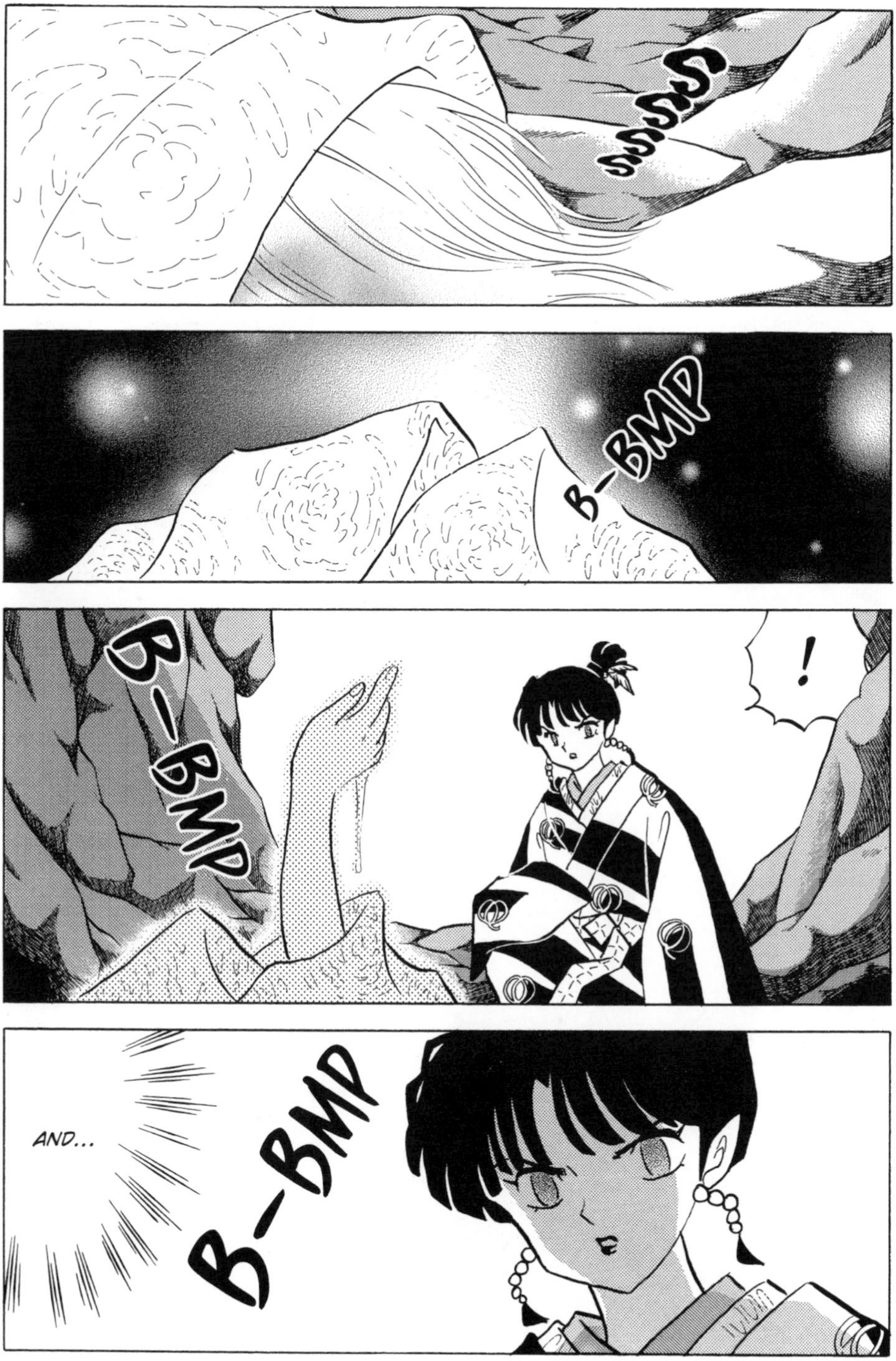
SSSSS
B-BMP
!
B-BMP
B-BMP
AND...

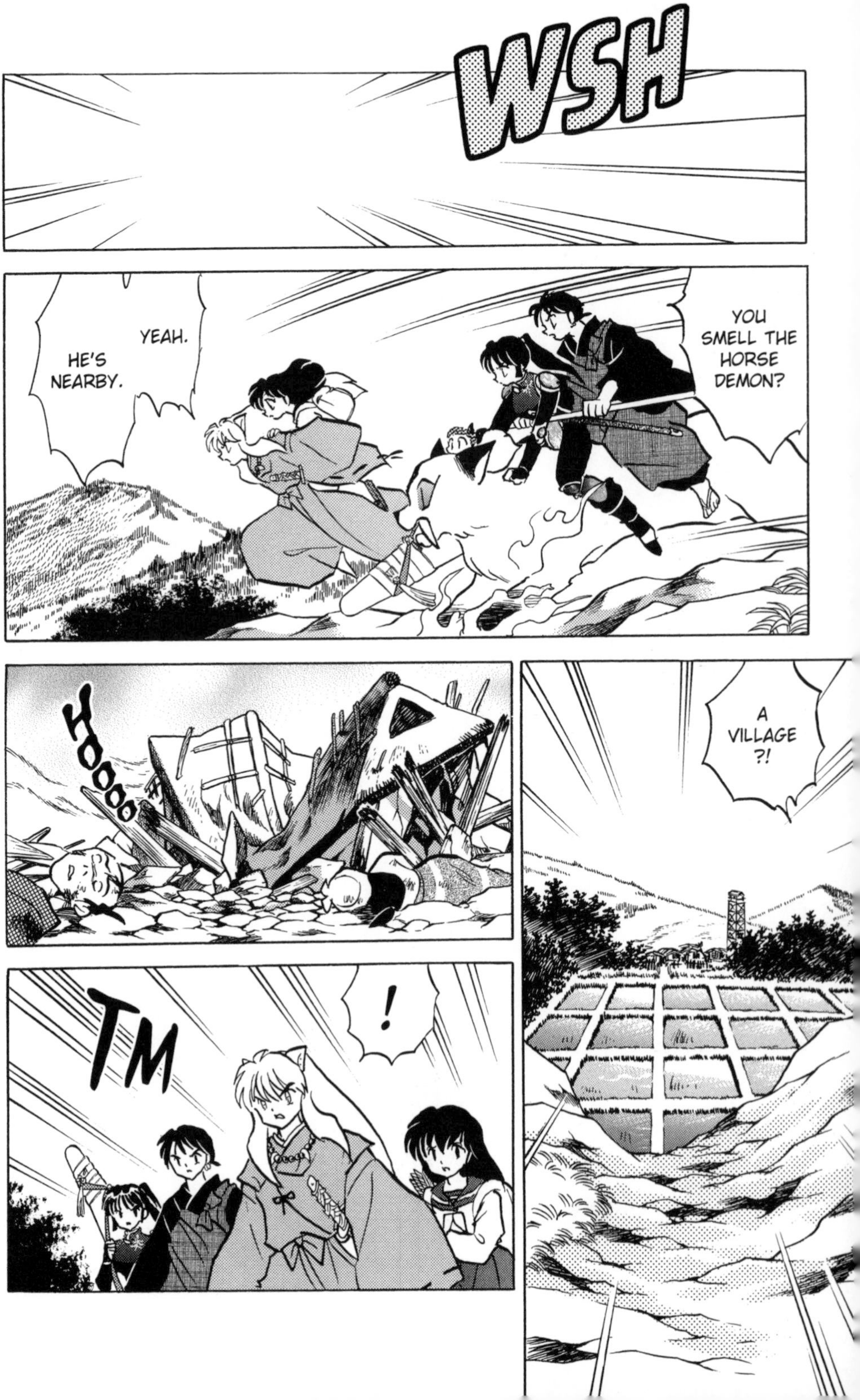
WSH
YOU SMELL THE HORSE DEMON?
YEAH.
HE'S NEARBY.
A VILLAGE ?!
HOOOO
!
TM

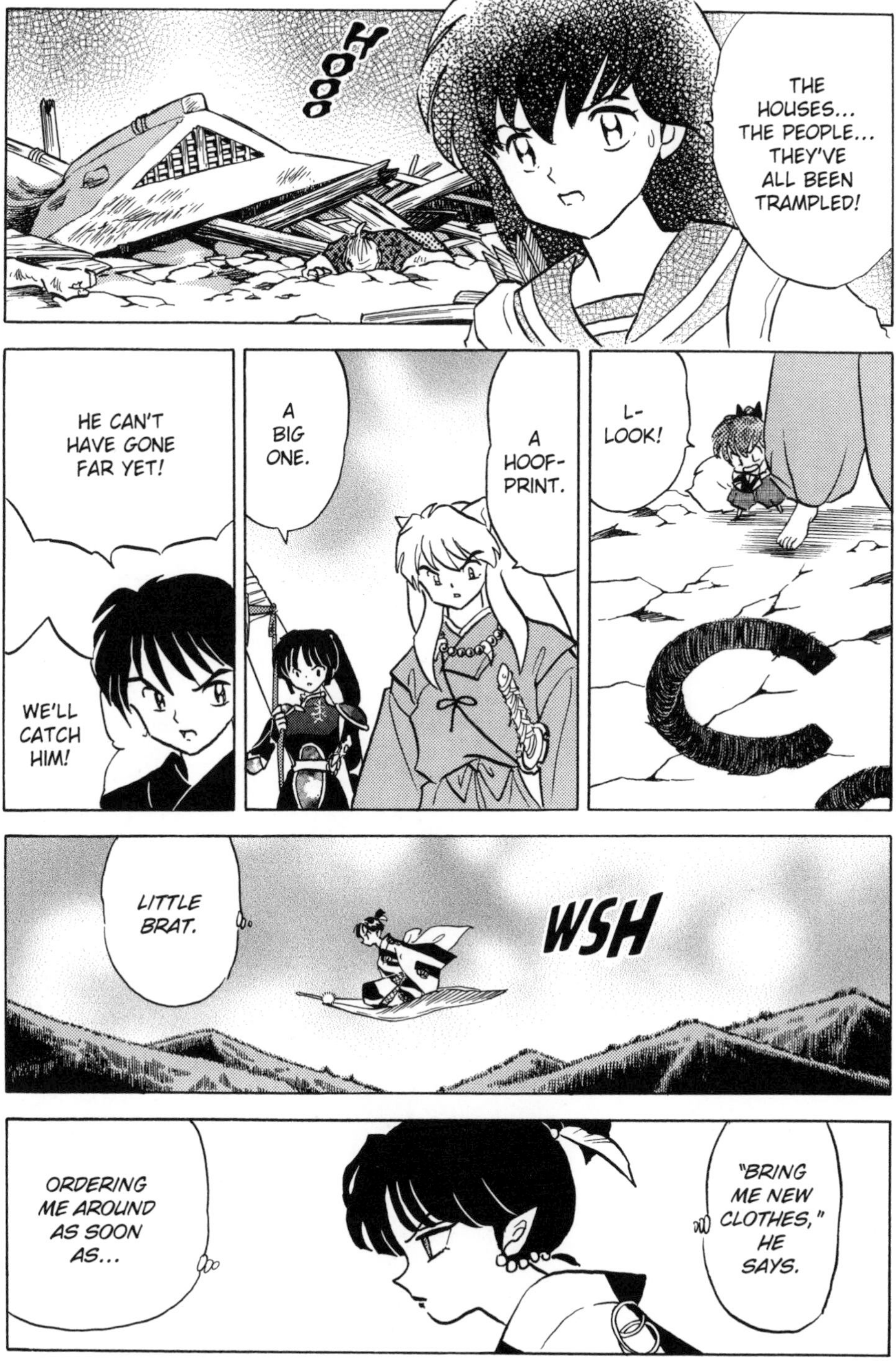
THE HOUSES... THE PEOPLE... THEY'VE ALL BEEN TRAMPLED!
HOOO
L-LOOK!
A HOOF-PRINT.
A BIG ONE.
HE CAN'T HAVE GONE FAR YET!
WE'LL CATCH HIM!
WSH
LITTLE BRAT.
"BRING ME NEW CLOTHES," HE SAYS.
ORDERING ME AROUND AS SOON AS...

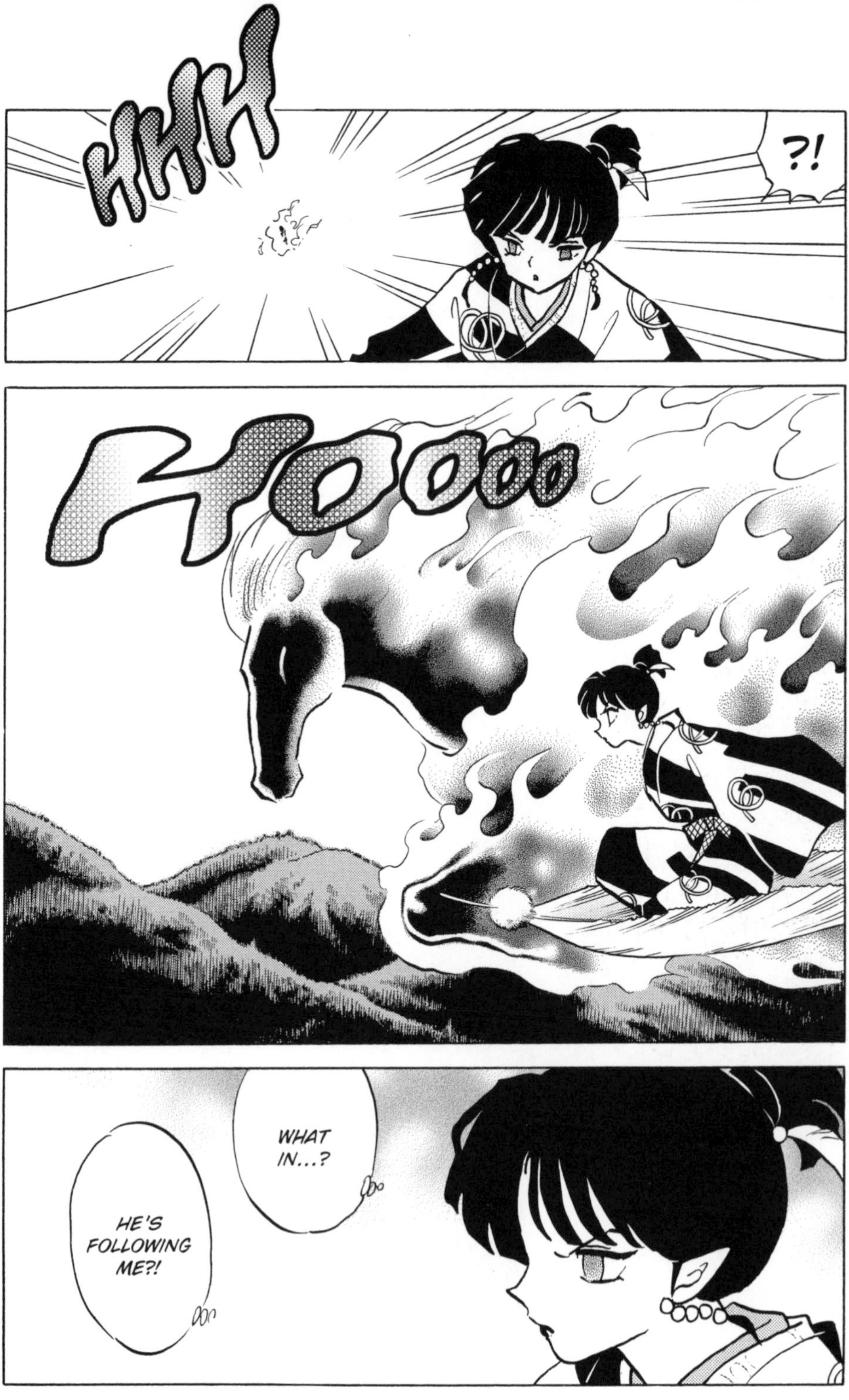
?!
HHH
HOOOO
WHAT IN...?
HE'S FOLLOWING ME?!

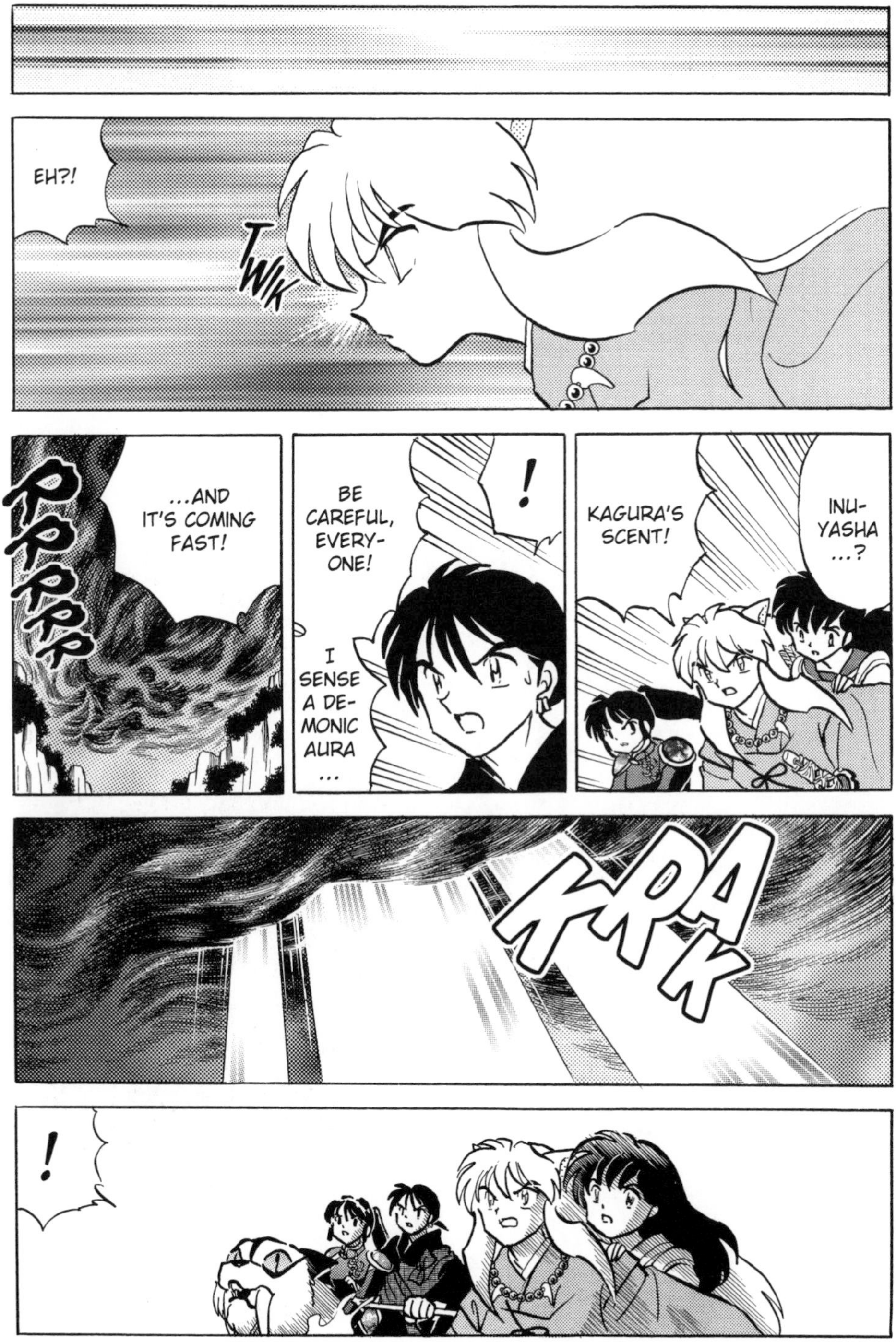
EH?!
TWIK
INU-YASHA ...?
KAGURA'S SCENT!
!
BE CAREFUL, EVERY-ONE!
I SENSE A DEMONIC AURA ...
...AND IT'S COMING FAST!
RRRRRR
KRAK
!

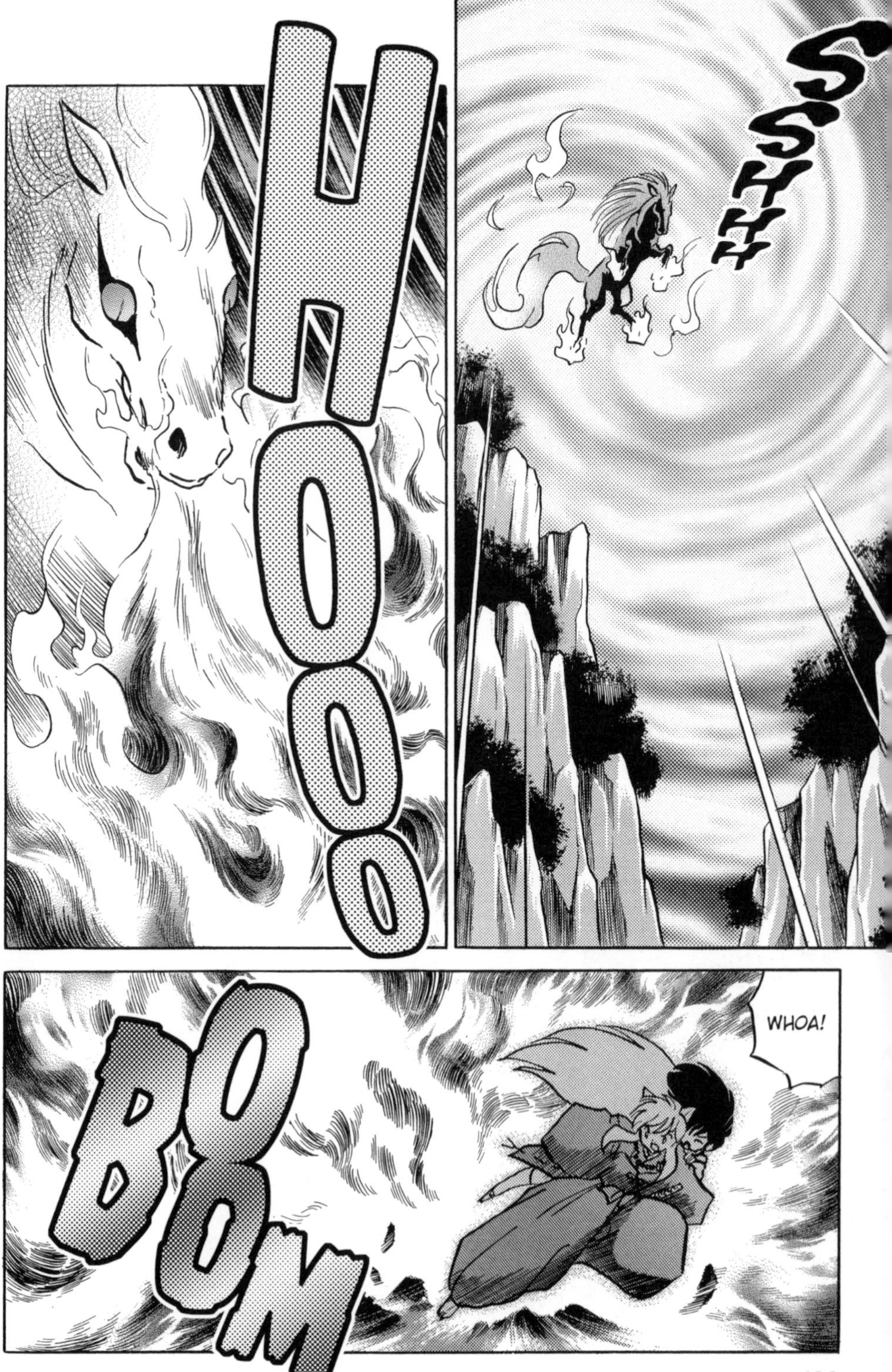
SSHHH
HOOOO
WHOA!
BOOM

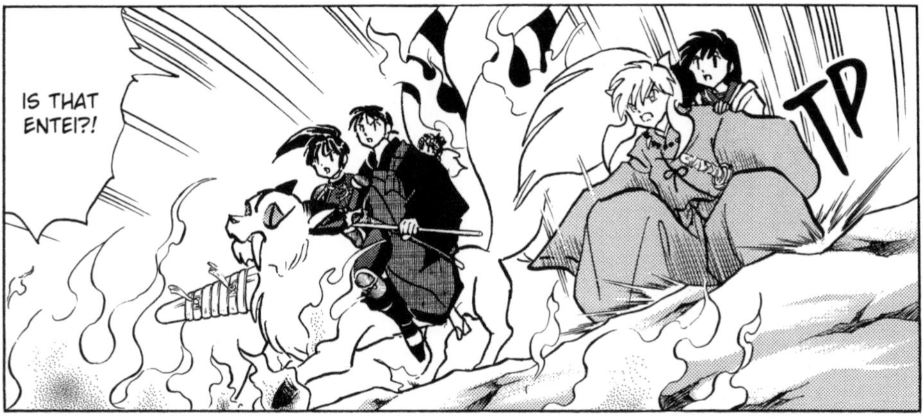
TP
IS THAT ENTEI?!

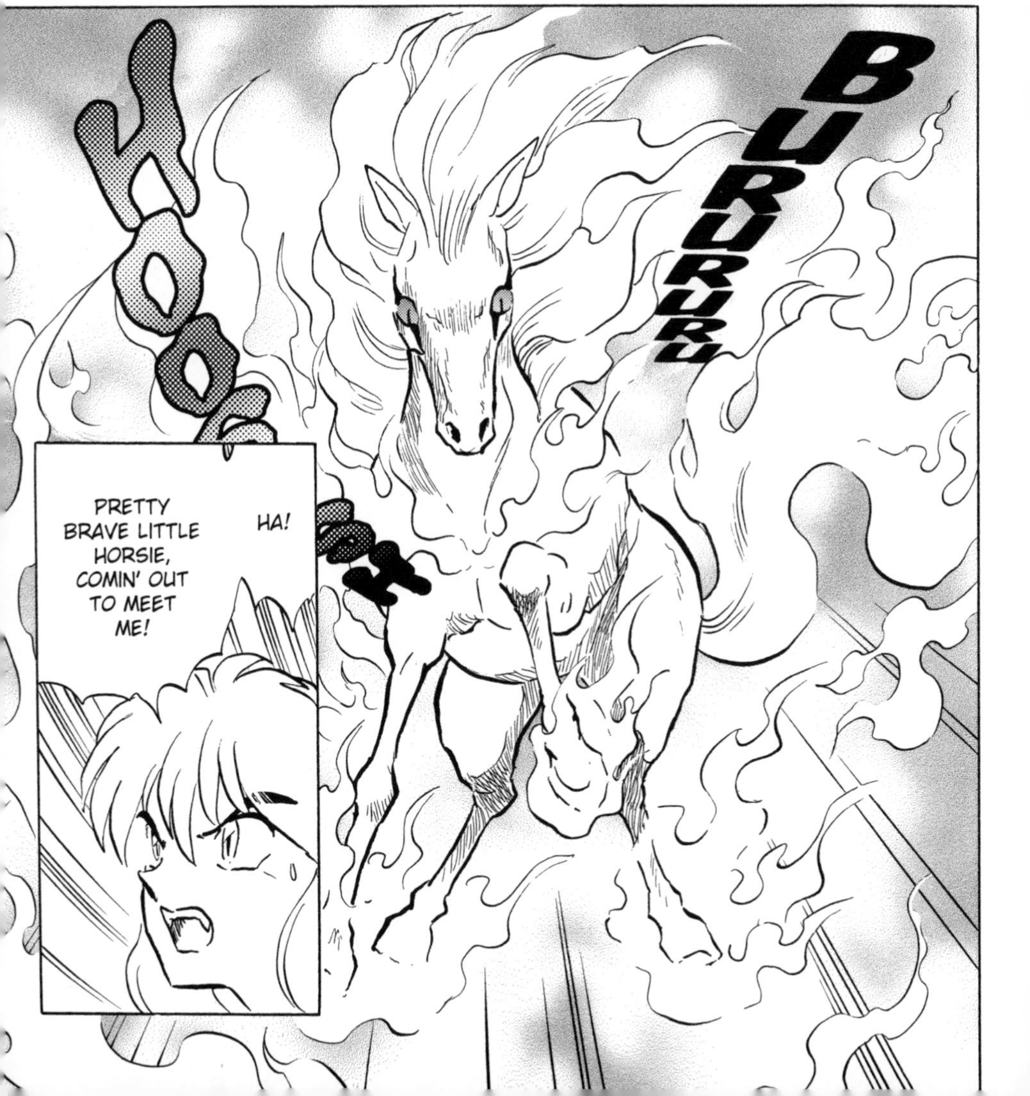
BURURURU
HA!
PRETTY BRAVE LITTLE HORSIE, COMIN' OUT TO MEET ME!

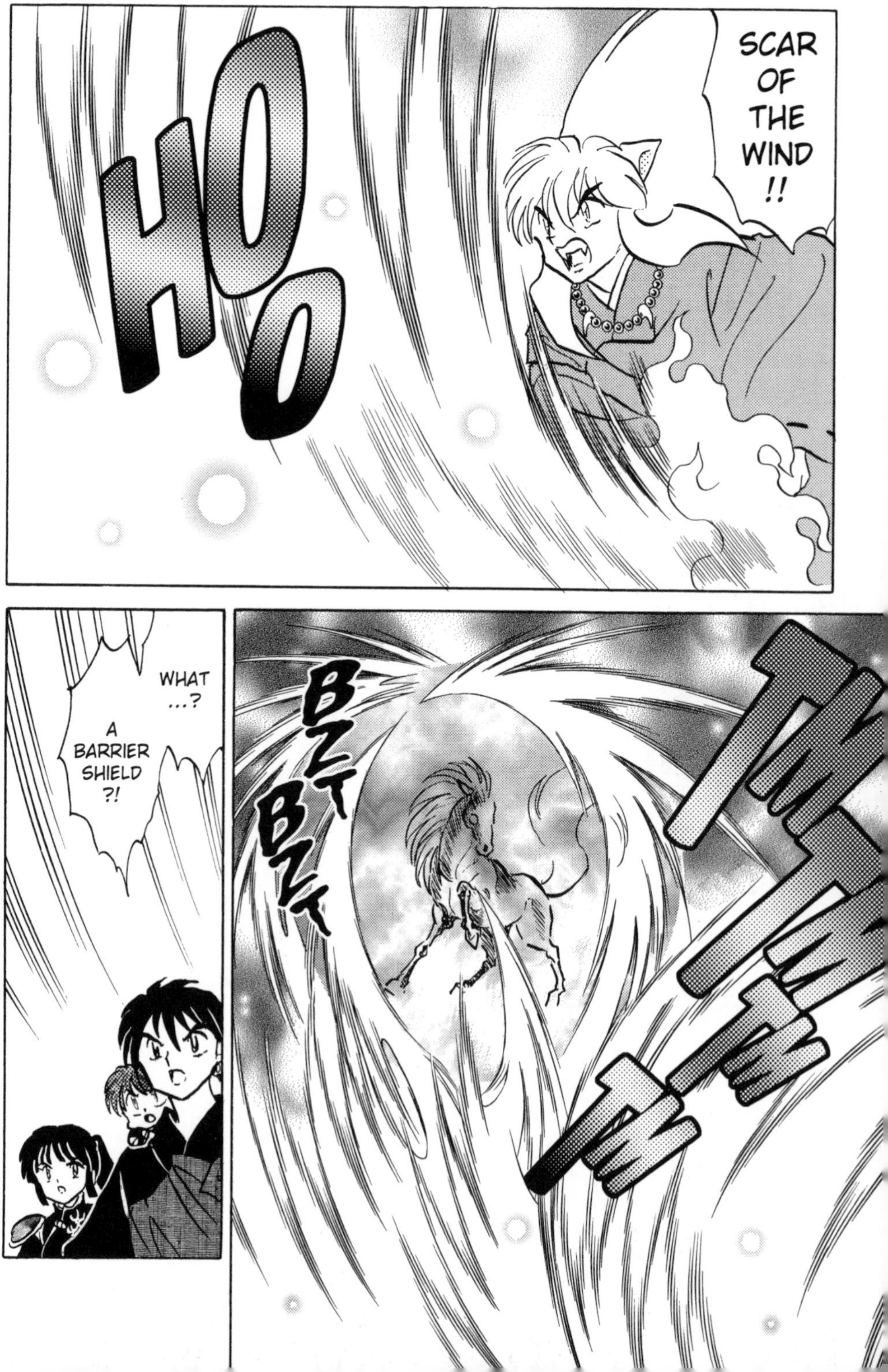
HOOO
SCAR OF THE WIND!!
TMTMTM
BZZT BZZT
WHAT...?
A BARRIER SHIELD?!

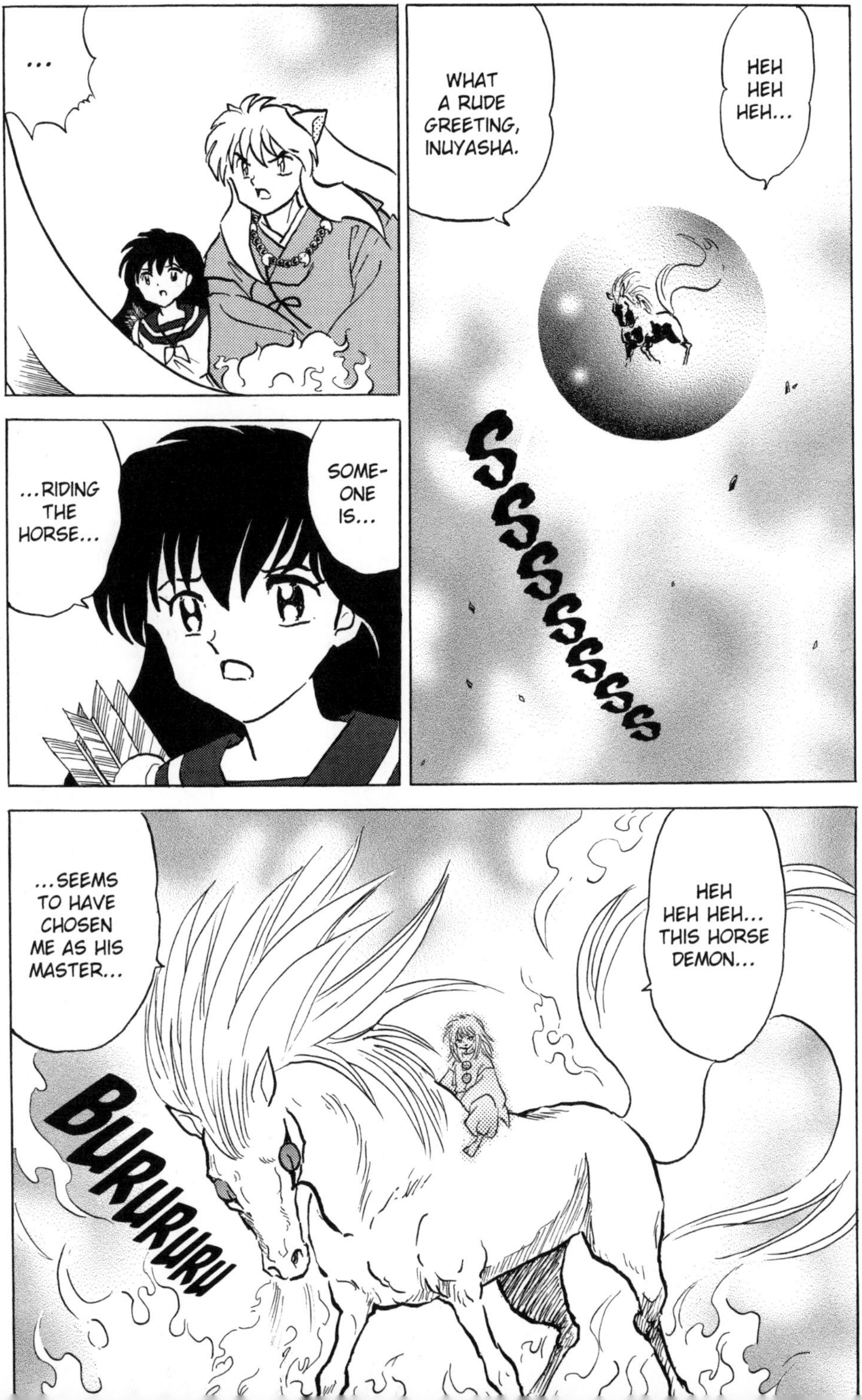
HEH HEH HEH...
WHAT A RUDE GREETING, INUYASHA.
SSSSSSSSS
...
SOME-ONE IS...
...RIDING THE HORSE...
HEH HEH HEH... THIS HORSE DEMON...
...SEEMS TO HAVE CHOSEN ME AS HIS MASTER...
BURURURU

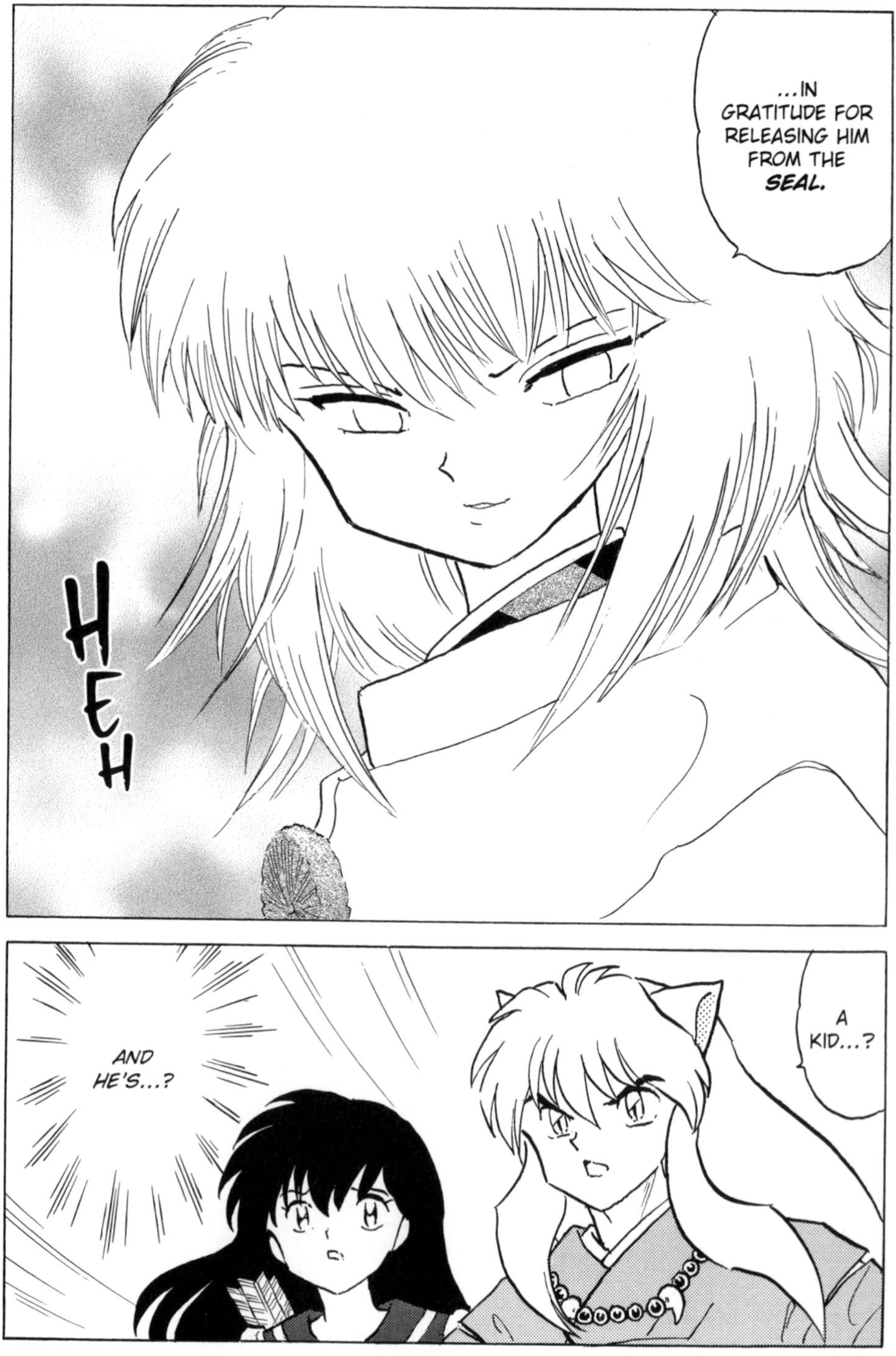
...IN GRATITUDE FOR RELEASING HIM FROM THE **SEAL.**
HEH
A KID...?
AND HE'S...?

SCROLL SEVEN
HAKUDOSHI

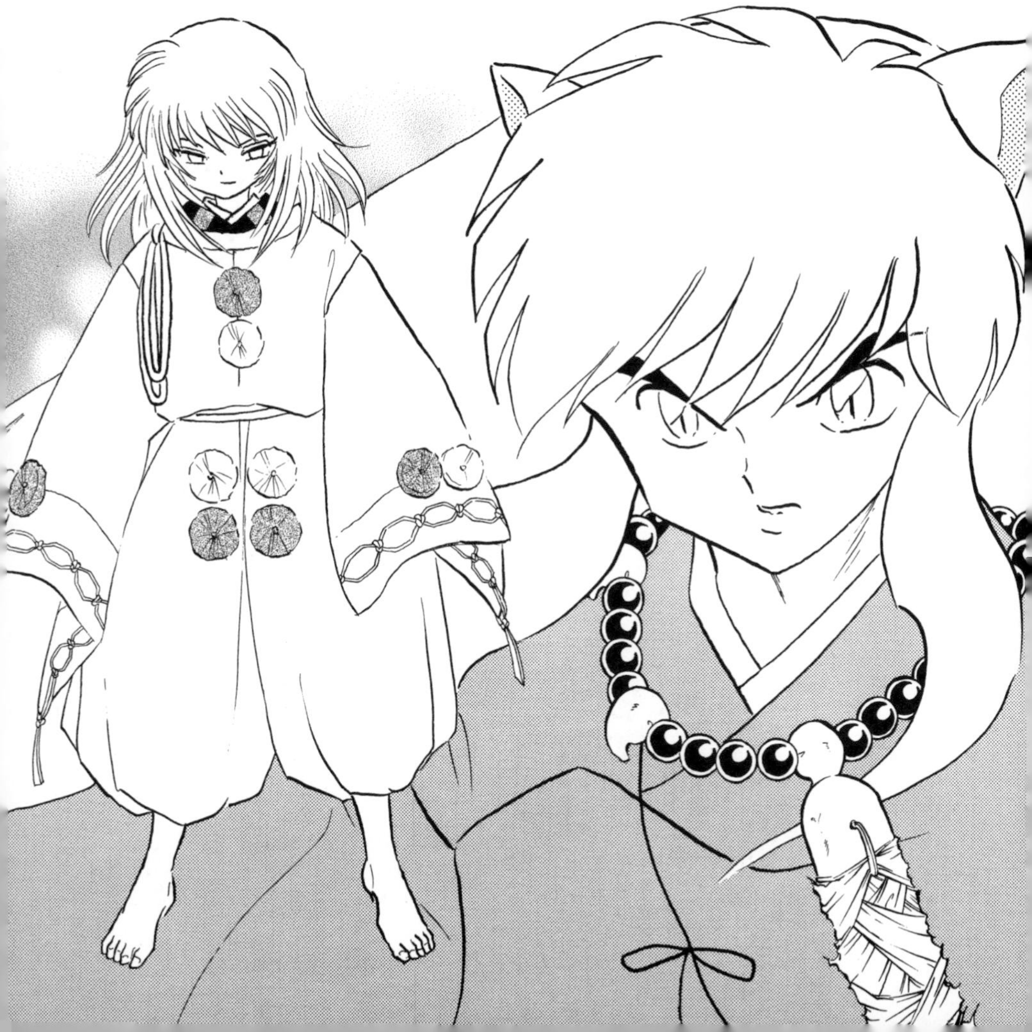

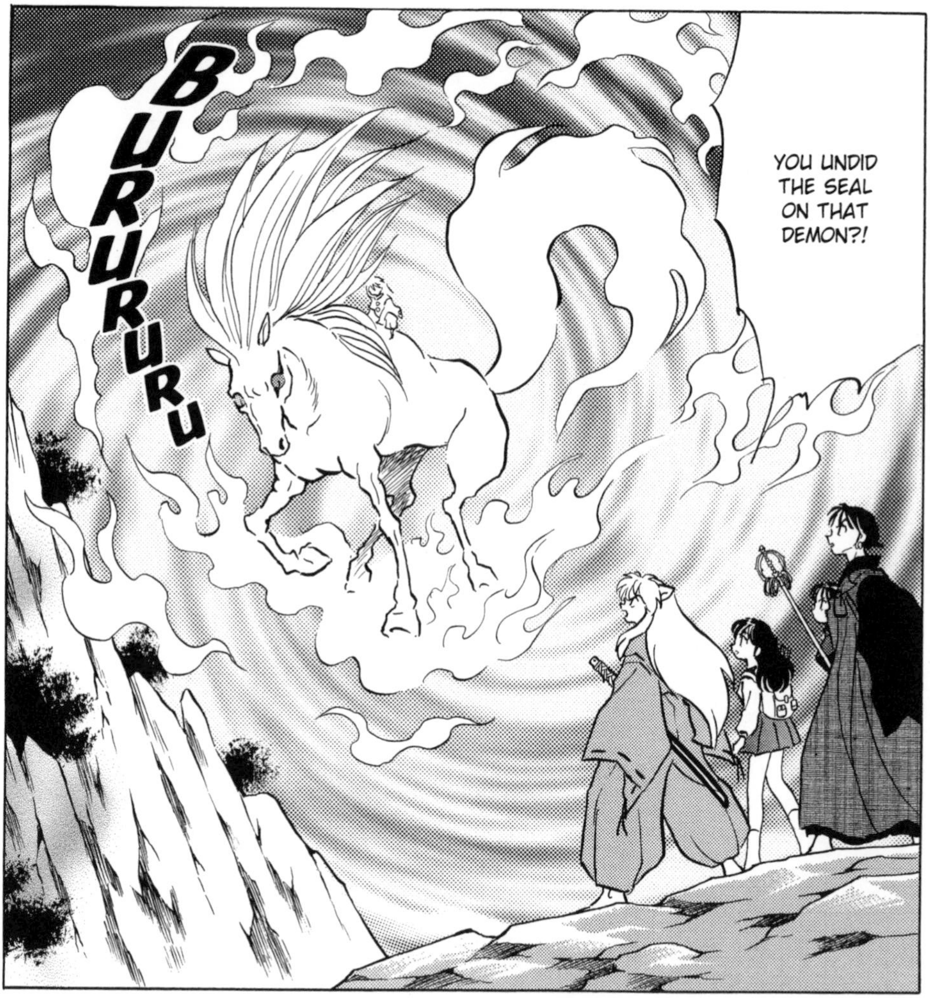
YOU UNDID THE SEAL ON THAT DEMON?!
BURURURURU

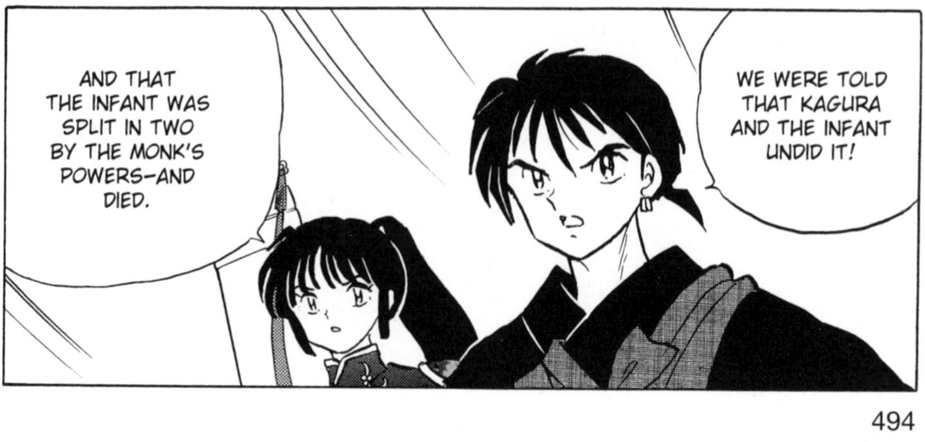
WE WERE TOLD THAT KAGURA AND THE INFANT UNDID IT!
AND THAT THE INFANT WAS SPLIT IN TWO BY THE MONK'S POWERS—AND DIED.

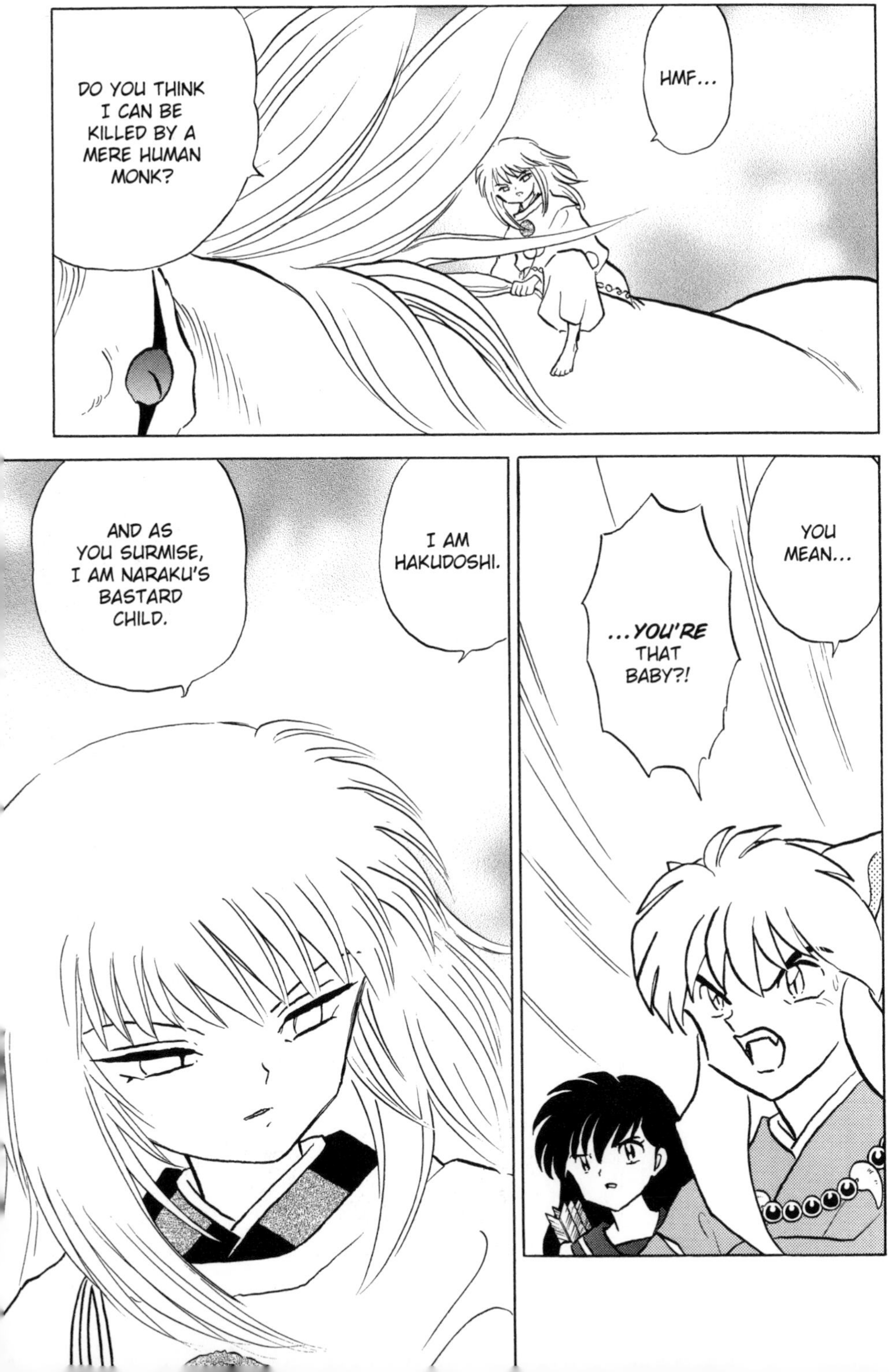
HMF...
DO YOU THINK I CAN BE KILLED BY A MERE HUMAN MONK?
YOU MEAN...
...*YOU'RE* THAT BABY?!
I AM HAKUDOSHI.
AND AS YOU SURMISE, I AM NARAKU'S BASTARD CHILD.

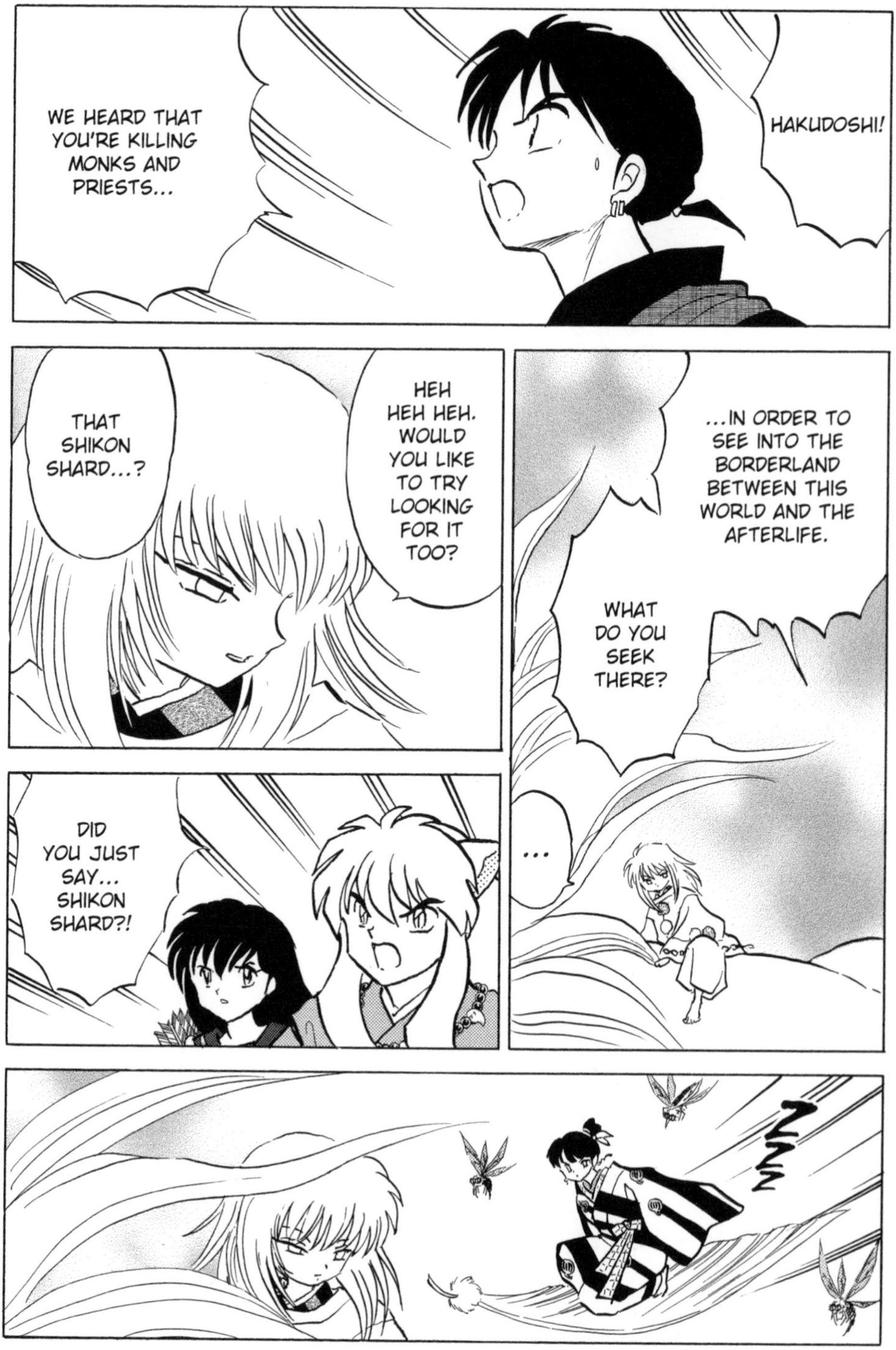
HAKUDOSHI!
WE HEARD THAT YOU'RE KILLING MONKS AND PRIESTS...
...IN ORDER TO SEE INTO THE BORDERLAND BETWEEN THIS WORLD AND THE AFTERLIFE.
WHAT DO YOU SEEK THERE?
...
HEH HEH HEH. WOULD YOU LIKE TO TRY LOOKING FOR IT TOO?
THAT SHIKON SHARD...?
DID YOU JUST SAY... SHIKON SHARD?!

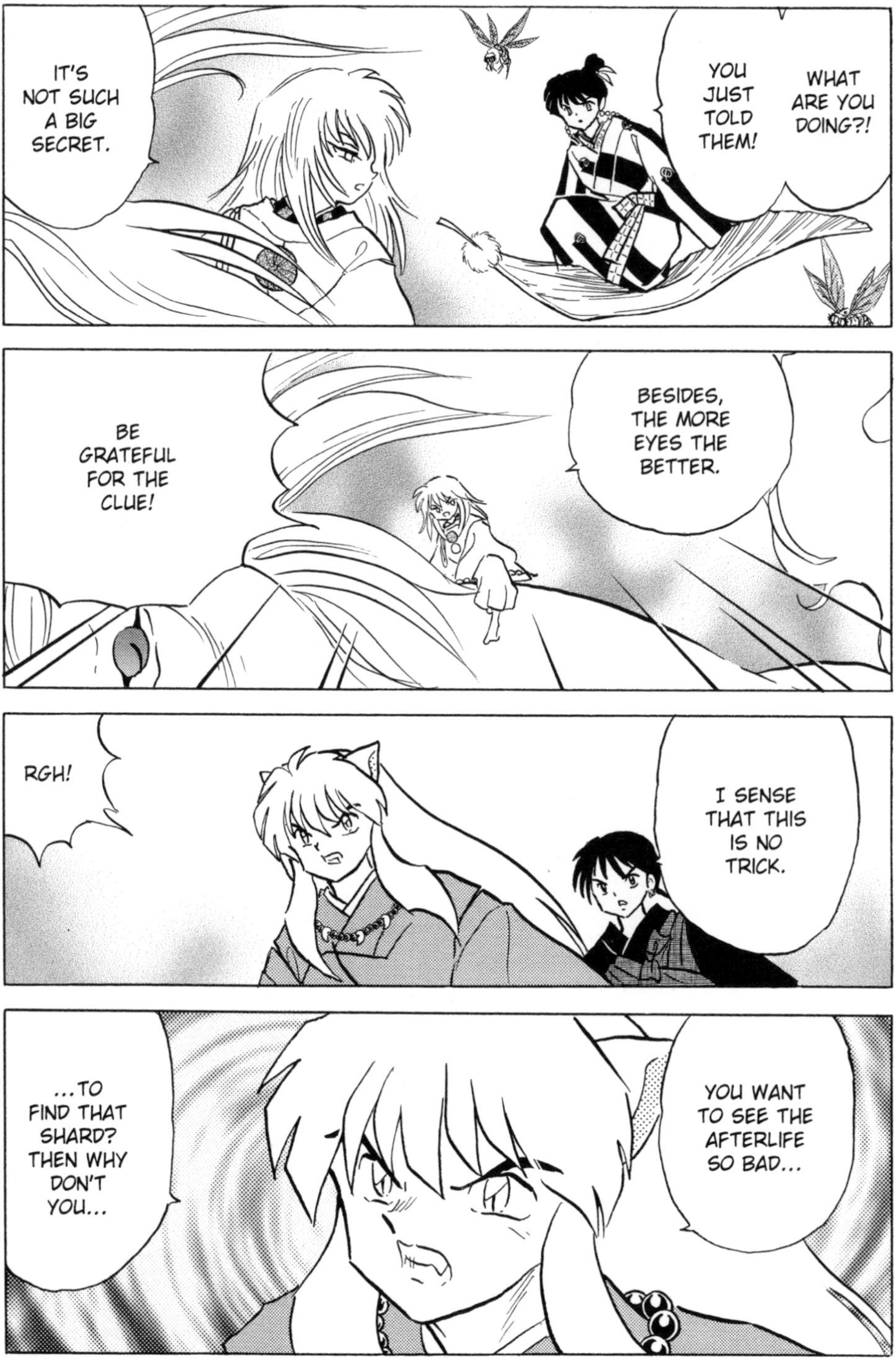
WHAT ARE YOU DOING?!
YOU JUST TOLD THEM!
IT'S NOT SUCH A BIG SECRET.
BESIDES, THE MORE EYES THE BETTER.
BE GRATEFUL FOR THE CLUE!
I SENSE THAT THIS IS NO TRICK.
RGH!
YOU WANT TO SEE THE AFTERLIFE SO BAD...
...TO FIND THAT SHARD? THEN WHY DON'T YOU...

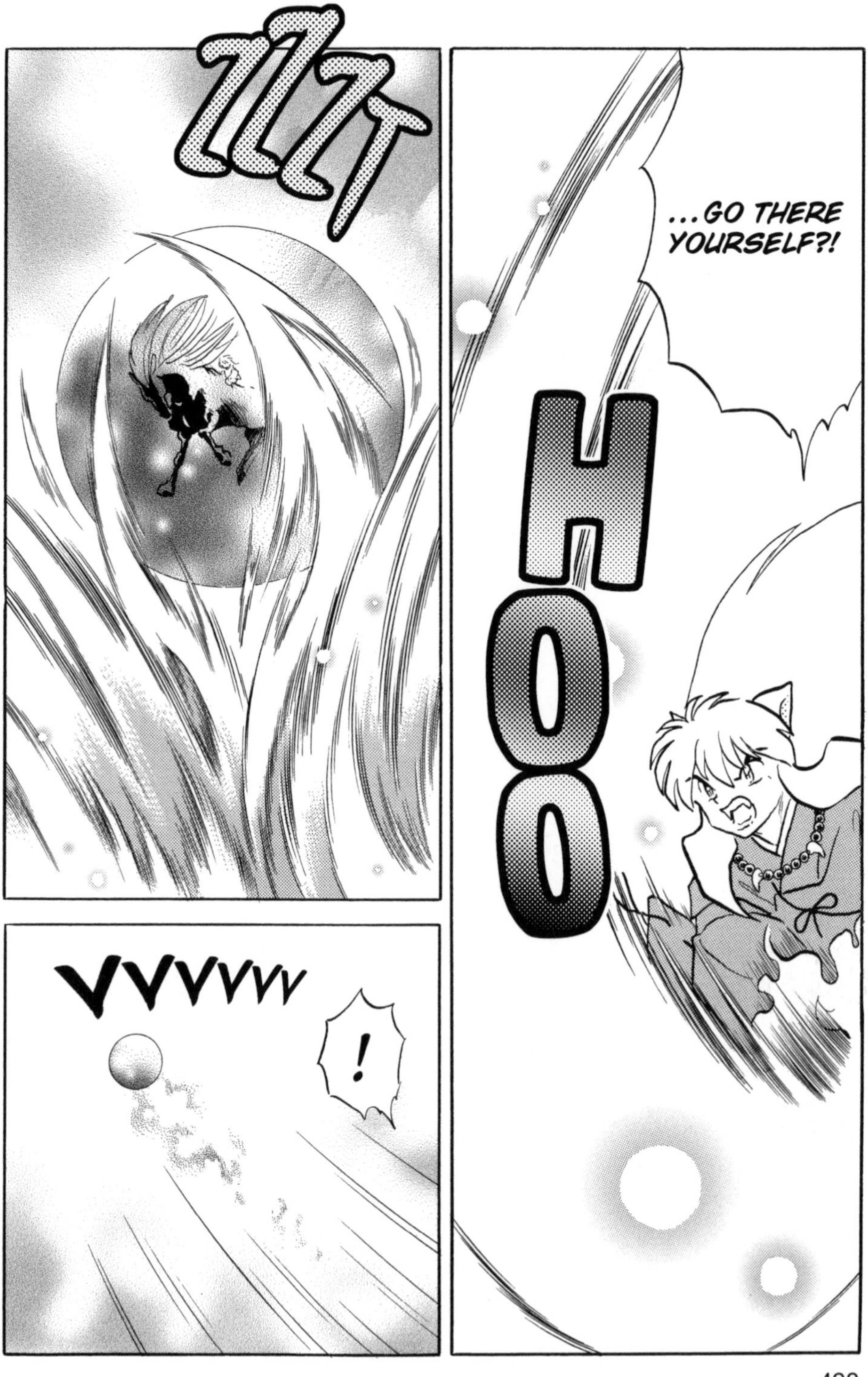
...GO THERE YOURSELF?!
HOO
ZZZT
VVVVVVV
!

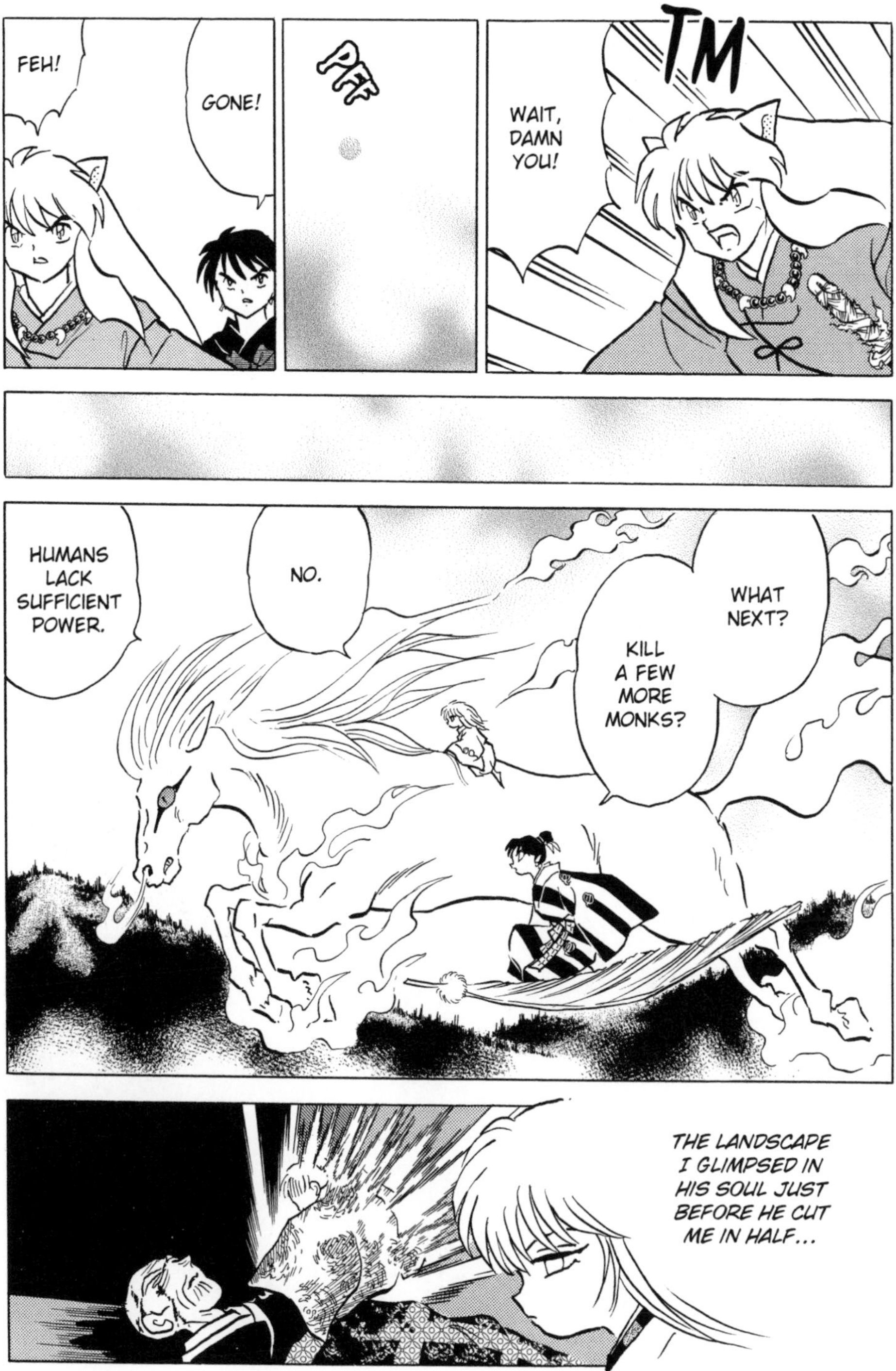
TM
WAIT, DAMN YOU!
PFF
GONE!
FEH!
WHAT NEXT?
KILL A FEW MORE MONKS?
NO.
HUMANS LACK SUFFICIENT POWER.
THE LANDSCAPE I GLIMPSED IN HIS SOUL JUST BEFORE HE CUT ME IN HALF...

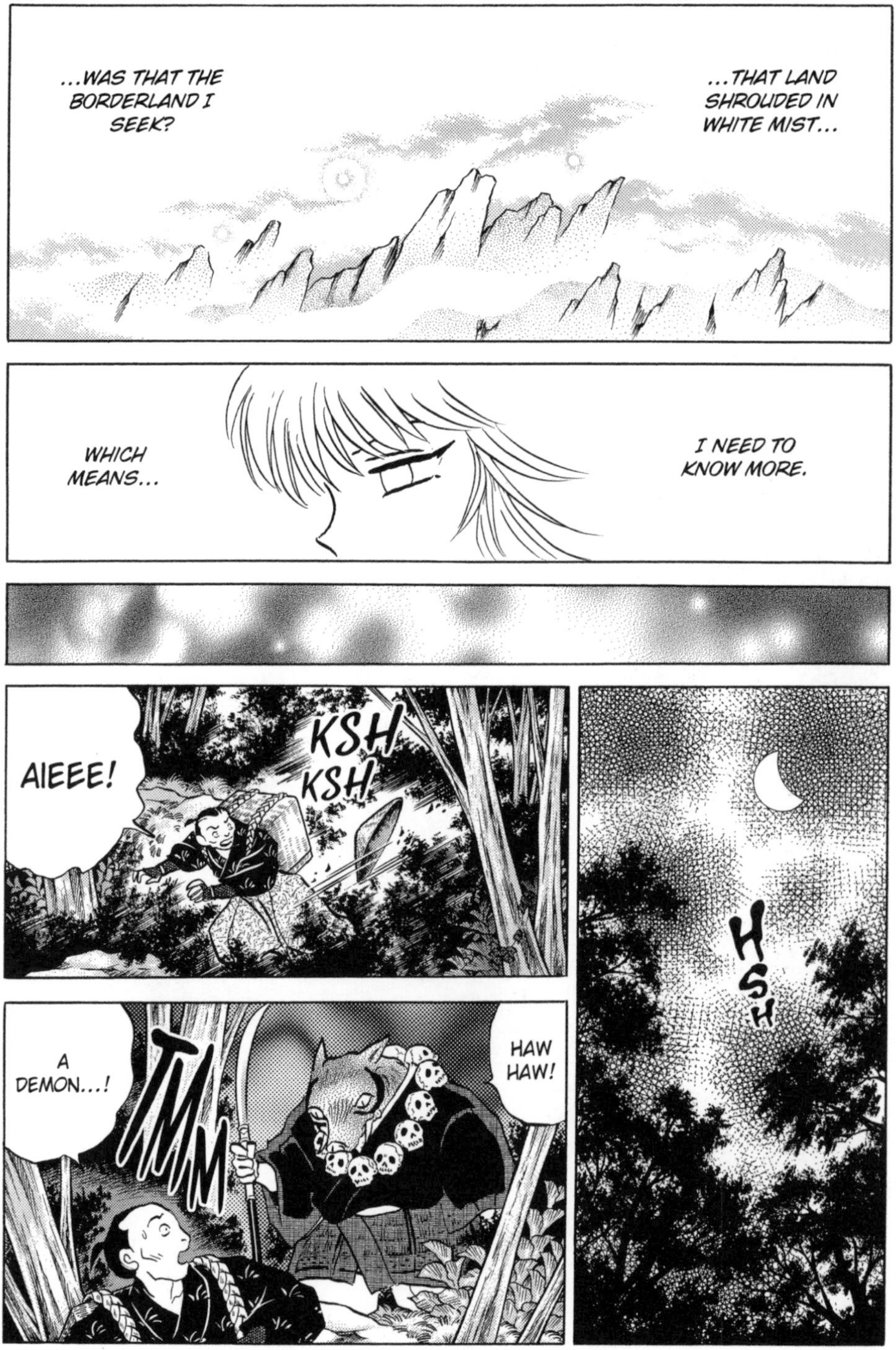
...THAT LAND SHROUDED IN WHITE MIST...
...WAS THAT THE BORDERLAND I SEEK?
I NEED TO KNOW MORE.
WHICH MEANS...
HSH
KSH KSH
AIEEE!
HAW HAW!
TMM
A DEMON...!

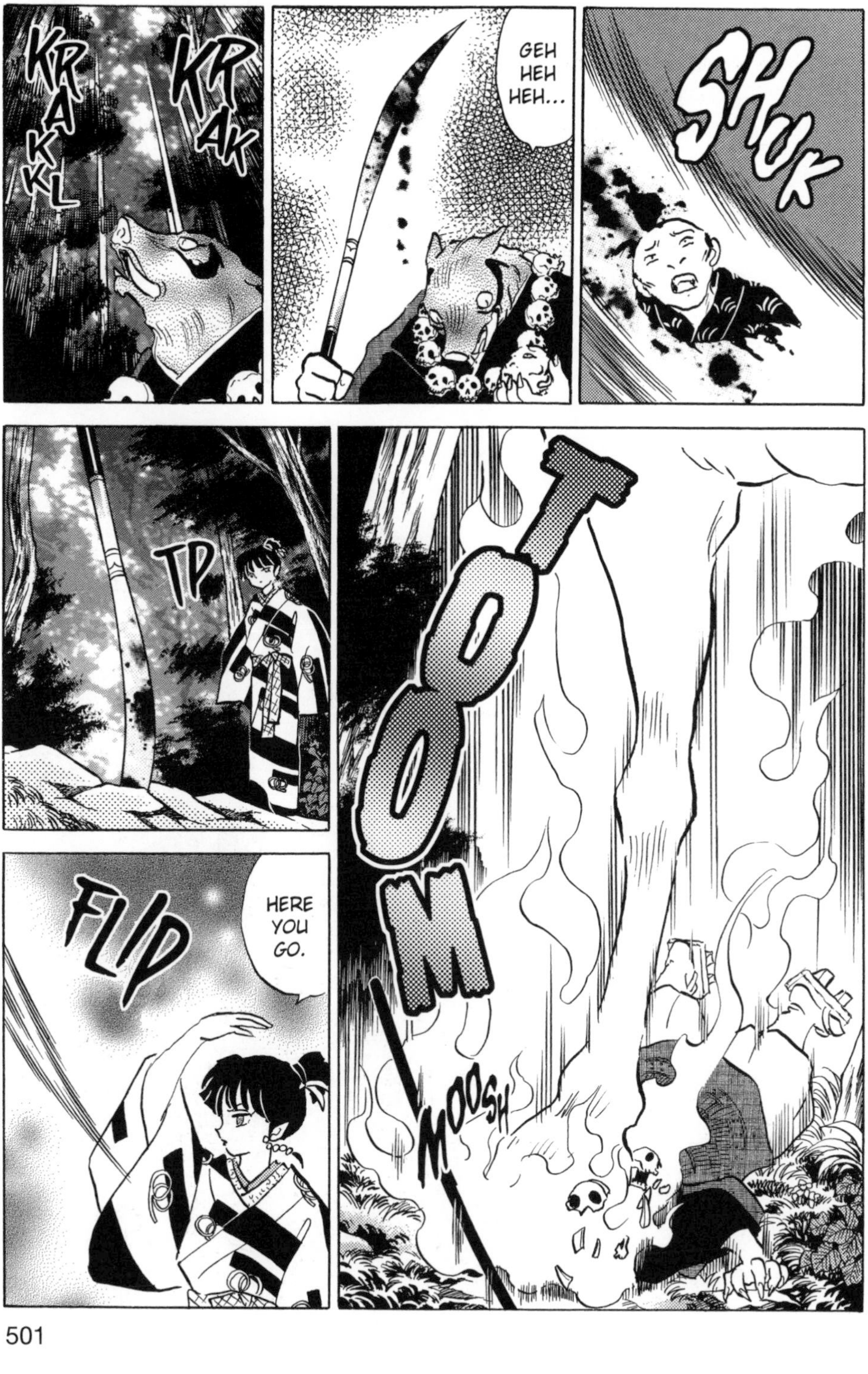
SHUK
GEH HEH HEH...
KRAK
KRAKKL
TOOM
MOOSH
TP
HERE YOU GO.
FLIP

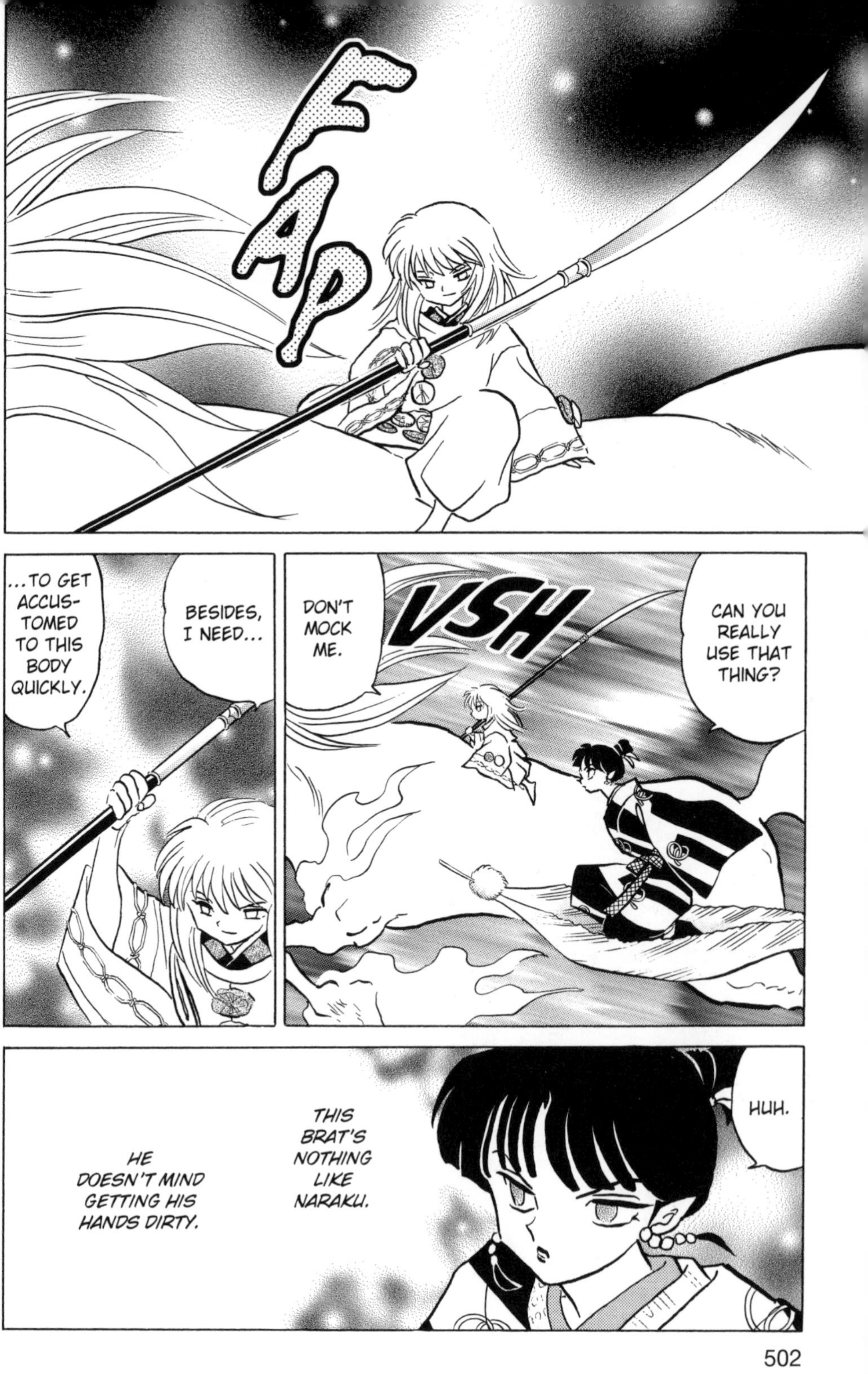
FAP
CAN YOU REALLY USE THAT THING?
VSH
DON'T MOCK ME.
BESIDES, I NEED...
...TO GET ACCUSTOMED TO THIS BODY QUICKLY.
HUH.
THIS BRAT'S NOTHING LIKE NARAKU.
HE DOESN'T MIND GETTING HIS HANDS DIRTY.

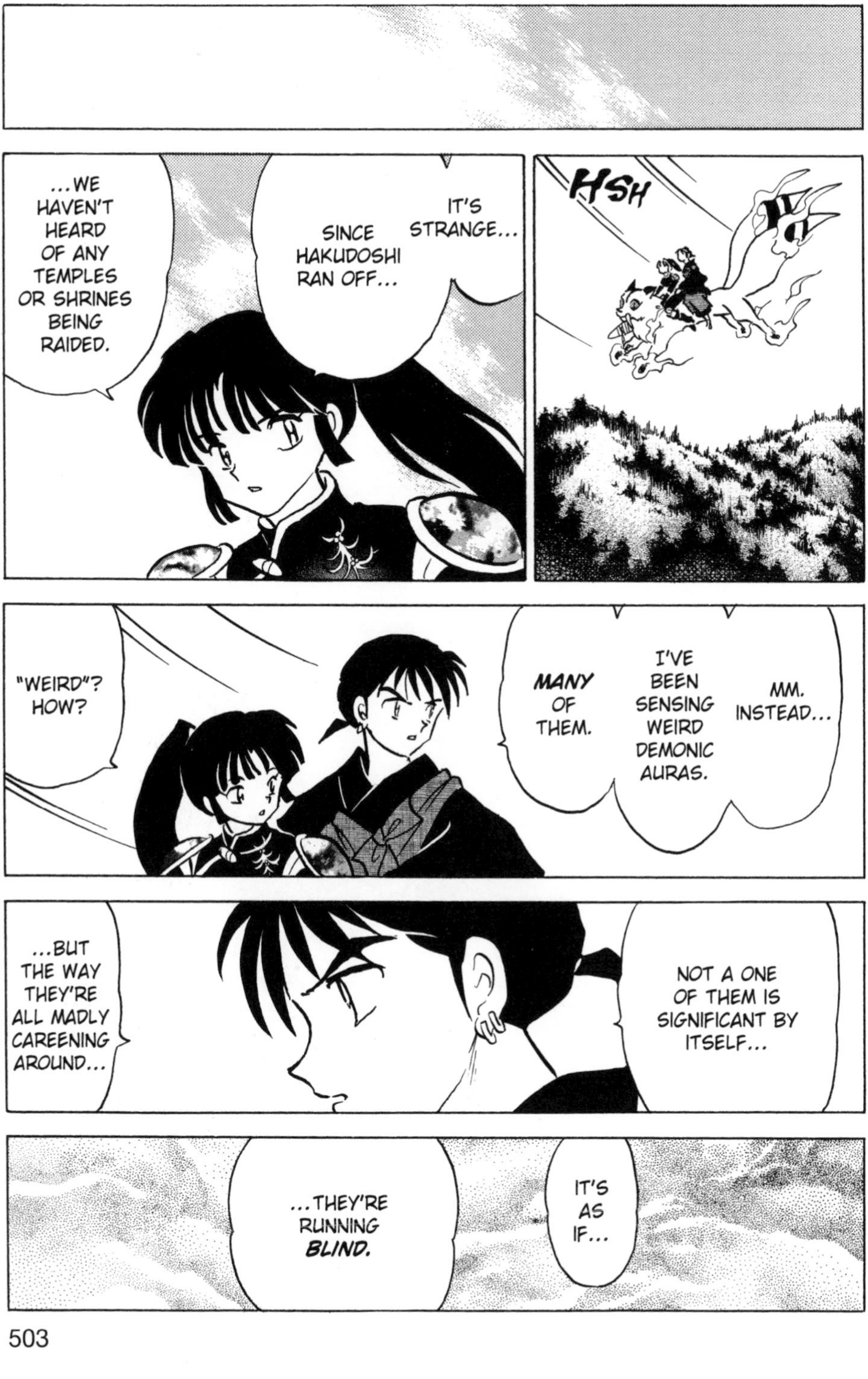
HSH
IT'S STRANGE...
SINCE HAKUDOSHI RAN OFF...
...WE HAVEN'T HEARD OF ANY TEMPLES OR SHRINES BEING RAIDED.
MM. INSTEAD...
I'VE BEEN SENSING WEIRD DEMONIC AURAS.
MANY OF THEM.
"WEIRD"? HOW?
NOT A ONE OF THEM IS SIGNIFICANT BY ITSELF...
...BUT THE WAY THEY'RE ALL MADLY CAREENING AROUND...
IT'S AS IF...
...THEY'RE RUNNING *BLIND.*

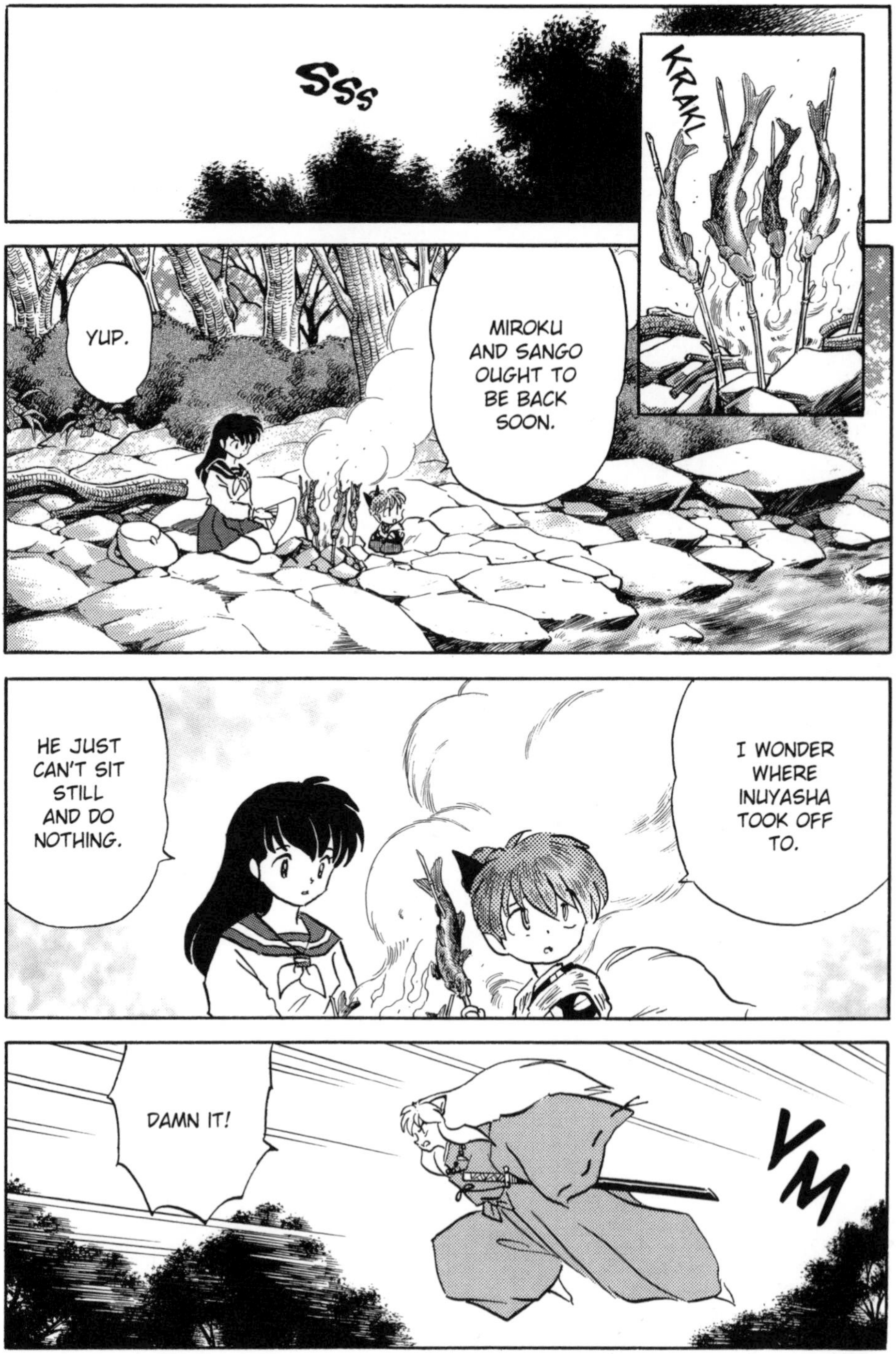

SSS
KRAKL
MIROKU AND SANGO OUGHT TO BE BACK SOON.
YUP.
I WONDER WHERE INUYASHA TOOK OFF TO.
HE JUST CAN'T SIT STILL AND DO NOTHING.
VM
DAMN IT!

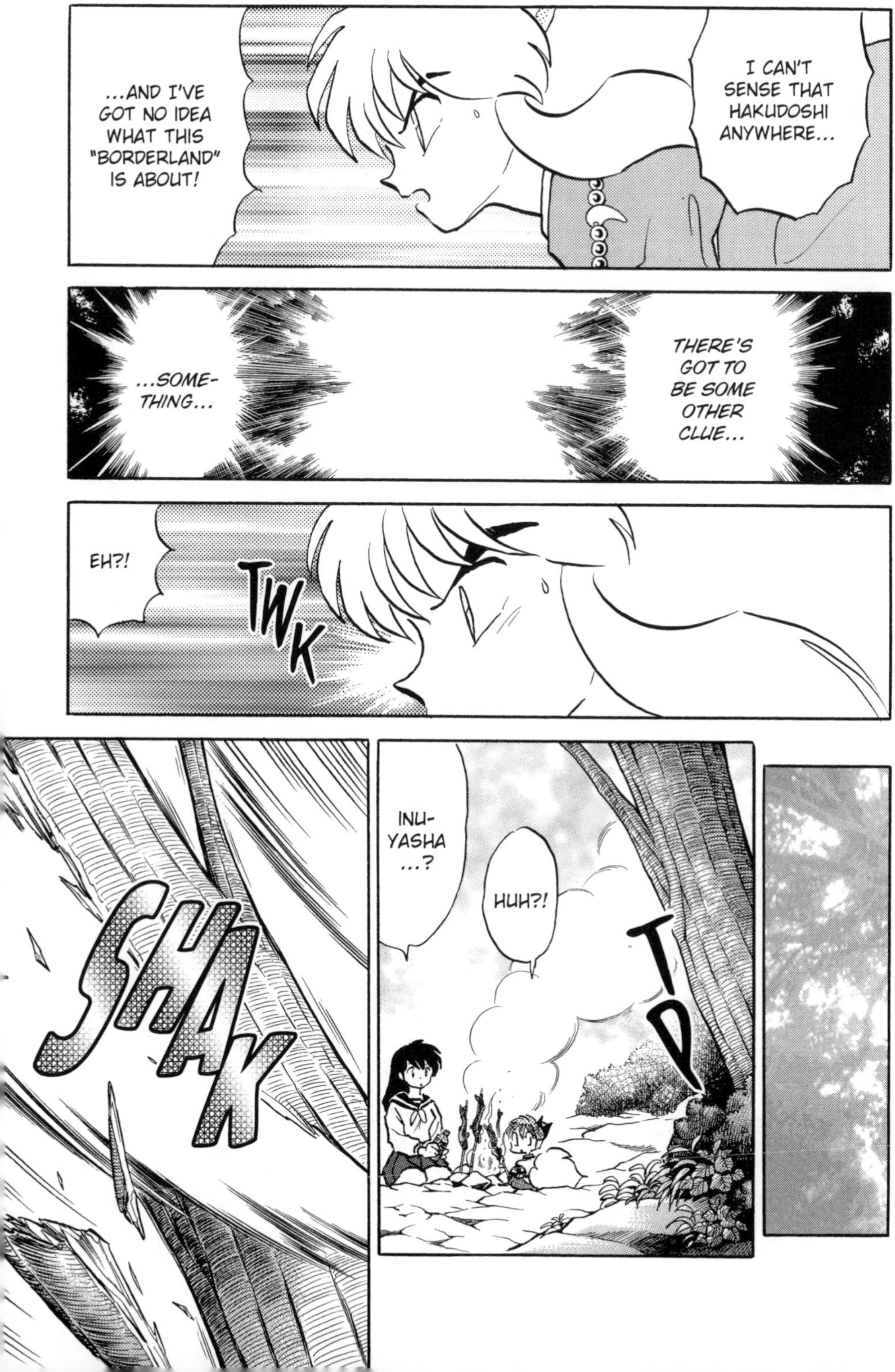
I CAN'T SENSE THAT HAKUDOSHI ANYWHERE...
...AND I'VE GOT NO IDEA WHAT THIS "BORDERLAND" IS ABOUT!
THERE'S GOT TO BE SOME OTHER CLUE...
...SOME-THING...
TWK
EH?!
TD
HUH?!
INU-YASHA ...?
SHAK

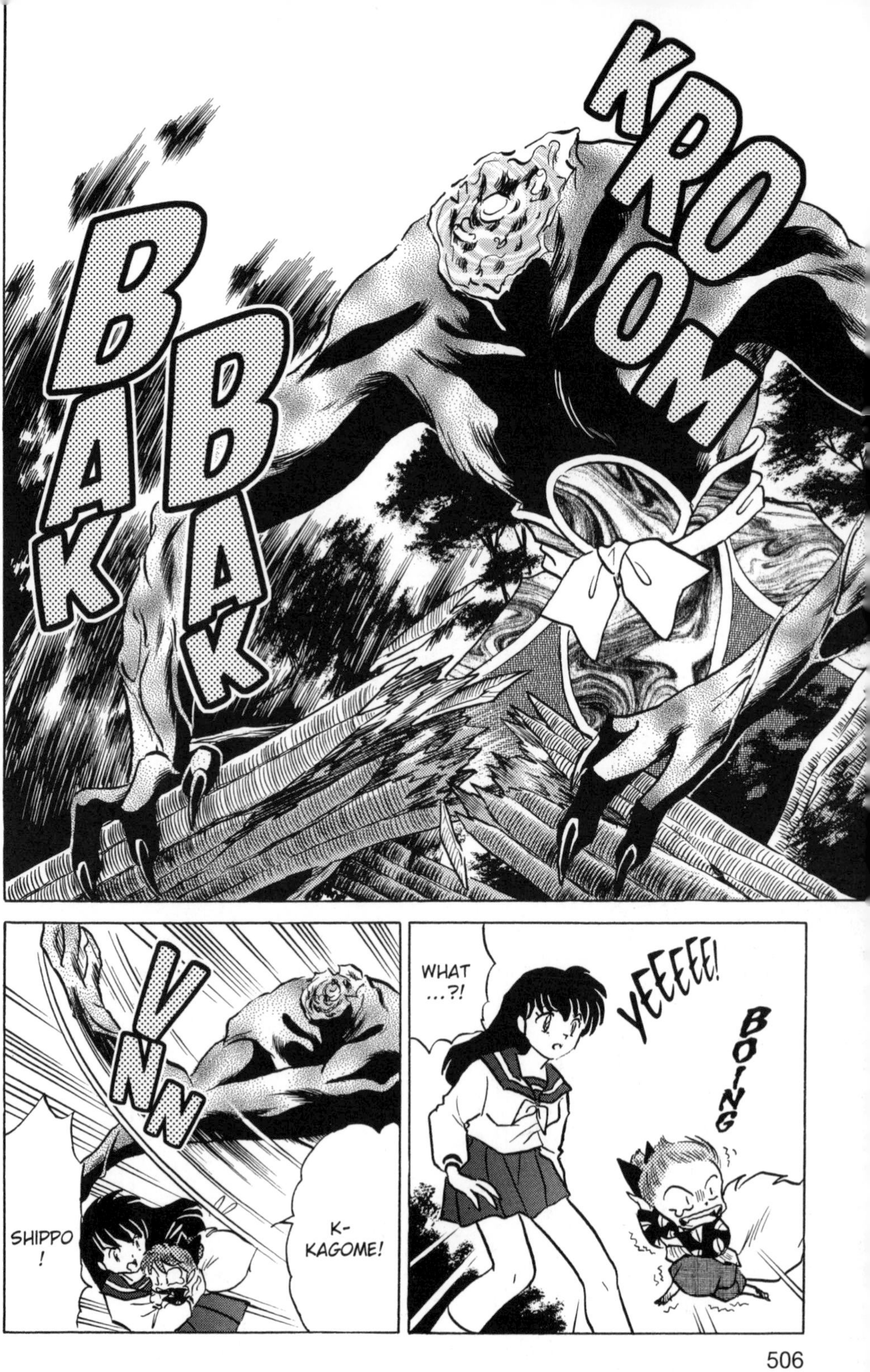
KROOM
BAK
BAK
WHAT ...?!
YEEEEE!
BOING
VNNN
K-KAGOME!
SHIPPO!

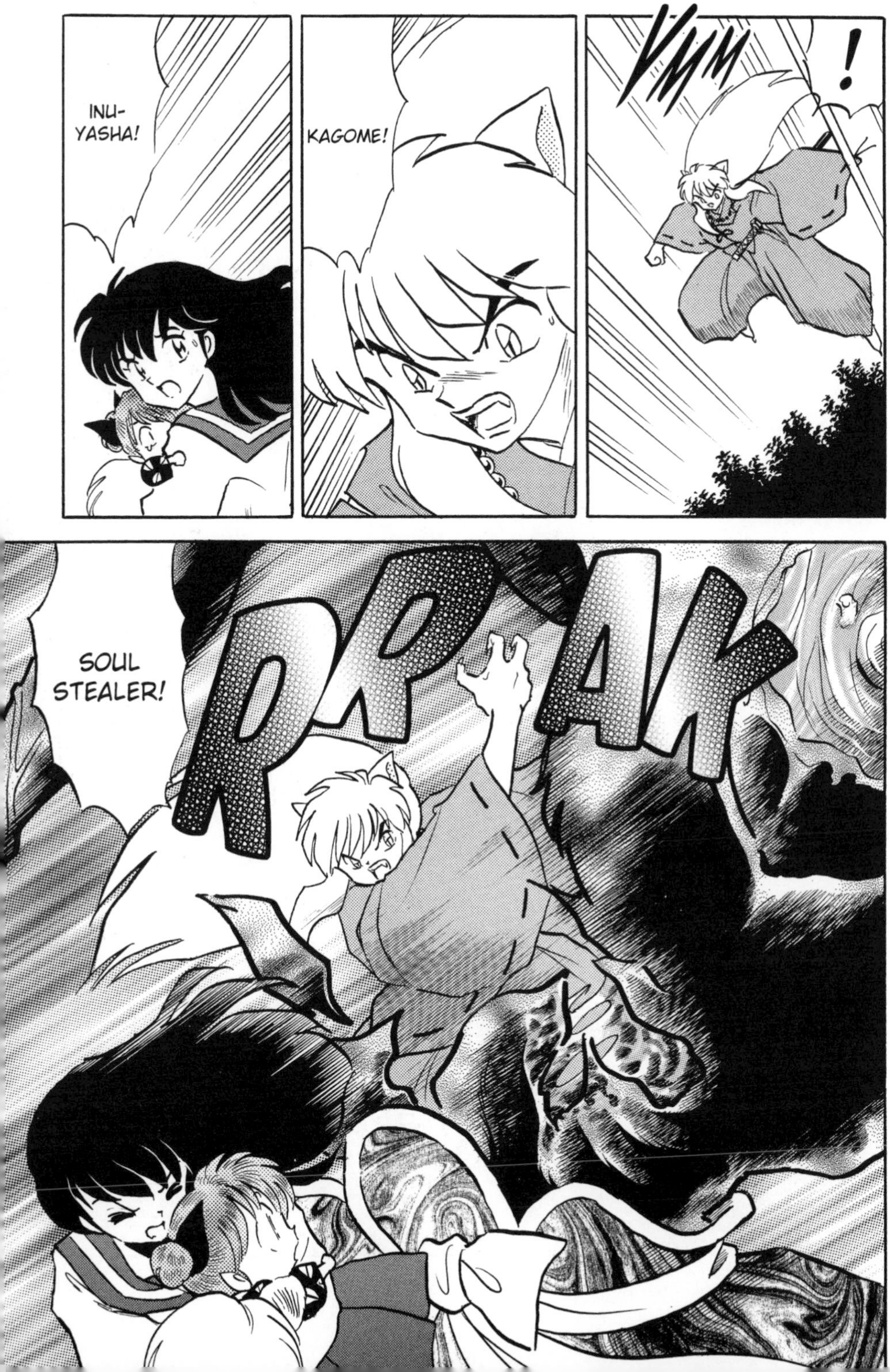
VMM
!
KAGOME!
INU-YASHA!
SOUL STEALER!
DRAK

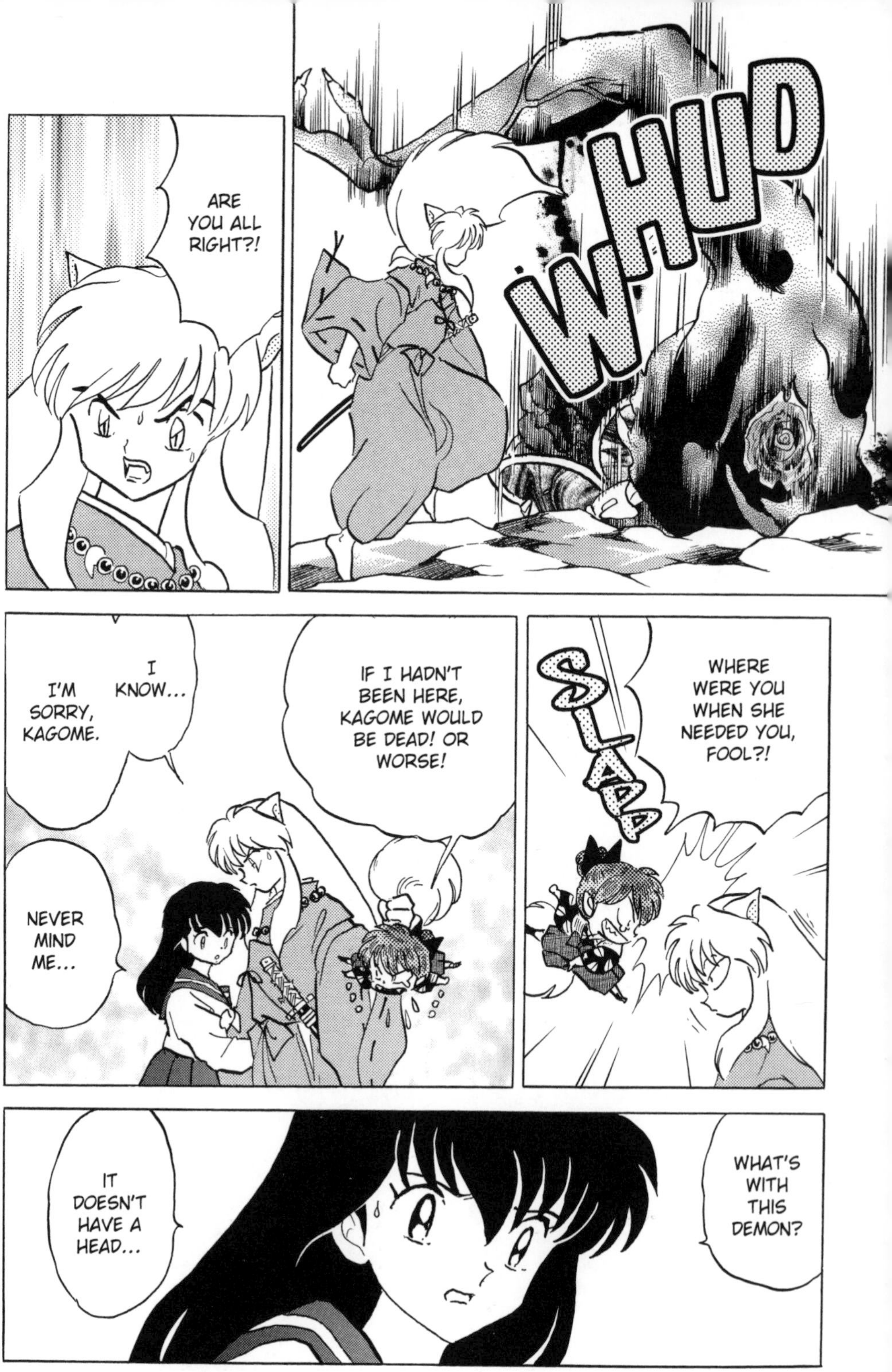
WHUD
ARE YOU ALL RIGHT?!
SLAAA
WHERE WERE YOU WHEN SHE NEEDED YOU, FOOL?!
IF I HADN'T BEEN HERE, KAGOME WOULD BE DEAD! OR WORSE!
I KNOW...
I'M SORRY, KAGOME.
NEVER MIND ME...
WHAT'S WITH THIS DEMON?
IT DOESN'T HAVE A HEAD...

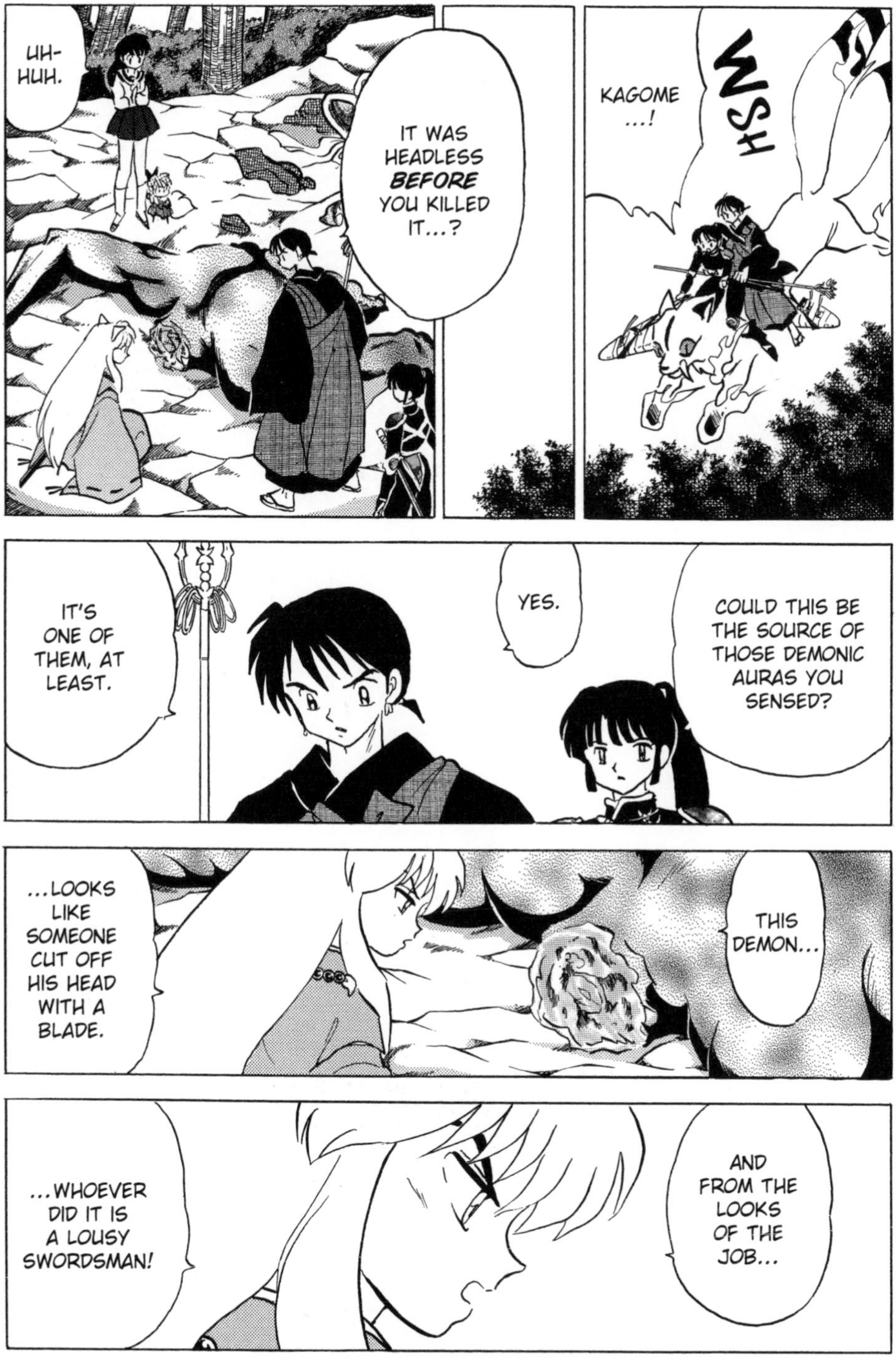
WSH
KAGOME ...!
IT WAS HEADLESS **BEFORE** YOU KILLED IT...?
UH-HUH.
COULD THIS BE THE SOURCE OF THOSE DEMONIC AURAS YOU SENSED?
YES.
IT'S ONE OF THEM, AT LEAST.
THIS DEMON...
...LOOKS LIKE SOMEONE CUT OFF HIS HEAD WITH A BLADE.
AND FROM THE LOOKS OF THE JOB...
...WHOEVER DID IT IS A LOUSY SWORDSMAN!

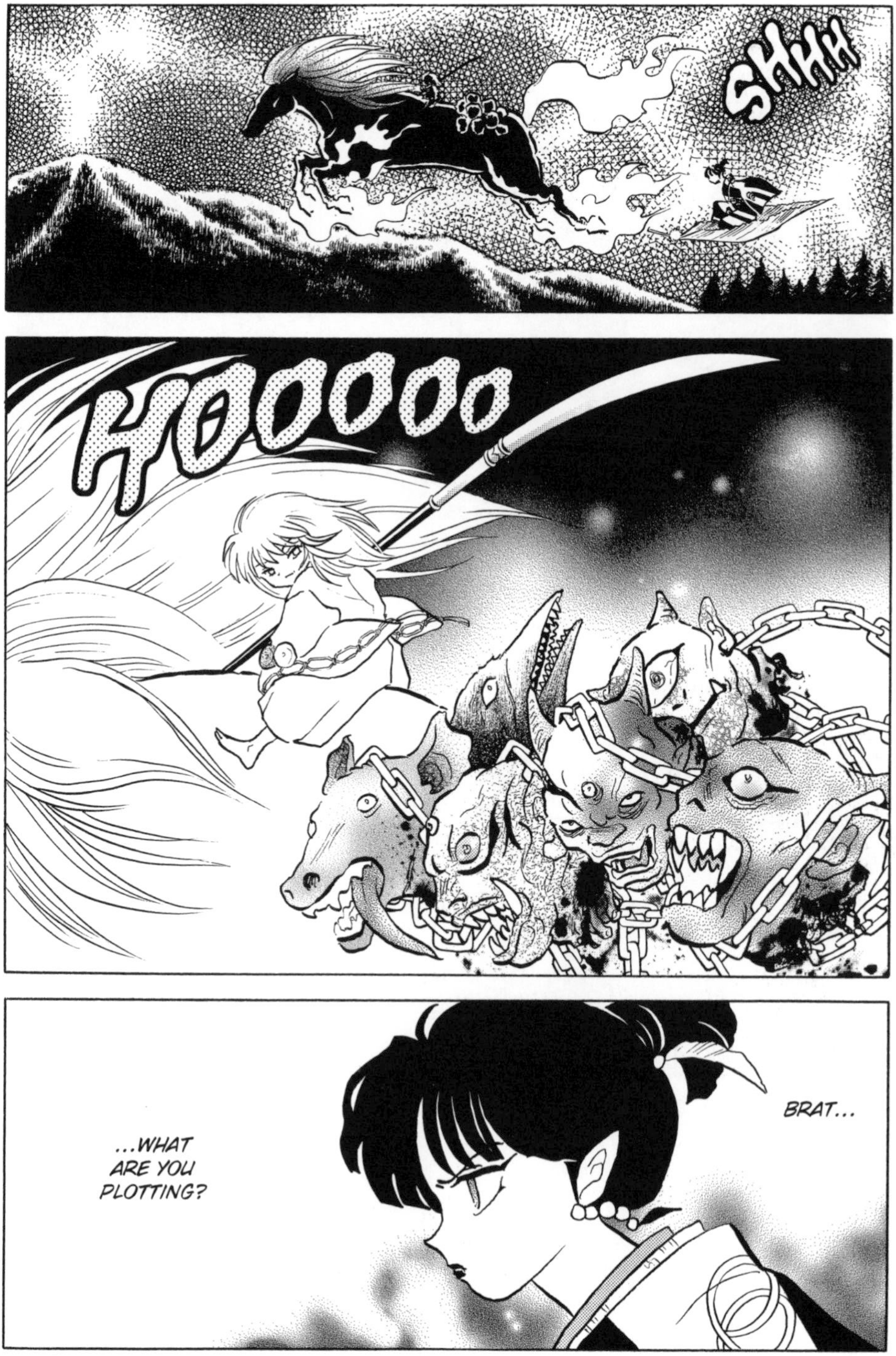
SHHH
HOOOOO
BRAT...
...WHAT ARE YOU PLOTTING?

SCROLL EIGHT
THE HEADLESS DEMONS

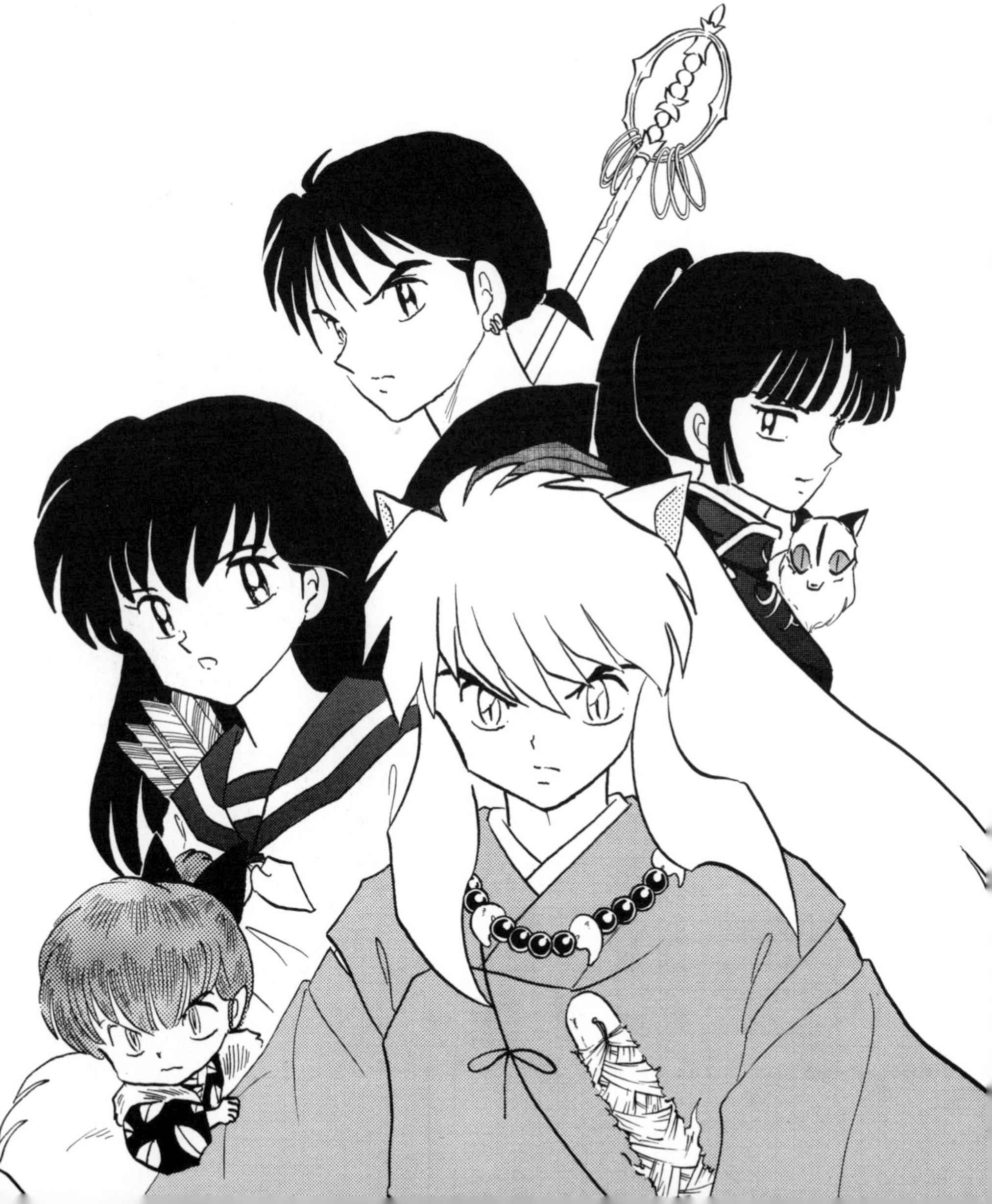

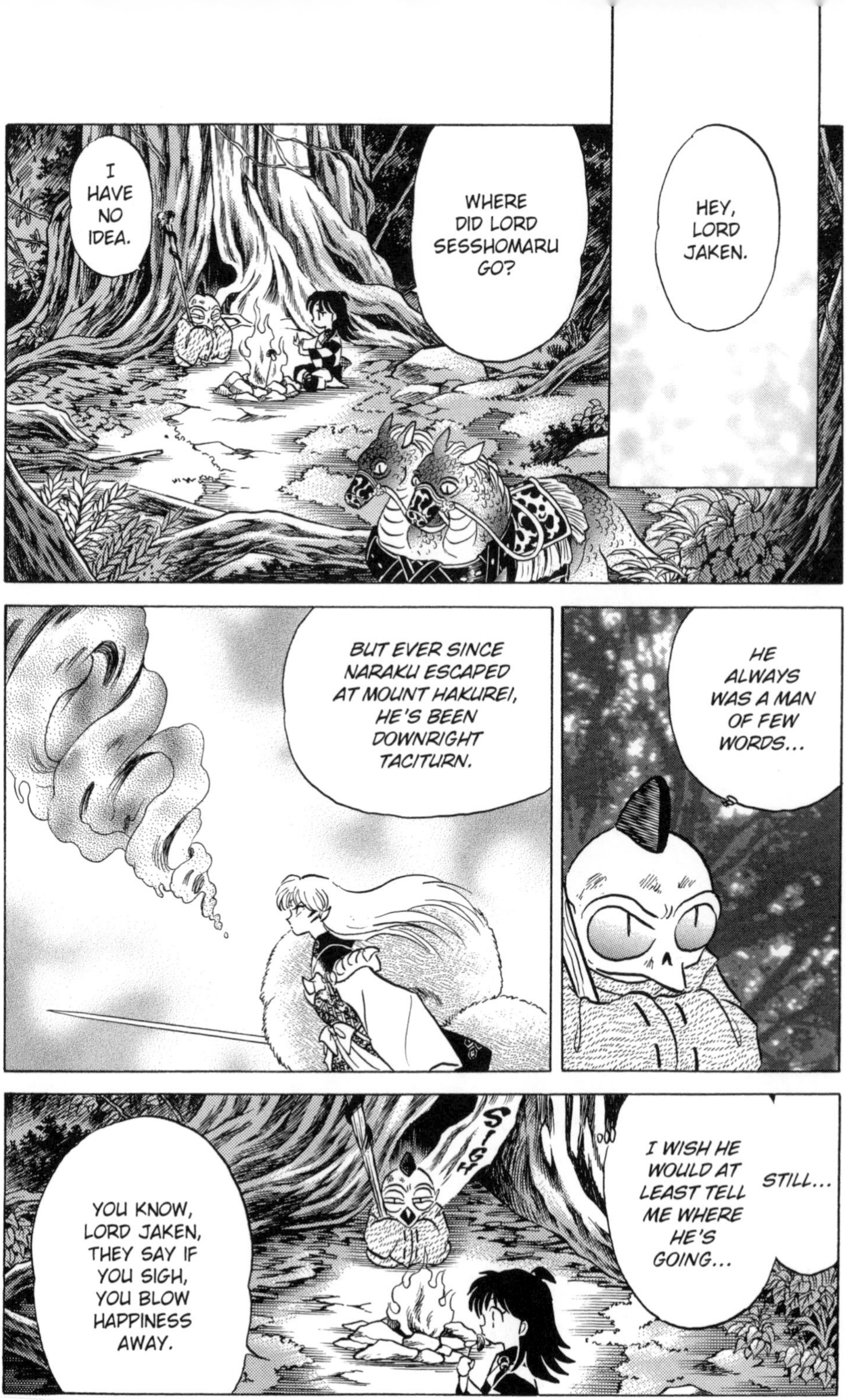
HEY, LORD JAKEN.
WHERE DID LORD SESSHOMARU GO?
I HAVE NO IDEA.
HE ALWAYS WAS A MAN OF FEW WORDS...
BUT EVER SINCE NARAKU ESCAPED AT MOUNT HAKUREI, HE'S BEEN DOWNRIGHT TACITURN.
STILL...
I WISH HE WOULD AT LEAST TELL ME WHERE HE'S GOING...
SIGH
YOU KNOW, LORD JAKEN, THEY SAY IF YOU SIGH, YOU BLOW HAPPINESS AWAY.

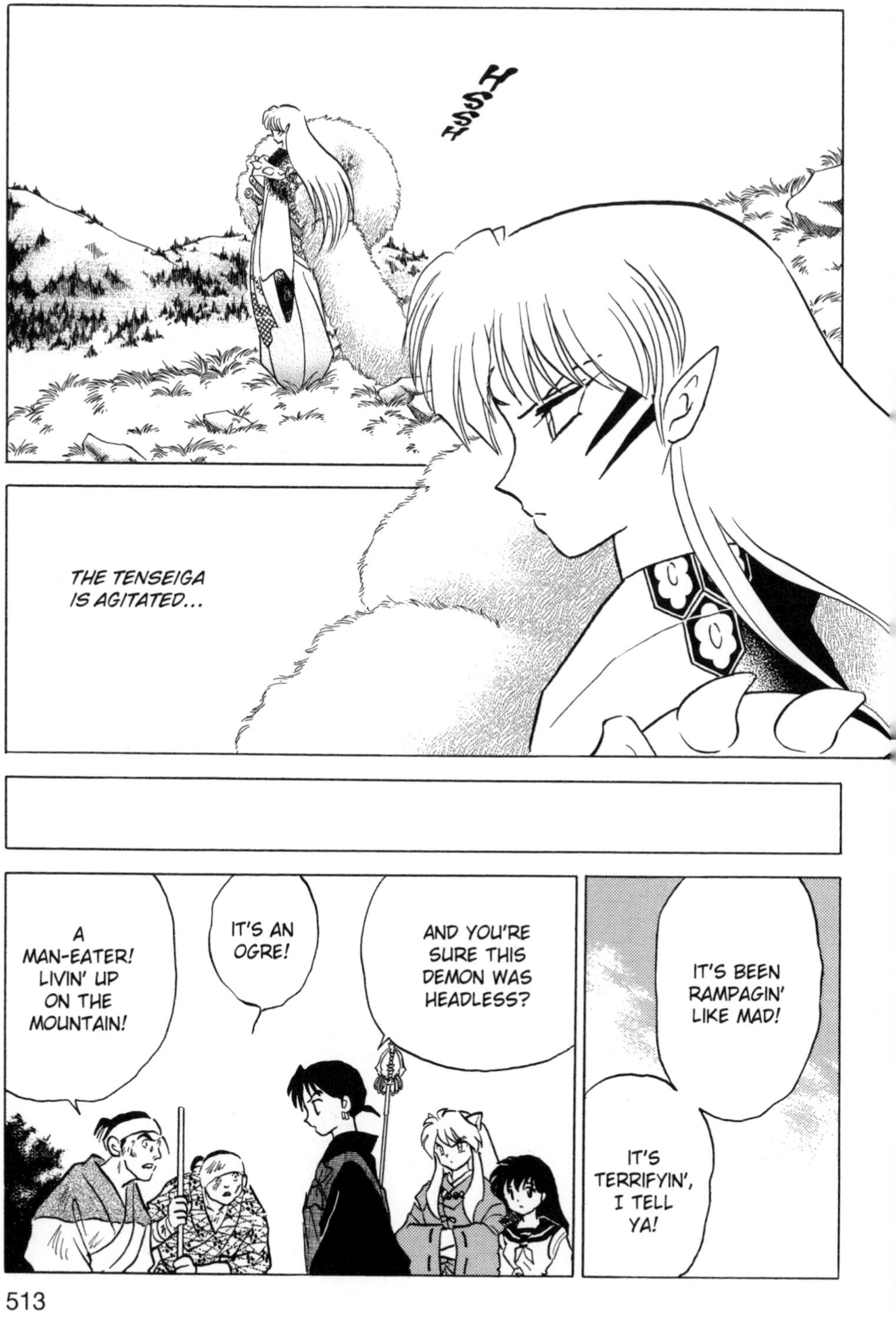
HSSH
THE TENSEIGA IS AGITATED...
IT'S BEEN RAMPAGIN' LIKE MAD!
IT'S TERRIFYIN', I TELL YA!
AND YOU'RE SURE THIS DEMON WAS HEADLESS?
IT'S AN OGRE!
A MAN-EATER! LIVIN' UP ON THE MOUNTAIN!

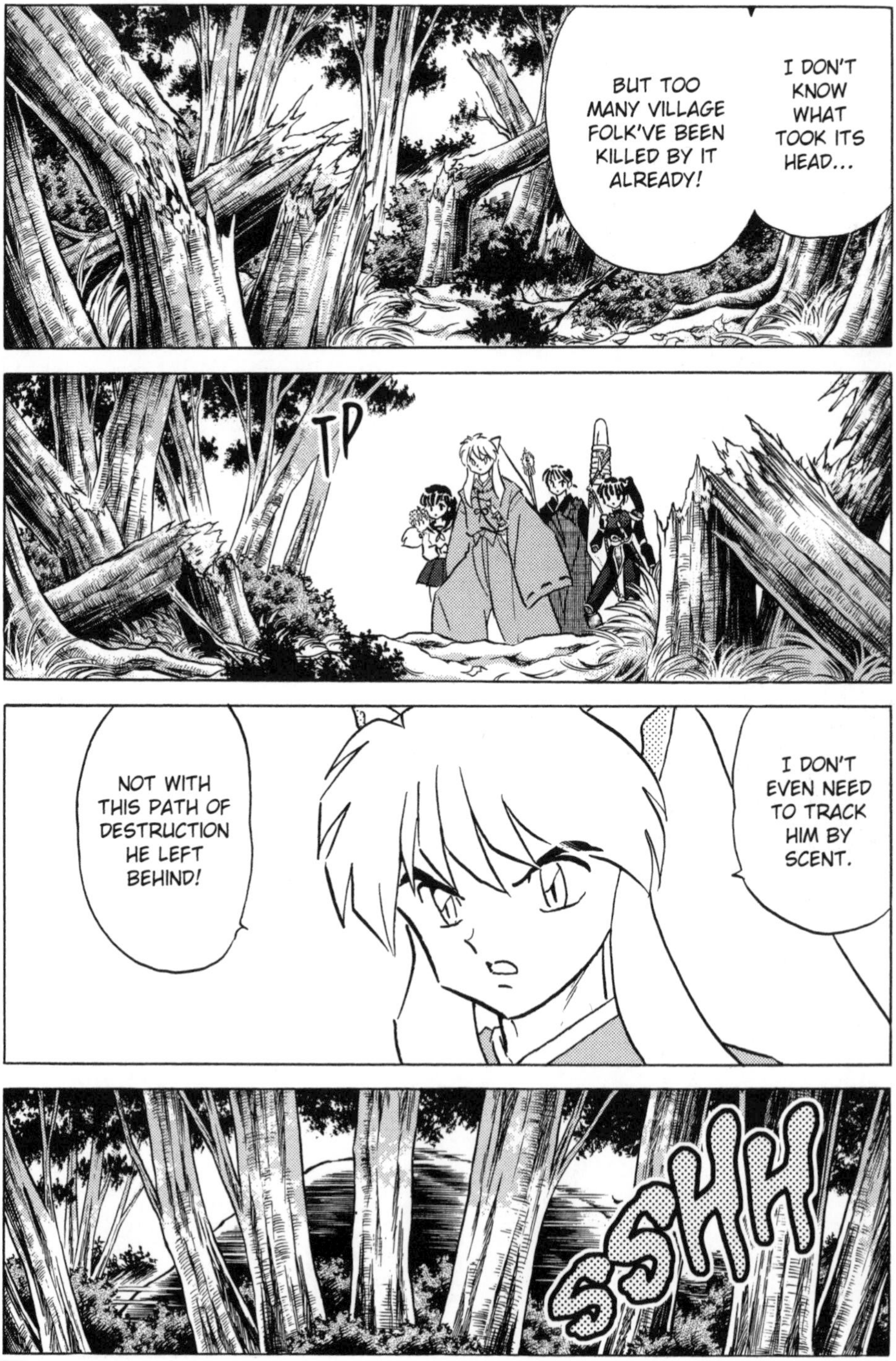
I DON'T KNOW WHAT TOOK ITS HEAD...
BUT TOO MANY VILLAGE FOLK'VE BEEN KILLED BY IT ALREADY!
TP
I DON'T EVEN NEED TO TRACK HIM BY SCENT.
NOT WITH THIS PATH OF DESTRUCTION HE LEFT BEHIND!
SSHH

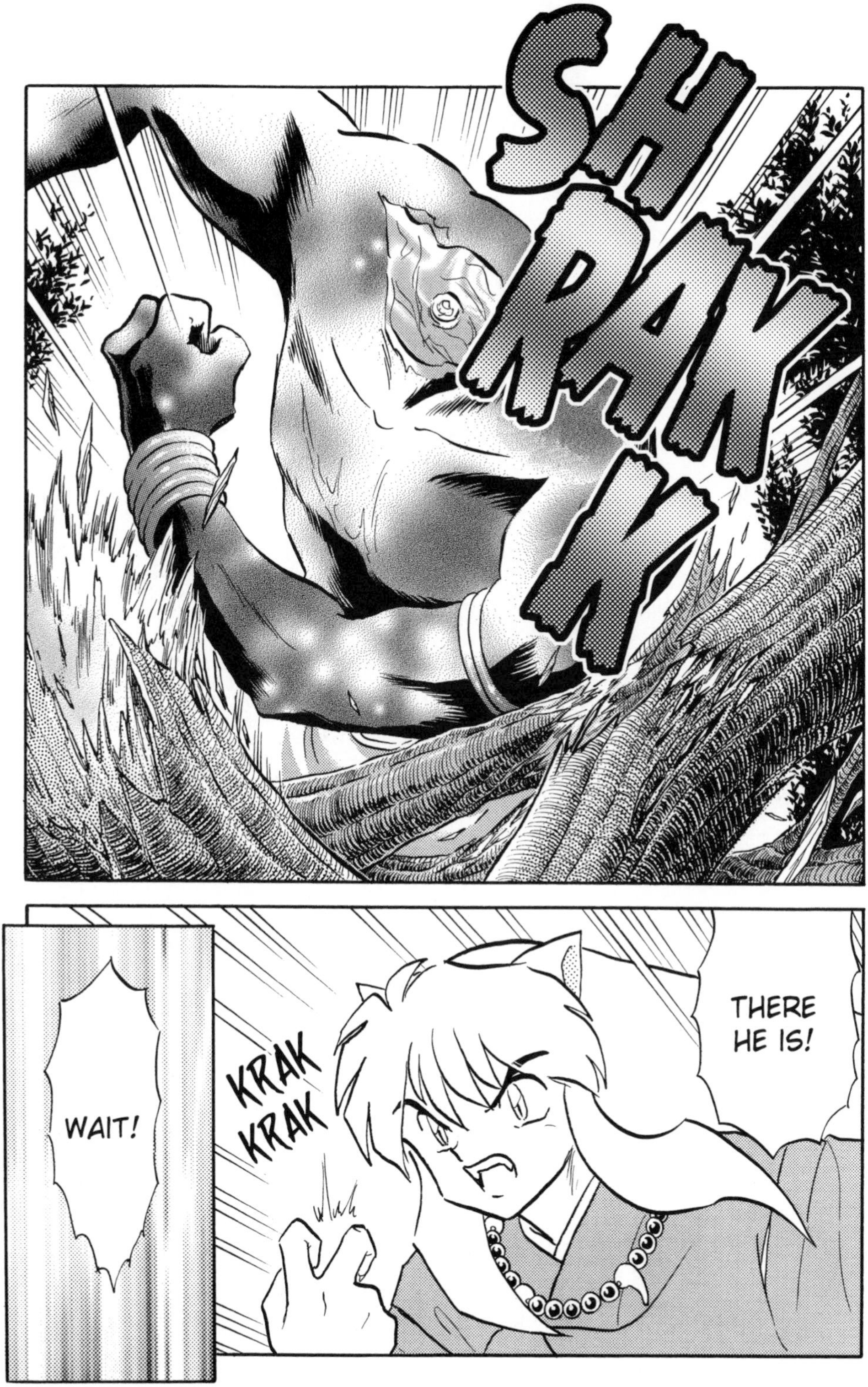
SHRAKK
THERE HE IS!
KRAK KRAK
WAIT!

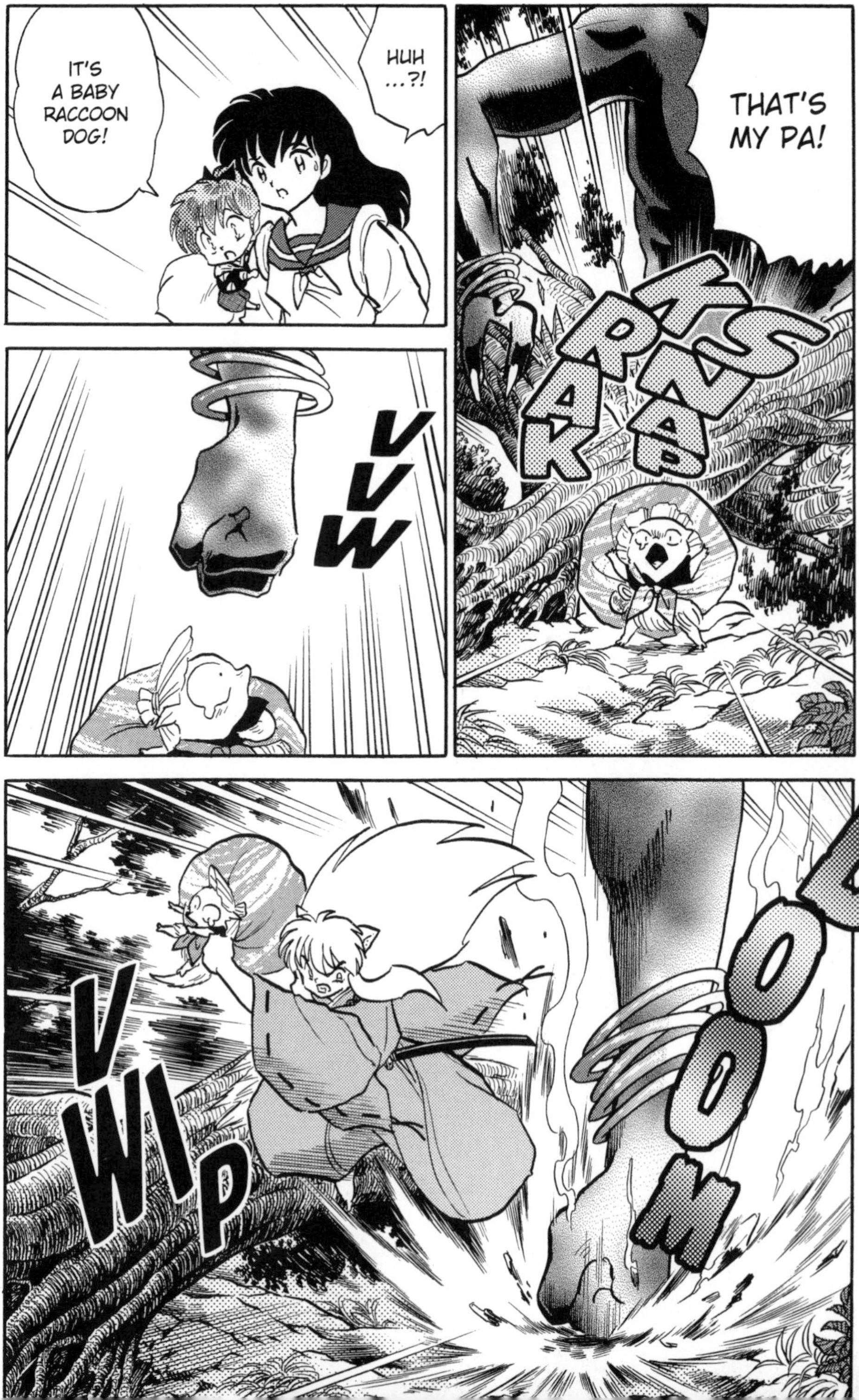
THAT'S MY PA!
SNAP
KRAK
HUH ...?!
IT'S A BABY RACCOON DOG!
VVVW
DOOOM
VWIP

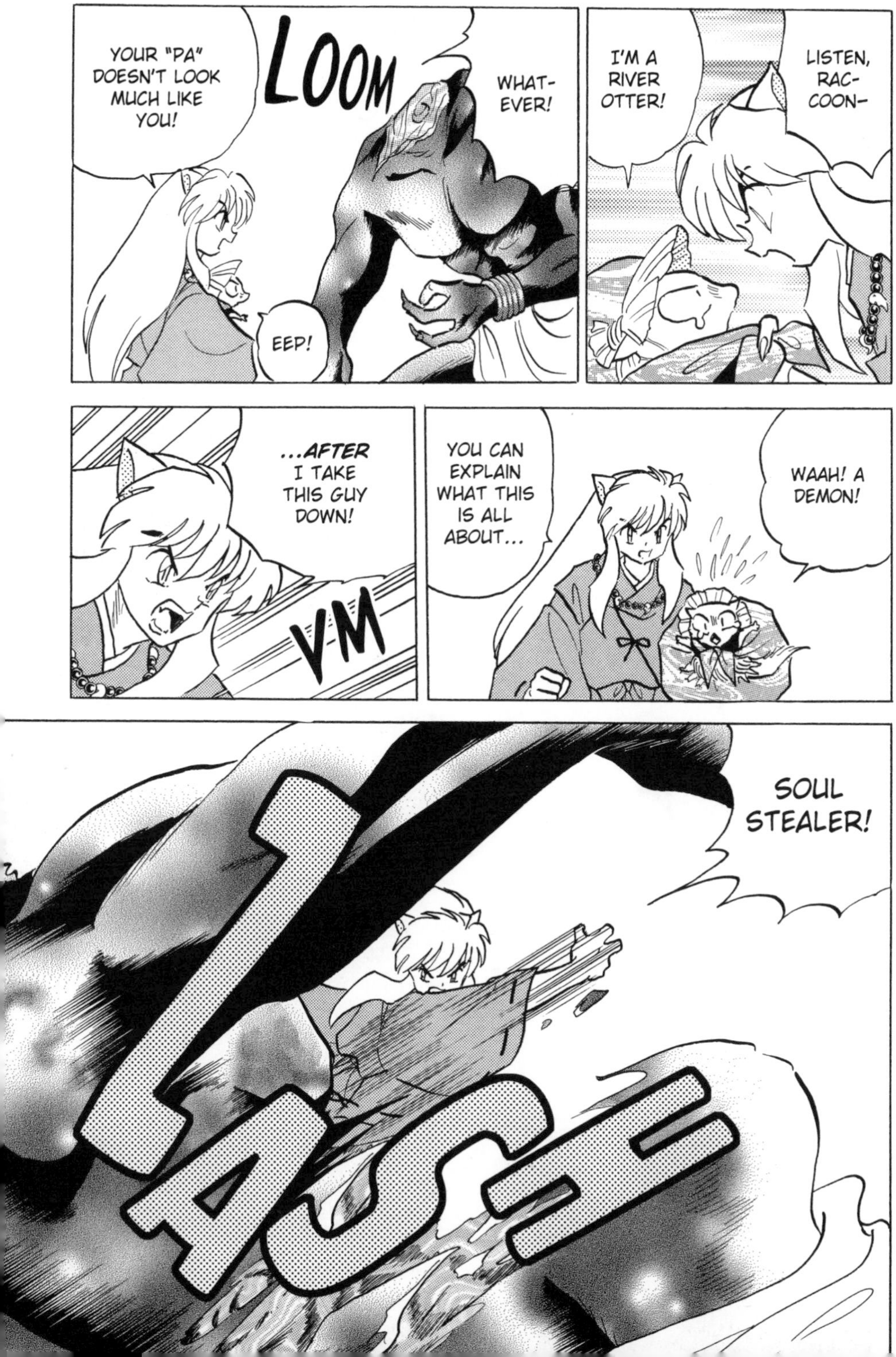
LISTEN, RAC-COON–
I'M A RIVER OTTER!
WHAT-EVER!
LOOM
YOUR "PA" DOESN'T LOOK MUCH LIKE YOU!
EEP!
WAAH! A DEMON!
YOU CAN EXPLAIN WHAT THIS IS ALL ABOUT…
…*AFTER* I TAKE THIS GUY DOWN!
VM
SOUL STEALER!
ZASCH

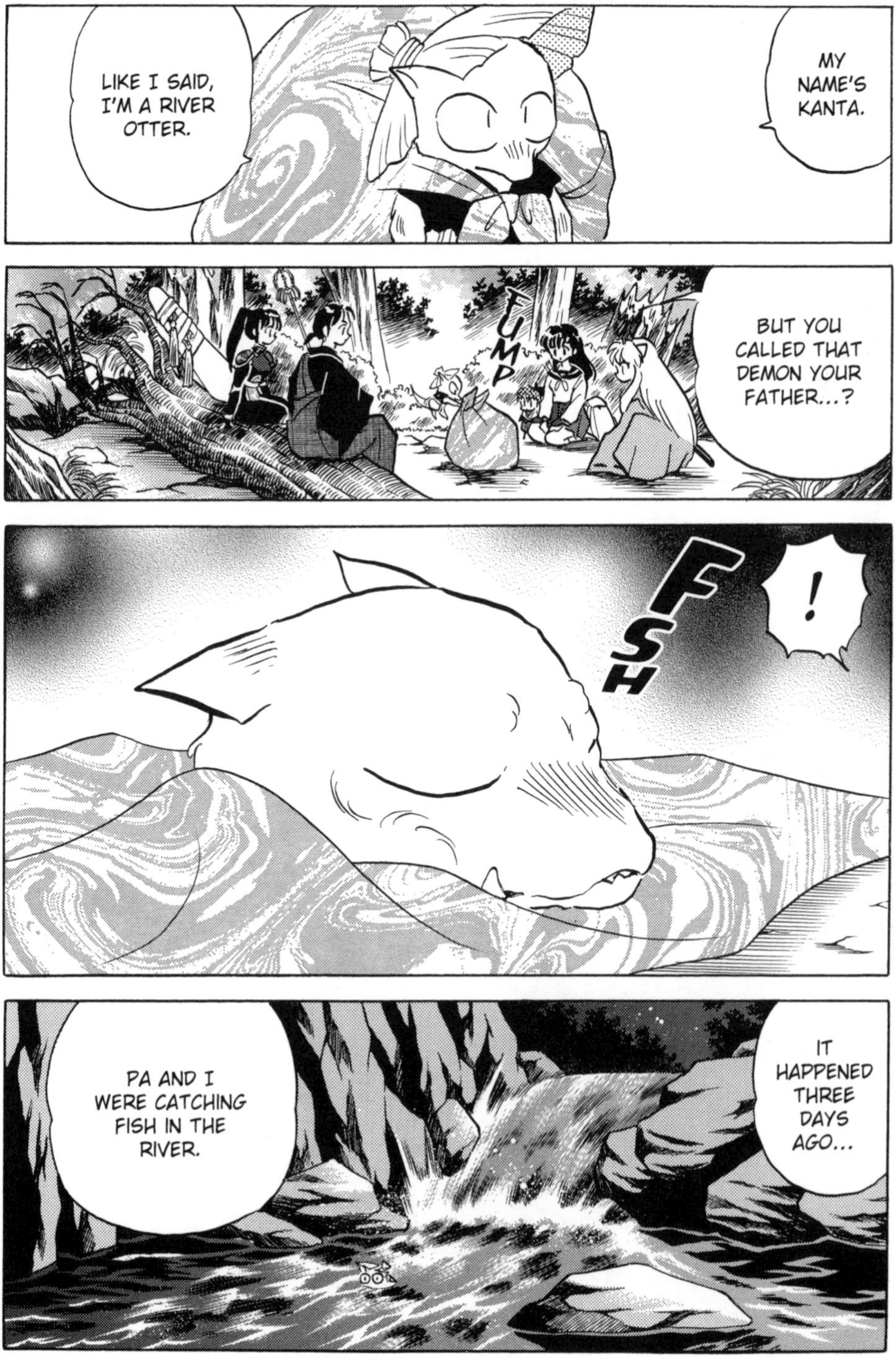
MY NAME'S KANTA.
LIKE I SAID, I'M A RIVER OTTER.
BUT YOU CALLED THAT DEMON YOUR FATHER...?
FUMP
!
FSH
IT HAPPENED THREE DAYS AGO...
PA AND I WERE CATCHING FISH IN THE RIVER.

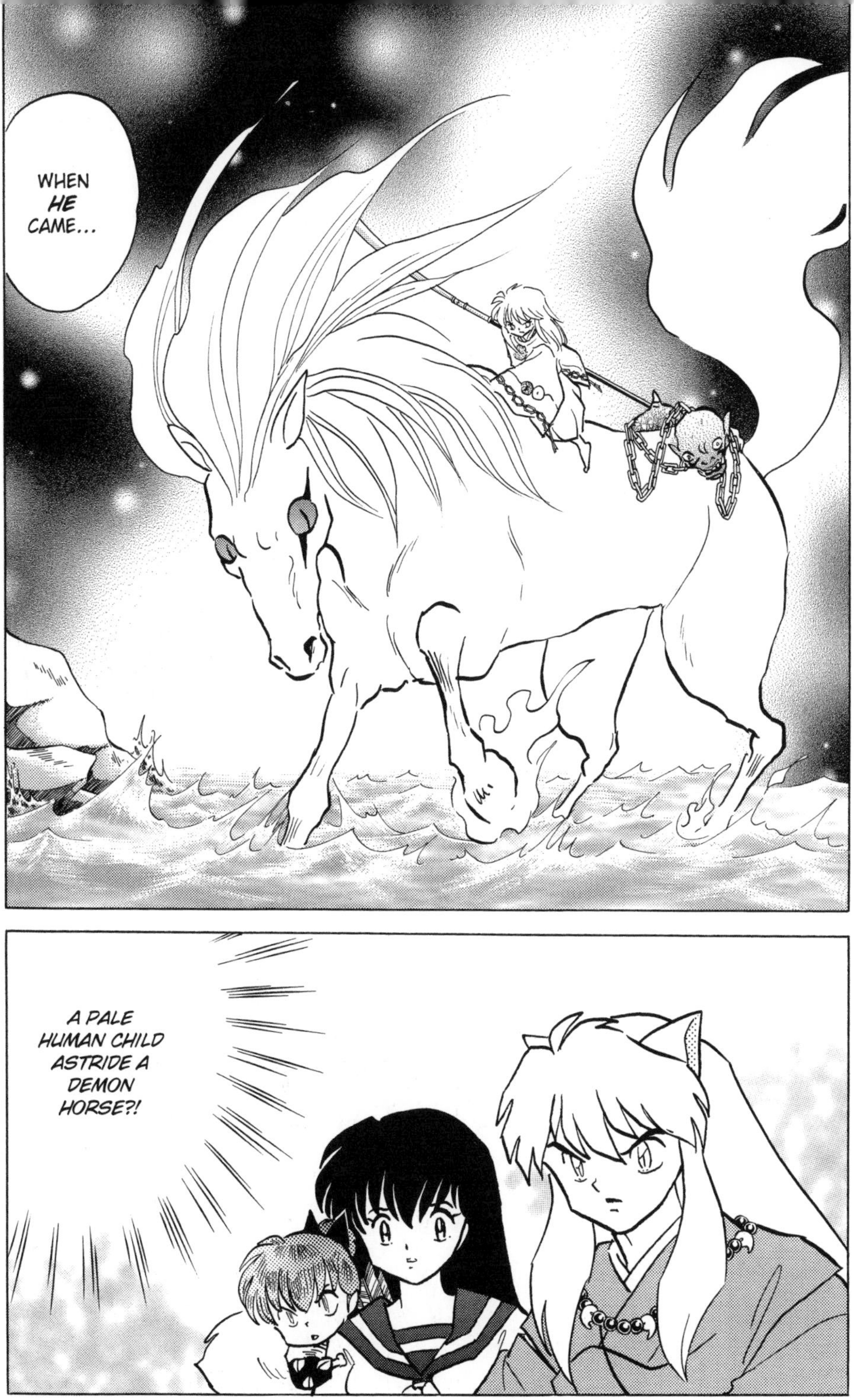
WHEN HE CAME...
A PALE HUMAN CHILD ASTRIDE A DEMON HORSE?!

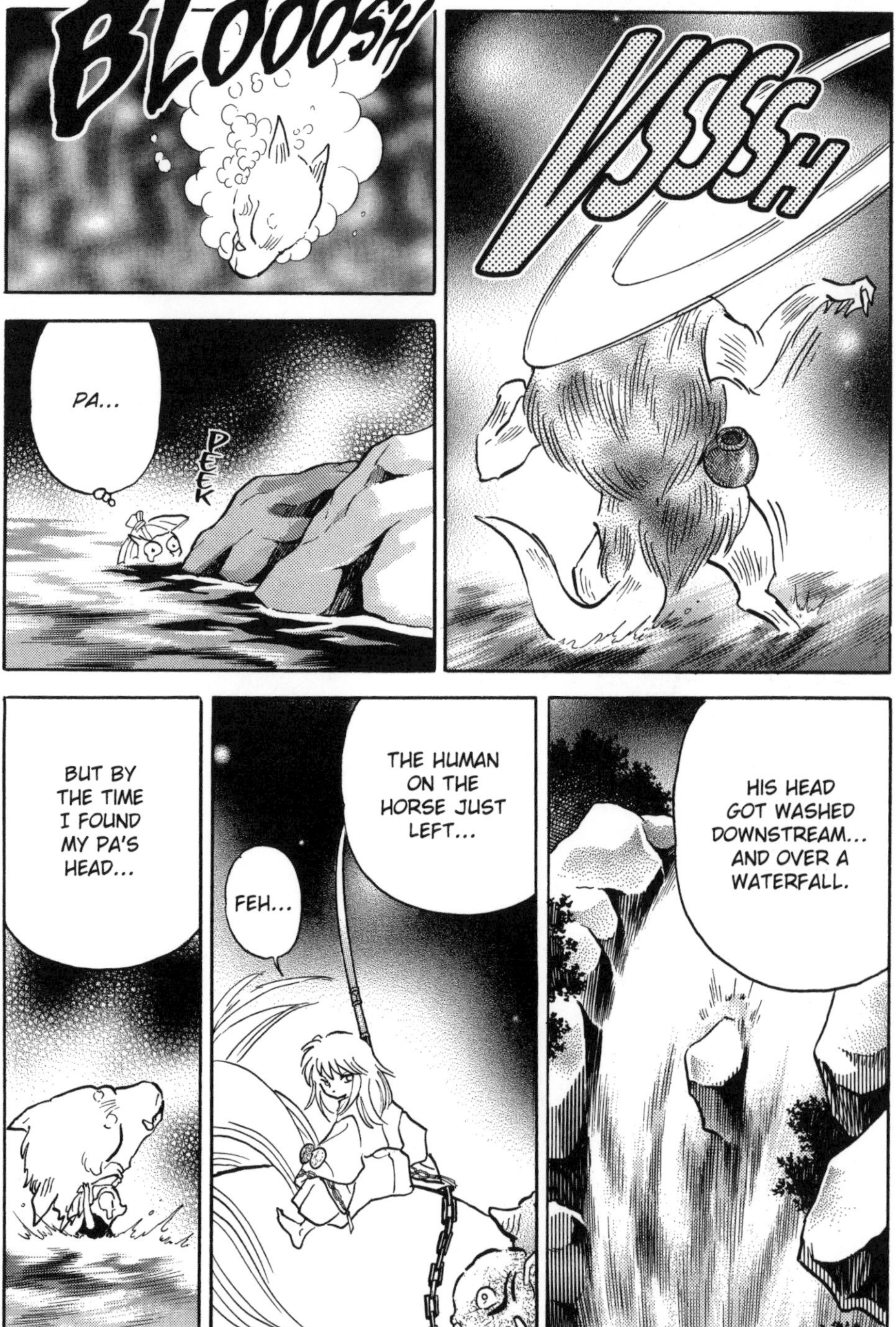
VSSSH
BLOOOSH
PA...
PEEK
HIS HEAD GOT WASHED DOWNSTREAM... AND OVER A WATERFALL.
THE HUMAN ON THE HORSE JUST LEFT...
FEH...
BUT BY THE TIME I FOUND MY PA'S HEAD...

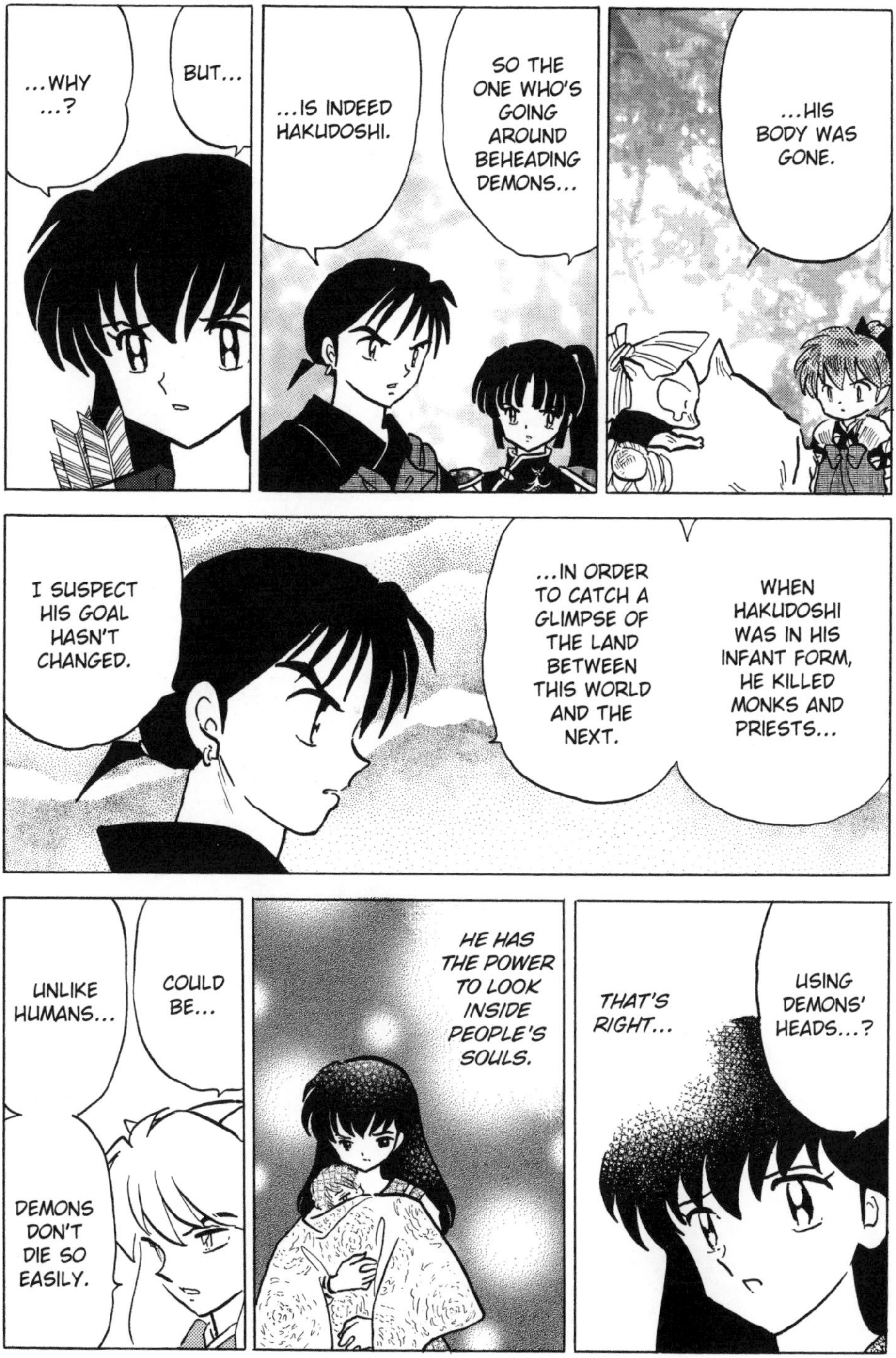
...HIS BODY WAS GONE.
SO THE ONE WHO'S GOING AROUND BEHEADING DEMONS...
...IS INDEED HAKUDOSHI.
BUT...
...WHY ...?
WHEN HAKUDOSHI WAS IN HIS INFANT FORM, HE KILLED MONKS AND PRIESTS...
...IN ORDER TO CATCH A GLIMPSE OF THE LAND BETWEEN THIS WORLD AND THE NEXT.
I SUSPECT HIS GOAL HASN'T CHANGED.
USING DEMONS' HEADS...?
THAT'S RIGHT...
HE HAS THE POWER TO LOOK INSIDE PEOPLE'S SOULS.
COULD BE...
UNLIKE HUMANS...
DEMONS DON'T DIE SO EASILY.

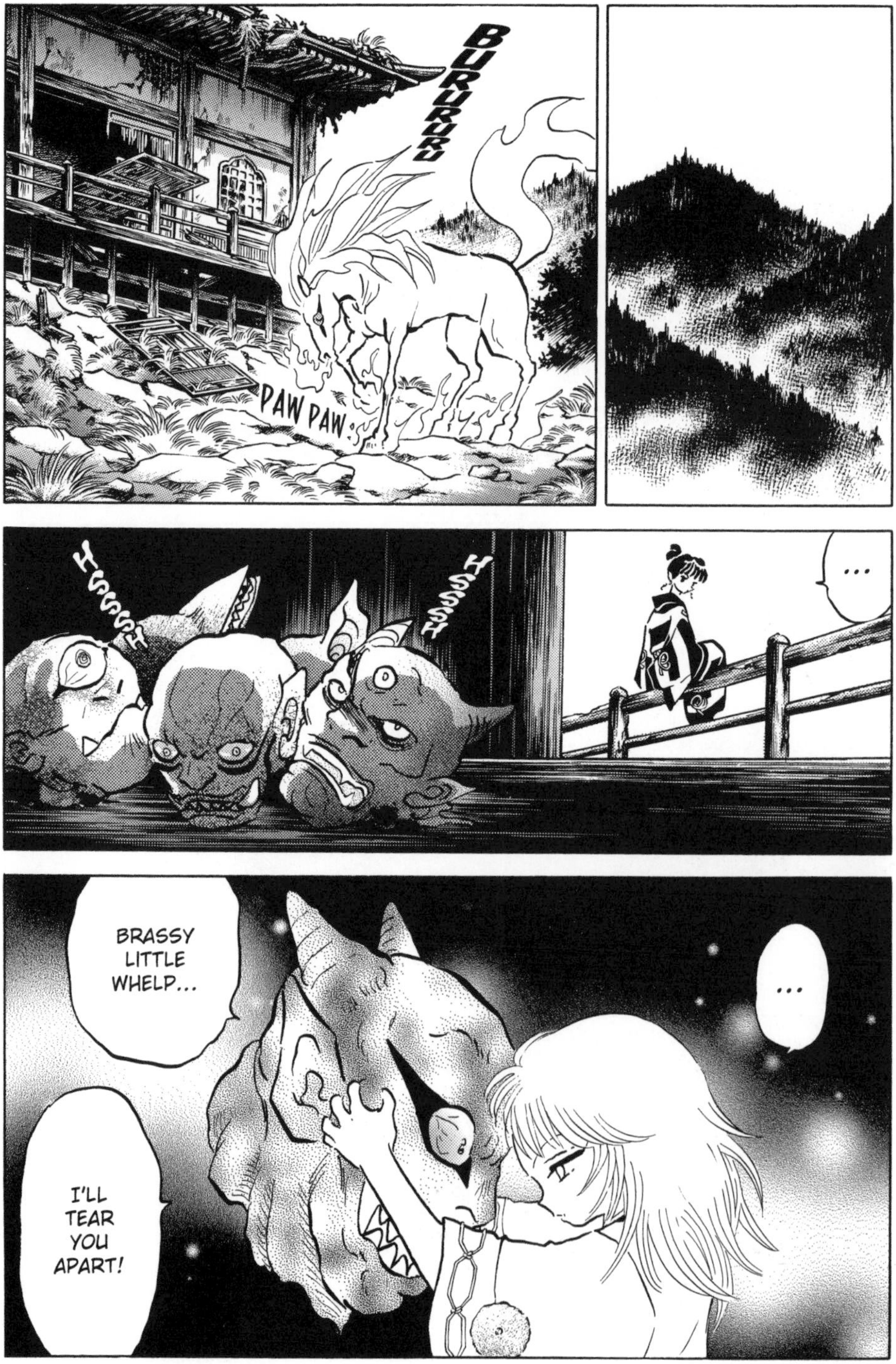
BURURURU
PAW PAW
...
HSSSSH
HSSSSH
...
BRASSY LITTLE WHELP...
I'LL TEAR YOU APART!

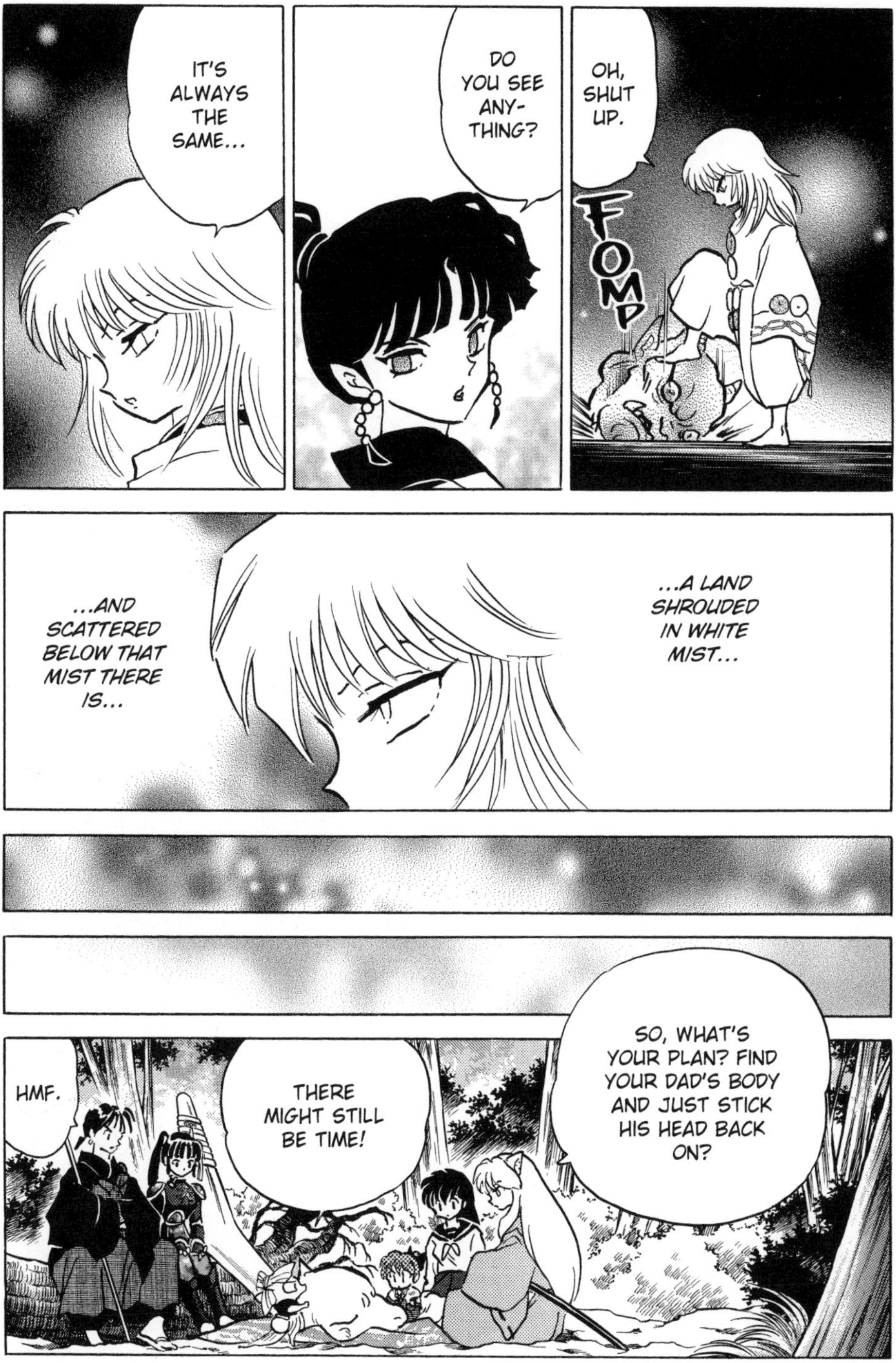
OH, SHUT UP.
FOMP
DO YOU SEE ANY-THING?
IT'S ALWAYS THE SAME...
...A LAND SHROUDED IN WHITE MIST...
...AND SCATTERED BELOW THAT MIST THERE IS...
SO, WHAT'S YOUR PLAN? FIND YOUR DAD'S BODY AND JUST STICK HIS HEAD BACK ON?
THERE MIGHT STILL BE TIME!
HMF.

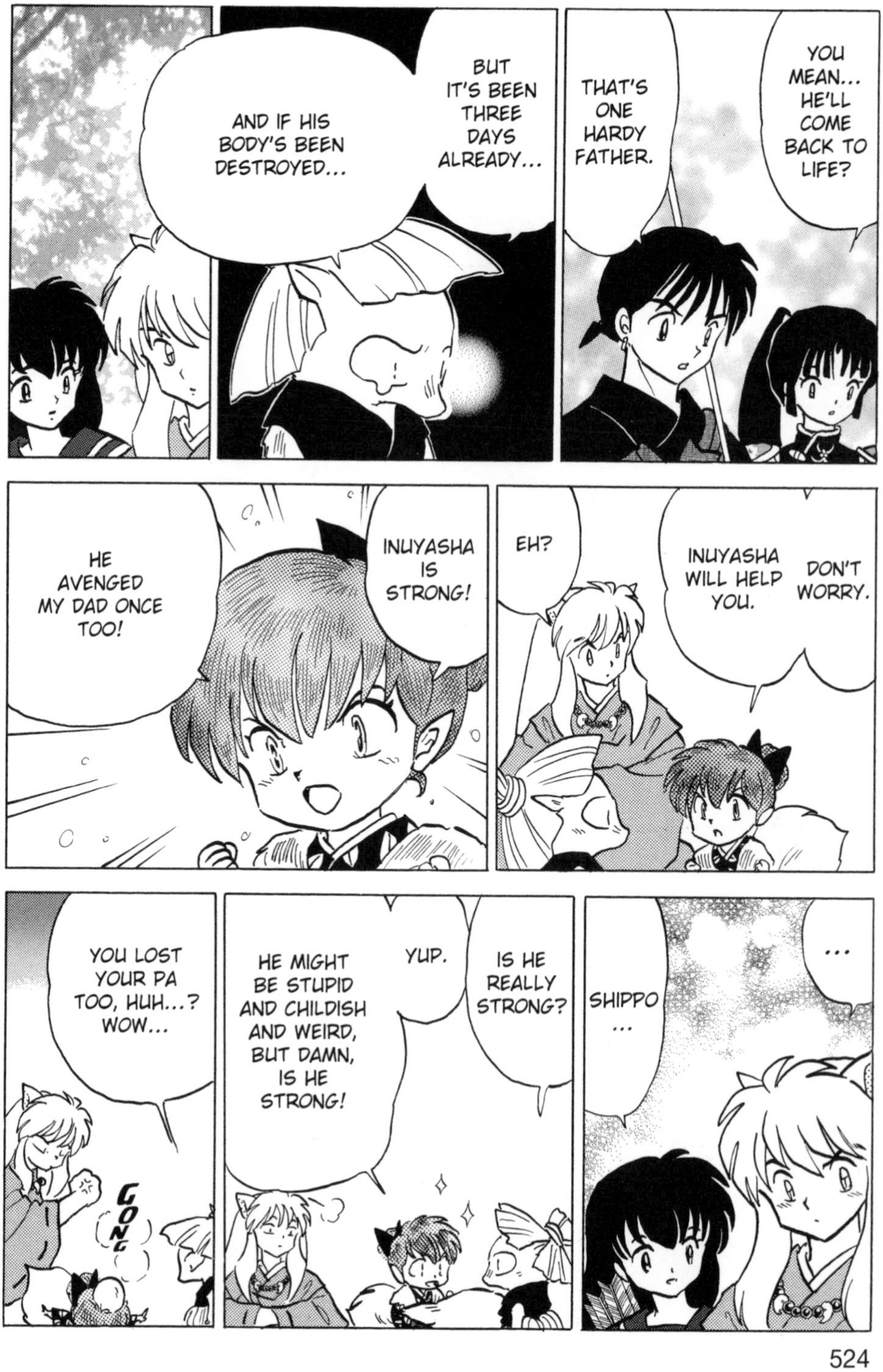
YOU MEAN... HE'LL COME BACK TO LIFE?
THAT'S ONE HARDY FATHER.
BUT IT'S BEEN THREE DAYS ALREADY...
AND IF HIS BODY'S BEEN DESTROYED...
DON'T WORRY.
INUYASHA WILL HELP YOU.
EH?
INUYASHA IS STRONG!
HE AVENGED MY DAD ONCE TOO!
...
SHIPPO...
IS HE REALLY STRONG?
YUP.
HE MIGHT BE STUPID AND CHILDISH AND WEIRD, BUT DAMN, IS HE STRONG!
YOU LOST YOUR PA TOO, HUH...? WOW...
GONG

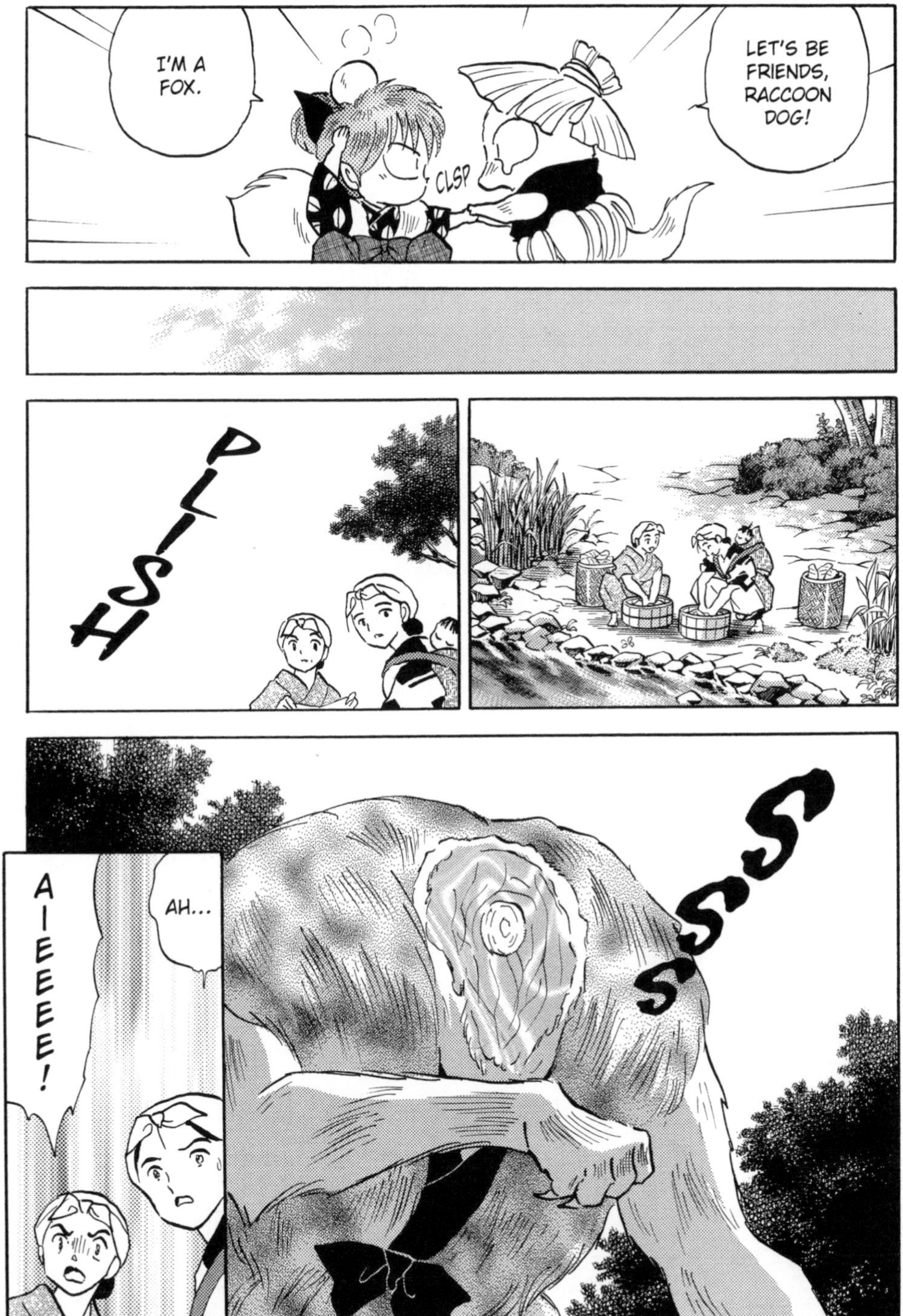
LET'S BE FRIENDS, RACCOON DOG!
CLSP
I'M A FOX.
PLISH
SSS
AH...
AIEEEEE!

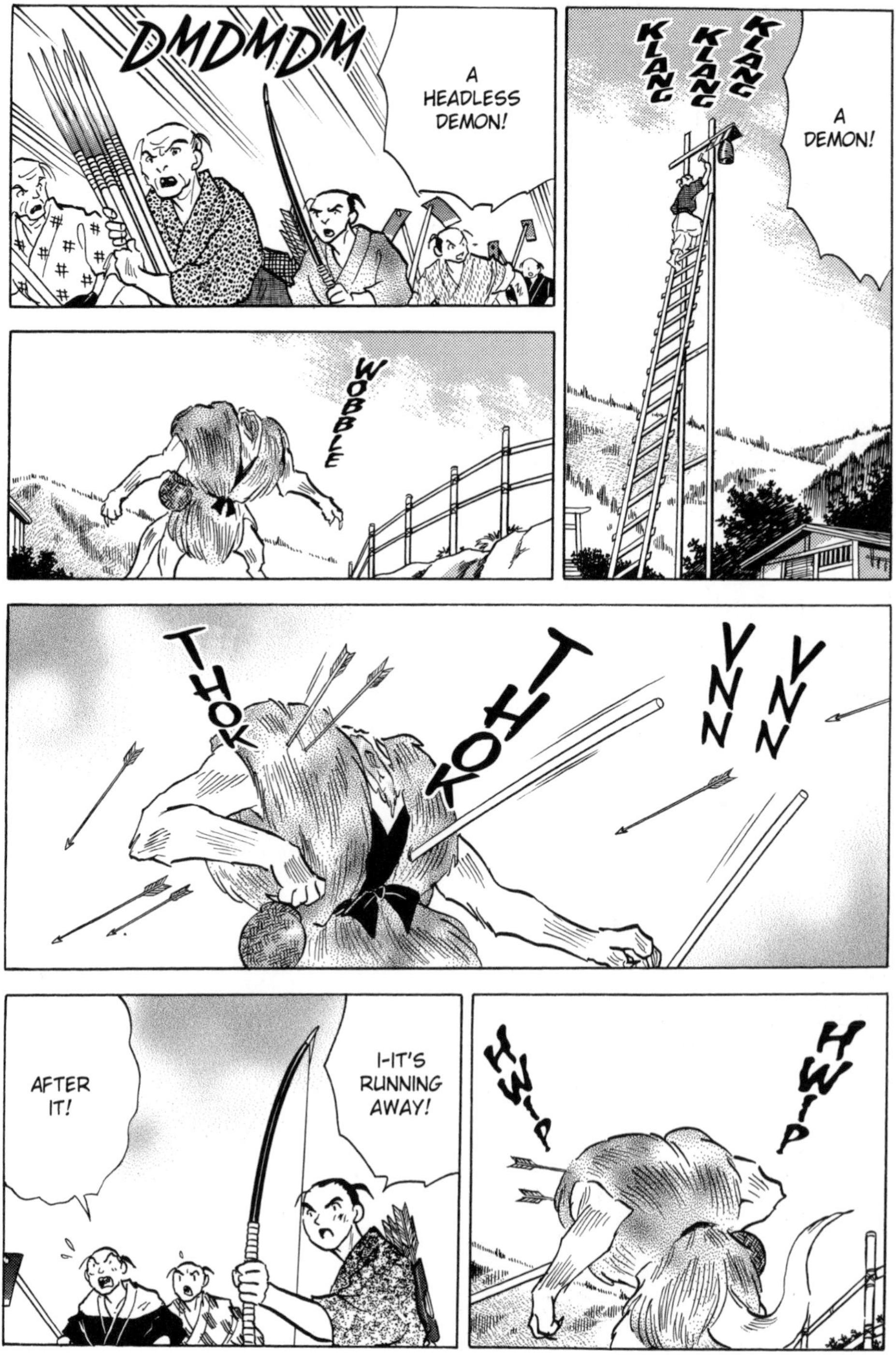
KLANG
KLANG
KLANG
A DEMON!
DMDMDM
A HEADLESS DEMON!
WOBBLE
VNN
VNN
THOK
THOK
HWIP
HWIP
I-IT'S RUNNING AWAY!
AFTER IT!

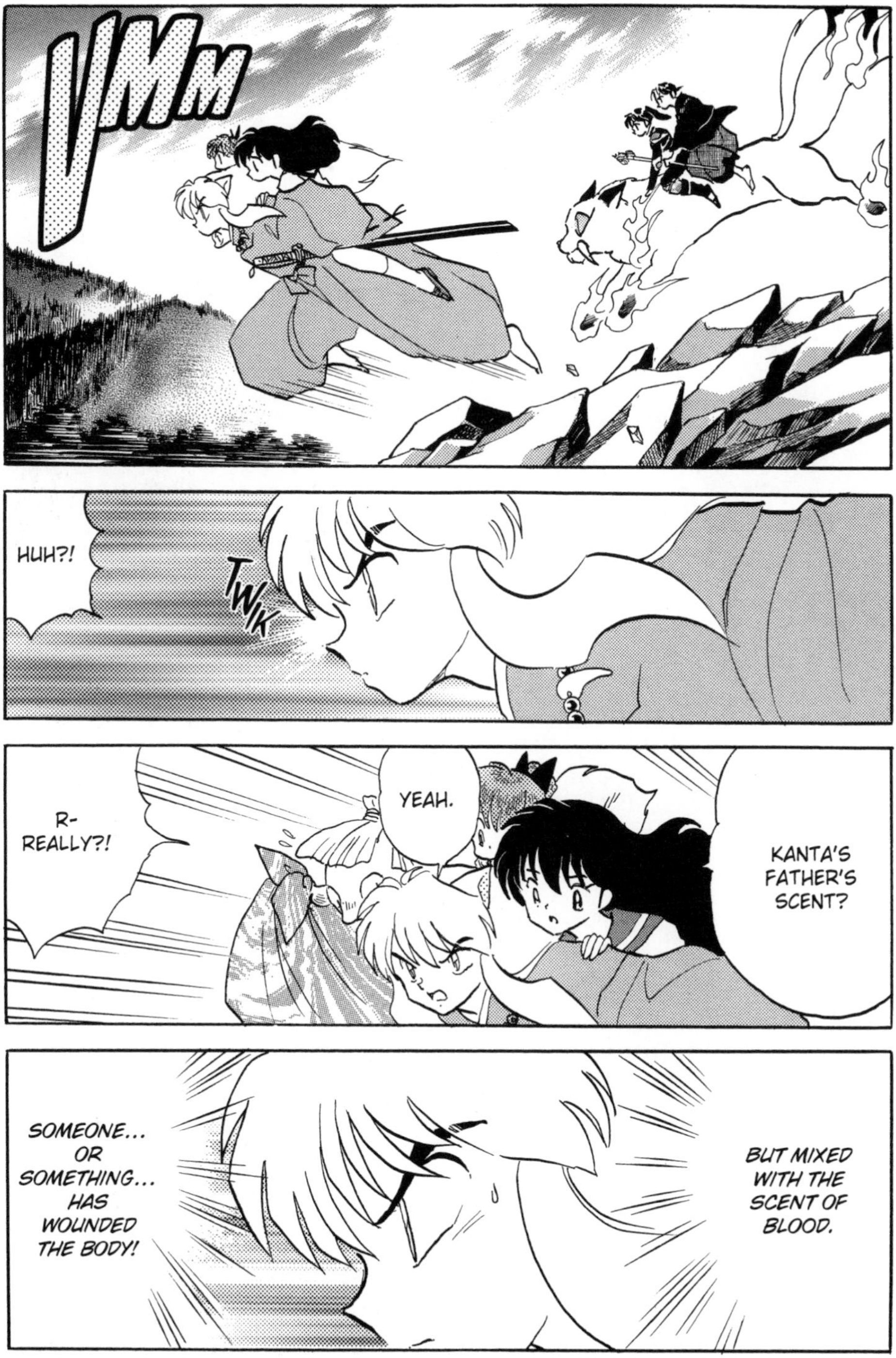
VMM
HUH?!
TWIK
KANTA'S FATHER'S SCENT?
YEAH.
R-REALLY?!
BUT MIXED WITH THE SCENT OF BLOOD.
SOMEONE... OR SOMETHING... HAS WOUNDED THE BODY!

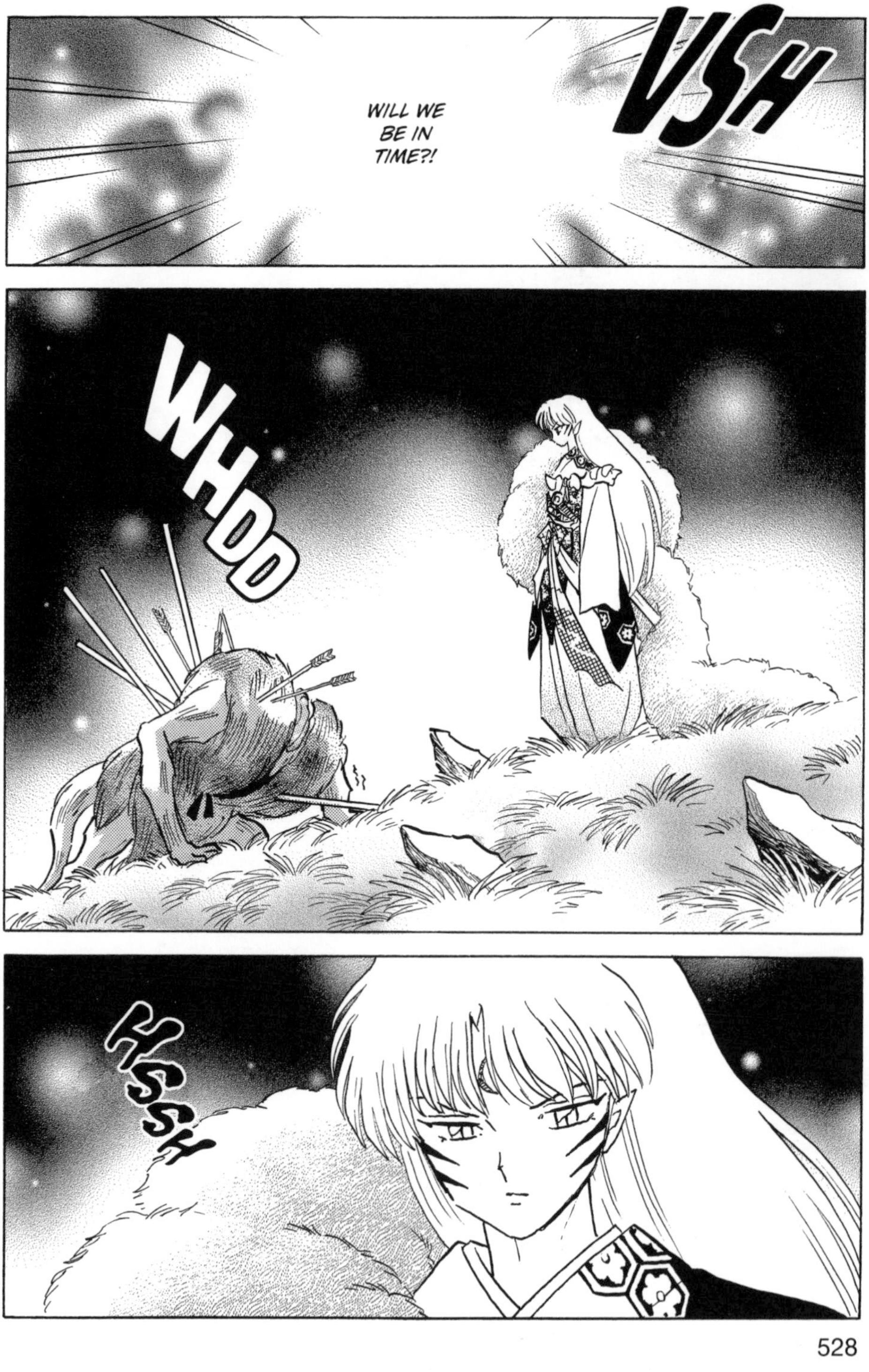
VSH
WILL WE BE IN TIME?!
WHDD
HSSH

SCROLL NINE
BETWEEN THIS WORLD AND THE NEXT

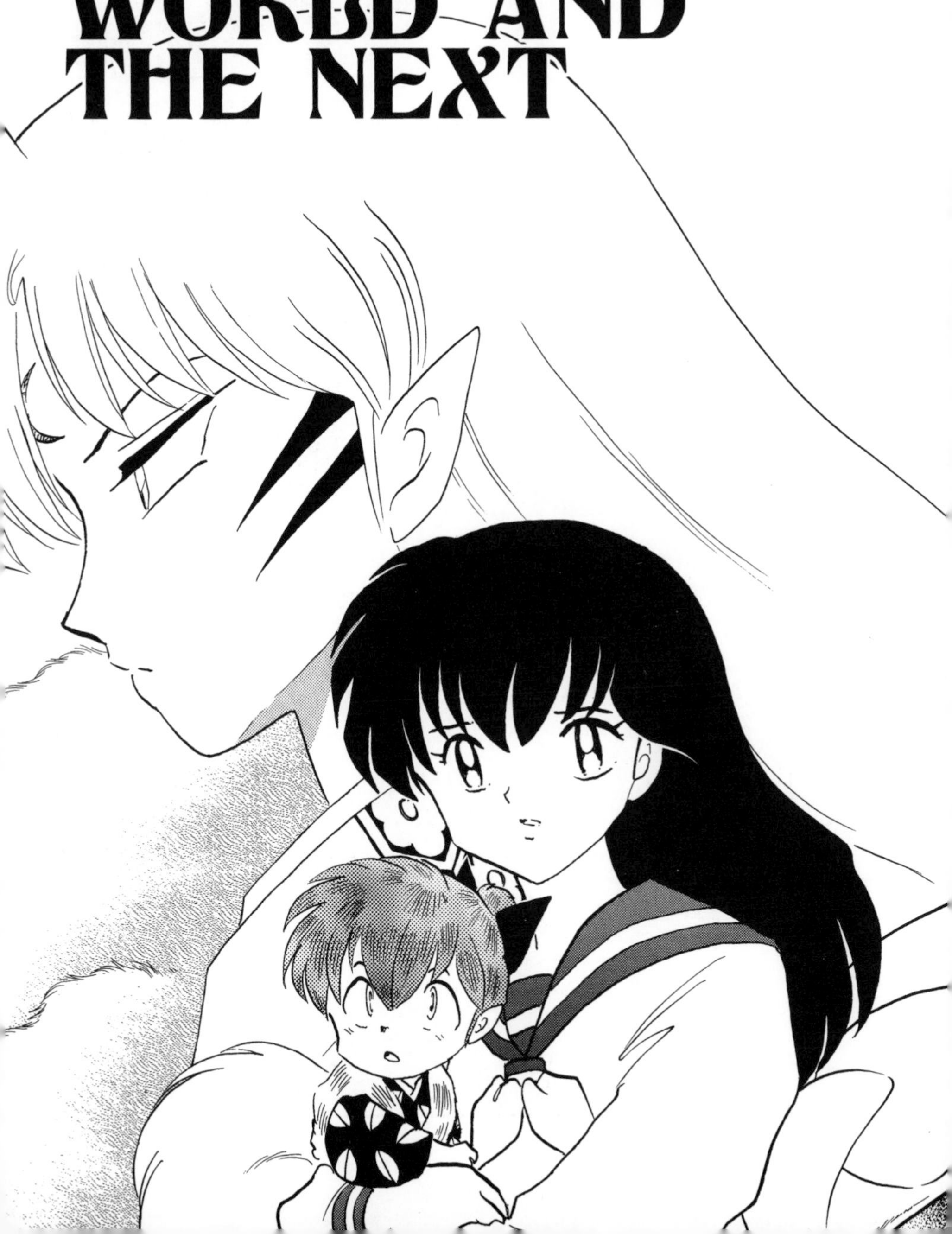

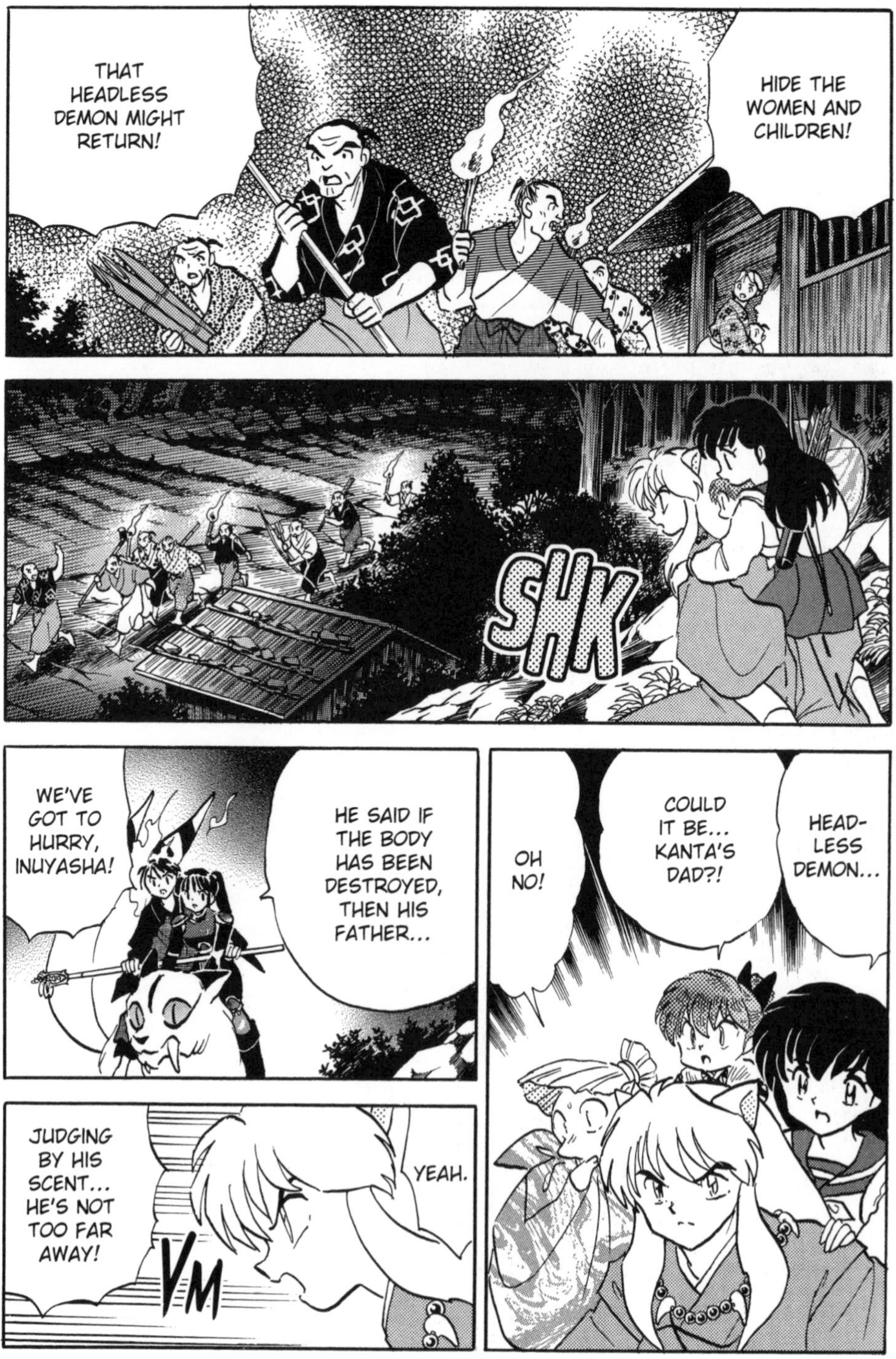
HIDE THE WOMEN AND CHILDREN!
THAT HEADLESS DEMON MIGHT RETURN!
SHK
HEAD-LESS DEMON...
COULD IT BE... KANTA'S DAD?!
OH NO!
HE SAID IF THE BODY HAS BEEN DESTROYED, THEN HIS FATHER...
WE'VE GOT TO HURRY, INUYASHA!
YEAH.
JUDGING BY HIS SCENT... HE'S NOT TOO FAR AWAY!
VM

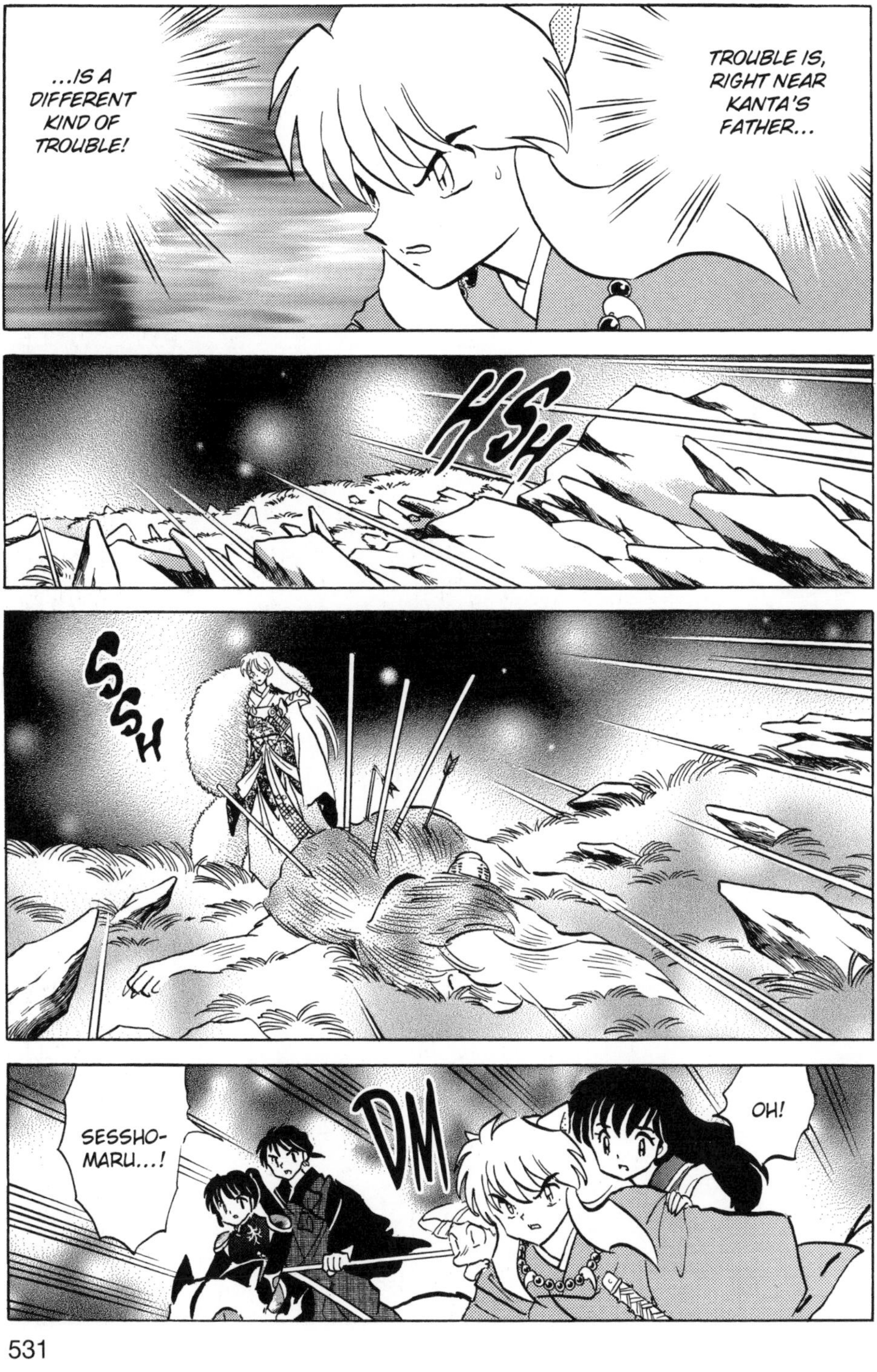
TROUBLE IS, RIGHT NEAR KANTA'S FATHER...
...IS A DIFFERENT KIND OF TROUBLE!
HSH
SSSH
OH!
DM
SESSHO-MARU...!

...

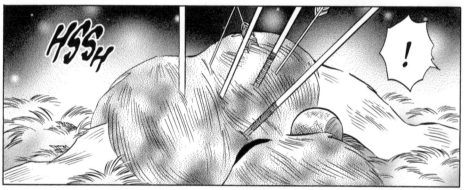

HSSH

!

LET'S GET HIS HEAD, KANTA!

YEAH.

H-HANG ON, PA-!

OH...

PA-!

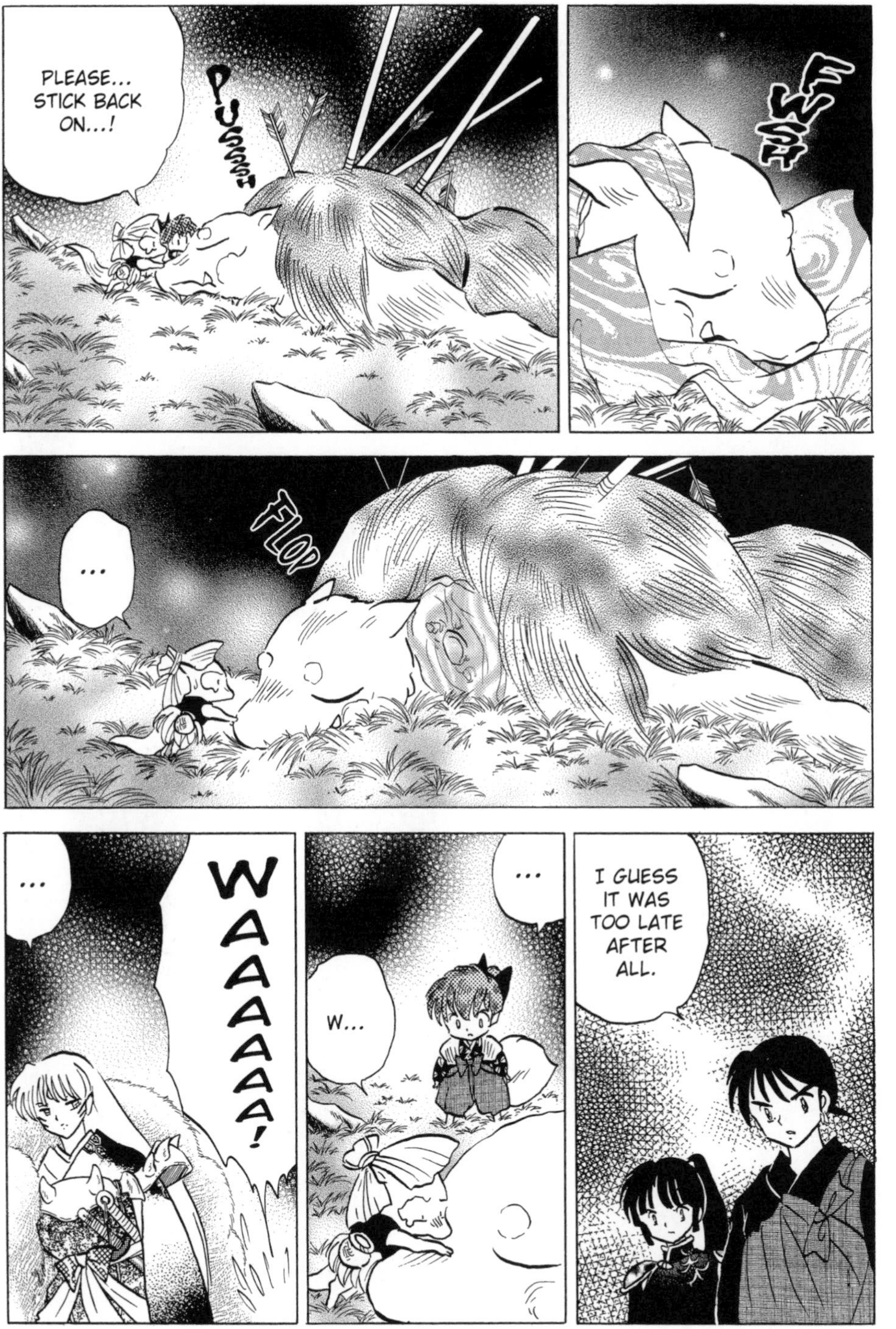
FWSH
PUSSSH
PLEASE... STICK BACK ON...!
FLOP
...
I GUESS IT WAS TOO LATE AFTER ALL.
...
W...
WAAAAAAA!
...

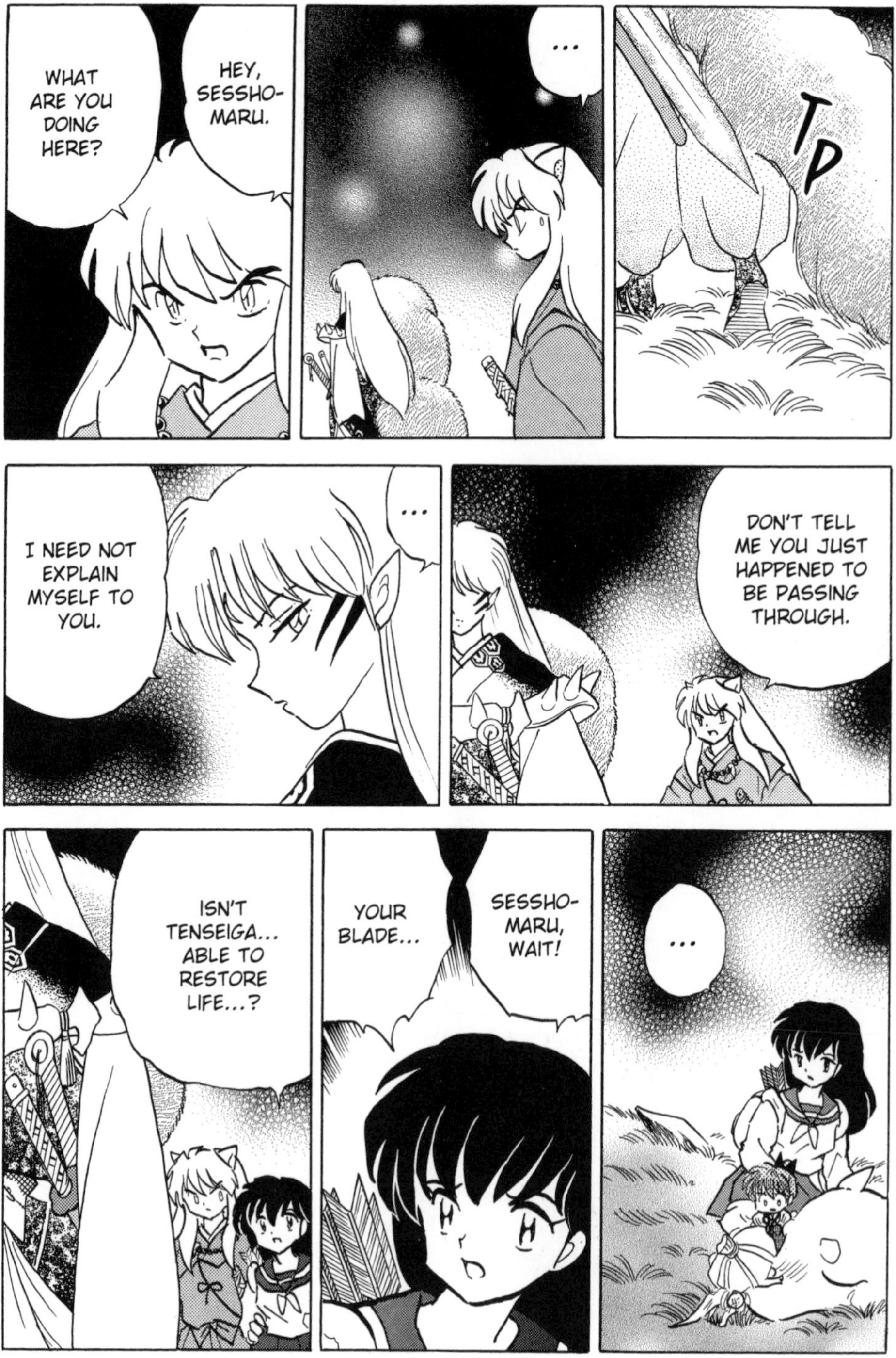
TP
...
HEY, SESSHO-MARU.
WHAT ARE YOU DOING HERE?
DON'T TELL ME YOU JUST HAPPENED TO BE PASSING THROUGH.
...
I NEED NOT EXPLAIN MYSELF TO YOU.
...
SESSHO-MARU, WAIT!
YOUR BLADE...
ISN'T TENSEIGA... ABLE TO RESTORE LIFE...?

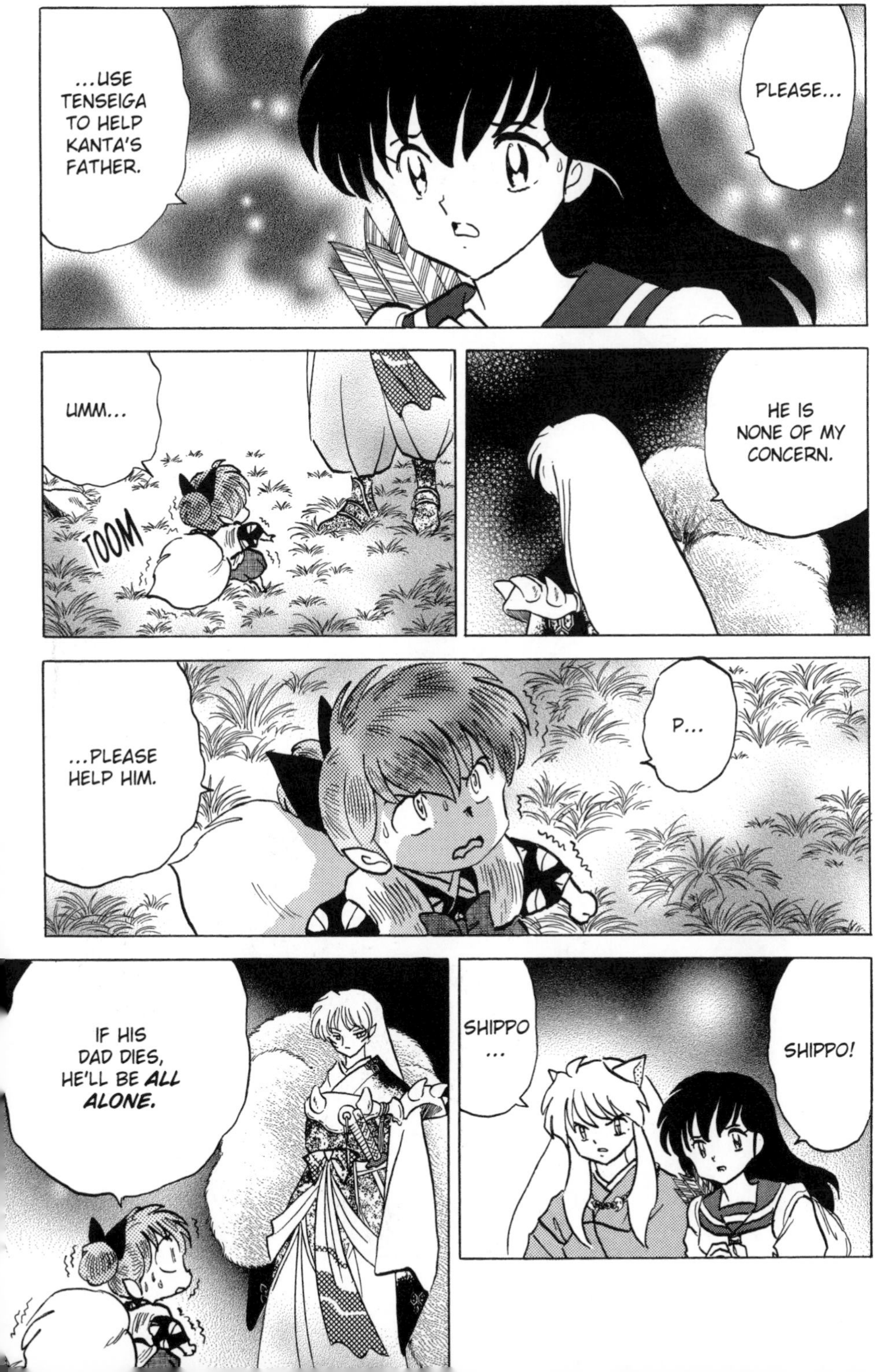
PLEASE...
...USE TENSEIGA TO HELP KANTA'S FATHER.
HE IS NONE OF MY CONCERN.
UMM...
TOOM
P...
...PLEASE HELP HIM.
SHIPPO!
SHIPPO ...
IF HIS DAD DIES, HE'LL BE ***ALL ALONE.***

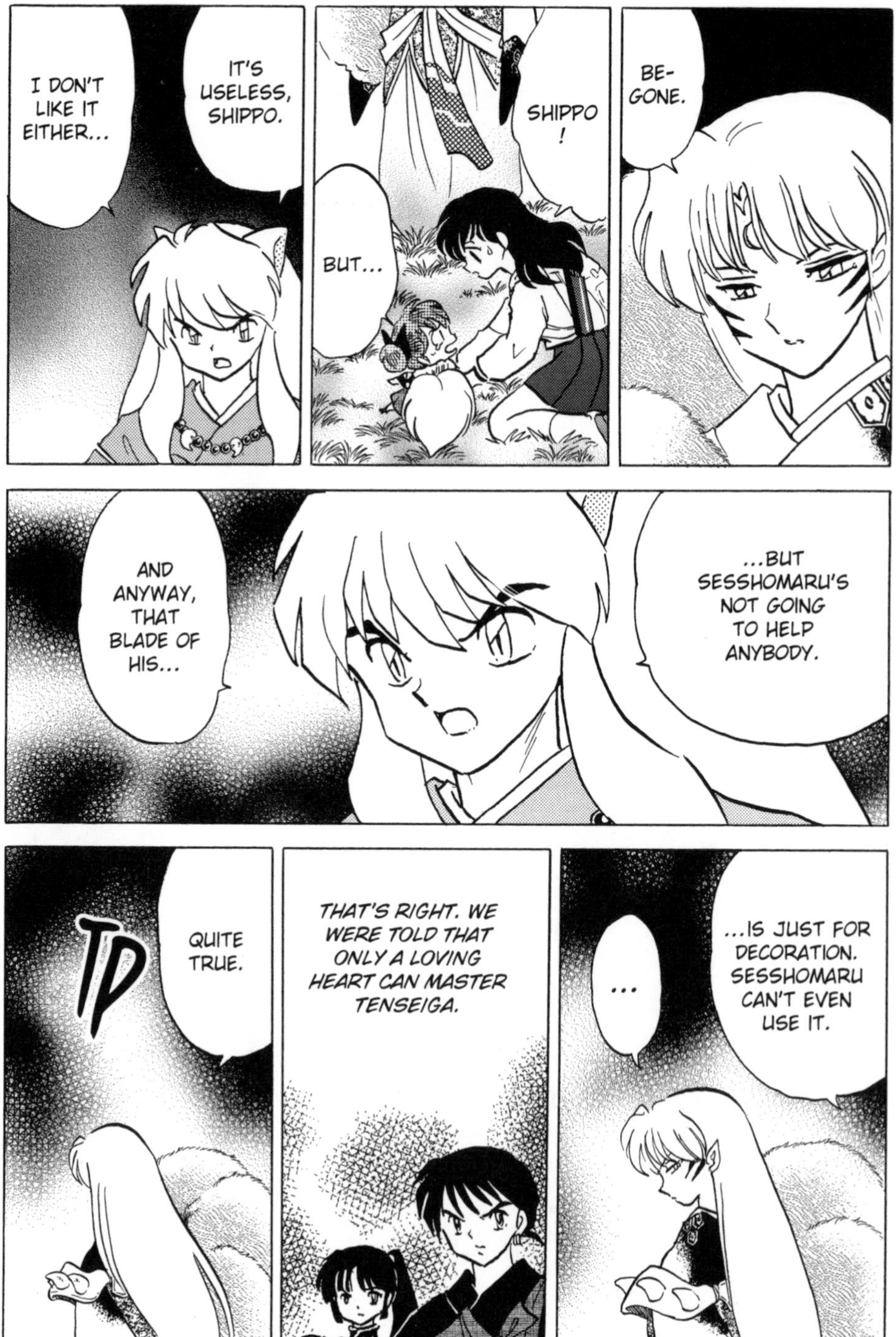
BE-GONE.
SHIPPO!
BUT...
IT'S USELESS, SHIPPO.
I DON'T LIKE IT EITHER...
...BUT SESSHOMARU'S NOT GOING TO HELP ANYBODY.
AND ANYWAY, THAT BLADE OF HIS...
...IS JUST FOR DECORATION. SESSHOMARU CAN'T EVEN USE IT.
...
THAT'S RIGHT. WE WERE TOLD THAT ONLY A LOVING HEART CAN MASTER TENSEIGA.
QUITE TRUE.
TP

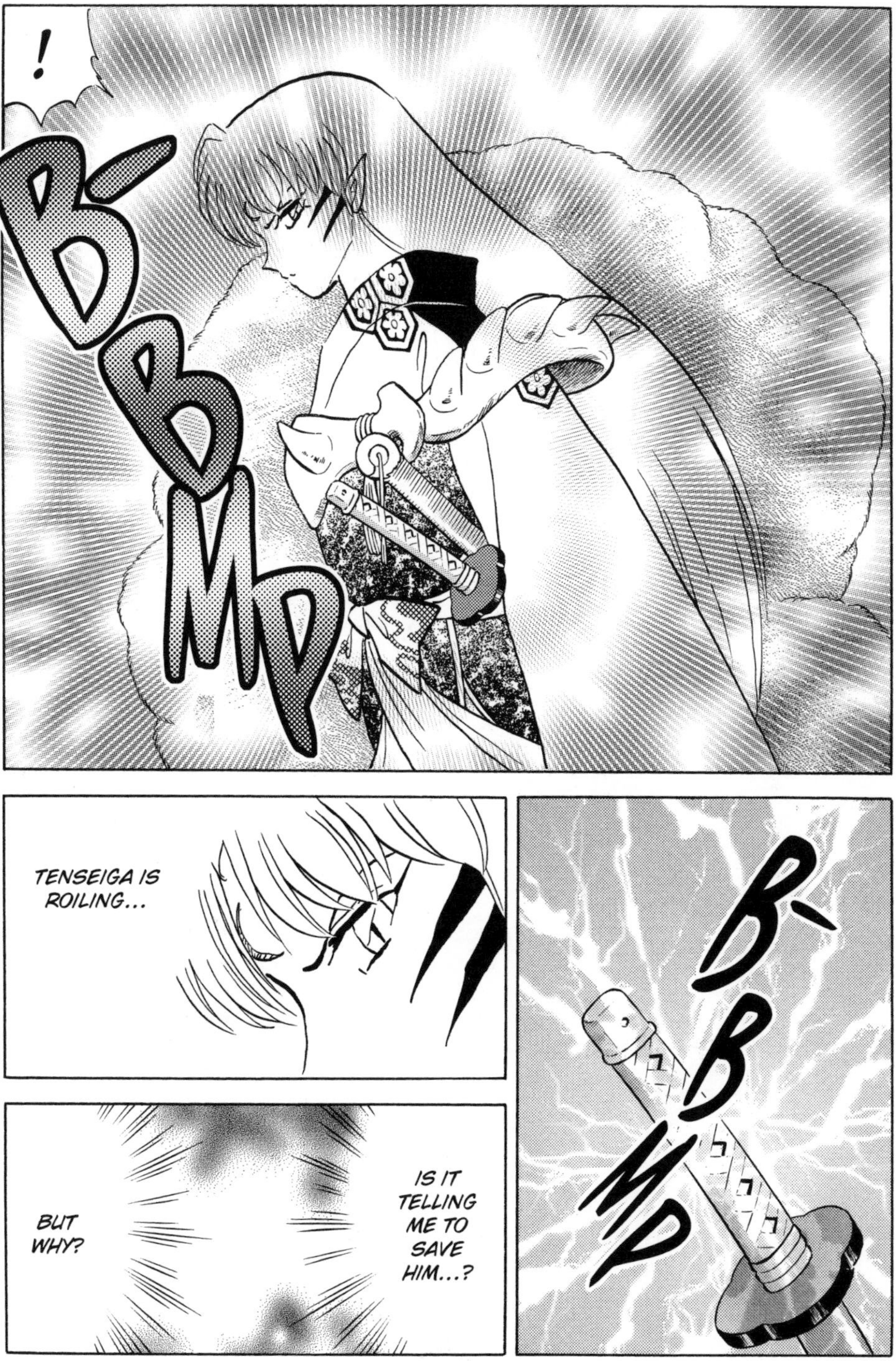
!
BBMP
BBMP
TENSEIGA IS ROILING...
IS IT TELLING ME TO SAVE HIM...?
BUT WHY?

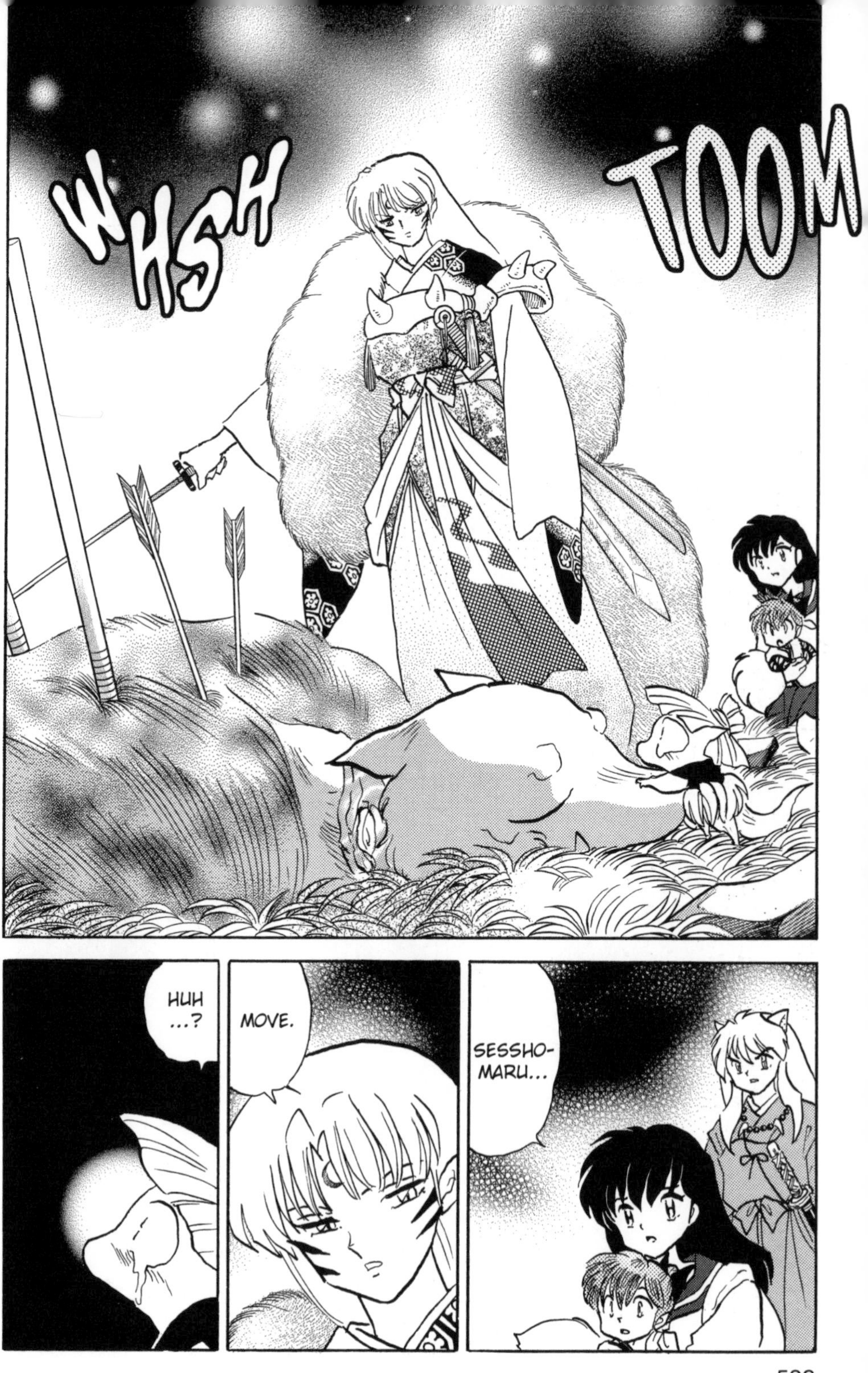
TOOM
WHSH
SESSHO-MARU...
MOVE.
HUH ...?

I CAN SEE THEM... THE MINIONS OF THE AFTERLIFE.

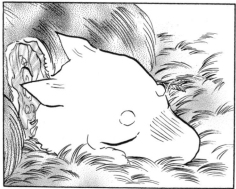

HE CUT SOMETHING ...?!

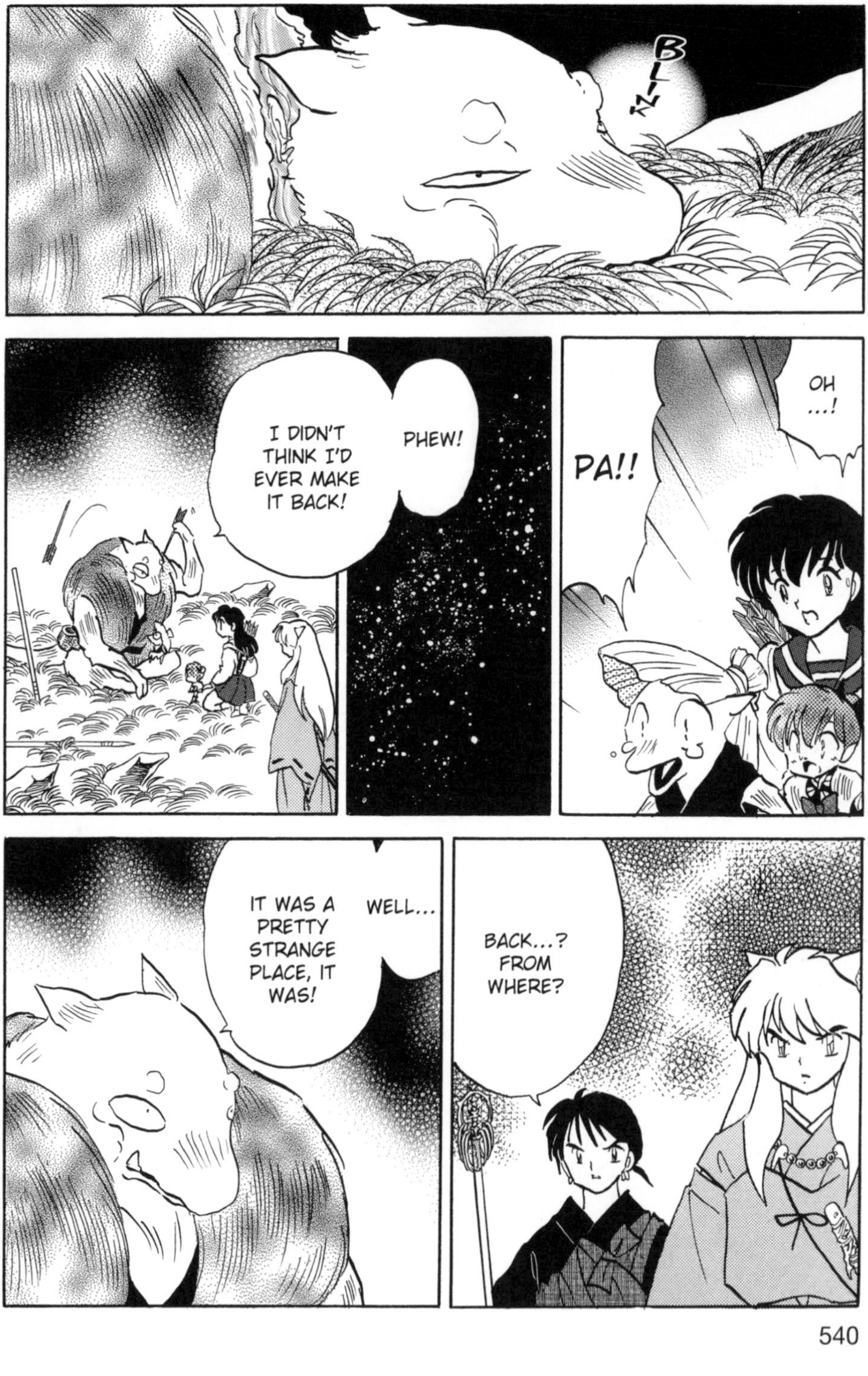
BLINK
OH ...!
PA!!
PHEW!
I DIDN'T THINK I'D EVER MAKE IT BACK!
BACK...? FROM WHERE?
WELL...
IT WAS A PRETTY STRANGE PLACE, IT WAS!

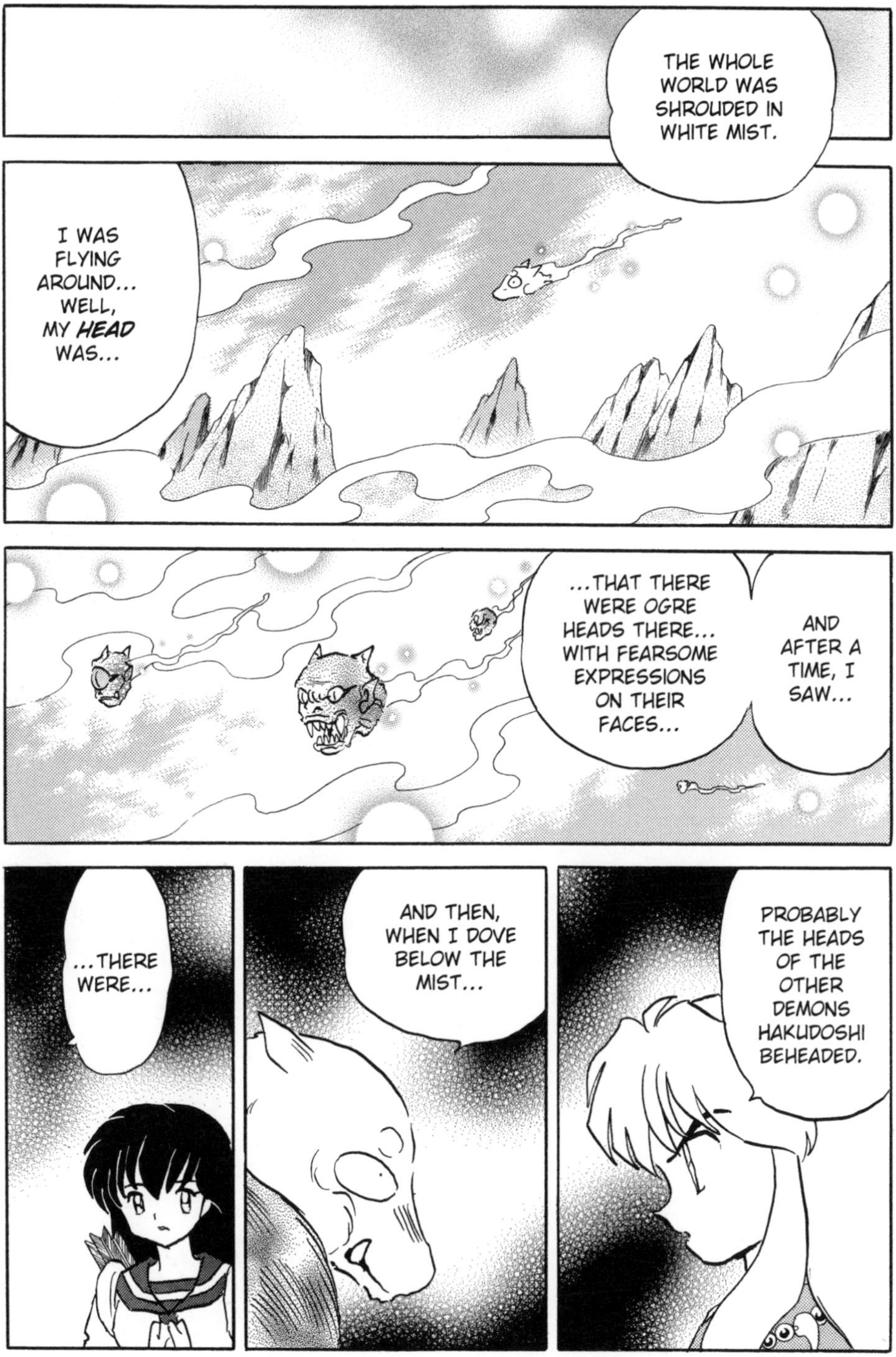
THE WHOLE WORLD WAS SHROUDED IN WHITE MIST.
I WAS FLYING AROUND... WELL, MY **HEAD** WAS...
AND AFTER A TIME, I SAW...
...THAT THERE WERE OGRE HEADS THERE... WITH FEARSOME EXPRESSIONS ON THEIR FACES...
PROBABLY THE HEADS OF THE OTHER DEMONS HAKUDOSHI BEHEADED.
AND THEN, WHEN I DOVE BELOW THE MIST...
...THERE WERE...

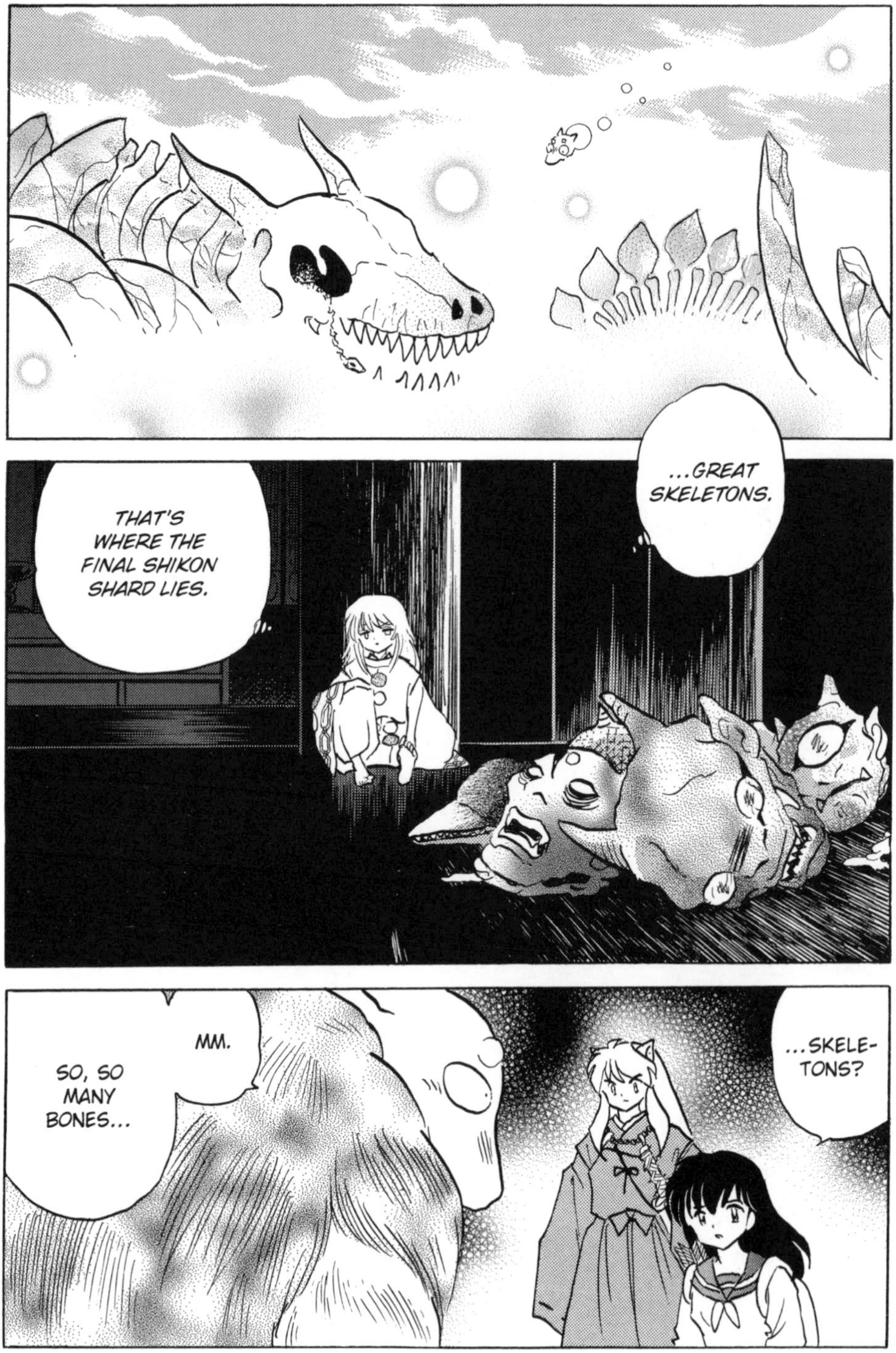
...GREAT SKELETONS.
THAT'S WHERE THE FINAL SHIKON SHARD LIES.
...SKELE- TONS?
MM.
SO, SO MANY BONES...

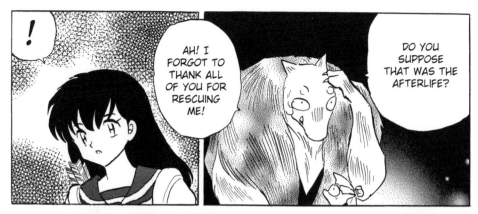

DO YOU SUPPOSE THAT WAS THE AFTERLIFE?
!
AH! I FORGOT TO THANK ALL OF YOU FOR RESCUING ME!
OH...
THANK YOU, SESSHO...
HM ...?
HE JUST LEFT.
WHAT IS TENSEIGA...
...TRYING TO TELL ME...?

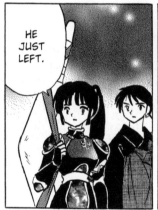

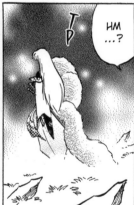

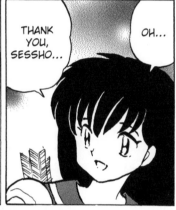

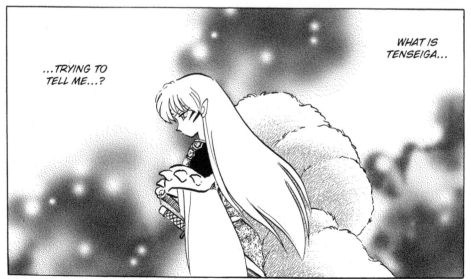

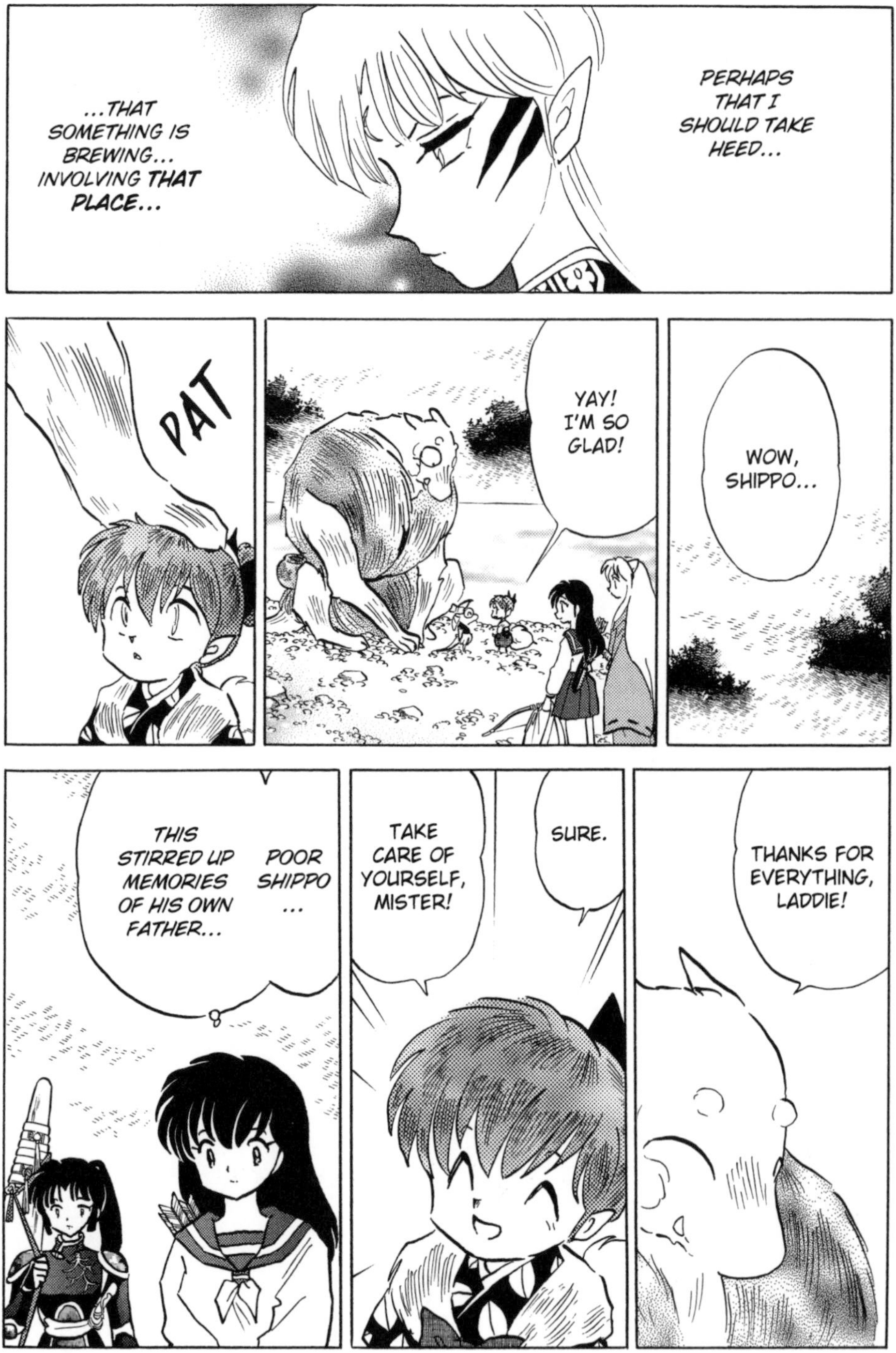
PERHAPS THAT I SHOULD TAKE HEED...
...THAT SOMETHING IS BREWING... INVOLVING THAT PLACE...
WOW, SHIPPO...
YAY! I'M SO GLAD!
PAT
THANKS FOR EVERYTHING, LADDIE!
SURE.
TAKE CARE OF YOURSELF, MISTER!
POOR SHIPPO...
THIS STIRRED UP MEMORIES OF HIS OWN FATHER...

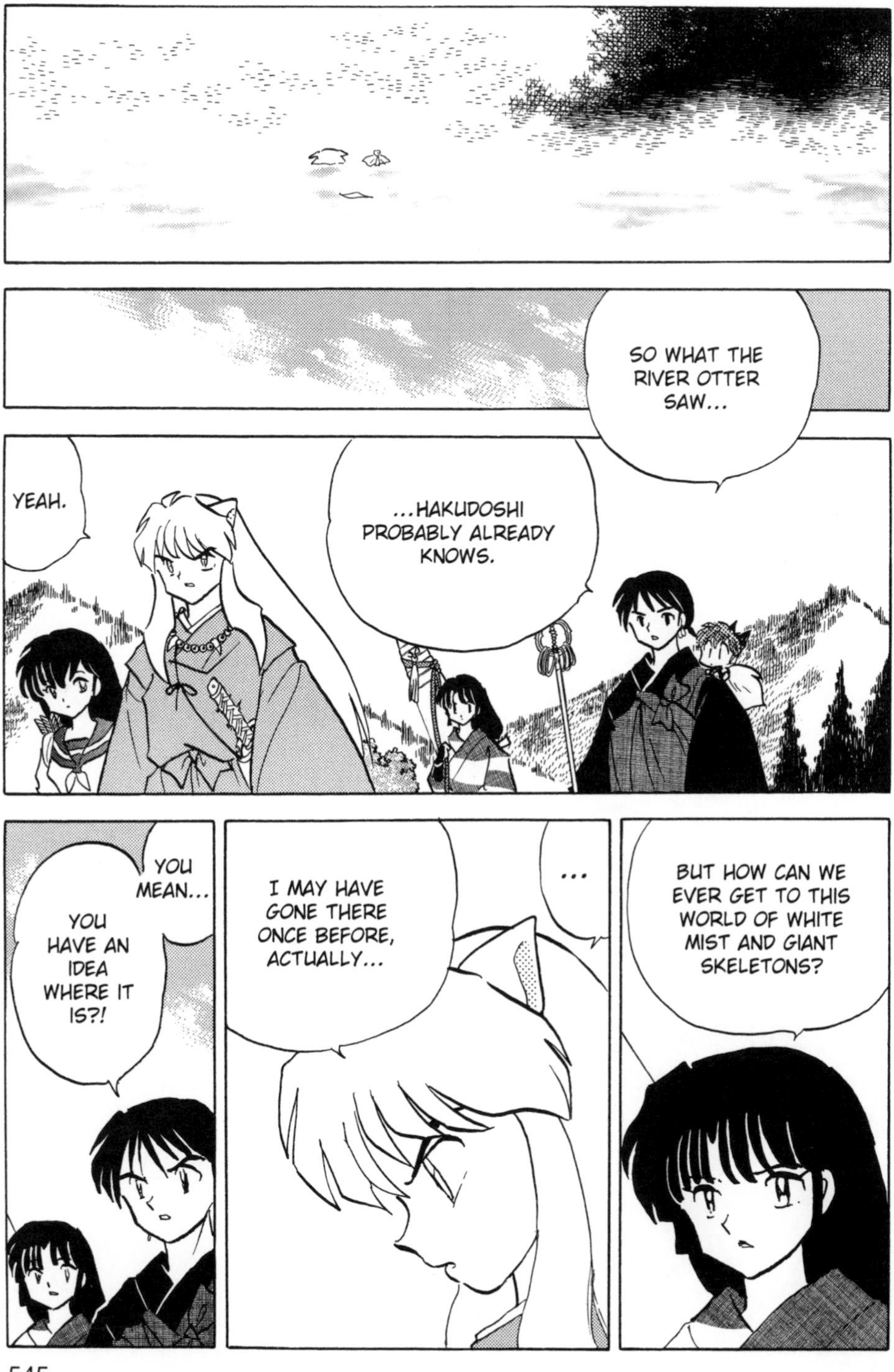
SO WHAT THE RIVER OTTER SAW...
...HAKUDOSHI PROBABLY ALREADY KNOWS.
YEAH.
BUT HOW CAN WE EVER GET TO THIS WORLD OF WHITE MIST AND GIANT SKELETONS?
...
I MAY HAVE GONE THERE ONCE BEFORE, ACTUALLY...
YOU MEAN...
YOU HAVE AN IDEA WHERE IT IS?!

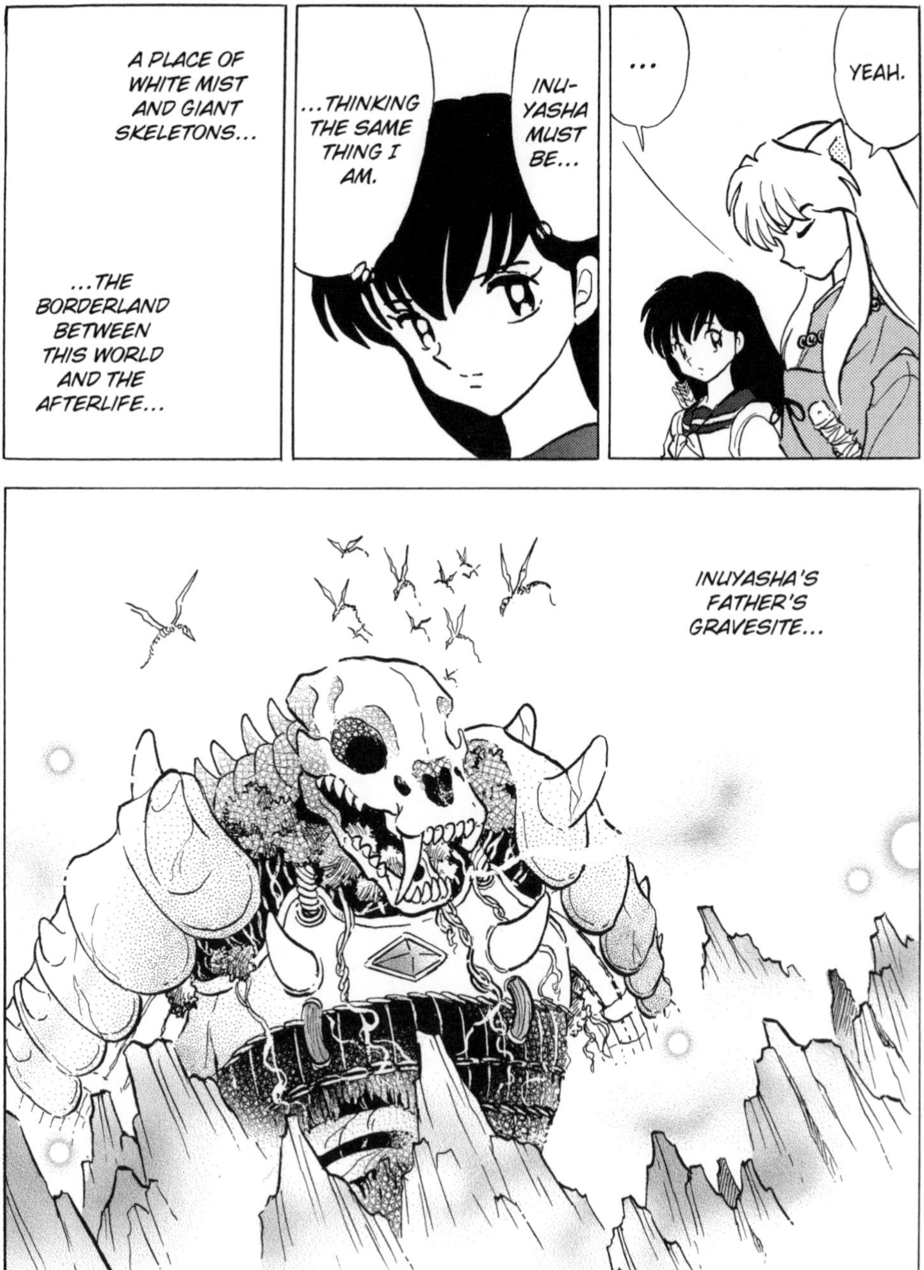
YEAH.
...
INU-YASHA MUST BE...
...THINKING THE SAME THING I AM.
A PLACE OF WHITE MIST AND GIANT SKELETONS...
...THE BORDERLAND BETWEEN THIS WORLD AND THE AFTERLIFE...
INUYASHA'S FATHER'S GRAVESITE...

SCROLL TEN
HOSENKI

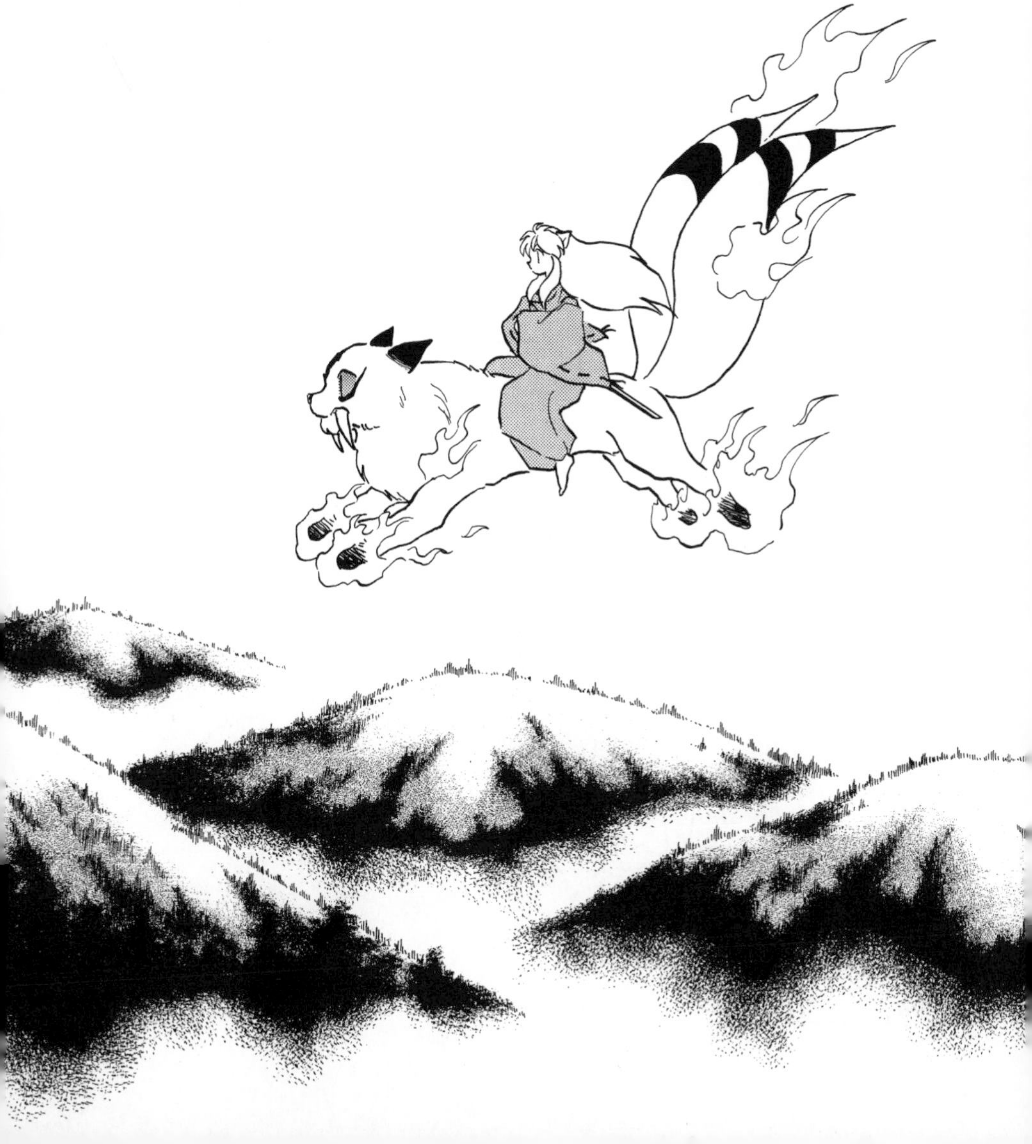

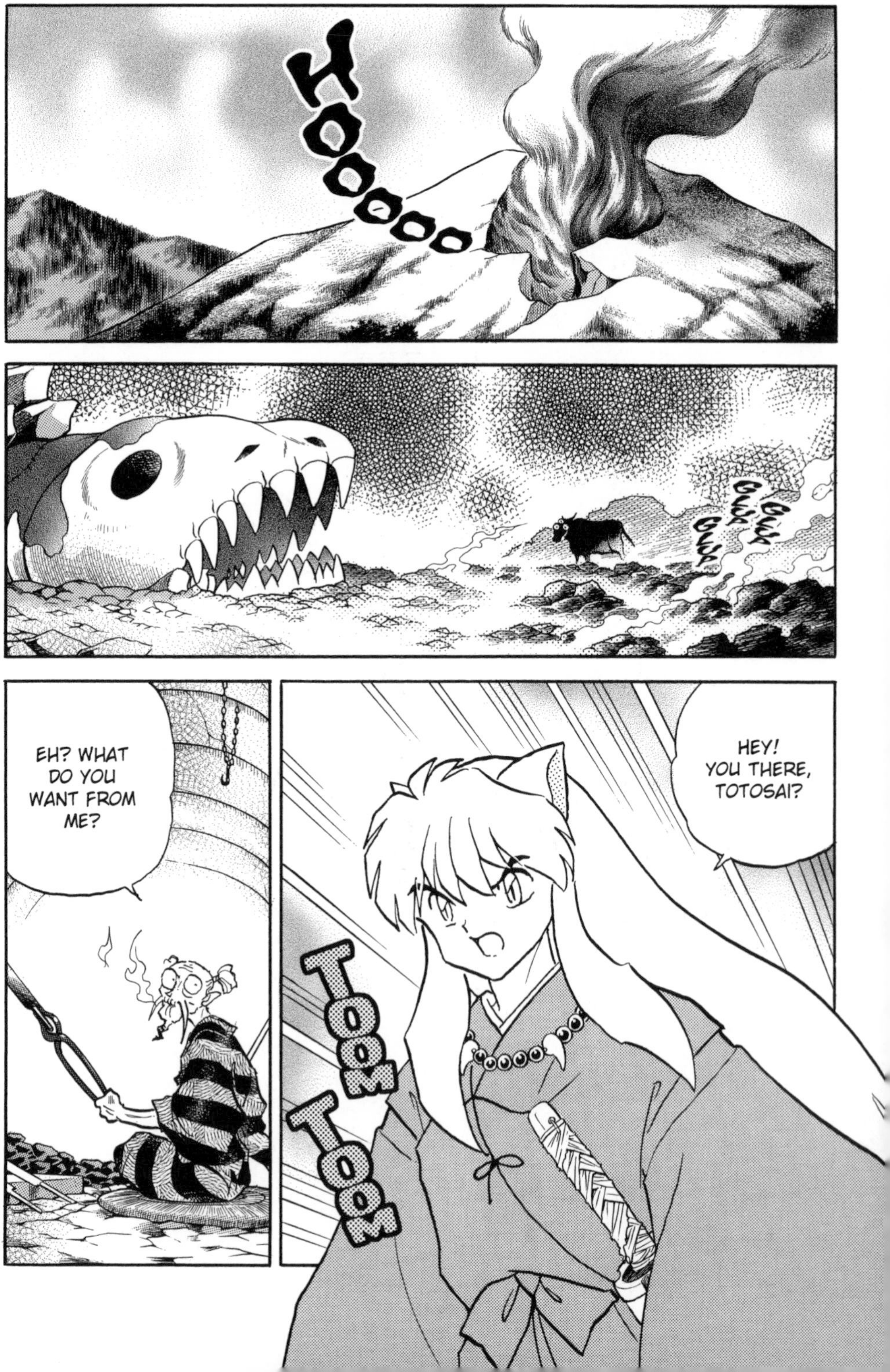
HOOOOOO
GUSH GUSH GUSH
HEY! YOU THERE, TOTOSAI?
TOOM TOOM
EH? WHAT DO YOU WANT FROM ME?

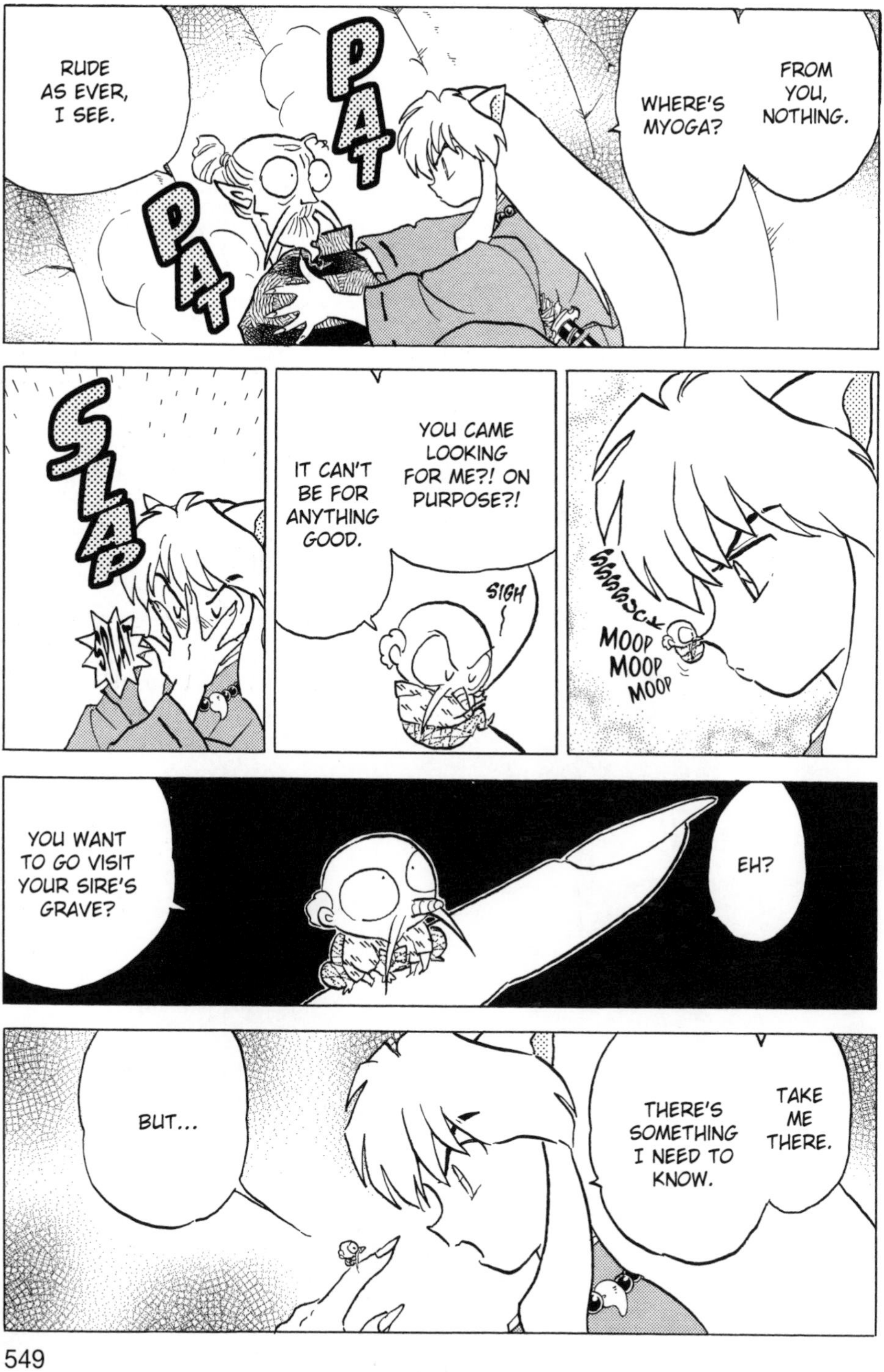
FROM YOU, NOTHING.
WHERE'S MYOGA?
PAT
PAT
RUDE AS EVER, I SEE.
MOOP MOOP MOOP
YOU CAME LOOKING FOR ME?! ON PURPOSE?!
IT CAN'T BE FOR ANYTHING GOOD.
SIGH
SLAP
SPLAT
EH?
YOU WANT TO GO VISIT YOUR SIRE'S GRAVE?
TAKE ME THERE.
THERE'S SOMETHING I NEED TO KNOW.
BUT...

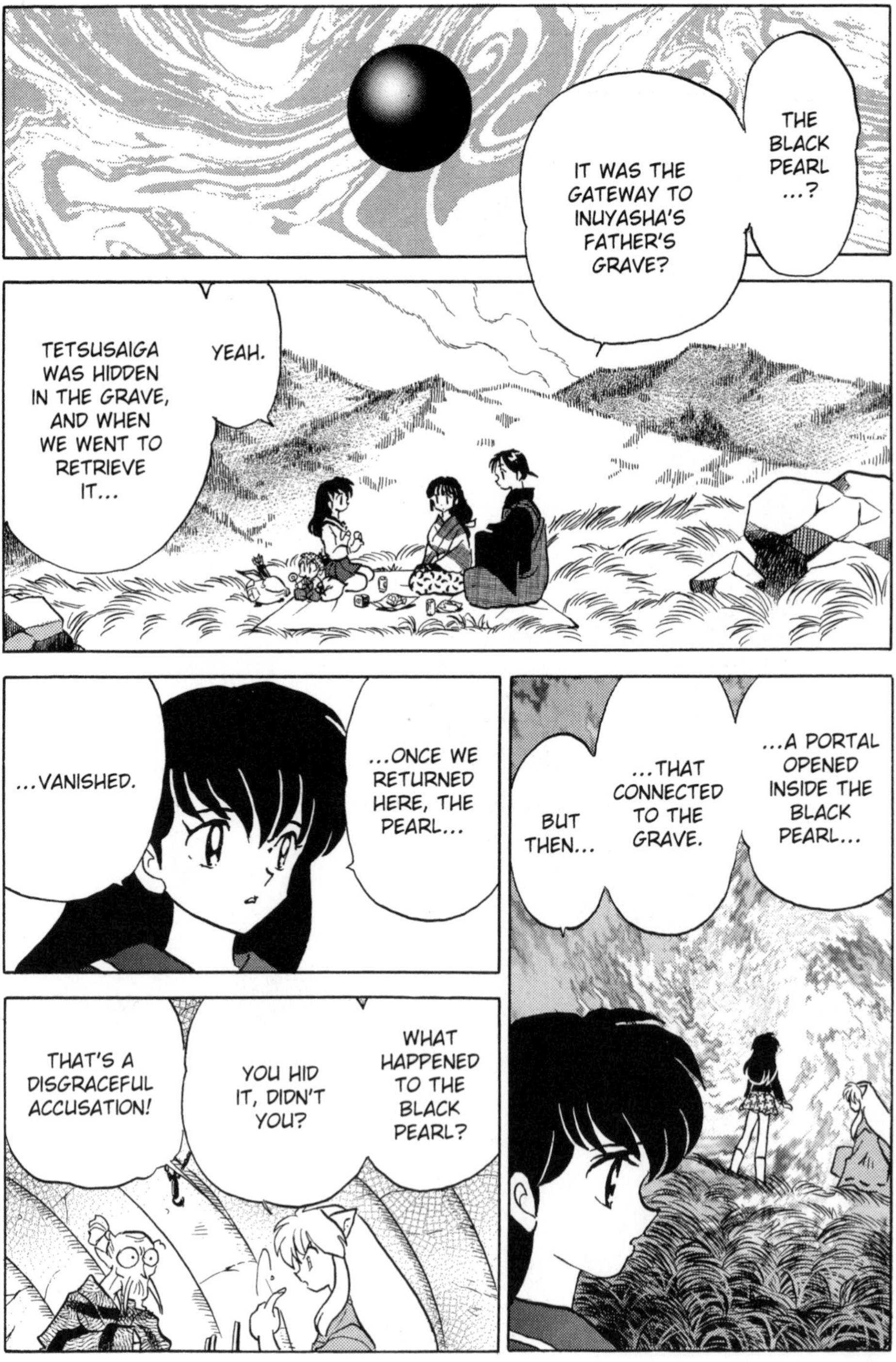
THE BLACK PEARL ...?
IT WAS THE GATEWAY TO INUYASHA'S FATHER'S GRAVE?
YEAH.
TETSUSAIGA WAS HIDDEN IN THE GRAVE, AND WHEN WE WENT TO RETRIEVE IT...
...A PORTAL OPENED INSIDE THE BLACK PEARL...
...THAT CONNECTED TO THE GRAVE.
BUT THEN...
...ONCE WE RETURNED HERE, THE PEARL...
...VANISHED.
WHAT HAPPENED TO THE BLACK PEARL?
YOU HID IT, DIDN'T YOU?
THAT'S A DISGRACEFUL ACCUSATION!

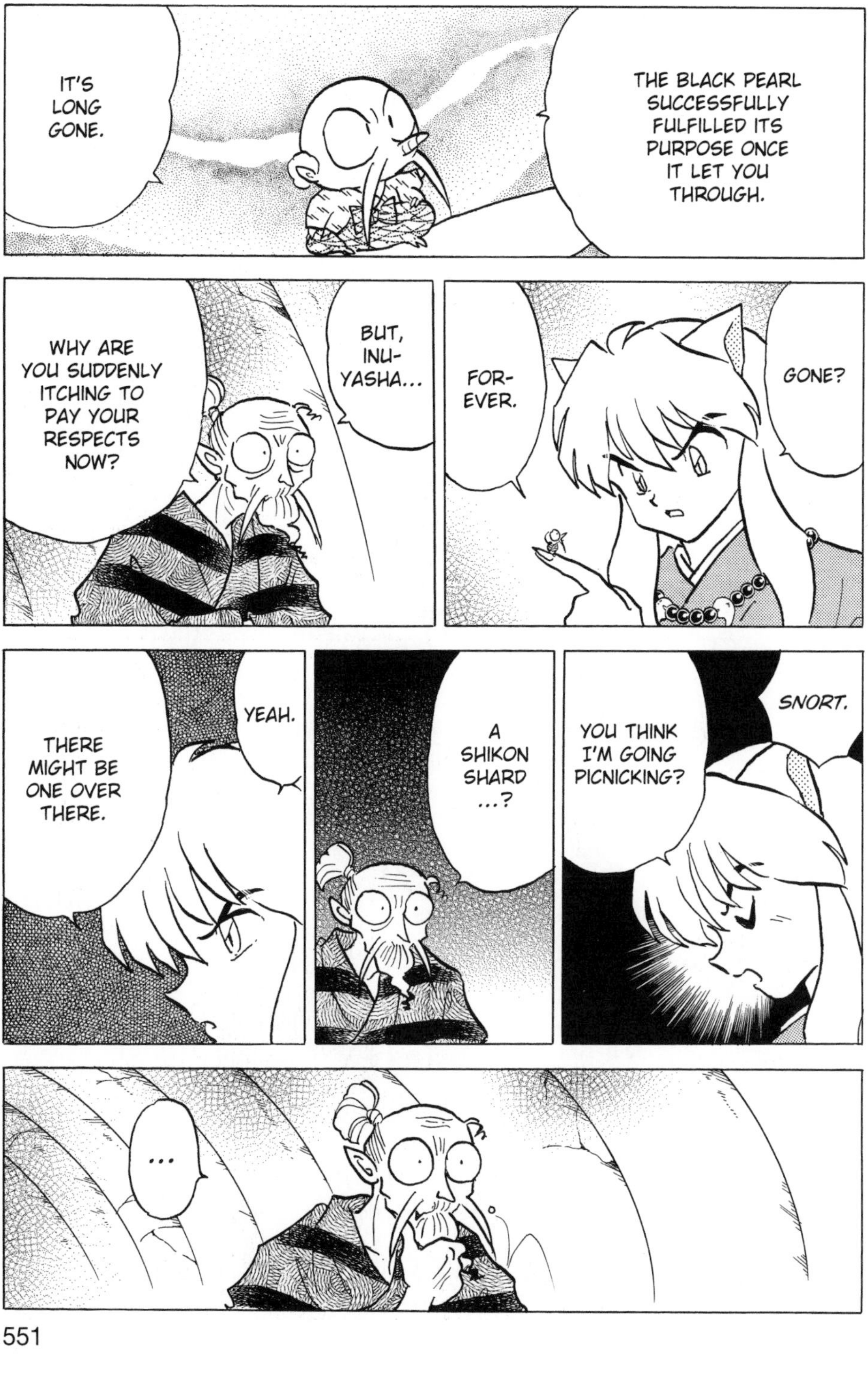
THE BLACK PEARL SUCCESSFULLY FULFILLED ITS PURPOSE ONCE IT LET YOU THROUGH.
IT'S LONG GONE.
GONE?
FOR-EVER.
BUT, INU-YASHA...
WHY ARE YOU SUDDENLY ITCHING TO PAY YOUR RESPECTS NOW?
SNORT.
YOU THINK I'M GOING PICNICKING?
A SHIKON SHARD ...?
YEAH.
THERE MIGHT BE ONE OVER THERE.
...

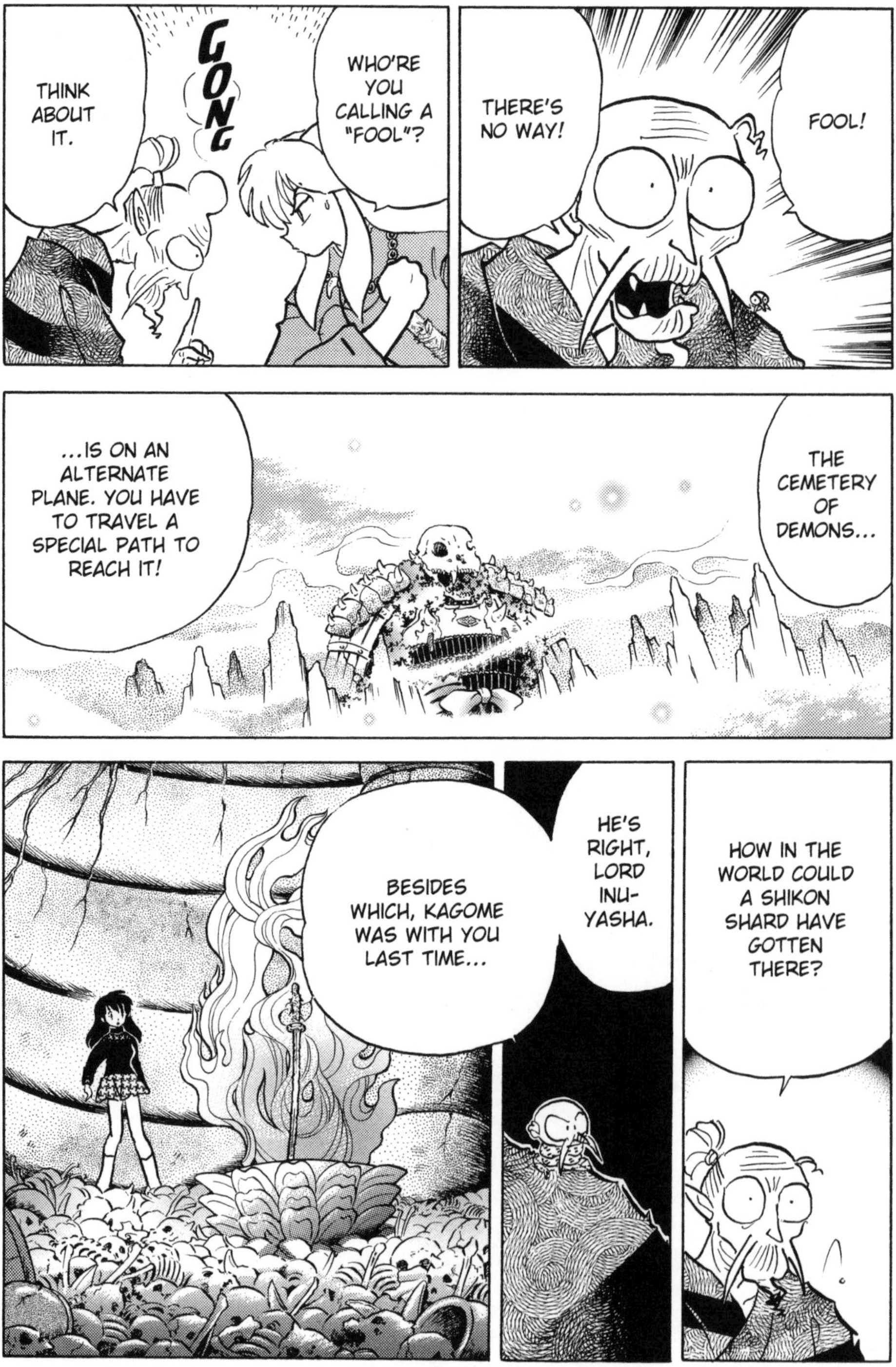
FOOL!
THERE'S NO WAY!
WHO'RE YOU CALLING A "FOOL"?
GONG
THINK ABOUT IT.
THE CEMETERY OF DEMONS...
...IS ON AN ALTERNATE PLANE. YOU HAVE TO TRAVEL A SPECIAL PATH TO REACH IT!
HOW IN THE WORLD COULD A SHIKON SHARD HAVE GOTTEN THERE?
HE'S RIGHT, LORD INU-YASHA.
BESIDES WHICH, KAGOME WAS WITH YOU LAST TIME...

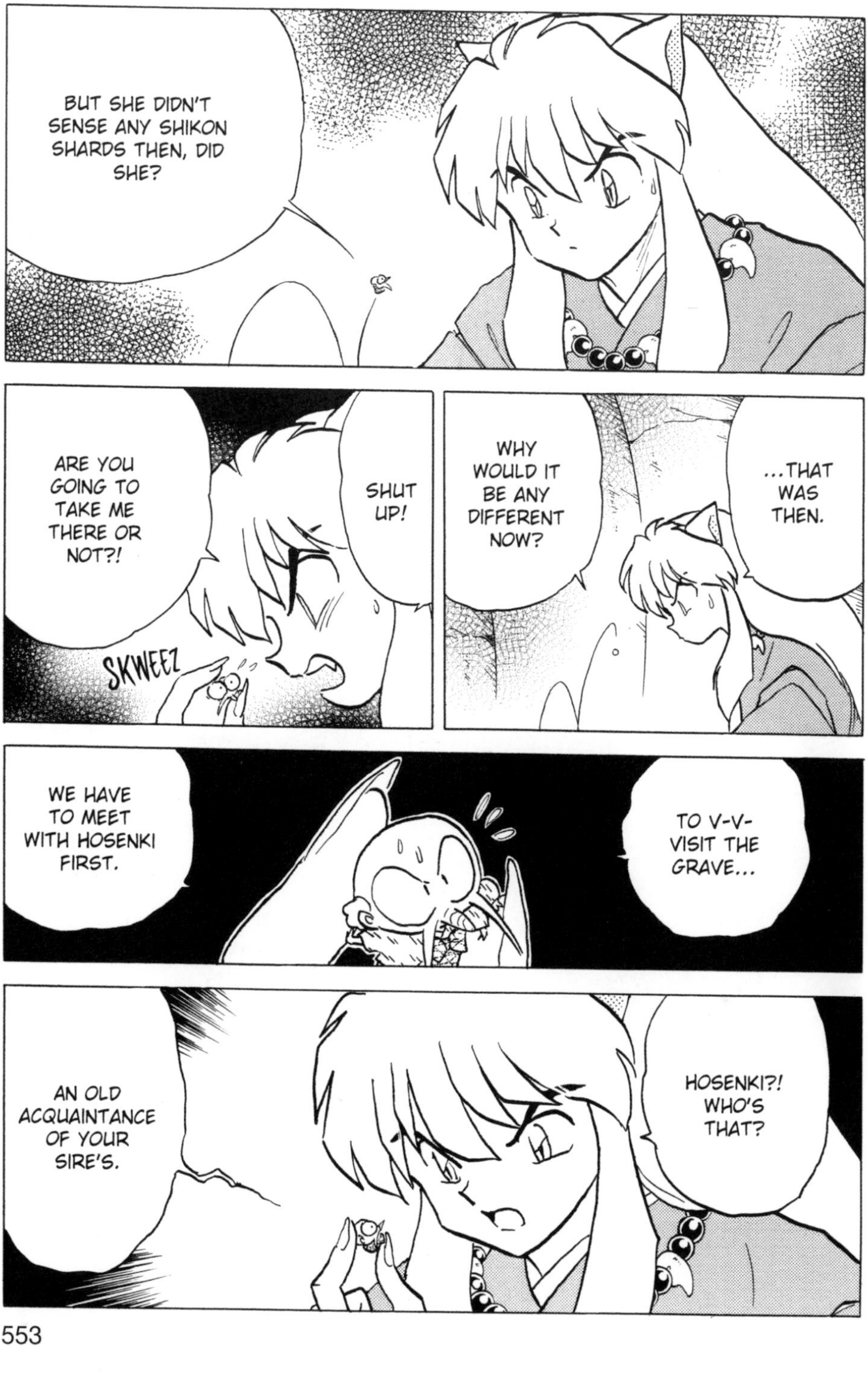
BUT SHE DIDN'T SENSE ANY SHIKON SHARDS THEN, DID SHE?
...THAT WAS THEN.
WHY WOULD IT BE ANY DIFFERENT NOW?
SHUT UP!
ARE YOU GOING TO TAKE ME THERE OR NOT?!
SKWEEZ
TO V-V-VISIT THE GRAVE...
WE HAVE TO MEET WITH HOSENKI FIRST.
HOSENKI?! WHO'S THAT?
AN OLD ACQUAINTANCE OF YOUR SIRE'S.

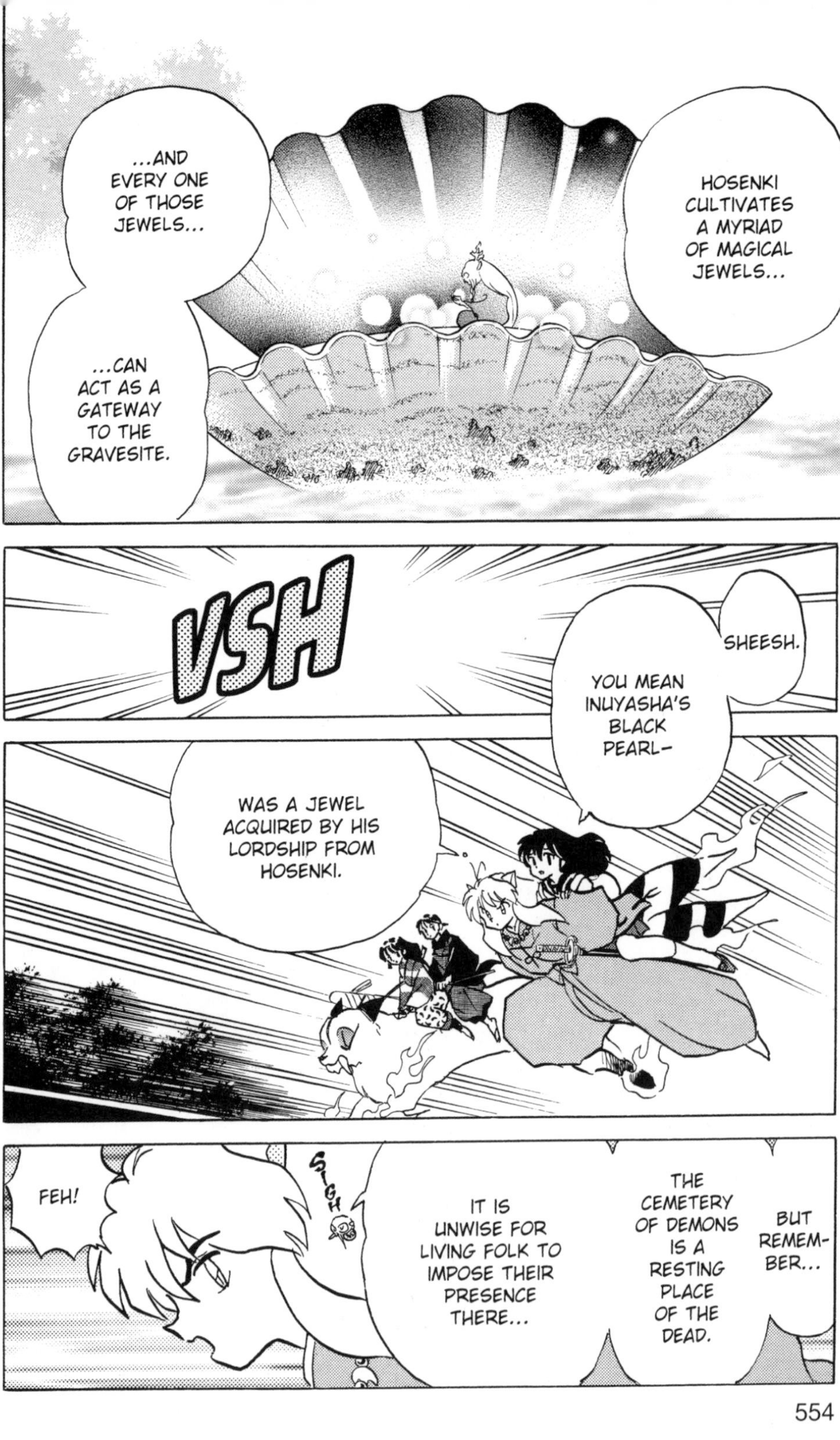
HOSENKI CULTIVATES A MYRIAD OF MAGICAL JEWELS...
...AND EVERY ONE OF THOSE JEWELS...
...CAN ACT AS A GATEWAY TO THE GRAVESITE.
VSH
SHEESH.
YOU MEAN INUYASHA'S BLACK PEARL—
WAS A JEWEL ACQUIRED BY HIS LORDSHIP FROM HOSENKI.
BUT REMEMBER...
THE CEMETERY OF DEMONS IS A RESTING PLACE OF THE DEAD.
IT IS UNWISE FOR LIVING FOLK TO IMPOSE THEIR PRESENCE THERE...
SIGH
FEH!

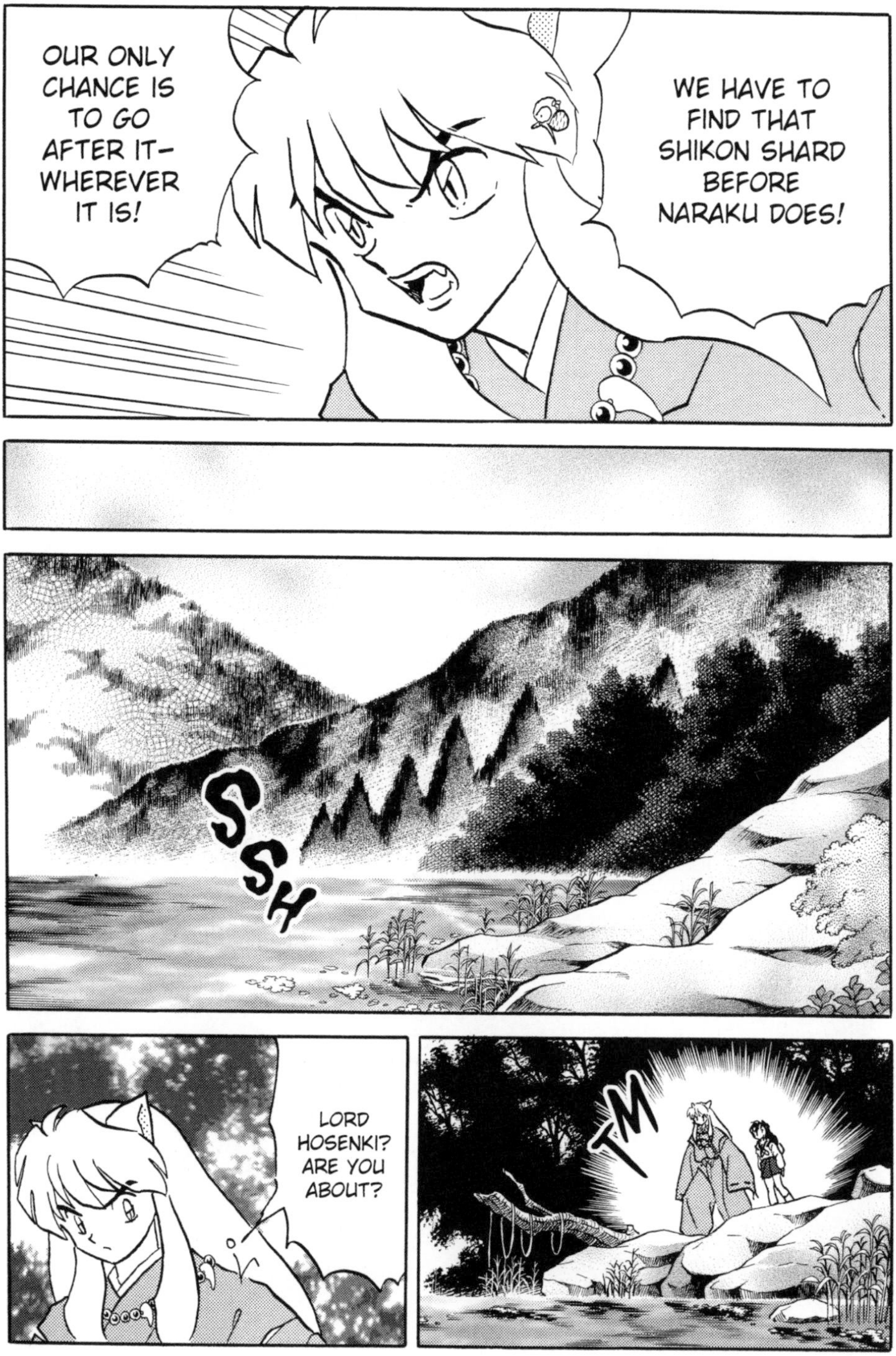
WE HAVE TO FIND THAT SHIKON SHARD BEFORE NARAKU DOES!
OUR ONLY CHANCE IS TO GO AFTER IT- WHEREVER IT IS!
SSSH
TM
LORD HOSENKI? ARE YOU ABOUT?

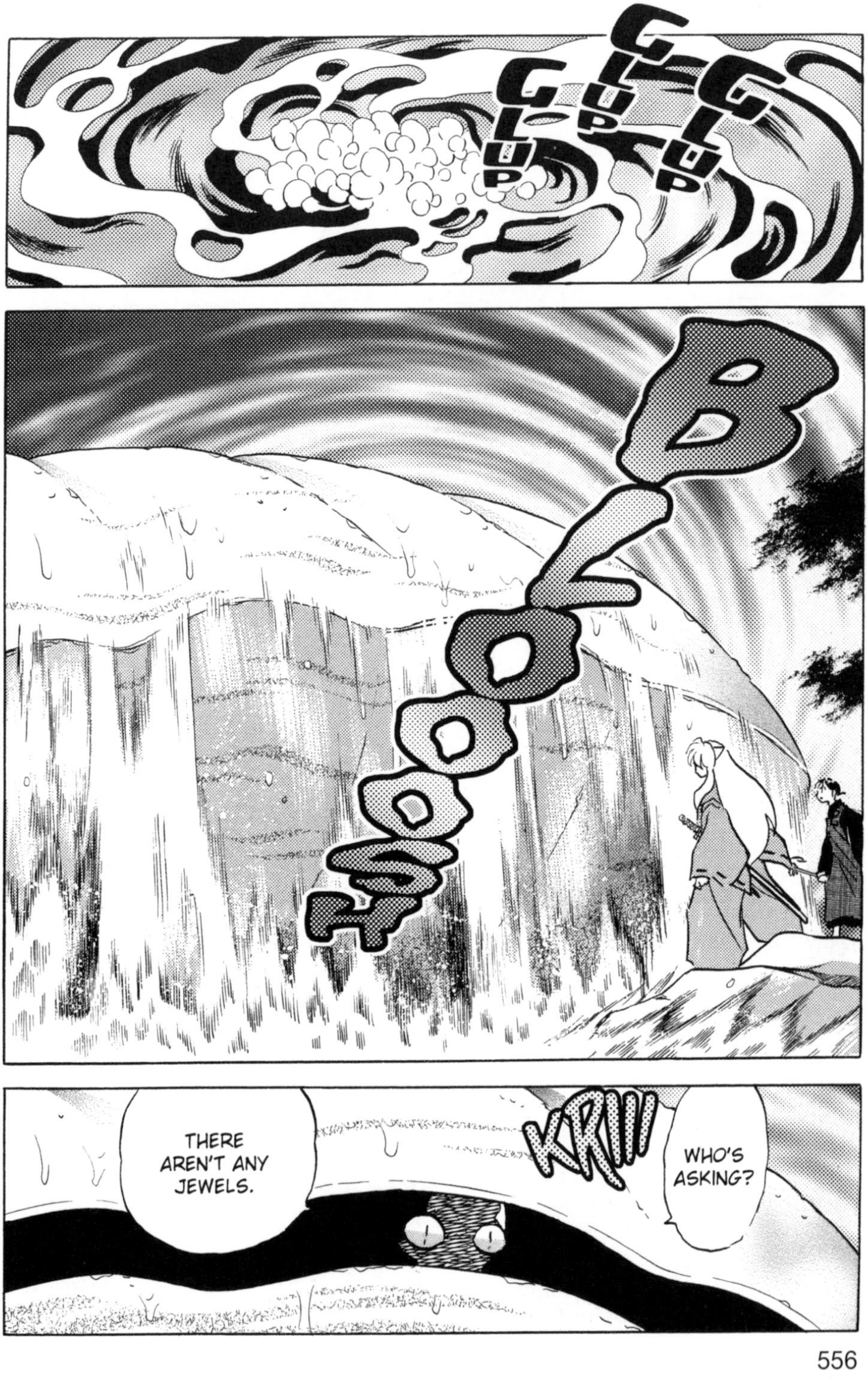
GLUP
GLUP
GLUP
BLOOOSH
WHO'S ASKING?
KRIII
THERE AREN'T ANY JEWELS.

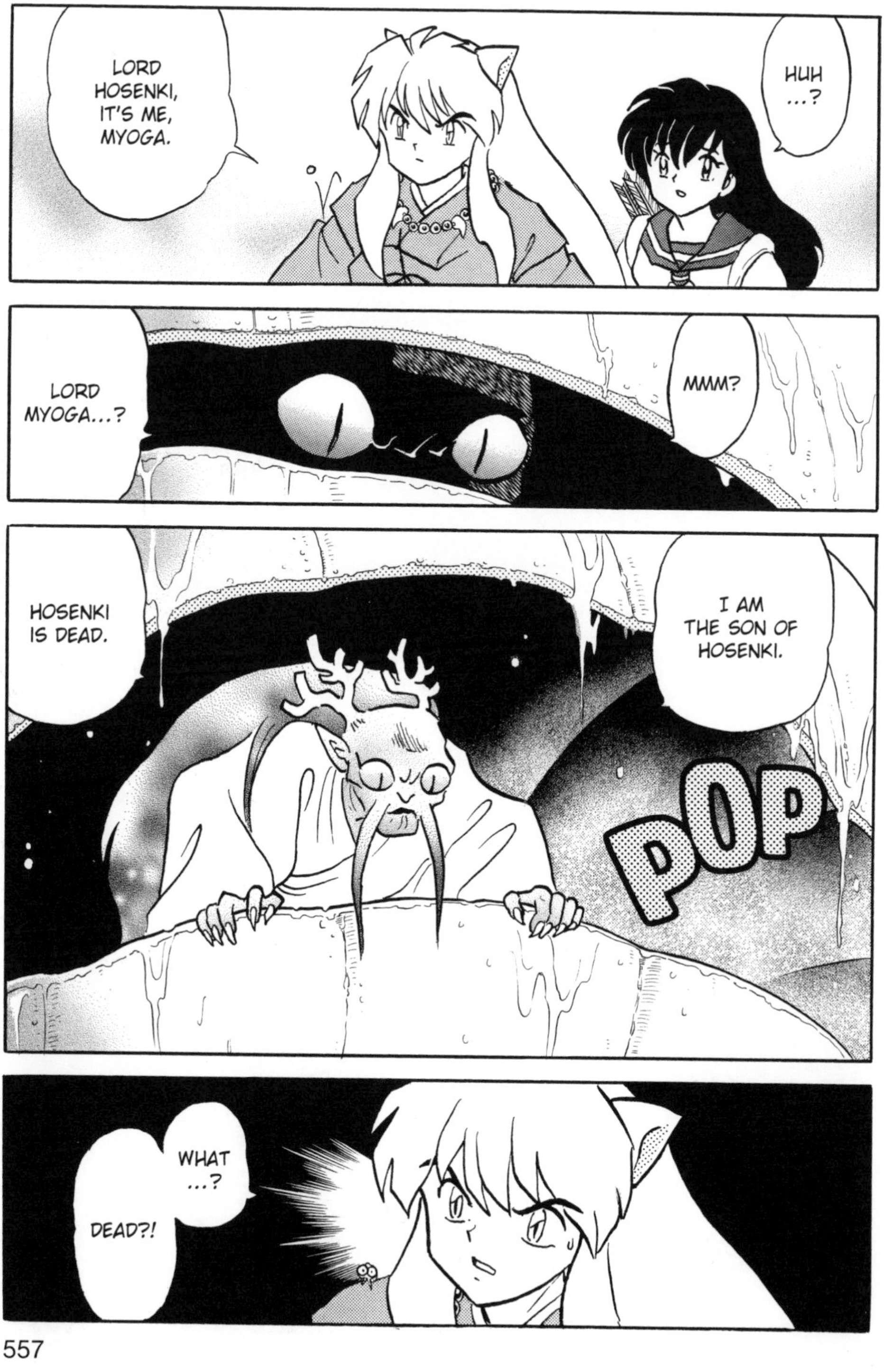
HUH ...?
LORD HOSENKI, IT'S ME, MYOGA.
MMM?
LORD MYOGA...?
I AM THE SON OF HOSENKI.
POP
HOSENKI IS DEAD.
WHAT ...?
DEAD?!

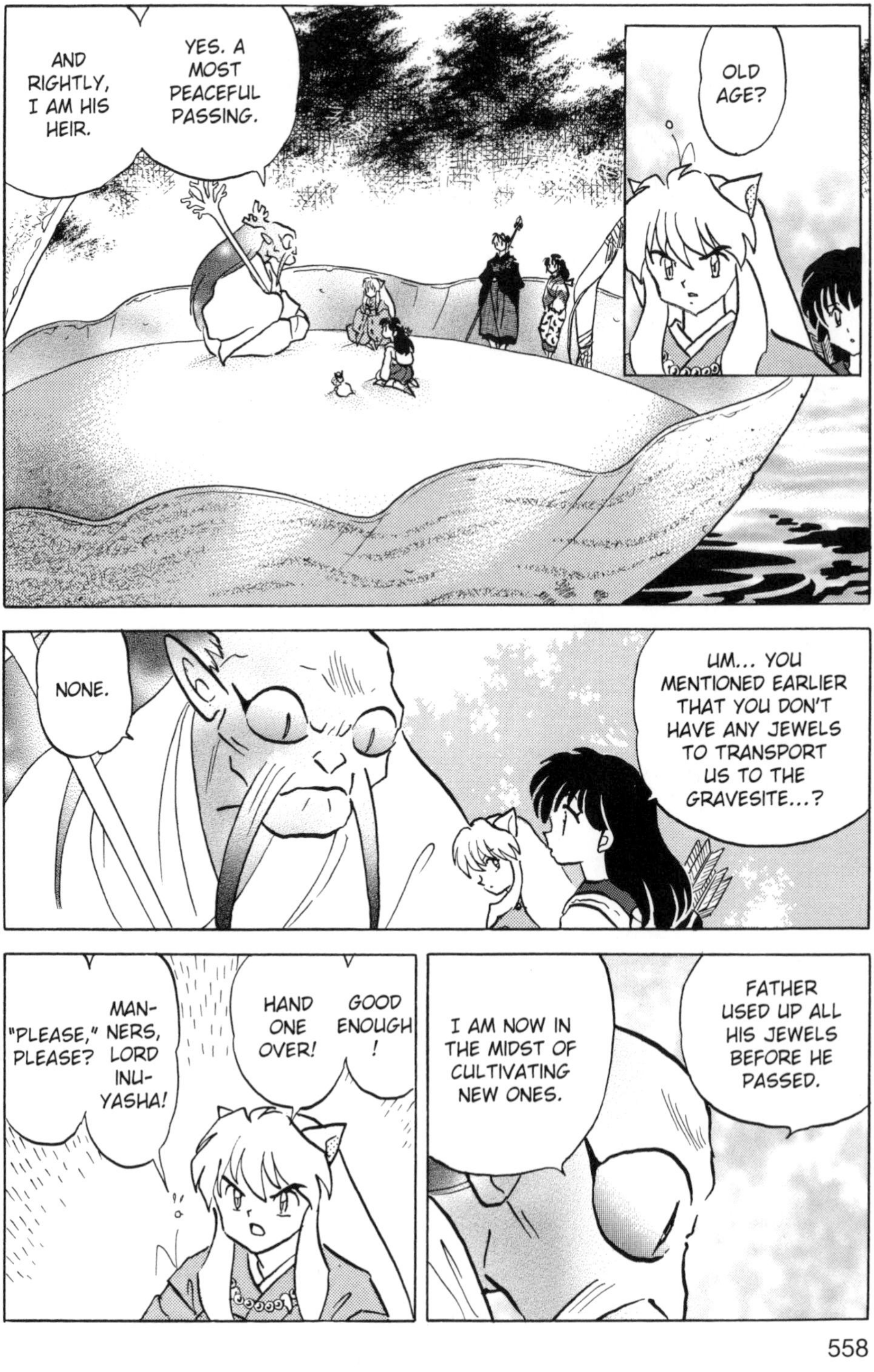
OLD AGE?
YES. A MOST PEACEFUL PASSING.
AND RIGHTLY, I AM HIS HEIR.
UM... YOU MENTIONED EARLIER THAT YOU DON'T HAVE ANY JEWELS TO TRANSPORT US TO THE GRAVESITE...?
NONE.
FATHER USED UP ALL HIS JEWELS BEFORE HE PASSED.
I AM NOW IN THE MIDST OF CULTIVATING NEW ONES.
GOOD ENOUGH!
HAND ONE OVER!
MAN-NERS, LORD INU-YASHA!
"PLEASE," PLEASE?

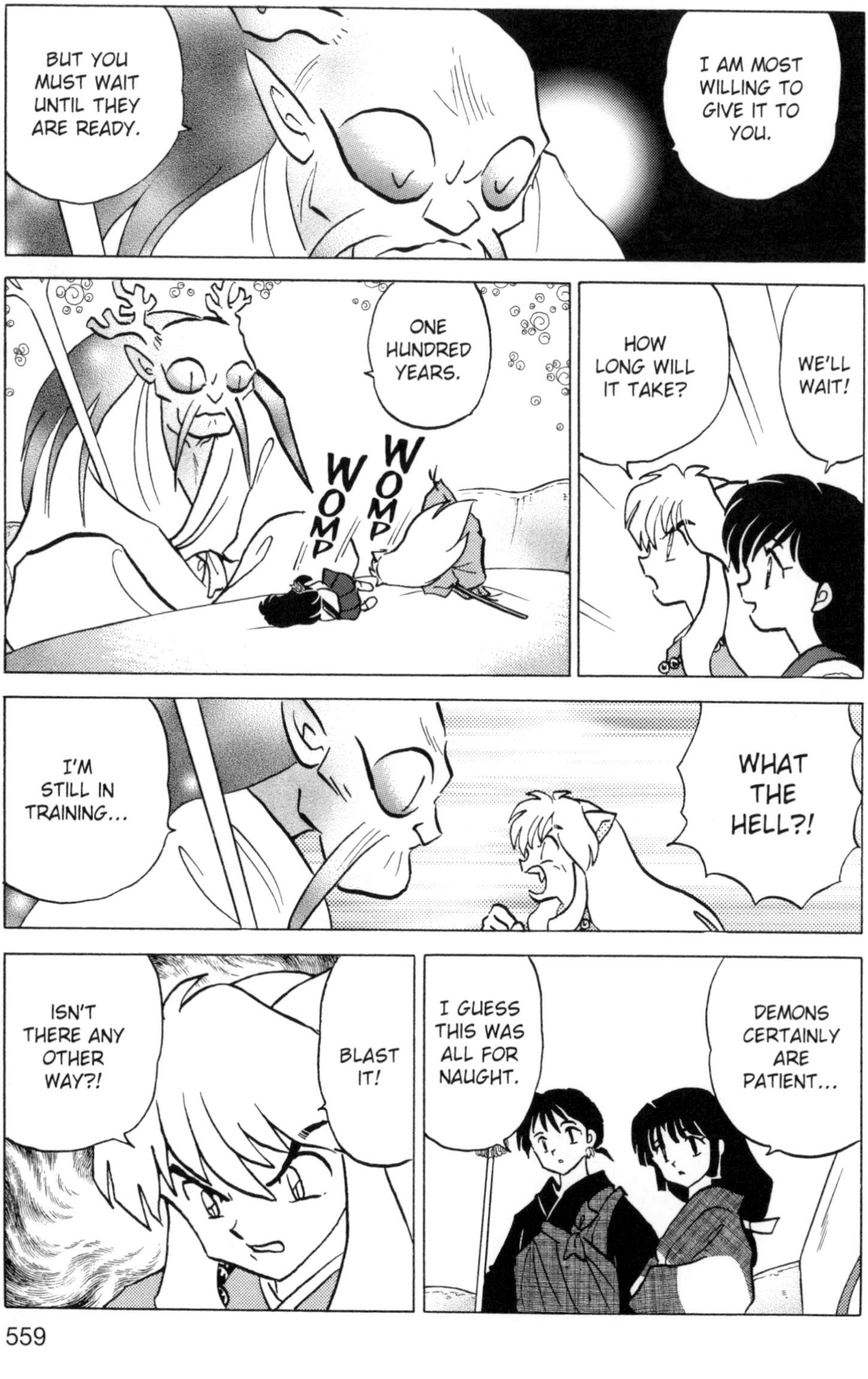
I AM MOST WILLING TO GIVE IT TO YOU.
BUT YOU MUST WAIT UNTIL THEY ARE READY.
WE'LL WAIT!
HOW LONG WILL IT TAKE?
ONE HUNDRED YEARS.
WOMP
WOMP
WHAT THE HELL?!
I'M STILL IN TRAINING...
DEMONS CERTAINLY ARE PATIENT...
I GUESS THIS WAS ALL FOR NAUGHT.
BLAST IT!
ISN'T THERE ANY OTHER WAY?!

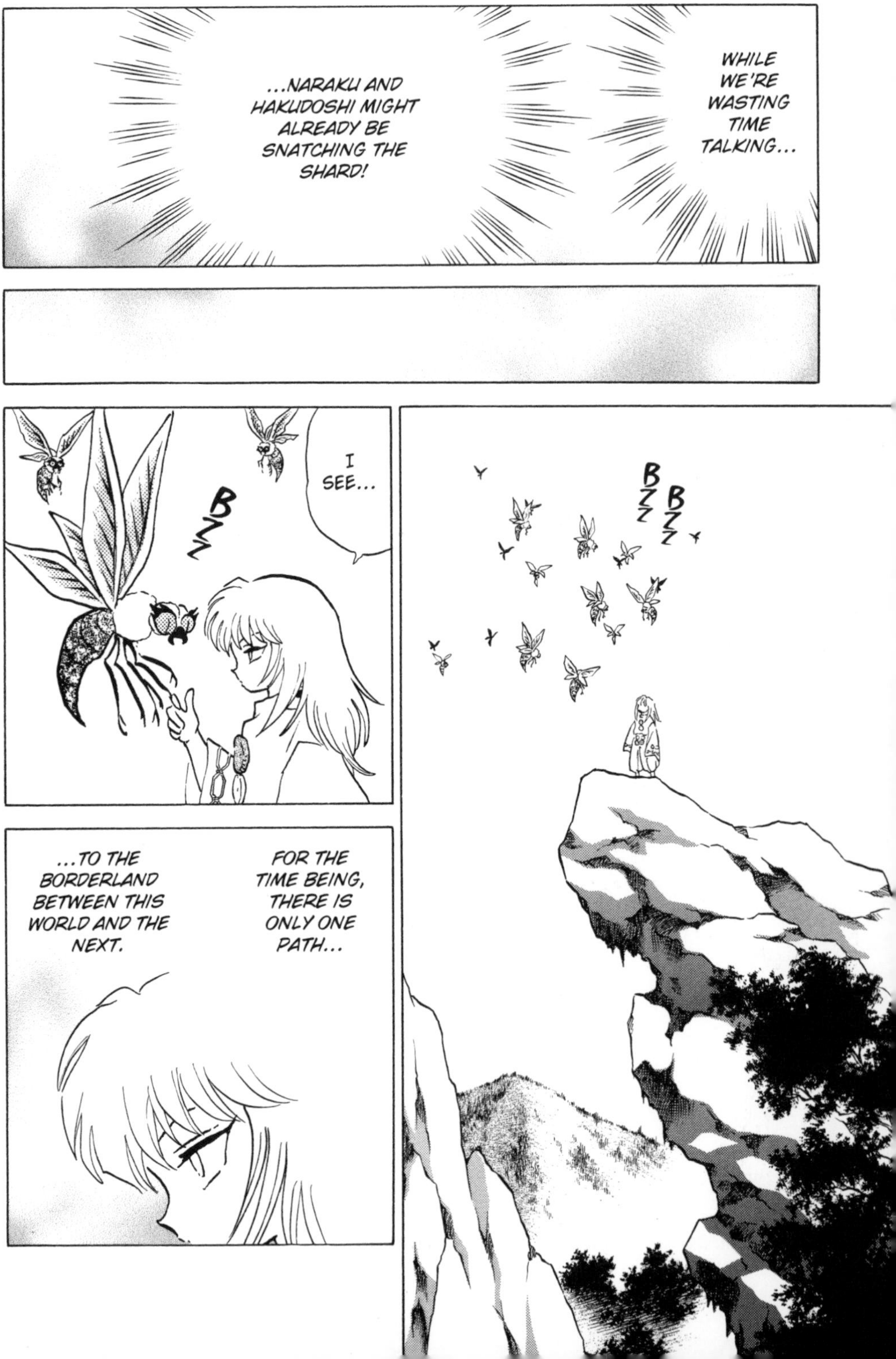
WHILE WE'RE WASTING TIME TALKING...
...NARAKU AND HAKUDOSHI MIGHT ALREADY BE SNATCHING THE SHARD!
BZZ BZZ
I SEE...
BZZ
FOR THE TIME BEING, THERE IS ONLY ONE PATH...
...TO THE BORDERLAND BETWEEN THIS WORLD AND THE NEXT.

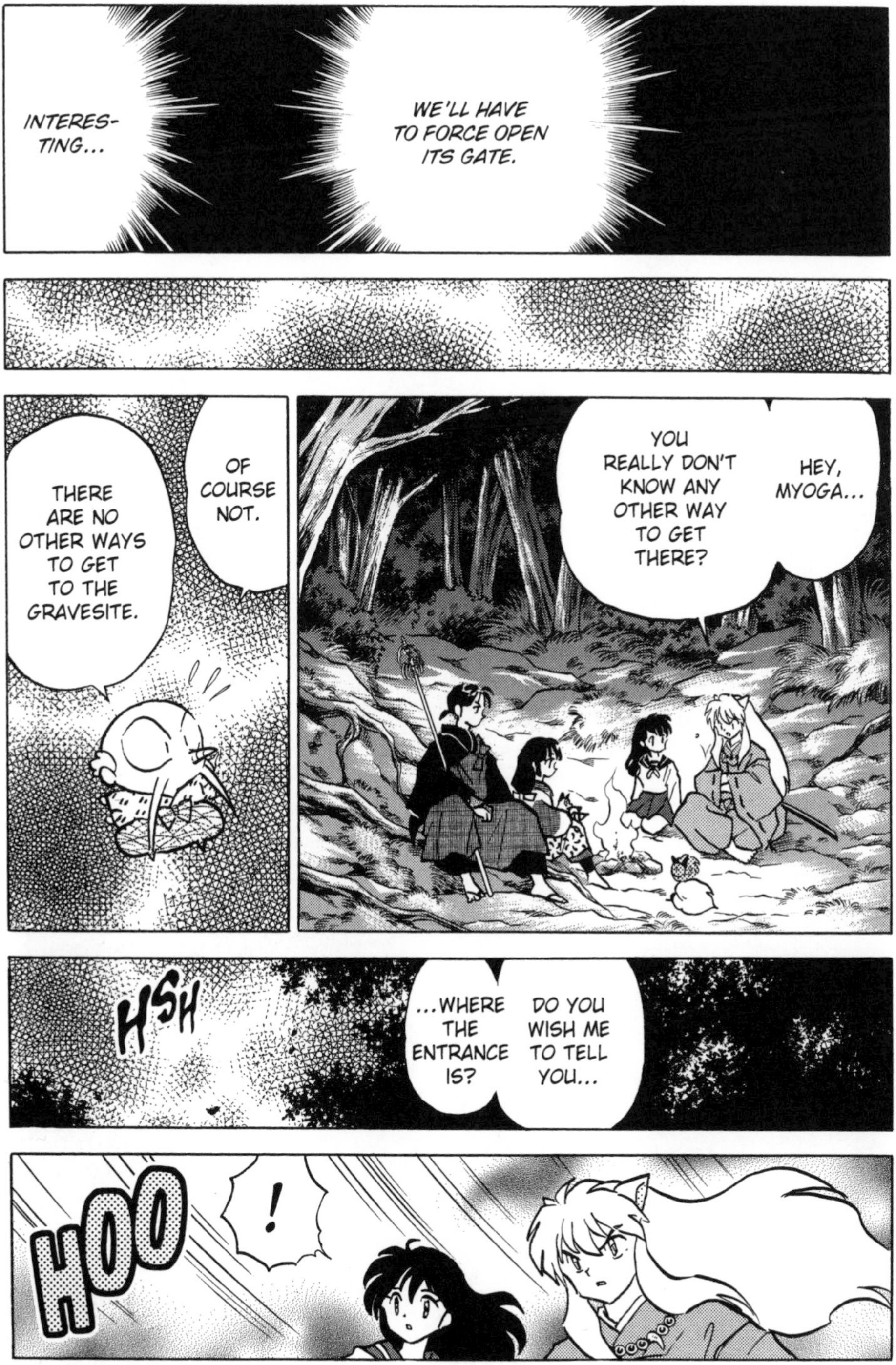
WE'LL HAVE TO FORCE OPEN ITS GATE.
INTERES-TING...
HEY, MYOGA...
YOU REALLY DON'T KNOW ANY OTHER WAY TO GET THERE?
OF COURSE NOT.
THERE ARE NO OTHER WAYS TO GET TO THE GRAVESITE.
DO YOU WISH ME TO TELL YOU...
...WHERE THE ENTRANCE IS?
HSH
!
HOO

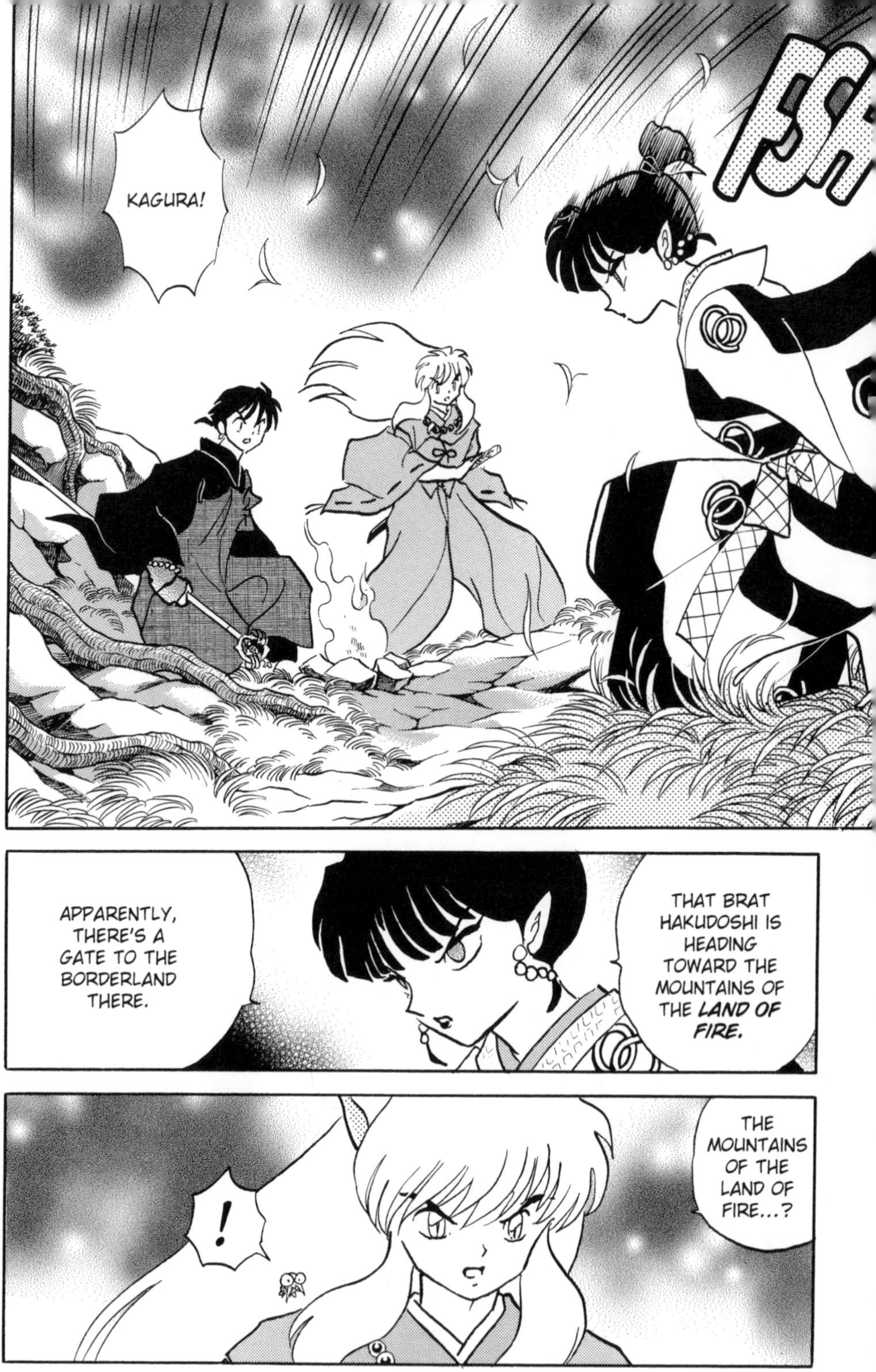
FSH
KAGURA!
THAT BRAT HAKUDOSHI IS HEADING TOWARD THE MOUNTAINS OF THE ***LAND OF FIRE.***
APPARENTLY, THERE'S A GATE TO THE BORDERLAND THERE.
THE MOUNTAINS OF THE LAND OF FIRE...?
!

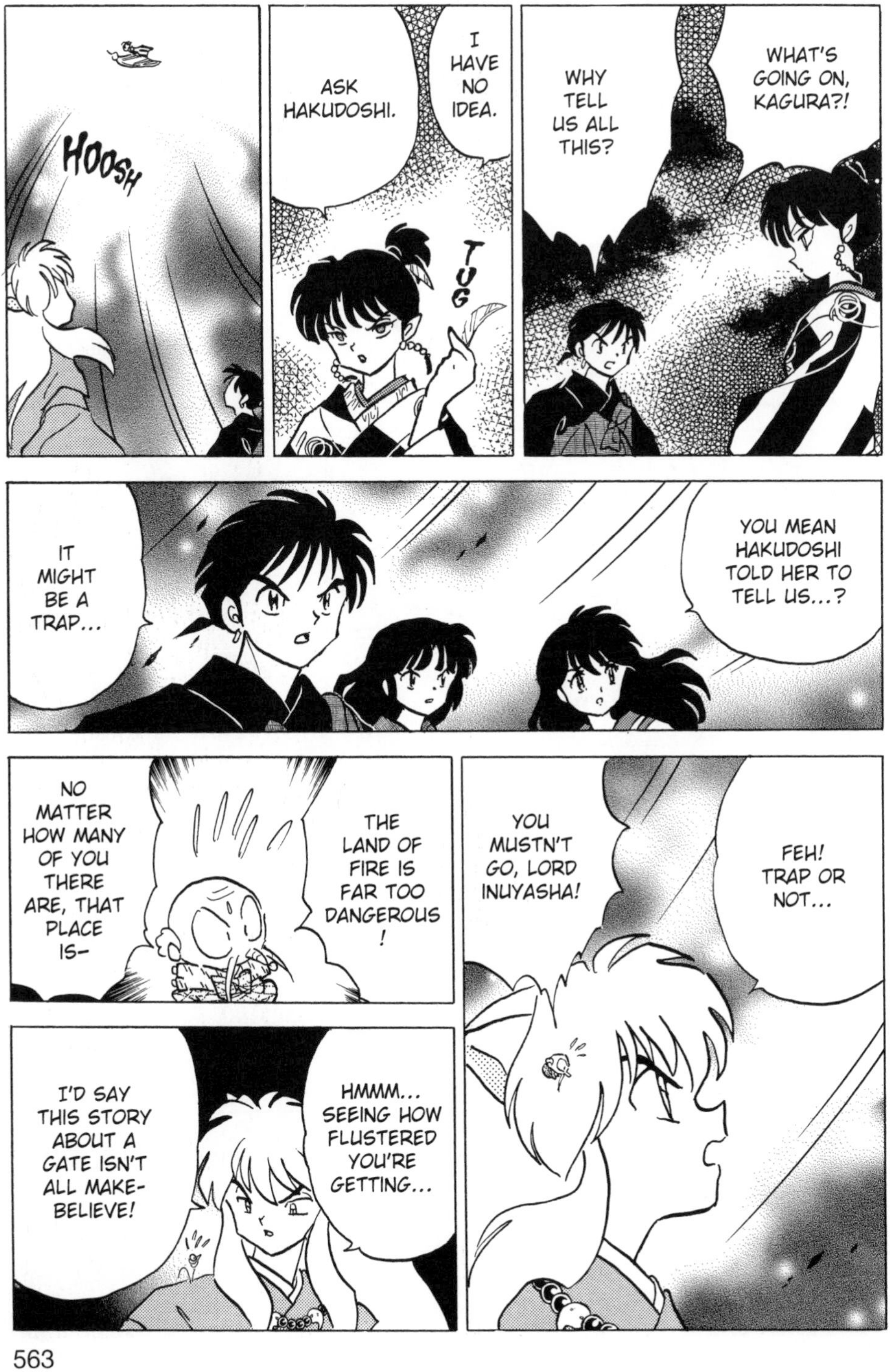
WHAT'S GOING ON, KAGURA?!
WHY TELL US ALL THIS?
I HAVE NO IDEA.
ASK HAKUDOSHI.
TUG
HOOSH
YOU MEAN HAKUDOSHI TOLD HER TO TELL US...?
IT MIGHT BE A TRAP...
FEH! TRAP OR NOT...
YOU MUSTN'T GO, LORD INUYASHA!
THE LAND OF FIRE IS FAR TOO DANGEROUS!
NO MATTER HOW MANY OF YOU THERE ARE, THAT PLACE IS-
HMMM... SEEING HOW FLUSTERED YOU'RE GETTING...
I'D SAY THIS STORY ABOUT A GATE ISN'T ALL MAKE-BELIEVE!

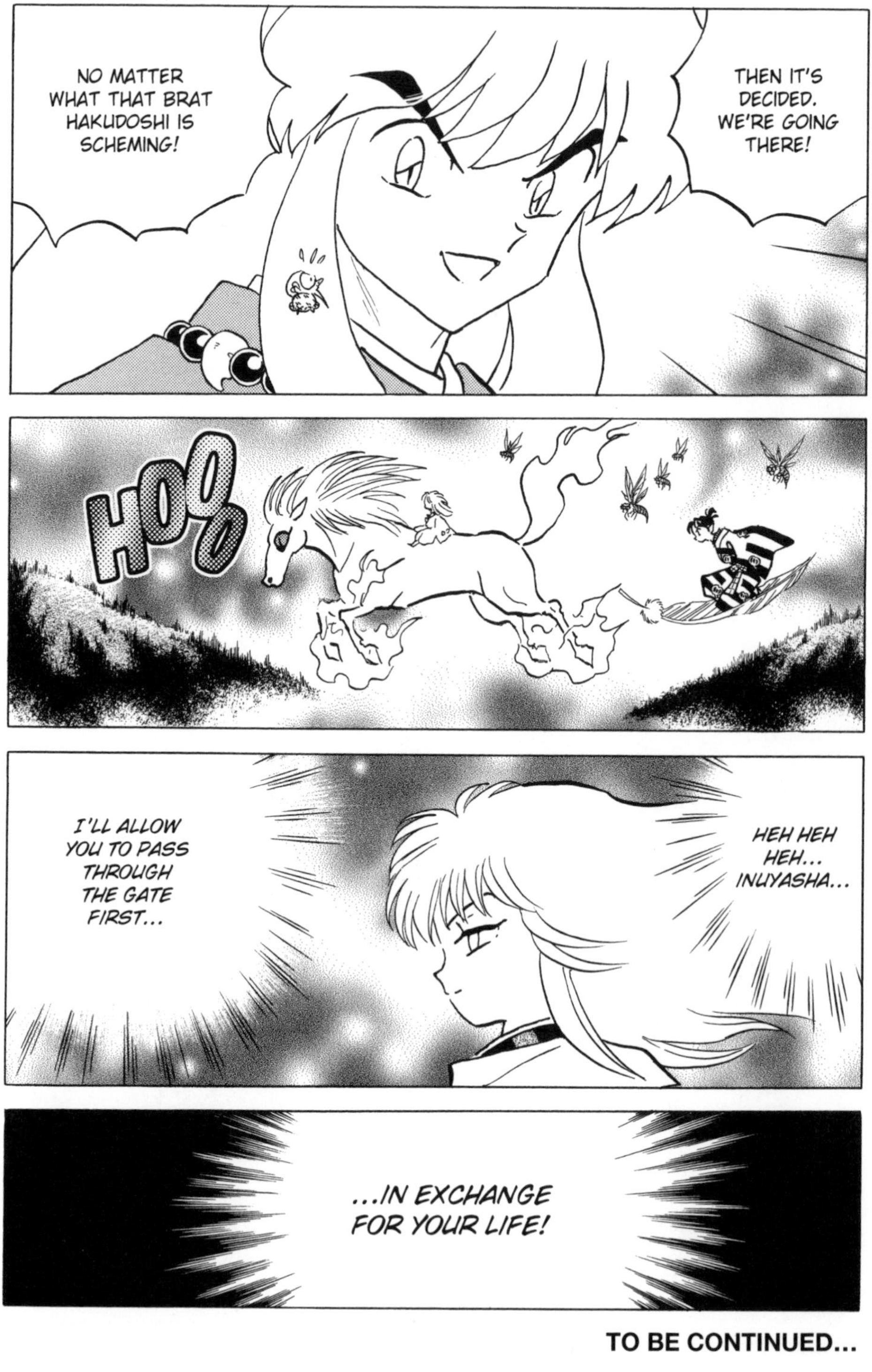
THEN IT'S DECIDED. WE'RE GOING THERE!
NO MATTER WHAT THAT BRAT HAKUDOSHI IS SCHEMING!
HOO
HEH HEH HEH... INUYASHA...
I'LL ALLOW YOU TO PASS THROUGH THE GATE FIRST...
...IN EXCHANGE FOR YOUR LIFE!

TO BE CONTINUED...

Original Cover Art Gallery

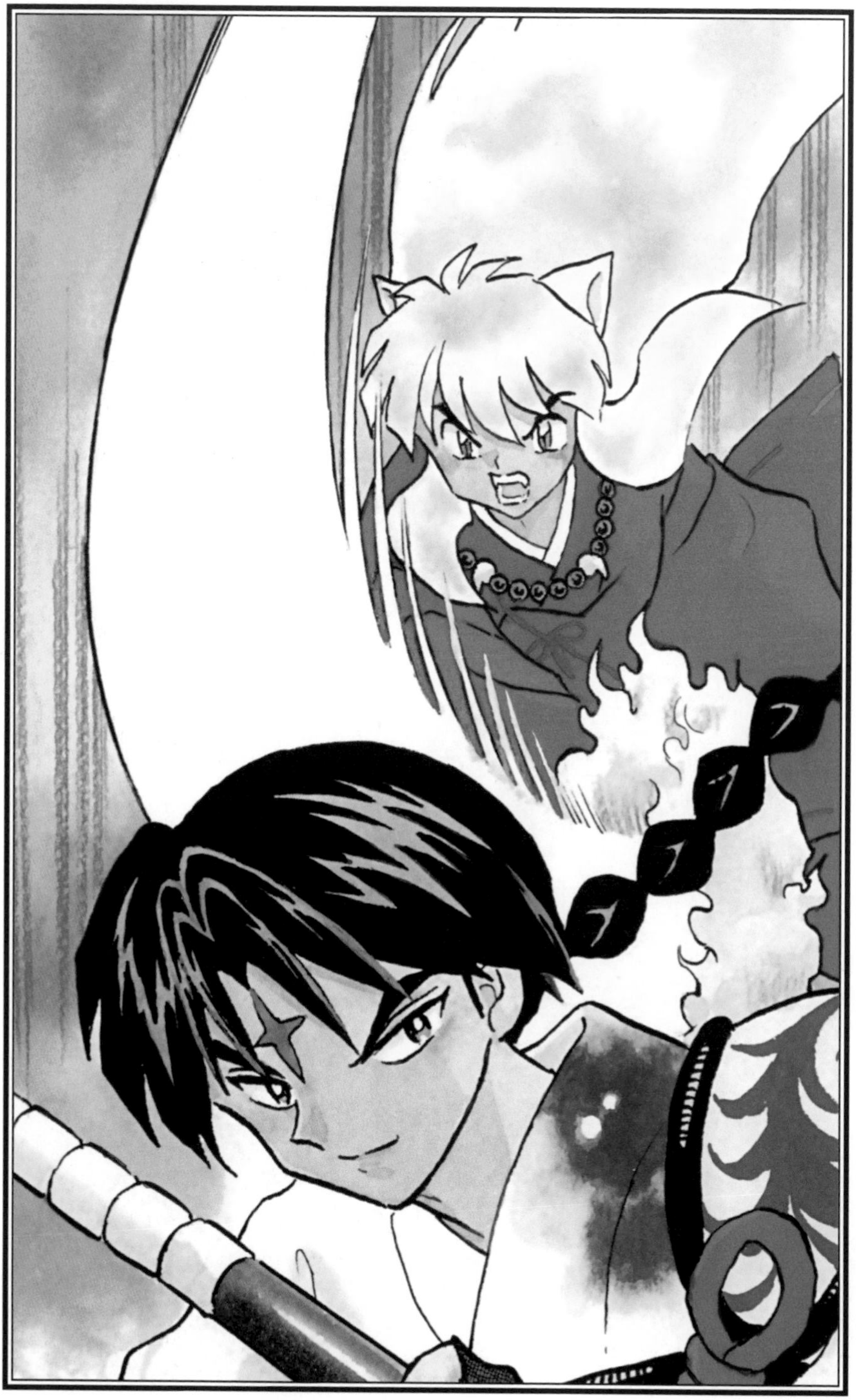

Original cover art from volume 28, published 2007

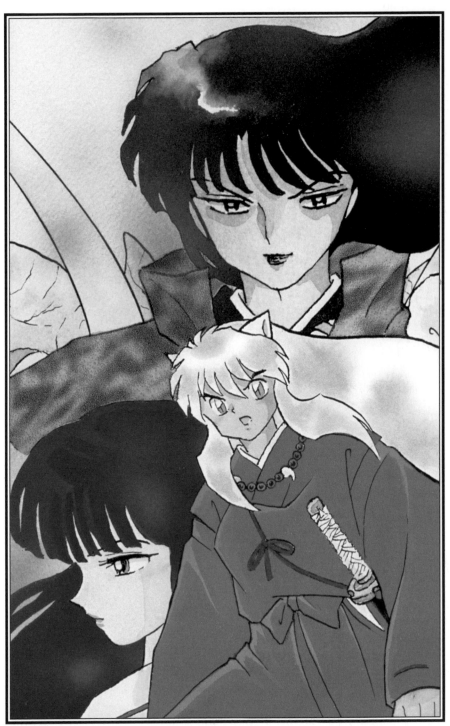

Original cover art from volume 29, published 2007

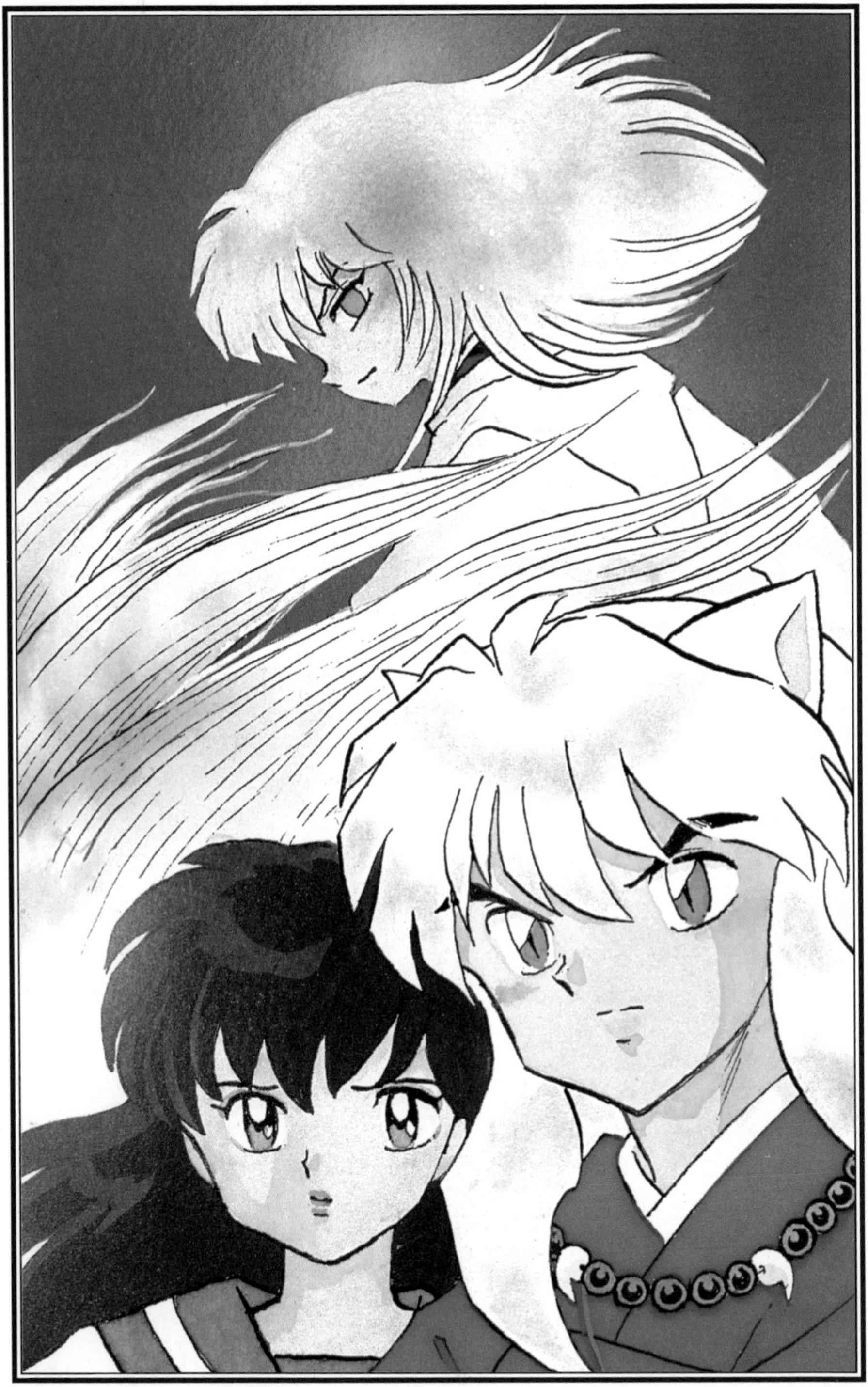

Original cover art from volume 30, published 2007

Coming Next Volume

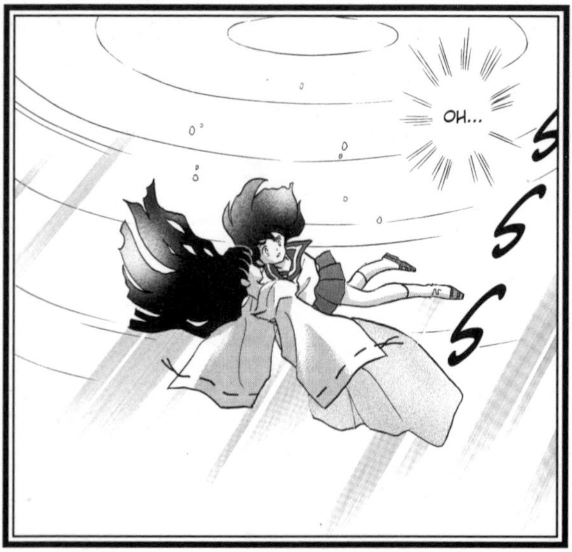
OH...

The search for the final shard of the Shikon Jewel leads Inuyasha and the gang to a mountain fortress...but only the *dead* may enter. Meanwhile, Naraku teams up with a demon who hunts the blood of innocent villagers—just his type!

Then Kagome faces a moral dilemma. Only she can rescue her rival Kikyo from Naraku's miasma. Will she make the right choice? Elsewhere, Naraku sends Kohaku on an evil errand...

Now a fierce battle rages in the borderland between the world of the living and the afterlife. A mysterious force attacks Inuyasha and claims to act on behalf of the Shikon Jewel itself! Naturally, Naraku joins the fray. Then, when all hope seems lost, Inuyasha receives unexpected help from his half brother!